Footprint Scotland

Alan Murphy

3rd edition

There is a story of the tourist who hails a passing crofter on a lonely Hebridean road and asks for directions. "Well", says the crofter, "if I was going there, I wouldn't start from here."

Sunday Herald, 7 September 2003

1 Edinburgh's Hogmanay
Join in the biggest New Year party on the planet

2 Glentress Forest
Have a go on one of the world's best mountain bike single tracks

3 Kirkcudbright
Visit arty little Kirkcudbright, on the beautiful Solway Firth

4 Fingal's Cave
Sail from Mull to this cave which echoes to the rhythm of Mendelsohn's romantic overture

5 Glasgow School of Art
Witness the genius of Charles Rennie Mackintosh, Scotland's answer to Gaudí

6 Jura
Take a ferry to Jura, where George Orwell wrote *1984*, and trek to the legendary Corryvreckan, the second largest whirlpool in the world

7 West Highland railway
Climb aboard, for one of the world's great train rides

8 Inverewe
Enjoy over 50 acres of horticultural heaven

9 Sandwood Bay
Sit on the beach and watch the sun set with a bottle of single malt and a loved one

Scotland Highlights

See colour maps at back of book

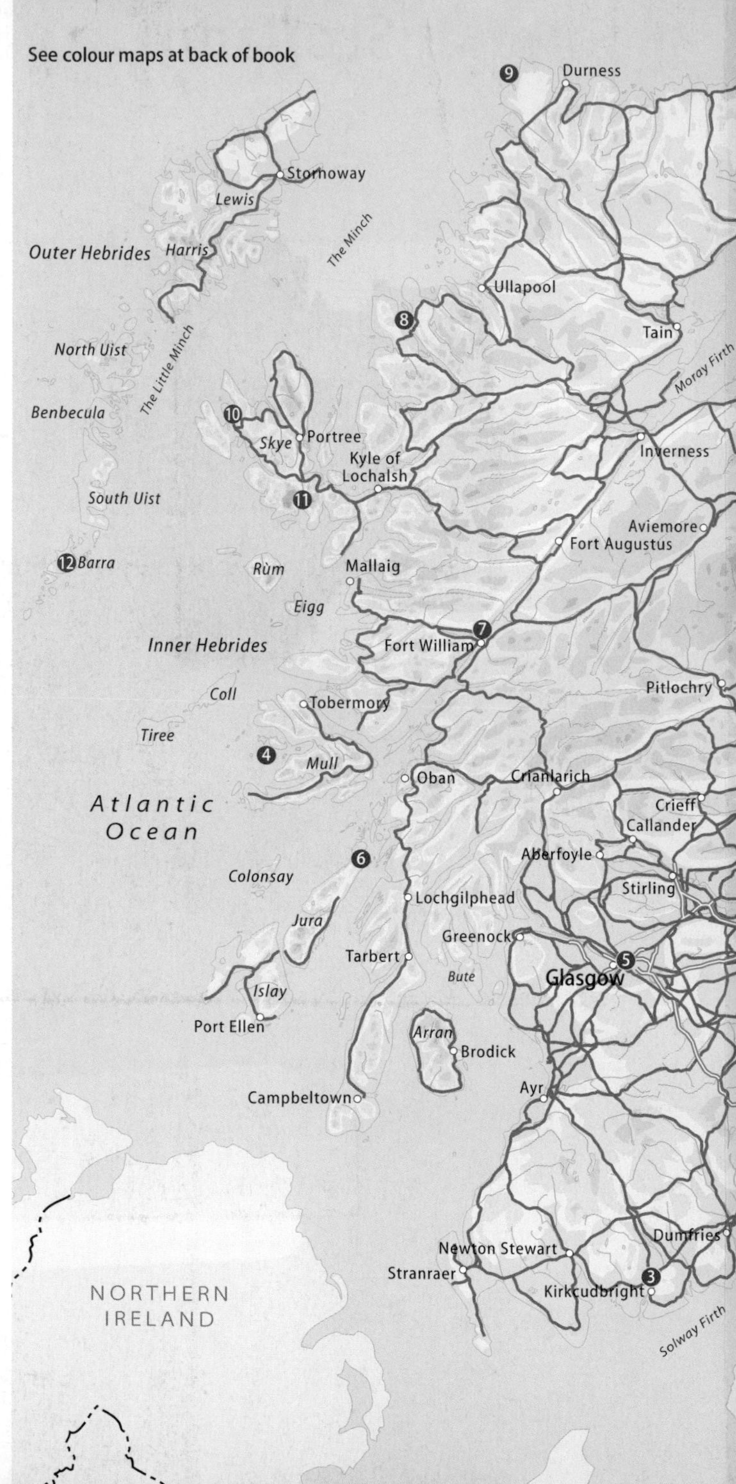

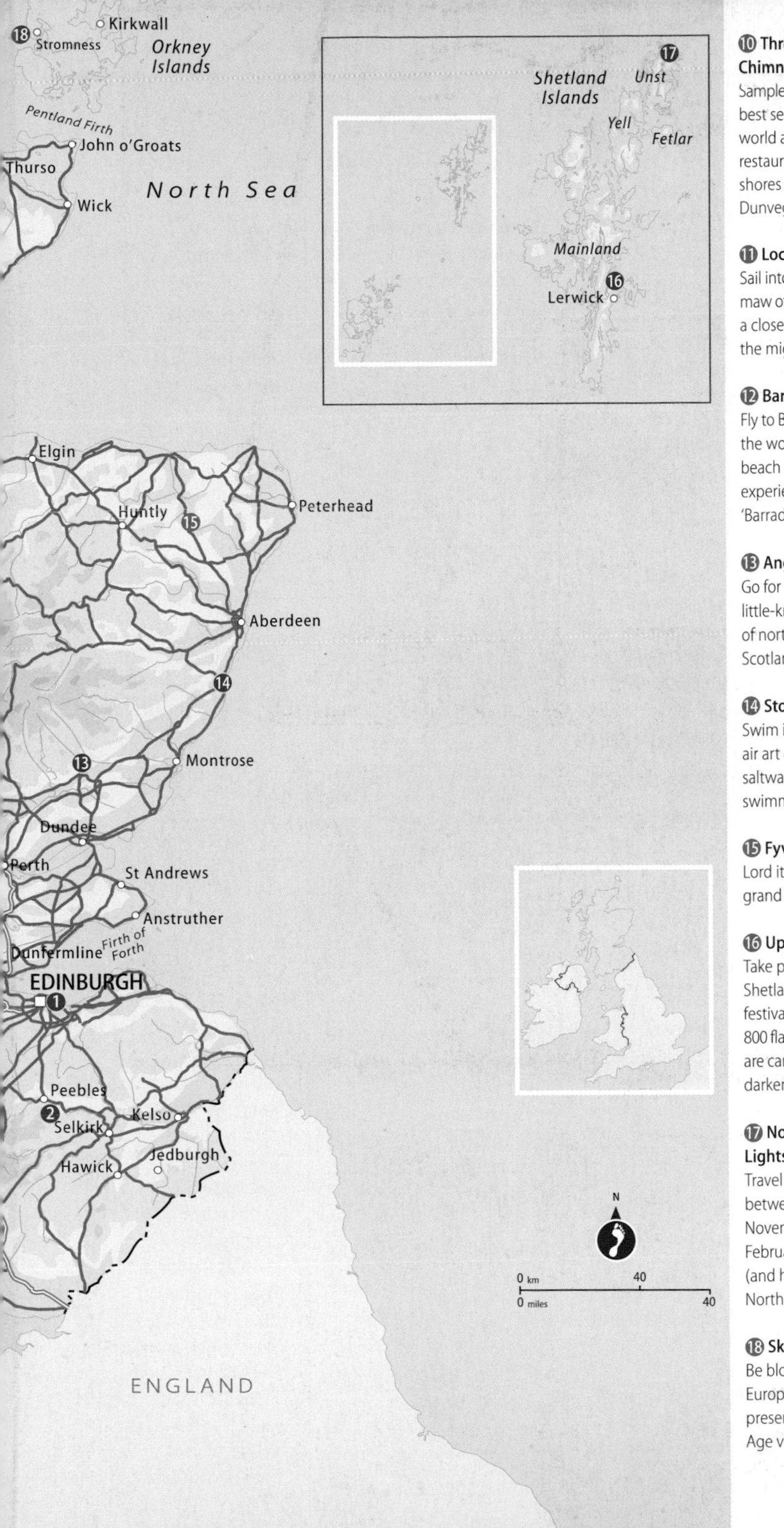

10 Three Chimneys
Sample some of the best seafood in the world at this restaurant on the shores of Loch Dunvegan

11 Loch Coruisk
Sail into the gaping maw of this loch for a close up view of the mighty Cuillins

12 Barra
Fly to Barra, land on the world's only beach runway and experience 'Barradise'

13 Angus glens
Go for a hike in this little-known corner of northeast Scotland

14 Stonehaven
Swim in the open-air art deco heated saltwater swimming pool

15 Fyvie Castle
Lord it up in this grand baronial pile

16 Up Helly-Aa
Take part in Shetland's fire festival, when over 800 flaming torches are carried through darkened streets

17 Northern Lights
Travel to Shetland between November and February to see (and hear) the Northern Lights

18 Skara Brae
Be blown away at Europe's best-preserved Stone-Age village

Contents

Central Scotland

Argyll & Inner Hebrides

Highlands

Skye & the Small Isles

Outer Hebrides

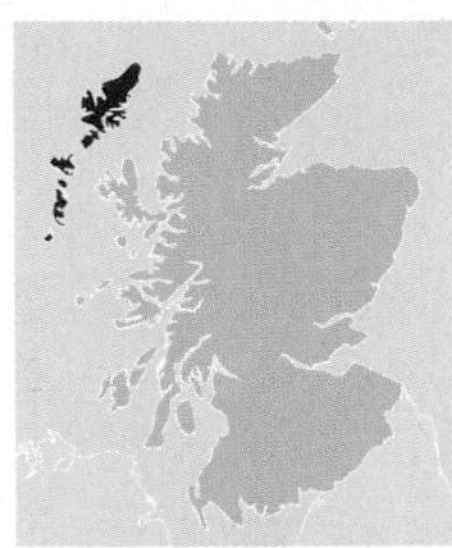

Northeast Scotland

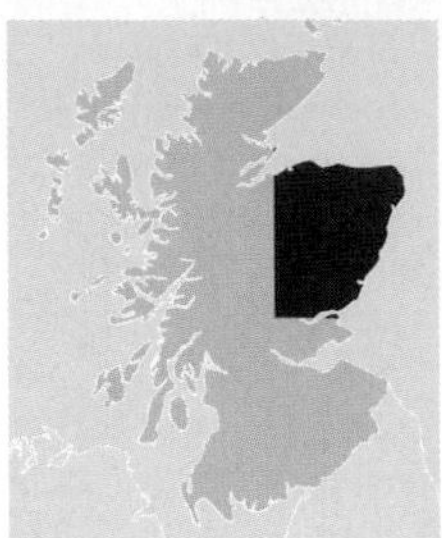

Orkney and Shetland

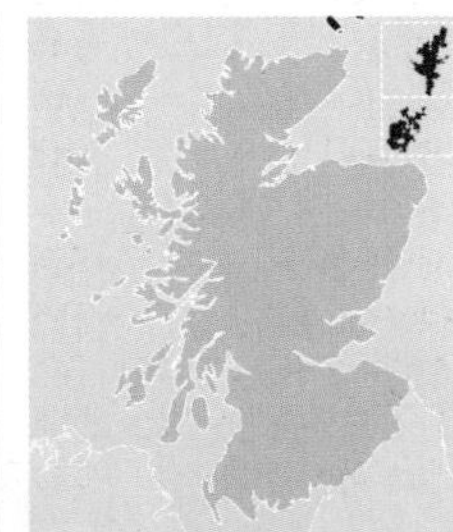

Snow business
The hardworking northeastern corner, around Aberdeen, has castles and whisky aplenty, but without the hordes.

Background

Footnotes

Inside front cover

Sleeping and eating price codes

Inside back cover

Author biography

Any port in a storm?
Oban, set in a cresent-shaped bay, backed by sheer hills, even caused Queen Victoria to praise its charms.

A foot in the door

Every self-respecting Scot comes over all proprietorial when introducing the glories of their country to a friend or loved one for the first time. So much so, you'd think they'd designed the whole place themselves. As if the jaw-dropping scenery of Wester Ross, or the Trossachs, was some kind of DIY makeover: 'oh, yes, we got rid of all that woodchip and planted the hillsides in Caledonian pine forest. The native woodland look is in this year.' The Scots have every right to be proud. When the rain stops falling and the mist clears, there is no more beautiful place on Earth. If there is a heaven, it probably looks like this, but let's hope the petrol's cheaper.

Scotland is one of the least densely-populated countries in Europe. Not much smaller than its southern neighbour, England, it has only a tenth of its population – and most of those are crammed into the narrow central belt, leaving two-thirds of the country virtually empty. The Highlands and Islands, in particular, are Europe's last great wilderness; one of the few places in this increasingly cluttered continent where you can really get away from it all.

About the only thing Scotland doesn't have going for it is a dependable climate. If you want to lie on a beach all day, then you ought to try somewhere else. Another perennial problem has been the clichéd image of bagpipes, haggis and shortbread. In an attempt to kill two birds with one stone, the tourist board promoted the country as the perfect destination for a romantic break – if the weather's rubbish then you'll have more time to stay in bed – thus giving a whole new meaning to the term Highland fling. It scandalized the more puritanical elements of the Scottish establishment. Heaven forfend that Scotland should become a sexy destination.

10 Pride and prejudice

The tired old clichés of haggis, whisky and tartan have done little to enhance the image of Scotland over the years but arguably the country's greatest handicap has been its crippling lack of self-confidence. No doubt induced by the all-pervading influence of a much larger neighbour, the Scots have been ambivalent about national identity; the wanton pride so often on display only serving to hide the cringing embarrassment of being Scottish. That embarrassment has been ebbing away over the past few decades with the reawakening of Scottish culture. Gaelic language is being revived, thanks to investment in broadcasting and publishing, and the popularity of Gaelic folk/ rock bands such as Runrig and Capercaillie. Lowland Scots, too, has been making a cultural comeback. Generations of Scottish children were taught that the language their parents speak is a debased form of speech but since James Kelman won the Booker prize writing in his own dialect, Scottish writers have had the confidence to express themselves in their native tongue.

Highland icon
Photographers, movie-makers and tourists alike, flock to Eilean Donan Castle.

Power to the people

Following in the wake of the cultural and artistic renaissance has been the gradual development of a separate political identity. After a 300-year adjournment, the Scottish Parliament is up and running and even indulging in coalition politics, which has seen the involvement of small parties such as The Greens, Scottish Socialists and various Independents. Of course, there are problems, not least of which is the vexed question of Scottish MPs in the British Parliament voting on matters which affect England when English MPs cannot have the same influence over Scottish affairs. Then there's the small matter of the new Scottish Parliament building itself, now subject to a public inquiry into the reasons why its costs increased tenfold and why it will open three years later than planned. Constitutional matters and the occasional financial and sexual scandal notwithstanding, the Scottish Parliament has got to be an improvement. At least the Scots can finally stop moaning about the English.

Creature feature
Known locally as the Armadillo, The Clyde Auditorium, one of Sir Norman Foster's creations, sits on the banks of the Clyde.

1
2
4
5
7
8
10
11

3

6

9

12

1 *Kilchurn Castle is a wonderfully romantic ruin.* ▸▸ *See page 294.*

2 *The Spey, one of Scotland's great rivers, has its source near Ben Crunachan.* ▸▸ *See page 533.*

3 *The Forth Rail Bridge is perhaps the most impressive Victorian engineering feat in Britain.* ▸▸ *See page 103.*

4 *The northeast is littered with standing stones, such as these, at Loanhead of Daviot, near Inverness.* ▸▸ *See page 531.*

5 *An unsung hero, Alexander 'Greek' Thompson did as much to shape Glasgow as the exalted Charles Rennie Mackintosh.* ▸▸ *See page 147.*

6 *The maze at Scone Palace is found in the grounds of one of the most historical and fascinating houses in Scotland.* ▸▸ *See page 240.*

7 *Founded by Cistercian monks in 1273, the red, crumbling sandstone ruins of Sweetheart Abbey have an interesting history behind their name.* ▸▸ *See page 213.*

8 *Little visited, peaceful Loch Awe is the longest freshwater loch in Scotland.* ▸▸ *See page 294.*

9 *Scotland is full of lighthouses but few were designed by Mackintosh with views of the Glasgow cityscape.* ▸▸ *See page 137.*

10 *With some of Europe's most wild and outstanding scenery, even the most exercise-shy would be foolish not to don a pair of boots and take to the hills.* ▸▸ *See page 59.*

11 *A tiny settlement on the Isle of Skye, Elgol is reached by a mind-blowing road from Broadford, and nearby is a dramatic boat ride into Loch Coruisk.* ▸▸ *See page 441.*

12 *The most accessible and renowned of all lochs in Scotland, Loch Lomond lives up to the hype, especially if you are lucky enough to enjoy it when the daytrippers have gone home.* ▸▸ *See page 263.*

Food for thought

One of the images Scotland still has to overcome – worse than the drizzle or midges – is that the food is disgusting. The country that gave the world the deep-fried pizza and Irn-bru is finally putting things right. Now you don't have to visit Paris, Madrid or Barcelona to taste melt-in-the-mouth smoked salmon, the freshest scallops, mussels, prawns and langoustines, and the best beef in Europe. The Scots are keeping it for themselves. Edinburgh and Glasgow are the best cities in the UK, outside London, for fine dining, but world-class cuisine is not confined to major urban centres. These days you don't have to look far for a good meal in Scotland.

Take a hike

Scotland has never been a place for softies. Its challenging weather and dramatic scenery really do convey a sense of being in the big outdoors. There are mountains galore to climb, lochs to fish and wildlife to watch, or you can just sit back and take in all that stunning scenery. In the Highlands in particular, there are countless opportunities to leave civilization a long way behind. You could explore Scotland's long-distance footpaths which snake through some of the country's finest scenery. These include the West Highland Way, the less well known Speyside Way and the Southern Upland Way. The more adventurous can try their hand (or feet) at 'Munro Bagging', which is not some dubious public school practice but the name given to the popular pursuit of climbing Scotland's 284 mountains higher than 3,000 feet.

Nature at its best. The Quiraing, on the Isle of Skye, is reached by a demanding 4-mile hike.

Britain's second highest range, the stunning Cairgorms, are extremely popular with those who love the outdoors – with hiking, mountain biking and skiing aplenty.

This offers the chance to explore wild areas of unparalleled beauty such as Glen Coe, Torridon, Kintail or the Cairngorms.

Horsing around

You'd have to be very unlucky not to experience at least one local festival. The calendar is bursting with them. Many have their roots in pagan ceremonies, others, such as Up Helly-Aa on Shetland, are of Viking origin, while some are downright crazy, like the Jedburgh Hand Ba' game – a weird mixture of basketball, rugby and mud-wrestling. Amongst the most colourful events are the Highland Games, traditional gatherings involving dancing, massed pipes and various sporting competitions. There are over a hundred of these gatherings held in towns and villages up and down the country. In summer the Borders towns of Hawick, Selkirk, Jedburgh and Lauder are alive to the sound of horses hooves as they celebrate their own particular version of the Common Ridings, a cross between Pamplona's Bull Run, Siena's Palio and the Munich Oktoberfest. But you don't have to attend organized events to have a good time. One of the most unforgettable experiences of a Scottish holiday is to find yourself in a pub in the the middle of nowhere, consuming copious quantities of whisky and then being hurled by a bunch of total strangers around the room, to the accompaniment of a fiddle and accordion.

On reflection
Loch Gamha, on the Rothiemurchus Estate, near the busy tourist town of Aviemore, one of Scotland's main adventure sports centres.

Essentials

Footprint features

Planning your trip

Where to go

Scotland is a small country but there's a lot to see and trying to cram everything into a first visit can be very frustrating. There are many, many places of great natural beauty and the country's long, turbulent history has left a rich heritage of medieval castles, cathedrals, palaces, abbeys and historic towns and cities. So, where do you begin?

Those arriving by air will start in Edinburgh, the capital, or Glasgow, Scotland's largest city. Edinburgh is one of the world's truly great cities and deserves at least a few days to explore its castle, palace, medieval streets, fine Georgian architecture, art galleries and museums, and enjoy its liberal licensing laws. Glasgow is less than an hour from Edinburgh and though it lacks the capital's tourist credentials, it is worth a visit for its elegant Victorian architecture, the genius of Charles Rennie Mackintosh – Scotland's very own Gaudí – and its friendly and quick-witted citizens.

One- to two-week trip

If you only have a week and you want to see some Highland scenery, you can head straight for the hills from Glasgow and Edinburgh. A short distance north of Glasgow is Loch Lomond, gateway to the Western Highlands and a beautiful introduction to the spectacular sights which lie in wait farther north. From Loch Lomond you should head north through Glencoe, one of the main highlights of a visit to Scotland, to Fort William, the main tourist centre for the Western Highlands. From Fort William there are two routes to another of Scotland's most popular attractions, the Isle of Skye. The quickest route is by road and bridge, via Kyle of Lochalsh, but by far the most romantic and scenic route is by train from Fort William to Mallaig, and by ferry from there to Armadale. You should then leave at least three days to explore the island, or more if you plan to do any walking.

Alternatively, it's only a short drive north from Edinburgh to Perthshire. Though not as dramatic as the northwest, the mountains, rivers, lochs and glens of the Perthshire Highlands are very beautiful and easily accessed. If you also want a slice of history thrown in, then you could make a round trip from Perth to the historic town of Stirling, with its important castle, and return via the Trossachs, a thick wedge of lochs, forests and mountains forever associated with Sir Walter Scott, tucked in between Stirling and Loch Lomond. Also near Perth is the medieval town of St Andrews, home of Scotland's oldest university and the world's most famous golf course. From St Andrews, it's an easy day trip to the charming fishing villages of the East Neuk of Fife.

An alternative to Fort William and Skye, or in addition if you have more time, would be to head from Glasgow or Edinburgh to Oban, the main ferry port of the west coast, and make the short trip to the beguiling Isle of Mull, which tends to be attract fewer visitors than Skye in the summer months, and from where you can pop across to its divine neighbour, Iona, or explore the inspirational Fingal's Cave on Staffa. Or you could head south from Oban, through Argyll, with its many prehistoric sites, and take a ferry to the little-visited islands of Islay, famous for its malt whiskies, and Jura. Both are great places for walking holidays. Also within reach of Argyll, or Ayrshire, is the island of Arran, described as 'Scotland in miniature' and ideal for walking or cycling.

Three- to four-week trip

If you have three or four weeks at your disposal then you can follow the long and winding road north from Kyle of Lochalsh, as it twists and turns along the coast to Ullapool. Most visitors don't make it north of Ullapool but those who do are rewarded

The long and winding road

It is easy enough to visit the main towns and tourist sights by bus or train, but getting off the beaten track without your own transport requires careful planning and an intimate knowledge of rural bus timetables. Even if you're driving, getting around the remote Highlands and Islands can be a time-consuming business as much of this region is accessed only by a sparse network of tortuous, twisting, single-track roads. Be sure to allow plenty of time for getting around the Highlands and Islands, especially for the countless impromptu stops you'll be making to admire the views, and book ferries in advance during the busy summer season. All this is covered in greater detail in Getting around page 39.

with the starkly beautiful, almost primeval landscapes of the far northwest. You can sail from Ullapool across to the Outer Hebrides, a long, narrow archipelago stretching from Lewis and Harris in the north to Barra in the south. Alternatively, you could include a trip to the Orkney Islands, littered with important Stone Age ruins and also one of the world's best dive sites. If time and money really are no object, then head for culturally-distinct Shetland Isles, home to Viking festivals and millions of seabirds, and which are so far north of the mainland that they can only be included on maps as an inset.

When to go

The high season is from May to September, and this is when Scotland receives the vast majority of visitors. Though the weather tends to be better during the summer months, prices for accommodation are higher in the high season and hotels and guest houses in the most popular places need to be booked in advance. It's also a good idea to make reservations at this time on ferries to the islands, especially to Skye and Mull. A major advantage to visiting in the summer months is the long hours of daylight, especially farther north, where the sun doesn't set till around 2200 or later in June and July.

During the low season, from October to Easter, many tourist sights are closed, and travelling around the Highlands and Islands can be difficult as public transport services are limited. Many of the smaller tourist offices are also closed during the low season. Though some hotels and guest houses close during the low season, the majority are now open all year round, as are most restaurants. Taking everything into consideration, May and September are probably the best months to visit Scotland, though Glasgow and Edinburgh are worth visiting at any time of the year.

Climate

The Scottish climate is notoriously unpredictable, especially on the west coast, where a bright, sunny morning can turn into a downpour in the time it takes to butter your toast. Predicting the weather is not an exact science and tables of statistics are most likely a waste of time. There's an old saying in Scotland that if you don't like the weather, then wait 20 minutes, and this just about sums it up. The west coast receives far more rain than the rest of the country and the east coast gets more sunshine. The west coast is also milder in the winter due to the relatively warm waters of the Gulf Stream.

For a seven-day weather forecast service, call Weather Check, T0891-3331111 plus 101 for the northwest, 102 for the northeast, and 103 for Glasgow, Edinburgh and southern Scotland.

On the buses

A great and cheap way to get around Scotland is on one of the jump-on-jump-off backpacker bus tours. These leave from Edinburgh daily, except Sunday, and stop off at independent hostels in Perth, Pitlochry, Inverness, Loch Ness, Isle of Skye, Fort William, Glencoe, Oban and Glasgow. You can hop on and off whenever you please, and you don't need to stay at any of the hostels. Prices range from around £69. The same companies also run excellent-value Highland tours, leaving from Edinburgh. Prices start at around £79 for three days, up to around £139 for six days. Prices do not include accommodation or food. See Tour operators below for details of companies offering these tours.

Winters in the north can be very harsh, especially in the mountains and glens, making hiking conditions treacherous. Winter storms also make it difficult to travel around the islands as ferry services are often cancelled. Generally speaking, May to September are the warmest months, with an average summer high of around 18-19°C and, though they are often the driest months, you can expect rain at any time of the year, even in high summer. So, you'll need to come prepared, and remember the old hikers' adage that there's no such thing as bad weather, only inadequate clothing.

Tour operators

There are many companies offering general interest or special interest tours of Scotland. Travel agents will have details, or you can check the small advertisements in the travel sections of newspapers, or contact the British Tourist Authority or Scottish Tourist Board for a list of operators.

In the UK

Assynt Guided Holidays, Birchbank, Knockan, Elphin, Sutherland, T/F01854-666215. Specialize in walking tours of this rugged corner of the northwest.
Avalon Trekking Scotland, Bowerswell Lane, Kinnoull, Perth, PH2 TDL, T/F01738-624194. Good all-round hillwalking tours.
Classique Tours, Glasgow, T0141-8894050, www.classiquetours .co.uk. 5-day tours start at £275 and their 7-day Grand Hebridean Tour is £485. For those who prefer something a wee bit different, tartan-free tours of the 'real Scotland' in a vintage bus.
Go Blue Banana, Edinburgh, T0131-5562000, www.gobluebanana.com. Backpacker bus tour operators, see box.
Haggis Backpackers, 11 Blackfriars St, Edinburgh EH1 1NB, T0131-5579393, www.haggis-backpackers.com. Backpacker bus tour operators, see box.
Heart of Scotland Tours, T0131-558 8855, www.heartofscotlandtours.co.uk. Runs 1- and 2-day coach tours, £27-57, departing from Edinburgh Backpackers Hostel.
Lomond Walking Holidays, 34c James St, Riverside, Stirling, FK8 1UG, T/F01786-447752, www.biggar-net.co.uk/lomond. Offer a variety of walking packages.
Macbackpackers, Edinburgh, T0131-5589900, www.macbackpackers.com. Backpacker bus tour operators, see box.
North-West Frontiers, 18A Braes, Ullapool, IV26 28Z, T/F01854-612628, www.nwfrontiers.com. Walking tours, a bit more hardcore than the rest.
Ossian Guides, Sanna, Newtonmore, Inverness, PH20 1DG, T/F01540-673402. Reliable walking guide company.
Rabbie's Trail Burners, 207 High St, Edinburgh, T0131-226 3133, www.rabbies.com. Run 1-5 day coach tours of the Highlands, from £22 up to £159 per person.

Saga Holidays, Saga Building, Middelburg Sq, Folkestone, Kent CT20 1AZ, T0800-300 500. Sightseeing tours for the older people.
Scottish Border Trails, Venlaw High Rd, Drummore, Peebles, EH45 8RL, T01721-720336, arthur@trails.scotborders.co.uk. Cycling and walking tours in the borders.
Scottish Cycle Safaris, 29 Blackfriars St, Edinburgh, EH1 1NH, T0131-5565560. Offers a range of 1-day tours around Edinburgh and Lothians and longer tours as far as the Highlands.
Scottish Cycling Holidays, 87 Perth St, Blairgowrie, Perthshire, PH10 6DT, T01250-876100, www.sol.co.uk/s/scotcycl/. Various two-wheeled packages.
Shearings Holidays, Miry Lane, Wigan, Lancs WN3 4AG, T01942-824824. Large road-clogging coach tour empire.
Timberbush Tours, 555 Castlehill, Edinburgh, T0131-226 6066, www.timberbush-tours.co.uk. Run a variety of 1-3 day guided coach tours around the country, £22-£90.
Walkabout Scotland, 2 Rossie Place, Edinburgh, T0131-661 7168, www.walkaboutscotland.com. Walking tours around Edinburgh and the Highlands.
Wild in Scotland, 9 South St Andrew St, Edinburgh, T0131-478 6500, www.wild-in-scotland.com. Run various coach tours from 3 days (£65) to 6 days (£119).

In North America

Abercrombie & Kent, T1-800-3237308, www.abercrombiekent.com. General sightseeing tours.
Above the Clouds Trekking, T800-2334499, www.gorp.com/abvclds.htm. Walking tours.
British Coastal Trails, T800-4731210, www.bctwalk.com. Walking tours.
Cross-Culture, 52 High Point Dr, Amherst MA01002-1224, T800-4911148, www.crosscultureinc.com. General sightseeing tours.
Especially Britian, T1-800-8690538. General sightseeing tours.
Golf International Inc, T1-800- 8331389, golfing tours from the USA offered.
Jerry Quinlan's Celtic Golf, T1-800-5356148, www.jqcelticgolf.com, organizes golfing packages from the USA.
Prestige Tours, T1-800-8907375. General sightseeing tours.
Saga, 222 Berkeley St, Boston, MA 02116, USA. General sightseeing tours.
Sterling Tours, T1-800 -7274359, www.sterlingtours.com. General sightseeing tours.

In Australia and New Zealand

Adventure Specialists, 69 Liverpool St, Sydney, T02-92612927. Adventure tours.
Adventure Travel Company, 164 Parnell Rd, Parnell, East Auckland, T09-3799755. New Zealand agents for **Peregrine** Adventures. Offers a range of activity tours.
Peregrine Adventures, 258 Lonsdale St, Melbourne, T03-96638611, www.peregrine.net.au; also branches in Brisbane, Sydney, Adelaide and Perth. Offers a wide range of activity tours throughout Scotland.
Saga, Level 1, 10-14 Paul St, Milsons Point, Sydney 2061. General sightseeing tours.

Finding out more

The best way of finding out more information for your trip to Scotland is to contact the British Tourist Authority (BTA), who represent the Scottish Tourist Board abroad. Their website, www.bta.org.uk, is very useful as a first stop directory for accommodation. Alternatively, you can write (or email) direct to the head office of the Scottish Tourist Board (STB). Both organizations can provide a wealth of free literature and information such as maps, city guides, events calendars and accommodation brochures. Travellers with special needs should also contact their nearest BTA office. If you want more detailed information on a particular area, contact the area tourist boards.

BTA offices

Australia, Level 16, The Gateway, 1 Macquarie Pl, Circular Quay, Sydney NSW 2000, T02-93774400, F93774499.
Belgium and Luxembourg, 306 Av Louise, 1050 Brussels, T2-6463510, F6463986.

Canada, 111 Avenue Rd, Suite 450, Toronto, Ontario MR5 3J8, T416-9256326, F9612175.
Denmark, Montergade 3, 1116 Copenhagen K, T33-339188, F140136.
France, Maison de la Grande-Bretagne, 19 Rue des Mathurins, 75009 Paris, T1-44515620, F44515621.
Germany, Austria and Switzerland, Taunustrasse 52-60, 60329 Frankfurt, T69-2380711.
Ireland, 18/19 College Green, Dublin 2, T1-6708000, F6708244.
Italy, Corso Vittorio Emanuele II No 337, 00186 Rome, T6-68806821, F6879095.
Netherlands, Stadhouderskade 2 (5e), 1054 ES Amsterdam, T20-6855051, F6186868.
New Zealand, 17th floor, Fay Richwhite Building, 151 Queen St, Auckland 1, T09-3031446, F3776965.
South Africa, Lancaster Gate, Hyde Park Lane, Hyde Park 2196, Johannesburg, T011-3250342.
USA, 7th floor, 551 Fifth Av, New York, NY 10176-0799, T212-986-2200/ 1-800-GO-2-BRITAIN. 10880 Wilshire Blvd, Suite 570, Los Angeles, CA 90024, T310-4702782.

Scottish Tourist Boards

Scottish Tourist Board Central Information Department, 23 Ravelston Terr, Edinburgh EH4 3EU, T0131-3322433, www.visitscotland.com; and 19 Cockspur St, London SW1 5BL, T020-7930 2812.
Aberdeen & Grampian Tourist Board, 27 Albyn Pl, Aberdeen AB10 1YL, T01224-632727, www.castlesandwhisky.co.uk.
Angus & City of Dundee Tourist Board, 7-21 Castle St, Dundee DD1 3AA, T01382-527527, www.angusanddundee.co.uk.
Argyll, the Isles, Loch Lomond, Stirling & Trossachs Tourist Board, 7 Alexandra Par, Dunoon, Argyll PA23 8AB, T01369-701000, www.scottish.heartlands.org.
Ayrshire & Arran Tourist Board, Burns House, Burns Statue Sq, Ayr KA7 1UP, T01292-288688, www.ayrshire-arran.com.
Dumfries & Galloway Tourist Board, 64 Whitesands, Dumfries, DG1 2RS, T01387-253862, www.galloway.co.uk.
Edinburgh & Lothians Tourist Board, 3 Princes St, Edinburgh EH2 2QP, T0131-4733800, www.edinburgh.org.
Greater Glasgow & Clyde Valley Tourist Board, 11 George Sq, Glasgow G2 1DY, T0141-2044400, seeglasgow.com.
The Highlands of Scotland Tourist Board, Peffery House, Strathpeffer IV14 9HA, T01479-810363, UK T0870-5143070, www.host.co.uk.
Kingdom of Fife Tourist Board Tourist Information Centre, 70 Market St, St Andrews KY16 9NU, T01334-470021, www.standrews.com.
Orkney Tourist Board, 6 Broad St, Kirkwall, Orkney KW15 1NX, T01856-872856, www.visitorkney.com.
Perthshire Tourist Board, Lower City Mills, West Mill St, Perth PH1 5QP, T01738-627958, www.perthshire.co.uk.
Scottish Borders Tourist Board Tourist Information Centre, Murray's Green, Jedburgh TD8 6BE, T01835-863435, www.scot-borders.co.uk.
Shetland Islands Tourism, Market Cross, Lerwick, Shetland ZE1 0LU, T01595-693434, www.visitshetland.com.
Western Isles Tourist Board, 26 Cromwell St, Stornoway, Isle of Lewis HS1 2DD, T01851-703088, www.witb.co.uk.

Useful websites

The official Scottish Tourist Board site and the various area tourist board sites have information on accommodation, transport and tourist sights as well as outdoor activities such as walking, skiing, fishing etc.

Travel and leisure

www.britannia.com A huge UK travel site. Click on 'Scotland guide' for a massive selection of subjects plus links to various sites including newspapers.
www.bbc.co.uk The UK's most popular site with an excellent what's on guide.
www.whatsonwhen.com Has a huge range of upcoming events around the world.
www.scotland.net Scotland online with good information on golf, walking and climbing and also features.
www.travelscotland.co.uk Run in conjunction with the Scottish Tourist Board, with magazine-style features and reviews.
www.scotland-info.co.uk Good for local information on hotels, shops and restaurants.

www.aboutscotland.co.uk Useful for accommodation.
www.uktrail.com Provides comprehensive information on transport and hostels.
www.go-edinburgh.co.uk The official site for the all the Edinburgh festivals.
www.edinburghevents.com Lists everything taking place in the capital.
www.clyde-valley.com/glasgow Covers all Glasgow sights and updated regularly.
www.hebrides.com Comprehensive site for the islands.

Outdoors
www.walkscotland.com Suggested walks, contacts and practical information for hikers and climbers.
www.walkingworld.com Perhaps the best directory of British walks though you have to pay to download their detailed maps.
www.golfscotland.co.uk Everything you need to know on golf in Scotland.
www.ski.scotland.net Information on ski conditions at all centres, updated daily.
www.born2ski.com and **www.ifyouski.com** Sites have Scotland pages with useful ratings.
www.sustrans.org.uk Official site of the charity that co-ordinates the National Cycle Network. The clickable map lets you zoom in on sections of the route.
www.cycling.visitscotland.com Excellent site; even shows how steep the climbs are.
www.goodbeachguide.co.uk How to check your kids won't be bathing in sewage, lists facilities and activities for over 400 recommended UK beaches.

History, politics and culture
www.electricscotland.com Massive directory with lots of information on clans, travel etc. In-depth history pages.
www.ceolas.org Celtic music site with lots of information and sounds.
www.scotchwhisky.net Everything you ever wanted to know about the 'water of life'.
www.scotland.gov.uk Updates on government affairs in Scotland.
www.scottish.parliament.uk Easy to use guide to the Scottish Parliament.
www.geo.ed.ac.uk/home/scotland/scotland/html Background information on history, politics and geography.

Language

Though the vast majority of Scots speak English, to the untutored ear the Scottish dialect can be hard to understand, as many words and expressions are derived not from English but from Lowland Scots, or lallans, which is now recognized as a separate language as opposed to simply a regional dialect. In the Highlands and Islands, the accent is very clear and easy to understand.

Scotland's oldest surviving language is Scottish Gaelic (*Gaidhlig*, pronounced 'Gallic'). Often referred to as the national language, it has been spoken the longest. Introduced to the country by Irish immigrants in the third and fourth centuries, its use soon spread and became well established. The language is spoken by about 85,000 people in Scotland (about two per cent of the population). This is in the Gaidhealtachd, the Gaelic-speaking areas of the Outer Hebrides, parts of Skye, and a few of the smaller Hebridean islands. Some road signs in the Highlands and Islands are in Gaelic. Gaelic is one of the Celtic languages, which has included Irish Gaelic, Manx, Welsh, Cornish and Breton. Today only Scottish and Irish Gaelic, Welsh and Breton survive. Those wishing to teach themselves Gaelic could start with the BBC *CanSeo* cassette and book. A good phrasebook is *Everyday Gaelic* by Morag MacNeill (Gairm). Also, the Celtic Heritage Centre, based on Arran, has a great store of Gaelic and Celtic information and documents; they publish a quarterly newsletter. *Macbain's Etymological Dictionary of the Gaelic language* contains a wealth of words and information.

More people in Orkney speak Cantonese than Gaelic; and it is widely believed that people from Inverness speak the clearest English in the UK.

Disabled travellers

For travellers with disabilities, visiting Scotland independently can be a difficult business. While most theatres, cinemas and modern tourist attractions are accessible to wheelchairs, accommodation is more problematic. Many large, new hotels do have disabled suites, but will charge more, and most B&Bs, guest houses and smaller hotels are not designed to cater for people with disabilities. Public transport is just as bad, though newer buses have lower steps for easier access and some ScotRail intercity services now accommodate wheelchair-users in comfort. Taxis, as opposed to minicabs, all carry wheelchair ramps, and if a driver says he or she can't take a wheelchair, it's because they're too lazy to fetch the ramp.

Wheelchair users, and blind or partially sighted people are automatically given 30-50 per cent discount on train fares, and those with other disabilities are eligible for the Disabled Person's Railcard, which costs £14 per year and gives a third off most tickets. There are no reductions on buses however.

If you are disabled you should contact the travel officer of your national support organization. They can provide literature or put you in touch with travel agents specializing in tours for the disabled. The **Scottish Tourist Board** produces a guide, *Accessible Scotland*, for disabled travellers, and many local tourist offices can provide accessibility details for their area. A useful website is www.atlholidays.com which specializes in organizing holidays for disabled travellers, recommends hotels with good facilities and can also arrange rental cars and taxis.

Useful organizations include: **Disability Scotland**, Princes House, 5 Shandwick Place, Edinburgh EH2 4RG, T0131-2298632; **The Royal Association for Disability and Rehabilitation (RADAR)**, Unit 12, City Forum, 250 City Road, London, EC1V 8AF, T020-72503222, www.radar.org.uk, is a good source of advice and information, and produces an annual guide on travelling in the UK (£7.50 including P&P); and **The Holiday Care Service**, second floor, Imperial Building, Victoria Road, Horley, Surrey RH6 7PZ, T-1293-774535, provides free lists of accessible accommodation and travel in the UK.

Gay and lesbian travellers

Scotland is generally tolerant of homosexuality, though overt displays of affection outside 'gay' venues are not advised. Edinburgh in particular has a flourishing gay scene and is a relativley easy place for gay travellers to feel safe and comfortable. Don't assume that because men are wearing skirts in the Highlands that people take a relaxed attitude to homosexuality. The same prejudices apply as elsewhere in rural parts of the UK.

The magazine, *Gay Scotland*, is a good source of information, as is the **Gay Switchboard**, T0131-5564049, or the **Lesbian Line**, T0131-5570751. For a good selection of gay events and venues, check out www.whatsonwhen.com or the UK gay-scene index at www.queenscene.com which has news on clubs, gay groups, accommodation, events, HIV/AIDS and cultural and ethical issues. Other good sites include: www.gaybritain.co.uk and www.gaytravel.co.uk. For nightlife, see pages 112 and 167.

Student travellers

Discount passes

There are various official youth/student ID cards available. The most useful is the **International Student ID Card (ISIC)**. For a mere £6 the ISIC card gains you access to the exclusive world of student travel with a series of discounts, including most forms of local transport, up to 30 per cent off international airfares, cheap or free admission to museums, theatres and other attractions, and cheap meals in some restaurants. There's also free or discounted internet access, and a website, www.usitworld.com, where you can check the latest student travel deals. You'll also receive the ISIC handbook, which ensures you get the most out of services available. ISIC cards are available at student travel centres, see page 30. US and Canadian citizens are also entitled to emergency medical coverage, and there's a 24-hour hotline to call in the event of medical, legal or financial emergencies.

If you're aged under 26 but not a student, you can apply for a **Federation of International Youth Travel Organisations (FIYTO)** card, or a **Euro 26 Card**, which give you much the same discounts. If you're 25 or younger you can qualify for a **Go-25 Card**, which gives you the same benefits as an ISIC card. These discount cards are issued by student travel agencies and hostelling organizations, see page 45.

Studying in Scotland

If you want to study in Scotland you must first prove you can support and accommodate yourself without working and without recourse to public support. Your studies should take up at least 15 hours a week for a minimum of six months. Once you are studying, you are allowed to do 20 hours of casual work per week in the term time and you can work full-time during the holidays. In North America full-time students can obtain temporary work or study permits through the **Council of International Education Exchange (CIEE)**, 205 E 42nd Street, New York, NY 10017, T212-8222600, www.ciee.org. For more details, contact your nearest British embassy, consulate or high commission, or the **Foreign and Commonwealth Office** in London, T020-7270 1500.

Travelling with children

Visiting Scotland with kids is no different from other parts of the UK, though you may find that the locals are just that little bit more tolerant and helpful, especially in the Highlands and other rural parts. Teenagers in particular should have no reason to moan as there are all manner of thrill-a-minute adventure sports to try, see Activities and sports on page 55 for more details.

If you're travelling with babies and/or toddlers you may find eating out a frustrating experience in some establishments, though the days of families being banished to some grubby room at the back, well out of the way of other diners, are, thankfully, a thing of the past in most places. The attitude to breastfeeding, while some way behind the likes of Scandinavia, is more relaxed than the US and becoming ever more civilized and progressive. In major towns and cities, Italian restaurants are generally more child-friendly. The child may not be quite be king here, but at least they are allowed to be seen and heard.

If you are flying inform the airline in advance that you're travelling with a baby or toddler, and check out the facilities when booking as these vary with each aircraft. British Airways now has a special seat for under 2s; check which aircraft have been fitted with them when booking. Pushchairs can be taken on as hand luggage or stored in the hold. Skycots are available on long-haul flights. Take snacks and toys for in-flight entertainment, and remember that swallowing food or drinks during take-off and landing will help prevent ear problems.

A recommended website is www.babygoes2.com, while www.mumsnet.com/bigissues/travel.html, is useful for parents with older kids. If you're visiting Edinburgh check out www.edinburgh.org/kids/intro.html, which was designed by kids at a local school.

Women travellers

Travelling in Scotland is neither easier nor more difficult for women than travelling in other parts of the UK. Generally speaking, Scots are friendly and courteous and even lone women travellers should experience nothing unpleasant, however, common sense dictates that single women would do well to avoid hitching on their own in the middle of nowhere. In the main cities and larger towns, the usual precautions need to be taken and you should avoid walking in quiet, unlit streets and parks at night.

Working in Scotland

Citizens of European Union (EU) countries can live and work in Britain freely without a visa, but non-EU residents need a permit to work legally. This can be difficult to obtain without the backing of an established company or employer in the UK. Also, visitors from Commonwealth countries who are aged between 17 and 27 may apply for a working holiday-maker's visa which permits them to stay in the UK for up to two years and work on a casual basis (ie non-career oriented). These certificates are only available from British embassies and consulates abroad, see page 27, and you must have proof of a valid return or onward ticket, as well as means of support during your stay. Commonwealth citizens with a parent or grandparent born in the UK can apply for a Certificate of Entitlement to the Right of Abode, allowing them to work in Britain.

Pick up a copy of What Scotland, a free guide for independent travellers living and working in Scotland; T020-7384 9330.

An option for citizens of some non-commonwealth countries is to visit on an au pair placement in order to learn English by living with an English-speaking family for a maximum of two years. Au pairs must be aged between 17 and 27, and come from one of the following countries: Andorra, Bosnia-Herzegovina, Croatia, Cyprus, Czech Republic, The Faroes, Greenland, Hungary, Macedonia, Malta, Monaco, San Marino, Slovak Republic, Slovenia, Switzerland or Turkey. This can be a good way to learn English, but check out the precise conditions of your placement before taking it up.

Those wishing to devote their time helping the environment, or simply gain some valuable experience can begin their search with the following organizations: **The British Trust for conservation volunteers**, 33 St Mary's Street, Wallingford, Oxon, OX10 OEU, T01491-821600, www.btcv.org, get fit in the 'green gym', planting hedges, creating wildlife gardens or improving footpaths; **Earthwatch**, 57 Woodstock Road, Oxford, OX2 6HJ, T01865-318838, team up with scientists studying our furry friends; **Jubilee Sailing Trust**, Hazel Road, Southampton, T023-8044 9108, www.jst.org.uk, work on deck on an adventure holiday; and **Waterway Recovery Group**, PO Box 114, Rickmansworth, WD3 1ZY, T01923-711114, www.wrg.org.uk, help restore a derelict canal.

Also check out the organizations listed on page 63, as well as the Scottish Youth Hostel Association (SYHA), see page 45.

Before you travel

Getting in

Visas

Visa regulations are subject to change, so it is essential to check with your local British embassy, high commission or consulate before leaving home. Citizens of all

European countries – except Albania, Bosnia, Bulgaria, Macedonia, Romania, Slovakia, Yugoslavia and all former Soviet republics (other than the Baltic states) – require only a passport to enter Britain and can generally stay for up to three months. Citizens of Australia, Canada, New Zealand, South Africa or the USA can stay for up to six months, providing they have a return ticket and sufficient funds to cover their stay. Citizens of most other countries require a visa from the commission or consular office in the country of application.

The **Foreign Office**'s excellent website, www.fco.gov.uk, provides details of British immigration and visa requirements. Also the **Immigration Advisory Service (IAS)**, County House, 190 Great Dover Street, London SE1 4YB, T020-7357 6917, www.vois.org.uk, offers free and confidential advice to anyone applying for entry clearance into the UK.

For visa extensions contact the **Home Office, Immigration and Nationality Department**, Lunar House, Wellesley Road, Croydon, London CR9, T020 86860688, before your existing visa expires. Citizens of Australia, Canada, New Zealand, South Africa or the USA wishing to stay longer than six months will need an Entry Clearance Certificate from the British High Commission in their country. For more details, contact your nearest British embassy, consulate or high commission, or the Foreign and Commonwealth Office in London, T020-72701500.

Customs

Visitors from EU countries do not have to make a declaration to customs on entry into the UK. The limits for duty-paid goods from within the EU are 800 cigarettes, or 1kg of tobacco, 10 litres of spirits, 20 litres of fortified wine, 90 litres of wine and 110 litres of beer. There is no longer any duty-free shopping. Visitors from non-EU countries are allowed to import 200 cigarettes, or 250 grams of tobacco, two litres of wine, and two litres of fortified wine or one litre of spirits. There are various import restrictions, most of which should not affect the average tourist. There are tight quarantine restrictions which apply to animals brought from overseas (except for Ireland). For more information on British import regulations, contact HM Customs and Excise, Dorset House, Stamford Street, London SE1 9PJ, T020-79283344, www.hmce.gov.uk.

Many goods in Britain are subject to a Value Added Tax (VAT) of 17.5 per cent, with the major exception of books and food. Visitors from non-EU countries can save money through the Retail Export Scheme, which allows a refund of VAT on goods to be taken out of the country. Note that not all shops are participants in the scheme and that VAT cannot be reclaimed on hotel bills or other services.

British embassies

For details of foreign consulates in Scotland, see pages 121 and 177.

Australia, High Commission: Commonwealth Av, Yarralumla, Canberra, ACT 2600, T02-62706666, www.uk.emb.gov.au.

Canada, High Commission: 80 Elgin St, Ottowa, K1P 5K7, T613-2371530, www.bis-canada.org.

France, 9 Av Hoche, 8e, Paris, 01-42663810.

Germany, Friedrich-Ebert-Allee 77, 53113, Bonn, T0228-234061.

Ireland, 29 Merrion Rd, Ballsbridge, Dublin 4, T01-2053700.

Israel, 192 Hayarkon St, Tel Aviv, T3-7251222, www.britemb.org.il/.

Japan, 1 Ichiban-cho, Chiyoda-ku, Tokyo 102-8381, T(3) 5211 1100.

Netherlands, Koningslaan 44, 1075AE Amsterdam, T20-6764343.

New Zealand, High Commission: 44 Hill St, Wellington, T04-4726049, www.brithighcomm.org.nz.

South Africa, High Commission: 91 Parliament St, Cape Town 8001, T21-4617220.

Spain, C/Fernando el Santo 16, 28010 Madrid, T91-7008200.

USA, 3100 Massachusetts Av NW, Washington DC 20008, T202-4621340, www.britain-info.org.

What to take

You'll be able to find everything you could possibly need for your trip in Scottish cities, so if you wish you can pack light and buy stuff as you go along. Given the climate, you will more than likely need warm and waterproof clothing, whatever the time of year. Also bring light clothes in the summer, preferably long-sleeved to protect you from the midges, see page 62. If you're planning on doing some hillwalking you should come properly prepared, as the weather can change rapidly in the mountains, see also page 56. It's worth treating your boots with a waterproofing agent as some of the trails cross boggy ground.

If you are backpacking, a sleeping bag is useful in hostels, and a sleeping sheet with a pillow cover is needed if staying in Scottish Youth Hostel Association (SYHA) hostels (or you can hire one there). A padlock can also be handy for locking your bag if it has to be stored in a hostel for any length of time. Other useful items include an alarm clock (for those early ferry departures), an adaptor plug for electrical appliances, an elastic clothes line and, if you're hillwalking or camping, a Swiss Army knife, torch (flashlight) and compass are essential.

Insurance

It's a good idea to take out some form of travel insurance, wherever you're travelling from. This should cover you for theft or loss of possessions and money, the cost of all medical and dental treatment, cancellation of flights, delays in travel arrangements, accidents, missed departures, lost baggage, lost passport, and personal liability and legal expenses. There are a variety of policies to choose from, so it's best to shop around to get the best price. Your travel agent can also advise you on the best deals available. **STA Travel**, www.statravel.co.uk, with branches nationwide, and other reputable student travel organizations often offer good-value travel policies. Another company worth calling for a quote is **Columbus Direct**, T020-7375 0011. Older travellers should note that some companies won't cover people over 65 years old, or may charge high premiums. The best policies for older travellers are offered by **Age Concern**, T01883-346964. Travellers from North America can try the **International Student Insurance Service (ISIS)**, which is available through **STA Travel**, T1-800-7770112, www.sta-travel.com. Some other recommended travel insurance companies in North America include **Travel Guard**, T1-800-8261300, www.noelgroup.com; **Access America**, T1-800-2848300; **Travel Insurance Services**, T1-800-9371387; and **Travel Assistance International**, T1-800-8212828.

Points to note: you should always read the small print carefully. Some policies exclude 'dangerous activities' such as scuba diving, skiing, horse riding or even trekking. Not all policies cover ambulance, helicopter rescue or emergency flights home. Find out if your policy pays medical expenses direct to the hospital or doctor, or if you have to pay and then claim the money back later. If the latter applies, make sure you keep all records. Whatever your policy, if you are unfortunate enough to have something stolen, make sure you get a copy of the police report, as you will need this to substantiate your claim. See page 66 for details of medical insurance.

Money

The British currency is the pound sterling (£), divided into 100 pence (p). Coins come in denominations of 1p, 2p, 5p, 10p, 20p, 50p, £1 and £2. Bank of England banknotes are legal tender in Scotland, in addition to those issued by the Bank of Scotland, Royal Bank of Scotland and Clydesdale Bank. These Scottish banknotes (bills) come in denominations of £5, £10, £20, £50 and £100 and are legal tender in the rest of Britain, though some less intelligent shopkeepers south of the border may be reluctant to accept them.

Banks

Most towns and villages in Scotland have a branch of at least one of the big four High Street banks – **Bank of Scotland, Royal Bank of Scotland, Clydesdale** and **TSB Scotland**. Bank opening hours are Monday to Friday from 0930 to between 1600 and 1700. Some larger branches may also be open later on Thursdays and on Saturday mornings. Banks are usually the best places to change money and cheques. You can withdraw cash from selected banks and ATMs (or cashpoints as they are called in Britain) with your cash card. In the Highlands, and especially on the islands, ATMs are few and far between and it is important to keep a ready supply of cash at all times. Outside the ferry ports on most of the smaller islands, you won't find an ATM.

In small and remote places, and on some islands, there may only be a mobile bank which runs to a set timetable. This timetable will be available from the local post office.

Your bank will give you a list of locations where you can use your card. **Bank of Scotland** and **Royal Bank** take **Lloyds** and **Barclays** cash cards; **Clydesdale** takes **HSBC** and **National Westminster** cards. **Bank of Scotland, Clydesdale** and most building society cashpoints are part of the Link network and accept all affiliated cards. See also Credit cards below. In addition to ATMs, bureaux de change can be used outside banking hours. These can be found in most city centres and also at the main airports and train stations. Note that some charge high commissions for changing cheques. Those at international airports, however, often charge less than banks and will change pound sterling cheques for free. Avoid changing money or cheques in hotels, as the rates are usually very poor.

Credit cards

Most hotels, shops and restaurants in Scotland accept the major credit cards such as MasterCard and Visa and, less frequently, Amex, though some places may charge for using them. They may be less useful in more remote rural areas and smaller establishments such as B&Bs which will often only accept cash or cheques.

Visa card holders can use the **Bank of Scotland, Clydesdale Bank, Royal Bank of Scotland** and **TSB** ATMs; Access/MasterCard holders can use the Royal Bank and Clydesdale; Amex card holders can use the Bank of Scotland.

Travellers' cheques

The safest way to carry money is in travellers' cheques. These are available for a small commission from all major banks. **American Express (Amex), Visa** and **Thomas Cook** cheques are widely accepted and are the most commonly issued by banks. You'll normally have to pay commission again when you cash each cheque. This will usually be one percent, or a flat rate. No commission is payable on Amex cheques cashed at Amex offices. Make sure to keep a record of the cheque numbers and the cheques you've cashed separate from the cheques themselves, so that you can get a full refund of all uncashed cheques should you lose them. It's best to bring sterling cheques to avoid changing currencies twice. Also note that in Britain travellers' cheques are rarely accepted outside banks, so you'll need to cash them in advance and keep a good supply of ready cash.

Though using a credit/debit card is by far the easiest way of keeping in funds, you must check with your bank what the total charges will be; this can be as high as 4-5 per cent in some cases.

Money transfers

If you need money urgently, the quickest way to have it sent to you is to have it wired to the nearest bank via **Western Union**, T0800-833833, or **Moneygram**, T0800-894887. Charges are on a sliding scale; ie it will cost proportionately less to wire out more money. Money can also be wired by **Thomas Cook** or **American Express**, though this may take a day or two, or transferred via a bank draft, but this can take up to a week.

Cost of travelling

Scotland can be an expensive place to visit, though there is plenty of budget accommodation available and backpackers will be able to keep their costs down. Edinburgh is the most expensive city, and prices are also higher in more remote parts of the Highlands and Islands. Petrol in particular is very expensive in the Highlands and Islands, where it can cost up to 10p per litre more than in the central Lowlands. Accommodation and restaurant prices also tend to be higher in more popular destinations and during the busy summer months.

The minimum daily budget required, if you're staying in hostels or cheap B&Bs, cycling or hitching, and cooking your own meals, will be around £25-30 per person per day. If you start using public transport and eating out occasionally that will rise to around £35-40. Those staying in slightly more upmarket B&Bs or guest houses, eating out every evening at pubs or modest restaurants and visiting tourist attractions, such as castles or museums, can expect to pay around £45-60 per day. If you also want to hire a car and use ferries to visit the islands, and eat well, then costs will rise considerably and you'll be looking at least £75 per person per day. Single travellers will have to pay more than half the cost of a double room in most places, and should budget on spending around £60 per person of what a couple would spend.

Getting there

Air

Generally speaking, the cheapest and quickest way to travel to Scotland from outside the UK is by air. There are good links to Edinburgh and Glasgow, with direct flights from many European cities, and direct flights from North America to Glasgow. There are also flights from a few European cities to Aberdeen and Inverness. There are no direct flights from North America to Edinburgh; these are usually routed via London or Dublin. There are also daily flights from Ireland and regular flights to most Scottish airports from other parts of the UK. There are no direct flights to Scotland from Australia, New Zealand, South Africa or Japan. You will have to get a connection from London. Those wishing to visit England as well should note that it is generally cheaper to fly to Scotland from the rest of Britain if you use an Airpass bought in your own country. This is offered by British Airways and British Midland. Airpasses are valid only with an international scheduled flight ticket.

Buying your ticket

There is a mind-boggling number of outlets for buying your plane ticket, and finding the best deal can be a confusing business. Fares will depend on the season. Ticket prices to Scotland are highest from around early June to mid-September, which is the tourist high season. Fares drop in the months either side of the peak season – mid-September to early November and mid-April to early June. They are cheapest in the low season, from November to April, when very few visitors are willing to brave the Scottish winter. The exception is during Christmas and New Year when seats are at a premium and prices rise sharply. It's also worth noting that flying at the weekend is normally more expensive. It is always worth spending a bit of time researching the various options available and starting early, as some of the cheapest tickets have to be bought months in advance and the most popular flights sell out quickly. One of the best ways of finding a good deal is to use the internet. The following **websites** are worth trying: www.expedia.co.uk, www.lastminute.com, www.cheapflights.co.uk, www.travelocity.com, wwww.ebookers.com and www.opodo.com.

Return tickets are usually a lot cheaper than buying two one-way tickets. **Round-the-World (RTW) tickets** can also be a real bargain, and may even work out cheaper than a return fare. RTW prices start at around £900 (US$1,500), depending on the season. Note that it's easy to include London on a Round-the-World itinerary, but a stop in Scotland may be harder to arrange and may involve backtracking. It may be cheaper and easier to buy the London to Scotland leg separately or to travel overland to Scotland from London.

When trying to find the best deal, make sure you check the route, the duration of the journey, stopovers allowed, any travel restrictions such as minimum and maximum periods away, and cancellation penalties. Many of the cheapest flights are sold by small **agencies**, most of whom are honest and reliable, but there may be some risks involved with buying tickets at rock-bottom prices. You should avoid paying too much money in advance, and you could check with the airline directly to make sure you have a reservation. You may be safer choosing a better-known travel agent, such as **STA**, 27 Forrest Road, Edinburgh, T0131-2267747; 86 Old Brompton Road, London, SW7 3LH, T020-73616161, www.statravel.co.uk, or **Trailfinders**, 194

Getting there

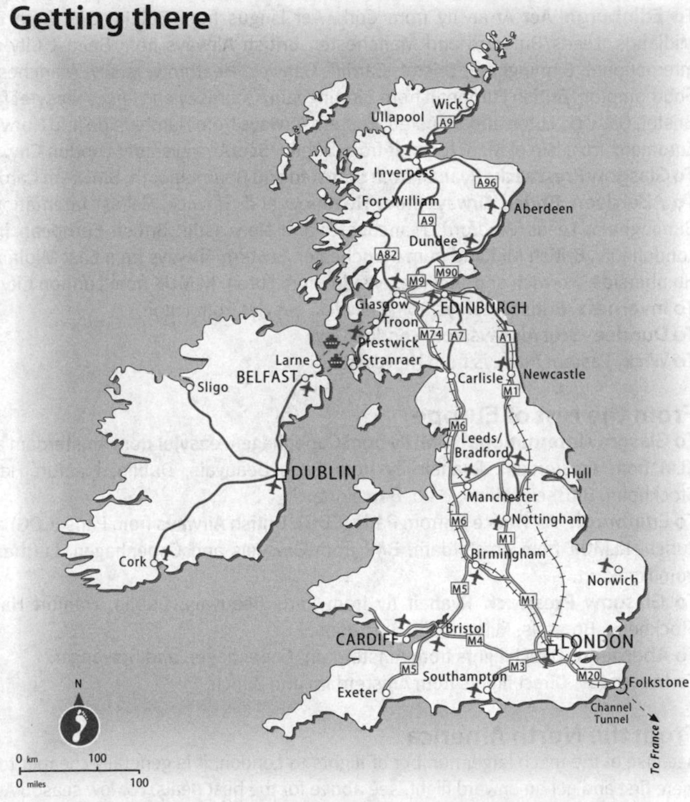

 Kensington High Street, London W8 6FT, T020-79383939. Both are specialists in low-cost student/youth flights and tours, also good for student IDs and insurance. **STA** have other branches in London, as well as in Brighton, Bristol, Cambridge, Leeds, Manchester, Newcastle-upon-Tyne and Oxford and on many university campuses.

From the UK and Ireland

There are direct flights to Scotland's three main airports – Glasgow, Edinburgh and Aberdeen – almost hourly from London Heathrow, Gatwick, Stansted and Luton airports. There are also daily flights from provincial UK airports and from Dublin. To fly on to the smaller airports, you'll need to change planes, see page 39 for domestic flights. The cheapest flights leave from London Luton or Stansted, plus a few provincial airports, with **Ryanair** and **easyJet**. If you book on-line, fares can be as little as £5 one-way during promotions, but usually you can expect to fly for under £50 return. These tickets are often subject to rigid restrictions, but the savings can make the extra effort worthwhile. Cheaper tickets usually have to be bought at least a week in advance, apply to only a few midweek flights, and must include a Saturday night stayover. They are also non-refundable, or only partly refundable, and non-transferable. A standard flexible and refundable fare from London to Glasgow or Edinburgh will cost at least £150-200 return. London to Glasgow and Edinburgh is roughly one hour.

To Glasgow International **British Airways** fly from Gatwick, Heathrow, Bristol, Southampton, Birmingham, Manchester, Cork and Isle of Man. **BMI** from Manchester, Heathrow, Leeds/Bradford. **easyJet** from Bristol, Belfast, Luton, Stansted. **BMI baby** from East Midlands.

To Edinburgh **Aer Arran** fly from Cork. **Aer Lingus** from Dublin. **BMI** from East Midlands, Leeds/Bradford and Manchester. **British Airways** from Belfast City and International, Birmingham, Bristol, Cardiff, Gatwick, Heathrow, Jersey, Manchester, Southampton. **British European** from Birmingham, Guernsey and Jersey. **easyJet** from Bristol, Gatwick, Luton and Stansted. **Eastern Airways** from Humberside and Norwich. **Euromanx** from Isle of Man. **Ryanair** from Dublin. **ScotAirways** from London City.

To Glasgow Prestwick **Ryanair** from Stansted and Bournemouth, **BMI** from Cardiff.

To Aberdeen **British Airways** from Heathrow and Gatwick, Belfast International, Birmingham, Leeds/Bradford, Manchester and Newcastle. **British European** from London City. **British Midland** from Manchester. **Eastern Airways** from East Midlands, Humberside, Norwich and Teeside. **easyJet** from Luton. **KLMUK** from London City.

To Inverness **British Airways** from Gatwick. **easyJet** from Luton.

To Dundee **Scot Airways** from London City.

To Wick **Eastern Airways** from Newcastle.

From the rest of Europe

To Glasgow International **BMI** fly from Copenhagen, **easyJet** from Amsterdam and **KLM** from Amsterdam. **Ryanair** fly from Paris Beauvais, Dublin, Franfurt Hahn, Stockholm, Brussels, Milan, Oslo, Barcelona.

To Edinburgh **Air France** fly from Paris (CDG). **British Airways** from Paris (CDG) and Zurich. **KLMUK** from Amsterdam. **BMI** from Brussels and Copenhagen. **Lufthansa** from Frankfurt.

To Glasgow Prestwick **Ryanair** fly from Paris Beauvais, Dublin, Franfurt Hahn, Stockholm, Brussels, Milan, Oslo, Barcelona.

To Aberdeen Direct flights from Amsterdam, Copenhagen and Stavangar.

To Inverness Direct flights from Amsterdam and Zurich.

From the North America

Because of the much larger number of flights to London, it is generally cheaper to fly there first and get an onward flight, see above for the best deals. For low season Apex fares expect to pay around US$400-600 from New York and other East Coast cities, and around US$500-700 from the West Coast. Prices rise to around US$700-900 from New York, and up to US$1,000 from the West Coast in the summer months. Low season Apex fares from Toronto and Montreal cost around CAN$600-700, and from Vancouver around CAN$800-900, rising to CAN$750-950 and CAN$950-1150 respectively during the summer. East Coast USA to Glasgow takes around six to seven hours direct. To London it takes seven hours. From West Coast an additional four hours.

To Glasgow International Continental Airlines fly from New York, **American Airlines** fly from Chicago and **Air Canada** from Toronto.

Airline contact details

Aer Arran, T0800-5872324, www.skyroad.com.
Aer Lingus, T08450-844444, www.aerlingus.com.
Air Canada, T1-800-7763000, www.aircanada.ca.
Air France, T08450-845444, www.airfrance.com.
American Airlines, T1-800-4337300, www.americanair.com.
BMI, T0870-6070555, www.flybmi.com.
British Airways, T0870-8509850, www.britishairways.com.
British European, T0870-5676676, www.flybe.com.
Continental, T1-800-2310856, www.flycontinental.com.
Eastern Airways, T01652-680600, www.easternairways.com.
easyJet, T0870-60 0000, www.easyjet.com.
Emirates, T0870 243 2222, www.emirates.com/uk.
Euromanx, T0870-1660102, www.euromanx.com.
Icelandair, T08457-581111, www.icelandair.com.
KLMUK, T0870-5074047, www.klm.com.
Lufthansa, T08457-737747, www.lufthansa.com.
Ryanair, T0871-2460016, www.ryanair.com.
ScotAirways, T0870-6060707, www.scotairways.com.

Rail

There are fast and frequent rail services from London and other main towns and cities in England to Glasgow, Edinburgh, Aberdeen and Inverness. Journey time from London is about 4½ hours to Edinburgh, five hours to Glasgow, seven hours to Aberdeen and eight hours to Inverness. Two companies operate direct services from London to Scotland: **GNER** trains leave from Kings' Cross and run up the east coast to Edinburgh, Aberdeen and Inverness; and **Virgin** trains leave from Euston and run up the west coast to Glasgow. **Scotrail** operate the *Caledonian Sleeper* service if you wish to travel overnight from London Euston to Aberdeen, Edinburgh, Glasgow, Inverness and Fort William. This runs nightly from Sunday to Friday.

Eurostar, T08705-186186, www.eurostar.com, operates high-speed trains through the Channel Tunnel to London Waterloo from Paris (three hours), Brussels (two hours 40 minutes) and Lille (two hours). You then have to change trains, and stations, for the onward journey north to Scotland. If you're driving from continental Europe you could take *Le Shuttle*, which runs 24 hours a day, 365 days a year, and takes you and your car from Calais to Folkestone in 35-45 minutes. Fares range from £84 to £165 per carload, depending on how far in advance you book or when you travel, T08705-353535 for bookings.

Enquiries and booking

National Rail Enquiries, T08457-484950, are quick and courteous with information on rail services and fares but not always accurate, so double check. They can't book tickets but will provide you with the relevant telephone number, see also below. The website **www.qjump.co.uk** is a bit hit-and-miss but generally fast and efficient and shows you all the various options on any selected journey, while **www.thetrain line.co.uk** also has its idiosyncrasies but shows prices clearly. For advance credit/debit card bookings, T08457-550033. **GNER**, T08457-225225, www.gner.co.uk; **Virgin**, T08457-222333; and **ScotRail**, T08457-550033, www.scotrail.co.uk.

Fares

To describe the system of rail ticket pricing as complicated is a huge understatement and impossible to explain here. There are many and various discounted fares, but restrictions are often prohibitive, which explains the long queues and delays at ticket counters in railway stations. The cheapest ticket is a Super Apex, which must be booked at least two weeks in advance, though this is not available on all journeys. Next cheapest is an Apex ticket which has to be booked at least seven days before travelling, and again tickets are restricted in number. Other discount tickets include a Saver return, which can be used on all trains, and a Super Saver, which costs slightly less but cannot be used on a Friday or during peak times. For example, a GNER London-Edinburgh Saver return costs £82.50, while an Apex is £51. A standard return with Scotrail on this route is £65. All discount tickets should be booked as quickly as possible as they are often sold out weeks, or even months, in advance, especially Apex and Super Apex tickets. The latter tickets guarantee seat reservations, but Saver and Super Saver tickets do not. These can be secured by paying an extra £1. A Caledonian Sleeper Apex return ticket from London to Edinburgh or Glasgow costs £89, while an open return is £125.

Railcards

There are a variety of railcards which give discounts on fares for certain groups. Cards are valid for one year and most are available from main stations. You need two passport photos and proof of age or status.

Young Person's Railcard For those aged 16-25 or full-time students in the UK. Costs £18 and gives 33 per cent discount on most train tickets and some ferry services.

Senior Citizen's Railcard For those aged over 60. Same price and discount as above.

Disabled Person's Railcard Costs £14 and gives 33 per cent discount to a disabled person and one other. Pick up application form from stations and send it to Disabled Person's Railcard Office, PO Box 1YT, Newcastle-upon-Tyne, NE99 1YT. It may take up to 21 days to process, so apply in advance.

Family Railcard Costs £20 and gives 33 per cent discount on most tickets (20 per cent on others) for up to four adults travelling together, and 81 per cent discount for up to four children.

Road

Bus/coach

Road links to Scotland are excellent, and a number of companies offer express coach services day and night. This is the cheapest form of travel to Scotland. The main operator between England and Scotland is **National Express**, T08705-808080, www.nationalexpress.com. There are direct buses from most British cities to Edinburgh, Glasgow, Aberdeen and Inverness. Tickets can be bought at bus stations or from a huge number of agents throughout the country. Fares from London to Glasgow and Edinburgh with **National Express** start at around £28 return for an economy advance return. Fares to Aberdeen and Inverness are a little higher. The London to Glasgow/Edinburgh journey takes around eight hours, while it takes around 11-12 hours for the trip to Aberdeen and Inverness. From Manchester takes around 6½ hours and costs from £21. See also pages 72 and 126.

Touching down

Business hours 0900-1700.
Electricity The current in Britain is 240V AC. Plugs have three square pins and adapters are widely available.
Emergencies For police, fire brigade, ambulance and, in certain areas, mountain rescue or coastguard, dial 999.
Laundry Most towns have coin-operated launderettes. The average cost for a wash and tumble dry is about £3. A service wash, where someone will do your washing for you, costs around £4-5. In more remote areas, you'll have to rely on hostel and campsite facilities.
Time Greenwich Mean Time (GMT) is used from late October to late March, after which time the clocks go forward an hour to British Summer Time (BST). GMT is five hours ahead of US Eastern Standard Time and 10 hours behind Australian Eastern Standard Time.
Telephone To call Scotland from overseas, dial 011 from USA and Canada, 0011 from Australia and 00 from New Zealand, followed by 44, then the area code, minus the first zero, then the number.
Useful numbers: operator T100; international operator T155; directory enquiries T192; overseas directory enquiries T153.
Toilets Public toilets are found at all train and bus stations and motorway service stations. They may charge 20p, but are generally clean, with disabled and baby-changing facilities. Those in town centres are often pretty grim.
Weights and measures Imperial and metric systems are both in use. Distances on roads are measured in miles and yards, drinks poured in pints and gills, but generally, the metric system is used elsewhere.

Car

There are two main routes to Scotland from the south. In the east the A1 runs to Edinburgh and in the west the M6 and A74(M) runs to Glasgow. The journey north from London to either city takes around eight to 10 hours. The A74(M) route to Glasgow is dual carriageway all the way. A slower and more scenic route is to head off the A1 and take the A68 through the Borders to Edinburgh. There's an Autoshuttle Express service to transport your car overnight between England and Scotland and vice versa while you travel by rail or air. For further information T08705-133714; reservations T08705-502309. See also Getting around page 41.

Sea

There are direct routes to Scotland from Europe on the **Smyril Line** (Aberdeen, T01224-572615; Lerwick, T01595-690845, www.smyril-line.com) service to Lerwick (Shetland) from Norway (Bergen), Iceland (Seydisfjordur) and the Faroe Islands (Torshavn). It sails from mid-May to early September only once a week and takes 12 hours. A sleeping berth one way from Norway and Faroe Islands costs from £68 in high season. You then have to get from Lerwick to Aberdeen. **Northlink Ferries,** www.northlinkferries.co.uk, sail from Lerwick to Aberdeen, see page 590.

Ferries also sail from Zeebrugge in Belgium to Rosyth in Fife, with **Norse Merchant Ferries,** T0870-6004321, www.norsemerchant.com.

P&O Irish Sea, T0870-2424777, www.poirishsea.com, has several crossings daily from Larne to Cairnryan (one hour) fares from £60 single for car and driver, and from Belfast to Troon (2½ hours) fares from £70 singles for car and driver). **Stena Line,**

 T0870-707070, www.stenaline.co.uk, run numerous ferries (three hours) and high-speed catamarans (1½ hours) from Belfast to Stranraer, fares from £90 single for car and driver. **Seacat Scotland** run daily services from Belfast to Troon (2½ hours; £250 for two adults and a car), T0870-5523523, www.seacat.co.uk.

Touching down

Airport information

Glasgow International, T0141-8871111, is eight miles west of the city, at junction 28 on the M8. It handles domestic and international flights. Terminal facilities include car hire, bank ATMs, currency exchange, left luggage, tourist information, T0141-8484440, and shops, restaurants and bars. There's also a Travel Centre, T0141-8484330, in the UK Arrivals concourse (open daily 0800-2200 in summer and till 1800 in winter), and a First Options Hotel and Travel Reservations desk in the International Arrivals concourse, T0141-8484731. **Glasgow Prestwick**, T01292-511000, www.gpia.co.uk, is 30 miles southwest of the city. For more details, see page 126. **Edinburgh airport**, T0131-3331000, has all facilities, including a tourist information desk, currency exchange, ATMs, restaurants and bars (first floor), shops (ground floor and first floor) and car hire desks in the terminal in the main UK arrivals area. For more details, see page 72. Scotland's other main airports are Aberdeen, T01224-722331, Inverness, T01463-232471, Prestwick, T01292-511006, Dundee, T01382-643242, and Wick, T01955-602215. See the relevant chapter for more information.

Tourist information

Tourist Information Centres

Tourist offices – called tourist information centres (TICs) – can be found in most Scottish towns. Their addresses, phone numbers and opening hours are listed in the relevant sections of this book. Opening hours vary depending on the time of year, and many of the smaller offices are closed during the winter months. All tourist offices provide information on accommodation, public transport, local attractions and restaurants, as well as selling books, local guides, maps and souvenirs. Many also have free street plans and leaflets describing local walks. They can also book accommodation for you, see page 43, for a small fee. Addresses of the main office of the Scottish Tourist Board and the Area Tourist Boards are given on page 21.

Museums, galleries and historic houses

Most of Scotland's tourist attractions, apart from the large museums and art galleries in the main cities, are open only from Easter to October. Full details of opening hours and admission charges are given in the relevant sections of this guide.

Over 100 of the country's most prestigious sights, and 185,000 acres of beautiful countryside, are cared for by the **National Trust for Scotland (NTS)**, 26-31 Charlotte Square, Edinburgh EH2 4ET, T0131-2439300, www.nts.org.uk. National Trust properties are indicated in this guide as 'NTS', and entry charges and opening hours are given for each property. If you're going to be visiting several sights during your stay, then it's worth taking annual membership. This costs £33, £12 for 25 years and under, and a family ticket £54. Touring passes for three, seven and 14 days; a 14-day pass costs £22 for an adult. YHA and HI members and student-card holders get 50 per cent discount on NTS admission charges.

Historic Scotland (HS), Longmore House, Salisbury Place, Edinburgh EH9 1SH, T0131-6688800, www.historic-scotland.gov.uk, manages more than 330 of Scotland's most important castles, monuments and other historic sites. Historic Scotland properties are indicated as 'HS', and admission charges and opening hours are also given in this guide. **Historic Scotland** offer an Explorer Ticket which allows free entry to 70 of their properties including Edinburgh and Stirling castles. A three-day pass (can be used over five consecutive days) costs £16 adult, £12 concession, family £32, seven-day pass (valid for 14 days) £22/16.50/44, 10-day pass (valid for 30 days) £25/19/50. It can save a lot of money, as entry to Edinburgh Castle alone is £8.50 per adult.

Many other historic buildings are owned by local authorities, and admission is cheap, or in many cases free. Most municipal art galleries and museums are free, as well as most state-owned museums, including those in Edinburgh and Glasgow. Most fee-paying attractions give a discount or concession for senior citizens, the unemployed, full-time students and children under 16 (those under five are admitted free everywhere). Proof of age or status must be shown. Many of Scotland's stately homes are still owned and occupied by the landed gentry, and admission charges are usually between £4 and £6.

Local customs and laws

Visitors will generally find their Scottish hosts to be friendly and obliging. In fact, the level of hospitality should be a significant part of the enjoyment of your trip. Those visiting the Outer Hebrides, need to be aware of the strict observance of the Sabbath on those islands.

Tipping

Believe it or not, people in Scotland do leave tips. In a restaurant you should leave a tip of 10-15 per cent if you are satisfied with the service. If the bill already includes a service charge, you needn't add a further tip. Tipping is not normal in pubs or bars. Taxi drivers will expect a tip for longer journeys, usually of around 10 per cent; and most hairdressers will also expect a tip. As in most other countries, porters, bellboys and waiters in more upmarket hotels rely on tips to supplement their meagre wages.

Responsible tourism

Sustainable or ecotourism has been described as: "...ethical, considerate or informed tourism where visitors can enjoy the natural, historical and social heritage of an area without causing adverse environmental, socio-economic or cultural impacts that compromise the long-term ability of that area and its people to provide a recreational resource for future generations and an income for themselves...".

Offset your flight's carbon emissions by paying to have the appropriate number of trees planted in sustainable forests through Future Forests, www.futureforests.com.

The Highlands and Islands of Scotland are beautiful, dramatic and wild, but also a living, working landscape and a fragile and vulnerable place. By observing the simple guidelines outlined on the previous page and behaving responsibly, you can help to minimise your impact and protect the natural and cultural heritage of this unique island environment so that it can continue to be appreciated by other visitors. Adhering to the Countryside Code will go along way in achieving this, see box.

For further information on what action is being taken either in Scotland, throughout UK or across the world to control against the negative aspects of tourism on the natural

The Countryside Code

1 Drive carefully and behave courteously to other motorists and cyclists on narrow, winding island roads. Park vehicles where they will not be a hazard or disruption to other motorists, residents or businesses.
2 Keep to public paths through farmland to minimise crop damage, and avoid 'short-cuts' on steep terrain to prevent soil erosion and damage to natural vegetation.
3 Litter is an eye-sore, harmful to farm animals, wildlife and the water supply – leave no waste and take all your rubbish home.
4 Protect wildlife, plants and trees.
5 Respect ancient monuments, buildings and sites of religious importance – do not vandalise or cause graffiti.
6 Many of the abandoned crofts are derelict and dangerous – keep out for your own safety.
7 Avoid damaging crops, walls, fences and farm equipment; fasten all gates.
8 Do not collect wildflowers, seabird eggs or historical artefacts.
9 Avoid pollution of water supplies - there are few toilets outside of villages so when walking in the countryside bury human waste and toilet paper in the ground and at least 30 metres from water courses.
10 Guard against risk of fire from matches, cigarettes, stoves and campfires.
11 Keep dogs under careful control, especially when near to sheep at lambing-time, seabird nesting sites at cliff edges and avoid dog-fouling in public places.
12 Respect the peace, solitude and tranquillity of the islands for others to enjoy – keep noise to a minimum.
13 The landscape can be spectacular but dangerous – take particular care along precipitous cliff edges, hilltops and slippery coastal rocks.
14 Stay away from working areas on the moors and hills during grouse-shooting, lambing season, deer culling and heather burning, and respect other locally or nationally imposed access restrictions.
15 Report any damage or environmental concerns to the landowner or the Scottish Environment Protection Agency (SEPA) (T01851-706477).
16 Be adequately prepared when you walk in the hills – check the weather forecast, carry warm, waterproof clothing and adequate food and water supplies, and know how to use a map and compass.

environment and traditional cultures, contact Tourism Concern in London, T020-77533330, or the Tourism and Environment Forum www.greentourism.org.uk.

Safety

Though Scottish cities have their fair share of crime, much of it is drug-related and confined to the more deprived peripheral areas. However, visitors to Scotland should take heed of the usual advice and avoid wandering around unlit city centre streets or parks alone at night. The major saftey issue when visiting the Highlands and more remote parts relates to the unpredictable weather conditions. Everyone should be aware of the need for caution and proper preparation when walking or climbing in the mountains. For more information on mountain safety, see page 56.

Getting around

Public transport is generally good and efficient. With a combination of buses, trains, ferries, walking, hiring a bike, plenty of time and careful planning, you can get almost anywhere. Most places in the Central Lowlands, between Glasgow, Edinburgh, Stirling, Perth and Dundee, are easily reached by bus and train. Services in the north and south of Scotland are less efficient and it can be a slow and difficult process getting to more remote parts of the Highlands and Islands and Argyll. Public transport can also be expensive, but there's a whole raft of discount passes and tickets which can save you a lot of money. Hiring a car can work out as a more economical, and certainly more flexible, option, especially for more than two people travelling together. It will also enable you to get off the beaten track and see more of the country.

Air

As well as the main airports of Glasgow, Edinburgh and Aberdeen, Scotland has many small airports, many of them on islands (one of them, on Barra, uses the beach as an airstrip). Internal flights are expensive, however, and not really necessary in such a small country, unless you are short of time and want to visit the Outer Hebrides or Orkney and Shetland. For example a return flight from Edinburgh or Glasgow to Shetland costs over £250. There are discounted tickets available, such as Apex fares, which must be booked at least 14 days in advance, and special offers on some services. BA's **Highland Rover** costs £189 and allows you to take any five flights within seven days (except inter-island flights within Orkney or Shetland). There is no departure tax on flights form Highlands and Islands airports.

The majority of flights are operated by **British Airways/Loganair**, T0870-8509850, www.british-airways.com. For inter-island flights in Shetland, you should book direct through **Loganair**, T01595-840246. For information on flight schedules, call the airports listed on page 34, or **British Airways**. The British Airports Authority (BAA) publishes a free Scheduled Flight Guide.

Rail

The rail network in Scotland is limited and train travel is comparatively expensive, but trains are a fast and effective way to get around and also provide some beautifully scenic journeys. The West Highland line to Fort William and Mallaig and the journey from Inverness to Kyle of Lochalsh are amongst the most beautiful rail journeys in the world and well worth doing. Services in the central belt, between Glasgow, Edinburgh, Stirling, Perth, Dundee and Aberdeen are fast and frequent, and there are frequent trains to and from Inverness.

ScotRail operates most train services. You can buy train tickets at the stations, from major travel agents, or over the phone with a credit/debit card. For information and advance credit/debit card bookings call T0845-7550033, or visit www.scotrail.co.uk. Details of services are given throughout the guide. For busy long-distance routes it's best to reserve a seat. Seat reservations to Edinburgh, Glasgow, Aberdeen or Inverness are included in the price of the ticket when you book in advance. If the ticket office is closed, there's usually a machine on the platform. If this isn't working, you can buy your ticket on the train. Cyclists should note that though train companies have a more relaxed attitude to taking bikes on trains, reservations for bikes (£3.50) are still required on some services.

Eurorail passes are not recognized in Britain, but **ScotRail** offers a couple of worthwhile travel passes. The most flexible is the **Freedom of Scotland Travelpass,** which gives unlimited rail travel within Scotland. It is also valid on all **CalMac** ferries on the west coast, many **Citylink** bus services in the Highlands, some regional buses, and Glasgow Underground. It also gives 33 per cent discount on **P&O Ferries** from Scrabster to Orkney and 20 per cent discount on **Northlink Ferries** from Aberdeen to Orkney and Shetland. It costs £89 for four days' travel out of eight consecutive days, £119 for eight in 15. The **Highland Rover** is more limited. It allows unlimited rail travel in the Highlands region, plus the West Highland line from Glasgow, and travel between Aberdeen and Aviemore. It also allows free travel on **Citylink** buses between Oban, Fort William and Inverness. It costs £59 for any four out of eight consecutive days.

Road

Bus and coach

Travelling around Scotland by bus takes longer than the train but is much cheaper. There are numerous local bus companies, but the main operator is **Scottish Citylink,** T08705-505050, www.citylink.co.uk. Bus services between towns and cities are good, but far less frequent in more remote rural areas. Note that long-distance express buses are called coaches. There are a number of discount and flexible tickets available and details of these are given on the **Citylink** website which is fast and easy to use.

The **Tourist Trail Pass** offers unlimited travel on all **Scottish Citylink** and **National Express** services throughout Britain. Passes cost from £49 for two days' travel out of three, up to £190 for 14 days' travel out of 30. They can be bought from major travel agents, at Gatwick and Heathrow airports, as well as from bus stations in Scottish towns and cities. **National Express Explorer Pass** offers unlimited travel within a specified period on **Scottish Citylink** buses. It is available to overseas visitors but must be bought outside Britain. **Smart Card** and **Discount Coach Card** holders can get a 30 per cent discount on these prices. In North America these passes are available from **British Travel International,** T1-800-3276097, www.britishtravel.com, or from **US National Express,** T502-2981395. The **SYHA** sells its own **Explore Scotland bus pass,** which allows free travel on **Citylink** services. It costs £155 for five days and £250 for eight days, and includes seven nights' hostel accommodation, free **SYHA** membership and free entry to many Historic Scotland properties. They also sell a **Scottish Wayfarer ticket** which is similar but also includes rail travel and **CalMac** ferries.

Various companies offer backpacker bus tours operating on a jump-on-jump-off basis. They are an affordable option for those on a modest budget, see page 20.

Many rural areas, particularly in the Highlands and Islands, can only be reached by Royal Mail **postbuses.** These are minibuses that follow postal delivery routes and carry up to 14 fare-paying passengers. They set off early in the morning from the main post office and follow a circuitous route as they deliver and collect mail in the most far-flung places. They are often very slow on the outward morning routes but quicker on the return routes in the afternoons. It can be a slow method of getting around, but you get to see some of the country's most spectacular scenery, and it is useful for walkers and those trying to reach remote hostels or B&Bs. There's a restricted service on Saturdays and none on Sundays. A free booklet of routes and timetables is usually available from local tourist information centres, or visit www.postbus.royalmail.com/RouteFinder.asp for a comprehensive route-planning service.

Car

Travelling with your own private transport is the ideal way to explore the country. This allows you to cover a lot of ground in a short space of time and to reach remote places. The main disadvantages are traffic congestion and parking, but this is only a problem in the main cities and on the motorways in the central belt. Roads in Scotland are generally a lot less busy than those in England, and driving is relatively stress-free, especially on the B-roads and minor roads. In remote parts of the country, in the Highlands and Islands in particular, many roads are single track, with passing places indicated by a diamond-shaped signpost. These should also be used to allow traffic behind you to overtake. Remember that you may want to take your time to enjoy the stupendous views all around you, but the driver behind may be a local doctor in a hurry. Don't park in passing places. A major driving hazard on single track roads are the huge numbers of sheep wandering around, blissfully unaware of your presence. When confronted by a flock of sheep, slow down and gently edge your way past. Be particularly careful at night, as many of them sleep by the side of the road (counting cars perhaps).

Note that petrol in the Highlands and Islands is a lot more expensive than in other parts of the UK, and that petrol stations and garages are few and far between.

To drive in Scotland you must have a current **driving licence**. Foreign nationals also need an international **driving permit**, available from state and national motoring organizations for a small fee. Those importing their own vehicle should also have their vehicle registration or ownership document. Make sure you're adequately **insured**. In all of the UK you drive on the left. **Speed limits** are 30 miles per hour (mph) in built-up areas, 70 mph on motorways and dual carriageways, and 60 mph on most other roads.

It's advisable to join one of the main UK motoring organizations during your visit for their 24-hour breakdown assistance. The two main ones in Britain are the **Automobile Association (AA)**, T0800-448866, www.theaa.co.uk, and the **Royal Automobile Club (RAC)**, T0800-550550, www.rac.co.uk. One year's membership of the AA starts at £46 and £39 for the RAC. They also provide many other services, including a reciprocal agreement for free assistance with many overseas motoring organizations. Check to see if your organization is included. Both companies can also extend their cover to include Europe. Their emergency numbers are: AA T0800-887766; RAC T0800-828282. You can call these numbers even if you're not a member, but you'll have to a pay a large fee. In remote areas you may have to wait a long time for assistance. Also note that in the Highlands and Islands you may be stranded for ages waiting for spare parts to arrive.

Car hire can be expensive in Scotland and you may be better off making arrangements in your home country for a fly/drive deal through one of the main multi-national companies. The minimum you can expect to pay is around £150-180 per week for a small car. Local hire companies often offer better deals than the larger multi-nationals, though **easycar** can offer the best rates, at around £10 per day, if you book in advance and don't push up the charges with high mileage. They are based at Glasgow airport and there are plans to open a branch in Edinburgh. Some companies such as **Melvilles** offer the flexibility of picking up in Glasgow and leaving in Edinburgh, and vice versa. Most companies prefer payment with a credit card, otherwise you'll have to leave a large deposit (£100 or more). You'll need a full driver's licence (one or two years) and be aged over 21 (23 in some cases).

Car hire companies

Arnold Clark, T0131-2284747 (Edinburgh); T0141-3399886 (Glasgow), www.arnoldclark.co.uk.

Avis, T08705-900500, www.avis.co.uk, in the US T800-3311084.

Budget, T0800-181181, www.budgetrentacar.co.uk, in the US T800-5270700.

Discount Car Hire Scotland, T0870-

2430733, www.discount-car-hire-scotland.co.uk.
easycar, www.easycar.com.
Europcar, T08457-222525.
Hertz, T08705-996699, www.hertz.co.uk, in the US T800-6543001.
Holiday Autos, T8705-300400, www.holidayautos.co.uk, in the US T800-4227737, www.holiday/colauto.com.
National Car Rental, T08705-365365, in the US T800-CAR-RENT, www.nationalcar.com.
Thrifty, T0131-3371319 (Edinburgh), T0141-4454440 (Glasgow), in the US T800-3672277, www.thrifty.com.

Hitching

As in the rest of the UK, hitching is never entirely safe, and is certainly not advised for anyone travelling alone, particularly women travellers. Those prepared to take the risk should not find it too difficult to get a lift, especially in the Highlands and Islands, where people are far more willing to stop for you. Bear in mind, though, that you will probably have to wait a while even to see a vehicle in remote parts.

Sea

There are around 60 or so inhabited islands off the coast of Scotland, and nearly 50 of them can be reached by a scheduled ferry service. Most ferries carry vehicles and can be booked in advance. If you're travelling to the islands by car, it's a good idea to book ferries in advance whatever the time of year, particularly to the more popular islands.

The majority of ferry services on the west coast are operated by **Caledonian MacBrayne,** T08705-650000, www.calmac.co.uk, or **CalMac** as they're more commonly known. They sail from Oban, Mallaig and Ullapool to over 20 islands in the Inner and Outer Hebrides. They also run services on the Firth of Clyde. Fares are expensive, especially with a car, but if you're planning on using ferries a lot, you can save a lot of money with an **Island Hopscotch ticket**, which offers reduced fares on 17 set routes. The ticket is valid for one month and you need to follow your set itinerary, though this can be changed en route without too much fuss. For more details and some sample fares, see under the relevant destination. A more flexible option is the **Island Rover**, which offers unlimited travel on **CalMac** ferries for a set period, though you still need to make reservations. An eight-day pass costs £46.50 per passenger and £222 for a car, and a 15-day pass costs £67 per passenger and £332 for a car. **CalMac** schedules are complicated, but details of sailings are given under each relevant destination in this guide. **Western Ferries**, T0141-3329766, runs services between Gourock and Dunoon and Islay and Jura.

Northlink Ferries, T01856-851144, www.northlinkferries.co.uk, run car ferries to Orkney and Shetland. Ferries to Orkney depart from Aberdeen or from Scrabster, near Thurso. There's also a passenger ferry from John O' Groats to Orkney which sails daily during the summer only (May-September) and is run by **John O' Groats Ferries,** T01955-611353. Ferries to Shetland sail from Aberdeen.

The Orkney islands are linked by services run by **Orkney Ferries**, T01856-872044, while Shetland's inter-island ferries are run by **Shetland Islands Council,** T01595-744866, www.shetland.gov.uk. There are also numerous small operators offering day-trips to various islands. Details of these are given in the relevant chapters.

Maps

You'll find a good selection of maps of Scotland in many bookshops and at the main tourist offices. Road atlases can be bought at most service stations. The best of these are the large-format ones produced by the AA, Collins and Ordnance Survey which cover all of Britain at a scale of around three miles to one inch and include plans of the major towns and cities. The Michelin and Bartholomew fold-out maps are also excellent, as are the official regional tourist maps published by Estate Publications, which are ideal for driving and which are available from most tourist offices.

The best detailed maps for walking are the Ordnance Survey maps, which are unsurpassed for accuracy and clarity. These are available at different scales. The Landranger series at 1:50,000 (1¼ inches to a mile) covers the whole of Britain and is good for most walkers. The new Explorer and Outdoor Leisure series are 1:25,000 and offer better value for walkers and cyclists. An excellent source of maps is **Stanfords** at 12-14 Longacre, London WC2E 9LP. Branches in Bristol and Manchester too.

Sleeping

Staying in Scotland can mean anything from being pampered to within an inch of your life in a baronial mansion to roughing it in a tiny island bothy with no electricity. If you have the money, then the sky is very much the limit in terms of sheer splendour and excess. We have listed many of the top class establishments in this book, with a bias towards those that offer that little bit extra in terms of character. In Glasgow and Edinburgh there are now several superb boutique hotels offering style and sophistication at a fraction of what it would cost in London. Those spending less may have to forego the four-posters and Egyptian cotton sheets but there are still many good value small hotels and guest houses with that essential wow factor – especially when it comes to the views. At the bottom end of the scale, there are also some excellent hostels in some pretty special locations.

If you'd like to stay in a Scottish castle as a paying guest of the owner, contact Scotts Castle Holidays, T0131-2297111, www.scottscastles.com.

We have tried to give as broad a selection as possible to cater for all tastes and budgets but if you can't find what you're after, or if someone else has beaten you to the draw, then the tourist information centres (TICs) will help find accommodation for you. They can recommend a place within your particular budget and give you the number to phone up and book yourself, or will book a room for you. Some offices charge a small fee (usually £1) for booking a room, while others ask you to pay a deposit of 10 per cent which is deducted from your first night's bill. Most tourist offices also offer a Book-a-Bed-Ahead service, which reserves accommodation for you at your next destination. This costs £3 per booking and is particularly useful in July and August, or if you'll be arriving in a town late. Details of town and city TICs are given throughout the guide. There are also several websites that you can browse and book accommodation. Amongst the best are www.aboutscotland.com/ and www.s-h-systems.co.uk/shs.html.

Accommodation in Scotland will be your greatest expense. Particularly if you are travelling on your own. Single rooms are in short supply and many places are reluctant to let a double room to one person, even when they're not busy. Single rooms are usually more than the cost per person for a double room and in some cases cost the same as two people sharing a double room.

Hotels, guest houses and B&Bs

Area tourist boards publish accommodation lists which include campsites, hostels, self-catering accommodation and STB-approved hotels, guest houses and Bed and breakfasts (B&Bs). Places participating in the STB system will have a plaque displayed outside which shows their grading, determined by a number of stars ranging from one to five. These reflect the level of facilities, as well as the quality of

Hotel price codes explained

Accommodation prices in this book are graded with the letters below and are based on the cost per person for two people sharing a double room with en suite bathroom during the high season. Cheaper rooms with shared bathrooms are available in many hotels, guest houses and B&Bs. Many places, particularly larger hotels, offer substantial discounts during the low season and at weekends. All places listed are recommended as providing good quality and value within their respective price category. Note that price codes for youth hostels are not given in the accommodation listings, as they all cost under £15 per person per night.

L £80 plus
A £66-80
B £46-65
C £36-45
D £26-35
E £16-25
F £15 and under

hospitality and service. However, do not assume that a B&B, guest house or hotel is no good because it is not listed by the tourist board. They simply don't want to pay to be included in the system, and some of them may offer better value.

Hotels

At the top end of the scale, there are some fabulously luxurious hotels, often in spectacular locations. Many of them are converted baronial mansions or castles and offer a chance to enjoy a taste of aristocratic grandeur and style. At the lower end of the scale, there is often little to choose between cheaper hotels and guest houses or B&Bs. The latter often offer higher standards of comfort and a more personal service, but many smaller hotels are really just guest houses, and are often family-run and every bit as friendly. Note that some hotels, especially in town centres or in fishing ports, may also be rather noisy, as the bar can often be the social hub. Rooms in most mid-range to expensive hotels almost always have bathrooms en suite. Many upmarket hotels offer excellent room-only deals in the low season. An efficient last-minute hotel booking service is www.laterooms.com, which specializes in weekend breaks. Also note that many hotels offer cheaper rates for online booking through agencies such as www.lastminute.com.

Guest houses

Guest houses are often large, converted family homes with up to five or six rooms. They tend to be slightly more expensive than B&Bs, charging between £25 and £35 per person per night, and though they are often less personal, usually provide better facilities, such as en suite bathroom, colour TV in each room and private parking. In many instances they are more like small budget hotels. Many guest houses offer evening meals, though this may have to be requested in advance.

Bed and breakfasts (B&Bs)

B&Bs provide the cheapest private accommodation. At the bottom end of the scale you can get a bedroom in a private house, a shared bathroom and a huge cooked breakfast for around £17-20 per person per night. Small B&Bs may only have one or two rooms to let, so it's important to book in advance during the summer season and on the islands where accommodation options are more limited. More upmarket B&Bs have en suite bathrooms and TVs in each room and usually charge from £21-26 per person per night. In general, B&Bs are more hospitable, informal, friendlier and offer better value than hotels. Many B&B owners, particularly in the Highlands and Islands, are a great source of local knowledge and can even provide OS maps for local walks. B&Bs in the Outer Hebrides also offer dinner, bed and breakfast, which is useful as eating options are limited, especially on a Sunday.

Some places, especially in ferry ports, charge room-only rates, which are slightly cheaper and allow you to get up in time to catch an early morning ferry. However, this means that you miss out on a huge cooked breakfast. If you're travelling on a tight budget, you can eat as much as you can at breakfast time and save on lunch as you won't need to eat again until evening. This is particularly useful if you're heading into the hills, as you won't have to carry so much food. Many B&B owners will even make up a packed lunch for you at a small extra cost.

Hostels

For those travelling on a tight budget, there is a large network of hostels offering cheap accommodation. These are also popular centres for backpackers and provide a great opportunity for meeting fellow travellers. Hostels have kitchen facilities for self-catering, and some include a continental breakfast in the price or provide cheap breakfasts and evening meals. Advance booking is recommended at all times, and particularly from May to September and on public holidays, and a credit card is often useful.

Scottish Youth Hostel Association (SYHA)

The Scottish Youth Hostel Association (SYHA), 7 Glebe Cresent, Stirling FK8 2JA, T01786-451181, www.syha.org.uk, is separate from the YHA in England and Wales. It has a network of over 60 hostels, which are often better and cheaper than those in other countries. They offer bunk-bed accommodation in single-sex dormitories or smaller rooms, kitchen and laundry facilities. The average cost is £9-12 per person per night. Though some rural hostels are still strict on discipline and impose a 2300 curfew, those in larger towns and cities tend to be more relaxed and doors are closed as late as 0200. Some larger hostels provide breakfasts for around £2.50 and three-course evening meals for around £4-5. For Scottish residents, adult membership costs £6, and can be obtained at the SYHA National Office, or at the first SYHA hostel you stay at. SYHA membership gives automatic membership of Hostelling International (HI). The SYHA produces a handbook (free with membership) giving details of all their youth hostels, including transport links. This can be useful as some hostels are difficult to get to without your own transport. You should always phone ahead, as many hostels are closed during the day. Phone numbers are listed in this guide. Many hostels are closed during the winter. Details are given in the SYHA Handbook. Youth hostel members are entitled to half-price entry to all National Trust for Scotland properties. The SYHA also offers an **Explore Scotland** and **Scottish Wayfarer** ticket, which can save a lot of money on transport and accommodation, especially if you're not a student, see page 40.

Independent hostels

The Independent Backpackers Hostels of Scotland is an association of nearly 100 independent hostels/bunkhouses throughout Scotland. They charge between £6 and £15 per person per night, though the average is around £8-10. They tend to be more laid-back, with fewer rules and no curfew, and no membership is required. They all have dormitories, hot showers and self-catering kitchens. Some include continental breakfast, or provide cheap breakfasts. All these hostels are listed in the *Blue Hostel Guide*, which is available from tourist offices, or send an A5 SAE to: Pete Thomas, Croft Bunkhouse & Bothies, Portnalong, Isle of Skye, IV47 8SL. They also have a website, www.hostel-scotland.co.uk.

Campsites, self-catering and campuses

Campsites

There are hundreds of campsites around Scotland. They are mostly geared to caravans, and vary greatly in quality and level of facilities. The most expensive sites, which charge up to £10 to pitch a tent, are usually well-equipped. Sites are usually only open from April to October. If you plan to do a lot of camping, you should buy *Scotland: Camping & Caravan Parks* (£3.95), available from most tourist offices. It lists around 150 camping and caravan parks graded by the STB.

North Americans planning on camping should invest in an international camping carnet, which is available from home motoring organizations, or from Family Campers and RVers (FCRV), 4804 Transit Road, Building 2, Depew, NY 14043, T1-800-2459755. It gives you discounts at member sites.

Self-catering

One of the most cost-effective ways to enjoy Scotland is to hire a cottage with a group of friends. There are lots of different types of accommodation to choose from, to suit all budgets, ranging from luxury lodges, castles and lighthouses to basic bothies with no electricity.

The minimum stay is usually one week in the summer peak season, though many offer shorter stays of two, three or four nights, especially outside the peak season. Expect to pay at least £150-200 per week for a two-bedroom cottage in the winter, rising to £300-500 in the high season, or more if it's a particularly nice place. City houses and apartments range from around £350 to over £1000 per week. A good source of self-catering accommodation is the STB's guide (£5.95), which lists over 1,200 properties and is available from any tourist office, but there are also dozens of excellent websites to browse. Amongst the best are www.cott ages -and-castles.co.uk; www.scottish-country-cottages.co.uk; www.cottages4you. co. uk; and www.ruralretre ats.co.uk. If you want to tickle a trout or feed a pet lamb, www.farmstay.co.uk/ offer over a thousand good value rural places to stay around the UK, all clearly listed on a clickable map. Highland Hideaways has a range of more individual self-catering properties, mainly in the Highlands and Islands. For a free brochure write to them at 5-7 Stafford Street, Oban, Argyll PA34 5NJ, T01631-526056.

The National Trust for Scotland owns many historic properties which are available for self-catering holidays. Prices start at around £250 per week in high season rising to £1000 for the likes of the sumptuous **Mar Lodge**. Contact them at 5 Charlotte Square, Edinburgh EH2 4DU, T0131-2265922, www.nts.org.uk.

Campuses

Many Scottish universities open their halls of residence to visitors during the summer vacation (late June to September), and some also during the Easter and Christmas breaks. Many rooms are basic and small with shared bathrooms, but there are also more comfortable rooms with private bathrooms, twin and family units, and self-contained apartments and shared houses. Full board, half board, B&B and self-catering options are all available. Prices for bed and breakfast tend to be roughly the same as most B&Bs, but self-catering can cost as little as £50 per person per week. Local tourist offices have information, or contact the **British Universities Accommodation Consortium,** T0115-9504571, for a brochure. Details are given in this guide under the relevant section.

Eating

While Scotland's national drink is loved the world over, Scottish cooking hasn't exactly had a good press over the years. This is perhaps not too surprising, as the national dish, haggis, consists of a stomach stuffed with diced innards and served with mashed tatties (potatoes) and neeps (turnips). Not a great start. And things got even worse when the Scots discovered the notorious deep-fried Mars bar.

But Scottish cuisine has undergone a dramatic transformation in recent years and Scotland now boasts some of the most talented chefs, creating some of the best food in Britain. The heart of Scottish cooking is local produce, which includes the finest fish, shellfish, game, lamb, beef and vegetables, and a vast selection of traditionally made cheeses. What makes Scottish cooking so special is ready access to these foods. What could be better than enjoying an aperitif whilst watching your dinner being delivered by a local fisherman, knowing that an hour later you'll be enjoying the most delicious seafood?

Modern Scottish cuisine is now a feature of many of the top restaurants in the country. This generally means the use of local ingredients with foreign-influenced culinary styles, in particular French. International cuisine is also now a major feature on menus all over the country, influenced by the rise of Indian and Chinese restaurants in recent decades.

Food

Fish, meat and game form the base of many of the country's finest dishes. Scottish beef, particularly Aberdeen Angus, is the most famous in the world. This will, or should, usually be hung for at least four weeks and sliced thick. Game is also a regular feature of Scottish menus, though it can be expensive (dear), especially venison (deer), but delicious and low in cholesterol. Pheasant and hare are also tasty, but grouse is, quite frankly, overrated.

Fish and seafood are fresh and plentiful, and if you're travelling around the northwest coast you must not miss the chance to savour local mussels, prawns, oysters, scallops, langoustines (called prawns here), lobster or crab. Salmon is, of course, the most famous of Scottish fish, but you're more likely to be served the fish-farmed variety than 'wild' salmon, which has a more delicate flavour. Trout is also farmed extensively, but the standard of both remains high. Kippers are also a favourite delicacy, the best of which come from Loch Fyne or the Achiltibuie smokery, see page 398. Arbroath smokies (smoked haddock) are a tasty alternative.

Haggis has made something of a comeback, and small portions are often served as starters in fashionable restaurants. Haggis is traditionally eaten on Burns Night (25 January) in celebration of the great poet's birthday, when it is piped to the table and then slashed open with a sword at the end of a recital of Robert Burns' 'Address to the Haggis'. Other national favourites feature names to relish: **cock-a-leekie** is a soup made from chicken, leeks and prunes; **cullen skink** is a delicious concoction of smoked haddock and potatoes; while at the other end of the scale of appeal is **hugga-muggie**, a Shetland dish using fish's stomach. There's also the delightfully named **crappit heids** (haddock heads stuffed with lobster) and **partan bree** (a soup made form giant crab's claws, cooked with rice). Rather more mundane is the ubiquitous **Scotch broth**, made with mutton stock, vegetables, barley, lentils and split peas, and stovies, which is a mash of potato, onion and minced beef.

“” So prevalent are exotic Asian and Oriental flavours that curry has now replaced fish and chips (fish supper) as the nation's favourite food. In Scotland, proper fish and chips use only haddock – cod is for Sassenachs and cats...

Waist-expanding puddings or desserts are a very important part of Scottish cooking and often smothered in butterscotch sauce or syrup in order to satisfy a sweet-toothed nation. There is a huge variety, including **cranachan**, a mouth-watering mix of toasted oatmeal steeped in whisky, cream and fresh raspberries, and **Atholl Brose**, a similar confection of oatmeal, whisky and cream.

Eaten before pudding, in the French style, or afterwards, are Scotland's many home-produced cheeses, which have made a successful comeback in the face of mass-produced varieties. Amongst the tastiest examples are **Lanark Blue**, made from unpasteurized ewe's milk and similar to Roquefort, and **Teviotdale** and **Bonchester**, which both come from the Borders. Many of the finest cheeses are produced on the islands, especially Arran, Mull, Islay and Orkney. **Caboc** is a creamy soft cheese rolled in oatmeal and is made in the Highlands.

Anyone staying at a hotel, guest house or B&B will experience the hearty **Scottish breakfast**, which includes bacon, egg, sausage and black pudding (a type of sausage made with blood), all washed down with copious quantities of tea, Scotland's staple drink. Although coffee is readily available everywhere, do not expect cappuccinos and café lattes: filter coffee is the staple 'tea-substitue' in most hotels and B&Bs. You may also be served kippers (smoked herring) or porridge, an erstwhile Scottish staple, which is now eaten by few people. Made with oatmeal and has the consistency of Italian polenta. It is traditionally eaten with salt, though heretics are offered sugar instead. Oatcakes (oatmeal biscuits) may also be on offer, as well as potato scones, baps (bread rolls), bannocks (a sort of large oatcake) or butteries (butter-laden bread similar to a croissant). These local baked goodies can be spread with marmalade, brought to the world's breakfast tables by the city of Dundee, see page 495.

After such a huge cooked breakfast you probably won't feel like eating again until dinner, or tea, taken between 1700 and 1800, and a national institution consisting of a cooked main course (usually fish and chips) and a smorgesbord of scones and cakes, washed down with more pots of tea.

Drink

Beer

Beer is the staple alcoholic drink in Scotland. The most popular type of beer is lager, which is generally brewed in the UK even when it bears the name of an overseas brand and is almost always weaker than in both strength and character than the lagers in mainland Europe. However, examples of the older and usually darker type of beers, known as ales, are still widely available, and connoisseurs should try some of these as they are far more rewarding. Indeed, the best of them rival Scotland's whiskies as gourmet treats.

Traditionally, Scottish ales were graded by the shilling, an old unit of currency written as /-, according to strength. This system is still widely used by the older

Turn water into whisky

Malt whisky is made by first soaking dry barley in tanks of local water for two to three days. Then the barley is spread out on a concrete floor or placed in cylindrical drums and allowed to germinate for between eight and 12 days, after which it is dried in a kiln, heated by a peat fire. Next, the dried malt is ground and mixed with hot water in a huge circular vat called a 'mash tun'. A sugary liquid called 'wort' is then drawn from the porridge-like result and piped into huge containers where living yeast is stirred into the mix in order to convert the sugar in the wort into alcohol. After about 48 hours the 'wash' is transferred to copper pot stills and heated till the alcohol vaporizes and is then condensed by a cooling plant into distilled alcohol which is passed through a second still. Once distilled, the liquid is poured into oak casks and left to age for a minimum of three years, though a good malt will stay casked for at least eight years.

established breweries, though many of the newer independents and 'micros' have departed from it. 70/- beers at around 3.5% ABV (alcohol by volume), known as 'heavy', and 80/- beers (4.5 per cent sometimes known as 'export', are the most popular, while 60/-, 'light' (3-3.5 per cent) is harder to find. Very strong 90/- beers (6.5 per cent + ABV), known as 'wee heavies', are also brewed, mainly for bottling.

The market is dominated by the giant international brewers: Scottish Courage with its McEwans and Youngers brands; Interbrew with Calders and Carslberg; and Tetley with Tennents lagers. Tennents, the first British brewery to produce a continental-style lager commercially back in the 19th century, is today best known for its bland but very strong canned lagers popular with winos and those who like to get drunk very quickly and cheaply.

Much better are the ales from smaller independent breweries. Edinburgh's Caledonian is a world-class brewer producing many excellent beers, including a popular 80/- and a renowned golden hoppy ale, Deuchars IPA. Belhaven, an old, established family brewery in Dunbar, has some superb traditional beers including a malty 80/-, once marketed as the Burgundy of Scotland. Broughton, a micro-brewery in the Borders, produces the fruity Greenmantle and an oatmeal stout. Another micro, Harvieston of Clackmannanshire (once an important brewing country) offers a wide and adventurous range of specialities, including Ptarmigan 80/- and a naturally brewed cask lager, Schiehallion. The Heather Ale Company, near Glasgow, has the spicy and unusual Fraoch (pronounced 'Frooch') which is flavoured with real heather as well as hops.

Draught beer in pubs and bars is served in pints, or half pints, and you'll pay between £1.50 and £2.50 for a pint. In many pubs the basic ales are chilled under gas pressure like lagers, but the best ales, such as those from the independents, are 'real ales', still fermenting in the cask and served cool but not chilled (around 12C) under natural pressure from a handpump, electric pump or air pressure fount. All Scottish beers are traditionally served with a full, creamy head.

Whisky

No visit to Scotland would be complete without availing oneself of a 'wee dram'. There is no greater pleasure on an inclement Highland evening than enjoying a malt whisky in front of a roaring log fire whilst watching the rain outside pelt down relentlessly. The roots of Scotland's national drink (*uisge beatha*, or 'water of life' in Gaelic) go back to the late 15th century, but it wasn't until the invention of a patent still

Which whisky?

Opinions vary as to what are the best single malts and as to when you should drink them. As a rough guide, we would recommend a Speyside malt such as Glenmorangie or Glenlivet before dinner and one of the Islay malts – Ardbeg, Bowmore, Bunnahabhain (pronounced 'bun-a-haven'), Lagavulin, or the very wonderful Laphroaig (pronounced 'la-froig') – after dinner.

If the Islays are not to your taste, then you could try instead the versatile Highland Park from Orkney or perhaps Tamdhu or Aberlour from Speyside. Those eternal favourites, Glenfiddich and The Macallan, can be enjoyed at any time.

in the early 19th century that distilling began to develop from small family run operations to the large manufacturing business it has become today. Now more than 700 million bottles a year are exported, mainly to the United States, France, Japan and Spain.

There are two types of whisky: single malt, made only from malted barley; and grain, which is made from malted barley together with unmalted barley, maize or other cereals, and is faster and cheaper to produce. Most of the popular brands are blends of both types of whisky – usually 60-70 per cent grain to 30-40 per cent malt. These blended whiskies account for over 90 per cent of all sales worldwide, and most of the production of single malts is used to add flavour to a blended whisky. Amongst the best-known brands of blended whisky are *Johnnie Walker*, *Bells*, *Teachers* and *Famous Grouse*. There's not much between them in terms of flavour and they are usually drunk with a mixer, such as water or soda.

Single malts are a different matter altogether. Each is distinctive and should be drunk neat to appreciate fully its subtle flavours, though some belive that the addition of water helps free the flavours. Single malts vary enormously. Their distinctive flavours and aromas are derived from the peat used for drying, the water used for mashing, the type of oak cask used and the location of the distillery. Single malts fall into four groups: Highland, Lowland, Campbeltown and Islay. There are over 40 distilleries to choose from, most offering guided tours. The majority are located around Speyside, in the northeast. The region's many distilleries include that perennial favourite, *Glenfiddich*, which is sold in 185 countries. A recommended alternative is the produce of the beautiful and peaceful Isle of Islay, whose malts are lovingly described in terms of their peaty quality. Scots tend to favour the 10 year-old *Glenmorangie*, while the most popular in the USA is *The Macallan*.

Soft drinks

Scotland's national soft drink is Irn-Bru, a sugar-loaded, rust-coloured beverage that is consumed in great quantities by the sweet-toothed Scots. Connoisseurs argue that it is best from bottles. Irn-Bru is also used as a mixer for whisky.

Eating out

There are places to suit every taste and budget. In Edinburgh and Glasgow in particular you'll find a vast selection of eating places, including Indian, Chinese, Italian and French restaurants, as well as Thai, Japanese, Mexican, Spanish and, of course Scottish. More and more restaurants, however, are moving away from national culinary boundaries and offering a wide range of international dishes and

Restaurant price codes explained

The prices ranges in this book are based on a two-course meal (main course plus starter or dessert) without drinks. We have tried to include an equal number of choices in each category, though this is not always possible. All places listed are recommended as offering relatively good value, quality and standards of service within their respective price category.

£££ over £20 a head
££ £10-20 a head
£ under £10 a head

flavours, so you'll often find Latin American, Oriental and Pacific Rim dishes all on the same menu. This is particularly the case in the many continental-style bistros, brasseries and café-bars, which now offer a more informal alternative to traditional restaurants. Not surprisingly, other parts of Scotland do not offer the same choice as Edinburgh and Glasgow, two cities with the greatest selection of places to eat in the UK outside London. Vegetarians are increasingly well catered for, especially in the large cities, where exclusively vegetarian/vegan restaurants and cafés are often the cheapest places to eat. Outside the cities, vegetarian restaurants are thin on the ground, though better-quality eating places will normally offer a reasonable vegetarian selection.

For a cheap meal, you're best bet is a pub, hotel bar or café, where you can have a one-course meal for around £5-7 or less, though don't expect gourmet food. The best value is often at lunchtime, when many restaurants offer three-course set lunches or business lunches for less than £10. You'll need a pretty huge appetite to feel like eating a three-course lunch after your gigantic cooked breakfast, however. Also good value are the pre-theatre dinners offered by many restaurants in the larger towns and cities (you don't need to have a theatre ticket to take advantage). These are usually available from around 1730-1800 till 1900-1930, so you could get away with just a sandwich for lunch. At the other end of the price scale are many excellent restaurants where you can enjoy the finest of Scottish cuisine, often with a continental influence. Outside Edinburgh and Glasgow, these are often found in hotels. You can expect to pay from around £25 a head up to £40 or £50 in the very top establishments.

The biggest problem with eating out in Scotland, as in the rest of the UK, is the ludicrously limited serving hours in most pubs and hotels. These places only serve food between 1230 and 1400 and 1700 and 1900, seemingly ignorant of the eating habits of foreign visitors, or those who would prefer a bit more flexibility during their holiday. In small places especially it can be difficult finding food outside these strictly enforced times. Places which serve food all day till 2100 or later are restaurants, fast-food outlets and the many chic bistros and café-bars, which can be found not only in the main cities but increasingly in smaller towns. The latter often offer very good value and above-average quality.

Entertainment

Bars and clubs

As in the rest of Britain, pubs are the main focus of social life and entertainment for most Scots. These vary greatly, from traditional old inns full of character (and often full of characters) to chic and trendy bars where you can order foccacia bread with sundried tomatoes washed down with your bottle of continental lager whilst you dance to Djs. Most city pubs are owned by the large breweries and only serve their own particular beers. There is also a growing number of chain pubs appearing on the high streets of many towns. In remote parts of the Highlands and Islands the local hotel bar is often the only watering hole for miles around. Many pubs close for a couple of hours between 1400 and 1600, which can be very annoying on a wet afternoon. Pubs generally are open from 1100 till 2300 Monday-Saturday and Sunday from 1100-1200 till 2230. In towns and cities many pubs are open till 2400 or 0100 on Friday and Saturday nights, or even later in Edinburgh, which has more relaxed licensing laws.

Glasgow and Edinburgh have lively club scenes, but you'll also find nightclubs outside the major cities. For a comprehensive guide to what's on in Glasgow and Edinburgh, look out for the fortnightly listings magazine *The List*.

Cinema

Scotland, like the rest of the UK, has succumbed to the rise of home entertainment and many of the finest cinemas have long gone, replaced by bingo halls and out-of-town leisure and entertainment complexes showing a vast array of Hollywood blockbusters and little else. That's not to say that independent cinema is dead. Edinburgh in particular has some excellent art house cinemas, which come into their own during the International Film Festival, see page 118, while Glasgow boasts the wonderful GFT, see page 170. Dundee, Aberdeen and Stirling also have very fine art house cinemas.

Dance

Edinburgh plays host to the world's top dance companies during the Festival but the arrival of the £6 million lottery-funded National Centre for Dance, see page 115, means that the capital attracts national and international dance companies throughout the year.

At a more grassroots level, one of the most vibrant expressions of Celtic culture is the ceilidh (pronounced 'kay-lee') an evening of Scottish music and dance, the music provided by a ceilidh band, which normally consists of a fiddler, an accordionist, a drummer and a singer. Here you can spend the evening sampling the delights of Gay Gordons or Dashing White Sergeants. In case you're wondering, these aren't people who frequent these events – they are actually Scottish country dances which, along with eightsome reels, figure prominently in the ceilidh dance-band repertoire. Beware the well-meaning local lad or lassie bearing gifts of whisky, however – an excellent evening enjoying the music can often lead to a spectacular hangover the following morning. The local TIC, or newspaper, will have details of what's on where.

Music

Edinburgh may stage the biggest arts festival on the planet but Glasgow is the home of Scottish Opera and the National Symphony Orchestra. Glasgow is also the main centre for all things pop and rock, especially indie music, and produces world-class bands with almost monotonous regularity. On almost any given night you can listen to a vast range of styles and levels of talent and, who knows, may even witness the arrival of the next Franz Ferdinand.

Folk music clubs still thrive in Scotland although, sadly, seem to be restricted to an 'early-in-the-week' slot of a Monday or Tuesday evening in bars, as landlords attempt to bring in customers on what are generally quieter nights for business. Even the Scots, with their fearsome (and well-earned) reputation for partying, can't do it every night of the week. Visiting the larger cities, look out for boards outside pubs which proclaim 'Live Music Tonight' or 'Folk Music Session – All Welcome', as the venues occasionally change from one week to the next, although the musicians tend to remain the same and are relatively easy to be found in both Edinburgh and Glasgow.

Theatre

The main focal points of Scottish theatre are, not surprisingly, the cities of Edinburgh and Glasgow. The latter in particular stages some of the UK's most exciting and innovative drama in its Citizens' and Tramway Theatres. Outside the big two, Dundee's Repertory Theatre has a well-deserved reputation for its range and quality, while Perth, Pitlochry and Inverness all have thriving summer programmes.

Festivals and events

There is a huge range of organized events held throughout Scotland every year, ranging in size and spectacle from the Edinburgh Festival, the largest arts festival in the world, to more obscure traditional events featuring ancient customs dating back many centuries. The Scottish Tourist Board publishes a comprehensive list, *Events in Scotland*, twice a year. It's free and is available from the main tourist offices. The most popular tourist events are the **Highland Games (or Gatherings)**, a series of competitions involving lots of kilts, bagpipes and caber-tossing, which are held across the Highlands and Islands, the northeast and Argyll from June to September. The best known is the **Braemar Gathering**, see page 527, which is attended by various members of the Royal Family. Those at Oban and Dunoon are large events, but smaller gatherings are often more enjoyable and 'authentic'. Details of Highland Gatherings are listed throughout the guide.

Details of local festivals are given in the listings sections of individual towns and cities; also visit www.whatsonwhen.com.

Folk festivals take place all over the country, from Arran to Shetland, and are great fun. Musicians from all over Scotland gather to play the tunes, sing the songs and maybe, just maybe, drink the odd beer or two. Amongst the best of the folk festivals are the **Celtic Connections**, held in Glasgow over three weeks in January, and the **Shetland Folk Festival**, held over a long weekend in mid-April. Also recommended are those held in Edinburgh before Easter, in Inverness in July and August, Stonehaven in mid-July, Auchtermuchty in mid-August, Girvan in early May, Killin at the end of June, Islay during the last two weeks in May, Arran in early June, Skye at the end of July and Kirriemuir on the first weekend in September. Details of these festivals, and many others, are available from the Scottish Area Tourist Boards, see page 36.

Festivals

Jan New Year's Day: A variety of ancient local celebrations take place, including the Kirkwall Ba' Game, a mixture of football and mud wrestling.

Up Helly-Aa: Re-enactment of the ancient Viking fire festival held on Shetland on the last Tue in Jan, see p578.

Celtic Connections: Huge celebration of Celtic music from around the world, held in various venues throughout Glasgow over 2 weeks in Jan.

Burns Night: Burns suppers held on 25th Jan all over the country to celebrate the poet's birthday. Lots of haggis, whisky and poetry recitals.

Apr Scottish Grand National: Held at Ayr racecourse in Apr.

Rugby Sevens: Seven-a-side rugby tournament held throughout the Borders.

May Scottish FA Cup Final: Held at Hampden Park in Glasgow in May.

Spirit of Speyside Whisky Festival: Held on Speyside in May.

The Highland Festival: Held over 2 weeks from late May till early Jun at venues throughout the Highland region. For details, T01463-719000, www.highlandfestival.org.uk.

Jun Royal Highland Show: Scotland's largest agricultural show, held at Ingliston, near Edinburgh, in Jun.

Jun-Aug Riding of the Marches: Horse riding, parades, brass bands etc commemorating the wars between the Scots and the English. Held in various towns in the Borders from Jun to Aug, see p190.

Jul International Jazz Festival: Held in Glasgow in Jul.

T in the Park: Scotland's largest outdoor music festival featuring many of the best pop and rock bands. Held at Balado Airfield at Kinross in Jul.

Aug Edinburgh International and Fringe Festival: The greatest arts extravaganza on the planet, held over 3 weeks in Aug. At the same time is the **Edinburgh Military Tattoo**, a massed pipe bands and military pageantry on the esplanade of Edinburgh Castle.

World Pipe Band Championships Held in Glasgow in Aug.

Sep Braemar Highland Gathering Attended by the Royal Family in Sep.

Oct National Mod: Competitive Gaelic music festival held at various locations.

Tour of Mull Rally: The highlight of the Scottish rally season, run over the island's public roads (no wonder they're in such appalling condition) in Oct.

Aberdeen Alternative Festival The north-east's major arts and culture fest, held in Oct.

Dec-Jan Hogmanay: Old year's night, and the most important national celebration. Possible derivations of the word include Holag Monath, Anglo Saxon for 'holy month',and Hoog min dag, which is Dutch for 'great love day'. Edinburgh's huge street party is the largest such celebration in the northern hemisphere.

Bank holidays

New Year's Day and **2 Jan**, **Good Friday** and **Easter Monday**, **May Day** (the first Mon in May), **Victoria Day** (the last Mon in May), **25 and 26 Dec** (Christmas Day, Boxing Day). There are also local public holidays in spring and autumn. Dates vary from place to place. Banks are closed during these holidays, and sights and shops may be affected to varying degrees. Contact the relevant Area Tourist Board for more details.

Shopping

The shelves of gift shops in every tourist attraction from John O' Groats to Jedburgh are stuffed full of dreadful tartan tat such as 'See-you-Jimmy' wigs and bonnets, Loch Ness monster replicas and those scary-looking tartan dolls with flickering eyelashes. All very harmless (except for the dolls which give you nightmares), but not doing much for Scotland's image. But amongst all this tourist kitsch are many excellent high-quality goods on offer.

Scottish textiles, especially the **tartan** variety, are popular and worth buying. Everything from a travelling rug to your own kilt outfit. Shops up and down the country, and especially in Edinburgh and Inverness, can tell which clan your family belongs to and make you a kilt in that particular tartan. For the full outfit, including kilt, sporran, jacket, shoes and skeann dhu dagger, expect to pay in the region of £600, or more if you want more elaborate accessories. There are mill shops making tweeds and cloths in many parts of Scotland. Most are in the Borders, though it is not necessarily cheaper to buy at source. **Harris Tweed** is also a good buy and you can watch your cloth being woven on the Hebridean islands of Harris and Lewis.

Knitwear is also good value and sold throughout Scotland, though the cashmere industry in the Borders is suffering from high trade tariffs. Shetland is a good place to find high-quality wool products. Note that Aran jumpers are not from the island of Arran, but from Aran (with one 'r') in Ireland. **Jewellery** is another popular souvenir and there are many excellent craft shops throughout the Highlands and Islands making beautiful jewellery with Celtic designs. **Glassware** is also popular, particularly Edinburgh crystal and Caithness glass, as well as pottery.

Food is another good souvenir and not just the ubiquitous shortbread sold in tartan tins. If you haven't far to travel home, smoked salmon, or any other smoked product, is good value. One of the best places for food products is the island of Arran, where you can buy their delicious local mustards and preserves, smoked fish and game, and cheeses. And, of course, there's **whisky**. Most distilleries will refund the cost of their guided tour in the form of a discount voucher on a bottle of their brand whisky.

Shop hours in Scotland are generally Monday to Saturday from 0900-1730 or 1800. In larger towns and cities, many shops also open on Sundays and late at night, usually on a Thursday and Friday. Large supermarkets and retail complexes found outside large towns are open till 2000 or later Monday-Saturday and till 1600 on Sunday. In the Highlands and Islands, few shops are open on Sunday, most notably in the Outer Hebrides where nothing is open on a Sunday. Also note that in many rural areas there is an early-closing day when shops close at 1300. This varies from region to region, but the most common day is Wednesday.

Sport and activities

Scotland has never been a place for softies. Its challenging weather and dramatic scenery really give you a sense of being in the great outdoors. Many visitors come specifically to enjoy the magnificent scenery as they walk in the hills, cycle through forests, ski down mountains or head off in search of rare wildlife. The coastline, lochs and rivers are ideal for fishing and offer plenty of opportunities for a whole range of watersports, including windsurfing, sailing and scuba diving. Aside from the more traditional outdoor pursuits, however, Scotland's rivers, mountains and coast are fast making it a centre for extreme activities. So before you head off to the other side of the world for a spot of whitewater rafting, check out Scotland to see what's on offer. At the end of this section is a list of organizations that are able to provide further information on sports and activities in Scotland, see page 63.

A weather phone-line service is available from the following numbers: East Highlands T0891-333197; West Highlands T0891-333198.

Canoeing, kayaking and rafting

Scotland's rivers, lochs and deeply indented coastline offer great opportunities canoeing, kayaking and the highlands has also gained a reputation for being one of the most exciting locations for whitewater rafting. Rapids are ranked from grade one (paddling pool standard) to grade six (stupidly scary). **Monster Activities**, 25 miles from Fort William, run trips on a dam-released river, which ensures that flows are kept even in the summer months, with grade 3 rapids, which are serious but safe enough for children aged 10 and over. Scotland's other main rafting centre is Perthshire, where companies offer fun yakking, which is like whitewater rafting but in boats for two people without a guide. See page 63 for details organizations and companies offering information, courses and trips.

Canyoning

Head downriver in a gorge, dropping several hundred feet by swimming, jumping into plunge pools, sliding down log flumes and abseiling. In Perthshire you can also go cliff-jumping form heights of up to 60 ft into rock pools combined with headfirst descents of waterfalls. If that's too tame then try the Tyrolean Traverse, which

Mountain safety

Visitors to Scotland should be aware of the need for caution and safety preparations when walking or climbing in the mountains. The nature of Scottish weather is such that a fine sunny day can turn into driving rain or snow in a matter of minutes. Remember that a blizzard can be raging on the summit when the car park at the foot of the mountain is bathed in sunshine. It is essential to get an up to date weather forecast before setting off on any walk or climb. Whatever the time of year, or conditions when you set off, you should always carry or wear essential items of clothing. A basic list for summer conditions would be: boots with a good tread and ankle support and a thick pair of socks; waterproof jacket and trousers, even on a sunny day; hat and gloves are important if the weather turns bad; warm trousers should be worn or carried, tracksuit bottoms are okay if you also have waterproof trousers; spare woolly jumper or fleece jacket will provide an extra layer; map and compass are essential to carry and to know how to use. Other essentials are food and drink, a simple first aid kit, a whistle and a torch. A small 25-30 litre rucksack should be adequate for carrying the above items. Also remember to leave details of your route and expected time of return with someone, and remember to inform them on your return.

In the winter extra warm clothing is needed, as well as an ice axe and crampons, and the ability to use them. The skills required for moving over ice or snow should be practised with an experienced and qualified mountain guide/instructor.

involves crossing a gorge at a height of 300 ft. See page 63 for companies offering canyoning trips.

Climbing

Scotland is a great place to try rock climbing and its arduous winter cousin, ice climbing. The Cairngorms and Cuillins offer the most challenging climbing, as do Glencoe and Torridon. Most mountaineering clubs have regular weekend meets in the hills as well as social gatherings closer to home. Some useful websites are: www.winternetscotland.co.uk, www.scotclimb.org.uk and www.nae-limits.com.

Cycling

The bicycle was invented in Scotland, near Dumfries, so it seems appropriate that travelling by bike is one of the best ways to explore the country. Most towns and cities, however, are not particularly cycle-friendly. Very few have proper cycle routes, and there's the added problem of security. It's best to stick to rural backroads, especially unclassified roads and country lanes, which are not numbered but are signposted and marked on OS maps. There are also forest trails and dedicated routes along canal towpaths and disused railway tracks. The main problem in rural areas, though, is the availability of spare parts.

The south of Scotland is particularly good for cycle touring due to the quiet roads, gentle gradients and large number of B&Bs and pubs. The wild and remote Highlands are popular with cyclists, but this is also walking country, and cyclists should stick to tracks where a right to cycle exists and be considerate towards walkers. The Forestry Commission has 1,150 miles of excellent off-road routes up and down the country. These are detailed in a series of *Cycling in the Forest leaflets*, which are available from Forestry Enterprise offices and from most tourist offices.

You can cut down on the amount of pedalling you have to do by transporting your bike by train. Bikes can be taken free on most local rail services on a first come-first served basis (call ScotRail bookings, T08457-550033). On long-distance routes you'll have to make a reservation and pay a small charge (£3.50). Space is limited on trains so it's a good idea to book as far in advance as possible. Bus and coach companies will not carry bikes, unless they are dismantled and boxed. Ferries transport bikes for a small fee and airlines will often accept them as part of your baggage allowance. Check with the ferry company or airline about any restrictions.

Bike rental is available at cycle shops in most large towns, cities and tourist centres. Expect to pay from around £6 to £15 per day, or from £50 a week, plus a refundable deposit. There's also the option of a cycling holiday package, which includes transport of your luggage, prebooked accommodation, route instructions and food and backup support. A list of specialists is given above.

The STB publishes a free booklet, *Cycling in Scotland*, which is useful and suggests routes in various parts of the country, as well as accommodation and repair shops. Many area tourist boards also provide cycling guides for their own areas. For a list of useful cycle guides and books, see page 623. The website www.spokes.org.uk is useful.

There is also some extreme cycling to be done. Scotland is one of the hottest **mountain-bike** destinations in the world. According to who? According to the Colorado-based **International Mountain Biking Association**, that's who. Further evidence is that the 2002 World Cup Downhill was held on the bottom ski slopes of the Nevis Range near Fort William. This black run is Britain's biggest downhill and is open May to September. Hook your bike up to the gondola and climb up to 2,050 ft before beginning the 1.6 mile steep and rough course. The lift operates 1045-1445 and a single run costs £9.75 (day access £17.50). Bike hire from **Off Beat Bikes** in Fort William, www.offbeatbikes.co.uk. The jewel in Scotland's mountain biking crown is Glentress Forest near Peebles, see page 189. It will form part of the new £2 million 7 Stanes Project, which will see another six mountain bike centres developed in southern Scotland, including Mabie Forest and Dalbeattie, where riders can enjoy everything from classic single track to cross-country race courses.

Diving

Scotland may not have the Great Barrier Reef but it does have some of the finest diving locations in the world, featuring shipwrecks, reefs, sheer underwater cliffs, soft corals and abundant sea life. The West Coast offers the best diving, as the water is warmed by the effects of the Gulf Stream and is not cold, even without a dry suit. Among the best sites are the west coast of **Harris**, the **Summer Isles** and the remote island of **St Kilda**. There are lots of wrecks in the **Sound of Mull**, and the chance to find a Spanish Galleon off **Tobermory**. **Scapa Flow** in Orkney is world-renowned as the burial site of the German World War I fleet. On the East Coast, there is a great marine reserve off **St Abb's Head**, with some spectacular rock formations. For a list of organizations, see page 63.

Fishing

Scotland's rivers, streams, lochs and estuaries are among the cleanest waters in Europe and are filled with salmon, trout (sea, brown and rainbow) and pike. Not surprisingly, then, fishing (coarse, game and sea) is hugely popular in Scotland.

Munros, Corbetts and Grahams

There are 284 mountains over 3,000 ft (914 m) in Scotland, known as 'Munros', after Sir Hugh Munro, first president of the Scottish Mountaineering Club (SMC), who published the first comprehensive list of these mountains in 1891. In the 1920s a further list was published, of the 221 summits between 2,500-3,000 ft, by J Rooke Corbett, and these became known as 'Corbetts'. A third list, of summits between 2,000-2,500 ft was compiled by Fiona Graham and published in 1992. This list was subsequently revised and corrected and now all peaks that are between 2,000-2,500 ft are called 'Grahams'.

This is where the term Munro-bagging comes from – one of Scotland's favourite pastimes – climbing as many peaks over 3,000 ft as possible

There is no close season for coarse fishing or sea angling. For wild brown trout the close season is early October to mid-March. The close season for salmon and sea trout varies from area to area and between net and rod fishing. It is generally from late August to early February for net fishing, and from early November to early February for rod fishing. No licence is required to fish in Scotland, but most of the land and rivers are privately owned so you must obtain a permit from the owners or their agents. These are often readily available at the local fishing tackle shop and usually cost from around £15, though some rivers, such as the Tweed, can be far more expensive.

The STB's booklet *Fish Scotland* is a good introduction and a source of all kinds of information. It is available free from tourist offices, or by post, see page 21. For a list of organizations, see page 63.

Golf

Scotland has over 400 golf courses, with more being built all the time, and, therefore has more courses per head of population than any other country in the world. Any decent sized town in Scotland will have a golf course nearby and most, if not all, are available for play. There are many public courses, which tend to be both cheap and extremely busy, often have excellent layouts. The majority of private clubs allow visitors, although many have restrictions as to what days these visitors can play. Weekends are usually reserved for club competitions for the members so it is best to try to play on a weekday. All private clubs have a dress code and it is inadvisable to turn up for a round in a collarless shirt and jeans. These minor caveats aside, you are more than likely to receive a warm and courteous welcome. To arrange golfing holidays visit www.scotland-golf-tours.co.uk.

One of the unique attractions of golf in Scotland is the accessibility of its famous venues. The average football fan will never get the chance to play at Wembley Stadium, likewise the club tennis player is unlikely to play a few sets on the Centre Court at Wimbledon, but any golfer can, for example, play at Carnoustie or St Andrews. This represents a unique opportunity to follow in the footsteps of golf's legendary players and compare your own game, however unfavourably, with theirs. Green fees for one of the top championship courses will cost from around £40 upwards. Many clubs offer a daily or weekly ticket. A Golf Pass Scotland costs between £46 and £70 for five days (Monday to Friday) depending on the area. Golf in Scotland is a free brochure listing 400 courses and clubs with accommodation details. For a copy contact the Scottish Tourist Board. The British Tourist Authority

(BTA) has a very useful *Golfing Holidays booklet* which provides details of golfing holidays and major golf tournaments in Britain. BTA and STB address on page 21. For a list of recommended golf books, see page 623. For a list of organizations, see page 63.

Health and beauty

Nothing can be more relaxing after a hard day's sightseeing than spending an hour or two being preened and pampered in a spa. Here are a few which really know how to do it style. **OneSpa** at the **Sheraton Grand Hotel**, see page 104. The number one spa in Scotland. Enjoy breathtaking views of the city while you immerse yourself in the ozone pool or sample one of a bewildering range of treatments, including the Balinese Synchronized Massage. Other excellent facilities can be found at and **Stobo Castle Health Spa**, see page 201, and **Gleneagles Hotel Spa**, see page 248.

Hillwalking

Scotland is a walker's paradise. Throughout the country there are numerous marked trails, ranging from short walks to long-distance treks from one side of the country to the other. Whatever your taste or level of fitness and experience, you'll find plenty of opportunities to get off the beaten track and explore the countryside.

Walking routes, ranging from a coastal stroll to an arduous mountain trek, are denoted throughout the guide by ▲

The best time for hiking in the mountains is usually from May to September, though in the more low-lying parts, April to October should be safe. Winter walking in the Highlands requires technical equipment such as ice axes and crampons and a lot of experience. July and August are the busiest times, though only the most popular routes, such as Ben Nevis, get really crowded. Another problem during these months are midges, see page 62. May to mid-June is probably the most pleasant time overall, as the weather can often be fine and the midges have yet to appear. September is also a good time, though it can be a lot colder. For a list of helpful organizations, see page 63.

Access

Scotland has a long tradition of generally free responsible access to mountain and moorland. This free access, of course, relies on walkers behaving responsibly and recognizing that the countryside is a place of work as well as recreation. Most land in Scotland is privately owned and at certain times of the year, such as the main shooting seasons, walkers may be asked to respect certain restrictions on access. The main deer stalking season runs from mid-August to 20 October and the grouse shooting season is between 12 August (referred to as the 'Glorious Twelfth') and 10 December. For more information on this, see *Heading for the Scottish Hills* which is published by the Mountaineering Council of Scotland, see page 56, and the Scottish Landowners Federation and gives estate maps and telephone numbers to call for local advice. There may also be restricted access during the lambing season from March to May.

It is not an offence to walk over someone's land in Scotland but, especially during the stalking and shooting seasons, you may be asked to take a different route, though this rarely happens. Scotland's first national parks opened in recent years: Loch Lomond and the Trossachs National Park (www.lochlomond-trossachs.org) in 2002 and Cairngorms National Park (www.cairngorms.co.uk). There is free access at all times of the year to areas owned by the National Trust for Scotland. These areas include Torridon and Glencoe. There is also free access to most land owned by the Forestry Commission, and there is good public access to land owned by the John Muir

 Trust, Scottish Natural Heritage, the Royal Society for the Protection of Birds and the Woodland Trust, though these areas are not marked on Ordnance Survey (OS) maps. Also not shown on OS maps are Rights of Way, which are signposted by the Scottish Rights of Way Society's green metal signs. The society publishes maps of rights of way, many of which follow ancient 'drove roads' through the hills.

Information and advice

The Scottish Tourist Board is a useful source of information for walkers and local tourist information centres have details of interesting local walks. Many walk descriptions and maps are given in this guidebook, but these should ideally be used in conjunction with a good map, such as the Ordnance Survey (OS) Landranger series. The relevant map numbers have been listed, where possible, with the route description. OS maps can be found at tourist information centres and also at outdoor shops, which are usually staffed by experienced climbers and walkers who can give good advice about the right equipment. The best-equipped shops are **Tiso**, www.tiso.co.uk, who have branches in the main towns and cities; and **Nevisport** in Fort William. For a list of recommended walking guidebooks and maps, see page 623.

Long-distance walks

There is a network of long walking trails across Scotland which are carefully prepared to provide ideal walking conditions together with sufficient places for accommodation and supplies en route. These walks can be attempted in full, or sampled in part by less experienced walkers. Area tourist boards and local tourist offices can provide information and advice for their own particular sections. Two of the three main trails, the **Southern Upland Way**, see page 220, and the **Speyside Way**, see page 540, are covered in the relevant sections of this guide.

The best-known, and busiest, long-distance trail is the **West Highland Way**, which runs for 95 miles from Milngavie (pronounced 'mull-guy'), just north of Glasgow, to Fort William. The route progresses steadily from the Lowlands, along the eastern shore of Loch Lomond and the traverse of the western edge of Rannoch Moor, to enter Glencoe at White Corries. It continues over the Devil's Staircase, past Kinlochleven, and through Glen Nevis to Fort William. Many walkers finish off with an ascent of Ben Nevis (4,406ft), the highest mountain in Britain, see page 362. Further information, including a trail leaflet with accommodation and facilities guide, is available from **West Highland Way Ranger Service**, Balloch Castle, Balloch G53 8LX, T01389-758216.

There are several other long-distance trails, including **St Cuthbert's Way**, see page 192, and the **Pilgrim's Way** in southern Scotland. Two newly-completed trails are the **Clyde Walkway**, which runs from the heart, which will eventually run from the heart of Glasgow to New Lanark, and the **Fife Coastal Path**, which runs for 60 miles along the Fife coastline, from North Queensferry, at the foot of the Forth Bridge, to the Tay Bridge at Dundee. Leaflets covering the trails are available from the Greater Glasgow and Clyde Valley and Fife area tourist boards, see Scottish Tourist Boards page 22.

Short walks

Many of the most popular short walks, including the ascent of Ben Nevis, are described in this guidebook. These range from gentle strolls through forest glades to strenuous hikes, steep hills and mountains, and also include some beautiful coastal trails. One of the most popular pastimes in Scotland is Munro-bagging, see also box page 58, which involves climbing as many peaks over 3,000 ft as possible. The best area for this is the Highlands, which provide many challenging peaks, and it's possible to climb several in a day. Many of these hills are straightforward climbs, but many also require a high level of fitness and experience, and all require proper clothing, see next page 56. You should never attempt walks beyond your abilities.

Other good areas for walking include the Isles of Arran, Mull, Islay and Skye, Perthshire, Stirling and the Trossachs and Galloway. The mighty Cairngorms are better known as a winter ski area, but provide excellent year-round hillwalking and climbing. This is extremely wild terrain, however, and suitable only for experienced walkers. There are many opportunities for less experienced walkers in Rothiemurchus Estate and Glenmore Forest Park around Aviemore. Other areas which are best left to serious climbers are Torridon, Kintail and Glencoe, though the latter also offers a few more straightforward walks through spectacular scenery, see page 369.

Kite surfing

The newest adrenaline sport is kite surfing, which involves whizzing over the sea with your surfboard attached to a giant kite at speeds of up to 50mph. One of the best places in the country is the windy Hebridean island of Tiree. See page 63 for details of companies offering courses.

Paragliding

If you fancy getting high during your visit, you can try your hand at the exciting sport of paragliding. The Isle of Arran offers some of the best sites in the Uk for both beginners and experts. See page 63 for details of companies offering flights.

Pony trekking and horse riding

Pony trekking is a long-established activity in Scotland and miles of beautiful coastline, lochsides, and moorland are accessible on horseback. There are numerous equestrian centres around the country catering to all levels of riders. The Scottish Tourist Board produces a *Trekking & Riding* brochure listing riding centres around the country, all of them approved by the **Trekking and Riding Society of Scotland (TRSS)** or the **British Horse Society (BHS).** Centres offer pony trekking (leisurely strolls at walking pace for novices), hacks (short rides at a fast pace for experienced riders) and trail riding (long distance rides at no more than a canter). The **Buccleuch Country Ride** is a four-day route through the Borders, using private tracks, open country and quiet bridleways. For more information, contact the **Scottish Borders Tourist Board.** For general information contact the TRSS. For a list of organizations, see page 63.

Skiing

Conditions in Scotland are not as good or reliable as anywhere in the Alps, but on a clear, sunny day, and with good snow, you can enjoy some decent skiing. However, at weekends, in conditions like these, expect the slopes to be very busy. Scotland offers both alpine (downhill) and nordic (cross-country) skiing, as well as the increasingly popular snowboarding. The high season is from January to April, but it is possible to ski from as early as November to as late as May. Ski packages are available, but it's easy to arrange everything yourself and there's plentiful accommodation and facilities in and around the ski centres.

Check out www.born 2ski.com for everything from snow reports to

Small but effective

The major problem facing visitors to the Highlands and Islands of Scotland during the summer months is *Culicoides Impunctatus* – or the midge, as it's more commonly known. These tiny flying creatures are savage and merciless in the extreme and hunt in huge packs. No sooner have you left your B&B for a pleasant evening stroll, than a cloud of these bloodthirsty little devils will attack from nowhere, getting into your eyes, ears, nose and mouth – and a few places you forgot you even had. The only way to avoid them is to take refuge indoors, or to hide in the nearest loch.

Midges are at their worst in the evening and in damp, shaded or overcast conditions, and between late May and September, but they don't like direct sunlight, heavy rain, smoke and wind. Make sure you're well covered up and wear light-coloured clothing (they're attracted to dark colours). Most effective is a midge net, if you don't mind everyone pointing and laughing at you. Insect repellents have some effect, particularly those with DEET, but herbal remedies such as bog myrtle, lavender, citronalla or eucalyptus are considered equally effective. Once you've been attacked the best treatments are antihistamine creams or dock leaves – and don't scratch the bites!

Ski centres

There are five ski centres in Scotland. The largest are **Glenshee**, which has the most extensive network of lifts and selection of runs, as well as snow machines, and **Cairngorm**, which has almost 30 runs spread over an extensive area. **Glencoe** is the oldest of the ski resorts, and the **Nevis Range**, at Aonach Mor near Fort William, has the highest ski runs and only gondola in Scotland, as well as a dry slope. **The Lecht** is the most remote centre, and is good for beginners and families and for nordic skiing. Access to all five centres is easiest by car. Each resort has a ski patrol and facilities for snowboarding.

Costs

Ski equipment and clothing can be hired at all resorts, but lessons should be booked in advance. Prices vary from centre to centre, but on average expect to pay around £13 per day for hire of skis, sticks and boots, and around £12 per day for ski clothes. Snowboard hire is around £16-17 per day for board and boots. Lift passes cost around £18-20 per day, or £68-80 for five days. Ski lessons are around £18 for four hours. Packages including ski hire, tuition and lift pass cost from around £125 to £155 for five days. These prices are for adults; prices for juniors are less.

Information

Details for each of the five resorts, including phone numbers, are given in the appropriate place in the main text. For further general information contact the **Scottish Tourist Board** for its Ski Scotland brochure and accommodation list, or visit their website, www.ski.scotland.net, which is updated daily. Or you can contact the **Scottish National Ski Council**.

The Ski hotline weather-report service gives the latest snow and weather conditions plus a five-day forecast: T0891-654 followed by 655 for Cairngorm; 656 for Glenshee; 657 for The Lecht; 658 for Glencoe; 660 for Nevis Range; and 659 for cross country skiing.

Surfing

Scotland has some of the best surfing beaches in Europe. But this is no Hawaii, with its sunbleached hair and bronzed bodies: surfing in Scotland is strictly for the hardy, with water temperatures rarely above 15°C and often as low as 7°C. A good wet suit is therefore essential. The waves, though, make up for the freezing waters and compare with those in Hawaii and Australia. The main season is September to December.

The best beaches on the West Coast are to be found at the northern tip of the Isle of Lewis and at Machrihanish, down near the Mull of Kintyre. On the North Coast the top spot is Thurso, especially at Dunnet Head to the east of town. Another recommended place is Strathy Bay, near Bettyhill, halfway between Thurso and Tongue. On the East Coast the best beaches are Pease Bay, south of Dunbar, near Cockburnspath on the A1, and Nigg Bay, just south of Aberdeen, between Montrose and Arbroath. There is a bi-monthly surf magazine, *Surf*, which is a good source of information. Also try the surf shops, which sell equipment and provide information on the best breaks. Useful websites, www.sas.org.uk and www.hebrideansurf. co.uk.

Wildlife watching

Almost anywhere around the northern coasts of Scotland there is a chance to see dolphins and occasionally porpoises, seals and whales. The most popular place to see **dolphins** is in the Moray Firth area which has a resident population of about 150, most frequently seen in the summer months. Other good places to catch glimpses of the creatures are at the entrance to the Caledonian Canal at Inverness, Nairn beach, Arderseir, Fort George, Fortrose and Cromarty. **Seals** can be seen in abundance. They can often be observed lolling about on sandbanks when the tide is out, and there are plenty of seal-spotting boat trips on offer from spring to autumn. **Otters** are more elusive. They tend to live on undisturbed remote stretches of the seashore or quiet areas of a river. If you are determined to spot the creatures, for further information contact **Skye Environmental Centre**, home to the International **Otter Survival Fund**, T01471-822487. **Whales**, Minke and Orcas, inhabit the Atlantic, Pentland Firth and the Moray Firth. Contact the **Highlands of Scotland Tourist Board**, T0870-5143070, www.highlandfreedom.com, for details of boat trips. See also page 322.

Scotland is great for **birdwatching**. Over 450 species have been recorded, including vast colonies of seabirds, birds of prey and many rare species. Among the best places in Scotland to see birds are Handa Island off the coast of Sutherland, and the Treshnish Islands, off Mull, where you'll see colonies of shags, razorbills, guillemots and puffins. Details of how to get there are given in the relevant sections. Other excellent places for birdwatching include Caerlaverock near Dumfries, the Isle of May off the coast of Fife, the Bass Rock off North Berwick, Fowlsheugh near Stonehaven, and Loch Garten by Boat of Garten, where you can see ospreys. Many of the Hebridean islands, such as Islay and Mull, are home to a rich variety of seabirds and you can also see golden eagles. Orkney and Shetland are famous for their rich variety of birdlife and are home to large colonies of seabirds and migratory birds. There are puffins, kittiwakes, fulmars, shags, razorbills, guillemots and even auks.

Useful organizations

Birdwatching Royal Society for the Protection of Birds, 17 Regent Terr, Edinburgh EH7 5BT, T0131-5573136. **Scottish Ornithologists Club**, 21 Regent Terr, Edinburgh EH7 5BT, T0131-5566042. **Scottish Wildlife Trust**, Cramond House, Cramond Glebe Rd, Edinburgh EH4 6NS, T0131-3127765, which owns and runs over 100 nature reserves.

Canoeing Scottish Canoe Association, Caledonia House, South Gyle, Edinburgh EH12 9DQ, T0131-3177314, www.scot-canoe.org. Organizes tours including introductory ones.
Splash Rafting, Aberfeldy, splashraft@compuserve.com.
Canyoning Nae Limits, T0771-8918275, www.nae-limits.com, in Blairgowrie, Perthshire has half-day canyoning for £35 and the Tyrolean Traverse for £25.
Vertical Descents, T01855-821593, www.activities-scotland.com, 8 miles south of Fort William has 2 hrs canyoning for £30.
Climbing Mountaineering Council of Scotland, The Old Granary, West Mill St, Perth, T01738-638227, www.mountaineering-scotland.org.uk.
Cycling Cyclists' Touring Club (CTC), Cotterell House, 69 Meadrow, Godalming, Surrey GU7 3HS, T01483-417217, www.ctc.org.uk, is the largest cycling organization in the UK, providing a wide range of services and information on transport, cycle hire and routes including day rides and longer tours.
Scottish Cyclists' Union (SCU), The Velodrome, Meadowbank Stadium, London Rd, Edinburgh EH7 6AY, T0131-6520187, www.btinternet.com/~scottish.cycling, produces an annual handbook and calendar of events for road racing, time trialling and mountain biking.
SUSTRANS, 53 Cochrane St, Glasgow G1 1HL, T0141-5720234, www.sustrans.co.uk, provides information on new cycle trails.
Diving The Puffin Dive Centre, see p293, is the UK's most comprehensive diving facility and runs intensive PADI courses.
Scottish Sub Aqua Club, 40 Bogmoor Place, Glasgow, G51 47Q, T0141-4251021.
Fishing Scottish Federation of Sea Anglers, Brian Burn, Flat 2, 16 Bellevue Rd, Ayr, KA7 2SA, T01292-264735.
Scottish National Anglers Association, David Wilkie, Administration Office, Caledonia House, South Gyle, Edinburgh EH12 9DQ, T0131-3398808.
General Forestry Commission, 231 Corstorphine Road, Edinburgh EH12 7AT, T0131-3340303.
Forestry Enterprise, 21 Church St, Inverness, IV1 1EL, T01463-232811, will provide information on Scotland's extensive network of forest trails for walking or cycling.
John Muir Trust, 41 Commercial St, Edinburgh EH6 6JD, T0131-5540114.
National Trust for Scotland (NTS), 26-31 Charlotte Sq, Edinburgh EH2 4ET, T0131-2439300, www.nts.org.uk.
Scottish Natural Heritage, 12 Hope Terr, Edinburgh EH9 2AS, T0131-4474784, www.snh.org.uk.
Scottish Rights of Way Society www.scotways.com/.
Scottish Tourist Board Central Information Department, 23 Ravelston Terr, Edinburgh EH4 3EU, T0131-3322433, www.visitscotland.com; and 19 Cockspur St, London SW1 5BL, T020-7930 2812.
Woodland Trust, Glenruthven Mill, Abbey Rd, Auchterarder, Perthshire PH3 1DP.
Horse riding British Horse Society Scotland, Woodburn Farm, Crieff, T01764-656334.
Trekking and Riding Society of Scotland (TRRS), Horse Trials Office, Blair Atholl, Perthshire, T01796-481543.
Kitesurfing Wild Diamond, T01879-220399, www.tireewindsurfing.com, offers a 2-day introductory course costing £120, which includes equipment, insurance and transfers to and from the island. Accommodation is extra.
The Wind Wizard, Glasgow, T0141-332 8407, www.windspells.com, runs courses.
Paragliding Flying Fever, Isle of Arran, www.flyingfever.net, offers a tandem flight for £45, or elementary pilot's course for £295 for 4-5 days. Chief instructor Zabdi Keen was a former Scotland female champion.
Skiing Scottish National Ski Council, T0131-3177280, www.snsc.demon.co.uk. They produce a useful *Snowsport Scotland Handbook*.
Surfing British Surfing Association, Champions Yard, Causewayhead, Penzance, Cornwall, T01736-360250.
Scottish Surfing Federation is being re-vamped, in the meantime, contact Andrew Bain of Surf Thurso, T01847-841300. Good shops include:
Boardwise, 1146 Argyle St, Glasgow, T0141-3345559;
Clan Surf, 45 Hyndland St, Partick, Glasgow, T0141-3396523;
Granite Reef, 45 Justice St, Aberdeen, T01224-621193; and
Momentum, 22 Bruntsfield Place, Edinburgh, T0131-2296665.

Whitewater rafting **Monster Activities**, T01809-501340, www.monsteractivities.com, run trips on a dam-released river near Fort William.

Freespirits, the Riverside Inn, Grandtully, by Pitlochry, T01887-840400, www.freespirits.co,uk, daily 0930-1630, prices range from £25-35 for a half-day trip.

Spectator sports

Football

Football (soccer) is Scotland's most popular spectator sport. The Scottish Football League, established in 1874, is the main competition, with three divisions of 10 teams and one of 12. Scottish football is dominated, and always has been, by the two main Glasgow teams, **Rangers** and **Celtic**, known collectively as the 'Old Firm', who regularly attract crowds of over 50,000. For a brief period in the 1980s this stranglehold was broken by **Aberdeen** and **Dundee United**, but events since have proved this an aberration rather than a trend. Money is the main reason for this and the Old Firm have seemingly endless pots of the stuff, which is why they have been able to fill their team with expensive foreign imports and win most of the domestic competitions. Though neither side has fared too well in European competition in recent years, Celtic were the first British side to win the **European Cup,** in 1967.

Scotland's top 12 teams make up the **Premier League,** which has become a battle between the big two for the championship. Teams in the lower divisions mostly exist on a shoestring budget, though the other major competition, the **Scottish FA Cup,** still throws up occasional upsets, such as Celtic's defeat at the hands of lowly Inverness Caledonian Thistle in 1999. The domestic football season runs from early August to mid-May. Most matches are played on Saturdays at 1500, and there are often games through the week, on Tuesday and Wednesday evenings at 1930. There is usually a match on a Sunday afternoon, which is broadcast live on satellite TV. Tickets range from £10 up to £20 for big games.

The national team play at the recently renovated Hampden Park in Glasgow. Their passionate supporters, known as the 'Tartan Army', have gained something of an international reputation for their fun-loving attitude and self-deprecating humour in the face of defeat. This has stood them in good stead over the years for, despite qualifying for most **World Cup Finals** since 1974, Scotland have never managed to reach the second round, failing against such footballing giants as Iran and Costa Rica along the way. The patience of the Tartan Army has been severely tested, however, in recent times as the national side have struggled to a 2-2 with the Faroe Islands and a 4-0 drubbing at the hands of Wales.

Rugby Union

Rugby is one of the major sports of the country but lags a long, long way behind football in terms of popularity. The national team plays at Murrayfield in Edinburgh, and during match weekends there's always a great atmosphere in the city. Every year, in February and March, Scotland takes part in the **Six Nations Championship**, along with the other home teams, plus France and Italy. The most important game, though, is the clash with the 'Auld enemy', England. Tickets for games are hard to come by, but you can contact the **Scottish Rugby Union (SRU),** T0131-3465000, for details of upcoming home fixtures and where to find tickets.

The game in Scotland has been in a state of disarray ever since the advent of professionalism and the national side's performances in the 2004 Six Nations championship were nothing short of a joke. Things can only get better. The Borders town of Melrose is home of seven-a-side rugby, a variation of the 15-a-side game, and the **Melrose Sevens**, is the biggest tournament of the year in Scotland. The club rugby season runs from September to May.

Shinty

Shinty (or camanachd in Gaelic) is an amateur sport similar to Ireland's hurling. It's a physical game played at a fast and furious pace, and is a bit like hockey, but with more blood. The game is played mostly in the Highlands, and the highlight of the season is the **Camanachd Cup Final**, which attracts a large crowd and is televized on STV.

Health

Medical emergency: dial T999 or T112 (both free) for an ambulance.

No vaccinations are required for entry into Britain. Citizens of EU countries are entitled to free medical treatment at National Health Service hospitals on production of an E111 form. Also, Australia, New Zealand and several other non-EU European countries have reciprocal health-care arrangements with Britain. Citizens of other countries will have to pay for all medical services, except accident and emergency care given at Accident and Emergency (A&E) Units at most (but not all) National Health hospitals. Health insurance is therefore strongly advised for citizens of non-EU countries.

Pharmacists can dispense only a limited range of drugs without a doctor's prescription. Most are open for normal shop hours, though some are open late, especially in larger towns. Local newspapers will carry lists of which are open late. Doctors' surgeries are usually open from around 0830-0900 till 1730-1800, though times vary. Outside surgery hours you can go to the casualty department of the local hospital for any complaint requiring urgent attention. For the address of the nearest hospital or doctors' surgery, T0800-665544. See also individual town and city directories throughout the book for details local medical services.

You should encounter no major problems or irritations during your visit to Scotland. The only exceptions to this are the risk of hypothermia if you're walking in the mountains in difficult conditions, see page 56, and the dreaded midge, see box page 62.

Keeping in touch

Communications

Internet

It is now de rigeur amongst travellers to get an email address you can access through the internet, such as hotmail or yahoo. As in many places, internet access in Scotland is extensive. Every major town now has at least one internet café, with more springing up daily. Email works out much, much cheaper than phoning home and is also useful for booking hotels and tours and for checking out information on the web. Many hotels now have internet and many hostels also offer internet access to their guests. Websites and email addresses are listed where appropriate in this guide. The Scottish Tourist Board and area tourist boards have their own websites and these are given on page 22. Cybercafés are also listed under each relevant section. Most of these can be found in Edinburgh and Glasgow. In the absence of any cybercafés listed under a particular town try the public library for internet access or ask at the tourist office.

Post

Most post offices are open Monday-Friday 0900 to 1730 and Saturday 0900 to 1230 or 1300. Smaller sub-post offices are closed for an hour at lunch (1300-1400) and many of them operate out of a shop. Post offices keep the same half-day closing times as shops.

Stamps can be bought at post offices, but also from vending machines outside, and also at many newsagents. A first-class letter to anywhere in the UK costs 27p and should arrive the following day, while second-class letters cost 19p and take between two to four days. Airmail letters of less than 20g cost 37p to Europe. To the USA and Australia costs 45p for 10g and 65p for 20g. For more information about Royal Mail postal services, call T08457-740740 or www.royalmail.com.

Telephone

Most public payphones are operated by British Telecom (BT) and are fairly widespread in towns and cities, though less so in rural areas. BT payphones take either coins (20p, 50p and £1) or phonecards, which are available at newsagents and post offices displaying the BT logo. These cards come in denominations of £2, £3, £5 and £10. Some payphones also accept credit cards.

Useful numbers include: operator T100, international operator T155; directory enquiries T192; overseas directory enquiries T153.

For most countries (including Europe, USA and Canada) calls are cheapest between 1800 and 0800 Monday-Friday and all day Saturday and Sunday. For Australia and New Zealand it's cheapest to call from 1430 to 1930 and from midnight to 0700 every day.

Phone codes for towns and cities are given in the margin by the town's heading throughout this book. You don't need to use the area code if calling from the same area. Any number prefixed by 0800 or 0500 is free to the caller; 08457 numbers are charged at local rates and 08705 numbers at the national rate.

To call Scotland from overseas, dial 011 from USA and Canada, 0011 from Australia and 00 from New Zealand, followed by 44, then the area code, minus the first zero, then the number. To call overseas from Scotland dial 00 followed by the country code. Country codes include: Australia 61; Ireland 353; New Zealand 64; South Africa 27; USA and Canada 1.

Media

Newspapers and magazines

The main British daily and Sunday newspapers are widely available in Scotland and some of them publish special Scottish editions, among them the *Scottish Daily Mail*, *Scottish Daily Express* and Rupert Murdoch's notorious scandal sheet, *The Sun*.

The Scottish press produces two main 'quality' newspapers, the liberal-leaning *The Scotsman*, published in Edinburgh, and *The Herald*, published in Glasgow, which is the oldest daily newspaper in the English-speaking world, dating from 1783. The biggest-selling daily is the *Daily Record*, a tabloid paper (or red top as they are known). The Sunday equivalents of the dailies are *Scotland on Sunday* from the Scotsman stable, the *Sunday Herald* and the *Sunday Mail*, published by the *Daily Record*. Provincial newspapers are widely read in Scotland. The two biggest-selling titles are the parochial *Press and Journal* from Aberdeen and *The Courier & Advertiser*, published by Dundee's giant DC Thomson group, who also produce *The Beano* and *Dandy* kids' comics. DC Thomson publish Scotland's most successful Sunday newspaper, the *Sunday Post*, famous for its Oor Wullie and Broons cartoon charaters. In the Highlands the main papers are the weekly *Oban Times* and the radical, crusading *West Highland Free Press* published on Skye. Visitors to Glasgow and Edinburgh should buy a copy of the fortnightly listings magazine, *The List*, with lively features and previews, and reviews of all events in both cities.

Foreign newspapers and magazines, including *USA Today* and the *International Herald Tribune*, are available in larger newsagents, especially in central Edinburgh and Glasgow. *Time* and *Newsweek* are also available in larger newsagents and bookstores.

TV and radio

There are five main television channels in Scotland; the publicly funded BBC 1 and 2, and the independent commercial stations, Channel 4, Channel 5 and ITV. The ITV network in Scotland is formed by STV, which serves central Scotland and parts of the West Highlands, the Aberdeen-based Grampian TV which produces a lot of Gaelic programmes, and Border TV which covers Dumfries and Galloway and northwest England.

The BBC network also broadcasts several radio channels, most of which are based in London. These include: Radio 1 aimed at a young audience; Radio 2 targeting a more mature audience; Radio 3 which plays mostly classical music; Radio 4 which is talk-based and features arts, drama and current affairs; and Radio 5 Live which is a mix of sport and news. Radio Scotland (92-95FM, 810MW) provides a Scottish-based diet of news, sport, current affairs, travel and music. It also provides a Gaelic network in the northwest, and local programmes in Orkney and Shetland. There are also a large number of local commercial radio stations, stretching from Shetland in the north to the Borders. The local Glasgow station is Clyde 1 (102.5FM), while in Edinburgh it is Radio Forth (97.3FM). You also have Beat 106 fm (105.7-106.1 FM) who covers all of central Scotland and offers listeners a mix of urban and rock music.

Edinburgh

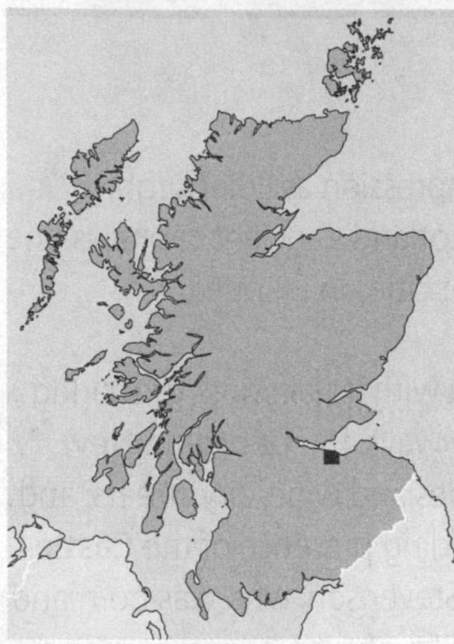

Footprint features

Introduction

Few cities make such a strong impression as Edinburgh. Dubbed the 'Athens of North', Scotland's ancient capital is one of the most beautiful and elegant cities in Europe.

There is the **medieval Old Town** with its labyrinth of soaring tenements and dark, sinister alleyways; the **Georgian New Town** with its genteel grey façades and wide, airy streets; and dominating everything, the brooding presence of the **Castle**. The great novelist, Robert Louis Stevenson, who was born and bred here, described the city as a "profusion of eccentricities, this dream in masonry and living rock", and went on to express his astonishment that it was "not a dropscene in a theatre, but a city in the world of everyday reality". Its urban parts are separated by parks and gardens and, most stunning of all, cliffs, rocks and grassy hills – even a few dormant volcanoes. This is real nature rather than the manicured stuff which you get in most other cities.

Fittingly, such a setting provides the stage for the **Edinburgh International Festival** and its various offshoots, which together comprise the biggest arts event on the planet. It also has many excellent museums and art galleries: the **National Gallery of Scotland**, the **Scottish National Gallery of Modern Art** and the **Museum of Scotland** all boast the finest collections outside London. But Edinburgh is more than just the sum of its arts. Its **Hogmanay party** is the biggest celebration in the northern hemisphere, and the arrival of the new **Scottish Parliament** has brought confidence and vitality to a city that was always thought of as being rather straight-laced. Edinburgh, once the most puritanical of places, has learned how to have fun, how to be stylish, and, heaven forbid, even how to be just a wee bit ostentatious.

★ Don't miss...

1. **Water of Leith** Take a walk along the river from the Scottish Gallery of Modern Art to the Botanic Gardens, page 98.
2. **Arthur's Seat** Climb Arthur's Seat for the wonderful views then descend to the Sheep's Heid Inn in Duddingston village for lunch, page 88.
3. **Ghost tour** Be very afraid... when you visit the haunted underground city vaults on one of the city's many ghost tours, page 120.
4. **Museum of Scotland and Sir Jules Thorn Exhibition** Visit the state-of-the-art museum, then head round the corner to the ghoulishly entertaining exhibition of the History of Surgery, page 91.
5. **Royal Yacht Britannia** Don't miss this vessel where you can take a peek at the Queen's bedroom and admire all that chintz, page 100.

Ins and outs ➔ *Phone code: 0131. Colour map 6, grid B1-2. Population 443,600.*

Getting there

Edinburgh international airport, T0131-333 1000 (general enquiries), T0131-344 3136 (airport information), is eight miles west of the city centre. Terminal facilities include a tourist information desk, Bureau de Change, ATMs, restaurants and bars (first floor) and shops (ground floor and first floor). The tourist information desk is in the international arrivals area, and will book accommodation and car hire. The main international car hire companies are in the main UK arrivals area. ➔ *For flight information, see page 120.*

There is an Airlink bus to the airport from Waverley Bridge, T0131-555 6363, www.flybybus.com. Fares are £3.30 single for adults, £2 for children. An open return is £5 for adults, £3 for children. Tickets can be bought from the driver or at the tourist information centre, see below. The journey time is 25 minutes, though this will be longer during the rush hour. Buses leave from Waverley Bridge every 10-20 minutes and every 10-20 minutes from the airport to the city centre from 0450 till 0025. The main pick up/drop off points in town are at the West End of Princes Street and Haymarket Station. Outside these times the N22 night bus service runs to the airport from St Andrew Square bus station. One of the white airport taxis to the city centre from the airport will cost around £16, while a black taxi cab will cost around £13-14. Journey time is roughly 20-30 minutes.

There are direct buses from most British cities to Edinburgh. The main operator is National Express, T0870-5808080, www.nationalexpress.com. Tickets can be bought at bus stations or from a huge number of agents throughout the country. Fares

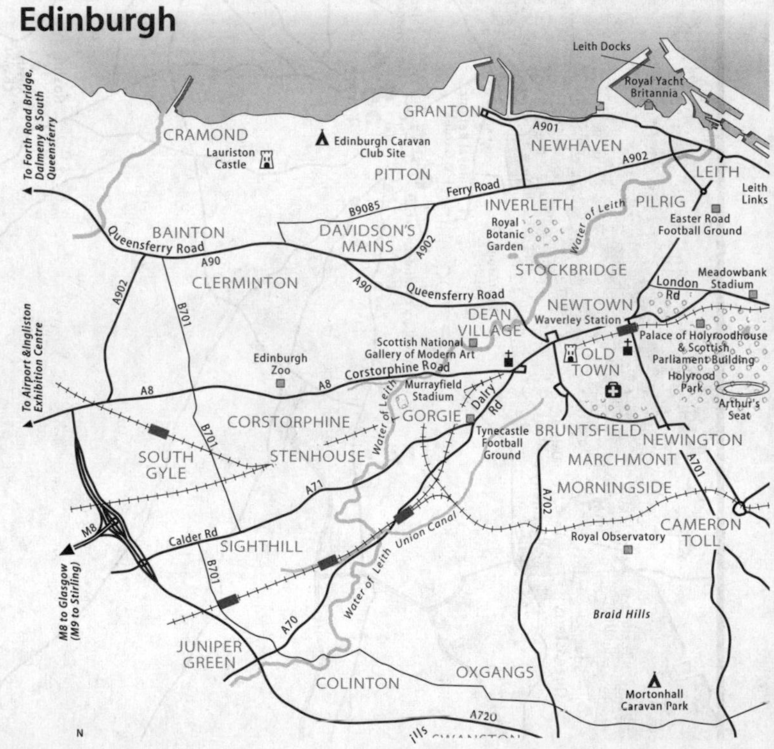

Come rain or shine

To describe Edinburgh's weather as changeable would be a huge understatement. The popular refrain states that if you don't like the weather, then just wait 20 minutes. Perhaps Robert Louis Stevenson best summed up the climatic conditions in his home town, "The weather is raw and boisterous in winter, shifty and ungenial in summer, and downright meteorological purgatory in spring". So, before you leave your hotel or guest house, be sure to pack your rain jacket, sunglasses, sunblock, thermals, gloves, woolly hat and snow shoes – and maybe an ice axe and crampons in case you fancy a walk up Arthur's Seat.

from London to Edinburgh start at £28 for an economy advance return. From Manchester it takes 6½ hours and costs from £21 return. There are also student discounts and passes for families and those travelling over a period of days that offer substantial savings. The new bus station in St Andrew Square is the terminal for all regional and national buses.

There are two main road routes to Edinburgh from the south: the M1/A1 in the east; and the M6 in the west. The journey from London takes around eight to 10 hours. A slower but more scenic route is to head off the A1 and take the A68 through the Borders.

All trains to Edinburgh go to Waverley station, off Waverley Bridge at the east end of Princes Street. Two companies operate direct services from London King's Cross to Edinburgh Waverley: GNER, T0845-7225225, www.gner.co.uk; and Virgin, T0845-7222333, www.virgin.com. Fares vary widely depending on time of travel and prior booking. For example from London prices start at £29 return rising to £186 for an open return. Trains from Birmingham take 5½ hours and cost from £29 return, from Newcastle take 1½ hours and cost from £18 return, and from Manchester take around 3½ hours and cost from £22 return. Scotrail, T0845-7550033, www.scotrail.co.uk, operate the Caledonian Sleeper service which travels overnight from London Euston to Edinburgh and takes seven hours. The main ticket booking office is located at Waverley Station, at which during peak periods a wait of 30-40 minutes is not unusual. Leave at least 10 minutes to buy tickets for immediate travel at other times. Taxis collect passengers from the station concourse, but if the queue is depressingly long, there's another taxi rank on Waverley Bridge. All trains to the north and to the west coast, including Glasgow, also stop at Haymarket station. ▸▸ *For further details, see Transport page 120.*

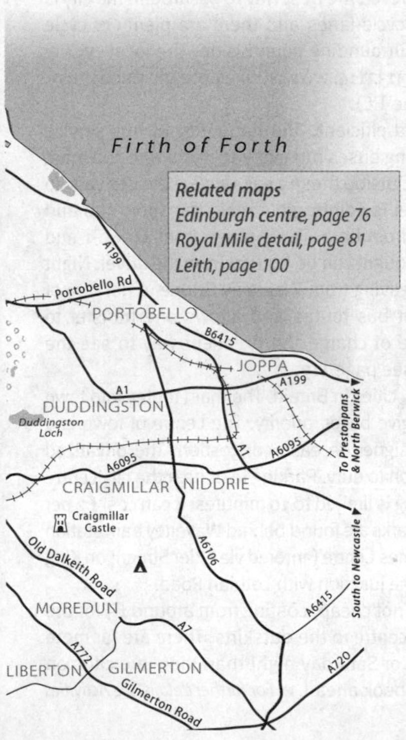

24 hours in the city

For those unlucky enough to have only a day to spend in Edinburgh, the following itinerary should give a taste of why it is the most visited British city outside London.

Start the day at the **Castle**, after which you'll need a breather and a well-earned coffee break at the **Elephant House**, on George IV Bridge. Afterwards, head across the road to the excellent **Museum of Scotland** in Chambers Street.

If you're feeling peckish, take a wee stroll down to **Black Bo's** on Blackfriars Street for a superb vegetarian lunch.

Then head down towards Princes Street and pop into the **National Gallery of Scotland**, the city's finest art gallery. If you've still got plenty of energy, head up **The Mound** and down the **Royal Mile** to the **Palace of Holyroodhouse**.

If the weather's fine, you may fancy a walk up to **Calton Hill** for the wonderful views, then head down to the nearby **Pivo Caffe** for a drink.

Then it's into a taxi and down to **Leith** for a superb seafood dinner at **Fishers**, before heading back uptown for some late-night action in one of the New Town's hip and groovy bars.

Getting around

Although Greater Edinburgh occupies a large area relative to its population of less than half a million, most of what you'll want to see lies within the compact city centre which is easily explored on foot. Though most of the main sights are within walking distance of each other, Edinburgh is a hilly city and a full day's sightseeing can leave you exhausted. Despite the hilly terrain however, the best way to get around the city is by bicycle. Many of the main roads have cycle lanes and there are plenty of cycle routes around the town and out into the surrounding countryside. The local cycling association, Spokes, 232 Dalry Road, T131-3132114, www.spokes.org.uk, publishes a very good cycle map (£4.95, available at the TIC).

Public transport is generally good and efficient. The frequency of bus service depends on the route, but generally speaking buses run every 10-15 minutes on most main routes Monday to Friday 0700-1900. Outside these peak times, services vary so it's best to check timetables. Princes Street is Edinburgh's main transport hub and you can get a bus to any part of the city from here. Fares range from £0.60-1 and there's a raft of saver tickets which can be bought can be bought from the driver. Night buses run every hour from 0015 till 0315, leaving from Waverley Bridge. A flat fare of £2 (£1 with Ridacard) applies on all night bus routes and allows one transfer to another Night Bus at Waverley Bridge free of charge. An excellent way to see the sights is to take one of the city bus tours, see page 119.

Edinburgh is one of the least car-friendly cities in Britain. The main routes into town have been turned into 'greenways', which give buses priority. The centre of town is a complicated system of one-way streets designed to ease congestion. The privatized traffic wardens are ruthless in their dedication to duty. Parking in or near the city centre is expensive and restrictive. On-street parking is limited to 10 minutes; it can cost £2 per hour to park in George Street. Large NCP car parks are found behind Waverley train station (entered via East Market Street), beside St James Centre (entered via Elder Street), on King Stables Road and on Morrison Street, near the junction with Lothian Road.

The council-imposed city taxi fares are not cheap, costing from around £3 for the shortest of trips up to around £6 from the centre to the outskirts. There are far more people wanting to get home late on Friday or Saturday night than there are cabs on the streets, so be prepared to wait, walk or book ahead. » *For further details, see Activities and tours page 119 and Transport page 120.*

Tourist information

Edinburgh's main **tourist office** ⓘ *3 Princes St on top of Waverley Market, T0131-473 3800, www.edinburgh.org, Apr and Oct Mon-Sat 0900-1800, Sun 1100-1800, May and Sep Mon-Sat 0900-1900, Sun 1100-1900, Jun Mon-Sat 0900-1900, Sun 1000-1900; Jul and Aug Mon-Sat 0900-2000, Sun 1000-2000, Nov-Mar Mon-Sat 0900-1800, Sun 1000-1800*. It gets very busy during the peak season and at Festival time, but has the full range of services, including currency exchange, and will book accommodation, provide travel information and book tickets for various events and excursions. There's also a tourist information desk at the **airport** ⓘ *T0131-333 2167, Apr-Oct Mon-Sat 0830-2130, Sun 0930-2130, Nov-Mar Mon-Fri 0900-1800, Sat 0900-1700, Sun 0930-1700*, in the international arrivals area. Another useful tourist information resource is the **Backpackers Centre** ⓘ *6 Blackfriars St, T0131-557 9393*, which will provide information about hostels and tours and will book coach tickets. The City Council has produced a free map of the different bus routes around Edinburgh. This is available from the TIC or from the **LRT ticket centres** ⓘ *31 Waverley Bridge, T0131-2258616, Easter-Oct Mon-Sat 0800-1800, Sun 0900-1630, Nov-Easter Tue-Sat 0900-1630, or 27 Hanover St, T0131-5556363, Mon-Sat 0830-1800*. Both offices sell travel cards. **Traveline** ⓘ *2 Cockburn St, near Waverley Station, T0800-232323 (local calls) or T0131-2253858 (national calls), Mon-Fri 0830-2000*, runs a public-transport information service for Edinburgh, East Lothian and Midlothian.

History

Edinburgh's early history begins on the Castle Rock, which was occupied in the Bronze and Iron Age. Following a brief visit by the Romans, the Angles of Northumbria came, saw, conquered and hung around for a while. In the seventh century, their king, Edwin, rebuilt the earlier fortress of Dun Eadain – the Fortress on the Slope – and changed its name to Edwin's Burgh.

The town only began to develop beyond the fortress during the 11th century; the pace of growth quickening when the new king, David I, moved his capital from Dunfermline to Edinburgh in 1124. Four years later he founded his abbey at Holyrood and the Burgh's continued progress was marked in 1329 by the granting of a charter by Robert the Bruce.

From the reign of James II to James IV (1437-1513) the city flourished. The first town wall was built in 1437 (the Wellhouse Tower at the northern foot of Castle Rock is the only remaining trace), followed by the construction of Holyrood Palace. This Renaissance period also saw much patronage of the arts and education, including the granting of a charter to the Royal College of Surgeons in 1506, and the establishment of Scotland's first printing press in 1508.

The Renaissance era was brought to a sudden end, however, by the disastrous defeat at Flodden in 1513, and there followed more than a century of darkness and despair. During the years of the 'Rough Wooing' – when Henry VIII took exception to the Scots' refusal to ratify a marriage treaty between his son and the infant Mary Stuart – in 1544 and 1547, the king, never a man to cross, devastated the city. Edinburgh suffered further in 1561, following the return of Mary, Queen of Scots from France, in what were seven turbulent and tragic years. When Mary's son, James VI, became James I of England with the Union of Crowns in 1603, he moved his court to London and Edinburgh entered a period of obscurity. Obscurity did not bring peace, however. The bitter and bloody religious struggle that began in Mary's short reign reached its climax in the 17th century. First, the National Covenant was signed at Greyfriars in 1638, then Cromwell occupied the city in 1650, and in the same year Montrose was executed. Meanwhile, witches continued to be burned on the castle esplanade and over 100 Covenanters were martyred in the Grassmarket.

Edinburgh centre

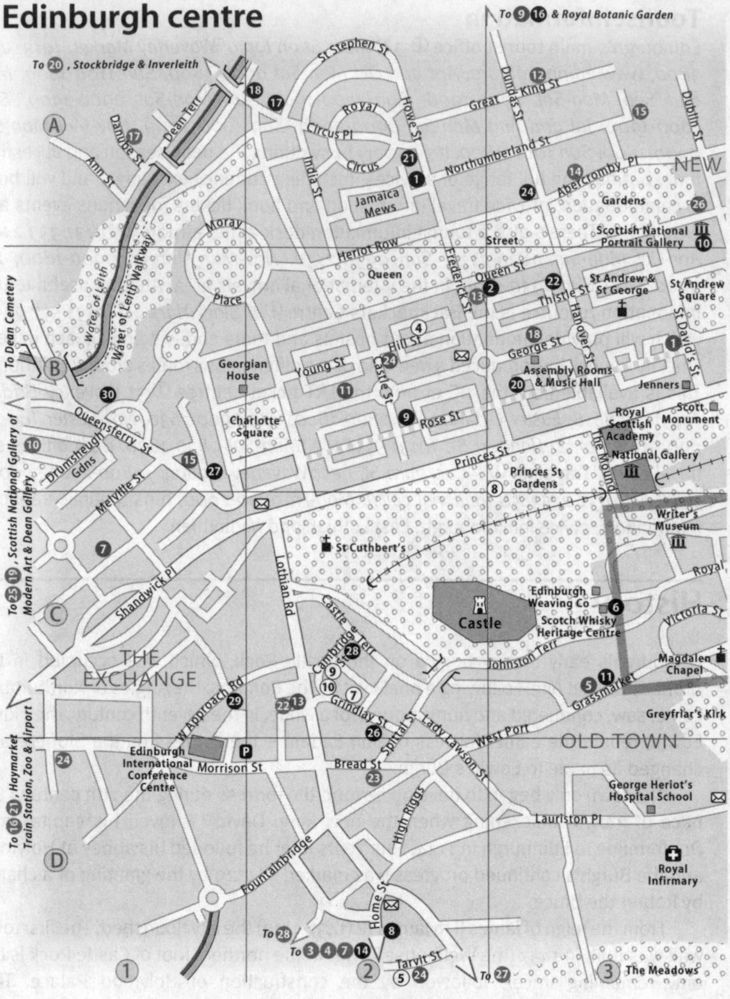

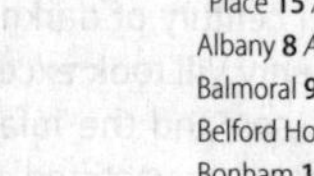

Sleeping

16 Lynedoch Place **19** *B1*
17 Abercromby Place **14** *A3*
24 Northumberland Place **15** *A3*
Albany **8** *A4*
Balmoral **9** *B4*
Belford Hostel **25** *B1*
Bonham **10** *B1*
Bruntsfield **3** *D2*
Bruntsfield Youth Hostel **4** *D2*
Edinburgh First **5** *D6*
Eglinton Youth Hostel **21** *C1*
Glasshouse **11** *A4*
Greenhouse **7** *D2*
Howard **12** *A3*
Orginal Raj **16** *C1*
Point & Mondobbo Bar **23** *D2*
Prestonfield House **2** *D6*
Ricks **13** *B2*
Royal Garden Apartments **26** *A3*
Scotsman **1** *B4*
Seven Danube Street **17** *A1*
Sheraton Grand **22** *C2*
Six Mary's Place **20** *A1*
Stuart House **18** *A4*
Teviotdale House **27** *D2*
Town House **28** *D2*
Travel Inn **24** *D1*
Witchery by the Castle **6** *C3*

Eating

A Room in the Town **1** *A2*
Atrium & blue **28** *C2*
Bar Roma **27** *B1*
Bell's Diner **17** *A2*
Blue Moon **23** *A4*
Café Royal Oyster Bar **15** *B4*
Café St-Honoré **2** *B3*
Duck's at Le Marche Noir **16** *A3*
Fruitmarket Café **3** *B4*
Glass & Thompson **24** *A3*
Henderson's Salad Table **22** *B3*
Home Bistro **5** *D4*
Howies **18** *A2*
Kalpna **6** *D5*
La Cuisine D'Odile **30** *B1*
Librizzi's **7** *D4*
Loon Fung **19** *A5*
Lost Sock Diner **31** *A4*
Mussel Inn **20** *B3*
Ndbele **8** *D2*

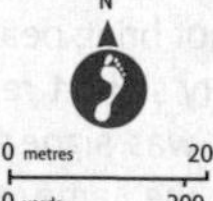

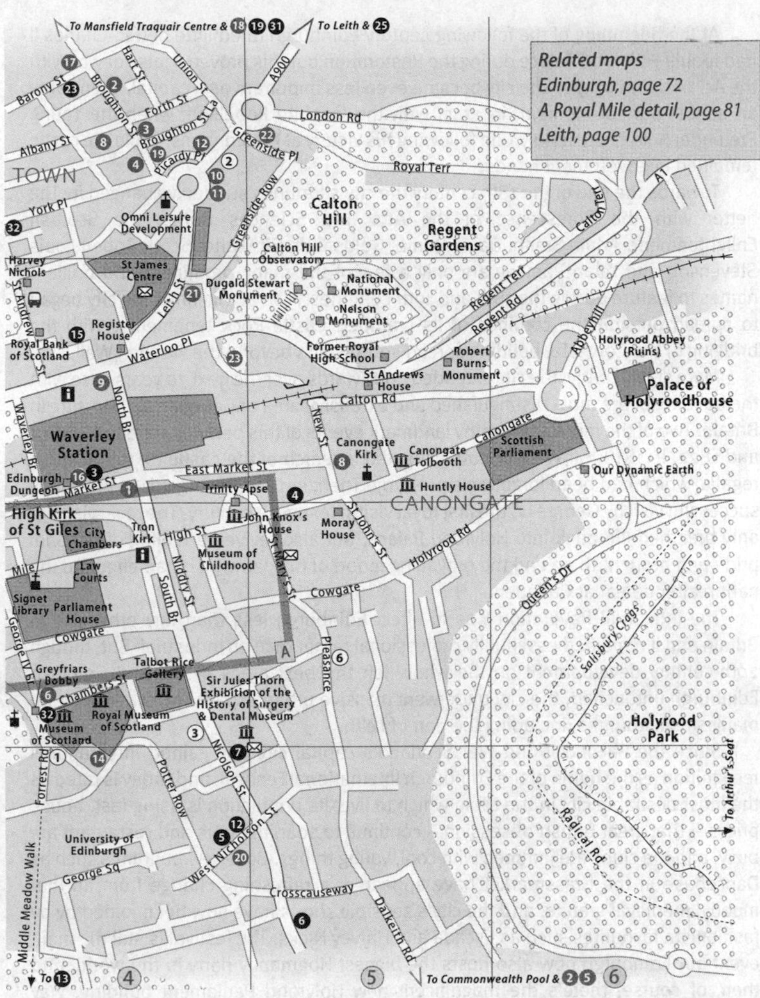

Oloroso **9** *B2*
Petit Paris **11** *C3*
Plaisir du Chocolat **4** *B5*
Queen Street Café **10** *A3*
Santini & One Spa **29** *C1*
Siam Erawan **21** *A2*
Stac Polly **26** *C2*
Susie's Diner **12** *D4*
Sweet Melindas **13** *D4*
Thai Lemongrass **14** *D2*
Tower **32** *C4*
Valvona & Crolla **25** *A5*
Zest **32** *A3*

Bars & clubs
Abbotsford **1** *B3*
Barony Bar **2** *A4*
Baroque **3** *A4*
Basement **4** *A4*
Beehive Inn **5** *C3*
Beluga Bar **6** *C4*
Bennet's Bar **24** *D2*
Bert's Bar **7** *C1*
Bongo Club **8** *B5*
Candy Bar **11** *B2*
CC Blooms **10** *A4*
Cumberland Bar **9** *A3*
Ego **12** *A4*
Filmhouse Café Bar **13** *C2*
Hurricane Bar & Grill **24** *B2*
Iguana & Negociants **14** *D4*
Indigo Yard **15** *B1*
Massa **16** *C4*
Nexus Café **17** *A4*
Opal Lounge **18** *B3*
Outhouse **19** *A4*
Pear Tree **20** *D4*
Pivo Caffé **21** *B4*
Planet Out **22** *A5*
Venue **23** *B4*

Entertainment
Bedlam Theatre **1** *D4*
Edinburgh Playhouse **2** *A4*
Festival Theatre **3** *C4*
Hill Street Theatre **4** *B2*
King's Theatre **5** *D2*
Pleasance Theatre **6** *C5*
Ross Open Air Theatre **8** *B3*
Royal Lyceum Theatre **7** *C2*
Traverse Theatre **9** *C2*
Ushers Hall **10** *C2*

At the beginning of the following century Edinburgh fared little better. Charles II had rebuilt Holyrood Palace during the Restoration but this proved a false dawn. With the Act of Union of 1707 the city became even less important as a capital. Then came an almost surreal moment, in 1745, with the Jacobite Rebellion, when the Young Pretender held court at Holyrood following his victory at Prestonpans, while the castle remained in government hands.

Towards the end of the 18th century the city's fortunes suddenly changed for the better with the florescence of the Arts and Sciences during the Scottish Enlightenment. Adam Smith, David Hume, Goldsmith, Sir Walter Scott, Robert Louis Stevenson and Allan Ramsay are only a few of the many prominent and brilliant names to feature during the 18th and 19th centuries. Also at this time, the city began to spread outside the confines of its cramped Castle Rock tenements. With the bridging of the Cowgate, building spread southwards beyond the Flodden Wall.

More significantly, the city extended northwards over the next 70 years or so with the building of the most distinguished and extensive area of Georgian architecture in Britain. Two of the most noteworthy landmark events of this period happened in 1818 and 1822. In 1818, Sir Walter Scott instigated a search of the castle for the Scottish regalia, which had been forgotten since 1707. Then, in 1822, he organized the highly successful visit by George IV, the first royal visitor for over a century. The royal visit not only breathed life back into Holyrood Palace, but also revived a feeling of national pride and brought to an end the prevailing mood of despair which had engulfed the nation after defeat at Culloden.

The Industrial Revolution was to affect Edinburgh less than any other city in Britain and it remained essentially professional rather than an industrial. But, though 20th-century development on the whole left the best areas of old and Georgian Edinburgh untouched, the city underwent massive urban expansion, swallowing up many smaller burghs, including the port of Leith.

Since the Second World War Scotland's capital city has gained international recognition as the home of the Edinburgh International Festival, and today is rated as the most desirable city in the UK in which to live. Its population is rising fast, house prices – that great British obsession – continue to soar, the bars and restaurant are busy, and the clubs are jammed with cool, young things. Bold new buildings such as Dancebase in the Grassmarket have appeared, a refreshing change from all that moody, medieval granite, and the city's sensible shops have now been joined by by fashionista favourites such as Escada and Harvey Nicks. The festival is still the main event but Edinburgh now also hosts the biggest Hogmanay party in the world, and then, of course, there's the magnificent new Holyrood Parliament building, way behind schedule and hugely over budget at a staggering £400 million and rising, but sure to be the country's most important architectural statement for many centuries.

Sights

The city centre is divided in two. North of Princes Street is the elegant neoclassical New Town, built in the late 18th and early 19th centuries to improve conditions in the city. South of Princes Street, across the beautiful Princes Street Gardens, is the Old Town, a rabbit warren of narrow alleys and closes, inhabited by the ghosts of Edinburgh's seamy past, and the inspiration for Stevenson's famous Dr Jekyll and Mr Hyde. *This medieval Manhattan of high-rise tenements runs from the castle down to the Palace of Holyroodhouse. Overlooking the palace is Edinburgh's largest and most impressive extinct volcano, Arthur's Seat, an authentic piece of mountain wilderness within a stone's throw of the city centre.* ▸▸ *For Sleeping, Eating and other listings, see pages 104-122.*

Old Town

The best place to start a tour of Edinburgh is in the medieval Old Town, where you'll find most of the famous sights from the castle, down through the Royal Mile, to the Palace of Holyroodhouse. South of the Royal Mile is the Grassmarket, the Cowgate and Chambers Street, site of the University of Edinburgh and two of the city's best museums, the Royal Museum of Scotland and the Museum of Scotland. ▸▸ *For Sleeping, Eating and other listings, see pages 104-122.*

Edinburgh Castle

ⓘ T0131-225 9846 (HS), Apr-Sep daily 0930-1800, Oct-Mar 0930-1700, last entry 45 mins before closing, £8.50, concessions £6.25, children £2.

The city skyline is dominated by the castle, Scotland's prime tourist attraction and the most visited sight in Britain outside London. The castle sits on top of an extinct volcano, protected on three sides by steep cliffs, and is well worth a visit, if only for the great views over the city from its battlements.

Not surprisingly, such a strategic site has been the focus of much attention over the centuries. The Picts, Scots, British (Welsh) and Angles disputed ownership of the Castle Rock until the Scots finally came out on top. Edinburgh then went on to become established as Scotland's capital but, due to its proximity to England, was under constant threat of invasion from south of the border. Since 1174, when it was held by the English for 12 years, the castle defences have hardly had a moment's rest. In 1296 King Edward I occupied this prime piece of real estate, then, in 1314, the Earl of Moray famously climbed the north face and drove out the English incumbents to reinstate King Robert the Bruce. The castle has withstood many sieges since then – the longest from 1570 to 1573, in defence of Mary, Queen of Scots – but has also been breached on a few occasions. In 1650 it succumbed to Cromwell's New Model Army, and in 1689, when the Duke of Gordon tried, but failed, to hold out against the Protestant army of William of Orange. Today, the castle is still 'invaded' on a regular basis, this time by crowds of a rather more benign nature, namely tourists.

❢ You can easily wander round the castle yourself, but for a more colourful introduction to its eventful past, you can join one of the first-rate guided tours.

The castle is entered from the top of the Royal Mile, via the Esplanade, which was built in the 18th and 19th centuries as a parade ground. During the Festival, the Esplanade is the setting for the Military Tattoo, see page 117, and from the south wall there are excellent views across to the Pentland Hills. Dotted around the Esplanade are various memorial plaques to members of the Scottish regiments who fell in overseas wars, and several military monuments, including one of Field Marshall Earl Haig, one of the city's most notorious sons, whose insane trench warfare strategy in the First World War led to such horrific casualties.

A drawbridge, the last ever built in Scotland, leads to the 19th-century Gatehouse, which is flanked by modern statues of Sir William Wallace and Robert the Bruce. The main path then leads steeply up, through the **Portcullis Gate**, to the **Argyll Battery** then the **Mill's Mount Battery**. Every day (except Sundays, Christmas Day and Good Friday) since 1851, the 'one o' clock gun' has been fired from the Mill's Mount Battery as a time-check for the city's office workers. From both batteries there are wonderful views across Princes Street, the New Town and the Firth of Forth.

The steep and winding road continues up past the Governer's House and the **New Barracks**, both built in the 18th century (many of the buildings within the castle walls date from the 18th century or later). Then the road turns once more, through Foog's

Stone of Destiny

Edinburgh Castle is the home of the famous Stone of Destiny, the subject of much controversy and rumour throughout the country's troubled past.

According to legend, the Stone of Destiny was the biblical 'Jacob's Pillow', on which Jacob dreamed of a ladder of angels leading from earth to heaven. The stone is said to have arrived in Scotland from the Holy Land, via Spain and Ireland. The king, Kenneth MacAlpin, moved it to Scone, near Perth, where the ancient coronation custom continued. Rumour has it that the supposed original, stolen by Edward I in 1296, which remained under lock and key in Westminster Abbey until 1996, is a poor substitute made of Perthshire sandstone, and that the real article was hidden, to reappear when Scotland regained her sovereignty. Some say Bruce was crowned on it, after which it went with his great ally, Angus Og of the Isles, to Islay for safekeeping.

Students removed the stone from Westminster in 1950 and returned it, briefly, to Scotland. Thereafter, unfolds a farcical tale of substitutes, replicas, claims and counter-claims. Some say the real stone was discovered around 100 years ago buried in Macbeth's ruined fort on Dunsinnan. Could this be the hiding place chosen by the monks of Scone in 1296, or did Macbeth hide it centuries earlier? If the stone – returned so ceremoniously from Westminster to Scotland in 1996 in a vain attempt to restore flagging Tory fortunes north of the border – is a fake, where is the real one? Somebody knows and isn't telling.

Gate, to the summit of Castle Rock and **St Margaret's Chapel**, the oldest surviving building in the castle, and probably in the city itself. The tiny, simple yet beautiful building is said to have been built by Margaret herself, but the Norman style suggests it was constructed later, most likely as a memorial by her son, King David I. Following Cromwell's capture of the Castle in 1650, the chapel was used as an ammunition store, until Queen Victoria had it restored, and it was eventually rededicated in 1934. In front of the chapel is the **Half Moon Battery**, which offers the best panoramic views over the city.

South of the chapel is Crown Square, the most secure and most important section of the entire complex. The eastern side is taken up by the **Palace of Holyrood house**, begun in the 15th century and remodelled in the 16th century for Mary, Queen of Scot's. Above the main doorway are the initials of Mary and her husband Henry, Lord Darnley. Here, in 1566, Queen Mary gave birth to James VI, later to become James I of England. Rumour has it that her child was stillborn, and the newborn baby of a serving maid was put in its place, but like much else in Scottish history, the truth remains elusive.

Later, in 1617, the Palace buildings were extended with the addition of the Crown Room, where the **Honours of Scotland** are now displayed – the royal crown, the sceptre and the sword of state. There is no more potent symbol of Scottish nationhood than these magnificent crown jewels, which were last used for the coronation of Charles II in 1651, an event which incurred the wrath of one Oliver Cromwell, who made repeated but unsuccessful attempts to get rid of the jewels. Then, in 1707, the crown jewels were locked away in a chest and forgotten about. They were presumed lost for over a century, until Sir Walter Scott initiated a search and rediscovered them in 1818. The oldest of the Honours is the **sceptre**, bestowed on James IV by Pope Alexander VI and later remodelled for James V. The even more impressive **sword of state** was presented to James IV by Pope Julius II in 1507. The jewel-encrusted **crown** contains the circlet of gold with which Robert the Bruce was crowned at Scone in 1306, and was remade for James V in 1540. Also housed in the Crown Room is the recently-installed **Stone of Destiny** (see box), the seat on which the ancient kings of Scotland were crowned. However, no one knows whether this is, in fact, the real stone.

On the south side of the square is James IV's Great Hall. Once the seat of the Scottish Parliament and later used for state banquets, it now houses a display of arms and armour. On the west side of the square is the 18th-century **Queen Anne Barracks**, which now contains the **Scottish United Services Museum**. On the north side stands the neo-Gothic **Scottish National Monument**, designed by Sir Robert Lorimer and a dignified testament to the many tens of thousands of Scottish soldiers killed in the First World War.

From the western end of Crown Square you can descend into the Vaults, a series of dark and dank chambers, once used as a prison for French captives during the Napoleonic Wars. One of the rooms contains **Mons Meg**, the massive iron cannon forged here in the reign of James IV (1488-1513). It was said to have had a range of nearly 1½ miles and was used for salutes on royal occasions. It was taken to the Tower of London in 1754, where it stayed until Sir Walter Scott persuaded George IV to return it during the latter's state visit to Scotland in 1822.

Royal Mile

Running through the heart of the medieval Old Town, from the castle down to the **Palace of Holyroodhouse**, is the Royal Mile, where you'll find a greater concentration of historic buildings than almost anywhere else in Britain. This street was described by Daniel Defoe (who lived in Edinburgh at the beginning of the 18th century) as "perhaps the largest, longest and finest Street for buildings, and Number of Inhabitants, not in

 Britain only, but in the world". It is now also one of the busiest tourist thoroughfares in the world, especially during the Festival. Consequently, it's full of shops selling tacky souvenirs, but not even these can detract from its sheer magnificence.

The 1,984 yards of the Royal Mile, from the Castle Keep to the Palace, comprises four separate streets: (from top to bottom) **Castlehill**, **Lawnmarket**, the **High Street** and the **Canongate**. Branching out from these is a honeycomb of *wynds* and *closes*, entered via archways known as pends. A close is the entrance to a 'land' or high-rise tenement block, and *wynds* are the narrow and winding alleyways giving access to the main street. These were the scene of many important – and sinister – events over the centuries and are certainly worth exploring in detail.

Here, the city's aristocracy, gentry, merchants and commoners lived together, often in the same building, with the upper classes at the bottom and the hoi polloi at the top. Until the end of the 18th century, the Old Town was the hub of fashionable society. Indeed, such was the concentration of talent that John Amyat, the King's chemist, remarked that he could stand at the Mercat Cross and "in a few minutes take fifty men of genius by the hand".

At the turn of the 19th century the Old Town was gradually abandoned by the Great and the Good of Edinburgh, who moved lock, stock and barrel to the New Town in what was called 'The Great Flitting'. The Old Town deteriorated into an overcrowded slum. People would throw their refuse and sewage out of the tenement windows onto the street, shouting to the passers-by, below with the traditional warning of 'Gardyloo' (from the French *garde a l'eau*). Not surprisingly, such a place of filth and squalor was highly vulnerable to epidemics and it is only in the past century that the Royal Mile has been cleaned and turned into one of the most fascinating and picturesque streets in the world.

Castlehill

The narrow uppermost part of the Royal Mile nearest the castle is known as Castlehill. Just below the Castle Esplanade is an iron fountain which marks the spot where more than 300 Edinburgh women were burned as witches between 1479 and 1722. Behind the fountain rises **Ramsay Gardens**, a distinctive and picturesque late 19th-century apartment block which grew around the octagonal **Goose Pie House**, home of 18th-century poet Allan Ramsay, author of *The Gentle Shepherd*. These early apartments were designed by Sir Patrick Geddes, a pioneer of architectural conservation and town planning, who created them in an attempt to regenerate the Old Town. At the corner of Castlehill and Castle Wynd is **Cannonball House**, which takes its name from a cannonball embedded in the west wall. According to legend, the cannonball was fired from the Castle during the '45 rebellion, but in fact it marks the high-water level of the city's first piped water supply in 1681.

At 354 Castlehill is the **Scotch Whisky Heritage Centre** ⓘ *T0131-2200441, www.whisky-heritage.co.uk, daily Jun-Sep 0930-1800, Oct-May 1000-1730, £7.50, children £3.95, concessions £5.50*, where you can find out everything you ever wanted to know about Scotland's national drink. The best part is the **Bond Bar**, where you can sample some of the vast range of malt whiskies on offer before buying a bottle in the gift shop. Across the street is the **Edinburgh Old Town Weaving Company** ⓘ *T0131-2261555, daily 0900-1730, free entry to mill and a small charge for the exhibition*, which has a real working mill where you can see tartan being woven and a small exhibition.

A few doors further down, on the corner of Ramsay Lane, is the **Outlook Tower** ⓘ *T0131-2263709, daily Apr-Oct 0930-1800 (later in Jul/Aug), Nov-Mar 1000-1700, £5.75, children £3.70, concessions £4.60*, which has been one of the capital's top tourist attractions since a **camera obscura** was set up in the hexagonal tower by optician, Maria Theresa Short, in 1854. The device consists of a camera which sweeps around the city and beams the live images onto a screen, accompanied by a running commentary of the city's past. There's also an exhibition of photographs taken with a variety of home-made pinhole cameras and the rooftop viewing terrace offers fantastic views of the city.

A little further down, on the opposite side of the street is the **Tolbooth Kirk**, whose distinctive spire is the highest in the city and a distinctive feature of the Edinburgh skyline. It was originally intended to house the General Assembly of the Church of Scotland, but they moved across the street in the 1850s. The Tolbooth Kirk was where the city's Gaelic speakers used to worship, until it was closed in 1981. It has since been converted into **The Hub**, which houses the ticket centre for Edinburgh International Festival, see Festivals and events page 117. The Hub also stages various events and is home to the excellent **Café Hub**, see Eating page 107. Opposite is the neo-Gothic **New College and Assembly Hall**. Built in 1859, it is the meeting place of the annual General Assembly of the Church of Scotland and is also used during the Festival to stage major drama productions. It is now the temporary home for the Scottish Parliament. You can arrange tickets to visit the Debating Chamber when Parliament is sitting (Wednesday afternoons and Thursdays) at the visitor centre, on the corner of the Royal Mile and George IV Bridge.

Lawnmarket

The Tolbooth Kirk and Assembly Hall mark the top of the Lawnmarket, a much broader street named after the old linen market which used to be held here. At the northern end is **Milne's Court**, built in 1690 and skilfully renovated in 1971 as student residences. Next comes **James Court**, a very prestigious address, where the philosopher David Hume lived and where Boswell entertained Dr Johnson in 1773. Back on Lawnmarket itself, at number 477b, is **Gladstone's Land** ⓘ *T0131-2265856 (NTS), 1 Apr-end-Oct Mon-Sat 1000-1700, Sun 1400-1700, £5, concessions £3.75, children free*, the most important surviving example of 17th-century tenement housing in the Old Town, where the cramped conditions meant that extension was only possible in depth or upwards. The magnificent six-storey building, completed in 1620, contains remarkable painted ceilings and was the home of an Edinburgh burgess, Thomas Gledstanes. The reconstructed shop booth on the ground floor has replicas of 17th-century goods and the first floor of the house has been refurbished as a typical Edinburgh home of the period.

Further down Lawnmarket, steps lead down to Lady Stair's Close, where you'll find **Lady Stair's House**, another fine 17th-century house, though restored in pseudo-medieval style. It is now the home of the **Writer's Museum** ⓘ *T0131-5294901, Mon-Sat 1000-1700 and Sun 1400-1700 during the Festival only, free* dedicated to the three giants of Scottish literature, Burns, Scott and Stevenson.

Opposite Gladstone's Land is **Riddle's Court**, another of David Hume's residences. Here also is the late-16th-century house of Bailie McMorran, who was shot dead by pupils of the Royal High School during a riot in 1595 against the proposed reduction in school holidays. Further down the street on the opposite side is **Brodie's Close**, named after the father of one of Edinburgh's most nefarious characters, Deacon Brodie. He was an apparent pillar of the community by day and a burglar by night, until his eventual capture and hanging in 1788. Robert Louis Stevenson co-wrote a play about his life, which was to provide the inspiration for *Dr Jekyll and Mr Hyde*.

High Kirk of St Giles and Parliament Square

ⓘ *T0131-2259442, Easter-Sep Mon-Fri 0900-1900, Sat 0900-1700, Sun 1300-1700, Oct-Easter Mon-Sat 0900-1700, Sun 1300-1700, free (donations welcome).*

Across George IV Bridge, at the top of the High Street, stands the High Kirk of St Giles, the only parish church of medieval Edinburgh and the home of Presbyterianism, where the firebrand preacher John Knox launched the Scottish Reformation. The Kirk is mistakenly called St Giles Cathedral. This is because Charles I called it so when he introduced bishops into the Church of Scotland and the name stuck, even after Presbyterianism was re-established. The church was given a major face-lift in the 19th century, covering most of its Gothic exterior, but parts of the original medieval building still survive, most notably the late-15th-century crowned tower. The four huge octagonal pillars which support the central tower are thought to date back to the previous Norman church, built in 1120 and razed to the ground by English invaders in the late 14th century.

The church has had a colourful past ever since medieval times when the Scottish Parliament met here. It was the launchpad for the Scottish Reformation, as mentioned above, then, around the turn of the 16th century, it was divided up and used as law courts, the town clerk's office, a school and a prison. When the High Kirk returned to its religious function it was partitioned into four different churches, each serving its own congregation, finally being reunified after its Victorian restoration.

One of the most celebrated incidents in the church's history happened in 1637, when an attempt to read from the English prayer book so incensed Jenny Geddes, a humble stallholder, that she launched her stool at the bishop's head, shouting (according to tradition): "False thief, will ye no say mass about my lug?", which roughly translates as "stop saying mass or you're in big trouble, mate!". A plaque marks the spot where the stool landed and recounts the ensuing riot. Such disturbances led to the National Covenenant of 1638, establishing the Presbyterian Church of Scotland in defiance of Charles I. This in turn led to Civil War, during which many Covenanters were imprisoned in the church. Two of the most famous figures of the war, the royalist Marquis of Montrose and the convenanting Marquis of Argyll, were both executed outside the church and now lie entombed within its walls, facing each other from opposite aisles.

There have been many additions to the High Kirk since its restoration. One of these is the very beautiful **Thistle Chapel**, the Chapel of the Most Ancient and Most Noble Order of the Thistle (Scotland's foremost order of chivalry). It was designed by Sir Robert Lorimer and built in 1911. The elaborate ornamentation and fine carvings are exquisite (look out for the angel playing the bagpipes). There are also several Pre-Raphaelite stained-glass windows in the church, and above the west door is a memorial window to Robert Burns, rather surprising given that the great bard was hardly an upholder of Presbyterian values. There's a good café in the church crypt.

Outside the High Kirk of St Giles, on Parliament Square, is an imposing equestrian statue of **King Charles II** and, nearby, a flat stone bearing the legend 'I.K. 1572' marks the reputed burial place of **John Knox**. In front of the west door of the church is the site of the city Tolbooth, demolished in 1817. The Tolbooth entrance is marked by a heart-shaped pattern in the cobblestones, known as the Heart of Midlothian, and made famous by Sir Walter Scott in his eponymous novel. Should you see passers-by spitting on it, it's not a sign of disrespect, but supposed to bring good luck. Behind the church is the Mercat Cross, where public proclamations are traditionally read. The present cross is a replica, gifted to the city by the then prime-minister, W.E. Gladstone.

The High Kirk of St Giles forms the northern side of Parliament Square which is also surrounded by the Law Courts, Parliament House and the Signet Library. The **Law Courts**, where Sir Walter Scott practised as an advocate, were originally planned by architect Robert Adam (1728-1792), who contributed so much to the grace and elegance of the New Town, but, due to lack of funds, built to designs by Robert Reid (1776-1856). On the west side of the square is the **Signet Library**, centre for the Society of Her Majesty's Writers to the Signet, an organization that originated from the 15th-century Keepers of the King's Seal, or signet. It boasts one of the finest neoclassical interiors in the city, but unfortunately can only be seen by prior written application, except on very occasional open days. **Parliament House**, facing the south side of St Giles, was the meeting place of the Scots Parliament between 1639 and 1707. It is now used by the city's lawyers in between court sittings, but is readily accessible during the week. The most notable feature is the magnificent **Parliament Hall** with its 17th-century hammerbeam roof.

Cockburn Street and Market Street

The steep, cobbled slope of Cockburn Street presents a grungier side of Edinburgh, with fetish clothing shops, piercing parlours and second-hand record shops. There are also some good bars and restaurants as well as the **Stills Gallery** ⓘ *T0131-622 6200, Tue-Sat 1000-1700*, and the **Collective Gallery** ⓘ *T0131-220 1260*. On Market Street, next to Waverley Station, is the **Edinburgh Dungeon** ⓘ *T0870-8460666, www.thedungeons.com, Nov-Mar Mon-Fri 1100-1600, Sat and Sun 1030-1630, Apr-Jun daily 1000-1700, Jul-Aug 1000-1900, Sep-Oct 1000-1700, £7.95, concessions £5.95*, an entertaining trawl through some of the more sinister and infamous characters in Scottish history and there's an Edinburgh section on the likes of Burke and Hare and Deacon Brodie. It's all very scary and not for the squeamish, but tends to paint its historical detail with a very broad brush.

Also on Market Street is the **City Arts Centre** ⓘ *T0131-529 3993, www.cac.org.uk, Mon-Sat 1000-1700, also Sun 1400-1700 in Jul and Aug, free (charges for special exhibitions)*, an excellent municipal art space with a large collection of Scottish works, including those by McTaggart, Fergusson, Peploe and Eardley. There's also an ever-changing programme of exhibitions. Directly opposite is the **Fruitmarket Gallery** ⓘ *T0141-225 2383, Mon-Sat 1100-1800, Sun 1200-1700, free,* a smaller and more contemporary gallery.

High Street

Opposite St Giles is **Edinburgh City Chambers**, built in 1753 as the Royal Exchange. In the early 19th century it became the headquarters of the city council. Beneath the city chambers is **Mary King's Close**, closed off for many years after the 1645 plague which killed most of the inhabitants. When the plague struck, the Close was abandoned and the houses sealed to prevent the spread of the disease. The building of the Royal Exchange was welcomed as an opportunity to end the fear and superstition associated with the Close's legacy. The infamous street remains virtually intact and has recently been re-opened as a tourist attraction, **Real Mary King's Close** ⓘ *High St, entrance on Warriston's Close, T08702-430160, www.realmarykings close.com, tours daily every 20 mins from 1000, Apr-Oct last tour at 2100; Nov-Mar last tour at 1600, £7, concessions £6, children 5-15 £5, under 5s are not allowed*. It's an eerily evocative experience and offers an authentic insight into the trials and tribulations of 17th-century Old Town life. A little further down is **Anchor Close**, where the first editions of *Encyclopaedia Britannica* and of Robert Burns' poems were printed at the printing works of William Smellie.

At the junction of the High Street and South Bridge is the **Tron Kirk**, founded in 1637, and named after the Tron, a public weighing beam which stood close by and which was a popular place for merchants to sell their wares. If they were found guilty of selling short measures, they were nailed to the Tron by their ears. The church was built to accommodate the Presbyterian congregation ejected from St Giles during the latter's brief period as a cathedral and continued in use until it was closed in 1952. It now houses the Old Town Tourist Information Centre, and recent excavations have revealed sections of Marlin's Wynd, which ran from the High Street down to the Cowgate.

Past the junction of the North and South Bridges, on the north side of the High Street, is **Carruber's Close**, where Sir James Simpson, the discoverer of chloroform, ran a medical dispensary in the 1860s. Above the entrance to Paisley Close is the bust of a boy saved from beneath the rubble when the tenement collapsed in 1861, killing 35 inhabitants, an incident which helped to hasten the much-needed improvement of the Old Town's buildings.

In Chalmers Close, just to the west, is **Trinity Apse**, a sad reminder of the Holy Trinity Church, one of Edinburgh's finest pieces of Gothic architecture, demolished in 1848 to make room for the railway line to Waverley. The stones from the original were carefully numbered for rebuilding on the present site, but pilfering depleted the stock so much that only the apse could be reconstructed, in 1852, on the present site. It is now a **Brass Rubbing Centre** ⓘ *Apr-Sep Mon-Sat 1000-1700, Sun 1200-1700 during the Festival only, free, T0131-5564364,* where you can make your own rubbings.

On the opposite side of the High Street, in Hyndford's Close, is the **Museum of Childhood** ⓘ *Mon-Sat 1000-1700, Sun 1400-1700 during the Festival, free, T0131-5294142*, which is full of kids screaming with excitement at the vast collection of toys, dolls, games and books, and nostalgic adults yelling "I used to have one of those!" There's even a video history of the various Gerry Anderson TV puppet series such as *Thunderbirds* and *Fireball XL5*. The museum also covers the serious issues of childhood, such as health and education, but that doesn't spoil the sheer fun of the place.

Almost directly opposite is the early 16th-century **Moubray House**, thought to be the oldest inhabited building in Edinburgh, but closed to the public. This is where Daniel Defoe was based when he came to Edinburgh in 1706 as an English agent to help negotiate the Act of Union. Next door is **John Knox's House** ⓘ *Mon-Sat 1000-1700 (in Aug also Sun 1200-1700), £2.25, £1.75 concession, £0.75 child, T0131-5569579*, one of the Royal Mile's most distinctive buildings and dating from the late 15th and 16th centuries. It's not known for sure whether or not the Calvinist preacher actually lived here, but the house did belong to James Mossman, goldsmith to Mary, Queen of Scots. Today, the house is a rather austere museum devoted to the life and career of John Knox.

Canongate

The High Street ends at the junction of St Mary's Street and Jeffrey Street, where the city's eastern gate, Netherbow Port, once stood. The remaining part of the Royal Mile, the Canongate, was a separate burgh for over 700 years, taking its name from the canons (priests) of Holyrood Abbey. As it was near the Palace of Holyroodhouse, the area developed as the court quarter with several fine residences being built there. Though the Canongate went into decline once the court moved to London in the early 17th century, it could still boast an impressive number of aristocrats among its inhabitants, even in the late 18th century.

The most lavish of Canongate's mansions is **Moray House**. Charles I visited here on several occasions and Cromwell used it as his headquarters in 1648. And if that weren't enough historical significance, in 1707 the Treaty of Union was signed in a summerhouse in the garden. A little further east is the 16th century **Huntly** House ⓘ *T0131-5294143, Mon-Sat 1000-1700 and Sun 1400-1700 during the Festival, free*, the city's main local history museum, but disappointing nevertheless. Among the highlights is the original copy of the National Covenant of 1638.

Opposite Huntly House is the late-16th-century **Canongate Tolbooth**, the original headquarters of the burgh administration, as well as the courthouse and burgh prison. It now houses **The People's Story** ⓘ *T0131-5294057, Mon-Sat 1000-1700 and Sun 1400-1700 during the Festival, free*, a genuinely interesting museum which describes the life and work of the ordinary people of Edinburgh from the late 18th century to the present day. The museum is filled with the sights, sounds and smells of the past and includes, among others, reconstructions of a prison cell, a workshop and a pub.

Next door to the Tolbooth is the **Canongate Kirk**, built in 1688 to house the congregation expelled from Holyrood Abbey when it was taken over by James VII (II of England) to be used as the chapel for the Order of the Thistle. More interesting, though, is the churchyard, burial place of many famous people. Among the list of notable names is Adam Smith, the father of political economy, who lived in Panmure House nearby, the philosopher Dugald Stewart and Robert Fergusson, arguably Edinburgh's greatest poet who died tragically at the tender age of 23 after being forced into the local madhouse during a bout of depression. Robert Burns, who was greatly inspired by Fergusson's poetry, donated the headstone in 1787, inscribed with his own personal tribute.

Abbey Strand

The last few yards of the Royal Mile, which forms the approach to the precincts of Holyrood Abbey and Palace, is known as the Abbey Strand. The strange little turreted 16th century building here is known as **Queen Mary's Bath House**, where, legend has it, Mary, Queen of Scots bathed in sweet white wine. However, it is more likely that it was a summer pavilion or dovecot.

Palace of Holyroodhouse

ⓘ *T0131-5561096, www.royal.gov.uk, 1 Apr-31 Oct daily 0930-1800, 1 Nov-31 Mar 0930-1630 (guided tour), closed to public during state functions and the annual royal visit in Jun and Jul, £6.50, £3.30 child, £5 concession, £16.50 family.*

At the foot of the Royal Mile lies Holyrood, Edinburgh's royal quarter. The palace began life as the abbey guest house, until James IV transformed it into a royal palace at the beginning of the 16th century. The only remaining part of the Renaissance palace is the northwest tower, built as the private apartments of his son James V. Most of the original building was damaged by fire in 1543 and further in 1650 during its occupation by Cromwell's troops, never the most considerate of guests.

The present palace largely dates from the late 17th century when the original was replaced by a larger building for the Restoration of Charles II, although the newly crowned monarch never actually set foot in the place. It was built in the style of a French chateau, around a large arcaded quadrangle and is an elegant, finely proportioned creation. Designed by William Bruce, it incorporates a castellated southwest tower that balances perfectly the northwest original.

Inside, the oldest part of Holyroodhouse is open to the public and is entered through the Great Gallery, which takes up the entire first floor of the north wing. Here, during the '45 rebellion, Bonnie Prince Charlie held court, and it is still used for big ceremonial occasions. The walls are adorned with over 100 portraits of Scottish Kings, most of them mythical, beginning with 'Fergus I, BC 330' and ending with James VI. Commissioned from the Flemish artist, Jacobus de Wet, they have been described as "paltry daubings [...] painted either from the imagination, or porters hired to sit for the purpose". They certainly make for some amusing viewing.

The Royal Apartments, in the northwest tower, are mainly of note for their association with Mary, Queen of Scots and in particular for the most infamous incident in the palace's long history. It was here that the queen witnessed the brutal murder, organized by her husband, Lord Darnley, of her much-favoured Italian private secretary, David Rizzio. He was stabbed 56 times, on a spot marked by a brass plaque and, until it was removed quite recently, by a distinctly unsubtle fake bloodstain.

The later parts of the palace, known as the State Apartments, are less interesting, though decorated in Adam Style, with magnificent white stucco ceilings, particularly the Throne Room and Dining room. These are associated with later monarchs, such as George IV, who paid a visit in 1822, dressed in flesh-coloured tights and the briefest of kilts, rather appropriately perhaps, given the length of time he actually spent here. But it was Queen Victoria and Prince Albert who returned the palace to royal favour, as a stopover on their way to and from Balmoral. This custom has been maintained by her successors and the present queen still spends a short while here every year at the end of June and beginning of July.

Holyrood Abbey

In the grounds of the palace are the ruins of Holyrood Abbey. According to legend King David I, son of Malcolm Canmore and St Margaret, was out hunting here one day in 1128, when he was charged by a huge stag and thrown from his horse. The stag then tried to gore him, and the king grabbed hold of its antlers to protect himself, only to find that he was instead holding a crucifix set between the horns. The stag then disappeared, leaving the crucifix in his hands. That night in a dream he was commanded to build a "house for Canons devoted to the Cross", and so he founded an Augustinian abbey of the Holy Rood (another word for Cross) on the site of his miraculous escape. The only surviving part of King David's Norman church is a doorway in the far southeastern corner. Most of the remains date from the early 13th century.

The abbey was, at its height, a building of great importance and splendour, and this is hinted at in the surviving parts of the west front. Much of it was destroyed, as were many of the county's finest ecclesiastical buildings, during the Reformation. During the reign of Charles I it was converted to the Chapel Royal and later to the Chapel of the Order of the Thistle, but it suffered severe damage once more, this time during the 1688 revolution. Some restoration work was attempted in the 18th century, but this only caused the roof to collapse in 1768, and since then the building has been left as a ruin. In the Royal Vault beneath the abbey are buried several Scottish Kings, including David II (son of Robert the Bruce), James II, James V and Lord Darnley, 'King Consort' to Mary, Queen of Scots.

Scottish Parliament

Opposite the Palace of Holyroodhouse is the new Scottish Parliament building, now in its final phase of development and due for completion in 2004. The controversial building was designed by visionary Barcelona architect, Enric Miralles, who died in 2000, the same year that Donald Dewar, political architect of the Scottish Parliament and the first First Minister of Scotland, also died. It incorporates symbols of Scottish economic and artistic heritage: the roof is a series of up-turned fishing boats, while the windows are based on an abstract shape of Sir Henry Raeburn's *Skater on Duddingston Loch*, and the crow-stepped gables are a paradigm of Scots vernacular architecture married to modernist principles. The parliament building has not been without its critics, however, in particular over the spiraling costs, which now stand at nearly £400 mn. The adjoining visitor centre ⓘ *1000-1600, free*, includes the original architectural designs and models and a 15-minute film of its development from the conceptual stage. Until the building is complete, the Scottish Parliament sits in the Church of Scotland headquarters in Milne's Court. A visitor centre on George IV Bridge provides information about the workings of the parliament.

Our Dynamic Earth

ⓘ *Holyrood Rd, T0131-5507800, www.dynamicearth.co.uk, Apr-Oct daily 1000-1800, Nov-Mar Wed-Sun 1000-1700. £8.45, children and concessions £4.95, family £22.50.* South of the Scottish Parliament is Edinburgh's very own mini-dome is multi-million pound, multi-media exhibition which takes you on a journey through space and time. Using the state-of-the-art technology and special effects, you'll experience every environment on Earth and encounter many weird and wonderful creatures. An absolute must if you've kids in tow and you're guaranteed to find out things about our planet that you never knew.

Holyrood Park and Arthur's Seat

Edinburgh is blessed with many magnificent green, open spaces, and none better than Holyrood Park (Queen's Park) – a 650-acre rugged wilderness of mountains, crags, lochs, moorland, marshes, fields and glens – all within walking distance of the city centre. This is one of the city's greatest assets, and it's easy to wander around till you're lost from the eyes and ears of civilization.

The park's main feature, and the city's main landmark, is **Arthur's Seat**, the igneous core of another extinct volcano, and the highest of Edinburgh's hills (822 ft). It is probably named after Arthur, Prince of Strathclyde, rather than King Arthur of legend, as is commonly thought. The best walk in the city is to the summit of Arthur's Seat, from where you get the very best view of the city, as well as the Pentland Hills to the south, the Firth of Forth and of Fife to the north, and, on a clear day, to the Highland peaks, 70 or 80 miles away. The walk to the top is a popular one, and easier than it looks. There are several different routes, all of which take less than an hour. A good circular walk that takes in the wilder bits and the lochs, starts from **St Margaret's Loch**, little more than an artificial pond, at the far end of the park from the palace. To reach the loch, follow Queen's Drive east (left) from the palace for about two-thirds of a mile (1 km) and it's on the right. Leave the car park beside the loch and head around the loch up towards the 15th-century ruin of **St Anthony's Chapel**. Pass the ruined chapel on your right and after a few hundred yards you'll see the main summit towering above you on the right. Keeping the summit to your right, climb over a saddle which joins the path up from **Dunsapie Loch**, which you can see below you on the left, and continue up a rocky path to the top. Dunsapie Loch is overshadowed by Dunsapie Hill, which makes a great place for an evening picnic and from here it's an easy drop down to **Duddingston Village**, just outside the park boundary, and one of the most attractive and unspoilt of the old villages that have become part of the city suburbs. The village **Kirk** dates back to the 12th century and the **Sheep Heid Inn**, see Eating page 107, is a great place to stop off for some liquid sustenance and a bite to eat. Adjoining the village, on the south side of Arthur's Seat, is **Duddingston Loch**, the largest of the park's lochs, which is a sanctuary for waterfowl. It can also be reached via Queen's Drive, heading right from the palace for about four miles.

There are other routes to the top of Arthur's Seat. One starts opposite the palace car park and winds up by the foot of the precipitous Salisbury Crags, another dominating feature of the Edinburgh skyline, lying directly opposite the south gates of the palace. This is the **Radical Road**, built in 1820 and so called because Sir Walter Scott suggested it be constructed by a group of unemployed weavers from the west, who were believed to hold radical political views. This is also where James Hutton is said to have dreamt up the idea of geology by looking at the rock formations. The road traverses the ridge below the crags and continues on grass through **Hunter's Bog** and up to the summit. You can also walk along the top of the crags, though there is no path.

South of the Royal Mile

Although the Royal Mile is the main tourist attraction, there are some interesting, and sometimes even quiet, corners of the Old Town to be found not so very far away from the hordes, not to mention the Museum of Scotland, one of the city's 'must-see' attractions.

Grassmarket is one of the city's main nightlife streets, with lots of busy restaurants and bars lining its north side. One of these, the White Hart Inn, was patronized by Robert Burns.

Cowgate, Grassmarket and Victoria Street

Holyrood Road runs from the palace back to the Old Town, running parallel to and south of the Canongate. It continues west till it's crossed by the Pleasance and becomes the **Cowgate** is one of Edinburgh's oldest streets and one of its least salubrious. It runs almost parallel to the High Street, but on a much lower level and when the South and George IV bridges were built over it, linking the Old and New Towns, it was half-buried below street level and reduced to a dark, desolate canyon of neglect and decay. In recent years the Cowgate has become one of the Old Town's main drinking streets, with many good pubs and clubs, but it was partly destroyed in a massive fire in December 2002 and several of its nocturnal attractions have moved elsewhere in the city.

There are, however, a couple of very notable and very interesting buildings here. At the corner of Niddry Street is the exquisite **St Cecilia's Hall** ⓘ *Wed and Sat 1400-1700, £3*, built in 1763 for the Edinburgh Musical Society. The interior is beautiful, with a music hall and concave elliptical ceiling. In the 18th century it was the city's main concert hall, and since its restoration in 1966 has again been used as a venue for concerts, especially during the Festival, see box page 118. The Hall also houses the **Russell Collection** of early keyboard instruments for Edinburgh's University's Music Department. Further west along the Cowgate is **Magdalen Chapel** ⓘ *Mon-Fri 0930-1630, other times by arrangement, T0131-2201450, free*, founded in 1541. The unremarkable façade is Victorian but the interior is Jacobean and worth a look, to see the pre-Reformation Scottish stained glass still in its original position.

The Cowgate passes beneath George IV bridge to become the **Grassmarket**, a wide cobbled street closed in by tall tenements and dominated by the castle looming overhead. The Grassmarket, formerly the city's cattle market, has been the scene of some of the more notorious incidents in the city's often dark and grisly past. The public gallows were located here and over a hundred hanged Covenanters are commemorated with a cross at its east end. It was in the Grassmarket, in 1763, where Captain Porteous was lynched by an angry mob after he had ordered shots to be fired at them as they watched a public execution. At the west end, in a now vanished close, is where **Burke and Hare** lured their hapless murder victims, whose bodies they then sold to the city's medical schools. The gruesome business finally came to an end when Burke betrayed his partner in crime, who was duly executed in 1829.

At the northeastern corner of Grassmarket are the few remaining buildings of the old West Bow, which once zigzagged up to the Royal Mile. It was swept away in the early 19th century and replaced by **Victoria Street**, an attractive two-tiered street with arcaded shops below and a pedestrian terrace above. This curves up from the Grassmarket to George IV Bridge and the **National Library of Scotland** ⓘ *Mon-Sat 1000-1700*, founded in 1682 and one of the largest public libraries in the UK. It holds a rich collection of early printed books and manuscripts, historical documents and the letters and papers of notable national literary figures, which are displayed for the public.

Greyfriars and around

At the southwestern end of George IV Bridge, at the top of Candlemaker Row, is the statue of **Greyfriars Bobby**, the faithful little Skye terrier who watched over the grave of his master John Gray, a shepherd from the Pentland Hills, for 14 years until his own death in 1872. During this time Bobby became something of a local celebrity and was cared for by locals who even gave him his own collar (now in the Huntly House Museum, see page 86), and every day, on hearing the one o'clock gun, he would go to the local pub (now named in his honour) to be fed. By the time of his death, his fame had spread to such an extent that Queen Victoria herself suggested that he be buried beside his master.

The little statue, modelled from life and erected soon after his death, is one of the most popular, and sentimental, of Edinburgh's attractions. The grave that Bobby watched over is the nearby **Greyfriars Kirkyard**, one of Edinburgh's most prestigious burial grounds. Here lie the poet Allan Ramsay, the architects John and Robert Adam, the philanthropist George Heriot (see below), James Douglas, Earl of Morton and Regent of Scotland during James VI's minority, and the poet Duncan Ban McIntyre (1724-1812) whose epic *Beinn Doruin* is considered one of the greatest poems in the

Gaelic language. Greyfriars also has its its sinister tales. Some of the memorials are protected with metal lattices. This was to defeat the efforts of body-snatchers. One woman was buried here while in a trance and awoke when body-snatchers tried to remove the rings from her fingers. Most notorious of all is the tale of George 'Bloody' Mackenzie, former Lord Advocate, who is interred here. Greyfriars is particularly associated with the long struggle to establish the Presbyterian church in Scotland. The kirkyard was the first place where the National Covenant was signed, on 28 February 1638. Later, in 1679, over 1,200 Covenanters were imprisoned by Mackenzie in a corner of the kirkyard for three months, and many died of exposure and starvation. The prison, known as the 'Black Mausoleum', behind the church on the left, is said to be haunted by Mackenzie's evil presence and is visited as part of one of the city's ghost tours, see Activities and tours page 119. **Greyfriars Kirk**, somewhat overshadowed by the graveyard, dates from 1620 and was the first church to be built in Edinburgh after the Reformation.

West of Greyfriars Kirkyard, and reached from Lauriston Place, is **George Heriot's Hospital School**, one of the finest pieces of Renaissance architecture in Scotland. It was founded as a school for the teaching of 'puir fatherless bairns' in 1659 by 'Jinglin Geordie' Heriot, James VI's goldsmith, although it had previously been used as a hospital by Cromwell during the Civil War. It is now one of Edinburgh's most prestigious fee-paying schools. You can't go inside but you can wander round the quadrangle and admire the towers, turrets and carved doorways of this fine palatial building. West of George Heriot's, leading north off Lauriston Place, is the **Vennel**, a narrow passage of steps that descends to the Grassmarket. On the eastern side is the best surviving section of the **Flodden Wall**, the old city wall built to prevent an English invasion in the wake of Scotland's disastrous defeat at Flodden in 1513.

Museum of Scotland and the Royal Museum

ⓘ *T0131-2474422, www.nms.ac.uk, Mon-Sat 1000-1700 (Tue 2000), Sun 1200-1700, free, full disabled access to all floors, free guided tours at 1415 (and 1800 on Tue).*

Across the road from Greyfriars Bobby, running between George IV Bridge and South Bridge, is Chambers Street, home of two of the best museums in Scotland. The **Museum of Scotland** is a striking contemporary building housing a huge number of impressive Scottish collections which were transferred from the National Museum of Antiquities. The museum is a veritable treasure trove of intriguing and important artefacts, including Roman gold and silver, Pictish and Gaelic carved stones and medieval armour. One of the most popular exhibits is 'The Maiden', Edinburgh's once-busy guillotine. The museum also contains an excellent rooftop restaurant, **The Tower**, see Eating page 108.

Next door is the **Royal Museum of Scotland**. The extensive and eclectic range of collections on display include everything from Classical Greek sculptures to stuffed elephants, from whale skeletons to Native North American totem poles. It's all here, beautifully presented in a wonderful Victorian building, designed by Captain Francis Fowkes of the Royal Engineers (architect of the Royal Albert Hall in London) and built in 1888 in the style of an Italianate palace. The magnificent atrium soars high above and makes a very impressive entrance to what is probably the most complete museum in the country.

Around Edinburgh University Old College

Hemmed in by Chambers Street, South Bridge, West College Street and South College Street is Edinburgh University Old College, whose main courtyard is reached through the massive arch on South Bridge. Built between 1789 and 1834, the Old College, was originally designed by Robert Adam, but on his death in 1792 very little had been completed and his grandiose plans had to be abandoned due to lack of funds. Nevertheless, it is magnificent architectural achievement and one of the finest neoclassical interiors in Scotland. It is now mainly used for ceremonial occasions but can be viewed by guided tour in the summer. The Upper Museum, which housed the Royal Museum before it moved to its present site, is now the home of the **Talbot Rice Gallery** ⓘ *T0131-650 2210, Tue-Sat 1000-1700 (daily during the Fesitval), free*, which features the University's collection of Renaissance European painting as well as several temporary exhibitions every year. There are also free, lunchtime guided tours of the Old College ⓘ *daily except Sun mid-July to end-Aug*. For more details of University tours, contact the **University of Edinburgh Centre** ⓘ *7-11 Nicolson St, T0131-650 2252, Mon-Fri 0915-1700*.

Almost opposite the Festival Theatre, at 18 Nicolson Street, is the Royal College of Surgeons, which houses the **Museum of Pathology and Anatomy** ⓘ *T0131-5271649, open only by booking well in advance and to groups of at least 12*, a gruesome freak show of various diseased and abnormal body parts. Around the corner, at 19 Hill Square, is the **Sir Jules Thorn Exhibition of the History of Surgery and Dental Museum** ⓘ *Mon-Fri 1400-1600, free, T0131-5271600*, a bit of a mouthful but a hidden gem which outlines the history of surgery in the city since the early 16th century. It's all a bit ghoulish but great for kids.

New Town

The neoclassical New Town, one of the boldest schemes of civic architecture in the history of Europe, is what makes Edinburgh a truly world-class city, every bit as impressive as Paris or Prague, Rome or Vienna. Built in a great burst of creativity between 1767 and 1840, it was the product of the Scottish Enlightenment. Even today, it is still inconceivable how, in the words of one historian, "a small, crowded, almost medieval town, the capital of a comparatively poor country, expanded in a short space of time, without foreign advice or foreign assistance, so as to become one of the enduringly beautiful cities of western Europe." ›› *For Sleeping, Eating and other listings, see pages 104-122.*

Princes Street to Queen Street

The southernmost terrace of the New Town plan was never intended to be the most important, but Princes Street has developed into the city's main thoroughfare. It is also one of the most visually spectacular streets in the world, because the south side has remained undeveloped, allowing superb uninterrupted views of the Castle Rock, across the valley now occupied by Princes Street Gardens. The north side of the street has lost any semblance of style and is now an undistinguished jumble of modern architecture. Princes Street may be Edinburgh's equivalent of Oxford Street in London, but at least the magnificent view makes walking its length a more pleasant experience. Everything worthwhile in Princes Street is on the south side, with a few notable exceptions outlined below.

Register House

ⓘ *T0131-3340380, www.gro-scotland.gov.uk, Mon-Fri 0900-1630, £17 for a day's search, must be booked in advance.*

At the far northeast end of the street is Register House, one of Adam's most glorious buildings and now the headquarters of the Scottish Record Office. It stores historical and legal documents – including birth, marriage and death certificates, wills and census records – dating as far back as the mid 16th century. Those wishing to trace their family roots should start here.

North Bridge

Directly opposite is North Bridge, originally built in the 1760s as the main artery between the Old and New Towns and completely rebuilt in the late 19th century to span Waverley station. North Bridge runs between the city's main post office and the **Balmoral Hotel**, see Sleeping page 104, one of the most luxurious of the city's hotels and a major landmark. Beside the hotel, the **Waverley Market** is a tasteful modern shopping complex, sunk discreetly below street level, and in stark contrast to the St James Centre. The roof gives access to the TIC and forms a nice open-air piazza.

East Princess Street Gardens

Running along most of the south side of Princes Street are the sunken **Princes Street Gardens**, which were formed by the draining of Nor' Loch in the 1760s and are now a very pleasant place to sit and relax during the summer. Standing in East Princes Street Gardens, is the towering **Scott Monument** ⓘ *Mar-May and Oct Mon-Sat 0900-1800, Sun 1000-1800, Jun-Sep Mon-Sat 0900-2000, Sun 1000-1800, Nov-Feb 0900-1600, £2.50*, over 200 ft high and resembling a huge Gothic spaceship, and built in 1844 as a fitting tribute to one of Scotland's greatest literary figures. Beneath the archway is a statue of Sir Walter Scott, and there are also 64 statuettes of characters from his novels. The monument is open to the public, and a 287-step staircase climbs to a platform near the top of the spire, from where you get wonderful views. Opposite the Scott Monument is the other notable building on the north side of Princes Street, the elegant 19th-century department store, **Jenners**, Edinburgh's answer to **Harrods**.

A little further west, Princes Street gardens are divided in two by **The Mound**, a huge artificial slope that runs from George IV Bridge in the Old Town down to Princes Street, and was formed by dumping the earth excavated during the building of the New Town.

National Gallery of Scotland and Royal Scottish Academy

ⓘ *T0131-624 6200, www.nationalgalleries.org, daily 1000-1700, Thu till 1900, free (charge made for special loan exhibitions), wheelchair access, lifts.*

At the junction of The Mound and Princes Street are two of Edinburgh's most impressive neoclassical public buildings, the Royal Scottish Academy and the National Gallery of Scotland both designed by William Playfair between 1822 and 1845 in the style of Greek temples. The **National Gallery of Scotland** houses the most important collection of Old Masters in the UK outside London. Begun originally by the old Royal Institution in the 1830s, the collection was given international credibility in 1946 by the loan of the Duke of Sutherland's collection, one of the finest in the UK. There are paintings by Raphael, Rubens, El Greco, Titian, Goya, Vermeer and Rembrandt. Also featured are Gaugin, Cezanne, Renoir, Degas, Monet, Van Gogh and Turner, and the Scottish collection is unrivalled with important works by Raeburn, Ramsay, Wilkie and James Drummond. If you visit the gallery in January you have the rare opportunity to see its excellent collection of Turner watercolours.

The National Gallery's neighbour, the **Royal Scottish Academy**, was built to house the Society of Antiquaries and the Royal Society. In 1911 it was converted into the headquarters for the royal Scottish Academy and now, following a massive refurbishment programme, the £30 million Playfair Project, is a world-class gallery in its own right. It re-opened with a major Monet exhibition and in 2004 will host 'The Age of Titian', focussing on the Venetian Renaissance. The final phase of the Playfair Project is an underground link between the two galleries, with a lecture theatre, IT gallery, restaurant and cafe and large concourse, due for completion in 2005.

West Princes Street Gardens

On the other side of The Mound is West Princes Street Gardens, beautifully located right under the steep sides of Castle Rock. At the entrance is the world's oldest **Floral**

Shock of the new

The New Town was essentially conceived by Edinburgh's forceful Lord Provost (Lord Mayor), George Drummond, who wanted his city to be a tribute to the Hanoverian-ruled United Kingdom, which he had helped create. His plan was to extend the city northwards onto a rectangular plateau known as Barefoot Parks, on the far side of the Nor' Loch (north loch) under the Castle Rock. Work began on draining the loch in 1759, to make way for Princes Street Gardens. The following year a competition was announced for the plans and the winner was an unknown 22-year-old architect, James Craig. His design symbolized the union of Scotland and England, reflected in many of the street names. The grand central thoroughfare of the First New Town, as the area came to be known, is George Street, named in honour of the king. It links two great civic squares, St Andrew in the east and St George's in the west. On either side of George Street, and running parallel to it, are two long lanes, Thistle Street and Rose Street, symbolizing the national emblems of the two countries. Traversing George Street are Hanover Street and Frederick Street.

The grid-iron pattern is a model of unity, simplicity and regularity, but its overriding success is the use made of the available space. Princes Street and Queen Street are both singles terraces, facing respectively south to the Castle and north towards the Firth of Forth. The beautiful symmetry of the plan and great views on offer were exploited fully by architect Robert Adam, who contributed greatly to the later phases of the work with many elegant neoclassical buildings. The speed with which the New Town was built is astonishing, considering the quality of the building. By the end of the century most of George Street, Castle Street, Frederick Street and Princes Street was in place as well as Register House, the north side of Charlotte Square, the Assembly Rooms and Music Hall, and St Andrew's Church.

Clock, which is laid out every year with over 20,000 plants. Further west is the **Ross Open Air Theatre**, used for various musical events, particularly during the Festival and at Hogmanay. Behind it, a footbridge crosses the railway line and a path leads to the ruined **Wellhouse Tower**, one of the oldest buildings in the city, dating from the reign of David II (1329-1371). At the far western corner, below the junction of Princes Street and Lothian Road, is **St Cuthbert's Church and Churchyard**. This is the oldest church site in the city, dating back to the reign of Malcolm III, though the present church was mostly built in the 1890s. The churchyard is worth visiting and a peaceful refuge from the Princes Street traffic. Here lies Thomas de Quincey (1785-1859), author of *Confessions of an English Opium Eater*, a classic account of drug addiction in the early 19th century. De Quincey spent the last years of his life in Edinburgh.

George Street and Queen Street

Running to the north and parallel to Princes Street is once venerable **George Street**, which has made the move from finance to fashion and is now lined with upmarket shops, bars and restaurants. At the eastern end is **St Andrew Square**, surrounded by insurance companies and financial institutions. The most impressive building, on the eastern side of the square, is the headquarters of **The Royal Bank of Scotland**. This handsome 18th-century town house was originally the home of Sir Laurence Dundas, but was remodelled in the 1850s when the wonderful domed ceiling was added. In the centre of the square is the massive 100-ft pillar, carrying the statue of the lawyer and statesman Henry Dundas, first Viscount Melville (1742-1811) chief ally of William Pitt the Younger and once described as the "absolute dictator of Scotland".

A few hundred yards along George Street are the **Assembly Rooms and Music Hall** (1787) once the social hub of the New Town and now a major Fringe venue. Opposite is the oval-shaped St Andrew's Church, now known as the **Church of St Andrew and St George**. The church is famous as the scene of the 'Great Disruption' of 1843, when the Church of Scotland was split in two. The 'evangelicals', led by Thomas Chalmers, went on to form the Free Church of Scotland, which proclaimed a much stricter but more democratic form of Presbyterianism.

At the western end of the street is **Charlotte Square**, designed by Robert Adam in 1791 and considered by most to be his masterpiece. Like its counterpart, St Andrew Square, Charlotte Square was originally purely residential, but is now the heart of the city's financial community, home to bankers, investment-fund managers, stockbrokers, corporate lawyers, accountants and insurance executives. At Number seven is the **Georgian House** ⓘ *T0131-2263318 (NT),1 Mar-31 Oct Mon-Sat 1000-1700, Sun 1400-1700, Nov-Dec Mon-Sat 1100-1600, Sun 1400-1600, £5, £3.75 concession*, which gives a fascinating insight into how Edinburgh's gentry lived in the late 18th century. The house has been lovingly restored by the NTS and is crammed with period furniture and hung with fine paintings, including portraits by Ramsay and Raeburn. The National Trust for Scotland has its head offices on the south side at number 27.

On the west side of the square is **St George's Church**, originally designed by Adam but following his death in 1792 the plans were abandoned on grounds of cost and the building you see today was built in 1811 by Robert Reid. In the 1960s it was refurbished as **West Register House** ⓘ *Mon-Fri 1000-1600, free* (part of the Scottish Record Office). It is open to the public and features displays of historical documents.

Parallel to George Street, and slightly downhill from it, is **Queen Street**, the most northerly terrace of James Craig's New Town plan, bordered by Queen Street Gardens to the north. This was a prime residential area of the New Town, with excellent views across the Firth of Forth towards Fife, and the air of exclusivity has been maintained, in that the gardens are accessible only to key holders who live nearby. The only public building of interest here is the **Scottish National Portrait Gallery** ⓘ *T0131-6246200, Mon-Sat 1000-1700, Sun 1400-1700 (till 1800 and from 1100 on Sun during the festival, free*, at the far eastern end of the street, a huge late-19th-century red sandstone building, modelled on the Doge's Palace in Venice. The gallery contains a huge range of pictures of notable Scots from the 16th century to the present day. It also has a good café.

Calton Hill and around

In the first few decades of the 19th century there were major extensions to the original New Town, spreading to the north, west and east, and all in keeping with the neoclassical theme. Perhaps the most interesting of the New Town extensions is the area around Calton Hill, another of Edinburgh's dead volcanoes, which grew beyond the east end of Princes Street.

The slopes of Calton Hill are covered with many fine buildings, which probably earned Edinburgh the epithet 'Athens of the North'. You could take a circular route, clockwise right round the hill, starting from Leith Walk and heading along **Royal Terrace**, **Calton Terrace**, **Regent Terrace**, **Regent Road** and **Waterloo Place**, which leads into the east end of Princes Street. The best of the buildings are to be found in the magnificent sweep of Regent Terrace, hailed as the most beautiful of all Regency terraces in Britain, with fantastic views across to Arthur's Seat and Salisbury Crags.

On Regent Road, 200 yds east of the junction with Regent Terrace, is the former **Royal High School**, perhaps the finest of all Edinburgh's Greek temples. It was built in 1825-1829 by Thomas Hamilton, a former pupil of the school and architect of the **Robert Burns Monument**, which stands on the opposite side of the road. The Royal High is the oldest school in Scotland, dating back to the 12th century (the previous premises were near the Cowgate in the Old Town), and its long list of famous former pupils includes Robert Adam, Sir Walter Scott and Alexander Graham Bell. The school moved premises in 1970, to the western outskirts of the city. Further west on Regent Road, on the south side, is **St Andrews House**, a massive art deco structure housing government offices, built on the site of **Calton Jail**. Until 1864, public executions were carried out on top of the jail, watched by crowds who stood opposite on the slopes to the south of the City Observatory (see below). The only part of the jail that remains is the castellated Governor's House, which looks onto the Old Calton Burial Ground, on the south side of Waterloo Place. The slightly spooky cemetery contains Robert Adam's tower built for the great empiricist David Hume, Thomas Hamilton's obelisk to the political martyrs of 1793 and a memorial to the Scottish-American soldiers who fought in the American Civil War, complete with a statue of Abraham Lincoln. You may come across a mausoleum to Robert Burns, but this is for the architect of the Nelson Monument and not to be confused with the poet Robert Burns.

An absolute must for visitors to Edinburgh is to climb to the top of Calton Hill. It is the site of anarchic pagan festivities at the feast of Beltane in May, and at night a popular cruising area for the nearby gay community. The views from the top are stunning.

Carlton Hill can be climbed via the stairs at the east end of Waterloo Place. The views from the top are simply stunning, especially up the length of Princes Street and the sweep of the Forth Estaury. The monuments at the top are also worth the climb. They form the four corners of a precinct and make for a strange collection. Most famous is the **National Monument**, built to commemorate the Scots who died in the Napoleonic Wars. The project was carried out on a massive scale and, not surprisingly, in 1822, three years after it had begun, funds ran out with only 12 columns built. However, this was in keeping with the original contract drawing, so what we see today was the architect's intention – a deliberate folly. Though it caused much controversy and was labelled 'Scotland's disgrace', it did serve to inspire all subsequent building in the 'Athens of the North'. On the west side of the hill, overlooking the St James Centre, is the old **Calton Hill Observatory**, also built by Playfair in 1818. It was abandoned in 1894 when light pollution became too great, and relocated to Blackford Hill. Since 1953 it has been home to the **Astronomical Society of Edinburgh** ⓘ *www.astronomyedinburgh.org*. It is open most Friday nights, if the skies are clear enough, and visitors with an interest in astronomy are welcome.

Southwest of the observatory is the **Monument to Dugald Stewart** (1753-1828), a Playfair construction commemorating an obscure University professor. Completing the quartet of monuments is **Nelson's Monument** ⓘ *Apr-Sep Mon 1300-1800, Tue-Sat 1000-1800, Oct-Mar Mon-Sat 1000-1500, £2.50*, a 108-ft tower in the shape of an upturned telescope, built in 1816 to celebrate Nelson's victory at the Battle of Trafalgar. In the mid-19th century the Astronomer Royal for Scotland introduced a time signal for sailors at Leith.

Broughton Street and around

Broughton Street and the streets around it form Edinburgh's so-called 'pink triangle', heart of the city's thriving gay scene. With an atmosphere redolent of New York's East Village, Broughton Street is home to many of the city's hippest bars, clubs, cafés and restaurants. On the corner of Broughton Street and East London Street is the **Mansfield Traquair Centre** ⓘ *www.mansfieldtraquairturst.org.uk*, a late 19th-century neo Norman edifice which is home to a stunning series of Pre-Raphaelite murals by Phoebe Traquair, a leading light in the Scottish Arts and Crafts Movement. She created them over an eight-year period (1893-1901), and though they suffered badly due to years of neglect, they have been restored to their original glory thanks to the dedication of the Mansfield Traquair Trust. Contact them for details of public viewing days and guided tours. Her work can also be seen on the walls of the Song School at St Mary's Cathedral.

Northern New Town

The earliest of the New Town extensions, begun in 1803, was the Northern New Town, which extends downhill from Queen Street Gardens as far as Fettes Row to the north and bounded to the west by the Water of Leith and Broughton Street to the east. This area is the best preserved of the New Town extensions and has retained its residential character. The latest, and finest, part of the northern development, begun in 1822, is the **Moray Estate**, to the east of Queensferry Street, designed by James Gillespie Graham, another of Edinburgh's architectural geniuses. This part of the New Town is characterized by gracious curves and circles, none finer than **Moray Place**, a magnificent twelve-sided circus. From Moray Place you can head east into **Heriot Row**, the southernmost avenue of the Northern New Town, where Robert Louis Stevenson spent most of his life (at number 17).

Over the years, Edinburgh's New Town spread out beyond its original plan to swallow up a series of quaint little villages. One of these, the once bohemian **Stockbridge**, is the perfect antidote to all that perfect symmetry and neoclassical grandeur. Stockbridge has been home to many artists and writers over the years, among them the painter Sir Henry Raeburn (1756-1823) and 19th-century junkie Thomas de Quincey (1785-1859), author of *Confessions of an English Opium Eater*. The residential streets on the far side of the river were developed by Raeburn. The most notable of these is **Ann Street**, named after Raeburn's wife and described by the poet Sir John Betjeman as "the most attractive street in Britain". It is now one of the most prestigious addresses in the city and is the only street in the New Town whose houses each have a front garden. Nearby is **Danube Street**, once home to Edinburgh's most notorious brothel, and now the epitome of middle-class decency. Though Stockbridge has all but lost its rakish charm, it remains one of Edinburgh's most beguiling corners and is an interesting place to explore with its jumble of antique shops and secondhand bookstores, and a fair number of good restaurants and bars.

Further north, beyond the northern boundary of the New Town and the Water of Leith, is the district of **Inverleith**, where you'll find Edinburgh's gorgeous **Royal Botanic Garden** ⓘ *Inverleith Row, T0131-5527171, Nov-Feb daily 1000-1600, till 1800 Mar-Apr and Sep-Oct, till 2000 May-Aug, free, but voluntary donations welcome, buses 8, 17, 23 and 27 from city centre.* Contained within its 72 acres is a mind-boggling variety of plants and trees, as well as walkways, ornamental gardens, various hothouses and huge open spaces. There's an awful lot to enjoy, but particularly notable are the **outdoor rock garden**, the huge **Victorian Palm House**, the amazing **Glasshouse Experience** and the new **Chinese Garden**, featuring the largest collection of Chinese wild plants outside China.

The Terrace Café is a good place for lunch, with stupendous views across the New Town to the castle.

West Edinburgh

Princes Street to the Water of Leith

Stretching from Princes Street and Lothian Road out towards the city bypass and the airport is West Edinburgh, an indefinable sprawl of mostly residential streets, which on the surface appears to offer little to visitors. This part of the city was once its main engine room, with dozens of breweries and the water-borne trade from the Union Canal. The old industries have mostly disappeared and the area around Lothian Road and the West Approach Road, called **The Exchange**, has reinvented itself as Edinburgh's new financial district. Queensferry Street follows the old coaching route to South Queensferry. Just beyond the western end of Princes Street is **Melville Street**, the most impressive thoroughfare in the West End. At its western end in Palmerston Place, is **St Mary's Cathedral**, the second-largest church in Scotland, designed by George Gilbert Scott in Gothic style, and featuring a set of murals by Phoebe Traquair, see page 96.

Queensferry Street soon reaches the wooded valley of the **Water of Leith**, the little river which flows from the Pentland Hills to the port of Leith where it enters the Firth of Forth. The road crosses the steep valley along the 100-ft-high Dean Bridge, a remarkable feat of engineering, built by Thomas Telford in the 1830s. At one time, the Water of Leith powered over 70 mills and below the bridge is Dean Village, a picturesque old milling community which has been revitalized with the conversion of some of the mills into designer flats.

▲ One of the best ways to escape the traffic fumes is to take a stroll along the Water of Leith, which can be walked beside for most of its length. The walkway runs from Roseburn, past the Gallery of Modern Art, through Dean Village, past the Royal Botanic Garden, then a short walk along the road at Canonmills before passing Warriston cemetery and on down to Leith docks. Particularly charming is the walk upstream from Stockbridge, into the verdant gorge under the Dean Bridge, where the running water blocks out any traffic noise. The path passes St Bernard's Well, a mineral spring covered by a mock Doric temple. It has recently been restored and is sometimes open to the public, but take note that the waters were once described as having "a slight resemblance in flavour to the washings of a foul gun barrel". At Dean Village you can turn right, up the steep slope of Dean Path to **Dean Cemetery**, one of Edinburgh's finest places of final rest. The cemetery houses the graves of the likes of architect William Playfair, pioneering photographer Octavius Hill, and Dr Joseph Bell, who is said to have been the flesh-and-blood inspiration for Arthur Conan Doyle's character Sherlock Holmes. It also contains many excellent examples of 19th-century sculpture. Alternatively, continue for about another ten minutes along the the riverside path to the Gallery of Modern Art.

Scottish National Gallery of Modern Art and Dean Gallery

ⓘ *Both open Mon-Sat 1000-1700, Sun 1400-1700, free. A free bus leaves the National Gallery (at 1100 and every hour on the hour till 1600) and visits the Portrait Gallery then these galleries, for more details T0131-624 6200.*

The Scottish National Gallery of Modern Art is definitely worth visiting, even if you know *nada* about Dada. It opened to the public in 1984 as the first ever gallery in Britain devoted to 20th-century art. The hugely impressive permanent collection features everything from the Impressionists to Hockney and is now second in Britain only to the Tate Museums in London. It is particularly strong on Expressionism, with works by Picasso, Cezanne, Matisse, Magritte, Mondrain, Henry Moore, Kandinsky, Klee, Giacometti and Sickert all displayed, among many other important names, including many contemporary Scottish artists. Don't miss the excellent café, especially if the sun is shining. Across the street is the new **Dean Gallery** (same times as above), featuring the work of Edinburgh-born artist Sir Eduardo Paolozzi. It also houses a major Dada and Surrealist collection and exhibitions of contemporary art.

Edinburgh Zoo

ⓘ *T0131-3349171, www.edinburghzoo.org.uk, Apr-Sep daily 0900-1800, Oct and Mar 0900-1700, Nov-Feb 0900-1630, £8, concessions £6, children £5, numerous buses from Haymarket and Princes St.*

Three miles west of the city centre, is Edinburgh Zoo, by far the largest in Scotland, set in 80 acres on the side of Corstorphine Hill. Whatever you think of zoos, this one is highly respected for its serious work as well as being an enormous amount of fun. There are over 1,000 animals from all over the world, but the zoo is best known for its penguins – the largest breeding colony of Antarctic penguins anywhere outside Antarctica itself. You can watch the famous penguin parade at 1400 daily (March to October weather permitting) and see them swimming underwater in the world's largest penguin pool. The latest attractions are the endangered Asiatic lions and the Magic Forest, full of marmosets and tamarins. There are also animal handling sessions, available at an extra £1 per person, and afternoon animal talks (ask for details at the zoo entrance).

South Edinburgh

The city also developed south from the Old Town, creating a district which became known as Southside and which today forms the heart of the **University quarter**. Beyond this area, and the open parkland of the **Meadows and Bruntsfield Links**, are the residential suburbs of Merchiston, Marchmont, Newington and Morningside. The latter has traditionally been the home of Edinburgh's elite, or 'crème de la crème', as Miss Jean Brodie might have put it in her Morningside accent, renowned for its 'rifained zenzitivity'.

To the south of Marchmont are the **Braid Hills**, which are mostly occupied by two golf courses, part of a great ring of golf courses that almost completely encircle the city. The hills are ideal for a Sunday walk. Beyond Morningside, Comiston Road leads south past Blackford Hill (539 ft), at the top of which stands the city's **Royal Observatory** ⓘ *T0131-6688405, Mon-Sat 1000-1700, Sun 1200-1700, £3.50, £2 .50 child, £2 concession, take buses 40 or 41 from The Mound and get off at Blackford Av, or walk from Comiston Rd*, where visitors can find out all about the mysteries of the solar system, play with various hands-on exhibits and enjoy the panoramic views of the city. At the foot of Blackford Hill, on Blackford Glen Road, is the starting point for the **Hermitage of Braid nature trail**, a lovely gentle walk along the Braid Burn. The track is easy to follow and although the hill is within the city, there's a real sense of being out in the countryside. The path takes you to **Hermitage House** ⓘ *Mon-Fri 1000-1600, Sun (Apr-Sep only) 1100-1800*, an 18th-century mansion which now serves as an information centre.

Leith and Newhaven

Leith Walk leads from Princes Street down to the port of **Leith**, which has a distinct flavour all of its own. There has been a settlement here for over 800 years and the harbour has been used commercially since Edward I captured Berwick for England in 1296. Leith became a burgh in its own right in 1833 and only became integrated into the city of Edinburgh in 1920. In its heyday, Leith was Scotland's major port. Ships exported coal, salt, fish, paper, leather and local ale and returned with grain, timber, wine and foreign delicacies, from Northern Europe and as far afield as North America and Australia.

Up until the 1950s, Leith and nearby **Granton** supported large deep-sea fishing fleets and were landing thousands of whales every year. Between the two ports the shoreline was lined with shipyards, dry docks, breaking yards and repair yards. When the fishing and shipping trade decanted south, the heart was ripped out of Leith.

Much of its old centre was replaced with grim housing schemes and the port area fell into decay. However, the old port's fortunes have changed in recent years and Leith has been turned around. Millions have been spent on restoring many of its fine historic buildings, and it is now one of the best parts of the city for eating and drinking, with scores of fashionable restaurants, bistros and bars, see Eating page 107 and Bars and clubs page 112. At the same time private developers have been converting old warehouses and office buildings into expensive dockside flats.

The old port still has its rough edges, and you'll need to be careful after dark, but it's worth a visit, especially **The Shore**, the road which follows the last stretch of the Water of Leith before it reaches the Firth of Forth. In the adjoining streets are some of the most notable buildings to have been given a face-lift, such as the old **Customs House** on Commercial Street, **Trinity House** on Kirkgate and the former **Town Hall** on Constitution Street. Set back from The Shore is **Lamb's House**, a well-preserved Renaissance house, which was the home of Andro Lamb, the merchant with whom Mary, Queen of Scots spent her first night on her return to Scotland in 1561. It is now used as an old people's day centre.

Leith's main attraction is the **Royal Yacht Britannia** ⓘ *T0131-5555566, www.royalyachtbritannia.co.uk, Oct-Mar daily 1000-1530, Apr-Sep daily 0930-1630, closes 1½ hrs after last admission, £8, concessions £6, children £4, family £20, Brittania Tour bus from Waverley Bridge or buses 11, 22, 34, 35 and 36 from Princes Street*, which is now moored at its own purpose-built Ocean Terminal, complete with swanky restaurants, bars and shops. The old ship is well worth visiting, despite the rather steep entrance charge, offering a genuine insight into the lives of the royals. It's like stepping into a 1950s time warp and you'll be amazed (or appalled) at the sheer ordinariness of it all.

A mile west of Leith is the little port of **Newhaven**, once a busy fishing community and one of the most colourful and interesting parts of Edinburgh. The fishing has now gone and though the little fishermen's cottages have been restored, there is no life

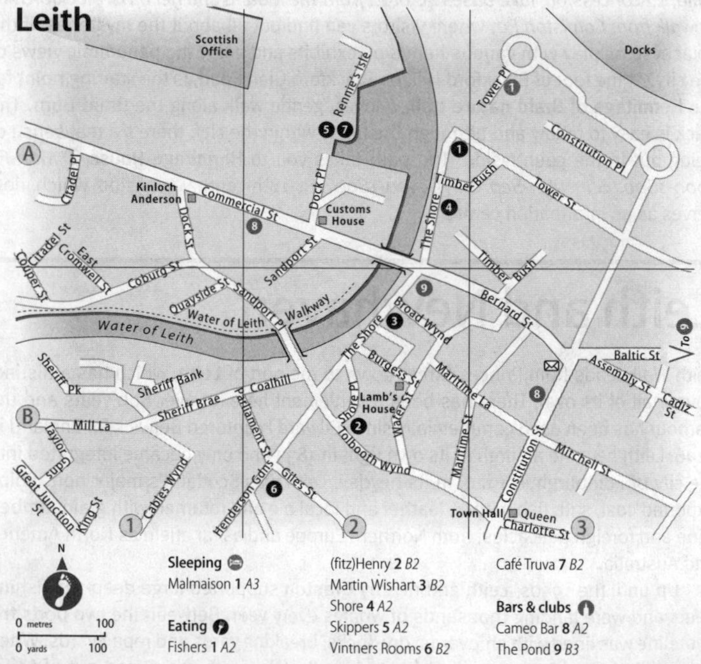

left in the place, other than the occasional pleasure yacht in the harbour. The village's proud maritime past is told in the excellent **Newhaven Heritage Museum** ⓘ *24 Pier Place, T0131-551 4165, daily 1200-1700, free, take bus 7, 10, 11 or 16 from Leith Walk.* The little, one-room museum has hands-on exhibits, a dressing-up box, evocative living history recordings and various activities for children.

Excursions

There are some worthy places to visit in East Lothian, just a short trip for Edinburgh. See page 182 for details.

Beyond the city limits are several worthwhile excursions. Each can be easily done in a morning or afternoon though if the weather's fine you may prefer to extend your jaunt or, better still, combine some of them. You could visit Lauriston Castle, Cramond, Dalmeny House and Hopetoun House in a leisurely day's outing, or perhaps follow up a morning walk in the Pentlands with a visit to Rosslyn Chapel in the afternoon.

Pentland Hills

South of the Braid Hills, beyond the City Bypass, are Edinburgh's Pentland Hills, a serious range of hills, remote in parts, rising to almost 2,000 ft and which stretch around 16 miles from the outskirts of Edinburgh to Lanarkshire. The hills offer relatively painless climbs and you'll be rewarded with magnificent views once you reach the top.

There are many paths up to the various Pentland summits and round the lochs and reservoirs. One of the many walks is described below, but if you want to explore more fully there are many books about the Pentlands, including *25 Walks in Edinburgh and Lothian* (HMSO, 1995). Ordnance Survey Landranger Map no 66 covers the area.

A relatively easy walk which provides great views and varied scenery starts at **Boghall Farm**, headquarters of the Pentlands Regional Park, on the A702 to Biggar. There are regular buses from the city centre, including the 4, 15 and 100. The circular walk covers five miles and takes around three hours. There's a map of the route in the car park at Boghall. Follow the **Farm Trail** signs from the corner of the car park, through the gates and along a fenced path. Cross the main track and follow the path past a pond and up **Boghall Glen**. Cross the burn by a footbridge and continue along the path. Follow the yellow arrows through a gate, up the side of a field and through another gate. Then head left to pick up the main track heading into the hills. Follow the track steadily upwards, passing through several gates. Then it curves right and climbs to **Windy Door Nick**, the pass between **Allermuir Hill** (91,618 ft) and **Caerketton Hill** (1,499 ft). Turn left and follow the clear path to the top of Allermuir Hill. The views from here, north to the Forth bridges and beyond, and south to the main Pentland ridge, are magnificent. From here, retrace your steps to the Nick and continue up Caerketton Hill. The views from the top are equally good, and extend further east to Berwick Law and the Bass Rock. Head east from the summit. Stay by the fence to pass a large cairn, then descend steeply to a fence corner. On your left you can see the **Hillend ski slope**. At the fence corner, cross the stile and continue down to the wood. Turn right here and you'll see the yellow arrows again, taking you along the top edge of the wood. When the wood ends, walk through gorse to a stile, then across open ground past a large mast and back to the cottage. Three miles south of Boghall is the **Flotterstone Inn**, which does a decent pub lunch or evening meal from 1800-2000. This is also the starting point for further walks in the Pentlands, most notably the one to Glencorse.

The main access is by the A702, which passes the Midlothian Ski Centre at **Hillend**. There's a marked walking trail up to the ski slope, or you can take the chair lift. At the top of the slope it's a short walk to **Caerketton Hill** for fantastic panoramic views of Edinburgh, the Firth of Forth and the hills of Fife and Stirlingshire. On the northern slopes of the Pentlands is the village of **Swanston**, a huddle of 18th-century thatched, whitewashed cottages. The largest of these, Swanston Cottage, was the holiday home of the Stevenson family, where the sickly young Robert Louis spent his summers.

Lauriston Castle, Cramond and Dalmeny

About five miles northwest of town is **Lauriston Castle** ⓘ *T0131-3362060, Apr-Oct Sat-Thu 1100-1300 and 1400-1700, Nov-Mar Sat/Sun 1400-1600, £7.50, concession £5,* a fine Edwardian country mansion set in lovely grounds overlooking the Firth of Forth. The original tower house is late 16th century, with many neo-Jacobean additions by William Burn in the 19th century. It was once the home of John Law, who founded the first bank in France and obtained sole trading rights in the Lower Mississippi, which he christened Louisiana in honour of the French King. The interior contains fine collections of period furniture and antiques.

One mile further west is the lovely little coastal village of **Cramond**, situated where the River Almond flows into the Forth. The 18th-century village of whitewashed houses is the site of an ancient Roman fort, a large part of which has been excavated. The most recent discovery was a magnificent sandstone sculpture of a lioness dating from the second century BC. In addition to being steeped in ancient history, Cramond boasts a pleasant promenade, a golf course and a lovely, wooded walk along the banks of the Almond river towards the 16th century **Old Cramond Brig**. And if that weren't enough to tempt you, there's also **Cramond Island**, which can be reached via a raised walkway when the tide is out. Just make sure you keep an eye on the time or you may find yourself stuck there for longer than you anticipated. Tide times are posted on the shore, and are also available from the tourist information centre. A local passenger **ferry service** ⓘ *0900-1300 and 1400-1700 in summer, till 1600 in winter, closed Fri*, still crosses the River Almond at Cramond. From the other side of the river it's a two-mile walk to **Dalmeny House** ⓘ *T0131-3311888, Jul and Aug Sun 1300-1730, Mon and Tue 1200-1730 (last admission 1645), £4, £2 children*, the Earl of Rosebery's home for over 300 years. The present house, built in 1815 in Tudor Gothic, contains a superb collection of 18th-century French furniture, porcelain and tapestries and paintings including portraits by Gainsborough, Raeburn, Reynolds and Lawrence. There is also a fascinating collection of Napoleon Bonaparte memorabilia, assembled by the fifth Earl of Rosebery, a former Prime Minister. The house can also be reached via the village of Dalmeny, eight miles west of Edinburgh, on the A90 then B924. There's a bus service from St Andrew Square to Chapel Gate, one mile from the house, or you can take a train which stops at the village station. The main point of interest in the village is the wonderful 12th-century **church**.

Once you've seen the chapel, there are some pleasant walks in nearby Roslin Glen, for great views of Roslin Chapel.

Roslin

Seven miles south of Edinburgh, in the county of **Midlothian**, just off the A701 to Penicuik, lies the little village of Roslin, home of the mysterious 15th-century **Rosslyn Chapel** ⓘ *Mon-Sat 1000-1700, Sun 1200-1645. £4, £3.50 concession. T0131-440 2159, www.rosslynchapelt.org.uk*. Perched above the North Esk, the magnificent and unique chapel has a richly carved interior full of Biblical representations and pagan and masonic symbols and has been described as "a fevered hallucination in stone". Foundations were laid in 1446 for a much larger church which was never built. What exists is the Lady Chapel, inspiration of Sir William Sinclair, who himself supervized masons brought from abroad who took 40 years to complete it to his design. According to legend, his grandfather, the adventurer Prince Henry of Orkney, set foot in the New

World a century before Columbus. This is backed up by the carvings of various New World plants. One of the most fascinating sights in the church, and the most elaborate carving, is the **Prentice Pillar**. Legend has it that while the master mason was away in Rome making additional drawings to complete the pillar, an apprentice finished it for him. On the mason's return he murdered the apprentice in a fury. Speculation as to the purpose of the chapel dwells on esoteric secrets and a plethora of recent books claims that the **Holy Grail**, supposedly brought from the East by the Knights Templar, is buried here. Whether or not you believe this, you'll still find its architecture and atmosphere fascinating. To get here, take one of the regular buses for Penicuik from St Andrews Square.

South Queensferry

Less than a mile from Dalmeny is the ancient town of South Queensferry, which gets its name from the 11th-century St Margaret, who used the town as the crossing point during her trips between her palaces in Edinburgh and Dunfermline, which was Scotland's capital at that time. The town's narrow main street is lined with picturesque old buildings, most striking of which is the row of two-tiered shops. If you fancy a drink, or a meal, or perhaps a bed for the night, try the historic **Hawes Inn**, which was featured in Stevenson's *Kidnapped*.

The town is dominated by the two great bridges that tower overhead on either side, spanning the Firth of Forth at its narrowest point. The massive steel cantilevered **Forth Rail Bridge**, over a mile and a half long and 360 ft high and is a staggering monument to Victorian engineering. It was built in 1883-90 and 60,000 tons of steel were used in its construction. Beside it, is the **Forth Road Bridge**, a suspension bridge built between 1958 and 1964, which ended the 900-year-old ferry crossing between South and North Queensferry. The Road Bridge is open to pedestrians and it's worth walking across for the views of the Rail Bridge.

From Hawes Pier, right underneath the Rail Bridge, you can take a variety of **pleasure boat cruises** on the Forth. See Activities and tours, see page 119.

Inchcolm Abbey

The most interesting cruise of all, and the most popular, is the cruise to the island of Inchcolm, whose beautiful ruined abbey, founded in 1123 by King Alexander I, is the best-preserved group of monastic buildings in Scotland. The oldest surviving building is the 13th-century octagonal chapter house. You can also climb the tower for great views of the island, which is populated by nesting seabirds and a colony of seals. See Activities and tours, see page 119.

Hopetoun House

ⓘ *T0131-3312451, www.hopetounhouse.com, daily Apr-end of Sep, every weekend in Oct, 1000-1730, £6, concessions £5, children £3.*

Two miles west of South Queensferry is Hopetoun House, which thoroughly deserves its reputation as 'Scotland's finest stately home'. Set in 100 acres of magnificent parkland, including the Red Deer park, the house is the epitome of aristocratic grandeur and recently celebrated its 300th birthday. Hopetoun House is perhaps the finest example of the work of William Burn and William Adam. It is, in fact, two houses in one. The oldest part was designed by William Bruce and built between 1699 and 1707. In 1721 William Adam began enlarging the house by adding the facade, colonnades and grand State Apartments. It was built for the Earls of Hopetoun, later created Marquesses of Linlithgow and part of the house is still lived in by the Marquess of Linlithgow and his family. The house contains a large collection of art treasures and the grounds are also open to the public. You could come here and pretend you're a member of the aristocracy for the day, then go back to your tiny B&B and weep.

Sleeping

As you'd expect in Scotland's major tourist city, Edinburgh has a huge selection of places to stay. Many of the hotels are concentrated in the New Town and the West End, particularly around Princes St, Calton Hill and the streets north of Haymarket station. There are also hundreds of guest houses and B&Bs dotted all over the city. There are several areas which have a particularly high concentration, all within about 2 miles of the centre and all on main bus routes, such as Bruntsfield and Mayfield, both south of the centre, Pilrig, east of the city centre heading towards Leith, and west from Haymarket along the Corstorphine Rd.

There are also four official SYHA hostels and several independent hostels, most of which are convenient, and a couple of campsites which are not too far from the centre. Most of the universities and colleges offer campus accommodation, but this is neither cheap nor centrally located. Another option, if you're staying a week or more, is self-catering, which is cost-effective, or you can rent a room or flat.

If you arrive in Edinburgh without a reservation, particularly during the Festival, or at Hogmanay, the chances are you won't find a room anywhere near the centre. It pays to book well in advance. The tourist information centre sends out its accommodation brochure for free so that you can book a place yourself, or their Central Reservations Service, T0131-4733855, centres@eltb.org, will make a reservation for you, for a non-refundable fee of £5.

Old Town *p79, maps p76 and p81*

L Scotsman Hotel, North Bridge, T0131-5565565, www.scotsmanhotel.co.uk. 68 rooms and suites. Each room has been furnished with attention to detail, with original art, DVD and internet. Services and facilities include valet parking, screening room, bar, brasserie and restaurant, breakfast room, private dining rooms and a Health Club and Spa with a stainless steel pool. Their restaurant, **Vermillion**, is jaw-droppingly expensive but memorable for the quality of the food as well as the bill. Its brash little brother, **North Bridge Brasserie**, is more affordable, see Eating, p107.

L The Witchery by the Castle, Royal Mile, T0131-225 0973, www.thewitchery.com. Upstairs from the acclaimed restaurant are 6 suites of Gothic theatrical excess, with velvet drapes, 4-poster beds, 18th-century oak paneling, marble bathrooms, antiques and historic portraits. Additional touches include a complimentary bottle of champers, home-made cookies, DVD and CD library. Four new suites have recently been opened across the road in 17th-century Sempill's Court.

B Bank Hotel, 1 South Bridge, T0131-556 9043, www.festival-inns.co.uk. Nine individually themed rooms, each based on a famous Scot, from the poetry of Robert Burns to the designs of Charles Rennie Mackintosh, and all tastefully done. Hotel reception is in **Logie Baird's** bar at street level and this is also where breakfast is served. A good deal for this part of town.

B Jurys Inn, 43 Jeffrey St, T0131-200 3300, bookings@jurysdoyle.com. 186 en suite rooms. Huge converted office block. Functional but comfortable and an unbeatable location close to the Royal Mile, Princes St and Waverley Station. Some rooms have been adapted for disabled visitors. On-street parking. Cheaper during the week (Sun-Thu) when the stags and hens have departed.

F Brodie's Backpacker Hostel, 12 High St, T/F0131-556 6770, www.brodieshostels.co.uk. Smaller and cosier than the other city centre hostels, with only four dorms. Friendly and good range of facilities.

F Castle Rock Hostel, 15 Johnston Terr, T0131-225 9666, castle-rock@scotlands-top-hostels.com. Prime location below the castle. Vast building with 250 beds in 20 dorms. No singles or doubles.

F High Street Hostel, 8 Blackfriars St, T0131-557 3984, high-street@scotlands-top-hostels.com. Long-established backpacker hang-out. 16 dorms. Cheap, lively and right in the thick of the action, between the sights of the Royal Mile and nightlife of the Cowgate. They also run their own (free) Old Town tour.

F Royal Mile Backpackers, 105 High St, T0131-557 6120, royalmile@scotlands-top-hostels.com. Small, cosy hostel with 38 beds in 5 dorms. Same group as the Castle Rock and High St hostels (see above). Open 24 hrs and offer an optional breakfast for under £2.

New Town *p92, map p76*

L-A **Albany Hotel**, 39-43 Albany St, T0131-5560397, 1237@compuserve.com. 21 rooms. New Town Georgian elegance and bourgeois charm only a few minutes from Princes Street. High degree of intimacy created by the rich furnishings and discreet attention. Excellent basement restaurant, **Haldane's**.

L **Balmoral Hotel**, 1 Princes St, T0131-5562414, www.roccofortehotels.com/ balmoral. 188 en suite rooms. Century-old Edinburgh landmark above Waverley station. From the modern and luxurious entrance hall to the magnificent city views in the upper rooms, the Balmoral oozes class. Its main restaurant, **Number One**, is excellent and the brasserie, **Hadrian's**, less grand but good value.

L **The Glasshouse**, 2 Greenside Pl, T0777-6003890, www.theetongroup.com. 65 rooms. This luxury boutique hotel, which opened in May 2003, is on the top floor of the Omni leisure complex and is entered via the original façade of a Victorian church. Most rooms have their own balconies and great views. Features a 2-acre roof garden with superb views and a rooftop bar. The rooms are stylish and contemporary, complementing the sleek glass exterior.

L **The Howard**, 34 Great King St, T0131-5573500, www.thehoward.com. 18 en suite rooms. Beautiful Georgian townhouse, the epitome of quiet, understated New Town elegance and famous for its chintzy luxury. Such privilege doesn't come cheap, however, and **The Howard** is more expensive than most. Its basement restaurant, **36**, serves the very best of modern Scottish cuisine in contemporary, minimalist surroundings.

B **Ricks**, 55a Frederick St, T0131-622 7800, www.ricksedinburgh.co.uk. Not so much a hotel as a restaurant with rooms. The 10 very sleek and stylish rooms are accessed via a staircase at the rear of the bar-restaurant, but sound-proofing means that late-night revellers don't keep you awake. Decor is subtle, furnishings unfussy and in-room entertainment includes CD and DVD players and minibar. Book well ahead during the Festival and Hogmanay.

B **17 Abercromby Place** 17 Abercromby Pl, T0131-5578036, F5583453. 9 rooms. Classic townhouse hotel and former home of renowned New Town architect, William Playfair. Sumptuous style and superb views.

B **24 Northumberland Place**, 24 Northumberland Pl, T0131-556 8140, www.ingrams.co.uk. Run by David and Theresa Ingram, very friendly, welcoming and engaging hosts who offer a quality of service lacking in most B&Bs. Three en suite rooms, all very comfortable and tastefully decorated, as you'd expect from a former antique dealer. Crucially, there's parking at the rear, a rarity in the New Town. No sign outside so very discreet. Booking ahead essential.

B **Seven Danube Street**, 7 Danube St, T0131-332 2755, seven.danubestreet@virgin.net. Three en suite rooms. Exceptional, award-winning B&B in a salubrious part of town. Big and airy rooms, despite being in the basement; double and twin have 4-poster beds. The single is the same price per head. They have a self-contained basement flat round the corner which sleeps up to 6. As with everywhere else in the area, parking is an issue. Booking essential.

B **Stuart House**, 12 East Claremont St, T0131-5579030, www.stuartguesthouse.co.uk. Five en suite rooms. Comfortable, well-furnished rooms in Georgian-style townhouse. A short walk from Broughton St and New Town.

C **Six Mary's Place**, 6 Mary's Pl, Raeburn Pl, T0131-3328965, info@sixmarysplace.co.uk. 8 rooms. Non-smoking guest house on busy Stockbridge St. Handy for shops and restaurants. Friendly, informal atmosphere. Offers good vegetarian cooking. Internet access in rooms.

F **Eglinton Youth Hostel**, 18 Eglinton Cres, West End, T0131-3371120. SYHA hostel in a quiet street about 1 mile west of the centre, near Haymarket train station. 160 beds, most in dorms but also 12 rooms for 4. Includes continental breakfast. Doors closed at 0200 and hostel closed in Dec.

For an explanation of sleeping and eating price codes used in this guide, see inside the front cover. Other relevant information is found in Essentials, see pages 43-51.

West Edinburgh *p97*

L The Bonham, 35 Drumsheugh Gdns, T0131-226 6050, www.thebonham.com. 48 rooms. This trio of Victorian townhouses was turned into a hotel in 1998. Rooms are all decorated individually in cool, yet elegant contemporary styles. The suites have lofty ceilings and the baths and 4-poster beds are so big you could get lost in them. The superb restaurant serves Scottish cuisine with an international twist.

L Sheraton Grand Hotel, 1 Festival Sq, T0131-229 9131, www.sheraton.com/grand edinburgh. 261 rooms. Enormous business hotel with few aesthetic qualities, but since the creation of The Exchange it has become less incongruous. Very central and with excellent facilities and service. Some rooms have great views of the Castle. Their **Grill Room** restaurant is highly acclaimed and the equally acclaimed **Santini**, see Eating p107, is on its doorstep. The new **One Spa** is the best in the city and the ultimate in pampering.

B The Original Raj, 6 West Coates, T0131-346 1333, originalrajhotel@aol.com. 17 rooms. A mile from Princes St on the airport road. Indian theme hotel, which is immediately apparent from the large white elephants guarding the entrance. Indian furniture and soft furnishings grace the airy, spacious rooms. The suites are a bit more expensive but very large and good value. Staff are friendly and accommodating. No car park, but being this far out of town street parking is not a great problem.

B Point Hotel, 34 Bread St, T0131-2215555, www.point-hotel.co.uk. 140 en suite rooms. This former Co-op department store has been stylishly refurbished and is now the height of contemporary chic and minimalist elegance. The suites are huge and some have jacuzzis. Handily placed for the castle and Royal Mile. Its bar and grill, **Mondobbo**, is equally stylish.

B 16 Lynedoch Place, 16 Lynedoch Pl, T0131-225 5507, www.16lynedochplace.co.uk. Three rooms. Great location between the West End and New Town, though parking might be an issue. Lovely Georgian townhouse with a double, twin and single room, plus small sitting room for guests. Excellent breakfast and hospitality sets it apart from the competition.

E Travel Inn, 1 Morrison Link, T0131-228 9819, www.travelinn.co.uk. 128 en suite rooms. Huge, converted office block offering the kind of facilities you get at motorway service stations. Not pretty, but to secure a bed at this price in the city centre requires sacrificing a few frills. Some rooms adapted for wheelchair users. Parking.

E-F Belford Hostel, 6-8 Douglas Gdns, T0131-225 6209, info@hoppo.com. 98 beds in small dorms (**F**), also double rooms (**E**). Huge red sandstone ecclesiastical edifice about a mile from the West End near Dean Village and the Gallery of Modern Art. Plenty of entertainment and facilities and no curfew. It may be a converted church, but don't expect any quiet reflection.

South Edinburgh *p99*

L-A Prestonfield House Hotel, Priestfield Rd, Prestonfield, T0131-6683346. Recently restored magnificent 17th-century mansion with period features, set in its own 13 acres of gardens below Arthur's Seat with Highland cattle and peacocks strutting around. All this only 5 mins from Princes St. A new wing was added recently, increasing the number of rooms to 31. Their newly opened restaurant, **Rhubarb**, has opened to mixed reviews. It is worth popping your head in to witness the lavish decoration.

L-B The Bruntsfield Hotel, 69 Bruntsfield Pl, T0131-2291393, bruntsfield@queensferry-hotels.co.uk. 50 rooms. Large, comfortable hotel in a quiet area overlooking Bruntsfield Links, one mile south of Princes St. Its restaurant, **The Potting Shed**, serves excellent modern Scottish cuisine.

C Teviotdale House Hotel, 53 Grange Loan, T0131-6674376, teviotdale.house@btinternet.com. 7 rooms. No smoking. Victorian townhouse offering quiet refinement and wonderful breakfasts. Some rooms have four-poster beds. Great value. Quiet refinement, great value and wonderful breakfasts.

C-D Edinburgh First, University of Edinburgh, 18 Holyrood Rd, T0131-651 2007, www.edinburghfirst.com. 800 single rooms, 120 doubles, 475 en suite. Open Mar-Apr and Jun-Sep. Massive student residence block offering functional but decent and good value accommodation. Overlooked by

Arthur's Seat and handy for the Old Town and Southside. Free parking.

D The Greenhouse, 14 Hartington Gdns, T0131-622 7634, www.greenhouse-edin burgh. com. 6 rooms. Closed Nov-Feb, except New Year. No smoking. Very comfortable and friendly award-winning vegetarian/vegan guest house on a quiet street. The breakfasts are superb and, as they rightly state, a breath of fresh air after so much of the standard artery-clogging fare. Minimum 2 nights stay. Booking essential.

D The Town House, 65 Gilmore Pl, T0131-2291985, www.thetownhouse.com. 5 rooms. No smoking. Former Victorian manse retaining many of the original features. Nicely furnished rooms and guest lounge. Stands out in a street full of similar accommodation.

E Bruntsfield Youth Hostel, 7 Bruntsfield Cres, T0131-4472994. Reliable and well-run SYHA hostel in quiet area overlooking the links, but within easy reach of the centre (takes buses 11, 15 or 16 from south side of Princes St). Doors locked at 0200. Book ahead at peak times.

Leith and Newhaven *p99, map p100*

L-A Malmaison Hotel, 1 Tower Place, Leith, T0131-4685000, www.malmaison.com. 101 rooms. Parking. Award-winning and designer hotel in Leith's waterfront quarter, still providing the benchmark for urban style. Rooms are the epitome of sleek sophistication and cool, contemporary chic with CD in every room (good selection at reception). Suites at front are the most expensive but have the best views. Stylish brasserie and café-bar on ground floor.

Camping

E Edinburgh Caravan Club Site, Marine Dr, T0131-3126874. Open all year. Run by the Caravan Club of Great Britain, with good facilities. 5 miles northwest of the centre in Silverknowes. Take a 28 bus from town.

D-E Mortonhall Caravan Park, 38 Morton-hall Gate, Frogston Rd East, T0131-6641533, enquiries@mortonhallcp.demon.co.uk. Open Mar-Oct. Well-equipped site about 6 miles southwest of town. From the city bypass take the Lothianburn or Straiton junction, or take a 7 or 11 bus from Princes St.

Serviced apartments

A Royal Garden Apartments, York Buildings, Queen St, T0131-625 1234, www.royalgarden.co.uk. Opposite the Scottish National Portrait Gallery and handy for Broughton village and George St. Sumptuously furnished self-catering apartments with bags of space, satellite TV, a CD player, designer fitted kitchen and views across the Firth of Forth, and access to Queen Street Gardens. Limited parking. Café serving breakfast and snacks. Great for families.

Eating

Edinburgh has a wide range of culinary options, everything from Creole to Cantonese. Scottish cuisine is also well represented from traditional fare to more contemporary eclectic cuisine. Most of the upmarket restaurants are in the New Town, though there are also some excellent places to be found around the Royal Mile and in Leith, with its many fish restaurants and bistros located around the refurbished dockside. The area around the University campus, in Southside, is where you'll find the best-value eating in town, especially for vegetarians. BYOB is a commonly used abbreviation meaning bring your own bottle.

Old Town *p79, maps p76 and p81*

£££ Bann UK, 5 Hunter Sq, T 0131-226 1112. Daily 1100-2300. Bann's is still one the city's leading vegetarian eateries with an effortlessly cool, minimalist look and a lifestyle menu to match. They offer an imaginative and adventurous range of dishes, taking veggie food far away from the tedious, sandal-wearing days of old. This is a popular street performing venue during the Festival, so great for an al fresco lunch, if that's your cup of herbal tea. Busy but laid-back and generally good value.

£££ The Grain Store, 30 Victoria St, T0131-2257635. Mon-Thu 1200-1400, 1800-2200, Fri and Sat 1200-1500, 1800-2300, Sun 1200-1500, 1800-2200. High quality Scottish ingredients in the exuberant menu featuring fish, game and meat. Wide selection of less orthodox starters which can be eaten combined with each other, tapas-style. A real find, and popular with those in the know.

£££ Iggs, 15 Jeffrey St, T0131-5578184. Mon-Sat 1200-1430, 1800-2230. Closed Sun. Superb Spanish restaurant with a formidable reputation. Combines the flavour of the Mediterranean with contemporary Scottish cuisine. Excellent tapas at lunch, though you may be better off trying the cheaper tapas bar, **Barioja**, next door (Mon-Sat 1100-2400).

£££ Librizzi's, 22a Nicolson St, T0131-6681997. Mon-Sat 1200-1400, 1730-2300. At the lower end of this category and great value. If you like Italian food, especially fish, there are few, if any, better places to eat.

£££ Off the Wall, 105 High St, T0131-558 1497. Mon-Sat 1200-1400, 1730-2200. Closed Sun. Combines the finest Scottish produce with flair and imagination, so the fillet of beef with soft braised fennel and crisp Parma ham is tender and pink (as all good Scottish beef must be). Vegetarians are also well-catered for and the puddings are luscious in the extreme. The wine list is upmarket but with low mark-up.

£££ Plaisir du Chocolat, 251-253 Canongate, T0131-556 9524. Tue, Wed and Sun 1000-1800, Thu-Sat 1000-2230. No smoking. Not content to be one of the city's best French restaurants, it is also its finest tea room, offering some 180 varieties of tea, hot chocolate, cakes and biscuits, sandwiches, brioche and petit fours. Now open in the evenings at weekends when the menu includes such classics as tarte tatin, fondue and superb foie gras. Their bread, is for sale in the *épicerie* across the road, along with the many other temptations.

£££ The Tower, Museum of Scotland, Chambers St, T0131-225 3003. Daily 1200-2300. No smoking. Still the place to be seen among the corporate set, the superb Scottish menu and magnificent views across the city skyline from the rooftop terrace are hard to beat. This is modern dining at its sophisticated best.

£££ The Witchery by the Castle, 352 Castlehill, T0131-225 5613. Daily 1200-1600, 1730-2330. The reputation here has spread far and wide and is frequented by the likes of Jack Nicholson and Michael Douglas. But though eating here is more of a life experience than simply a meal, style does not take precedence over content. The wine list is phenomenal, with over 900 available. Downstairs, in a converted schoolyard, is the impossibly romantic Secret Garden, which shares the same glorious Scottish menu.

££ Black Bo's, 57-61 Blackfriars St, T0131-5576136. Mon-Sat 1200-1400, 1800-2230, Sun 1800-2230. Vegetarian restaurant that is one of the city's truly great culinary experiences. So good even the most fanatical carnivore might even give up meat. Supremely imaginative use of various fruits gives the delicious dishes a real splash of colour. Their lunch is superb value at under £10. The bar next door serves the same food.

££ Creelers, 3 Hunter Sq, T0131-220 4447. Sun, Mon and Thu 1200-1400, 1700-2230; Tue-Wed 1200-1400 (May-Oct only), 1700-2230; Fri-Sat 1200-1400, 1700-2300. No smoking. From the owners of the famous Arran restaurant and smokehouse, the capital version serves the same wonderfully fresh seafood, with outdoor seating in the summer. Highlights include the sensational smoked or cured salmon and lip-smacking langoustines grilled in garlic butter.

££ North Bridge Brasserie, 20 North Bridge, T0131-662 2900. Daily 1215-1430, 1815-2230. Bar open Sun-Thu 1000-2300, Fri-Sat till 0100. No smoking. Located in the swanky **Scotsman Hotel**, erstwhile home of *The Scotsman* newspaper. Excellent brasserie menu features grilled meats and seafood, plus sushi and vegetarian choices, though a definite minus is the highly priced starters.

££ Petit Paris, 38-40 Grassmarket, T0131-226 2442. Daily 1200-1500, 1730 till late. Francophiles will fall in love with this place. Everything about it is French to the core, from the chequered tablecloths to the coquettish waitresses. The food is delectable and includes classic dishes such as Toulouse sausages and coq au vin. All in all, a wonderful experience, despite the squeeze. Great lunchtime bargains with a selection of mains for only £5 and pre-theatre deals. BYOB Sun-Thu £2 corkage.

Cafés

Café Hub, Castlehill, T0131-473 2015. Sun-Mon 0930-1800, Tue-Sat 0930-2200. No smoking. The relaxing blues and yellows of this stylish, chilled-out café provide a soothing backdrop to the tasty and inventive food. Seating outside on the terrace in summer.

Elephant House, 21 George IV Bridge, T0131-220 5355. Daily 0800-2300. Very studenty – a great place to linger over coffee and bagels or one of many cheap snacks and main courses. Café-bar by evening with live music. Mellow vibe and lots of pachyderms but not a mahout in sight.

Elephant's Sufficiency, 170 High St, T0131-220 0666. Mon-Fri 0800-2200, Sat and Sun 0900-2200, till 1700 in winter months. Perennial favourite with locals and tourists. Great value, with a huge selection of breakfasts and lunches. It gets totally crazy at lunchtimes, so prepare to wait or try somewhere a less popular.

Fruitmarket Café, Fruitmarket Gallery, 45 Market St, T0131-2261843. Mon-Sat 1100-1700, Sun 1200-1700. One of the coolest cafés in town with windows large enough to guarantee being seen. A great place for a quick, cheap and tasty lunch, or just for coffee and chat. No smoking.

New Town *p92, map p76*

£££ Café Royal Oyster Bar, 17a West Register St, T0131-5564124. Daily 1200-1400, 1900-2200. An Edinburgh institution and much-loved by numerous celebrities. The ornate tiles and stained-glass windows create an atmosphere of Victorian elegance and opulence. There are better (and cheaper) seafood restaurants in town but none is as classy. The adjoining **Bistro Bar** is just as impressive and less damaging on the bank balance.

£££ Café Saint-Honoré, 34 Thistle Street La, T0131-2262211. Mon-Fri 1200-1415, 1900-2200, Sat 1900-2200 only. Tucked away in a little side street, this place couldn't be any more French. An authentic corner of Paris in the heart of Scotland's capital.

£££ Duck's at Le Marche Noir, 2-4 Eyre Pl, T0131-558 1608. Mon-Fri 1200-1430, 1800-2230, Sat 1800-2230, Sun 1800-2130. Classic French provincial cooking married to the best of Ecossais served with precision in sumptuous surroundings. Perhaps Edinburgh's finest French? Complemented by an extensive wine list.

£££ Oloroso, 33 Castle St, T0131-2267614. Daily 1200-1430, 1800-2230 (bar open till 0100). No smoking. This relative newcomer is now the place to be seen around town. A lift takes you up to the cool penthouse eating space which has earned an enviable reputation for the doing the simple things with style and considerable attention to detail. A place this good is also rammed so book well ahead.

££ Bell's Diner, 7 St Stephen St, Stockbridge, T0131-225 8116. Mon-Fri 1800-2300, Sat/Sun 1200-2300. The best burgers and steaks in town. This diner is popular with the locals, students and tourists alike who come for its honest, filling and great value food in an informal atmosphere.

££ Howies, 4-6 Glanville Pl, T0131-225 5553. Daily 1200-1430, 1800-2230. Something of an Edinburgh institution, this chain of bistros hits the spot every time with imaginative Scottish food that is always tasty and great value (BYOB), in an informal atmosphere. The others are at 29 Waterloo Pl, 208 Bruntsfield Pl, and 10-14 Victoria St.

££ Loon Fung, 2 Warriston Pl, T0131-5561781. Mon-Thu 1200-2330, Fri 1200-0030, Sat 1400-0030, Sun 1400-2330. Still one of the great Oriental eating experiences in town, this Cantonese restaurant is an old favourite, with a wide selection of dim sum and seafood dishes.

££ Lost Sock Diner, 11 East London St, T0131-5576097. Mon 0900-1600, Tue-Sat 0900-2200, Sun 1000-1700. By day this relaxed little café is ideal for a quick snack while you wait for your smalls to spin dry next door in the laundrette (hence the name); by night it's a buzzing bistro offering a wide range of dishes at reasonable prices.

££ The Mussel Inn, 61-65 Rose St, T0131-225 5979. Mon-Thu 1200-1500, 1800-2200, Fri and Sat 1100-2200. What could be better than a huge pot of steaming fresh mussels and a bowl of fantastic chips? Not much, judging by the popularity of this place, in the heart of pub-land. A must for seafood-lovers.

££ A Room in the Town, 18 Howe St, T0131-228204. Daily 1200-1500, 1730 till late. Excellent quality Scottish produce presented with flair and imagination in a friendly atmosphere. Exceptional value. BYOB.

££ Siam Erawan, 48 Howe St, T0131-226 3675. Daily 1200-1430, 1800-2245. Edinburgh's original Thai restaurant and still the best, according to many. The cosy basement ambience encourages you to take your time. The same people have two other branches: Erawan Express, 176 Rose St, T0131-220 0059; and Erawan Oriental, 14 South St Andrew St, T0131-556 4242.

££ Zest, 15 North St Andrew St, T0131- 556 5028. Daily 1200-1400, 1730-2330. The decor in this most untypical of Indian restaurants is every bit as crisp, fresh and innovative as the food. It's curry, Jim, but not as we know it. A welcome addition to the scene. Superb.

£ Henderson's Salad Table, 94 Hanover St, T0131-225 2131. Mon-Sat 0800-2230. This basement vegetarian self-service restaurant is the oldest in the city and still one of the best. It can get very busy but manages to combine efficiency with comfort. Excellent-value 2-course set lunch. Upstairs is their deli and takeaway and round the corner is **Henderson's Bistro**, which provides the same excellent food but in more intimate surroundings, with table service and at only slightly higher prices.

Cafés

Blue Moon, 1 Barony St, T0131-5562788. Mon-Fri 1100-0030, Sat and Sun 0900-0030. Gay café in the city's 'pink triangle'. Good selection of cakes, also snacks and meals. Gets busy later in the evening with pre-clubbers.

Glass & Thompson, 2 Dundas St, T0131-5570909. Mon-Fri 0830-1830, Sat 0830-1730, Sun 1100-1630. Coffee shop and deli with the emphasis on quality food. Popular with local residents who know a good thing when they see (and taste) it.

The Queen Street Café, The Scottish National Portrait Gallery, 1 Queen St, T0131-5572844. Mon-Sat 1000-1630, Sun 1400-1630. The best scones and caramel shortcake in town, not to mention excellent value snacks and light meals, served in grand surroundings. No smoking.

Terrace Café, Royal Botanic Garden, Inverleith Row, T0131-5520616. Daily 0930-1800. Set in the grounds next to Inverleith House, this is little more than a school canteen, but the views of the castle, Old Town and Arthur's Seat take some beating. No smoking.

Valvona & Crolla, 19 Elm Row, T0131-556 6066. Mon-Sat 0800-1700. More authentically Italian than almost anything you'd find in New York. Great home cooking and the best cappuccino in town. Needless to say, somewhere this good is very, very popular. No smoking.

West Edinburgh *p97*

£££The Atrium, 10 Cambridge St (same building as the Traverse Theatre), T0131-228 8882. Mon-Fri 1200-1400, 1800-2200, Sat 1800-2200. Award-winning Scottish cooking in elegant modern surroundings. This outstanding restaurant is one of the best in town, but by no means the most expensive.

£££ Stac Polly, 8-10 Grindlay St, T0131-229 5405. Mon-Fri 1200-1430, 1800-2200, Sat/Sun 1800-2200. Elegant Scottish restaurant famous for its now legendary haggis in filo pastry, as well as numerous other mouth-watering native dishes with a gallic touch. Also has a subterranean sister at 29-33 Dublin St.

££ Bar Roma, 39a Queensferry St, T0131-2262977. Mon-Thu and Sun 1200-2400, Fri and Sat till 0100. Traditional Italian serving a huge variety of pasta and pizza to huge numbers of late-night revellers in a fun atmosphere.

££ blue, 10 Cambridge St, T0131-2211222. Tue-Sat 1200-0100, Sun and Mon till 1200. The stylish and minimalist interior of this leading city bistro attracts the arty and media types as well as the more sober suits. Sister to the outstanding **Atrium** (downstairs) so not surprisingly the food on offer is a substantial cut above the rest. Also a great place for a drink, its well-stocked bar boasts a satisfying selection of malts. Excellent service.

££ Santini, 8 Conference Sq, T0131-221 7788. Mon-Fri 1200-1430, 1830-2230, Sat 1830-2230. Bar Mon-Fri 1200-1500, 1700-2400, Sat 1700-2400. With such a sleek, chic interior, this is the smartest Italian restaurant in town. With two branches in London and one in Milan, Mr Santini knows how to wow the punters. Everything is cooked to perfection. The bistro, **Santini Bis**, is more informal with its own menu.

£ La Cuisine D'Odile, 13 Randolph Cres, T0131-225 5685. Tue-Sat 1200-1400 only. Hidden away in the French Institute, this is a real find. Genuine quality French cuisine at amazingly low prices. Great views from the terrace in the summer.

Cafés

The Gallery Café, Scottish Gallery of Modern Art, 74 Belford Rd, T0131-3328600. Mon-Sat 1000-1630, Sun 1400-1630. There are few better ways to spend a couple of hours on a sunny afternoon than to sit outside in the walled sculpture garden enjoying a coffee and cake, a light snack, or something more substantial washed down with a glass of wine. This is one of the city's great delights.
Ndbele, 57 Home St, T0131-2211141. Daily 1000-2200. A real taste of southern Africa in the Tollcross. Huge selection of sandwiches with some unusual fillings such as smoked ostrich. Nice, friendly atmosphere.

South Edinburgh *p99*

££ The Apartment, 7-13 Barclay Pl, T0131-2286456. Mon-Fri 1800-2300, Sat/Sun 1200-1500, 1800-2300. Caused a stir when it opened a few years back, this is still a happening place where the portions are as big as the owner's personality. A truly different eating experience with dishes divided into 'CHLs' (Chunky Healthy Lines), 'Slabs', 'Fish Things' etc. All in all, a great night out.
££ Home Bistro, 41 West Nicolson St, T0131-6677010. Tue-Sat 1200-1500, 1800-2200, Sun 1130-1530. Tasty and affordable comfort food such as steak and eggs, macaroni cheese and beer-battered cod and chips. Everything about this place is understated, as all great British things should be.
££ Sweet Melindas, 11 Roseneath St, T0131-2297953. Mon 1900-2200, Tue-Sat 1200-1400, 1900-2200. No smoking. This neighbourhood restaurant is a little out of the way but well worth seeking out for its excellent fish and seafood. It's not salubrious, the food does the talking here.
££ Thai Lemongrass, 40-41 Bruntsfield Pl, T0131-2292225. Mon-Thu 1700-2330, Fri-Sun 1200-2330. BYOB. This newcomer to the already wide range of Thai eateries has already established itself as a firm favourite so book early.

£ Kalpna, 2-3 St Patrick's Sq, T0131-6679890. Mon-Fri 1200-1400, 1730-2300, Sat 1730-2300. This popular and imaginative Indian vegetarian is one of the best of its kind in the UK, using fantastically inventive and sophisticated sauces. Buffet lunch is a bargain at £4.50, but not quite the same as the full dinner experience. Don't leave town without trying it. No smoking.
£ Susie's Diner, 51-53 West Nicolson St, T0131-6678729. Tue-Sat 0900-2100, Mon till 2000, Sun 1200-1900. Self-service vegetarian/vegan diner offering a broad range of dishes, including Mediterranean and Middle Eastern. Popular with students and lecturers from the nearby University. Also belly dancing nights and live music at weekends. Good food and atmosphere.

Leith and Newhaven *p99, map p100*

£££ (fitz)Henry, 19 Shore Pl, T0131-555 6625. Mon-Fri 1200-1430, 1830-2230, Sat 1830-2230. This stylish warehouse brasserie is incongruously located close to some seedy looking tenements but don't be put off. It has received awards for its genuinely original and excellent Scottish cooking and is up there with the city's finest.
£££ Restaurant Martin Wishart, 54 The Shore, T0131-553 3557. Tue-Fri 1200-1400, 1900-2200, Sat 1900-2200. Multi award-winning restaurant serving French-influenced cuisine at its very finest. A meal here is a truly memorable experience, as you'd expect from such a renowned chef as Martin Wishart, the only one in the city to receive a coveted Michelin star.
£££ Skippers, 1a Dock Pl, T0131-554 1018. Mon-Sat 1230-1400, 1900-2200. This nautical bistro is small and intimate, and very popular, so you'll need to book. Many in the know would say this is the best place to eat seafood in town.
£££ The Vintners Rooms, 87 Giles St, T0131-554 6767. Mon-Sat 1200-1400, 1900-2230. These former wine vaults dating from the 17th century now house a restaurant and bar, both lit by candlelight and oozing historic charm and romance. The food is French provincial and excellent, as is the service. Meals in the bar at lunchtime are cheaper.

££ Fishers, 1 The Shore, T0131-5545666. Daily 1215-2230. This is one of Edinburgh's finest fish restaurants, in an area packed full of them. It's housed in the tower at the end of The Shore.

££ Malmaison Brasserie, 1 Tower Pl, T0131-468-5000. Mon-Fri 0700-1000, 1200-1400, 1800-2230 (Sat from 0800, Sun till 2200). Attached to the acclaimed Malmaison Hotel (see Sleeping). Excellent French brasserie food in stylish surroundings.

££ The Shore, 3-4 The Shore, T0131-5535080. Mon-Sat 1100-2400, Sun 1230-2300. One of the city's best fish restaurants with a real fire and huge windows overlooking the Water of Leith. No smoking. You can eat from the restaurant menu in the adjoining bar.

Cafés

Café Truva, 77 The Shore, T0131-5545502. Mon-Fri 0800-1830, Sat 0900-1800, Sun 1000-1800. Great little Turkish café serving national specialities in cosy, unpretentious surroundings. An authentic Turkish coffee will perk you up.

Bars and clubs

Edinburgh boasts an inordinate amount of watering holes, from centuries-old pubs brimming with history, to the latest in contemporary chic. There's a bar for everyone in this town. And if that weren't enough, the city is blessed with liberal licensing laws, which are relaxed even further during the Festival in Aug and over Christmas and New Year. It is not a problem finding bars open till past midnight any night of the week and some are open till 0300 at weekends.

A good area for bars is around the Grassmarket, in the Old Town, which gets very lively at weekends and is particularly popular with students. Those looking for more hip and happening places should head for George St, or the area between George IV Bridge and the High St in the old town, or the cluster of cool bars around Broughton St, at the east end of the New Town. This is in the 'pink triangle', the centre of the city's gay scene, though many of the bars are not exclusively gay. See also p115. Most bars are open from 1100-0100 Mon-Fri and 1230-0100 Sun. During the Festival and the Xmas/New Year period all premises get the opportunity to open an extra 2 hours, so many stay open till 0300.

Old Town *p79 maps p76 and p81*

The Beehive Inn, 18-20 Grassmarket, T0131-225 7171. Typically rowdy Grassmarket pub downstairs, but the restaurant upstairs is surprisingly intimate and serves good Scottish fare. Starting point for Literary Edinburgh tours, see p120.

Beluga Bar, 30a Chambers St, T0131-624 4545. Vast basement drinking den, regularly rammed with the city's toothsome 20-somethings. Stylish decor and furnishings but the clientele are more interested in getting trousered than admiring each others' gear. Food in the ground floor bistro is fairly predictable and a tad pricey. DJs at weekends and live jazz on Sun.

City Café, 19 Blair St, T0131-220 0125. The daddy of Edinburgh's style bars and still the busiest and most vibrant pre-club venue in town. Done out like an American diner with chrome-topped bar and booth seating. Humungous platefuls of food served all day (chilli, burgers, etc) and a couple of pool tables. Set on two floors with a large bar area with pool tables to the rear on the top (ground) floor and smaller bar downstairs where funky House/Garage DJs play at weekends.

EH1, 197 High St, T0131-2205277. Attracts workers from the High St area during week and popular with tourists sitting in the sun. In the vicinity of the main clubs which are situated around the Cowgate/Royal Mile area and is a modern furbished bar with a small area at the back where DJ's play on Fri-Sat nights.

Iguana, 41 Lothian St, T0131-2204288. Refurbished from old student haunt the Bristo Bar. Smart deco and DJ's Fri/Sat night. Large video screens. Can be too noisy to maintain any form of conversation. Popular with clubbers going to Potterrow which is a Student Venue. The food is excellent and the menu imaqinative, but it qets busy at night, so book if you want to be sure of a table.

Negociants, 45-47 Lothian St, T0131-2256313. Is it a bar, is it a bistro? Both, actually. Great for a relaxing lunch-time beer or coffee and popular with students and professionals alike. At night it's a fave late-night watering hole with DJs and dancing downstairs. The menu is international in flavour, excellent value and available till 0230. Good place for a relaxing Sun brunch too.

Clubs

The Bongo Club, 14 New St, T0131-556 5204. Cabaret-style venue for a wide variety of performing artists, aimed very much at the arty, bohemian crowd. Innovative, eccentric and pretentious in equal measure. Music nights include funky breakbeat, trip hop and Latin. Operates a full and varied list of live acts every evening Mon-Thu.

Cabaret Voltaire, 36 Blair St. Formerly home of The Honeycomb and **Peppermint Lounge**. Now refurbished and aiming to host a variety of performance art and avant garde acts during the week with club nights at weekends. The funky house Ultragroove has relocated from the burnt-out **La Belle Angèle** and runs fortnightly Sat.

The Honeycomb, 15 Niddry St. Formerly **The Vaults**, some £100 million has been spent on its refurbishment. It was set to be sold early this year until most of its surrounding opposition was destroyed in the great fire of December. Hosts on alternative Saturdays Audio Deluxe and Do This Do That (the latter night which often sees big name DJs visiting Edinburgh once again). The long-running Friday drum'n'bass night, Manga, has relocated from the fire-ravaged **La Belle Angèle**.

The Liquid Room, 9c Victoria St (top end), T0131-225 2564. Now a very popular venue. Attracting many acts for gigs Mon-Thu (particularly old punk acts) and hosting some of the city's biggest club nights at the weekends. Sat rotate between the long-running gay-friendly night Luvely, 70's cheese Rewind, live acts and Colours (which attracts many big name DJs). Sun host the popular gay-friendly night Taste.

Massa, 36-39 Market St. There are two sides to this venue, on a Friday from 1700 onwards its TFI Friday night is the most popular post-work venue for the city's office workers, and half price drinks are served till 2000 to a backdrop of Wham, Abba, young secretaries and leering bosses – not for the faint hearted. It also hosts the gay nights, Eye Candy and Tackno.

New Town *p92, map p76*

The Abbotsford, 3 Rose St, T0131-2255276. Big, old reliable pub in a street that's largely lost its drinking appeal. Good, solid pub lunches and a restaurant upstairs that's open in the evenings.

Barony Bar, 81-85 Broughton St, T0131-5570546. Stylish and lively place where you won't feel like you've gatecrashed your young nephew's party. Very busy at weekends. Good bar food.

Baroque, 39-41 Broughton St, T0131-5570627. Brightly coloured decor that's not quite as loud as the young party lovers who frequent this popular bar. Usual range of trendy grub and a great selection of juices.

The Basement, 10-12a Broughton St, T0131-5570097. This Broughton St original feels like it's been around for ever and is just as hip and happening as ever. Good bistro food with a mainly Mexican flavour.

Café Royal Circle Bar, 19 West Register St, T0131-5564124. You can't help feeling spoiled in these elegant and civilized surroundings. Adjacent to the **Café Royal Oyster Bar**, see Eating p107. Treat yourself to the seafood menu.

Café Royal Bistro Bar, next door upstairs, is thea big favourite with the rugger fraternity.

Candy Bar, 113-115 George St, T0131-225 9179. Cosy and classy subterranean bar with a warm, unpretentious feel and good cocktail list. Simple, clean lines and an attractive design make it easy on the eye.

CC Blooms, 23-24 Greenside Pl, T0131-556 9331. Ever-popular gay bar and club next to the Playhouse Theatre. Upstairs is the bar – lots of mirrors and neon; downstairs is the sweaty dance floor. Packed to the gunnels late at night and weekends.

The Cumberland Bar, 1 Cumberland St, T0131-5583134. Classic New Town bar that oozes refinement and respectability. Fine selection of real ales, a beer garden and some decent nosh. A good place to kick back and while away an hour or several.

Hurricane Bar and Grill, 46 North Castle St. Supremely cool and stylish bar serving the best cocktails in the city. The grill is also receiving plaudits for its flavoursome food.

Opal Lounge, 51a George St, T0131-226 2275. Cavernous subterranean bar and bistro with three other bar areas, sunken lounges for dining and dancing. Comfortable and relaxed vibe despite the high pose quotient, created by the sultry lighting, dark wood decor and chocolate furnishings. The menu is Oriental in flavour and decent value.

The Outhouse, 12a Broughton St La, T0131-557 6668. Under the same management as Ego night club, this small dark bar is not very plush but does fill up quickly and has a good atmosphere. A firm fave with pre-clubbers. Good beer garden in the summer months.

Pivo Caffé, 2-6 Calton Rd, T0131-5572925. At the top of Leith Walk opposite the St James Centre. Czech-themed bar offering a thick slice of Prague. Very good czech beer and huge portions of grub. Lively buzz in evenings when it's full of students on their way to **The Venue**.

Planet Out, Greenside Pl, T0131-524 0061. Friendly, happy, award-winning gay bar which attracts a loyal following for its various weekly activities including DJs and a quiz. Voted 'Best Pub in Scotland' by *NOW UK*.

Clubs

Ego, 14 Picardy Pl. Refurbished casino hosting various well-established club nights such as Velvet, a monthly lesbian night, Vibe (every Tue), the monthly Wiggle and long-running gay night Joy. Fri tend to host new clubs in the smaller Cocteau Lounge. Club nights in the summer months sometimes utilize **The Outhouse's** beer garden.

The Venue, 17-23 Calton Rd (behind Waverley Station), T0131-557 3073. Recently refurbished and under new management, Venue now hosts a variety of new up and coming soul, hip hop and house nights with a variety of live acts on week nights.

West Edinburgh *p97*

Bert's Bar, 29-31 William St, T0131-2255748. A better class of rugby bar which attracts the more refined aficionado as well as the occasional Charlotte Street mafioso. A pie and a pint doesn't get much better than this.

Filmhouse Café Bar, 88 Lothian Rd, T0141-2295932. Comfortable place to relax whether or not you're catching a movie. Busy at lunchtimes and evenings with a wide mix of people who come for coffee and chat or to enjoy the excellent-value vegetarian food. A good place for star-spotting during the film festival.

Indigo Yard, 7 Charlotte La, T0131-220 5603. This converted and covered courtyard has been transformed into an immensely popular bar and restaurant. The menu is cosmopolitan (Thai, Mexican, French, Italian etc) and the food excellent. It has a good cocktail list and popular with weekend pre-clubbers. One of the places to be seen drinking in.

Mondobbo, 34 Bread St, T0131-2215555. Part of the supremely stylish **Point Hotel**, and don't it show. Popular with local office workers for a sophisticated light lunch or after work for happy-hour cocktails.

Traverse Bar Café, Traverse Theatre, 10 Cambridge St, T0131-2285383. Very stylish bar that's popular with luvvies, suits and students. Excellent and affordable food served at all times and regular special drinks offers.

South Edinburgh *p99*

Bennet's Bar, 8 Leven St, T0131-2295143. Next to the King's Theatre. Marvel at the carved wooden gantry, the stained-glass windows, the huge mirrors, and the glass-topped tables with inlaid city maps while you enjoy a great pint of beer and perhaps some good old-fashioned (and cheap) food (served in the back room at lunchtimes only). One of the city's finest traditional pubs.

The Canny Man's, 237 Morningside Rd. Part museum/part pub that's been serving good real ale and a vast smorgasbord of sandwiches in most interesting surroundings since Victoria was on the throne, and probably to the same bunch of regulars. A word of caution. If the publican doesn't like the look of you, you'll be out on yer ear.

The Pear Tree, 38 West Nicolson St, T0131-6677533. Near the Uni, so a favourite student haunt, once a focal point for the city's crusties but now the occasional suit can be spotted.

Boasts Edinburgh's only decent- sized beer garden, which gets packed in summer. Also serves amazingly cheap food.

Sheep Heid Inn, 43 The Causeway, Duddingston, T0131-656 6951. An 18th-century coaching inn that makes a pleasant stop for a drink after a walk over Arthur's Seat. You could make a day of it and include Duddingston Loch and village and lunch here in the restaurant upstairs or in the bar. Either way it's good. In summer there's the added attraction of the open-air barbecue.

Leith and Newhaven *p99, map p100*

Cameo Bar, 23 Commercial St, T0131- 554 9999. An unexpected find which, though the decor is perhaps a tad oppressive, serves very good and is fantastic value at under a tenner for 2 courses.

The Pond, 2 Bath Rd, T0131-467 3825. Make no mistake, this place looks weird, but makes for an interesting drinking experience, and also effortlessly laid-back.

Entertainment

As host of the world's premiere arts festival, Edinburgh is well endowed with various cultural venues. But don't be mistaken in thinking that when the Festival packs its bags and leaves in early Sep the city hibernates till Aug comes round again. The city's cultural scene is thriving throughout the year, catering equally well for the avid culture vulture or hedonistic night owl.

The many fine theatres and concert halls have full and varied programmes. Club culture in the capital has improved greatly in the last few years and Edinburgh now boasts some of the UK's best club nights, many of which go on until 0400 or 0500. These change frequently but tend to use the same venues, which are listed below. Those who prefer their music live, can take advantage of the liberal licensing laws and check out jazz, folk and rock bands any night of the week in many of city's 700-plus bars. The main live music venues are listed below, but also see under Bars and clubs, p112.

The city's vibrant gay scene has been centred around the Playhouse Theatre at the top of Leith Walk, the 'pink triangle', for many years. It has continued to develop around Broughton St, with new places constantly opening up, be they exclusively gay or gay-friendly. A large percentage of the city's trendiest bars, cafés and clubs can now be found on or around Broughton St, making Edinburgh an easy city for the gay tourist to visit.

To find out what's on in the city, pick up a copy of *The List*, the fortnightly listings magazine that tells you what's happening and where in both Edinburgh and Glasgow. Alternatively, the local evening paper, the *Edinburgh Evening News*, appears daily except Sun and gives details of what's going on the city on that day. Tickets and information on all events are available at the tourist information centre. You can also find flyers (promotional leaflets) for various events at the main concert halls and theatres and in many of the bars and cafés in the centre of town. For a full list of what's on, visit www.edinburghevents.com.

Cinema

The Cameo, 38 Home St, T0131-2284141. In the Tollcross. 3 screens showing new arthouse releases and cult classics. Late showings at weekends and a good bar with video screen showing short films, comfy seating and snacks. Great place for movie buffs to hang out. Bar open Sun-Wed 1230-2300, Thu-Sat till 0100.

Filmhouse, 88 Lothian Rd, T0131-2282688. Three screens showing a wide range of movies, including new arthouse releases, obscure foreign films and old classics. Good café-bar. Hosts the annual Film Festival, so you never know who you might bump into.

UGC Cinemas, Fountainpark, Dundee St, T0870-9020417. Vast 13-screen complex which also includes bars, restaurants, gym and nightclub.

Comedy

During the 80s, alternative comedy was king and any aspiring comedian had to play the Edinburgh Festival if they wanted to make an impact. This is now less so, as more and more comedians preview their Edinburgh shows in London, but playing The Fringe is still de rigueur for any self-respecting funny person and the Perrier Award, given to the brightest new comedy talent, remains the ultimate goal for all budding comedians. The legendary Gilded Balloon Theatre was tragically burned down in the terrible fire of Dec 2002, but it lives on in spirit at a series of alternative venues.

Jongleurs Comedy Club, Unit 6/7, Omni Leisure Developent, Greenhouse Pl, T0870-7870707, www.jongleurs.com. Thu-Sun till 2300. Opened in 2003.

The Stand Comedy Club, 5 York Pl, T0131-558 7272, www.thestand.co.uk. Mon-Thu 1200-2400, Fri 1200-1900, 1930-0100, Sat 1930-0100, Sun 1230-2400. This is the showcase for emerging comedy talent 7 nights a week. By day it's a popular café-bar serving budget lunches, and on Sun there's free comedy with your lunch.

Concert halls

For details of current performances, see *The List* or Sat's *Scotsman* newspaper.

Classical music played by one of the national orchestras can be heard at the main civic concert hall, the **Usher Hall**, Lothian Rd and Grindlay St, T0131-2281155. Smaller classical ensembles, as well as jazz, blues, folk, rock and pop groups, play at **Queen's Hall**, 89 Clerk St, T0131-6682019. Less frequent performances are held at **Reid Concert Hall**, Bristo Sq, T0131-6504367, **St Cecilia's Hall**, Cowgate and Niddry St, T0131-6502805.

Dance

Dance Base, T0131-225 5525, www.dance base.co.uk. Four studios and the largest dance space available for public use in the UK.

Gay clubs and bars

There are many gay or gay-friendly cafés, bars and restaurants on Broughton St and several of these are listed elsewhere in Eating p107 and Bars and clubs p112.

Café Kudos, 22 Greenside Pl (at the front of the Playhouse Theatre), T0131-5564349. Outside seating in summer. Popular with bright young things. Open daily till 0100.

CC Blooms, 23 Greenside Pl, next to the Playhouse, T0131-5569331. Packed almost every night on the dancefloor. This is where everyone ends up. Open daily till 0300.

New Town Bar, 26 Dublin St, T0131-5387775. Fairly mixed crowd upstairs. Downstairs is called **Intense** – appropriately named and full-on. The bar daily till 0130, weekends till 0230. Intense Thu-Sun.

Nexus Café, 60 Broughton St, T0131-478 7069. Comfortable and laid-back spot overlooking the garden behind the Gay and Lesbian Centre. Good all-day breakfasts and reasonably priced snacks. Good pre-club meeting place. Daily 1100-2300.

Live music venues

Good places to catch up-and-coming young indie bands are **The Liquid Room** and **The Venue**, listed under Bars and clubs p112.

Henry's Cellar Bar, Morrison St, T0131-2211228. Also know as the **Jazz Joint**, this tiny cellar bar shows a vast range of acts. Occasional jazz concerts, as well as a growing number of top rock and pop gigs, also take place at the Queen's Hall, see above.

The Liquid Room has established itself as good place to see touring acts such as Moby and Mogwai. They also host the T on The Fringe music festival.

The Playhouse Theatre, a favourite with old codgers like Lou Reed and Van Morrison.

The Royal Oak, 1 Infirmary St. One of the best places to hear authentic grassroots folk.

Tron Ceilidh House, 9 Hunter Sq, T0131-220 1550. Below the ground floor bar are 2 basement levels, regular folk sessions and comedy. Open Sun-Thu till 2400, Fri/Sat till 0100.

Whistlebinkies, Niddry St, T0131-5575114, Nighthawks should head here, where you can listen to raucous folk till 0300.

Theatre

Festival Theatre, Nicolson St, T0131-529 6000. The city's showcase theatre with a varied programme including the world's leading companies.

King's Theatre, 2 Leven St, T0131-2291201. Refurbished Edwardian theatre showing everything from Shakespeare to panto.

Netherbow Arts Centre, 43 High St, T0131-5569579. Home to the Scottish Storytelling Centre, with children's shows in the day and drama for adults in the evenings.
Playhouse Theatre, 18-22 Greenside Pl, T0131-5572950. Vast 3,000-seater theatre for all the West End productions as well as the occasional rock star. Used during the official Festival for dance and opera.
Pleasance Theatre, 60 The Pleasance, T0131-5566550. One of the top Fringe venues staging comedy and drama. The outdoor cobbled courtyard is a great place to star-spot during the Festival.
Royal Lyceum, 30 Grindlay St, T0131-2299697. Lovely old Victorian theatre staging mainstream drama all year round.
Theatre Workshop, 34 Hamilton Place, T0131-2265425. Small and amenable theatre in bohemian Stockbridge with a reputation for innovative and daring productions.
Traverse Theatre, 10 Cambridge St, T0131-2281404. Internationally renowned theatre dedicated to new writing talent. Consistently good entertainment. Also blessed with the excellent restaurant, **The Atrium**, in the foyer and **blue** bistro upstairs, see Eating p107, as well as a good bar, see Bars and clubs p112.

Festivals and events

For full information about the International Festival events, and the myriad of all other websites of all the Festivals visit the official festival site: www.go-edinburgh.co.uk. The free daily listings magazine, *The Guide*, is a good way to find out what's on and where. *The List* and *The Scotsman* also give comprehensive coverage.
Dec: **Edinburgh's Hogmanay** Edinburgh not only hosts the world's greatest arts festival, but also stages several other notable events throughout the rest of the year. The most renowned of these is Edinburgh's Hogmanay, which has grown to become one of the world's major winter events and which was the largest Millenium celebration in the northern hemisphere. It starts on the 29 Dec with a torchlit procession through the city centre followed by four days of various events, including pop and rock concerts. The highlight is the giant street party on 31 (which is for ticket holders only). Accommodation is always fully booked at this time. For information contact **The Hub**, or www.edinburghshogmanay.org.
Apr: **Folk Festival**, at the beginning of the month is this massive event drawing performers from near and far, T0131-5543092.
May: **Scottish International Children's Festival** is the UK's largest performing arts festival for children and is held at the end of the month. For further information contact the box office, 45a George St, T0131-2258050 or www.imaginate.org.uk.
Jun: **Royal Highland Show**, at the Royal Highland Centre, Ingliston, T0131-3356200, is held at the end of the month. It's a sort of display of the best of rural Scotland, with pedigree livestock competitions, flower shows, craft fairs and showjumping, amongst other things.
Caledonian Beer Festival, held in the 1st week, usually at Edinburgh's own Caledonian Brewery on Slateford Rd (see Bars and clubs). The event features dozens of real ales, food and live music (mostly jazz) in the brewery's Festival Hall. See local press for details, or T0131-3371286.
Jul-Aug: **Edinburgh Festival**. See the box for information and contact details below for further information.
Edinburgh International Festival Box office: The Hub, Castlehill, T0131-4732000, www.eif.co.uk.
Edinburgh Festival Fringe Box office: 180 High St, T0131-2265257, www.edfringe.com.
Edinburgh International Film Festival Box office: Filmhouse, 88 Lothian Rd, T0131-2292550, www.edfilmfest.org.uk.
Edinburgh International Jazz & Blues Festival Box office: 29 St Stephen St, T0131-2252202, www.jazzmusic.co.uk.
International Book Festival Box office: 137 Dundee St, T0131-2285444, www.edbookfest.co.uk.
Edinburgh Military Tattoo Box office: 32 Market St, T0131-2251188, www.edintattoo.co.uk.
International Science Festival Box office: Roxburgh's Court, off 323 High St, T0131-2605860, www.sciencefestival.co.uk.

Fun of the festival

Every year Edinburgh plays host to the world's biggest arts festival when the capital bursts into life in a riot of entertainment unmatched anywhere. Edinburgh during its Festival has been variously described as "simply the best place on Earth" and "the cultural hub of the world". There's a unique buzz about the place as over a million tourists descend on the city to experience a mind-blowing variety of performances. Dance groups, opera and theatre companies, orchestras, string quartets, comedians and puppeteers play to audiences in concert halls, theatres, church halls, pubs, clubs, hotels, Masonic lodges and big tents all across the city. Meanwhile, outdoors, the streets, parks and squares are filled with fire-eaters, jugglers, clowns, musicians, trapeze artists and escapologists all vying for your attention and to relieve you of your small change.

The Edinburgh Festival is actually a collection of different festivals running alongside each other, from the end of July through to the beginning of September. The **International Festival** tends to be a fairly highbrow affair and features large-scale productions of opera, ballet, classical music, dance and theatre performed in the larger venues. It ends with an open-air concert and spectacular fireworks display in Princes Street Gardens. The **Festival Fringe** began life in 1947 as an adjunct to the International, or 'official' festival, but has since grown so large it now overshadows its big brother and threatens to outgrow the city. Over the years the Fringe has been a major showcase for fresh talent and the likes of Billy Connolly, Maggie Smith, Emma Thompson, Rowan Atkinson and Harry Enfield all started out here. The Fringe continues to be the launching pad for many of our greatest actors, comedians, writers and directors as well as pushing back the boundaries of art and entertainment. A good opportunity to preview many of the Fringe performers for free is Fringe Sunday, which takes place in Holyrood Park, at the foot of the Royal Mile.

The **International Jazz and Blues Festival** kicks the whole thing off in July and features some of the world's leading performers, as well as many lesser known ones, playing in just about every pub in the city centre. The **International Film Festival** is the UK's most important film festival and screens many brilliant new movies long before they reach London and the rest of the country. It is also the longest continually running event of its kind in the world. The **International Book Festival**, meanwhile, may look like a just a bunch of tents in Charlotte Square, but the marquees are full of some of the biggest names in literature holding readings, discussions, interviews and a whole range of workshops for adults and children. Although it's a separate event, the **Military Tattoo**, set against the magnificent backdrop of Edinburgh Castle, is very much part of the Festival. It's an unashamedly kilt-and-bagpipes event, featuring Massed Pipes and Drums, display teams, dancers and bands from all over the world.

During the Festival, many of Edinburgh's tourist attractions have longer opening hours.

Shopping

Edinburgh's shops are best known for traditional Scottish souvenirs and upmarket goods, food products in particular.

The main shopping street is Princes St, where you'll find all the main department stores such as **Debenhams**, **Frasers**, **BHS**, **Marks & Spencers**. Two independent department stores are **Jenners**, also on Princes St, and **Aitken & Niven**, at 77-79 George St.

George St is the place for fashionistas as it's lined with chic clothes shops, with that temple to conspicuous consumption, **Harvey Nicks**, now open in St Andrews Sq. Good places to look for second-hand and antique art, jewellery and books are around the **New Town** (St Stephen St, Northwest Circus Pl, Thistle St), **Broughton St**, **Victoria St** and the **Grassmarket**.

There are more food outlets than any other type of shop in the capital, so you won't have trouble finding your haggis, whisky and shortbread. **Peckhams**, 155-159 Bruntsfield Pl, T0131-2297054. Fine vintners and victualers that leave you salivating and a few quid lighter. They sell the famed MacSween haggis. Open daily till 2200. **Valvona & Crolla**, 19 Elm Row (see also Eating p107). Superb Italian deli importing fresh produce direct from Italy. Mon-Wed and Sat 0800-1800, Thu/Fri till 1930. **Royal Mile Whiskies**, 379 High St, T0131-2253383. Over 300 types of whisky to choose from and all kinds of attractive gift packages. Mon-Sat 1000-1900, Sun 1200-1900. **Ian Mellis**, 30a Victoria St, T0131-2266215. An overwhelming selection of cheeses, in every sense of the word. Mon-Sat 0930-1730.

Activities and tours

Boat tours

Jet Boat Tours, South Queensferry, T0131-3314777, for 'Bridge Tours' and 'Jet-Boat fun rides' on the Forth as well as cruises up the River Almond at Cramond, looking out for dolphins, seals and porpoises en route. Prices are around £5-10 per person, cruises run Apr/May/Sep/Oct weekends and public holidays 1000-1800; Jun-Aug daily 0930-2000.
Sealife Cruises on *Maid of the Forth*, T0131-3314857, sailings from Easter to Oct, evening jazz and ceilidh cruises throughout the summer on Fri, Sat and Sun evenings, £11, £9 concession, £4.50 child, as well as Evening Cruises beneath the bridges with jazz and folk accompaniment. Contact for cruises to Inchcolm Abbey too.

Bus tours

One of the best ways to see the city sights is to take a guided bus tour on board an open-top double decker bus. These depart from Waverley Bridge every 15 mins, the first one leaving around 0900 and the last one between 1730 and 2000, depending on the time of year. The complete tour lasts an hour, stopping at the main tourist sights, but tickets are valid for the full day and you can hop on and off any of the company's buses at any of the stops.
Guide Friday tours are recommended and cost £8.50 per person (students £7/children £2.50); Guide Friday Tourism Centre, 133-135 Canongate, Royal Mile, T0131-5562244, www.guidefriday.com.
Lothian Regional Transport (LRT) runs similar guided bus tours; £7.50 (students £6/children £2.50). Tickets and further information from their city centre offices.

Climbing

Adventure Centre, Ratho village, off A8, 10 mins west of airport, T0131-229 3919, www.adventurescotland.com. Massive rock climbing and sports training venue based in a converted quarry. This is the largest climbing arena in the world, with outdoor rock cliffs and wall. Home to the National Rock Climbing Centre. Includes Air Park, a suspended aerial adventure ropes ride, and an adventure sports gym. Bars, restaurant and accommodation.

Football

Edinburgh has 2 Scottish Premier League teams, who play at home on alternate Sat during the league season. **Heart of Midlothian**, or Hearts, play at Tyncastle, on the Gorgie Rd about a mile west of Haymarket, and **Hibernian** (Hibs) play at Easter Rd, east of the centre near Leith. Rivalry between the two is fierce, but thankfully free from the religious bigotry of their Glasgow counterparts.

Health and fitness

Escape, Scotsman Hotel, see Sleeping p104, T0131-622 3800, www.escapehealthclubs.com. State-of-the-art gym, beauty spa, sauna and 16-m stainless steel pool.
One Spa, Sheraton Hotel, 8 Conference Sq, T0131-221 7777, www.one-spa.com. The ultimate in pampering, from a simple back massage (£38) to the full Ayurverdic Holistic Body Treatment (£110).

Horse riding

Edinburgh & Lasswade Riding Centre, Kevock Rd, Lasswade, T0131-6637676.
Pentland Hills Icelandics, Rodgersrigg Farm, Carlops, Midlothian, T01968-661095.
Tower Farm Riding Stables, 85 Liberton Drive, T0131-6643375.

Rugby

Scotland's national side play at Murrayfield Stadium, a few miles west of the centre and reached from Corstorphine Rd or Roseburn St. For tickets T0131-3645000, though these are scarce for major internationals.

Skiing

Midlothian Ski Centre, Hillend, take the A702 off the City Bypass at the Lothianburn exit, T0131-4454433. Open Mon-Sat 0930-2100, Sun 0930-1900. Artificial ski slope for ski and snowboarding practice and instruction. Also downhill mountain bike trail and chairlift.

Walking tours

There are various guided walking tours of Edinburgh, which fall into roughly two categories: historical tours of the medieval closes and wynds of the Royal Mile during the day, and spooky, nocturnal tours of the city's dark and grisly past. Some of the latter tours include a visit to the 200 year-old haunted vaults hidden deep beneath the city streets. There are several versions of these but most walking tours last around 2 hrs and cost £6-7 per person.
City of the Dead Haunted Graveyard Tour, T0771-5422750, leaves from the Mercat Cross nightly at 2030 and involves being locked in a haunted graveyard with the notorious Mackenzie poltergeist.
Edinburgh Literary Pub Tour, a witty exploration of the city's distinguished literary past, which starts at the **Beehive Inn** in the Grassmarket. The 2-hr tour costs £7 per person (students £5). Tickets can be booked at the tourist office or direct from **The Scottish Literary Tour Company**, T0131-226 6665, www.scot-lit-tour.co.uk.
Mercat Tours, T/F0131-225 6591, the main ghost tour operator, tours leave from the Mercat Cross by St Giles Cathedral.

Transport

Air

There are flights to Edinburgh from Europe, Ireland and the UK. Flights from North America arrive via Glasgow. For flight details, see p). There is one daily flight from Edinburgh to **Inverness**, 45 mins.

Bus

Buses leave from St Andrew Square bus station to most of the major towns in Scotland. Most west coast towns are reached via Glasgow. There are buses to and from **Glasgow**. There are also regular daily buses to: **Aberdeen** (4 hrs); **Dundee** (2 hrs 10 mins, or 1 hr 25 mins direct); **Perth** (1½ hrs, or 1 hr direct); **Inverness** (4½ hrs, or 3 hrs 40 mins direct), via Pitlochry and Aviemore. One of the main operators is **Scottish Citylink**, T08705-505050, with buses to virtually every major town in Scotland. For bus services to and from English towns and cities, contact **National Express**.

There are numerous bus services from London and prices are very competitive.

There are also links with other English cities, such as **Newcastle**, **Manchester**, **Birmingham** and **York**. For further details, see p72.

Car hire

The main national car-hire companies can all be found at the airport. Here are local companies which may offer better deals: **Arnold Clark**, Lochrin Pl, T0131- 2284747; **Condor Self Drive**, 45 Lochrin Pl, Tollcross, T0131-229 6333, sales@condorselfdrive.com; **Enterprise Rent-a-Car**, Block B, Unit 15, Sighthill shopping Centre, T0131-442 4440; and **Melville's**, 9 Clifton Terr, Haymarket, www.melvilles.co.uk.

Cycle hire

Central Cycle Hire, 13 Lochrin Pl, T0131-2286333, F2283686. £15/day. Open Mon-Fri 0930-1800, Sat 0930-1730, Sun 1200-1700.

Edinburgh Cycle Hire, 29 Blackfriars St, T0131-5565560. £10-12 per day. 0900-2100.

Train

ScotRail runs regular daily train services to **Inverness** (3¾ hrs), via **Stirling** (45 mins), **Perth** (1¼ hrs), **Pitlochry** and **Aviemore** (3 hrs). Also to **Aberdeen** (2¾ hrs), via **Kirkcaldy** and **Dundee** (1¾ hrs). There are trains every 30 mins to and from **Glasgow** (50 mins; £8-10 day return). There is also a regular service to **North Berwick** (35 mins).

There are regular daily services to and from most major English cities. For further details, see p72.

Directory

Banks

Bank opening hours are Mon-Fri from 0930 to between 1600 and 1700. Some larger branches may also be open later on Thu and on Sat mornings. You can withdraw cash from selected banks and ATMs (or cashpoints as they are called in Britain) with your credit/debit card. Visa card holders can use the **Bank of Scotland**, **Clydesdale Bank**, **Royal Bank of Scotland** and **TSB** ATMs; Access/MasterCard holders can use the **Royal Bank** and **Clydesdale**; Amex card holders can use the **Bank of Scotland**.

Consulates

Australia, 37 George St, T0131-6243333.
Canada, 30 Lothian Rd, T0131-2204333.
Denmark, 4 Royal Terr, T0131-5564263.
France, 11 Randolph Cres, T0131-2257954.
Germany, 16 Eglinton Cres, T0131-3372323.
Italy, 32 Melville St, T0131-2263631.
Japan, 2 Melville Cres, T0131-2254777.
Netherlands, 53 George St, T0131-2203226.
Spain, 63 North Castle St, T0131-2203226.
Sweden, 22 Hanover St, T0131-2206050.
Switzerland, 66 Hanover Pl, T0131-2265660.
USA 3 Regent Terr, T0131-5568315.

Gay and lesbian

Lothian Gay and Lesbian Switchboard, T0131-556 4049. Daily 1930-2200.

Hospitals

The Royal Infirmary of Edinburgh, 1 Lauriston Place, T0131-5361000. Edinburgh's 24-hr walk-in accident and emergency department. If it's not an emergency but you still need to see a doctor look in the *Yellow Pages*, or call the Primary Care department, T0131-5369000.

Internet

There are cybercafés throughout the city, but these are two of the best:

Cyberia, 88 Hanover St, T0131-2204403, open Mon-Sat 1000-2200, Sun 1100-2000, prices from £2.50 per ½ hr (£2 concession); and **Web 13**, 13 Bread St, T0131-2298883, open Mon-Fri 0900-2200, Sat 0900-2000, Sun 1100-2000, prices from £2.50 per ½ hr at peak times (1200-1700 Mon-Sat) and £3.50 all other times.

Easy Everything, Hanover Buildings, 58 Rose St, T0131-2203580. Open 24 hrs and cheap at £1 per hr.

Libraries

Central Library, George IV Bridge, T0131-2255884. Open Mon-Fri 0900-2100, Sat 0900-1300. Excellent Scottish and local reference sections.

Map Room, 33 Salisbury Pl. Open Mon-Fri 0930-1700, Sat 0930-1300. Reference.

National Library of Scotland, George IV Bridge, T0131-2264531. Open Mon-Fri 0930-2030, Sat 0930-1300. Superb copyright library, for research purposes only.

Pharmacies

Boots, 48 Shandwick Pl, T0131-2256757. Open Mon-Sat 0800-2100, Sun 1000-1700. Outside these times, go to the Royal Infirmary.

Police

If you are robbed or assaulted and need to report the crime, call 999. The police information centre is at 188 High St, T0131-2266966, open daily 1000-2200.

Post office

The central post office, at 8-10 St James Centre, is open Mon 0900-1730, Tue-Fri 0830-1730, Sat 0830-1800. There's also a main office at 7 Hope St. Other post offices are open Mon-Fri 0900 to 1730 and Sat 0900 to 1230 or 1300. Smaller sub-post offices are closed for an hour at lunch (1300-1400) and keep the same half-day closing times as local shops. There is a late collection from the post box at the Royal Mail head office, 10 Brunswick Rd (one third of the way down Leith Walk). For further information see p66.

Glasgow

Footprint features

Introduction

There's an old saying that Edinburgh is the capital but Glasgow has the capital. This dates back to the late 19th century, when Glasgow was the 'Second City of the Empire'. It was a thriving, cultivated city grown rich on the profits from its cotton mills, coal mines and shipyards, and a city that knew how to flaunt its wealth. The heavy industries have long gone, but Glasgow has lost none of its energy and excitement, and its people possess a style and swagger that makes their Edinburgh counterparts look staid and stuffy by comparison. Just take a stroll round the revived Merchant City or along Byres Road in the West End, and sit in one the countless stylish bars and you'll witness a degree of posing that is Continental in its fervency. The licensing laws may not be Continental but they're more liberal than they are in London and the atmosphere is infused with those vital Glasgow ingredients missing from so many large British cities – warmth and humour. Perhaps that's because it doesn't feel British. Glasgow is often described as European in character; for the diversity of its architecture, accessibility of its art and optimism of its people. It's also compared with North America; for its gridiron streets and its wisecracking streetwise citizens.

It's no accident that Glasgow was chosen as both City of Culture and, more recently, UK City of Architecture and Design. Its main attractions are its magnificent Victorian buildings. Sir John Betjeman, Poet Laureate and architectural enthusiast, described Glasgow as the "greatest Victorian city in Europe" and many examples of its rich architectural legacy can be found in the commercial centre. The River Clyde has been added to the list of visitor attractions. The Clydeside Walkway, running from Victoria Bridge in the east to the River Kelvin in the west, is an attempt to direct Glasgow's great river towards a post-industrial future of leisure and tourism.

★ Don't miss...

1. **Citizens' Theatre** See an amazing show at this world-renowned theatre, page 171.
2. **People's Palace** Find out all about the city's fascinating history through the eyes of its people at this palace, page 135.
3. **School of Art** Take a tour around Charles Rennie Mackintosh's art nouveau masterpiece, page 140.
4. **Barras Market** For a slice of real Glaswegian life, take a stroll around this East End market, page 135.
5. **Transport Museum** One of the city's less obvious attractions and a delight to young and old alike, page 144.
6. **The Arches** Get your freak on at the home to some of Glasgow's best club nights, page 168.
7. **New Lanark** A fascinating restored village, the site of a revolutionary social experiment circa late eighteen century, page 155.

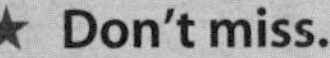

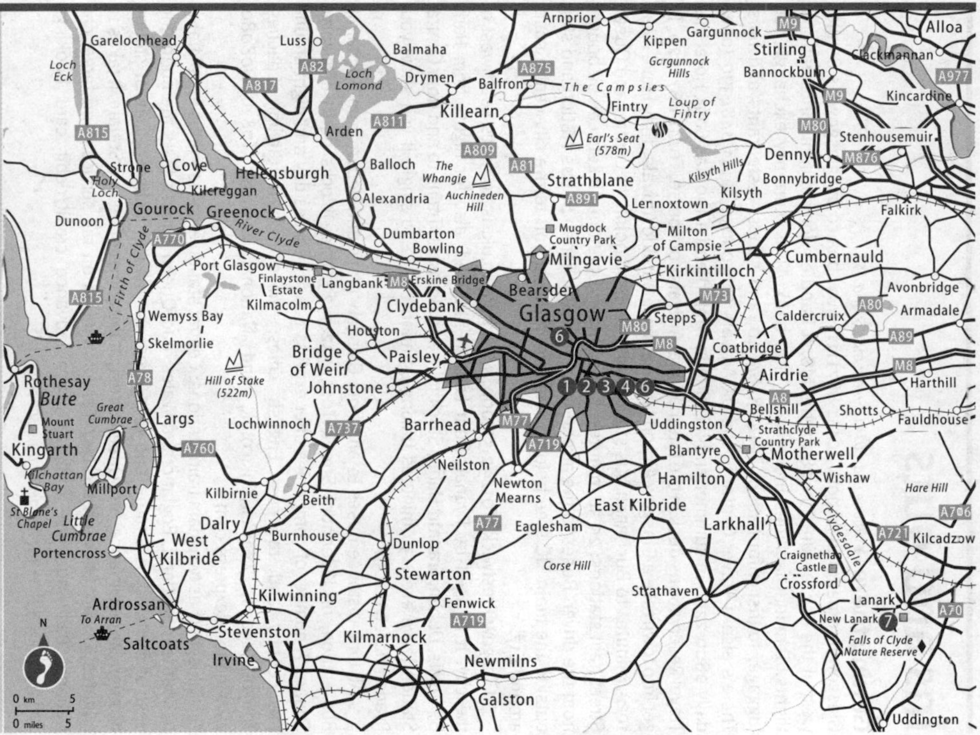

Ins and outs

Getting there → *Phone code: 0141. Colour map 5, grid A5.*

Glasgow International Airport, T0141-8871111, www.baa.co.uk/glasgow, is 8 miles west of the city, at junction 28 on the M8. It handles domestic and international flights. Terminal facilities include car hire, bank ATMs, currency exchange, left luggage, tourist information, T0141-8484440, and shops, restaurants and bars. There's also a Travel Centre in the UK Arrivals concourse, T0141-8484330 (open daily 0800-2200 in summer and till 1800 in winter) and a Thomas Cook Hotel and Travel Reservations desk in the International Arrivals concourse, T0141-8877220. To get into town take a Glasgow Airport Link bus from outside Arrivals. They leave every 10-15 minutes to Buchanan bus station, with drop-off points at Central and Queen Street train stations; 25-30 minutes, £3.30 single, £5 return. Tickets can be bought from the driver. Buses to the airport leave from Buchanan St bus station and stop outside the main TIC (see below). A taxi from the airport to the city centre costs around £17.

Glasgow Prestwick, T01292-511000, www.gpia.co.uk, is 30 miles southwest of the city. It is used by Ryanair from London Stansted, also for flights from Paris Beauvais, Dublin, Franfurt Hahn, Stockholm and Brussels. Trains to and from Central Station leave every 30 minutes (taking 45 minutes; £2.50 single if you show your Ryanair ticket, or £5).

All long-distance buses to and from Glasgow arrive and depart from Buchanan Bus station, on Killermont Street, T0141-332 7133, three blocks north of George Square. A number of companies offer express coach services day and night around the country and to most English cities; these include Citylink Coaches, T08705-505050, www.citylink.co.uk, and National Express, T08705-808080, www.nationalexpress.com.

Glasgow has two main train stations: Central station is the terminus for all trains to southern Scotland, England and Wales; and Queen Street serves the north and east of Scotland. A shuttle bus runs every 10 minutes between Central station (Gordon Street entrance) and Queen Street, at the corner of George Square. It takes 10 minutes to walk between the two. For information on rail services and fares, call National Rail Enquiries, T08457-484950 (advance credit/debit card bookings T08457-550033). ⏩ *For further details, see page 175.*

Getting around

The best way to get around the city centre sights is by walking, although some of the hills are very steep. If you want to explore the West End or South Side, you'll need to use the public transport – which is generally good, efficient and reasonably priced – or taxis.

Buses in the city are run by First Glasgow and use white buses with a pink stripe. Arriva operate buses linking the city centre to Paisley and Braehead and use white and green buses. The frequency of bus services depends on the route, but generally speaking buses run every 10-15 minutes on most main routes Monday-Friday 0700-1900. Outside these peak times services vary so it's best to check timetables with Traveline Scotland, T0870-6082608. The areas around Queen Street and Central stations are the city's main transport hubs. There's a useful bus map of the city, mapmate, produced by First Glasgow available from SPT travel outlets, the TIC and various shops in the city, price £1.

It is relatively easy to get around Glasgow by car, especially as the M8 runs right through the heart of the city. Parking is not a problem either. There are sufficient street meters and 24-hour multi-storey car parks dotted around the centre, at the St Enoch

Ticket to ride

There are some useful saver tickets available that can save you money and are very flexible.
FirstDay Tourist ticket allows visitors to hop on and off any First bus in Glasgow all day, before 1000 it's £2.50, after £2.20.
Roundabout Glasgow ticket covers all Underground and train transport in the city for one day and costs £4. Valid Monday to Friday after 0900 and weekends.
Discovery ticket gives unlimited travel on the Underground for a day (valid after 0930 Monday to Friday and weekends). It costs £1.70.
Daytripper ticket gives unlimited travel on all transport networks throughout Glasgow, the Clyde coast and Clyde Valley. It's valid for one day and costs £8 for 1 adult and 2 children, or £14 for two adults and up to four children.

Centre, Mitchell Street, Oswald Street, Waterloo Street and Cambridge Street. Taxis are plentiful and reasonably priced and can be hailed from anywhere in the city. There are taxi ranks at Central and Queen Street train stations and Buchanan bus station. Minimum fare around the city centre is £2. To the Burrell collection from the city centre (about three miles) should cost around £8-9.

The best way to get from the city centre to the West End is to use the city's Underground, or subway as it's also known, whose stations are marked with a huge orange 'U' sign. This is less effec\\tive for the South Side but for that there's a vast range of buses from the city centre. There's also an extensive suburban train network run by SPT, www.spt.co.uk, which is a fast and efficient way to reach the suburbs south of the Clyde. ⏩ *For further details, see Activities and tours page 173 and Transport page 175.*

Orientation

Glasgow city centre covers the large area from Charing Cross train station and the M8 in the west to Glasgow Green in the east, near the cathedral. It is built on a grid system across some steep hills on the north side of the River Clyde. The heart of the city is **George Square**. Here you'll find the tourist office, and the two main train stations (Central station and Queen Street) and the Buchanan bus station are all within a couple of blocks. Immediately to the east of George Square is the renovated **Merchant City** which, together with the streets west of George Square, forms the commercial and business centre. Here the Palladian mansions of the Tobacco Lords have been cleaned up and reclaimed by the professional classes as a fashionable place to eat, drink and play. Further east, in almost surreal contrast, is the **East End**, a traditional working-class stronghold, and to the north is the oldest part of Glasgow, around the medieval **cathedral**. The main shopping streets in the city centre are **Sauchiehall Street**, which runs parallel to the river, west as far as **Kelvingrove Park**, the pedestrianized **Buchanan Street**, which runs south from the east end of Sauchiehall Street, and **Argyle Street**, at the south end of Buchanan Street. From here the streets rise towards **Blythswood Square**, a much quieter area of elegant late Georgian buildings filled with office workers.

The **West End** begins across the ugly scar of the M8, which cuts a swathe through the city. This is the home of the University and is the city's main student quarter, with many of its best bars, cafés and restaurants. An area of grand Victorian townhouses and sweeping terraces it is also home of some of the city's best museums. The West End is well connected with the city centre by the Underground. South of the Clyde are the more sedate suburbs, known as the **South Side**. To the southwest, in **Pollok Country Park**, are two of Glasgow's main tourist attractions, Pollok House and the Burrell Collection, which can easily be reached from the city centre by train or bus.

Tourist information

The main tourist information centre ⓘ *11 George Sq, T0141-2044400, F2213524, www.seeglasgow.com, May daily 0900-1800, Jun and Sep daily 0900-1900, Jul and Aug daily 0900-2000, Oct-Apr Mon-Sat 0900-1800*, provide an excellent service with a wide selection of maps and leaflets and a free accommodation booking service. You can also buy travel passes, theatre tickets, arrange car rental and exchange currency at their bureau de change.

South of George Square, in front of the giant St Enoch Centre, is the Strathclyde Travel Centre ⓘ *T0141-2264826, Mon-Sat 0830-1730*. They can provide maps, leaflets and timetables. Their free Visitor's Transport Guide includes a particularly useful map of the city. Travel information is also available from Traveline Scotland ⓘ *T0870-6082608, www.travelinescotland.com.*

History

Glasgow was founded in 543 AD when St Mungo built a church in what was then called Glas-ghu (meaning "dear green place"). The establishment of a cathedral in the 12th century and Scotland's second university in the 15th century brought status to the city and it was made a royal burgh in 1454.

But Glasgow played little part in the political or economic history of medieval Scotland. It was largely ignored during the bitter wars with England and most of the country's trade was with the Low Countries via the east coast ports.

The city's commercial prosperity came in the 17th century, when it began importing tobacco, sugar, cotton and other goods from the Americas. It began to expand westwards from the medieval centre of the High Street (with the exception of the cathedral, nothing of medieval Glasgow remains). Glasgow's location in the Clyde valley, surrounded by developing coalfields and with deep-water docks only 20 miles from the sea, ensured its development during the Industrial Revolution, in the late 18th century. The city grew rapidly with an influx of immigrants, mainly from the West Highlands, to work in the cotton mills. The deepening of the Clyde up to the Broomielaw, near the heart of the city, and the coming of the railway in the 19th century made the city one of the great industrial centres of the world.

It continued to expand rapidly between the late 18th and early 19th centuries, growing five-fold in only 50 years, and was further swelled by thousands of Irish immigrants fleeing Ireland to escape famine and to seek work. By the mid-19th century Glasgow's population had reached 400,000 and it could justifiably call itself the "second city of the empire". The Victorians built most of the city's most notable buildings, along with the acres of congested tenements that would later become notorious slums.

Since the Second World War and the decline of shipbuilding and heavy industries, Glasgow's population has fallen from over a million to less than 700,000: the result of planning policies designed to decant its population from slum tenements into "new towns" such as East Kilbride and Cumbernauld outside the city. During the recession of the late 1970s, Glasgow suffered more than most but instead of confronting central government, Glasgow embarked on a bold plan to reinvent

24 hours in the city

Twenty-four hours in Glasgow is just not enough, but if you're really pushed for time the following suggested itinerary will give a brief indication of why this is now considered one of the most exciting cities in Europe.

Start the day at the **People's Palace** on Glasgow Green for an introduction to the city's history. Head across to **Sauchiehall Street** for mid-morning coffee in the **Willow Tea Rooms** and admire the elegant interior design of Charles Rennie Mackintosh. Down to **Princes Square** for a spot of shopping, followed by a walk around the **Merchant City**. Lunch in **Babbity Bowster**.

After lunch, head up to the **School of Art**, take a tour and find out what all the fuss is about. Then head across the M8 to St George's Cross Underground and take the subway to Hillhead for a browse round the trendy shops of **Byres Road**. Stop for an aperitif in one of the many cool bars and cafés then it's off for dinner to the one-and-only **Ubiquitous Chip**. Take a cab back to the city centre for a cruise round some of the hip pre-club bars before hitting one of the city's legendary clubs for a good, old boogie.

itself and shake off the shackles of its industrial past. With its customary energy and wit, the city launched the "Glasgow's Miles Better" promotional campaign in 1983 which led to the 1988 Garden Festival, 1990's year as European City of Culture and, most recently, City of Architecture and Design, in 1999. Glasgow may still suffer the problems of urban deprivation, but it has regained its old confidence and transformed itself into a thriving, post-industrial city with a bright future.

Sights

Those who have come to see the sights won't be disappointed, for there are some world-class museums and galleries, many of which are free. To see and do everything recommended below would take five or six days, without rushing around too much. Top of everyone's list, and the city's most popular visitor attraction, is the Burrell Collection, a state-of-the-art building stuffed with priceless antiquities from around the world. In the West End are the Kelvinhall Museum and Art Gallery and the Transport Museum. Across the other side of town, in the East End, is the fascinating People's Palace, which tells the story of this great city, while on the north side of the city centre is the strangely beguiling Tenement House, a time capsule of life in pre-war Glasgow.

And then, of course, there's Charles Rennie Mackintosh, Glasgow's answer to Gaudí. Many visitors come solely to admire the genius of the man, and his masterpiece, the Glasgow School of Art, is not to be missed. Most of the Mackintosh sights are in and around the city centre, with the exception of Hill House in Helensburgh, and can be visited comfortably in two or three days. Lovers of fine buildings will also want to see some examples of Alexander 'Greek' Thomson, Glasgow's other great architect, especially Holmwood House, which has been described as a 'sonnet in stone'. ▸▸ *For Sleeping, Eating and other listings, see pages 156-177.*

City centre and the East End

George Square

The heart of modern Glasgow is George Square, which makes the obvious starting point for a tour of the city centre, as the tourist information centre is located here, on the south side. Amongst the many statues which adorn the square are those of Queen Victoria, Prince Albert, Sir Walter Scott, Robert Burns, Sir Robert Peel and James Watt. The square was named after George III and laid out in 1781. However for several years it was not much more than a watery patch of ground where horses were taken to be slaughtered and puppies to be drowned. The plan was to make it an upmarket, elegant square with private gardens at its centre. However many of the buildings – designed by the Adam brothers – were never built, while the gardens didn't last long as Glaswegians objected to such an obvious display of privilege and ripped the railings down in disgust. The square only became the heart of the city when the council decided to make it the location for the **City Chambers** ⓘ *T0141-2872000, free guided tours, Mon-Fri at 1030 and 1430*, the most visible symbol of Glasgow's position as Second City of the Empire. Among the other fine Victorian building on the square the grandiose chambers fill the east side and are a wonderful testament to the optimism and aspiration of Victorian Glasgow. The building was designed in Italian Renaissance style by William Young and the interior is even more impressive than its façade. The imposing arcaded marble entrance hall is decorated with elaborate mosaics and a marble staircase leads up to a great banqueting hall with a wonderful arched ceiling, leaded glass windows and paintings depicting scenes from the city's history. One wall is covered by a series of murals by the Glasgow Boys, see page 141.

On the northwest corner of George Square, opposite Queen Street station, is another fine building, the **Merchants' House** ⓘ *T0141-2218272, free, entry by appointment only*, now the home of Glasgow Chamber of Commerce. The interior is worth a look as it boasts some beautiful stained glass windows and chocolate brown wood panelling.

Gallery of Modern Art

ⓘ *T0141-2291996, www.glasgow.gov.uk, Mon-Thu and Sat 1000-1700, Fri and Sun 1100-1700, free.*

Just to the south of George Square, facing the west end of Ingram Street, is **Royal Exchange Square**, which is almost completely filled by the Gallery of Modern Art (GOMA). The building dates from 1778, when it was built as the Cunninghame Mansion, home to one of Glasgow's wealthy Tobacco Lords. It passed to the Royal Bank of Scotland in 1817 and 10 years later the magnificent portico was added to the front and the building then became the Royal Exchange, the city's main business centre. It then housed a library, until its reopening in 1996 as one of the city's newest, and its most controversial, art venues, drawing the ire of many a critic for its unashamed eclecticism and populism.

The gallery features contemporary works from artists worldwide over three themed levels: the **Earth Gallery** on the ground floor; the **Water Gallery**; and the **Air Gallery**. It's a bold, innovative art space, making excellent use of the fabulous original interior. The works you can see are varied and include powerful paintings by Peter Howson, the Imperial War Museum's war artist in Bosnia; photographs by Henri Cartier-Bresson, and Beryl Cook's jolly work *By the Clyde*.

Although there's a statue of Burns in George Square, the poet did not have very strong links with Glasgow. On the few times he did come to the city he seems to have gone shopping, buying, on various visits, some books, some cocoa and some black silk for his wife.

Merchant City

The grid-plan of streets to the east of George Square as far as the High Street form the Merchant City, where the Tobacco Lords built their magnificent Palladian mansions. They made Glasgow the most important tobacco trading city in Europe and can also take the credit for it being one of the lung cancer capitals of the world by the mid-20th century.

This part of the city was once a bustling trade centre and money has been poured into the restoration of its 18th century warehouses and homes in an attempt to revitalize and regenerate the city's old historic core. Though many of the buildings are little more than façades, the investment has succeeded in attracting expensive designer clothes shops and a plethora of stylish bistros, cafés and bars, which are packed with the city's young professionals and media types. It's a very pleasant and interesting area to explore, and when all that neoclassical architecture gets too much, you can pop into one of the trendy café-bars for some light relief.

A good place to start is **Hutchesons' Hall** ⓘ *158 Ingram St, T0141-5528391, www.nts.org.uk, Mon-Sat 1000-1700, free*, a distinguished Georgian building which is now the National Trust for Scotland's regional headquarters. It was built by David Hamilton in 1805 in neoclassical style with a traditional Scottish 'townhouse' steeple. It was once home of the Scottish Educational Trust, a charitable institution founded by the 17th-century lawyer brothers George and Thomas Hutcheson which provided almshouses and schools for the city. Their statues gaze down towards the site of the original almshouse in Trongate. Upstairs is the ornate hall where you can see a film on the Glasgow Style, the distinctive style of art that evolved from the works of artists such as Charles Rennie Mackintosh. Downstairs there's an exhibition, also on Glasgow Style, featuring jewellery, textiles, furniture and prints by contemporary Glasgow artists and craftspeople. All the works are for sale – for anything from a few pounds to several hundred pounds.

In nearby Glassford Street is Glasgow's oldest secular building, the **Trades Hall** ⓘ *T0141-5522418, www.bbnet.demon.co.uk/thall, entry subject to availability Mon-Fri 0900-1800, Sat 0900-1300, guided tours by appointment only*, designed by Robert Adam and built in 1794 as the headquarters of the city's trade guilds. It still serves its original purpose. The Grand Hall is an impressive sight, lined with a Belgian silk tapestry depicting the work of a range of former city trades such as bonnetmakers (not much call for them nowadays) and cordiners (bootmakers). At the corner of Ingram Street and Glassford Street is the lavish **Trustee Savings Bank** building, designed by that prodigious talent, JJ Burnet in 1900. Nearby, on Ingram Street, is another fine building, **Lanarkshire House**, designed by his father, John Burnet, along with two more of Glasgow's greatest architects, David Hamilton and James Salmon Junior. It dates from 1879 and has now been opened as The Corinthian, a combination of bars, restaurants and meeting rooms.

Running off Ingram Street is Virginia Street, whose name recalls Glasgow's trading links with America. Here you'll find a rather dilapidated collection of early 19th-century buildings, **Virginia Buildings**. Parallel to Virginia Street is Miller Street, where you'll find the Merchant City's oldest surviving house (No 42), the **Tobacco Lord's House**, dating from 1775.

Glasgow Cross and around

The Merchant City is bounded to the east by the High Street and to the south by Trongate. These two streets meet at Glasgow Cross, once the centre of trade and administration and regarded as the city centre, until the coming of the railway in the mid-19th century. In the centre of the intersection stands the 126 ft-high **Tolbooth Steeple**, one of only three crowned steeples in the country. This is the only remnant of the original tolbooth built in 1626, which housed the courthouse and prison

Glasgow centre

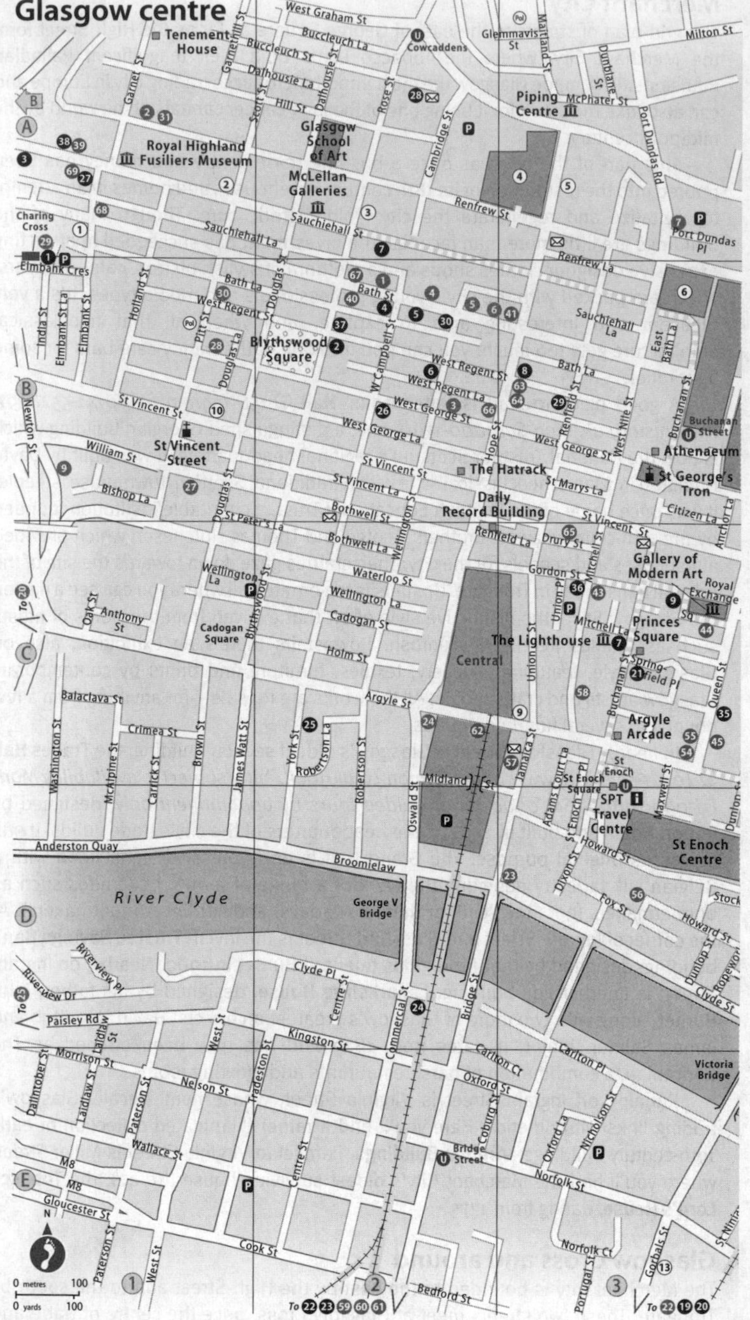

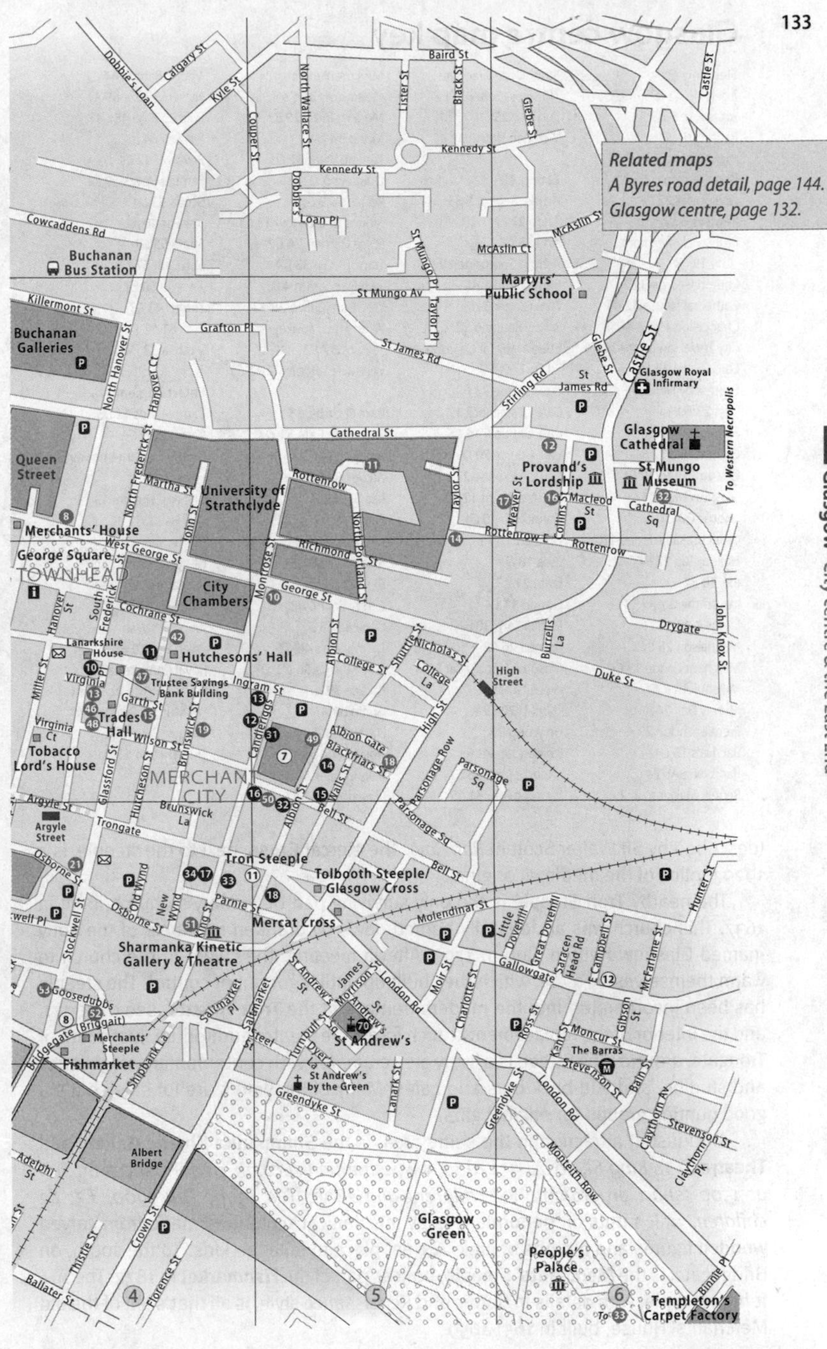
Related maps
A Byres road detail, page 144.
Glasgow centre, page 132.
Buchanan Bus Station
Buchanan Galleries
Queen Street
Merchants' House
George Square
TOWNHEAD
City Chambers
University of Strathclyde
Martyrs' Public School
Glasgow Royal Infirmary
Glasgow Cathedral
Provand's Lordship
St Mungo Museum
To Western Necropolis
Lanarkshire House
Hutchesons' Hall
Trustee Savings Bank Building
Trades Hall
Tobacco Lord's House
MERCHANT CITY
Argyle Street
High Street
Tron Steeple
Tolbooth Steeple/ Glasgow Cross
Mercat Cross
Sharmanka Kinetic Gallery & Theatre
Merchants' Steeple
Fishmarket
St Andrew's
St Andrew's by the Green
The Barras
Albert Bridge
Glasgow Green
People's Palace
Templeton's Carpet Factory
Dobbie's Loan
Calgary St
Kyle St
Baird St
North Wallace St
Lister St
Black St
Glebe St
Castle St
Kennedy St
Cowcaddens Rd
Dobbie's Loan Pl
Couper St
St Mungo Pl
McAslin St
McAslin Ct
Killermont St
St Mungo Av
Taylor Pl
Grafton Pl
St James Rd
Stirling Rd
North Hanover St
Hanover Ct
Cathedral St
North Frederick St
Martha St
John St
Rottenrow
North Portland St
Taylor St
Weaver St
Collins St
Macleod St
Cathedral Sq
Rottenrow E
West George St
Richmond St
Montrose St
George St
Drygate
John Knox St
Hanover St
South Frederick St
Cochrane St
Albion St
Shuttle St
Nicholas St
College St
College La
Burrells La
Duke St
Miller St
Virginia Pl
Ingram St
Garth St
Virginia Ct
Brunswick St
Wilson St
Candleriggs
Albion Gate
Blackfriars St
High St
Parsonage Row
Parsonage Sq
Glassford St
Hutcheson St
Walls St
Bell St
Argyle St
Brunswick La
Trongate
Osborne St
Old Wynd
New Wynd
Parnie St
King St
Stockwell St
Molendinar St
Little Dovehill
Great Dovehill
Saracen Head Rd
E Campbell St
McFarlane St
Hunter St
Gallowgate
Goosedubbs
Bridgegate (Briggait)
Saltmarket Pl
Saltmarket
St Andrew's St
James Morrison St
London Rd
Moir St
Charlotte St
Ross St
Kent St
Gibson St
Moncur St
Stevenson St
Bain St
Shipbank La
Steel St
Turnbull St
Dyer's La
Greendyke St
Lanark St
Claythorn Av
Claythorn Pk
Monteith Row
Adelphi St
Crown St
Thistle St
Florence St
Ballater St
Binnie Pl
To 33

Glasgow centre map key

Sleeping
Adelaide's **1** *B2*
Art House **5** *B2*
Babbity Bowster & Schottische **18** *C5*
Best Western Ewington **22** *E3*
Bewleys **6** *B2*
Brunswick Merchant City **19** *C4*
Carlton George **3** *B2*
Cathedral House **32** *B6*
Chancellors Hall **14** *C5*
City Travel Inn Metro **10** *C5*
Euro Hostel **23** *D3*
Express by Holiday Inn **21** *D4*
Forbes Hall **17** *B6*
Garnett Hall **12** *B6*
Glasgow Hilton **9** *B1*
Glasgow Moat House **20** *C1*
Groucho Saint Judes **4** *B2*
Holiday Inn **27** *B1*
Ibis **30** *B1*
Inn on the Green **33** *E6*
Langs **7** *A3*
Malmaison **28** *B1*
Merchant Lodge **13** *C4*
Millennium **8** *B4*
Murray Hall **16** *B6*
Premier Lodge **29** *A1*
Rab Ha's **15** *C4*
Radisson SAS **24** *C2*
Rennie Mackintosh **2** *A1*
Strathclyde Graduate Business School **11** *B5*
Swallow **25** *D1*
Victorian House **31** *A1*

Eating
Amber Regent **8** *B3*
Arigo **22** *E2*
Arta **15** *C5*
Ashoka Southside **19** *E3*
Baby Grand **1** *A1*
Bleu Ginger **3** *A1*
Bouzy Rouge **6** *B2*
Brian Maule at Chardon d'Or **2** *B2*
Buongiorno **23** *E2*
Café Cossachock **17** *D4*
Café Gandolfi **14** *C5*
Café Source **70** *D5*
Canton Express **27** *A1*
City Merchant **12** *C5*
Corinthian **10** *C4*
Dhabba **16** *C5*
Esca **18** *D5*
Etain **21** *C3*
Frango **11** *C4*
Fratelli Sarti **30** *B2*
Gamba **26** *B2*
Glasgow Noodle Bar **38** *A1*
Greek Golden Kebab **20** *E3*
Ho Wong **25** *C2*
Ichiban Japanese Noodle Café **35** *C3*
Metropolitan **31** *C5*
Miss Cranston's Tearooms **36** *C3*
Modern India **29** *B3*
Mono **34** *D4*
Pancho Villas **32** *D5*
Quigleys **5** *B2*
Rogano's **9** *C3*
Smiths of Glasgow **13** *C5*
Spice Garden **24** *D2*
Trattoria Gia **33** *D4*
Two Five Seven **4** *B2*
Wee Curry Shop **28** *A2*
Where the Monkey Sleeps **37** *B2*
Willow Tea Rooms **7** *A2, C3*

Bars & clubs
13th Note Café **51** *D4*
Archaos **54** *C3*
Arches **62** *C2*
Bar 10 **58** *C3*
Bargo **49** *C5*
Bennet's **47** *C4*
Blackfriars **50** *C5*
Bloc **41** *B3*
Candy Bar **66** *B2*
Cube **45** *C3*
Delmonica's **46** *C4*
Fury Murry's **56** *D3*
Garage **39** *A1*
Griffin **68** *A1*
Havana **63** *B3*
Horse Shoe **65** *C3*
Kelly Cooper & Lowdown **67** *B2*
MAS & Babaza **44** *C3*
Nice 'n' Sleazy **69** *A1*
Polo Lounge **48** *C4*
Pot Still **64** *B3*
Revolver **42** *C4*
Samuel Dow's **59** *E2*
Scotia **53** *D4*
Spy Bar **40** *B2*
Strata **55** *C3*
Sub Club **57** *C3*
Taverna **60** E2
Tunnel **43** *C3*
Tusk **61** *E2*
Victoria **52** *D4*

Entertainment
Barrowlands **12** *D6*
Cathouse **9** *C3*
Centre for Contemporary Arts **2** *A1*
Citizens' Theatre **13** *E3*
City Hall **7** *C5*
Clutha Vaults **8** *D4*
Glasgow Film Theatre **3** *A2*
Kings Theatre **1** *A1*
King Tut's Wah Wah Hut **10** *B1*
Royal Concert Hall **6** *B3*
Royal Scottish Academy of Music & Drama **4** *A3*
Theatre Royal **5** *A3*
Tron Theatre **11** *D5*

(described by Sir Walter Scott in *Rob Roy*). The **Mercat Cross**, next to the steeple, is a 1929 replica of the medieval original.

The nearby **Tron Steeple** is the only surviving part of St Mary's Church, built in 1637. This church was accidentally burned down by drunken members of the aptly -named Glasgow Hellfire Club in 1793. After a meeting, they went to the church to warm themselves by a fire, which they built up until it got out of control. The steeple has been incorporated into the modern frontage of the **Tron Theatre**, see page 171, and the interior of the replacement church forms the theatre auditorium. Just south of Trongate, around King Street, is a lively area crammed with contemporary art galleries and studios, and laid-back bars and cafés. Many of the works are for sale so it's a good hunting ground for original gifts.

An unusual attraction in the same area, is the **Sharmanka Kinetic Gallery and Theatre** ⓘ *14 King St, T0141-5527080, www.sharmanka.co.uk, performances on Sun at 1500 (short programme for children) and 1800, Tue 1300, Thu 1900, £3, £2 children*, which puts on performances by mechanical sculptures made from carved wooden figures and old bits of junk. A great place to take the kids. To the south, on Bridgegate, is the **Merchants' Steeple**, built as part of the **Fishmarket** in 1872. The 164 ft-high steeple, with details in Gothic and Renaissance style, is all that's left of the old Merchants' House, built in 1651-1659.

The East End

East of Glasgow Cross, Gallowgate and London Road lead into the city's East End, only a stone's throw from the Merchant City. It may look shabby and rundown by comparison but this is where you can sample a slice of pure Glasgow, especially in **The Barrows ('The Barras')** ⓘ *weekends, 1000-1700, entrance is marked by the red gates on Gallowgate*, a huge market spread out around the streets and alleys south of Gallowgate. You could spend days rummaging around through acres of cheap, new and second-hand goods. A lot of it's junk (dodgy computer games, pirate videos etc) but there are plenty of bargains to be found and there's every chance of unearthing some valuable antique. The real attraction, though, is the distinctive atmosphere of the place and wit and repartee of the market traders.

South of The Barras is the wide expanse of **Glasgow Green**, said to be the oldest public park in Britain. It has been common land since at least medieval times and Glaswegians still have the right to dry their washing here. There are various **monuments** dotted around the park, including a 144 ft-high monument to Lord Nelson, erected in 1806, and one to James Watt. Just to the north of the Green are two of the city's oldest churches, dating from the mid-18th century. In St Andrew's Square is **St Andrew's Church**, one of the finest classical churches in Britain. Sadly neglected for many years, it has now been restored to its Georgian splendour. It no longer functions as a church but has been cleverly converted to house the sleek **Café Source**, see page 160, downstairs and a Scottish music venue upstairs. You can go upstairs and see the stunning original stained-glass windows and intricate plaster work. Concerts and ceilidhs are staged throughout the year – tickets available from the café. Nearby is the episcopal **St Andrew's-by-the-Green**, once known as the Whistlin' Kirk because of the introduction of its organ, a radical move in those days.

On the edge of the green, to the east of the People's Palace, see below, is **Templeton's Carpet Factory**, a bizarre but beautiful structure designed in 1889 by William Leiper in imitation of the Doges' Palace in Venice. Once described as the 'world's finest examples of decorative brickwork, it's Britain's best example of polychromatic decoration (in other words, very colourful). The building is now used as a business centre.

On the northern end of the green, approached from London Road, is the **People's Palace** ⓘ *T0141-5540223, Mon-Thu and Sat 1000-1700, Fri and Sun 1100-1700, free*, opened in 1898 as a folk museum for the East End. The recently refurbished museum gives a real insight into the social and industrial life of this great city from the mid-18th century to the present day. Its galleries display a wealth of artefacts, photographs, cartoons and drawings, and a series of films, music and people's anecdotes. There's a reconstructed 'steamie' (communal laundry) from nearby Ingram Street; brochures extolling the delights of a trip 'Doon the watter' on the Clyde, and video displays on 'the patter' – Glaswegian a la Rab C Nesbitt. The museum doesn't shrink from covering the less salubrious aspects of city history either. There's a display on 'the bevvy' (drink) which includes a barrow once used regularly by the police to wheel drunks home. There's also a small display on the sectarian divide in city football – evidenced by a t-shirt protesting at Rangers' signing of Mo Johnston (their first Catholic player). A visit to the People's Palace should be on everyone's itinerary, particularly if you're interested in scratching beneath the city's surface and getting to know it better. Equally recommended is the **Winter Gardens**, a huge conservatory at the rear of the museum, where you can enjoy a cup of tea or coffee and a snack in tropical surroundings.

Bonnie Prince Charlie reviewed his troops on Glasgow Green in 1745 before they were hung out to dry by the English at Culloden. The Green has always been dear to the people of Glasgow and some of the city's major political demonstrators have held meetings here, including the Chartists in the 1830s and Scottish republican campaigners in the 1920s.

More Mackintosh

Aside from the Mackintosh buildings listed separately, there are a number of his lesser known works scattered around the city centre.

These include the former **Daily Record Building** (1901), at 20-26 Renfield Lane (external viewing only), the **Royal Fusiliers Museum** (circa 1903), at 518 Sauchiehall Street (ring for opening times, T0141-3320961), **Ruchill Church Hall**, Shakespeare Street (open from Monday to Friday 1030-1430, closed July and August, free) and the former **Glasgow Society of Lady Artists' Club** (1908), at 5 Blythswood Square (external viewing only).

Glasgow Cathedral and Precinct

Until the 18th century Glasgow consisted only of a narrow ribbon of streets running north from the river past the Glasgow Cross and up the High Street to the cathedral. Then came the city's rapid expansion west and the High Street became a dilapidated backwater. At the top of the High Street stand the two oldest buildings in the city, Glasgow Cathedral and Provand's Lordship.

Glasgow Cathedral ⓘ *T0141-5526891, www.historic-scotland.gov.uk, Apr-Sep Mon-Sat 0930-1800, Sun 1400-1700, Oct-Mar Mon-Sat 0930-1600, Sun 1400-1600, free*, is a rather severe-looking early Gothic structure and the only complete medieval cathedral on the Scottish mainland. It was built on the site of St Mungo's original church, established in AD 543, though this has been a place of Christian worship since it was blessed for burial in AD 397 by St Ninian, the earliest missionary recorded in Scottish history. Most of the building was completed in the 13th century though parts were built a century earlier by Bishop Jocelyn. The choir and crypt were added a century later and the building was completed at the end of the 15th century by Robert Blacader, the first Bishop of Glasgow. During the Reformation, the city's last Roman Catholic Archbishop, James Beaton, took off for France with most of the cathedral treasures, just ahead of the townsfolk who proceeded to rid the building of all traces of 'idolatry' by destroying altars, statues, vestments and the valuable library. The present furnishings mostly date from the 19th century and many of the windows have been renewed with modern stained glass. The most outstanding feature in the cathedral is the fan vaulting around St Mungo's tomb in the crypt, one of the very finest examples of medieval architecture in Scotland. There's also fine work in the choir, including a 15th-century stone screen, the only one of its kind left in any pre-Reformation secular (non-monastic) church in Scotland.

Behind the cathedral looms the **Western Necropolis**, a vast burial ground overlooking the city from the top of a high ridge. It was modelled on Pere-Lachaise cemetery in Paris. Around 3,500 tombs have been built here and around 50,000 burials have taken place. Most of the burials took place in the 19th century and the ornate nature of many of the tombs makes it appear as if the city worthies buried here really were trying to take their money with them when they died. It's the ideal vantage point from which to appreciate the cathedral in all its Gothic splendour and many of the tombs are wonderfully-ornate. Interred here are the great and the good (and not so good) of Victorian Glasgow – there was no discrimination; anyone could be buried here as long as they could afford it. The graveyard is overseen by a statue of John Knox, the 16th-century firebrand reformer. There's also a monument to William Miller who penned the nursery rhyme Wee Willie Winkie. Look out for a monument to Alexander McCall. A Celtic Cross, it's the first solo work by Charles Rennie Mackintosh.

In front of the cathedral is the weetabix-coloured **St Mungo Museum of Religious Life and Art** ⓘ *T0141-5532557, Mon-Thu and Sat 1000-1700, Fri and Sun 1100-1700, free*, which features a series of displays of arts and artefacts representing the six major world religions, as well as a Japanese Zen garden in the courtyard outside – great for a few moments of quiet contemplation. Highlights include **Salvador Dalí**'s astounding *Christ of St John of the Cross*, purchased by the city from the artist in 1951. You can also see a Native American ceremonial blanket depicting sacred animals; masks used in African initiation rites, and as Islamic prayer rug. Displays on religion in the west of Scotland cover everything from the Temperance movement of the late 19th century, to the religious life of the modern city's vibrant ethnic communities. Don't miss the extremely interesting comments on the visitors' board. There's also a bookshop and café serving hot meals, snacks and drinks.

Across the street the **Provand's Lorship** ⓘ *same phone number and opening hours as above*, the oldest remaining house in Glasgow, built in 1471 as part of a refuge for the city's poor and extended in 1670. It has also served as an inn of rather dubious repute in its time. Now it's a museum devoted mainly to medieval furniture and various domestic items. In the grounds is a specially created medieval garden.

A short walk north from these ancient buildings is **Martyrs' Public School** ⓘ *Parson St (off Stirling Rd), T0141-5522356, Mon-Sat 1000-1600, Sun 1100-1600, free*. This school, which was opened in 1897, was one of the first buildings designed by Charles Rennie Mackintosh.

Buchanan Street to The Lighthouse

At the bottom end of Buchanan Street is St Enoch Square, dominated by the **St Enoch Centre**, a gigantic glass-covered complex of shops, fast-food outlets and an ice rink. There's also a subway station and transport centre in the square. St Enoch Square looks onto **Argyle Street**, one of Glasgow's most famous shopping streets. Though its status has been usurped in recent decades by the more fashionable streets to the north, it does boast the **Argyle Arcade**, Scotland's first ever indoor shopping mall, built in 1827 in Parisian style, at the junction with Buchanan Street.

Argyle Street runs west from here under the railway bridge at **Central station**. The bridge has always been known as the 'Heilanman's Umbrella', owing to the local joke that Highlanders would stand under it for shelter rather than buy an umbrella.

A short walk north on Buchanan Street is **Princes Square**, one of the most stylish and imaginative shopping malls in Britain. Even if you're not buying or looking, it's worth going in to admire this beautifully-ornate art nouveau creation, or to sit at the top-floor café and watch others spend their hard-earned cash in the trendy designer clothes shops below. A little further north, on the opposite side of the street, is a branch of the famous **Willow Tea Rooms**, with replicas of Mackintosh designs. Almost opposite is **Borders Bookshop**, housed in the huge and impressive former Royal Bank of Scotland (1827), which backs onto Royal Exchange Square.

The Lighthouse

ⓘ *T0141-2216362, Mon, Wed, Fri and Sat 1030-1730, Tue 1100-1700, Thu 1030-1700, Sun 1200-1700, £2.50, £2 concession.*

Lovers of architecture should head west into Gordon Street and then south (left) into Mitchell Street, where you'll find The Lighthouse, a tardis-like building full of surprises. It was designed by the ubiquitous Charles Rennie Mackintosh in 1893 to house the offices of the Glasgow *Herald*. *The Herald* vacated the premises in 1980

Glasgow's commercial heart is the area between Buchanan Square and the M8. This vast grid-plan, home to the city's main shopping streets, businesses and financial institutions, inspired town planners in the USA. It is also where you'll find many of its architectural treasures.

Glasgow's Gaudí

To say that Barcelona has Gaudí and Glasgow has Rennie Mackintosh is not overstating the case. He is not only one of Scotland's most celebrated architects, but one of the creative geniuses of modern architecture.

Charles Rennie Mackintosh was born in Glasgow in 1868 and at 15 began work as a draughtsman with a local firm of architects. At the same time, he continued to pursue his studies at the Glasgow School of Art where his talent as an artist soon earned him recognition, and his experimental, decorative style brought him into contact with kindred spirits Herbert MacNair and two sisters, Frances and Margaret MacDonald. They became known as 'The Four' and together they developed their unique form of art and design, which became known as the 'Glasgow Style'.

Mackintosh was as much an artist and interior designer as an architect but he saw no conflict in this. He considered architecture to be "...the synthesis of the fine arts, the commune of all the crafts", and he used his diverse talents to great effect, designing every detail of a building, down to furniture, carpets and decoration. This can be seen to greatest effect in his most important building, the Glasgow School of Art.

In the late 1890s he began his Argyle Street tea room project for Miss Cranston, and developed his distinctive, elegant high-backed chairs, for which he is probably best known today. In 1900 he married Margaret Macdonald (Herbert MacNair and Margaret's sister were married the previous year) and they began to design the interior of their own flat, creating their distinctive colour schemes of white and grey, pink and purple, and the light and dark interiors representing the masculine and feminine.

Throughout his career, Mackintosh's talents were far better understood abroad than at home, where his designs were often criticized as being iconoclastic and too modern. He was forced to leave Glasgow in 1914 due to lack of work and soon became depressed and alcoholic, and though his fortunes improved after moving to London, he died, a tragic but romantic figure, in 1928.

It is only in the past few decades that his genius has been fully recognized and serious efforts made to preserve his artistic legacy. The restoration of the Willow Tea Rooms, Scotland Street School, Queen's Cross Church and the Mackintosh House at the Hunterian Art Gallery, as well as The Hill House in Helensburgh, are all testimony to his prodigious talents.

and it lay empty, until its recent transformation into **Scotland's Centre for Architecture, Design and the City**, a permanent legacy of the Glasgow's role as UK City of Architecture and Design in 1999. The Lighthouse offers a programme of lively temporary exhibitions associated with architecture and design. In the past these have included an exhibition on the work of Japanese architects, and one on Glasgow's favourite buildings. This stunning 21st-century building also contains the **Mackintosh Interpretation and Review Gallery**, on the third floor, which features original designs and information on the life and work of the great architect. There are interactive displays telling the story of his life and scale models of his works. From this gallery you can reach the **Mackintosh Viewing Tower**. Reached by a 135-step spiral staircase, it was part of the original building and offers unbeatable, panoramic views of the city. There's also a shop and café on the fifth floor and another café on the ground floor.

Buchanan Street north and St Vincent Street

Further north on Buchanan Street, close to Buchanan Street Underground, are two more interesting buildings: **St George's Tron Church**, designed in 1808 by William Stark and the oldest church in the city centre; and the **Athenaeum**, designed in 1886 by JJ Burnet and showing early signs of his later modernism. Running west from George Square, between Argyle Street and Sauchiehall Street, is St Vincent Street, where you'll find two of the city's extraordinary buildings. **The Hatrack**, at No 142, was designed in 1902 by James Salmon Junior. It's a very tall, narrow building, like many in the city centre, with a fantastically-detailed roof which looks like an old hat stand.

Further along St Vincent Street, near the intersection with Pitt Street, is one of the jewels in Glasgow's architectural crown, the **St Vincent Street Church**, designed in 1859 by Alexander 'Greek' Thomson, the city's 'unknown genius' of architecture. Much of his work was destroyed in the 1960s and this is his only intact Romantic Classical church, now on the World Monument Fund's list of the 100 most endangered sites. The Presbyterian church is fronted by Ionic columns like those of a Greek temple and the church also shows Egyptian and Assyrian decoration. The main tower is Grecian in style while the dome could have come straight out of India during the Raj. At the time of writing, this magnificent church remains under threat. To allow it to deteriorate further would be a national disgrace.

A series of streets climb northwards from St Vincent Street up to Sauchiehall Street, another of the city's main shopping thoroughfares. If there's one thing Glaswegians like to do it's spend money and Glasgow is second only to London in the UK in terms of retail spending. The newest of the city's shopping centres is the upmarket **Buchanan Galleries**, next door to the **Royal Concert Hall**, see page 170, at the north end of Buchanan Street, where it meets the east end of Sauchiehall Street.

Sauchiehall Street

There are a few notable places of interest here, including Charles Rennie Mackintosh's wonderful **Willow Tea Rooms** ⓘ *No 217, above Henderson's the Jewellers, www.willowtearooms.co.uk, 0930-1630, see also Eating page 160*. This is a faithful reconstruction on the site of the original 1903 tea room, designed by CRM for his patron Miss Kate Cranston, who already ran three of the city's most fashionable tea rooms, in Argyle Street, Buchanan Street and Ingram Street. The tea room was very much peculiar to Glasgow, promoted by the Temperance Movement as a healthy alternative to the gin palaces, popular throughout the country in the late 19th century, and Miss Cranston's were the *crème de la crème* of tea rooms. They offered ladies-only rooms, rooms for gentlemen and rooms where both sexes could dine together. In addition, her tea rooms offered a reading room, a billiards room for the gentlemen and a smoking room, not forgetting the unrivalled splendour of the decoration. Mackintosh had already worked with Miss Cranston on her other tea rooms, but Sauchiehall Street was their *tour de force*. Sauchiehall means 'alley of the willows' and this theme was reflected not only in the name, but throughout the interior. Mackintosh was allowed free rein to design the fixtures and fittings; everything, in fact, right down to the teaspoons. The exclusive Salon de Luxe, on the first floor, was the crowning glory, and the most exotic and ambitious part of the tea rooms, decorated in purple, silver and white, with silk and velvet upholstery. Visitors today can relive the splendour of the original tea rooms as they relax in the distinctive high-backed chairs with a cup of tea, brought to them by the specially selected high-backed waitresses.

A few yards west, on the opposite side of the street, are the **McLellan Galleries** ⓘ *T0141-5654137, www.glasgowmuseums.com, Mon-Thu and Sat 1000-1700, Fri and Sun 1100-1700, free*, another fine example of classical architecture. While Kelvingrove Art Gallery and Museum is closed for refurbishment (until late 2005) these galleries are hosting a display of the most important artworks from the collection.

Further down the street, on the same side, is the **Centre for Contemporary Arts (CCA)** ⓘ *T0141-3327521, www.cca-glasgow.com, centre open Mon-Sat 0900-2400, Sun 1200-1900, galleries open Mon-Sat 1100-1800, Sun 1200-1700, free*, housed in the Grecian Buildings, a former commercial warehouse designed by Alexander 'Greek' Thomson in 1867-1868. The centre presents a changing programme of contemporary theatre, dance and other cultural events. It also has two excellent café-bars, see Eating page 160.

Glasgow School of Art

ⓘ *167 Renfrew St, T0141-3534526, www.gsa.ac.uk, guided tour Oct-Jun Mon-Fri at 1100 and 1400, Sat 1030 and 1130, Jul-Sep Mon-Fri 1100 and 1400, Sat and Sun 1030, 1130 and 1300 (booking advised), closed late Jun for graduation and Christmas to New Year, £5, £3 students.*

Barcelona has the Sagrada Familia, New York the Empire State Building and Glasgow has its School of Art. A very steep walk up from Sauchiehall Street is the city's defining monument, and one of the most prestigious art schools in the country. The building was designed by Charles Rennie Mackintosh, after his proposal won a competition set to find a design for the school, in 1896. It was built in two stages from 1897-1899 and completed in 1907.

Much of the inspiration for his design came from nature and from his drawings of traditional Scottish buildings. He was also influenced by the art nouveau style, particularly the illustrations of Aubrey Beardsley. The school is now regarded as Mackintosh's architectural masterpiece and gives full expression to his architectural ideals. It is rooted in tradition, with a thoroughly modern-looking exterior of extreme austerity, and there are medieval, castle-like features such as turrets and curving stairwells. The interior is both spacious and utilitarian and shows perfectly his desire to create a unified and harmonious working environment for both students and teachers. The studio walls and high ceilings are painted white, with huge windows allowing light to pour into the spaces. The corridors and staircases are decorated with glazed coloured tiles to help guide students and staff around the massive building. In the famous two-storey library Mackintosh also designed the light fittings, bookcases and the oak furniture. There are symbols of nature everywhere throughout the building, used to inspire the students to produce their own works of art. And who could fail to be inspired in such a stunning environment.

Entry to the school is by guided tour only which visits the main rooms containing many of the well-known pieces of furniture. It is still a working art school, so take note of the annual closing.

Tenement House

ⓘ *T0141-3330183, www.nts.org.uk, 1 Mar-31 Oct, 1300-1700, £4, £3 concession.*

A few hundred yards northwest of the School of Art, down the other side of the hill, at 145 Buccleuch Street, is the Tenement House, a typical late Victorian tenement flat. This was the home of Miss Agnes Toward, a shorthand typist, for 50 years until she moved out in 1965. It's a fascinating time-capsule of life in the first half of the 20th century and retains most of the original features such as the bed recesses, kitchen range and coal bunker. The whole experience is a little voyeuristic, as the flat includes many of Agnes' personal possessions, and in the parlour the table is set for afternoon tea, lending a spooky atmosphere redolent of the Marie Celeste. On the ground floor is an exhibition on tenement life.

On the other side of Cowcaddens Road, behind the huge Royal Scottish Academy for Music and Drama, is the **Piping Centre** ⓘ *30-34 McPhater St, T0141-3530220, www.thepipingcentre.co.uk, May-Sep daily 1000-1630, Oct-Apr Mon-Sat 1000-1630, £3, £2 concession.* It's a kind of centre for the promotion of the bagpipes and contains rehearsal rooms, performance spaces and accommodation for aficionados of the instrument which divides opinion so sharply. There's also a very fine café and a

Glasgow Boys

With the coming of the industrial age, Glasgow had grown rapidly from a small, provincial town into the 'Second City of the Empire'. This sudden growth in size and wealth led to the beginnings of the famous and long-standing rivalry between Glasgow and Edinburgh, and, by the 1880s, to a new departure from the cultural mainstream, when a group of students nicknamed the Glasgow Boys, united in protest against Edinburgh's dominance of the arts.

This group of five painters – Guthrie, Hornel, Lavery, Henry and Crawhall – rejected the traditional concept of art which was confined to historical melodrama, sentimental 'poor but happy' cottagers and grandiose visions of the Highlands inspired by Sir Walter Scott. They referred to these paintings as 'gluepots' for their use of megilp, a treacly varnish that lent the paintings a brown patina of age. Instead, they experimented with colour and, inspired by the European Realists, chose earthy, peasant themes. This not only shocked and offended the genteel Edinburgh art establishment, but also scandalized their fellow citizens.

The Glasgow Boys left Scotland to study in Paris, where their work met with great acclaim. Subsequently their art began to fetch high prices from the new rich of Glasgow, eager to buy status through cultural patronage. But once the group had achieved the artistic respect and commercial success its members craved, they sadly lost their freshness.

museum which features a collection of antique pipes. It also has audio visual displays and gives you headsets so you can listen bagpipe music as you go round.

West End

On the other side of the M8 is the West End, an area which contains many of the city's major museums, as well some of its finest examples of Victorian architecture. During the course of the 19th century the West End grew in importance as wealthy merchants moved here, away from the dirt and grime of the industrial city. By the middle of the 19th century the **Park Conservation Area** had been established and was described as one of the finest pieces of architectural planning of the century. Perhaps the most impressive of all the terraces in the conservation area are **Park Quadrant** and **Park Terrace**, with glorious views across **Kelvingrove Park.** Soon after, in 1870, the **university** also moved west, to its present site overlooking Kelvingrove Park, and in 1896 the Glasgow District Subway was extended west. In 1888 the park was used to stage an international exhibition and the profits were used to build the **Kelvingrove Art Gallery and Museum** (closed for refurbishment until late 2005 – artworks from the collection are temporarily on display at the McLellan Galleries in Sauchiehall Street, see page 139), which housed the second international exhibition in 1901. The bustling hub of the West End is Byres Road, running south from the Great Western Road past Hillhead Underground. ▸▸ *For Sleeping, Eating and other listings, see pages 156-177.*

It's an area populated mostly by students and full of fashionable shops, bars, cafés and restaurants.

Queen's Cross Church

ⓘ *870 Garscube Rd, T0141-9466600, www.crmsociety.com, Mon-Fri 1000-1700, Sun Mar-Oct 1400-1700, £2, £1 concession, buses 21, 61 and 91 from Hope St, or Underground to St George's Cross and walk 10 mins on Maryhill Rd.*

West End

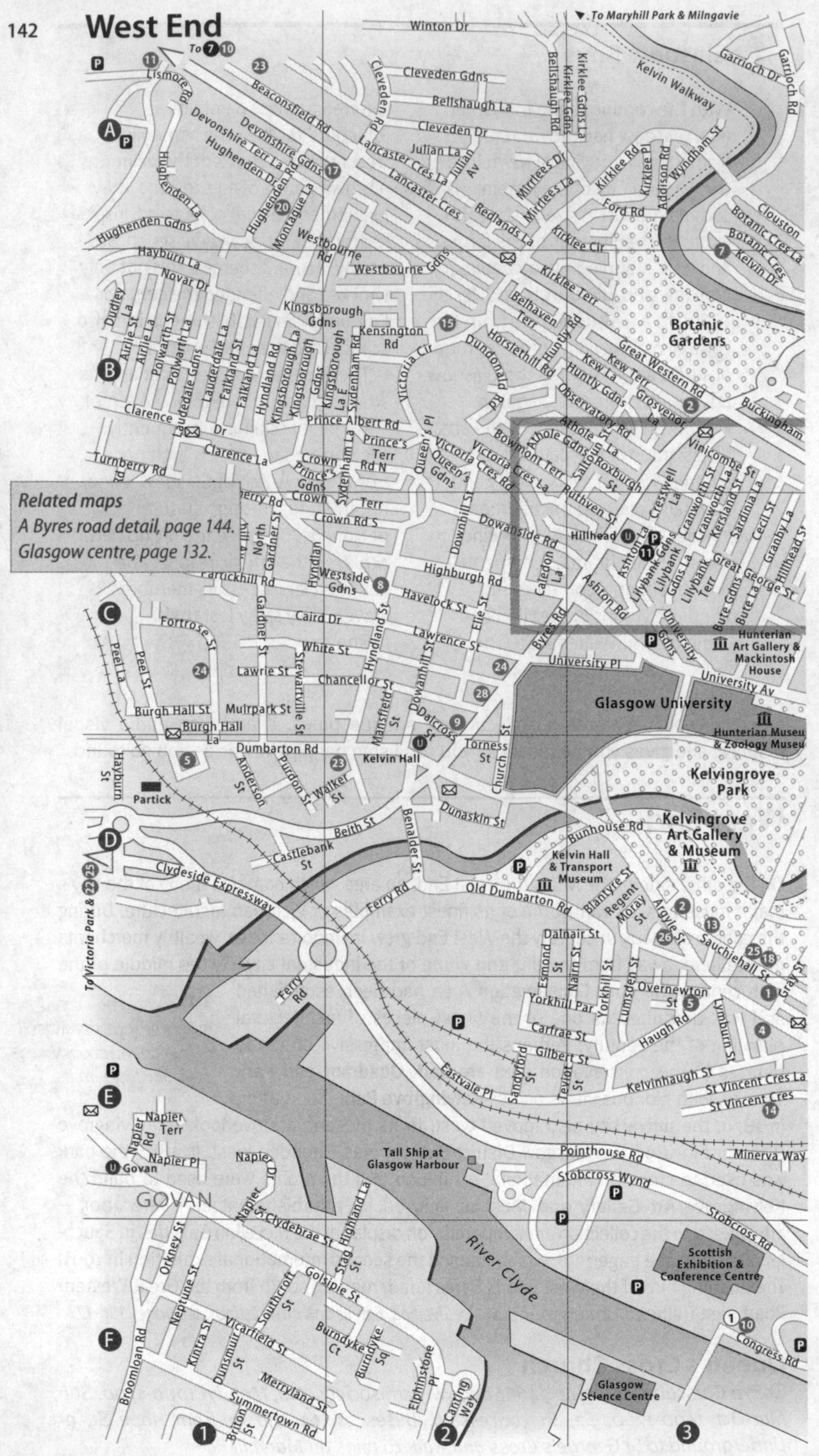

Related maps
A Byres road detail, page 144.
Glasgow centre, page 132.
Botanic Gardens
Glasgow University
Hunterian Art Gallery & Mackintosh House
Kelvingrove Park
Kelvingrove Art Gallery & Museum
Kelvin Hall & Transport Museum
Kelvin Hall
Partick
Govan
GOVAN
Tall Ship at Glasgow Harbour
River Clyde
Scottish Exhibition & Conference Centre
Glasgow Science Centre
To Maryhill Park & Milngavie
To Victoria Park & 22 25
Great Western Rd
Byres Rd
Dumbarton Rd
Clydeside Expressway
Argyle St
Sauchiehall St
University Av

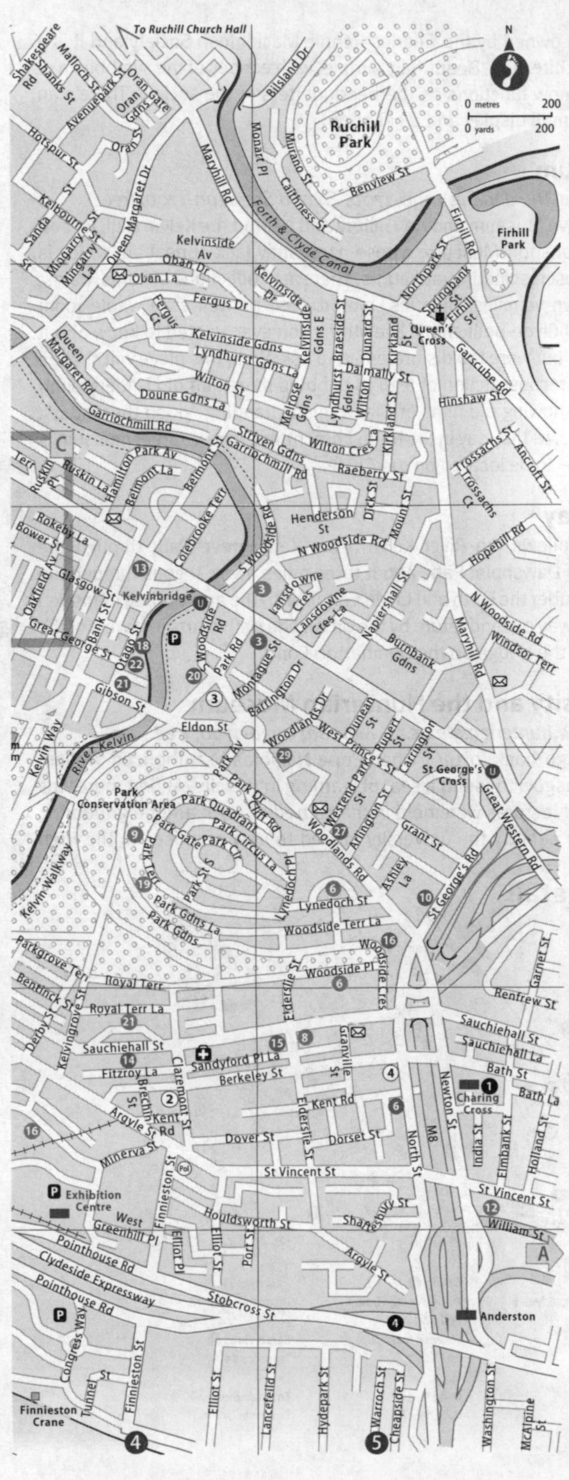

Sleeping
Argyll 1 *E3*
Cairncross House 4 *E3*
City Apartments 3 *C5*
Dreamhouse Inc 6 *D5*
Embassy Apartments 7 *B3*
Glasgow Backpackers Hostel 9 *D4*
Glasgow Hilton & Cameron's Restaurant 12 *E5*
Glasgow Moat House 10 *F3*
Hilton Glasgow Grosvenor 2 *B3*
Greek Thomson 8 *E5*
Jury's Glasgow 11 *A1*
Kelvingrove 13 *D3*
Kelvinhaugh Gate 5 *E3*
Kirkland House 14 *E3*
Kirklee 15 *B2*
Manor Park 25 *D1*
Number Thirty Six 16 *E4*
One Devonshire Gardens 17 *A2*
Park House 22 *D1*
Sandyford 18 *D3*
SYHA Youth Hostel 19 *D4*
Townhouse 20 *A1*
Townhouse Hotel 21 *E4*
White House 23 *A1*
Wickets 24 *C1*

Eating
Ashoka West End 2 *D3*
Baby Grand 1 *E5*
Bay Tree 3 *C5*
Buttery 4 *F5*
Cabin 5 *D1*
Café India 6 *E5*
Cooks Room 16 *D5*
Cottier's 8 *C2*
Dining Room 9 *C2*
Gingerhill 7 *A1*
Grassroots Café 10 *D5*
Grovsvenor Café 11
La Parmigiana 13 *C4*
Mother India 14 *E4*
Mr Singh's India 15 *E5*
Otago 18 *C4*
Shish Mahal 20 *C4*
Stravaigin 21 *C4*
TchaiOvna 22 *C4*
University Café 24 *C2*

Bars & Clubs
Firebird 26 *D3*
Halt Bar 27 *D5*
Lock 27 12
Tap 25 *D3*
Uisge Beatha 29 *D5*

Entertainment
Clyde Auditorium 'Armadillo' 1 *F3*
Henry Wood Hall 2 *E4*
Mitchell Theatre 4
Stand Comedy Club 3 *C4*

This is the only church owned by the Charles Rennie Mackintosh Society and it is a fascinating piece of architecture. Beautifully simple, with echoes of the symbolism of his other buildings, it now functions as the headquarters of the society. There's an information centre, a small display and a gift shop.

Transport Museum

ⓘ *T0141-2872720, Mon-Thu and Sat 1000-1700, Fri and Sun 1100-1700, free.*

Opposite the Kelvingrove Museum and Art Gallery and behind the Kelvin Hall, just off Argyle Street, is the Transport Museum, whose name may lack appeal but which is one of the country's most fascinating museums. There are collections of trams, trains, motor cars, horsedrawn vehicles, bicycles, motorbikes, as well as a whole room dedicated to models of Clyde-built ships. Everything you ever wanted to know about the history of transport but were too disinterested to ask. Well, this place will change all that. There's also a reconstruction of a 1938 cobbled street, an old Underground station and a cinema showing old films of Glaswegians heading "doon the watter". Something for everyone, as they say in the tourist brochures. A new, larger museum is planned for the future – to be located on the Clyde.

▲ Kelvin Walkway

The Kelvin Walkway follows the River Kelvin from Kelvingrove Park through the northwest of the city to Dawsholm Park, about three miles away. It goes through the Botanic Gardens and under the Forth and Clyde Canal. With the appropriate maps you could follow one waterway out and return by the other. The path starts just west of the Transport Museum, by the bridge on the Dumbarton Road.

Glasgow University and the Hunterian Museum

ⓘ *T0141-3304221, www.hunterian.gla.ac.uk, Mon-Sat 0930-1700, free.*

The university's roots go back to 1451 when Pope Nicholas V authorized William Turnbull, Bishop of Glasgow to found a seat of learning in the city. At first there was just an arts faculty and lectures were held in the cathedral crypt and neighbouring monastery. In the 17th century the university moved to new premises in the High

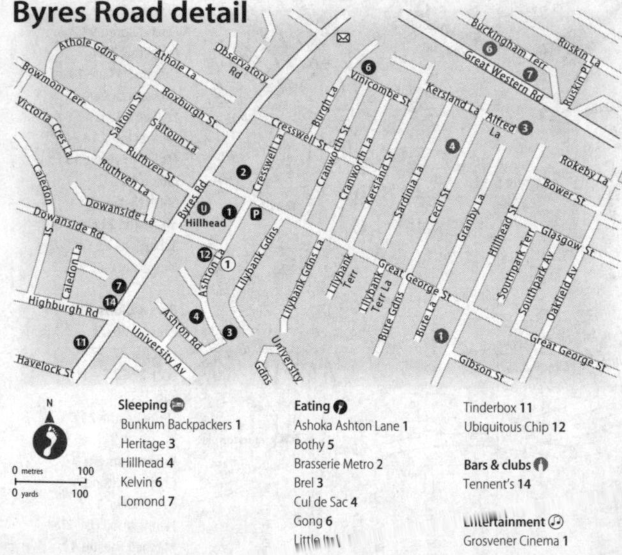

Street, but these became too small and, in 1870, it moved to its present site, on Gilmorehill, overlooking Kelvingrove Park. The Gothic buildings were designed by Sir George Gilbert Scott, though the Lion and Unicorn balustrade on the stone staircase opposite the Principal's Lodging is a relic of the old High Street colleges, as is the stonework of the lodge gateway. Bute Hall, which is now used for graduation and other ceremonies, was added in 1882. The **university chapel** is also worth seeing.

Contained within the university buildings is the **Hunterian Museum**, named after William Hunter (1718-1783), a student at the university in the 1730s. His bequest to the university of his substantial collections led to the establishment of the Hunterian Museum in 1807, Scotland's oldest public museum. It has displays of social history, archaeology and geology and includes Roman relics from the Antonine Wall and one of the largest coin collections in Britain. Beneath the museum is the **University Visitor Centre**, which features interactive displays on the university and a coffee bar. There's also a **Zoology Museum**, housed in the Graham Kerr Building, a few minutes' walk from the main museum.

Hunterian Art Gallery and Mackintosh House

ⓘ *T0141-3304221, www.hunterian.gla.co.uk, Mon-Sat 0930-1700 (Mackintosh House closes daily 1230-1330), free, buses 44 and 59 from the city centre (Hope St), or the Underground to Hillhead and walk.*

Opposite the University is the Hunterian Art Gallery, a modern building containing the more interesting part of Hunter's bequest, the fabulous art collection. The gallery holds an important collection of European paintings including works by **Rembrandt**, **Koninck**, **Rubens**, **Pissaro** and **Rodin**, as well as 18th-century British portraits by **Ramsay** and **Reynolds**. There is also a fine collection of Scottish 19th- and 20th-century paintings including works by **McTaggart**, **Guthrie** and **Fergusson**. The *piece de resistance* is the huge collection of works by the American painter, **James McNeill Whistler**. There are some 70 paintings and a selection of his personal possessions (including his specially made long-handled paintbrushes) on show, making it the largest display of his work outside the USA. Among the works are many of his distinctive full-length portraits and some moody depictions of the Thames.

Attached to the gallery is the **Mackintosh House**, a stunning reconstruction of the main interiors from 78 Southpark Avenue, the Glasgow home of Charles Rennie Mackintosh and his wife, Margaret MacDonald, from 1906 to 1914. A stairway leads to an introductory display containing numerous drawings and designs, including those for his major buildings, furniture and interiors. From there you are led into the cool, soothing rooms, lovingly reconstructed and exquisitely furnished with some 80 original pieces of his furniture. These give the perfect example of just why this innovative designer and architect is so revered. Among the highlights are the Studio Drawing Room, decorated in white and flooded with natural light, and the guest bedroom from Northampton, a later commission, with its bold and dazzling geometric designs. When George Bernard Shaw, a guest, was asked if the decor would disturb his sleep, he replied, "No, I always sleep with my eyes closed.".

Botanic Gardens

ⓘ *0700 till dusk, free, Kibble Palace and all glasshouses open daily 1000-1645 in summer, 1000-1615 in winter.*

At the top of Byres Road, where it meets the Great Western Road, is the entrance to the Botanic Gardens, a smallish but perfectly formed park where you can lose yourself along the remote paths that follow the wooded banks of the River Kelvin. They were created to provide medical and botanical students at the university with fresh plant material, but soon became a fashionable place to promenade. There are two large hothouses in the park, one of which is the **Kibble Palace**, built as a conservatory for the Clyde Coast home of Glasgow businessman, John Kibble, and then shipped to its present site in 1873. It was once used for public meetings and British Prime Ministers William Gladstone and Benjamin Disraeli both gave their rectorial addresses here when they became Rectors of the University. The domed glasshouse, contains the national collection of tree ferns and temperate plants from around the world. The **main glasshouse** is more attractive, and has 11 sections featuring plants such as cacti, palms, insectivorous plants and palms. Its collections of orchids and begonias are outstanding. There is also a herb garden with five beds growing medicinal, culinary, dye and scented plants. The central bed has plants that have been used in the past in Scotland. Look out for Meadowsweet, used for headaches; Coltsfoot used for coughs and chest complaints, and Yellow Flag iris – the leaves of which give a bright green dye and the rhizomes a black dye which were traditionally used in the Harris tweed industry. In the Outer Hebrides the black dye was used for the cloth for the suits worn on Sundays.

South Side

South of the River Clyde is a part of Glasgow largely unknown to most visiting tourists, except for three of the city's most notable attractions, the **Burrell Collection** and **Pollok House**, both set in the sylvan surrounds of **Pollok Country Park**. There are other reasons to venture south of the river, however, not least of these being to see Charles Rennie Mackintosh's **House for an Art Lover** in nearby Bellahouston Park. Further east is another stop on the Mackintosh trail, the **Scotland Street School Museum of Education**. To the south, in Cathcart, is **Holmwood House**, Alexander 'Greek' Thomson's great architectural masterpiece. » *For Sleeping, Eating and other listings, see pages 156-177.*

Govan

Flanking the Clyde is Govan, forever associated with shipbuilding and not worth a trip, unless you're visiting Ibrox, home of **Glasgow Rangers**, or looking for **Govan Old Parish Church** ⓘ *Govan Rd, T0141-4451941, 1st Wed in June to 3rd Sat in Sept, Wed 1030-1230, Wed, Thu, Sat 1300-1600, other times by appointment, free, near Govan Cross underground.* Not only does the church stand on an ancient Christian site, it also has a unique collection of carved stones dating back to the ninth century. There's also a sarcophagus which is covered in fine carvings and a good collection of stained glass windows.

Scotland Street School Museum of Education

ⓘ *T0141-2870500, Mon-Thu and Sat 1000-1700, Fri and Sun 1100-1700, free. Underground to Shields Rd, or buses 89, 90, 96 and 97 from the city centre.*

Directly opposite Shields Road Underground is another of Charles Rennie Mackintosh's great works, the Scotland Street School, which opened in 1906 and closed in 1979. The entire school has been preserved as a museum of education and is a wonderfully evocative experience. The school has been refurbished and now includes an audio-visual theatre and has computer activities for children. There's a collection of school memorabilia and reconstructed classrooms from Victorian times up to the 1960s, as well as changing rooms, science room and headmaster's office.

This was the most modern of Mackintosh's buildings and is notable for its semi-cylindrical glass stair towers, the magnificent tiled entrance hall and his customary mastery of the interplay of light and space. There's also a café, but don't worry, they don't serve authentic school food.

Alexander the Great

Alexander Thomson was the greatest architect of Victorian Glasgow, who did as much to shape the city as the famous Charles Rennie Mackintosh. In the middle of the 19th century, when the "Second City of the Empire" was a growing, dynamic place, he brought a distinctive flair to all manner of buildings: warehouses and commercial premises, terraces and tenements, suburban villas and some of the finest Romantic Classical churches in the world.

Despite his nickname he never visited Greece and was not a conventional Greek Classicist. In fact, he thought the architects of the Greek revival had failed "because they could not see through the material into the laws upon which that architecture rested. They failed to master their style, and so became its slaves". Instead, Thomson evolved a distinctive manner of building using a Greek style but in an unconventional way and incorporating modern inventions such as iron beams and plate glass. Thomson was struck by "the mysterious power of the horizontal element in carrying the mind away into space and into speculations on infinity". This dominance of horizontality has led to comparisons with Frank Lloyd Wright, though Thomson predates him by 40 years.

Thomson was a truly original and brilliant architect yet was shamefully neglected after his death in 1875. In the 1960s, in a frenzy of destruction, the city planners did their best to wipe out this man's amazing achievements completely. Finally, though, the city paid tribute to one of their most talented sons with a major exhibition about his work as part of the City of Architecture and Design year.

For more information on Alexander 'Greek' Thomson and his surviving buildings, see the tourist office's Glasgow architectural guide 1. The only building open to the public is Holmwood House, in Cathcart, see page 149.

Burrell Collection

ⓘ *T0141-6497151, www.glasgow.gov.uk, Mon-Thu and Sat 1000-1700, Sun 1100-1700, free. Buses 45, 47 and 57 from the city centre (Union St) pass the park gates on Pollokshaws Rd, from the gates it's a 10-min walk to the gallery or there's a twice hourly bus service; regular trains from Central station to Pollockshaws West station; or a taxi from the city centre costs £6-7.*

Three miles southwest of the city centre is Glasgow's top attraction and a must on any visit, the Burrell Collection, standing in the extensive wooded parklands of Pollok Country Park. The magnificent collection contains some 8,500 art treasures, donated to the city in 1944 by the shipping magnate, William Burrell (1861-1958) who sold his shipping interests in order to devote the remainder of his life to collecting art. He began collecting in the 1880s, and in 1917 bought Hutton Castle near Berwick-on-Tweed to house his collection. There it stayed, even after his bequest to the city, as he stipulated that all the works in his collection be housed in one building in a rural setting – since he was concerned about the possible damage caused by the pollution that then blackened Glasgow. It wasn't until the Clean Air Act of the 1960s and the council's acquisition of Pollok Park that a suitable site was found and the modern, award-winning gallery could be built – with the £450,000 donated by Burrell. The building opened to the public in 1983.

The collection includes ancient Greek, Roman and Egyptian artefacts, a huge number of dazzling oriental art pieces, and numerous works of medieval and post-medieval European art, including tapestries, silverware, textiles, sculpture and exquisitely-lit stained glass. The tapestries are particularly fine and date from the late 15th and 16th centuries. There's also an impressive array of paintings by **Rembrandt**, **Degas**, **Pissaro**, **Bellini** and **Manet** amongst many others. Look out too for **Rodin**'s famous sculpture *Thinker* which, like many film stars and TV personalities you've only seen in pictures, is smaller than you expect in real life.

The gallery is a stunning work of simplicity and thoughtful design, which allows the visitor to enjoy the vast collection to the full. The large, floor-to-ceiling windows afford sweeping views over the surrounding woodland and allow a flood of natural light to enhance the treasures on view. Some sections of the gallery are reconstructions of rooms from Hutton Castle and incorporated into the structure are carved stone Romanesque doors. There's also a café and restaurant on the lower ground floor.

Pollok House

ⓘ *T0141-6166410, www.nts.org.uk, house daily 1000-1700, Apr-Oct £6, £4 child/concession and Nov-Mar free. Entry to the park is from Pollokshaws Road, or Haggs Road if you're on foot. Car parking is at the Burrell Collection and costs £1.50.*

Also in Pollok Country Park, a 10-minute walk from the Burrell, is Pollok House, designed by William Adam and finished in 1752. This was once the home of the Maxwell family, who owned most of southern Glasgow until well into the last century. It contains one of the best collections of Spanish paintings in Britain, including works by **Goya**, **El Greco** and **Murillo**. There are also paintings by **William Blake**, as well as glass, silverware, porcelain and furniture. The most interesting part of the house are the servants' quarters downstairs, which give you a real insight into life 'below stairs' – with rows of bells waiting to summon servants to any part of the house. There's a good tea room in the old kitchens. If the weather's fine, the park is worth exploring. There are numerous trails through the woods and meadows and guided walks with the countryside rangers. There are two golf courses within the park grounds, as well as a herd of highland cattle.

House for an Art Lover

ⓘ *T0141-3534770, www.houseforanartlover.co.uk, Apr-Sep Mon-Wed 1000-1600, Thu-Sun 1000-1300, Oct-Mar Sat-Sun 1000-1300, call for weekday access times, £3.50, £2.50 concession. Take the Underground to Ibrox station and walk (15 min), or bus 91 from Renfrew St (every 20 mins Mon-Sat, every 30 mins Sun).*

A short distance north of Pollok Park is Bellahouston Park, site of the most recent addition to the Charles Rennie Mackintosh trail, the House for an Art Lover. Although the building was designed in 1901 as an entry to a competition run by a German design magazine, the brief being to create a lavish country house for an art lover. The interior and exterior had to be a coherent work of art. Building never went ahead during Mackintosh's lifetime and it was not until 1989 that construction began following his original drawings. It was not completed until 1996, when it became a centre for Glasgow School of Art postgraduate students, though a number of rooms on the lower floor are open to the public. Mackintosh worked closely with his wife on the design of the house and there is distinctive evidence of her influence, especially in the exquisite **Music Room** with its elaborate symbolism, particularly the rose motif, which is used throughout. But though the detail is, as ever, intense, the overall effect is one of space and light. The exterior of the house is equally impressive and totally original. On the ground floor is an excellent café, which is popular with locals, see page 160.

Queens Park and around

To the east of Pollok Country Park, by Pollokshaws Road, is **Queen's Park**, named after Mary, Queen of Scots, whose reign ended after defeat here, at the Battle of Langside, in 1568. A memorial outside the park marks the site of the battle. It's a pleasant place for a stroll and the views north across the city make it even more enjoyable. Close by, in Mount Florida, is **Hampden Park**, home of Scottish football and now also the home of the new **Scottish National Football Museum** ⓘ *T0141-6166139, www.scottishfootballmuseum.com, Mon-Sat 1000-1700, Sun 1100-1700, £5, £2.50 concession, tour of the stadium £2.50 (£5 if not visiting museum). Regular trains to Mount Florida station from Central station (turn left out of station and head straight downhill till you see the stadium (there are no signs), buses 5, 12, 31, 37 or 44A.* The museum describes the history of the game in Scotland. This may strike some as a rather masochistic idea given some of the more infamous and embarrassing episodes, but there have been highs (Wembley '67 and Lisbon '69) as well as lows (Argentina '78, Faroe Islands 2002 and Cardiff 2004). The museum is very large and includes a huge range of football memorabilia, from Jimmy medals and jerseys to teapots. It even has the minutes of the very first meeting of Scotland's first football club – dated 9th July 1867. You can also get a guided tour of Hampden Park.

Holmwood House

ⓘ *T0141-6372129, Apr-31 Oct, daily 1200-1700, but access may be restricted at certain times, phone in advance, £4, £3 child/concession.*

South of Queens Park and Hampden, at 61-63 Netherlee Road in Cathcart, is Holmwood House, designed by Alexander 'Greek' Thomson, Glasgow's greatest Victorian architect. Holmwood was built for James Couper, a paper manufacturer, between 1857 and 1858 and is the most elaborate and sumptuously decorated of all the villas Thomson designed for well-to-do industrialists on the outskirts of Glasgow. It was rescued from decline by the National Trust for Scotland in 1994 and is well worth a visit.

The building is a work of genuine originality and has become a monument of international importance, as Thomson was the first modern architect to apply a Greek style to a free, asymmetrical composition. The house also includes features reminiscent of Frank Lloyd Wright, which pre-date the great American architect by some forty years. Thomson designed everything in the house and conservation work is revealing very beautiful and elaborate stencilled decoration and friezes with Greek motifs. The best description of Holmwood comes from Thomas Gildard who wrote in 1888: "If architecture be poetry in stone-and-lime – a great temple an epic – this exquisite little gem, at once classic and picturesque, is as complete, self-contained and polished as a sonnet".

To visit Holmwood House there are trains every 30 minutes to Cathcart from Central station, or you can take buses 44 and 46 from the city centre to Cathcart bridge, turn left onto Rannon Road and walk 10 minutes to gates.

Along the Clyde

Glasgow Science Centre and around

ⓘ *50 Pacific Quay, T0141-4205000, www.gsc.org.uk. Science Mall daily 1000-1800, £6.95, £4.95 concession, IMAX Theatre Sun-Wed 1100-1700, Thu-Sat 1000-2030 (hours subject to change) £5.95, £4.45 concession, Glass Tower £5.95, £4.45 concession, discounts available for more than one attraction. Arriva buses 23 and 24 go to the Science Centre from Jamaica St.*

After all the years of neglect, it is good to see that Glasgow's newest, most dazzling development is to be found on the Clyde. The £75 million Glasgow Science Centre opened late in 2001 on the south side of the Clyde on the former garden festival site. This enormous complex aims to demystify science, bringing it life with imaginative displays and interactive exhibits covering everything from the human body to the internet. The kids love it – as do their fathers.

The heart of the centre is the **Science Mall**, with three floors of themed exhibits. The first floor looks at how we experience the world, the second floor looks at science in action and the third floor looks at how science affects your daily life. You can find anything here from laboratories where you can study your own skin or hair through a microscope, to an infra-red harp which you play with a beam of light.

The **Glasgow Tower**, the tallest free-standing building in Scotland at 300 ft, has experienced some engineering problems and at the time of writing it's shut. But when it reopens it's worth a look as each of its floors has a theme and takes a serious look at aspects of science, from the basic rules of nature to cloning and genetic modification. At the top there's a viewing cabin and great views over Glasgow and the Clyde. The centre also contains an IMAX theatre.

Opposite the Science Centre is the **Scottish Exhibition and Conference Centre (SECC)**, built in 1987 on the site of the former Queen's Dock and now the country's premier rock and pop venue. Next door is the controversial **Clyde Auditorium**, known locally as the 'Armadillo', which was designed by Sir Norman Foster and built in 1997. Its used as a venue for major pop and rock acts and a business and conference centre.

Tall Ship at Glasgow Harbour

ⓘ *100 Stobcross Rd, T0800 3281373, www.thetallship.com, Mar-Oct daily 1000-1700, Nov-Feb daily 1100-1600, £4.50, £3.95 concession.*

Further west, also on the north bank of the Clyde, is a romantic looking sailing ship, the *SS Glenlee*, otherwise known as the Tall Ship at Glasgow Harbour. Launched in 1896, this three-masted ship was built on the Clyde and is one of only five Clydebuilt sailing ships that remain afloat in the world. She circumnavigated the globe four times and carried cargo as varied as coal, grain – and even guano, which was transported from Chile to the European ports of Antwerp and Rotterdam to be used as fertilizer. The ammonia fumes from the guano were so pungent they corroded the lining of sailor's noses and even killed the occasional ship's cat. The *Glenlee* was saved from the scrapyard in 1992 and has now been restored. Exhibitions on board provide a vivid insight into the daily lives of the sailors and the conditions on board ship in 1896.

Clydebuilt

ⓘ *Junction 25a (westbound) off the M8 or reached on the Clyde waterbus (see page 173), T0141-8861013, Mon-Thu and Sat 1000-1800, Sun 1100-1700, £3.50, £1.75 concession.*

Further west still, at Braehead, is Clydebuilt, a museum charting the close relationship between Glasgow and the Clyde. There's an audio-visual presentation on the history of shipbuilding and displays on a whole range of themes related to the river from the cotton and tobacco trades to emigration and immigration. There are also plenty of 'hands-on' activities for kids and temporary exhibitions throughout the year. The museum is very close to Braehead Shopping Centre which has all the usual high-street outlets as well as cafés, and skating and curling rinks.

Clyde Walkway

The Clyde Walkway is a 40-mile walking route which is being developed to link the centre of Glasgow to the Falls of Clyde at Lanark, via the Clyde Valley, see page 153. Sections of the waterfront walk are still rather empty and depressing but the central part, between Victoria Bridge and the SECC, is interesting and takes in some of the more distinguished bridges and much of Glasgow's proud maritime heritage.

Start the walk at **Victoria Bridge**, built in 1854 to replace the 14th century Old Glasgow Bridge, and continue past the graceful **Suspension Bridge**, built in 1851 as a grand entrance to the 'new town' on the south bank. You can cross from here to **Carlton Place**, whose impressive Georgian façades have been restored and which

A fishy tale

Though it is many years since salmon were caught in the Clyde, two appear in the city's coat of arms. Each fish has a ring in its mouth, recalling an old local legend.

The Queen of Strathclyde was given a ring by her husband but then promptly gave it to her lover. The king found the lover wearing the ring as he slept beside the Clyde. He took the ring and threw it into the water, and then went to his wife and asked her to show it to him. The Queen prayed to St Mungo for help, and immediately, one of her servants miraculously found the ring in the mouth of a salmon he had caught. The king then had to accept his wife's pleas of innocence, despite knowing something fishy was going on.

were designed to front the never-completed 'new town'. Back on the north bank is **Customs House Quay** and, further west beyond George V Bridge, **Broomielaw Quay**. From here, Henry Bell's Comet inaugurated the world's first commercial passenger steamboat service. This was also the departure point for many Scottish emigrants to North America, and, later, for thousands of holidaying locals heading "doon the watter" to the Firth of Clyde seaside resorts. Further west, at Anderston Quay, is the **P.S. Waverley Terminal** (see above). Between here and the SECC is the huge 175ft high **Finnieston Crane**, which was once used for lifting railway locomotives at a time when Glasgow was the largest builder of these in the world outside North America. Close by is the **Rotunda** (1890-1896) which was once the northern terminal of the complex of tunnels which took horse-traffic and pedestrians under the river, until the building of a new road tunnel in the 1960s. The Rotunda has been restored as a restaurant complex. Soon you come to the **Scottish Exhibition and Conference Centre (SECC)** and the **Clyde Auditorium** (the "Armadillo"), sitting opposite the new **Glasgow Science Centre**.

Other walkways

The **Kelvin Walkway** follows the River Kelvin from Kelvingrove Park through the northwest of the city to Dawsholm Park, about three miles away. See page 144.

The **Forth and Clyde Canal** was opened in 1790 and provided a convenient short-cut for trading ships between Northern Europe and North America, linking both coasts of Scotland. The towpath starts at **Port Dundas**, just north of the M8 by Craighall Road, and runs to the main canal at the end of Lochburn Road, off Maryhill road. It then runs east all the way to Kirkintilloch and Falkirk, and west, through Maryhill and Drumchapel to Bowling and the River Clyde. It passes through sections of bleak industrial wasteland, but there are many interesting sights along the way and open, rural stretches. A series of 'Walk Cards' are available from *British Waterways* ⓘ *T0141-3326936, www.scottishcanals.co.uk*.

At **Mugdock Country Park** ⓘ *Craigallian Rd, T0131-9566100, www.mugdock-country-park.org.uk*, in the select suburb of Milngavie you can pretend that you're in the country as there are 750 acres of unspoilt grounds and ancient woodlands to explore. It's open from dawn to dusk every day.

Other country parks with walks and nature trails are **Clyde Muirshiel Park** ⓘ *Lochwinnoch, 30 mins drive from the centre, T01505-842803, www.clydemuirshiel.co.uk*. It covers 102 square miles of land and has walks in woods and over moorland. Also here is an **RSPB Nature Reserve** ⓘ *T01505 842663, www.rspb.org.uk/reserves/lochwinnoch*. There's also a new **Glasgow-Edinburgh** route, which incorporates part of the Clyde Walkway. The **West Highland Way**, see page 60, begins in Milngavie, eight miles north of the city centre, and runs for 95 miles to Fort William.

Excursions

Glasgow is surrounded by a series of drab satellite towns, once major centres of coal and steel, or shipbuilding, which are struggling to recover their identity. It's tempting to pass through this depressed hinterland, especially as the delights of the West Highlands lie northwest just beyond the city's boundary, but there are some interesting sights for those with the time or the inclination. The 18th-century model community of New Lanark and the spectacular Falls of Clyde nearby are well worth the trip from Glasgow, and there are a couple of interesting historical sights near Hamilton, namely Bothwell Castle and Chatelherault. ›› *For Sleeping, Eating and other listings, see pages 156-177.*

Mugdock Country Park

Within easy reach of the city, north of the suburb of Milngavie (pronounced 'Mullguy'), is Mugdock Country Park, sitting between Glasgow and the Campsie Fells. It offers some fine walking along marked trails and includes the first section of the **West Highland Way**, which starts in Milngavie, see page 60. There are regular trains from Central station to Milngavie. You can either walk from here for three miles across Drumclog Moor or take the Mugdock bus from the station.

Paisley

West of Glasgow, close to the airport, is the town that gave its name to the famous fabric design copied from Kashmiri shawls. Paisley grew up around its 12th-century roots and by the 19th century was a major producer of printed cotton and woollen cloth, specializing in the production of the eponymous imitation shawls.

In the town centre, opposite the town hall, is **Paisley Abbey** ⓘ *T0141-8897654, www.paisleyabbey.org.uk, Mon-Sat 1000-1530, free*, founded in 1163 but destroyed during the Wars of Independence in the early 14th century. It was rebuilt soon after, but fell into ruin from the 16th century. Successive renovations took place, ending with a major restoration in the 1920s. The façade doesn't do justice to the wonderfully spacious interior, which includes exceptional stained-glass windows and an impressive choir. Also of note is the 10th-century Barochan Cross, at the eastern end of the north nave. Once or twice a year the 150-ft high tower is open to the public. The views from the top are great. There's also a gift shop and tea room.

In the High Street is the **Museum and Art Gallery** ⓘ *T0141-8893151, Tue-Sat 1000-1700, Sun 1400-1700, free*, with a huge collection of the world famous Paisley shawls and an interesting display of the history of weaving. Also on the High Street is another imposing ecclesiastical monument, the **Thomas Coats Memorial Church** ⓘ *T0141-8899980, viewing by appointment*, built by the great Victorian thread maker and one of the grandest Baptist churches in Europe. The **Coats Observatory** ⓘ *Oakshaw St, T0141-8892013, Tue-Sat 1000-1700, Sun 1400-1700, free, public telescope viewing Thu 1930-2130 Oct-Mar*, has some interesting displays on climate, seismology and astronomy. Another interesting sight is the **Sma' Shot Cottages** ⓘ *George Place, off New St, T0141-8891708, Wed and Sat 1200-1600 Apr- Sep*. These are fully restored and furnished 18th-century weavers' cottages, with photographs and various artefacts. There's also a tea room with home baking. To the south of Paisley is the **Gleniffer Braes Country Park**, which is a great place for a walk in the hills. To get there, take the B775 south of town.

The tourist information centre ⓘ *9A Gilmour St, T0141-8890711*, will help you find a place to stay though there's no reason to as it's so close to Glasgow.

Firth of Clyde

West of Glasgow, the banks of the Clyde are still lined with the hulking ghosts of this great river's shipbuilding heritage. West of the Erskine Bridge, which connects the north and south banks of the Clyde, is **Port Glasgow**, the first of a series of grim towns which sprawl along the southern coast of the Firth of Clyde. It was developed as the city's first harbour in the late 17th century, but there's little to detain visitors today. Just before Port Glasgow, however, west of Langbank, just off the M8/A8, is **Finlaystone Estate** ⓘ *T01475-540505, www.finlaystone.co.uk, gardens all year 1030-1700, tea room Apr-Sep 1100-1630, £3, £2 concession,* a Georgian mansion house set in sprawling landscaped grounds and featuring a walled garden, woodland play area, visitor centre and conservatory tea room. There are great views across the Clyde.

Greenock About 30 miles west of Glasgow, Greenock was the first dock on the Clyde, back in the early 18th century and was the birthplace, in 1736, of James Watt, whose development of the steam engine contributed so much to the Industrial Revolution. Greenock today doesn't look particularly appealing, but it has its attractions. On the quay is the **Customs House Museum** ⓘ *T01475-726331, Mon-Fri 1000-1600, free,* housed in the 19th-century neoclassical former Customs House, where Robert Burns and Adam Smith were once employees. The museum charts the history of the Customs and Excise service, which is a lot more interesting than it sounds. While you're here, you should also visit the **McLean Museum and Art Gallery** ⓘ *15 Kelly St, near Greenock West station, T0131-723 741, www.inverclyde.gov.uk/museums, Mon-Sat 1000-1700, free.* The museum contains a collection of items belonging to the town's most famous son, James Watt, including a precursor to the photocopier which he patented around 1790 and was used in offices right up until the 1940's. There is also an Egyptology collection featuring items brought back from 19th century explorations. The small gallery on the ground floor has works by the Glasgow Boys as well as Fergusson, Cadell and Peploe.

Gourock and Wemyss Bay Three miles west of Greenock is the shabby old seaside resort of Gourock. Gourock is the terminal for the CalMac ferry to Dunoon, on the Cowal Peninsula, see page 301. Eight miles south of Gourock is Wemyss Bay, departure point for ferries to Rothesay, on the Isle of Bute. Every summer this place used to be packed full of holidaying Glaswegians heading "doon the watter" to Rothesay, and the magnificent Victorian train station is a proud legacy of those days. CalMac ferries run frequently, see page 175, and trains run every hour to Glasgow.

Dumbarton Once the capital of the ancient Britons of Strathclyde, Dumbarton dates back as far as the fifth century, when it was an important trading centre and of strategic importance. Today, though, it's a pretty awful place, and of little importance to tourists. It's best to avoid the town and head straight for the spectacular **Dumbarton Castle** ⓘ *T01389-732167, Apr-Sep daily 0930-1830, Oct-Mar Mon-Thu and Sat 0930-1630 (not Thu afternoon), Sun 1400-1600, £2.20, £1.50 concession, get off at Dumbarton East station,* perched on top of Dumbarton Rock, which is surrounded by water on three sides and commands excellent views over the Clyde estuary. This has been a strategic fortress for 2,000 years, though most of the current buildings date from the 18th century or later. If you're interested in shipbuilding then you should visit the **Scottish Maritime Museum** ⓘ *Castle St, T0141-763444, Mon-Sat 1000-1600. £1.50.* It has a working ship model experiment tank; the oldest one in the world, in fact.

The Clyde Valley

The River Clyde undergoes a series of changes as it begins the journey from its source, 80 miles southeast of Glasgow, through the orchards and market gardens of pretty Clydesdale and the abandoned coal mines of North Lanarkshire on its way to the former shipyards of Glasgow. The M74 motorway follows the course of the river, straddled by the valley's two largest towns, **Hamilton** and **Motherwell,** the latter still reeling from the recent closure of its steelworks. Sandwiched between them is **Strathclyde Country Park**, a huge recreational area which features a 200-acre man-made loch and is massively popular with watersports enthusiasts. The M74 then turns south towards the border with England, while the A72 takes up the task of shadowing the river to **Lanark**, the most interesting focus of this area, standing as it does beside the fascinating village of **New Lanark**.

Blantyre This town, now more of a suburb of Hamilton, is famous as the birthplace of **David Livingstone**, the notable Victorian missionary and explorer, who felt the white man's burden more than most and took off to Africa in 1840 to bring Christianity to the natives. He was born in the humble surroundings of a one-roomed tenement, in 1813, and worked in the local cotton mill before educating himself and taking a medical degree. The entire tenement block has been transformed into the **David Livingstone Centre** ⓘ *165 Station Rd, T01698-823140, Apr-Dec Mon-Sat 1000-1700, Sun 1230-1700, £4, £3 child/concession*, which tells the story of his life, including his battle against slave traders and that famous meeting with Stanley. There's also an African-themed café, gift shop and garden. The centre is a short walk from the train station.

A 30-minute walk down the river towards Uddingston brings you to the substantial red sandstone ruin of **Bothwell Castle** ⓘ *T01698-816894, Apr-Sep Mon-Sun 0930-1830, Oct-Mar Mon-Wed 0930-1630, Thu morning only, Sun 1400-1630, £2.20, £0.75 children*. This is commonly regarded as the finest 13th-century stronghold in the country and was fought over repeatedly by the Scots and English during the Wars of Independence. It has withstood the ravages of time well and is still hugely impressive.

Southwest of Blantyre is the **Museum of Scottish Country Life** ⓘ *Philipshill Rd, Wester Kittochside, East Kilbride, T01355-224181, www.nms.ac.uk, daily 1000-1700, £3.00, £1.50 concession, children free*, which gives an insight into the lives of people in rural Scotland. Situated on a 170-acre site complete with Georgian farmhouse, the land was gifted by the Reid family who farmed here for 400 years. The Reids resisted intensive farming methods, so the land is still rich in wild plants that have disappeared from much farming land in Britain. The Exhibition Building has galleries on the environment, rural technologies and people and has thousands of exhibits, including the oldest threshing machine in the world, dating back to circa 1805. The Historic Farm will be worked to demonstrate traditional agricultural methods of the 1950s, and will follow the seasons to show ploughing, seed time, haymaking and harvest. There is also an Events Area where there will be demonstrations of the working collection, plus a shop and café. It's enough to make you start tuning in to The Archers every day.

Hamilton This town has the longest history of any in the area, with associations with Mary, Queen of Scots, Cromwell and the Covenanters, who were defeated by Monmouth at nearby Bothwell Bridge, in 1679. The town today is unremarkable but a mile or so south, at Ferniegair, are the gates to **Chatelherault** ⓘ *T01698-426213, visitor centre Mon-Sat 1000-1700, Sun 1200-1700, free, house Mon-Thu and Sat 1030-1630, Sun 1230-1630, free*, an extensive country park and impressive hunting lodge and summer house, built in 1732 by William Adam for the Dukes of Hamilton. There are ornamental gardens and 10 miles of trails to explore along the deep wooded glen of the Avon, past the 16th-century ruins of **Cadzow Castle** and into the surrounding countryside. The Ranger service offers guided walks around the park.

Within the bounds of nearby Strathclyde Park is the **Hamilton Mausoleum** ⓘ *tours Apr-Sep on Wed, Sat and Sun at 1500, Oct-Mar Sat, Sun and Wed 1400, £1.15, £0.80 children*, a huge burial vault of the Hamilton family. It's an eerie place with an amazing 15-second echo: the longest in Europe, Europe, Europe...

Lanark and New Lanark The little market town of Lanark, 25 miles southeast of Glasgow, sits high above the River Clyde. Most people come here to visit the immaculately restored village of **New Lanark** ⓘ *T01555-661345, www.newlarnark.org, visitor centre 1100-1700, tickets to all attractions, £5.95, £3.95, concession/children, access to the village at all times*, one of the region's most fascinating sights, a mile below the town, beside the river. The community was founded in 1785 by David Dale and Richard Arkwright as a cotton-spinning centre, but it was Dale's son-in-law, Robert Owen, who took over the management in 1798 and who pioneered the revolutionary social experiment. He believed in a more humane form of capitalism and believed the welfare of his workers to be crucial to industrial success. He provided them with decent housing, a co-operative store (the forerunner of the modern co-operative movement), adult educational facilities, the world's first day nursery and the social centre of the community, the modestly-titled Institute for the Formation of Character. Here, in the visitor centre, you can see an introductory video about New Lanark and its founders, join the Millennium Ride (an atmospheric 'dark ride') and see original textile machinery. In Robert Owen's School for Children audio visual technology allows you to see the 'ghost' of Annie McLeod (an imaginary mill girl) on stage, telling you the story of life in 19th-century New Lanark. The programme lasts 15 minutes. There is also a reconstruction of an early classroom. You can wander through the village and see the 1920s shop, a restored mill-worker's house and even **Robert Owen's House**. There's also a tea room and gift shop. It takes about 45 minutes to get here from the city and there is enough to keep you occupied for the day.

Just beyond the village lies the wooded **Falls of Clyde Nature Reserve**, managed by the Scottish Wildlife Trust (SWT). You can visit the SWT Wildlife Centre ⓘ *T0141-665262, daily 1100-1700, (1200-1600 Jan, Feb), free*, housed in the old dyeworks, which provides information about the history and wildlife of the area.

▲ You can walk from the village to the stunning **Corra Linn** waterfalls and beyond. The total distance, including the extension, is 5½ miles. Allow three to four hours there and back, and wear boots or strong shoes as some parts can be muddy. Starting from the village, walk past the SWT centre and up the stone steps into the nature reserve above Dundaff Linn, the smallest of the three waterfalls on the walk. A riverside boardwalk takes you past a 200-year-old weir, and just beyond the end of the boardwalk go right at a junction to pass Bonnington power station. Steps then lead up to a viewing platform above the dramatic Corra Linn, the highest falls on the Clyde, where the river plunges 90 ft in three stages. Continue up the steps and follow the path through woodlands to reach another set of falls at **Bonnington Linn**. You can retrace your steps back to the village, or extend the walk by crossing the weir at Bonnington Linn and turning right down the track on the opposite bank, taking a narrow path on the right after a few hundred yards. Take care here as the path is very close to the lip of the gorge! After about a mile, the path leads you to the crumbling ruin of **Corra Castle**. To return to Bonnington Linn, retrace your steps for about 100 yards and then follow the vehicle track on the right.

There's a tourist information centre in Lanark ⓘ *Horsemarket, 100 yards west of the train station, T0141-661661, open year round*, who can book accommodation.

Crossford Five miles northwest of Lanark is the village of Crossford, from where you can visit **Craignethan Castle** ⓘ *Apr-Sep Mon-Sat 0930-1630, Sun 1400-1630, Mar and Oct Mon-Wed, Sat and Sun 0930-1630, Thu 0930-1230, £1.50*, an ornate tower house standing over the River Nethan. It was built by Sir James Hamilton for James V, in 1530, and was last major castle to be built in Scotland. Mary, Queen of Scots left from here to do battle at Langside (at Queen's Park in Glasgow), where she was defeated and fled to France before her eventual imprisonment. The castle, like so many others in Scotland, is said to be haunted by her ghost. To get there take a bus from Lanark to Crossford, then it's a 15-minute walk.

Sleeping

Glasgow has a good range of accommodation. Most of the hotels, guest houses, B&Bs and hostels are in the city centre and the West End or south of the river, around Queen's Park. The best area to find good value mid-range accommodation is the West End, around Kelvingrove Park and the university. This is a good area to stay in, as it's convenient for several of the city's major sights as well as many of the best bars and restaurants. Glasgow has undergone something of a revolution on the hotel front in recent years and the market is highly competitive. A large number of big chains have opened up in the city, offering everything from deluxe accommodation to simple low cost lodging – meaning that there are often good deals available to travellers prepared to shop around. The city also has several boutique hotels, offering stylish accommodation with more character than the international chains. Finding a decent room for the night can be difficult during the major festivals (see p171) and in Jul and Aug and it's best to book ahead at these times. The tourist information centre can help find somewhere to stay and also publishes a free accommodation guide.

There is plenty of **Scottish Tourist Board** approved self-catering accommodation available. The minimum stay is usually 1 week in the summer peak season, or 3 days or less at other times of the year. Expect to pay from around £300 to over £1000 per week in the city. Much of this self catering and serviced accommodation in the city is quite upmarket.

A good option for those on a budget is campus accommodation. The universities open their halls of residence to visitors mainly during the summer vacation (late Jun to Sep) but some all year. Many rooms are basic and small, with shared bathrooms, but some are more comfortable with private bathrooms, twin and family units and self-contained apartments and shared houses. Full-board, half-board, B&B and self-catering options are all available. Prices for bed and breakfast tend to be roughly the same as for most B&Bs, but self-catering can cost as little as £50 per person per week. Local tourist offices have information, or contact the **British Universities Accommodation Consortium**, T0115-9504571, for a brochure.

Craigendmuir Park, Campsie View, Stepps, T0141-7794159, www.craigendmuir.co.uk, is 4 miles northeast of the centre and a 15-min walk from Stepps station. It's the nearest to the city.

City centre and the East End *p130, map p132*

There is a good range of accommodation in Glasgow. The luxurious, the atmospheric and backpacker options have been joined by a bewildering number of large, no frills, chain hotels, all doing just what it says on the tin. There are many more guest houses along Renfrew St than we list here.

L-A Glasgow Hilton, 1 William St, T0141-2045555, www.hilton.co.uk. 319 rooms. Gigantic, futuristic-looking luxury hotel regarded as one of the city's best. Full facilities include leisure centre and shopping mall. Their restaurant, **Cameron's**, is also widely held to be one of the finest around, see Eating p160.

L-A Glasgow Moat House, Congress Rd, T0141-3069988, www.moathousehotels.com. 283 rooms. Massive glass structure next to the SECC and 'Armadillo' on the banks of the Clyde and conveniently situated opposite the glittering new Science Centre. A bit out of the city centre but good views of the river 2 excellent restaurants, **Mariner's** and **Dockside No 1**.

L-A Radisson SAS, 301 Argyle St, T0141-2043333, www.radisson.com/glasgowuk. Shiny glass branch of this reliable chain with 247 rooms. It's handily placed for the shops and other city centre sights and also has a health club with a 20-m swimming pool.

L-B Langs Hotel, 2 Port Dundas Pl, T0141-3331500, www.langshotel.co.uk. Has 110 contemporary bedrooms which have CD players and power showers, a funky bar and Californian inspired restaurant. *Sex and the City* comes to Glasgow.

A The Art House, 129 Bath St, T0141-2216789, www.arthousehotel.com. Stylish, sleek and individual hotel in a refurbished former education authority building. It's well located – **Sarti's** the excellent Italian restaurant is down below – and good value. The hotel itself features Scotlands's first Japanese Teppan-yaki grill.

A The Brunswick Merchant City Hotel, 106-108 Brunswick St, T0141-5520001, www.scotland2000.com/brunswick. 21 rooms. Chic minimalism in the heart of the Merchant City. Ideal for cool dudes wishing to sample the delights of Glasgow nightlife. Their excellent bar-restaurant, **Brutti ma Buoni** (that's 'ugly but good' in Italian), is stylish and relaxed – and does a particularly good line in ice cream.

A Millennium Hotel, George Sq, T0141-3326711, www.millennium-hotels.com. 117 rooms. Huge 18th-century hotel in the heart of the city, next to Queen St station – you can't miss it. It's an ideal location for those wanting to explore both the Merchant City and the shops in Buchanan St, while the conservatory bar on the ground floor provides great people-watching potential.

B The Carlton George Hotel, 44 West George St, T0141-3536373, www.carlton hotels.co.uk. Established chain with 65 rooms and a rooftop restaurant. No surprises, just a traditional, plush hotel very close to George Sq and the shops.

B Groucho Saint Judes, 190 Bath St, T0141-3528800, www.saintjudes.com. An intimate and stylish boutique hotel with just 6 bedrooms and a fine dining restaurant. It's a good place for a romantic break, perhaps combined with a bit of shopping in the Italian Centre. Unlike its London namesake, you don't have to be a member.

B Malmaison, 278 West George St, T0141-5721000, www.malmaison.com. 72 rooms. One of the high quality designer chain that can now be found in several UK cities. Stylish urban accommodation, perfect for 30-somethings taking a short break. The chic rooms have CD players and the hotel's brasserie attracts plenty of diners.

B-C Cathedral House, 28/32 Cathedral Sq, T0141-5523519, www.cathedralhouse.com. 8 rooms. Overlooking the cathedral, this is wonderfully atmospheric. An old turretted building with comfortable rooms and a very good restaurant (**££**).

C Bewleys Hotel, 110 Bath St, T0141-3530800, www.bewleyshotel.com, one of the well-known Irish chain hotels which opened in Jul 2000. It's a good central location and the 103 rooms, all priced at £59 year-round, represent great value.

C City Travel Inn Metro, 187 George St, T0141-2383320, www.travelinn.co.uk, has 254 rooms and is close to Glasgow Cathedral.

C Express by Holiday Inn, 122 Stockwell St, T0141-5485000, www.hiexpress.com/glasgowtyct. Another chain.

C Holiday Inn, Bothwell St, T0870 400 9032, www.holiday-inn.co.uk. 275 rooms. Basic, reliable chain.

C The Inn on the Green, 25 Greenhead St, T0141-5540165, www.theinnonthegreen.co.uk. Well-established small hotel in the East End featuring hand-crafted furniture quirky rooms. It's by the striking Templeton buildings (modelled on the Doges' Palace) and very convenient for visiting the family friendly People's Palace.

C Rab Ha's, 83 Hutcheson St, T0141-5720400, www.rabhas.com. Just 4 rooms available at this central Merchant City institution best known for its food. Very stylish decor with light, bright contemporary rooms, crisp sheets and white bathrobes. It's above the pub so could be noisy at night. Rab Ha, in case you're wondering, was a famous Glasgow glutton.

C-D Adelaide's, 209 Bath St, T0141-2484970, www.adelaides.co.uk. 8 rooms. Beautiful 'Greek' Thomson restoration, with 8 rooms in the heart of the city centre. A chance to stay somewhere a bit different at a reasonable price. Good budget option, especially for lovers of architecture.

C-D Babbity Bowster, 16-18 Blackfriars St,T0141-5525055. 6 rooms. A local institution and one of the first of the Merchant City townhouses to be renovated. Typical Glaswegian hospitality, a near-legendary pub (see p167) and an excellent restaurant. Babbity Bowster, in case you were wondering, is an old Scottish country dance.

For an explanation of sleeping and eating price codes used in this guide, see inside the front cover. Other relevant information is found in Essentials, see pages 43-51.

C-D Premier Lodge, 10 Elmbank Gardens, T0870 9906312, www.premierlodge.com. Standard lodge accommodation. 278 rooms.

C-D The Townhouse Hotel, 21 Royal Cres, T0141-3329009, www.hotels.glasgow.com. 19 rooms. Elegantly-restored Victorian town house, set back off Sauchiehall St. A 10-min walk from the city centre. Good value.

D Greek Thomson, 140 Elderslie St, T0141-3326556, www.renniemackintosh hotels.com. 17 rooms. Named after Glasgow's less-famous architectural son. Good value city centre guest house.

D Ibis, 220 West Regent St, T0141-225 6000, www.ibishotel.com. One of the cheapest and most basic of the chain hotels.

D Kelvingrove Hotel, 944 Sauchiehall St, T0141-3395011, www. kelvingrove-hotel. co.uk. Traditional 4-star guest house with 22 en suite rooms. Non smoking.

D The Merchant Lodge, 52 Virginia St, T0141-5522424, www.themerchantlodge. sagenet.co.uk. 40 rooms. Renovated old building that's tucked away in quiet side-street close to the Merchant City's stylish bars and restaurants. It's very clean and contemporary and the staff are friendly. Great value.

D Rennie Mackintosh Hotel, 218-220 Renfrew St, T0141-3339992, www.rennie mackintoshhotels.com. 24 rooms. A small hotel offering friendly service and superb value for money.

D The Victorian House, 212 Renfrew St, T0141-3320129, www.thevictorian.co.uk. 50 rooms in a friendly lodge close to the art college and Tenement House. Superb location. About the best value in the city centre.

Self-catering and serviced accommodation

Number 52 Charlotte St, T01436-810264, www.52charlottestreet.co.uk, a former tobacco merchant's mansion now converted into 6 apartments in the East End. Weekly rates start at £415.

The Serviced Apartment Company, SACO House, 53 Cochrane St, T0845 1220405, www. sacoapartments.co.uk. 12 apartments in the Merchant City. Weekly rates from £525-630.

The Spires, The Pinnacle, 1/10 160 Bothwell St, T0141-5720022, www.thespires.co.uk, offers 22 city centre apartments, nightly rates from £135, weekly rates from £945.

Hostels

E-F Euro Hostel, 318 Clyde St, T0141-2222828, www.euro-hostels.com. 364 beds, all rooms with en suite facilities, includes continental breakfast. A huge multi-storey building overlooking the Clyde.

Campus accommodation

The University of Strathclyde, T0141-5534148, www.rescat.strath.ac.uk, also has a wide range of B&B lodgings available in its various halls of residence across the city, mostly in Jun-Sep, though a few are open all year round, including:

C Strathclyde Graduate Business School, 199 Cathedral St, T0141-5536000, www. rescat.strath.ac.uk. 40 en suite rooms. Open all year. This one is the most salubrious of the campus choices.

D Chancellors Hall, Cathedral St (on campus). 218 en suite rooms;

E Forbes Hall, Cathedral St, 104 single rooms B&B or self-catering flats. £300-355 per week;

E Garnett Hall, Cathedral St (on campus). 124 single rooms. Also self-catering, around £260-330 per week; and

E Murray Hall, Cathedral St (on campus). 70 single rooms.

West End *p141, maps p142 and p144*

L One Devonshire Gardens, 1 Devonshire Gdns, T0141-3392001, www.onedevonshire gardens.co.uk. 36 rooms. Highly-acclaimed hotel which is still the very last word in style and comfort, with fragrant fresh flowers, deep baths to wallow in and staff who pay attention to every detail. There are few, if any, classier places to stay in the country. It's the hotel of choice for Tina Turner, George Clooney, in fact almost every big name who comes to Glasgow.

L-B Hilton Glasgow Grosvenor, 1-10 Grosvenor Terrace, Great Western Rd, T0141-3398811, www.hilton.co.uk. A smaller, 4-star, version of the city centre Hilton situated in a traditional West End terrace. A good one for nature lovers as about half their rooms have views of the Botanic Gardens opposite.

B-C Manor Park Hotel, 28 Balshagray Dr, T0141-3392143, F3395842. 10 rooms. This West End hotel in a cosy, traditional building is unusual in Glasgow in that Gaelic is spoken and actively promoted. Good for anyone wanting a rich taste of Scottish culture.

C **Argyll Hotel**, 973 Sauchiehall St, T0141-3373313, www.argyllhotelglasgow.co.uk. 38 rooms. A traditional hotel in a refurbished Georgian building.

C **Kirklee Hotel**, 11 Kensington Gate, T0141-3345555, www.kirkleehotel.co.uk. 9 rooms. Lovely clean Edwardian town house with a beautiful garden that's widely admired. Close to bars and restaurants on Byres Rd and the Botanic Gardens.

C **Park House**, 13 Victoria Park Gardens South, T0141-3391559, www.parkhouseglasgow.co.uk. Victorian townhouse with 3 rooms offering 4-star B&B.

C **The Sandyford Hotel**, 904 Sauchiehall St, T0141-3340000, www.sandyfordhotelglasgow.co.uk. 55 rooms. Comfortable and good value lodge convenient for the SECC and art galleries.

C **Wickets Hotel**, 52 Fortrose St, T/F0141-3349334, www.wicketshotel.co.uk. 11 rooms. Quiet comfort overlooking the west of Scotland cricket ground and close to Partick rail station and Underground.

C-D **Heritage Hotel**, 1 Alfred Terr, 625 Great Western Rd, T0141-3396955, www.goglasgow.co.uk. 26 rooms. Good value Victorian town house close to the West End action.

C-D **Hillhead Hotel**, 32 Cecil St, T0141-3397733, www.hillheadhotel.co.uk. 11 rooms. Small, friendly hotel ideally placed for the Byres Rd nightlife and close to Hillhead Underground.

C-D **Jury's Glasgow Hotel**, Great Western Rd, T0141-3348161, www.jurysdoyle.com. 137 rooms. Nothing too fancy, but comfortable rooms and good facilities (pool, sauna and gym). Free parking. Very good value.

C-D **Kelvin Hotel**, 15 Buckingham Terr, Great Western Rd, T0141-3397143, www.kelvinhotel.com. 21 rooms. Comfortable guest house in lovely Victorian terrace near Byres Rd and Botanic Gardens.

C-D **Kirkland House**, 42 St Vincent Cres, T0141-2483458, www.kirkland.net43.co.uk. 5 rooms. Small, family-run guest house with that little bit extra. Close to Kelvingrove Park.

C-D **Lomond Hotel**, No 6 Buckingham Terr, Great Western Rd, T0141-3392339, www.scotland 2000.com/lomond. Smaller option than the nearby Kelvin Hotel, but friendly and comfortable.

C-D **Number Thirty Six**, St Vincent Cres, T0141-2482086, www.no36.co.uk. A worthwhile guest house option.

C-D **The Townhouse**, 4 Hughenden Terr, T0141-3570862, www.thetownhouseglasgow.com. 10 rooms. Just off the Great Western Rd. Lovely Victorian town house offering comfort, hospitality and great value.

Hostels

F **Bunkum Backpackers**, 26 Hillhead St, T0141-5814481, www.bunkumglasgow.co.uk. It has 32 beds and kitchen facilities.

F **Glasgow Backpackers**, T0141-2217880, www.glasgowhostels.com. Until early 2005 there is a temporary hostel sleeping 26 at 163 North St, Charing Cross (57 bus from the city centre; get off near the Mitchell Library), while other hostels are being renovated. After that two large hostels on Berkeley St, Charing Cross, will open up, together with a proposed new hostel near Central Station.

F **Glasgow Backpackers Hostel**, 17 Park Terr, T0141-3329099, www.scotlands-top-hostels.co.uk. 90 beds. Open Jul-Sep. Independent hostel housed in university halls of residence.

F **SYHA Youth Hostel**, 7/8 Park Terr, T0870-0041119, www.syha.org.uk. 135 beds. This former hotel has been converted into a great 4-star hostel, all rooms with en suite facilities (being refurbished, opens Jun 2004). Price includes continental breakfast. It gets very busy in Jul/Aug so you'll need to book ahead. Open 24 hrs. It's a 10-min walk from Kelvinbridge Underground station, or take bus 44 or 59 from Central station and get off at the first stop on Woodlands Rd, then head up the first turning left (Lynedoch St).

Self-catering and serviced accommodation

City Apartments, 401 North Woodside Rd, T0141-3424060, www.glasgowhotelsandapartments.co.uk. Close to Kelvinbridge Underground. Have 4 apartments to let from £330 per week, £48 per night.

Dreamhouse Inc, T0141-3323620, www.dreamhouseapartments.com, have several luxury serviced apartments in Lynedoch Cres. Nightly rates range from £120-215.

Embassy Apartments, 8 Kelvin Dr, T0141-9466698, www.glasgowhotelsand

apartments.co.uk. 6 apartments in a converted Victorian terrace house in the West End, about a mile from the city centre. All are en suite and sleep between 1 and 5 people. Weekly rates from £330.

The White House, 12 Cleveden Cres, T0141-3399375, www.whitehouse-apartments.com. This has 32 suites with a country house atmosphere. Weekly rates from £300-620.

Campus accommodation

University of Glasgow, contact the Conference and Visitor Services, 3 The Sq, T0141-330 5385, www.cvso.co.uk. There is a range of self-catering accommodation, available Jul-Sep, including:

Cairncross House, 20 Kelvinhaugh Pl, off Argyle St, near Kelvingrove Park, has rooms to let, and Kelvinhaugh Gate and Murano St Village have flats and rooms. It also has B&B accommodation (**E**) at Dalrymple Hall in the West End, available Mar-Apr and Jul-Sep;

St Andrews Campus, 6 miles from the West End, available Apr-May and mid-Jun to mid-Aug; and

Wolfson Hall, a modern block by Kelvin Conference Centre, available Mar-Apr and May-Sep.

South Side *p146*

A-B Sherbrooke Castle Hotel, 11 Sherbrooke Av T0141-4274227, www.sherbrooke.co.uk. Small hotel (25 rooms) with a bit more character than the chains. It's a good base for exploring the attractions of the south side as it's only about a mile from the Burrell collection.

B Best Western Ewington, Balmoral Terr, 132 Queen's Dr, T0141-4231152, www.countryhotels.net. 43 rooms. Friendly and comfortable hotel in a secluded terrace facing Queen's Park. Their restaurant, Minstrels, is superb value and worth a visit in its own right.

B-C Swallow Hotel, 517 Paisley Rd West, T0141-4273146, www.swallowhotels.com. This chain hotel has 117 rooms and is conveniently close to the new Science Centre and has its own pool.

Excursions *p152*

Thoses listed are in New Lanark. There are plenty to choose in both Lanark and New Lanark, though the most interesting places to stay are in New Lanark. If you wish to stay in any other of the towns covered in Excursions, see the relevant TIC.

B New Lanark Mill Hotel, T01555-667200, www.newlanark.org. 38 en suite rooms. Converted 18th-century mill with great views. Its restaurant serves lunch and dinner (**££**). Also has 8 self-catering cottages.

F New Lanark Youth Hostel, T0870-155 3255, new.lanark@syha.org.uk. Beautifully situated in Wee Row by the river. It's open Mar-Oct and includes continental breakfast.

Eating

Forget the deep-fried Mars bar. OK, it was invented here – and is still available in some establishments – along with other Caledonian culinary delights like the deep-fried pizza, deep-fried black pudding and the deep-fried Cadbury's creme egg (yes, you heard). These may be the headline grabbing foods that everyone associates with Glasgow, but they really don't reflect the quality and variety of food that the city has to offer. Glasgow has undergone a culinary renaissance and it continues unabated. Glasgow has always boasted a wide selection of ethnic eateries, particularly Indian, Chinese and Italian restaurants, and these have been joined by a growing number of cuisines from around the globe. Scottish cuisine is also well represented, reflecting the growing trend of marrying traditional Scottish ingredients with continental and international flavours and styles. Meats like venison, pheasant, lamb and beef are often on the menu, and haggis may feature too – often as a starter so as not to frighten the uninitiated. Fresh local fish is also widely available. Look out for salmon, halibut, scallops, langoustines, mackerel and Loch Fyne kippers. Vegetarians are also well catered for. Though there aren't too many exclusively vegetarian or vegan restaurants, most places now offer substantial and imaginative vegetarian menus.

66 99 Forget the deep-fried Mars bar. OK, it was invented here – and is still available in some establishments – along with other Caledonian culinary delights like the deep-fried pizza, deep-fried black pudding and the deep-fried Cadbury's creme egg...

The greatest concentration of eating places is around Byres Rd in the West End, which is heavily populated by students and therefore the best area for cheap but stylish places to eat. Merchant City contains most of the designer brasseries, which are more expensive. The city centre has the main share of pricey but superb restaurants. For those on a tight budget, many city restaurants offer cheap business lunches. Pre-theatre dinner menus also provide an opportunity to sample some of the finest food at affordable prices, if you don't mind eating before 1900. Many of the restaurants are open 7 days a week.

Glasgow prides itself on its café society and many of the new, trendy designer cafés make it seem more like Barcelona or Greenwich Village than the west coast of Scotland. Glasgow is also full of authentic Italian cafés where you can enjoy a cheap fry-up washed down with frothy cappuccino. Whatever your preference, you won't have any trouble finding the right place for that essential caffeine shot during a hard day's sightseeing or shopping. Glasgow is also the home of the tea room and those who insist on their mid-afternoon infusion won't be disappointed. Most cafés also serve food and are often the most economical option for a midday snack or meal.

City centre and the East End *p130, map p132*

£££ Brian Maule at Chardon d'Or, 176 West Regent St, T0141-2483801. Opulent venue catering very much to well lunched businessmen. Head chef was formerly at Le Gavroche in London.

£££ The Buttery, 652 Argyle St, T0141-2218188. Victoriana abounds in this old favourite with its clubby atmosphere. Consistently rated as one of the best in the city, with an emphasis on the finest Scottish fish, seafood and game. Good high-quality wine list. Tue-Fri 1200-1400, 1900-2200; Sat 1800-2200.

£££ Cameron's, 1 William St, T0141-2045511. In **Glasgow's Hilton Hotel**. Sublime Scottish/French cuisine with starters like mussels and scallops, and mains that include excellent Aberdeen Angus beef. Pricey but well worth it. No smoking area. Mon-Fri 1200-1400, 1900-2200; Sat 1900-2200.

£££ Etain, The Glass House, Springfield Court, T0141-2255630. This is Terence Conran's fine dining 'destination' restaurant, offering French dishes like roast pigeon with Puy lentils. Set lunches make it a more affordable option than in the evening. Mon-Fri 1200-1430, 1900-2200; Sat, Sun 1900-2200.

£££ Gamba, 225a West George St, T0141-5720899. Popular fish restaurant, where you get the freshest fish cooked with flair and imagination. The decor is cool and discreet, and it's a great special occasion place. Try the fish soup to start. Mon-Sat 1200-1430, 1700-2230.

£££ Groucho St Judes, 190 Bath St, T0141-3528800. Part of the chic small hotel but open to non residents. Very much the in-place for Glasgow's movers and shakers. Modern Scottish food with lots of char-grilled fish and meat but be sure to leave room for those scrummy puddings. Mon-Fri 1200-1500; Mon-Sun 1800-2230.

£££ Ho Wong, 82 York St, T0141-2213550. Tucked away just off Argyle St, this Chinese restaurant doesn't look much from the outside but inside awaits a memorable Cantonese culinary experience and the city's finest Szechuan food. Not cheap but worth every penny. Try their fish or seafood. BYOB. Mon-Sat 1200-1400, 1800-2330; Sun 1800-2330.

£££ Quigleys, 158 Bath St, T0141-3314060. Contemporary restaurant in the old Christie's showroom, offering imaginative fusion food for the slick set in a relaxed atmosphere. Good value pre-theatre menu served 1700-1900. Mon-Sat 1200-1500, 1700-2300.

£££ Rogano's, 11 Exchange Pl, T0141-2484055. A Glasgow culinary institution. Designed in the style of the Cunard liner, Queen Mary, and built by the same workers. Looks like the set of a Hollywood blockbuster and you'll need a similar budget to pay the bill, but the seafood is truly sensational. Daily 1200-1430, 1830-2230. Downstairs is:

£££ Café Rogano, which offers a less stylish alternative, but it's a lot easier on the pocket. Sun-Thu 1200-1430, 1830-2230.

£££ Two Five Seven, 257 West Campbell St, T0141-5724052. Scottish produce with a French twist is on the menu at this new restaurant, on the site of Gordon Yuill's former eaterie. The chef is the same and the interior chic, though the service could be improved. Open Mon-Sat 1200-1430, 1800-2200.

££ Amber Regent, 50 West Regent St, T0141-3311655. Plush and very upmarket restaurant serving classic Chinese cuisine. Those on a tight budget can also indulge themselves, with half price main courses before 1900 Wed-Fri and all night Mon/Tue. BYOB. Mon-Thu 1200-1415, 1730-2300; Fri 1200-1415, 1730-2330; Sat 1200-2330.

££ Arta, housed in the Old Cheesmarket, 13-19 Walls St, T0141-5522101. Stylish Spanish restaurant serving tapas, tortillas and meaty stews. Housed in the Old Cheesmarket, the decor is faux-Spanish with mosaics and huge candelabras. Wed, Thur and Sun 1700-2300, Fri, Sat 1700-2400. Bar open later.

££ Baby Grand, 3-7 Elmbank Gardens, T0141-2484942. Chic jazz-café offering good bistro-style food when most other places have shut up shop. Enjoy late night drinks and food and soothing jazz piano. Mon-Thu 0800-2400; Fri 0800-0200; Sat 1000-0200; Sun 1000-2400.

££ Bleu Ginger, 441 Sauchiehall St, T0141-3325999. This new Chinese restaurant offers classy dining in elegant surroundings - a large chandelier hangs from the ceiling and contemporary prints line the walls. Lots of 'chilli' dishes and several choices for veggies. Mon-Sat 1200-1430, 1730-0200; Sun 1730-0200.Mon-Sat 1200-1430, 1730-0200; Sun 1730-0200.

££ Bouzy Rouge, 111 West Regent St, T0141 -2218804. One of a chain offering two types of dining – casual and gourmet. Gourmet choices are things like posh Scottish (venison and the like), casual has steaks and veggie options. Sleek wooden interior. Sun-Thu 1200-2130, Fri, Sat 1200-2230.

££ Café Cossachock, 10 King St, T0141-5530733. Near the Tron Theatre. Cosy, authentic-feeling Russian restaurant with a relaxed, informal atmosphere. Try a bowl of crimson borscht (beetroot and cabbage soup) – great on a damp Glasgow day, or a blini (pancake) stuffed with meat, spinach or even ice cream. The art gallery upstairs features the work of artists from around the world and exhibits change regularly. More than just a good meal, it's an entire cultural experience. Tue-Sat 1130-2230; Sun 1600-2230.

££ Café Gandolfi, 64 Albion St, T0141-5526813. The first of Glasgow's style bistro/brasseries back in 1979, which almost makes it antique by today's contemporary design standards. Still comfortably continental, relaxed and soothing. Good place for a snack or a leisurely late breakfast. Mon-Sat 0900-2330, Sun 1200-2330.

££ City Merchant, 97-99 Candleriggs, T0141-5531577. The best of Scottish meat and game but it's the fish and seafood which shine. Absolutely superb. It's at the top end of this price range but their two- and three-course set menus are more affordable and excellent value (available 1200-1830). Very popular and a good atmosphere. No smoking area. Mon-Sat 1200-2230.

££ Corinthian, 191 Ingram St, T0141-5521101, Mon-Thu 1700-2230, Fri and Sat,

For an explanation of sleeping and eating price codes used in this guide, see inside the front cover. Other relevant information is found in Essentials, see pages 43-51.

1700-2300, bar open from 1200 Mon-Sat, 1230- on Sun. There's a sense of occasion about going to the popular **Corinthian**. There are several bars, a nightclub and private club as well as the restaurant. Food tends to be traditional with a modern twist and the puddings are very good.

££ The Dhabba, 44 Candelriggs, T0141-5531249. Stylish new Indian restaurant with lots of polished wood and gleaming cutlery offering authentic Northern Indian cuisine. Daily 1200-2300.

££ Esca, 27 Chisholm St, T0141-5530880. Sleek, contemporary restaurant with a friendly, relaxed atmosphere, serving Mediterranean with a strong emphasis on pastas and steaks. Mon-Fri 1200-1500, 1700-2200, Sat 1200-2230, Sun 1700-2200.

££ Frango, 15 John St T0141-5524433, Mon-Sat noon-2230. Conveniently located in the Italian Centre this place is popular with business people and fashion conscious shoppers. There's an all day menu, with lots of fish dishes such as fish soup, tuna, and monkfish. Pudding might include a scrummy rosemary panacotta. Relaxed atmosphere.

££ Fratelli Sarti, 121 Bath St, T0141-2040440. Everything you'd expect from a great Italian restaurant, and a lot more besides. It's a real Glasgow institution, practically everyone in the city must have eaten here at some time. Good value food in authentic Italian surroundings – lots of chatter and bustle. Their pizzas are delicious. No wonder it's always busy – but be warned, service can be slow. No smoking area. Mon-Sat 0800 2230; Sun 1200-2230.

££ The Green Room, Glasgow Royal Concert Hall (see Entertainment p169), 2 Sauchiehall St, T0141-3538000. Much more than a good place to eat before the show. A superb restaurant in its own right where you can indulge in the finest of Scottish produce at reasonable prices. Good vegetarian selection. No smoking area. Open performance days only 1700-2130.

££ Metropolitan, Merchant Sq, T0141-5529402. Housed the huge covered courtyard of the city's old Fruitmarket, this is a stylish, but slightly self-consciously trendy, restaurant and bar – leather sofas and fashion TV on wide screen in the bar, and a sleek clientele – perfect for metrosexuals. You can drink outside in the covered courtyard. Food is contemporary with dishes like jerk chicken, steaks and pastas.

££ Modern India, 51 West Regent St, T0141-3311980. Contemporary Indian restaurant featuring many dishes from Goa. Business lunches are a great bargain. Mon-Thu 1200-2330, Fri, Sat 1200-0100, Sun 1600-2330.

££ Pancho Villas, 26 Bell St, T0141-5527737. Mon-Thu 1200-2230, Fri, Sat 1200-2300, Sun 1800-2230. Cheery Mexican eaterie with good, adventurous food and colourful decor inspired by the Mexican festival, the Day of the Dead. Come here to sip Margaritas, slam tequilas and feast on fajitas.

££ Schottische, 16-18 Blackfriars St, T0141-5527774. Upstairs from the legendary Babbity Bowsters (see below). Good French/Scottish food at very affordable prices. They use seasonal produce and you might find venison as well as haggis on the menu, so if you've never tried it, here's your chance. Leave room for their diet-busting puddings. Tue-Sat 1830-2300.

££ Smiths of Glasgow, 109 Candleriggs, T0141-5526539. There's a French tang to this Merchant City favourite which functions as a café by day and a restaurant by night. Tue-Sat 0930-2200, Sun, Mon 0930-1730.

££ Tron Theatre, Chisholm St, T0141-5528587. Refurbished restaurant offers a dining experience that's worth applauding. No smoking area. The effortlessly stylish bar is perfect for that pre-prandial tipple. Mon-Sat 1000-late; Sun 1100-late.

£ Babbity Bowster, 16-18 Blackfriars St, T0141-5525055. You can't get away from this place, and why would you want to? Buzzing café-bar housed in a magnificent 18th-century building in the heart of the Merchant City. Traditional Scottish and French dishes served with flair. Outrageously good value. The bar is one of the city's perennial favourites (see Bars and clubs, p167). Mon-Sat 1200-2300; Sun 1000-2300.

£ Café Source, 1 St Andrews Sq, in the church, T0141-5486020. Great contemporary café offering everything from fishcakes to savoury vegetarian tart. Or just chill out with a latter and read the papers. Mon-Thu 1100-2300, Fri, Sat 1100-2400, Sun 1200-2300, no food 1500-1700 Mon-Fri. Live music every Wed from 2100.

£ Canton Express, 407 Sauchiehall St, T0141-3320145. No-frills, cheap and filling Chinese fast food at any hour of the day or night. Daily 1200-0400.

£ Glasgow Noodle Bar, 482 Sauchiehall St, T0141-3331883. Oriental fast food eaten from disposable containers with plastic chopsticks or forks. Very cheap chow and great after a heavy night on the town. Daily 1200-0500.

£ Ichiban Japanese Noodle Café, 50 Queen St, T0141-2044200. Excellent value, healthy Japanese specialities in cool, modern surroundings. No smoking. Mon-Wedi 1200-2200, Thu-Sat 1200-2300; Sun 1300-2200.

£ Mono, Kings Court, King St, T0141-5532400. Clean and simple, this contemporary vegan restaurant is a welcome addition to the Glasgow culinary scene. No, it's not knit your own nut loaf territory, instead you'll find things like smoked tofu wantons with spicy apricot conserve or a delicate Thai curry. All the beers and wines are vegan so you can eat and drink with a sparkling clear conscience. Daily 1200-220.

£ Tempus at the CCA, 350 Sauchiehall St, T0141-3327959. Set in the recently refurbished Centre for Contemporary Arts, this café/restaurant serves contemporary Scottish dishes. The menu is flexible and you can just drop in for a coffee and a snack if you don't want lunch.

£ CCA Bar, upstairs from Tempus at the CCA, Sauchiehall St, serves sandwiches and coffees. It is notable for its decor, designed by artist Jorge Pardo, which is a psychedelic creation with lots of bright colours and carved wood. Daily 1100-midnight (last order for food 2130).

£ Trattoria Gia, 17 King St, T0141-5527411. Very good value Italian eaterie near the Merchant City. Service is friendly and supremely efficient. Tue-Sat 1200-1400, 1700-2230, Sun 1700-2230.

£ Wee Curry Shop, 7 Buccleuch St, T0141-3530777. Son of **Mother India** (see below). Small in every sense except flavour and value. Quite simply the best cheap curry this side of the Hindu Kush. Cosy, relaxed atmosphere. Good vegetarian options and incredible value 3-course buffet lunch. BYOB. Mon-Sat 1200-1400, 1730-2230.

Cafés

Café Cosmo, 12 Rose St. T0141-3326535. Part of the Glasgow Film Theatre (see Entertainment p169) and definitely worth knowing about, even if you're not a movie buff. It's a great cheap lunch venue, especially for vegetarians. Daily 1200-1700, bar open till 2100.

Miss Cranston's Tearooms, 33 Gordon St T0141-2041122. You could miss this traditionally run tea shop as it's hidden above a baker's shop. This is the place to come for a full blown afternoon tea with sandwiches, scones, cakes and gallons of tea.

The Doocot Café and Bar, The Lighthouse, 11 Mitchell La, T0141-2211821. There's a 1950s retro look at this café on the top of The Lighthouse (see Sights p137). Stop for soups, sandwiches and light meals before immersing yourself in the world of architecture.

Willow Tea Rooms, 217 Sauchiehall St, T0141-3320521. A recreation of the original Miss Cranston's Tearooms, designed by Charles Rennie Mackintosh and filled with many of his original features. Most visitors come here for the interior design, but they also offer a good selection of reasonably priced teas, sandwiches, cakes and scones, as well as hot meals. Mon-Sat 0900-1630, Sun noon-1530. There's also a sister branch at 97 Buchanan St, T0141-2045242, which is licensed. No smoking area. Mon-Sat 0930-1700, Sun 1200-1700.

Where the Monkey Sleeps, 182 West Regent St, T0141-2263406, is a relaxed exhibition space/café. Good cappuccinos and sandwiches, as well as soups from **Eurasia** (see above). Exhibits and sells works of new artists, including graduates of Glasgow and Londón schools of art. Mon-Sat 0700-1900, Sat 1000-1900

West End *p141, maps p142 and p144*

£££ The Cabin, 996-998 Dumbarton Rd, T0141-5691036. If you're idea of a good night out is piles of the finest Scottish food followed by a post-dinner cabaret by Wilma, the legendary singing waitress, then this is the place for you. A truly one-off experience and great fun. The only drawback is there's only one dinner sitting, at 1930, Tue-Sat, also Tue-Fri 1200-1400. BYOB.

£££ The Cook's Room, 13 Woodside Cres, T0141-353 0707. This former southside favourite has now moved to the West End, taking over Nick Nairn's old premises. They serve good modern Scottish food in clean blue and cream surroundings. Look out for dishes like tarragon chicken and leave room to try their great puddings. Sunday brunch is good value and you can eat more cheaply at lunchtime than in the evening. Mon-Sat 1200-14.30 and 1800-2200.

£££ Dining Room, 41 Byres Rd, T0141-339 3666. Acclaimed, imaginative food at this snug West End restaurant. Mains might include a creamy asparagus and pea risotto, but try to leave room for desert - the warm carrot cake with marmalade ice cream is a winner.

£££ La Parmigiana, 443 Great Western Rd, T0141-3340686. This sophisticated Italian restaurant is one of Glasgow's finest eating establishments. Recommended for a special occasion. Open Mon-Sat 1200-1430, 1800-2300.

£££ Stravaigin, 28-30 Gibson St, T0141-3342665. Hard to define but difficult to resist. An eclectic mix of flavours and prime Scottish ingredients to produce the most sublime results. Expensive but you won't get better value for money in this category and totally justifies its many awards. Upstairs is a café-bar where you can sample some of that fabulous food at more affordable prices. Tue-Thu, 1700-2230, Fri-Sun 1200-1430, 1700-2300.

£££ The Ubiquitous Chip, 12 Ashton La, T0141-3345007. A ground-breaking, multi award-winning restaurant and still the city's favourite place for Mactastic Scottish food, especially venison and seafood. All served in a plant-filled, covered courtyard patio. Mon-Sat 1200-1430, 1730-2300, Sun 1230-1500, 1830-2300. Upstairs is their bistro, **Upstairs at the Chip**, which doesn't make you feel quite as special but is much easier on the wallet (daily 1200-2300).

££ Ashoka Ashton Lane, 19 Ashton La, T0141-3371115. First-class Indian restaurant, part of the famous west coast chain. Very popular with students and Byres Rd trendies. Mon-Thu 1200-2400, Fri and Sat 1200-0030, Sun 1700-2400.

££ Ashoka West End, 1284 Argyle St, T0141-3393371. The oldest in this ever-popular chain of excellent Indians. Great value and a vegetarian-friendly menu. Sun-Thu 1700-0030, Fri and Sat 1700-0100.

££ The Bothy, 11 Ruthven La, T0141-334-4040. Only just opened and owned by the same people at Corinthian, offers traditional Scottish food in rustic surroundings – all done in a modern, ironic West End sort of way. Daily 1200-2400.

££ Brel, 39-43 Ashton La, T0141-3424966. Another stylish continental eating establishment in Glasgow's hippest culinary quarter. This time it's Belgian. Great food and great value, especially during the half price happy hour (1700-1900). Daily for food 1200-2230, bar open longer.

££ Café India, 171 North St, T0141-2484074. Cavernous Indian restaurant that's big on style and has a deserved reputation for fine food. Good value buffet downstairs (1200-1400 Mon-Fri, daily 1800-2230). Mon-Thu 1200-2400, Fri and Sat 1200-0030, Sun 1500-2400.

££ Cottier's, 93-95 Hyndland St, T0141-3575825. Very elegant Caribbean style restaurant housed in a converted church. The food is heavenly and the ambience spiritually rewarding. These dear souls are also great with kids, bless them. Stylish bar and theatre downstairs on the ground floor where you can often hear live music (see p169). Mon-Thu 1200-1600, 1700-2230, Fri and Sat 1200-1600, 1700-2300, Sun 1200-2230.

££ Cul de Sac, 44-46 Ashton La, T0141-3346688. Effortlessly fashionable, laid back and oh, so boho. A great place to sit back, soak up the atmosphere and enjoy good French-style food. Their famous crêpes are half price between 1700 and 1900, as are the tasty burgers and pasta. Good vegetarian choices, too, and it's a great place to work of last night's excesses with a hearty Sun brunch. Sun-Thu 1200-2300, Fri and Sat 1200-2400.

££ Gingerhill, 1 Hillhead St, T0141-9566515. Well off the beaten track in posh Milngavie, but well worth the trip. Has a reputation as one of Glasgow's best seafood restaurants. It's an awfy wee place so you'll have to book well in advance. Wed -Sun 1930-2130. No smoking. BYOB (no licence).

££ Gong, 17 Vinicombe St T0141-5761700. Sleek new venture housed in an old cinema that is already proving popular with the locals. Lots of sharing platters and Italian and Mexican influences. Brunch served at weekends. Mon-Thu 1700-2230, Fri and Sat 1200-1500, 1700-0200, Sun 1200-1500, 1700-2230, bar open longer.

££ **Mother India**, 28 Westminster Terr, Sauchiehall St, T0141-2211663. Exquisite Indian cooking at affordable prices. Friendly and informal atmosphere. Strong vegetarian selection. Cheap set lunch and good banquet menus. BYOB. Mon, Tue 1730-2230, Wed and Thu 1200-1400, 1730-2230, Fri 1200-1400, 1700-2300, Sat 1300-2300, Sun 1630-2200.

££ **Mr Singh's India**, 149 Elderslie St, T0141-2040186. Imagine good Punjabi cooking brought to you by kilted waiters with a background wallpaper of disco music. If that sounds like your cup of char then get on down here and join in the fun. Many celebs have, so you never know who might pop in for a popadum. Very child friendly. Mon-Sat 1200-2400, Sun 1430-2400.

££ **Shish Mahal**, 66-68 Park Rd T0141-3398256. 'The Shish' has long been a byword for great curry in Glasgow. The Pakistani food's imaginative and there's loads of choice. Mon-Thu 1200-1400, 1700-2330, Fri and Sat 1200-1145, Sun 1700-2330. You can BYOB.

£ **The Bay Tree**, 403 Great Western Rd, T0141-3345898. Rather basic self-service café serving food with a Middle Eastern emphasis. Mon-Sat 0930-2100; Sun 1000-2000.

£ **Grassroots Café**, 97 St George's Rd, T0141-3330534. Vegetarian and vegan food at this intimate café near St Georges Cross. Lots of soups and salads and filling main courses. Daily 1000-2200.

£ **Otago**, 61 Otago St T0141-3372282. There's a cool, minimalist look to this Mediterranean bistro that offers lots of veggie choices. Good selection of wines too. Daily 1100-2200.

Cafés

Brasserie Metro, 8 Cresswell La, T0141-3388131. Big and bright West End café/deli just off Byres Rd that's popular with students. Wide-ranging menu makes it a good, cheap choice for lunch. No smoking area. Mon 0800-1800, Tue-Sat 0800-2200, Sun 0900-1800.

Grosvenor Café, 31 Ashton La, T0141-3391848. Behind Hillhead Underground. A perennial favourite with local students who come for the wide selection of cheap food (filled rolls, soup, burgers, pizzas, etc). Cosy and friendly atmosphere. Mon and Tue 0900-1600, Wed-Sat 0900-2200, Sun 1000-1800.

Little Italy, 205 Byres Rd, T0141-3396287, is a convenient and buzzy refuelling stop that never seems to close. Great pizza and strong espresso. Mon-Thu 0800-2200, Fri and Sat 0800-1145, Sun 1000-2200.

North Star, 108 Queen Margaret Dr, T0141-9465365. Portugeuse café/deli that has an extremely loyal following. Good speciality treats. Mon 0800-1800, Tue-Thu 0800-1900, Fri and Sat 0800-2000, Sun 1100-1800.

TchaiOvna, 42 Otago La, T0141-3574524. Laid back Eastern inspired café, with a huge selection of teas. Daily 1100-2300.

Tinderbox, 189 Byres Rd, T0141-3393108. Coffee shop which looks and feels more like a style bar. Great coffee, good magazines to read and a large no smoking, child-friendly area. Mon-Sat 0745-2300, Sun 0845-2300.

University Café, 87 Byres Rd, T0141-3395217. Authentic Italian art deco caff, where grannies and students sit shoulder-to-shoulder enjoying real cappuccino, great ice cream and good, honest and cheap mince and tatties, pie and chips and all the other golden oldies. A glorious evocation of a world before sundried tomatoes. Mon-Thu 0900-2200, Fri and Sat 0900-2230, Sun 1000-2200.

South Side *p146*

££ **Arigo**, 67 Kilmarnock Rd, T0141-6366616. Good Italian restaurant offering high quality fresh food. The sort of place that doesn't need to advertise. Mon-Fri 1200-1430, 1700-2230, Sat and Sun 1200-2230.

££ **Ashoka Southside**, 268 Clarkston Rd, T0141-6370711. Small and intimate Southside version of this venerable chain of Indian restaurants. Fri and Sat 1700-2400, Sun-Thu 1700-2300.

££ **The Cook's Room**, 205 Fenwick Rd, Giffnock T0141-6211903. Good modern Scottish cooking and some great puddings. Sunday brunch is good value. Mon-Fri

1800-2130, Sat and Sun 1200-1500, 1800-2130.

££ The Greek Golden Kebab, 34 Sinclair Dr, T0141-6497581. It might sound like a takeaway but this is a restaurant and an enduring favourite with those who come for the home cooked Greek food. Thu-Sun 1700-0100.

££ Spice Garden, 11-17 Clyde Pl, T0141-4294422. There's an enormous choice at this popular Indian restaurant that prides itself on its cleanliness. It's conveniently open all night so good for those desperate for a post-club curry. Daily 1800-0430.

£ Buongiorno, 1021 Pollokshaws Rd, T0141-6491029. The best pizza in Glasgow - at these prices? Impossible, surely. Well, check it for yourself. Impeccable Italian family cooking, with cosy ambience to match. They even have a pre-theatre 2-for-1 deal! Are they crazy? Simply unbeatable, so book ahead. Mon-Sat 0900-2300, Sun 1000-2200.

Cafés

Art Lovers' Café, Bellahouston Park, Drumbreck Rd, T0141-3534779. Housed in CRM's exquisite **House for an Art Lover**. A nice place to chill and a good selection of light snacks and hot and cold meals. Also live jazz on Sat nights in the bar. No smoking. Sun-Fri 1000-1700, Sat also 1830-2400.

Excursions *p152*

££ Ristorante La Vigna, 40 Wellgate, Lanark, T0141-630351, an Italian of some renown. It's open daily for lunch and dinner, but is popular, so book in advance.

£ Market Bar and Restaurant, Lanark Market, Hyndford Rd. If you're in town on a Mon, market day, it's well worth trying this place.

Bars and clubs

Forget all the tired old clichés about Glasgow and Glaswegians, a night out in Scotland's largest city is a memorable experience – for all the right reasons. Glasgow is bursting at the seams with bars and pubs to suit all tastes from ornate Victorian watering holes to the coolest of designer bars, where you can listen to thumping dance beats before heading off to a club. Most pubs and bars open till 2400, though a few are open later, and many of them close at 2300 on weekdays and Sun. DJs normally start at 2100 till 2400 and entry is usually free, with some places charging after 2300 when they transform into clubs.

One of the best areas for the sheer number and variety of pubs and bars is the West End, with its large student population. The city centre has a great choice too. A number of style bars have also opened up along Bath St and Glasgow's gay scene has grown around the trendy bars and cafés of the Merchant City, especially Virginia St, Wilson St and Glassford St. Glasgow's club scene, much of which is found in the city centre, is amongst the most vibrant in the UK. Opening times are pretty much the same all over with doors opening from 2300-0300. Entry costs vary from £2-5 for smaller mainstream clubs and £5-10 for the bigger venues, up to £20 for some of the special club nights with top class DJs.

City centre and the East End *p130, map p132*

Bars

13th Note Café, 50-60 King St, T0141-5531638, established East End hang out serving veggie food. Live music venue.

Arches Café Bar, 253 Argyle St. Part of the legendary club, this stylish basement bar is the perfect place to linger over a Belgian beer or enjoy their food.

Babbity Bowster, 16-18 Blackfriars St. Prime Merchant City pub that has everything; lively atmosphere, wide selection of real ales and good food, see also Eating p160.

Bar 10, 10 Mitchell St. This converted warehouse is Glasgow's original style bar and still as cool as ever. Good food on offer and a popular pre-club meeting place at weekends with regular Djs.

Bargo, 80 Albion St. Stylish and spacious Merchant City bar/bistro with surprisingly good food and a high posing quotient, see also Eating p156.

Blackfriars, 36 Bell St. Merchant city favourite which pulls in the punters with its vast range of international beers and lagers. Also a wide range of excellent grub, live music and comedy at weekends and that inimitable Glasgow atmosphere, see Entertaiment p169.

Bloc, 117 Bath St, T0141-5746066. Another Bath St style bar, with food that's a mix of Eastern European and Far Eastern flavours.

Candy Bar, 185 Hope St, T0141-3537240. Billed as one of the city's coolest bars, this is the place to flaunt those new clothes you splashed out on in Princes Sq. A long way from spit and sawdust.

The Griffin, 226 Bath St. Opposite the King's Theatre. Turn-of-the-century pub (not the most recent one) recently renovated but losing none of its style. Still the best place in the city for pie and chips and a drink. Other traditional dishes, plus vegetarian, at amazing value.

The Horse Shoe Bar, 17 Drury La, between Mitchell St and Renfield St, near the station. Classic Victorian Gin Palace that is still one of the city's favourites. Its much-copied island bar is the longest continuous bar in the UK, so it shouldn't take long to get served, which is fortunate as it gets very busy. Incredibly good-value food served Mon-Sat 1200-1930, Sun 1230-1700 and perhaps the cheapest pint in town. If you only visit one pub during your stay, then make sure it's this one.

Kelly Cooper Bar, 158-166 Bath St, T0141-3314060. Style conscious newcomer on the Glasgow scene – dress to impress. Downstairs is **Lowdown**, which is another cool hangout that majors on cocktails.

Nice 'n' Sleazy, 421 Sauchiehall St, T0141-3330900. Great bar and music venue with an eclectic mix of people and music (see below). The upstairs bar is a favourite with musos who take advantage of the fine jukebox.

The Pot Still, 154 Hope St. Edwardian traditional pub justly famous for its massive range of malts (around 500 of them). They also have a selection of cask ales and decent pub grub during the day.

Rab Ha's, 83 Hutcheson St. This old Merchant City stalwart still packs 'em in. It has an enviable reputation for its food and is above the restaurant of the same name.

The Scotia Bar, 112 Stockwell St. This old East End pub also claims to be the oldest in town, and its low ceilings and wooden beams support a convincing argument. Its also the best place in town for folk music, see Entertainment p169, and much-frequented by writers, poets and drinking thinkers (or thinking drinkers).

Spy Bar, 153 Bath St T0141-221 7711. Another sleek style bar on Bath St and popular with a pre club crowd. Food ranges from sandwiches and soups to more substantial fare (food until 2000).

Strata, 45 Queen St T0141-2211888. Another horizontally cool city bar where you can strut your stuff before heading off to the clubs. Food until 2200.

The Victoria Bar, 159 Bridgegate. Real traditional howff in one of Glasgow's oldest streets. Seemingly unchanged since the late 19th century and long may it stay that way. One of the city's great pubs, where entertainment is provided free, courtesy of the local wags.

Clubs

Alaska, 142 Bath La, T0141-2481777. Everything from funk and soul to house music.

Archaos, 25 Queen St, T0141-2043189. A younger more dressy crowd come here for house, techno and club classics in this massive venue.

Arches, 253 Argyle St, T0901-0220300, www.thearches.co.uk. Cavernous space under Central station. Glasgow's finest and always at the cutting edge of the UK dance scene.

Babaza, 24 Royal Exchange Sq, T0141-2040101. Unusual interior, up-for-it crowd who love their R&B and hip hop.

Cube, 34 Queen St, T0141-2268990. Increasingly popular plays host to a musical mix of club nights 5 nights a week.

Fury Murry's, 96 Maxwell St, T0141-2216511. Behind the St Enoch Centre. An eclectic crowd get down to a mix of dance and student faves.

The Garage, 490 Sauchiehall St, T0141-3321120. Downbeat, sticky student haunt featuring the usual cheesy retro stuff that they seem to love, and cheap drinks, which always go down well. Occasional live bands. More of an old-fashioned getting bevvied up and copping off kind of place.

Havana, 50 Hope St, T0141-2484466. More of a bar with dancing, and only open till

0100 at weekends, but they play the hottest Latin grooves you can find.

MAS, 29 Royal Exchange Sq, T0141-2216381. Fool's Gold on Wed is indie and rock n' roll night, techno and house mix on Thu.

The Sub Club, 22 Jamaica St, T0141-2484600. One of the city's favourite clubs. House, techno, dance and anything else.

The Tunnel, 84 Mitchell St, T0141-2041000. A new Millennium and still going strong as one of the city's prime club venues.

Gay venues

Bennet's, 90 Glassford St, T0141-5525761. The main gay club. Wed-Sun 2300-0330.

Delmonica's, 68 Virginia St, T0141-5524803. Daily 1200-2400. Free. Fun with a very up-for-it crowd. DJs weekends, karaoke Sun nights.

Merchant Pride, 20 Candleriggs, T0141-5641285, Mon-Sun 1200-2400. Sociable bar with karaoke nights and jazz sessions on Sat.

Polo Lounge, 84 Wilson St, T0141-5531221. Mon-Thu 1700-0100, Fri-Sun 1700-0300. Happy Hour. Very classy bar popular with young professionals. Very busy at weekends.

Revolver, 6a John St, T0141-5532456. Mon-Sun 1200-2400. Free jukebox. Sexy new bar with interesting theme nights.

Sadie Frost's, 8-10 West George St, underneath Queen St station, T0141-3328005. Mon-Sat 1200-2400, Sun 1300-2400. Free. Very busy and noisy.

West End *p141, maps p142 and p144*

Bars

Firebird, 1321 Argyle St. Yet another of the city's style bars, but this one has the distinct advantage of providing excellent food, especially their pizzas. DJs most nights.

The Halt Bar, 160 Woodlands Rd. T0141-5641527. This erstwhile tram stop (hence the name) is one of Glasgow's great unspoiled pubs with many of the original Edwardian fixtures intact. Also a good place to see live music two or three times a week (see below).

Lock 27, 1100 Crow Rd. If the weather's fine (and it sometimes is), there are few nicer places to enjoy a spot of al fresco eating and drinking than this place by the Forth and Clyde Canal in Anniesland. Good food served until 2100 and kids are made welcome. You could take a stroll along the towpath afterwards.

The Tap, 1055 Sauchiehall St. Classic student haunt, within skiving distance of the university. Convivial atmosphere, cheap food and a good selection of ales on tap are all major attractions.

Tennent's, 191 Byres Rd. Big, no-nonsense, old West End favourite, serving a range of fine ales to a genuinely mixed crowd. It's also a great place for a chat (no loud music) and some very cheap food.

Uisge Beatha, 232 Woodlands Rd. The 'water of life' is one of those pubs you go into for a wee drink and you're still there many hours later, the day's plans in ruins around your feet. Looks and feels like a real Highland hostelry. Cosy and welcoming and serving ridiculously cheap food. Scottish in every sense, and 135 whiskies to choose from too.

South Side *p146*

Bars

Samuel Dow's, 69-71 Nithsdale Rd. Or Sammy Dow's as it's known by its many Shawlands regulars. A friendly Southside local serving good ale and cheap bar food. Also regular live folk music nights.

The Taverna, 778 Pollokshaws Rd. Popular Southside venue near the Tramway Theatre and Queen's Park. Nice, bright Mediterranean look and feel which extends to their love of kids. Good selection of ales and European beers and good value food, especially their pre-theatre dinner.

Tusk, 18 Moss Side Rd, T0141-6499199. Opulent Asian interior at this popular Southside style bar – a huge Buddha watches over proceedings.

Entertainment

It's been a few years now since Glasgow was chosen as City of Culture but the legacy lives on and the city continues to enjoy a wide span of art, theatre, film and music. The majority of the larger theatres, concert halls and cinemas are concentrated in the city centre, though its two most renowned theatres, **the Citizens'** and **the Tramway**, are to be found south of the Clyde.

Details of all the city's events are listed in the two local newspapers, *The Herald* and the *Evening Times*. Another excellent source of information is the fortnightly listings magazine *The List*, www.list.co.uk, which also covers Edinburgh and which is on sale in most newsagents. To book tickets for concerts or theatre productions, call at the **Ticket Centre**, City Hall, Candleriggs, Mon-Sat 0900-1800; Sun 1200-1700. Phone bookings T0141-2874000, Mon-Sat 0900-2100; Sun 0900-1800. Note that some of the live music venues don't have their own box office. For tickets and information go to **Tower Records**, Argyle St, T0141-2045788.

Cinemas

There are mainstream multiplexes throughout the city and a few art house cinemas.

Glasgow Film Theatre (GFT), 12 Rose St, T0141-3328128, an excellent programme of art house movies and a good bar for discussion later.

Grosvenor, Ashton La, off Byres Rd in the West End, T0141-3398444. An old 2-screen cinema recently refurbished, showing art house and mainstream films.

Odeon Cinema, 56 Renfield St, T0870-5050007. A 9-screen multiplex.

Comedy

Blackfriars, 36 Bell St, T0141-5525924. Regular slots on Sun nights. Also live jazz (see below).

The Stand Comedy Club, 333 Woodlands Rd, T0870-6006055, www.thestand.co.uk. Top notch comedy Thu-Sun.

The State Bar, 148 Holland St, T0141-3322159. Good comedy club on Sat nights. Also live blues on Tue and a good selection of real ales. Not a bad pub, actually.

Concerts

City Halls, Candleriggs, T0141-3538000. Smaller-scale classical music events. Home of the Scottish Chamber Orchestra.

Henry Wood Hall, 73 Claremont St, T0141-2253555, www.rsno.org.uk. HQ of the Royal Scottish National Orchestra.

Royal Concert Hall, 2 Sauchiehall St, T0141-3538080, www.grch.com. Prestigious venue for orchestras and big-name rock, pop and soul acts.

Royal Scottish Academy of Music and Drama, 100 Renfrew St, T0141-3324101, www.rsamd.ac.uk. Varied programme of international performances.

Theatre Royal, Hope St, T0141-3323321, www.theatreroyalglasgow.com. The home of the generally excellent Scottish Opera and Scottish Ballet, also regularly hosts large-scale touring theatre and dance companies and orchestras.

Live music

Barrowlands, Gallowgate, T0141-5524601. Famous old East End ballroom and now Glasgow's liveliest and best-loved gig venue. Popular with acts breaking through and big names trying to rediscover what it's about.

Cathouse, 15 Union St, T0141-2486606. Glasgow's only rock club. Ideal for seeing bands before they make it big.

Clutha Vaults, 167 Stockwell St, T0141-5527520. Well-known pub which has live music nights from a wide range of local talent.

Cottier's, 93-95 Hyndland St, T0141-3575825. Good venue for more esoteric music acts, also jazz and blues, see also Eating p160.

The Garage, 490 Sauchiehall St, T0141-3321120. Medium-sized venue for bands on the verge of a breakthrough.

The Halt Bar, 160 Woodlands Rd, T0141-5641527. Popular bar featuring live indie/pub rock bands two or three times a week, see also Bars and clubs p167.

King Tut's Wah Wah Hut, 272a St Vincent St, T0141-2215279. Glasgow's hallowed live music venue. Many a famous band has made the break in this cramped, sweaty club. Good bar downstairs for a pre-gig drink.

Nice 'n' Sleazy, 421 Sauchiehall St, T0141-3330900. Great bar and music venue. Everything from indie to rock.

The Scotia Bar, 112 Stockwell St, T0141-5528681. A Glasgow institution and home of Glasgow's folk scene.

Scottish Exhibition and Conference Centre (SECC), Finnieston Quay, T0141-2483000. Gigantic multi-purpose venue with all the atmosphere of a disused aircraft hangar. Plays host to the likes of Robbie Williams and Pavarotti.
13th Note Café, 50-60 King St, T0141-5531638. A major player on the alternative live music scene. Popular and lively venue for up-and-coming indie/rock bands.

Theatre

The Arches, 30 Midland St, T0141-5651023. In the railway arches under Central station. Presents more radical and experimental theatre. Also home to one of the city's major clubs, see Bars and clubs p167.
Centre for Contemporary Arts (CCA), 350 Sauchiehall St, T0141-3524900. Hosts contemporary dance and theatre, as well as staging various art exhibitions.
Citizens' Theatre, 119 Gorbals St, T0141-4290022, www.citz.co.uk. Just across the river. Home to some of the UK's most exciting and innovative drama. Main auditorium and two smaller studios. Big discounts for students and the unemployed.
King's Theatre, 294 Bath St, T0141-2401300, www.kings-glasgow.co.uk. The city's main traditional theatre presenting musicals, panto and that kind of thing.
Mitchell Theatre, 6 Granville St, T0845-3303501. At Charing Cross. Stages various drama productions as well as occasional jazz concerts. Theatre Royal (see Concert halls above). Primarily a concert hall but also stages high-brow theatre, darling.
Tramway Theatre, 25 Albert Dr, T0845-3303501. Just off Pollokshaws Rd. Internationally-renowned venue with varied programme of innovative and influential theatre, dance, music and art exhibitions.
Tron Theatre, 63 Trongate, T0141-5524267. Major contemporary theatre productions. Also musical performances and big-name comedy acts. Home to a very fine bar and restaurant, see Eating p160.

Festivals and events

Glasgow doesn't like to be overshadowed by Edinburgh, and has a few notable festivals.
Jan: **Celtic Connections music festival** features artists from around the world. It is held in the various venues, T0141-3538000, www.celticconnections.co.uk.
Jun: **West End Festival**, 2 weeks of music, theatre and various free events, T0141-3410844, www.westendfestival.co.uk.
Jun: **RSNO Proms**, at the Royal Concert Hall.
Jul: **Glasgow International Jazz Festival**, T0141-5523552, www.jazzfest.co.uk.
Mid-Aug: **World Pipe Band Championships**, T0845 241 4400.
Late Oct to early Nov: **Lesbian and gay arts festival** held in various venues, T0141-3347126, www.glasgay.co.uk, is Britain's largest. See also www.seeglasgow.com.

Shopping

Glasgow is a shopaholic's paradise – particularly for anyone seeking clothes. Locals love fashion and are happy to spend their money on good clobber – so were staggered when **Harvey Nicks** chose to locate their first Scottish store in staid old Edinburgh rather than streetwise Glasgow. Despite that snub, Glasgow is still the best shopping city in the UK after London and there are endless opportunities for retail therapy.

Merchant City is the city's most upmarket shopping area, and fashionistas should click their Manola clad feet over to the classy **Italian Centre**, which has branches of Armani and Versace. There are some huge shopping malls too, like the Buchanan Galleries near Queen St station, which has a large branch of the **John Lewis** department store, as well as all the usual high street suspects. There's also the ever classy Princes Sq, which has a good mix of designer stores and gift shops. Buchanan St is the most upmarket of the city's central retail thoroughfares, while cheaper outlets are focused on Sauchiehall St and Argyle St. The

West End is the place to go for more off-beat and quirky purchases, with designer jewellers, vintage and individual clothes shops, and second-hand bookshops. Often overlooked is the area round King St which has loads of individual galleries and is a great place for anyone looking for contemporary artworks to take home.

Art and antiques **Glasgow Print Studio Galleries**, 22-25, King St, T0141-5520704, www.gpsart.co.uk. Tue-Sat 1000-1730. One of the largest publishers of original prints in the UK. They display and sell etchings, lithographs and screenprints by over 300 artists including well known names like Elizabeth Blackadder, Ken Currie, Peter Howson and Adrian Wiszniewski.

Hutcheson's Hall, 158 Ingram St, T0141-552 8391. A good place to find original crafts by Scottish designers. Worth browsing for unusual gifts – real Glasgow Style.

Victorian Village, 93, West Regent St, T0141-332 0808, Mon-Sat 1000-1700. Covers several floors and has a selection of individual traders who sell lovely costume jewellery, antiques and retro clothing.

Books **Borders**, 98 Buchanan St, T0141-222 7700, Mon-Sat 0830-2200, Sun 1000-2000. Great selection of books on Glasgow and Scotland, as well as hefty sections on travel and fiction. Lots of magazines and newspapers and there's a café and toilet too, so you can spend an hour or two here easily.

Ottakars, 6 Buchanan Galleries, T0141-3531500, Mon-Wed, Fri, Sat 0900-1800, Thu 0900-2000, Sun 1100-1730. Good children's section and a coffee shop with squashy sofas.

Voltaire and Rousseau, 12-14 Otago La, T0141-3391811, Mon-Sat 1000-1800, is an old established antiquarian bookstore and a favourite with students. The two resident cats are an added attraction and have their own unofficial fan club.

Clothes and shoes Pedestrianized Buchanan St has plenty of good clothes and shoe shops like **Dune**, **Nine West**, **Diesel**, **Hobbs**, **Karen Millen**, **Miss Sixty**, **Planet**, **Boss** and **Office**.

Urban Outfitters, No 157, T0141-2489203, which is full of '70s items and retro gear. Mon-Wed and Fri, Sat 0930-1830, Thu 0930-1800, Sun 1200-1800.

Designer Exchange, 17 Royal Exchange Sq, near **Roganos**, T0141-221 6898, Tue-Sat winter 1030-1630, summer 1000-1700. Has loads of nearly new designer clothes, samples and accessories. Great place for a bargain.

Moon, 10 Ruthven lane, T0141-339 2315. Mon-Sat 1000-1730. Good outlet for women's designer clothes, stocking names like Betty Jackson.

Mr Ben, Studio 6 Kings Court, Kings St, T0141-5531936, Mon-Sat 1030-1730, Sun 1230-1700. Good range of retro clothing. They'll fit you out with jeans, ballgowns – or even old nylon Y-fronts.

Pink Poodle, 181 Byres Rd, T 3573344, Mon-Sat 1000-1800, Sun 1200-1700, women's fashion labels like Miss Sixty and others which will really put some va va voom into your wardrobe.

Saratoga Trunk, Unit 10, 61 Hydepark St, T0141-2214433. Mon-Fri 1030-1700. Also has a small outlet in Victorian Village. For the widest range of vintage and retro clothing. It's an enormous Aladdin's cave of a warehouse stuffed with the most extraordinary range of clothes from beautiful beaded dresses to swirly 1960s gear. The staff are very friendly and they also have brilliant jewellery and accessories. They supply gear for film and TV crews. Well worth the journey if you like a good rummage.

Slaters, 165 Howard St T0141-5527171. Mon-Wed, Fri, Sat 0830-1730, Thu 0830-1930, Sun 1130-1630. A famous and enormous menswear store which has become something of a Glasgow institution.

Starry Starry Night, 19 Dowanside La, T0141-3371837. Mon-Sat 1000-1730. Has a wide range of old and vintage clothes from the 1980s back to Victorian times.

The Italian Centre, 19 John St, Merchant City, T0141-5522277. Mon-Wed, Fri 1000-1800, Thu 1000-1900, Sat 1000-1830. Has branches of Armani and other upmarket shops, cafés, restaurants. Friendly Glaswegian staff make these less intimidating than they are in other cities – though you still wouldn't want to come on a 'fat day'.

There's also a Cruise, 180 Ingram St, T0141-5723232. Mon-Wed 0930-1800, Thu 1000-1900, Fri 0930-1900, Sat 0900-1800 and Sun 1200-1700. The hottest outlet for designer gear in the city stocking everything from Prada and Gucci to Oki-ni and Boyd.

Food and drink **Heart Buchanan**, Byres Rd, T0141-3347626, Mon-Sat 0830-2130, Sun 1200-1900. Brilliant deli with lots of fresh sandwiches and cakes. They specialize in restaurant quality takehome meals to reheat – there's a veggie meal each day.

Ian Mellis, 492 Great Western Rd, T0141-339 8998. 0930-1800 Mon-Wed, Thu 0930-1830, Fri 0930-1900, Sat 0900-1800, Sun 1100-1700. Wonderful cheese shop full of unusual varieties of cheese ranging from strong blues, to creamy bries. Choose from around 45 types. Great range of Scottish cheeses like Isle of Mull cheddar or Criffel, a soft cheese, and plenty of Irish cheeses too such as the unusual Coolea.

Peckham's, 124 Byres Rd, T0141-3571454, 0900-2400 daily. Great outlet stocking fine wines and all sorts of scrummy foods for posh picnics and treats.

Jewellery **Bethsy Gray** is a jewellery designer specializing in silver with a shop/workshop in **Starry Starry Night** (see above).

De Courcey's Arcade, 5-21 Cresswell La, T0141-3346673. Has a brilliant selection of goods from different traders. You can find jewellery, as well as antiques, pottery, 'Glasgow Style' artefacts, etc.

Orro, 49 Bank St, West End T0141-3576999, Tue-Sat 1030-1730, is a sleek contemporary jewellers'. There's also a branch in the Merchant City, 12 Wilson St, T0141-552 7888, Tue-Sat 1100-1730.

Kilts **Geoffrey (Tailor) Kiltmakers**, 309 Sauchiehall St, T0141-3312388, Mon-Wed, Fri, Sat 0900-1730, Thu 0900-1900, Sun 1100-1700. Not just traditional kilts but contemporary numbers too.

Hector Russell (soon to be renamed RJ Lawrie), 110 Buchanan St, T0141-2210217. Mon-Sat 0900-1730, Sun 1100-1700. Well-known kiltmakers who will measure you up for a kilt in your tartan. Kilts for hire too.

Markets **The Barras**, London Rd. Sat, Sun 0900-1700. This is Glasgow's famous East End market with over 1,000 traders flogging their wares. Worth coming if only to hear their patter.

Music **Avalanche Records**, 34 Dundas St, T0141-332 2099. Mon-Sat 0930-1800, Sun 1200-1800. Lots of obscure labels and vintage vinyl.

Fopp Records, 358 Byres Rd, T0141-357 0774. Mon-Sat 0930-1900, Sun 1100-1800. The successful chain flogging the chart hits for discounted prices.

Outdoor gear **Graham Tiso**, 129 Buchanan St, T0141-2484877. Mon-Tue, Thu-Sat 0930-1730, Wed 1000-1730, Sun 1200-1700. The outdoor shop, which has 5 floors of boots, waterproofs, maps and anything else you'll need for exploring the hills.

Shopping malls **Buchanan Galleries**, T0141-333 9898. Mon-Wed, Fri, Sat 0900-1800, Thu 0900-2000, Sun 1100-1700. Has a large branch of the **John Lewis** department store, and clothes shops like Mango, Morgan, Gap and **H&M**.

Princes Square, Buchanan St, T0141-221 0324. Mon-Wed and Fri 0930-1800, Thu 0930-2000, Sat 0900-1800, Sun 1200-1700. Classy shopping centre with a Rennie Mackintosh theme. Clothes and shoe shops here include **French Connection, Whistles, Calvin Klein, Monsoon** and **Jo Malone** for women and **Ted Baker, Hugo** and **Lacoste** for men. For unusual gifts there's Illuminati and for cosmetics and perfumes there's **Space NK** and **Penhaligons**. There's also a branch of **Bo Concept** for all sorts of cool homewares.

St Enoch Centre, Argyle St, T0141-2043900, Mon-Sat 0900-1800 (Thu till 2000), Sun 1100-1730. Huge mall crammed with all the usual high-street suspects and places to re-fuel.

▲ Activities and tours

Boat trips

Seaforce, T0141-2211070, www.seaforce.co.uk. 0800-2200. Trips all year, must be booked. Next to the **Tall Ship**, a company offering high speed powerboat trips along the Clyde. Trips range from a 15 min 'taster' (£3.00) to a 4-hr trip to the village of Kilcreggan (includes a chance to visit the village), costs £35, £15 concession. There's also a mystery tour which goes to, well, it's a surprise, costs £50, lunch included, £25 concession.

The Clyde Waterbus, T07711-250 969, www.clydewaterbusservices.co.uk. Trips go about every 1½ hrs and include a commentary on the history of the river. Services run Mon-Fri from 1045-1815, Sat from 1115, Sun from 1145. £3, £5 return, concession £2/£3.50. *Pride of the Clyde*, is a riverbus that runs along the Clyde between Broomielaw and Braehead (where there is the large Braehead shopping centre and Clydebuilt maritime museum).

The Waverley, T0141-2218152, www.waverleyexcusions.co.uk. Sailings take place from Easter-mid May and from Office open summer Mon-Fri 0900-1700, Sat 0900-1300, winter Mon-Fri 0900-1700. Trips range from £10-30. At Anderston Quay, east of the Science Centre is the world's last ocean going paddle steamer and one of a former fleet of pleasure boats that used to take Glaswegians on trips 'doon the watter' to Clyde coast resorts. She has now completed a £7 mn refit and has been restored to her original glory. You can take still take day-trips on the *Waverley* along the Clyde to Dunnoon, Largs, the Kyles of Bute and Arran, etc.

Bus tours

City Sightseeing Glasgow, T0141-2040444, www.CitySightseeingGlasgow.co.uk, costing £8, £6 concession, £3 children, £19.50 family (2 adults, up to 4 children). The complete tour takes in Glasgow Cathedral, the Merchant City, the People's Palace, the Tall Ship and the Transport Museum. It lasts 1 hr 20 mins, although you can hop on and off as you please. Tours leave from George Sq and run every 15 mins (from 0930 in summer).

Glasgow Corporation Transport, T0845-1208091, £6, £3.50 concessions/children, tickets valid for 2 days. Open-top bus tour that runs from George Sq every 30 mins. The tour last 1 hr 20mins and again covers all the main sites like the Cathedral and the Tall ship. You can hop on and off all day.

Cycling

There are several scenic cycle paths in and around the city, giving the visitor the opportunity to escape the noise and traffic and to stretch their legs. There are also several long-distance cycle routes which start in Glasgow. The tourist office has a wide range of maps and leaflets detailing these routes, which follow quiet back streets, public parks and disused railways for much of the way. Many of the routes start at Bell's Bridge (by the SECC). For the most up to date information on the expanding network of cycle routes in the area, and throughout the country, contact **Sustrans**, 162 Fountainbridge, Edinburgh, T0131-624 7660, www.sustrans.org.uk or www.cyclingscotland.com. A useful book is *25 Cycle Routes In and Around Glasgow*, E.B. Wilkie (HMSO). For bike hire, see p177.

The Clyde Coast Cycle Routes run from Bell's Bridge at the SECC through some of the city's parks and closely follows the old Paisley-Ardrossan Canal to Greenock, Gourock and on to Ardrossan, for ferries to the Isle of Arran. It's 28 miles one way as far as Gourock and the route is covered by the *Glasgow and Clyde Coast Cycle Routes* leaflets; Glasgow to Paisley and Paisley to Greenock sections. There is also a **Clyde to Forth Cycle Route**, a Millennium cycle route that runs between Edinburgh and Gourock.

The **Glasgow-Loch Lomond Cycle Way** is for both walkers and cyclists. It runs for 21 miles from the centre of Glasgow, following a disused railway track to Clydebank, the Forth and Clyde Canal towpath to Bowling, then a disused railway to Dumbarton, and finally reaching Loch Lomond by way of the River Leven. The route continues all the way to Killin, in the heart of the Perthshire Highlands, via Balloch, Aberfoyle and Callander.

Football

The two main Glasgow teams are **Rangers** and **Celtic**, who regularly attract crowds of over 50,000 and are two of the wealthiest clubs in Britain. The domestic football season runs from Aug to mid-May. Most matches are played on Sat and there are also games during the week on Tue and Wed evenings. Ticket prices are around £20.

Celtic FC are based at Celtic Park, Parkhead, T0141-5562611, www.celticfc.net, while their bitter rivals **Rangers FC** are based at Ibrox Stadium, T0870-600 1972, www.rangers.co.uk. The national team plays at Hampden Park, which is also the location of the **National Football Museum**, see p149.

Golf

There are many municipal courses in and around Glasgow, as well as several top-class championship courses within easy reach of the city. Green fees will often cost from £40

upwards. Among the courses are:
Haggs Castle, 70 Dumbreck Rd, an 18-hole course. Visitors Mon-Fri;
Knightswood Golf Course, Lincoln Ave, T0141-959 6358, a 9-hole course;
Lethamhill Golf course, 1240 Cumbernauld Rd, T0141-770 6220, www.glasgow.gov.uk, which also has 18 holes; and
World of Golf centre, 2700 Great Western Rd, Clydebank, T0141-944 4141, www.worldofgolf-uk.co.uk, which has a large driving range and a teaching academy.
Loch Lomond, Luss, T01436 860223, www.lochlomond.com;
Prestwick, Prestwick, T01292 477404, www.prestwickgc.co.uk;
Royal Troon, Troon, T01292 311555; and
Turnberry, Ayrshire, T01655 331000, www.turnberry.co.uk.

Taxi tours

Glasgow Taxis, T0141-4297070, www.glasgowtaxisltd.co.uk. Glasgow taxi drivers are known for their patter and knowledge of the city, so a taxi tour is a option worth considering. City tours last 1 hr and take you round all the main places of interest, £25 per taxi (maximum 5 passengers), available 24 hrs. There's also a 2-hr tour, which also takes you past Southside attractions like Scotland St School Museum, House for an Art Lover and the Burrell Collection (where you can finish the tour if you choose), £45 per taxi. Pick- ups can be at any point on the route.

Walking tours

Journeyman Tours, T0800-0939984, www.journeymantours.co.uk. If you fancy a night out as well as an informative tour, try Journeyman's Glasgow Fling. It's a night time tour that takes you round the Merchant City, stopping for refreshment at various pubs along the way and ends up at a ceilidh club. Starts from the war memorial in George Sq at 1900 on Fri, Sat and ends around midnight. Price of £15 per adult includes some drinks and entry to ceilidh club. They also do a history tour **Secrets of the Merchant City** that leaves George Sq at 1930 Thu-Sun. £5, £4 concession, £2.50 children, under 12s free.
Mercat Glasgow, T0141-5865378, www.mercat-glasgow.co.uk. Their Horror Walks leave from George Sq and they also offer themed walks on various aspects of Glasgow's history. £7.
Walkabout Tours, T0141-2432437, www.walkabout-tours.com. This is a great option to those who hate that feeling of being herded around the city .You pick up one of their audio machines from the Tourist Office in George Sq, then use it to guide you around, with a running commentary giving you the background to the sights. £5 per day, family £15 - 2 adults, 2 children – proof of ID required.

Transport

Glasgow *p129*

Air

Glasgow International airport is the main departure point in Scotland for flights to North America. There are also regular flights to several European destinations and many domestic flights. There are also flights to Glasgow Prestwick. See also p30 and p126.

Airlines include: **Aer Lingus**, T0845-084 4777, www.aerlingus.com; **BMI Baby**, T0870-264 2229, www.bmibaby.com; **British Airways**, T08457-733377, www.britishairways.com; **Easy Jet**, T0870-600 0000, www.easyjet.com; **Emirates**, T0870-243 2222, www.emirates. com/uk; **Fly Be**, T0870-567 6676; **Icelandair**, T0845-7581111, www.icelandair.com; **KLM**, T0870-507 4047, www.klm.com.

Bus

For short trips in the city fares are £0.80, all-day tickets £2.50. On most buses you'll need to have exact change. After midnight till 0400, there's a limited night bus service (more frequent at weekends). A good way to get around town is to buy a ticket for one of the guided bus tours, see p173.

For longer journeys, **Scottish Citylink**, T08705 505050, www.citylink.co.uk, runs services to most major towns in Scotland. There are buses to **Edinburgh** every 20 mins (1¼ hrs, £4 single, £6 return); half hourly buses to **Stirling** (45 mins, £4 single) and hourly **Inverness** (4 hrs, £15.50); 13 buses daily to **Aberdeen** (4 hrs, £16); 3 daily to **Oban** (3 hrs, £12.20); 4 daily to **Fort William** (3 hrs, £13); 3 daily to **Portree** (7 hrs, £22); and half hourly to **Perth** (1½ hrs, £8.80 day return) and **Dundee** (2¼ hrs, £8.80 single). **First Glasgow** (T0141-423 6600, www.firstgroup.com) runs buses to **Milngavie**, at the start of the West Highland Way (40 mins, £1.15 single).

Car hire

Arnold Clark, 188 Castlebank St, T0141-339 98861 (also at the airport, T0141-8480202), www.arnoldclark.com. **Avis**, 70 Lancefield St, T0141-2212877 (also at the airport, T0141-8872261), www.avis.co.uk. **Hertz**, 138 Hydepark St, T0141-2487736 (also at the airport, T0141-8877845), www.hertz.co.uk. Enterprise, 45 Finnieston St, Unit 4, T0141-2212124, www.enterprise.com.

Cycle hire

West End Cycles, 16 Chancellor St, T0141-3571344, south end of Byres Rd. £12 per day for mountain bikes, £50 per week. ID and £50 deposit required. For bike tours, see p173.

Taxi

There are taxi ranks at Central and Queen St train stations and Buchanan bus station. To call a cab, try Glasgow Taxis, T0141-4292900, who also run city tours. Minimum fare around the city centre is £2. To the Burrell collection from the city centre (about 3 miles) should cost around £8-9.

Train

Trains leave from Glasgow Central mainline station to all destinations south of the Clyde, including to **Greenock** (for ferries to Dunoon), **Wemyss Bay** (for ferries to Rothesay), **Ardrossan** (for ferries to Arran) and to Prestwick airport. There's a low-level station below Central station which connects the southeast of the city with the northwest. This cross-city line serves the SECC and a branch runs north to **Milngavie**, at the start of the West Highland Way. There's also a line from Queen St which runs west all the way to **Helensburgh**, via **Partick** and **Dumbarton**. Branches of this line run to **Balloch**, at the south end of **Loch Lomond**, and **Milngavie**.

Scotrail also operates the West Highland line from Queen St north to **Oban** (3 daily, 3 hrs), **Fort William** (3 daily, 3¾ hrs) and **Mallaig** (3 daily, 5¼ hrs). ScotRail also run services to **Edinburgh** (every 15 mins, (30 mins between 1900-0700) 50 mins, £7.90 cheap day return), **Perth** (hourly, 1 hr), **Dundee** (hourly, 1 hr 20 mins), **Aberdeen** (hourly, 2½ hrs), **Stirling** (every 30 mins, 30 mins) and **Inverness** (3 daily, 3½ hrs).

Underground

Locals affectionately call it the 'Clockwork Orange', as there's only one circular route serving 15 stops and the trains are bright orange. It's easy to use and there's a flat fare of £0.90, or you can buy a day ticket for £2.50. Trains run roughly every 5-8 mins from approximately 0630 till 2235 Mon-Sat and from 1100 till 1750 on Sun.

Excursions *p152*

Paisley

There are frequent buses, which stop at the abbey. Buses depart from Gilmour St station every 10 mins for Glasgow Airport, 2 miles north of town. There are frequent **trains** to Gilmour St station from Glasgow Central.

Firth of Clyde

There are buses every hour from Buchanan bus station and regular trains to **Greenock** from Glasgow Central.

At **Gourock and Wemyss Bay** ferries leave frequently every day on the 20-min crossing. For details call CalMac T0870-5650000. Western Ferries, T01369-704452, also runs a ferry service (every ½ hr) between **Gourock** and **Dunoon**. They leave from McInroy's point, 2 miles from the train station, from where Citylink buses also depart. Clyde Marine, T01475-721281, www.clyde-marine.co.uk, runs a frequent passenger-only ferry service to **Kilcreggan** (10 mins) and a less frequent service (40 mins) to **Helensburgh** (see p303), daily. Clyde Marine also run cruises on the Firth of Clyde to **Brodick on Arran**, **Tighnabruaich**, or **Tarbert** on Loch Fyne (Jun-Aug). Note that these leave from Victoria Harbour by the station. Trains and buses to Glasgow are the same as for Greenock. Gourock train station is next to the CalMac ferry terminal.

To **Dumbarton** there are trains to Dumbarton Central and Dumbarton East stations running regularly from Helensburgh, Balloch, and Glasgow Queen St.

The Clyde Valley

Trains to **Blantyre** leave from **Glasgow Central** every ½ hr. It's a 20-min journey. Buses run regularly from Buchanan bus station; take nos 63 or 67 for **Blantyre** and nos 55 or 56 for **Bothwell**.

For **East Kilbride**, take First Bus 31 from the St Enoch Centre in Glasgow to Stewartfield Way, or a train.
To **Lanark** there are hourly trains from Central station. There's an hourly bus service from Lanark train station to **New Lanark**, but the 20-min walk is recommended for the wonderful views. The last bus back uphill from the village leaves at 1700. To book a taxi, call **Clydewide**, T01555-663813.

Directory

Banks

Bank of Scotland, 235 Sauchiehall St, 2 Trongate; **Royal Bank of Scotland**, 339 Byres Rd, 393 Sauchiehall St; **Clydesdale Bank**, 1 Woodside Cres, Charing Cross. English banks include **Barclays**, 90 St Vincent St and **Lloyds TSB**, Ingram St.

Consulates

Germany, 158 West Regent St, T0141-2210304.
Italy, 24 St Enoch Sq, T0141-2263000.
Norway, 80 Oswald St, T0141-2041353.
Spain, 389 Argyle St, T0141-2216943.
Sweden, 16 Robertson St, T0141-2217845.

Currency exchange

American Express, 115 Hope St, T0870 6001060, open Mon-Fri 0830-1730, Sat 0900-1200; **Thomas Cook**, Central station, T0141-207 3400/3407, open Mon-Wed and Sat 0800-1900, Thu and Fri 0800-2000, Sun 1000-1800.

Dentists

For dental emergencies go to the **Glasgow Dental Hospital**, 378 Sauchiehall St, T0141-2119600.

Gay and lesbian

Lesbian and Gay Switchboard, T0141-8470447, open daily 0700-2200; **Stonewall Scotland**, LGBT Centre, 11 Dixon St, T0141-2040746.

Hospitals

Glasgow Royal Infirmary, 84 Castle St, T0141-2114000, near the cathedral; **The Southern General Hospital**, Govan Rd, T0141-2011100, main South Side hospital.

Internet

EasyEverything, 57 St Vincent St, T0141-2222365, huge facility and the cheapest service in town.

Post

The main post office, 47 St Vincent St, T0345-222344. Services include poste restante, currency exchange and cash withdrawal at the **German Savings Bank**. Open Mon-Fri 0830-1745, Sat 0900-1900. Also branches at 85-89 Bothwell St, 228 Hope St and 533 Sauchiehall St. Post offices in some supermarkets are open on Sun.

Left luggage

There's an office at **Buchanan bus station**, daily 0630-2230. Also lockers at Central and Queen St train stations (£2 per day).

Pharmacies

Superdrug, Central station, T0141-2218197; Mon-Fri, till 2130, Sat, Sun till 1700; **Munroes'**, 693 Great Western Rd, T0141-3390012; open daily till 2100.

Police

945 Argyle St, T0141-5323200. Free emergency numbers are T999 or T112.

Travel agents

STA Travel, 184 Byres Rd, T0141-3386000 and at 112 George St, T0141-5526505; **Flight Centre UK**, 280 Sauchiehall St, T0141-3531351.

Southern Scotland

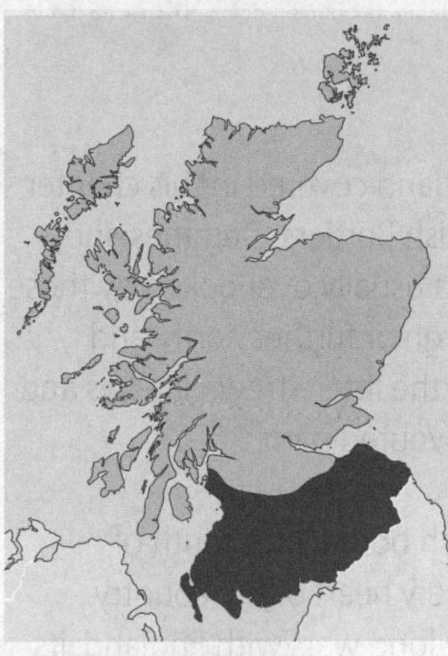

Footprint features

Introduction

The vast swathe of Southern Scotland covered in this chapter comprises East Lothian, the Scottish Borders, Dumfries and Galloway and Ayrshire. It's an area usually overlooked by those on their way to Glasgow, Edinburgh or further north, and consequently relatively free from the litter-strewn lay-bys and crowded beauty spots of more favoured parts.

Despite its proximity to the English border, the south of Scotland is in many ways at the very heart of the country. Under constant threat during the long wars with England, its people were at the front line in the defence of Scottish nationhood. It is therefore no coincidence that Scotland's two greatest literary figures, **Robert Burns** and **Sir Walter Scott**, were born and lived here.

Southern Scotland is divided neatly by the A74(M), the main route from England to Scotland. To the east of this line the main tourist focus is the **Borders region**, with its peaceful little mill towns, in particular lovely little **Melrose**. To the north are the narrow ranges of the **Lammermuir**, **Moorfoot** and **Pentland Hills**. North of the Lammermuirs is **East Lothian**, with its sandy bays and rugged coastline.

The landscape becomes ever more wild and mountainous as you head west from the **Tweed Valley** across the **Southern Uplands**. The most spectacular scenery is west of Dumfries, in the **Galloway Forest Park**. The **Solway coast**, from Dumfries to the Mull of Galloway, is equally appealing. North of Galloway is the **Ayrshire coast**, lined with seaside resorts and some great golf courses, and best known for its associations with Robert Burns, especially **Alloway**, where he was born.

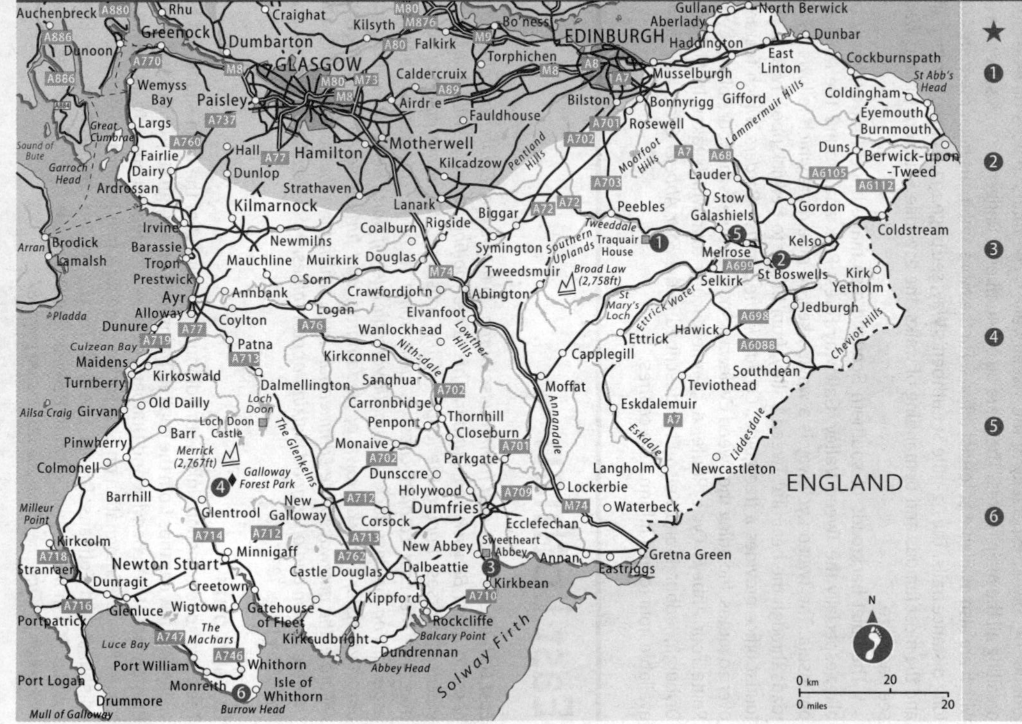

★ Don't miss...

1. **Traquair House** Take a trip back in time with a visit to one of Scotland's great country houses, page 190.
2. **Dryburgh Abbey** Set among ancient cedars, this is one of the most beautiful and evocative of the border abbeys, page 193.
3. **Sweetheart Abbey** Lose your heart in this romantic ruin, on the beautiful Solway coast, page 213.
4. **Galloway Forest Park** Explore this wild and rugged park, where you can see red deer and even golden eagles, page 217.
5. **Eildon Hills** Take a walk on the magic side, in this enchanted area, which overlooks the lovely border town of Melrose, page 192.
6. **Isle of Whithorn** On a balmy summer evening have dinner at the Steampacket Inn in this atmospheric old fishing village, page 219.

Ins and outs

Getting there and around

Bus services are good around Ayrshire, East Lothian and between the main towns in the Borders, and there are also regular services between Dumfries and Stranraer, along the A75, but services to more remote parts are limited. Train services are limited to the line north from Berwick-upon-Tweed to Edinburgh on the east coast, and lines from Dumfries and Stranraer to Ayrshire in the west, with links to Glasgow. Details of all public transport services are given under the relevant towns and villages. Phone numbers of travel information lines and the main operators are also given. Bus timetables are available at local tourist offices.

There aren't any organized Burn's tours as such. The Burns Heritage Centre in Alloway, see page 230, has literature to help you with an independent trail.

The south of Scotland is excellent walking country, and there are numerous marked trails through the forests and hills and circular walks around the towns, especially in the Tweed Valley. The tourist offices have leaflets detailing all the main routes. There are also a number of Ranger-led walks, details of which are also available at tourist offices. For the more ambitious hiker there are two long-distance trails. The 62-mile St Cuthbert's Way, see page 192, a cross-border trail, and the most famous and demanding of walks, the 212-mile Southern Upland Way, see page 220.

The quiet backroads of southern Scotland also make it ideal for exploring by bike, especially the Tweed Valley, Galloway Forest Park and around The Machars peninsula. The Tweed Cycleway is a waymarked 90-mile route which follows minor roads through the beautiful Tweed Valley, from Biggar to Berwick-upon-Tweed. The tourist office provides a free guide, *Cycling in the Scottish Borders*, which features over 20 routes, including the Tweed Cycleway. Another route is the Four Abbeys Cycle Route Four Abbeys Cycle Route, a 55-mile circular tour which takes in Melrose, Dryburgh, Jedburgh and Kelso. It is described in the *Four Abbeys Cycle Way* guide available from tourist information centres.

East Lothian

East Lothian stretches east from Musselburgh, to the east of Edinburgh, along the coast to North Berwick and Dunbar. This is real golfing country, with a string of excellent courses running the length of the coast, and there are miles of sandy beaches. The East Lothian coast is also home to huge colonies of seabirds, especially on the Bass Rock, a dramatic volcanic islet off North Berwick. Inland is the attractive historic market town of Haddington, and further south the village of Gifford is the gateway to the Lammermuir Hills, which form the boundary with the Borders region and offer good walking opportunities. ▸▸ *For Sleeping, Eating and other listings, see pages 186-187.*

Ins and outs

There are good transport links with Edinburgh and most of the main sights can be visited in a few day trips from the capital. Trains from Edinburgh stop in Musselburgh, Prestonpans, North Berwick and Dunbar. There are also regular buses to all the main towns. For more information on East Lothian and for a free accommodation, contact Edinburgh and Lothians Tourist Board ⓘ *T0131-4733800*, *www.eltb.org*, or East Lothian TICs in Musselburgh, North Berwick and Dunbar. ▸▸ *For further public transport information call Traveline, T0800-232323, and see page 187.*

Musselburgh to North Berwick

→ *Phone code: 0131. Colour map 6, grid A2.*

Musselburgh

Six miles east of Edinburgh, across the River Esk, is the town of Musselburgh. It's a fairly humdrum place, but may be of interest to golfing enthusiasts as the original home of golf; **Royal Musselbugh** is one of the oldest clubs in the country. It is also a target for naturalists who come to see the huge populations of migrating waders, ducks and seabirds which flock to the mouth of the River Esk. Ice cream lovers may also be interested to note that **Luca's** on the High Street has most of the competition licked and is definitely worth a stop if you're passing by. There's also a TIC ⓘ *just off the A1 at Old Craighall, T0131-6536172, daily in summer, Oct-Mar Mon-Sat only.*

Aberlady and around

Ten miles east of Musselburgh is the conservation village of Aberlady, at the mouth of the River Peffer. A row of Georgian cottages lines the main street and there's a lovely old church which hints at Aberlady's erstwhile importance as a port. The old harbour is silted up and now forms part of the mudflats and salt marshes of the **Aberlady Bay Nature Reserve**, which is the home of numerous seabirds.

A couple of miles north of Aberlady is **Gullane**, a resort town with an exclusive air which is hopelessly devoted to golf. There are no fewer than four golf courses surrounding Gullane; Nos 1, 2 and 3 and the world-famous **Muirfield**, where you need an introduction to play. Golf may be Gullane's raison d'être, but windsurfing has recently been gaining in popularity.

Dirleton and around

Between Gullane and North Berwick is the attractive little village of Dirleton, dominated by the ruins of **Dirleton Castle**. The original castle dates from the 12th century and was added to over the following three centuries, until it was destroyed by Cromwell's army. The very lovely gardens ⓘ *T01620-850330 (HS), Apr-Sep 0930-1830, Oct-Mar Mon-Sat 0930-1630, Sun 1400-1630, £2.80, £2 concession,* which date from the 16th century, are well worth a visit. At the eastern end of the village a road runs north for a mile or so to **Yellowcraigs**, one of the very best beaches in the country, with great views across to **Fidra island**. Access is from the car park (£1.50), an easy five-minue walk along the woodland and dune path.

North Berwick and around

→ *Phone code: 01620. Colour map 6, grid A2. Population: 4,850.*

The dignified and slightly faded Victorian seaside resort of North Berwick, 23 miles east of Edinburgh, is easily visited as a day trip from the capital. The town's chief attractions are its fine sandy beaches and the two excellent golf courses, the West Links and the Glen, but there are several other points of interest for visitors.

Sights

The biggest attraction is on the harbour, the **Scottish Seabird Centre** ⓘ *T01620-890202, www.seabird.org, summer daily 1000-1800, winter Mon-Fri 1000-1600, Sat, Sun 1000-1730. £4.50.* It's a bit like a hi-tech hide, with remote control cameras on the Bass Rock transmitting live pictures to screens placed in the visitor centre. You can control the cameras yourself, rotating, panning and zooming so that you can get the best view possible. Cameras are also trained on Fidra, so that you can watch the puffins too. If you come during the winter, when the gannets and puffins have left, you can watch the grey seals that pup on the nearby Isle of May in December. There's also a very popular café here, with great views across the water.

Next to the harbour are the remains of the **Auld Kirk**, the 12th-century Church of St Andrews, scene of one of the strangest events in Scottish history. In 1590, while King James VI was returning from Europe with his new wife, Anne of Denmark, Francis Stewart, Earl of Bothwell was plotting against him. The Earl summoned the witches of East Lothian to the church to meet the 'Devil' (actually Bothwell in disguise) and attempted by means of witchcraft to cause a storm in the Firth of Forth in order to drown King James and his new wife. The attempt failed and, when James got wind of this satanic treachery, several witches were tried and executed. Bothwell himself was imprisoned but later escaped. There is a tourist information centre ⓘ *Quality St, T01620-892197, daily in summer, Apr and May Mon-Sat, Oct-Mar Mon-Fri.*

North Berwick is overlooked by **Berwick Law**, a 613-ft volcanic crag, topped by the ruins of a watchtower built during the Napoleonic Wars, and an arch made from a whale's jawbone. It's an easy walk to the top and the views on a clear day are rewarding. Take Law Road out of town and then follow the signs.

Around North Berwick

Three miles east of town, off the A198, are the mid-14th-century ruins of **Tantallon Castle** ⓘ *T01620-892727 (HS), Apr-Sep daily 0930-1830, Oct-Mar Mon-Wed and Sat 0930-1630, Thu 0930-1200, Fri and Sun 1400-1630. £2.80, £2 concession*, perched dramatically on the edge of the cliffs, looking out to the Bass Rock. This formidable fortress was the stronghold of the 'Red Douglases', Earls of Angus, until Cromwell's attack in 1651, which left only the massive 50-ft high curtain wall intact. To get there, take the Dunbar bus from North Berwick. There's a great beach a few miles south of Tantallon which is well worth the slight detour. Turn left off the A198 at Auldhame farm, follow the road for about a mile to the gate (£1 toll charge) and beyond to the car park, then walk.

Three miles offshore is the 350-ft high **Bass Rock**, a massive, guano-covered lump of basalt, used as a prison in the 17th century but now home to millions of nesting gannets and other seabirds including guillemots, razorbills and fulmars. There are also puffins nesting on the nearby island of **Fidra**.

Dunbar → *Phone code: 01368. Colour map 6, grid A3. Population: 5,800.*

Twelve miles southeast of North Berwick, just off the main A1 from Edinburgh to the south, is the little fishing port of Dunbar. The town's main claim to fame is as the birthplace of John Muir, the explorer naturalist who founded Yellowstone National Park in the USA and became known as the father of the conservation movement.

John Muir House ⓘ *128 High St, T01368-860187, Jun-Sep Mon-Sat 1100-1300 and 1400-1700, Sun 1400-1700, free*, is his childhood home. It has been refurbished in period detail and contains a small museum dedicated to his life and work.

Dunbar is also well known as the home of **Belhaven beers**, which are still brewed on the original site (signposted off the Edinburgh road). Guided tours can be arranged if you contact them in advance ⓘ *T01368-864488.*

▲ The scant remains of **Dunbar Castle** stand beside the old harbour. A two-mile clifftop trail leads west from the castle to **John Muir Country Park** ⓘ *T01620-827318*, a vast area comprising the Tyne estuary and Belhaven Bay, and covering a variety of habitats which are home to numerous bird species. As well as the excellent beachcombing possibilities, there's also fishing and horse riding in the park. For more details contact the TIC in town.

A few miles south of Dunbar on the A1, past Torness Nuclear Power Station, is the turn-off for the beautiful long strand of **Thorntonloch Beach**, almost hidden behind the rocky outcrop of Torness Point and backed by shallow dunes. Here, you can windsurf, swim or just admire the views south to the Berwickshire cliffs. A geology trail starts from the car park at Whitesands Bay and there's lots to interest the keen twitcher. The TIC ⓘ *143 High St, T863353. May Mon-Sat, daily Jun-Sep.*

Haddington and around

→ *Phone code: 01620. Colour map 6, grid A2. Population: 8,000.*

Handsome Haddington is the archetypal prosperous country town. It sits on the River Tyne, 15 miles east of Edinburgh, making it ideal for a pleasant day out from the rigours of city life. The town dates from the 12th century but most of it was built during the 17th to 19th centuries, when Haddington benefited from its role as the driving force behind the Agricultural Revolution which transformed farming in East Lothian.

There's no tourist office, but information boards are found at places of interest, and a booklet, A Walk Around Haddington *(£1.50), is available from newsagents.*

Sights

The compact town centre is very attractive and makes for a pleasant stroll. No fewer than 129 buildings have been listed as historically interesting, including the graceful **Town House**, in tree-lined Court Street, which was built in 1748 by William Adam, father of Robert. At the east end of the High Street, Church Street leads to **St Mary's Collegiate Church** ⓘ *T01620-823109, Apr-Sep Mon-Sat 1100-1600, Sun 1400-1630, free (donations welcome)*, the largest parish church in Scotland, dating from the 14th century and restored in the 1970s. It's a particularly beautiful ecclesiastical building, with lots of interesting nooks and crannies, and enjoys a lovely setting on the river. There are public services, brass rubbings on Saturday, concerts on Sunday afternoons in the summer and also a tearoom.

Nearby at Haddington House are the peaceful medicinal gardens of **St Mary's Pleasance**, which are free and open during daylight hours. Buried in the churchyard is Jane Welsh (1801-1866), wife of essayist and historian Thomas Carlyle. The **Jane Welsh Carlyle House** ⓘ *2 Lodge St, T01620-823738, Apr-Sep Wed-Sat 1400-1700, £1.50, £1 concession*, was her home until her marriage, and part of it is open to the public.

Around Haddington

A mile south of Haddington is **Lennoxlove House** ⓘ *T01620-823720, Easter-Oct Wed, Thu and some Sat and Sun 1400-1630, £4, £2 concession*, seat of the Duke of Hamilton. The sprawling confection of styles consists of a medieval tower house with gradual extensions and additions over the centuries. Inside the house are some fine paintings and furniture, but the pièce de résistance is the death mask of Mary, Queen of Scots, and a silver casket in which she kept her letters, given to her by her first husband, Francis II of France.

About four miles northeast of Haddington, on the B1347 at East Fortune, is the excellent **Museum of Flight** ⓘ *T01620-880308, Apr-Jun, Sep and Oct daily 1030-1700, Jul and Aug daily 1030-1800, Nov-Mar Mon-Fri 1100-1500, £3, children free.* Scotland's national museum of aviation is housed in a complex of Second World War

Haddington was the birthplace of firebrand preacher John Knox, founder of the Presbyterian Church in Scotland, whose famous tract, The First Blast of the Trumpet Against the Monstrous Regiment of Women, *did little to endear him to either Mary of Guise, regent of Scotland, Mary, Queen of England or Elizabeth I, see page 599. Also born here where Alexander II of Scotland, in 1198, and Samuel Smiles, in 1812, author of the first self-help book.*

hangars and nissen huts. There is a vast and impressive collection of old aircraft – from the Tigermoth to the Vulcan bomber – and wartime memorabilia.

Six miles east of Haddington, at **East Linton**, is the very photogenic **Preston Mill** ⓘ *T01620-860426, Easter and May-Sep Mon-Sat 1100-1300 and 1400-1700, Sun 1330-1700, weekends in Oct 1330-1600, £2.50, £1.75 concession*, an 18th-century water wheel and grain mill, which includes an exhibition on milling. Just to the south of East Linton is **Traprain Law,** which offers fantastic views of the coast and hinterland of East Lothian as well as being the site of a prehistoric hillfort. Near the foot of Traprain Law are the extensive 13th-15th-century ruins of **Hailes Castle.**

Five miles south of Haddington, on the B6369, is the pretty little village of **Gifford,** birthplace of the Reverend John Witherspoon, in 1723, who was a signatory to the American Declaration of Independence. Gifford makes a good base for hiking in the **Lammermuir Hills** to the south. It's possible to follow trails across the hills and meet up with the **Southern Upland Way,** see page 220.

Sleeping

Musselburgh to North Berwick *p183*

L **Greywalls Hotel**, Gullane, T01620-842144, open Apr-Oct, a supremely charming and elegant Edwardian country house designed by Sir Edwin Lutyens. It overlooks Muirfied golf course and has an enviable reputation for superb cuisine (**£££**). If you can't afford a meal, call in for tea and shortbread. It's not cheap (£7.50), but it does give you a chance to enjoy the house – and the lovely gardens.

A **Open Arms Hotel**, Dirleton, T01620 -850241. A traditional country house hotel opposite the castle, it's a friendly and comfortable place with a highly rated restaurant (**£££**).

C-D **Old Aberlady Inn**, on the main street in Aberlady, T01875-870503. A cosy wee place, with good food and ales in its traditional bar.

D **Castle Inn**, Dirleton, T01620-850221, friendly with a small beer garden.

Camping

There's a campsite, T01875-870666, open Mar-Oct, on the Haddington Rd, Aberlady.

North Berwick and around *p183*

A-B **The Marine Hotel**, Cromwell Rd, T01620-892406, F894480. 83 rooms. North Berwick's premier hotel, overlooking the seafront and with an open-air pool.

C **Craigview**, 5 Beach Rd, T01620-892257. 3 rooms, overlooking West Beach, friendly, healthy breakfasts with vegetarian options.

D **The Glebe House**, Law Rd, T/F01620-892608, excellent central guest house.

E **The Studio**, T01620-895150, Grange Rd, is another good choice in North Berwick.

Camping

Tantallan Caravan Park, T01620-893348, open Mar-Oct, on Dunbar Rd, campsite overlooking the Glen golf course.

Dunbar *p184*

C-D **Muirfield House**, 40 Belhaven Rd, T/F01368-862289. A popular choice.

Camping

Belhaven Bay Caravan & Camping Park John Muir Country Park, just off the A1087 to the west of town, T01368-8659568.

Haddington and around *p185*

B **Browns Hotel**, 1 West Rd, Haddington, T/F01620-822254, www.browns-hotel .com, an elegant Regency town house.

B **Maitlandfield House Hotel**, 24 Sidegate, Haddington, T01620-826513, www.maitlandfieldhotel.fsnet.co.uk, top-class hotel which boasts 2 very fine restaurants.

C **Abbey Mains**, a couple of miles out of town, T01620-823286, a large stone farmhouse with its own kitchen garden. Evening meals also available.

E **Plough Tavern**, 11 Court St, Haddington, T01620-823326, a traditional inn serving decent food.

Eating

Musselburgh to North Berwick *p183*

£££ La Pontinière, T01620-843214, on the main street, Gullane. This cosy French bistro was the best place to eat in Gullane but has changed hands.

North Berwick and around *p183*

£££ The Grange, 35 High St, T01620-895894. Good contemporary Scottish cuisine in classy surroundings.
££-£ Millennium Spice, High St, T01620-895418, serves good Indian food.
££-£ Poonthai, 7 High St, is a good Thai restaurant.
£ Scottish Seabird Centre, see Sights p183. The café here is worth trying.
£ Westgate Gallery, Westgate, for a good cup of tea and a cake.

Dunbar *p184*

££ The Creel, near the harbour, T01368-863279. The best place to eat in town, serves good seafood and other dishes. Open Tue-Sun.

Haddington and around *p185*

££ Drover's Inn, East Linton, T01620-860298. A great place for a pub lunch where you can sit outside on a sunny day, or stay inside in the cosy bistro. Either way, the food is excellent and worth the trip alone.
££ Poldrate's, T01620-826882, in a converted mill on the road to Gifford. A decent choice.
££ Tweedale Arms, High St, Gifford, T01620-810240, serves tasty bar food 1100-2300 and good ales, also has rooms.
££ The Waterside, T01620-825674, by the river near Nungate Bridge, where you can enjoy excellent French bistro-style food. Open 1200-1400, 1730-2200 (1200-2200 at weekends).
£ Victoria Inn, T01620-823332, Court St, Haddington, also does decent bar meals as well as hosting the Haddington Folk Club on Wed nights.

Activities and tours

North Berwick and around *p183*

Fred Marr, T01620-892838, runs boat trips from North Berwick, weather permitting, to the Bass Rock and Fidra, daily between May and Sep. Trips cost £5.00 per person and last about 1¼ hrs. You can also arrange in advance to be dropped off on Bass Rock and picked up 3 hrs later for £10 per person, but you'll need to be a dedicated birdwatcher to put up with the stench of guano.

Transport

North Berwick and around *p183*

There are also regular buses (X5, 124) from **Edinburgh** (via **Aberlady** and **Gullane**). These stop on the High St. **First Edinburgh** buses, T0131-6639233. The train station is a 10-min walk east of the town centre. There's a frequent rail service to and from **Edinburgh** (30 mins).

Dunbar *p184*

There are regular buses from **Edinburgh** to Dunbar via Haddington (X6/106). First **Edinburgh** buses, T0131-6639233. Dunbar is on the main London-Edinburgh rail line and there are regular trains to and from **Edinburgh** (40 mins) and south to **England**.

Haddington and around *p185*

The regular buses from **Edinburgh** travelling to Dunbar go via Haddington (X6/106). First **Edinburgh** buses, T0131-6639233, and buses from **East Linton** to Haddington. There are also hourly buses to **North Berwick** (Mon-Sat, less frequently on Sun; 45 mins) and hourly buses to **Gifford** (20 mins).

Scottish Borders

The Scottish Borders covers a huge swathe of southern Scotland to the east of the M74. It's an unspoiled wilderness of green hills, rushing rivers and bleak, barren moors, and it has an austere beauty which would surprise those who think that real Scotland starts somewhere north of Perth. The Borders' proximity to England also gives it a romantic edge and makes it even more essentially Scottish. This is a region which is drenched in the blood of countless battles with the English, and its many ruined castles and abbeys bear witness to Scotland's long, turbulent relationship with its belligerent southern neighbour. It should come as no surprise, then, that this southern corner of Scotland has so inspired the country's greatest poets and writers. Robert Burns and John Buchan often spoke of its rare charms, but it is Sir Walter Scott, inspired not only by the stark beauty of the countryside but also by its lore and legends, who is most closely associated with the region.

The wildest and most spectacular scenery is to be found in the southern part of the region, along the Yarrow Water, between Selkirk and Moffat, the upper reaches of the Tweed valley, south of Peebles, and in Liddesdale, southwest of Jedburgh. But it is along the central valley of the River Tweed, between Peebles in the west and Kelso in the east, where you'll find most of the historic attractions, including the fascinating Traquair House, Sir Walter Scott's mansion at Abbotsford. Together with Selkirk, and the textile-producing towns of Galashiels and Hawick, these towns form the heart of the Borders. ▸▸ *For Sleeping, Eating and other listings, see pages 201-206.*

Ins and outs

Getting there and around

There's a good network of buses serving the region's main towns. For all bus information, call the Borders Council Transport Division, T01835-825200. The main operator is First Edinburgh, T0131-6639233. There are numerous buses running between the main towns of Galashiels, Melrose, Peebles, Hawick, Selkirk, Jedburgh and Kelso. There are also buses connecting the Border towns with Edinburgh and Berwick-upon-Tweed. There are regular buses from Berwick-upon-Tweed, Traveline T0870-6082608. National Express, T08705-808080, runs services from Newcastle to Edinburgh via Jedburgh, Galashiels and Melrose. The regular bus service is supplemented during the summer months (July to September) by the Harrier Scenic Bus Services. Buses make round-trip tours once a week on the following routes: Melrose-Moffat, via Galashiels, Selkirk, Bowhill House, Yarrow, St Mary's Loch (on Thursday); Selkirk-Eyemouth via Galashiels, Melrose, Kelso, Coldstream, Berwick-upon-Tweed; Hawick-Eyemouth via Jedburgh, Town Yetholm, Berwick-upon-Tweed. ▸▸ *For further information, contact the various operators, local TICs and Transport page 205.*

The main London-Edinburgh railway line follows the east coast from Berwick-upon-Tweed north to Dunbar in East Lothian. There is no rail link with the Border towns, so you'll have to get off at Berwick and take a bus from there. There's a good road network which allows you to explore the region easily by car. The best way to see the Borders, though, is on foot or by bike. The 90-mile Tweed Cycleway runs past the most important sights, while the Southern Uplands Way takes you through the region's most beautiful and spectacular scenery. ▸▸ *For further details and cycle paths and walks, see page 182.*

Tourist information

There are nine tourist information centres throughout the region. The ones in Jedburgh and Peebles are open all year, and the others (in Coldstream, Eyemouth, Galashiels, Hawick, Kelso, Melrose and Selkirk) are open from April to October. Details are given under each town. Visit www.scot-borders.co.uk, or call the information line, T01835-863435. For any of their free publications call T0870-6070250, and for information on Borders festivals, such as the Melrose Rugby Sevens or the Ridings, call the Events Line, T01750-20054.

Peebles and the Tweed Valley

Due south of Edinburgh is the neat and tidy town of Peebles, on the banks of the river Tweed, surrounded by wooded hills. The river here is wide and fast, whereas the pace of life on the town's broad High Street is altogether more sedate. Things liven up somewhat during the week-long Beltane Fair, the great Celtic festival of the sun which is held in June and marks the beginning of summer. Another good time to visit is during the Peebles Arts Festival, which is held over two weeks at the end of August and beginning of September. Peebles is only a 45-minute drive from Edinburgh, and makes a convenient base for a tour of the Tweed Valley. ➡ *For Sleeping, Eating and other listings, see pages 201-206.*

Peebles and around → *Phone code: 01721. Colour map 6, grid B1. Population: 7,000.*

Tweeddale Museum ⓘ *High St, Apr-Oct Mon-Fri 1000-1200 and 1400-1700, Sat 1000-1200, 1400-1600, winter hours vary, free*, is housed in the Chambers Institute, which was a gift to the town from William Chambers, a native of Peebles and founding publisher of the **Chambers Encyclopaedia**. It houses two notable friezes: one is a copy of the Elgin marbles taken from the Parthenon in Athens (and yet to be returned to their rightful home); the other is the 19th-century Triumph of Alexander. Temporary exhibitions are also staged throughout the year.

Just to the west of town, on the A72, is **Neidpath Castle** ⓘ *T01721-720333. 3-6 and 25-28 May, mid June-early Sep, Mon-Sat 1030-1630, Sun 1230-1630, £3, £2.50 concession, £1 children*, perched high on a rocky bluff overlooking the Tweed. The medieval tower house enjoys an impressive setting, but there's little to see inside which would justify the entrance fee. The castle can be reached by following the trail along the River Tweed from Hay Lodge Park in town. The walk passes a beautiful picnic spot beneath the castle and you can swim in the river (but take care). The trail continues through lovely wooded countryside and you can cross the river and return at Manor Bror (a three-mile round trip) or further on at Lyne footbridge (an eight-mile round trip). Details of this and other local walks can be found in the *Popular Walks around Peebles* leaflet available at the tourist office.

Two miles east of town on the A72 is **Glentress Forest**, which is fast becoming a top mountain biking destination with some of the best singletrack anywhere in the UK. There are dozens of tracks through the forest, graded according to level of difficulty. **The Hub in the Forest** ⓘ *T01721-721736, www.thehubintheforest.co.uk, Mon-Fri 1000-1800, Wed till 2200, Sat and Sun 0900-1900*, is an official partner of Forest Enterprise and hires out ountain bikes for £12 per half day and £16 per day, as well as providing route maps and spares. There's also a good café where your bike can have a post-ride hosedown while you tuck into coffee and cake.

On the B7062 to Traquair, see below, about two miles east from Peebles, is **Kailzie Gardens** ⓘ *T01721-720007, Apr-Oct daily 1100-1730, Nov-Mar 1100-1700 £2.50*, with a walled garden, greenhouses, woodland walks, trout fishing pond, CCTV coverage of nesting ospreys nearby and an excellent courtyard tearoom.

Eight miles southwest of Peebles, a mile beyond the village of Stobo on the B712, is **Dawyck Botanic Gardens** ⓘ *T01721-760254, mid Feb-mid Nov daily 1000-1800, till 1600 in Feb and Nov*, an outstation of Edinburgh's Royal Botanic Garden, which contains a fine collection of trees and shrubs and landscaped wooded paths.

Peebles TIC ⓘ *High St, T01721-720138, peebles@scot-borders.co.uk, Apr-Oct daily, Nov and Dec hours vary.*

Innerleithen → *Phone code: 01896. Colour map 6, grid B1.*

Seven miles east of Peebles is the village of Innerleithen, home of **Robert Smail's Printing Works** ⓘ *T01896-830206 (NTS), Mar-Jun and Sep-Oct Thu-Mon 1200-1700, Sun 1300-1700, Jun-Aug Thu-Mon 1000-1800, Sun 1300-1700, £3.50, £2.50 child/concession*, on the main street, where you can see how printing was done at the beginning of the 20th century. You can watch the printer at work on the original machinery and even try your hand at typesetting.

There are many graded cycle routes through the Glentress, Cardrona and Elibank and Traquair forests. At Walkerburn, east of Innerleithen, you can link up to the fully

Riding of the Marches

The Border people's passion for rugby is matched only by their enthusiastic celebration of the Riding of the Marches, which takes place throughout the early summer months in each of the major towns. This ancient ritual dates back to the Middle Ages, when the young men – or 'Callants' – would ride out to check the boundaries of common lands owned by the town.

Each town has its own variations of the Riding ceremonies, with other activities including concerts, balls, and festivities lasting several days. Others also commemorate local historical events. For instance, the Selkirk Gathering, the oldest and largest of the Ridings, ends with the Casting of the Colours, which commemorates Scotland's humiliating defeat at the Battle of Flodden.

signposted 90-mile **Tweed Cycleway**. See the tourist board leaflet *Cycling in the Scottish Borders*.

Traquair House → *Phone code: 01896. Colour map 6, grid B1.*

ⓘ T01896-830323, www.traquair.co.uk, Apr, May and Sep daily 1200-1730, Jun-Aug 1030-1730 Oct 1100-1600, £5.60, £5.30 concession, £3.10 child.

The big attraction in these parts is the amazing Traquair House, one of Scotland's great country houses. It lies about a mile south of Innerleithen, on the south side of the Tweed. Traquair is the oldest continually inhabited house in the country and is still owned by the Maxwell Stuarts, who have been living here since 1491. Its history goes much further back, however, and parts of the house are believed to date from the 12th century. The original tower house was added to over the next five centuries, and most of what you see today dates from the mid-17th century. It has been visited by no fewer than 27 monarchs, including Mary, Queen of Scots, who stayed here with her husband, Darnley, in 1566. The place is steeped in Jacobite history, but the family paid for its Catholic principles. The fourth earl was imprisoned in the Tower of London, and sentenced to death, for his part in the Jacobite rising of 1715, but managed to escape with the help of his wife who smuggled him out disguised as a maid. The fifth earl served two years in the Tower of London for his support of Bonnie Prince Charlie in 1745 and the famous Bear Gates, which have remained closed ever since the Pretender passed through them on his way south, bear testament to his undying support. By the turn of the 18th century the family had lost most of its estates and had neither the money nor the motivation to undertake any major rebuilding.

As a result, visiting Traquair is genuinely like stepping back in time, and there's a uniquely nostalgic and spooky atmosphere missing from so many other historic houses. One of the most interesting rooms is the **priest's room**, where a succession of resident priests lived in hiding until the Catholic Emancipation Act of 1829 allowed them to give mass. Amongst the many fascinating relics is the cradle used by Mary, Queen of Scots for her son, James VI, and some letters written by the Stuart pretenders. Also worth seeing are the **gardens**, where you'll find a maze, craft shops, a cottage tearoom and an 18th-century working **brewery** producing several ales including Bear Ale and Jacobite Ale, which can be purchased in the tearoom and gift shop. There's also B&B accommodation available. A **craft and music fair** is held in the grounds of the house every August.

Galashiels → *Phone code: 01896. Colour map 6, grid B2. Population: 13,700.*

At the junction of the A72 and A7 Edinburgh-Carlisle road is the gritty, workmanlike textile town of Galashiels, strung out along the banks of the Gala River for more than two miles. Galashiels is one the largest towns in the Borders region, and a transport hub, but there's precious little to detain passing tourists. Galashiels has played a vital role in the Borders economy for over 700 years as a major weaving town, producing tartans, tweeds and woollens, and is the home of the **Scottish College of Textiles,** though the industry has gone into decline in recent times. The only real attraction is **Lochcarron Cashmere and Wool Centre** ⓘ *Huddersfield St, open all year round daily for guided tours, phone for times T01896-751100*, a working mill with a visitor centre, textiles museum and reasonable mill shop. Galashiels TIC ⓘ *3 St John's St, T01896-755551, Apr-Jun and Sep-Oct Mon-Sat, daily Jul and Aug.*

Melrose and around

➔ *Phone code: 01896. Colour map 6, grid B2. Population: 2,300.*

Nestled at the foot of the mystical Eildon Hills, by the banks of the Tweed, is little Melrose, the loveliest of all the Border towns. It's an engaging mix of cute little shops and cottages and dignified Georgian and Victorian houses, and boasts one of the most famous ruins in Scotland. The normally soporific atmosphere is shattered every April during the week-long Melrose Sevens, when the town is taken over by rugby fans from all over the world for the acclaimed seven-a-side rugby tournament which has been going since 1883. Melrose makes a great base for exploring the beautiful landscapes of the middle stretch of the Tweed which so inspired Sir Walter Scott, the famous son of the Borders. Two of the area's main sights, Dryburgh Abbey and Abbotsford House, are inextricably linked with the writer's life and work. They can be reached by public transport, but you'll need your own transport if you want to get off the beaten track. ⏩ *For Sleeping, Eating and other listings, see pages 201-206.*

The much longer Southern Upland Way also passes through the town. For more details, *see page 220.*

Sights

The bitter wars that ravaged the Scottish borders for centuries did irrevocable damage to **Melrose Abbey** ⓘ *T01896-822562 (HS), Apr-Sep daily 0930-1830, Oct-Mar Mon-Sat 0930-1630, Sun 1400-1630, £3.30, £2.50 concession*, but even in ruins it remains toweringly beautiful and impressive. It was founded in 1136 by the prolific David I (who helped to found all four of the great Border Abbeys) and was the first Cistercian monastery in Scotland. It was attacked in 1322 by Edward II, but soon restored thanks to the financial assistance of Robert the Bruce. In 1385 it was largely destroyed by Richard II of England, then completely rebuilt, only to be ravaged again, this time by Henry VIII, in the mid-16th century. The abbey as it stands today dates from the 14th and 15th centuries, and was preserved by the money of the Duke of Buccleuch and the energy and talent of Sir Walter Scott. His great narrative poem *The Lay of the Last Minstrel* painted an eloquent picture of the abbey and helped him on the road to fame. The red sandstone ruins show an elaborate Gothic style and some of the finest figure sculpture in Scotland. Of particular note are the humorous gargoyles, which include a pig playing the bagpipes on the roof of the south side of the nave. The abbey's real claim to fame is that the **heart of Robert the Bruce** was buried here, at his request, after it had been taken to the Holy Land to help in the Crusades. The lead casket believed to contain the heart was finally excavated in 1996 and now takes pride of place in the abbey museum, in the **Commendator's House,** next to the church.

Next to the abbey is **Priorwood Garden** ⓘ *T01896-822493 (NTS), Apr-Sep Mon-Sat 1000-1730, Sun 1330-1730, Oct-Dec Mon-Sat 1000-1600, Sun 1330-1600, £2.50, £1.90 concession, £1 child*, where plants are grown specifically for dried flower arrangements. There's also a dried flower shop on site. Also next to the abbey is Melrose Tourist ⓘ *Abbey St, T822555, daily Apr-Oct.*

Legends of the Eildons

The three-peaked Eildon Hills were considered a sacred place by the ancient Celts and have long been shrouded in mystery and associated with a number of legends. For a start, they are believed to have been created by the wizard/alchemist Michael Scott, and it was here that the mystic Thomas the Rhymer was given the gift of prophecy by the Faerie Queen. Most startling of all, though, is the claim that King Arthur and his knights lie asleep beneath the hills, victims of a terrible spell.

On Market Square is the **Trimontium Exhibition** ⓘ *T01896-822651, Apr-Oct daily 1030-1630, Sat, Sun closed 1300-1400, £1.50, £1 concession*, a small but interesting centre which tells the story of the Roman occupation of the area and includes some archaeological finds. The more adventurous can follow the **Trimontium Walk** ⓘ *T01896-822651, Apr-Oct Thu 1330-1700. £2*, a four-mile guided tour of Roman sites in the area, including the site of the Trimontium (Three Hills) fort at Newstead.

Eildon Hills

The three peaks of the Eildon Hills can be seen from all parts of the Central Borders region and can be climbed quite easily from Melrose. Starting from Market Square, head along the B6359 to Lilliesleaf, and after 100-yds the path is signed to the left and leads to the saddle between the North and Mid hills (Mid Hill is the highest, at 1,385 ft). The path leads to the summit of North Hill, then Mid Hill, and finally West Hill, to the south. There are several routes back to town, but heading via the golf course makes a nice circular walk of two miles. Allow about 1½ hours. The route is detailed in the Eildon Hills Walk leaflet available from the tourist office.

St Cuthbert's Way

The 62-mile St Cuthbert's Way is a cross-border trail which links several places associated with St Cuthbert, who started his ministry at Melrose in the mid-seventh century and ended it at Lindisfarne (Holy Island), on the Northumberland coast. The waymarked route starts at **Melrose Abbey** and climbs across the Eildon Hills before joining the River Tweed. Highlights include Dere Street, a Roman Road, the Cheviot foothills, St Cuthbert's Cave and the causeway crossing to Lindisfarne. They can also provide a trail pack which includes maps and route descriptions.

Abbotsford House

ⓘ *T01896-750043, mid-Mar to May and Oct Mon-Sat 0930-1700, Sun 1400-1700, Jun-Sep daily 0930-1700, £4, £2 child.*

One of the Borders' top tourist attractions is Abbotsford House, home of Sir Walter Scott from 1812 to 1832 and a must for the novelist's many admirers. For an account of his life, see page 611. Scott spent a small fortune transforming the original farmhouse into a huge country mansion befitting a man of his status and, though Abbotsford may not be to everyone's taste, the house is an intriguing mix of styles and enjoys a beautiful setting. The house is still lived in by Scott's descendants, and the library and study have been preserved much as they were when he lived here, including the collection of over 9,000 antiquarian books. There's also an amazing assortment of Scottish memorabilia, including Rob Roy's purse, Bonnie Prince Charlie's drinking cup and Flora MacDonald's pocketbook. The house is well worth visiting and sits in pleasant grounds, about three miles west of Melrose between the Tweed and the B6360. Take the Melrose-Galashiels bus and get off at the Tweedbank traffic island. From there it's a 15-minute walk.

Dryburgh Abbey

ⓘ *T01835-822381, Apr-Sep 0930-1830, Oct-Mar Mon-Sat 0930-1630, Sun 1400-1630, £2.80, £2 concession.*

Five miles southeast of Melrose on the B6404, near the village of St Boswells, is Dryburgh Abbey. Its setting amongst ancient cedars on the banks of the Tweed, also make it the most beautifully idyllic, romantic and evocative of the Border abbeys. It dates from around 1150, when it was founded by Hugh de Morville for Premonstratensian monks from Alnwick in Northumberland. The 12th- and 13th-century ruin is remarkably well-preserved and complete, and was chosen as the burial place for Sir Walter Scott. His final resting place is in the north transept of the church. Close by lies Field Marshal Earl Haig, the disastrous First World War Commander.

If you're travelling by public transport from Melrose, take the **Jedburgh** bus as far as St Boswells (10 minutes), then walk north from the village for about a mile. If you're driving, make sure you pass **Scott's View**, on the B6356, which offers a sweeping view of the Eildon Hills and Tweed valley. Scott came here many times to enjoy the view (hence its name) and to seek inspiration. There's an even better view from the hill on the other side of the road.

Thirlestane Castle

North of Melrose on the main A68 is the stolid market town of **Lauder**, which merits inclusion because of **Thirlestane Castle** ⓘ *T01578-722430, end Mar-end Oct daily (except Sat) 1030-1700, last admission 1615, £5.30, £3 child*, one of Scotland's oldest and finest castles, which stands on the eastern edge of town. The castellated baronial house is the seat of the Earls of Lauderdale and has been owned by the Maitland family since the 16th century. Inside, the 17th-century plaster ceilings are particularly notable.

Selkirk and around

→ *Phone code: 01750. Colour map 6, grid B2. Population: 6,000.*

About six miles southwest of Melrose, on the A7 to Hawick, is the little town of Selkirk, standing on the edge of the Ettrick Forest which rises steeply from the Ettrick Water. Selkirk has been a textile centre since the early 19th century when the growing demand for tweed could no longer be met by the mills of Galashiels. Those mills are closed now and Selkirk is a quiet, unassuming place that only comes to life during the **Selkirk Gathering** in June, the largest of the Border Ridings, see page 190. That said, Selkirk is handily placed for visiting the other Border towns and sights, and makes a good base for touring the area. ⏩ *For Sleeping, Eating and other listings, see pages 201-206.*

Sights

Halliwell's House Museum and Robson Gallery ⓘ *T01750-20096, daily Apr-Oct, free,* features an 18th-century ironmongers and tells the story of the town and its industry. The gallery has a changing programme of temporary exhibitions. Also on Market Square is **Walter Scott's Courtroom** ⓘ *Apr-end Sep Mon-Sat 1000-1600, Jun-Aug also Sun 1400-1600, Oct Mon-Sat 1300-1600, free*, where Sir Walter Scott served as Sheriff of Selkirk from 1799 to 1832. It houses an exhibition on his life and writings. Outside the courtroom is a statue of the great novelist, and at the other end of the High Street is a statue of **Mungo Park** (1771-1805), the famous explorer and anti-slavery campaigner who was born in Selkirkshire.

At the northern end of town, on the A7 to Galashiels, is **Selkirk Glass** ⓘ *T01750-20954, Mon-Sat 0900-1700, Sun 1100-1700, free*, a thriving local industry, where you can see glass-blowing displays. Selkirk TIC ⓘ *Market Sq, T01750-20054, daily Apr-Oct*, is next to Halliwell's House.

Bowhill House and Country Park

ⓘ *House open Jul daily, 1300-1630, £4.50. £2 child, wheelchair users free; country Park Apr-Jun and Aug daily except Fri 1200-1700, Jul daily 1200-1700, £2.*

Three miles west of Selkirk, where the B7009 turns south off the A708, is the entrance to Bowhill House and Country Park, home of the Scotts of Buccleuch and Queensberry since 1812. They were once the largest landowners in the Borders and fabulously wealthy, a fact made evident by the fantastic collection of French antiques and European paintings on display. There are works by Canaletto, Guardi, Reynolds and Gainsborough. The wooded hills of the Country Park can be explored via a network of footpaths and cycle trails. There's no public transport to Bowhill, but the weekly Harrier Scenic Bus Service runs near Bowhill from Selkirk and Melrose in the morning, returning in the afternoon. It runs from July to September, see page 188.

Yarrow Water and Ettrick Water → *OS Landranger Nos 73 and 79.*

The A707 heads southwest from Selkirk to Moffat, following the beautiful Yarrow Water to **St Mary's Loch**, where the road is crossed by the Southern Upland Way. A few miles west of Selkirk is the turning south on to the B7009 which follows the course of the Ettrick Water to meet the B709, which continues south, past the village of **Ettrick** to Eskdalemuir and on to Langholm, see page 196.

This is one of the most remote and beautiful parts of Scotland, and an area inextricably linked with **James Hogg** (1770-1835), 'The Ettrick Shepherd', who was a great friend of Sir Walter Scott. Hogg was a notable writer himself and his most famous work, *The Confessions of a Justified Sinner*, is important in Scottish literature. Hogg was born in Ettrick and spent his entire life in the Ettrick and Yarrow valleys. He and Scott would often meet in **Tibbie Shiels Inn**, see Sleeping page 201. From **Tibbie Shiels Inn** you can follow the Southern Upland Way south to Ettrick Water, where an unclassified road leads east to the village of Ettrick, or continue southwest all the way down to Moffat, see page 208. Alternatively, head north along the eastern shore of St Mary's Loch to the A708, then continue north to **Traquair House**, see page 190, then east towards Yair Hill Forest, where you can turn south to the **Broadmeadows Youth Hostel**, see Sleeping page 201. These are strenuous hikes and you should be fit and well equipped, see page 56.

At **Cappercleuch**, on the west shore of St Mary's Loch, a spectacular single-track road twists and turns its way up to the Megget Reservoir and then down past the Talla Reservoir to the tiny village of **Tweedsmuir**, on the A701, see page 209.

Jedburgh → *Phone code: 01835. Colour map 6, grid B2. Population: 4,000.*

Ten miles from the English border is the attractive little town of Jedburgh, straddling the Jed Water at the edge of the northern slopes of the wild, barren Cheviot Hills. Jeburgh was strategically the most important of the Border towns, due to its proximity to England, and as a result received the full brunt of invading English armies. These days the only invaders are tourists. Jedburgh is the most visited of the Border towns and there are a number of interesting sights. » *For Sleeping, Eating and other listings, see pages 201-206.*

Ins and outs

Jedburgh TIC ⓘ *Murray's Green, T01835-863435, Apr, May and Oct Mon-Sat 1000-1700, Sun 1100-1600, Jun and Sep Mon-Sat 0930-1800, Sun 1100-1700, Jul and Aug Mon-Fri 0900-2000, Sat 1000-1900, Sun 1000-1800, Nov-Mar Mon-Sat 1000-1700, hours may vary*, iss a large and well-stocked office with leaflets detailing local walks.

Sights

The town is dominated by **Jedburgh Abbey** ⓘ *T01835-863925, May-end Sep daily 0930-1830, Oct-Mar Mon-Sat 0930-1630, Sun 1400-1630, £3.30, £2.50 concession, £1.20 child*, founded in 1138 by David I for Augustinian canons from northern France. The site had much older religious significance, however, and stonework in the abbey's museum dates from the first millennium AD. Malcolm IV was crowned here and Alexander III married his second wife in the abbey in 1285. Their wedding feast was held at nearby Jedburgh Castle (see below) and, like the castle, the abbey came under attack during the many English invasions, most devastatingly in 1523 when it was bombarded and burned. Despite this, the abbey church is remarkably complete, particularly the tower. Excavations have recently uncovered the remains of the cloister buildings, and among the finds is the priceless 12th-century 'Jedburgh comb', which is on display in the excellent visitor centre which brilliantly tells the abbey's long and fascinating history.

Nearby, at the top of the Castlegate, is **Jedburgh Castle Jail and Museum** ⓘ *T01835-864750, Easter-end Oct Mon-Sat 1000-1630, Sun 1300-1600 £1.50, £1 concession*, which was formerly the county jail. It was built in 1823 on the site of the 12th-century castle, which changed hands many times until it was destroyed by the Scots because of its value to the English. The displays in the cell blocks depict prison life in the 19th century, and there's an exhibition on the town's history.

At the other end of the town centre is **Mary, Queen of Scots House** ⓘ *T01835-863331, Mar-Nov Mon-Sat 1000-1630, Sun 1200-1630, £2.60, £1.50 concession*, a beautiful 16th-century building of rough-hewn stone which contains a small bedroom occupied by Mary during her stay at Jedburgh in 1566. She spent several weeks here recovering from illness after her famous 30-mile ride to Hermitage Castle, see page 196, to visit her injured lover, the Earl of Bothwell. The ensuing scandal was only exacerbated by the murder of her husband Darnley the following year at Holyrood Palace in Edinburgh. Many years later, during her long incarceration, Mary regretted the fact that she hadn't died while staying in Jedburgh. This episode in Scottish history is told through a series of displays, and there are various artefacts associated with Mary.

Hawick and around

➔ *Phone code: 01450. Colour map 6, grid B2. Population: 15,700.*

Hawick (pronounced 'Hoyk'), 14 miles southwest of Jedburgh and 12 miles south of Selkirk, is the largest town in the Borders and centre of the region's knitwear and hosiery industry for over 200 years. Hawick is not a place noted for its great beauty, but it does attract lots of visitors who come to shop at its many factory outlets where you can buy all the classic brand names in knitwear. A list of knitwear suppliers is available at the TIC. » *For Sleeping, Eating and other listings, see pages 201-206.*

Ins and outs

Hawick TIC is in Drumlanrig Tower ⓘ *High St, T01450-372547, Easter-May and Oct Mon-Sat 1000-1700, Sun 1200-1700, Jun and Sep Mon-Sat 1000-1730, Sun 1200-1730, Jul and Aug Mon-Sat 1000-1800, Sun 1200-1800*. Hours may vary.

Sights

In the same building as the TIC is a **museum** ⓘ *same hours as the tourist office, £2.50, £1.50 concession*, which outlines the tower's role in Anglo-Scottish wars from the 16th century. In Wilton Lodge Park is the **Hawick Museum and Scott Art Gallery** ⓘ *T01450-373457, Oct-Mar Mon-Fri 1300-1600, Sat closed, Sun 1400-1600, Apr-Sep Mon-Fri 1000-1200 and 1300-1645, Sat, Sun 1400-1645, free*, which has an interesting collection of mostly 19th-century textile exhibits.

Around Hawick

The A7 runs southwest from Hawick through the dramatic scenery of Teviotdale to the tiny village of **Teviothead**, where it then exchanges the valley of the River Teviot for the **Ewes Water**. The Ewes then meets the River Esk at **Langholm**, in Dumfries and Galloway. The A7 continues its route south, to meet the A74(M) just north of Carlisle.

A much more beautiful route south is to take the A698 northeast out of Hawick, then turn off on to the A6088 which heads southeast. Just beyond the tiny village of **Bonchester Bridge**, take the B6357 which leads you into lovely **Liddesdale**. The B6357 follows the course of the Liddel Water all the way south to the village of **Canonbie**, see page 208, where it meets the A7.

A few miles north of Newcastleton, the B6357 meets the B6399 which runs north back to Hawick. Four miles north of the junction is the turning to **Hermitage Castle** ⓘ *T01387-376222 (HS), Apr-Sep daily 0930-1830. £2, £1.50 concession*, one of the great Border strongholds. The oldest part of the castle dates from the 13th century and it was in the hands of the Earls of Douglas until 1492, when it passed to the Earls of Bothwell. The fourth Earl of Bothwell, James Hepburn, was the third husband of Mary, Queen of Scots, following the murder of her second husband, Darnley, and is thought to have been behind the plot to murder him. It was to Hermitage that Mary made her famous ride to visit her future husband who had been injured in a border raid. Mary's marriage to Bothwell in 1566 was ill-advised and only succeeded in uniting their enemies; and led ultimately to her imprisonment in Lochleven Castle. Bothwell meanwhile fled to Norway, where he was captured and later died a prisoner himself, in 1578. Hermitage became largely irrelevant following the Union of Crowns in 1603 and fell into disrepair. Much of what you see today dates from the 19th century when the Duke of Buccluech ordered its repair. The vast and eerie ruin is said to be haunted, which is not surprising given its grisly past. One owner, William Douglas, starved his prisoners to death in the ghoulish dungeons, which can still be seen.There is no public transport service from Hawick to the castle.

Kelso and around

→ *Phone code: 01573. Colour map 6, grid B3. Population: 6,000.*

The little market town of Kelso, at the confluence of the Tweed and Teviot rivers, is one of the most picturesque of the Border towns, with its cobbled streets leading into a wide market square bounded by elegant, three-storey 18th- and 19th-century town houses. The countryside around Kelso is worth exploring, for here you'll find some of Scotland's finest stately homes. ⏩ *For Sleeping, Eating and other listings, see pages 201-206.*

Sights

Kelso Abbey ⓘ *Apr-end Dec daily (Sun afternoon only), free*, was once the largest and richest of the Border abbeys, but suffered the same fate as its counterparts, Jedburgh, Dryburgh and Melrose. Kelso was a strategic point in the Border wars between the Scots and the English and the abbey, founded in 1138 by King David, was laid to waste by successive English invasions, most devastatingly in 1545 by the Earl of Hertford. This latter attack was part of Henry VIII's so-called 'Rough Wooing', when the king took exception to the Scots' refusal to ratify a marriage treaty between his son and the infant Mary Stuart. Today, little remains of the abbey, and it is the least complete of those in the Borders. The nearby octagonal **Old Parish Church**, built in 1773, is unusual.

Aside from the abbey, the town's only other major attraction is the pleasant **Cobby Riverside Walk**, which leads along the banks of the Tweed to Floors Castle (see below). Leave The Square by Roxburgh Street, and follow the signposted alley to the start of the walk. The route passes the junction of the Tweed and Teviot rivers, a spot famous for its salmon fishing.

Kelso tourist information centre ⓘ *Town House, The Square, T01573-223464, d21aily Apr-Oct, winter Mon-Sat 1100-1600*. Hours subject to change.

Kirk Yetholm and Town Yetholm

Six miles southeast of Kelso on the B6352 are the twin villages of Kirk Yetholm and Town Yetholm, lying within a stone's throw of the English border on the edge of the Cheviot Hills. Two long-distance walks cut through the villages. They are at the northern end of the Pennine Way, which runs up the spine of northern England, and are on the St Cuthbert's Way, which runs from Melrose to Lindisfarne in Northumberland, see page 192.

Floors Castle

ⓘ *T01573-223333, mid Apr to end Oct daily 1000-1630 (last admission 1600), £5.50, £4.75 concession.*

The vast ancestral home of the Duke of Roxburghe stands imperiously overlooking the Tweed, about a mile northwest of the town centre. The original Georgian mansion was designed by Robert Adam and built in 1721-1726, though it was later remodelled by William Playfair in the 1840s, with the addition of many flamboyant features. Only 10 rooms are open to the public but they are undeniably elegant and palatial, and amongst the many priceless family items on display are outstanding collections of European furniture, porcelain and paintings by Picasso, Matisse and Augustus John, and a 15th-century Brussels tapestry. Floors is the largest inhabited castle in Scotland and the current occupier, the 10th Duke of Roxburghe, is a close personal friend of the royal family. The house also has a restaurant and a coffee shop.

Smailholm

Six miles northwest of Kelso on the B6397 is the village of Smailholm, where a turning leads to **Smailholm Tower** ⓘ *T01573-460365, Apr-Sep daily 0930-1830, Oct-Mar Sat 0930-1630, Sun 1400-1630, £2, £1.50 concession*, a classic Scottish tower house and an evocative place full of history and romance. The 15th-century fortified farmhouse, built by the Pringles, squires to the Earls of Douglas, stands on a rocky pinnacle above a small lake. Sir Walter Scott's grandfather owned the nearby farm and the young Scott came here as a sickly child in the 1770s to improve his health. So began the writer's long love affair with the lore and landscapes of the Scottish Borders which inspired so much of his poetry and prose. Scott would write a ballad about this gaunt tower house – *The Eve of St John* – as part of a deal with the owner to save it. Today Smailholm houses a small, unremarkable museum relating to some of Scott's works, but the views from the top of the tower are rewarding.

Mellerstain House

ⓘ *T01573-410225, Easter weekend and May-Sep Sun-Mon 1230-1700, last admission 1630, £5, £4.50 concession, café/shop 1130-1730.*

Northwest of Kelso, on the A6089 to Gordon, is the signpost for Mellerstain House, home of the Earl of Haddington and one of Scotland's great Georgian houses. This 18th-century architectural masterpiece was designed by William Adam and his son Robert and perfectly characterizes the elegant symmetry of the period. The superb exterior is more than matched by the exquisitely ornate interiors. There is also furniture by Chippendale and Hepplewhite, as well as paintings by Constable, Gainsborough, Veronese and Van Dyck. The formal Italian gardens, laid out in the early 20th century, are equally impressive.

Coldstream ➔ *Phone code: 01890. Colour map 6, grid B3.*

Standing on the north bank of the River Tweed, which marks the border with England, is the little town of Coldstream. The busy A697 linking Newcastle-

Not such a Dunce

Duns was also the birthplace of John Duns Scotus (1266-1308), a medieval scholar and theologian of some note, who taught at the universities of Oxford and Paris. He opposed the orthodox views of Thomas Aquinas, and his teachings divided the Franciscans and Dominicans. After his death his ideas quickly fell out of favour and those who held them were derided as being stupid, and so we now have the word 'dunce', derived from the heterodox views of John Duns Scotus.

upon-Tyne with Edinburgh runs through the centre of town, but Coldstream has little to offer visitors other than history. The town gave its name to the famous regiment of Coldstream Guards, formed by General Monck in 1659 before he marched south to support the restoration of the Stuart monarchy a year later. The regiment had originally been sent to Scotland as part of Cromwell's New Model Army, but Monck was persuaded to change allegiance. No doubt the offer of the title, first Duke of Albermarle, had something to do with his decision. The Guards remain the oldest regiment in continuous existence in the British army and you can find out all about their proud history in the **Coldstream Museum** ⓘ *T01890-882630, Market Sq, off the High St, Apr-Sep Mon-Sat 1000-1600, Sun 1400-1600; Oct Mon-Sat 1300-1600, free.*

Near the handsome five-arched bridge which spans the river at the east end of town is the 18th-century **Toll House**, where eloping couples from England were once granted 'irregular marriages'. On the western edge of town is the 3,000-acre **Hirsel Country Park** ⓘ *open all year during daylight hours*, seat of the Earls of Home. Hirsel House isn't open to the hoi polloi, but you can wander around the grounds.

Coldstream Tourist Information Centre ⓘ *Town Hall on the High St, T01890-882607, Apr-Jun and Oct Mon-Sat, daily Jul-Aug*. Winter hours vary.

Flodden Field

Four miles southeast of Coldstream, across the border near the village of Branxton, is Flodden Field. In 1513 James IV crossed the Tweed at Coldstream to attack the English, while Henry VIII was busy fighting in France. The invasion was a diversion to assist the French, but Henry sent an army north to meet the threat and James IV's army was routed. The king, his son and some 9,000 men were slain in one of Scotland's greatest military disasters.

Duns and around → *Phone code: 01361. Colour map 6, grid B3.*

The quiet market town of Duns lies in the middle of Berwickshire, surrounded by the fertile farmland of the Merse. Duns is best known as the birthplace of Jim Clark (1936-1968), a former farmer who went on to become world motor racing champion twice in the 1960s and who remains one of Britain's greatest ever racing drivers. His successful career was tragically cut short when he was killed in a crash while practising at Hockenheim in Germany.

The **Jim Clark Room** ⓘ *44 Newton St, T01361-883960, Apr-Sep Mon-Sat 1000-1300 and 1400-1630, Sun 1400-1600, Oct Mon-Sat 1300-1600, £1.30, child free*, is a museum dedicated to this moter racing champions life

▲ There are some good local walks, detailed in the leaflet *Walks Around Duns*. The best walk is to the top of **Duns Law** (714 ft), from where there are terrific views of the Merse and the Lammermuir Hills to the north. Also at the top is the **Covenanter's**

Stone, which marks the spot where the Covenanting army camped in 1639, awaiting the arrival of Charles I's troops. Duns Castle was used for many of the Highland scenes in the film, Mrs Brown.

Duns lies only a few miles south of the **Lammermuir Hills**, a low-lying range running east to west and acting as a natural boundary between the Borders and East Lothian. The hills are criss-crossed by numerous paths and ancient droving trails, including the easterly section of the **Southern Upland Way** from Lauder, on the A68, to Cockburnspath by the A1 on the coast. You can walk the final 10 miles of the route, starting from the hamlet of **Abbey St Bathans**, northwest of Duns on the Whiteadder Water.

Two miles east of Duns, on the A6015, is **Manderston House** ⓘ *T01361-883450, www.manderston.co.uk, mid-May to Sep Thu and Sun 1400-1700, £6.50, £3 concession (house and gardens), £3.30, £1.50 concession (gardens only)*, described as the finest Edwardian country house in Scotland. No expense has been spared in the design and decoration and the whole effect, from the silver staircase to the inlaid marble floor in the hall, is one of quite staggering opulence. Take a good look at the staircase – it had tarnished badly over the years (one panel is left to show how black it was) and was voluntarily and lovingly cleaned up by a retired couple. The 56 acres of beautiful gardens should not be missed. There are wonderful displays of rhododendrons late in May.

Twelve miles east of Duns, and five miles west of Berwick-upon-Tweed off the B6461 to Swinton, is **Paxton House** ⓘ *Easter-Oct daily 1115-1700, 1615 last tour, £5, £4.75 concession (house), Apr-Oct 1000 till sunset (grounds)*, a grand neoclassical mansion designed by John and James Adam, the less-famous brothers of Robert, for Patrick Home, who had fallen in love with a Prussian aristocrat at the court of Frederick the Great. She was a great favourite of Frederick's and he strongly opposed the marriage, which never went ahead. She and Patrick corresponded for years and vowed never to marry anyone else while the other was alive. Both kept their promise. Inside there's an impressive display of Chippendale and Regency furniture, and the Picture Gallery is an outstation of the National Gallery of Scotland. In the 80 acres of grounds beside the River Tweed is a Victorian boathouse and a salmon-fishing museum.

Berwickshire Coast

The Berwickshire Coast is not exactly a name on the tip of every Scottish tourist's tongue. Tucked out of the way, these wild and woolly cliffs are often deserted and home to a number of excellent coastal walks, particularly the seven-mile Burnmouth to St Abbs walk described below. The waters around Eyemouth are excellent for scuba diving. They form part of the St Abbs and Eyemouth Voluntary Marine Reserve, one of the best dive sites in Scotland, with a wide variety of marine life and the spectacular Cathedral Rock. » *For Sleeping, Eating and other listings, see pages 201-206.*

Eyemouth → *Phone code: 018907. Colour map 6, grid B3. Population: 3,500.*

Five miles north of the border on the Berwickshire Coast is the busy fishing port of Eyemouth. Fishing has been the life and soul of Eyemouth since the 13th century and the **Eyemouth Museum** ⓘ *same hours as tourist office, £1.75, £1.25 concession*, in the Auld Kirk on Market Place, has displays on the town's fishing heritage. The centrepiece is the Eyemouth Tapestry, made by local people in 1981 to mark the centenary of the Great Disaster of 1881, when 189 local fishermen were drowned during a violent storm. Eyemouth TIC ⓘ *T018907-50678, daily Apr-Sep, Oct Mon-Sat, hours subject to change*, is in the same building as the museum.

St Abb's Head → *Phone code: 018907. Colour map 6, grid B3.*

Three miles north of Eyemouth on the A1107 is the village of **Coldingham**, notable only for its medieval **priory**, founded by King Edgar in 1098, then rebuilt in the 13th century before suffering further attacks in 1545 and 1648. The remaining sections have been incorporated into the present parish church. Here the B6438 turns north and winds its way down to the picturesque little fishing village of St Abbs, nestled beneath steep cliffs. There's a little museum and a visitor centre for the Marine Reserve in the Old School House – open summer, hours vary with volunteer staff. St Abbs is also a good base for divers wishing to explore the St Abbs and Eyemouth Voluntary Marine Reserve, see below.

Just north of the village is the **St Abb's Head National Nature Reserve** (NTS), which comprises almost 200 acres of wild coastline with sheer cliffs inhabited by large colonies of guillemots, kittiwakes, fulmars and razorbills. To get to the reserve, follow the trail from the car park at Northfield Farm on the road into St Abbs. The path ends at the lighthouse, about a mile from the car park. An excellent coastal walk, from Burnmouth, south of Eyemouth, to St Abbs is described below. A side road turns off the B6438 at Coldingham and leads a mile down to the coast at **Coldingham Sands**, a tiny resort with a fine sandy beach. It's a popular spot for surfing and diving.

▲ Burnmouth to St Abbs coastal walk → *OS Landranger No 67.*

The Berwickshire coast offers some good walking opportunities along high cliffs with lots of birdlife to see. This walk starts at **Burnmouth**, a few miles south of Eyemouth. To get there, take the hourly bus service from Coldingham, which connects in Berwick with services to other Border towns. The seven-mile route is waymarked and is mostly on good paths, though there is some rough ground. Allow about four hours and take care at some points along the clifftop. To get to the cliff path, get off the bus at Burnmouth primary school, go through the gate by the houses and walk up the side of the field. Continue along the path towards Eyemouth, past some dramatic scenery at **Fancove Head**, the highest point of the cliffs, at 338 ft. When you reach the golf course, follow the signs around the seaward edge and then left across the golf course, then right towards **Eyemouth harbour**.

Cross the bridge near the lifeboat mooring and walk along the quayside to the end of the promenade, where you cross a short section of beach and then climb the steps to the headland and the remains of Eyemouth Fort. Walk around the seaward side of the Caravan Park and turn right to cross the fields and then return to the cliff path. The path descends to **Linkum Shore** and crosses the beach. Follow it around Yellow Craig to reach **Coldingham Bay**. At the far end of the bay, climb the steps and then follow the tarmac path which leads to the village of **St Abbs**. From here you can follow Creel Path to reach the B6438, and from there it's a short walk into Coldingham.

Berwick-upon-Tweed → *Phone code: 01289.*

Yes, we know, Berwick-upon-Tweed is in England, but the town has strong historical ties with Scotland, and its football team plays in the Scottish league. It also makes a convenient stopping point if you've had a long journey north. The town, which takes its name from a river which has its source in Scotland, wasn't always in England. It changed hands more than a dozen times between 1147 and 1482, when it was finally taken for England by Richard, Duke of Gloucester, later Richard III. Berwick was a strategic base for English attacks on the Borders and large sections of the town wall, built by Edward I to repel the Scots, still survive. It has also retained its medieval street plan, and many of its steep, cobbled streets are worth exploring. The TIC ⓘ *106 Marygate, T01289-330733, Oct-Mar Mon-Sat 1000-1200 and 1300-1600, longer hours from Easter to Oct.*

Sleeping

Peebles and the Tweed Valley *p188*
L Stobo Castle Health Spa, Stobo, 7 miles outside of Peebles, T01721-725300, www.stobocastleco.uk. This luxury hotel housed in an early 19th-century baronial castle offers more than 70 treatments for face and body, as well as an exercise pool complex and high-tech gym, and various exercise and relaxation activities. Above all, though, it's a great place to unwind or even meditate. Price (around £150 per person) includes a back massage, breakfast, lunch and dinner and use of all health suites.
A Cringletie House Hotel, T01721-730233, www.cringletie.com. 2 miles north of Peebles just off the A703 to Edinburgh. Lovely 19th-century baronial house set in 28 acres of grounds, with an excellent restaurant, see Eating, and friendly service.
A Peebles Hotel Hydro, Innerleithen Rd, Peebles, T01721-720602, www.peebleshotel hydro.co.uk. One of Scotland's oldest and grandest hotels, the Hydro has made a concerted effort to meet modern demands with an excellent pool and a health and beauty suite offering a huge range of therapies. Also provides a whole host of activities for kids and baby-sitting service. Prices include dinner in the grand, but rather formal dining room. Their bistro, **Lazels**, is more realxed. Various deals on offer so best to call and ask for the best prices.
B-C Castle Venlaw Hotel, on the Edinburgh Rd, T01721-720384, www.venlaw.co.uk, a lovely old baronial castle with good views.
C-D Kingsmuir Hotel, Springhill Rd, Peebles, T01721 720151, www.kinsmuir.com. 10 rooms, friendly, does good bar meals.
C-D Traquair Arms Hotel & Restaurant, Traquair Rd, Innerleithen, T01896-830229, traquair.arms@scotborders.com. Good place to stay and a local favourite for its fine food and real ales.
D Glentress Hotel and Country Inn, at the entrance to Glentress Forest, T01721-720100. Cosy with a good restaurant.
E Grey Gables, on Springwood Rd, Peebles, T01721-721252, uses organic produce.
E Rowanbrae, Northgate, which runs off the east end of the High St, Peebles, T01721-721630, excellent B&B.

Camping
Rosetta Caravan & Camping Park, on Rosetta Rd, a 15-min walk north of the High St, Peebles, T01721-720770. Open Apr-Oct.
Tweedside Caravan Park, Montgomery St, Innerleithen, T01896-831271, open Apr-Oct. Note that accommodation is usually fully booked during the **Traquair Fair** in Aug (see below).

Melrose and around *p191*
There's not a huge amount of accommodation in Melrose, considering its appeal, so it's best to book in advance during the summer and especially during the Melrose Sevens in mid-Apr. The following options are all in Melrose.
B-C Burts Hotel, Market Sq, T01896-822285, www.burtshotel.co.uk. This refurbished traditional 18th-century inn is the best option, very comfortable and renowned locally for its excellent modern Scottish cuisine, see Eating p203.
C Millars Hotel, Market Sq, T01896-822645. Small and comfortable.
D Kilkerran House, High St, T01896-822122, www.kilkerran.net. One of the best B&Bs. Nicely furnished, in the centre.
E Braidwood, Buccleuch St, T01896-822488. Another good choice of B&B. Very good value.
F Youth Hostel, in a large mansion on the edge of town, overlooking the abbey from beside the A6091 bypass, T01896-822521, Very good and very popular. Open all year.

Camping
Gibson Park, T01896-822969, at the end of the High St, the campsite is opposite the Greenyards rugby ground.

Selkirk and around *p193*
A Philipburn Country House Hotel, Linglie Rd, Selkirk, T01750-720747,

For an explanation of sleeping and eating price codes used in this guide, see inside the front cover. Other relevant information is found in Essentials, see pages 43-51.

www.philipburnhouse hotel.co.uk. Upmarket accommodation and good food.

D Glen Hotel, Yarrow Terr, Selkirk, T/F01750-20259, www.glenhotel.co.uk, refurbished Victorian house with good views of the hills and river.

D-E Tibbie Shiels Inn, T01750-42231, on the narrow strip of land separating St Mary's Loch from the ethereal Loch of the Lowes. It's still a famous watering hole and popular stop along the Southern Upland Way. It also serves bar meals (Easter-Nov daily; Nov-Easter closed Mon, Tue, Wed).

E Gordon Arms Hotel, east of St Mary's Loch, at the junction of the A708 and B709 which runs north to Innerleithen and south and then east to Hawick, T01750-82232. Said to be the last meeting place of Scott and Hogg. It's a popular stopping point for walkers, and offers bar food and local ales.

E Hillholm, 36 Hillside Terr, Selkirk, T01750-21293. Good value. 5 mins walk from town.

E Sunnybrae House, 75 Tower St, Selkirk, T01750-21156. Dinner also available. Bed-rooms with adjoining private sitting room.

F SYHA Broadmeadows Youth Hostel, Yarrowford, T01750-76262; open end-Mar to end Sep, 5 miles west of Selkirk on the A708, beyond Bowhill (see below).

Camping

Victoria Park Caravan & Camping Site, Selkirk, T01750-20897, beside the river next to the indoor swimming pool.

Jedburgh *p194*

B Jedforest Hotel, in the village of Camptown, 6 miles south of Jedburgh, on the A68, and only 5 miles from the border, T01835-840222, www.jedforesthotel.free serve.co.uk. This is the most luxurious place to stay. It is the self-proclaimed 'First Hotel in Scotland' and is very comfortable, with a fine restaurant. Halfboard is (**A**).

D Glenfriars House, The Friars, Jedburgh, T01835-862000, www.edenroad.demon. co.uk. A lovely Georgian house near the north end of the High St. Recommended.

D-E Ancrum Craig, T/F01835-830280, ancrumcraig@clara.net. Open Jan-Dec. A quiet 19-century country house 2 miles from the A68 near Ancrum. Great value.

E Hunalee House, T/F01835-863011, sheila. whittaker@btinternet.com. Open Mar-Oct. There are several B&Bs in and around town, but few can match the sheer style and value-for-money of this early 17th-century house, a mile south of town on the A68, set in 15 acres of gardens and woodlands.

E Kenmore Bank Guest House, Oxnam Rd, T01835-862369, www.hotelsjedburgh.co.uk, overlooking the Jed Water in town.

E Meadhon House, 48 Castlegate, Jedburgh, T/F01835-862504, meadhon@aol.com. More characterful than most.

Camping

There are a few campsites close to Jedburgh.

Elliot Park Camping & Caravanning Club, T01835-863393, open Apr- Oct, is a mile north of town.

Jedwater Caravan Park, T01835-840219, open Apr-Oct. 4 miles south of town on the A68.

Lilliardsedge Holiday Park and Golf Club, T01835-830271, open Easter-end Oct, 5 miles to the north of Jedburgh.

Hawick and around *p195*

B-C Glenteviot Park, Hassendeanburn, Hawick, T01450-870660. 5 rooms. New, purpose-built hotel overlooking the Teviot River, faultless design and exceptional service, strictly for grown-ups in search of some indulgence and pampering.

C Mansfield House Hotel, 1 mile from town, on the A698 to Kelso, T01450-373988, www.mansfield-house.com. A traditional mansion house hotel offering good food (lunch **£**; dinner **££**).

D Kirklands Hotel, West Stewart Pl, T01450-372263.

D-E Borders Honey Farm, T/F01387-376737, 3 miles north of Newcastleton on the B6357. Definitely the place to 'bee'.

E Liddlesdale Hotel, Newcastleton, 5½ miles south of Hermitage Castle, T/F01387-375255, also serves local specialities such as pleasant and salmon.

E Oakwood House, Buccleuch Rd, T01450-372814. Decent value B&B.

Kelso and around *p196*

L Roxburghe Hotel & Golf Course, at the village of Heiton, a few miles from Kelso on the A698 to Hawick, T01573-450331, www.roxburghe.net. This country mansion, owned by the Duke of Roxburgh, is the most luxurious place to stay hereabouts. It stands in hundreds of acres of park and woodlands on the banks of the Teviot, and offers grand style, superb cuisine and a championship golf course.

B Ednam House Hotel, Bridge St, Kelso, T01573-224168, F226319. Less salubrious but nevertheless highly recommended and slightly more affordable. A family-run Georgian mansion overlooking the Tweed and close to the town centre. Excellent food served all day (lunch **£**; dinner **££**) in a restaurant with great views over the river.

C Border Hotel, T01573-420237, Kirk Yetholm, overlooking the village green, which marks the end of the Pennine Way. Kirk Yetholm was once the home of the king of the gypsies (you can still see his pretty little cottage by the green) and the bar is full of pictures of the former gypsy inhabitants. It serves a welcome pint of ale and good food, too.

D Bellevue House, Bowmont St, Kelso, T/F01573-224588, bellevue.kelso@virgin.net. Fine non-smoking guest house.

D-E Valleydene, High St, Kirk Yetholm, T01573-420286, valleydene@rdplus.net. Cosy B&B with log fire in guest lounge.

F Youth Hostel, Kirk Yetholm, T01573-420631, open mid-Mar to end Oct.

Camping

Kirkfield Caravan Park, Grafton Rd, Town Yetholm, T01573-420346, open Apr- Oct. A caravan park, does not take tents.

Springwood Caravan Park, T01573-224596, admin@springwoodcaravanpark.co.uk, open Mar-Oct. Overlooking the Tweed on the A699 heading west towards St Boswells, this is the nearest campsite to Kelso.

Duns and around *p198*

B Chirnside Hall Hotel, a mile east of Chirnside on the road to Berwick, T01361-818219, www.chirnsidehallhotel.com. This Victorian mansion house offers luxurious accommodation and excellent food all day at mid-range prices (booking essential).

D Wellfield House, Preston Rd, T01361-883189, www.wellfieldhouse.com, a traditional Georgian house offering great value (no smoking) in Duns.

D-E St Albans, T01361-883285, www.scottishbordersbandb.co.uk, on Clouds, a lane behind the police station in Duns. Recommended and non-smoking.

Berwickshire Coast *p199*

L Churches, Albert Rd, Eyemouth, T018907-50401, www.churcheshotel.co.uk. 6 rooms. Such a serious wow factor is suprising here. Stylish without a hint of pretension. The restaurant, see Eating, is the best for miles.

B Marshall Meadows Country House Hotel, Berwick-upon-Tweed, T01289-331133, is a Georgian mansion set in 15 acres of grounds only a few hundred yards from the border. Highly recommended.

C Dunlaverock Country House Hotel, at Coldingham Sands, T018907-71450, a small, comfortable hotel offering excellent food.

D Castle Rock Guest House, Murrayfield, on the cliffs above the harbour in St Abbs Head, T018907-71715, is excellent.

D-E Dervaig Guest House, 1 North Rd, Berwick-upon-Tweed, T01289-307378, only a few mins from the train station.

E Brown's B&B, 1 Hallydown Cottages, Eyemouth, T018907-51242. Also good value .

E Hillcrest, Coldingham Rd, Eyemouth, T018907-50463. A good-value B&B.

E Wilma Wilson's B&B, 7 Murrayfield, St Abbs Head, T018907-71468. Former fisherman's cottage.

F The Rock House Dive Centre, St Abbs Head, T018907-71288, bunkhouse accommodation right on the harbour.

F Youth hostel, Coldingham Sands, on the cliffs above the south end of the bay, T018907-71298, open mid-Mar to end Sep.

Camping

Eyemouth Holiday Park, T01890-751050, overlooking the beach at the north end.

Scoutscroft Holiday Centre, St Abb's Head, T018907-71338, open Mar-Nov, which also rents diving equipment and offers courses. One of several campsites in the area.

Eating

Peebles and the Tweed Valley *p188*

£££-££ Cringlethie House Hotel, see Sleeping, is the best place to eat. It serves delicious Scottish cuisine. Open 1230-1400, 1900-2100.

££ Horse Shoe Inn, T01721-730225, at Eddleston, about 5 miles north of Peebles on

the A703. It serves very good food throughout the day and evening.
££ The Sunflower Restaurant, 4 Bridgegate, T01721-722420. A great place in the centre of Peebles which serves coffee, cakes and Mediterranean style lunches – as well as evening meals on Thu, Fri and Sat.
£ The Olive Tree, 7 High St, Peebles. An excellent deli in town selling a wide selection of continental delicacies and local produce and specializes in cheeses.
£ Park Hotel, Innerleithen Rd, does decent bar meals.

Melrose and around *p191*
£££ Burt's Hotel, see Sleeping, Melrose. Best of all. Dine in style in the dining room or opt for their excellent pub grub.
££ Hoebridge Inn Restaurant, on the other side of the river, in the village of Gattonside, T01896-823082, offers good quality Scottish fare, and well worth the walk.
££ King's Arms, High St, Melrose, T01896-822143. Another hotel recommended for food.
££ Marmions Brasserie, T01896-822245, on Buccleuch St near the abbey, Melrose. A good French-style bistro, daily 0900-1800, 1830-2200.

Selkirk and around *p193*
Possibilities for eating in Selkirk are limited.
££ County Hotel, T01750-21233, on the High St, Selkirk, serves decent bar meals.
£ Jackie Lunns, Market Sq, Selkirk. Buy the local speciality, Bannock bread, from here.

Jedburgh *p194*
There's not a great deal of choice for eating in Jedburgh or Hawick, apart from the hotel bars and restaurants.
££-£ Simply Scottish, High St, Jedburgh, T01835-864696, offers modern, bistro-style Scottish fare all day.
££ Carter Bar, 11 miles south of Jedburgh, the first/last pub in Scotland, standing on the border with England in the Cheviot Hills.

Kelso and around *p196*
£££-££ Roxburghe and **Ednam House Hotels**, see Sleeping above, are the best places to eat.
£ Black Swan Hotel, T01361-224563, on Horsemarket, Kelso. Offers cheap bar meals.
£ Cottage Garden Tea Room, opposite the abbey, Kelso, offers tea, coffee and light lunches (closed Sun and Wed, Nov-Easter, and Mon Jan, Feb).
£ Queens Head, 24 Bridge St, Kelso, T01361-224636, is a decent hotel in which to grab a bite.

Duns and around *p198*
£££ Wheatsheaf at Swinton, in the village of Swinton, about 5 miles south of Duns on the A6112, T01361-860257, www.wheatsheaf-swinton.co.uk. The best place to eat in the area. The food is first-class. Open Tue-Sun 1200-1400, Tue-Sat 1800-2100.

Berwickshire Coast *p199*
£££ Churches, Albert Rd, Eyemouth, T018907-50401. Run by Rosalind and Marcus, who also have the eponymous hotel, see Sleeping. Superior cooking served with aplomb in chic surroundings. Dishes feature local fish and game.
££ Northfield Farm Visitor Centre is a good place to eat if you're going to St Abb's Head. Has a pleasant tea room with tables outside.
££ The Ship, Eyemouth, T018907-50224, best of a string of pubs and hotels along the harbour serving fresh fish and standard bar meals.

Entertainment

Melrose and around *p191*
The Wynd Theatre, T01896-823854, is a tiny theatre which stages regular drama.

Festivals and events

Jedburgh *p194*
Jedburgh's Common Riding, the Callant's Festival, takes place in **late Jun/early Jul**, see also p190.
In **early Feb** is the **Jedburgh Hand Ba' game**, a bruising and exhausting contest between the 'uppies' (those born above the Market Place) and the 'downies' (those born below), who endeavour to get a leather ball from one end of the town to the other. Visitors from south of the border may wish to note that the game used to be played with the heads of vanquished Englishmen.

Kelso and around *p196*
The main festivals are the **Border Union Agricultural Show** and the town's **Riding of the Marches**, both of which take place in **Jul**. Kelso also hosts its own **Rugby Sevens** in early **Sep**.
productions and musical events. Check at the TIC for the current programme.

Berwickshire Coast *p199*
The main events in Eyemouth's calendar naturally has a fishing theme. The week-long **Herring Queen Festival** takes place late **Jul**.

Activities and tours

Jedburgh *p194*
Ferniehurst Mill Lodge, T01835-863279, 2 miles south of Jedburgh on the A68. Horse riding is available for experienced riders here. They also offer accommodation and tailor-made riding holidays.

Berwickshire Coast *p199*
There are a number of boats offering dive charters as well as birdwatching boat trips.
Alistair Crowe, T018907-71412.
Billy Atkinson, T018907-71288.
Peter Gibson, T018907-71681.
Alternatively ask down at the harbour.
All based in St Abb's Head.
Scoutscroft Holiday Centre, T018907-71669, see Sleeping. Dive shop here which rents out equipment and runs diving courses.

Transport

Peebles and the Tweed Valley *p188*
There are hourly buses from **Peebles** to **Edinburgh** (1 hr), **Galashiels** and **Melrose** and, less frequently, to **Selkirk** and **Biggar**, with First Edinburgh, T01721-720181. Buses stop outside the post office, near the TIC, on Eastgate. Bus No C1 runs once a day to **Traquair** from **Peebles**. First Edinburgh, T01721-720181, bus No 62 runs regularly to **Innerleithen** and **Peebles** from **Edinburgh**. From **Galashiels** there are frequent buses to and from **Edinburgh** (1 hr 25 mins); **Peebles**, **Melrose** (20 mins), **Hawick** (40 mins), **Selkirk** (15 mins) and **Carlisle** (2 hrs).

Bikes can be hired from **Crossburn Caravan Cycle Hire**, T/F720501, on the Edinburgh Rd, Peebles, from £8-14 per day.

Melrose and around *p191*
From Melrose there are regular buses to **Galashiels** (15 mins), **Kelso** (several daily; 35 mins), **Jedburgh** (30 mins), **Peebles** (several daily; 1 hr 10 mins), and **Selkirk** (hourly Mon-Sat, less frequently on Sun; 40 mins). To get to **Hawick**, it's easier to catch a bus to Galashiels and then change (see p611). Buses to Melrose stop in Market Square, close to the abbey and tourist office. First Edinburgh bus No 95 runs frequently to and from **Edinburgh** and **Hawick**, via **Selkirk** and **Galashiels**. There are also regular daily buses to **Langholm** and **Carlisle**. There's a bus to **Moffat**, on Sat only. All buses leave from Market Sq. Those who wish to explore the area by bike can hire cycles in Galashiels, at Gala Cycles, T01896-757587, at 58 High St.

Selkirk and around *p193*
See Melrose above for details.

Jedburgh *p194*
The bus station in Jedburgh is close to the abbey and there are good connections around the Borders. **First Edinburgh**, T0131-6639233, runs frequent daily buses to **Hawick**, **Kelso** and **Galashiels**. There are also buses daily to and from **Edinburgh**. From **Hawick** there are regular daily buses to and from **Selkirk** (20 mins), **Edinburgh** (2 hrs) and **Carlisle** (1¼ hrs). There's also a service to **Melrose** (40 mins), but it may be quicker to go to **Galashiels** and change there.

Kelso and around *p196*
Kelso bus station is on Roxburgh St, a short walk from The Square. There are regular buses to and from **Galashiels**, **Melrose**, **Jedburgh**, **Coldstream** and **Kirk Yetholm** (20 mins). Services are less frequent on Sun. For more details, contact the main bus operator **First Edinburgh**, T0131-663 9233, or Traveline, T0870-6082608. There are also several buses (Mon-Sat) to and from **Berwick-upon-Tweed** which pass through **Duns** and **Coldstream**.

Berwickshire Coast *p199*
There are several buses daily to **Eyemouth** from **Edinburgh** (1 hr 40 mins), and there are a couple of daily buses (Mon-Fri) to and from **Kelso**, via **Duns**. There's also a daily service to and from **Berwick-upon-Tweed**.

First Edinburgh, T01896-752237, and Swan's Coaches, T01289-306436. Buses between **Edinburgh** and **Berwick-upon-Tweed** pass through **Coldingham** several times daily. There's also an hourly service between **St Abbs**, **Coldingham**, **Eyemouth** and **Berwick**. Traveline, T0870-6082608.

Berwick is on the main **London-Aberdeen** rail line and there are fast and frequent trains to and from Edinburgh.

If you're driving, the best route north is the scenic A1107 which joins the fast A1 near Cockburnspath.

Directory

The main border towns all have banks, post office, petrol stations and a decent range of shops, as well as internet access in the local library, details of which are available from the TICs.

Dumfries and Galloway

Dumfries and Galloway is one of Scotland's forgotten corners, forsaken by most visitors for the cities of Edinburgh and Glasgow or the grandeur of the Highlands. But the southwest has much to offer those prepared to leave the more-beaten track. Away from the main routes west from Dumfries to Stranraer and north to Glasgow, traffic and people are notable by their absence, leaving most of the region free from the tourist crush of more popular parts. Some of the most beautiful scenery is to be found along the Solway Coast, west from Dumfries to the Mull of Galloway. Here you'll find the romantic ruins of Caerlaverock Castle, Threave Castle and Sweetheart Abbey, along with Whithorn Priory, known as the 'Cradle of Christianity' in Scotland. Also on this lovely coast is the beguiling town of Kirkcudbright, inspiration for some of Scotland's most famous artists and still a thriving artistic colony. Rising behind the coastline are the Galloway Hills which form part of the 150,000-acre Galloway Forest Park, a vast area of mountains, moors, lochs and rivers, criss-crossed by numerous trails and footpaths suitable for all levels of fitness. Running right through the heart of the Galloway Hills is the 212-mile Southern Upland Way, one of the country's great long-distance walks, see page 220. The southwest also has strong literary associations. The great poet, Robert Burns, lived and died here, in Dumfries, and the town boasts several important Burns sights. » *For Sleeping, Eating and other listings, see pages 221-228.*

Ins and outs

Getting there and around

The region has a good network of buses. The main operators are Stagecoach Western, T01387-253496, and McEwan's, T01387-256533. National Express, T08705-808080, has long-distance coaches from London, Birmingham, Glasgow and Edinburgh to Stranraer, for the ferry crossing to Belfast and Larne in Northern Ireland. There are two train routes from Carlisle to Glasgow, via Dumfries and Moffat. There's also a line from Stranraer to Glasgow. For rail information, T08457-484950. Dumfries and Galloway council has a travel information line, T08457-090510, for all public transport services. Open Monday to Friday 0900-1700. » *For further details, see Transport page 227.*

Tourist information

Dumfries and Galloway Tourist Board has its head office in Dumfries ⓘ *64 Whitesands, T01387-245550, www.visit-dumfries-and-galloway.co.uk*. They have a range of free brochures and guidebooks for the region, including accommodation, birdwatching, cycling, fishing, walking and golfing. There are also tourist offices in Stranraer, Castle Douglas, Gatehouse of Fleet, Gretna Green, Kirkcudbright, Moffat and Newton Stewart.

Wedding bellows

In Scotland, a marriage declaration made before two witnesses used to be legally binding, and anyone could perform the ceremony. This meant that eloping couples from south of the border came to Scotland to have their weddings witnessed by whomever came to hand. As Gretna Green was the first available community on the main route north, it became the most popular destination for runaway lovers. In their desperation, many tied the knot at the first place to hand after getting off the stagecoach, and in Gretna this happened to be the local blacksmith's shop, situated at the crossroads. The marriage business boomed in the village, until 1940 when marriage by declaration was made illegal. However, under Scots law young couples can still marry at 16 without parental consent, and Gretna Green still attracts its fair share of Romeos and Juliets.

Annandale, Eskdale and the Lowther Hills

Cutting through the eastern reaches of Dumfires and Galloway is the A74(M), the congested main route from England to Scotland. Most people whizz straight through this area on their way north, but away from the main roads there are a few interesting places to visit.

Gretna Green → *Phone code: 01461 Colour map 6, grid C1.*

The first place you encounter across the border is the nondescript little village of Gretna Green. It's not a particularly interesting place to visit, but Gretna Green has been synonymous with marriage ceremonies for many years and thousands of couples still come here to tie the knot. **World Famous Old Blacksmith's Shop** ⓘ *T01461-338224, www.gretnagreen.com, Jan-Mar and Nov-Dec daily 0900-1700, Apr-May and Oct daily 0900-1800, Jun and Sep daily 0900-1900, Jul and Aug daily till 2000, £2, £1.50 concession*, houses a visitor centre with a small exhibition on Gretna Green's history as well as gift shops. Opposite is the tourist office which opens daily. There's also a rival blacksmith's shop, **Gretna Hall Blacksmith's Shop** ⓘ *T01461-337635, Apr-Oct daily 0900-2000, Nov-Mar daily 0900-1700, £0.80, children free*, at the **Gretna Hall Hotel**. This was where better-off runaway couples would come to maintain a class distinction.

Ecclefechan and Lockerbie → *Phone code: 01576. Colour map 6, grid C1.*

Nine miles northwest of Gretna Green on the A74(M) is the neat little village of Ecclefechan, birthplace of the great writer and historian **Thomas Carlyle** (1795-1881), one of the most powerful and influential thinkers in 19th-century Britain. His old home, The Arched House, is now a tiny museum known as **Carlyle's Birthplace** ⓘ *T01461-300666, Apr-30 Sep Fri-Mon 1330-1700. £2.50/£1.70*, and features a collection of personal memorabilia.

About eight miles north of Ecclefechan is **Lockerbie**, a quiet, unassuming little town which hit the headlines on 21 December 1988 when a Pan-Am jumbo jet, flying from Frankfurt to New York, was blown up by a terrorist bomb, killing all 196 passengers and crew. The plane's fragments fell on the town, killing a further 11 people. After many months of exhausting diplomatic efforts, the two suspects were extradited from Libya, tried in a Scottish court set up in the Netherlands, and sentenced to life imprisonment. But for the people of Lockerbie life has never been the same.

Langholm → *Phone code: 01387. Colour map 6, grid C2.*

Langholm sits at the confluence of three rivers – the Esk, Lewes and Wauchope – on the A7, one of the main routes north to Edinburgh, and a less stressful alternative to the A74(M). During the 18th century Langholm became a thriving textile town and is still a major centre of the Scottish tweed industry. This is clan Armstrong country and the **Clan Armstrong Trust Museum** ① *T01387-380610, Easter-Oct Tue-Sun 1400-1700, £1.50*, is a must for anyone with that particular surname. Neil was here, but we don't know if Gary has ever been.

Langholm was also the birthplace of the great **Hugh McDiarmid** (1892-1978), poet and co-founder of the Scottish National Party. He is also buried here, against the wishes of the local nobs, who took great exception to his radical views. On the hill above the town is the **McDiarmid Memorial**, a stunning modern sculpture which looks like a giant metallic open book. A path leads for about half a mile to another memorial, from where there are wonderful views across the Southern uplands and the Solway Firth. A signed single-track road leads off the A7, about half a mile north of Langholm, to a path which leads to the memorials.

North from Langholm

The A7 runs north to Hawick and on to Edinburgh. It also runs south to Carlisle, via **Canonbie**, through an area known as the Debatable Land until the border was settled in 1552. From Canonbie, the B6357 provides a more scenic alternative route to the Borders running through lovely **Liddesdale** towards Hawick and Jedburgh, see page 196. A shorter route to Liddesdale is to take the single-track road heading east off the A7 just to the north of Langholm, which joins the B6357 at Newcastleton.

Another scenic route from Langholm to the Borders region is the B709. It runs northwest to the tiny village of **Eskdalemuir**, 14 miles from Langholm, then north through the Eskdalemuir and Craik forests to **Ettrick**, where it follows the valley of the Ettrick Water to Selkirk, see page 193. About 1½ miles north of Eskdalemuir is the **Kagyu Samye Ling Tibetan Monastery** ① *T01387-373232, www.samyeling.org, daily 0900-1800 (tearoom and shops daily 1000-1700 and 1900-2200 at weekends), tours prices vary from £2-5, all inclusive 8-day retreats £300, weekend courses £45*. This Tibetan Buddhist centre was founded in 1967 for study, retreat and meditation, and incorporates the Samye Temple, the first Tibetan Buddhist monastery in the west. There are guided tours for visitors, regardless of faith, and a programme of retreats and weekend courses. There's also a café for vegetarian meals (pre-booking advised) and shops on site and pleasant walks through the gardens. Bus No 112 from Lockerbie stops at the centre.

Moffat → *Phone code: 01683. Colour map 6, grid C1. Population: 2,000.*

Just to the east of the A74(M), at the northern end of Annandale, is the neat and tidy market town of Moffat. Once a fashionable spa town, Moffat is now a centre for the local woollen industry, as clearly evidenced by the statue of a ram on its wide High Street. The tourist information centre is on Ladyknowes, off the A701 heading into town from the A74 ① *T01683-220620, daily Apr-Oct*. It has a selection of leaflets detailing the many local walks. Near the TIC is the **Moffat Woollen Mill** ① *T01683-220134, Mar-Oct daily 0900-1730, Nov-Feb daily till 1700, free*, where you can see a demonstration of traditional weaving and trace your Scottish ancestry. There's also a shop selling woollens and tartans. Nearby is the **Moffat Museum** ① *T01683-220868, Easter to end Sep Mon, Tue and Thu-Sat 1030-1300 and 1430-1700, Sun 1430-1700, £1*, which tells the town's eventful history.

Around Moffat

Moffat makes a convenient base from which to explore the Lowther Hills to the west and the wild and barren southwest Borders to the east, either by car or on foot. The

A708 to Selkirk is a very beautiful route which passes through the most stunning parts of the Southern Uplands. Ten miles northeast of Moffat on this road is the spectacular **Grey Mare's Tail** waterfall, which plunges 200 ft from a glacial hanging valley. It's only a five-minute walk from the car park up a series of steps to the base of the falls. More serious walkers can take the path which crosses the stream and climbs steeply up to **Loch Skeen**, the source of the falls. It's about an hour to the loch. From Loch Skeen experienced walkers can climb to the summit of **White Coomb** (2,696 ft). This is also a popular birdwatching area. The A708 carries on into the Borders region and passes the famous **Tibbie Shiels Inn**, see Sleeping page 201, on the shores of **St Mary's Loch**, see page 194.

Another scenic route from Moffat is the A701 which runs north towards Edinburgh. En route it meets the A72, which heads east to Peebles and along the Tweed Valley, see page 188. Six miles north of Moffat on the A701 you get a great view of the **Devil's Beef Tub**, a vast, deep natural bowl once used by Border *reivers* (rustlers) for hiding stolen cattle. The Tub was also used as a hide-out by persecuted Covenanters during Charles II's 'killing times'.

Further north the road enters **Tweeddale** and passes through tiny **Tweedsmuir**, where a spectacular side road climbs up into the hills to meet the A708 at St Mary's Loch, see page 194. Just to the north of Tweedsmuir is the historic **Crook Inn**. The old country inn has strong literary associations. **Robert Burns** wrote his poem *Willie Wastle's Wife* in what is now the bar, and Sir Walter Scott used to pay the occasional visit. From the inn you can climb **Broad Law** (2,756 ft), the second highest hill in southern Scotland.

Stagecoach Western bus No 199 runs along this route to Edinburgh on Fridays and Saturdays, T01387-253496.

Biggar → *Phone code: 01899. Colour map 5, grid B6.*

North of Moffat, is the old market town of Biggar, just across the regional border, in South Lanarkshire. Biggar stands on the A702, the main route from the M74 to Edinburgh, and makes a pleasant and convenient stopping-point for those driving to the capital from the south. The town centre has had a recent makeover and there are enough places of interest to warrant a few hours here. The tourist information centre ⓘ *155 High St, T01899-221066, Easter-Sep Mon-Sat 1000-1700, Sun 1200-1700.*

Moat Park Heritage Centre ⓘ *T01899-221050, Easter-Oct Mon-Sat 1030-1700, Sun 1400-1700. £2/£1.50*, is housed in a renovated church near the foot of Kirkstyle, off the High Street. It includes displays on local history, archaeology and geology as well as some very interesting tapestries. Ask here about details of **Hugh McDiarmid's Cottage**, which is three miles north of town. It was the home of the poet until his death and can be viewed by appointment only.

There are four other museums in Biggar. Close by, on North Back Road, is **Gladstone Court Museum** ⓘ *Apr-Oct Mon-Sat 1030-1700, Sun 1400-1700. £2/£1.50*, which features a Victorian street with shops, a bank and schoolroom preserved just as they were 150 years ago. The Gladstone family, ancestors of the 19th-century Liberal Prime Minister, William Ewart Gladstone, are buried in the churchyard of St Mary's Church. **Greenhill Covenanters' Museum** ⓘ *May-Sep daily 1400-1700, £1, £0.70 concession*, on Burnbrae, traces the development of the Covenanting movement. Nearby is the **Gasworks Museum** ⓘ *Jun-Sep daily 1400-1700, £1, £0.50 concession*, the only surviving coal-fired gasworks in Scotland. On Broughton Street is the **Puppet Theatre** ⓘ *T01899-220631, museum open Easter-end Aug Mon-Sat 1000-1630, Sun 1400-1630*, set up by Purves Puppets, a touring theatre company. The museum features puppets from all over the world, including some very strange ones indeed. There are also regular workshops, backstage tours and shows are held all year round in the Victorian theatre. All seats £5.

Biggar is overlooked by **Tinto Hill** (2,333 ft), near the village of Symington, four miles southwest of town at the junction of the A72 and A73. It's a fairly easy walk from the village to the summit, from where the views are fantastic. There's also a Druidic Circle and Bronze-Age burial cairn. A good track starts from near the Tinto Hill farm shop on the A73. Allow about three hours. Regular Biggar-Lanark buses pass through Symington.

The Lowther Hills

West of Moffat, between the A74(M) and Nithsdale, are the wild and bare Lowther Hills. About 13 miles north of Moffat, at Elvanfoot, the B7040 leaves the A74(M) and crosses the hills, passing through the old lead-mining villages of Leadhills and Wanlockhead to meet the A76 a few miles south of Sanquhar, see page 213.

Leadhills is a rather forlorn-looking place, but a few miles south is **Wanlockhead**, the highest village in Scotland at 1,500 ft and home of the **Museum of Lead Mining** ⓘ *T01659-74387, www.leadminingmuseum.co.uk, 1 Apr -31 Oct daily 1000-1630, £3.95, £2.75 concession.* The visitor centre gives an introduction to the mining industry and there's a guided tour of an old lead mine, miners' cottages and the 18th-century library. Wanlockhead was also a gold mining centre and you can try your hand at gold panning at the museum. From Leadhills **Britain's highest adhesion railway** ⓘ *T01555-820778, www.leadhillsrailway.co.uk, £3, concession £2.50, child £1*, runs to Wanlockhead, passing through the old mine workings.

Dumfries and around

➔ *Phone code: 01387. Colour map 5, grid C6. Population: 31,000.*

Dumfries is the largest town in southwest Scotland, straddling the River Nith, a few miles from the Solway Firth. Known as the 'Queen of the South', Dumfries has long been a thriving market town and seaport for a large agricultural hinterland, and its strategic position made it a prime target for English armies. Its long history of successive invasions began in 1306, when Robert the Bruce committed the first act of rebellion against Edward I by capturing Dumfries Castle, which led to the Wars of Independence. But it was town planners in the 1960s who did more to destroy the town centre than invading armies. Nevertheless, Dumfries is a pleasant and convenient base from which to explore the beautiful Solway Coast, and its associations with Robert Burns, who spent the last years of his life here, also make it worth a visit in its own right. There are many interesting sights lying within easy distance of Dumfries, including Caerlaverock Castle to the southeast, Drumlanrig Castle to the north in Nithsdale as well as some of the best mountain biking trails in Scotland, particularly in Mabie Forest, south of town on the road to New Abbey. » *For Sleeping, Eating and other listings, see pages 221-228.*

Ins and outs

Getting there and around The bus station is a short walk west of the High Street, at the top of Whitesands beside the river. The train station is on the east side of town, a five-minute walk from the centre. If driving, there's parking by the river opposite the TIC. Collect a disc from the TIC for three hours' free parking. For all bus times, call the Travel Information Line, T08457-090510, or Traveline T0870-6082608. » *For further details, see Transport page 227.*

Tourist information TIC ⓘ *64 Whitesands, on the corner of Bank St, T01387-253862. Apr, May and Oct daily 1000-1700, Jun-Sep daily 0930-1800.*

Sights

Most of the town's attractions and facilities are on the east side of the river. A tour of the main sights should begin on the pedestrianized High Street, at the **Burns Statue**, at its northern end. It shows the great bard sitting on a tree stump with his faithful dog at his feet. A few minutes' walk along the High Street is the **Midsteeple**, built in 1707 to serve as a courthouse and prison. Nearby, at 56 High Street, is the **Globe Inn**, one of Burns' regular drinking haunts, where you can sit in the poet's favourite chair and enjoy a drink, see Eating page 224. Continue down the High Street and follow the signs for **Burns' House** ⓘ *T01387-255297, Apr-Sep Mon-Sat 1000-1700, Sun 1400-1700, Oct-Mar Tue-Sat 1000-1300, 1400-1700, free*, in Burns Street, where the poet spent the last few years of his life, and died in 1796. It contains some interesting memorabilia, including original letters and manuscripts. Just to the south is the red sandstone **St Michael's Church**. In the churchyard is the **mausoleum** where Burns lies buried. Pick up a copy of the free Burns Trail leaflet from the TIC.

On the other side of the river is the award-winning **Robert Burns Centre** ⓘ *Mill Rd, T01387-264808, Apr-Sep Mon-Sat 1000-2000, Sun 1400-1700, Oct-Mar Tue-Sat 1000-1300 and 1400-1700, free, audio-visual £1.50, concession £0.75*, housed in an old water mill. It tells the story of Burns' last years in the town. On the hill above, centred around an 18th-century windmill tower, is **Dumfries Museum** ⓘ *T01387-253374, Apr-Sep Mon-Sat 1000-1700, Sun 1400-1700, Oct-Mar Tue-Sat 1000-1300 and 1400-1700, free*, which has good local history, natural history and anthropology displays. On the top floor of the windmill tower is a **Camera Obscura** ⓘ *Apr-Sep, Mon-Sat 1000-1700, Sun 1400-1700, £1.50, £0.75 concession*. Also on the west bank of the river, at the west end of the 15th-century Devorgilla Bridge, is the dinky **Old Bridge House** ⓘ *T01387-256904, Apr-Sep Mon-Sat 1000- 1700, Sun 1400-1700, free.* Built in 1660 and the town's oldest house, it is now a rather disjointed museum.

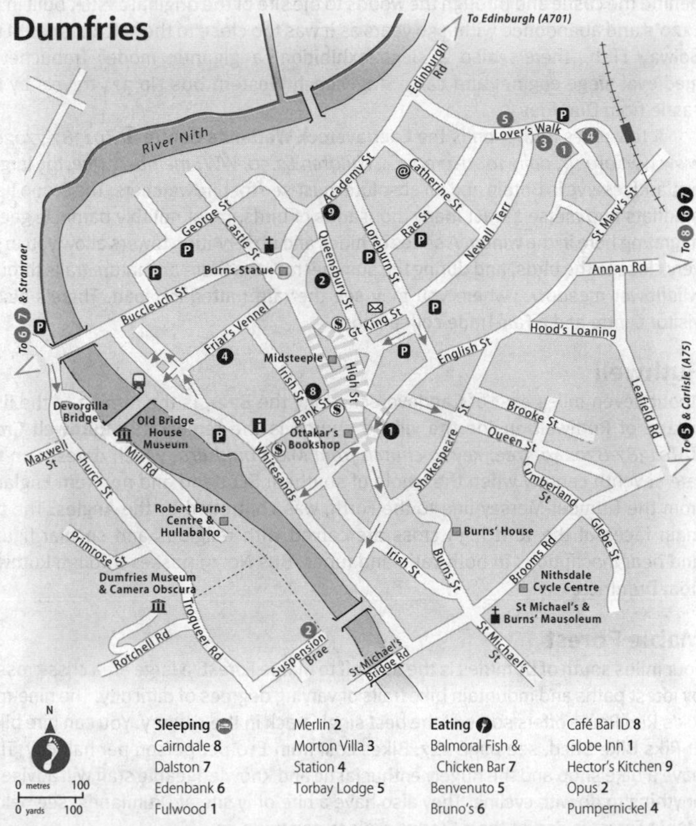

On the outskirts of town is the **Dumfries and Galloway Aviation Museum** ⓘ *Heathhall Industrial Estate, T01387-259546, www.dumfriesaviationmuseum.com, Easter-Oct Sat and Sun 1000-1700, Jul-Aug Wed-Fri 1100-1600, £2.50, concession/ child £1.50, family £7*, a diverting collection of old aircraft and memorabilia based around the original control tower of RAF Dumfries, and staffed by volunteers. It's all very hands-on and you can even sit in the cockpit of a jet fighter.

Caerlaverock Castle

ⓘ *T01387-770244 (HS), Apr-Sep 0930-1830, Oct-Mar Mon-Sat 0930-1630, Sun 1400-1630, £3, concession £2.30, child £0.80.*

Eight miles from Dumfries, on the east bank of the Nith estuary where it enters the Solway Firth, is the magnificent ruin of Caerlaverock Castle, the ultimate defensive fortress and one of the best-preserved medieval castles in Scotland. The unusual triangular-shaped castle, which dates from around 1277, was the stronghold of the Maxwells, the Wardens of the Western Marches. But though surrounded by a moat and impregnable-looking, it has fallen several times over the course of its long history. It was first besieged and captured in 1300 by Edward I of England during the Wars of Independence, then destroyed by Robert the Bruce. It was repaired in the 1330s, then 300 years later refurbished in the trendy Renaissance style by Robert Maxwell, first Earl of Nithsdale. But several years later it was attacked again, this time by the Covenanters, who captured it after a 13-week siege and proceeded to trash the place. Caerlaverock was never occupied again. A nature trail runs behind the castle and through the woods to the site of the original castle, built in the 1220's and abandoned within 50 years as it was too close to the salt marshes of the Solway Firth. There's also a siege exhibition, a gigantic model Trebuchet (a medieval siege engine) and café. Stagecoach Western bus No 371 travels by the castle from Dumfries.

A few miles further on is the **Caerlaverock Wetlands Centre** ⓘ *T01387-770200, www.wwt.org.uk, daily 1000-1700, £4, children £2.50, WWT members free*, the largest wetland reserve in Britain and an absolute must-see for birdwatchers. The 8,000 ha of mudflats and merse attract many thousands of birds, most notably barnacle geese, migrating here in the winter. A series of hides and observation towers allow you to get very close to the birds, and during the summer months there are nature trails through wildflower meadows, where you may see the rare natterjack toad. There's also a visitor centre and a Fair-Trade coffee shop.

Ruthwell

About seven miles east of Caerlaverock along the B724 is the turning to the little village of Ruthwell. Inside the village church is the remarkable **Ruthwell Cross** ⓘ *T01387-870249, free, key to church from Mrs Coulthard*, which dates from the late seventh century when the whole of southern Scotland and northern England, from the Humber-Mersey line to the Forth, was controlled by the Angles. The two main faces of the 18-ft high cross are carved with religious and secular figures and bear inscriptions in both Latin and runes. Bus No 79 passes through Ruthwell from Dumfries.

Mabie Forest

Four miles south of Dumfries is the turn-off to Mabie Forest, a large area criss-crossed by forest paths and mountain bike trails of varying degrees of difficulty. The nine-mile Rik's Red Route offers some of the best single track in the country. You can hire bikes at **Riks Bike Shed**, see page 227. Bikes cost from £10 per person per half day. They have a bike shop and the hugely enthusiastic and knowledgeable staff will advise on anything to do with cycling. They also have a hire-only site at Drumlanrig, see below. Mabie Forest is part of the 7 Stanes project, see page 57.

West of Dumfries

Off the A75 to Castle Douglas, is **Glenkiln Reservoir**, where you'll find an extraordinary collection of sculptures scattered amongst the hills, woods and meadows of Glenkiln Estate. There are six works in all, the easiest ones to find being *John the Baptist* by Rodin, which stands at the head of the reservoir, and *Standing Figure* by Henry Moore. There are other works by Moore as well as one by Epstein, which is hidden in a copse of Scots Pine. Heading west on the A75, take the turning right for Shawhead, about nine miles west of Dumfries. From Shawhead, follow signs for the reservoir.

Ellisland Farm

ⓘ *T01387-740426, www.ellislandfarm.co.uk, Apr-Sep Mon-Sat 1000-1300 and 1400-1700, Sun 1400-1700, Oct-Mar Tue-Sat 1000-1700, £2.50, £1 concession, child free.* Six miles northwest of Dumfries, on the A76 at Hollywood, is Ellisland Farm. This was the home of Robert Burns from 1788 to 1791, during which time he built the farmhouse and tried to introduce new farming methods. Ultimately, this venture collapsed and he moved to Dumfries, but not before writing his famous ghost story, *Tam o' Shanter*, and Hogmanay favourite, *Auld Lang Syne*. The farmhouse is now a museum displaying various personal items.

North of Dumfries

About 14 miles north of Dumfries is **Thornhill**, where the A702 heads eight miles west to the peaceful little conservation village of **Moniaive**. Bus No 202 runs to Moniaive from Dumfries. Four miles north of Thornhill is the turning for **Drumlanrig Castle** ⓘ *T01848-330248, www.drumlanrigcastle.org.uk, castle Easter and May to early Sep Mon-Sat 1100-1600, Sun 12001600, gardens Easter-end Sep daily 1100-1700, £6, concessions £4, child £2*, more French château than Scottish castle. This sumptuous stately home of the Duke of Buccleuch and Queensberry is renowned for its superb art collection, which reflects the mind-boggling wealth of its owners. Included are works by such luminaries as Rembrandt, Leonardo Da Vinci, Holbein, Breughel and Van Dyck, as well as numerous family portraits by Allan Ramsay and Godfrey Kneller. After all that you may need to clear your head with a stroll round the extensive country park. You can also hire mountain bikes and explore a network of trails. There's also a **bicycle museum**, commemorating the fact that the bicycle was invented nearby, at Keir Mill.

Seven miles north of Drumlanrig, the B797 turns right (east) off the A76 and climbs up to **Wanlockhead**, the highest village in Scotland, see 210. A few miles further, on the A76, is the neat little town of **Sanquhar**, which lies on the Southern Upland Way.

New Abbey and around

→ *Phone code: 01387. Colour map 5, grid C6.*

Seven miles south of Dumfries, in the endearing little village of New Abbey, are the graceful red sandstone ruins of **Sweetheart Abbey** ⓘ *T01387-850397 (HS), Apr-Sep daily 0930-1830, Oct-Mar Mon-Wed and Sat 0930-1630, Thu 0930-1200, Fri and Sun 1400-1630, £1.80, concession £1.30, child £0.75*, founded by Cistercian monks in 1273. The abbey gets its name from the extreme marital devotion of its patron, Lady Devorgilla de Balliol, wife of John, who founded Balliol College, Oxford. On his death she had his heart embalmed and carried it around with her, until her own death in 1290. Now both she and the heart are buried in the presbytery. The ruins can be appreciated just as easily from outside the perimeter fence, or even better, from the patio of the **Abbey Cottage tearoom**, see page 224. On the northern edge of the village is **Shambellie House Museum of Costume** ⓘ *T01387-850375, Apr-Oct daily 1100-1700, £2.50, concession £1.50*, a Victorian country house set in beautiful

Drumlanrig Castle became front page news on 27 August 2003 when thieves walked off with Leonardo Da Vinci's Madonna with Yarnwinder*, worth a cool £40 million.*

gardens, which houses a collection of period costumes from the late 18th to the early 20th centuries. New Abbey is dominated by **Criffel Hill** (1,867 ft). One and a half miles south of the village take the turning for Ardwell Mains Farm, from where a track leads to the summit. The views from the top are magnificent, stretching all the way south to the lakes and across to the Borders.

A few miles south of New Abbey, at **Kirkbean**, is the turning for the **John Paul Jones Cottage** ⓘ *T01387-880613, Apr-Jun Tue-Sun 1000-1700, Jul and Aug daily 1000-1700, £2 (£1)*, birthplace of the US naval hero. It's now a small museum and includes an exhibition and audio visual of his amazing life. While you're here don't miss a visit to the **Steamboat Inn**, see page 224, in the tiny hamlet of Carsethorn, at the end of the single-track road. South of Kirkbean, at **Southerness**, there's an excellent championship golf course ⓘ *T01387-880677*, overlooking Sandyhills Bay.

Rockcliffe and Kippford → *Phone code: 01556. Colour map 5, grid C6.*

The A710 turns west south of Kirkbean and parallels the Solway Coast, past the wide expanse of the perfectly-named **Sandyhills Bay** to **Colvend**. About a mile beyond, a side road turns off to the impossibly cute little village of **Rockcliffe**, its row of whitewashed cottages facing a rocky cove and beach at the mouth of the Urr estuary. On a sunny day it's almost too perfect.

From Rockcliffe you can walk about 1½ miles to neighbouring Kippford, a popular sailing centre, along the **Jubilee Path** (NTS). The path passes the **Mote of Mark**, an ancient Celtic hillfort. Another path runs south from Rockcliffe along the cliff tops, to **Castlehill Point**. From Kippford, at low tide, you can walk across the causeway to **Rough Island**, a 20-acre offshore bird sanctuary owned by the NTS. During May and June, when the terns and oystercatchers are nesting, it's out of bounds.

Kirkcudbright, Castle Douglas and around

→ *Phone code: 01557. Colour map 5, grid C5. Population: 3,500.*

Kirkcudbright (pronounced 'kir-koo-bree') sits at the mouth of the River Dee and is, without doubt, the most attractive town in the southwest. It has an airy and spacious feel to it, its wide streets lined with elegant Georgian villas and Victorian town houses. The Glasgow Boys, see below, started to come here in the late 19th century and established an artists' colony, and ever since then Kirkcudbright has been a favourite haunt of artists – the Scottish equivalent of St Ives in Cornwall. Several miles northeast of Kirkcudbright, Castle Douglas couldn't be more different, geared as it is towards to more active outdoor pursuits such as cycling, golf and watersports on nearby Loch Ken. ⏩ *For Sleeping, Eating and other listings, see pages 221-228.*

Ins and outs

Getting there and around Kirkcudbright, 25 miles west of Dumfries, can be reached via the A75 or A711. It is 50 miles east of Stranraer on the A75. Bus 500 runs between Dumfries and Stranraer passing through Castle Douglas and Newton Stewart. Bus Nos 501, 502 and 505 run between Kirkcudbright and Dumfries. ⏩ *For further information, see page 227.*

Tourist information Kirkcudbright TIC ⓘ *beside the harbour, T01557-330494, Apr-Jun, Sep and Oct 1000-1700; Jul and Aug 0930-1800*, will book accommodation for you during the busy summer season, and sell the leaflet *Walks Around Kirkcudbright*, which details many local walks. See also www.kirkcudbright.co.uk.

Kirkcudbright

Near the harbour is **MacLellan's Castle** ⓘ *T01557-331856 (HS), Apr-Sep 0930-1830, £2, concession £1.50, child £0.75*, which is a castellated town house rather than a

The good, the bad and the nautical

John Paul Jones (1747-92) was a hero to the Americans, but the British saw him as a pirate. Early on in his nautical career, as plain John Paul, he was imprisoned in Kirkcudbright Tolbooth for the manslaughter of his ship's carpenter. His fortunes changed, along with his name, in later life when he joined the US fleet in 1775. Four years later, during the American War of Independence, in command of a few American and French ships, he won a dramatic victory against a powerful British force off the English coast and became an American hero. He is generally regarded as the father of the modern US Navy.

defensive fortress. It was built in the 1570s by the then-provost, Thomas MacLellan of Bombie, using stone from the adjoining ruined monastery. The castle is relatively complete, except for the roof, and inside there's a warren of rooms to explore.

Nearby, at 12 High Street, is the wonderful **Broughton House** ⓘ *T01557-330437 (NTS), house closed for restoration (may open 2004, check at TIC), garden open Apr-Oct daily 1300-1700 (1100 in Jul), £2, concession £1 (honesty box)*, the Georgian town house which was bought in 1901 by E A Hornel, the renowned artist and member of the 'Glasgow Boys', an influential late 19th-century group of painters who established an artists' colony in Kirkcudbright, see also page 141. Many of Hornel's works are on display here, in the excellent **Hornel Gallery**. The artist also designed the beautiful **Japanese Garden**, which leads from the house down to the river.

Only a few minutes' walk along the High Street is the early 17th-century tolbooth, which now houses the **Tolbooth Art Centre** ⓘ *T01557-331556, all year Mon-Sat 1100-1600 and Sun 1400-1700, free*. As well as featuring a display of works by Hornel and his fellow 'colonists', including local artist Jessie King, the centre also tells the story of the town's artists colony from the late 19th century to the present day, and there are temporary exhibitions of local arts and crafts and photography. Another of the town's art galleries is the **Harbour Cottage Gallery** ⓘ *Mar-Nov Mon-Sat 1030-1230, 1400-1700, Sun 1400-1700, £0.80, concession £0.50, child free*, which hosts a variety of shows throughout the year. From art to artefact, one of the town's more eclectic attractions is the **Stewartry Museum** ⓘ *St Mary St, T01557-331643, all year Mon-Sat 1100-1600 and Sun 1400-1700, free*, an extraordinarily diverse collection of exhibits reflecting the social and natural history of this part of the Solway coast, once known as the Kirkcudbright Stewartry because it was administered by the kings' stewards during the 14th and 15th centuries.

A few miles northwest of town, off the A75 at Twynholm, is a **museum** dedicated to Formula 1 star **David Coulthard** ⓘ *T01557-860050, Apr-Oct Mon-Tue, Thu-Sat 1000-1600, open Wed 1000-1600 in Jun, £2.50, £1.50 concessions*, who was born in the area. The collection includes memorabilia from his go-carting days up to the present. There's a popular tearoom too called **The Pit Stop**.

Dundrennan Abbey and Orchardton Tower

About seven miles southeast of Kirkcudbright are the ruins of **Dundrennan Abbey** ⓘ *T01557-500262 (HS), Apr-Sep daily 0930-1830, Oct-Mar Sat 0930-1630 and Sun 1400-1630, £1.80, concession £1.30, child £0.75*, a 12th-century Cistercian establishment standing in a beautifully bucolic setting in a secluded valley. You may not be too surprised to learn that the abbey has associations with Mary, Queen of

Kirkcudbright's name comes from the now-vanished Kirk of Cuthbert, which relates to St Cuthbert, who converted much of southern Scotland to Christianity

 Scots. She spent her last night on Scottish soil here. Although Bus No 505 travels between Kirkcudbright and Dumfries passing through Dundrennan, if you're feeling energetic, the better option is the lovely five-mile walk along quiet country roads.

A mile further east is the lovely wee village of Auchencairn and, between here and Palnackie, see Festivals and events page 226, is the turn-off for the 15th-century **Orchardton Tower** ⓘ *(HS) Apr-Sep daily 0930-1830, Oct-Mar Mon-Sat 0930-1630, free, key available locally*, the only circular tower house in Scotland. A few miles north of Palnackie is **Dalbeattie**, a distinctly unremarkable town but with a wide range of shops and services. Just south of Dalbeattie, off the A710 to Kippford, is the start of the notorious **Hardrock Trail**, a must for all mountain-bike enthusiasts.

Castle Douglas

The neat little town of Castle Douglas, standing on the edge of lovely little **Carlingwark Loch**, was laid out in the 18th century by Sir William Douglas, a local lad who made his fortune in the Americas. There's nothing of note in the town itself, but it makes a good alternative base for exploring Galloway Forest Park, see page 217, and the surrounding sights. The A713 runs north from Castle Douglas along the shores of long and skinny **Loch Ken**, a popular watersports centre, with sailing, windsurfing, water-skiing, canoeing, rowing and fishing, see Activities and tours page 227. There's also an RSPB nature reserve on the west bank, and walking trails. Castle Douglas TIC ⓘ *Market Hill Car Park, T01556-502611, Apr-Jun, Sep and Oct daily 1000-1630, Jul and Aug daily 1000-1800.*

Threave Garden and Estate

ⓘ *T01557-502575 (NTS), gardens all year from 0930 till sunset; visitor centre Apr-Oct 0930-1730, Feb-Mar and Nov-Dec 1000-1600; house Mar-Oct Wed-Fri and Sun 1100-1600, guided tours only, £9, concession £6.50, garden only £5, concession £3.75.*
A mile southwest of town, off the A75 or reached by the lochside road, is this estate, the NTS horticultural school's magnificent floral extravaganza. The best time to visit is early spring when over 200 types of daffodils burst into bloom, but it's a very colourful experience at any time of the year. Now open to the public, the house can be viewed by guided tour only. There's a very good self-service restaurant in the visitor centre, see Eating page 224.

Threave Castle

ⓘ *T0131-6688800 (HS), 1 Apr-30 Sep daily 0930-1830, last boat back at 1800, £2.20, concession £1.60, child £0.75.*
Two miles further west at Bridge of Dee, a country lane branches north (right) and leads for about a mile to the start of a footpath which takes you to the gaunt tower of Threave Castle, standing alone on an island in the middle of the River Dee. Threave was built in the 14th century by Archibald 'the grim', third Earl of Douglas, and head of the 'Black' Douglas line. The Douglases were one of Scotland's most powerful baronial families and the main line, the 'Black' Douglases, were descended from 'the Good' Sir James, trusted friend of Robert the Bruce. The outer wall of the castle was added in 1450 in an unsuccessful attempt to defend it against King James II, who was determined to break the power of the maverick Border family. The Covenanters reduced Threave to its present ruinous state in 1640, and little remains of the interior. It's a romantic ruin nevertheless, especially as you have to be ferried across to the island. It's a 1-km walk from the car park, then ring the bell for the custodian to take you across in a small rowing boat. There's a tearoom at the car park.

Gatehouse of Fleet

The quiet little town of Gatehouse of Fleet lies 10 miles west of Kirkcudbright, a mile or so north of the A75. It's an attractive place on the banks of the Water of Fleet, surrounded by forested hills. On the main street, opposite the TIC, is the **Mill on the Fleet Museum** ⓘ *T01557-814099, Easter-Oct daily 1030-1700, £1.50, concession £1, child £0.50*, housed in a restored 18th-century cotton mill complete with working waterwheel. The museum traces the history of the town's cotton industry which lasted from the mid-18th century until the early 19th century. There's also a bookshop and a pleasant café with riverside terrace.

There are several pleasant walks in the surrounding countryside, including to **Cardoness Castle** ⓘ *T01557-814427 (HS), Apr-Sep daily 0930-1830, Oct-Mar Sat 0930-1630 and Sun 1400-1630, £2.20, concession £1.60, child £0.75, about 1½ miles to the south, standing on a hill overlooking the B796 which connects Gatehouse with the main A75*. The remarkably well-preserved ruin was the home of the MacCullochs and is a classic example of a 15th-century tower house. There are excellent views across Fleet Bay from the top floor. Details of other local walks are given in a leaflet which is on sale at the tourist office. Gatehouse of Fleet TIC ⓘ *in the car park on the High Street, T01557-814212, Mar, Apr and Oct daily 1000-1630, Jun and Sep till 1700, Jul and Aug till 1800*.

Galloway Forest Park

Between the Solway Firth and the Ayrshire coast lies Galloway Forest Park, the largest forest park in Britain, covering 300 square miles of forested hills, wild and rugged moorland and numerous lochs. It's a vast and beautiful area crisscrossed by waymarked Forestry Commission trails and longer routes, such as the Southern Upland Way, see page 220. It's also home to a rich variety of fauna, such as feral goats, red deer, falcons and even golden eagles. ▸▸ *For Sleeping, Eating and other listings, see pages 221-228.*

Ins and outs

Getting there Newton Stewart is the main service town for Galloway Forest Park. It lies on the main A75 between Dumfries and Stranraer and there are regular buses to and from each of these destinations. ▸▸ *For further details, see Transport page 227.*

Getting around The best way to see the park is on foot or by bike. Those wishing to hike in the park should be properly equipped and buy the relevant Ordnance Survey maps. As well as the OS map, *The Galloway Hills: A Walker's Paradise*, by George Brittain, is also useful. National Cycle Route 7, incorporates 30 miles of off-road trails through the park, as well as the Raider's Road, see below.

Tourist information Newton Stewart TIC ⓘ *Dashwood Sq, just off the main street and opposite the bus station, T01671-402431, Apr and Oct daily 1000-1630, May, Jun and Sep till 1700, Jul and Aug till 1800*. They can book accommodation for you (for a £3 fee) as well as provide lots of information on walking and cycling in Galloway Forest Park. See also their free guide to Ranger led walks and activities. There are visitor centres at Glentrool, Kirroughtree and Clatteringshaws (see below). The Forestry Commission regional office is at Creebridge, east of Newton Stewart, T01671-402420, www.forestry.gov.uk/gallowayforestpark.

▲ The park → *Phone code: 01556. Colour map 5, grid C5. OS Outdoor Leisure Map No 32.*

The A712 runs northwest from Newton Stewart, cutting through the southern section of the Galloway Forest Park, to New Galloway. This 19-mile stretch of scenic road is known as **The Queen's Way**. Seven miles southwest of New Galloway the road skirts **Clatteringshaws Loch**, hidden amongst the pine trees, with a 14-mile footpath running round it. This path joins the Southern Upland Way which winds its way north towards the **Rhinns of Kells**, a range of hills around 2,600 ft that form the park's eastern boundary. On the shores of the loch is the **Clatteringshaws Forest Wildlife**

 Centre ⓘ *T01556-420285, Apr-Oct daily 1030-1700, free*, which gives an introduction to the park's flora and fauna. From the centre you can follow the lochside trail to **Bruce's Stone**, a huge boulder marking the spot where Robert the Bruce is said to have rested after yet another victory over those troublesome southern neighbours.

About a mile southwest of the centre, opposite the massive Clatteringshaws dam, is the turning for the **Raiders' Road**, a 10-mile timber road and erstwhile cattle rustlers' route which runs from the A712 and follows the Water of Dee southeast to Stroan Loch and then turns north to meet the A762 just north of Mossdale. About halfway along the trail is the otter's pool, in a clearing in the forest, a great place for a picnic. The Raider's Road is only open between April and October, and there's a toll charge. It can be driven but is best enjoyed on two wheels. The A762 heads north along the western shore of Loch Ken back to New Galloway, making a circuit of about 20 miles, starting and ending in New Galloway. About three miles southwest of Clatteringshaws Loch along The Queen's Way is the **Galloway Red Deer Range** ⓘ *T07771-748401, end of Jun to mid-Sep Tue and Thu 1100 and 1400, Sun 1430, £2.50, £1 child*, where you can get close up to the deer, stroke them and take photos.

About three miles east of Newton Stewart, near Palnure, is the **Kirroughtree Visitor Centre** ⓘ *T01671-402165, Apr-Sep daily 1030-1700, Oct closes at 1630*, the southern gateway to Galloway Forest Park. A series of waymarked trails and cycle routes lead from here into the forest. There's also a tea room serving light meals. One of the most accessible and loveliest parts of Galloway Forest Park is **Glen Trool**. Ten miles north of Newton Stewart at Bargrennan, on the A714, a narrow road winds its way for five miles past Glen Trool Village to **Loch Trool**, hemmed in by the wooded slopes of the glen. Halfway up the loch is **Bruce's Stone**, which marks the spot where Robert the Bruce's guerrilla band ambushed the pursuing English force in 1307, after they had routed the main army at Solway Moss.

There are a number of excellent hiking trails which start out from here, including the one to the summit of **Merrick** (2,766 ft), the highest peak in southern Scotland. It's a tough climb of about four hours, but fairly straightforward and well worth the effort. There are also numerous Forestry Commission trails for the less fit/experienced/adventurous. Part of the **Southern Upland Way**, see page 220, runs through Glen Trool and along the southern shores of Loch Trool, then continues east towards Clatteringshaws Loch. On the road to Loch Trool, about a mile from the village, is the **Glen Trool Visitor Centre** ⓘ *T01671-402420, Apr-Oct daily 1030-1730.*

New Galloway and around → *Phone code: 01644. Colour map 5, grid C5.*

One of the most convenient entry points for Galloway Forest Park is New Galloway, a pleasant little village of whitewashed houses nestled in the valley of **The Glenkens**, which runs north from Loch Ken. A few miles north of New Galloway is the village of **Dalry**, or St John's town of Dalry, to give it it's full name, sitting beside the Water of Ken and giving access to the Southern Upland Way. About five miles farther north on the A713 is the turning to **Polmaddy Settlement**, a reconstructed Galloway village dating from before the Clearances of the 18th and 19th centuries.

Newton Stewart and around → *Phone code: 01671. Colour map 5, grid C4.*

Population: 3,200.

The amiable little town of Newton Stewart is a popular base for hiking in the hills of Galloway Forest Park, especially around **Glen Trool**. Set on the west bank of the River Cree at the junction of the main A75 and the A714, amidst beautiful wooded countryside, Newton Stewart is also a major centre for salmon and trout fishing. The season runs from March till mid-October. Permits, guides and the hire of fishing gear can all be arranged at the fishing tackle shops in town.

Four miles north of town, reached via the A714, is the **Wood of Cree Nature Reserve** ⓘ *T01671-402861*, the largest ancient woodland in southern Scotland. This

RSPB reserve is home to a huge variety of birdlife, including pied flycatchers, redstarts and wood warblers. There are nature trails running for two miles through the forest in the Cree Valley. Southeast of town, just beyond Palnure, on the A75, is **Creetown**, standing on the east shore of Wigtown Bay, overlooked by the distinctive bulk of Cairnsmore of Fleet hill (2,330 ft). Creetown is most notable for its **Gem Rock Museum** ⓘ *T01671-820357, www.gemrock.net, Easter-Sep daily 0930-1800, Oct and Nov daily 1000-1600, Dec-Feb Sat and Sun 1000-1600, £3.25, concession £2.75, child £1.75, family £8.25*, which has a wide range of precious stones on display.

The far southwest → *Colour map 5, grid C3-5.*

South of the A75 is the peninsula of fertile rolling farmland known as the Machars. It's a somewhat neglected corner of the southwest but has strong early-Christian associations, and there are many important sites. The main town in the far southwest, Stranraer, wins no prizes for beauty or tourist appeal, but as Scotland's main ferry port for Northern Ireland it's an important town which sees a lot of through traffic. It sits on the shores of sheltered Loch Ryan on the Rhinns of Galloway, a windswept peninsula shaped like the head of a pick-axe at the end of the Solway Coast. Nine miles southwest of Stranraer on the windswept and rugged west coast of the Rhinns is the extremely photogenic old port of Portpatrick. ▸▸ *For Sleeping, Eating and other listings, see pages 221-228.*

The Machars

The disconsolate little town of **Wigtown** sits on the northwesterly shore of Wigtown Bay and is notable for its large number of bookshops (18 at the last count). It is now gaining a reputation as Scotland's National Book Town with festivals held throughout the year, www.wigtown-booktown.co.uk. If you need to buy a book in the southwest, then this is the place to do it.

Eleven miles south from Wigtown is the village of **Whithorn**, which occupies a crucially place in Scotland's history. It was here in the fifth century, that **St Ninian** established a mission and built the first Christian church north of Hadrian's Wall. The tiny church, which he called **Candida Casa** (bright shining place), has not survived but after Ninian's death a priory was built to house his tomb. This became a famous seat of learning and an important place of pilgrimage for penitents from England and Ireland, as well as from Scotland. **Whithorn Story** ⓘ *T01988-500508, Apr-Oct daily 1030-1700, £2.70, concessions £1.50*, features artefacts uncovered by the archaeological dig in the ruins of the 12th-century priory and an audio-visual display telling the story of the area's development. The adjacent **Priory Museum** contains some important interesting archaeological finds and early-Christian sculpture, including the Latinus Stone which dates from AD 450 and is the earliest Christian memorial in Scotland.

Four miles away is the misnamed **Isle of Whithorn**, which isn't an island at all but an atmospheric old fishing village built around a natural harbour. The village is the site of the ruined 13th-century **St Ninian's Chapel**, built for pilgrims who landed here from England and Ireland. Along the coast to the west of the village is **St Ninian's Cave**, said to have been used by the saint as a private place of prayer. It is reached via a footpath off the A747 before entering the Isle of Whithorn.

From Whithorn the A747 heads west to meet the coast and then runs northwest along the east shore of **Luce Bay** for 15 miles till it meets the A75 at the pretty little village of Glenluce. Two miles north of the village, signposted off the A75, is **Glenluce Abbey** ⓘ *Apr-Oct 0930-1830, Oct-Mar Sat 0930-1630, Sun 1400-1630, £1.80, £1.30 concession*, founded in 1192 by Roland, Earl of Galloway for the Cistercian order. The remains, set in a beautiful and peaceful valley, include a handsome early

16th-century Chapter House with a vaulted ceiling noted for its excellent acoustics. The abbey was visited by Robert the Bruce, James IV and, you guessed it, Mary, Queen of Scots. Buses 430 and 500 between Newton Stewart and Stranraer stop in Glenluce village and you can walk from there.

Stranraer

The main attraction here is the medieval tower which is all that remains of the 16th-century **Castle of St John** ⓘ *T01776-705544, Apr-mid Sep Mon-Sat 1000-1300 and 1400-1700, £1.20, concession £0.60,* one of the main headquarters of Graham of Claverhouse, the fanatical persecutor of the Protestant Covenanters in the late 17th century. Many of them died in the castle dungeons. It was later used as a prison in the 19th century. Inside, an exhibition traces the castle's history. Also worth a peek is the **Stranraer Museum** ⓘ *T01776-705088, Mon-Fri 1000-1700, Sat 1000-1300, 1400-1700, free,* which features displays on local history and has a section devoted to the life of Arctic explorer Sir John Ross (1777-1856), whose expeditions to find the Northwest Passage to the Pacific led to the discovery, in 1831, of the North Magnetic Pole. His house, called North West Castle, is now a hotel (see below). The tourist information centre ⓘ *28 Harbour St, T01776702595, Apr-Jun, Oct and Nov Mon-Sat 0930-1730, Sun 1000-1600, Jul-Sep Mon-Sat 0930-1730, Sun 1000-1630, Dec-Mar Mon-Sat 1000-1600.*

Three miles east of Stranraer are **Castle Kennedy Gardens** ⓘ *T01776-702024, Apr-Sep daily 1000-1700, £3, £2 concession,* famous for their riotous rhododendrons and magnificent monkey puzzle trees. The 75 acres of landscaped gardens are set on a peninsula between two lochs and two castles – Castle Kennedy and Lochinch Castle.

Portpatrick to the Mull of Galloway

Until the mid-19th century it was the main departure point for Northern Ireland but is now a peaceful little holiday resort and a good base from which to explore the southern part of the peninsula. You can arrange sea fishing trips from Portpatrick ⓘ *£8 for half a day, T01776-810468.* Portpatrick is also the starting point for the **Southern Upland Way,** the 212-mile coast-to-coast route which ends at Cockburnspath on the Berwickshire coast, see below.

From Portpatrick the road runs south to the Mull of Galloway through lush, green farmland which receives high average rainfall. The Rhinns are also warmed by the Gulf Stream which gives the peninsula the mildest climate in Scotland and means it's almost frost-free. This is beautifully demonstrated at **Logan Botanic Garden,** ⓘ *T01776-860231, Apr-Sep daily 1000-1800, Mar/Oct 1000-1700, £3, concession £2.50, children £1,* an outpost of Edinburgh's Royal Botanic Garden, about a mile north of the tiny village of Port Logan. The garden boasts a vast array of exotic, subtropical flora from the southern hemisphere, including tree ferns and cabbage palms. Bus No 407 from Stranraer passes through Port Logan on its way to Drummore.

Five miles further south is the **Mull of Galloway**, a dramatic, storm-lashed headland and Scotland's most southerly point, only 25 miles from Ireland and the Isle of Man. The narrow isthmus is an **RSPB nature reserve** and the home of thousands of seabirds such as guillemots, razorbills and puffins. There's a small information centre ⓘ *T01671-402861, late May-Aug.*

▲ Southern Upland Way

This is most famous and demanding of walks, the 212-mile Southern Upland Way, running from Portpatrick to Cockburnspath on the Berwickshire coast in the east, south of Dunbar. The route passes through a great variety of scenery from the Rhinns of Galloway to the wild heartland of Southern Scotland to the gentler eastern Borders. The most picturesque sections are the beginning and the end, but in between the highlights include Glen Trool, the Lowther Hills, St Mary's Loch and the River Tweed. A route leaflet is available from the **Countryside Ranger Service** ⓘ *Scottish Borders Council, Harestanes Visitor Centre, Ancrum, Jedburgh TD8 6UQ, T/F01835-830281.* There is also a trail pack, available from the Dumfries and Galloway or Scottish Borders tourist boards. See also www.dumgal.gov.uk/southernuplandway.

Sleeping

Annandale, Eskdale and the Lowther Hills *p207*

There's plenty of accommodation in Moffat but it's a busy place in Jul and Aug and you'll have to book ahead.

C **Best Western Moffat House Hotel**, Moffat, T01683-220039, www.moffathouse.co.uk. 20 rooms. This impressive mansion is the best of several hotels lining the High St. Has a good restaurant, the Adam Library, which does a 3-course dinner for £24.

C **Riverside Inn**, Canonbie, near Langholm, T01387-371512, www.langholm.com/riverside, serves superb pub food and is also a good place to stay.

C **Well View Private Hotel**, Ballplay Rd, Moffat, T01683-220184, www.wellview.co.uk. Overlooking the town is this lovely Victorian house with an excellent restaurant, see Eating.

D **Skirling House**, at Skirling, about 3 miles northeast of Biggar, T01899-860274, www.skirlinghouse.com, open Mar-Dec, a wonderful B&B with superb home cooking.

D **Star Hotel**, 44 High St, Moffat, T01683-220156, www.famousstarhotel.com. Claims to be the narrowest hotel in the UK, so not for the large of waist.

D-E **Hartfell House**, Hartfell Cres, Moffat, T01683-220153, robert.white@virgin.net. Elegant and supremely comfortable guest house which is about a 10-min walk from the High St.

D-E **Lindsaylands House**, 1 mile west of Biggar, T01899-220033. An excellent B&B.

D-E **The Reivers Rest**, 81 High St, Langholm, T01387-381343, www.reivers-rest.demon.co.uk. Serves bar meals and real ales.

E **Border House**, 28 High St, Langholm, T01387-380376, cairns@borderhouse.fsnet.co.uk, one of several B&Bs in town.

E **Kirkland House**, Well Rd, Moffat, T01683-221133, www.kirkland-moffat.co.uk. 4 spacious rooms, 2 en suite. Former manse, only a few mins from the High St. Parking. Friendly and comfortable. Caters for vegetarians.

F **Lotus Lodge**, Wanlockhead, T01659-74252, open Apr-Oct, on the Southern Upland Way, is this youth hostel.

Camping

Ewes Water Caravan & Camping Park, T01387-380386, open Apr-Sep, close to Langholm.

Hammerlands Farm, T01683-220436, open Mar-Nov, about a mile east of Moffat by the A708, has a campsite.

Dumfries and around *p210, map p211*

A **Comlongon Castle**, T01387-870283, www.comlongon.com. For a bit of luxury, try this 14th-century, family-owned castle and adjacent mansion house hotel. To get there, head north from Ruthwell for about a mile to Clarencefield, where a signposted road turns left (west) for another mile to the castle.

B **Cairndale Hotel**, English St, Dumfries, T01387-254111, www.cairndalehotel.co.uk. 91 rooms. Popular with business visitors with excellent leisure facilities as well as a good restaurant, hosts a ceilidh on Sun nights (May-Oct).

B **Cavens**, Kirkbean near New Abbey, T01387-880234. Country house hotel, once owned by tobacco baron, Robert Oswald. The perfect place to get away from whatever it is you want to get away from, and superb food, see Eating p224.

B **Station Hotel**, 49 Lovers Walk, Dumfries, T01387-254316, www.stationhotel.co.uk. 32 rooms. Refurbished classic Victorian hotel, very handy for the train station and has a good restaurant.

C **Millbrae House**, Rockcliffe, T01556-630217. Just a short walk from the sea. Also have studio flat for rent. Open Mar-Oct.

C **Trigony House Hotel**, Closeburn, Thornhill, 01843-331211, www.trigonyhotel.co.uk. Former shooting lodge for Closeburn Castle, Trigony combines the traditional estate living with the cosy hospitality of a family home. Ideal base for fishing and walking holiday but it is the food that really sets it apart. Everything is home-made, using organic produce from their own garden and the best in local game and fish. Highly recommended.

C-D **Speddoch**, large country house, a short drive from the sculptures at Glenkiln Reservoir, T01387-820342, www.wolsey-lodges.co.uk. Has been owned by the same family for 300 years. The family is very hospitable, there are cosy log fires and good home cooking – if you choose to eat there you'll dine with the family at night. It's a Wolsey Lodge – private homes offering accommodation where you're treated like a family guest.

D **Buccleuch and Queensberry Hotel**, 112 Drumlanrig St, Thornhill, T/F01848-330215, www.buccleuchhotel.co.uk. 19th century coaching inn in the centre of the village. Very good restaurant.

D **Cairngill House Hotel**, Kippford, T01387-780681. Comfortable

D **Craigbittern House**, at Sandyhills, about a mile east of Colvend, T01387-780247. Baronial splendour at affordable prices. Also has self-contained cottage for rent.

D **Edenbank Hotel**, 17 Laurieknowe, Dumfries, T01387-252759, www.edenbankhotel.co.uk. 10 en suite rooms. A short walk west of the town centre, where you'll find several places to stay.

D **Kirkland Country House Hotel**, next to the church in Ruthwell, T01387-870284. Very comfortable, family-run establishment.

D **Redbank House**, New Abbey Rd, Dumfries, T01387-247034, www.redbankhouse.co.uk. 5 en suite rooms. Lovely country house set in 3 acres of gardens. Non-smoking.

E **Fulwood Hotel**, 30 Lovers Walk, Dumfries, T01387-252262. Another good guest house close to the train station.

E **Hazeldean House**, 4 Moffat Rd, Dumfries, T01387-266178, www.hazeldeanhouse.com. 6 en suite rooms. Private parking. Good value.

E **The Merlin**, 2 Kenmure Terr, Dumfries, T01387-261002. Nicely-located overlooking the river near the Burns Centre.

E **Morton Villa**, 28 Lovers Walk, Dumfries, T01387-255825. Lovely Victorian house opposite the train station. Caters for vegetarians.

E **Rosemount Guest House**, Kippford, T01556-620214, with good views of the bay.

Self-catering accommodation is plentiful in Rockliffe. Contact the tourist board for further details, see p210. **National Trust for Scotland** have a lovely cottage right on the beach, sleeps 5, £250-550 per week, see p36 for details.

Camping

There are some good campsites in the Rockcliffe/Kippford area.

Castle Point Caravan Site, T01556-630248, open Mar-Oct, near Rockcliffe.

Kippford Holiday Park, T/F01556-620636, www.kippfordholidaypark.co.uk.

Sandyhills Bay Leisure Park, T01387-780257, open Apr-Oct. Pick of the bunch is this wonderfully-sited option.

Kirkcudbright, Castle Douglas and around *p214*

A-B **Balcary House Hotel**, Auchencairn, T01556-640217, www.balcary-bay-hotel.co.uk. 20 rooms. Open Mar-Oct. Luxurious, family-run country house hotel set in 3 acres of garden, overlooking lovely Auchencairn Bay. Excellent restaurant, see Eating p224.

B **Cally Palace Hotel**, Gatehouse of Fleet, T01557-814341, www.callypalace.co.uk. Set in 500 acres of its own grounds, this very exclusive Georgian mansion and former home of local laird James Murray who amassed a massive fortune from the cotton industry, offers impeccable luxury and top-class facilities, including private 18-hole golf course and indoor pool.

B **Selkirk Arms Hotel**, High St, Kirkcudbright, T01557-330402, www.selkirkarmshotel.co.uk. 17 rooms. The top hotel in town. Beautifully refurbished Georgian building with attractive rooms and also has the town's finest restaurant, see Eating p224.

C **Craigadam**, 11 miles out Castle Douglas, on the A712 near Crockettford, T/F01556-650233, www.craigadam.com. 6 en suite rooms. Elegant country house and working farm where you can enjoy good home cooking (**B** with evening meal).

C **Gordon House Hotel**, 116 High St, Kirkcudbright, T01557-330670, gordonhousehotel@yahoo.co.uk. 8 en suite rooms. A solid and reliable option, good food, see Eating p224.

C **Murray Arms Hotel**, Ann St, Gatehouse of Fleet, T01557-814207, www.murrayarms.com. A bit more down-to-earth but lots of character and good bar meals (see Eating).

D **Baytree House**, 110 High St, Kirkcudbright, T01557-330824, www.baytreehouse.net. 3 en suite rooms, 1 on ground floor. Unmissable peach-coloured Georgian house with nice touches throughout. Good food available. No smoking. Great value.

D **Crown Hotel**, 25 King St, Castle Douglas, T01556-502031, www.thecrownhotel.co.uk. 11 rooms. Comfortable with good food on offer, see Eating p224.

D **Imperial Hotel**, 35 King St, Castle Douglas, T01556-502086. 12 rooms. Caters mostly for golfing packages. Serves good bar food, see Eating p224.

D **Fresh Fields**, Arden Rd, Twynholm, a few miles north of Kirkcudbright, T01557-860221, open Jan-Oct. 5 en suite rooms. Friendly, attractive rooms, guest lounge, good breakfasts.

D **Gladstone House**, 48 High St, Kirkcudbright, T01557-331734, hilarygladstone@aol.com. 3 en suite rooms. This wonderful, superior guest house has a secluded garden and also offers afternoon tea. No smoking. A cracking place to stay, fantastic value.

D **Mrs McLaughlin**, 14 High St, Kirkcudbright, T01557-330766. 2 en suite rooms, open Apr-Sep. Very comfortable rooms and good views of the river.

D **Number 3**, 3 High St, Kirkcudbright, T01557-330881, www.number3-bandb.co.uk. 3 rooms. 'B' listed Georgian house. No smoking.

D-E **The Greengate**, 46 High St, Kirkcudbright, T01557-331895, www.thegreengate.co.uk. 1 en suite room. Former home of artists Jessie M King and E A Taylor. No smoking.

D-E **High Auchenlarie Farmhouse**, Gatehouse of Fleet, T01557-840231, open Mar-Oct. A little way out of town but highly recommended. No smoking.

E **Albion House**, 49 Ernespie Rd, Castle Douglas, T01556-502360, open Mar-Oct. Best of the B&Bs in town.

E **The Bobbin Guest House**, 36 High St, Gatehouse of Fleet, T01557-814229. 6 en suite rooms. Reliable, family-run.

E **Emharoo**, 109a High St, Kirkcudbright, T01557-331279, open Mar-Oct. 2 rooms. Nicely-decorated. No smoking.

E **Millburn House**, Millburn St, Kirkcudbright, T01557-339166. Lovely old house, good breakfasts. No smoking.

E **Mrs Caygill**, at 'The Marks', Kirkcudbright, T01557-330854, www.marksfarm.co.uk. Set in countryside out of town, provides evening meals.

E **The Rossan**, Auchencairn, T01556-640269, www.the-rossan.co.uk. 3 rooms. Vegetarian-friendly B&B offering dinner at a modest extra charge. Easy-going and informal atmosphere, ludicrously cheap considering the levels of cuisine and comfort. Carnivores and special diets also catered for. No smoking. Recommended.

Camping

Lochside Caravan & Camping Site, beside the loch, Castle Douglas, T01557-503806, open Easter-late Oct.

Loch Ken Holiday Park, by the village of Parton, T01644-470282, www.lochkenholidaypark.freeserve.co.uk, open late Mar-early Nov (see also Activities and tours below).

Seaward Caravan Park, Kirkcudbright, T01557-870267, open Mar-Oct, is part of a new leisure complex at Brighouse Bay, with a wide range of facilities including heated pool, 9-hole golf course and pony trekking.

Silvercraigs Caravan & Camping Site, T01557-503806, open Easter to late-Oct, is on an elevated site overlooking the Kirkcudbright, about a 10-min walk from the centre.

Galloway Forest Park *p217*

L **Kirroughtree House**, Newton Stewart, T01671-402141, www.kirroughtreehouse.co.uk. 17 rooms. This grand 18th-century country mansion is set in its own grounds and offers impeccable standards of comfort and service. It's superb restaurant has a well-deserved reputation for its gourmet Scottish cuisine.

A **Creebridge House Hotel**, across the river in the village of Minnigaff, near Newton Stewart, T01671-402121, www.creebridge.co.uk. 19 rooms. Nice location, good food in restaurant or bistro.

D **Leamington Hotel**, High St, New Galloway, T01644-420327, www.Leamington-hotel.com. Small and comfortable, does evening meals.

D **Oakbank**, Corsbie Rd, Newton Stewart, T01671-402822, open Feb-Nov. 3 rooms.

Very comfortable Victorian house, good breakfasts. Evening meals by arrangement. No smoking.

D Stables Guest House, Corsbie Rd, Newton Stewart, T01671-402157, www.stablesguesthouse.com. 6 rooms. Comfortable. No smoking.

D-E Kilwarlin, 4 Corvisel Rd, Newton Stewart, T01671-403047, open Apr-Oct. Friendly and welcoming, caters for cyclists.

E High Park, a few miles to the east, in the village of Balmaclellan, near New Galloway, T01644-420298. A farmhouse B&B.

E SYHA Youth Hostel, Newton Stewart, T01671-402211, open mid-Mar to end-Oct, in the village of Minnigaff, which is on the other side of the river, across the bridge.

E Youth Hostel, Kendoon, T01644-460680, 5 miles north of Dalry on the B7000, close to the Southern Upland Way and the A713. It's open mid-Mar to early Oct. Take the Castle Douglas-Ayr bus and ask to get off near the hostel.

Camping

Glen Trool Holiday Park, T01671-840280, open Mar-Oct, near Glen Trool village, just off the A714.

The far southwest *p219*

L Corsewall Lighthouse Hotel, 11 miles northwest of Stranraer at Corsewall Point, T01776-853220, corsewall-lighthouse@msn.com. 6 rooms. This cosy hotel is housed in a working lighthouse, set in 20 acres of its own grounds on the wild and windy clifftops, a surreal experience. The owners can arrange transport from Stranraer.

L Knockinaam Lodge Hotel, Portpatrick, T01776-810471. By far the best place to stay in this area, a wonderful place which offers great sea views, exquisite and unmatched cuisine, see Eating p224, and impeccable service. It is rated as one of the best hotels in the south of Scotland.

B Corsemalzie House Hotel, 11 miles west of Whithorn, near the village of Port William, T01988-860254, www.corsemalzie-house.ltd.uk. Sumptuous and highly rated hotel and restaurant. Open Mar-Jan.

B Fernhill Hotel, Stranraer, T01776-810220, www.fernhillhotel.co.uk. Those without the means to enjoy the splendours of Knockinaam Lodge can try the Fernhill which overlooks the village. Its restaurant has a fine reputation.

B North West Castle Hotel, Stranraer, T01776-704413, www.northwestcastle.co.uk. 73 rooms. This is the most luxurious choice in the area. The former home of Sir John Ross (see p193) also offers full leisure facilities and excellent cuisine. Superb.

D-E Steam Packet Inn, Isle of Whithorn, T01988-500354, a popular fishermen's pub with rooms on the quayside, which serves good, cheap bar meals.

F Sally's Hoose, Balyet Farm, Cairnryan Rd, Stranraer, T01776-703395. It only has 6 beds but is open all year.

Eating

Annandale, Eskdale and the Lowther Hills *p207*

£££ Well View Private Hotel, see Sleeping, locally-renowned for its excellent use of the best of local produce. 6-course dinner is lavish and expensive, lunch is mid-range and served Sun-Thu.

££ Claudio's Restaurant, in the old police station at Burnside, Moffat, T01683-220958. Sun-Thu till 2130, Fri/Sat till 2200, Sep-May closed Mon. Serves a range of Italian dishes.

££ The Lime Tree, High St, Moffat, T01683-221654, www.limetree-restaurant.co.uk. Open for dinner Tue-Sat. Very popular restaurant with a varied menu that always hits the mark. Best to book in advance.

£ The Weavers Restaurant, Moffat Woollen Mill, Ladyknowe. Self-service. Open daily 0900-1730 for wholesome cheap meals.

Dumfries and around *p210, map p211*

££ Abbey Arms Hotel, New Abbey, T01387-850489. Directly opposite the **Criffel Inn**, see below. Less adventurous menu but good value. Free internet access. Food daily 1200-1400, 1700-1945.

££ Anchor Hotel, Kippford, T01556-620205. Serves superb pub food and is the perfect spot for a great pint of real ale after the walk from Rockcliffe.

££ Benvenuto, 42 Eastfield Rd, Dumfries, T01387-259890. Very popular Italian-style restaurant some way from the centre of town. Tue-Sun 1700-late. Pizza and pasta under £5 1700-1830. Home delivery service next door, daily 1600-2200, T01387-256211.

££ Bruno's, 3 Balmoral Rd, Dumfries, T01387-255757. Good, honest Italian food. Pizza/pasta supper special at £9 for 2 courses. Open 1700 till late.

££ Criffel Inn, New Abbey, T01387-850244. Great village pub serving good bar meals. Beer garden and good selection of ales. Food daily 1200-1400 and 1700-2000.

££ Hector's Kitchen, 20a Academy St, Dumfries, T01387-256263. International menu featuring such diverse temptations as Tempura vegetable salad and pan-crusted sea bass, also tex-mex and pasta. Cheap lunches. Shiny, happy decor matched by the friendliness of the owners. Mon-Sat 0900-1500 and 1730-2130. No smoking.

££ Hullabaloo, Mill Rd, Dumfries, T01387-259679, above the Burns Centre in a converted old water mill. Chilled atmos by day with good selection of wraps, baguettes and bagels, by night menu features pastas, steaks and salads plus daily specials and decent wine list. Beer garden for those rare summer rays. Mon 1100-1600, Tue-Sat 1100-1600 and 1800-2200, Sun 1100-1500.

££ Opus, 95 Queensbury St, Dumfries, T01387-255752. One of the few vegetarian eateries. Mon-Sat 0900-1630, Thu till 1415.

££ Steamboat Inn, Carsethorn, near New Abbey, T01387-880631, www.steamboatinn carsethorn.co.uk. Location alone would be enough for the **Steamboat** to be included, sitting at the end of a dead-end road looking across the Solway Firth, but blow me if they don't go and serve some of the best pub grub this side of Hadrian's Wall. And don't take our word for it – they were voted best pub for food by the *Good Pub Guide*. On top of all that, they have a good selection of beers and malts. And that beer garden out front. People drive 100s of miles for this sort of thing. Food daily 1200-1430, 1830-2300.

£ Balmoral Fish & Chicken Bar, Dumfries, next door to **Bruno's** and run by the same family. Sells the best chips in town. Mon-Fri 1200-1400, 1600-2230, Sat 1200-2230, Sun 1200-2200.

£ Pumpernickel, 60-62 Friars Vennel, Dumfries, T01387-254475. A good place for coffees and light lunches. Mon-Sat 0830-1730. No smoking area.

Kirkcudbright, Castle Douglas and around *p214*

£££ Balcary House Hotel, Auchencairn, see Sleeping p221. Enjoy the modern Scottish dinner menu or Sunday lunch in the conservatory. Either way, this is a rare treat. Mon-Sat dinner by arrangement, Sun 1200-1400.

£££ Selkirk Arms Hotel, see Sleeping p221. The best place to eat in Kirkcudbright, the highly skilled chef is something of local celebrity. Restaurant specializes in local fish and seafood while the bistro offers a more affordable alternative. Food served daily 1200-1400 and 1800-2130.

££ Auld Alliance Restaurant, 5 Castle St, Kirkcudbright, T01557-330569. As the name suggests, it's a mixture of Scottish and French culinary styles, and features delights such as local queen scallops in garlic butter with smoked Ayrshire bacon and Galloway cream, also whisky, honey and oatmeal ice cream. Their 3-course Sunday lunch is a steal at £10.50. Open Easter-Oct Mon-Sat 1830-2130, Sun also 1200-1400.

££ Carlo's, 211 King St, Castle Douglas, T01556-503977. Italian restaurant offering the only real alternative to the town's hotel dining rooms or bars.

££ Crown Hotel, Castle Douglas, see Sleeping p221. Probably the best option for a bar meal in town. Lunch is particularly good value.

££ Imperial Hotel, Castle Douglas, see Sleeping p221. Another good option for for a pub lunch.

££ Murray Arms Hotel, Gatehouse of Fleet, see Sleeping p221. Extensive dinner menu featuring local beef, fish and seafood, lunch a little less adventurous but cheaper. Food served 1200-1400, 1700-2130.

££-£ Gordon House Hotel, Kirkcudbright, see Sleeping p221. **Marshall's Restaurant** offers a decent Modern Scottish menu while the bar meals served next door are very good value. Food served 1200-1400, 1800-2100.

£ Designs Café, 179 King St, Castle Douglas, T01556-504552. Downstairs, at rear of gallery and shop, very relaxed, attentive service and good, healthy lunch specials served Mon-Sat 1200-1500.

For an explanation of sleeping and eating price codes used in this guide, see inside the front cover. Other relevant information is found in Essentials, see pages 43-51.

£ Purdie's Delicatessen & Sandwich Bar, 173 King St, Castle Douglas. Best sandwiches in town (to take away). Mon-Sat 0830-1600.
£ Riverside Café, Mill on the Fleet, see p217. Salads and other typical lunchtime dishes, good value. Daily 1030-1630.
£ The Terrace, Threave Garden and Estate, see p216. Self-service restaurant in NTS Visitor Centre using the finest produce from their own garden. Great spot for lunch but food served all day during opening hours.

Galloway Forest Park *p217*
£££ Kirroughtree House, Newton Stewart, see Sleeping p223. The best place to eat for miles. Worth the expense.
££-£ Black Sheep Inn, T01671-404326, about ½ mile out of Newton Stewart on the A714 heading south is this licensed restaurant and bar.
££-£ The Brig End Pantry, a tearoom and restaurant overlooking the Cree bridge, Newton Stewart, T01671-402003.
££-£ The Riverbank, Newton Stewart, a popular lunch stop near the main car park, T01671-403330
£ Kitty's Tearoom, main street, New Galloway. Tue-Sun 1100-1700. A local insitution and the best place around for lunch or a coffee break. Great cakes.

The far southwest *p219*
As well as these options, you can try hotel bar meals or the numerous fast food outlets.
£££ Knockinaam Lodge, see Sleeping p224. The best place to eat in Portpatrick and one of the very best in the south of Scotland.
£££ North West Castle Hotel, Stranraer, see Sleeping p221. The most expensive place to eat in the area.
£££ Waterfront Hotel and Bistro, seafront, Portpatrick, T01776-810800. Good value lunch and dinner featuring local seafood.
££ The Bay House, Ladies Walk, Stranraer. For good Scottish food.
££ L'Aperitif, London Rd, Stranraer, T01776-702991. Serves good Italian food Mon-Sat 1200-1400 and 1730-2100.

Bars and clubs

Dumfries and around *p210, map p211*
Caffe Bar Identity, 23 Bank St, Dumfries, type of trendy bar that will probably have changed hands by the time you read this. Big-screen sports and bar menu. Open till 0100 at weekends.
Globe Inn, 56 High St, Dumfries. Atmospheric old place, famous as the favourite watering hole of a certain poet of this parish.

Entertainment

Dumfries and around *p210, map p211*
RBC Film theatre, Burns Centre, Dumfries, T01387-264808. Good programme of arthouse and mainstream cinema. £4, concession £3.

Festivals and events

Annandale, Eskdale and the Lowther Hills *p207*
In Langholm, local festivals include the town's **Common Riding**, which takes place on the last weekend in **Jul**, the **Langholm & Eskdale Festival of Music and Arts** which is held in the last week in **Aug**, and the **Esk- dale Agricultural Show** held at the end of **Sep**.

Amongst the local festivals held in Moffat is the **Moffat Agricultural Show**, held on the last Sat in **Aug**.
In the Lowther Hills, the **Scottish and British Gold Panning Championships** are held in Wanlockhead during the second last weekend in **May**.

Dumfries and around *p210, map p211*
Dumfries Book Fair at the beginning of **May**, and **Guid Nychburris Festival** in the middle of **Jun**, which features a week of entertainment and ceremonies. On the second Sat in **Aug** is the **Dumfries & Lockerbie Agricultural Show**. For a full list of dates, check with the tourist office. On the first Sat in **Aug** Palnackie hosts the **World Flounder Tramping Championships**, an unusual event which involves trying to catch the biggest flounder – with your feet!

Kirkcudbright, Castle Douglas and around *p214*
In Kirkcudbright, the **Kirkcudbright Arts Festival**, takes place over 2 weeks in late **Aug** and early **Sep** in venues throughout the town. **Kirkcudbright Jazz Festival** is held in mid **Jun**. Check out www.summerfestivities.com.

Castle Douglas now hosts the **Scottish Alternative Games** on the first Sun in **Aug**. The various traditional Scottish games include the world finals of the Gird'n'Cleek competition, spinnin' the peerie and snail racing. More details at www.lochkenholidaypark.freeserve.co.uk.

Shopping

Dumfries and around *p210, map p211*
Ottakar's, 79-83 High St, Dumfries, T01387-254288. Best bookshop in town, strong on contemporary Scottish writers. Daily 0900-1730.

Activities and tours

Kirkcudbright, Castle Douglas and around *p214*
Galloway Sailing Centre, Parton, T01644-420626, www.lochken.co.uk, offers tuition and hire for windsurfers, canoes and dinghies, as well as other activities such as quad biking and gorge scrambling. Also hot showers, hot and cold snacks and basic dormitory accommodation (**F**). Apr-Oct daily 0900-1900, Nov-Mar daily till 1700.
GM Marine Services, Kirkcudbright, T01557-331557. Run wildlife cruises up and down the River Dee on the Lovely Nellie. Leave from the marina (behind Broughton House). Contact TIC for times. £5, concession/child £2.50.
Loch Ken Marina, near the village of Parton, hires boats (£15 per day), canoes (£5 per day), bikes (£12 per day) and issues fishing permits (£5 per day). Easter-31 Oct daily 0900-1700.
Longsheds Equestrian, Kelton, 2 miles from Castle Douglas, past Threave Garden, T01556-680498. For horse riding.

Transport

Annandale, Eskdale and the Lowther Hills *p207*
To **Gretna** and **Ecclefechan**, there are buses from Dumfries. Gretna Green is also on the Dumfries-Carlisle rail line and there are regular trains in either direction. Ecclefechan is served by buses that run between Lockerbie and Annan.

Langholm is on the No 95 bus route between Carlisle and Galashiels, and buses pass through several times daily. Bus No 124 (**Yellow Bus**) runs between Langholm and Eskdalemuir, and No 112 (**MacEwans**) runs betwenn Eskdalemuir and Lockerbie.

From **Moffat**, there are frequent buses to Edinburgh, Glasgow (No X74) and Dumfries (Nos 114 and 199). Bus No 199 also runs to Edinburgh, via the A708, on Fri and Sat. Bus No 382 runs to Carlisle, via Lockerbie and Gretna Green, and bus No 130 runs to Galashiels, via Selkirk, along the scenic A708. The main operator is **Stagecoach Western Buses**, T01387-253496. There's also the **Harrier Scenic Bus Service**, which runs once or twice a week between Jul and Sep – useful for walkers (see also p188). For Harrier Service bus times call **First Edinburgh**, T0131-6639233.

From **Biggar** there are several daily buses to Edinburgh.There are also regular daily buses to Lanark. A **postbus** service, T01752-494527, runs to Tweedsmuir, Abington and Wanlockhead.

For the **Lowther Hills** there's a bus (No 223) to Leadhills from Sanquhar which passes through Wanlockhead.

Dumfries and around *p210, map p211*
From **Dumfries** there are regular buses to **Kirkcudbright** (Nos 76, 501, X74). No 500 and X75 go twice daily to **Newton Stewart** (1 hr 20 mins) and **Stranraer** (2 hrs), for the ferry to **Belfast**. National Express, T08705-808080, runs a daily service between **London** and **Belfast**, via **Dumfries** and **Stranraer** and towns in between. Stagecoach Western, T01292-613500, has 2 buses daily to and from **Edinburgh** (No 100; 2 hrs 20 mins). There are also regular buses to **Carlisle** (No 79; 50 mins) and to **Moffat** (No 114 or X74; 1 hr). Bus No 500 runs to **Castle Douglas** (45 mins) and No 246 to **Cumnock**, via **Sanquhar** (50 mins). There are also buses to **Thornhill**, **Dalbeattie** via **Rockcliffe**, **Moniaive**, **Glencaple/ Caerlaverock Castle** and **Annan** via **Ruthwell**. Bus No 372 runs from **Dumfries** to **Dalbeattie**, stopping in **New Abbey**, **Kirkbean**, **Rockcliffe** and **Kippford**, T710357. There are frequent trains Mon-Sat to and from Carlisle (35 mins) and several

daily (Mon-Sat) to and from **Glasgow** (1½ hrs), via **Kilmarnock**, where you change for trains to **Stranraer**. There's a reduced service on Sun.

Car hire from **Arnold Clark**, New Abbey Rd, Dumfries, T01387-247151. Open Mon-Fri 0800-1800, Sat 0830-1700, Sun 1100-1700. From £18 per day.

Cycle hire from **Nithsdale Cycle Centre**, 46 Brooms Rd, Dumfries, T01387-254870. Daily 1000-1700. For bike repairs and parts go to **Kirkpatrick Cycles**, 13-15 Queen St, Dumfries, T01387-254011. In Mabie Forest is **Riks Bike Shed**, T01387-270275, rik@riksbikes.co.uk, open Mon-Sat 1000-1800, Sun 1000-1600, see p212, for hire and trips out.

Kirkcudbright, Castle Douglas and around *p214*

Bus No 500 travels between **Dumfries** and **Stranraer** stopping in **Gatehouse of Fleet**. No 500 and X75 run between Gatehouse of Fleet and **Newton Stewart**. McEwan's bus Nos 501 and 505 run frequently from **Dumfries** to **Kirkcudbright**, stopping in **Castle Douglas**. Bus No 520 runs north along the east shore of **Loch Ken** from Castle Douglas to **New Galloway** and **Dalry**.

Cycle hire from W Law, 19 St Cuthbert St, Kirkcudbright, T01557-330579, and **Castle Douglas Cycle Centre**, 11 Church St, Castle Douglas, T01556-504542. £10 per day for mountain bikes and hybrids. Mon-Wed, Fri, Sat 0900-1230, 1330-1700.

Galloway Forest Park *p217*

Buses X75 and 500 run between **Dumfries** and **Stranraer**, stopping in **Newton Stewart** and other towns en route. There's also a No 430 bus to Stranraer. **Newton Stewart** is the departure point for buses south to **Wigtown** and **Whithorn** (No 415). There's a service (No 359) north along the A714 to **Girvan**, via Bargrennan and **Glen Trool** village several times a day Mon-Sat (less frequently on Sun). Yellow Bus S2, **Castle Douglas** to **Dalry**, stops in **New Galloway**. Some of these buses continue to **Ayr**. There are also regular buses to **Dumfries**, nos 503 and 501.

The far southwest *p219*

In **Stranraer**, the main transport hub, transport links are all conveniently located close to each other. The train station is on the ferry pier, close to the **Stena Line** ferry terminal (T08705-707070), from where car and passenger ferries leave for Belfast. A few mins' walk south is the bus station.

P&O ferries to Larne, T08705-980666, www.poirishsea.com, leave from **Cairnryan**, 5 miles north of Stranraer on the A77. Bus No 358 and X58 runs to Cairnryan from Stranraer. For details on services to Northern Ireland, see p30.

National Express, T08705-808080, www.gobycoach.com, No 920 runs between **London** and **Belfast** via **Stranraer** at 0945 and overnight. Ulster Bus has services between **Belfast** and **Glasgow/Edinburgh** via **Stranraer**. Booking is essential on all these services. Stagecoach Western has a service from **Glasgow** (3 hrs) to Ayr (X77), change at **Ayr** for **Stranraer**. There are regular buses to **Newton Stewart**, **Kirkcudbright**, **Dumfries** and other towns along the A75. There are also regular daily buses to Ayr (2 hrs), and daily buses to **Portpatrick** (25 mins), **Port Logan** (35 mins) and **Drummore** (45 mins).

There are several trains daily to **Belfast** via **Larne**. There's also a daily service to and from **Glasgow** (2 hrs) and Ayr (1 hr 20 mins). For all rail enquiries call T08457-484950.

Directory

Dumfries and around *p210, map p211*

Banks All the major banks have branches with ATMs in the centre.

Internet **Ewart Library**, Catherine St, T01387-253820. Free access. Mon-Wed and Fri 0915-1930, Thu and Sat 0915-1700.

Kirkcudbright, Castle Douglas and around *p214*

Internet **Library**, Sheriff Court House, High St, Kirkcudbright, T/F01557-331240. Free access. Mon 1400-1930, Tue, Fri 1000-1930, Wed 1200-1930, Thu, Sat 1000-1700. **Library**, King St, Castle Douglas, T01557-502643. Free access. Mon-Wed and Fri 1000-1930, Thu and Sat 1000-1700.

Laundry **Shirley's Laundrette**, 20 St Cuthbert St, Kirkcudbright, T01557-332047. Mon-Fri 0900-1600, Sat 0900-1300. £5 per load.

Ayrshire

→ *Colour map 5, grid A4-B4.*

The region of Ayrshire is best known as the birthplace of Robert Burns, Scotland's great poet, loved and revered the world over. The vast majority of visitors come here to visit the many sights associated with the great bard, but the Ayrshire Coast is also famed for its excellent golf courses such as Turnberry, Troon and Prestwick. There are a few other reasons for visiting Ayrshire, most notably Culzean Castle to the south of Ayr, one of Scotland's top tourist attractions. ▸▸ *For Sleeping, Eating and the listings, see pages 232-233.*

Ins and outs

The main TIC is in Ayr ⓘ *22 Sandgate near the Town Hall, at the opposite end of the main shopping street from the bus and rail stations, T01292-678100*. There are also seasonal offices in Irvine, Largs, Girvan and Millport ⓘ *open Easter-Oct*. ▸▸ *For Transport details, see page 233.*

Ayr and around

The largest town in southwest Scotland, looking west out on to the Firth of Clyde and Arran, Ayr has been a popular seaside resort since Victorian times. The town's 2½ miles of sandy beach, together with Scotland's most important racecourse, continue to attract hordes of visitors from nearby Glasgow. Ayr is best known for its many

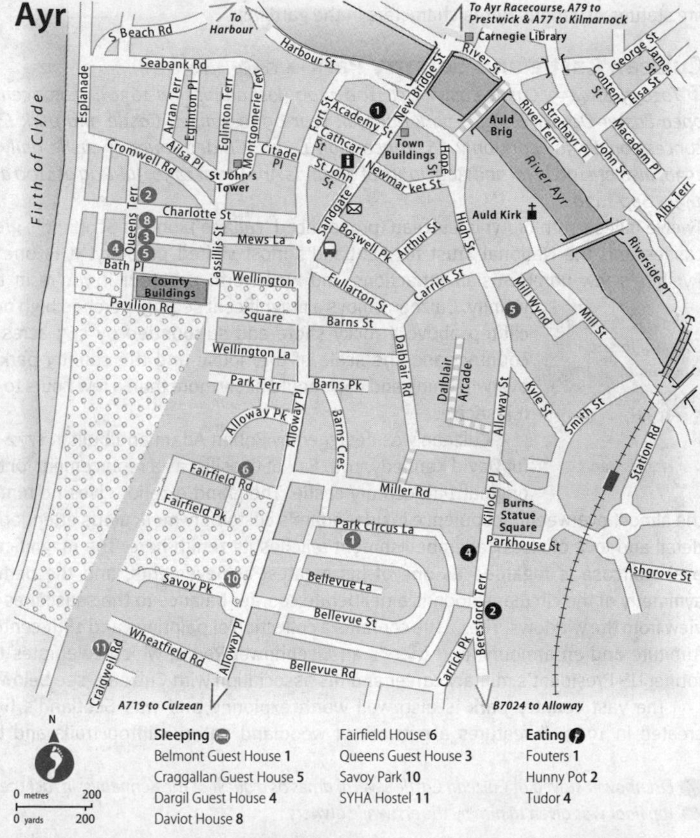

connections with Scotland's national poet, **Robert Burns**, who was born in the neighbouring village of **Alloway** and who famously praised the town for its 'honest men and bonnie lasses'.

Most of Ayr's important sights are contained within the **Burns National Heritage Park** ⓘ *www.burnsheritagepark.com, Apr-Sep daily 0930-1730, Oct-Mar daily 1000-1700, combined ticket (valid for 3 days) £5, concessions £2.50, family £12.50, audio guide £0.50*, in Alloway a few miles south of the town centre. Buses run from Alloway to Ayr (No 361) regularly. The best place to start is the **Burns Cottage and Museum**, the low, thatched, whitewashed 'auld clay biggin' where the poet was born on 25 January 1759 and spent the first seven years of his life. The museum contains original manuscripts, books, paintings and other memorabilia, plus a brief history of his life. Nearby is the **Tam o' Shanter Experience**, a modern building housing an audio-visual theatre telling the story of *Tam o' Shanter*, a funny and frightening poem and a cautionary tale of the consequences of alcoholic over-indulgence. There's also a well-stocked gift shop and a restaurant.

Across the road are the ruins of **Alloway Kirk**, where Robert Burns' father, William, is buried. This was the setting for the famous scene in *Tam o' Shanter* when Tam stumbles across a wild orgy of witches, warlocks and demons. When he gets carried away watching one particularly winsome witch, Nannie, and screams out his encouragement, the ghouls give chase and Tam and his mare, Meg, narrowly escape, minus Meg's tail, across the **Brig o' Doon**, the 13th-century humpbacked bridge which still stands nearby, spanning the River Doon. Overlooking the bridge is the ostentatious **Burns Monument**, a Neoclassical temple which houses a display. There are statues of various Burns characters in the gardens.

Culzean Castle and Country Park → *Colour map 5, grid B4.*

ⓘ *T01655-884455, Castle Easter-Oct 1100-1700 (last admission 1630); visitor centre open Easter-Oct 1030-1730; park open all year 0900-sunset. Castle and park £10, concession £7.50; park only £6, concession £4.50. Guided tours of castle daily at 1530, also at 1100 in Jul and Aug, tours of grounds Apr-Jun at 1430, Jul-Aug at 1100 and 1430, Sep 1430.*

Twelve miles south of Ayr is Culzean (pronounced 'cullane'), one of Scotland's great castles and the National Trust for Scotland's most visited property. It is one of Ayrshire's few non-Burnsian attractions and well worth a detour if you're in the vicinity. Culzean enjoys a magnificent setting, perched high on a clifftop above a rocky shore and surrounded by 563 acres of country park. The scale of the house and the country park is overwhelming and you should allow more than a few hours to do it justice.

You can stay here for a night in one of the six double bedrooms on the top floor for top rates. There's also a top-class, and very expensive, restaurant for residents.

Culzean was designed by Robert Adam and built in 1772-90 for David Kennedy, 10th Earl of Cassilis, as a replacement for the original 15th-century castle. The grand exterior gives no hint of the almost overweening opulence inside. Adam's customary meticulous attention to detail and love of classical embellishment reaches its zenith here. The magnificent oval staircase is regarded as one of his greatest achievements, and the perfect symmetry of the circular saloon is a deliberate counter-balance to the seascapes on view from the windows. The castle contains a collection of paintings and 18th-century furniture and an armoury, and there's an Eisenhower Room, which celebrates the former US President's military career and his association with Culzean, see below.

The vast **country park** is also well worth exploring and was Scotland's first, created in 1969. It features a network of woodland paths, clifftop trails and the

Eisenhower stayed at Culzean Castle several times as a guest of the Kennedys; in fact the top floor was given to him by the erstwhile owners.

Beans means crimes

One of the southwest's most horrific legends is that of Sawney Bean and his monstrous tribe.

Sawney Bean and his young wife ran away from East Lothian in the late 16th century and settled in a cave somewhere near Girvan in Ayrshire. They lived there for some 25 years, during which time they raised an incestuous family of 8 sons, 6 daughters, 18 grandsons and 14 granddaughters. The entire clan survived by killing and eating passing travellers. It is claimed some 1,000 poor souls were murdered on the road and their bodies taken to the Bean's cave to be consumed.

Amazingly, the Beans went undetected, though other, innocent, victims were tried and hanged for the many of the disappearances, until one couple, riding home from a local fair, were ambushed on the road. The wife was killed but the husband managed to escape, thanks to the arrival of a group returning from the same fair.

With the authorities alerted, a huge posse of men and hounds were dispatched to track down the cannibal clan. They eventually found the Beans' lair, with human parts cured and smoked like hams and suspended from ropes, or lying pickled in barrels, along with a huge pile of the victims' clothing and valuables.

They were taken to Edinburgh and executed without trial; the men by having their hands and feet severed to bleed to death and the women burned in three great bonfires.

shoreline below, formal gardens, the ice house, pagoda and the beautiful Swan Pond. There's also a walled garden with a Victorian vinery. The best place to start is the visitor centre housed in the Home Farm buildings, with a café, shop and exhibits. Here you can pick up free leaflets and maps to help you find your way around, or you can take a guided tour.

Kirkoswald and Crossraguel Abbey

A few miles inland from Culzean, on the A77, in the tiny village of Kirkoswald, is the refurbished **Souter Johnnie's Cottage** ⓘ *T01655-760603, Apr-Sep daily 1130-1700, also weekends in Oct 1130-1700, £3, concession £2*, which was the home of John Davidson, village souter (shoemaker), who was the original Souter Johnnie of Robert Burns' *Tam o' Shanter*. Life-sized stone figures of the souter, Tam himself, the innkeeper and his wife are in the restored ale-house in the garden, and there are Burns' relics in the cottage. An hourly bus service between Ayr and Girvan stops in Kirkoswald.

Two miles south of Maybole on the A77 are the ruins of **Crossraguel Abbey** ⓘ *T01655-883113, Apr-Sep daily 0930-1830, £2.20, concession £1.60*, a Clunaic establishment founded in the 13th century by the Earl of Carrick, and much rebuilt during the next three centuries. The remarkably complete remains include the church, cloister, chapter house and much of the domestic premises. About five miles northwest of Maybole on the A719 coastal road to Ayr, you'll pass a curious local phenomenon known as the **Electric Brae**. Because of an optical illusion, it appears that you're travelling uphill rather than down.

Largs and Great Cumbrae

The most attractive town on the North Ayrshire Coast is the resort of Largs, backed by high wooded hills and facing the island of Great Cumbrae, a few miles offshore and reached by ferry from Largs. The town is not only a traditional family holiday centre, but its extensive marina is popular with yachties, and the **Sportscotland National Centre** at Inverclyde ⓘ *T01475-674666*, hosts numerous national indoor competitions.

The award-winning **Vikingar!** ⓘ *T01475-689777, www.vikingar.co.uk, Apr-Sep Mon-Fri and Sun 1030-1730, Sat 1230-1530, Oct and Mar Mon-Fri and Sun 1030-1530, Sat 1230-1530, Nov and Feb Sat 1230-1530, Sun 1030-1530, £3.80, children £2.90*, at the north end of the promenade is a multi-media exhibition which fully describes the Viking influence in Scotland, which ended with the Battle of Largs in 1263 (see below). Hidden away in Largs' Old Kirk on Bellman's Close, just off the High Street, is **Skelmorlie Aisle** ⓘ *Jun-Aug Mon-Fri 1400-1700, keys from museum next door, free*, an absolute gem of Renaissance architecture unique in Scotland.

Only a few minutes from Largs by ferry is the hilly island of **Great Cumbrae**. At only four miles long and a couple of miles wide, it's ideally suited for a day or half-day trip from Largs and is best explored on foot or by bike. Great Cumbrae is a major water sports centre and Millport beach is a popular place for windsurfing. The only settlement of any size is **Millport**, which is home to Europe's smallest cathedral, the beautiful **Cathedral of the Isles** ⓘ *daily 1100-1600 except during services.* built in the mid-19th century. About a mile east of town is the **Marine Life Museum** ⓘ *T01475-530581, Mon-Fri 0930-1215 and 1400-1645; Jul-Sep also Sat. £1.50, £0.75 children*, part of Glasgow University Marine Biology department, which contains an excellent aquarium. The nicest parts of the island are away from Millport and are best explored by bike. The 14-mile main road runs right round the edge of the island, or there's a narrow Inner Circle Road which passes **The Glaidstone** (417 ft), the highest point on the island. More information on these cycle routes is available from the TIC.

Sleeping

Ayrshire *p229*

In Ayr, there are numerous comfortable guest houses and B&Bs in the Victorian new town, in the streets and squares between Alloway Pl and the Esplanade, especially along Queens Terr.

L Turnberry Hotel, 5 miles north of Girvan, T01655-331000, www.turnberry.co.uk, one of the most luxurious and prestigious hotel in the country, overlooking the world-famous gold course.

L-A Fairfield House Hotel, 12 Fairfield Rd, Ayr, T01292-267461, www.fairfieldhotel.co.uk. 45 rooms. Near the seafront, luxury facilities, excellent restaurant, conservatory brasserie.

A Ivy House, Alloway, T01292-442336, www.theivyhouse.uk.com. 5 rooms. This comfortable country house is convenient for the Burns Trail and has a good restaurant.

B Brisbane House Hotel, on the seafront promenade, Largs, T01475-687200, www.maksu-group.co.uk. Comfortable and offers very fine Scottish cuisine (**££**).

B Savoy Park Hotel, 16 Racecourse Rd, T01292-266112, www.savoypark.com. 15 en suite rooms. Homely feel but high-class service and standards.

E Belmont Guest House, 15 Park Circus, T01292-265588, www.belmontguesthouse.co.uk. 5 en suite rooms. Victorian terraced house in quiet street. Excellent value.

E Craggallan Guest House, 8 Queens Terr, T01292-264998, www.craggallan.com. 4 en suite rooms. Comfortable guest house in the Victorian new town.

E Dargil Guest House, 7 Queens Terr, T01292-261955, www.dargil.co.uk. 5 rooms, 3 en suite. Another good choice on a street lined with guest houses and B&Bs.

E Daviot House, 12 Queens Terr, T01292-269678, thedaviot@aol.com. 4 en suite rooms. Friendly, can provide evening meal on request.

E Queens Guest House, 10 Queens Terr, T01292-265618, www.queensguesthouse.com. 5 well-appointed en suite rooms.

F SYHA Youth Hostel, 5 Craigweil Rd, T01292-262322, www.syha.org.uk. About a 20-min walk south of the town centre, off Alloway Pl, open Mar-Dec.

For an explanation of sleeping and eating price codes used in this guide, see inside the front cover. Other relevant information is found in Essentials, see pages 43-51.

Eating

Ayrshire *p229*

£££ Brisbane House Hotel, Largs, see Sleeping, best place in town for big meal.

£££ Fouters, 2a Academy St, Ayr, T01292-261391. This bistro/restaurant in a converted bank basement opposite the town hall offers superb French-influenced cuisine using the very best of local fish, seafood, game and beef.

££ Tudor Restaurant, 8 Beresford Terr, Ayr, T01292-261404. More of a café really and serves great home-cooked meals and high teas. Mon-Sat 0900-2000, Sun 1200-2000.

££ Nardini's, on the promenade, Largs, T01475-674555. This authentic 1950s Italian café is an institution and is reckoned by some to be the best café in Scotland. Though it has recently changed hands the ice cream is still a truly magical experience. Also good Italian food and coffee.

£ Hunny Pot, 37 Beresford Terr, T01292-263239, Mon-Sat 0900-2200, Sun 1030-2100. A great place for cheap, no-nonsense snacks.

£ Ritz Café, Great Cumbrae, Largs, has been serving great ice cream, chips and cappuccino for almost a century. Fine choice.

Activities and tours

Ayrshire *p229*

Ayr Racecourse, 2 Whitletts Rd, T01292-264179, www.ayr-racecourse.co.uk. It's the premier racecourse in Scotland and holds 25 days of racing throughout the year, including the Scottish Grand National in mid-Apr.

Transport

Ayrshire *p229*

There are frequent buses and trains to Ayr from **Glasgow**, **Dumfries** and **Stranraer**. There are trains every 30 minutes to and from Glasgow Central (50 mins), and several daily to Stranraer (1¼ hrs).

There's a bus service (No 923) between **Glasgow** and **Stranraer**which passes through Ayr.

Ferries leave **Largs** every 15 mins during the summer and every 30 mins in winter for the 10-min sailing to the slip on the northeast shore. Buses meet the ferry for the 4-mile trip to Millport. The return fare is £3.15 per person and £13.35 per car, or £3.60 and £15.70 respectively at peak times. Bikes cost £2 return. For more information, contact **CalMac**, T08705-650000, or at Largs pier.

Bike hire in Millport at **Mapes & Son**, 3-5 Guildford St, T01475-530444, for £4 per day.

Directory

Ayrshire *p229*

Internet Carnegie Library, 12 Main St, Ayr, T01292-286385, jcastle@lib.south.ayrshire.gov.uk.

Central Scotland

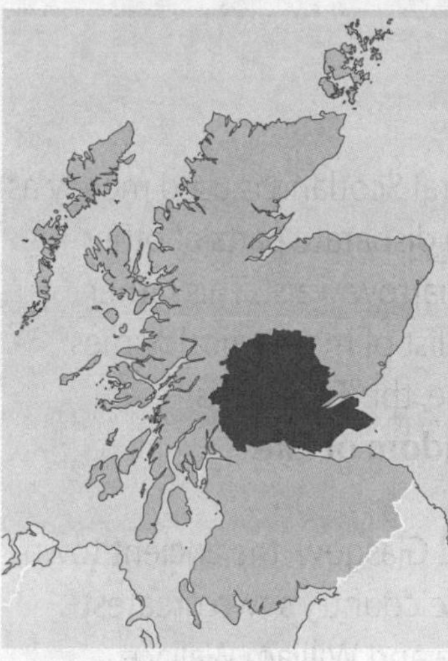

Footprint features

Introduction

The distinctly prosaic title of Central Scotland is used merely as a convenient blanket to cover the disparate parts of other regions that make up Scotland's narrow waist. This rather Soviet-sounding moniker hides a list of more lyrical names: **Perthshire**, **Stirling**, **Breadalbane**, the **Trossachs**, **Clackmannanshire** and the **Kingdom of Fife**.

Standing between Edinburgh and Glasgow, the ancient town of **Stirling** is synonymous with the country's two greatest historical heroes, Robert the Bruce and William Wallace. Stirling is the gateway to the **Trossachs**. Strictly speaking, the Trossachs is the narrow wooded glen between Loch Katrine and Loch Achray, but the name is now used to describe a much larger area stretching north from the **Campsies** and west from **Callander** to the eastern shore of **Loch Lomond**. It's a very beautiful and diverse area of sparkling lochs, craggy mountains and deep, forested glens, and so is often referred to as the 'Highlands in minature'. Visit in the autumn when the hills are purple and the trees are a thousand luminous hues.

Northeast of Stirling is the town of **Perth**, one of the main gateway towns the highlands, whose hinterland is steeped in the rich broth of Scottish history and seasoned with lochs and mountains. In the far west of the region, on the eastern shores of Loch Lomond, is the **West Highland Way**, Scotland's most popular long-distance hike. To the east is the **Kingdom of Fife**, once isolated from the rest of the country. Even since the building of the Forth and Tay bridges, the region has managed to retain its own peculiar flavour. The small peninsula juts out into the North Sea like the head of a terrier dog. Rather apt, given the proud Fifers' fight to preserve the identity of their own 'Kingdom' when it was threatened by local government reorganization in 1975 and 1995.

★ Don't miss...

1. **Fortingall** Find the Roman in the gloamin' at this lovely Perthshire village, said to be the birthplace of Pontius Pilate, page 244.
2. **Glen Lyon** Take a picnic to this glorious glen and try, if you can, to imagine a more perfect place, page 244.
3. **St Andrews** Stand on the first tee at the St Andrews Old Course on a misty morning, knees shaking in nervous anticipation of tackling the world's most famous golf course, page 273.
4. **Duke's Pass** Travel the road from Aberfoyle to Callander, through the spectacular pass, one of the most beautiful routes in the country, page 261.
5. **Stirling** Explore historic Stirling, home of Braveheart and scene of Scotland's greatest military triumph, page 252.
6. **East Neuk of Fife** Meander through the string of pretty fishing villages in this area, page 277.

Perthshire

Perth is the main gateway to the eastern side of the Highlands and the A9, the road north, is a gentle introduction to the wild northern reaches of Scotland. The Perthshire Highlands may lack the sheer magisterial grandeur of the northwest but have their own serene beauty. Numerous remnants from the highland's troubled past are scattered around the glens of Perthshire, including Blair Castle and Scone Palace.

Ins and outs

Getting there Perth is accessible from almost anywhere in the country. It's only 1½ hours from Edinburgh or Glasgow, and half an hour from Dundee, by road, and on the main train lines to these cities, as well as on the main lines north to Aberdeen and Inverness. » *For further details, see Transport page 251.*

Getting around Though the more remote northerly parts of Perthshire are difficult to reach by public transport, much of the region is easily accessible. The main road north to Inverness, the A9, runs through the heart of the region. Dunkeld and Pitlochry are on the Perth-Inverness rail line and there are several daily trains to Perth. Strathtay Scottish, T01382-228054, buses run hourly (less frequently on Sunday) from Perth to Blairgowrie and Glenshee on the A93.

Tourist information The region, from Kinross in the south to Blair Atholl in the north and from Glenshee in the east to Rannoch Moor in the west, is covered by the Perthshire Tourist Board ⓘ *www.perthshire.co.uk*, with tourist offices in Aberfeldy, Auchterarder, Blairgowrie, Crieff, Dunkeld, Kinross, Perth and Pitlochry.

Perth and around

→ *Phone code: 01738. Colour map 4, grid B-C3. Population: 48,000.*

'The Fair City' of Perth is aptly named. Situated on the banks of Scotland's longest river, the Tay, Perth and its surrounding area boasts some of the most beautiful scenery in the country. Perth was once the capital of Scotland, and there are many interesting sights to visit. The jewel in Perth's crown, though, is undoubtedly Scone (pronounced 'scoon') Palace, on the outskirts of town. Scone was the home of the Stone of Destiny for nearly 500 years, and the site where every Scottish king was crowned. The city is also well-placed for other outdoor activities such as walking, cycling and skiing. » *For Sleeping, Eating and other listings, see pages 248-251.*

Ins and outs

Getting around The train and bus stations are almost opposite each other at the west end of town, where Leonard St meets Kings Place. The town centre is very compact and it's easy to get around on foot, but Scone Palace and many of the B&Bs are on the eastern bank of the river, so you may wish to take a bus. Local buses are run by Stagecoach, T01738-629339. An enjoyable way to see the sights is to use the Guide Friday bus tour of Perth. Tour tickets are valid all day, so you can get on and off as often as you please and you can join the tour at various locations throughout the city. For more details, T0131-5562244, or contact the tourist office.

Tourist information Perth TIC ⓘ *Lower City Mills, West Mill St, T01738-450600. Apr-Jun, Sep and Oct Mon-Sat 0900-1730, Sun 1100-1600, Jul and Aug Mon-Sat 0900-1830, Sun 1100-1700, Nov-Mar Mon-Sat 0900-1600.*

Sights

A few minutes' walk north of the High Street, on North Port, is the **Fair Maid's House**, the fictional home of Sir Walter Scott's virginal heroine in his novel, *The Fair Maid of*

Perth. Close by, at the corner of Charlotte Street and George Street, is the **Museum and Art Gallery** ⓘ *T01738-632488, Mon-Sat 1000-1700, free*, with displays on local history, art, archaeology, natural history and whisky.

In the 18th century the world-famous Black Watch regiment was raised in Perth, and the **Black Watch Museum** ⓘ *T0131-310 8530, May-Sep Mon-Sat 1000-1630, closed last Sat in Jun, Oct-Apr Mon-Fri 1000-1530, free*, housed in the 15th-century Balhousie Castle, is well worth a visit even to the most un-military minded. The museum is on Hay Street, on the edge of the North Inch, to the north of the town centre. Back in the town centre, in West Mill Street is Lower City Mills (also home to the tourist office), a restored and working 19th-century oatmeal mill powered by a huge water wheel (closed to visitors at the time of writing). Perth's other museum contains the excellent **Fergusson Gallery** ⓘ *T01738-441944, Mon-Sat 1000-1700, free*, a display of works by the renowned Scottish colourist, John Duncan Fergusson. The gallery is found at the south end of Tay Street, near South Inch, in a splendid neo-classical building which was once Perth's waterworks.

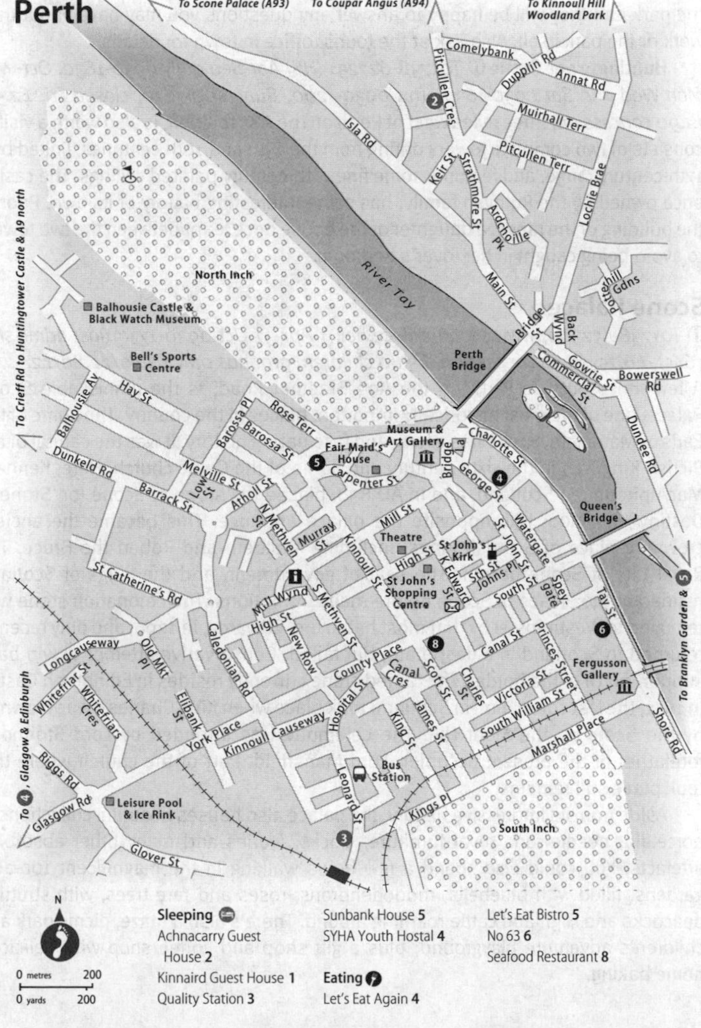

For those with more horticultural leanings, **Branklyn Garden** ⓘ *116 Dundee Rd, T01738-625535 (NTS), Mar-Oct daily 0930-sunset, £5, £3.75 concession*, has been described as "the finest two acres of private garden in the country". With an impressive collection of rare and unusual plants, it includes superb examples of Himalayan poppies. Well worth a visit at any time of year, many of the plants grown there are on sale in the shop.

Kinnoull Hill Woodland Park is a beautiful wooded area on the outskirts of the city. The trip to the top of Kinnoull Hill (783 ft) itself affords an astounding view across Perth, down to the Tay estuary and through Fife to the Lomond hills. To the north, the views stretch from Ben More in the west to Lochnagar in the northeast. There are four walks through the Woodland Park – Nature Walk, Tower Walk, Jubilee Walk and Squirrel Walk – and each of these is graded according to how difficult it is and what type of conditions the walker can expect. However, none of the walks are extremely strenuous, though the Squirrel Walk is most suitable for the less able. If you're feeling particularly energetic, cycling and horse riding take place in specific zones in the park, principally in the Deuchny Wood area. There is a Countryside Ranger Service in the park and they will be happy to answer any questions you may have about their work or the park itself. Also ask at the tourist office in town for details.

Huntingtower Castle ⓘ *T01738-627231 (HS) Apr-Sep daily 0930-1830, Oct- Mar Mon-Wed and Sat 0930-1630, Thu 0930-1200, Sun 1400-1630, closed Fri, £2.50, £1.90 concession*, three miles west of Perth on the A85 to Crieff, is also worth a visit. It consists of two complete towers dating from the 15th and 16th centuries, linked by a 17th-century range, and features some fine 16th-century painted ceilings. The castle, once owned by the Ruthven family, has some interesting history of its own. Prior to the building of the range, a daughter of the house once leapt between the two towers to avoid being caught in her lover's bedroom.

Scone Palace

ⓘ *T01738-552300, www.scone-palace.net, 1 Apr-31 Oct 0930-1730 (last admission 1645), £6.75, £5.70 concession, £3.80 children, grounds only £3.40/£2.80/£2.*

A few miles outside Perth on the A93 Braemar Road, is the unmissable Scone Palace, one of the most historically important places in the country. The home of the Earls of Mansfield, Scone has a long and fascinating history. It was the capital of the Pictish Kingdom in the sixth century and home of the Celtic church. Here, Kenneth MacAlpin united Scotland, and in AD 838, placed the stone of Scone (or 'Stone of Destiny') on Moot Hill, opposite the palace entrance. This became the ancient crowning place of Scottish kings, including Macbeth and Robert the Bruce. The Royal City of Scone became the seat of government, and the kings of Scotland resided at the Palace of Scone before their coronations. The coronation stone was removed to Westminster by that most hated foe, Edward I, in 1296, and only recently returned to Scotland in a desperate, but failed, Conservative attempt to win back support north of the border. The famed stone currently resides in Edinburgh Castle. In 1651, the last coronation in Scotland took place when King Charles II was crowned by the Scots on the Moot Hill. The ceremony was attended by Lord Stormont, forefather of the present occupier, Lord Mansfield. Part of the church where this took place still remains.

Aside from its impressive history, the palace also houses beautiful collections of porcelain, needlework, royal furniture, clocks, ivories and many other absorbing artefacts. You could also spend a few hours walking in the magnificent 100-acre gardens, filled with bluebells, rhododendrons, roses and rare trees, with strutting peacocks and Highland cattle roaming around. There's also a maze, picnic park and children's adventure playground, plus a gift shop and coffee shop with delicious home baking.

Dunkeld and Birnam

Twelve miles north of Perth is the attractive village of **Dunkeld**, standing right on the Highland line. It's definitely worth making a stop here, if only to admire the **cathedral** ⓘ *Apr-Sep 0930-1830, free*, in the most idyllic situation on the banks of the fast-flowing, silvery Tay. Half of it is still in use as a church and the other half is in ruins. The oldest part of the cathedral is the 14th-century choir, which now forms the parish church, while the 15th-century nave and tower are also still standing. Much of the original was damaged during the orgy of ecclesiastical destruction that accompanied the Reformation. It was damaged again in the Battle of Dunkeld in 1689, fought between supporters of the protestant William of Orange and the Stuart monarch James VII. Dunkeld offers excellent walking opportunities, details of which are available from the TIC at The Cross ⓘ *T01350-727688*.

Across the bridge from Dunkeld is **Birnam**, made famous in Shakespeare's *Macbeth*. Birnam was the inspiration for another famous literary figure, **Beatrix Potter**, who spent her childhood summers here. Visitors can explore the origins of the *Peter Rabbit* stories at the **Beatrix Potter Exhibition** ⓘ *daily 1000-1700, free*.

▲ A short distance north of Dunkeld on the A9 is the turning to **The Hermitage**. A marked woodland walk starts from the car park and follows the river Braan to the Black Linn Falls, overlooked by Ossian's Hall, an 18th-century folly built by the Duke of Atholl. It's a lovely spot, which has inspired the likes of Wordsworth and Mendelssohn. Further on is Ossian's Cave. Buses to Pitlochry stop at the turning for The Hermitage.

A few miles northeast of Dunkeld, off the A923 to Blairgowrie, is the **Loch of the Lowes Visitor Centre** ⓘ *Apr-Sep daily 1000-1700, free but donation advised*, managed by the Scottish Wildlife Trust. There's a hide with binoculars for viewing a pair of ospreys which breed here and which can be seen on the loch from early April to early September.

Pitlochry and around

→ *Phone code: 01796. Colour map 4, grid B2-3. Population: 2,500.*

Despite being one of the busiest Highland tourist towns in the summer, Pitlochry's setting on the shores of the River Tummel, overlooked by Ben y Vrackie, makes it a pleasant enough base for exploring the area, especially out of season. The town also has a few notable attractions of its own. ▸▸ *For Sleeping, Eating and other listings, see pages 248-251.*

Sights

Pitlochry's main attraction is the **fish ladder**, part of the power station and dam which formed man-made **Loch Faskally** when it was constructed on the River Tummel. The ladder allows salmon to swim up to their spawning grounds and you can watch them leaping spectacularly in the spring and summer. The best months are May and June. The fish ladder is across the river, a short distance from the **Pitlochry Festival Theatre**, see Entertainment page 250.

Also here is **Scottish Plant Collector's Gardens** ⓘ *T01796-484626, www.scottishplantcollectorsgardens.com, Apr-Oct Mon-Sat 1000-1700, Sun 1100-1700, £3, £2.50 concession, £1 child*. Scotland's newest public garden features a programme of visual arts, sculpture, music and drama throughout the summer.

There are two excellent whisky distilleries to visit. The larger of the two is Bell's **Blair Atholl Distillery** ⓘ *T01796-482003, www.malts.com, Easter-Sep Mon-Sat 0930-1700, Sun 1200-1700, Oct Mon-Fri 1000-1600, Nov-Easter Mon-Fri 1300-1600, tours every 20 mins, £4, redeemable in shop*, at the southern end of town, heading towards the A9 to Perth. A couple of miles east of town, on the A924, is the **Edradour Distillery**

 ⓘ *T01796-T472095, www.edradour.com, Jan and Feb Mon-Sat 1000-1600, Sun 1200-1600, Mar-Oct Mon-Sat 0930-1800, Sun 1130-1700, Nov and Dec Mon-Sat 0930-1700, Sun 1200-1700, free*, the smallest in Scotland, which can be a blessing or a curse, depending on how busy it is.

The tourist office sells a useful leaflet *Pitlochry Walks* which describes four long local walks, and there are many other fine walks in the surrounding area. The greatest walking attraction is **Ben y Vrackie** (2,758 ft), a steep six-mile walk (there and back) from the tiny hamlet of Moulin, a mile north of Pitlochry on the A924 (turn left at the **Moulin Inn**). The path is well trodden and the going is relatively easy, across bleak moorland, until the steep final ascent on scree. On a clear day the views from the summit of the Trossachs are wonderful, so it's best not to attempt this on a cloudy day. In spite of its proximity to Pitlochry, you need to be properly equipped and take the usual safety precautions, see page 56.

OS Landranger maps Nos 43 and 52 cover all the walks, and the OS Explorer map No 21 (Pitlochry and Loch Tummel) covers them in greater detail.

Another excellent walk from Pitlochry, described in the tourist office leaflet, leaves town on the north road and turns left past the boat station. It then crosses the Cluanie footbridge and follows the road to Loch Faskally and up the River Garry to Garry Bridge over the Pass of Killiecrankie, see below. The path returns to Pitlochry along the west bank of the River Garry, before turning west up the River Tummel, passing close by the Linn of Tummel, then crossing the Tummel and following the west shore of Loch Faskally to the dam and fish ladder.

Pass of Killiecrankie

Four miles north of Pitlochry the A9 cuts through the Pass of Killiecrankie, a spectacular wooded gorge which was the dramatic setting for the Battle of Killiecrankie in 1689, when a Jacobite army led by Graham of Claverhouse, Viscount 'Bonnie Dundee', defeated the government forces under General Hugh Mackay. One government soldier allegedly evaded capture by making a jump of Olympic gold medal-winning proportions across the River Garry at **Soldier's Leap**. The NTS visitor centre ⓘ *T01796-473233, Apr-Oct daily 1000-1730, free (honesty box £1 donation advised)*, has displays on the battle and the local natural history.

Blair Castle

ⓘ *T01796-481207, Apr-Oct 1000-1800 (0930 in Jul and Aug), house and grounds £6.25, grounds only £2.*

Seven miles from Pitlochry, and a mile from the village of Blair Atholl, is Blair Castle, the traditional seat of the Earls and Dukes of Atholl. This whitewashed, turreted castle dates from 1269 and presents an impressive picture on first sight. This is the headquarters of Britain's only private army, the Atholl Highlanders, and one of them usually pipes in new arrivals. Thirty-two rooms in the castle are open for public viewing and are packed full of paintings, furniture, armour, porcelain and much else besides, presenting a startling picture of aristocratic Highland life in previous centuries. The surrounding landscaped grounds are home to peacocks and Highland cattle, and there are woodland walks and a walled Japanese water garden to enjoy.

Falls of Bruar

Eight miles from Blair Atholl, just off the A9, are the Falls of Bruar. A well-maintained path leads from the lower falls along the gorge of the Bruar River to the upper falls and back down the other side. It's a 1½-mile round trip.

From the House of Bruar, turn right by the adventure playground, then left up the river bank. The path passes under a railway arch and through a kissing gate. It then heads through open forest to a rocky outcrop, from where you can see the lower falls. A series of wooden steps leads down from the outcrop, then a ricky path climbs up till it forks. Go right, then cross the bridge, from where there's a good view of the lower falls. From here a clear path leads up the far side till it reaches a deer fence. Climb up to the gate, go through it and continue uphill through trees till the path levels out high above the gorge. Further on there's a picnic area, then the path curves left down to the upper bridge, which is a great vantage point from which to admire the stunning view. The path heads left through more trees. It then crosses a stream before descending to thelower bridge and then back to the car park.

By the car park is the excellent **House of Bruar**, a huge shopping emporium designed like a Victorian hunting lodge where you can buy just about any kind of souvenir and enjoy some very fine Scottish cooking.

From Blair Atholl to Kinloch Rannoch

The B8019 turns off the B8079 road from Pitlochry to Blair Atholl and runs west along the shores of beautiful lochs Tummel and Rannoch, best seen in the autumn when the trees change their colours. At the eastern end of Loch Tummel is **Queen's View**, a spectacular viewpoint which looks down the loch and across to Schiehallion. There's a visitor centre ⓘ *T01796-473123, Apr-Oct daily 1000-1730, free, £1 parking charge*, with displays and audio-visual programmes about the area.

▲ **Schiehallion** (3,547 ft) is one of Scotland's best-loved mountains, whose distinctive conical peak made it ideal for use in early experiments in 1774 to judge the weight of the earth. These were not an unqualified success, but led to the invention of contour lines as an aid to surveying the mountain. The walk to the summit is fairly straightforward, except for the very rocky final stretch. You'll need to be properly clothed and equipped and take a map and compass. The route to the summit starts at the car park on the B846 Kinloch Rannoch to Aberfeldy road, near Braes of Foss. OS sheet No 51 covers the route.

Beyond Loch Tummel is the little village of **Kinloch Rannoch**, where hikers can stock up on supplies before heading into the hills. Sixteen miles west of the village the road ends at Rannoch station, where you can catch trains north to Fort William or south to Glasgow.

Aberfeldy and Loch Tay

→ *Phone code: 01887. Colour map 4, grid B2.*

The little town of Aberfeldy stands on the banks of the River Tay, on the A827 which runs between the A9 and Loch Tay. It's well placed geographically for exploring the northern part of Perthshire, though Pitlochry has better tourist facilities. The 14-mile-long Loch Tay is surrounded by some of the loveliest scenery in Perthshire and is well worth exploring. ▸▸ *For Sleeping, Eating and other listings, see pages 248-251.*

Aberfeldy

The River Tay is spanned by Wade's Bridge, built by General Wade in 1773 during his campaign to pacify the Highlands. Also in the town, building is underway on the new Aberfeldy Watermill development, which will comprise a bookshop, art gallery, music and coffee shop, planned for opening in Spring 2005.

Dewar's World of Whisky ⓘ *T01887-822010, www.dewars.com/worldofwhisky, Apr-end Oct Mon-Sat 1000-1800, Sun 1200-1600, Nov-Mar Mon-Fri 1000-1600, £5, concession £3, children £2.50*, just outside Aberfeldy, is one of a new breed of distillery visitor centres. The tour is always interesting, though the hard sell may not be to everyone's taste.

A mile west of Aberfeldy, across the Tay at Weem, is **Castle Menzies** ⓘ *T01887-820982, Apr-mid Oct Mon-Sat 1030-1700, Sun 1400-1700, £3.50, £3 concession*, an impressive, restored 16th-century 'Z-plan' fortified tower house, the former seat of the chief of Clan Menzies.

66 99 On a summer's day there can be few lovelier places on earth, as the River Lyon tumbles through corries and gorges and through flowering meadows, with high mountain peaks on either side and eagles soaring overhead...

▲▲A popular local walk is to the **Falls of Moness**, through the famous **Birks of Aberfeldy**, forever associated with the poet Robert Burns who was inspired by the birks (birch trees) to write his eponymous song. It's a fairly easy walk along a marked trail up to the impressive falls, and the views of Strathtay and the surrounding hills on the descent also make it worthwhile. It's about four miles there and back.

Loch Tay and around

At the northeast end of Loch Tay is **Kenmore**, a neat little village of whitewashed cottages dominated by a huge archway which stands at the gateway to Taymouth Castle, built by the Campbells of Glenorchy in the early 19th century and now a very fine golf course ⓘ *T01887-830228*. Near the village, on the southern bank of the loch, is the excellent **The Scottish Crannog Centre** ⓘ *T01887-830583, Mar and Nov daily 1000-1600, Apr to mid-Oct 1000-1730, £4.25, concession £3.85*, an authentic reconstruction of a *crannog*, an artificial Bronze-Age island- house built for the purpose of defence.

Loch Tay is a major watersports centre, see Activities and tours page 251, for details.

For those with their own transport, two of the least-known and loveliest routes in the country are at hand. The first is the spectacular road which winds its way south from Kenmore high up into the mountains, across a bleak and barren plateau and down the other side to the tiny hamlet of **Amulree**. This road is often closed in the winter and there are gates at either end. From Amulree you can continue south to Crieff (see below), through the gentler, but equally stunning scenery of the **Sma' Glen**. Alternatively, you could head north to Aberfeldy and then complete the circuit back to Kenmore.

A few miles west of Kenmore a minor road turns off the A827, which runs along the north bank of the loch, and heads to **Fortingall**, a tiny village of classic beauty which features on many a calendar. It's little more than a row of thatched cottages which wouldn't even get a mention were it not for two amazing claims. The 3,000-year-old yew tree in the churchyard is claimed to be the oldest living thing in Europe. More astonishing is the claim that this is the birthplace of **Pontius Pilate**, said to be the son of a Roman officer who was stationed here. Furthermore, it is believed that Pilate returned here to be buried, and a gravestone in the churchyard bears the initials 'PP'. If you have your own transport, make a detour up **Glen Lyon**, one of the most beautiful of all Scottish glens. On a summer's day there can be few lovelier places on earth, as the River Lyon tumbles through corries and gorges and through flowering meadows, with high mountain peaks on either side and eagles soaring overhead. It's no surprise that Wordsworth and Tennyson waxed lyrical over its qualities. The road from Fortingall runs all the way to the head of the glen, at Loch Lyon. This is walking and fishing paradise. There are several Munros to 'bag' and fishing permits are available at the **Fortingall Hotel**, see Sleeping page 248.

Ben Lawers → *OS sheet No 51 covers the area.*

The highest mountain in Perthshire, Ben Lawers (3,987 ft), dominates the north side of Loch Tay. Its massif of seven summits includes six Munros which are linked by an eight-mile ridge which can be walked in one day by fit and experienced hillwalkers. The best access to the ridge is from Glen Lyon. The trek to the main summit starts from the NTS Visitor Centre, two miles along a track which turns off the main A827 about halfway between Kenmore and Killin. This track continues over a wild pass to Bridge of Balgie in Glen Lyon. Leaflets describing the climb are available from the visitor centre. It's a seven-mile walk there and back, and though the route is straightforward and easy to follow, it's a very steep, tough climb of 2,700 ft from the centre to the summit. Allow five to six hours. You should be fit, properly clothed, see page 56, and have some previous hillwalking experience, but the views from the top on a clear day are amazing, across to the North Sea in the east and the Atlantic Ocean in the west. There's also a much easier one-mile nature trail, and an accompanying booklet describing the rare Alpine flora is available at the centre.

Blairgowrie and Glenshee → *Phone code: 01250. Colour map 4, grid B3.*

The other major road running north from Perth is the A93, soon reaching the respectable town of **Blairgowrie**, or Blairgowrie and Rattray to give it its full title. It lies amidst the raspberry fields of Strathmore and is conveniently placed to serve as an accommodation centre for **Glenshee Ski Centre**, see Activities and tours page 251. The TIC ⓘ *26 Wellmeadow, T01250-872960, Apr-Oct daily, Nov-Easter Mon-Sat.* There's little of real interest to detain passing tourists, but **Keathbank Mill** ⓘ *Apr to early Oct daily 1030-1700, £4.25*, off the A93 to Braemar, is worth a look. This huge 19th-century jute mill has a steam turbine dating from 1862 driven by the largest water wheel in Scotland. There's also a heraldry museum, model railway and woodcarving workshops.

The A9s continues north passing the Glenshee ski resort on its way to Braemar and then heads east through Deeside to Aberdeen, see page 510.

Strathearn → *Phone code: 01764. Colour map 4, grid C2-3.*

Strathearn is the wide valley (or *strath*) of the River Earn, which stretches west from Perth to Loch Earn, on the border of the Perthshire and Stirling regions. The Highladns officially begin in the western part of Strathearn and the Highland Boundary Fault runs through the village of Comrie, near Crieff. The well-groomed town of Crieff sits on the slopes of the Grampian foothills overlooking the wide Strathearn Valley. It's a popular tourist centre and a good base for exploring the western part of Perthshire and the Trossachs. » *For Sleeping, Eating and other listings, see pages 248-251.*

Crieff

The superb **Glenturret Distillery** ⓘ *T01764-656565, www.glenturret.com, Jan-Dec daily 0900-1800 (last tour 1630), Jul and Aug daily 0900-1830 (last tour 1730), £6, concessions £5, under 12s free*, is Scotland's oldest distillery, established in 1775, and is also the most visited whisky distillery in Scotland. Its easy to see why, combining as it does the best of tradition and modernity. It has a good restaurant which serves food all day. It is a mile from town, just off the A85 to Comrie.

Three miles south of Blairgowrie, just off the A93 by Meikleour, is a 100-ft-high beech hedge – the highest hedge in the world!

Two miles south of Crieff, on the A822 to Muthill, is the turning to the very wonderful **Drummond Castle Gardens** ⓘ *T01764-681257, Easter weekend and May-Oct daily 1400-1800 (last entry 1700), £3.50, £2.50 concession, take bus No 47 towards Muthill and get off at the gates, then walk a mile up the castle drive*, one of the finest formal gardens in Europe. Even the most horticulturally ignorant of people could not fail to be amazed by the graceful harmony and symmetry, in particular the magnificently laid-out flower beds celebrating family and Scottish heraldry. If you have the feeling you've seen them before, that's because they were featured in the film *Rob Roy*.

Comrie and around

Seven miles west of Crieff is the pleasant village of **Comrie**, which has the distinction of being the most earthquake-prone place in Britain due to its position on the Highland Boundary Fault. The world's first seismometer was set up here, in 1874, at the **Earthquake House** ⓘ *Apr-Oct daily*, which is at The Ross, about one mile west of the village, just off the A85. A great place for kids is the **Auchingarrich Wildlife Centre** ⓘ *T01764-679469, all year daily 1000 till dusk, £4, £3 children*, a few miles south of Comrie on the B827 on a windy hillside. It has a large collection of wild and exotic animals which you can feed and pet.

A recommended walk from Comrie is to the **Devil's Cauldron**, a spectacular waterfall in Glen Lednock which extends six miles into the hills northwest of Comrie. It's a pleasant mile-long woodland walk to the waterfall, and from there you can climb up to **Melville Monument**, at the top of Dunmore Hill (840 ft), from where there are excellent views across Strathearn and the Ochil Hills.

Five miles further west is the village of **St Fillans**, at the east end of Loch Earn. The A85 runs along the northern shore of the loch to Lochearnhead, where it continues northwest towards Crianlarich, see page 263.

Auchterarder and Dunning

South is the trim little town of Auchterarder, overlooked by the Ochil Hills to the south and surrounded by rich farmland. There's a tourist information centre on the High Street ⓘ *T01764-663450, check opening hours*. The adjacent heritage centre tells of centuries of local history – from agriculture to education – including information on the local textile industry which has been going here since the 16th century. Most people come here to play golf at the world-renowned **Gleneagles Hotel**, see Sleeping page 248.

Five miles east of Auchterarder, and eight miles southwest of Perth, is the historically interesting little village of Dunning, once the capital of the Picts and the place where Kenneth I, king of the Picts and Scots, died in 860. The village was burned to the ground by the Jacobites in 1716 and the only surviving building is the 12th-century Norman tower of St Serf's church. A mile west of the village, by the B8062, is **Maggie Walls Monument**, which commemorates the burning of a local witch in 1657.

The Ochil Hills

The Ochils rise sharply from the flat flood-plain of the River Forth and stretch northeast, through Clackmannanshire, into Perth and Kinross. This unfashionable and little-known range of hills is characterized by the shapely, rounded tops divided by steep-sided glens. There are good walking opportunities and some surprisingly dramatic scenery. At their feet, the pretty little towns and villages known collectively as 'the Hillfoots' were once Scotland's second-largest wool-producing region, after the Borders. Today visitors can explore the region's tweedy heritage on the Mill Trail, starting in Alva and linking the main mill centres along the A91, which runs east all the way to St Andrews in Fife.

Blairlogie and Alva

A few miles northeast of Stirling, in the village of Blairlogie, is the crumbling 16th-century **Logie Old Kirk** and its ancient graveyard full of fascinating old stones, beautifully located by Logie Burn. A few miles further east is the little town of **Alva**, home to the Mill Trail Visitor Centre ⓘ *Glentana Mill, Stirling St, T01259-769696, Jan-Jul and Sep-Dec 1000-1700, Aug 0900-1700, free*. Here you'll see what life was like for mill workers in the mid-19th century (pretty grim apparently), and learn about the history of textile production from the Industrial Revolution onwards.

Alva Glen → *OS Landranger No 58.*

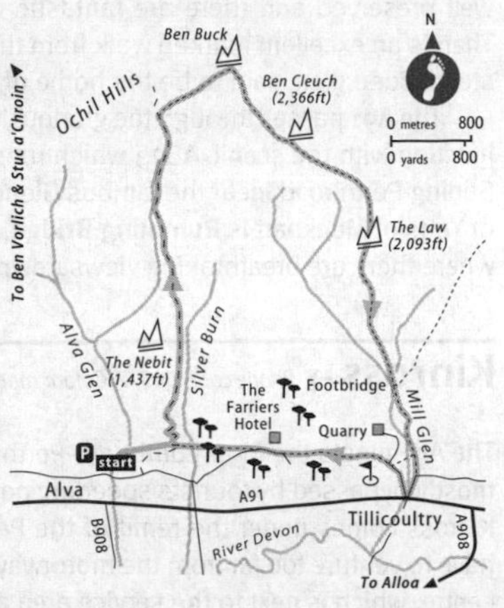

A fine walk from Alva heads up Alva Glen to the summit of **Ben Cleuch** and then down Mill Glen to Tillicoultry. It's a total distance of eight miles and should take around four to five hours. It's mostly on good paths and tracks, but walking boots are recommended, as well as waterproofs, warm clothing, food and drink. Starting from the car park head up the glen, cross the bridge, climb a series of steps and then go under a large pipe and past the water works to reach a gate giving access to the open hill. Follow a clear path across the hill until it reaches a track. Follow this track up to the head of the glen and, just before it turns left, leave it and take a path on the right which climbs towards the summit of Ben Buck. First, you'll reach a false summit, from where there are great views north to the mountains of Breadalbane, near Callander and Loch Earn. Follow the fence line to the right and, after a fence junction, take a clear path up to the rocks at the summit of Ben Cleuch. Having taken in the views, leave the summit along the same fence line. Near a fence junction, keep to the right and take the path which climbs up to The Law (2,093 ft), from where there is a wonderful view across the Forth. Follow the path which descends steeply and is eroded, taking care especially near the foot of the hill. Cross the burn by the footbridge and, at the path junction beyond, take the right-hand lower path, which winds down the steep-sided Mill Glen, re-crossing the burn several times. Once you reach the road, go down Upper Mill Street as far as the main road. You can head left into Tillicoultry to catch a bus back to Alva, or enjoy a pint at **The Woolpack**. To continue the walk, head right and take the next right along a rough road heading up to the quarry. Continue straight ahead on a clear track leading up beside the golf course and through woodland until you reach **The Farriers Hotel**, restaurant and craft shop complex. At the entrance to the Woodland Park car park, go right and follow a broad path uphill through the trees. The path levels out then crosses the Silver Burn, where silver was mined in the 18th century. Go through a kissing gate and then head back to the start of the walk.

A few miles south of Alva is the unappealing brewery town of **Alloa**, notable only for the beautifully restored **Alloa Tower** ⓘ *T01259-211701, Apr-Sep daily 1330-1730, Oct weekends only 1330-1730, £3.50, £2.60 concession*, which stands in a park a short walk from the town centre. The 15th-century tower house, one of the largest surviving medieval tower houses in Scotland, is the ancestral home of the Erskine family, Earls of Mar and Kellie, who were custodians of the young Mary, Queen of Scots. Of particular note is the Italianate staircase, the original oak rood beams and the pit dungeon. There are also excellent views from the parapet walk.

Dollar and around

Top of the bill in these parts is the well-heeled little town of Dollar, 11 miles east of Stirling and well worthy of a day trip. Looming above the town at the head of magical Dollar Glen, is the spectacularly sited **Castle Campbell** ⓘ *T01259-742408 (HS), Apr-Sep daily 0930-1830, Oct-Mar Mon-Wed and Sat 0930-1630, Thu 0930-1230, Sun 1400-1630, £3, £2.30 concession*, standing between two deep ravines and formerly known as Castle Gloom, until it passed into the hands of the Campbells in the 15th century. The castle was sacked by Cromwell's troops in 1654, but the tower is well preserved and there are fantastic views down Dollar Glen from the parapet. There's an excellent marked walk from the town up to the castle through the narrow, steep-sided glen, said to be the home of fairies and other woodland spirits.

The A91 passes through the gloriously named hamlet of **Yetts o' Muckhart**, at the junction with the scenic A823 which runs north through Glen Devon to meet the A9 Stirling-Perth road, near the famous **Gleneagles Hotel**, see Sleeping page 248. South of Yetts o' Muckhart is **Rumbling Bridge**, at the junction of the A823 and A977, from where there are breathtaking views down into a deep gorge.

Kinross → *Phone code: 01577. Colour map 4, grid C3.*

The A91 meets the M90 Edinburgh-Perth motorway by the town of Kinross, which is mostly bypassed by tourists speeding north to the Highlands or south to the capital. Kinross comes under the remit of the Perthshire Tourist Board and you don't even have to venture too far from the motorway to visit the helpful local tourist information centre, which is next to the service area at Junction 6 ⓘ *T01577-863680, Apr-Oct.*

On an island in the middle of Loch Leven, is the lonely tower of **Loch Leven Castle** ⓘ *T07778-040483 (HS), Apr-Oct daily 0930-1715, £3.50, concession £2.50*, where Mary, Queen of Scots was imprisoned for almost a year at the behest of Queen Elizabeth. She made a dramatic escape in May, 1568, with the help of her young, impressionable jailer. There's not much left of the 14th-century ruin, but it's an evocative place full of romance and history. During the summer a ferry leaves from Kinross to the island.

Not far from Loch Leven – Junction 5 off the M90 – is the RSPB reserve at **Vane Farm** ⓘ *T01577-862355, daily 1000-1700, £3, £2 concession*. There are several nature trails to follow and three hides from which to observe the rich bird life of the loch. In autumn and winter you can see thousands of geese, as well as birds such as tufted duck, teal and peregrine. In September you may also see ospreys hunting for fish on the loch.

Sleeping

Perth and around *p238, map p239*

L Hilton Dunkeld, Dunkeld, T01796-727771, www.dunkeld.hilton.com. Luxurious former home of the Duke of Atholl, now with full leisure and outdoor activity facilities.

L Kinnaird House, Dalguise, about 8 miles north of Dunkeld via the A9 and the B898, T01796-482440. The top hotel in the area. The setting, the style, the service and the restaurant are all excellent.

A Ballathie House Hotel, Kinclaven, near Stanley, 2 miles north of Perth, just off the A9, T01250-883268, www.ballathiehouse hotel.com. 43 rooms. Pick of the bunch. This elegant, award-winning 19th-century former hunting lodge has a reputation for superb Scottish cuisine (**£££**).

B Huntingtower Hotel, T01738-583771, F583777, www.huntingtowerhotel.co.uk, 1 mile west of Perth off the A85 to Crieff, 34 rooms. Another excellent option. Elegant country house hotel in its own landscaped gardens, good food in the dining room (**££**) and bar meals in the conservatory (**£**).

B Quality Station Hotel, next to the train station, Leonard St, Perth, T01738-624141,

admin@gb628-u-net.com. 70 rooms. A grand old Victorian edifice close to the town centre.
C Sunbank House Hotel, 50 Dundee Rd, Perth, T01738-624882, F442515. 9 rooms. A lovely little hotel overlooking the Tay and close to Branklyn Garden and Kinnoull Hill, great value.
D The Bridge B&B, 10 Bridge St, Dunkeld, T01796-727068, www.visitscotland.com/thebridge; and
D The Pend, 5 Brae St, Dunkeld, T01796-727586, www.thepend.com, are two of several B&Bs in Dunkeld.
E Achnacarry Guest House, 3 Pitcullen Cres, on the A94 Coupar Angus road, T01738-621421. Good choice on a road full of B&Bs.
E Kinnaird Guest House, 5 Marshall Pl, overlooking the South Inch, Perth, T01738-6280121, www.kinnaird-guesthouse.co.uk.
F SYHA Youth hostel, 107 Glasgow Rd, T01738-623658, open Mar-Oct, about half a mile west of the town centre (take bus No 7).
F Western Caputh Independent Hostel, at Caputh, 5 miles east of Dunkeld, on the A984 to Coupar Angus, T01738-710617. It has 18 beds and is open all year.

Camping

Cleeve Caravan Park, on Glasgow Rd, near the ring road, about 2 miles from town, T01738-639521, open Apr-Oct.
Scone Palace Camping & Caravan Club Site, T01738-552308, open Apr-Oct.

Pitlochry and around *p241*

There are numerous guest houses and B&Bs in Pitlochry, far too many to list here. The tourist office will provide a full list.
B Killiecrankie Hotel, a few miles north of Pitlochry, in the village of Killiecrankie, T01796-473220, www.killiecrankiehotel.co.uk. Open Mar-Dec. 10 rooms. It's a quiet, cosy country house hotel which offers quite possibly the very finest food in the area.
B Pine Trees Hotel, Strathview Terr, Pitlochry, T01796-472121, wwwpinetreeshotel.co.uk. The best hotel in town is this superb Victorian country house set in 10 acres of gardens away from the tourist bustle. Its Garden Restaurant has a fine reputation.
C Atholl Arms Hotel, near the train station in Blair Atholl village, T481205, does B&B and serves bar meals.
C Dunfallandy Country House Hotel & Restaurant, T01796-472648, dunfalhse@aol.com. A mile out of Pitlochry on the road to Logierait. 8 rooms. Top-class hotel. Georgian mansion offering great views, peace and quiet and superb cuisine, no smoking, excellent value.
D Craigroyston House, 2 Lower Oakfield, T1796-472053. Recommended guest house.
E Arrandale House, Knockfarrie Rd, Pitlochry, T1796-472987. Comfortable.
E Bunrannoch House, Kinloch Rannock, T01882-632407, www.bunrannoch.co.uk, a former Victorian shooting lodge which offers good cooking.
E Craigatin House & Courtyard, 165 Atholl Rd, Pitlochry, T1796-472478. Good value.
F SYHA Youth Hostel, T1796-472308, on Knockard Rd overlooking the town centre of Pitlochry, open all year.

Aberfeldy and Loch Tay *p243*

L-A Farleyer House Hotel, Weem, a mile west from Aberfeldy, T01887-820332, 100127.222@compuserve.com. Best of the hotels around town. Magnificent 15th-century building.
B Guinach House, Aberfeldy, T01887-820251. Family run country house in a lovely setting by the Birks, with a superb restaurant (**£££**).
C Ailean Chraggan, Weem, a mile or so west from Aberfeldy, T01887-820346. Serves very good food in the bar (**££**).
C Kenmore Hotel, Kenmore, T01887-830205. Claims to be Scotland's oldest coaching inn, dating from 1572. Whether or not this is true, there's no denying that it's full of character and very comfortable. Excellent food is to be had in the lovely bar (**££**).
C Weem Hotel T01887-820381, in Weem, about a mile west of Aberfeldy on the B846 to Strathtummel. Very friendly welcome.
D Fortingall Hotel, next to the churchyard in Fortingall, T01887-830367, hotel@fortingall.com. Wonderful and very popular.
E Tigh'N'Eilean Guest House, Taybridge Dr, Aberfeldy, T01887-820109. Recommended.

For an explanation of sleeping and eating price codes used in this guide, see inside the front cover. Other relevant information is found in Essentials, see pages 43-51.

Strathearn *p245*

L **Crieff Hydro**, turn off the High St at the Drummond Arms Hotel, then continue uphill and follow the signs, Crieff, T01764-655555, www.crieffhydro.com. First opened in 1868 as the Strathearn Hydropathic. The best place to stay in Crieff. It offers a huge range of leisure activities and a fine restaurant.

L **Gleneagles Hotel**, Gleneagles, T01764-662231, www.gleneagles.com. A luxury 5-star hotel and leisure resort with 3 top-class golf courses. If you can afford it, there is no better way to pamper yourself. The restaurant, **Andrew Fairlie**, T01764-694267, is equally impressive (**£££**).

B **Royal Hotel**, Melville Sq, Comrie, T01764-679200, www.royalhotel.co.uk. Very comfortable, has a good restaurant and great pub round the back serving real ales.

E **Merlindale**, Perth Rd, Crieff, T01764-655205. Best of the cheaper accommodation.

F **Braincroft Bunkhouse**, T01764-670140, an independent hostel 2 miles east of Comrie on the road to Crieff.

The Ochil Hills *p246*

F **SYHA Youth Hostel**, a few miles north of Yetts o' Muckhart, at the village of Glendevon, T01259-781206, open mid-Mar to early Oct, provides information on walks in the Ochil Hills.

Eating

Perth and around *p238, map p239*

££ Let's Eat Bistro, Kinnoull St, T01738-643377. Tue-Sat 1200-1400, 1830-2130. Very classy establishment which provides a modern Scottish menu with Mediterranean influences, all meals cooked fresh to order. Its sister restaurant, **Let's Eat Again**, 33 George St and open till 2145.

££ No. 63, 63 Tay St, T01738-441451. Tue-Sat 1200-1400, 1830-2100. Swish restaurant down by the river. Serves contemporary Scottish food.

££ The Seafood Restaurant, 168 South St, T01738-449777. Specializes in fish and game.

Pitlochry and around *p241*

£££ East Haugh Country House Hotel & Restaurant, a couple of miles south of Pitlochry on the old A9 road, T01796-473121, www.easthaugh.com. A 17th-century country house with excellent and elegant dining and great bar lunches.

£££ Killiecrankie Hotel, see Sleeping, is expensive but the best place to eat.The bar is less formal and cheaper than the restaurant.

£££ Loft, Golf Course Rd, Blair Atholl, T01796-481377, www.theloftrestaurant.co.uk. The best food hereabouts. Superior Modern Scottish/Mediterranean food.

££ Port-na-Craig Inn & Restaurant, T01796-472777, which is just below the Festival Theatre on the banks of the River Tummel. It offers great Scottish cooking in a bistro ambience.

£ Moulin Inn, a few miles north of Pitlochry, at Moulin on the A924, T01796-472196, www.moulin.u-net.com. Food daily till 2130. Serves good, cheap pub food and fine real ales (try their 'Braveheart') in a great atmosphere.

Strathearn *p245*

££ The Bank, 32 High St, Crieff, T01764-656575. Other than the hotels in town and the Glenturret Distillery, see above, there isn't a huge choice of good places to eat. This is the pick of the lot and offers modern food.

Entertainment

Perth and around *p238, map p239*

Perth Theatre, 185 High St, Perth, T01738-621031, is a beautiful Victorian-era theatre with an excellent reputation for high-class productions.

Playhouse, 6 Murray St, Perth, T01738-623126, offers a dose of escapism on the big screen.

Pitlochry and around *p241*

Pitlochry Festival Theatre, T01796-484626, is across the river from the town centre. It stages a different play every night for 6 nights a week from May to Oct.

Festivals and events

Perth and around *p238, map p239*

Perth Highland Games are held on the second Sun in Aug, on the same weekend as the **Perth Show**, which takes place on South Inch.

Perth Racecourse, near Scone Palace, T01738-551597, has regular jump racing events during the summer.

Strathearn *p245*
Crieff Highland Gathering takes place on the penultimate Sun in Aug.

Activities and tours

Perth and around *p238, map p239*
Fishing Sandyknowes fly-fishery at Bridge of Earn, T01738-813033, a few miles southeast of Perth. Located between the rivers Earn and Tay, there are facilities for the novice, right up to the most experienced angler with great fishing in a beautiful landscape. The season runs from Mar-Dec and currently costs £10 per day. Details of all the Perthshire fisheries are available from the TIC.
Leisure centres Bell's Sports Centre, Hay St, T01738-622301, daily 0900-2200, covers virtually every sport and leisure activity imaginable.
Dewar's Rinks, next door to the pool, T01738-624188, where the visitor can curl, ice skate or bowl.
Perth Leisure Pool, T01738-492410, open daily 1000-2200, west of the town centre on the Glasgow Rd, claims to have the best leisure swimming pool in Scotland.

Pitlochry and around *p241*
Cycling Atholl Mountain Bikes, Blair Atholl, 01796-T473553, have a leaflet listing various cycle routes, including the Glen Tilt route above.
Escape Route, 8 West Moulin Rd, Pitlochry, T/F01796-473859. Touring and off-road bikes for £14 per day.

Aberfeldy and Loch Tay *p243*
Croft-Na-Caber, near the Crannog Centre, Kenmore, T01887-830588, Scotland's best watersports and activities centre, where you can try water-skiing, windsurfing, sailing, rafting, jet biking, river sledging, fishing, parascending, clay-pigeon shooting, walking and Nordic skiing.
Loch Tay Boating Centre, Kenmore, T01887-830291, open Apr-Oct, hires speedboats, fishing boats and canoes, as well as bicycles.

Blairgowrie and Glenshee *p245*
Glenshee ski centre, T01339-741320, www.ski.scotland.net, is at the crest of the Cairnwell Pass (2,199 ft), the highest main road pass in Britain. It is the most extensive skiing area in Scotland, with 38 pistes, as well as Nordic skiing. Ski rental is £13 per day (£12 for snowboards) and lessons £18 for 4 hrs. A 1-day lift pass costs £18, or £72 for 5 days, including tuition and hire. For the latest weather conditions, call Ski Hotline T0900-1-654656.

Transport

Perth and around *p238, map p239*
Stagecoach run local buses to **Dunkeld**, **Pitlochry**, **Aberfeldy** and **Crieff**; and Strathtay Scottish (T01382-228054) buses serve **Blairgowrie** (via Dunkeld), **Alyth** and **Dundee**. Citylink buses between Perth and Inverness stop at the train station by **Birnam** several times daily in either direction. Scottish Citylink buses, T08705-505050, run frequently to **Glasgow** (1 hr 25 mins), **Edinburgh** (1½ hrs), **Dundee** (35 mins), **Aberdeen** (2½ hrs) and **Inverness** (2½ hrs).
Arnold Clark, St Leonard's Bank, Perth, T01738-442202, hires cars.
There are also hourly trains to **Stirling** (30 mins), **Dundee** (25 mins) and **Aberdeen** (1 hr 40 mins), and several daily to **Inverness** via **Pitlochry** (30 mins) and **Aviemore**. There's an hourly train service (Mon-Sat; 2-hourly on Sun) to **Glasgow Queen St** (1 hr); and frequent trains to **Edinburgh** (1 hr 20 mins).

Pitlochry and around *p241*
From Pitlochry not all trains stop at Blair Atholl. **Elizabeth Yule Transport**, T01796-472290, runs a service between Pitlochry and **Blair Atholl**, via Killiecrankie, a few times daily, except Sun. See also section above.

The Ochil Hills *p246*
There are regular buses to **Dollar** from **Stirling**. There are also buses to and from **Alloa**.

Blairgowrie and Glenshee *p245*
The only public transport to the ski resort is a daily postbus service (Mon-Sat only) from **Blairgowrie** to **Spittal of Glenshee**, or from **Braemar** and **Ballater**.

Stirling and around

Standing between Edinburgh and Glasgow, yet only a short distance from some of the country's most beautiful scenery, the ancient town of Stirling is synonymous with the country's two greatest historical heroes, Robert the Bruce and William Wallace. It was once said that whoever controlled Stirling held the key to Scotland. Consequently the town and its surrounds have witnessed many crucial struggles between the Scots and the English. As you'd expect with such a strategically important town, Stirling has a long and fascinating history and is packed with major historical sights. It was here that the Scots under William Wallace defeated the English at the Battle of Stirling Bridge in 1297. A more famous battle was fought just a few miles away, at Bannockburn in 1314, when Robert the Bruce's small army routed Edward II's much larger English force. Being so close to both Edinburgh and Glasgow, the sights of Stirling can be visited in a day from either city, but it's also a very pleasant place to stay. It may lack the cosmopolitan feel of Edinburgh but has a lively buzz of its own during the busy summer months and there is a wide range of accommodation and other tourist facilities. ▸▸ *For Sleeping, Eating and other listings, see pages 257-258.*

Ins and outs

Getting there Stirling is easily reached from Edinburgh, Glasgow, Perth and most other main towns and cities by regular bus and train services. The train station is on Station Road, near the town centre, and the bus station is close by, on Goosecroft Road, behind the Thistle Shopping Centre. ▸▸ *For further details, see Transport page 258.*

Getting around Most of the important sights, except Bannockburn and the Wallace Monument, are within easy walking distance of each other. There's an open-topped 'hop on, hop off' Heritage Bus Tour which runs from June to September and includes the castle and Wallace Monument. There are tours every 30 minutes from 1000 till 1700. A day ticket costs £6.50. Check details at the TIC. There are regular buses to Doune from Stirling, via Blair Drummond.

Tourist information Stirling TIC ⓘ *41 Dumbarton Rd, T01786-475019, daily Jun-Sep Mon-Sat Oct-May*. It is the main office for Loch Lomond, Stirling and the Trossachs and stocks a wide range of books, guides, maps and leaflets. It also has information on the guided walks of the town, including the popular ghost walks which take place Tuesday to Saturday at 1930 and 2130. Dunblane TIC ⓘ *Stirling Rd, T01786-824428, May-Sep*. Linlithgow TIC ⓘ *Burgh Halls, The Cross, T01506-844600, Easter-Sep daily 1000-1700.*

Stirling → *Phone code: 01786. Colour map 4, grid C2. Population: 37,000.*

Stirling Castle

ⓘ *T01786-450000 (HS), Apr-Oct daily 0930-1800 (last entry 1715), Nov-Mar till 1700 (last entry 1615), £8, £6 concession (includes admission to Argyll's Ludging).*

The obvious place to begin a tour is the immensely impressive castle which stands 250 ft above the flat plain atop the plug of an extinct volcano. From the west there's a sheer drop down the side of the rocky crag, making the castle seem a daunting prospect to would-be attackers, and now presenting visitors with fantastic views of the surrounding area. There's been a fortress here since the Iron Age, though the current building dates mostly from the 15th and 16th centuries, when it was the favourite residence of the Stuart kings.

On the esplanade is a visitor centre which shows an introductory film giving a potted history of the castle. There are great views from the esplanade, across the valley floor to the Wallace Monument, with Stirling Old Bridge clearly visible, and the Ochil hills rising behind the monument. From the visitor centre you proceed to the **Upper Square**, where you can see the magnificent **Great Hall**, built by James IV and which was recently restored to its original condition. He also built the royal residence known as the **King's Old Building**, which now houses the museum of the Argyll and Sutherland Highlanders, which traces the history of this famous regiment from its inception in 1794 to the present day. James V, whose wives were both French, brought masons from France to create the spectacular **Palace** (1540-1542), the finest Renaissance building in Scotland. This was where the young Mary, Queen of Scots spent much of her life until her departure for France, in 1548. The interior of the royal apartments is largely bare but you can still see the **Stirling Heads**, 56 elegantly carved oak plaques which once decorated the ceiling of one of the rooms. Also impressive is the interior of the **Chapel Royal**, built by James VI in 1594 for the baptism of his son. The 16th- century **kitchens** are also interesting and have been restored to recreate the preparations for a royal banquet.

Other sights

The Old Town grew from around the 12th century, when Stirling became a royal burgh, and spread from the castle down the hill towards the flood-plain of the River Forth. Most of the historic sights are clustered around these medieval cobbled streets. The **town walls** are the best surviving in Scotland and can be followed along a path known as the **Back Walk**, which starts near the tourist office in Dumbarton Road and runs up the side of the walls and up to the Castle esplanade. Five minutes' walk downhill from the castle is **Argyll's Lodging** ⓘ *T01786-450000, same opening hours as the castle, £3.30, or joint ticket with the castle*, the finest and most complete surviving example of a 17th-century town house in Scotland. In the 18th century the house became a military hospital, and in the 1960s was used as a youth hostel. It has recently been restored to its former glory and rooms are furnished as they would have been in the late 17th century.

Further down Castle Wynd, at the top of Broad Street, is **Mar's Wark**, the extravagant renaissance façade of a dilapidated town house, started by the first Earl of Mar, Regent of Scotland, in 1569 but left to fall into ruin following his death two years later. Next door is the medieval **Church of the Holy Rude**, an imposing, brooding cliff of dark grey stone, where the infant James VI was crowned in 1567. A short way down St John Street is the impressively refurbished **Old Town Jail** ⓘ *T01786-450050, Apr-Sep daily 0930-1800, Oct daily till 1700, Nov-Feb daily till 1600, Mar till 1700, £5, £3.75 concession*, where the rigours of life behind bars in times gone by is brilliantly brought to life by enthusiastic actors. A glass lift then takes you up to the roof for spectacular views across the town and Forth Valley.

At the bottom of Broad Street is **Darnley's House**, where Mary, Queen of Scots' second husband, Lord Darnley, is said to have stayed. It now houses a coffee shop. In the Thistle Shopping Centre you can visit **The Bastion Jail** ⓘ *Mon-Sat 0900-1800, Sun 1200-1500, free*, which is all that remains of a defensive tower that formed part of the old town wall. You can look down into the Thieves Pit where prisoners were kept.

At the bottom of Spittal Street, where it joins King Street, turn into Corn Exchange Road and then head west up Dumbarton Road to reach the **Smith Art Gallery and Museum** ⓘ *T01786-471917, all year Tue-Sat 1030-1700, Sun 1400-1700, free*, which houses some interesting displays about the town's history and culture, as well as a fine collection of paintings and the world's oldest football(!).

At the north end of the town, a 20-minute walk from the town centre, is the 15th-century **Old Bridge**, which was the lowest crossing point on the River Forth, and

Stirling is a derivation of 'the striveling', meaning place of strife in Gaelic, evidence of its strategic importance in Scottish history.

Stirling

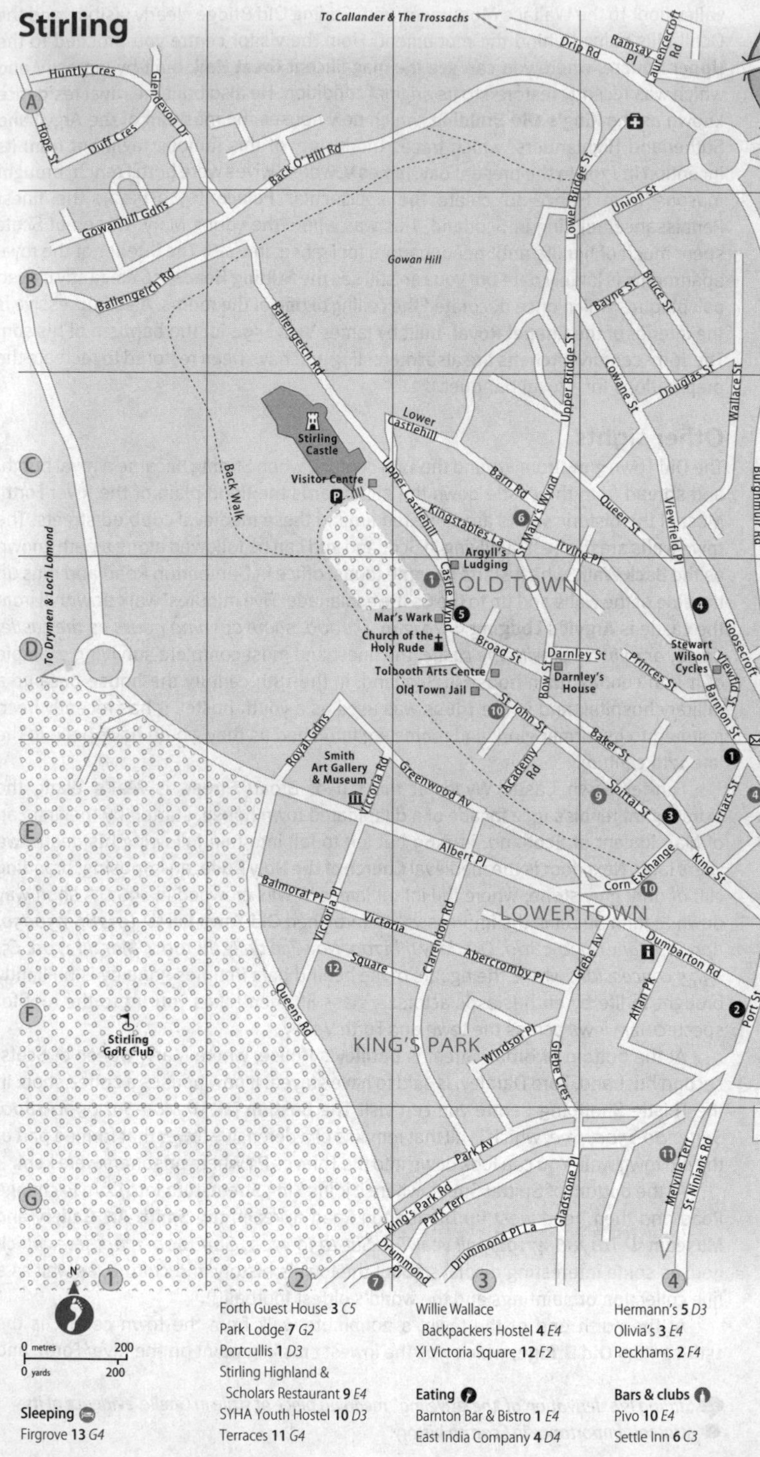

Sleeping
Firgrove 13 *G4*
Forth Guest House 3 *C5*
Park Lodge 7 *G2*
Portcullis 1 *D3*
Stirling Highland & Scholars Restaurant 9 *E4*
SYHA Youth Hostel 10 *D3*
Terraces 11 *G4*
Willie Wallace Backpackers Hostel 4 *E4*
XI Victoria Square 12 *F2*

Eating
Barnton Bar & Bistro 1 *E4*
East India Company 4 *D4*
Hermann's 5 *D3*
Olivia's 3 *E4*
Peckhams 2 *F4*

Bars & clubs
Pivo 10 *E4*
Settle Inn 6 *C3*

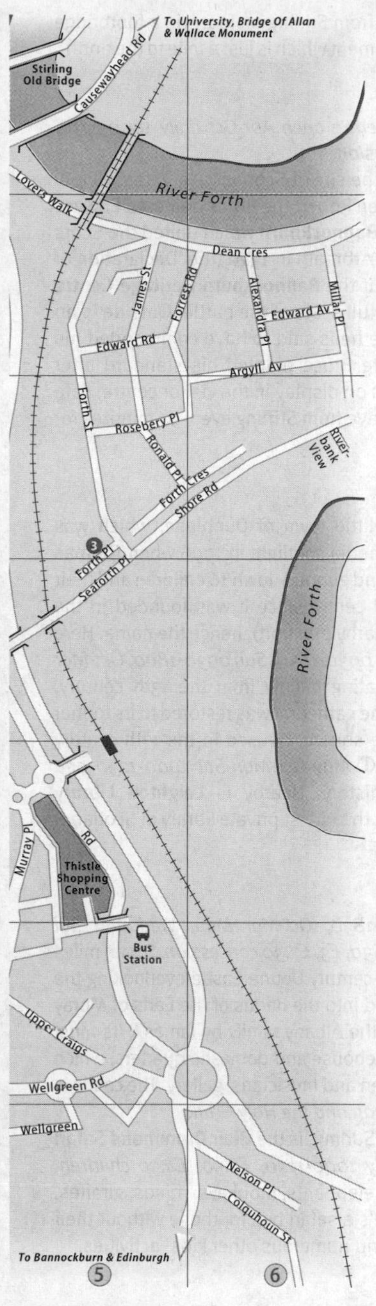

one of the most important bridges in Scotland until Kincardine Bridge was built in 1936. The bridge was built to replace earlier structures, including the famous wooden bridge, scene of the battle in 1297 in which William Wallace defeated the English.

Around Stirling

➔ *Colour map 4, grid C2.*

Wallace Monument

ⓘ *T01786-472140, Jan, Feb, Nov and Dec daily 1030-1600, Mar-May and Oct 1000-1700, Jun 1000-1800, Jul, Aug and Sep 0930-1830, £3.95, £2.75 children.* Two miles northeast of the town, near the University and Bridge of Allan, is this impressive Victorian Gothic tribute to Sir William Wallace, hero of the successful but hugely inaccurate film, *Braveheart*. Wallace was knighted by Robert the Bruce for his famous victory at Stirling Bridge, but following defeat later at Falkirk he went off to Europe in search of support for the Scottish cause. During his absence he was betrayed by the Scots nobles and on his return found guilty of treason and cruelly hanged, drawn and quartered in London. Inside the monument are various exhibits including a Hall of Scottish Heroes and Wallace's mighty two-handed sword (5 ft 4 ins long – about the same height as the actor who played him in the film). There are fantastic views from the top of the 220-ft tower. There's a shuttle bus which runs from the foot of the hill up to the tower every 15 minutes. An open-topped tour bus runs to the monument from Stirling Castle every half hour.

Cambuskenneth Abbey

ⓘ *Open all year, free.* A mile east of Stirling are the ruins of Cambuskenneth Abbey, founded in 1147 by David I for Augustinian canons, and once one of the richest abbeys in the country. Robert the Bruce held his parliament here in 1326, and King James III (1451-1488) and his wife, Queen Margaret of Denmark, are buried in the grounds. The only substantial surviving feature is the

14th-century belfry. The abbey can be reached from Stirling on foot, via a footbridge over the River Forth, and from the Wallace Monument which is just a mile to the north.

Bannockburn

ⓘ *T01786-812664 (NTS), site open all year, centre open Apr-Oct daily 1000-1730, Oct-Mar 1030-1600, £3.50, £2.60 child/concession.*
A few miles south of Stirling is Bannockburn, the site of Scotland's greatest victory over the English (apart from Wembley '67), when Robert the Bruce defeated Edward II's army, on 24 June 1314. It was the **Battle of Bannockburn** which united the Scots and led to the declaration of independence at Arbroath in 1320 (the 'Declaration of Arbroath'). There's not an awful lot to see, but the **Bannockburn Heritage Centre** puts flesh on the bones and brings to life the full scale of the battle. Outside is an equestrian statue of Bruce, on the spot where he is said to have commended his forces, and the site of the bore stone, where Bruce planted his standard after victory. What's left of the original bore stone is on display in the visitor centre, safe from souvenir hunters. Buses Nos 51 and 52 leave from Stirling every 30 minutes for the site.

Dunblane

Four miles north of Stirling is the attractive little town of Dunblane, which was suddenly and horrifyingly catapulted into the media spotlight in 1996 when Thomas Hamilton walked into the local primary school and gunned down 16 children and their teacher. The town has been an ecclesiastical centre since it was founded in the seventh century by St Blane who lived at the nearby *dun* (fort), hence the name. Here also is **Dunblane cathedral** ⓘ *Apr-Sep Mon-Sat 0930-1830, Sun 0930-1800, Oct-Mar Mon-Sat 0930-1630, Sun 1400-1630, free*, dating mainly from the 13th century, though the lower part of the tower is Norman. The cathedral was restored to its former glory in the late 19th century. Close by on the square, housed in the 17th-century Dean's house, is the tiny cathedral **museum** ⓘ *May-Oct Mon-Sat 1000-1230 and 1400-1630, free*, with a display on local history. Nearby is **Leighton Library** ⓘ *May-Oct Mon-Fri 1000-1230 and 1400-1630*, the oldest private library in Scotland, now open to the public.

Doune Castle

ⓘ *T01786-841742 (HS), Apr-Sep daily 0930-1830, Oct-Mar Mon, Wed and Sat 0930-1630, Thu 0930-1230, Fri and Sun 1400-1630, £3, £2.30 concession.* Seven miles northwest of Stirling, is the well-preserved 14th-century Doune Castle overlooking the River Teith. Built for the Regent Albany, it passed into the hands of the Earls of Moray (who still live there) following the execution of the Albany family by James I. Its most striking feature is the combination of tower, gatehouse and domestic quarters, which includes the Lord's Hall with its carved oak screen and musicians' gallery. The castle is better known for its role in the film, *Monty Python and the Holy Grail*.

A few miles south of Doune, off the A84 to Stirling, is the **Blair Drummond Safari Park** ⓘ *T01786-841203, Mar to early Oct daily 1000-1730, £8.50, £4.50 children*, Scotland's only wildlife park, with lions, tigers, elephants, monkeys, rhinos, giraffes, zebras and various other exotic animals. There's a safari bus for those without their own transport. There are also sea lion shows and numerous other kids' activities.

Falkirk and Linlithgow

Near Falkirk is the amazing **Falkirk Wheel** ⓘ *www.falkirkwheel.co.uk, Apr-Oct daily 0930-1700, Nov-Mar 1000-1500, boat trips cost £8, concessions £6, children £4, family £21*, the world's first and only rotating boat lift. This huge steel structure, which resembles two gigantic ring-pulls, transfers craft from the Forth and Clyde Canal to the Union Canal and you can book a 45-minute boat trip to experience it for yourself.

Halfway between Falkirk and Edinburgh is the pleasant little West Lothian town of Linlithgow, home of the magnificent Renaissance **Linlithgow Palace** ⓘ *T01506-842896 (HS), Apr-Sep daily 0930-1830; Oct-Mar Mon-Sat 0930-1630, Sun 1400- 1630, £3, £2.30 concession*, one of the most impressive historic buildings in Scotland. It's off the beaten track, relatively little-visited and well worth the detour. The 15th-century ruin is set on the edge of Linlithgow Loch and is associated with many of Scotland's main historical players, including James V (1512) and Mary, Queen of Scots (1542), who were both born here. James V was also married here, to Mary of Guise, and Bonnie Prince Charlie popped in for a visit during the 1745 rebellion. One year later the palace was badly damaged by fire during its occupation by General Hawley's troops, prior to their defeat by Jacobite forces under Prince Charles at the Battle of Falkirk. The ruin still conveys a real sense of the sheer scale of the lavish lifestyle of the court, from the ornate fountain in the inner courtyard to the magnificent Great Hall with its massive kitchens.

Sleeping

Stirling *p252, map p254*

L Stirling Highland Hotel, Spittal St, T01786-272727, F272829. 78 rooms. Converted school refurbished to high standards with full facilities, including a pool and saunas. Ask for a room with a view. Their Scholars Restaurant is recommended.

C Park Lodge Hotel, 32 Park Terr, T01786-474862, www.parklodge.net. 10 rooms. Luxurious Georgian/Victorian town house beautifully situated close to town centre, overlooking the park and castle, with a very fine restaurant.

C The Portcullis, Castle Wynd, T01786-472290, F446103. 6 rooms. 200-year-old hotel near the castle, some rooms have great views over the town. Busy bar below so not for light sleepers but great location.

C Terraces Hotel, 4 Melville Terr, T01786-472268. 17 rooms. Quiet hotel set off the main road with parking.

D X1 Victoria Square, 11 Victoria Sq, T01786-475545. Extremely comfortable with great views of the castle.

E Firgrove, 13 Clifford Rd, T01786-475805. Large, comfortable, Victorian house.

E Forth Guest House, 23 Forth Pl, T01786-471020. A short walk north of the train station. Recommended.

F SYHA youth hostel, in a converted church on St John St at the top of the town, T01786-473442, open all year.

F Willie Wallace Backpackers Hostel, 77 Murray Place, T01786-446773. 54 beds. More laid-back alternative to the SYHA. Good info on best nightlife.

Around Stirling *p255*

L Cromlix House, 4 miles north of Dunblane, near Kinbuck on the B8033, T01786-822125. One of Scotland's best country-house hotels, with its own loch and chapel. It's worth coming here for dinner or Sun lunch.

A Hilton Dunblane Hydro, Dunblane, T01786-825403. Overlooking the town, set in 44 acres of woodland, luxurious and exclusive.

Camping

Witches Craig Caravan Park, at Blairlogie, 3 miles east of Stirling on the A91, T01786-474947, Apr-Oct.

Eating

Stirling *p252, map p254*

£££ Scholars Restaurant, Stirling Highland Hotel, see Sleeping, has an excellent reputation for modern Scottish cuisine.

£££-££ Hermann's, 32 St John St, T01786-450632. At the Tolbooth on the road up to the castle, is an upmarket choice. It offers excellent Scottish/Austrian cuisine.

££ Olivia's Restaurant, 5 Baker St, T01786-446277. Modern Scottish and Thai food cooked with flair and imagination and served in an informal atmosphere. Mon-Sat 1200-1430 and 1830-2200.

££ Peckhams, 52 Port St, T01786-463222. Mon-Fri 1000-2200, Sat and Sun 0930-2300. Deli out front and booth seating at rear. Good quality modern Scottish cuisine, also snacks and sandwiches.

£Barnton Bar & Bistro, opposite the post office on Barnton St, T01786-461698. A favourite with students. Open till 2400 (0100 at weekends) and serves great breakfasts.
£East India Company, 7 Viewfield Pl, T01786-471330. The best curry in town.

Around Stirling *p255*
£££Champany Inn, 2 miles northeast of Stirling, at the junction of the A904 and A803, T01506-834532. Seriously good dining, their steaks are legendary.
££Boozy Rouge at the Sheriffmuir Inn, on the wild moors of Sheriffmuir, south of Dunblane, T01786-823285. The inn dates from the early 18th century and serves fine food and ales. A wonderful place in summer.
££Four Marys, 65 High St, Linlithgow, T01506-842171. Renowned in these parts for their bar meals and real ales. Food served daily 1200-1430, 1730-2030, 1230-2030 Sun. Booking essential.

Bars and clubs

Stirling *p252, map p254*
Pivo, Corn Exchange, T01786-451904, is a trendy Czech bar which serves light meals.
Portcullis, on Castle Wynd, below the castle, T01786-472268, one of the best in Stirling.
Settle Inn, St Mary's Wynd. The oldest hostelry in town (1773) and very popular with Stirling's large student population.

Entertainment

Stirling *p252, map p254*
The Tolbooth, just off Broad St, T01786-274000, is a multi-purpose arts centre with a lively programme of events and a good café and restaurant.

Transport

Stirling *p252, map p254*
Local buses are run by **First Edinburgh**, T01324-613777. There are frequent services to **Dunblane**, **Doune** via Blair Drummond (30 mins), **Callander** (45 mins), **Dollar** (35 mins), **Falkirk** (30 mins) and **Linlithgow** (1 hr), and several daily to **Aberfoyle** (45 mins). Long-distance service are run by **Scottish Citylink** who have buses at least every hour to and from **Dundee** (1½ hrs) and at least every 30 mins to **Perth** (50 mins) and **Glasgow** (1 hr). There are also regular buses to **Inverness** (3½ hrs) and **Aberdeen** (3½ hrs), but you'll probably need to change at Perth and Dundee respectively. Buses also run to **Edinburgh**, but as the journey takes 1½ hrs you might prefer to take the train.

There are **ScotRail** trains, every 30 mins (Mon-Sat; hourly on Sun) to **Edinburgh** (45 mins) and **Glasgow** (45 mins), and regular services to **Perth** (35 mins), **Dundee** (1 hr) and **Aberdeen** (2¼ hrs).

Car hire from **Arnold Clark**, Kerse Rd, T01786-478686. Cycle hire from **Wildcat Bike Tours**, Stirling Enterprise Park, Unit 102, John Player Building, T/F01786-464333. **Stewart Wilson Cycles**, Barnton St, T01786-465292.

Around Stirling *p255*
There are regular buses to **Dunblane** from Stirling (see above). There are also hourly trains to and from **Edinburgh** (20 mins), **Glasgow Queen Street** (30 mins) and **Stirling** (35 mins). Regular buses from Stirling and Edinburgh stop at The Cross in **Linlithgow**. The train station is at the southern end of town.

The Trossachs and Loch Lomond

Strictly speaking, the Trossachs is the narrow wooded glen between Loch Katrine and Loch Achray, but the name is now used to describe a much larger area between Argyll and Perthshire, stretching north from the Campsies and west from Callander to the eastern shore of Loch Lomond. It's a very beautiful and diverse area of sparkling lochs, craggy mountains and deep, forested glens, and for this reason is often called the 'Highlands in miniature', best visited in the autumn when the hills are purple and the trees are a thousand luminous hues, from lustrous gold to flaming scarlet and blazing orange. The Trossachs was one of the country's first holiday regions, and remains a major tourist destination. Its enduring appeal is due in no small measure to Sir Walter Scott, who eulogized its great natural beauty in his epic poem, Lady of the Lake, *and whose historical novel,* Rob Roy, *brought to public attention the region's other great attraction, Rob Roy MacGregor, one of the great romantic Highland figures.*

West of the Trossachs is Loch Lomond, Britain's largest inland waterway, measuring 22 miles long and at certain points up to five miles wide. Its once 'bonnie' banks are now one of the busiest parts of the Highlands, due to their proximity to Glasgow (only 20 miles south along the congested A82). During the summer the western shore in particular becomes a playground for day-trippers who tear up and down the loch in speedboats and on jet skis, obliterating any notion visitors may have of a little peace and quiet. The eastern shores are altogether less hectic and form part of the new Loch Lomond National Park, the first to be established in the country. ⏩ *For Sleeping, Eating and other listings, see pages 264-266.*

Ins and outs

Getting there There are regular buses from Stirling to Aberfoyle and Callander, T0870-6082608. There are also daily services to Aberfoyle from Glasgow, via Balfron. There's a Scottish Citylink service once daily in summer between Edinburgh and Fort William which stops in Callander. There's a postbus service, T01752-494527, www.royalmail.com/postbus, from Aberfoyle to Inversnaid on Loch Lomond. A postbus leaves Callander daily, except Sunday, at 0915 to Trossachs Pier and connects with cruises on Loch Katrine, see page 261. There's also a postbus during the week in the afteroons between Callander and Aberfoyle, via Port of Menteith. ⏩ *For further details, see Transport page 265.*

Getting around The Trossachs Trundler is a bus which makes a circuit of the Trossachs, linking Stirling, Callander, Aberfoyle and Port of Menteith, and stopping off at various scenic places en route. It also connects with departures of the *SS Sir Walter Scott* on Loch Katrine. It runs from June to September except Wednesdays and costs £8 for a day ticket. Contact the local TIC for details, see below.

Tourist information Aberfoyle TIC ⓘ *on the main street, T01877-382352, Apr-Jun, Sep and Oct daily 1000-1700, Jul and Aug 0930-1900, weekends only Nov-Mar.* Callander TIC ⓘ *Ancaster Sq, T01877-330342, Mar-May and Oct-Dec daily 1000-1700, Jun 0930-1800, Jul and Aug 0900-2000, Sep 1000-1800, Jan and Feb weekends only 1000-1600*, shares the same building as the Rob Roy and Trossachs Visitor Centre. Loch Lomond Shores ⓘ *T01389-721500*, is a large visitor centre and orientation centre as you come into town, which operates as the gateway to the National Park. At the 100-acre site you can see a film celebrating the area in addition to shops, restaurants and the restored steamer *Maid of the Loch*. Tarbet TIC ⓘ *T01301-702260, Apr-Oct.*

The Campsies

→ *Phone code: 01360. Colour map 4, grid C2.*

Running southeast from Loch Lomond, and bordered by the broad farmlands of the Carse of Stirling to the north and the northern suburbs of Glasgow to the south, are the Campsies. This is an area of gently rolling hills and fertile farmland, comprising the Fintry, Gargunnock, Strathblane and Kilsyth Hills and the Campsie Fells. Other than weekend hikers from Glasgow, the Campsies attract few visitors and their unspoiled peace and beauty is their main attraction. There's a string of picturesque villages nestled in the hills, amongst them Killearn, Kippen, Gargunnock and Balfron, birthplace of Alexander 'Greek' Thomson, Glasgow's great Victorian architect, see box page 147. There's also plenty of good walking to be done here.

Lying at the heart of the Campsies is the attractive little village of **Fintry**, at the head of the Strathendrick Valley, and regular winner of the 'Scotland in Bloom' competition. Two miles east of the village is the 90-ft-high **Loup of Fintry waterfall**. At the western end of the Campsie Fells is the village of **Drymen**, the busiest of the Campsie villages due to its proximity to the eastern shores of Loch Lomond. Drymen also lies on the **West Highland Way**. There's a seasonal tourist office in the library on The Square ⓘ *T01360-660068*. South of Killearn on the A81 is the excellent **Glengoyne Distillery** ⓘ *T01360-550254, tours hourly on the hour Mon-Sat 1000-1600, Sun 1200-1600, £3.95*.

▲Glengoyne is also the starting point for two excellent walks in the Strathblane Hills, to the top of both **Dumgoyne Hill** (1,400 ft), and **Earl's Seat** (1,896 ft), the highest point in the Campsies. Further west, on the other side of Strathblane, is **Queen's View** on Auchineden Hill, from where there are wonderful views up Loch Lomond as far as Ben Ledi. Queen Victoria was particularly impressed with the view – hence its name. The path to the top starts from the busy car park on the A809 Bearsden to Drymen road. It takes about 45 to 50 minutes each way. From the car park a path also leads up to The Whangie, a deep cleft in the rock face with sheer walls rising over 30 ft on either side. A path runs for 100 yds through the narrow gap.

The Trossachs → *Phone code: 01877. Colour map 4, grid C1-2.*

▲ Walking in the Trossachs → *OS Landranger maps 56 and 57 covers these routes.*

The Trossachs is superb walking country. The two most challenging peaks are Ben Venue and Ben A'an around Loch Katrine and Loch Achray, about 10 miles west of Callander. **Ben Venue** (2,385 ft) is the more difficult climb. It starts from behind the **Loch Achray Hotel** and is waymarked, but it's a strenuous climb which requires hillwalking experience, proper clothing and all the usual safety precautions. Allow about five hours for the return trip. **Ben A'an** (1,520 ft) isn't a giant of a hill, but it's a steep climb from the start, from the car park of the former **Trossachs Hotel** (now a timeshare development) on the north bank of Loch Achray, and there's a bit of scrambling involved near the summit. It takes about 1½ hours to the top. The views from both hills are stupendous on clear days, but remember that the weather is as unpredictable in the Trossach mountains as anywhere else in the Highlands. A useful guide is Collins' *Walk Loch Lomond and the Trossachs*.

Both these mountains lie within the **Queen Elizabeth Forest Park**. This vast and spectacular wilderness of 75,000 acres borders Loch Lomond to the west and incorporates Loch Ard, Loch Achray and Loch Lubnaig, as well as Ben Venue, Ben A'An and **Ben Ledi**, which overlooks Callander. The park is run by the Forestry Commission and is criss-crossed by a network of less difficult waymarked trails and paths which start from the **Queen Elizabeth Park Visitor Centre** ⓘ *T01877-382258, Mar-Oct daily 1000-1800, Oct-Dec 1100-1600 (parking £1)*, about half a mile north of Aberfoyle on the A821. Available at the centre are audio-visual displays on the park's flora and fauna and information on the numerous walks and cycle routes around the park. Full details of the park are available from the Forest Enterprise in Aberfoyle.

Aberfoyle

The sleepy village of Aberfoyle suddenly bursts into life in the summer with the arrival of hordes of tourists. It lies on the edge of the Queen Elizabeth Forest Park and, along with Callander to the east, is one of the main tourist centres for the Trossachs. It makes an ideal base for walking and cycling in the surrounding hills. There's plentiful accommodation, though you'll have to book during the busy summer season.

Three miles east of Aberfoyle is the **Lake of Menteith**, the only lake in Scotland (as opposed to loch). On **Inchmahome Island** in the middle of the lake are the beautiful and substantial ruins of **Inchmahome Priory** ⓘ *T01877-385294 (HS),*

The Highland Man

As the tourist board never tires of reminding us, the Trossachs is Rob Roy country. Rob Roy ('Red Robert' in Gaelic) was one of Scotland's most notorious outlaws or one of the bravest Highland heroes, depending on your point of view. It is true that he was a freebooter, but he was also defending Highland clan culture and more specifically fighting for the very survival of his own clan against proscription and persecution by the government and its supporters.

Rob Roy MacGregor (1671-1734) was born in Glengyle, to the northwest of Loch Katrine. The MacGregors' lands included those previously owned by the rival Campbells but bestowed on the MacGregors for services rendered to Alexander II in his conquest of Argyll. For a long time the clan kept possession of their lands by right of the sword, but the constant attempts by neighbouring clans to displace them led to retaliation by the MacGregors and earned them a reputation for being aggressive. Rob Roy did little to change this image, and his bitter feud with the powerful Duke of Montrose led to his being outlawed and eventually captured and sentenced to transportation. He was pardoned and returned to Balquhidder, where he stayed for the rest of his life. He now lies buried in the churchyard.

The Rob Roy story was first popularized by Sir Walter Scott's eponymous 19th-century novel, and his life continues to be romanticized, most recently in the 1995 film starring Liam Neeson and Tim Roth. Like Robin Hood before him, his courage in refusing to bow to the forces of authority seems to strike a chord with people.

Apr-Sep Mon-Sun 0930-1830, £3.30, £2.60 concession, the 13th-century Augustinian priory where the four-year-old Mary, Queen of Scots was sent in 1547, safe from the clutches of Henry VIII. A ferry takes visitors over to the island from **Port of Menteith**.

To the north of Aberfoyle is Doon Hill, better known as the **Fairy Knowe**. The tree at the top is said to be the home of the 'People of Quietness', and in 1692 a local minister was less than discreet in telling the world of their secrets. As punishment he was taken away to fairyland, and his spirit has languished there ever since. If you go round the tree seven times, your wish will be granted, but go round it backwards and... well, we won't be held responsible. It's about an hour and a half up and back. Follow the road across the bridge south of the car park by the Vistitor Centre, then follow the road till it forks – take the left fork, a waymarked path, to the hilltop.

Aberfoyle to Callander

The A821 route north from Aberfoyle, through the spectacular **Duke's Pass**, and then east past Loch Achray and Loch Vennachar, is one of the most beautiful routes in the country and not to be missed. There are a couple of worthwhile diversions along the way. About five miles north of Aberfoyle, a track branches to the right and runs through Achray Forest and along the shores of **Loch Drunkie**, before rejoining the A821 further north. A few miles further on, a road turns left to **Trossachs Pier** on the eastern shore of **Loch Katrine**. This is the departure point for cruises on the *SS Sir Walter Scott*, see Activities and tours page 265. In the mornings (daily except Wednesday) it sails to the remote settlement of **Stronachlachar** on the far western shores of the loch and back. In the afternoons it only sails around the loch for an hour. There's a road and cycle path around the loch as far as Stronachlachar, and you could take the morning cruise there and then cycle back to the pier. For cycle hire, see page 265.

Callander and around

Callander sits at the eastern end of the Trossachs, 14 miles northwest of Stirling, its main street totally and unashamedly devoted to tourism and lined with tearooms, restaurants and craft shops. The town is a good base for exploring the Trossachs. The overworked tourist information centre shares the same building as the **Rob Roy and Trossachs Visitor Centre** ⓘ *Mar-May and Oct-Dec daily 1000-1700, Jun 0930-1800, Jul and Aug 0900-2000, Sep 1000-1800, Jan and Feb weekends only 1000-1600, £3.25,* which gives an entertaining account of the life of Rob Roy MacGregor.

A recommended local walk is to Bracklinn Falls, reached by a woodland trail which leads from Bracklinn Road. It's about 30 minutes each way. Another trail from Bracklinn Road leads up to Callander Crags, from where there are great views of the surrounding area. Allow 1½ hours there and back. The most challenging walk in the area is to the summit of Ben Ledi (2,857 ft), but it's a tough climb and you'll need to be fit, experienced and prepared

Two miles north of Callander, on the A84 route to the Highlands, are the **Falls of Leny**, in the narrow and dramatic Pass of Leny. The falls are accessible from the car park by the roadside or via the **Callander to Strathyre Cycleway**, which follows the old train line to Oban, from Callander north along the west bank of **Loch Lubnaig**. This forms part of the **Glasgow to Killin Cycleway**, which runs from the centre of Glasgow, via Balloch, Aberfoyle, Callander, Balquhidder and Lochearnhead, to Killin. This is the best way to see the Trossachs.

The A84 heads north from Callander along the east bank of Loch Lubnaig, and beyond towards **Loch Earn**. A few miles further north, a side road branches left to the tiny village of **Balquhidder**, famous as the burial place of Rob Roy. His grave in the churchyard, where his wife and two of his sons are also buried, is thankfully understated.

North of Callander to Lochearnhead and Killin

A few miles north of the turning to Balquhidder, where the A84 meets the A85 from Crieff to Crianlarich, is **Lochearnhead**, at the western tip of Loch Earn. The loch is a highly popular watersports centre, see Activities and tours page 265. Lochearnhead is also a good base for walking in the surrounding hills. In the far northwestern corner of Stirling region, just to the west of Loch Tay, is **Killin**, a pleasant little village which makes a good base for walkers wishing to explore the wild mountains and glens of the ancient district of **Breadalbane** (pronounced Bread-albinn). Killin's picture-postcard setting, with the beautiful **Falls of Dochart** tumbling through the

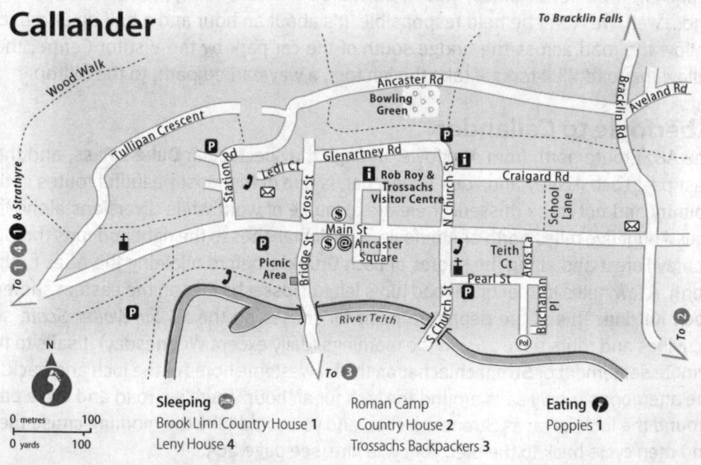

〝〞 Luss is to the genuine Highland experience what Ozzy Osbourne is to philosophical debate...

centre of the village, makes it a popular destination for tourists. The TIC overlooks the falls ⓘ *Mar-Oct daily*.

Twelve miles west of Killin is **Crianlarich**, at the crossroads of the A82 Glasgow-Fort William road and the A85 to Perth, and at the junction of the Glasgow to Fort William and Oban rail lines. It is a staging post on the **West Highland Way**. Six miles further north is tiny **Tyndrum**, which shot to prominence a few years ago after the discovery of gold in the surrounding hills. There's a seasonal TIC ⓘ *Main Rd, T01838-400246, Apr-Nov daily*.

Loch Lomond → *Colour map 4, grid C1.*

Britain's largest inland waterway, measuring 22 miles in length and at certain points up to five miles wide, is one of Scotland's most famous lochs, thanks to the Jacobite ballad about its 'bonnie banks'. These same banks are now one of the busiest parts of the Highlands, due to their proximity to Glasgow (only 20 miles south along the congested A82). During the summer the loch becomes a playground for day-trippers who tear up and down the loch in speedboats and on jet skis, obliterating any notion visitors may have of a little peace and quiet.

At the southern end of the loch is the resort town of **Balloch**, packed full of hotels, B&Bs, caravan parks and any number of operators offering boat trips around the loch's overcrowded waters. At the northern end of the town is **Loch Lomond Shores**, a huge visitor centre-cum-shopping mall, which includes the tourist information centre and National Park Gateway Centre ⓘ *T01389-722199, daily year round*, as well as shops, restaurants, bars and cafés. Here you can pick up all the information you need on the national park, as well as book a loch cruise, hire bikes, kayaks or sailing dinghies, or simply enjoy the views from the Drumkinnon Tower. See Activities and tours page 265 for further information.

The west bank of the loch, from Balloch north to Tarbet, is one long, almost uninterrupted development of marinas, holiday homes, caravan parks and exclusive golf clubs. The most picturesque village here is **Luss**, though it is more of theme park than a real village. It is to the genuine Highland experience what Ozzy Osbourne is to philosophical debate. One and a half hour boat trips leave from Luss pier. Further north, things begin to quiten down a bit. At **Inverbeg**, you can take a pedestrian ferry across the loch to Rowardennan (T01360-870273 for times). North of Tarbet, at the narrow northern end of the loch, things quieten down a great deal more and the road to **Ardlui**, at its northern tip, is very beautiful and peaceful. The A82 continues north of Ardlui, past Inverarnan, to meet the A85 at **Crianlarich**.

▲The tranquil east bank of Loch Lomond is a great place for walking. The **West Highland Way** follows the east bank all the way from **Drymen**, through **Balmaha**, **Rowardennan** and **Inversnaid**. Beyond Rowardennan this is the only access to the loch's east bank, except for the road to Inversnaid from the Trossachs. From Rowardennan you can climb **Ben Lomond** (3,192 ft), the most southerly of the Munros.

Loch Lomond, along with a large chunk of the Cowal Peninsula, the Campsies and the Trossachs, are all part of the Loch Lomond and the Trossachs National Park, which become Scotland's first National Park, as late as 2002.

 It's not too difficult and the views from the top, in good weather, are astounding. An easier climb is **Conic Hill**, on the Highland fault line and very close to Glasgow. The route starts from the Loch Lomond Visitor Centre car park at Balmaha. It takes about 1½ hours to reach the top, from where the views of the loch are stunning.

Sleeping

The Campsies *p259*
See Eating for details.

The Trossachs *p260*
A Lake Hotel, in Port of Menteith, on the lakeshore overlooking Inchmahome, T01877-385258, www.lake-of-menteith-hotel.com. The best place to stay in the area. It's stylish, comfortable, very romantic and boasts a fine restaurant (lunch **££**; dinner **£££**).
A Roman Camp Country House Hotel, Callander, T01877-330003, www.roman-camp-hotel.co.uk. An exquisite 16th-century hunting lodge set in extensive grounds by the river, away from the hoi polloi. Queen Victoria was quite taken with the place. Also serves superb Scottish cuisine (**£££**).
B The Four Seasons, in the village of St Fillans, a few miles east of Lochearnhead, T01764-685333, www.thefourseasonshotel.co.uk. Spectacular setting on the shores of Loch Earn, this 19th-century house, surrounded by wooded hills, also delivers on the food and service fronts.
B Leny House, Callander, T01877-331078, www.lenyestate.com. Open Apr-Oct. A 5-star B&B in the parkland of the Leny Estate.
C Creagan House, at the northern end of Loch Lubnaig, in Strathyre, T01877-384638, a family run 17th-century farmhouse offering excellent food (**£££-££**) and comfortable accommodation, open Mar-Jan.
C Monachyle Mhor Hotel, Callander, T01877-384622, on the road to Inverlochlarig. It offers great views of the loch, peace and quiet and fabulous Scottish/French cuisine (**£££**).
D Brook Linn Country House, Callander, T01877-330103, open Easter-Oct, a fine Victorian house overlooking the town.
D Creag-Ard House, in Milton, 2 miles west of Aberfoyle overlooking Loch Ard, T01877-382297. Lovely place with fishing and boat hire available.
D Dall Lodge Country House Hotel, Killin, T01567-820217, www.dallodgehotel.co.uk, open Mar-Oct. The best place to stay in the village, offers idiosyncratic style and very good food.
F Trossachs Backpackers, a couple of miles out of Callander, along the Invertrossachs Rd which turns off the A81, T01877-331200, trosstel@aol.com. 30 beds, with dorms and family rooms. Relaxed and peaceful independent hostel which also rents bikes.

Camping
Cobeland Campsite, T01877-382392, open Apr-Oct, 2 miles south of Aberfoyle on the edge of the Queen Elizabeth Forest Park.
Trossachs Holiday Park, T01877-382614, open Mar-Oct. An excellent site set in 40 acres with mountain bike hire.

Loch Lomond *p263*
C Rowardennan Hotel, Rowardennan, T01360-870273, comfortable choice, serves bar meals.
D Inversnaid Hotel, on the northeast shore, and only accessible by road via the B829 from Aberfoyle, T01877-386223. Splendidly isolated.
F Loch Lomond SYHA Youth Hostel, Arden, T01389-850226, www.syha.org.uk Grand 19th-century turreted mansion complete with the obligatory ghost.

Camping
There's a good campsite at **Lomond Woods Holiday Park at Tullichewan** T01389-755000, on the Old Luss Rd, where you can hire mountain bikes.

Eating

The Campsies *p259*
££ Castle Bar, Culcreuch Castle, Fintry, T01360-860555. Very good Scottish cooking brought to you in the informal bar of this refurbished historic castle. Dinner and B&B available in the hotel (**A-B**).
££ Clachan Inn, 2 The Square, Drymen, T01360-660824. Good spot for lunch

(£ for 2 courses) or dinner. Mostly steaks and standard pub fare. Also has B&B.

The Trossachs *p260*

£££ Roman Camp Hotel, Callander, see Sleeping. The best place to eat by far, simply superb.

££ Braeval Old Mill, T01877-382711, a few miles east on the A873 to Port of Menteith. The best place to eat, excellent and very popular.

££ Brig O' Turk Tearoom, Brig O' Turk, Callander. Look out for the shabby green hut with peeling paint and tired-looking hanging baskets outside. Inside it's like a scout hut with higgledy-piggeldy chairs and mismatching crockery and table-cloths. Wonderfully informal and very good food.

££ Byre Inn, just before Brig o' Turk, on the A821 from Aberfoyle direction, T01877-376292. A cosy bar serving good ales and hearty food, ideally placed for walkers and cylists. Open 1200-1430 and 1800-2300. Also has 3 rooms for B&B.

££ Poppies, Leny Rd, Callander, T01877-330329. Small, unassuming restaurant that surprises with the depth and quality of the dishes on offer, all using local ingredients.

Loch Lomond *p263*

££ Coach House Coffee Shop, Luss, T01436-860341. Huge portions of good, wholesome food. Try their excellent home baked goodies. This is the only reason for stopping here but it's a pretty good one anyway.

££ Inverbeg Inn, a few miles north of Luss, at Inverbeg, T01436-860678. Good food.

Bars and clubs

Loch Lomond *p263*

Drover's Inn, Inverarnan, T01301-704234. The famous Highland watering hole, with smoke-blackened walls, low ceilings, bare floors, open fires, a hall filled with stuffed animals, barman in kilt and a great selection of single malts. The perfect place for a wild night of drinking in the wilderness. It simply doesn't get any better than this.

Activities and tours

The Trossachs *p260*

Lochearnhead Watersports, T01567-830330, has water-skiing, canoeing and kayaking on the loch.

SS Sir Walter Scott, T01877-376316, www.incallander.co.uk/steam.htm, £6.80 return, concession £4.80, children under 5 free. Cruises leave from Loch Katrine daily, except Wed, Apr-Oct, at 1100, 1345 and 1515. Bikes can be taken on the 1100 cruise (book in advance), allowing you to return along the private North Shore Road. For bike hire see Transport below.

Loch Lomond *p263*

Can You Experience, T01389-602576, www.canyouexperience.com. Offers guided walks around Loch Lomond, £18 for 3 hrs, full-day walks also. Canoe, kayak and pedalo hire, £10 for 30 mins, £15 for 1 hr, also available as well as guided canoe trips.

Lomond Adventure, T01360-870218, Balmaha House, Balmaha. Canoe/kayak hire from £20 per day, sailing in dinghys/catamarans from £35 a day, watersking £45 for 1 hr.

Lomond Shores National Park Gateway, T08707-200631, open daily is the centre for all activities on Loch Lomond. See p263.

Sweeney's Cruises, T01389-722406, www.sweeney.uk.co, are based at **Lomond Shores** and offer a wide range of trips, starting at around £4-5 for an hour. A daily 2½-hr cruise from Balloch to Luss leaves at 1430 (£7).

Walk Wild Loch Lomond, T01360-870476, www.walkwildlochlomond.co.uk. Offer day guided walks in the National Park, pick up from Balloch or Drymen. £29 per person including lunch and possible boat trip.

Transport

The Campsies *p259*

There are several buses daily to **Drymen** from **Glasgow**, via **Queen's View**. There are also buses through the region from **Stirling**. A postbus service, T01752-494527, www.royalmail.com/postbus, leaves from **Denny**, 5 miles south of Stirling, to **Fintry**

For an explanation of sleeping and eating price codes used in this guide, see inside the front cover. Other relevant information is found in Essentials, see pages 43-51.

(Mon-Sat at 0955), from where 2 buses (Mon-Sat) run to **Balfron**. There are regular buses to **Denny** from Stirling bus station.

The Trossachs *p260*

There are buses to **Killin** from Stirling via **Callander** (1¾ hrs). There's a postbus from **Callander** once daily Mon-Fri (1 hr), which continues to **Crianlarich** and **Tyndrum**. There's also a postbus service from **Aberfeldy** (see p). Scottish Citylink buses, between **Glasgow** and **Oban** and **Fort William** stop in both villages. There's also a postbus service between **Crianlarich** and **Tyndrum** and **Killin** (Mon-Sat).

There are 2 train stations at **Tyndrum** and **Crianlarich**. One serves the **Glasgow** to **Oban** line and the other the **Glasgow** to **Fort William** line.

Cycle hire from **Wheels**, Invertrossachs Rd, Callander, T01887-331100. **Trossachs Cycle Hire**, at Loch Katrine, T01877-376316, Apr-Oct daily 0900-1700, £8 per ½ day, tandems and trailers available.

Loch Lomond *p263*

Scottish Citylink buses run regularly from Glasgow to **Balloch** (45 mins), and on to **Luss** and **Tarbet** (1 hr 10 mins). Some buses go to **Ardlui** (1 hr 20 mins) and on to **Crianlarich**.

There's a passenger ferry service across the loch between **Inverbeg** and **Rowardennan**, T01360-870273, 3 times daily (Apr-Sep).

There are 2 rail lines from Glasgow to **Loch Lomond**. One runs to **Balloch** every 30 mins (35 mins) the other is the West Highland line to **Fort William** and **Mallaig**, with a branch line to Oban. It reaches Loch Lomond at **Tarbet** and there's another station further north at **Ardlui**.

Directory

The Trossachs *p260*

Internet DOT Computers, Main St, Callander, Mon-Sat 1000-2100, Sun 1300-2100.

Fife

For such a small region, Fife is a very diverse place. The difference between the blighted industrial landscape of the southwest and the prosperous-looking rural northeast couldn't be more marked. Northeast Fife consists of St Andrews and the East Neuk and if you only have a few days in which to visit, then this is the area to see. St Andrews, in particular, is important and attractive enough to visit on its own. The ruins of its cathedral and castle bear witness to its former importance, while the Royal and Ancient Golf Club is the sport's spiritual home and stands on the world's most famous links course. It also has the oldest university in Scotland. The East Neuk of Fife is a string of picture-postcard old fishing villages. Those with more time on their hands could also venture inland to explore Falkland, Cupar and the Howe of Fife. Here, you'll find Falkland Palace, one of Scotland's most remarkable historic buildings. » *For Sleeping, Eating and other listings, see pages 280-282.*

Ins and outs

Getting there and around The train line north from Edinburgh follows the coast as far as Kirkcaldy and then cuts inland towards Dundee, stopping at Cupar and Leuchars. From Leuchars a bus can be taken to St Andrews. There are frequent buses between Dundee and Kirkcaldy, stopping in St Andrews and the East Neuk villages along the way, and between Kirkcaldy and Edinburgh, stopping in Dunfermline. There are also buses from Dundee to Cupar. It is possible to explore the peninsula using public transport, but it can be a slow and time-consuming business as buses to the more remote parts are few and far between.

Tourist information Dunfermline TIC ⓘ *13/15 Maygate (next to the Abbot House). T01383-720999*. Kirkcaldy TIC ⓘ *19 Whytescauseway, T01592-267775, Mon-Fri 1000-*

1700, Sat 1000-1300 and 1400-1700. St Andrews TIC ⓘ *70 Market St, T01334-472021, daily Apr-Sep, Oct-Mar Mon-Sat*. Anstruther TIC ⓘ *next to the Fisheries museum, T01334-311073, Easter to mid-Sep*.

Southwest Fife → *Phone code: 01383. Colour map 4, C3-4.*

The southwest part of the Kingdom suffers by comparison with the star-blessed Northeast but this gritty poor relation still has its own pleasurable diversions. Dunfermline is steeped in history, while nearby Culross, one of Scotland's most precious assets, is a medieval village preserved in aspic. Further east things are less appealing, though Kirkcaldy boasts a very fine art collection and one of the country's biggest and best street fairs. ›› *For Sleeping, Eating and other listings, see pages 280-282.*

Dunfermline

Dunfermline was once the capital of Scotland, from the 11th century to the Union of Crowns in 1603, and its great abbey and royal palace still dominate the skyline. Until the late 19th century, Dunfermline was one of Scotland's most important linen producers and a major coal-mining centre.

Dunfermline Abbey ⓘ *T01383-739026 (HS), Apr-Sep daily 0930-1830, Oct-Mar Mon-Wed and Sat 0930-1630, Thu 0930-1230, Sun 1400-1630, £2.50, £1.90 concession, £0.75 children*, stands on the site of the Benedictine Priory, built by Queen Margaret in the late 11th century. When she endowed the priory, she set up a shrine, with a relic of the 'True Cross' and encouraged pilgrims to come from miles away to venerate it. Her son, David I, raised the priory to the rank of abbey and began building the new abbey church in 1128, on the foundations of Margaret's church. Frequently sacked and burned over the centuries, today's building is a combination of different tastes and styles. Much of the present abbey was built long after King David's death but the superb Norman nave, with its massive pillars, is still there to be admired. The Norman decorations above the west doorway are rare examples of such work in Scotland. The north porch, northwest tower, west front and massive buttresses are all the work of William Shaw, Master of works to Anne of Denmark in the 16th century. The other part of the abbey church was added in the 19th century and today serves as the parish church.

Close to the east gable of the parish church are the foundations of the shrine of St Margaret where she and her husband are buried. But they were not the only royal persons to be buried in the abbey. Six Scottish kings also lie there, with the grave of Robert the Bruce beneath the pulpit. He was buried in the abbey in 1329 but over the years the exact position of his grave became uncertain. Then, in 1818, when the foundation of the new church was being prepared, Bruce's tomb was rediscovered, the skeleton covered in a shroud of gold and the breast bone severed where his heart had been removed in order to take it to the Holy Land, in accordance with his wishes. Unfortunately, it never made it and now lies in Melrose Abbey. In 1889, Robert the Bruce's descendent, the Earl of Elgin, gifted a memorial brass to mark the tomb. To celebrate the historic find, an over-enthusiastic architect designed the vast inscription round the top of the square tower, which no one can fail to notice.

The Abbey church stands adjacent to the ruined **monastery** building and the **Royal Palace**, built when Malcolm and Margaret married. It has fallen into ruins, but what little remains still hints at its undoubted magnificence. For centuries, it was a favourite residence of the Kings of Scotland. David II, James I and Charles I were all born here, the latter being the last monarch to be born in Scotland.

It was at Rossend Castle that the impetuous French poet, Chastelard, propositioned Mary, Queen of Scots in 1563, and was promptly beheaded for his impertinence.

The beautiful and lavishly endowed **Pittencrief Park**, known locally as 'the glen', is opposite the west door of the Abbey. Inside the park is **Pittencrief House Museum** ⓘ *T01383-722935, Apr-Sep daily 1100-1700, Oct-Mar daily 1100-1600, free*, built in 1610 and also bought by Carnegie for the people of Dunfermline. It features displays of local history, costumes and an art gallery. The glasshouses are filled with tropical plants and flowers, and the art deco pavilion has a restaurant. Here also stands the ruin of **Malcolm's Tower**, where King Malcolm and his bride lived before the building of the palace. Dunfermline – which means 'fort by the crooked pool' – takes its name from the tower's location.

In the Maygate is the **Abbot House** ⓘ *T01383-733266, all year daily 1000-1700, £3, £2 concession, children free*, which was the home of Robert Pitcairn, the post-Reformation Abbot of the Abbey. The house is one of the oldest in Scotland, possibly 14th century, and was restored in 1963. There's a café serving snacks and light lunches. The 19th-century **Town House** in Bridge Street was designed in the French and Scottish Gothic style, said to be very fashionable at the time. Among its interesting features are the gargoyles and grotesques, depicting the heads of King Robert the Bruce, King Malcolm, Queen Margaret and Queen Elizabeth.

Incongruously housed in the stone building in Chalmers street car park is the entrance to **Saint Margaret's Cave** ⓘ *Easter to end-Sep daily 1100-1600, free.* The saintly queen often retired here for moments of secret devotion. Her husband, suspicious of her frequent visits to the cave, followed and discovered her kneeling in prayer. Overjoyed that his suspicions were groundless, he had the cave fitted up for her as a place of devotion.

Dunfermline Museum ⓘ *Viewfield Terr, south of the East Port, T01383-313838, all year, Mon-Fri, free, phone 24 hrs in advance for admission*, has displays concentrating on local history, including the weaving and damask linen industries, for which the town was famous and which greatly contributed to Fife's economic well-being. **Andrew Carnegie Birthplace Museum** ⓘ *T01383-724302, Apr-Oct Mon-Sat 1100-1700, Sun 1400-1700, groups in winter by appointment only, £2, £1 concession, children free*, is the small cottage in Moodie Street where the famous steel magnate and great philanthropist was born.

Culross

Culross (pronounced 'kooros') is a beautifully restored village containing the finest surviving examples of Scottish vernacular architecture from the 16th and 17th centuries. At this time Culross was one of the largest ports in Scotland, and enjoyed a flourishing trade in coal and salt with other Forth ports and the Low Countries. Following the industrial revolution, however, the little town went into near-terminal decline until the National Trust rescued it from decay in 1932.

To appreciate the town's unique sense of history fully, explore its narrow cobbled streets on foot.

A good starting point on a walking tour of Culross is the **National Trust Visitor Centre**, in the **Town House** ⓘ *T01383-880359, www.nts.org.uk, Palace and Town House daily Apr, May, Sep and weekends in Oct 1230-1630, Easter weekend and Jun-Aug 1000-1700, combined ticket for the Palace, Town House and Study £9, £6.50 child/concession, £23 family*, or Tolbooth, on the main road beside the palace, which dates from 1626. Here you can watch an excellent video charting the history of the town. The **Palace** was built between 1597 and 1611 by local merchant, Sir George Bruce, who made his fortune from coal and salt panning. It's not so much a palace as a grand house, but its crow-stepped gables and pan-tiled roofs give a delightful example of Scottish architecture from this period. Inside, the main features are the wonderful original painted ceilings and wood panelling.

Along the shore, is the ruin of **St Mungo's Chapel**, built in 1503 by Archbishop Blackadder. It was here, in the sixth century, that St Kentigern was born. Affectionately nicknamed 'Mungo', he went on to build Glasgow Cathedral, around which the city later grew. About 10 km east of Culross is Charlestown, an 18th-century village with a picturesque harbour, built by the 5th Earl of Elgin for sailing vessels trading with Europe. It was the 7th Earl of Elgin who took the ancient Greek marble sculptures from the Parthenon in Athens and sold them to the British Museum in 1816 for £35,000. These became known as the 'Elgin Marbles' and continue to be a bone of contention between Britain and Greece. One-and-a-half kilometres further east lies the charming village of Limekilns, which takes its name from the lime kilns that used to be one of its main industries. If you fancy a drink, try the **Ship Inn**, which featured in Robert Louis Stevenson's *Kidnapped*.

North Queensferry and Inverkeithing

At the foot of the Forth Rail Bridge is North Queensferry home to the popular **Deep Sea World** ⓘ *T01383-411880, www.deepseaworld.com, Apr-Oct 1000-1800, Jul/Aug 1000-1830, Nov-Mar daily 1100-1700, £8.95*, Scotland's award-winning national aquarium, which boasts the world's largest underwater viewing tunnel, through which you pass on a moving walkway, coming face-to-face with sharks, conger eels and all manner of strange creatures. There is also a display of species from the Amazon rainforest.

The desolate shipbreakers yards at Inverkeithing, a stone's throw from North Queensferry, give no hint that this is one of the oldest Royal Burghs in Scotland. Granted a charter by King William the Lion around 1165, Inverkeithing was for centuries a place of trade and commerce with a small harbour and local coal workings. Born in the town in 1735 was Samuel Greig, often described as the founder of the Russian Navy. The son of a local shipmaster, he initially had a career in the British Navy, but following secondment to Russia he organized the Russian fleet for Catherine the Great, for which he received a knighthood.

Aberdour, Burntisland and Kinghorn

Five miles east of the Forth bridges, on the A921, is **Aberdour**. The **castle** ⓘ *T01383-860519, Apr-Sep daily 0930-1800, Oct-Mar Mon-Wed and Sat 0930-1600, Thu 0930-1200, Sun 1400-1600, £2.50, £1.90 concession, £0.75 children*, at the southern end of the main street, was built by the Douglas family on lands originally granted to Thomas Randolph, Earl of Moray, by King Robert the Bruce in 1325. The 14th-century tower is the oldest part of the castle, the other buildings having been added in the 16th and 17th centuries, including the unusual Dovecote (pronounced doocot) and the attractive walled garden. Nearby is **St Fillan's Church**, which is part Norman, part 16th century. The church has a peaceful, timeless quality which entices the visitor to linger in quiet contemplation. Note the leper-squint in the west wall, formerly used by sufferers who were not allowed to worship within the church.

Three miles east of Aberdour is **Burntisland**, once famous for shipbuilding but now more popular as a holiday resort. The **Highland Games**, held in mid-July, are reputed to be the second oldest in the world and take place, like most of the town's summer activities, on the busy seafront Links. The **church of St Columba** was the first to be built in Scotland after the Reformation. The General Assembly of the Kirk of Scotland was held here in 1601, when in the presence of James VI, it was proposed that there should be a new translation of the Bible, the Authorised version, published in 1611. **Rossend Castle** is a 15th-century tower house that was recently restored and is now occupied by a firm of architects.

A few miles along the coast from Burntisland, at **Kinghorn**, you'll pass a monument beside the road in the shape of a Celtic cross. This is where Alexander III was thrown from his horse and killed, an event that completely changed the course of Scottish history. The king had been heading home from Edinburgh to his new wife, whom he had married only six months earlier in an attempt to provide himself with an heir. There was a violent storm that night, but he insisted on being ferried across the Forth before galloping east towards Pettycur, where his still-barren queen was waiting. His horse stumbled on the cliff edge and the king was thrown to his death, thus plunging the country into many years of bitter conflict and power struggles. Today, Kinghorn is a busy summer resort with a sandy beach, a golf course and a wide range of guest houses.

Kirkcaldy and around → *Phone code: 01592.*

Fifteen miles east of the Forth bridges is Kirkcaldy (pronounced kirkoddy), called the 'Lang Toon' because of its main street which, running along the seafront, is all of four miles long. It's perhaps unkind to say that Kirkcaldy was once famous (or infamous) for its terrible stench, but at the height of its thriving linoleum industry you could smell the place for miles around. Nowadays, the town's economy has diversified and the smell has thankfully gone. Also gone is much of its shipping trade, and the area around the harbour bears witness to a once thriving sea port. Some of the little streets and *wynds* (steep alleyways) opposite the harbour are worth exploring, such as Kirk Wynd or Sailor's Walk, which have been lovingly restored by the NTS. Today, the town is best known as Fife's main shopping centre, but if you're passing through there are a few other attractions aside from the many high street chain stores.

Museum and Art Gallery ⓘ *T01592-412860, all year daily Mon-Sat 1030-1700, Sun 1400-1700, free*, is in the War Memorial Gardens next to the railway station. There is a good archaeological collection and you can learn about the area's social, industrial and natural history. The small art gallery has an excellent collection of Scottish colourists, including work by William McTaggart, Peploe, Lowry, Sickert and Raeburn. There are also displays of the local Wemyss Ware pottery. Across from the War Memorial Gardens is the **Adam Smith Centre**, see page 281, named after one of the town's most famous sons, the pioneer economist and author of *The Wealth of Nations* in 1776. In the High Street among the many shops, you'll find the birthplace of Adam Smith. At the old burgh school there's a plaque recording that both he and Robert Adam, the famous architect, were pupils there in the 1730s, and that Thomas Carlyle, the historian and essayist, taught there nearly 100 years later.

Ravenscraig Castle towers dramatically above the park of the same name, at the east end of the town, on a rocky promontory guarding the wide bay. The ruin dates from 1460, when James II intended it as a dower house for his wife. The castle was the first in Britain to be designed specifically for defence by and against cannon fire and you can see the wide gun loops in the massive thick walls. Near the castle, the steps that lead from the high-rise flats in Nether Road down to the beach should number 39 and are said to have inspired John Buchan to write his famous novel.

Dysart, the eastern suburb of Kirkcaldy, is a little burgh dating back to the 16th century and is full of character, with its delightful little *wynds* and courtyards and old houses with crow-stepped gables and pan-tiled roofs. Dysart was once a busy trading port with the Netherlands. Now all that remains is the little harbour, perfectly set below the ancient battlements of St Serf's church. The Pan Ha', an area of 17th-century houses, was restored by the NTS, as was the **McDougall Stuart Museum** ⓘ *T01592-412860, Jun-Aug daily 1400-1700, free*. This house, dated 1575, was the birthplace of John McDougall Stuart, the first man to cross Australia from north to south, in 1866. The award-winning museum charts the story of Stuart and his fascinating and often dangerous expedition.

A few miles east along the coast from Dysart are the villages of **East** and **West Wemyss**, so called from the many 'weems', or caves, found on this particular stretch of Fife coast. The famous caves lie along the foreshore of East Wemyss, below the ruins of **MacDuff's Castle**, reputed to be the home of Macduff of Shakespeare's *Macbeth*. Within the caves you'll find Britain's earliest picture of a boat, as well as

The 14th-century Balgonie Castle was described as one of the scariest places on earth in an American TV show.

hunting scenes, portrayed by craftsmen of Pictish times. King James IV was so impressed by one of the caves that he held court there and it is now known, unsurprisingly, as Court Cave.

The A92 runs from the northeastern outskirts of Kirkcaldy to **Glenrothes**, a sprawling new town, developed since 1950, which was originally designed to meet the housing needs of new colliery workers. Coal mining, however, declined in Fife, and Glenrothes instead attracted the trailblazers of Scotland's new light electronics industries. Two miles east of Glenrothes on the B921 off the A911, is the splendid 14th-century **Balgonie Castle** ⓘ *daily 1000-1700, for a personal guided tour*. This was the 17th-century home of Field Marshall Sir Alexander Leslie, Lord General of the Scottish Covenanting Army and First Earl of Leven, and was garrisoned by Rob Roy MacGregor with 200 clansmen in 1716. Restoration continues in this family home and living museum.

The Howe and North Fife → *Colour map 4, grid C4-5.*

In stark contrast to the industrial landscape of Southwest Fife, the Howe of Fife (*howe* means valley) is a low-lying area of patchwork fields, woodlands and farming communities which runs from the attractive market town of Cupar in the east to Falkland, at the foot of the Lomond Hills. To the north, the rich agricultural lands gently slope towards the banks of the River Tay, marking the county's northern boundary. ⏩ *For Sleeping, Eating and other listings, see pages 280-282.*

Falkland

Tucked away at the foot of the Lomond Hills, off the A912, the ancient and beautiful village of Falkland is the most royal of Fife's Royal Burghs and holds a unique place in Scottish history, as it is the site of **Falkland Palace** ⓘ *T01337-T857397, Apr-Oct Mon-Sat 1000-1730, Sun 1330-1730, £9, £6.50 child/concession, £23 family*, the favourite residence of the Stuart monarchs. The great Royal Palace stands in the heart of the village, which is a surprise in itself as it shows a remarkable lack of class distinction; rare in medieval Scotland. But it is not only the location of the palace that is exceptional. It is one of the grandest buildings in the country and its variety of styles is part of its charm. Facing the street, the south front is a splendid example of Scottish Gothic with its buttresses, niches and statues of Christ and the saints. The magnificent courtyard frontage in the classical style, with pillars and medallions, strikes an altogether different mood and an air of gracious living. Scotland has few surviving buildings that were in the mainstream of Renaissance architecture, but this one is by far the best. Though the building shows a strong French influence, there is a flavour about it that is unmistakably Scottish. Most of the existing palace was built In the early 16th century by James IV and his son James V. It was designed as a hunting lodge and was much loved by the Stuart kings and queens who came here to hunt deer and wild boar in the surrounding forests. There was also royal (or real) tennis to ease the strains of government. The royal tennis court, built in 1539 and the oldest in Britain, is still in use. But though the monarchy, from James II to Charles II, spent some of their happiest days at Falkland, the best known event to happen there was the tragic death of King James V. He had come to the palace after his defeat at Solway Moss in 1542 and died of a broken heart on hearing of the birth of a daughter, the future Mary, Queen of Scots. When the news was broken to him he exclaimed "Fareweil, it cam with ane lass and it will pass with ane lass". He then turned his face to the wall and died. The king's bedchamber is one of the many attractions inside the palace, morbid though it may be. A guided tour lasts 40 minutes and includes the Chapel Royal (still used for Mass), the superb Flemish Tapestry Gallery, the King's Bedchamber and Queen's Room, as well as the gardens and Tennis Court.

Cupar and around

The main centre in the Howe of Fife is Cupar, a thriving market town that was once the administrative centre of Fife. There's an air of relative well-being about the place, verified by an array of shops catering to the retail connoisseur. One of the main reasons for stopping off at Cupar is to visit **Hill of Tarvit** ⓘ *open Easter and May-Sep, weekends in Oct, £5, £3.75 child/concession, garden and grounds only £2/1*, two miles south of the town and one mile from Ceres (see below). This Edwardian mansion house was beautifully remodelled by Robert Lorimer in 1906. Among the fine collection of treasures inside are Flemish tapestries, Chinese porcelain, Dutch paintings and 18th-century French, Chippendale and vernacular furniture. The gardens are laid out in the French style, with box hedges and yew trees, and there is a woodland walk to a hilltop toposcope with a lovely view of the house.

Scottish Deer Centre ⓘ *T01337-810391, Easter-31 Oct daily 1000-1800, Nov-Easter daily 1000-1700, £4.50, £3.50 children, three miles west of Cupar on the A91*, is both enjoyable and educational. Here you can see many species of deer at close hand, and even feed, stroke or photograph them during a ranger-led tour. There are indoor and outdoor adventure parks for the kids as well as a restaurant and winery.

Once described as the most attractive village in Scotland, **Ceres** lies three miles south of Cupar. Whether or not you agree with that assertion, the village does present an appealing picture with its pan-tiled cottages surrounding a historic village green. Tradition says that the village and ancient cobbled bridge have been there for more than 650 years, that the men of Ceres marched across the bridge on their way to the battle of Bannockburn and on their return celebrated their victory with games on the village green. The **Highland Games** are still an annual event, on the last Saturday in June, with the Ceres Derby the highlight of the day. Another special feature of Ceres is the **Fife Folk Museum** ⓘ *T01334-T828250, Easter and mid-May to Oct daily 1400-1700, £2.50, £2 concession, children free*, housed in part of the 17th-century Tolbooth Weigh House and two adjoining cottages. The award-winning museum displays crafts and trades, costumes, tools and utensils of a bygone age in rural Fife.

Also worth visiting is the **Griselda Hill Pottery** ⓘ *T01334-828273, summer and Christmas Mon-Fri 0900-1630, Sat and Sun 1400-1700, Mon-Fri 0900-1630 in winter, free*, at Kirkbrae. Here you can see a revival of the production of Wemyss Ware, the best-known Scottish pottery.

North Fife

Four miles northwest of St Andrews is **Leuchars**, best known as an RAF base, but in the centre of the village is one of the oldest churches in Scotland. The 12th-century chancel and apse, incorporated into the parish church, are exceptional examples of Norman architecture. One mile east of Leuchars is the privately owned **Earlshall Castle** built in 1546 by Sir William Bruce, ancestor of the present owners. This is a fine example of a 16th-century Scottish castle, very strongly built with five-feet thick walls, battlements and gun loops. The castle is set among beautiful gardens with unusual topiary chessmen, but is not open to the general public.

Just beyond Leuchars is the B945 turning for **Tentsmuir Forest**, on the northeastern tip of Fife, where there is an excellent broad sandy beach – the perfect spot for a picnic – as well as a nature reserve where you can see wildfowl waders and a large colony of seals sunning themselves on the sands. In 1957, on a site near **Morton Farm** on the Tentsmuir Peninsula, evidence was found of a settlement visited seasonally by hunter-gatherers about 8,000 years ago. This remarkable site is one of the earliest human habitations in Scotland. Finds from the site are in the Dundee Museum and the Museum of Scotland in Edinburgh.

Nearby, on the shores of the Tay, is the unremarkable village of **Tayport**, from where a ferry used to cross the river to Dundee. Tayport's church tower dates from the 17th century and a plaque commemorates General Ullysses Grant's visit on his way to see the first Tay Rail Bridge, which was blown down in 1879 while a train was passing over it. A new bridge has been built since, along with the Tay Road Bridge, which carries you from Fife into the city of Dundee.

Five miles west of the Tay Rail Bridge, off the A914, is **Balmerino Abbey**, on a hill overlooking the river. It was founded in the 13th century by Alexander II, whose mother Ermengarde, widow of William the Lion lies buried there. Little of the abbey remains today. In 1547 it was set on fire by the English Army during the 'Rough Wooing', see page 75, and in 1559 Knox's Reformers completed the destruction on their way back to St Andrews after 'reforming' Lindores (see below). Some of the pillars and part of the cloisters are still visible and in the orchard is a great Spanish chestnut tree, planted by the monks some 700 years ago. Unfortunately, the buildings are unsafe and inaccessible.

Lying on the south shore of the River Tay, close to Fife's western boundary, is **Newburgh**, a Royal Burgh with a pretty little harbour and a long history. On the hill to the south of the town are the remains of **MacDuff's Cross**, the legendary place of sanctuary for any MacDuff who had committed a murder in hot blood. To achieve pardon, the murderer had to touch the cross, wash himself nine times at Ninewells nearby and forfeit nine cows, each of which had to be tied to the cross. If you're passing through, it's worth stopping to visit the **Laing Museum** ⓘ *T01337-840223, Apr-Sep, Mon-Fri 1000-1700, Sat-Sun 1400-1700, Oct-Mar, Wed and Fri 1200-1600, Sun 1400-1700, free*, which shows excellent exhibitions including fossilized fish discovered in the area, a feature on Scottish emigration and Victorian displays. Standing above the town are the ruins of **Lindores Abbey**, founded in the 12th century by David, Earl of Huntingdon. Not much of the great abbey now remains – only the gateway, part of the tower and fragments of the great walls. The abbey never recovered form the devastation visited upon it in 1559 by John Knox and his 'Congregation of the Godly'. Its ruins became a quarry whenever any building stone was needed. The views from the ruins across the Tay are lovely, especially on a summer evening. The story of Newburgh, however, dates back much further than its abbey. A thousand years earlier, history was already being made on the eastern outskirts of the town, at Carpow. Here, in AD 208, the Romans built a great fortress which was to be the base for their campaign against the tribes of Angus and Mearns. Unlike England, Scotland never became Romanized, and the fortress at Carpow was eventually demolished by the Romans when they withdrew to the south. Evidence of human settlement around Newburgh extends even further back in time. People built and lived in the hillfort on top of Norman's Law during the last four centuries BC. Today, its remains are accessible by public footpath from the roads north and south of the Law. Three circles of fortification can easily be traced.

St Andrews → *Phone code: 01334. Colour map 4, grid C5. Population: 13,000.*

This well-groomed seaside resort on the northeastern coast of Fife is the 'Home of Golf' and a mecca for aficionados of the sport the world over. Here is the headquarters of the game's governing body, the Royal and Ancient Golf Club, and the world's most famous golf course, the Old Course. But it's not all Pringle sweaters and five irons. St Andrews has an air of calm dignity tinged with an inherent sense of history, as you'd expect from a place that was once the ecclesiastical capital of Scotland and the country's oldest seat of learning. ▸▸ *For Sleeping, Eating and other listings, see pages 280-282.*

History

St Andrews is, of course, synonymous with Scotland's patron saint. Andrew was the first of the disciples and among his many converts was the wife of the Roman Governor of Patras in Western Greece. The governor was so furious and jealous of his wife's conversion that he had Andrew crucified. Andrew asked to be tied to an X-shaped cross so that he would not appear to be emulating Christ – thus giving the Scottish flag its distinctive Saltire Cross. According to legend, a saintly monk called Rule, or Regulus, who lived in Patras, was divinely inspired to take some of the Apostle's bones and make a journey far to the west. St Rule set off and was shipwrecked on the rocks just to the west of St Andrews harbour. After converting the Pictish king to Christianity, St Rule enshrined the sacred relics on the headland where the ruins of the 12th-century cathedral now stand. The shrine became a place of worship for Christian pilgrims from far and wide and a special ferry was kept on the river Forth to transport them. St Andrew became Scotland's patron saint and his city the ecclesiastical capital of the country.

Sights

History envelops St Andrews; every street and building has its own story. So it's a real pleasure just to wander aimlessly through its narrow alleyways (or *closes*) that connect the medieval streets and discover its many hidden delights. A good example is Louden's Close, between Blackfriars and the West Port. Alternatively, stroll down The Pends by the Cathedral to the quaint old harbour; here, during term time, you might see the Sunday Parade of University students processing from the chapel in their scarlet medieval gowns that were introduced so that they could be spotted easily when entering the local brothels.

St Andrews' street plan has not changed since the Middle Ages. It basically consists of three main streets – North Street, Market Street and South Street – which still converge on the **cathedral** ⓘ *T01334-472563, Apr-Sep daily 0930-1830, Oct-Mar Mon-Sat 0930-1630, Sun 1400-1630, joint ticket with castle £4, £1.25 child, £3 concession,* standing proudly, overlooking the harbour at the eastern end of the town.

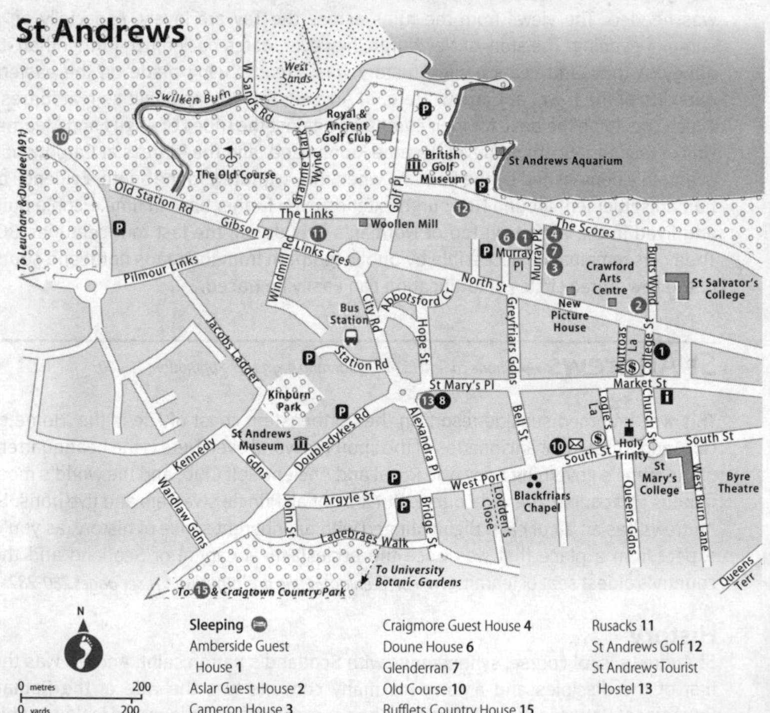

Founded in 1160, it was consecrated 160 years later, in 1318, by Robert the Bruce. Medieval pilgrims came in their thousands to pray at its many altars. This explains the exceptional width of North Street, which enabled the vast numbers to proceed to the cathedral. Though devastated over the years by fire and by religious reformers, the Cathedral ruins are still impressive, giving proof that this was by far the largest ecclesiastical building ever to be erected in Scotland. The Romanesque **St Rule's Tower** is where the holy relics of the Apostle were kept until the Cathedral was completed. It's a hard climb to the top of the tower, but the view on a clear day is worth the effort. The Cathedral visitor centre has a fine collection of early Christian sculptured stones from the church of St Mary of the Rock. Of particular interest is the unique eighth century Pictish sarcophagus.

Poised on a rocky headland overhanging the sea stands the ruin of **St Andrews Castle** ⓘ *T01334-477196, opening times as for the Cathedral, joint ticket with cathedral*. It was built at the end of the 12th century as the place and stronghold of the Bishops of St Andrews and has witnessed many violent incidents in the blood-stained history of the Scottish Church. Many reformers suffered imprisonment here, including George Wishart, whom the infamous Cardinal Beaton had burnt at the stake in front of the castle in 1546. His initials can be seen picked out in cobble-stones on the roadway near the entrance. Following the martyrdom of Wishart, a group of avenging Protestants gained entry to the castle disguised as stone masons and brutally murdered Beaton. His body was then hung over the battlements for all to see. After the murder the reformers held the castle against siege for a year until they capitulated to the French fleet. The castle fell into ruin in the 17th century, but two very notable features remain. In the northwest tower is the grim bottle dungeon, hollowed out of solid rock and from which death was the only release. Also of note is the mine and countermine, tunnelled through the rock during the siege that followed Cardinal Beaton's murder. The besiegers started their tunnel, but were thwarted by the defenders who tried to intercept them. Uncertainty about who was there led to its abandonment. A fascinating exhibition in the visitor centre brings the history of the castle to life.

The **University of St Andrews**, founded in 1410 by Henry Wardlaw, Bishop of St Andrews, is the third-oldest in Britain after Oxford and Cambridge. Among its many fine buildings is the **Church of St Salvator** in North Street. The first of its colleges, **St Salvator's** was founded by Bishop Kennedy in 1450. The Bishop's niece, Kate, was said to be so beautiful that all the students were in love with her. Today's students still pay homage to her pulchritude in the Kate Kennedy Pageant, see page 282. The bishop's tomb is in the church, along with a magnificent mace from his time, which is still carried on special occasions. The pulpit is the very one from which John Knox delivered his firebrand sermons in the Parish Church. The initials PH laid in the pavement outside the entrance mark the spot

Eating 7
Brambles 1
New Balaka Bangladeshi 8
The Vine Leaf 10

God's way or the fairway

The Royal and Ancient Golf Club of St Andrews is the ruling house of golf worldwide and a mecca for all who play or follow the game. On any one day during the summer, you'll see many addicts staring reverentially across the most famous stretch of golf course in the world. The imposing 1854 clubhouse overlooks the first and 18th holes and you can enter by invitation only. Anyone, however, can play on the six courses at St Andrews, including the historic Old Course itself.

The citizens of St Andrews have been playing golf on these Links for a very long time, even before 1457 when the Scottish Parliament tried to ban the game. No one in the town took the ban seriously and by 1553 they had an inalienable right to play golf on the Links. The game developed and acquired popularity in the highest circles – even Mary, Queen of Scots was known to indulge in the odd round or two.

The new craze was getting out of hand, however, and towards the end of the 16th century there was a spate of church absenteeism caused by people slipping off for a quick 18 holes. Two men were brought before the Kirk session in 1598 for "prophaning of the Saboth day in playing at the gouf eftir nune". As it was a first offence they got off with an admonition.

By the 17th and 18th centuries St Andrews was very much in decline, but exciting things were happening in the world of golf. In 1754 some 22 noblemen, mostly landowners in Fife, decided to move their golfing activities from Edinburgh to St Andrews. And so the exclusive Society of St Andrews Golfers, the forerunner of the Royal and Ancient Golf Club, came into existence. It was that fortunate decision that saved St Andrews turning into a ghost town and it has never looked back since.

where Patrick Hamilton, one of the early reformers, was burned in 1528. Other parts of the University include **St Mary's College,** in South Street, founded in 1537 by Archbishop James Beaton, uncle of the notorious cardinal. **Queen Mary's House,** in South Street by the Cathedral, is where the ill-fated queen stayed in 1563. Charles II also stayed here, in 1650. The house was restored in 1927 and is now used as St Leonard's school library. During her stay Queen Mary planted a thorn tree that still flourishes in the quadrangle of St Mary's college. **St Leonard's College,** on Pends Road which leads from the end of South Street down to the harbour, was founded in 1512 but then amalgamated with St Salvator's in 1747. The present buildings now house a private girls' school.

St Andrews has many other notable historic buildings and monuments. **The West Port** (circa 1580) at the west end of South Street, was the main entrance to the old town and is one of the few surviving city gates in Scotland. All that remains of **Blackfriars Chapel,** a small Dominican church, is a single apse. Rebuilt around 1515, its remains are in South Street, beside Madras College. Opposite the tourist information centre in South Street is the **Holy Trinity Church,** rebuilt in 1410, which was modified in the late 18th century and restored in the 20th century. Inside, Archbishop Sharp's monument graphically records his brutal murder in 1679 on Magus Muir.

As well as an impressive history, St Andrews has other attractions. There are two fine sandy beaches, the **East** and **West Sands,** that enclose the town like golden

Royal superstar, William, studied art history at St Andrews University, leading to a sudden rise in the number of applicants from young girls from across the Atlantic.

bookends. The latter provided the setting for the opening sequence in the film *Chariots of Fire*. If you've got children, then the huge **St Andrews Aquarium** ⓘ *T01334-474786, www.standrews aquarium, daily in summer 1000-1800, phone for winter opening hours, £5.50, £3.75*, is a must. Situated on The Scores, at the west end of town near the Golf Museum, this is where you can legally indulge in any number of piscean pleasures with an array of weird and wonderful sea creatures.

The history of golf, and the town's intimate association with it, are all to be discovered in the **British Golf Museum** ⓘ *T01334-460046, www.britishgolfmuseum .co.uk, Easter to mid-Oct daily 0930-1730, mid-Oct to Easter Thu-Mon 1100-1500, £3.75, £1.50 children, £2.75 concession, £9.50 family*, standing directly behind the Royal and Ancient Clubhouse on Bruce Embankment. It is the most exciting of its kind, and audio-visual displays and touch activated screens bring the game to life and trace its development through the centuries. The **Botanic Gardens** ⓘ *Canongate, daily all year 1000-1600, £2, £1 child/concession*, offer a peaceful retreat from all that golf and history, only 10 minutes walk south of South Street.

The East Neuk → *Phone code: 01333. Colour map 4, grid C5.*

Here, on Fife's easternmost stretch of coastline are some of the kingdom's greatest attractions. From Earlsferry to Fife Ness lies a string of picturesque villages, each with its own distinctive character and charm. These were once thriving seaports trading with the Low Countries. The Dutch influence lives on in their architectural styles. The red pan-tiled roofs and crow-stepped gables lend a particular continental feel to one of the most attractive corners of Scotland. A path, part of the Fife Coastal Path, links all of the East Neuk villages. ▸▸ *For Sleeping, Eating and other listings, see pages 280-282.*

Lower Largo

Though not technically part of the East Neuk (despite what other guide books and the tourist board may try to tell you), Lower Largo is nevertheless worth a look. It is best known as the birthplace of Alexander Selkirk, the real-life *Robinson Crusoe*. His statue can be seen in the main street running behind the **Crusoe Hotel**. This was once an important fishing centre. Now it is a popular holiday resort with its golden crescent of sand and picturesque little harbour, framed by an impressive railway viaduct.

Elie and Earlsferry

Westernmost of the East Neuk villages are Elie and Earlsferry, which are really two halves of the same place. This is one of Fife's most popular resorts, with a mile of lovely sandy beaches, and is very popular with sailors and windsurfers. There is an exclusive air about Elie, which is only enhanced by the tale that, at one time, fish and chips were banned from the town! Like its neighbours, though, it shares the distinctive Dutch-influenced architecture. The **Lady's Tower**, a short walk from the harbour, recalls a more aristocratic past. The tower was built as a bathing box for Lady Janet Anstruther, a noted beauty of the 18th century. The whole town knew when Lady Janet was bathing, for she sent a bellman round the streets to warn the inhabitants to stay away.

Elie's westerly neighbour is the much older burgh of **Earlsferry**. There are three caves in the rock face at Kincraig Point, the headland at the far end of a broad sandy beach: Deil's (Devil's) Cave; Doo's (dove's) Cave; and the spectacular MacDuff's Cave.

St Monans and Pittenweem

Further along the coast is St Monans once one of Scotland's busiest fishing ports, a fact that is emphasized by the presence of Miller's boatyard by the harbour. This is one of the oldest surviving boat-builders, established in 1747 and still producing

Desert island tiffs

In a humble cottage down by the shore at Lower Largo, Alexander Selkirk spent his boyhood. By the age of 15 he was a strapping lad with a fierce temper, and in one particular incident the Minister and Kirk session were appalled to hear that he had threatened to blow out both his brother's and father's brains.

Young Alex went to sea after that and, in 1704, he set off for the South Seas as a sailing master in the vessel Cinque Ports. Eight months had elapsed when Selkirk had a violent quarrel with the captain and, at his own request, went ashore on the uninhabited island of Juan Fernández, off the coast of Chile.

Four years and four months later, Selkirk saw two ships approaching the island and, lighting a fire to attract their attention, ran along the shore to meet them. He was dressed completely in goat skins. However, by the time he returned home to Lower Largo, he had amassed a small fortune in pirate booty and his clothes were somewhat more elegant. So much so that his mother didn't even recognize him.

This was the story that was related to Daniel Defoe when the two met in a London coffee house in 1715 – the fiery-tempered Fifer was later immortalized in Defoe's tale of *Robinson Crusoe*.

traditional fishing boats. Other reminders of the town's sea-faring past remain. The tiny fishermen's church stands so close to the sea that during winter storms the spray rises over the churchyard wall to wash the gravestones in the cemetery. The present foundations of the church date from 1362, but the original church dates from a century earlier.

Pittenweem, a few miles east, is the home of the East Neuk fishing fleet with a thriving fish market and harbour crammed with fishing boats. It is well worth rising early to come here and witness the landing of the catch. At the east end of the harbour is **The Gyles**, an attractive group of 16th- and 17th-century houses beautifully restored by the National Trust of Scotland and boasting some fine examples of Dutch-style gables. The oldest house by far in Pittenweem is in **Cove Wynd**, which climbs steeply up to the High Street from the East Shore overlooking the harbour. In the seventh century the early Christian missionary, St Fillan lived here in a cave, dug deep into the rock. All through the middle ages pilgrims came to visit the cave. This primitive dwelling gave the town its name, for in the Pictish tongue, the word means 'place of the cave'. To visit the cave, collect the key from the **Gingerbread Horse** in the High Street ⓘ *T01333-311495*.

Three miles inland from Pittenweem, on the B9171, stands **Kellie Castle** ⓘ *Easter to end-Sep, and weekends in Oct, 1330-1730, garden and grounds open Apr-Sep daily 0930-2100, Oct-Mar till 1630, £5, £3.75 concession/child, £14 family*, one of the oldest and most magnificent of Scottish castles. This is 16th- and 17th-century domestic architecture at its best, though the oldest part of the castle dates from 1360. The interior is notable for its superb plasterwork ceilings, which were then the height of fashion.

Anstruther and around

Anstruther is the largest of the East Neuk villages. Today, it is best known as the home of the Scottish Fisheries Museum, but it was Scotland's main fishing port at the end of the 19th century, with almost 1,000 boats in its fleet. This proud heritage has been well preserved in the **Scottish Fisheries Museum** ⓘ *T01334-310628, Apr-Sep Mon-Sat 1000-1730, Sun 1100-1700, Oct-Mar Mon-Sat 1000-1630, Sun 1200-1630,*

£3.50, £2.50 concession/child, which faces the harbour on the site of the pre-Reformation St Ayles chapel. The museum, established in 1969, gives a fascinating insight into the life and work of a fishing community and is well worth a visit. There's also a fine collection of actual and model fishing boats, equipment, maps and compasses, as well as an aquarium.

Three miles north of Anstruther, just off the B9131 to St Andrews at Troy Wood, is **Scotland's Secret Bunker** ⓘ *T01334-310301, www.secretbunker.co.uk, Apr to end- Oct daily 1000-1700, £7.20, £3.95 child, £5.75 concession*, one of Fife's most fascinating attractions. This was to have been the government HQ for Scotland in the event of nuclear war and was only opened to the public in 1994. In fact, part of the complex is still operational and remains secret, as do the equivalent centres in England and Wales. The approach is through an innocuous-looking farmhouse, then visitors descend via a huge ramp to the bunker, 30 m underground and encased in 5 m of reinforced concrete. The bunker could house 300 people and was to be fitted with air filters, an electricity generator and its own water supply. It even had a couple of cinemas, which are now used to show a rather frightening 1950s newsreel giving instructions to civilians on what to do in the event of nuclear attack. Aside from the café and gift shop, the bunker has been left exactly as it was in the 1950s. The direct St Andrews to Anstruther bus takes you to the turn-off for Troy Wood. From here it's a one-mile walk.

During the summer months boats from Anstruther visit the **Isle of May** ⓘ *T01333-310103, one sailing daily from May to end-Sep (not on Fri from May-mid Jul), £14*, five miles offshore, guarding the mouth of the Firth of Forth. The approach to the island's impressive cliffs is spectacular. The island became a national nature reserve in 1956 and is home to a large population of puffins, shags, guillemots, razorbills and kittiwakes as well as seals. The island has an intriguing history. It was home to the Benedictine Priors who came in remembrance of St Adrian, the Christian missionary who was murdered there in AD 870 and the remains of whose chapel can still be seen. The first lighthouse in Scotland, built here in 1636, can also be seen. The present lighthouse was built by Robert Louis Stevenson's grandfather in 1816.

Crail

Three miles northeast of Anstruther and 10 miles from St Andrews is the most ancient and picturesque of all Fife's Royal Burghs, Crail. This was once the largest fishmarket in Europe and for centuries its ships returned from the Low Countries and Scandinavia laden with cargo. Today you're more likely to see tourists than fishermen, but you can still buy fresh lobster and shellfish here. Crail's real attraction is its beautiful harbour, surrounded by whitewashed cottages with pan-tiled roofs and crow-stepped gables. It is one of the most photographed locations in all of Scotland and a favourite with artists. To reach the old harbour you go down the steep, winding Shoregate. At the foot of the Shoregate is the 19th-century customs house.

Centuries ago, the town's rich merchants built their handsome houses round the market place. At the far end of the Marketgate, is the **Collegiate Church of St Mary**, whose origin goes back to the 12th century. During the building of the church the Devil is said to have hurled a great boulder at it from the Isle of May. The boulder split as it flew through the air and one part landed only 30 m from the churchyard gate. It still sits there, bearing the Devil's thumbprint. At the other end of the Marketgate is the **Tolbooth**, dating from the early 16th century, now serving as the town hall. In the striking Dutch tower is a bell dated 1520, cast in Holland. Also in the Marketgate is the **Museum and Heritage Centre** ⓘ *Apr-May weekends and public holidays 1400-1700, Jun-Sep Mon-Sat 1000-1300 and 1400-1700, Sun 1400-1700, free*, which shows much of the history of the town.

Sleeping

Southwest Fife *p267*
L **Balbirnie House Hotel**, Balbirnie Park, Markinch, near Kirkcaldy, T01592-610066, www.balbirnie.co.uk. This magnificent Georgian mansion is set in 400 acres of country park with its own 18-hole golf course and is the height of luxury, 30 en suite rooms and restaurant.
B **Davaar House Hotel**, 126 Grieve St, Dunfermline, T01383-721886, F623633. 10 en suite rooms, within walking distance of the town centre and bus and rail stations, good restaurant.
B **Garvock House Hotel**, St John's Dr, Transy, near Dunfermline, T01383-621067, www.garvock.co.uk. 12 rooms with bathroom, elegant country house in woodland setting, short break deals available. Excellent.

The Howe and North Fife *p271*
B **Fernie Castle Hotel**, near Letham, 5 miles north of Cupar, T01337-810381, www.ferniecastle.demon.co.uk. A beautifully restored 14th-century castle set in 17 acres of grounds with its own loch, 15 comfortable en suite rooms, lovely dining room and bar.
C **Covenanter Hotel**, near the palace, Falkland, T01337-857224, www.covenanterhotel.com. 6 comfortable en suite rooms, excellent food served in the restaurant (**££**) and bistro (**£**) downstairs.
C **Eden House Hotel**, 2 Pitscottie Rd, Cupar, T01334-652510, www.eden-group.com. Elegant Victorian town house with 11 en suite rooms and excellent restaurant, also arranges golfing packages.
F **Burgh Lodge**, Back Wynd, Falkland, T01337-857710, www.burghlodge.co.uk. 37 beds. Open all year.

St Andrews *p273, map p274*
Most of the guest houses are around Murray Pk and Pl between The Scores and North St.
L **Old Course Hotel**, T01334-474371, www.oldcoursehotel.co.uk. Internationally renowned golf resort and spa overlooking the 17th hole, 125 en suite rooms, bar and restaurants.
L **The Parkland Hotel**, Kinburn Castle, Double Dykes Rd, T01334-473620, www.parklandstandrews.com. A 19th-century castle in the town centre, its restaurant is highly-praised.
L **Rufflets Country House Hotel**, Strathkinnes Low Rd, T01334-472594, www.rufflets.co.uk. Small country house set in 10 acres of grounds on the outskirts of town by the B939, with 25 en suite rooms and good restaurant.
L **St Andrews Golf Hotel**, T01334-472611, www.standrews-golf.co.uk. 22 comfortable en suite rooms, good restaurant with extensive wine list, specialize in golf breaks.
C **Craigmore Guest House**, 3 Murray Pk, T01334-472142, F477963.
D **Amberside Guest House**, 4 Murray Pk, T/F01334-474644, amberside@talk21.com.
D **Cameron House**, 11 Murray Pk, T01334-472306, www.cameronhouse-sta.co.uk.
D **Doune House**, 5 Murray Pl, T/F01334-475195, dounehouse@aol.com.
D **Glenderran**, 9 Murray Pk, T01334-477951, F477908, glenderran@ telinco.com.
F **St Andrew Tourist Hostel**, Inchcape House, St Mary's place, T01334-479911, www.hostelsaccommodation.co.uk. 40 beds. Open all year.

The East Neuk *p277*
B **Craw's Nest Hotel**, Bankwell Rd, Anstruther, T01334-310691, www.smoothhoud.co.uk/hotels/crawsnes.html. Very good hotel with restaurant and full range of facilities, 50 en suite rooms. Also serves very good food.
D **The Grange**, 45 Pittenweem Rd, Anstruther, T/F01334-310842, pamelarae@amserve.com. 4 rooms, 2 en suite. No smoking guest house, very friendly, sun deck with sea views.
D **Spindrift**, Pittenweem Rd, Anstruther, T01333-310573, www.thespindrift.co.uk. 9 rooms. Evening meals by arrangement (£15 a head).

Eating

Southwest Fife *p267*
££ Old Rectory, Dysart, a few miles east of Kirkcaldy, T01592-657211. Best restaurant by far in the area. Tue-Sat dinner, Tue-Sun lunch.
££ Stag, Mill Wynd, near Falkland, is a whitewashed 17th-century pub. A nice cosy place for lunch or a drink.

£ Kind Kyttock's Kitchen, Cross Wynd, opposite the palace. Good home baking.
£ Valente's, 73 Oventon Rd, east of town centre in Kirkcaldy. The best fish and chips here, or anywhere else. Open till 2300, closed Wed.

The Howe and North Fife *p271*
£££ Peat Inn, 3 miles southeast of Ceres on the B940, T01334-840206. This 18th-century inn is well worth a detour. Here you can sample some of the finest food in the entire country. The proprietors have a Michelin star to verify this and the French-influenced decor and ambience match the culinary excellence.
££ Ostler's Close, 25 Bonnygate, Cupar, T01334-655574. The best place to eat in town. Does a 3-course lunch for under £20.

St Andrews *p273, map p274*
Most of upmarket hotels have excellent restaurants, see Sleeping.
£££ The Grange Inn, Crail Rd, near Kinkell Braes overlooking the East Sands, T01334-472670, F462604. Excellent restaurant.
£££ The Vine Leaf, 131 South St, T01334-477497, has a deservedly high reputation which is matched by the prices.
££ New Balaka Bangladeshi Restaurant, at the corner of St Mary's Pl and Alexandra Pl, T01334-474825. The place to go for a curry. It was recently voted 'Best Curry in Scotland'.
£ Brambles, 5 College St, beside the Market Sq. One of the nicest places for lunch, a light snack or coffee and cakes.

The East Neuk *p277*
£££ The Cellar, 24 East Green, just behind the Fisheries Museum, Anstruther, T01334-310378. Peter Jukes' lauded seafood restaurant is among the finest in the country and will set you back around £30 for a 3-course dinner. Also has a really good wine list.
££ Bouquet Garni, High St, Elie, T01334-330374. Open for lunch and 1900-2100, closed Sun. No smoking. Highly acclaimed cooking in unassuming surroundings.
££ Seafood Restaurant, 16 West End, just off the A917, T01334-730327. Fife's answer to Rick Stein is set in an extended fisherman's cottage down by the harbour. Supremely excellent value at these prices. Try the hand-dived scallops with black truffle and cauliflower puree. 1200-1500 (1230 on Sun) and 1800-2300 Sat. Closed Mon.
££ Ship Inn, Elie, down by the harbour. Excellent food in the nautical bar or restaurant. Good selection of real ales tii.
£ Anstruther Fish Bar, on Shore St. One of the best fish suppers in the country, hence the long queues in the summer.

Entertainment

Southwest Fife *p267*
Adam Smith Centre, Kirkcaldy, T01592-412929, stages live theatre and concerts and also has a cinema and restaurant/bar.

St Andrews *p273, map p274*
Byre Theatre, Abbey St, T01334-475000, www.byretheatre.com, stages an excellent range of productions throughout the year and began its life in a cowshed of the old Abbey St Dairy Farm, hence its name.

Activities and tours

St Andrews *p273, map p274*
Golf As well as the legendary **Old Course**, there are no fewer than 5 other 18-hole courses in and around the town: **Duke's Course**, T01334-474371; **Eden Course**; **Jubilee**; **New**; and **Strathtyrum**. For information and reserving tee-times on all except the Duke's, T01334-466666. Green fees range from £17 up to £80 for the Old Course (day ticket).
Walking tours **Original St Andrews Witches Tour** run Apr-Sep on Fri at 2000 (also Sun in Jun and Thu and Sun in Jul/Aug), Oct-Mar Fri at 1930. St Andrews Guided Walks leave from Church Sq at 1100 on Wed till end-Oct. Details on all of these at the TIC.

The East Neuk *p277*
Elie Waterpsorts, by the harbour, Elie, T01333-330962, offers windsurfing, sailing, water-skiing and canoe hire and instruction and also hire out mountain bikes.

For an explanation of sleeping and eating price codes used in this guide, see inside the front cover. Other relevant information is found in Essentials, see pages 43-51.

Festivals and events

St Andrews *p273, map p274*
Kate Kennedy Pageant, usually held on the third Sat in **Apr**, is the other main event in the town's calendar.
Links Market, every **Apr** for 5 days, is when Kirkcaldy's esplanade is closed to traffic for 5 days during one of the largest and oldest street fairs in Britain.
Lammas Fair is Scotland's oldest surviving medieval market, with showmen from all over Britain setting up stalls and booths in the three main streets. This bright, lively carnival is held in early **Aug**.

Transport

Southwest Fife *p267*
Trains from **Edinburgh** connect with **Dunfermline**. Trains run hourly from **North Queensferry** to and from **Edinburgh** and there are 2 buses every hour to **Dunfermline**. **Kirkcaldy** is on the main **Edinburgh** to **Dundee** and **Aberdeen** rail line, with regular services each way.

The Howe and North Fife *p271*
The nearest train station to **Falkland Palace** is 5 miles away at Markinch, on the Edinburgh to Dundee line. **Cupar** is on the Edinburgh to Dundee rail line and trains depart in each direction roughly every hour, or every 2 hrs on Sun.

St Andrews *p273, map p274*
The bus station is on City Rd, at the west end of town. There are frequent buses to **Dundee** (30 mins), the **East Neuk** villages and **Cupar** (20 min). There is also a service to **Stirling**. Buses run from **Edinburgh** to St Andrews via **Kirkcaldy**. St Andrews is not on the train line. The nearest station is 5 miles away at **Leuchars**, on the Edinburgh-Dundee-Aberdeen line. Regular buses make the 15-min journey from there to St Andrews. A taxi costs around £7.

The East Neuk *p277*
The No 95 bus runs every hour between **Dundee** and **Leven**, via **St Andrews**, **Crail**, **Anstruther**, **Pittenweem**, **St Monans** and **Elie** (East Neuk).

Directory

St Andrews *p273, map p274*
Banks There are banks with ATMs in Market St and South St. Also bureau de change at the TIC.
Hospitals Accident and Emergency (A&E) 24 hrs at Memorial Hospital, Abbey Walk, T01334-472327. Health Centre, Pipeland Rd, T01334-476840, 24 hrs.
Police North St, T01334-418900.
Toilets Church Sq (disabled and baby changing facilities); on City Rd; at the Harbour; West Sands car park.

Argyll & Inner Hebrides

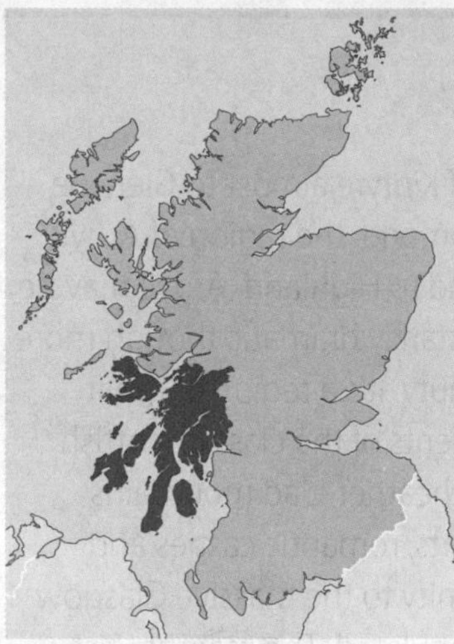

Footprint features

Introduction

Stretching north from the Mull of Kintyre almost to Glencoe and east to the shores of Loch Lomond, the region of Argyll marks the transition from Lowland to Highland. Argyll may be Highlands-like to some, it is less starkly dramatic though more lush and with its own special beauty. It's a region of great variety, containing all the ingredients of the classic Scottish holiday: peaceful wooded glens, heather-clad mountains full of deer, lovely wee fishing ports, romantic castles and beautiful lochs. Despite its proximity to the massive Glasgow conurbation, Argyll is sparsely populated. The main tourist centre and second largest town, **Oban**, has only 8,000 inhabitants. Oban is also the main ferry port for Argyll's Hebridean islands.

The **Inner Hebrides** comprise the great swathe of islands lying off the western coast of Argyll, each with its own distinct appeal. The most accessible, and most popular, is **Mull**, a short ferry ride from Oban. The variety of scenery on offer is astounding and its capital, **Tobermory**, is the most attractive port in western Scotland. A stone's throw from Mull is tiny **Iona**, one of the most important religious sites in Europe, with some divine beaches. Boat trips can be made to the dramatic island of **Staffa**, looming out of the sea like a great cathedral and the inspiration for Mendelssohn's *Hebrides Overture*. Further west, windswept **Coll** and **Tiree** offer miles of unspoilt beaches and great windsurfing and, to the south, **Colonsay** is a stress-free zone that makes Mull seem hectic. Those who enjoy a good malt whisky should head for **Islay**, famed for its distilleries, while neighbouring **Jura** is a wild and beautiful place, perfect for some off-the-beaten-track hiking. If you're after some peace and quiet on Jura then you're in good company, for this is where George Orwell came to write *1984*.

★ Don't miss...

1. **Loch Etive** Take a cruise on this hidden treasure, inaccessible except by boat, page 294.
2. **Kilmartin Glen** Explore the archaeological wonders of Argyll's very own pre-history park, page 297.
3. **Tighnabruaich** Best seen at the end of a drive down the southwest coast of Cowal, with wonderful views across the Kyles of Bute, page 302.
4. **Mount Stuart** Take a look around this magnificent Gothic fantasy, page 304.
5. **Inverawe Fisheries and Smokery** Sample the finest of piscine cuisine, preferably to take away for a picnic, page 295.
6. **Staffa** Take a boat to this spectacular island and witness the cathedral-like Fingal's Cave, which inspired Mendelssohn, page 316.
7. **Iona** Hire a bike and explore the most spiritual, and one of the loveliest, of Hebridean islands, page 319.
8. **Jura** Follow in the footsteps of George Orwell on one of Scotland's most remote islands, page 330.

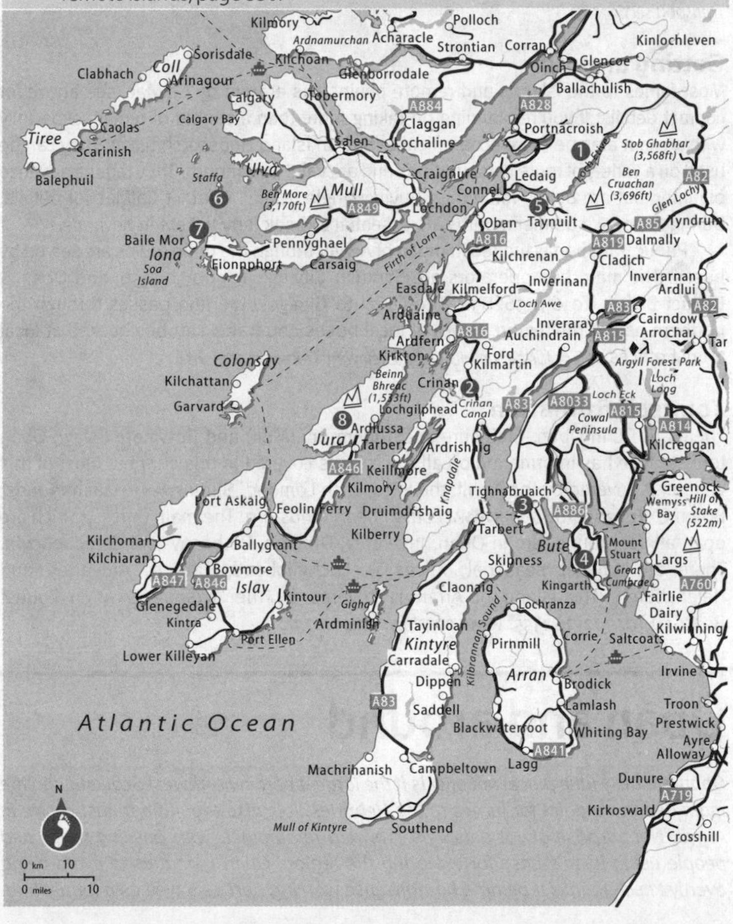

Ins and outs

Getting there

There are plenty of buses and trains from Glasgow and Fort William to Oban. For full details of bus connections contact Scottish Citylink, T08705-505050, or contact the TIC in Oban, T01631-563122. Bus, train and ferry times can be found in Argyll & Bute Council's free Area Transport Guides to Lorn, Mull and Islay & Jura, available at most tourist offices. There are flights from Glasgow to Port Ellen (Islay) and to Tiree. For full details of flight times and prices call British Airways Express, T08457-733377, the local TICs, or Port Ellen airport, T01496-302022, and Tiree airport, T01879-220309.

CalMac car and passenger ferries sail to and from Mull, Islay, Coll, Tiree, Colonsay and Gigha, and passenger-only ferries sail to Iona (and to the Small Isles, see page 451). The departure point for ferries to Mull, Coll, Tiree and Colonsay is Oban. Ferry times change according to the day of the week and time of the year. Services listed in the Transport sections for each separate island are for the summer period (2 April-16 October). For full details see the CalMac Ferry Guide or call CalMac, T01475-650100, www.calmac.co.uk (general enquiries), The departure point for ferries to Islay (and on to Jura), and some ferries to Colonsay, is Kennacraig. ▸▸ *For further details, see the relevant Transport sections.*

Getting around

Most ferries to the islands and remote peninsulas are run by CalMac, see above for contact details. If you're planning on taking more than a couple of ferries, especially with a car, it may be more economical to buy an Island Hopscotch ticket. They can be used on a variety of route combinations and are valid for a month. They require advance planning but are better value than buying single tickets. Contact CalMac for details. During the peak summer months it's essential to book ferry tickets in advance.

Public transport is limited in much of Argyll, though the main towns are served by buses. The main bus operators are Scottish Citylink, T0990-505050, and Oban & District Buses, T01631-562856. The Oban to Glasgow rail line passes through the northern part of the region. Times of local buses and trains can be checked at local tourist offices. ▸▸ *For further details, see the relevant Transport sections.*

Tourist information

There are TIC in Oban, Craignure and Tobermory (Mull) and Bowmore (Islay). Oban tourist office has information on all the islands covered in this chapter. Most of this chapter is covered by the Argyll, the Isles, Loch Lomond, Stirling & Trossachs Tourist Board ⓘ *T01369-706085, www.scottish.heart lands.org*. The main offices, which are open all year round, are in Oban, Inveraray, Dunoon, Rothesay and Campbeltown. There are smaller seasonal offices in Lochgilphead, Tarbert, Ardgarten and Helensburgh. The island of Arran is covered by the Ayrshire & Arran Tourist Board ⓘ *T01292-262555, www.ayrshire-arran.com*.

Oban and around

Oban is a busy little place: not only is it the largest port in northwest Scotland and the main departure point for ferries to the Hebrides, it is also the main tourist centre in Argyll. Not surprisingly, it gets very crowded in summer, with passing traffic and people using it as a base for exploring the region. Oban manages to avoid being overtly kitsch thanks it being a no-nonsense working port as a well as a tourist hub.

It has a wide range of hotels, guest houses, B&Bs, restaurants and shops, and a number of tourist attractions, which is useful to know if you're stuck here in bad weather. The town lies in the beautiful setting of a wide, crescent-shaped bay, backed by steep hills, with the island of Kerrera, just offshore, providing a natural shelter. Oban lies at the centre of the northerly part of Argyll, known as Lorn, which comprises several relatively peaceful islands including Lismore, Kerrera, Seil and Luing.
▸▸ For Sleeping, Eating and other listings, see pages 291-294.

Ins and outs

Getting there and around Oban is reasonably well served by buses and trains from Glasgow, Fort William and Inverness, and there are a number of west coast local bus services to and from Lochgilphead, Dalmally and Kilmartin. There are regular

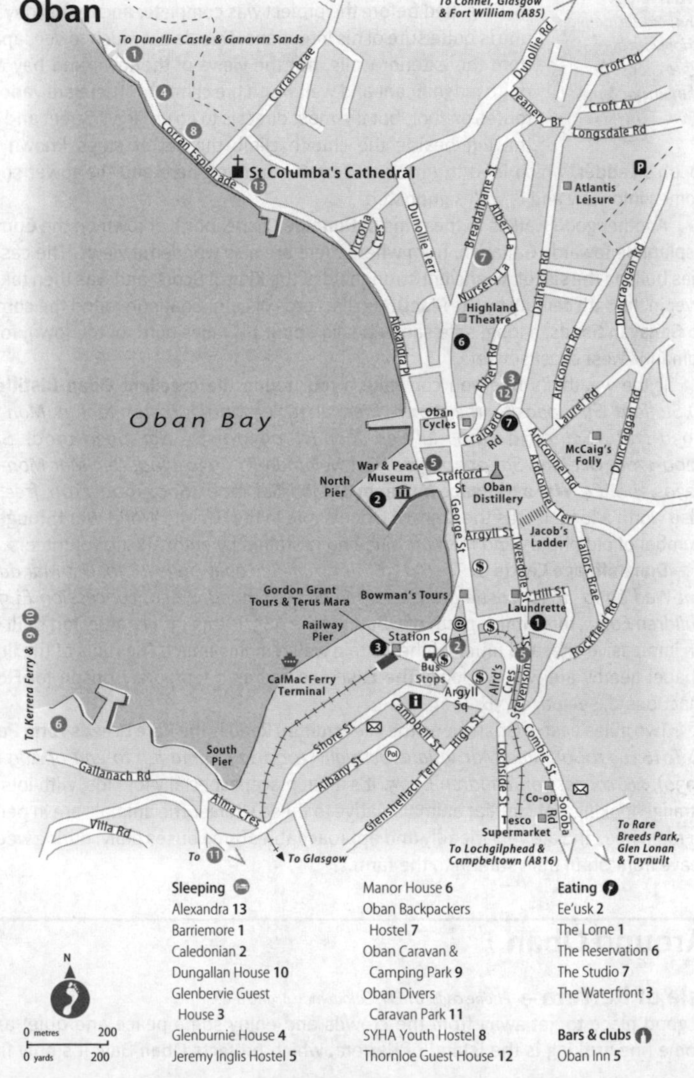

local buses around town and around Lorn, including to Clachan Seil, North Cuan, Isle of Luing, North Connel, Dalavich, Bonawe, and Ganavan Sands. These are mostly operated by Oban & District Buses or Royal Mail Postbuses, T01463-256200. » *For further details, see Transport page 293.*

Tourist information Oban Tourist Information Centre ⓘ *Argyll Sq, T01631-563122, open daily all year round, hours subject to variation*, has internet access.

Oban → *Phone code: 01631. Colour map 3, grid B5.*

The town's great landmark is **McCaig's Folly**, an incongruous structure that resembles Rome's Coliseum and which dominates the skyline. The tower was built by local banker John Stuart McCaig in the late 19th century, as a means of providing work for unemployed stonemasons. Unfortunately, McCaig died before the project was complete, and to this day no one is quite sure of his intentions. There's not much to see, apart from the exterior walls, but the views of the town and bay are quite magnificent and well worth the climb up. There are various routes on foot, but the most direct is to go up Argyll Street and on the left beside the church climb the set of steps known as Jacob's Ladder, which lead to Ardonnel Terrace. Turn left here and the tower soon comes into view and is well signposted.

Don't leave town without a visit to Sweeties, a glorious, old-fashioned sweet shop with over 350 varieties to choose from, most of them hand-made in Scotland.

Another good walk is to the ruins of **Dunollie Castle**, north of town on the Corran Esplanade towards Ganavan, from where there are also wonderful views. The castle was built on the site of an ancient stronghold of the King of Scots, and was then taken over in the 13th century by the MacDougalls, Lords of Lorn. Continue round the corner to **Ganavan Sands**, a long, safe sandy beach about 1½ miles north of the town, for a romantic west coast sunset.

If the weather's bad you can take a tour round the excellent **Oban Distillery** ⓘ *Stafford St, opposite the North Pier, T01631-572004, Easter to Jun Mon-Fri 0930-1700, Sat 0930-1700, Jul-Sep Mon-Fri 0930-1930, Sat 0930-1900, Sun 1200-1700, Oct Mon-Sat 0930-1700, Oct-Nov Mon-Fri 0930-1700, Dec-Mar Mon-Fri 1230-1700, £4.* **War and Peace Museum** ⓘ *Mon-Sat 1000-1600, 1900-2100, free*, is also worth a look. It tells the story of Oban's role in the Second World War through a number of old photos and memorabilia and is staffed by enthusiastic volunteers.

Dunstaffnage Castle ⓘ *T01631-562465, Apr-Sep daily 0930-1830, Oct-Mar daily Sat-Wed 0930- 1630, castle grounds open all year round, £2.50, concession £1.90, children £0.75*, three miles north of Oban, off the A85, is this 13th-century fort built on an impressive site, and much of the curtain wall remains intact. The ruins of the little chapel nearby are worth a look. The castle served as a temporary prison for Flora MacDonald, see page 436.

Two miles east of Oban along the Glencruitten Road is the **Rare Breeds Farm Park** ⓘ *T01631-770608, late Mar to late Oct daily 1000-1730 (mid-Jun to end of Aug till 1930), £6, concession/children £3.75*. It's a fun place, especially for kids, with lots of strange-looking, yet familiar animals native to these shores. The animals are in pens, or roam free, and are very friendly and approachable. Three buses daily, during week, leave from Oban train station to the farm.

Around Oban

Isle of Kerrera → *Phone code: 01631. Colour map 3, grid B-C5.*

A good place to get away from the crowds and enjoy some peace and quiet and some fine walking is the island of Kerrera, which protects Oban Bay. It's only five miles by two, so can be explored easily on foot or by bike. The highest point on the island is 600 ft, from where there are great views across to Mull, the Slate Islands, Lismore and Jura. Otherwise, there's a good trail down to the ruins of **Gylen Castle**, built by the MacDougall's in 1582, which is perched on a cliff-top on the south coast. A mile northwest of the ferry jetty is **Slatrach Bay**, a nice sandy beach and a great place for a picnic.

Connel to Barcaldine Castle → *Phone code: 01631. Colour map 3, grid B5.*

Five miles north of Oban an impressive steel cantilever bridge carries the A828 across the mouth of Loch Etive at Connel. It's worth stopping here to see the **Falls of Lora**, a wild tide-race created by the narrow mouth of the sea loch and the reef that spans most of it, thus restricting the flow of water. The result is the impressive rapids, which are best seen from the shore in the village or from halfway across the bridge.

Continue on this road to reach **Barcaldine Castle** ⓘ *T01631-720598, Jul-Aug Tue-Sun 1200-1700, £3.60*, built by the Campbells in the late 16th century. The tower house is still occupied by Campbells, having been sold in the mid-19th century and then bought back as a ruin 50 years later. It's now open to the public and, though there are no real treasures, there are interesting stories to be told, a dungeon (with obligatory ghost) and a tearoom where you can try Mrs Campbell's home baking.

Near Barcaldine Castle, on the main A828, is the **Oban Sealife Centre** ⓘ *T01631-720386, daily 0900-1800 (1000-1700 in the winter months), £6.95, children £5, buses to from Oban to Fort William pass by the Sealife Centre (see page 293)*, on the shore of Loch Creran. It's enormous fun and also environmentally friendly as they rescue seals and other aquatic life and then release them back into the wild at the end of the season. You can see lots of strange underwater creatures at close quarters and even touch some of them.

Appin → *Phone code: 01631. Colour map 3, grid B5.*

The road runs around Loch Creran and enters the district of Appin, made famous in Robert Louis Stevenson's *Kidnapped*, which was based on the 'Appin Murder' of 1752. A road turns southwest off the main Fort William road to **Port Appin**, on the western tip of the peninsula, the departure point for the passenger ferry to Lismore. To the north of Port Appin is the irresistibly photogenic **Castle Stalker**. Standing on its own tiny island with a background of islands and hills, it's probably second only to the famous Eilean Donan in its portrayal of Scotland's romantic image. It was built in the 16th century by the Stewarts of Appin before falling into Campbell hands after the ill-fated 1745 rebellion. The current owners open it to the public for a limited period in July and August. Check opening times at the tourist office in Oban.

Isle of Lismore → *Phone code: 01631. Colour map 3, grid B5.*

The island of Lismore lies only a few miles off the mainland, in Loch Linnhe, yet feels a world away. It makes an ideal day trip and offers great opportunities for walking and cycling, as well as wonderful views across to the mountains of Morvern and Mull, the Paps of Jura to the south and Ben Nevis to the north. It's a fertile little island (the name *leis mór* is Gaelic for the big garden) and once supported a population of 1,400, though the present population is about a tenth of that. Lismore has a long and interesting history. It was the ecclesiastical capital of Argyll for several centuries and the **Cathedral of St Moluag** was founded here in the 12th century, just north of Clachan. All that remains is the choir, which is now used as the parish church. The cathedral occupies the site of a church founded by the Irish saint, who established a religious community on the island about the same time as St Columba was busy at work in Iona. Legend has it that the two saints were racing to the island, in an attempt to be the first to land and found a monastery. Such was Moluag's religious zeal that he cut off his finger and threw it on to the shore, thus claiming possession. This sort of behaviour is, of course, frowned upon in Olympic rowing events. Not far from the church, is the 2,000-year-old **Broch of Tirefour**, one of the best-preserved prehistoric monuments in Argyll, with surviving circular walls up to 16-ft high. Other interesting sights include **Castle Coeffin**, a 13th-century fortress built by the MacDougalls of Lorn, on the west coast, and in the southwest of the island the 13th-century Achadun Castle, built for the Bishops of Argyll. It's a short walk from here to **Bernera Island**, which can be reached at low tide (but don't get stranded).

South Lorn and the Slate Islands → *Phone code: 01852. Colour map 3, grid C4-5.*

Eight miles south of Oban the B884 turns west off the A816 and wriggles its way round glassy lochs and knobbly, green hills studded with copper-coloured cattle to the tiny Slate Islands, so called because in the mid-19th century, the island's slate quarries exported millions of roofing slates every year. The quarrying industry has long since gone, leaving behind dilapidated old buildings as well as pretty little villages of whitewashed cottages built for the slate workers.

The most northerly of the Slate Islands is **Seil** (or Clachan Seil), which is reached from the mainland across the seriously humpbacked Clachan Bridge, better known as the 'Bridge over the Atlantic', built in 1792, with its elegant, high arch to allow ships to pass beneath. Beside the bridge is an old inn, **Tigh an Truish**, or 'House of the Trousers', where islanders would have to swap kilt for trousers in order to conform to the post-1745 ban on the wearing of Highland dress. There's also a petrol pump and souvenir shop here. Two miles south, at **Balvicar**, the road turns right and climbs up and over to the main village of **Ellanbeich**, an attractive wee place with rows of white cottages around the harbour. This was once a tiny island itself until the intensive slate quarrying succeeded in silting up the narrow sea channel. The village is also, rather confusingly, known by the same name as the nearby island of Easdale, so renowned was the latter for its slate deposits. Another road runs south from Balvicar to **North Cuan**, from where the car ferry sails across the treacherous Cuan Sound to **Luing**, see below.

❢ Seil is well worth a visit, for its walks and fascinating island history. It is also the departure point for exciting wildlife cruises, see page 292.

Endearingly tiny **Easdale** is separated from Seil by a 500-yd-wide channel which has to be dredged to keep it open. The island, only 800 yds by 700 yds, was the centre of the slate industry. There was once a population of over 450 here, but the quarries were flooded during a great storm in 1881 and the industry collapsed. The fascinating history of the island is explained at the **folk museum** ⓘ *T01852-300370, Apr-Oct daily 1030-1730, £2.25, children £0.50*, a few minutes' walk from the ferry pier. The whitewashed former slate workers' cottages have been refurbished and now house a burgeoining local population as well as a number of holiday homes and self-catering cottages. The island's lively social life revolves around the proud new community hall and neighbouring **Puffer Bar**. The old quarries can still be seen, now filled with water and venue for the world stone-skimming championships, see Festivals and events page 292. For more information on the island, visit www.easdale.org.

The long, thin island of **Luing** (pronounced 'Ling') once had a population of around 600 which was drastically reduced during the Clearances to make way for cattle. The island is still well known for its beef, and is the home of a successful new breed named after it. The island is small, six miles by two, and mostly flat, making it ideal for exploring by bike. Bikes can be hired in the pretty little village of **Cullipool**, a mile or so southwest of the ferry, see Transport page 293. The only other village is Toberonochy, three miles from Cullipool on the east coast. It's another village of attractive white cottages built for slate workers and nested below a ruined church.

South of the turn-off to the Slate Islands is **Arduaine Gardens** ⓘ *T01852-200366, daily all year 0930 till sunset, £5, concession £4*, a beautiful place and an absolute must for all gardening enthusiasts. The 20-acre garden, now owned by the National Trust for Scotland, is best visited in May and June when you can enjoy the spectacular rhododendrons, but there are also beautiful herbaceous borders, ponds filled with water lilies, woodland and sweeping lawns to admire, as well as great views across to Jura and the Slate Islands.

This is boating country, and just south of Arduaine, on the northern coast of the Craignish Peninsula, is surreal **Croabh Haven**, a yachting marina built in the style of a reproduction 18th-century fishing village. South of Croabh Haven is another yachting marina at **Ardfern**, where there's a hotel and B&Bs, a popular pub, restaurant and delicatessen. You can arrange boat trips from Ardfern around Loch Craignish and to the offshore islands, see Activities and tours page 292.

Sleeping

Oban *p286, map p287*

Oban is the main ferry port for the islands and gets busy in the summer with traffic. It's often an idea to get the tourist office to find a place, which costs more, but saves time and effort.

L **Caledonian Hotel**, Station Sq, T0871-2223415, www.go2oban.com. Huge landmark building overlooking the ferry pier. For a touch of luxury try one of the Captain's rooms, with prime views across the bay and all the requisite pampering facilities.

A **Alexandra Hotel**, Corran Esplanade, T01631-562381. Large hotel with well-equipped rooms and good facilities including pool, steam room and beauty salon.

A **Manor House Hotel**, Gallanach Rd, T01631-562087, F563053. 11 rooms, open Feb-Dec. Overlooking the bay on the road south out of town towards the Kerrera ferry. Offers comfort, style and superb cuisine.

C **Dungallan House Hotel**, Gallanach Rd, T01631-563799, www.dungallanhotel-oban.co.uk. 13 rooms, open Jan, Mar-Oct and Dec. A Victorian house set in 5 acres of woodland, offering great views, hospitality and fine food.

D **Barriemore Hotel**, Corran Esplanade, T/F01631-566356. 13 rooms, open Mar-Nov. More of a guest house, and a superior one at that. Great views and a friendly atmosphere.

D **Glenburnie House**, Corran Esplanade, T/F01631-562089. 15 rooms, open Apr-Oct. Another very good guest house along the seafront, which is lined with more upmarket guest houses and hotels.

D **Thornloe Guest House**, Albert Rd, T/F01631-562879, www.thornloeoban.co.uk. 7 rooms. Quiet and centrally located guest house run by Alan and Valerie Bichener. Friendly and welcoming, good-sized en suite rooms and limited off-street parking. Continental breakfast available.

E **Glenbervie Guest House**, Dalriach Rd, T01631-564770, F566723. 8 rooms. Lovely house high above the town on a street full of good accommodation, good value.

F **Jeremy Inglis Hostel**, T01631-565065, at 21 Airds Cres, opposite the TIC. Cheaper and with breakfast included, smaller and quirkier.

F **Oban Backpackers**, T01631-562107, on Breadalbane St. Mar-Oct and 21 Dec-14 Jan.

F **SYHA Youth Hostel**, T01631-562025, open all year from Mar, is on Corran Esplanade, just beyond St Columba's Cathedral.

Camping

Oban Caravan & Camping Park, T01631-562425, F566624, Apr to mid-Oct, Gallanach Rd, 2 miles south of town near the Kerrera ferry.

Oban Divers Caravan Park, T/F01631-562755, open Mar-Nov, on the Glenshellach Rd, 1½ miles south of the ferry terminal.

Around Oban *p288*

L **Airds Hotel**, Port Appin, T01631-730236, F730535. 12 rooms. This classy little roadside hotel boasts one of the very best restaurants in the whole country.

A **Loch Melfort Hotel**, Arduaine, T01852-200233, www.loch-melfort.co.uk. 26 rooms. Open all year. It enjoys great views and a reputation for the finest seafood.

A **Willowburn Hotel**, Seil, T01852-300276, www.willowburn.co.uk. Open Mar-Nov. 7 rooms. Great little hotel overlooking the Sound of Seil. As well as the peace and quiet you can also enjoy the superb food on offer.

C **Pierhouse Hotel**, Port Appin, T01631-730302, F730400. Sitting right by the tiny pier, this cosy little hotel has a deserved reputation for excellent, moderately priced local seafood.

E **Wendy Baldock**, Easdale island, T01852-300438. 2 rooms. Friendly B&B in refurbished quarry workers' cottage. Evening meals also available (**££**).

F **Kerrera Bunkhouse**, Isle of Kerrera, T01631-570223. Open Apr-Sep. 6 beds. Can arrange transport to and from ferry pier.

Eating

Oban *p286, map p287*

£££ **Ee'usk**, North Pier, T01631-565666. Glass-fronted fish restaurant which has the edge over its competitors in style, though the jury is still out on whether its food is the best in town. Superb fish and seafood. Open daily 1100-1600 and 1800-2130.

£££ **The Waterfront**, Ferry Pier, T01631-563110. Contender for the best seafood restaurant in town, with mouth-watering dishes such as sea bass fillets with ginger and coriander noodles. Open daily 1130-1400 and 1800-late.

££ **The Reservation**, 108 George St, T01631-563542. Very popular though the name refers to its North American theme. Mostly burgers, fajitas and other meat-based dishes. Open daily 1100-2200.

££ **The Studio**, Craigard Rd, T01631-562030. Good-value 3-course set dinner and good à la carte menu, popular with locals, so you'll need to book. Wide-ranging menu featuring fish, seafood and steaks. Open daily 1800-2200 (cheap 'early bird special' served 1800-1830).

£ **John Ogden** has his world-famous green shed by the ferry terminal. For a cheap snack look no further here. His prawn sandwiches are widely held to be the best on the planet (£2.50). Open 0930-1800.

£ **The Lorne**, Stevenson St, T01631-570021. Busy local pub with beer garden and a good selection of bar meals, including burgers and fish dishes. Food served all day. Fine value.

Around Oban *p288*

££ **The Barn**, Cologin, Lerags, T01631-564618. Good, wholesome pub grub served with a smile. Open daily Mar-Nov.

££ **Seafood and Oyster Bar**, Ellenabeich pier, Seil, T01852-300121. Wide range of fish and seafood dishes, from half-a-dozen oysters for £7.50 to scallops and lobster. Great fish and chips to take away and eat on the harbour wall.

££ **The Wide-mouthed Frog**, Dunstaffnage Marina, Connel, T01631-567005. Popular with the boating fraternity. Lots of fresh fish and seafood dishes, plus meat and game. Kids meals and cheap snacks too. Outdoor seating. Rooms available.

Bars and clubs

Oban *p286, map p287*

Not exactly the party capital of Scotland, so don't expect much in the way of late-night diversion.

Oban Inn, by the north pier, is the nicest pub in town and serves bar food.

Around Oban *p288*

In Ardfern is a popular pub, and in Easdale, **Puffer bar**, serves as a focal point of the community.

Entertainment

Oban *p286, map p287*

The Highland Theatre, at the north end of George St, T01631-562444, is confusingly the local cinema. It shows most of the popular current releases.

Festivals and events

Oban and around *p286, map p287*

Apr Highlands & Islands Music & Dance Festival is held at the end of Apr/beginning of May.

Aug Argyllshire Gathering (Oban Games) is held at the end of Aug in Mossfield Park.

Sep World stone-skimming championships are held on Easdale on the last Sun. Lots of drinking and merriment, there's even talk of a mariachi band circumnavigating the tiny island. For the lowdown on what's on, or the chance to defeat the Aussies, visit www.stoneskimming.com.

Activities and tours

Oban *p286, map p287*

Boat trips Boat trips can be made from Oban to Mull, Iona, Staffa and The Treshnish Islands with a variety of companies.

For an explanation of sleeping and eating price codes used in this guide, see inside the front cover. Other relevant information is found in Essentials, see pages 43-51.

Bowman's Tours, Queens Park Pl, T01631-566809, bowmanstours@supanet.com; **Gordon Grant Tours**, T01631-562842; and **Turus Mara**, T01631-566999, www.turusmara.com, both on Railway Pier, all offer offer a variety of island and wildlife cruises, ranging in price from £30-40.

Borro Boats, Dungallan Parks, Gallanach Rd, T01631-563292. Boats for rent.

Diving Puffin Dive Centre, Gallanach Port, Gallanach Rd, T01631-566088, or booking office at George St, T01631-571190. Diver training centre and facilities (open 0800-2000).

Swimming Atlantis Leisure, Dalriach Rd, T01631-566800, www.atlantisleisure.co.uk. Sports and leisure centre with pool.

Around Oban *p288*

Boat trips Craignish Cruises, T01852-500540, www.craignishcruises.co.uk, runs private charters and fishing trips from Ardfern Yacht Centre to the Sound of Jura, Corryvreckan and Firth of Lorne.

Kerrera Sea Adventures, T07786-963279, runs 1-hr trips around Kerrera on an rigid inflatable boats (RIB).

Seafari Adventures, T01852- 300003, www.seafari.co.uk, offers excitement from the harbour at Ellenabeigh on Seil (but can be booked in advance at Oban TIC). They use 300hp RIBS (rigid inflatable boats) to take you on a thrilling ride across the Corryvreckan (see p330). They also stop to check out the local wildlife; seals, porpoises and lots of seabirds, perhaps even a golden eagle. Trips cost £22 per person.

Horse riding Ardfern Riding Centre, Craobh Haven, T01852-500632, appaloosaholidays@talk21.com. Offers a variety of trails and pub rides, from £15 for 1 hr.

Watersports Linnhe Marine Watersports Centre, Lettershuna, just beyond Port Appin, T01631-730227, where you can hire motor boats, sailing dinghies or windsurfing boards, take sailing or windsurfing lessons, or try water-skiing, pony trekking or even clay pigeon shooting. May-Sep 0900-1800.

Transport

Oban *p286, map p287*

There are regular daily buses to and from **Fort William**, via **Benderloch** and **Appin** (1¾ hrs) with **West Coast Motors**, T01586-552319, **Highland Country Buses**, T01463-233371, and **Oban & District Buses**, T01631-562856. There's a regular daily service to and from Glasgow (3 hrs) with **Scottish Citylink Coaches**, T08705-505050, and to **Inverness** (1¼ hrs). There are regular daily buses to and from **Dalmally**, via **Cruachan Power Station**, **Lochawe** and **Taynuilt Hotel**, operated by **Oban & District**, **Scottish Citylink**, **Awe Service Station**, T01866-822612, and **LF Stewart**, T01866-833342. There's a service to **Lochgilphead**, via **Kilmartin**, a couple of times a day (Mon-Sat), operated by **Oban & District**, **Scottish Citylink** and **West Coast Motors**.

Oban is the main ferry port for many of the Hebridean islands. **CalMac** ferry terminal, T01631-566688, is on Railway Pier, to the south of the town centre. See the island's Transport sections for details.

Only 100 yds away is the train station which is next to the bus terminal. There are 3 trains daily to **Glasgow**, via **Crianlarich**, where the Oban train connects with the Mallaig/Fort William-Glasgow train.

Car hire from **Flit Van & Car Hire**, Glencruitten Rd, T/F01631-566553. From £33.50 per day. **Practical Car & Van Rental**, Robertson's Motor Repairs, Lochavullin Industrial Estate, T01631-570900. From £36 per day. **Hazelbank Motors**, Lynn Rd, T01631-566476, F566783. From £35 per day. You can rent bikes from **Oban Cycles**, 9 Craigard Rd, T01631-566966. For details of cycle routes through the forests of Argyll, see the Forest Enterprise leaflet, *Cycling in the Forest*, available at the tourist office.

Around Oban *p288*

The departure point for ferries to **Kerrera** is 1½ miles along the Gallanach Rd. They leave several times daily between 0845 and 1800 (between 1030 and 1700 on Sun).

The **CalMac** car ferry from Oban lands at **Achnacroish** on Lismore (2-4 daily Mon-Sat, 50 mins, £2.65 one way per passenger, £22.10 per car). A passenger ferry leaves from **Port Appin** pier to the island's north point (daily every 1-2 hrs, 10 mins). A tiny passenger ferry sails from **Ellanbeich** on Seil to **Easdale**, making the 5-min trip at regular intervals between 0745 and 2100 Mon-Sat (between 0930 and 1500 on Sun), partly to schedule, partly on request. Ring the bell in the shelter on the pier. A car ferry to **Luing** (South Cuan) sails from South Cuan on Seil (5 mins), Mon-Sat every 15-30 mins from 0745 to 1815 (later in summer) and on Sun every 30 mins from 1100 to 1800. Check times at Oban tourist office.

Cycle hire from Isle of Luing Bike Hire, Isle of Luing, T01852-314256. £10 per day.

Directory

Oban and around *p286, map p287*

Banks All the major banks have branches with ATMs in the centre and you can change foreign currency at the TIC.

Internet Oban Backpackers charge £1.50 for 15 mins. Also at Fancy That, George St, T01631-562996. Daily 0900-2200. £1.50 per 15 mins.

Mid-Argyll, Kintyre, Cowal and Bute

Further south from Oban the long finger of Mid-Argyll and Kintyre points south into the wild Atlantic Ocean, sheltering the Isle of Arran on the leeward side and Islay and Jura on its Starboard. This is a very attractive, slightly out-of-the-way region of sea lochs, rolling hills, huge forests and, in Kilmartin Glen, one of the most important prehistoric sites in Europe. Mull of Kintyre is the tip, barely a stone's throw from Northern Ireland, and one of the loneliest spots in the country. On the other side of Loch Fyne is the gaint claw of the Cowal Peninsula, looking like it's about to crush in its grasp the aptly-named Isle of Bute, home to one of Scotland's most fantastical stately homes.

▸▸ *For Sleeping, Eating and other listings, see pages 304-307.*

Ins and outs

Cowal's main TIC is in Dunoon ⓘ *Alexandra Parade, T01369-703785, Apr-Oct*; Helensburgh TIC ⓘ *clock tower on the waterfront, T01436-672642, Apr-Oct*; Bute TIC ⓘ *Promenade, Rothesay, T01700-502151*; Iveraray TIC ⓘ *Front St, T01499-302063*; Lochgilphead TIC ⓘ *Lochnell St, T01546-602344, Apr-Oct*; Tarbert TIC. ⓘ *Harbour St, T01880-820429*; and Campbeltown TIC ⓘ *Old Quay, T01586-552056.*

Loch Awe and Loch Etive

→ *Colour map 3, C5, grid B5-6.*

Loch Awe is the longest freshwater loch in Scotland and, further north, is the beautiful Loch Etive. There's enough here to justify a couple of days' exploration, particularly the little-visited west shore of Loch Awe, and there are plenty of other places to visit around Inveraray to the south.

At the northeastern tip of Loch Awe, between the villages of of **Dalmally** and **Lochawe**, is the romantic ruin of **Kilchurn Castle**, on a promontory jutting out into the loch. The castle ruin can be visited by boat from the pier in Lochawe village. A few miles west of Lochawe, and almost a mile inside Ben Cruachan (3,695 ft) is the underground **Cruachan Power Station** ⓘ *Apr- Nov 0930-1700, Jul-Aug 0930-1800, £3.50, children £1.50*, or "Hollow Mountain". From the visitor centre on the shores of Loch Awe, a bus trip takes you into the heart of the mountain through tunnels until you reach the generating room. The whole effect is somewhere between a Gerry Anderson production or an evil villain's lair in an early Bond movie.

Between Loch Awe and Loch Etive runs the River Awe, which squeezes through the dark and ominous Pass of Brander, so steep and narrow that legend has it that it was once held against an entire army by an old woman brandishing a scythe.

Piscine cuisine

The whole philosophy of smoking fish varies from one producer to another.

At **Inverawe Fisheries and Smokery**, see below, they buy smaller farmed salmon because they believe the lower fat content makes them tastier than larger ones. Traditional methods prevail here. The fish are dry salted, washed, smoked over oak logs for anything from 16 to 24 hours, depending on conditions, and then hand-sliced. The result is a rich and freshly oaky taste in a huge range of formats from a 112 grams sliced pack (£5.95) to a whole side (£20.65), as well as gravadlax, smoked trout, eel and halibut, plus a whole range of pre-packed hampers.

Knipoch Smokehouse, in South Lorn near Oban, T01852-316251, www.knipochsmokehouse.co.uk, on the other hand, believes that large salmon, weighing 6-7 kg, produce the best quality. Its approach involves a dry salt cure strengthened with sugar, whisky, juniper and rowan berries, plus a lengthy two to three day smoke. The fish comes out so black it has to be washed and trimmed to look presentable, and the taste is a rather unusual one: strong, sweet, sharp and almondy. A whole side costs £45, but it can be cut to any size: sliced at £17.60 per 500 grams, unsliced at £15.95.

Further west, and 12 miles east of Oban, is the tiny village of **Taynuilt**, near the shore of Loch Etive. Just before the village, at Bridge of Awe, is a sign for **Inverawe Fisheries Country Park** ⓘ *T01866-822777, www.smokedsalmon.co.uk, daily 0800-1800*, where you can take fishing lessons, learn about traditional smoking techniques, or wander along a series of nature trails. If the weather's fine, you can buy some of their delicious smoked products and have a picnic, see box. If you fancy more of the same delivered to you at home, make sure you sign up for their mailing list.

North of the village on the shores of Loch Etive is **Bonawe Iron Furnace** ⓘ *T01866-822432, Apr-Sep, daily 0930-1830, £2.80, concession £2, children £1.* Founded in 1753 by a group of Cumbrian ironmasters, Bonawe used the used the abundant woodlands of Argyll to make charcoal to fire its massive furnace. At its height, it produced 600-700 tons of pig-iron a year. This was then shipped out to the forges of England and Wales. Iron production ceased at Bonawe in 1876 and it has now been restored as an industrial heritage site, with displays explaining the whole production process. Beyond Bonawe is the pier from which Loch Etive Cruises depart. The loch is inaccessible except by boat, and the three-hour cruise of one of Scotland's great hidden treasures is definitely worth it, see Activities and tours page 306.

Running south from the village is the very lovely and very quiet Glen Lonan. About four miles along the Glen Lonan road is **Barguillean's Angus Garden** ⓘ *T01866-822333, daily 0900-1800, free*, one of Argyll's youngest and smallest gardens, but also one of the most peaceful and evocative, set around the shores of little Loch Angus. It was created in 1957, in memory of Angus MacDonald, a journalist and writer killed in Cyprus in 1956.

▲A single-track road runs southwest of Kilchrenan along the shores of Loch Awe to the tiny villages of **Dalavich** and **Ford**, through the very beautiful Inverinan Forest, a Forestry Commission property which has a series of undemanding marked trails running through the hills overlooking the loch. The first walk starts out from the little hamlet of **Inverinan**. Red waymarkers lead you from the car park into the woods surrounding the gorge of the River Inan. Part of the route follows the old drove road along which cattle were driven from the Highlands down to the markets in south and central Scotland. The walk is three miles long and should take around an hour and a half. Further along the road, half a mile north of Dalavich, is a car park at **Barnaline Lodge**, the starting point for a nine-mile bike route, a waymarked walk through the Caledonian Forest Reserve, and a couple of other woodland walks. The longest of the walks is the five-mile route that leads along the River Avich, then along the shores of Loch Avich before returning to the lodge. Two and a half miles south of Dalavich is a car park, which marks the starting point for a blue waymarked walk along the shores of Loch Awe. The route passes through Mackenzie's Grove, a sheltered gorge containing some of the largest conifers on the west coast. The route then runs along the shores of the loch, from where you can see the remains of a *crannog*, one of over 40 of these Iron-Age settlements on Loch Awe. The route then heads back to the car park; about three miles in total. These routes are all outlined, with accompanying maps, in the Forestry Commission leaflet, 'A Guide to Forest Walks and Trails in North Argyll', available at tourist offices.

Inveraray and around

Inveraray → *Phone code: 01499. Colour map 3, grid C6.*

Inveraray is the classic 18th-century planned town (don't call it a village), with its straight, wide streets and dignified Georgian houses, and enjoys the most stunning of settings, on the shores of Loch Fyne. It was rebuilt by the third Duke of Argyll, head of the Campbell clan, at the same time as he restored the nearby family home, which now attracts hordes of summer visitors. As well as its natural beauty and elegance, and fine castle, Inveraray has several other notable attractions in and around the town and you could quite happily spend a few days here, whatever the weather.

One of Argyll's most famous castles, **Inveraray Castle** ⓘ *T01499-302203, Apr-Jun, Sep-Oct Mon-Thu and Sat 1000-1300 and 1400-1745, Sun 1300-1745, Jul-Aug Mon-Sat 1000-1745, Sun 1300-1745, £5.50, concession £4.50, children £3.50,* has been the clan seat of the Campbells for centuries and is still the family home of the Duke of Argyll. The present neo-Gothic structure dates from 1745, and its main feature is the magnificent armoury hall, whose displays of weaponry were supplied to the Campbells by the British government to quell the Jacobite rebellion. The elaborately furnished rooms are also on display, as is the fascinating and troubled family history in the Clan room. There are extensive grounds with fine walks, particularly up to the hill-top folly. has been the clan seat of the Campbells for centuries and is still the family home of the Duke of Argyll.

Inveraray Jail ⓘ *T01499-302381, Apr-Oct daily, 0930-1800, Nov-Mar daily 1000- 1700, £5.75, concession £3.75, children £2.80, family £15.70,* the Georgian prison and courthouse in the centre of the village has been brilliantly restored as a fascinating museum that gives a vivid insight into life behind bars from medieval times up till the 19th century. You can sit in on an 1820 courtroom trial, then visit the cells below and learn all about some of the delightful prison pursuits, such as branding with a hot iron, ear nailing and public whipping. The whole experience is further enhanced by the guides, who are dressed as warders and prisoners. Makes you want to stay on the right side of the law, though, thankfully conditions have improved – as you will see for yourself.

Another worthwhile diversion, especially if you've got kids in tow, the **Inveraray Maritime Museum** ⓘ *T01499-302213, Apr-Sep daily 1000-1800, Oct-Mar daily 1000-1700, £3.60, concession £2.60, children £2,* housed in the *Arctic Penguin*, one of the world's last iron sailing ships, which is moored at the loch-side pier. Below decks are lots of interesting displays on Clyde shipbuilding and the Highland Clearances, as well as various 'hands-on' activities.

A few miles southwest of town, on the A83 to Lochgilphead, **Argyll Wildlife Park** ⓘ *T01499-T302264, daily 1000-1700, £4, concession £3, children £2,* is another great place for kids. Amongst the native wildlife wandering around the forest-clad hills are pine martens, badgers, foxes, deer, wildcats, wild goats, a variety of wildfowl and birds of prey, racoons and wallabies, though the more informed of you will have noted that the last two are not native to Scotland. There's also the obligatory tearoom and gift shop.

Three miles beyond Argyll Wildlife Park is **Auchindrain Township** ⓘ *T01499-500235, 1 Apr-30 Sep daily 1000-1700, £3.80, concession £3, children £1.80*, a complete reconstruction of an original West Highland village. The thatched cottages, barn and blacksmith have all been perfectly restored, and are all furnished and equipped to give a real insight into what rural life must have been like in the Highlands before the Clearances. There's also an informative visitor centre, with a bookshop and tearoom.

Four miles further down the A83 is **Crarae Gardens** ⓘ *T01546-886614, Mar-Oct 0900-1800, from dawn till dusk in winter, £5, concession £4*, one of Scotland's very best public gardens, dramatically set in a deep wooded glen on the shores of Loch Fyne. There are marked woodland walks winding their way through a spectacular array of rhododendrons, azaleas and numerous other exotic plants towards the tumbling waterfalls of the 'Himalayan Gorge'. May is a good time to see the gardens in full bloom, as is autumn for the vast variety of deciduous trees, but any time of year is worth it.

Kilmartin and around → *Phone code: 01546. Colour map 3, grid C5.*

Much of this region was once part of the ancient Kingdom of Dalriada, established by the Irish Celts (known as the Scotti, hence Scotland) who settled here in the fifth century. North of Lochgilphead, on the A816 to Oban, is **Kilmartin Glen**, an area of Neolithic and Bronze-Age chambered and round cairns, stone circles, rock carvings, Iron-Age forts and duns, Early-christian sculptured stones and medieval castles. Before exploring this fascinating area, it's a good idea to stop off at **Kilmartin House** ⓘ *T01546-510278, daily all year 1000-1730, £3.90, concession £3.10, children £1.20.* This multi award-winning interpretive centre is housed in the old manse next to the parish church in the tiny village of **Kilmartin**. Imaginative and interesting, it helps to explain the bewildering array of prehistoric sites lying all around, and includes artefacts from the various sites and prehistoric music. The café/restaurant does not disappoint either, and serves cheap snacks and meals, using local produce, and excellent coffee from 1230 till 1700. Next door in the church graveyard are the **Kilmartin crosses**, dating from as far back as the ninth and 10th centuries. Also within the graveyard is one of the largest collections of medieval grave slabs in the West Highlands.

Two miles north of Kilmartin, sitting high above the A816, is **Carnasserie Castle**, an imposing 16th-century tower house built by John Carswell, Bishop of the Isles, who translated *The Book of the Common Order* in 1567, the first book to be printed in Gaelic. Entry to the castle is free, but it's a little way from the car park.

Most notable of all is the **linear cemetery**, a line of burial cairns that stretch southward from Kilmartin village for over two miles. The largest and oldest of the group is the Neolithic cairn, Nether Largie South, which is over 5,000 years old and big enough to enter. The other cairns, Nether Largie North, Mid Nether Largie and Ri Cruin, are Bronze Age and the huge stone coffins show carvings on the grave slabs. Nearby are the Temple Wood Stone Circles, where burials took place from Neolithic times to the Bronze Age.

On the other side of the A816, and visible from the road, is a group of monuments which can all be reached from Dunchraigaig Cairn. This is a huge Bronze-Age cairn with some of the covering stones removed to reveal three stone coffins. From here a path is signed to **Ballymeanoch Standing Stones**, the tallest of which is 12-ft high. Two of the stones are decorated with cup marks, prehistoric rock carvings that can be found at numerous locations throughout the Kilmartin area. There's also a henge monument in the same field. These were generally round or oval platforms with an internal ditch, and it's thought they were used for ceremonial purposes. The best example of rock carvings is at Achnabreck, near Cairnbaan village, the largest collection anywhere in Britain. The purpose and significance of these cup- and ring-marked rocks is still a matter of debate.

A few miles south of Kilmartin village is the Iron-Age hill fort of **Dunadd,** which stands atop a rocky outcrop and dominates the surrounding flat expanse of **Moine Mhór** (Great Moss), one of the few remaining peat bogs in the country and now a nature reserve. Dunadd Fort became the capital of the ancient kingdom of Dalriada around AD 500 and is one of the most important Celtic sites in Scotland. The views from the top are wonderful and worth the visit alone, but you can also see carved out of the exposed rock, a basin and footprint, thought to have been used in the inauguration ceremonies of the ancient kings of Dalriada. There's also an inscription in *ogham* (a form of early writing from Ireland) and the faint outline of a boar, possibly of Pictish origin.

Crinan Canal → *Colour map 3, grid C5.*

Kilmartin Glen is bordered to the south by the Crinan Canal, a nine-mile stretch of waterway linking Loch Fyne at Ardrishaig with the Sound of Jura. It was designed and built by Sir John Rennie in 1801, with the assistance of the ubiquitous Thomas Telford, to allow shipping to avoid the long and often hazardous journey round the Mull of Kintyre and to help stimulate trade in the islands. These days you're more likely to see pleasure yachts and cruisers sailing on the canal than the cargo vessels which once transported coal and other goods to the islands and returned with livestock. You don't need to come in a boat to appreciate the canal. You can walk or cycle along the towpath that runs the entire length of the canal, from Ardrishaig to Crinan, and watch boats of all shapes and sizes negotiating a total of 15 locks. The best place to view the canal traffic is at **Crinan**, a pretty little fishing port on Loch Crinan at the western end of the canal, see Activities and tours page 306.

▲ Knapdale

Running south from the Crinan Canal down to Kintyre is Knapdale, a forested, hilly area that gets its name from its Gaelic description, *cnap* (hill) and *dall* (field). It's an area worth exploring, for there are many walking trails and superb views from the west coast across to the Paps of Jura. Immediately south of the canal is Knapdale Forest, which stretches from coast to coast over hills dotted with tiny lochs. The Forestry Commission has marked out several lovely trails. Three fairly easy circular trails start from the B8025 which runs south from **Bellanoch**, just east of Crinan.

One sets out from the car park at the Barnluasgan Interpretation Centre and runs up to a point beyond **Loch Barnluasgan**, with great views over the forest and the many lochs. It's a mile in total. A second trail, also a mile long, starts from a car park a little further along the B8025 and heads through the forest to the deserted township of **Arichonan**. The third trail starts out from the car park between the starting points for the first and second trails. It runs right around **Loch Coille-Bharr** and is three miles long. A more strenuous walk starts from a car park about 100 yds into the forest, off the B841, about half a mile west of Cairnbaan, and climbs up to the peak of **Dunardy** (702 ft).

At the Barnluasgan Interpretation Centre a little side road turns south down the eastern shore of beautiful Loch Sween, past the village of Achnamara, to the 12th-century **Castle Sween**. First impressions of the castle, situated on the shores of the lovely loch with the forested hills all around, are completely ruined by the criminally distasteful caravan park nearby. Unfortunately, the caravans were not there when Robert the Bruce attacked the castle, otherwise he might have done us all a favour by razing them. Three miles south is the ruined 13th-century **Kilmory Knap Chapel**. A new glass roof protects the carved stones inside. The most notable of these is the 8-ft high, 15th-century **MacMillan's Cross**, which shows the Crucifixion on one side and a hunting scene on the other.

Lochgilphead → *Colour map 3, grid C5.*

The main town in the area fo Mid-Argyll, and administrative centre for the entire Argyll and Bute region, is Lochgilphead, a sleepy little place at the head of Loch Gilp, an arm of Loch Fyne. Lochgilphead started life as a planned town, but the industries came and went, leaving it with the customary grid plan of wide streets but little else. Today it serves as a useful base for exploring the area, with a decent range of accommodation, a bank and supermarket. There's a nice easy walk from the car park at Kilmory Castle Gardens, about a mile east of town, up to Kilmory Loch. It takes about an hour there and back and is well marked. The gardens also make a pleasant stroll and there are other marked walks, including up to Dun Mór (360 ft).

Kintyre → *Phone code: 01880. Colour map 3, grid A-B2.*

The long peninsula of Kintyre is probably best known as the inspiration for Paul McCartney's phenomenally successful 1970s dirge, 'Mull of Kintyre', but don't let that put you off. Kintyre has all the usual Highland ingredients, such as great scenery, wildlife, bags of history, golf and whisky, but also has the added attraction of being one of Scotland's least explored spots. The peninsula would be an island, were it not for the mile-long isthmus between West and East Loch Tarbert, a fact not lost on King Magnus Barefoot of Norway. In the 11th century he signed a treaty with the Scottish king, Malcolm Canmore, giving him all the land he could sail round, and promptly had his men drag his longboat across the narrow isthmus, thus adding Kintyre to his kingdom. ▸▸ *For Sleeping, Eating and other listings, see pages 304-307.*

Ins and outs

Getting around Kintyre without your own transport requires time and patience. There's a bus service running up and down the west coast, and also a limited service from Campbeltown to places around the peninsula. There are buses from Tarbert to Kennacraig (for ferries to Islay) several times daily except Sunday. Also from Tarbert to Claonaig (for ferries to Lochranza on Arran) and Skipness (two to three daily Monday to Saturday). Details from Argyll & Bute Council, T01546-604695, or the TIC. ▸▸ *For further details, see Transport page 306.*

Tarbert

The fishing village of Tarbert sits at the head of East Loch Tarbert, in a sheltered bay backed by forested hills, and is one the most attractive ports on the west coast. Tarbert (the name derives from the Gaelic *An Tairbeart* meaning 'isthmus') has a long tradition of fishing, and in the 18th and 19th centuries was a major herring port. Today, prawns and other shellfish are the main catch and though there is still a sizeable fleet, fishing has declined in importance to the local economy. Tourism, meanwhile, is a growing source of income, and Tarbert attracts its fair share of yachties, particularly in May when the village hosts the second largest racing series in the UK after Cowes attracting hundreds of boats and thousands of visitors. The tourist information centre ⓘ *Harbour St, T01880-820429, Apr-Sep.*

Overlooking the harbour is the dramatically sited ruin of **Robert the Bruce's** 14th-century castle. There's not much left to see, other than the five-storey 15th-century keep. It's unsafe to investigate the ruins too closely, but the view alone is worth the walk. There are steps leading up to the castle, next to the Loch Fyne Gallery on Harbour Street. Behind the castle there are several marked trails leading up into the hills, with great views over Loch Fyne and the islands. Less strenuous is the short walk at the end of Garvel Road, on the north side of the harbour, which leads to the beach. At the end of East Pier road, beyond the Cowal Ferry, is another good walk, to the **Shell Beaches**. You can also explore the lovely gardens at **Stonefield Castle Hotel**, see Sleeping page 304.

Gigha

The small island of Gigha (pronounced 'Gee-a' with a hard 'g') translates from Norse as 'God's Island'. A grand claim, perhaps, but there's no question that this most accessible of islands is also one of the loveliest. It's only a 20-minute ferry ride away, and only six miles by one mile, so it can be visited easily in a day, which is just about enough time to appreciate why the Vikings loved it so much. Like so many of the Hebridean islands, Gigha has had a long list of owners, including various branches of the MacNeils and, more recently, in 1944, Sir James Horlick, he of bedtime drink fame. Now, though, the islanders are the new proud owners of their own little piece of paradise, thanks to a successful buy-out in 2001.

It was Horlick who created the island's single greatest attraction is the wonderful **Achamore Gardens** ⓘ *T01583-505254, daily all year 0900 till dusk, £2,* one mile south of the ferry terminal. Thanks to Gigha's mild climate, the 50-acre woodland garden has an amazing variety of tropical plants, including rhododendrons, azaleas, camellias as well as other, more exotic, species. There are two marked walks through the gardens, which start out from the walled garden. The gardens are best seen in early summer, when the rhodies are in full bloom.

The island's other delights include some good walks, white sandy beaches and fantastic views across to Jura on one side and Kintyre on the other. One of the best walks is to take the path left after the nine-hole golf course, signed Ardaily, past Mill Loch to the Mill on the west shore. The views from here are just magnificent. Another good idea is to walk, or cycle (see Transport page 306) to the peninsula of Eilean Garbh at the north of the island. About half a mile beyond Kinererach Farm a path leads left to the peninsula where two crescent-shaped beaches are separated by a thin spit of land. And if the weather's good enough for a picnic, make sure you try some of the island's famously distinctive cheese.

Campbeltown and around

At the southern end of the Kintyre Peninsula is **Campbeltown**. This may be the largest town by far in this part of Argyll, but it has a real end-of-the-line feel, due in part to its geographical isolation, but also because the town has long since lost its raison d'être – whisky. Six miles from Campbeltown, on the west coast of Kintyre, is **Machrihanish**, site of Campbeltown's airport and a magnificent beach – five miles of glorious unspoiled sand backed by dunes and washed by gigantic Atlantic breakers. Not surprisingly, this is a cracking place for windsurfing and surfing; one of the very best in the country, in fact. It also boasts a dramatic 18-hole championship golf course. The beach can be approached either by walking north from the village, or south from the car park on the main A83 to Tayinloan and Tarbert, where it leaves the coast.

If the weather's good, it's worth taking a walk up to **Beinn Ghulean**, which overlooks the town and loch. Follow the signs for the A83 to Machrihanish until you reach Witchburn Road. After passing the creamery on your left, turn left into Tomaig Road and continue till you come to a wooden gate. Cross over the stile and follow the track through the fields, crossing two more stiles, before you reach the Forest Enterprise sign which marks the start of the walk. It's about four miles there and back from the end of Tomaig Road.

One of the most popular day trips is to the uninhabited **Davaar Island**, connected to the peninsula by a tidal breakwater. Here you can see the cave painting of the Crucifixion, completed in secret by a local artist in 1877. The island can be visited at low tide from Kildalloig Point, a couple of miles east of town. Check tide times at the tourist office before setting out.

It's only a short drive south from Campbeltown to the tip of the peninsula, the Mull of Kintyre, eulogized by one-time resident Paul McCartney in the irritating eponymous hit single. There's nothing much to see in this bleak, storm-battered place, apart from the coast of Ireland, a mere 12 miles away and clearly visible on a good day. The road out to the lighthouse, built in 1788 and remodelled by Robert Stevenson, grandfather of Robert Louis, is pretty hairy, to put it mildly. It's possible to walk from here up to Machrihanish (about 10 miles), past the ruined township of **Balmavicar** and the **Largiebaan Bird Reserve**. The views are great and there's a chance of seeing golden eagles.

The southernmost village on Kintyre is **Southend**, a bleak, windswept place with a wide sandy beach. At the east end of the beach, jutting out on a rocky promontory, are the scant remains of **Dunaverty Castle**, once a MacDonald stronghold, where 300 Royalists were brutally massacred in 1647 by the Covenanting army of the Earl of Argyll, despite having already surrendered. To the west of Southend, below the cliffs, is the ruined 13th-century **Keil Chapel**, which is said to mark the spot where St Columba first set foot on Scottish soil, before heading north to Iona. Close by is a pair of footprints carved into the rock, known as Columba's footprints.

The slow and winding single track B842 meanders up the east coast from Campbeltown to Skipness and **Claonaig**, departure point for the ferry to Arran, see page 307. The scenery en route is gentle and pleasant, with nice views of Arran, and there are some worthwhile places to stop, but public transport is somewhat limited.

Ten miles up the coast are the idyllic ruins of **Saddell Abbey**, a Cistercian establishment founded by Somerled in 1160. The abbey fell into ruin in the early 16th century and much of the stone was used in the building of Saddell Castle for the Bishop of Argyll. Though little remains, there are some impressive medieval grave slabs, depicting knights, monks, ships, animals and other images.

A few miles further north is the village of **Carradale**, the only place of any size on the east coast, nestling in the sandy sweep of beautiful Carradale Bay. There are several pleasant marked walks through the woods between the B842 and the shore. The shortest of these walks (with green waymarkers) starts from the Network Centre (see below) and is a mile long. There's a three-mile walk with red waymarkers which starts at the Port Na Storm car park and follows the forest road to the left. After 150 yds the route turns left again at the road junction. A mile further on, you turn right off the road and follow the track up to the summit of Cnoc-nan Gabhor, from where there are great views of Kintyre and across to Arran. A third walk (six miles; blue waymarkers) also starts from the Port Na Storm car park. This time the route heads right at the junction 150 yds beyond the car park and then runs north along the shore, with a chance of seeing dolphins and basking shark. The path then swings west towards the road, then turns south with views of Carradale Glen.

Twelve miles north of Carradale the B842 ends at **Claonaig**, which is actually nothing more than a slipway for the ferry to Arran, see below. From here the B8001 heads west to meet the A83 near the Kennacraig ferry pier. A dead-end road runs north for a few miles to the tiny village of **Skipness**, where you can visit the substantial ruins of the 13th-century Skipness Castle and nearby chapel.

Cowal Peninsula and the Clyde Coast

→ *Colour map 3, grid C5-6.*

The Cowal Peninsula reaches out into the Firth of Clyde, framed by Loch Fyne and Loch Long. This is the most visited part of Argyll due to its proximity to Glasgow, but, despite the summer hordes, much of it is undisturbed. Most people head straight for Dunoon, the main ferry port and one of the major Clyde seaside resorts, leaving more adventurous souls to enjoy the forests and mountains of Argyll Forest Park in the north or the peace and tranquillity of the southwest coastline. ▸▸ *For Sleeping, Eating and other listings, see pages 304-307.*

Argyll Forest Park

The northern part of the peninsula is largely covered by the sprawling Argyll Forest Park which extends from Loch Lomond south to Holy Loch. This area contains the most stunning scenery in Cowal, and includes the **Arrochar Alps**, a range of rugged peaks north of Glen Croe which offer some of the best climbing in Argyll. The most famous of these is Ben Arthur (2,891 ft), better known as **The Cobbler**. Rather less imposing are the hills south of Glen Croe, between Loch Goil and Loch Long, in an area known as Argyll's Bowling Green (not because it's flat, but an English corruption of the Gaelic Baile na Greine, meaning 'Sunny Hamlet'). There are also numerous footpaths and cycle tracks threading their way through the park, and details of these can be found in the Forestry Commission leaflets available at the tourist office in Ardgarten.

Arrochar to Dunoon

The gateway to Cowal, Arrochar, sits at the head of Loch Long on the main A83, only a few miles west of Tarbet and the shores of Loch Lomond. It's a small, unremarkable place but the setting is dramatic, with The Cobbler towering overhead. A few miles beyond Arrochar, on the shores of Loch Long, is **Ardgarten**, where there's a tourist office and visitor centre ① *T01863-702342, daily Apr-Oct 1000-1700, till 1800 in Jul and Aug*, and provides useful advice and information on hillwalking and wildlife, as well as organizing various activities. From Ardgarten the A83 climbs steeply up Glen Croe to reach one of Scotland's classic viewpoints at the top of the pass, the **Rest and be Thankful**. The hordes of like-minded tourists, eager for that memorable photograph, cannot detract from the majestic views of the surrounding craggy peaks. Here the road forks. The A83 continues towards **Inveraray**, see page 296, and the single-track B828 heads southwest to meet the B839, which runs down to the village of Lochgoilhead, in a beautiful setting on Loch Goil. There are several hotels and B&Bs as well as an unsightly village of self-catering holiday chalets next door. At the end of the road, several miles down the west side of Loch Goil, are the ruins of 15th-century **Castle Carrick**.

The A83 meanwhile runs down through **Glen Kinglas** to reach the village of **Cairndow**, at the head of Loch Fyne. A mile or so further on towards Inveraray, at **Clachan**, at the head of Loch Fyne, is the highly acclaimed **Loch Fyne Oyster Bar**, see page 306. At the southern end of Loch Eck, at Benmore, is the **Younger Botanic Garden** ① *T01369-706261, 1 Mar-31 Oct daily 0930-1800, £3, concession £2.50, children £1*, a lovely woodland garden and offshoot of the Royal Botanic Garden in Edinburgh. Its 140 acres are laid out with over 250 species of rhododendrons and feature an avenue of Giant Redwoods.

Dunoon

The largest town in Cowal, and indeed the largest in Argyll, with 13,000 inhabitants, is Dunoon, one-time favourite holiday destination for Glaswegians, who came in their hordes on board the many paddle steamers that sailed "doon the watter" from Glasgow. Dunoon still attracts visitors, albeit in much smaller numbers, but the town has fallen on desperately hard times with the recent closure of the US nuclear submarine base on nearby Holy Loch, which was the town's life blood. Nevertheless, the town still comes to life during the **Cowal Highland Gathering**, see page 306.

The southwest

One of the most beautiful parts of Argyll is the southwest of Cowal, particularly the route down to the little village of **Tighnabruaich**. The A8003 runs down the west side of Loch Riddon and there are few lovelier sights than the view from this road across the **Kyles of Bute**, the narrow straits that separate Cowal from the island of Bute. Tighnabruaich gets busy in the summer with visitors who come here to enjoy the best sailing on the west coast. A few miles southwest of Kames, is **Portavadie**, on the west coast of Cowal. A CalMac car and passenger ferry sails from here to Tarbert, on the Kintyre Peninsula, saving a lot of time if you're heading for the islands of Islay, Jura or Colonsay.

Helensburgh

Overlooking the Clyde is the town of Helensburgh, its wide, grid-plan streets lined with elegant Georgian houses. The town is most famously known for its connection with the great Glasgow architect, **Charles Rennie Mackintosh**. In the upper part of the town is **Hill House** ⓘ *Upper Colquhoun St, T01436-673900, Apr-Oct daily 1330-1730, £8, concession £6*, one of the best examples of Mackintosh's work. The house was designed for Glasgow publisher Walter Blackie in 1902-1904, and is now owned by the National Trust for Scotland. The house is a masterpiece of balanced perfection and artistry and there's much to admire. The attention to detail, the use of natural light, the symbolism of the floral patterns and use of light and dark – hallmarks of his personal art nouveau style – are all very much in evidence. After exploring the house, you can visit the kitchen, which has been tastefully converted into a tearoom ⓘ *1330-1630*. To get there from the Central Train Station, walk about a mile and a half up Sinclair Street, then turn left at Kennedy Street and follow the signs. From Helensburgh Upper Station, it's a five-minute walk.

Isle of Bute

Barely a stone's throw off the south coast of Cowal is the island of Bute, another favourite holiday destination for people from Glasgow and Ayrshire, who come here in droves during the busy summer months. But though the island is small (15 miles long by five miles wide), it's deceptively easy to escape the hordes, who tend to congregate around the east coast resort of Rothesay, leaving the delights of the sparsely populated west coast free for those who enjoy a bit of peace and quiet. » *For Sleeping, Eating and other listings, see pages 304-307.*

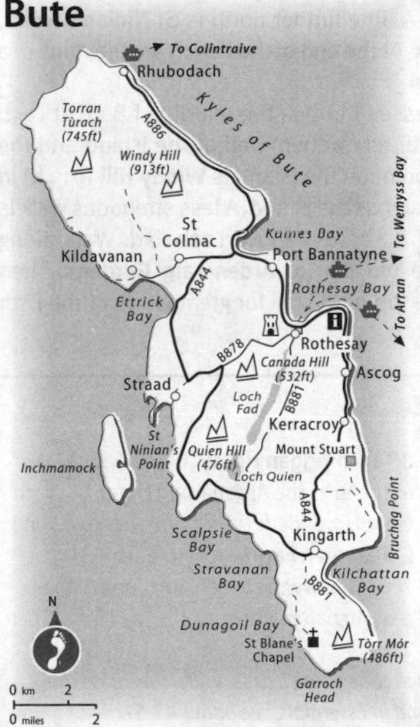

Rothesay

The sole town on Bute is Rothesay, with its handsome period mansions lining the broad sweep of bay, its elegant promenade lined with palm trees and the distinctive 1920s **Winter Gardens**, now refurbished and housing a cinema and restaurant, as well as the TIC. **Rothesay Castle** ⓘ *Apr-Sep Mon-Sat 0930-1830, Sun 1400-1830, Oct-Mar Mon-Sat 0930-1630, Sun 1400-1630 closed Oct-Dec Thu and Fri, Jan-Mar Thu afternoons, Fri and Sun morning, £2.50, concession £1.90, children £0.75*. One thing you must do before leaving Rothesay is spend a penny in the palatial **Victorian public toilets** ⓘ *Easter-Sep, 0800-2100, Oct-Mar 0900-1700, £0.15*. Rather more than that (£300,000 to be exact) has already been spent on restoring this architectural gem to its former glory. Gents get the best deal but the ladies can also take a peek.

Mount Stuart

ⓘ *T01700-503877, www.mountstuart.com, Easter weekend and May-Sep/Oct daily except Tue and Thu, gardens 1000-1800, house 1100-1700, hours vary every year so check in advance, house/gardens £7, children £3.*

One of Bute's main attractions is Mount Stuart, a unique Victorian Gothic house set in 300 acres of lush woodland gardens, three miles south of Rothesay. This magnificent architectural fantasy reflects the Third Marquess of Bute's passion for astrology, astronomy, mysticism and religion, and the sheer scale and grandeur of the place almost beggars belief. This is truly one of the great country houses of Scotland and displays breathtaking craftsmanship in marble and stained glass, as well as a fine collection of family portraits and Italian antiques. Much of the existing house dates from 1877, and was built following a terrible fire which destroyed the original, built in 1719 by the Second Earl of Bute. Equally impressive are the landscaped gardens and woodlands, established by the Third Earl of Bute (1713-1792), who advised on the foundation of Kew Gardens in London, and the stunning new visitor centre. It's worth spending a whole day here in order to take in the amazing splendour of the house and to explore the beautiful gardens. And if the weather's fine, why not bring a picnic and enjoy the wonderful sea views.

Other sights around the island

Just before Mount Stuart is the tidy little village of **Kerracroy**, designed by the wife of the Second Marquess of Bute and featuring an interesting mix of building styles. South of Mount Stuart and the village of Kingarth is **Kilchattan Bay**, an attractive bay of pink sands and the start of a fine walk down to Glencallum Bay, in the southeastern corner of the island.

Southwest of Kilchattan Bay is **St Blane's Chapel**, a 12th-century ruin in a beautifully peaceful spot near the southern tip of the island. The medieval church stands on the site of an earlier monastery, established in the sixth century by St Blane, nephew of St Catan, after whom Kilchattan is named. The ruin can be reached by road from Rothesay, or as part of the walk from Kilchattan Bay (see above). Four miles north of St Blane's, on the west coast, is **Scalpsie Bay**, the nicest beach on the island and a good place for seal-spotting. A little further north is **St Ninian's Point**, looking across to the island of **Inchmarnock**. At the end of the beach are the ruins of a sixth-century chapel, dedicated to St Ninian.

The Highland-Lowland dividing line passes through the middle of Bute at Loch Fad, which separates the hilly and uninhabited northern half of the island and the rolling farmland of the south. The highest point on the island is **Windy Hill** (913 ft) in the north, from where there are great views across the island. A less strenuous walk is up **Canada Hill**, a few miles southwest of Rothesay, above Loch Fad. Walk along Craigmore promenade and turn off at the old pier to **Ardencraig Gardens**. Then continue uphill along the golf course to the top of the hill for great views of the Firth of Clyde.

Sleeping

Loch Awe and Loch Etive *p294*

L **Ardanaiseig Hotel**, T01499-833333, www.ardanaiseig-hotel.com. 3 miles east of Kilchrenan village on an unclassified road. Open Feb-Dec. The most luxurious place to stay, and the best place to eat.

B **Taychreggan Hotel**, T01499-833211. Not as grand as the Ardanaiseig Hotel, but with equally wonderful views and superb cuisine.

C **Blarcreen Farm**, Archattan, T01631-750272, www.blarcreenfarm.com. A mile past Archattan Priory on the road from Oban

For an explanation of sleeping and eating price codes used in this guide, see inside the front cover. Other relevant information is found in Essentials, see pages 43-51.

to Bonawe. Elegant Victorian farmhouse standing on its own surrounded by lovely countryside. Beautiful rooms and superb cuisine. Recommended.

Inveraray and around *p296*

L Crinan Hotel, T01546-830261, www.crinanhotel.com. One of the most beautifully located hotels in the country, at the end of the Crinan canal with views across to Jura. Pampering at its most decadent and a sensational restaurant make it worth the expense.

A Fernpoint Hotel, T01499-302170, fernpoint.hotel@virgin.net. Lovely Georgian house overlooking the loch. Specializes in vegetarian food.

B Cairnbaan Hotel, T01546-603668, F606045. Lovely 18th-century coaching inn overlooking the Crinan Canal in the village of Cairnbaan, just north of Lochgilphead. Very good food in the restaurant.

B George Hotel, Main St, T01499-302111. 18th-century building with tasteful, spacious and comfortable rooms, a cosy bar and excellent food. Recommended.

D Bellanoch House, Bellanoch Bay, on the B841 near Crinan, T01546-830149, house@bellanoch.free-online.co.uk. Italian-owned Gothic mansion overlooking the canal basin. Great location. Dinner served on request.

D Kilmartin Hotel, opposite the church in Kilmartin village, T01546-510250, F606370. Comfortable and serves meals all day.

D Tigh-na-Glaic, Crinan, T01546-830245. On a hill behind the Crinan Hotel. Great views at a fraction of the cost. Friendly and comfortable.

Kintyre *p299*

L-A Stonefield Castle Hotel, 3 miles north of Tarbert, on the A82 to Lochgilphead, T01880-820836, F820929. Price includes dinner. A Baronial Victorian mansion set in acres of woodland garden, with great views across the loch.

B Columba Hotel, on East Pier Rd, Tarbert, T/F01880-820808, www.columbahotel.com. 10 rooms. On the waterfront with restaurant and bar.

C Gigha Hotel, Ardminish on Gigha, T01583-505254, F505244, open Mar-Oct, offers comfort, great views and good bar food.

C Kilberry Inn, west of Tarbert on the B8024, T01880-770223, www.kilberry inn.com. 3 rooms, open Easter-Oct. Offers superb food and perfect peace.

C Tayinloan Inn, at the ferry port of Tayinloan, 01583-T441233, a small and cosy 18th-century coaching inn.

E Post Office House, T01583-505251, a short walk from the ferry. The McSporrans also run the post office and general store, provide good home cooking and even rent out bikes.

Cowal Peninsula and the Clyde Coast *p301*

B Ardfillayne House, a mile south of Dunoon on the Innellan Rd, T01369-702267, www.argyll-business.directory.com. Atmospheric Victorian country house surrounded by 16 acres of woodland gardens and offering fine Scottish/French cooking (booking required).

C Kames Hotel, Kames, T01700-811489, tcandrew@aol.com. Great views and live music in the bar.

C The Royal Hotel, Tighnabruaich, T01700-811239, royalhotel@btinternet.com, on the waterfront, with a multi-gym and sauna, and restaurant.

F SYHA youth hostel, T01700-811622, open Apr-Sep, sits high above the village with great views across the Kyles and is often full.

Isle of Bute *p303*

A Balmory Hall, 3 miles south of Rothesay, at Ascog, T/F01700-500669, www.balmory hall.com. Superior guest house, with elegant and sumptuous rooms. The 7-course breakfast is an event in itself.

B Cannon House Hotel, Battery Pl, Rothesay, T01700-502819, F505725. A comfortable Georgian townhouse. Convenient for the ferry.

E Ascog Farm, 3 miles south of town, at Ascog, T01700-503372. Feng shui farmhouse offering excellent-value. Very friendly.

E Kingarth Hotel, Kingarth in the south of the island, T01700-831662, simon@kingarth hotel.com. Quiet, unassuming little hotel not far from the beach. Does good bar meals (**££**). Great value. Stella McCartney's hubby-to-be had his stag night here, attended by Macca himself and his rock-star chums.

Eating

Inveraray and around *p296*
££ Loch Fyne Oyster Bar, T01499-600264. About 9 miles east of Inveraray on the A83 near Clachan. This restaurant, shop and smokehouse is the best for miles and popular with many local celebs who travel all the way from Glasgow to sample their classy crustacea. Open Nov-Mar daily 0900-1800, from mid-Mar onwards 0900-2100 (booking essential at weekends).

Cowal Peninsula and the Clyde Coast *p301*
££ Chatters, 58 John St, Dunoon, T01369-706402. Aside from the hotels in town the best food can be found at this informal and outstanding little restaurant offering French-style Scottish cuisine. Mon-Sat.

Isle of Bute *p303*
££ The Bistro, Discovery Centre, Winter Gardens, T01700-505500. Handily placed for the ferry, this modern-style bistro serves up contemporary Scottish cooking in a relaxed atmosphere.
£ West End Café, 1-3 Gallowgate, Rothesay, T01700-503596. It is a must while you are on Bute to sample the fish and chips at this award-winning chippie. It's open all year round except Mon.

Festivals and events

May The **Isle of Bute Jazz Festival** is held during the May Bank Holiday weekend.
Jul There's also the **Isle of Bute International Folk Festival** and **World Ceilidh Band Championships**, a massive festival of music and dance held over the third weekend in Jul.
Aug If you're around Campbeltown at the end of Aug, don't miss the **Mull of Kintyre Music Festival**, 3 days of the best in traditional Celtic music, held throughout the town. **Dunoon Highland Games**, held on the last weekend of the month, are the world's largest and culminate in a spectacular march of massed pipes and drums through the streets.
Sep Tarbert hosts an excellent **folk music festival**, over a weekend at the end of the month. For details, call T01880-820343.

Activities and tours

Loch Awe and Loch Etive *p294*
Boat trips Loch Etive Cruises, T01866-822430, cruises depart at 1000 and 1200 (1 ½ hr cruise) and 1400 (3-hr cruise), Easter-Oct Sun-Fri, Apr and Oct at 1400 only. 1 ½ hr cruise £5, children £3; 3- hr cruise £9, children £5. No booking necessary but arrive in plenty of time. The departure point is beyond the Bonawe Heritage Site. The 3-hr cruise is very highly recommended.
Fishing Lochawe Boats, The Boat House, Ardbrecknish, by Dalmally, T01866-833256. From £15 per day for a rowing boat up to £45 for a motor boat with cabin. Canoes also for hire.

Inverary and around *p296*
Boat trips Gemini Cruises, based at Crinan harbour, T/F01546-830238, www.gemini-crinan.co.uk, take out boat trip offerering 2-hr wildlife spotting cruises round Loch Craignish or longer trips out to the Gulf of Corrievreckan. The trips cost £11 (2-hrs), children £7.50; £18/11 (4-hrs).
Vic 32, the last functioning Clyde 'puffer' on the west coast, are available through Rachel and Nick Walker, The Change House, Crinan Ferry, Lochgilphead, T01546-510232, www.highlandsteamboats.com. They run five-day summer cruises on the west coast on board this 85-ft vessel. Prices is £475 pp and includes all meals and bed linen.
Horse riding Argyll Riding, Dalchenna Farm, 2 miles south of Inveraray on A83, T01499-302611, www.horserides.co.uk. Riding school, trekking and hacking tours.
Argyll Trail Riding, Brenfield Farm, Ardrishaig, T01546-603274, www.brenfield.co.uk. Riding trails, pub trails and beach gallops, week-long stays and lessons. Also clay-pigeon shooting.
Walking tour Tales on the Hoof, www.ansgeulaiche.co.uk. Storytelling tours of Kilmartin Glen, £5, children £2.50. Book through the TIC in Oban or Lochgiphead.

Transport

Inverary and around *p296*
There are buses from **Lochgilphead** to **Cairnbaan**, **Crinan**, **Achnamara** and **Tayvallich** several times daily Mon-Sat.

There are buses and taxis to **Oban** via **Kilmartin** (Mon-Sat) and a postbus to **Inveraray** (Mon-Sat). There's a service to and from **Ardrishaig**. See also Kintyre below for buses from Glasgow.

Crinan Cycles, 34 Argyll St, Lochgilphead, T01546-603511. Bikes for rent from £12 per day, also parts and repairs and will advise on routes and provide maps. Mon-Sat 0930-1730.

Mid Argyll Taxis, 4 Slockavullin, Kilmartin, T01546-510318, for taxi hire.

Kintyre *p299*
There are 2 flights daily (35 mins), all year round from Glasgow to **Machrihanish** airport. For times and reservations, contact British Airways Express, T08457-733377.

There are several daily buses from Glasgow to **Campbeltown** (4½ hrs) (via **Inveraray**, **Lochgilphead**, **Kennacraig** and **Tarbert**). There are buses from Campbeltown to **Machrihanish** (hourly Mon-Sat, 3 on Sun; 15 mins), to **Carradale** (45 mins) and **Saddell** (4 daily Mon-Sat, 2 on Sun; 25 mins), to **Southend** (several daily; 25 mins).

There is a car and passenger ferry from Portavadie on the Cowal peninsula to **Tarbert** (25 mins, £2.90 per passenger, £13.15 per car), which leaves daily every hour in summer, less frequently in winter. There are ferries from **Lochranza** on Arran from **Claonaig** on the west coast of Kintyre, south of Kennacraig (see p) several times daily (30 mins, £4.25 per passenger, £19 per car). Ferries leave from **Kennacraig**, 5 miles south of Tarbert, to **Islay** (see p332) and to **Colonsay** (see p). A small car and passenger ferry leaves from Tayinloan to the ferry pier at Ardminish on Gigha, daily all year round (hourly 0800-1800 Mon-Sat, 1100-1700 Sun), 20 mins, £5 per passenger, £18.85 per car.

Cowal Peninsula and the Clyde Coast *p301*
To Dunoon there ferries every 30 mins from **Gourock**, with train connections to and from Gourock to **Glasgow Central**, 20 mins, £2.95 one way per person, £7.25 per car.

Isle of Bute *p303*
The service provided by Western Buses is fairly good, though limited on Sun. The best way to see Bute is by bike; the island is fairly flat, the roads are quiet and in good condition.

Bute is easily accessible from **Glasgow**. Take a train from Glasgow Central to the ferry terminal at **Wemyss Bay** (1 hr 10 mins), and from there it's a 35-min crossing to Rothesay. They leave every 45 mins from 0715 till 1945 (later on Fri, Sat and Sun), 35 mins, £3.45 one way per passenger, £13.85 per car. For times, T01700-502707.

There are also buses to Rothesay from **Tighnabruaich** in southwest Cowal once or twice a day Mon-Thu (1 hr). For times, contact Western Buses, T01631-502076. A car/passenger ferry makes the 5-min crossing from **Colintraive** to **Rhubodach**, at the northern end of Bute, daily every half hour or hour; from 0530-1955 Mon-Sat and 0900-1955 Sun in the summer (21 Apr-27 Aug). It costs £1.10 one way per person and £7 per car.

Isle of Arran

➔ *Phone code: 01770. Colour map 5, grid A-B3.*

In the wedge of sea between Ayrshire and Kintyre lies the oval-shaped and very beautiful island of Arran. It manages to combine the classic features of the Northwest Highlands with the more sedate pleasures of the Southern Lowlands, thus earning the sobriquet, 'Scotland in Miniature'. This obvious appeal, coupled with its easy accessibility, makes Arran a very popular destination, but it remains unspoiled, and at 25 miles long is big enough never to feel crowded. ➤➤ *For Sleeping, Eating and other listings, see pages 311-312.*

Ins and outs

Getting there The main ferry route to Arran is from the distinctly unappealing Ayrshire town of Ardrossan to the island's main town, Brodick. There are train connections from Glasgow and bus connections from Edinburgh to Ardrossan. The other ferry route is from Claonaig, near Skipness, to Lochranza in the north of the island. » *For further details, see Transport page 312.*

Getting around It's possible to explore the island using public transport, as there are regular bus and postbus services.

Tourist information Brodick Tourist Information Centre ⓘ *beside the pier and bus terminal, T01770-302140, www.ayrshire-arran.com, Mar-Sep Mon-Sat 0900-1930, Sun 0900-1700, also open daily in winter, all hours vary so check beforehand.*

Brodick

The largest and busiest settlement on Arran, and main ferry port, is Brodick, lying in a wide bay (hence its Norse name *breidr vik*, meaning 'broad bay') backed by a range of steep crags. It's not the most attractive village on the island, and consists of little more than one long street that sweeps round the bay, but you'll find a wide range of tourist facilities and services here.

A few miles north of town is the impressive **Brodick Castle** ⓘ *T01770-302202, castle and restaurant 1 Apr-30 Jun and 1 Sep-31 Oct, daily 1100-1630, 1 Jul-31 Aug, daily 1100-1700, garden and country park all year, daily 0930-1700 (park till sunset), castle, garden and country park £8, £6 concession, garden and country park only £3,* one of the island's top sights and a flagship NTS property. Until recently this was the family seat of the Dukes of Hamilton, erstwhile owners of the island. The oldest part of the castle dates from the 13th century, with extensions added in the 16th, 17th and

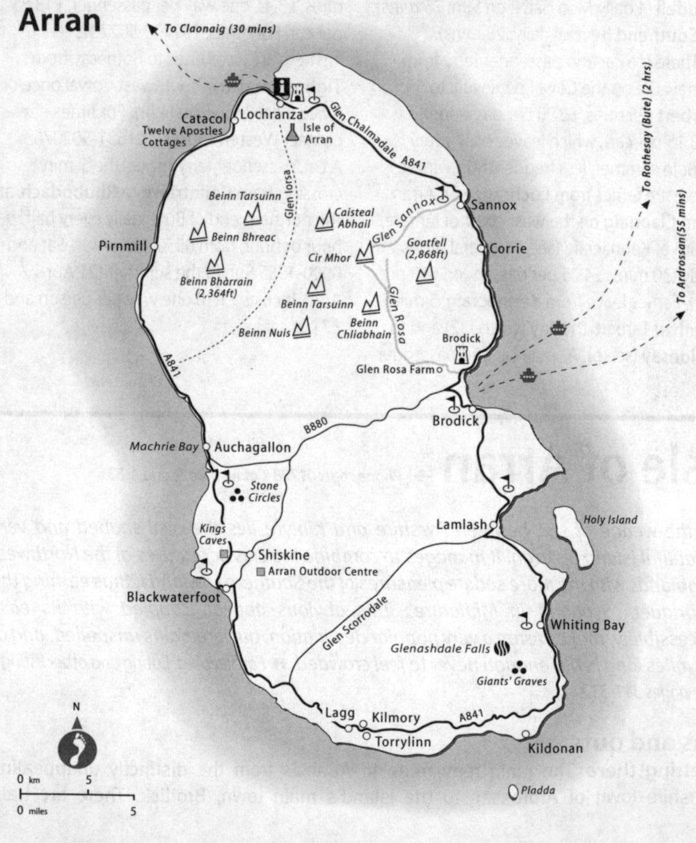

19th centuries. The hour-long tour of the sumptuously furnished rooms and kitchens is interesting and can be rounded off with a visit to the castle restaurant, where you can enjoy home-cooked meals or light snacks. On a good day you can sit outside on the castle terrace and have lunch whilst admiring the views. The walled garden is worth a look, and the surrounding country park includes 11 miles of way-marked trails.

Halfway between the village and the castle is the **Arran Heritage Museum** ⓘ *T01770-302636, www.arranmuseum.co.uk, Apr-Oct daily 1000-1630, £2.25, £1 children*, an interesting diversion which explains the island's archaeology, geology and social history. There's also a very good café.

South Arran

The south of Arran is a fertile landscape of rolling hills and pretty little seaside villages, where you'll find the bulk of the island's population and tourists. A few miles south of Brodick is **Lamlash**, a quiet and attractive place set in a wide, sheltered bay but with an unappealing mud beach.

Lying just offshore is the humpbacked **Holy Island**, which is owned by a group of Scottish Buddhists who have retired here for peace and meditation. A ferry runs to and from the island several times daily from 1 May to 4 September (limited service 5 September to 30 October). The first ferry departs Lamlash at 1000 and the last one returns at 1715, leaving you just enough time to climb up to the highest point, **Mullach Mór** (1,030 ft).

The little fishing village of **Blackwaterfoot** is set round a bay with a tiny harbour. Two miles north along the coast are the **King's Caves**, where, according to legend, Robert the Bruce watched a spider try, try and try again and was thus inspired to secure his own and Scotland's destiny. It's a 45-minute walk from where you leave the car to the cathedral-like main cave, which has an iron gate to keep out wandering sheep.

Four miles north of Blackwaterfoot, off the main coast road, is **Machrie Moor**, site of the most impressive of Arran's Bronze-Age **stone circles**. Park by the Historic Scotland sign and then walk for one and a half miles along the farm track to reach an area boasting no fewer than six stone circles. Many of them are barely visible above the ground, but the tallest is over 18 ft high. A few miles further on, just south of the turn-off to Machrie village, is another Historic Scotland sign, this time for **Moss Farm Road Stone Circle**, which lies about a half mile walk along the farm track.

North Arran

The north half of Arran contrasts sharply with the southern part. It looks and feels more like the Scottish Highlands – desolate, unspoiled and much of it accessible only to the serious hillwalker. But though the north is scenically more spectacular, it attracts few visitors. Six miles north of Brodick is Arran's loveliest village, **Corrie.** Corrie has a couple of hotels and B&Bs, a good pub, and makes an attractive alternative to Brodick as a starting point for the ascent of Goatfell. The main coastal road continues north from Corrie to **Sannox,** with its sandy beach, then it cuts inland and climbs northwest towards Lochranza. It's worth taking your time to admire the view and on the other side of the pass, in **Glen Chalmadale**, you can see red deer heading down to the shore at dusk.

The most spectacular introduction to Arran is to arrive at **Lochranza**, the most northerly village and second ferry port. This charming village is guarded by its ruined 13th-century castle and backed by looming mountains. **Lochranza Castle** can be visited free of charge (the key is available from the **Lochranza Stores**). Lochranza is also the site of Scotland's newest distillery, **Isle of Arran Distillers** ⓘ *T01770-830264, www.arranwhisky.com, Apr-Oct daily 1000-1800, £3.50, £2.50 concessions,* which opened in 1995 and is the first legal whisky distillery on the island for over 150 years. There are guided tours of the distillery, followed by the obligatory dram, and also an excellent restaurant, see Eating page 312.

Walks on Arran → *OS map No 69 covers these walks.*

Arran is a hill walker's paradise. The north part of the island boasts ten peaks of over 2,000 ft and dozens of ridge walks while the gentler south features a variety of less strenuous forest walks. Note that you should only attempt these routes in good weather and avoid climbing any rockfaces. Some ridge walks – A'Chir, Witches Step, Suidhe Fherghas and Cioch Na Oighe – involve quite a lot of scrambling and can be dangerous. They should only be attempted by fit and experienced climbers. Ropes and good OS maps should also be taken. Ask local advice during the deer stalking season (late August to late October).

The **Glenashdale Falls and Giants' Graves walk** is one of the most popular on the island. It's a steady, easy climb through woodland with the considerable incentive of a beautiful waterfall at the end of it. Both walks can be done together and should take around two to three hours in total, though you should allow some time to enjoy the falls. If you want to take a picnic, pop into the Village Shop which has a wide range of deli-type foods and local cheeses. The trail starts by the bridge over Glenashdale Burn, next to the Youth Hostel. There's a map board here showing the route. Walk up the track alongside the burn till you see the sign for the path leading to the left up to the Giants' Graves. It's about 40 to 45 minutes up to the graves and back to this point, but it's a stiff climb up a steep staircase of 265 steps. At the top continue left along a path through the trees, which then curves right till you reach a clearing and the graves, which are chambered tombs, believed to be around 5,000 years old. Depending on the light, this can be a very eerie, but almost magical place. Return back down the steps, and head left along the main path as it climbs steadily above the burn, past smaller falls, till you reach the main falls. The setting is stunning and the falls are spectacular as they plummet 140 ft into the pools below. You can rest and have a picnic at the top of the falls, or follow the paths down to the pools below which you can swim. The path back down to Whiting Bay passes the scant remains of an Iron-Age fort, then turns back uphill to reach a broad track. Turn right, cross a small burn by stepping stones, then follow the track downhill all the way to the main road, a short way along from the car park.

Arran's most popular peak, **Goatfell**, is also its highest, at 2,866 ft. There's a path leading up from Corrie, but most people begin the walk from the car park at Cladach sawmill, near Brodick Castle. The path is well marked, easy to follow and, apart from the final section, relatively easy. It runs initially through the Brodick Country Park,

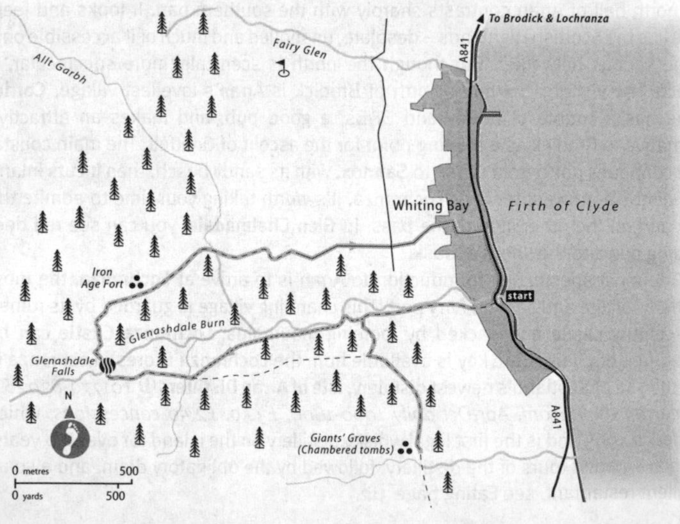

then follows the Cnocan burn as it rises steadily through woodland before crossing the Mill burn. Beyond the burn is a deer fence which runs across the entire island to keep the deer from the north away from the farming in the south. Above the deer fence the landscape changes to heather moorland and the path begins to climb the flanks of the mountain. The final 650 ft up to the top is steep and rocky and the path is not always clear. The last section requires some scrambling on loose scree but the views that greet you at the top on a clear day are magnificent, stretching right across from Ireland to Mull. The walk to the summit and back should take about five hours. Though it's considered a fairly straightforward ascent, remember that this should be treated with the same caution and respect as any Scottish mountain. You should be dressed and equipped appropriately and be prepared for any sudden change in the weather. There are also numerous ridge walks around Goatfell as well as other high peaks to climb.

Many of the walks start from Glen Rosa Farm. One of these takes in the three Beinns; **Beinn Nuis, Beinn Tarsuinn** (2,681 ft) and **Beinn A'Chliabhain**. Start at Glen Rosa Farm and go up the Wood Road to the High Deer Gate, then to Torr Breac and the 'Y' junction at the top of the Garbhalt and on to the path which runs round the Three Beinns. This is a full day's walk.

Another excellent walk is from Glen Rosa to the head of the Glen; then take the path up into the Coire Buidhe and on to the ridge between **Cir Mhor** (2,617 ft) and **A'Chir** (known as the Ceems Ridge). Then follow the path around the west side of A'Chir. This is not easy to find, but takes you around the back of A'Chir to Bowman's Pass and the north end of Beinn Tarsuinn. From here take the path to Beinn A'Chliabhan and down to the foot of Garbhalt Ridge and back down to Glen Rosa.

Cir Mhor can also be climbed from Glen Rosa. Before going over into Glen Sannox take the steep path straight up. On the way back down, head into Coire Buidhe and back down the glen. You can also continue from the top of Cir Mhor and take the path around the west side of A'Chir to the north end of the Bowman's Pass up on to Beinn Tarsuinn and along the ridge to Beinn Nuis, then down the path to the Garbhalt Bridge.

Finally, you can also climb **Caisteal Abhail** (2,818 ft) from Glen Rosa. Go straight up into Coire Buidge on to the Ceems Ridge. Then take the path round the west side of the A'Chir through the Bowman's Pass and on to Beinn A'Chliabhain down the side of the Garbhalt to Glen Rosa.

There are also several walks in and around lovely **Glen Sannox**. It's a pleasant walk just to make your way up the head of the Glen and return the same way. You can walk up the Glen to beyond the old mine then make your way up towards the Devil's Punchbowl until you reach the main path and follow that down into the Coire. Take the main path back down into Glen Sannox instead of trying to climb out of the Devil's Punchbowl. You can also walk from Glen Sannox to Glen Rosa, which takes around four hours.

Sleeping

Brodick *p308*

A Kilmichael Country House Hotel, T01770-302219, www.kilmichael.com. 7 rooms. Take the road north towards the castle, turn left at the golf course and follow the signs for about a mile. Refined elegance in the island's oldest house. Their award-winning restaurant is the best on the island. Booking is essential for non-residents. No children under 12.

A Auchrannie Country House Hotel, just beyond the turning to Kilmichael, T01770-302234, www.auchrannie.co.uk. 28 rooms (also self-catering and time-share lodges). May lack the charm of Kilmichael but makes up for it with superb facilities and leisure complex. It also has a 36-bedroom spa resort. Their **Garden Restaurant** is also highly rated and the **Brambles Bistro** offers less expensive bar meals.

C Glen Cloy Farmhouse, Glen Cloy Rd, T01770-302351. A B&B a cut above the rest.

Camping

Glen Rosa, T01770-302380, open Apr-Oct, 2 miles from town on the road to Blackwaterfoot, is the nearest campsite.

South Arran *p309*

A Argentine House Hotel, Whiting Bay, T01770-700662, www.argentinearran.co.uk. 5 rooms, on the seafront and recognizable by the flags flying outside. Excellent cooking.

A-B Burlington Hotel, T01770-700255, www.milford.co.uk/go/burlingtonarran.html. 9 rooms, open Easter-Oct. Comfortable rooms and a reputation for superb seafood; moderately priced set 3-course dinner in dining room or à la carte in bistro.

North Arran *p309*

B Apple Lodge, Lochranza, T/F01770-830229. A lovely country house with 4 double rooms, offering home cooking for residents.

B Corrie Hotel, Corrie, T01770-810273. Friendly and good value with a lively bar.

C Castlekirk, Lochranza, T01770-830202, a converted church opposite the castle.

Camping

There's a campsite next to the golf course in Lochranza, with facilities, T01770-820273, office@lochgolf.demon.co.uk, Apr-Oct.

Eating

Brodick *p308*

£££-££ Creelers Seafood Restaurant, at the Home Farm, a mile or so north of town on the road to the castle, T01770-302810. Some of the best seafood in the whole country.

££-£ Brodick Bar, behind Wooley's bakery and opposite the post office. Superior pub grub served in the bar or in the restaurant next door.

North Arran *p309*

££ Harold's Restaurant, T01770-830264, arranvc@aol.com, in the distillery visitor centre. Here you can enjoy innovative Scottish/Caribbean cuisine. Open till 2100.

Transport

Local There are regular daily buses from **Brodick** to **Blackwaterfoot** (30 mins) via 'The String'; to **Lamlash** (10 mins) and **Whiting Bay** (25 mins) and on to **Blackwaterfoot** (1 hr, 10 mins); to **Corrie** (20 mins), **Sannox** (25 mins), **Lochranza** (45 mins), **Catacol** (50 mins), **Pirnmill** (1 hr), **Machrie** (1 hr, 10 mins) and **Blackwaterfoot** (1 hr, 20 mins). There's also a postbus service from **Brodick** to **Corrie**, **Sannox**, **Lochranza**, **Catacol**, **Pirnmill**, **Machrie**, **Blackwaterfoot** and back to Brodick; and from Brodick to **Lamlash**, **'The Ross'**, **Kildonan**, **Whiting Bay** and back to Brodick. For details of bus services to Claonaig, T01546-604695.

Arran is best appreciated on a bike, however. **Whiting Bay Hires**, on the jetty in Brodick, T01770-700382, hires out bikes. Whiting Bay Garage, T/F01770-700345, for car hire, taxis, or island tours.

Long distance The main ferry route is from **Ardrossan** to **Brodick**. CalMac car/passenger ferry makes the 55-min journey 5-6 times daily Mon-Sat, 4 times on Sun, 55 mins, £4.70 one-way per passenger, £33.50 per car. There's a regular train connection between Ardrossan and **Glasgow Central**. There's also a bus connection to and from **Edinburgh**. By car, from the south the main route to Arran is from the M74 motorway, on to the A71 via Kilmarnock, to Irvine and Ardrossan. For more ferry information, contact Ardrossan ferry office, T01294-463470, or Brodick, T01770-302166. The other ferry route to Arran is from **Claonaig**, near **Skipness**, to **Lochranza** in the north of the island. The non-bookable car/passenger ferry makes the 30-min trip 7 to 9 times daily during the summer (Apr-Oct), less frequently in winter, £4.25 per passenger, £19 per car. For ferry times, T08705-650000, www.calmac. co.uk; for reservations on sailings to Lochranza, T01880-730253.

Directory

Brodick *p308*

Banks Brodick has banks with ATMs but these are the only ones on the island.

Post The post office is just off the seafront, opposite the petrol station and pharmacy.

Mull and Iona → *Colour map 3, grid B3-4, C3-4.*

The island of Mull, a short hop from Oban, is the third largest of the Hebridean islands and, after Skye, the most popular. Everyone has their own favourite island, but Mull has enough going for it to appeal to most tastes: spectacular mountain scenery, 300 miles of wild coastline, castles, wildlife, a narrow-gauge railway, some of the best fishing in Scotland, and some of the prettiest little villages, all in an area roughly 24 miles from north to south and 26 miles from east to west. It's worth spending time on Mull to fully appreciate its pleasures and take the time to make a pilgrimage to tiny Iona, the most spiritual of places and one of the loveliest. ▸▸ *For Sleeping, Eating and other listings, see pages 321-324.*

Ins and outs

Getting there and around Mull is served by regular car/passenger ferry services, mostly from Oban but also from Kilchoan on the Ardnamurchan Peninsula and Lochaline on the Morvern Peninsula. Once on the island you can get to most parts of the island by bus. Services given in the Transport section are for April to October. Winter services are less frequent. There are regular five-minute sailings to and fro Iona. ▸▸ *For further details, see Transport page 323.*

Tourist information Craignure TIC ⓘ *opposite the pier in the same building as the CalMac office, T01680-812377, Easter-end Oct*. Tobermory TIC ⓘ *at the far end of Main St, T01688-302182, Apr-Sep*, is also in the same building as the CalMac office.

Mull

Craignure to Tobermory

The arrival point for visitors is the village of Craignure. One and a half miles south of here is **Torosay Castle** ⓘ *T01680-812421, easter-mid Oct daily 1030-1730, gardens open all year daily 0900-1900, £5*, more of a baronial family home than a full-blown castle. The best way to arrive at the castle is by the **Mull and West Highland Railway** ⓘ *T01680-812494, Easter-mid Oct, £3.75 return.*

A couple of miles east of Torosay is **Duart Castle** ⓘ *T01680-812309, May-mid Oct daily 1030-1800, £4*, the 13th-century ancestral seat of the Clan Maclean stands imperiously at the end of a promontory, commanding impressive views over Loch Linnhe and the Sound of Mull. The castle's main feature is the tower house, built in the late 14th century when it became the main residence of the Macleans of Duart. Today it's a fascinating place to visit, with many relics and artifacts on display. There's also an excellent tearoom serving delicious home-baked scones.

Midway between Craignure and Tobermory on the main A849 is the pretty village of **Salen**. It stands on the east coast at the narrowest point on the island, and is only three miles from the west coast, making it a good base from which to explore the island. There are a couple of interesting sights around Salen. Just to the north, overlooking the bay, is the ruin of **Aros Castle**, built in the 14th century and one of the strongholds of the Lords of the Isles. Tradition holds that the treasure of the Spanish galleon sunk in Tobermory Bay in 1588, see page 317, was recovered by the Macleans and still lies buried beneath the ruins of Aros Castle.

Four miles southwest of Salen, near Gruline and Loch Ba, is the **MacQuarrie Mausoleum**, which houses the remains of Major-General Lachlan MacQuarrie (1761-1824). He took over as Governer-General of New South Wales from the unpopular William Bligh, formerly of the *Bounty*, and became known as the 'Father of Australia'. The mausoleum is maintained by the NTS, on behalf of the National Trust of Australia.

There is no prettier port in the west of Scotland than Tobermory, Mull's main village. The brightly painted houses that line the harbour front date from the late 18th century when the British Fisheries Society built Tobermory as a planned herring port. It never really took off as a fishing port, however, and nowadays you're more likely to see pleasure yachts anchored in the protected waters of the natural harbour. Lying at the bottom of the harbour is a galleon of the Spanish Armada, which sank in mysterious circumstances, along with its treasure of gold doubloons which has eluded salvage crews ever since, see box. Not only is Tobermory the only Highland town to have a Womble named after it, it is also the setting for the BBC's hugely popular TV show, *Balamory*.

The harbour front – known as Main Street – is where you'll find most of what you want: hotels, guest houses, restaurants, pubs and shops and the tourist office. Mercifully, though, it's free from the tartan tat that blights so many other tourist

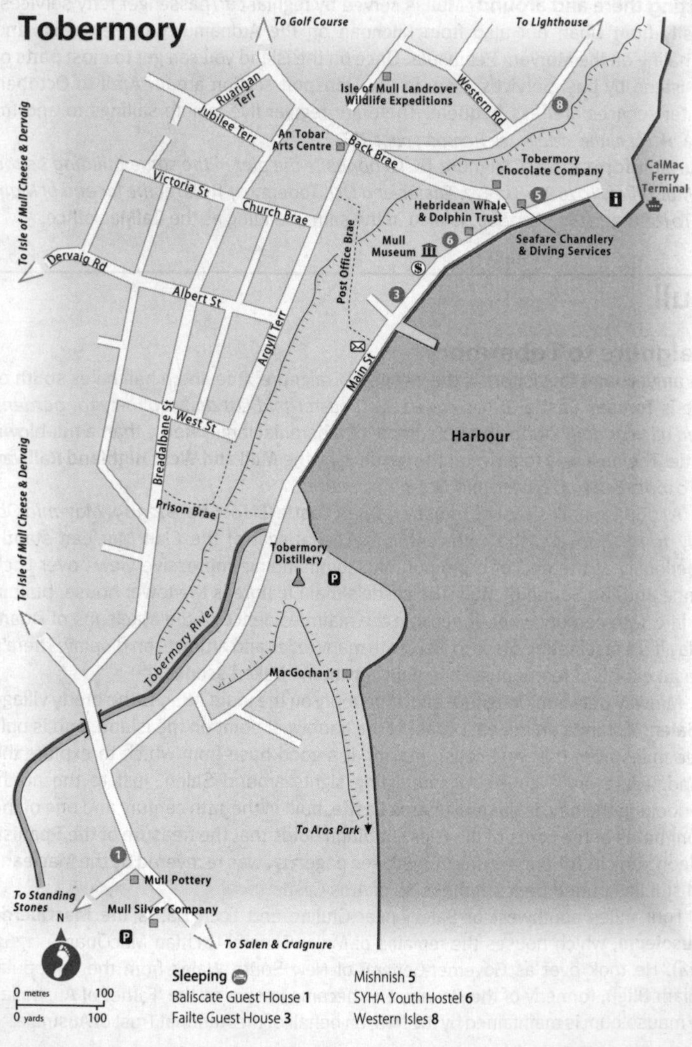

Things to do on Mull when it's wet

It rains a lot on Mull, but luckily there's a fairly large number of indoor options to keep you nice and dry until the weather changes. If you've just arrived off the ferry from Oban and it's chucking it down, then head straight for **Torosay Castle**, just to the south of Craignure. And if the weather changes whilst exploring the interior, don't miss the gardens. Just beyond the castle is **Wings Over Mull**, a bird of prey conservation centre which offers indoor hawk-handling and a chance to learn about the island's incredible bird life. Nearby is Mull's greatest fortification, **Duart Castle**, which is also worth a peek. If all that history gets too much then you could do worse than hole up in the bar of the **Craignure Inn** and relax in front of their roaring log fire.

In the north of the island, the most appealing option by far is the **Old Byre Heritage Centre**, not far from the picturesque village of Dervaig. When in Tobermory do as the locals do, and get yourself down to the **bar of the Mish**, though you shouldn't really need the excuse of inclement weather. Meanwhile, over in Fionnphort, the departure point for the pilgrimage to Iona, you can seek spiritual assistance with a wee dram in the cosy **Keel Row Bar**.

hot-spots. Here you'll find the **Mull Museum** ⓘ *T01688-302493, Easter-end Oct Mon-Fri 1030-1630, Sat 1030-1330, £1*, housed in an old bakery. It's worth visiting on a rainy day and you'll learn all about the island's history. At the foot of the main road down to the harbour is the tiny **Tobermory Distillery** ⓘ *T01688-302645, www.burnstewartdistillers.com, Easter to end-Oct Mon-Fri 1000-1700, Oct-Easter by appointment, £2.50, concession £1, children 18 free*, which offers a guided tour rounded off with a sampling of the island's single malt. At the top of Back Brae, on Argyll Terrace, is **An Tobar** ⓘ *T01688-302211, www.antobar.co.uk, Mon-Sat all year 1000-1800, free*, an excellent new arts centre housed in an old schoolhouse and featuring a varied programme of exhibitions, music and workshops. Or you can just have a coffee and admire the view.

The west coast

Mull's west coast is where you'll find some of the island's most stunning scenery. The B8073 winds its way anti-clockwise from Tobermory in a series of twists and turns as it follows the contours of the coastline. The road climbs west from Tobermory then makes a dramatic descent, with hairpin bends, to Dervaig.

Dervaig is a lovely village of whitewashed cottages, beautifully situated at the head of Loch Cuin. It has two very notable features. One is **Kilmore Church**, which has an unusual pencil-shaped spire. Dervaig's claim to fame, though, is the **Mull Little Theatre** ⓘ *T01688-400245, May-Sep*, the smallest professional theatre in Britain, with only 43 seats. It puts on an impressive programme of plays in the summer. One mile beyond Dervaig take the turn-off to Torloisk to reach the **Old Byre Heritage Centre** ⓘ *T01688-400229, Easter to end-Oct daily 1030-1830, £3, concession £2, children £1.50*, which stands out as one of the few genuinely interesting examples of these places. It also features a video of Mull's history and a tearoom, see Eating.

Five miles west of Dervaig is **Calgary Bay**, Mull's most beautiful beach ringed by steep wooded slopes with views across to Coll and Tiree. Calgary in Alberta, Canada was named after the former township. Many emigrants were forcibly shipped to Canada from here during the Clearances. There are some wonderful paths through Calgary Wood, just past **Calgary Farmhouse Hotel**, including a half hour circular walk.

Isle of Ulva

If you have the time and need to escape the hectic bustle of Mull, then take a day out on idyllic Ulva (meaning 'wolf island' in Norse), just off the west coast. You won't see any wolves around, but you're almost guaranteed to spot deer, golden eagles, buzzards and seals offshore. There are several woodland and coastal trails across the island, including one to the southwest where there are basalt columns similar to those on Staffa, or you can follow the trail to the top of the hill for views across to the Cuillins on Skye (on a clear day), or cross to Ulva's even smaller neighbour **Gometra** by a causeway. For more information on the island walks and on its history, visit the **Boathouse Heritage Centre** ⓘ *T01688-500241, ulva@mull.com, Easter-Oct Mon-Fri 0900-1700 and Sun Jun-Aug only, entry is included in the ferry fare (see Transport)*, close to the ferry slip on Ulva. There's also a tearoom where you can try the local oysters with Guinness.

Staffa

The tiny uninhabited island of Staffa, five miles off the west coast of Mull, is one of the most spectacular sights not just in Scotland but anywhere in the world. It consists of immense, hexagonal, basalt pillars which loom up out of the sea, like a giant pipe organ. Staffa was formed 60 million years ago by the slow cooling of Tertiary basalt lavas. These have been carved by the pounding sea into huge cathedral-like caverns such as the mightily impressive **Fingal's Cave**. The sound of the sea crashing against the black crystalline columns made such an impression on Felix Mendelssohn in 1829 that he immortalized the island in his *Hebrides Overture*. The composer was obviously aware of its original name in Gaelic, which means 'The Melodious Cave'. You can land on the island – if the weather is good enough – and walk into the cave via the causeway; an experience not be missed. But even if the seas are too rough, it's worth making the 90-minute boat trip just to witness the columns and cave.

Mull

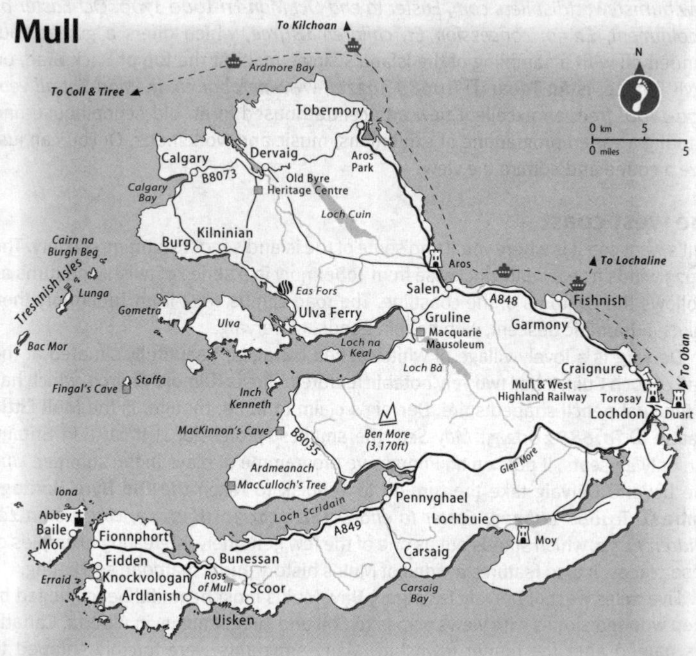

Shiver me timbers

The history of 16th-century Europe is littered with the remains of carefully forged and hastily broken political alliances between the various superpowers. One such deal between England and Spain was broken in 1588, prompting Philip II of Spain to send the Spanish Armada, a massive force of 130 ships, to take on the English navy. Originating in Cadiz, the Spanish force moved north and left Lisbon on 20 May. They met Queen Elizabeth's ships in the English Channel, where they were duly routed.

A number of Spanish ships fled up the east coast, chased by the British fleet as far as the Firth of Forth. Denied entry into the estuary by further British naval forces, the tattered remnants of these great Spanish galleons were no longer considered to pose a threat and were left to their own fate. Many continued up the east coast of Scotland, only to be wrecked in the perilous North Sea. Not all the crews drowned, however, and several integrated into local communites, where their descendants still live to this day. Most of their offspring were distinctively black haired and there is strong facial resemblance even today between some on the northeast coast of Scotland and the residents of Cadiz, from where the Armada originally sailed.

Some Spanish ships headed for the west coast, but were lost in a violent storm in the Hebrides. One galleon, the Florida, was lost in Tobermory harbour, reputedly carrying £300,000 worth of gold bullion. However, during recent dives all that was found on the seabed were rotted timbers, a sailor's bangle and a silver spoon.

South Mull

From Ulva Ferry the B8073 heads east along the north shore of **Loch na Keal** then enters a wide flat valley, where the road forks east to Salen and west along the south shore of Loch na Keal. This part of Mull is dominated by **Ben More** (3,170 ft), the island's highest mountain. All around is a spectacular region of high jutting mountains and deep glens, extending west to the **Ardmeanach Peninsula**. The peninsula may look impenetrable, but with the proper walking gear can be explored on foot. On the north coast, about a mile from the road, is the massive entrance to **MacKinnon's Cave**, which runs for about 100 yds back under the cliffs. Make sure to visit only at low tide. The area around the headland, now owned by the National Trust for Scotland, is known as **The Wilderness**. Near the headland is **MacCulloch's Tree**, a remarkable fossilized tree 40 ft high and thought to be 50 million years old, which was discovered in 1819. The tree is only accessible by a seven-mile footpath which begins at Burg Farm. You should have a map of the area and also time your arrival with low tide.

Mull's southernmost peninsula stretches west for 20 miles from the head of Loch Scridain as far as Iona. Most visitors use it merely as a route to Iona but there are a couple of interesting little detours along the way. A twisting side road leads south from Pennyghael over the hills and down to **Carsaig Bay**, from where you can head east or west along the shore for some dramatic coastal scenery. Two roads lead south from Bunessan. One leads to **Scoor**, near where is a great beach at Kilveockan. The other road splits near the coast: the left branch leads to **Uisken Bay**, where there's a nice beach; the righthand branch leads to **Ardlanish Bay**, which also has a good beach.

The story of St Columba

St Columba (*Colum Cille* in Gaelic), a prince of Ireland and grandson of the Irish King, Niall of the Nine Hostages, came to Scotland not as a missionary, but as an act of self-imposed penance for his actions. He stubbornly refused to hand over his copy of the Gospels, illegally copied from St Finian's original, which led to a bitter dispute with the king. This ended in a pitched battle in which Columba's supporters prevailed, but he was so overcome with remorse at the bloodshed he had caused that he fled Ireland, finally settling on Iona as it was the first place he found from where he couldn't see his homeland. Columba, however, was not retiring into obscurity. His missionary zeal drove him to begin work on building the abbey. He also banished women and cows from the island, declaring that "where there is a cow there is a woman, and where there is a woman there is mischief". Workers at the abbey had to leave their womenfolk on nearby Eilean nam Ban (Women's Island). Not content with that, he also banished frogs and snakes from Iona, though there are plenty on Mull. He is even said to have pacified the Loch Ness Monster during a visit to Inverness. He went on to found the Celtic Church, or the Church of the Culdees, with centres throughout Scotland, which differed in many ways from the Church of Rome.

The road ends at **Fionnphort**, the departure point for the small passenger-only ferry to Iona, just a mile across the Sound of Iona. The village is little more than a car park, a row of houses, a pub and a shop, but there are several inexpensive B&Bs for those arriving too late to make the crossing. Even if you're not staying, it's worth stopping off in the village to visit the **Columba Centre** ⓘ *mid-May to end-Sep Mon-Sat 1000-1800, Sun 1100-1800, £2, children £1*, a museum which relates the saint's life story.

A road runs south from Fionnphort to **Knockvologan**, opposite **Erraid Island**, which is accessible at low tide. The island has literary connections, for it was here that Robert Louis Stevenson is believed to have written *Kidnapped*. **Balfour Bay** on the south of the island is named after the novel's hero who was shipwrecked here.

Walks on Mull → *OS Landranger maps 47, 48 and 49 cover the entire island.*

Mull presents numerous walking opportunities, ranging from gentle forest trails to wild and dramatic coastal routes, or even a spot of Munro-bagging for the more intrepid. With the exception of the Cuillins on Skye, Mull's highest peak, Ben More (3,170 ft) is the only Munro not on the mainland.

The trail starts at a lay-by on the B8035, at Dishig, and is fairly clear, though it can be tricky near the top. Return the same way, or more experienced climbers could continue down the narrow ridge to the eastern summit, **A'Chioch**, then descend the eastern face to the road that skirts **Loch Ba**. The views from the top are magnificent, across the other Hebridean islands and even as far as Ireland. If it's a cloudy day, it's worth postponing the ascent until there's clear weather. Allow around six hours for the round trip.

There are a couple of excellent coastal walks which start out from Carsaig Bay. A good path heads west along the shore to **Carsaig Arches** at Malcom's Point. The path runs below the cliffs out to the headland and then around it, and after about a mile reaches **Nun's Cave**, a wide and shallow cave where the nuns of Iona took refuge after being expelled during the Reformation. The path continues for another mile or so, but becomes a bit exposed in places and traverses a steep slope above a sheer drop into the sea. The famous arches are columnar basalts worn into fantastic shapes. One is a free-standing rock stack and another is a huge cave with two entrances. You'll need to allow about four hours in total plus some time at the arches.

Heading east from Carsaig Bay is a spectacular 4½-mile walk to **Lochbuie**, past **Adnunan stack**. It starts out through woodland, then follows the shore below the steep cliffs, with waterfalls plunging straight into the sea. It's easy at first but then gets very muddy in places and there's quite a bit of wading through boggy marsh, so make sure you've got good walking boots. Allow about five to six hours in total.

A shorter walk takes you to the Bronze-Age **Lochbuie Stone Circle** at the foot of **Ben Buie**. Leave your car at the stone bridge before you reach the village. Look for the green sign on the gate to your left and follow the white marker stones across the field. The stone circle is hidden behind a wall of rhododendrons, so follow the marker stones across the plank bridge until you see it. It takes about 30 minutes.

There are a few marked trails through Forestry Commission land on Mull. The first walk is to **Aros Park**, on the south side of Tobermory Bay. Start out from the car park near the distillery in Tobermory and follow the shoreline for about a mile to Lochan a'Ghurrabain, which is good for trout fishing. From here there is also a marked path around the loch (one mile). A longer walk is to **Ardmore Bay**, three miles north of Tobermory. The trail/cycle path starts at the car park by the road that runs northwest from Tobermory. From here, it runs out almost to Ardmore point and back again, passing a couple of ruined villages on the way. There's a good chance of seeing seals and lots of sea birds in Ardmore Bay. The trail is four miles in total.

Four miles north of Craignure is the car park and picnic site at **Garmony Point**, where a two-mile trail leads to the ferry terminal at **Fishnish**, hugging the shore all the way. Another trail (four miles) runs out to Fishnish Point and back through the forest to the car park by the old harbour.

Iona → *Phone code: 01681. Colour map 3, grid C3. Population: 130.*

Iona is a small island – barely three miles long and a little over a mile wide – but its importance to Christianity is out of all proportion to its size. Iona's place in religious history was guaranteed when St Columba arrived with his 12 disciples and founded a monastery there in AD 563. The Irish monk then set about converting practically all of pagan Scotland and much of northern England. Iona went on to become the most sacred religious site in Europe and has been a place of pilgrimage for several centuries. Today that pilgrimage has turned into more of an invasion, with daytrippers making the five-minute ferry trip from Mull to visit the abbey. Few, however, venture beyond the main village, **Baile Mór**, and it's easy to find a quiet spot, particularly on the west coast with its sparkling silver beaches washed by turquoise sea. It's worth spending a day or two here to soak up the island's unique spiritual peace so well conveyed in the words of Dr Johnson: "that man is little to be envied whose...piety would not grow warmer among the ruins of Iona".

Background

Iona is known as the 'Cradle of Christianity in Scotland', and was a centre of the arts. The monks produced elaborate carvings, manuscripts, ornate gravestones and Celtic crosses. Their greatest work was the beautiful Book of Kells, which dates from AD 800, and which is now on display in Dublin's Trinity College. This proved to be the high point of the church's history. Shortly after came the first of the Viking raids, in AD 806, when many monks were slaughtered at Martyrs' Bay, followed by another in AD 986 which destroyed the work of many years. The relentless pressure from the established church ended with the suppression of the Celtic Church by King David in 1144.

In 1203 Iona became part of the mainstream church with the establishment of a nunnery for the Order of the Black Nuns, as well as a Benedictine Abbey by Reginald of the MacDonalds of the Isles. Iona became overshadowed by the royal city of Dunfermline, and its final demise came with the Reformation when buildings were demolished and all but three of the 360 carved crosses destroyed.

The abbey lay in ruins until in 1899 the island's owner, the eighth Duke of Argyll, donated the buildings to the Church of Scotland on condition that the abbey church was restored for worship. Then in 1938 the Reverend George Macleod founded the Iona Community as an evangelical Church of Scotland brotherhood, with the abbey buildings as its headquarters, and by 1965 had succeeded in rebuilding the remainder of the monastic buildings. Now the abbey complex has been completely restored and the island of Iona, apart from the abbey buildings, is owned by the National Trust for Scotland.

The abbey

ⓘ *Open all year and at all times, free but a donation at the entrance is appreciated.* The present abbey dates from around 1200, though it has been rebuilt over the centuries and completely restored in the 20th century. The oldest part is the restored **St Oran's Chapel**, to the south of the abbey on the right, which is plain and unadorned save for its splendid 11th-century Norman doorway. It is said that Columba was prevented from completing the building of the original chapel until a living person had been buried in the foundations. His friend Oran volunteered and was duly buried. Columba later asked for the face to be uncovered so that he could bid a final farewell to his friend, but Oran was found to be alive and claimed he had seen Heaven and Hell, describing them in such blasphemous terms that Columba ordered he be covered up immediately!

You get a good view of the whole complex from the top of the small grassy knoll opposite the abbey entrance.

Surrounding the chapel is the **Reilig Odhrain**, the sacred burial ground, which is said to contain the graves of 48 Scottish kings, including Macbeth's victim, Duncan, as well as four Irish and eight Norwegian kings. The stones you see today are not the graves of kings but of various important people from around the West Highlands and Islands. The most recent is that of John Smith, leader of the British Labour Party from 1992 until his untimely death in 1994.

Beside the Road of the Dead, which leads from the abbey church to St Oran's Chapel, stands the eighth-century **St Martin's Cross**. This is the finest of Iona's Celtic high crosses and is remarkably complete, with the Pictish serpent-and-boss decoration on one side and holy figures on the other. Standing in front of the abbey entrance is a replica of **St John's Cross**, the other great eighth-century monument. The restored original is in the **Infirmary Museum**, at the rear of the abbey, along with a fine collection of medieval gravestones.

No part of St Columba's original buildings survives, but to the left of the main entrance is **St Columba's Shrine**, the small, steep-roofed chamber which almost certainly marks the site of the saint's tomb. This is **Torr an Aba**, where Columba's cell is said to have been. The **Abbey** itself has been carefully restored to its original beautiful simplicity and inside, in a side chapel, are marble effigies of the eighth Duke of Argyll and his third wife, Duchess Ina.

Baile Mór

The passenger ferry from Fionnphort on Mull lands at Baile Mór, Iona's main village, which is little more than a row of cottages facing the sea. There are over a dozen places to stay but, as demand far exceeds supply during the busy summer season, it's best to book in advance at one of the tourist offices on Mull, or in Oban. There's also a post office, a very good craft shop and general store in the village. Just outside the village, on the way to the abbey, are the ruins of the **Augustinian nunnery**. Just to the north, housed in the parish church manse, built by Thomas Telford, is the **Iona Heritage Centre** ⓘ *Apr-Oct Mon-Sat 1030-1630, £1.50*, which features displays on the island's social history. Nearby stands the intricately carved 15th-century **Maclean's Cross**.

Around the island

On the west coast are some lovely beaches of white sand and colourful pebbles. The best of the lot is the **Bay at the Back of the Ocean**, beside the golf course, and only a mile and a half walk from the ferry. This was one of John Smith's favourite places and it's easy to see why. At the southern tip of the island is another sandy beach at **St Columba's Bay,** believed to be the spot where the saint first landed. Another good walk is to the top of **Dun I,** the only real hill, which rises to a height of 300 ft.To get there, continue on the road north from the abbey, past MacDougal's Cross, then go through a gate to the right of Bishop's Walk Farm and follow the fence up to where you join a footpath up to the top. It's only about half an hour up and down and there are great views from the top of the entire island and the coastline of Mull.

Sleeping

Mull *p313*

L Western Isles Hotel, Tobermory, T01688-302012, F302297. 23 rooms. Open all year, the biggest and grandest hotel on the island, set high above the harbour with great views from the comfortable rooms, has 3 excellent restaurants, including the lovely conservatory bar.

A Druimard Country House Hotel, Dervaig, T01688-400291, www.druimard.co.uk. 6 rooms, open end Mar-Oct. This Victorian country house is right beside the Mull Little Theatre; the room rate includes dinner.

D Calgary Farmhouse Hotel, Calgary Bay, T01688-400256. 9 rooms, open Apr-Oct. This farmhouse is one of Mull's gems, and the adjoining **Dovecote Restaurant** serves excellent food (**££**). There's also a tearoom, The Carthouse, which offers light lunches and home baking.

D Craignure Inn, Craignure, T01680-812305, www.craignure-inn.co.uk. 3 rooms, open all year. Its cosy bar serves decent food (**££-£**) and is a good place to seek refuge on a wet day.

D Mishnish Hotel, Main St, Tobermory, T01688-302009, www.mishnish.co.uk. Open all year, 10 rooms. Its bar is the live music focus of the town and social hub (see below).

D Old Mill Guest House & Restaurant, 3 miles south of Craignure, at Lochdon, T/F01680-812442. 3 rooms. Their cosy little restaurant has a deserved reputation for fine cuisine, so you'll need to book in advance.

D Pennyghael Hotel, Pennyghael, overlooking the loch, T01681-704288, F704205, which is open from Easter to Oct and has an excellent restaurant.

E Achaban House, just before Fionnphort, T01681-700205, www.achabanhouse.co.uk. 7 rooms. This former manse is comfortable and well-furnished, and also offers dinner.

E Baliscate Guest House, a short walk from Tobermory, T01688-302048, F302666. 4 en suite rooms. They also organize fishing and wildlife trips, see Activities and tours p322.

E Failte Guest House, Main St, Tobermory, T/F01688-302495. Open Mar-Oct, 7 rooms. Best of the guest houses, excellent.

E Uisken Croft, Uisken Bay, T01681-700307, open Apr-Oct. Idyllic.

Iona *p319*

B Argyll Hotel, T01681-700334, www.argyllhoteliona.co.uk. 17 rooms, open Apr-Oct. This is the better of the island's 2 upmarket hotels, and its good restaurant serves lunches 4-course dinners.

F Iona Hostel, T01681-700642. An exceptional hostel with views to the Treshnish Islands about a mile from the ferry along the path past the abbey. It's best to book ahead in summer.

Eating

Mull *p313*

£££-£ Western Isles Hotel, Tobermory, see Sleeping, offers the best eating in town. Here you can choose between 3 restaurants. A 3-course à la carte in the dining room or the oriental Spices Bistro (expensive to mid-range), while cheap bar meals are served in the Conservatory Bar.

Other places in Tobermory can be found on the harbour front, which is filled with places to eat, including the bar of the **Mishnish Hotel**. A worthwhile detour is to walk to the edge of town to the **Green Barn** which is run by Isle of Mull Cheese.

££ Dovecote Restaurant, adjoining Calgary Farmhouse Hotel, Calgary Bay, see Sleeping, serves excellent food. There can be no better way to end the day than dinner here followed by a stroll along the beach at sunset. There's also a tearoom, **The Carthouse**, which offers light lunches and home baking.

Entertainment

Mull *p313*

Mishnish Hotel, Main St, Tobermory. An absolute must when in town is a night in the 'Mish'. After one of their pub meals and several pints of ale, bending over the pool table is an effort, not to mention getting down to some good live folk music.

For the sake of choice, other pubs and live music venues are available, namely **MacGochan's**, at the other end of the harbour, near the distillery. There are also music events at **An Tobar**, Tobermory, see Sights p314.

Festivals and events

Mull *p313*

Apr Mull Music Festival, known as the Whisky Olympics, is held on the last weekend of the month. It is a great time to be on Mull when you can enjoy a feast of Gaelic folk music and, of course, whisky. The focus of the festival is the bar of the Mishnish Hotel, Tobermory. For details T01688-302383.

Jul Mendelssohn on Mull Festival, held over 10 days in early Jul, this is another great festival. It is held to commemorate the famous composer's visit here in 1829.

Jul Tobermory Highland Games, annually on the 3rd Thu in Jul.

Sep The Sound of Mull, a day long celebration of local rock and pop acts, takes place at the end of Sep.

Oct Tour of Mull Rally, held in early Oct, should not be missed by rally enthusiasts.

Shopping

Mull *p313*

Despite its popularity, Tobermory hasn't succumbed to the dreaded tartan disease that afflicts so many other tourist hot-spots. You're more likely to find shops selling fishing tackle or diving gear than tacky souvenirs, and the ones that do cater for the tourist market are tastefully done.

Isle of Mull Cheese, on the edge of town, 500 yds off the Dervaig Rd, at Sgriob-Ruadh Farm, T01688-302235. Here you can savour their award-winning traditionally made cheese and their wonderful glass barn. Open Apr to end-Sep Mon-Fri 1000-1600.

Mull Pottery, T01688-302057, tasteful pots in different shapes and sizes.

Mull Silver Company, T01688-302345, open 0900-1730, are tastefully done and enjoyable places to browse in on a wet afternoon.

Tobermory Chocolate Company, at the foot of Back Brae, which leads steeply up from the harbour to the upper part of the village, T01688-302526, open May-Oct Mon-Sat 0930-1730. Here you can try out their speciality – chocolate made with the local whisky.

Activities and tours

Boat trips

Alternative Boat Hire, T01681-700537, offer trips around the coastline and handline fishing on a traditional wooden boat. You can hire by the hour or for an afternoon, May-Oct, from Fionnphort and Iona.

Edge of the World, T01688-302808, www.edge-of-the-world.co.uk, operate powerboat trips from Tobermory around Mull and as far as Ardnamurchan. One-hour trips cost £12, 2-hr trips £20. Seals, porpoises, basking sharks and even minke whales can be seen.

Turus Mara, www.turusmara.com. Trips to Staffa and the Treshnish Isles leave from Oban, Dervaig, Ulva Ferry, Iona or

Fionnphort, weather permitting. A full-day cruise including Staffa and the Treshnish Isles costs £33 per person (£17 for children); a cruise to Staffa only costs around £15.

Diving

Seamore Diving offer diving trips and courses. Book through **Seafare Chandlery & Diving Service**, Main St, Tobermory, T/F01688-302277.

Fishing

Amidas Sea Fishing & Wildlife Trips, based at **Baliscate House**, see Sleeping, or book at **Tackle & Books**, T01688-302336, offers fishing trips. They cost around £15 for 3 hrs, or £30 for a full day.

A Brown & Son, 21 Main St, Tobermory, T01688-302020, F302454. Permits for trout fishing are available from here.

For more details pick up the *Tobermory Angling Association* leaflet from the tourist office.

Wildlife tours

Island Encounter Wildlife Safaris, Arla-Beag, Aros, T01680-300441. These can be made from Aros, just to the north of Salen, with Richard Atkinson. A full-day wildlife safari with a local guide costs £25 including lunch. You'll see golden eagles, white-tailed sea eagles, hen harriers, divers, merlins, peregrine falcons, seals and porpoises, to name but a few.

Sea Life Surveys, T01688-302787. Whale- and dolphin-watching trips can be made from Tobermory with this outfit. A full-day tour costs £45 (£48 in Jul/Aug), and there's a maximum of 12 people per trip. You can find out more at the **Hebridean Whale and Dolphin Trust**, 28 Main St, Tobermory, T01688-302620, www.hwdt.org, Apr-Oct daily 1000-1700, Nov-Mar Mon-Fri 1100-1700, a charity which aims to protect the marine environment through education, and at **Isle of Mull Landrover Wildlife Expeditions**, Ulva House Hotel, T01688-302044, David Woodhouse.

Transport

Mull *p313*

Local There's a bus from Tobermory post office to **Dervaig** and **Calgary**, 5 times a day Mon-Fri and twice on Sat (operated by **RN Carmichael**, T01688-302220). The **Craignure** to Tobermory via **Salen** service runs 5 times a day Mon-Fri, 8 times on Sat and 3 times on Sun (operated by **Bowman's Coaches**, T01680-812313, and **Highlands & Islands Coaches**, T01680-812510). There's a bus from **Craignure** to **Fionnphort** (for Iona) 6 times a day Mon-Fri, 4 times on Sat and 1 on Sun (**Bowman's and Highlands & Islands**). There's also a postbus service from **Salen** to **Burg** (Kilninian) via the Ulva Ferry twice a day Mon-Sat (**Royal Mail**, T01463-256200). For bus times, contact the operators or pick up the *Mull Area Transport Guide* at the tourist office in Oban, Tobermory or Craignure. This also includes ferry times.

Tobermory is a 30- to 40-min drive north from the ferry pier at **Craignure**. There are daily buses from Craignure which coincide with ferry arrivals. A small bicycle/passenger-only ferry makes the 2-min crossing on demand from Ulva Ferry, Apr-Oct Mon-Fri 0900-1700, and on Sun Jun-Aug. This includes entry to the **Boathouse Heritage Centre, Sheila's Cottage** (a musuem of island life) and access to all walks. At other times call to make arrangements, T01688-500226.

There are many places to rent bikes. In Tobermory there's **Tom-a' Mhuillin**, the Salen Rd, T01688-302164, **Brown's Hardware** shop on Main St, T01688-302020, or try the **youth hostel** in Tobermory. In Salen there's **On Yer Bike**, T01680-300501, which also has a shop by the ferry terminal in Craignure, T01680-812487.

Long distance From **Oban** to **Craignure** (45 mins) 5-7 times daily Mon-Sat and 5 times daily on Sun, £3.75 one way per passenger, £33.50 per car, £5 day return £6.45 and £45. **CalMac** offices: Oban, T01631-566688, and Craignure, T01680-812343. **Lochaline** on the Morvern Peninsula (see p375) to **Fishnish** (15 mins, £2.35 per passenger, £10.15 per car) hourly 0700-1830 Mon-Sat and 4 times on Sun. Some ferries from **Oban** to **Coll** and **Tiree** (see below) call in at **Tobermory**. There are also ferries from **Kilchoan** on the Ardnamurchan Peninsula (see p375) to **Tobermory** 7 times daily Mon-Sat and 5 times daily on Sun (Jun-Aug).

Iona *p319*
To Iona, a passenger-only ferry leaves from Fionnphort on Mull (5 mins) frequently 0845-1815 Mon-Sat and hourly 0900-1800 Sun, £3.50 per passenger, bicycles free.

Directory

Banks Clydesdale Bank, Main St, is Mull's only permanent bank. There's also a mobile bank which tours the island; for details T08457-826818.

Coll, Tiree and Colonsay

The low-lying, treeless and windswept island of Coll offers the simple pleasures in life. There's little to do here other than stroll along the magnificent, deserted beaches. Tourism, though, remains low on the list of priorities, and those who do come prefer it that way. Even by Hebridean standards there are few facilities, and accommodation is scarce. Tiree, meanwhile, claims to be the sunniest place in Scotland, but it's also one of the windiest places in the country. So windy, in fact, that Tiree has become the windsurfing capital of Scotland and is known as the 'Hawaii of the North'. Colonsay is the epitome of the island haven: remote, tranquil and undemanding. It has abundant wildlife, beautiful plants and flowers and glorious beaches. All this has become accessible to daytrippers, with a ferry round trip (see below), leaving you six hours ashore. This does scant justice to the island's peculiar charms, however, and judging by the ever-growing number of holiday homes and self-catering accommodation on Colonsay, it's a view shared by many. ▸▸ *For Sleeping, eating and other listings, see page 326.*

Coll → *Phone code: 01879. Colour map 3, grid B2-3.*

The best of Coll's beaches are on the west coast, at **Killunaig**, **Hogh Bay** and **Feall Bay**. The latter is separated from the nearby **Crossapool Bay** by giant sand dunes up to 100 ft high. These are now owned by the RSPB to protect the resident corncrake population. The CalMac ferry from Oban calls in at Coll's only village, **Arinagour**, where half of the island's population live and where you'll find the post office and a few shops. There's no petrol station, but you should leave the car behind anyway. The island is only 13 miles long by four miles wide and the best way to get around is on foot or by bike. It's worth taking a walk up **Ben Hogh** (341 ft), the island's highest point, overlooking Hogh Bay on the west coast, to get a good overview. The east coast, north from Arinagour to Sorisdale, is an uninhabited wilderness which is ideal for some gentle hillwalking.

Tiree → *Phone code: 01879. Colour map 3, grid B2.*

Tiree is a low, flat island, only about 11 miles long and six miles across at its widest, and is also known by the nickname *Tir fo Thuinn*, or 'Land below the waves'. When seen from a distance most of it disappears below the horizon, save its two highest hills, **Ben Hynish** (462 ft) and **Beinn Hough** (390 ft), on the west coast. Being flat and small, it obviously makes good sense to explore it by bicycle, but remember that the constant wind varies from strong to gale force. The ferry port is at **Gott Bay,** half a mile from **Scarinish**, the island's main village and home to a **Co-op** supermarket, post office and bank (there's a garage at the pier head). About four miles from Scarinish, is Vaul Bay, where the well-preserved remains of **Dun Mor**, a Pictish Broch built around the first century AD, stand on a rocky outcrop to the west of the bay.

The island's main road runs northwest from Scarinish, past the beautiful beach at **Balephetrish Bay** to Balevullin, where you can see some good examples of restored traditional thatched houses. Just to the south, at Sandaig, is the **Thatched House Museum** ⓘ *Jun-Sep Mon-Fri 1400-1600*, which tells of the island's social history.

In the southwestern corner of the island is the most spectacular scenery of all, at the headland of **Ceann a'Mara**, or Kenavara. The massive sea cliffs are the home of thousands of sea birds and you can see seals on the rocky shore. East from here, across the golden sands of Balephuil Bay, is the island's highest hill, **Ben Hynish**, topped by a radar-tracking station resembling a giant golf ball. Despite this, it's worth the climb to the top for the magnificent views over the island and, on clear days, across to the Outer Hebrides. Below Ben Hynish, to the east, is the village of **Hynish**, where you'll find the **Signal Tower Museum**, which tells the fascinating story of the building of the **Skerryvore Lighthouse** (1840-1844) by Alan Stevenson, an uncle of Robert Louis Stevenson. This incredible feat of engineering was carried out from Hynish, where a dry dock/reservoir was built for shipping materials by boat to the Skerryvore reef, 10 miles to the southwest.

If you are a windsurfing fan, you must come to Tiree – it is one of the best places to surf in the British Isles.

Colonsay → *Phone code: 01951. Colour map 3, grid C3.*

Colonsay's population lives in the three small villages, the largest of which is **Scalasaig**, the ferry port. A few miles north of the ferry, in the middle of the island, is **Colonsay House**, dating from 1772. The house was sold, along with the rest of the island, in 1904 to Lord Strathcona, who had made his fortune in Canada with the Hudson Bay Company and went on to found the Canadian Pacific Railway. The house is not open to the public but the lovely gardens and woods, full of rhododendrons, giant palms and exotic shrubs, are worth a stroll. The estate cottages are now self-catering holiday homes.

There are several standing stones, the best of which are **Fingal's Limpet Hammers**, at Kilchattan, southwest of Colonsay House. There are also Iron Age forts, such as **Dun Eibhinn**, next to the hotel in Scalasaig (see below). Colonsay is also home to a wide variety of wildlife. You can see choughs, one of Britain's rarest birds, as well as corncrakes, buzzards, falcons, merlins and perhaps even the odd golden eagle or sea eagle. There are also otters, seals and wild goats (said to be descended from the survivors of the Spanish Armada ships wrecked in 1588). The jewel in the island's crown, though, lies six miles north of Scalasaig, past Colonsay House, at **Kiloran Bay**. The beach here is described as the finest in the Hebrides, and who could argue. The magnificent half mile of golden sands, backed by tiers of grassy dunes, with massive breakers rolling in off the Atlantic, is worth the two-hour ferry crossing alone.

Just off the southern tip of Colonsay is the island of Oronsay, two miles square with a population of six and one of the highlights of a visit to Colonsay. The name derives from the Norse for 'ebb-tide island', which is a fitting description as Oronsay can be reached on foot at low tide, across the mud flats known as 'The Strand'. It takes about an hour to walk from the south end of Colonsay to the ruins of a 14th-century **Augustinian Priory**. This was the home of some of the most highly skilled medieval craftsmen in the Western Highlands. A surviving example of their work is the impressive Oronsay Cross and the beautifully carved tombstones, on display in the **Prior's House**. Make sure you take wellies for the walk across The Strand and check on the tides. Tide tables are available at the hotel or shop. Spring tides (new and full moon) allow about three to four hours to walk across and back, which is just enough time to see the priory but little else.

Sleeping

Coll *p324*

C **Coll Hotel**, Arinagour, T01879-230334. A family hotel with a good restaurant.

E **Achamore**, T01879-230430. A lovely old farmhouse a few miles west of the village.

Tiree *p324*

C **Kirkapol House**, in a converted church overlooking Gott Bay, T/F01879-220729.

D **The Glassary Guest House & Restaurant**, at Sandaig, T/F01879-220684. 4 en suite rooms, open all year, very good food (££).

Colonsay *p325*

Accommodation on Colonsay is limited and must be booked up well in advance.

B **Isle of Colonsay Hotel**, T01951-200316, www.colonsay.org.uk. A few 100 yds from the ferry, 11 rooms, a cosy inn with a friendly bar and excellent food; they also arrange various trips around the island.

E **Seaview**, T01951-200315, at Kilchattan, near the standing stones. Open Apr-Oct.

F **Colonsay Backpacker's Lodge**, T01951-200312, www.colonsay.org.uk. An old keeper's cottage 2km from the ferry, sleeps 16 and open all year, phone for lift from ferry.

Activities and tours

Tiree *p324*

Windsurfing tuition is available at Loch Bhasapol, T01879-220559 (summer only). The major windsurfing event is the **Wave Classic**, held annually in Oct.

Transport

Coll *p324*

Some 13 miles long by 4 miles wide, Coll is best navigated on foot or by bike. CalMac car/passenger ferries leave from **Oban**, 2 hrs 40 mins, 1 daily, £12 per person and £70 per car.

Tiree *p324*

Local There's a shared taxi service which operates on request Mon-Fri 0930-1500 (limited service on Sat), also Mon-Wed and Fri 1600-1730, and a Tue evening service for arriving ferries in the summer. For private taxi hire call **Island Cabs**, T01879-220344 (evenings and weekends only). There's a postbus service around the island, including to and from the airport. The timetable is available at **Scarinish Post Office**. Bicycle hire is available at the **Tiree Lodge Hotel**, or contact Mr N Maclean, T01879-220428.

Long distance Tiree has an airport with 1 flight daily Mon-Sat (45 mins), all year round to Glasgow. The airport is at The Reef, Crossapol, T01879-220309. CalMac car/passenger ferries sail to the island from **Oban**, via **Coll** and, occasionally, **Tobermory**. The ferry port is at Scarinish (T01879- 220337). From Oban to Tiree (3 hrs 50 mins via Coll) once daily.

Colonsay *p325*

Local There's a limited bus and postbus service around the island Mon-Sat, for those without their own transport. On Wed in the summer, a tour bus meets the ferry and takes visitors round the island. As the island is only 8 miles long by 3 miles wide, you might want to consider hiring a bicycle. Bike hire from **A McConnel**, T01951-200355.

Long distance There are ferry sailings from **Oban** (2 hrs, £10.65 one way per passenger, £52 per car) once daily Mon, Wed, Thu Fri and Sun, arriving at Scalasaig on the east coast. From **Kennacraig** there is 1 sailing (3 hrs 35 mins) on Wed. From **Port Askaig** there is 1 sailing (1¼ hrs, £4 per passenger, £20.65 per car) also on Wed. Ferries need to be booked well in advance during the summer months.

Islay and Jura

Islay (pronounced eye-la), the most southerly of the Hebridean islands and one of the most populous, with around 4,000 inhabitants, has one very important claim to fame – single malt whisky. Islay produces a very distinctive, peaty malt and connoisseurs

Weapon of Mass Drunkeness

The US Defence Threat Reduction Agency (DTRA), whose mission is "to safeguard the US and its allies from weapons of mass destruction" has been monitoring the Bruichladdich Distillery on Islay.

The distillery installed webcams to show the world that their whisky is made using traditional methods, but in September 2003 discovered that the DTRA was spying on them. According to the agency, it only takes a 'tweak' – their words – in the process of whisky making and Bruichladdich could be producing deadly chemical weapons, hence their interest. The DTRA had emailed the distillery to inform them that one of their webcams was faulty and when the distillery replied to thank them and inquire who they were, the agency went right ahead and revealed who they were and what they were doing.

Once they had been 'outed', the DTRA had to admit that the distillery posed no threat to world peace, though many would contest that excessive consumption of the amber liquid has been known to contribute to the occasional breach of peace in the island's bars.

Mark Reynier, the managing director of the Port Charlotte distillery, took it all in good humour: "we're a sinister-looking bunch, so I can see how we might be mistaken for Al-Qaeda", he quipped.

As they say, only in America.

are in for a treat, as the island has no fewer than seven working distilleries. Aside from whisky, people also come here to watch birds. The island is something of an ornithologists' wonderland, and from October to April plays host to migrating barnacle and white-fronted geese flying down from Greenland in their thousands for the winter. The short ferry crossing from Islay takes you to Jura, a primeval and uncompromising place; a lost world, pervaded by an almost haunting silence. The words 'wild' and 'remote' tend to get overused in describing the many Hebridean islands, but in the case of Jura they are, if anything, an understatement. Jura has one road, one hotel, six sporting estates and 5,000 red deer, which outnumber the 200 people by 25:1, the human population having been cleared to turn the island into a huge deer forest. Rather appropriately, the name Jura derives from the Norse 'dyr-ey', meaning deer island. ▸▸ *For Sleeping, Eating and other listings, see page 330-332.*

Ins and outs

Islay's only official tourist information centre is in Bowmore ⓘ *T01496-810254, Apr-Sep daily, Sep and Oct Mon-Sat, Oct-Mar Mon-Fri*. They'll find accommodation for you. ▸▸ *For Transport details, see page 332.*

Islay → *Phone code: 01496. Colour map 5, grid A1.*

Port Ellen and around

Port Ellen is the largest place on Islay and the main ferry port, yet it still has the feel of a sleepy village. There are many day trips from Port Ellen. A road runs east out to **Ardtalla**, where it ends. Along the way, it passes three distilleries, first **Laphroaig**, then **Lagavulin** and lastly, **Ardbeg**, all of which offer guided tours, see page 331. Between the Lagavulin and Ardbeg distilleries is the dramatically sited 16th-century ruin of **Dunyvaig Castle**, once the main naval base and fortress of the Lords of the Isles. A mile further on is the impressive **Kildalton Cross**, standing in the graveyard of the ruined 13th-century chapel. The eighth-century cross is well preserved and one of Scotland's most important Early Christian monuments, and the carvings depict biblical scenes.

Southwest of Port Ellen a road runs out to a little, rounded peninsula known as **The Oa**, an area of varied beauty, both wild and pastoral, and with a wonderful coastline. The road runs as far as **Upper Killeyan**, from where it's about a mile uphill to the spectacular headland at the **Mull of Oa**. Here you'll see the strange-looking **American monument**. The obelisk commemorates the shipwrecks offshore of two US ships, the *Tuscania* and the *Ontranto*, both of which sank in 1918 at the end of the war. There's a great walk north from the Mull of Oa up to Kintra, but it's best to start out from Kintra.

If you are a golfer then tee off at the Machrie golf course, for a memorable golfing experience.

A turn-off from the road to The Oa leads north to **Kintra**, at the south end of **The Big Strand** at Laggan Bay, with five miles of sands and dunes. There's a restaurant and accommodation here, and it's a great place for camping. The restaurant is at the end of the road, with the beach on one side and on the other a wild and spectacular coastal walk to the **Mull of Oa**. There's a detailed map of the route in the restaurant. Just to the north of Kintra is the **Machrie golf course**, a golfing experience that shouldn't be missed.

Bowmore and the Rinns of Islay

The A846 runs north from Port Ellen, straight as a pool cue, to Bowmore, the island's administrative capital and second largest village. Founded in 1768 by the Campbells, it's an appealing place, laid out in a grid plan with the main street running straight up the hill from the pier to the unusual round church, designed to ward off evil spirits, who can hide only in corners. Thankfully, the nice spirit stayed behind and can be found at the **Bowmore Distillery**, just to the west of Main Street. This is the oldest of the island's distilleries, founded in 1779, and the most tourist-friendly.

North of Bowmore, at **Bridgend**, the A846 joins the A847 which runs west to the hammerhead peninsula known as the Rinns of Islay ('rinns' is derived from the Gaelic for promontory). A few miles west of Bridgend the B8017 turns north to the **RSPB Reserve** at **Loch Gruinart**. The mudflats and fields at the head of the loch provide winter grazing for huge flocks of barnacle and white-fronted geese from Greenland, arriving in late October. There's an RSPB visitor centre at **Aoradh** (pronounced 'oorig') which houses an observation point with telescopes and CCTV, and there's a hide across the road. There are about 110 species of bird breeding on Islay, including the rare chough and corncrake.

The coastal scenery around the Rinns is very impressive, particularly at **Killinallan Point**, a beautiful and lonely headland at the far northeast of Loch Gruinart. Also impressive is **Ardnave Point**, west of Loch Gruinart, and further west along the north coast, **Sanaigmore.** The best beaches are at **Saligo** and **Machir Bay** on the west coast, past Loch Gorm. Both are lovely, wide, golden beaches backed by high dunes, but swimming is forbidden due to dangerous undercurrents.

Port Charlotte is without doubt the most charming of Islay's villages, with rows of well-kept, whitewashed cottages stretched along the wide bay. Here, the **Islay Wildlife Information and Field Centre** ⓘ *T01496-850288, Easter-Oct Mon, Tue, Thu, Fri and Sun 1000-1500, £2,* is a must for anyone interested in flora and fauna. It's very hands-on, with good displays on geology and natural history, a video room and reference library. It's also a great place for kids, and has activity days when staff take tours of the surrounding area. Also worth visiting is the compact **Museum of Islay Life** ⓘ *Easter-Oct Mon-Sat 1000-1700, Sun 1400-1700, £2*, to the east of the village, where you can find out all about illegal whisky distilling on the island. It also has interesting archival material. At the southern end of the Rinns is the picturesque little fishing and crofting village of Portnahaven, its Hebridean cottages rising steeply above the deeply indented harbour.

Port Askaig and around

Port Askaig is Islay's other ferry port, with connections to the mainland and to the islands of Jura and Colonsay. It's little more than a dock, a car park and a few buildings huddled at the foot of a steep, wooded hillside. A short walk north along the coast is the **Caol Ila distillery**, and a couple of miles further north, at the end of the road which branches left before you enter Port Askaig, is the beautifully situated **Bunnahabhain Distillery**.

The A846 runs east from Bridgend out to Port Askaig passing through **Ballygrant**, just to the south of **Loch Finlaggan**. Here, on two crannogs (artificial islands), were the headquarters of the Lords of the Isles, the ancestors of Clan Donald. The MacDonalds ruled from Islay for nearly 350 years, over a vast area covering all of the island off the west coast and almost the whole of the western seaboard from Cape Wrath to the Mull of Kintyre. There's a new **visitor centre** ⓘ *Easter-Oct Tue, Thu and Sun 1400-1630, £1.50*, to the northeast of the loch, where you can see some of the archaeological remains. You can walk across the fen to **Eilean Mor**, where there's a collection of carved gravestones near the ruins of a medieval chapel. A smaller island, **Eilean na Comhairle** (The Council of the Isle), is where the Lords of the Isles met to decide policy.

Islay

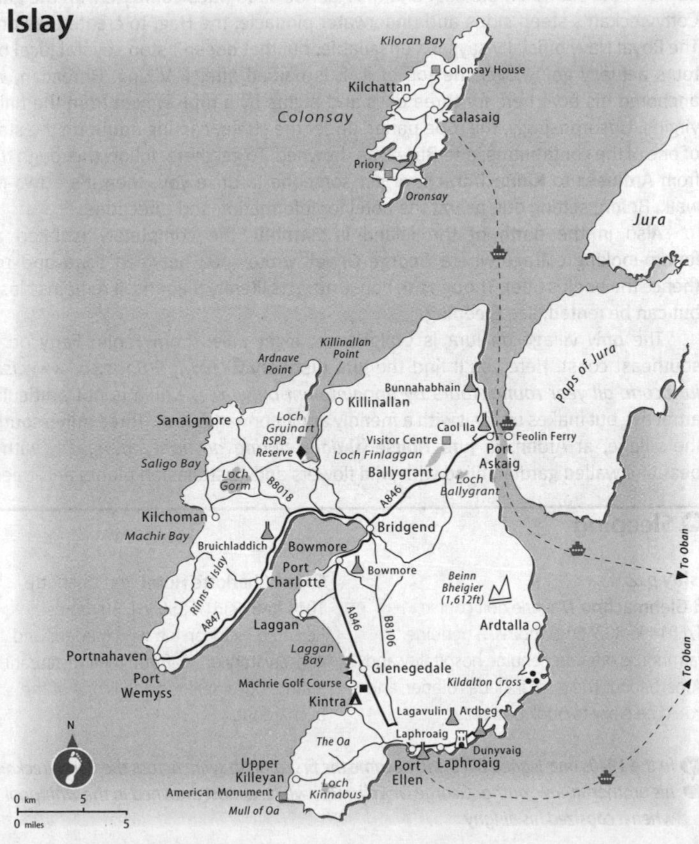

Jura → *Phone code 01496. Colour map 3, grid C4.*

Jura is one of the last, great wildernesses in the British Isles and perfect for some real off-the-beaten-track walking. Its main attractions are the beautiful **Paps of Jura**, three breast-shaped peaks that dominate not only the island itself but also the view for miles around. From Kintyre, Mull, Coll and Tiree, and from the mountains of mainland Scotland from Skye to Arran, they can be seen on the horizon. The Paps provide some tough hillwalking and require good navigational skills, or a guide. It takes a good eight hours to cover all three peaks, though during the Paps of Jura fell race they are covered in just three hours.

A good place to start is by the three-arch bridge over the Corran River, north of Leargybreack. The first pap you reach is Beinn a'Chaolais (2,408 ft), next is the highest, Beinn an Oír (2,571 ft) and the third is Beinn Shiantaidh (2,476 ft). To find out about guides, ask at **Jura Hotel**, see Sleeping. The island's west coast is completely uninhabited and inaccessible to all but the hardiest and most dedicated of walkers.

One of the island's main draws is the **Corryvreckan whirlpool** at the very northern tip, between Jura and the uninhabited island of **Scarba**. The notorious whirlpool, the second largest in the world, is in fact a tidal race that creates an action like a gigantic washing machine. It is seen at its awesome best during spring tides, especially with a westerly gale, when this most treacherous stretch of water creates oar falls of 25 ft and the terrible roar can be heard for up to 10 miles away. A two-hour tidal difference between the sound on the east and the Atlantic flood tides combine with the gulf of Corryvreckan's steep sides and underwater pinnacle, the Hag, to create the vortex. The Royal Navy officially says it's unsailable, but that doesn't stop several local boat tours actually going over the top of it. It is named after a Viking, Bhreacan, who anchored his boat here for three days and nights by a rope woven from the hair of virgins. Unsurprisingly, the rope parted under the strain, casting doubt on the status of one of the contributors, and Bhreacan drowned. To get there, follow the rough track from **Ardlussa** to **Kinuachdrach**, or get someone to drive you, then it's a two-mile walk. Before setting out, ask at the hotel for information and directions.

Also in the north of the island is **Barnhill**, the completely isolated and forlorn-looking cottage where **George Orwell** wrote *1984* between 1946 and 1948 (hence the book's title). Though the house attracts literary pilgrims, it remains closed, but can be rented, see Sleeping.

The only village on Jura is Craighouse, eight miles from Feolin Ferry on the southeast coast. Here you'll find the **Jura distillery** ① *T01496-820240, www.isleofjura.com, all year round, tours by appointment only, free*, which is not particularly attractive but makes up for it with a friendly and informative tour. Three miles south of the village, at Ardfin, is **Jura House** ① *daily during daylight hours, £2*, with its beautiful walled garden, filled with wild flowers and Australasian plants and trees.

Sleeping

Islay *p327*

B Glenmachrie, Machrie golf course, T/F01496-302560. 5 rooms. A genuine farmhouse offering genuine hospitality and superb food. The price includes dinner, and you'd be crazy to book B&B only.

C Port Charlotte Hotel, Port Charlotte, T01496-850361, F850361. 10 rooms. Restored Victorian inn with gardens and conservatory on seafront; their restaurant features local seafood and is one of the best around.

In the 1940s one-legged Bill Dunn became the first man to swim across the Corryvreckan, his brother-in-law, author George Orwell, meanwhile, almost drowned in the whirlpool when it capsized his dinghy.

Super highway

Though the whisky distilling process is basically the same everywhere, some distilleries have more beautiful locations and more interesting tours. Islay's seven distilleries enjoy the most scenically stunning settings and are full of character and history. Islay also offers the unique opportunity to visit several of Scotland's most impressive distilleries in one day, and their distinctive peaty malts are considered to be among the finest.

Laphroaig, *T01496-302418, www.laphroaig.com, tours all year by appointment only 1015 and 1415, free*, (pronounced 'la-froyg'), is the closest to Port Ellen, and its wonderful setting is summed up by its name, meaning 'The beautiful hollow by the broad bay' in Gaelic. According to many this is the ultimate in malt whisky and is at its best after dinner.

Lagavulin, *T01496-302400, www.malts.com, tours all year Mon-Fri by appointment 1000, 1130 and 1430, £4*, (pronounced 'laga-voolin') is a mile along the shore by the romantic ruin of Dunyveg Castle. Their 16-year-old single malt is one of the classics and also makes the ideal after-dinner tipple. A very interesting tour.

Ardbeg, *T01496-302244, www.ardbeg.com, tours all year Mon-Fri 1030, 1130, 1430 and 1530, Jun-Aug daily, £2*, is a mile further east and produces a robust and powerful single malt. Established in 1815, it was closed for a while, but was recently acquired by Glenmorangie.

Bowmore, *T01496-810441, www.bowmore.com, tours winter Mon-Fri 1030 and 1400, Sat 1030; summer Mon-Fri 1030-1130, 1400 and 1500, Sat 1030 and 1400, £2*, is the oldest distillery on Islay and still uses all the old traditional methods to produce its fine single malt, also at its best after dinner. Their hour-long tours are the most professionally done and even include a video.

Caol Ila, *T01496-302760, www.malts.com, tours by appointment Apr-Oct Mon-Thu 1000, 1115, 1330 and 1445, £4*, (pronounced 'coal-eela') was founded in 1846 and lies close to Port Askaig, with great views across the Sound of Islay to Jura. Unlike most of its island peers, this single malt is best before dinner.

Bunnahabhain, *T01496-840646, www.brunstewartdistillers.com, tours Mar-Oct Mon-Fri 1030, 1300 and 1500, other times by appointment only, free*, (pronounced 'bun a havan') is the most northerly of the distilleries, set in a secluded bay with great views across to Jura.

Bruichladdich, *T01496-850221, www.bruichladdich.com, tours Mon-Fri 1030, 1130 and 1430, Sat (booking required) 1030 and 1430, £3*, (pronounced 'brook-laddie') is in the village of the same name on the road south to Port Charlotte. Recently voted distillery of the year by the readers of America's Malt Advocate.

D Harbour Inn, Main St, Bowmore, T01496-810330, www.harbourinn.com. 4 rooms. Completely refurbished to a high standard, great views across the bay and superb food in their acclaimed restaurant (**£££**) where you can watch your seafood being landed.

D Kilmeny Farmhouse, near Port Askaig, T/F01496-840668. Comfort, style, excellent food and a warm, friendly atmosphere. The only drawback is that there are only 3 rooms, so book well in advance.

D Lochside Hotel, Shore St, Bowmore, T01496-810244, F810390. 8 rooms. Friendly and good-value hotel with a mind-boggling selection of single malts.

E The Bothy, 91 Lennox St, Port Ellen, T01496-302391, mickstuart@thebothyislay.

freeserve.co.uk. Run by Mick Stuart who hires out bikes and acts as a wildlife guide.

Jura *p330*

C Jura Hotel, T01496-820243, www.hometown.aol.com. The island's one and only hotel, overlooking the small isles bay. They'll provide information on island walks, and the pub is the social hub.

Barnhill, can be rented through Scotts Cottages, T0131-229 7111, www.scotts cottages.com, for £590 for 4 people, £710 for 5, and £830 for 6. Closed Nov-Mar.

Camping

Ask about camping at the **Jura Hotel**.

Activities and tours

Mike Richardson, T07899-912116, guides hill walks and Orwell trails from £20 per person (minimum charge of £55 if fewer than 3 people) and runs a landrover taxi service on Jura.

Transport

Islay *p327*

Local For those without their own transport, there's a regular bus service around Islay, with **Islay Coaches**, T01496-840273, and **postbuses**, T01246-546329. There are buses from **Portnahaven** to **Port Ellen**, via **Port Charlotte**, **Bridgend**, **Bowmore** and the airport; from **Port Askaig** to **Port Ellen** via **Ballygrant**, **Bridgend**, **Bowmore** and the airport; from **Port Ellen** to **Ardbeg**, **Bowmore**, **Port Askaig** and **Portnahaven**, and also a postbus to **Bunnababhain**. Buses run regularly at least from Mon-Sat, but only once on Sun.

Long distance Islay can be reached by air from Glasgow (for details, see p286). The airport is at Glenegedale, a few miles north of Port Ellen on the road to Bowmore.

The ferry to Islay (and Jura) from **Kennacraig** to **Port Ellen** (2 hrs 10 mins, £7.75 one way per passenger, £55 per car) sails twice daily on Mon, Tue, Thu, Fri and Sun, once on Wed and 3 times on Sat. A ferry also sails from **Kennacraig** to **Port Askaig** (2 hrs, same prices as above) once daily on Tue and Thu, twice daily on Wed, Fri, Sat and Sun, and 3 times on Mon. The Wed ferry sails via **Colonsay**. The ferry from **Oban** to Port Askaig sails on Wed (4¼ hrs). **CalMac** offices are in Kennacraig, T01880-730253; Port Ellen, T01496-302209.

Jura *p330*

There is a bus service on Jura, which runs from **Feolin Ferry** to **Craighouse** several times a day, Mon-Sat. A few buses continue to **Lagg** and **Inverlussa** and return to Craighouse. Note that some journeys are by request only and must be booked the day before. Contact Alex Dunnichie, T01496-820314, or visit www.scotland-inverness.co.uk/jura.htm, for an online timetable.

A small car and passenger ferry makes the regular 5-min crossing daily to Jura, from **Port Askaig** on Islay to Feolin Ferry. For times, contact **Cerco Denholm**, T01496-840681.

The Highlands

Footprint features

Introduction

The Highlands is the part of Scotland which best reflects most people's romantic image of the country, with mist-shrouded castles on every headland, a spooky tale around the next corner and an enthusiastic welcome waiting behind every door.

Inverness, the largest settlement in the region and 'capital of the Highlands', became a city in 2000. It lies at the north-eastern end of the **Great Glen**, which cuts diagonally across the southern Highlands to **Fort William**, like a surgical incision, linking deep and mysterious **Loch Ness** with the west coast and giving access to **Glencoe**, one of the most beautifully evocative Highland glens and a major climbing and skiing centre.

Inverness is also ideally situated for exploring the **north-east coast**, with its charming old fishing ports, and the storm-lashed north coast, running west from **John O'Groats** to **Cape Wrath**, as wild and remote a place as you could ever wish for.

The main town on the **northwest coast** is **Fort William**, which lies in the shadow of **Ben Nevis**, Britain's highest mountain. North from here stretches a dramatic shoreline of deep sea lochs and sheltered coves of pure white sand backed by towering mountains and looking across to numerous Hebridean islands. West of Fort William, via the lyrical '**Road to the Isles**', is **Mallaig**, the main departure point for ferries to Skye. Further north is **Ullapool**, one of the main ferry ports for the Outer Hebrides and the ideal base from which to explore the wild and near-deserted far northwest.

★ Don't miss...

1. **Moray Firth** Cruise with the dolphins in the Moray Firth, page 343.
2. **West Highland line** Get on board the Jacobite Steam Train and ride the West Highland line, one of the world's great train journeys, page 365.
3. **Glenelg** Drive from Shiel Bridge to this splendidly isolated village, home of Gavin Maxwell's famous otters, page 382.
4. **Applecross** Travel the vertigo-inducing route over the mountains to this village where you can sit with a pint of fresh prawns washed down with Red Cuillin ale in the cosy Applecross Inn, page 387.
5. **Sandwood Bay** Go for a walk along the beach here and watch the sun set with a bottle of single malt and a loved one, page 401.
6. **Aonoch Mhor** Take your bike on a gondola up to this ski resort and then test your nerve by riding it back down the steep mountain slopes, page 364.

Ins and outs

Getting there

There are daily flights to Inverness airport from London, Glasgow and Edinburgh. Inverness is linked to the south by the fast A9 from Edinburgh and Perth, to Aberdeen by the A96 and to Fort William by the A82, and is well served by buses. Wick, Thurso, Ullapool and Kyle of Lochalsh can all be reached by bus from Inverness. The rail line from Edinburgh closely follows the A9 to Inverness, and there are connections north to Wick and Thurso, west to Kyle of Lochalsh and east to Aberdeen. Fort William is easily reached from Glasgow by buses and trains which continue to Mallaig for the ferry to Skye.

Getting around

Getting around in the Highlands is a lot easier with your own transport, especially in the more remote parts, but it's not difficult to reach the main tourist centres by bus or train. Getting off the beaten track can be a little more complicated, but with forward planning is easily achievable. Much of the time you'll need to rely on the local postbus service, www.royalmail.com/postbus, which runs between the various remote post offices throughout the region. Timetables are available at most post offices or tourist information centres. A good idea is to purchase the *Public Transport Travel Guides for South Highland and/or North Highland and Orkney*. These are available at main tourist offices for £1. Details of ferries from the mainland ports to Skye, the Outer Hebrides and Orkney are given in the respective island chapters. Highlands Council produces guides showing timetables for all modes of transport for the Highland area, T01463 702458, public.transport@highland.gov.uk.

By far the most scenic route to the Highlands is the spectacular West Highland Railway, one of the world's great rail journeys, particularly the section from Fort William to Mallaig.

Tourist information

Roughly speaking, this chapter covers the northern half of mainland Scotland and is covered by the *Highlands of Scotland Tourist Board*, T01997-421160, www.visithighlands.com, T0845-2255121, which publishes free accommodation guides for the region. They will also book accommodation for a nominal fee. Note that many of the smaller offices are closed during the low season.

Climate

The beauty of the northwest Highlands is only enhanced by the notoriously unpredictable weather and that ever-present travelling companion, the midge. That's a lie. The midge is the scourge of many a Highland holiday: a ferocious, persistent and unbelievably irritating little beast who will drive you to the edge of sanity. For details on how best to combat this little terror, see page 62.

The only predictable thing about the weather is its unpredictability. You can have blazing sunshine in April, pouring rain in July and a blizzard in May. So, you'll need to be prepared for everything. Climbers and walkers especially must take heed of all weather warnings. It can be hot enough for bikinis in the car park at the foot of a 2,000-ft mountain, and two hours later near the summit you're faced with driving, horizontal hail, rain or snow and unable to see further than the end of your nose. People die every year on the Scottish mountains simply because they are ill-prepared, and it is essential to take proper precautions, see page 56. Even those who are not intent on bagging the odd Munro should remember the old adage, that there's no such thing as bad weather, only inadequate clothing.

Inverness

→ *Phone code: 01463. Colour map 2, grid C2. Population: 42,000.*

Inverness is the only city in the Highlands and the busy and prosperous hub of the region. All main routes through the Highlands pass through here at some point, so it's a hard place to avoid. The town's position at the head of the Great Glen and on the shores of the Moray Firth have made it a firm favourite with tourists, who flock here in their legions during the summer months to look for the evasive Loch Ness Monster. Though Inverness has little in the way of major sights, it's a pleasant place to base yourself as you explore the other, more visible attractions on offer in the surrounding area, including the resident population of dolphins in the Moray Firth. The city, though, is not without its own appeal, particularly the leafy banks of the River Ness, which runs through its heart, linking Loch Ness with the Moray Firth. ▸▸ *For Sleeping, Eating and other listings, see pages 340-345.*

Ins and outs

Getting there

There are daily flights to and from London Gatwick, Glasgow and Edinburgh with British Airways, and daily flights to and from London Luton and London Gatwick with easyJet. There are also flights to and from Birmingham and Manchester (Monday and Friday) with Eastern Airways, and to and from Stornoway (Monday to Saturday) with British Airways Express. The airport is seven miles east of the town at Dalcross (T01667-464000, www.hial.co.uk). A twice-daily airport bus to and from the town centre connects with London and Stornoway flights. It takes 20 minutes and costs £2.50. A taxi to/from the airport costs £10-13. The bus station is nearby, just off Academy Street, T01463-233371. Left luggage costs £2-3 per item, open Monday to Saturday 0830-1800, Sunday 1000-1800. The train station is at the east end of Academy Street, T01463-239026. Left-luggage lockers at the train station cost £2-4 per 24 hours. ▸▸ *For further details, see page 344.*

Getting around

Inverness town centre is compact and easy to explore on foot, and most of the hotels and guest houses are within a 15-minute walk of the TIC. Loch Ness is not within walkable distance, so you'll need your own transport, or alternatively book a tour, see pages 343 and 359.

Tourist information

Tourist information centre ⓘ *T01463-234353*, or National Contact Centre ⓘ *T0845-2255121*, is on Castle Wynd, near Ness Bridge, a five-minute walk from the train station. It stocks a wide range of literature on the area, can book accommodation and transport and gives out free maps of the town and environs. Tickets for all the tours listed on the next few pages are available from the TIC. Open daily Easter-November, Monday-Saturday November-Easter.

History

One of the old town's first visitors was that much-travelled cleric, St Columba, who came in AD 565 to confront the Pictish King Brude, whose fortress was reputedly at Craig Phadraig, a few miles west of Inverness. Around the mid-12th century King David I built the original castle and made Inverness a royal burgh on the strength of its

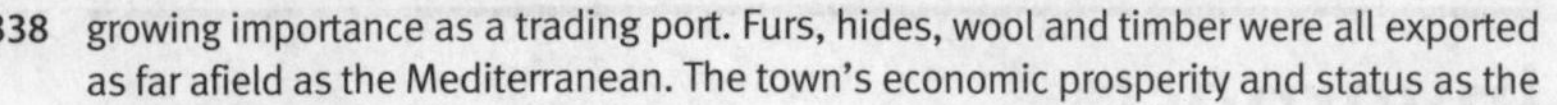

growing importance as a trading port. Furs, hides, wool and timber were all exported as far afield as the Mediterranean. The town's economic prosperity and status as the

Inverness

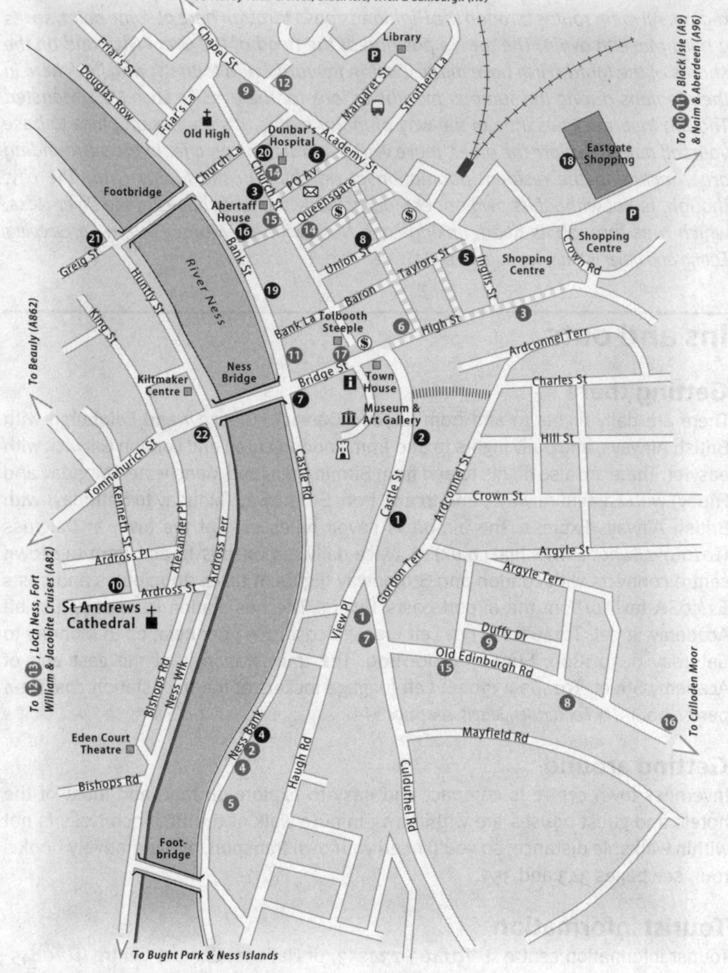

To Moray Firth Cruises, Black Isle, Wick & Edinburgh (A9)

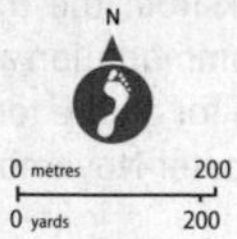

Sleeping
Bazpackers Hostel 1
Brae Ness 2
Culloden House 10
Dionard Guest House 16
Dunain Park 13
Eastgate Backpackers Hostel & Zanzibar 3
Felstead House 4
Glenmoriston Town House 5
Ho Ho Hostel 6
Inverness Hostel 7
Ivybank Guesthouse 8
Kinkell House 9
Melness Guest House 15
Moyness House 12
SYHA Hostel 11
Wetherspoon's Lodge 14

Eating
Café No 1 1
Castle 2
Chez Christophe 10
Dickens 3
Glen Mhor Hotel 4
Jimmy Chung's Chinese Buffet 8
Lemon Tree 5
Mustard Seed 16
Pizza Express 18
Raja 6
Red Pepper 20
River Café & Restaurant 19
River House 21
Rocpool 22
Shapla 7

Bars & clubs
Blackfriars 9
Chilli Palmers 14
Gellions 17
Hootenanny & Sofa Bar 15
Johnny Foxes 11
Phoenix Bar 13
Shot's 12

most important northern outpost, however, made it a prime target for marauding Highland clansmen, and during the Wars of Independence in the 13th century Inverness was also a regular target for both English and Scots armies.

The town's renaissance came with the completion of the Caledonian Canal and rail links with the south in the 19th century. These improved communications heralded something of a tourist boom amongst the wealthy and fashionable who came north to the Highlands to shoot anything that moved in the name of sport. In the mid-19th century Queen Victoria decided to embrace all things Scottish, which only boosted the town's popularity. Over recent decades Inverness has grown rapidly, not only as a prime base for visiting tourists, but also as the main administrative and commercial centre for the Highlands. In 2000 it was given city status, a move which has given it a considerable boost.

Sights

The city is dominated by its red sandstone **castle** ⓘ *T01463-243363, Mar-Nov Mon-Sat (Sun only in Jul/Aug) 1030-1730, £4, concession/child £3. Built in 1834*, this Victorian edifice is very much the new kid on the block in terms of Scottish castles. The original castle dates from the 12th century and was built on a ridge to the east of the present structure. Nothing remains of the old castle, which is unsurprising given its bloody and eventful history. It was here that King Duncan of Scotland was slain by Macbeth, an event dramatically (and erroneously) portrayed in Shakespeare's eponymous work. The castle was occupied three times during the Wars of Independence in the 13th century, and when Robert the Bruce recaptured it in 1307 he destroyed it. In the mid-17th century Cromwell ordered his men to build a stone version on the same site. In 1715 James Francis Edward was proclaimed king there, but not long after it was destroyed by the Jacobites to prevent it from falling into enemy hands following the defeat of Bonnie Prince Charlie at Culloden, see page 356. The present castle houses the Sheriff Court and also stages the Castle Garrison Encounter, where you can sign up as a mid-18th-century soldier. New recruits (that's you) pass through the Quartermaster's Store and are introduced to the Sergeant of the Guard, before being accosted by a female camp follower and finally led out through the garrison shop. On the castle terrace is a statue of Flora MacDonald, to honour her part in helping the prince to escape, see box page 436.

Nairn is only 5 miles from the airport and makes a pleasant alternative to staying in Inverness.

Below the castle is **Inverness Museum and Art Gallery** ⓘ *Mon-Sat 0900-1700, free, Castle Wynd beside the TIC*. The museum gives a decent overview of the history of the town and the region, while the gallery hosts some special exhibitions that have included paintings by the Scottish colourist JD Fergusson. Just around the corner, on High Street, is the Gothic-style **Town House**, where Prime Minister Lloyd George held an emergency cabinet meeting in 1921, the first ever to be held outside London.

Opposite, on the corner of Bridge Street and Church Street, is the **Tolbooth Steeple** which dates from 1791 and which had to be repaired after an earth tremor in 1816. Church Street also boasts the town's oldest building, **Abertarff House** ⓘ *T01463-250999*. Built around 1592, it is now a contemporary art and jewellery gallery. Almost opposite is the much-restored **Dunbar's Hospital**, built in 1688 as an almshouse for the town's poor. At the end of Church Street, where it meets Friar's Lane, is the **Old High Church** ⓘ *Fri 1245-1315, mid Jun-mid Sep Fri 1200-1400, guided tour at 1230*, founded in the 12th century and rebuilt in 1772, though the 14th-century vaulted tower remains intact. In the adjoining graveyard prisoners taken at Culloden were executed, and you can still see the bullet marks left by the firing squads on some of the gravestones.

At the corner of Huntly Street and Ness Bridge, is the **Kiltmaker Centre** ⓘ *T01463-222781, www.hector-russell.com, Mid-May-end Sep Mon-Sat 0900-2100, Sun 1000-1700, Oct-mid-May Mon-Sat 0900-1700, £2, concession £1*, where you can learn everything you ever wanted to know about tartan (including what Scotsmen wear under their kilts). You can also see kilts being made in the factory and, in the shop downstairs, be measured up for one of your own. Nearby, directly opposite the castle, is the neo-Gothic **St Andrews Cathedral** which dates from 1869, and is worth a peek if you're passing by. Continuing south along Ness Bank, past the **Eden Court Theatre**, see Entertainment page 342, you reach **Bught Park**, see Sleeping page 340, which overlooks the Ness Islands, joined by footbridge to both banks. The islands are attractively laid out as a park and are a favourite with local anglers. This also happens to be a lovely place for a peaceful evening stroll.

Sleeping

Inverness *p337, map p338*

You shouldn't have much trouble finding somewhere to stay in Inverness, though in Jul and Aug it's advisable to book ahead. This can be done through the TIC, or less cheaply, at the train station at the Thomas Cook booth; you'll be charged a booking fee, see p43.

There are several good quality hotels in and around town and plenty of B&Bs. The best places to look are along both banks of the river south of the Ness Bridge, Old Edinburgh Rd and Ardconnel St (east of the castle) and around Bruce Gardens, Ardross St, Kenneth St and Fairfield Rd(the west bank). There are also several budget hostels in and around the centre, and a couple of campsites.

L Culloden House Hotel, Milton of Culloden, 3 miles east of town near the A9. T01463-790461, www.cullodenhouse.co.uk. 28 rooms. Superb Georgian mansion with 1st-class facilities, service and restaurant.

A Dunain Park Hotel, about 3 miles southwest of the town centre, just off the A82 Fort William Rd, T01463-230512, www.dunainparkhotel.co.uk. 11 rooms. An elegant Georgian mansion house with its own grounds, lovely and peaceful with an excellent restaurant, see Eating p341, and its own indoor pool.

B Glenmoriston Town House Hotel, 20 Ness Bank, T01463-223777. 15 rooms. Recently refurbished and now one of the classiest places in town, with a superb Italian restaurant, see Eating p341.

B Inverness Marriot, Culcabock Rd, 1 mile south of the town centre near A9, T01463-237166, F225208. 82 rooms. Large, modern hotel with excellent rooms, service and facilities.

C Brae Ness Hotel, 17 Ness Bank, T01463-712266, www.braenesshotel.co.uk. 10 rooms. No smoking. Family-run Georgian hotel overlooking the river and Eden Court, with a licensed restaurant for residents.

C Felstead House, 18 Ness Bank. T/F01463-231634, felsteadgh@aol.com. 8 rooms, 5 with en suite. Family-run Georgian guest house, large and comfortable rooms, good breakfast and overall good value.

C Glenruidh House Hotel, Old Edinburgh Rd South, 2 miles from the town centre (phone for directions). T01463-226499, www.cozzee-nessie-bed.co.uk. 5 rooms. No smoking. Comfortable and peaceful hotel in secluded setting, with friendly service and excellent food.

C Highland Voyages, Eala Bhan tall ship, T01463-404441, www.highlandvoyages.co.uk. When moored at Seaport Marina has on board accommodation in 3 and 2 bunk cabins, evening meals available.

C Ivybank Guesthouse, 28 Old Edinburgh Rd, T/F01463-232796, www.ivybankguesthouse.com. 5 rooms, 3 with en suite bathroom. Georgian house with lots of character, nice garden and friendly welcome.

C Melness Guest House, 8 Old Edinburgh Rd, T01463-220963, www.melness@visit-inverness.com. 2 rooms, 1 en suite. Very clean and comfortable accommodation.

C Moyness House Hotel, 6 Bruce Gardens, T/F01463-233836, www.moyness.co.uk. Fine Victorian villa in a quiet area near the theatre, with very clean and comfortable en suite rooms and nice touches like Body Shop products in the bathrooms. No smoking.

D Dionard Guest House, 39 Old Edinburgh Rd, T01463-233557, www.dionardguest

house.co.uk. 4 rooms, friendly and comfortable B&B a few mins walk from the centre of the city.

D Kinkell House, 11 Old Edinburgh Rd, T01463-235243, clare@kinkell.freeserve.co.uk. 7 rooms, 3 with en suite bathroom. Comfortable Victorian family home with spacious rooms, decent value (£2 charge for credit card payment).

D Wetherspoon's Lodge, 72-74 Church St, T01463-251800, invernesslodge@jdwether spoon.co.uk. 27 en suite rooms. Great value central rooms, if rather lacking in character, breakfast not included but available in the bar.

F Bazpackers Hostel, 4 Culduthel Rd (at the top of Castle St), T01463-717663, bazmail@ btopenworld.com. 48 beds in dorms of 4-8, twin and double rooms available, cooking facilities and garden for barbecues, also has laundrette, good atmosphere.

F Eastgate Backpackers Hostel, 38 Eastgate T/F01463-718756, www.hostelsaccommod ation.com. 38 beds, free tea and coffee, and continental breakfast for £1.50.

F Ho Ho Hostel, 23a High St, T01463-221225, www.hohohostel.force9.com, is another cheap option.

F Inverness Student Hotel, 8 Culduthel Rd, next door to **Bazpackers**, T01463-236556. 9 dorms with 54 beds, some dorms have good views. Friendly and laid-back atmosphere with all the usual facilities.

F SYHA Youth Hostel, Victoria Drive, off Millburn Rd, T0871-3308529. 166 beds. Huge hostel in former school hall of residence.

Camping

Bught Caravan and Camping Site Bught Park, on the west bank of the river near the sports centre, T01463-236920. The largest and most centrally located campsite, with good facilities, £4.30-11.40 per pitch.

Eating

Inverness *p337, map p338*

As you'd expect in a major tourist centre, there's the usual plethora of pubs, cafés and restaurants serving cheap and basic food for the non-discerning palate, but those looking for a high standard of cuisine won't be disappointed either. Takeaways are plentiful particularly on Academy St, Eastgate, around the train station and on Young St, just across the Ness Bridge.

£££ Chez Christophe, 16 Ardross St, T01463-717126. High quality French cuisine a few minutes from the city centre.

£££ Dunain Park Hotel, see Sleeping. Award-winning Scots-French cuisine in elegant surroundings, with a superb list of malts. Take a stroll in the lovely gardens afterwards.

£££ Glen Mhor Hotel, 9-12 Ness Bank, T01463-234308. Their **Riverview** restaurant at the front is good, especially for seafood and the bistro, **Nico's** offers a cheaper alternative.

£££ La Riviera, **Glenmoriston Town House Hotel**, see Sleeping. Excellent Italian food.

£££ River House Restaurant, 1 Grieg St, T01463-22203. Green tartan outside is a clue to the fact that this restaurant serves good quality Scottish produce. Dishes might include sea bass, or Highland game stew. 3 courses for £27.95. Tue-Sat 1200-1400, 1830-late.

££ Café No 1, 75 Castle St, T01463-226200. Nice contemporary decor, good selection of vegetarian options. Mon-Sat 1200-1400 and 1800-2130.

££ Dickens, 77 Church St, T01463-713111. Offers a mix of oriental and international dishes with an emphasis on fish, set lunch for £6.50. Daily 1200-1400 and 1730-2300.

££ The Mustard Seed, 16 Fraser St, T01463-220220. Lovely contemporary restaurant, with cheery yellow walls and sculptural flowers as well as an imaginative menu. Lunch choices like spinach and gorgonzola polenta, dinner might include salmon or guinea fowl. Daily 1200-1500, 1800-2200.

££ Pizza Express, Falcon Sq, T01463-709700. New branch of the dependable pizza chain. Mon-Sat 1130-2200, Sun 1200-2200.

££ The River Café and Restaurant, 10 Bank St, T01463-714884. Offers high teas and traditional dishes like haggis. Mon 1000-2030, Tue-Sat 1000-2130, Sun 1200-2030.

For an explanation of sleeping and eating price codes used in this guide, see inside the front cover. Other relevant information is found in Essentials, see pages 43-51.

££ Rocpool, 1 Ness Walk, T01463-717274. Very popular contemporary restaurant with wooden floors and crisp white tablecloths. Serves dishes like fillet of beef or lemon and herb risotto. Daily 1200-1430, 1800-2200.
££ Shapla, 2 Castle Rd, T01463-241919. Good Indian restaurant with Tandoori and Balti menu and good views of the river in the upstairs lounge. Daily 1200-2330.
£ Castle Restaurant, 41 Castle St. Clean, no nonsense café serving huge portions of stodgy, filling grub at low prices, convenient for backpacker's hostels. Daily till 2100.
£ Jimmy Chung's Chinese Buffet, 28-36 Union St, T01463-237878. Cheap Chinese food served daily 1145-1445 and 1700-2300.
£ The Lemon Tree, 18 Inglis St. Located in the pedestrianized town centre, family-run café offering good home-baking and basic but filling meals.
£ The Red Pepper, Bow Court, 74 Church St, T01463-237111. Bustling little café/takeaway offering fresh paninis, sandwiches, soups and salads. Mon-Sat 1930-1630.
For picnic supplies check out **Gourmet's Lair**, 8 Union St, a great deli with all sorts of goodies. **Ashers**, Church St, is a good bakery.

Bars and clubs

Inverness *p337, map p338*
Blackfriars,Academy St, a decent pub.
Chilli Palmers, on the corner of Queensgate and Church St, is a trendy new bar offering decent food and a DJ at weekends, and you can enjoy a Jazz Lunch on Sun at No 27, on Castle St.
Gellions, Bridge St, has varied live music throughout the week.
Hootananny, 67 Church St. A great bet for atmosphere and all things Scottish, has live music every night and anyone is welcome to get involved with the Mon and Tue sessions. They have ceilidhs 1500-1700 on Sat and Gaelic speaking meetings 1930-2030 on Mon.
Johnny Foxes, 26 Bank St, features Irish folk music every night in summer as well as boasting one of the most unusual pub menus around.
Phoenix, 108 Academy St. One of the best pubs in town and always lively.
Shot's, Academy St, next door to Phoenix, a sports pub.
Sofa Bar, above **Hootenanny**, aims to please a younger crowd with live bands, DJs and comfy sofas.

Entertainment

Inverness *p337, map p338*
Cinema The cinema attached to Eden Court Theatre, see below, shows a programme of art house and newly released movies, for information: T01463-234234. Prices vary depending on the performance.
Warner Village, A96 Nairn Rd, about 2 miles from the town centre, The 7-screen. Tickets cost from £4.
Theatre Eden Court Theatre, Bishops Rd, overlooking the River Ness. It offers a varied programme of theatre, dance and all kinds of music. There's also a bar and self-service restaurant with good food and views over the river.

Festivals and events

Inverness *p337, map p338*
There are numerous events held in and around Inverness throughout the year. These range from a humble pub ceilidh and a food festival and to a full-blown Highland Games. For details contact the tourist information centre or visit their website.
Feb/Mar: **Inverness Music Festival**, T01463-716616.
Easter The best of the local folk festivals are held over the Easter weekend, T01738-623274.
Jun: **Highland Festival** is excellent and taking place over several days at the end of the month, T01463-711112, www.highlandfestival.demon.co.uk.
Jul: **The Inverness Tattoo** is held in the Northern meeting Park.

Shopping

Inverness *p337, map p338*
Inverness is a good place to buy a kilt, or practically anything else in tartan. To find your own clan tartan, head for the Scottish Kiltmaker Visitor Centre, see Sights.
Bookshops There are several bookshops in town.
Leakey's, Castle St, is a brilliant second-hand bookshop which has about 100,000 books

Big blue

The waters in this area are renowned for their populations of the well-loved mammal, the dolphin. Buckie is the home of the Moray Firth Wildlife Centre, which houses a dolphin exhibition, where you can find out evrything you ever wanted to know about them. There are various dolphin-spotting cruises around the Moray Firth, but there is a code of conduct for boat operators. Before you choose a cruise, make sure the company is part of the Accreditation Scheme.

Moray Firth Dolphin Cruises, Inverness, T01463-717900, morayfirth.cruises@virgin.net, are accredited and offer trips for £10 (£8 concession), last 1½ hours and leave from Shore Street Quay (at the far end of Chapel St). Buses run from the TIC 15 minutes before sailings.

McAuley Charters, Harbour offices, Longman Drive, Inverness, T01463-717337, are also accredited and offer dolphin-spotting cruises which leave from Cromarty (see page 413) and Buckie.

with a huge wood burning stove in the middle of the shop and a café upstairs.
Waterstone's, 50-52 High St.

Highland dress and traditional gifts
Chisholm's Highland Dress, 47-51 Castle St, T01463-234599, 0900-1730 and 1900-2130 in Jul and Aug.
Hector Russell, 4-9 Huntly St, T01463-222781.
James Pringle Weavers, Holm Mills, Dores Rd, T01463-223311.
Mall **Eastgate Shopping Centre** has all the usual high-street branches like Gap and Marks and Spencer.
Market **Victorian Market**, Church St, has a wide range of shops.

Activities and tours

Inverness *p337, map p338*
Boat tours **Fingal of Caledonia**, T01397-772167, www.fingal-cruising.co.uk, run all-inclusive 4- and 6-day cruises in a converted Dutch 'spitz' barge that gently ploughs its way through the 60-mile waterway of the Great Glen. During this time guests can make use of mountain bikes, canoes, sailing dinghies and windsurfers lashed to the deck. Guides and instructors are included. Cruises operate from Apr to Oct and cost from £250-525 per person.
Bus tours **Guide Friday** run open-topped bus tours around the city and to Culloden. Tours leave from Bridge St near the TIC at 1000 and then every 45 mins till 1645 from May to Oct. Tickets can be bought at their booth in the train station, T01463-224000, Mon-Fri 0900-1730, Sat 0830-1745, or on board the bus. Full-day tour costs £7.50, concession £6, children £2.50. They also run half-day bus tours around Loch Ness.
Cycling The recently opened **Great Glen Way** (see Walking below) can be cycled. The stretch alongside the **Caledonian Canal** is flat and good for families. For a free leaflet, T01320-366322.
Golf The best golf course in the area is at Nairn (see p348). There's an 18-hole municipal course at Torvean, 2 miles from town on the A82 to Fort William, T01463-711434.
Ghost tours **Inverness Terror Tour** leaves from outside the tourist office at 1900 nightly and tells the tale of the town's horrific past, complete with witches, ghosts, torture and murders.
Horse riding **Highland Riding Centre**, Borlum Farm, Drumnadrochit, T01456-450892, www.borlum.com.
Iceskating There's an Ice Centre at Bught Park, T01463-235711, www.inverness-ice-centre.org.uk.
Leisure centre **Aquadome Leisure Centre**, Bught Park, T01463-667500, Mon-Fri 0730-2200, Sat-Sun 0730-2100. Competition-sized pool, flumes, wave machine and kiddies' pool, also health suites, gym and other indoor sports facilities.
Loch Ness tours **Jacobite Cruises**, T01463-233999, www.jacobite.co.uk, run a

variety of coach tours, boat cruises and combined coach and cruise trips around the loch.

Discover Loch Ness, T0800-7315564 (freephone), www.discoverlochness.com, run cultural tours which include a cruise and entry to Urquhart Castle. Tours leave Inverness at 1030 all year round. Summer prices: half-day tour from £22, or £12 without a boat trip or castle entry; full-day tour £30.

George Edwards, contact Loch Ness Cruises, T01456-450395, www.lochness-cruises.com, or Original Loch Ness Monster Visitor Centre, see p352, takes would-be monster-spotters out on the loch in his boat, Nessie Hunter, which is based near Drumnadrochit. He not only once caught a glimpse of Nessie but also discovered the deepest part of the loch (812 ft), now known as Edward's Deep. Cruises run from Apr to Oct 0930-1800. They last 1 hr and cost £9 per adult and £5 per child.

Orkney tours Orkney Islands Day Tours leave from Inverness every day throughout the summer. The tour departs daily 1 Jun-2 Sep from Inverness bus station at 0730; returns 2100. Booking essential; £44 per person, under 16 half price. Details from the tourist office, or contact **John O'Groats Ferries**, Ferry Office, John O'Groats, Caithness. T01955-611353, F611301, www.jogferry.co.uk (for tours from John O'Groats, see p409).

Tennis and squash Inverness Tennis and Squash Club, Bishop's Rd, T01463-230751.

Ten-pin bowling Roller Bowl, 167 Culduthel Rd, T01463-235100, Mon-Fri 1200 till late, Sat-Sun 1100 till late.

Walking Great Glen Way is a new, waymarked walking trail that runs for 73 miles between Inverness and Fort William. Panoramic views of Loch Ness can be seen at many of the sections between Fort Augustus and Inverness. Although a relatively easy walk, there are some fairly tough sections around Loch Ness and you'll need to be properly equipped and have a good map. OS Landranger Nos 26, 34 and 41 cover the entire route. The route should take 4-5 days to complete, depending on your level of fitness. It is probably better to walk it in 'reverse', from Fort William to Inverness, as the easiest section is then at the start. The Great Glen Way also has its own website at www.greatglenway.com.

Transport

Inverness *p337, map p338*

Bus There are regular daily buses to **Glasgow** and **Edinburgh** (via **Aviemore**), **Pitlochry** and **Perth** with Scottish Citylink, T0990-505050. Change at Perth for **Dundee**. There are regular daily **Citylink** buses to **Ullapool**, connecting with the ferry to **Stornoway**; also to **Fort William** and **Oban**. There are daily Citylink buses to **Kyle of Lochalsh**, **Portree** and **Uig** (connecting with ferries to **Tarbert** and **Lochmaddy**). There are regular Citylink buses to **Fort Augustus** via **Drumnadrochit** and **Urquhart Castle** (also with Highland Bus & Coach, T01463-233371), and to **Scrabster**, for the ferry to **Stromness**, via **Wick** and **Thurso**; also with Morrison's Coaches, T01847-821241.

To **Ullapool** via **Gairloch** and **Aultbea**, there are daily buses with Spa Coaches, T01997-421311, Bluebird Northern, T01463-239292 and Westerbus T01445-712255. To **Tain** and **Lairg** there are daily services with Bluebird and Rapson's. To **Tain** and **Helsmdale**, via **Dornoch** there are regular daily buses with Citylink, Morrison's and Bluebird. To **Lochinver** via **Ullapool** there's a daily service with Spa coaches and Rapson's of Brora, T01408-621245. To **Durness** via **Lairg** and **Tongue**, or via **Ullapool** (not in winter) there's a daily service with Royal Mail postbuses, T0131-2287407. To **Grantown-on-Spey**, daily service with Highland Country Buses, T01463-233371, and Highland Bus & Coach. Inverness Traction and Highland Country Buses have services to places around **Inverness**, including **Nairn**, **Forres**, **Culloden**, **Beauly** and **Dingwall**. Bluebird have regular buses to **Aberdeen**, via **Nairn**.

Boat For details of connections to **Stornoway** (Lewis) see p458, or contact the CalMac office in Inverness, T01463-717681. For **Scrabster** to **Stromness**, run by Northlink Ferries, T01856-851144, www.northlinkferries.co.uk, see p550.

Taxi Rank Radio Taxis, T01463-221111; Tartan Taxis, T01463-233033. For a **Taxi Tour** of the area, T01463-220222.

Train For more information, T0845-7484950. There are direct trains to/from **Aberdeen**, **Edinburgh** (via **Aviemore**) and **Glasgow**. There are several daily services to/from **London King's Cross** (via **Perth**) and **Edinburgh**, and a Caledonian Sleeper service from **London Euston** to **Inverness** and **Fort William**, ScotRail, T08457 550033, www.scotrail.co.uk. There is also a regular service to **Wick** and **Thurso**, via **Tain**, **Lairg** and **Helmsdale**. The journey from Inverness to **Kyle of Lochalsh** (for Skye) is one of the most scenic in Britain. There are 3 trains daily (none on Sun).

Directory

Inverness *p337, map p338*

Banks All the major banks can be found in the town centre. The **Royal Bank** is on the High St; the **Bank of Scotland** is opposite the Town House on the High St; the **Clydesdale** is opposite the train station; and **Lloyds TSB** is on Church St.

Currency exchange Money can be changed at the TIC's bureau de change at 2.5% commission, see below for address and opening hours. Also **Thomas Cook**, 9-13 Inglis St, T711921, Mon-Fri 0900-1700; and **Alba Travel** (American Express agents), 43 Church St, T01463- 239188, Mon-Sat 0900-1700.

Car hire **Avis** is at the airport (T01667-462787); **Budget** is on Railway Terr behind the train station (T01463-713333); **Europcar** has an office at 16 Telford St (T0870-0500289), and at the airport (0870-8700120); **Sharps Reliable Wrecks**, Railway Station, Academy St, T01463-236694 and at the airport T01463-461212, www.sharpsreliablewrecks.co.uk.

Thrifty is at 33 Harbour Rd, T01463-T224466. Expect to pay from around £30 per day.

Cultural centres Inverness library is opposite the bus station. It has an excellent genealogical research unit. Consultations with the resident genealogist cost £12 per hr; T236463, for an appointment. The library also houses the Highland archives, where you can research the history and culture of the region. Open Mon-Fri 1100-1300 and 1400-1700; Oct-May 1400-1700 only.

Cycle hire **Barney's Bicycle Hire & Shop**, 35 Castle St, T01463-232249. Daily 0900-2100 in season. Mountain bike hire from £12 per day. **Highland Cycles**, Telford St, T01463-234789. Mon-Sat 0900-1730 all year, range of bikes available from £11 per day. Also bikes for hire from **Bazpacker's Hostel**, see Sleeping p340.

Hospitals **Raigmore Hospital**, on the southeastern outskirts of town near the A9, T01463-704000, for accidents and emergencies.

Internet Available from the **TIC**, the **Launderette**, Young St, **The Mail Box**, Station Sq and at the **library**. **The Gate café bar**, opposite the post office, has internet facilities and serves drinks and snacks, 1000-2100.

Pharmacies **Boots**, Eastgate Shopping Centre; daily 0900-1730, Thu till 1900. The main branch is at 14-16 Queensgate, T01463-234111. Mon-Thu 0900-1730, Fri 0930-1730, Sat 0900-1320.

Around Inverness

→ Colour map 2, grid C2.

East of Inverness along the Moray Firth stretches a long coastline of cliff-top walks, fine beaches, attractive old towns and many historic sites and castles. The Moray Firth is perhaps best known for its large resident population, the largest dolphins in the world. Over 100 of these beautiful and intelligent mammals live in the estuary, the most northerly breeding ground in Europe, and there's a very good chance of seeing them, particularly between June and August. The Moray Firth dolphins have become a major tourist attraction and several companies run dolphin-spotting boat trips. You can also see them from the shore. Two of the best places are, on the southern shore of the Black Isle, see page 412, and Fort George, on the opposite shore, see below. The Kessock Bridge, which crosses the Moray Firth to the Black Isle, is another good dolphin-spotting location and also has a visitor centre, where you can listen in to their underwater conversations.

The attractions that follow can be visited as day-trips from Inverness.

Battle of Culloden

The second Jacobite rebellion of 1745 was ill-fated from the start. Bonnie Prince Charlie's expedition south lacked sufficient support and was turned back at Derby. After their long and dispiriting retreat north, the half-starved, under-strength army – exhausted after an abortive night attack on Hanoverian forces at Nairn – faced overwhelmingly superior forces under the command of the ambitious Duke of Cumberland at Culloden.

The open, flat ground of Culloden Moor was hopelessly unsuitable for the Highlanders' style of fighting, which relied on steep hills and plenty of cover to provide the element of surprise for their brave but undisciplined attacks. In only 40 minutes the Prince's army was blown away by the English artillery, and the Jacobite charge, when it finally came, was ragged and ineffective. Cumberland's troops then went on to commit the worst series of atrocities ever carried out by a British Army. Some 1,200 men were slain, many as they lay wounded on the battlefield. Prince Charlie, meanwhile, fled west where loyal Highlanders protected him until he made his final escape to France.

But the real savagery was to come. Cumberland resolved to make an example of the Highlands. Not only were the clans disarmed and the wearing of Highland dress forbidden, but the Government troops began an orgy of brutal reprisals across the region. Within a century the clan system had ended and the Highland way of life changed forever. For further information see page 602.

West of Inverness, the Moray Firth becomes the Beauly Firth, a relatively quiet little corner despite its proximity to Inverness, as most traffic heading north crosses the Kessock Bridge on the main A9. The A862 west to Beauly offers a more scenic alternative, and the chance to visit a 13th-century priory and a distillery. South of Beauly, the A831 leads to two of Scotland's most beautiful glens, Glen Strathfarrarand Glen Affric. *» For Sleeping, Eating and other listings, see pages 350-351.*

The Moray Firth

Culloden → *Colour map 2, grid C2.*

ⓘ *T01463-790607. Site open daily all year. Visitor centre open Feb-31 Mar and 1 Nov to 31 Dec daily 1100-1600, 1 Apr-30 Jun, 1 Sep-31 Oct daily 0900-1800, Jul, Aug daily 0900-1900. Visitor centre, including audio-visual presentation, and Old Leanach cottage £5, concession £3.75, children £1. Wheelchair access, bookshop, restaurant.* The eerie and windswept Culloden Moor, five miles to the east of Inverness on the B9006, was the site of the last major battle fought on the British mainland. The Jacobite cause was finally lost here, on 16 April 1746, when the army of Prince Charles Edward Stuart was crushed by the superior Government forces, led by the Duke of Cumberland, whose savagery earned him the nickname 'Butcher'. Contrary to popular myth this was not a battle between the Scots and the English, more a civil war: there were actually English Jacobites while many Scots fought for the Government. It is now owned by the National Trust for Scotland.

The battlefield has been restored to its original state (minus the dead bodies). The visitor centre is the obvious starting point and gives a graphic audio-visual description of the gruesome episode. From the visitor centre paths lead across the field to the clan graves, marked by simple headstones which bear the names of the

“” Culloden is a melancholy place and by far the most painfully evocative of Scotland's battlefields, especially on a bleak and windy winter's day...

clans who fought. Next to the visitor centre, the restored cottage of Old Leanach – which was used by the Jacobites as a headquarters, and where 30 Highlanders were burnt alive – is arranged as it would have been at the time of the battle. A memorial cairn, erected in 1881, is the scene each April of a commemorative service organized by the Gaelic Society of Inverness.

Clava Cairns

This impressive and important Bronze-Age site lies only a mile southeast of Culloden and is well worth a short detour. The 5,000 year-old site consists of three large burial cairns encircled by standing stones, set in a grove of trees. The less imaginative visitor may see it as merely a pile of stones but no one can fail to be affected by the spooky atmosphere of the place. This is even more perceptible when no one else is around! To get there, continue on the B9006 past Culloden Moor, then turn right at the Culloden Moor Inn and follow the signs for Clava Lodge. Look for the sign on the right of the road.

Fort George → *Colour map 2, grid C2.*

ⓘ T01667-460232, Apr-Oct daily 0930-1830, Oct-Mar Mon-Sat 0930-1630, Sun 1400-1630, £6, concession £4.50, children £1.50. Wheelchair access, café.

Standing proudly on a sandy spit that juts out into the Moray Firth is Fort George, Europe's finest surviving example of 18th-century military architecture. Begun in 1748, it was the last in a chain of three such fortifications built in the Highlands – the other two being Fort Augustus and Fort William – as a base for George II's army to prevent any potential threats to Hanoverian rule. It was completed in 1769, by which time the Highlands were more or less peaceful, but was kept in use as a military barracks. Today it remains virtually unchanged, and there are even armed sentries at the main gate. You can walk along the ramparts to get an idea of the sheer scale of the place and also enjoy the sweeping views across the Moray Firth. You may even be lucky enough to see a school of dolphins. Within the fort are the barracks, a chapel, workshops and the Regimental Museum of the Queen's Own Highlanders, which features the fascinating Seafield Collection of arms and military equipment, most of which dates from the Napoleonic Wars.

Cawdor Castle → *Colour map 2, grid C2.*

ⓘ T01667-404401, May to mid-Oct daily 1000-1730, £6.50.

Though best known for its legendary association with Shakespeare's *Macbeth*, Cawdor Castle post-dates the grisly historical events on which the great Bard based his famous tragedy. The oldest part of the castle, the central tower, dates from 1372, and the rest of it is mostly 16th or 17th century. But despite the literary disappointment, the castle is still one of the most appealing in Scotland. It has been in the hands of the Cawdor family for over six centuries and each summer they clear off, leaving their romantic home and its glorious gardens open for the enjoyment of ordinary folks like us. There's also a nine-hole golf course.

! Highlights include the impressive paintings and tapestries, the fascinating kitchen and the genuinely witty captions that have visitors laughing all over the castle.

According to family legend, an early Thane of Cawdor, wanting a new castle, had a dream in which he was told to load a donkey with gold, let it wander around for a day and watch where it lay down, for this would be the best spot for his new castle. He duly followed these instructions and the donkey lay down under a thorn tree, the remains of which can still be seen in the middle of a vaulted chamber in the 14th-century tower.

Just to the west of Cawdor is **Kilravock Castle** ① *T01667-493258, gardens Mon-Sat 1000-1600, free*. This lovely 15th century stately home (pronounced 'Kilrawk') is still the seat of the Rose family and is closed to the public but can be visited by prior appointment. You can also stay here, in the guest house, which is run on strictly Christian principles. The castle gardens are open to the public and worth visiting.

Nairn and around → *Phone code: 01667. Colour map 2, grid C2. Population: 11,190.*

The genteel seaside resort of Nairn claims the driest and sunniest climate in the whole of Scotland. This alone should be reason enough to pay a visit, but there are other attractions besides the sunshine. There are miles of sandy beach stretching east to the Culbin Forest, a championship golf course (which hosted the 1999 Walker Cup), and two of the best castles in the country are within easy reach – Cawdor Castle, see above, and Brodie Castle, see below.

Nairn Museum ① *May-Sep Mon-Sat 1000-1630, £1*, at Viewfied House on Viewfield Drive, gives an insight into the area's history with interesting account of the building of the harbour and subsequent decline of the herring industry.

About two miles east of Nairn, in the little village of **Auldearn**, is a 17th-century *doocot* (dovecote) from where the royal standard was flown, in 1645, by the victorious troops of Charles I led by the Marquis of Montrose against the Covenanters. Displays in the *doocot* ① *£1.50*, tell of the battle.

Ten miles south of Nairn on the A939 to Grantown is **Dulsie Bridge**, a very popular local beauty spot which is a great place for a summer picnic or to swim in the River Findhorn. On the southern shores of the Moray Firth, just east of Nairn, is **Culbin Sands**, a stretch of sand home to a host of birdlife. The best time to visit is from autumn to spring when bar-tailed godwits, oystercatchers, knots, dunlins, ringed plovers, redshanks, curlews, shellducks, red breasted mergansers, greylag geese and snow buntings, to name but a few, come here in their droves.

Brodie Castle

① *T01309-641371. Castle Apr, Jul, Aug daily 1200-1600, May, Jun, Sep, Sun-Thu 1200-1600; grounds all year daily 0930-sunset. Castle £5, concession £3.75, children £1; grounds only £1 (honesty box).*

Brodie Castle, 8 miles east of Nairn, just off the main A96 to Forres, is one of Scotland's finest castles. The oldest part of the castle, the Z-plan tower house, is 16th-century, with additions dating from the 17th and 19th centuries, giving it the look of a Victorian country house. The interior of the house is the epitome of good taste, with some fabulous ceilings, and you can look round several rooms, including the huge Victorian kitchen. The collections of furniture and porcelain are wonderful but most notable are the outstanding paintings, which include Edwin Landseer and Scottish Colourists. The grounds, too, are a delight, especially in spring when the daffodils are in bloom. There's also a tearoom.

The Beauly Firth

Beauly and around → *Phone code: 01463. Colour map 2, grid C1.*

The sleepy little market town of Beauly is 10 miles west of Inverness, where the Beauly river flows into the Firth. It's a lovely wee place – hence its name. According to local legend, when Mary, Queen of Scots stayed here, at the priory, in 1564, she was so taken with the place that she cried (in French, of course) "Ah, quel beau lieu!" (What a beautiful place!).

At the north end of the marketplace is the ruin of **Beauly Priory** ⓘ *Jun-end 30 Sep daily 0930-1830, £1.20, concession £0.90, children £0.50*, founded in 1230 for the Valliscaulian order, but like so much else of Scotland's ecclesiastical heritage, destroyed during the Reformation.

Four miles east of Beauly, at Balchraggan just off the main Inverness road, is **Moniack Castle Winery** ⓘ *Mon-Sat 1000-1700 summer, 1100-1600 winter*, where you can try a whole range of wines, including elderflower and birch. Four miles to the north is the **Glen Ord Distillery** ⓘ *T01463-872004, www.malts.com, Nov-Feb, Wed-Fri 1130-1500, Mar-Jun, Mon-Fri 1000-1700, Jul-Sep Mon-Sat 1000-1700, Sun 1200-1600, Oct Mon-Fri 1100-1600, £4, take a bus or train from Inverness, on the outskirts of Muir of Ord*, just off the A832. It offers a fairly good basic tour and a wonderful de-luxe tour for whisky aficionados. The River Beauly is one of Scotland's best salmon-fishing rivers, and five miles south of Beauly at **Aigas** is a fish lift ⓘ *Mon-Fri 1000-1500*, where you can watch salmon bypass the dam with the aid of technology.

Glen Strathfarrar → *Colour map 1, grid C6.*

Southwest of Beauly are glens Affric and Strathfarrar. Glen Strathfarrar, the lesser known of the two, is unspoiled and considered by some to be the more beautiful. To get there, take the A831 nine miles south from Beauly to Struyand follow the signs. Access to the glen is restricted by the owners, Scottish Natural Heritage, to 12 cars at a time and you have to leave by 1900. The glen is also closed from mid-August to October. But once you're in there is a tremendous feeling of peace, and there's good climbing, fishing and walking. The little ungraded road runs for 14 miles all the way to the impressive **Monar Dam** at the head of the glen. Glen Strathfarrar can also be reached from Drumnadrochit, via Cannich (see below). Most of the walks and cycle routes here are covered by OS Landranger Nos 25 and 26.

Glen Affric → *Colour map 3, grid A6. OS Landranger Nos 25 and 26.*

The A831 continues south from Struy through Strathglass to the village of **Cannich**, gateway to glorious Glen Affric, a dramatic and beautiful gorge, with the River Affric rushing through it, and surrounded by Caledonian pine and birch forest – in fact this is one of the few places where you can still see the native Scots pine. There are few, if any, more stunning sights in the Scottish Highlands and it's perfect for walking, or even just to drive through and stop for a picnic on a nice, sunny day.

Glen Affric reaches west into the very heart of the Highlands and is great for a spot of Munro-bagging, see further page 58.

Beyond Loch Affric the serious walking starts. From **Affric Lodge**, nine miles west of Cannich, begins a 20 mile trail west to **Morvich**, near Shiel Bridge, on the west coast near Kyle of Lochalsh, see page 382. This strenuous walk is for experienced hikers only, and takes around 10 hours. You can stop off halfway at one of the most remote youth hostels in Scotland, **Glen Affric Youth Hostel**, at Allt Beithe (no phone, open mid-March till end October).

There are also many shorter, easier walks around Glen Affric. There are some short, circular marked trails at the end of the road which runs west from Cannich almost to Loch Affric, and also from the car park at the impressive **Dog Falls**, 4½ miles from Cannich and a great place to stop for a picnic and swim. Cycling in the forests around Cannich is good too – you can hire bikes at Cannich Caravan and Camping Park.

Glen Affric can also be reached from **Drumnadrochit**, see page 352, by heading west on the A831 through Glen Urquhartto Cannich. Just before Cannich, on the road from Drumnadrochit, a single track road leads left (south), past the Caravan and Camping Park, to the tiny village of **Tomich**. From here, it's a three-mile hike up a woodland trail to a car park. A few hundred yards down through the trees takes you to the lovely Plodda Falls. An old iron bridge affords a spectacular view of the waterfall as it plunges 150 yds into the foaming waters below.

Sleeping

Nairn and around *p348*

L The Golf View Hotel, Seabank Rd, next to the golf course, T01667-452301, scotland@ morton-hotels.demon.co.uk. 47 rooms. The most luxurious here, with pool, sauna, spa, gym, tennis courts and fine restaurant.

E Bracadale House, Albert St, T01667-452547, neil.macleod@lineone.net. Among the many guest houses and B&Bs, this option is very fine.

Camping

Spindrift Caravan & Camping Park, Little Kildrummie, T01667-453992, open Apr-Oct. A good campsite 1½ miles from town.

Beauly and around *p348*

L The Priory Hotel, on the main street, T01463-782309. The most expensive place to stay.

C Lovat Arms Hotel, at the opposite end of the main street from **The Priory Hotel**, T01463-782313, lovat.arms@cali.co.uk. A relaxed and comfortable place with an excellent restaurant and great bar food, lots of tartan and the occasional ceilidh. Best place to stay in town.

F Ellengowan, Croyard Rd, T01463-782273, open Apr-Oct. A cheaper B&B option.

Glen Affric *p349*

There are several options in and around Cannich.

B The Tomich Hotel, Tomich, T01456-415399, F415469. The price includes dinner, and it's a comfortable place with good food and free use of the nearby indoor heated pool; also great for fishing holidays.

C-D Kerrow House, Cannich village, T01456-415243, stephen@kerrow-house. demon.co.uk. An excellent B&B.

F Cougie Lodge, near Tomich, T01456-415459, www.cougie.org, Apr-Sep. An independent hostel with 6 beds. Valerie or John will pick you up from Tomich or Cannich if you phone ahead.

F Glen Affric Backpackers, Cannich, T/F01456-415263, which is open all year. Slightly cheaper than Cannich Youth Hostel and independent.

F SYHA Cannich Youth Hostel, Cannich, T01456-415244, open mid-Mar to end Oct. Clean hostel accommodation.

Eating

Cawdor Castle *p347*

££-£ Cawdor Tavern, in the village of Cawdor, close by the castle, T/F01667-404777, a traditional country pub serving excellent food in a friendly atmosphere. Perfect for lunch or dinner after visiting the castle.

Nairn and around *p348*

££ Boath House, T01463-455469, 2 miles east of Nairn in the little village of Auldearn. Aside from the hotels in town, this is one of the best places to eat.

£ Friar Tuck's, at 30 Harbour St, if you fancy a fish supper.

£ Asher's Bakery, 2 Bridge St, recommended for a hot snack. Run by the same folk as the one in Inverness.

Beauly and around *p348*

£££-£ Lovat Arms Hotel, serves up the best food around. Offers bar meals (**£**) or dinner in the restaurant (**£££**).

Beauly Tandoori, The Square, T01463-782221, for a cheap curry.

Friary for an even cheaper fish supper.

Activities and tours

Cycling The Bike Shop, High St, Nairn. For bike hire.

Horse riding Heatherfield Riding Centre, Lochloy Rd, Nairn, T01667-456682, offer pony trekking.

Transport

Culloden *p346*

Highland Country Bus No 7 leaves from Inverness – pick it up outside the Post Office

Mon-Sat (last bus back about 1830).
Guide Friday tour buses leave from Bridge St, Inverness, May-Sep (see p343).

Fort George *p347*
Fort Highland Bus and Coach No 11 from the Post Office in Inverness, several daily except Sun, also buses from Nairn.

Cawdor Castle *p347*
Highland Country Buses No 12 leaves from **Inverness** Post Office and runs several times daily (except Sun), the last bus returns around 1800, also regular buses from **Nairn**.

Brodie Castle *p348*
Bluebird buses run to Brodie from Inverness, via Culloden and Nairn, 45 mins.

Nairn and around *p348*
There are regular daily buses to Nairn from **Inverness** (30 mins) with **Highland Country Buses** and **Bluebird**, see p344. Nairn is on the **Inverness-Aberdeen** rail line, and there are several trains daily from **Inverness** (20 min).

Beauly and around *p348*
There are **Inverness Traction** buses, T01463-239292, every hour to **Beauly**, and on to **Muir of Ord**, from **Inverness** and from **Dingwall**. There's also a Ross's Minibus service from Beauly 3 days a week, T01463-761250.

The train station at Beauly (with the shortest platform in the UK, so take care getting off) is now open; trains between **Inverness** and **Thurso** stop here.

Glen Affric *p349*
Highland Bus & Coach, T01463-233371, runs buses 3 days a week Mon-Fri from **Inverness** to **Cannich** and **Tomich**, via **Drumnadrochit**. There are also buses from **Inverness** to **Cannich** and **Tomich**, via **Beauly** (2 on Tue and Fri, and 1 on Sat).

Loch Ness and around

One of Scotland's biggest attractions is the narrow gash of Loch Ness, Britain's deepest body of fresh water, stretching 23 miles from Fort Augustus in the south almost to Inverness in the north. The loch is scenic in its own right, with rugged hills rising steeply from its wooded shores, but visitors don't come here for the views. They come every year, in their hundreds of thousands, to stare across the dark, cold waters in search of its legendary inhabitant, the Loch Ness Monster. A huge tourist trade has grown up around 'Nessie', as the monster is affectionately known, and every summer the main A82 which runs along its western shore is jam packed with bus-loads of eager monster-hunters, binoculars trained on the loch surface, desperate for one glimpse of the elusive beast. ▸▸ *For Sleeping, Eating and other listings, see pages 357-360.*

Ins and outs

The best way to see the loch is on a cruise from Inverness, see page 359 and page 354. There are also boat trips from Drumnadrochit and Fort Augustus. Most of the tourist traffic uses the congested A82, which offers few decent views of the loch. By far the best views of the loch are from the quiet and picturesque B862/852 which runs along its eastern shore from Fort Augustus up to Inverness. It's possible to make a complete circuit of the loch, which is best done in an anti-clockwise direction heading south from Inverness on the A82, but you'll need your own transport (or take a tour), as there are no buses between Fort Augustus and Foyers. There are regular daily bus services between Inverness and Fort William, with additional buses between Invergarry and Fort Augustus. ▸▸ *For further details, see Activities and tours page 359 and Transport, page 360.*

Around the loch

Drumnadrochit → *Phone code: 01456. Colour map 2, grid C1.*

The Nessie tourist trade is centred on the village of Drumnadrochit, 15 miles south of Inverness, where the canny locals have cashed in on the enduring popularity of the monster myth. The monster hype is almost overpowering, with two rival Monster Exhibitions and the inevitable souvenir shops selling all manner of awful tartan tack, including those scary-looking tartan dolls with flickering eyelids, the "See-You-Jimmy" tartan bonnet, complete with ginger 'hair', and not forgetting the Loch Ness Monster novelty hat. There's a TIC in the car park ⓘ *T01456-459086*.

Of the two aforementioned Monster Exhibitions, the **Original Loch Ness Visitor Centre** ⓘ *T01456-450342, Apr to end of Oct daily 1000-1800 (Jul-Aug till 2100), £3.50, students £3, children/OAPs £2.75*, is the least worthwhile. It's a glorified gift shop with a rather amateurish audiovisual show attached. Loch Ness Cruises operate from here, see page 359. Those genuinely interested in the fascinating history of the search for 'Nessie' should visit the **Loch Ness 2000 Exhibition** ⓘ *T01456-450573, Easter-end May 0930-1700, Jun and Sep 0900-1800, Jul-Aug 0900-2000, Oct 0930-1730, Nov-Mar 1000-1530, £5.95, students/seniors £4.50, children £3.50*. Though it's considerably more expensive, it gives a detailed description of the many eye-witness accounts over the years and also explains the recent research projects carried out in the loch.

If it all gets too much, then fear not, for Drumnadrochit gives easy access to one of the most beautiful corners of Scotland. The A831 heads west from the village through **Glen Urquhartto Cannich**, about 12 miles away, at the head of Glen Affric, a great place for walking or enjoying a picnic, see page 349.

Castle Urquhart

ⓘ *T01456-450551, Apr-Sep 0930-1830, Oct-Mar 0930-1630, £6, concession £4.50, children £1.20.*

A few miles south of Drumnadrochit are the ruins of Castle Urquhart. The castle bears the scars of centuries of fighting but its setting, perched on a rocky cliff on the loch's edge, is magnificent and, not surprisingly, one of the most photographed scenes in Scotland. Dating from the 14th century, the castle was a strategic base, guarding the Great Glen during the long Wars of Independence. It was taken by Edward I, held by Robert the Bruce against Edward II, and was then almost constantly under siege before being destroyed in 1692 to prevent it from falling into Jacobite hands. Most of the existing buildings date from the 16th century, including the five-storey tower, the best-preserved part of the complex, from where you get great views of the loch and surrounding hills. There's also a new visitor centre, which is not to everyone's taste, so if you really like it, best keep it to yourself.

Invermoriston → *Phone code: 01320. Colour map 4, grid A1.*

Between Drumnadrochit and Fort Augustus is the tiny village of Invermoriston, probably the nicest spot on the entire Inverness to Fort Augustus stretch of the A82. It's a beautiful little piece of Highland scenery, with a photogenic old stone bridge over foaming river rapids. There are marked woodland trails leading off into the hills past some lovely waterfalls.

At Invermoriston the A887 heads west through Glen Moriston to meet the A87, which runs from Invergarry (below) all the way through the rugged and dramatic Glen Shielto, the awesome mountains of Kintailon to the west coast near Kyle of Lochalsh.

Fort Augustus → *Phone code: 01320. Colour map 4, grid A1.*

At the more scenic southern end of Loch Ness stands the village of Fort Augustus, originally set up as a garrison after the Jacobite rebellion of 1715, and headquarters of

Great Monster Hunt

In a country full of myths and legends, the Loch Ness Monster is the greatest of them all. As elusive as a straight answer from a politician, Nessie has single-handedly sold more tins of tartan-wrapped shortbread to foreign visitors than Edinburgh Castle.

Tales of Nessie go way back to the sixth century, when St Columba is said to have calmed the beast after she had attacked one of his monks. But the monster craze only really took off with the completion of the A82 road along the loch's western shore in 1933. Since then there have been numerous sightings, some backed up with photographic evidence, though the most impressive of these – the famous black-and-white movie footage of Nessie's humps moving through the water, and the classic photograph of her head and neck – have been exposed as fakes.

In recent decades determined monster hunters have enlisted the help of new technology, such as sonar surveys, but have failed to come up with conclusive evidence. Enter Cyber Nessie, the latest attempt to end the years of rumours, hoaxes and speculation. Nessie's very own website – www.lochness.scotland.net/ camera.htm – is a 24-hour real-time video watch of Loch Ness, and has already produced a couple of claimed sightings. But nothing could compare with the excitement of seeing the monster in the flesh.

General Wade's campaign to pacify the Highlands. Today, Fort Augustus is a busy little place, full of monster-hunting tourists and boats using the flight of five locks to enter or leave Loch Ness on their journey along the Caledonian Canal. The tourist information centre ⓘ *T01320-366367, Apr-Oct*, is in the car park next to the petrol station and Bank of Scotland.

On the shores of Loch Ness is **Fort Augustus Abbey**, a Benedictine Monastery founded in 1876 on the site of the original fort. The abbey closed in 1998. By the canal locks is **The Clansman Centre** ⓘ *T01320-366444, Apr, May, Jun and Sep daily 1100-1700, Jul-Aug 1000-1800, £3, concession £2.50*, where young guides in traditional dress provide a lively and entertaining presentation of 17th-century Highland family life in an old turf house. There follows a display of weaponry and a mock sword fight in the garden. You can even have your picture taken wearing traditional Highland costume. There's also a craftshop selling the more tasteful kind of souvenirs.

Fort Augustus to Dores → *Colour map 4, grid A1-2.*

A worthwhile detour from Fort Augustus is to take the B862/852 up the east shore of Loch Nesson, a mostly single-track road that skirts the loch for much of its length to the village of Dores. It's a much quieter and more scenic route than the busy A82 and follows General Wade's original (and very straight) military road which linked Fort Augustus with Fort George. Though it makes a more interesting alternative to the more popular A82 route from Inverness to Fort Augustus, it's best done from south to north, if you have the time.

The road winds its way up into rugged hills before returning to the lochside at **Foyers.** It's worth stopping here to see the impressive waterfall where the River Foyers plunges into Loch Ness. To get there, follow the steep (and slippery) track down from opposite the shops. Three miles further north, at **Inverfarigaig**, is the spooky and sinister **Boleskine House**, once home of Alastair Crowley, who is said to have practised devil worship here. In the 1970s the house was bought by Jimmy Page of

Old as the hills

The Great Glen, which splits the Scottish mainland from Fort William in the south to Inverness in the north, is one of the world's major geological fault lines. The Glen was formed millions of years ago when the northern part of the Caledonian mountains 'slid' more than 60 miles south, leaving behind a massive glen with four freshwater lochs – Loch Linnhe, Loch Lochy, Loch Oich and Loch Ness.

The most famous of these is Loch Ness, which attracts hordes of visitors eager to catch a glimpse of its elusive monster.The renowned engineer, Thomas Telford, succeeded in connecting all these lochs when he built the impressive Caledonian Canal. The canal took 22 years to complete, and when it was opened in 1822 was the first in Britain to take ships from one coast to the other. It remains the only canal in the country capable of carrying ships of up to 500 tons. The best way to appreciate the glen is by boat, through the 38 miles of natural lochs and rivers and the 22 miles of canal, and every summer pleasure craft of all shapes and sizes ply its length. The main A82 runs from Inverness south to Fort William. The southern section, from Fort Augustus, follows the original line of the road constructed in 1727 by General Wade to link the military garrisons at Fort William and Fort Augustus (hence their names).

Another way to travel through the Great Glen is along the excellent cycle route, which follows the canal towpaths, forest trails and quiet minor roads to avoid the busy main road. The route is outlined in the Forestry Commission leaflet, available from most tourist information centres.

Led Zeppelin, but sold some years later after the tragic death of his daughter. Those of a nervous disposition may wish to pass on quickly and continue to the little village of **Dores,** at the northeastern end of the loch, where you can enjoy a good pint of ale and some decent grub at the **Dores Inn**.

You can then continue to Inverness, or return via the beautiful hill road that leads up to **Loch Mhorand** back to Fort Augustus via the **Stratherrick Valley**. From **Errogie,** at the northern end of Loch Mhor, there's a dramatic section of road that winds down to the loch through a series of tight, twisting bends, reminiscent of an Alpine pass, and great for cyclists. There are also interesting marked woodland trails around Errogie.

Fort Augustus to Fort William

South of Fort Augustus, the A82 leaves behind Loch Ness and runs along the west shore of Loch Oich and then the east shore of Loch Lochy, till it reaches Spean Bridge. Here the A82 continues south to Fort William, while the A86 branches east through Glen Spean to join the A9 Perth to Inverness road finally at Kingussie . All along this route are many opportunities to get off the beaten track and explore huge chunks of real wilderness, deserted since the Clearances and soaked in the blood of history.

▸▸ *For Sleeping, Eating and other listings, see pages 357-360.*

Invergarry and around → *Phone code: 01809. Colour map 4, grid A1.*

The old village of Invergarry stands where the A82 turns west to meet the A87. There's not much to see or do in the village, but the surrounding area merits some exploring, particularly the route west through Glen Garry, and there are several places to stay.

Inside the entrance to the **Glengarry Castle Hotel**, see Sleeping page 360, stand the ruins of **Invergarry Castle**, once the stronghold of the MacDonnells of Glengarry and later destroyed by the Duke of Cumberland as he wreaked revenge on the Highlands in the aftermath of Culloden, see page 43. The hotel was later built as the main house of the Ellice family, who made their fortune from the Hudson Bay Company in Canada and who were the main driving force behind the creation of the Victorian planned village.

A mile or so south of the village, at **North Laggan**, is a monument by the side of the road standing over **The Well of the Seven Heads**. This tells the grisly story of the **Keppoch Murders**, one of the most infamous clan murders which took place at **Roy Bridge** (see below) in the 17th century. It all began when the chief of the clan MacDonnell died, leaving two young sons, who were sent away to complete their education before returning to Roy Bridge to celebrate the elder brother's accession to the chiefship. Another branch of the clan present at the celebrations started a fight in which both brothers were killed. Believing they had been murdered, one of their cousins persuaded a fellow clan member to raise 50 men and march on the murderers' house at nearby Inverlair. The accused murderers – a father and his six sons – were duly slaughtered and their heads cut off, to be displayed before the local laird at Glengarry. On the way to his lodge, the heads were washed here in this well.

A few miles further south, at **Laggan**, where the A82 crosses to the east bank of Loch Lochy, is the site of the **Battle of the Shirts**, see box. The A87 leads west from Invergarry through Glen Shiel to Shiel Bridge, on the way to Kyle of Lochalsh on the west coast, see page 382. About seven miles along the A87, past the turning for Kinloch Hourn (see below), is the **Glen Garry viewpoint**, from where you get one of the most stunning, and famous, of all Highland views. From this angle Loch Garry looks uncannily like a map of Scotland, so get out the camera for that classic holiday snap.

Glen Garry to Kinloch Hourn → *Colour map 3, grid A5-6.*

A mile or so before the Glen Garry viewpoint, where the A87 begins to leave the shores of Loch Garry, is the turning left for the road through Glen Garry, described as the longest and most beautiful cul-de-sac in Britain. The little single-track road turns and twists for 22 glorious miles along the shores of Loch Garry and Loch Quoich all the way to Kinloch Hourn, at the head of Loch Hourn, a sea loch on the west coast.

Glen Garry is now virtually deserted but was once home to some 5,000 people who were driven out during the infamous Highland Clearances in the 19th century. The road passes the tiny hamlet of **Tomdoun**, once the junction of the main road to Skye, until the massive post-war hydroelectric schemes changed the landscape. Experienced hillwalkers can still follow the old route to Skye, through Glen Kingie, along Loch Hourn and then across the wild Knoydart peninsula till they reach the tiny settlement of **Inverie**. From here a little ferry runs twice a day (Monday to Wednesday and Friday) to Mallaig, see page 378.

Beyond Tomdoun the road passes a huge dam, built in the 1950s, which raised the waters of **Loch Quoich** by over 100 ft, flooding many of the old settlements. Also flooded was **Glen Quoich Lodge**, which can count Edward VII and Sir Edward Landseer among its notable guests. It was reputedly Glen Garry that gave Landseer the inspiration for his famous painting *The Monarch of the Glen*. The road then reaches its highest point, at 1,200 ft, before descending to **Kinloch Hourn**, once a thriving fishing village but now remote and isolated. Incredible as it may seem, you can actually stay here, see Sleeping page 360.

Spean Bridge → *Phone code: 01397. Colour map 3, grid B6.*

The main A82 runs down the east shore of Loch Lochy to the village of Spean Bridge, at the head of Glen Spean, beneath the towering Lochaber Mountains. The village gets its name from Thomas Telford's bridge across the River Spean. Two miles west

Getting shirty

One the bloodiest battles in Scottish clan history was the Battle of the Shirts, fought in 1544. It was so named because it was fought on a hot day and the combatants took off their shirts before proceeding to butcher each other. One side – the Frasers – were almost wiped out and their opponents – a combined force of MacDonalds, MacDonnells and Camerons – suffered less heavy losses and claimed victory. In total over 1,000 were killed and a plaque beside the canal locks describes the terrible events.

are the remains of the old 'Highbridge', built in 1736 by General Wade, and the site of the first clash between Government troops and the Jacobites, three days before Prince Charles raised his standard at Glenfinnan.

Spean Bridge is only eight miles north of Fort William so gets busy in the summer, but it still makes a more peaceful and attractive alternative base for exploring this astoundingly beautiful part of the Highlands. There's a tourist information centre ⓘ *T01397-712576, Easter-Oct*, just off the main road behind the post office. Spean Bridge is also the starting point for the excellent **Grey Corries ridge walk** (OS Landranger Map No 41).

Loch Arkaig and around → *Phone code: 01397. Colour map 3, grid A6.*

A mile north of Spean Bridge on the A82 is the **Commando Memorial**, which commemorates the commandos who trained here during the Second World War. It's worth lingering for a few moments to appreciate the fantastic views all around. From here the B8004 branches west to **Gairlochy**, crossing the Caledonian Canal, then the B8005 heads north to Loch Arkaig, a long, deep and mysterious loch stretching west through the mountains. Bonnie Prince Charlie passed this way, before and after Culloden, through an area which has, for centuries, been the seat of the Camerons of Lochiel. The Camerons were fervent supporters of the Jacobite cause and when Prince Charles landed at Loch nan Uamh, on the road from Fort William to Mallaig, he called on Cameron of Lochiel to join him at Glenfinnan.

In the tiny township of **Achnacarry**, nestled between the shores of Loch Lochy and Loch Arkaig, you can find out all about the Camerons and their involvement in the Jacobite rebellion of 1745 at the **Clan Cameron Museum** ⓘ *T01397-712480, Easter to mid-Oct daily 1330-1700, Jul-Aug 1100-1700, £3, concession £1.50, children free*. This museum is housed in an old cottage rebuilt after being burned by government troops in 1746.

Beyond the turn-off to Achnacarry, the single-track road runs through the Clunes Forest and The Dark Mile, a long line of beech trees which completely cuts out daylight. At the east end of Loch Arkaig, a stone bridge crosses the Caig Burn. Beside the bridge is a car park, from where a path leads up to the spectacular **Cia-Aig Falls** which tumble into a deep, dark pool known as **The Witch's Cauldron**. It was here that an old hag was accused of casting her evil eye over Lochiel's cattle, causing them to fall ill and die. But when she fell into the pool and drowned, the cattle miraculously began to recover from their illness. The road runs along the north shore of Loch Arkaig all the way to the head of the loch, from where experienced and well-equipped hill walkers can hike through the glens to Loch Nevis and Knoydart.

Glen Roy and Loch Laggan → *Phone code: 01397. Colour map 4, grid A-B1.*

From Spean Bridge the A86 runs east through Glen Spean to meet the A9 Perth to Inverness road which leads to Aviemore, see page 423. The road passes through Roy

Bridge, which is the turn-off for Glen Roy, noted for its amazing 'parallel roads'. These are not in fact roads, but three gravel ledges etched on to the mountains at different heights. The 'roads' marked the shorelines of a glacial lake formed during the last Ice Age. Roy Bridge was also the site of the infamous Keppoch Murders, see page 354.

The road continues east towards Loch Laggan. After a couple of miles it passes **Cille Choirille**, an ancient church built by a 15th-century Cameron chief as penance for a life of violence. The church fell into disrepair but was restored and reopened in 1932 and now attracts people of all creeds as it's said to inspire peace and spiritual healing. Further east, at the eastern end of Loch Laggan, is the massive **Laggan Dam**, built in 1933 to provide water for the aluminium smelter at Fort William. The water is piped through tunnels up to 15 ft in diameter carved through the core of Ben Nevis. The road runs along the north shore of the loch, past the **Creag Meagaidh National Nature Reserve**, where you can see herds of red deer right by the reserve car park. A track leads from here up to **Lochan a' Choire** (about four hours).

Sleeping

Drumnadrochit *p352*

There's a wide range of accommodation in and around the village of Drumnadrochit.

B **Polmaily House Hotel**, 3 miles from Drumnadrochit on the A831 to Cannich, in Glen Urquhart, T01456-450343, polmailyhousehotel@btinternet.com. 10 rooms. If you can afford it, this is your best bet. A comfortable, child-friendly country house far enough away from the madding crowd to offer peace and quiet, many walks nearby, also tennis courts, horse riding and covered pool, and a good restaurant.

D **The Benleva Hotel**, T01456-450288, F450781. Small, family-run hotel with bar and dining room.

D **Gillyflowers**, T/F01456-450641, gillyflowers@cali.co.uk. Good value.

D-E **Woodlands**, East Lewiston, T01456-450356, www.woodlandsbandb.net. 3 en suite rooms. Open Mar-Oct. Refurbished to a high standard and very comfortable.

E **Drumbuie Farm**, T01456-450634, F450595. Modern farmhouse on the right as you enter the village from Inverness, with its own herd of Highland cattle. Recommended.

F **Loch Ness Backpackers Lodge**, Coiltie Farmhouse in East Lewiston, T01456-450807, immediately south of Drumnadrochit, on the left. It's open all year, has excellent facilities, and arranges boat trips and local walks.

Invermoriston *p352*

F **SYHA Loch Ness Youth Hostel**, T0871-3308537, mid-Apr to end Oct. A few miles to the north on the main A82 overlooking Loch Ness.

Loch Ness Caravan & Camping Park, 1½ miles south of Invermoriston, and 6 miles north of Fort Augustus, is the T01320-351207, right on the shores of the loch with great views and excellent facilities (open Easter-Oct).

Fort Augustus *p352*

There are lots of B&Bs to choose from here.

D **Lovat Arms Hotel**, T01320-366206, www.ipv.com/lovatarms. 23 rooms. This beautiful old mansion house standing above the village is the best place to stay around here. It also has a good restaurant (**££**).

D-E **Mrs Service**, Sonason the Inverness Rd, T01320-366291. A great named B&B.

E **Kettle House**, Golf Course Rd, T01320-366408, open Feb-Nov. Another B&B with a good name. Friendly too.

F **Morag's Lodge**, T01320-366289. Newly converted, this place offers backpacker accommodation between Mar and Oct.

Fort Augustus to Dores *p353*

E-F **Intake-House**, Foyers, T01456-482258, open Apr-Oct.

F **Foyers House**, Foyers, T01456-486623. Small independent youth hostel.

Invergarry and around *p354*

A **Glengarry Castle Hotel**, T01809-501254, www.glengarry.net, open Mar-Nov. Set in 60 acres of woodland running down to Loch Oich. 26 rooms. There are various options for sleeping in and around Invergarry, but none can match the splendour of this place. The hotel has been in the MacCallum family for over 40 years and continues to be one of the best in the Highlands.

C-D **Invergarry Hotel**, T01809-501206, hotel@invergarry.net. Rather less luxurious but still comfortable and good value.

D **Forest Lodge**, South Laggan, south of Invergarry, T01809-501219, www.flgh.co.uk. 7 rooms. Welcoming and comfortable B&B run by Janet and Ian Shearer. Well-equipped rooms with good views and a 4-course dinner is available.

F **SYHA Loch Lochy Youth Hostel**, South Laggan, T01809-501239, mid-Mar to end-Oct.

Camping

There are a couple of campsites near the village: **Faichem Park**, T01809-501226, open Easter-Oct; and **Faichemard Farm Camping Site**, T01809-501314, Apr-Oct, which is off the A87.

Glen Garry to Kinloch Hourn *p355*

B **Skiary**, T01809-511214, open May-Sep, phone ahead to arrange for a boat to meet you. This is perhaps the most remote guest house in the Highlands. It is accessible only by boat or foot and has no mains electricity. There are 3 rooms and prices are for full board, and include the boat trip both ways. The food is wonderful and the setting is simply magnificent.

Spean Bridge *p355*

There's no shortage of accommodation in Spean Bridge. There are lots more guest houses and B&Bs than are listed here.

A **Old Pines Restaurant with Rooms**, just past the Commando Memorial on the B8004, T01397-712324, www.oldpines.co.uk. 8 rooms, price includes dinner. Pick of the bunch in Spean Bridge. This Scandinavian- style chalet run by Bob and Sukie Barber is a great place to stay, especially if you have kids in tow, features include a large playroom, a barn with snooker and table tennis and a trampoline in the garden. Sukie's exceptional, award-winning Scottish cuisine is also a major draw. The 5-course dinner (**£££**) is also available to non-guests.

A **Corriegour Lodge Hotel**, 9 miles north of Spean Bridge on the A82, T01397-712685, www.courriegour-lodge-hotel.com. 9 rooms, open Feb-Dec. Lovely Victorian hunting lodge on the shores of Loch Lochy, with fine views and an excellent restaurant (non-residents dinner only **£££**).

D **Corriechoille Lodge**, T/F01397-712002, www.corrie1.demon.co.uk. Open Mar-Nov. A good stop for a night.

D **Invergloy House**, on the shores of Loch Lochy, T01397-712681. Very good B&B.

E **Smiddy House**, in Spean Bridge village, T01397-712335, F712043. A comfortable guest house with a bistro attached, serving good, cheap meals.

Camping

There are a couple of campsites, north of the village at **Stronaba Caravan & Camping**, T01397-712259, open Apr-Oct; and west towards Gairlochy at **Gairlochy Holiday Park**, T01397-712711, F712712, open Apr-Oct.

Glen Roy and Loch Laggan *p356*

There are several hotels in Roy Bridge and 3 independent hostels, listed below.

C **Stronlossit Hotel**, T0800-0155321, www.stronlossit.co.uk, which serves good meals all day from 1100 (**££-£**).

F **Aite Cruinnichidh**l, Achluachrach, a 1½ miles from the village, T01397-712315, is the cheaper hostel.

F **Grey Corrie Lodge**, T01397-712236, is handy for shops and transport, serves cheap bar meals and also has laundry facilities.

F **Station Lodge**, 5 miles east at Tulloch train station, T/F01397-732333, is this option which serves meals (including vegetarian).

Eating

Drumnadrochit *p352*

Bear in mind that the hotels all tend to serve decent bar food and some B&Bs offer evening meals.

££ **Fiddler's Bistro**, T01456-450678, which offers generous portions of staples such as salmon steak and good service. Open for lunch and dinner, last orders 2100.

For an explanation of sleeping and eating price codes used in this guide, see inside the front cover. Other relevant information is found in Essentials, see pages 43-51.

Fort Augustus *p352*

££-£ Bothy, T01320-366263, a cosy choice down by the canal bridge, which serves simple but tasty meals from 1000-2000.

£ Loch Inn, by the canal, is the best place for a drink, and also serves decent pub grub.

Spean Bridge *p355*

£££ Old Station Restaurant, T01397-712535. In a converted railway station. Has a very good reputation, lunch by prior arrangement only, open Apr-Oct, Tue-Sun 1800-2100.

£££-££ The Coach House Restaurant, 3 miles north of town on the right-hand side, at Glenfintaig, T01397-712680, crann_tara@bigfoot.com. It's a popular place and small, so you'll have to book ahead for lunch or dinner, open late Apr to late Oct, daily 1200-1500 and 1800-2100.

Glen Roy and Loch Laggan *p356*

£££-££ Glenspean Lodge Hotel, T01397-712223. Lunch served 1230-1430 and dinner 1830-2100. A good place to eat

Festivals and events

Fort Augustus *p352*

Late Jun and Jul, mid-Aug and early Sep is the period when Fort Augustus hosts **Highland Gatherings** featuring traditional dancing and piping competitions, tossing the caber and sheep dog trials.

Activities and tours

Climbing

Nevis Guides, Bohuntin, Roy Bridge, T01397-712356.

Cycling

Hiring bikes in Drumnadrochit and cycling into Glen Affric makes for a great day out. You can hire mountain bikes at **Fiddler's** Bistro, see Eating. In Fort Augustus you can hire bikes at **Loch Ness Ferry Co Ltd**.

Fishing

Fishing Scotland, T/F01397-712812, www.fishing-scotland.co.uk, runs fishing courses and trips on the surrounding lochs. Loch Arkaig in particular is renowned for its trout fishing.

Horse riding

Fort Augustus Riding Centre, Pier House, Fort Augustus, T01320-366418.

Highland Icelandic Horse Trekking, beyond the falls at Loch Arkaig, T01397-712427, hihot@compuserve.com, offers 1-hr, 2-hr and day rides in the surrounding hills.

Highland Riding Centre, T01456-450358, Borlum Farm, Drumnadrochit.

Loch Ness tours

There are various monster-spotting tours of Loch Ness which leave from the tourist office in Drumnadrochit.

Cruise Loch Ness, T01223-208939, on board the *Royal Scot*, set off from the canal in the centre of Fort Augustus, Apr-Oct hourly from 1000. The trip lasts 50 mins and costs £6 per adult. Also boat and bike hire.

Guide Friday, at the train station, Drumnadrochit, T01456-224000. Half-day coach trips right round the loch, at 1030 and 1430, lasting 3 hrs. Tickets cost adult £14.50, concession £11.50, children £6.50, available from booking office at the station or TIC.

Jacobite Cruises, Drumnadrochit, T01456-233999, jacobite@cali.co.uk, offers coach tours, boat cruises and combined coach and cruise trips round the loch. Half-day cruises cost £10, half-day coach and cruise trips cost £14.50 (including entry to the Loch Ness Monster Exhibition and Castle Urquhart). Trips run from Apr-Oct and leave from Tomnahurich Bridge on Glenurquhart Rd, 1½ miles south of the town centre in Drumnadrochit. Free buses leave from the TIC, 20 mins before sailing, if tickets are bought here. Otherwise, to get there take Inverness Traction buses Nos 3, 3A, 4 and 4A every 15 mins from Church St.

Tour companies

Glengarry Mini Tours, Invergarry, T01809-501297, runs various minibus day tours in Great Glen, Glen Coe and Glen Nevis.

Watersports

Great Glen Water Park, east shore of Loch Oich, near North Laggan, T01809-501381. An outdoor activities centre offering adventure sports including whitewater rafting, canoeing, mountain biking, rock climbing, sailing, windsurfing, hill walking and water skiing. Self-catering lodges for rent too.

Transport

Drumnadrochit *p352*
Citylink buses between **Inverness** and **Fort William** stop at here several times daily in either direction. Additional services run between **Inverness** and **Urquhart Castle** during the summer months. There are also buses from **Inverness** to **Cannich** and **Tomich**, via Drumnadrochit (see p351). **Citylink** buses between **Inverness** and **Kyle of Lochalsh** stop at Invermoriston.

Fort Augustus *p352*
Fort Augustus is a convenient stopover between **Fort William** and **Inverness**, and there are several buses daily in either direction. It takes 1 hr to both towns. There is an additional service between **Fort Augustus** and **Invergarry** (see below) once a day Mon-Sat.

Fort Augustus to Dores *p353*
This route is only possible if you have your own transport. There are buses south from **Inverness**, but they only run as far as **Foyers** (3 times Mon-Fri, twice on Sat). Alternatively, it can be done by bike, as a full-day circular trip from Fort Augustus or from Inverness.

Invergarry and around *p354*
Invergarry is on the **Fort William** to **Inverness** bus route (see Fort Augustus above). It is also on the main **Fort William** to **Kyle of Lochalsh** (and Skye) **Citylink** route, and a couple of buses pass through daily in both directions. For times T0990-505050.

Glen Garry to Kinoch Hourn *p355*
There's a postbusfrom **Invergarry** on Mon, Wed and Fri, which runs to **Kingie**, which is halfway to Kinloch Hourn. A 4-seater post car runs all the way to Kinloch Hourn from **Invergarry** on Tue, Wed, Thu and Sat. A more scenic return would be to take the ferry from Kinloch Hourn to **Arnisdale** (summer only; daily by arrangement) and then head to **Glenelg** (see p382), from where you can take a ferry across to **Kylerhea** on Skye.

Spean Bridge *p355*
There are regular buses to and from **Fort William** and **Inverness** (£6 single). Spean Bridge is also on the **Fort William-Glasgow** railline (see p368).

Loch Arkaig and around *p356*
There's no public transport beyond Achnacarry, and there's only 1 busa day to Achnacarry from Lochaber High School in Fort William.

Glen Roy and Loch Laggan *p356*
There are busesfrom **Fort William** to **Roy Bridge** (3 times daily Mon-Fri; 1 on Sat). **Roy Bridge** is also on the **Fort William-Glasgow** railline.

Fort William and around

Fort William is the gateway to the Western Highlands and one of the country's main tourist centres. It stands at the head of Loch Linnhe, with the snow-topped mass of Ben Nevis towering behind. You could be forgiven for assuming that it's quite an attractive place, but you'd be wrong. Despite its magnificent setting, Fort William has all the charm of a motorway service station. A dual carriageway runs along the lochside, over a litter-strewn pedestrian underpass and past dismal 1960s concrete boxes masquerading as hotels. Most of the good things about Fort William are outside the town. The surrounding mountains and glens are amongst the most stunning in the Highlands and attract hikers and climbers in their droves: Ben Nevis – Britain's highest peak at 4,406 ft – and also the very beautiful Glen Nevis, which many of you may recognize from movies such as Braveheart *and* Rob Roy. *There's also skiing and snowboarding at nearby Aonach Mor, one of Scotland's top ski areas and some good mountain biking around the Leanachan Forest.* *»» For Sleeping, Eating and other listings, see pages 366-368.*

Ins and outs

Getting there

Fort William is easily reached by bus, from Inverness, Glasgow and Oban, and by train, direct from Glasgow via the wonderful West Highland Railway, see page 365. The train station is at the north end of the High Street. The bus station is also here but closed for refurbishment at the time of going to press. Buses leave from temporary stances opposite the Nevis Centre. If you're driving, parking can be a problem. There's a big car park beside the loch at the south end of town, and another behind the tourist office. You can also walk to Fort William, if you have a week to spare, from just north of Glasgow, along the 95 mile-long West Highland Way, see page 59.

Getting around

The town is strung out for several miles along the banks of Loch Linnhe. The centre is compact and easy to get around on foot. Many of the guest housesand B&Bs, and a few youth hostels, are in Corpach, 1½ miles to the north, but there are frequent buses from the town centre. There are also buses to the youth hostel in Glen Nevis. » *For further details, see Transport page 368.*

Tourist information

The overworked TIC ⓘ *Cameron Sq, just off the High St, T01397-703781, F705184, open year round, Apr-late Oct daily, Nov-Mar Mon-Sat*, stocks a good range of books, maps and leaflets covering local walks. They will also help arrange transport to more remote Highland parts.

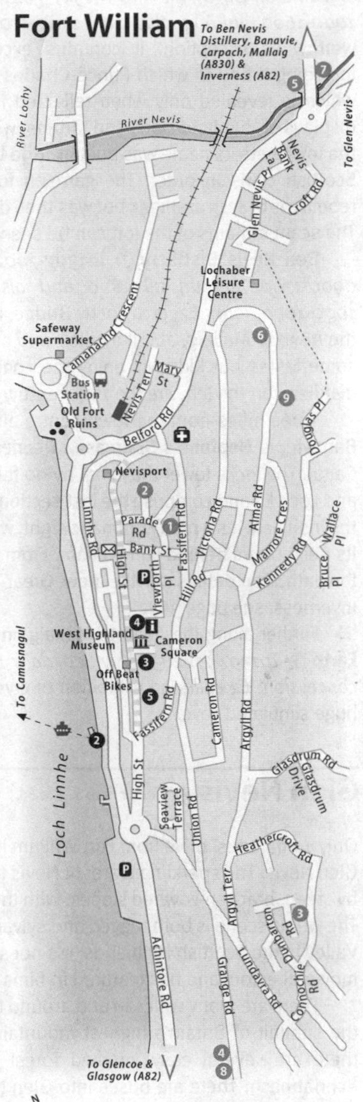

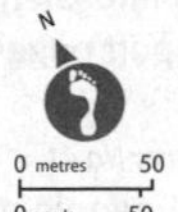

Sleeping
6 Caberfeidh 1
Alexandra Milton 2
Bank Street Lodge 6
Calluna 3
Crolinnhe 4
Distillery House 5
Lauriestone Guesthouse 7
Fort William Backpackers 6
Glenlochy Guesthouse 7
Grange 8
Guisachan House 9

Eating
Crannog Seafood 2
Grog & Gruel 3
McTavish's Kitchens 5
No 4 Cameron Square 4

Fort William → *Phone code: 01397.*

Colour map 3, grid B6. Population: 10,774.

Though it's not a pretty sight, Fort William is the largest town hereabouts and has all the services and facilities you'd expect. There are banks with ATMs on the pedestrianized High Street, as well as a couple of good supermarkets and well-stocked outdoor-equipment shops.

Sights

There's little of real interest in the town, though the **West Highland Museum** ⓘ *Cameron Sq by the TIC, T01397-702169, Jun-Sep Mon-Sat 1000-1700, Oct-May 1000-1600, Jul-Aug also Sun 1400-1700, £3, £2 concession, £0.50 child*, is a worthwhile exception. It contains excellent exhibits of Jacobite memorabilia, including a bed in which Prince Charles slept, and a 'secret' portrait of the prince which is revealed only when reflected in a cylindrical mirror. There are also fine displays of Highland clans and tartans, wildlife and local history. The fort from which the town gets its name was built in 1690 by order of William III to keep the rebellious Scottish clans in order. The garrison fought off attacks by Jacobites during the rebellions of 1715 and 1745 but was then demolished to make way for the railway line. The scant remains of the fort can be seen on the lochside, near the train station.

Ben Nevis Distillery ⓘ *T01397-700200, www.bennevisdistillery.com, Mon-Fri 0900-1700, Jul-Aug till 1800 and also Sun 1200-1600, Easter-Sep also Sat 1000-1600, tours £2*, is at Lochy Bridge, at the junction of the A82 to Inverness and the A830 to Mallaig, about a mile north of the town centre. It's a bit too polished for some tastes but kids will enjoy the company of Hamish McDram. Just before the distillery, on the left, are the 13th-century ruins of **Inverlochy Castle.**

Three miles from the town centre along the A830 to Mallaig, in the suburb of Banavie, is **Neptune's Staircase**, a series of eight linked locks on the Caledonian Canal. The locks lower the canal by 90 ft in less than two miles between Loch Lochy and Loch Eil and comprise the last section of the canal which links the North Sea with the Irish Sea. It's a pretty dramatic sight, with equally dramatic views of Ben Nevis and its neighbours behind Fort William. From here you can walk or cycle along the canal towpath. For details on the new Great Glen Way, which links Fort William with Inverness, see page 367.

Further along the A830 to Mallaig, in the village of Corpach, is **Treasures of the Earth** ⓘ *T01397-772283, May-Sep daily 0930-1900, Oct-Apr 1000-1700, £3.50, £3 concession, £2 child*, an exhibition of crystals, gemstones and fossils displayed in a huge simulated cave.

Glen Nevis → *Colour map 3, grid B6.*

Only 10 minutes' drive from Fort William is one of Scotland's great glens, the classic Glen Nevis. The sparkling Water of Nevis tumbles through a wooded gorge, closed in by steep, bracken-covered slopes, with the massive hulk of Ben Nevis watching over. The whole scene is both rugged and sylvan, and the nearest you'll get to a Himalayan Valley in the Scottish Highlands. It's not surprising, then, that this is a favourite with movie directors and has featured in films such as *Rob Roy* and *Braveheart*.

There are many walks in and around the glen, not least of which is the trek up to the summit of Britain's highest mountain. Aside from the walks described below, there are several easy, marked forest walks which start from the car park at Achriabhach. There are buses into Glen Nevis, as far as the youth hostel, from Fort William bus station, see Transport page 368.

▲ Ben Nevis → *OS Landranger No 41.*

Every year many thousands of people make the relatively straightforward ascent of Ben Nevis, and every year a frighteningly high percentage end up injured, or lost, or dead. More people die annually on the 'Ben' than Everest, so this is a mountain that needs to be taken seriously. Though it may be around 70°F in the car park when you set off, the weather changes with alarming speed and you can find yourself in a blizzard at the summit, or, as is usually the case, in a blanket of cloud or hill fog. It goes without saying that you need to be well prepared. You will need a good, strong pair of boots, warm clothing, waterproofs, food and drink. You should also take a map and a compass. Allow six to eight hours for the return trip. In the winter the top part of the mountain is covered in snow and you should not attempt the walk unless you are an experienced hill climber.

The main tourist path, built as a pony track to service the now-dilapidated observatory on the summit, starts from the car park at Achintee Farm, on the north side of the river, reached by the road through Claggan. It climbs gradually at first across the flank of Meal an t-Suidhe, before joining the alternative path from the youth hostel. This latter route is shorter but much steeper.

The trail continues to climb steadily as it begins to follow the Red Burn, until it reaches a junction, with Lochan Meal an t-Suidhe down to the left. Here, an alternative route down from the summit heads left under the north face of the mountain (see below).This is the halfway point of the main route. The path crosses the Red Burn and then climbs by a series of long and seemingly never-ending zigzags up to a plateau. The path splits in two, but both paths take you up to the summit, marked by a cairn and emergency shelter, on the ruins of the old observatory. Note that on the upper sloping plateau the path can 'disappear' in mist and snow, and some cairns and beacons have been removed by vandals masquerading as purists. If conditions deteriorate, a compass is a life-saver. There is a shelter on the summit and at least two others on the mountain.

To return simply retrace your steps all the way. If the weather is settled enough and you have time, you can follow the alternative route below the north face. This leads right round the mountain to the Charles Inglis Clark mountain hut, then heads down into the Allt a' Mhuilinnglen which leads all the way down to the distillery on the A82, a mile north of the town centre. Note that this route adds an extra three or four miles to the descent and should only be attempted by fit and experienced hillwalkers.

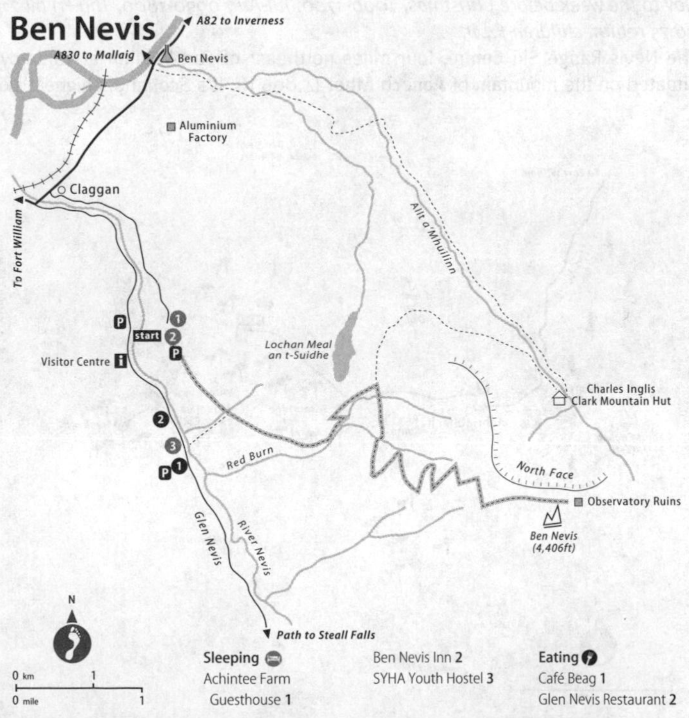

Steall Falls → *OS Landranger No 41.*

A fairly easy low-level walk is to the spectacular 300 ft-high Steall Falls at the head of the glen. It's a popular walk, especially in the summer when the trail can resemble the queue for the Ladies at a Tom Jones concert, but this doesn't detract from its stunning natural beauty.

The path starts at the end of the road, at the second car park. Before setting off you might like to note the sign by the steep waterfall that cascades down to the edge of the car park. It reads 'Warning! This is not the path to Ben Nevis'. If you need to be warned against attempting to climb up Ben Nevis through a waterfall, you probably shouldn't be left alone in possession of this book, never mind let loose on the Scottish mountains. Once you've shaken your head in disbelief at the apparent mind-numbing stupidity of some of your fellow travellers, follow the track alongside the Water of Nevis. The path climbs steadily through the woods and becomes rocky, with the river thundering below through the steep gorge. It runs close to the river before emerging from the gorge and opening up into a wide, flower-filled meadow, with a high waterfall at the far end. It's a beautiful, tranquil place and ideal for a picnic. Follow the path across the valley floor till it crosses the river via a precarious bridge that consists of three ropes of thick wire in a V-shape. The path then leads to the bottom of the falls. You can also head left at the bridge and continue up the valley to some ruins. From here the path leads to Corrour station, 14 miles away, but it's for fit and experienced hillwalkers only. You can then catch a train back to Fort William. It's a very popular route, and there's even accommodation at the end of it, near the train station, at the **SYHA Loch Lochy Youth Hostel**, T01809-501239, open mid-March to late October.

Nevis Range Ski Centre

ⓘ T01397-705825, www.ski.scotland.net, the gondola is open all year, except early Nov to the week before Christmas, 1000-1700, Jul-Aug 0930-1800, Thu-Fri till 2100, £6.75 return, children £4.15.

The Nevis Range Ski Centre, four miles northeast of Fort William at Torlundy, is situated on the mountain of **Aonach Mhor** (4,006 ft). It's Scotland's highest skiing

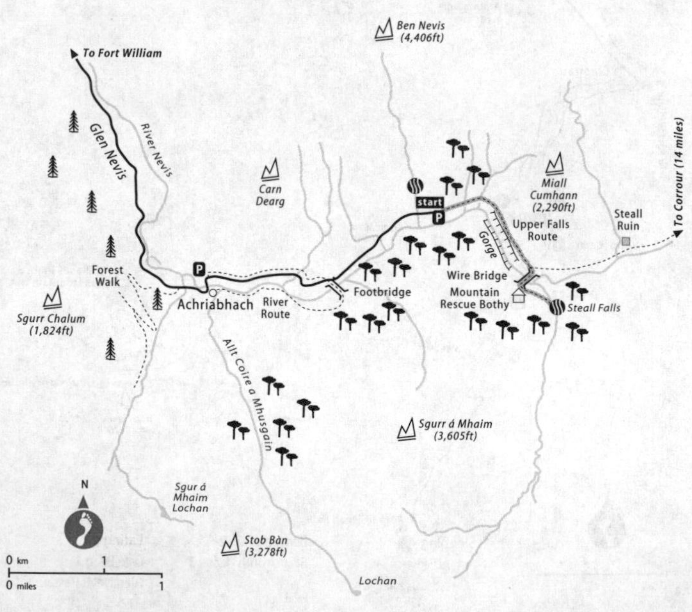

Riding the rails

Running from Glasgow to Mallaig via Fort William, the **West Highland Railway** is only 164 miles long but is widely acknowledged as one of the most scenic railway journeys in the world. The great thing about this journey is its variety, taking you from the distinctive red tenements of Glasgow and the former shipbuilding areas of the River Clyde, to the windy wilderness of Rannoch Moor and the chilly splendour of the hills. It's about an hour after leaving Glasgow that you get your first taste of highland scenery when the train hugs the eastern bank of sinewy Loch Long. Then it's on past the 'bonnie banks' of Loch Lomond, Britain's largest body of inland water. It's impossible not to pass this serene loch without thinking of the famous ballad about two Jacobite soldiers captured after the '45 rebellion. The soldier taking 'the low road' is due to be executed, his companion taking the 'high road' is due to be released.

After Ardlui, at the top of Loch Lomond, the countryside gets more rugged. Wherever you look you see something of interest: a waterfall gushing down a hillside, a buzzard surfing on the breeze, perhaps a herd of Highland Cattle wallowing in a river.

The **West Highland Way**, the long-distance footpath from Glasgow to Fort William, is close to the line now and at stations such as Crianlarich, Upper Tyndrum and Bridge of Orchy you can often spot footsore walkers with muddy boots – who get on the train looking slightly guilty and collapse on their seats with sighs of relief.

The landscape gets wilder and bleaker as the railway crosses the lonely, peaty wastes of Rannoch Moor and on to Corrour, which featured in the film version of Irvine Welsh's cult book *Trainspotting*. Then you descend to the lusher country around Tulloch, before pulling in to Fort William. This is a popular visitor centre as it's close to Ben Nevis, Britain's highest mountain, and beautiful Glen Nevis, which has featured in films such as *Braveheart* and *Rob Roy*. Now comes the most spectacular part of the journey, for the West Highland Line leaves the best till last. Leaving Fort William, the train crosses Thomas Telford's Caledonian Canal – where you can see an impressive series of eight locks known as 'Neptune's Staircase' – hugs the shore of Loch Eil, then crosses the magnificent Glenfinnan Viaduct, a masterpiece in concrete. You soon get superb views of the evocative Glenfinnan Monument that commemorates the start of the 1745 rebellion, before pulling in to Glenfinnan Station. The train now takes you through a landscape of craggy hills and glacial lochs etched with birch and pine trees. You pass Loch nan Uamh, from where Bonnie Prince Charlie fled for France after his defeat at Culloden, then draw in to Arisaig, the birthplace of the man who inspired RL Stevenson's *Long John Silver*. Next is beautiful Loch Morar, Britain's deepest inland loch and home – so legend has it – to a mysterious monster. Soon you get great views across the water to the craggy islands of Eigg and Rhum, before finally pulling in to the port of Mallaig.

and snowboarding area and has the longest ski season, running from Christmas to May. It also boasts the country's only cable-car system, built in 1989. The 1½-mile gondola ride is a popular attraction not only with skiers and snow- boarders in the winter but also during the summer off-season period, when it's used by hillwalkers to gain easy access to the mountains. For most tourists, though, it's an easy way to climb to over 2,000 ft and enjoy the wonderful views from the terrace of the self-service restaurant at the top. There are ski and snowboarding schools and also a dry slope for summer skiing in July and August, open Sunday-Thursday 1100-1230, £18 including gondola.

Leanachan Forest

The Leanachan Forest, below Aonach Mhor, is four miles north of Fort William. Access is via the road to the Aonach Mhor ski development. The forest covers a huge area with 25 miles of mountain bike trails, ranging from easy to demanding. You can even take your bike up on the gondola and ride it back down the 2.6-km course. For bike hire details, see page 367.

Sleeping

Fort William has plentiful accommodation, ranging from large luxury hotels to modest guest houses and B&Bs. Many of the B&Bs are in Corpachand Banavieto the north of town. Achintore Rd, which runs south along the loch, is packed with B&Bs and hotels, many of which are large and characterless. Running parallel is Grange Rd, which is lined with B&B accommodation. There are also plenty of B&Bs which are closer to the bus and train stations, mostly on and around Fassifern Rd and Alma Rd. As a main tourist centre, Fort William gets very busy in the high season and you'll need to book ahead at this time. The tourist office will book a room for you, for a small fee, or you can ask for their *Freedom of the Highlands Accommodation Guide* and phone around yourself.

South of Fort William, on the A82, are the villages of Onich and North Ballachulish, which make an attractive alternative to staying in the town.

Fort William *p361, map p361*

L **Inverlochy Castle Hotel**, 3 miles north of town on the A82 to Inverness, T01397-702177, www.inverlochy.co.uk. 16 rooms. One of the best hotels in the country, and everything you'd expect to find in a real castle: unsurpassed elegance, impeccable service and superb food (see Eating p367), all set in 500 acres of beautiful grounds.

B **Crolinnhe**, Grange Rd, T01397-702709, open Mar-Nov; and B **The Grange**, Grange Rd, T01397-705516, open Mar-Nov. Two of the best B&Bs on this road.

B **The Moorings Hotel**, 3 miles out of town in Banavie, on road to Corpach and Mallaig, T01397-772797, www.moorings-fortwilliam.co.uk. 21 rooms. Overlooks 'Neptune's Staircase'; well situated and comfortable with an excellent restaurant.

C **Alexandra Milton Hotel**, The Parade, T0808-1005556, www.miltonhotels.com. 97 rooms. Large established hotel right in the centre of town, with restaurant.

C **Glenloy Lodge Hotel**, about 6 miles from town on the B8004 north from Banavie, T/F701397-12700. 9 rooms. Open mid-Dec to late Oct. Friendly and comfortable little hotel tucked away in a quiet, secluded location, and with a good restaurant.

C **Highland Hotel**, Union Rd, T01397-702291, www.british-trust-hotels.com. Traditional Highland hotel overlooking the town, with great views across Loch Linnhe. Good restaurant, comfortable; cheaper off-season.

D **Distillery House**, across the road from the Glenlochy Guesthouse (opposite the road into Glen Nevis), T01397-700103, www.fort-william.net/distillery-house. 6 rooms. Comfortable, upmarket guest house.

D **Glenlochy Guesthouse**, Nevis Bridge, North Rd, T01397-702909, www.glenlochyguesthouse.co.uk, is recommended.

D **Guisachan House**, Alma Rd, T/F01397-703797; and D **6 Caberfeidh**, Fassifern Rd, T01397-703756, both of which are recommended.

D **Lawriestone Guesthouse**, Achintore Rd, T/F01397-700777, www.lawriestone.co.uk.

For an explanation of sleeping and eating price codes used in this guide, see inside the front cover. Other relevant information is found in Essentials, see pages 43-51.

More appealing than most of the other guest houses on this road.

F Bank Street Lodge, Bank St, T01397-700 070, www.accommodation-fortwilliam.com.

F Calluna, T01397-700451, calluna@westcoast-mountainguides.co.uk, is at Heathercroft, about a 15-min walk from the tourist office (see map). It's run by experienced mountain guide, Alan Kimber.

F Fort William Backpackers, Alma Rd, 500 yds from the train station, T01397-700711.

Glen Nevis *p362*

E Achintee Farm Guesthouse, T01397-702240, mcy@btinternet.com, by the start of the path to Ben Nevis. For details of how to get there, see Transport p368.

F Ben Nevis Inn, at Achintee Farm, across the river from the visitor centre (see above), T01397-701227, www.ben-nevis-inn.co.uk. This independent operation is a good bet.

F Farr Cottage Hostel is at the Farr Cottage Activity Centre, Corpach, T01397-772315, www.farrcottage.com, which also organizes hillwalking trips and rents out mountain bikes.

F SYHA Youth Hostel, T01397-702336, 3 miles out of town in Glen Nevis, near the start of the path up Ben Nevis, this large hostel gets very busy in summer.

Camping

Glen Nevis Caravan & Camping Park, T01397-702191, 2 miles up the Glen Nevis Rd, open mid-Mar to late Oct, has excellent facilities.

Eating

Fort William *p361, map p361*

Fort William isn't exactly the culinary capital of the Highlands, but there are some top quality restaurants and a decent choice across the range. Most of the hotels offer lunch and dinner.

£££ Crannog Seafood Restaurant, on the Town Pier, T01397-705589, www.crannog. net. By far the best option is this excellent restaurant housed in an old smokehouse. The seafood is as fresh as you can get and the surroundings are unpretentious. It gets very busy and service can be slow, so book ahead and take your time.

£££ Inverlochy Castle, see Sleeping. This is the best hotel to eat at. It's expensive but the food is superb and the surroundings are the last word in grandeur. Daily 1230-1345, 1900-2115.

££ An Crann, T01397-772077, 4 miles from town, take the A830 to Mallaig, turn right to Banavie on the B8004. This converted barn is a local favourite and offers good Scottish cooking in a friendly atmosphere. Mon-Sat 1230-1500, 1700-2100. Apr- mid Oct.

££-£ No 4 Cameron Square, Cameron Sq, T01397-704222, is good for a light lunch.

££ The Grog & Gruel, 66 High St, T01397-705078, is a pub-cum-restaurant offering good-value pizza, pasta and Tex Mex, and a wide range of superb cask ales. Open til 2400.

£ McTavish's Kitchens, High St, T01397-702406, a self-service restaurant serving steaks and seafood. In summer it hosts nightly Scottish music shows, with dancing and bagpipes, from 2030.

Glen Nevis *p362*

££-£ Glen Nevis Restaurant, near the SYHA hostel, T01397-705459, serves a 2-course lunch, 3-course dinner. Daily 1200-2200, Apr-Oct.

£ Café Beag, T01397-703601, a cosy place with log fire. Good vegetarian food.

Activities and tours

Canoeing

There are several good rivers around Fort William ranging in difficulty from Grade I to VI.

Nevis Canoe Club, T01397-705388.

Snowgoose Mountain Centre, attached to The Smiddy Bunkhouse, next to the Corpach train station, T01397-772467, runs canoe courses.

Day tours

Jacobite Steam Train, contact West Coast Railway Company, T01524-732100, www.westcoastrailway.co.uk, runs from Fort William to Mallaig during the summer months. Top of the pops as far as tours go.

Seal Island Cruises, T01397-705589, runs trips of 1½ hrs from Apr-Sep. One of several cruises which leave from the Town Pier in Fort William which give you the chance to spot local marine wildlife including seals, otters and seabirds.

Fishing

Torlundy Trout Fishery, Torlundy Farm in Tomacharich, 3 miles north off the A82, T01397-703015, has 3 lakes filled with rainbow trout and hires out rods. Also pony trekking from £15/hr, book in advance.

Hiking and climbing

Fort William is a mecca for hikers and climbers. For information on the climb up Ben Nevis and walks around Glen Nevis, see p362. Nevis Range offers some of the most accessible winter climbs in the country for experienced climbers. For details of the gondola ride see p364. If you want to hire a guide, try **Lochaber Walks**, 22 Zetland Av, T01397-703828; **Fort William Mountain Guides**, T01397-700451; **Alba Walking Holidays**, T01397-704964; and **Snowgoose Mountain Centre** (see above). Fort William has 2 excellent outdoor activity equipment shops: **Nevisport**, T013967-704921, is on the High St, and has a huge selection of books, maps and guides, a bureau de change and bar-restaurant. At the other end of the High St is **West Coast Outdoor Sports**, T01397-705777. There's an indoor climbing wall at the **Lochaber Leisure Centre** (see below).

Mountain biking

Great Glen Cycle Route, which is mainly off-road, runs all the way from Fort William to Inverness. See p366 and p344.

For the hire, sale or repair of bikes, and good advice, **Off Beat Bikes**, 117 High St, and **Nevis Range Ski Centre**, T01397-704 008, www.offbeatbikes.co.uk, open Jul-Aug.

Skiing

Nevis Range ski centre, see Sights. For ski equipment, try **Nevisport**, see above.

Swimming

There's an indoor pool at **Lochaber Leisure Centre**, off Belford Rd, T01397-704359.

Transport

Boat

There is a passenger-only ferry service to **Camusnagaul**, on the opposite bank of Loch Linnhe, from the Town Pier. It sails several times daily (Mon-Sat) and takes 10 mins. For further details contact Highland Council, T01463-702695, or ask at the TIC. The Corran Ferry to **Ardgour** (see p375) is 8 miles south of Fort William, just off the A82. The ferry makes the 5-min crossing every 30 min.

Bus

There are local buses every 10-20 mins to and from **Caol** and **Corpach**, and every hour on Sun and in the evening. There is an hourly service to **Glen Nevis**, Mon-Sat 0800-2300, Jun to Sep only (fewer on Sun). Four buses daily to **Aonach Mhor** during the ski season.

Long-distance services include several daily **Citylink** buses to **Inverness** (1 hr, £8.20); to **Oban** (1¾ hrs, £7.60) via **Glencoe** (30 mins); and to **Uig** (3½ hrs), via **Portree** and **Kyle of Lochalsh** (1 hr 50 mins). Citylink buses also go several times daily to **Glasgow** (3¼ hrs), via **Glencoe** and **Tyndrum**, and to **Edinburgh** (4 hrs, £18.50), via **Stirling** (3 hrs). There is a bus to **Mallaig** (1½ hrs, £4) daily except Sun with **Shiel Buses**, T01967-431272. **Highland Country Buses**, run several times a day to **Kinlochleven** (50 mins) via **Glencoe**. There is also a postbus service (Mon-Sat) to **Glen Etive**.

Car hire

Easydrive, at Lochy Bridge, T01397-701616; **Volkswagen Rental**, at Nevis Garage, Argour Rd, Caol, T01397-702432; **Budget**, at North Rd, T01397-702500, or **Practical Car & Van Hire**, at Slipway Autos, Corpach, T01397-772404. Prices start from around £35 per day.

Taxi

You can call a taxi on T01397-706070.

Train

There are 2-3 trains daily from **Glasgow** to **Fort William** (3¾ hrs) via **Crianlarich**. These continue to **Mallaig** (1 hr 20 mins) where they connect with ferries to **Armadale** on Skye (see p432). There are no direct trains to Oban; you need to change at Crianlarich. There is a sleeper service from **London Euston** (see p33), but you'll miss the views.

Directory

Fort William *p361, map p361*

Banks Plenty with ATMs on the High St.

Internet The **library** on the High St and **Thing King**, on High St.

Glen Coe

→ *Phone code: 01855. Colour map 3, grid B5-6.*

There are many spectacular places in the Scottish Highlands, but few, if any, can compare to the truly awesome scenery of Glen Coe. No one could fail to be moved by its haunting beauty, with imposing mountains, their tops often wreathed in cloud, rising steeply on either side from the valley floor. The brooding atmosphere of the landscape is only enhanced by the glen's tragic history. Once you've heard of the Glen Coe Massacre it sends a shiver down the spine every time you pass this way. Scotland's most famous glen is also one of the most accessible, with the A82 Glasgow to Fort William road running through it. Much of the area is owned by the National Trust for Scotland and virtually uninhabited, leaving huge tracts of glen and mountain which provide outstanding climbing and walking. There's also skiing at the Glencoe Ski Centre, and canoeing on the River Coe and River Etive. ▸▸ *For Sleeping, Eating and other listings, see pages 373-374.*

Onich, North Ballachulish and Kinlochleven

The A82 south from Fort William passes through the collection of guest houses and B&Bs known as Onich before the B863 turns east at North Ballachulish and heads to Kinlochleven, at the head of Loch Leven. It can also be reached on the same road from Glencoe Village, seven miles west. It's an unlikely place to find a huge aluminium factory, but it kept the village alive for many years, until its recent closure. It has since been turned into an indoor mountaineering centre (see Activities and tours below). You can find out all about the long and often tragic history of aluminium-working in Lochaber at **The Aluminium Story** ⓘ *Linnhe Rd, T01855-831663, Apr-Oct Tue-Fri 1030-1800, Sat-Sun 1100-1500, free*, in the Kinlochleven Visitor Centre and Library.

The **West Highland Way** passes through the village and many walkers spend the night here before setting out on the last stretch before Fort William. There are also good walks in the surrounding hills and glens, a few of which are described below.

Walks around North Ballachulish

About a mile north of the village of North Ballachulish, there's an easy 40-minute circular walk up to **Inchree Waterfall**. It starts from the car park at the end of the road beyond the tiny hamlet of Inchree and is clearly marked. The waterfall is impressive and divided into three sections. The views from the top, down the length of Loch Linnhe, are worth the walk alone. The path continues up past the waterfall to the forest road which leads back downhill to the car park.

Walks around Kinlochleven

→ *OS landranger No 41.*

There are some fairly easy short walks from Kinlochleven up the glen of the River Leven, including the one to the impressive **Grey Mare's Tailwaterfall**. It's a short walk of under an hour, signposted from the village.

A fairly easy but rewarding half-day walk is to follow the **West Highland Way** south from the village to the top of the **Devil's Staircase**, where it meets the A82 at the eastern end of Glen Coe. The route starts from the **British Aluminium Visitor Centre,** runs around the side of the aluminium factory, then crosses a wooden bridge and climbs gradually on a dirt jeep-track up to **Penstock House,** at 1,000 ft. At the top, near the house, the track forks to the right and continues on a rough footpath to the Devil's Staircase. The path is marked with the West Highland Way thistle sign, so it's easy to follow uphill to the top of the pass (1,804 ft), from where you get great views of Loch Eilde Mór and the

The Devil's Staircase was named by the 400 soldiers who had to endure severe hardship while building it in the 17th century.

 Mamores to the north. The path then descends down the staircase to Glen Coe, with breathtaking Buachaille Etive Mór in front of you all the way. You'll have to return to Kinlochleven by the same route, or you could carry on to the **Kingshouse Hotel** (see below). The return trip from Kinlochleven should take four to five hours, or you can start out from Glencoe (see below). This section of the West Highland Way was once part of the old military road which ran from Fort William to Stirling.

Another good hike, though more strenuous, is to **Beinn na Callich** (2,507 ft). You'll need to be fairly fit for this steep climb, and allow around six to seven hours for the return trip. The route is well marked and starts from the West Highland Way footpath opposite the school, which is on the road heading out of the village towards Fort William. The path climbs steeply at first, crosses the tarmac road to **Mamore Lodge**, then continues till it joins General Wade's old military road, which takes the West Highland Way on its final 11 miles to Fort William. From here, you'll see the path zigzagging up the mountain. Continue along the old military road for about 400 yds until you cross a wooden bridge. Then follow a path down to another wooden bridge, where the ground is quite boggy. Cross the bridge and the path begins to zigzag uphill till it levels out on to a plateau, before continuing relentlessly upwards through a long series of zigzags to the summit, marked by a couple of cairns and a commemorative plaque. The views from the top make the tiring climb worthwhile. You can see down on to Loch Leven, across to Glen Coe and the magnificent Mamores looming close by.

Fit and experienced hillwalkers can access the **Mamores** from the Mamore Lodge road. Once you're up there you have the opportunity to bag several Munros, via a series of excellent ridge walks connecting Am Bodach (3,386 ft) with Stob Coire a'

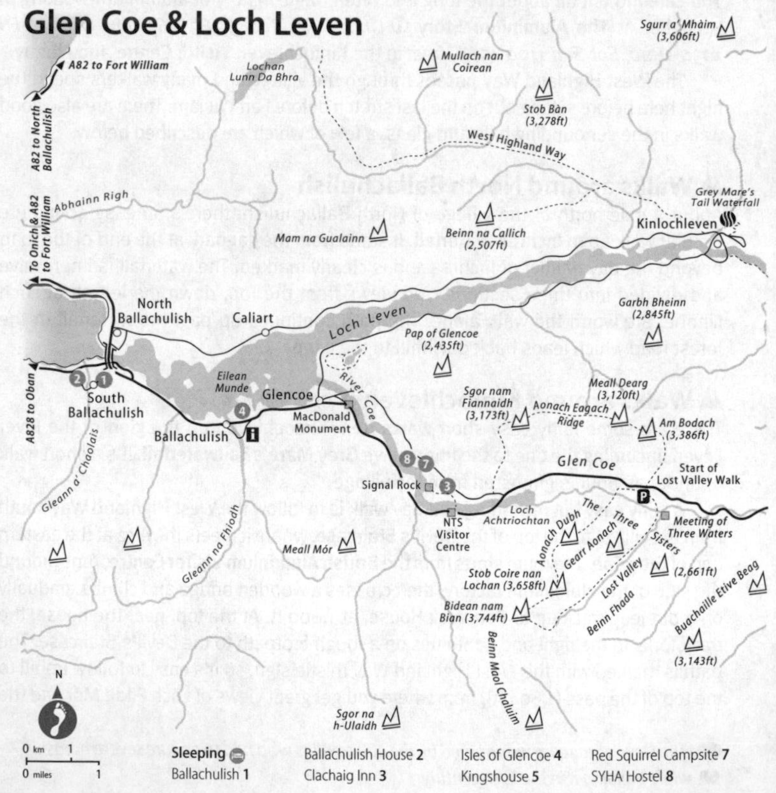

Chairn (3,219 ft), Na Gruagaichean (3,461 ft), An Gearanach (3,222 ft), Sgor An Iubhair (3,285 ft), Sgurr a'Mhaim (3,606 ft) and Stob Ban (3,278 ft). These peaks and ridges can also be reached from Glen Nevis, see page 362. As well as a good pair of lungs and the proper equipment, take a map and a compass.

Ballachulish

On the southern shore of Loch Leven, a mile or so west of Glencoe Village on the A82, is the old slate quarrying village of Ballachulish. There's a good range of accommodation here and many use the place as a base to visit Glencoe. In the car park just off the main road is the TIC ⓘ *T01855-811296, Apr-Oct*. As well as the usual accommodation booking service they have displays about the quarries.

Glencoe Village

At the western entrance to the glen, on the shores of Loch Leven, is Glencoe Village, 16 miles south of Fort William just off the A82. There are several places to stay in and around the village, as well as a general store, post office and the thatched **Glencoe Folk Museum** ⓘ *late May to Sep 1000-1730, £1.50*, which has collections of costumes, military memorabilia, and domestic and farm tools and equipment. There's a small **National Trust for Scotland Visitor Centre** ⓘ *T01855-811307, early Apr to mid-May and early Sep to end Oct daily 1000-1700, mid-May to end Aug 0930-1730, £4.50, concession £2.60*, at the western end of the glen, about three miles south of Glencoe Village. It shows a short video on the Glencoe Massacre and has a gift shop selling the usual stuff.

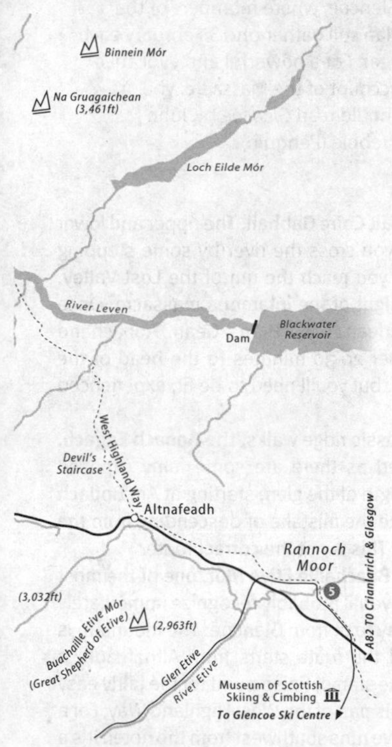

Climbing and hiking in Glen Coe → *OS Landranger No 41.*

Glen Coe offers some of Britain's most challenging climbing and hiking, with some notoriously treacherous routes and unpredictable weather conditions that claim lives every year. The routes described below are some of the least strenuous, but you'll still need a map, good boots, warm clothing, food and water, and you should take the usual precautions, see page 56.

One of the most popular walks is the relatively straightforward hike up to the **Lost Valley**, a secret glen where the ill-fated MacDonalds hid the cattle they'd stolen. Allow around three hours for the return trip. Start from the car park by the large boulder (see map), opposite the distinctive **Three Sisters**. Head down to the valley floor and follow the gravel path which leads down to a wooden bridge across the River Coe. Cross the bridge and follow the path up and over the stile. From here there's a choice of two routes. The less obvious route heads right and offers an easier climb into the valley. This eventually meets the lower, well-worn track, which involves a bit of scrambling but is more

A stab in the back

Glen Coe is probably best known as the scene of one of the most shameful and notorious incidents in Scottish history.

Following his succession to the throne, William III wanted all the clans to swear an oath of allegiance by 1 January 1692. After much hesitation, the Jacobite clans of the West Highlands agreed to do so. However, Maclain of Glencoe, chief of a small branch of the MacDonalds, was not only late in setting off on the journey, but mistakenly went to Fort William to sign, instead of Inveraray. By the time he reached Inveraray it was 6 January and the deadline had passed.

The government decided that the rebellious clan be punished, in order to set an example to other clans, some of whom had not taken the oath. A company of 120 soldiers, under the command of Cambell of Glenlyon, were sent to Glen Coe and, since their leader was related by marriage to Maclain, the troops were billeted in MacDonald homes, in keeping with the long-standing Highland tradition of hospitality.

There they stayed for almost two weeks, until the cold-blooded order came through to '... put all to the sword under seventy'. And so, on a cold winter's night, in the early hours of 13 February 1692, the Campbells ruthlessly slaughtered their hosts. Maclain and 37 men, women and children were slain in their beds, while many others fled into the hills, only to die of hunger and exposure. It was a bloody incident which had deep repercussions and proved to be the beginning of the end of the Highland way of life. For further information, see page 602.

There's a monument to the fallen MacDonalds in the village of Glencoe, where members of the clan still gather on 13 February each year. For a powerful and evocative account of the Massacre, you should read *Glencoe* by John Prebble (Penguin).

exciting as it follows the rushing waters of the **Allt Coire Gabhail.** The upper and lower paths meet a few miles further up and here you cross the river by some stepping stones. Proceed up the steep scree slope till you reach the rim of the **Lost Valley,** where many of the MacDonalds fled on the night of the infamous massacre. Once in the valley there are great views of Bidean nam Bian, Gearr Aonachand Beinn Fhadaand you can continue for a further 20-30 minutes to the head of the valley. From here it's possible to climb **Bidean**, but you'll need to be fit, experienced and well equipped.

Glen Coe also offers one of the world's classic ridge walks, the **Aonach Eagach**. It's not for the inexperienced or faint-hearted as there are some fairly exposed pinnacles. The ridge runs almost the entire length of the glen, starting at **Am Bodach** and ending at **Sgor nam Fiannaidh**. Don't make the mistake of descending from the last summit straight down to the Clachaig Inn. This is not the correct route.

Another difficult route is to the summit of **Buachaille Etive Mór,** one of the most photographed mountains in Scotland and one you'll probably recognize immediately the first time you see it from the A82 on the way to or from Glencoe. The mountain is best viewed from the **Kingshouse Hotel** and the route starts from Altnafeadh, a couple of miles west of the hotel. This is also the start or finish point for the fairly easy half-day walk over the **Devil's Staircase**, which is part of the West Highland Way. For a description of the route, see page 369. **Glen Etive** runs southwest from the hotel. It's a very beautiful and little-visited place, and great for wild camping. There's a postbus service once a day from Fort William.

Finally, there are some short, pleasant walks around **Glencoe Lochan**, an artificial loch created in the mid-19th century by Lord Strathcona for his homesick Canadian wife. Take the left turning off the minor road to the youth hostel just beyond the bridge over the River Coe. There's a choice of three walks of between 40 minutes and an hour, all detailed at the car park.

Glencoe Ski Centre

ⓘ *T01855-851226, www.ski.scotland.net, chair lift operates 0930-1700, full day pass with lifts, costs £17 (children £9.50), combined 5-day pass for Glencoe and Nevis Range.* The Glencoe Ski Centre is just over a mile from the **Kingshouse Hotel**, on the other side of the A82, on **Meall A'Bhuiridh** (3,636 ft). This is Scotland's oldest ski centre, established in 1956, and remains one of the best, with the longest single descent. At the base station is the **Museum of Scottish Skiing and Climbing** ⓘ *May-Sep 0900-1700, restaurant and café*, where you can see the ice axe used by Chris Bonnington, among other things.

Sleeping

Onich, North Ballachulish and Kinlochleven *p369, map p370*

There's a wide selection of places to stay in the villages of Onich and North Ballachulish, mostly with good views of the loch. They make an attractive alternative to Fort William.

L **Allt-nan-Ros Hotel**, Onich, T01855-821210, www.allt-nan-ros.co.uk. Price includes dinner. James and Fiona Macleod's Victorian country house overlooks Loch Linnhe with views across to Appin and the hills of Ardgour and Morvern, with pretty gardens and great food.

L **The Lodge on the Loch Hotel**, Onich, T01855-821237, www.freedomglen.co.uk, open Feb-Dec. High-quality hotel with great views and good restaurant (**£££**).

B **Cuilcheanna House**, Onich, T01855-821226, open Easter-Oct. A comfortable guest house just off the main road, a good place to dine, but for residents only.

B **Onich Hotel**, Onich, T01855-821214. Loch views and good meals (**££**) in its busy bar.

D **MacDonald Hotel**, Fort William Rd, Kinlochleven, T01855-831539, open Mar-Dec, serves cheap bar lunches and moderately priced dinners.

E **Tailrace Inn**, Riverside Rd, Kinlochleven, T01855-831777, does cheap bar meals all

F **Blackwater Hostel**, Lab Rd, Kinlochleven, T01855-831253, www.blsckwaterhostel.co.uk.

F **Inchree Hostel**, T/F01855-821287, at Inchree, on the A82 to Fort William.

Ballachulish *p371, map p370*

As well as one of the most historic hotels in Scotland, there's a wide selection of cheaper B&Bs and guest houses in the village.

L **The Isles of Glencoe Hotel**, T01855-811602, www.freedomglen.co.uk/ig. 39 rooms. A modern hotel and leisure complex on the shores of the loch, and facilities include heated pool, sauna and gym. The restaurant serves a 3-course lunch (**££**) and 3-course dinner (**£££**).

L **Ballachulish Hotel**, South Ballachulish by the bridge, T01855-821582, www.freedom glen.co.uk/bh. 54 rooms. Grand old hotel, handily placed for Glen Coe, Fort William or Oban, restaurant serves meals throughout the day (**£££-££**).

L **Ballachulish House**, T01855-811266, www.ballachulishhouse.com, open Mar-Oct. 7 rooms. Some 200 yds beyond the Ballachulish Hotel on the A828 to Oban. This comfortable and elegant hotel/guest house is steeped in history and said to be the most haunted house in Scotland. The seat of the Stewarts of Ballachulish since the 16th century, this was where the final order for the Glencoe Massacre was signed. Hospitality is second-to-none and the food is superb; even if you're not staying you can enjoy the experience of dining here (**£££**), but book ahead.

E **Fern Villa**, T01855-811393, a very good guest house.

For an explanation of sleeping and eating price codes used in this guide, see inside the front cover. Other relevant information is found in Essentials, see pages 43-51.

Glencoe Village *p371, map p370*
There are several B&Bs and guest houses in the village and quite a few options around.
C-D **Clachaig Inn**, about 3 miles south of the village, on the old road which leads from the village to the NTS visitor centre, T01855-811252, www.clachaig.com. 19 rooms. Good-value accommodation and one of the great Highland pubs. It's a favourite haunt of climbers and there's a lively atmosphere as well as some fine real ales and decent cheap food. There are also 3 chalets which can be rented on a weekly basis (phone for details), and mountain bike hire (see below).
D **Kingshouse Hotel**, at the east end of the glen, almost opposite the turn-off to the Glencoe Ski Centre, T01855-851259. 22 rooms. This is Scotland's oldest established inn and such a landmark that it even appears on maps, marked as 'hotel'. It's on the West Highland Way and is popular with hikers, climbers and skiers who frequently drop in for a refreshing drink in the bar and some good-value food.
E **The Glencoe Guesthouse**, T01855-811244. On the outskirts of the village, at Upper Carnoch.
E **Scorrybreac Guesthouse**, T/F01855-811354, www.scorrybreac.co.uk, open Dec-Oct. In the village, this is a pleasant guest house.
F **Glencoe Bunkhouses**, nearby SYHA Youth Hostel, T01855-811256, squirrels@amserve.net, offers cheap, basic accommodation in 2 bunkhouses and an alpine barn. The same people also run the **Red Squirrel Campsite** further along the road.
F **SYHA Youth Hostel**, on the same road as Clachaig Inn, about 2 miles from the village, T01855-811219. An excellent hostel, open all year and very popular with climbers, so you should book ahead.

Camping
Invercoe Caravans, T/F01855-811210. To the east of the village, on the shores of Loch Leven. See also **Glencoe Bunkhouses** above.

Eating

Onich, North Ballachulish and Kinlochleven *p369, map p370*
££ **Four Seasons Bistro and Bar**, Inchree, T01855-821393, a friendly and informal place that looks like a log cabin. It's open daily except Tue, 1800-2130.

Glencoe Village *p371, map p370*
Apart from the places listed under Sleeping:
££-£ **The Glencoe Hotel**, in the village T01855-811245, serves decent bar food.

Activities and tours

Climbing
Ice Factor, Kinlochleven, T01855-831100, www.ice-factor.co.uk. The world's largest indoor ice climbing facility has opened in the former aluminium factory with rock climbing wall, bouldering hall, outdoor equipment shop, café and restaurant, sauna, steam room and hot tub. Annual membership costs £5 and daily rates range from £6.50 to £14. Also climbing courses available. Mountain guides can be found at **Hadrian Mountaineering**, 19b Carnoch, T/F01855-811472, www.glencoe-mountain-sport.co.uk; **Glencoe Guides**, T01855-811402; **Dave Hanna**, Ballachulish, T01855-811620.

Cycling
Glencoe Mountain Bike Centre, at the Clachaig Inn (see Sleeping), has bike hire, £12 for a full day, £8 for a half day.

Outdoor activities
Alfresco Adventure, T01855-821248, just to the east of North Ballachulish on the B863 to Kinlochleven, offers boat hire and various outdoor activities such as mountain biking and canoeing.

Transport

Onich, North Ballachulish and Kinlochleven *p369, map p370*
Highland Country Buses, T01397-702373, runs 6 times a day (Mon-Sat) between **Fort William** and **Kinlochleven** (50 mins).

Glencoe Village *p371, map p370*
Highland Country Buses run several times daily from Fort William to Glencoe Village (30 mins, £3.40). There are **Citylink** buses to **Glasgow** (2½ hrs) and **Fort William**. The daily **postbus** service from **Fort William** to the Kingshouse Hotel and **Glen Etive** stops at the Glencoe crossroads.

West of Fort William

➔ *Colour map 3, grid B4-5 & A4.*

West of Fort William is one of the most remote parts of the Highland region, stretching south from Loch Ailort to the Morvern Peninsula, and west to the wild and beautiful Ardnamurchan Peninsula. To the north the area is topped off by 'The Road to the Isles', a stunning journey from Fort William through to Mallaig. ▸▸ *For Sleeping, Eating and other listings, see pages 379-382.*

Ardgour, Ardnamurchan and Morvern

This lonely, southwestern corner features a dramatic landscape of rugged mountains, desolate moorland and near-deserted glens, fringed by a coastline of sparkling white beaches and clear turquoise seas with wonderful views across to the isles of Mull and Skye. This is one of the least-populated areas in Britain, mainly due to the legacy of the Highland Clearances in the mid-19th century, when whole communities were evicted by landlords in favour of more profitable sheep. With so few people around, this is an area noted for its wildlife, with a huge variety of birds and animals, such as deer, pine martens, wildcats and eagles. If you have both the time and the energy, it's worth exploring on foot. There's a series of footpaths throughout the area, particularly around Ardnamurchan.

Ins and outs

Once you leave the A830 Fort William to Mallaig road, buses are few and far between, so it's not easy to get around quickly without your own transport. You'll need your own transport to reach Ardnamurchan Point and Sanna Bay as there are no buses beyond Kilchoan. Some 30 walks in the area are listed in a local guidebook available at tourist offices. You should also have OS Map numbers 40, 47 and 49, which cover the area It's an area of few roads. ▸▸ *For further details, see Transport page 375.*

Ardgour

➔ *Phone code: 01967. Colour map 3, grid B5.*

The name Ardgour means 'height of the goats', and you can still see feral goats in this huge, sparsely populated wilderness bordered by Loch Shiel, Loch Eil, Loch Linnhe and Loch Sunart. Access is via the A861 south from Kinlocheil, or on the Corran Ferry to the tiny lochside villages of **Corran** and **Clovulin**.

The attractive little village of **Strontian** on the shores of Loch Sunart gave its name to the element strontium, which was first discovered in the nearby lead mines in 1790. These now-abandoned mines also produced most of the lead shot used in the Napoleonic wars. Strontian is the largest settlement in these parts and has a couple of shops, a post office and a tourist information centre ⓘ *T01967-402131, Apr-Oct Mon-Fri 0900-1700, Sat 1000-1600, Sun 1000-1400*. About two miles north of the village is the **Ariundle Nature Reserve**, which offers a pleasant two-hour nature trail through the glen and a 40-minute forest walk.

Morvern

➔ *Phone code: 01967. Colour map 3, grid B6.*

Just east of Strontian the A884 leads south through the bleak, desolate landscape of Morvern to the tiny remote community of **Lochaline** on the Sound of Mull, departure point for the CalMac ferry to Fishnish. About three miles before Lochaline is the turning left for the track which leads down the side of Loch Aline to the 14th-century ruins of **Ardtornish Castle**. First you'll come to **Kinlochaline Castle** (keys available at the cottage) and **Ardtornish House**. This house stands on the site of

> ❢ *During the stalking season (1 July-20 October) check at the estate office before setting out on the walk to Loch Tearnait.*

the original house, which was visited on several occasions by Florence Nightingale, who was a family member of the original owners. The author John Buchan spent many summers here in the 1930s. There's a path which leads from the estate office uphill across open moorland for an hour till it reaches **Loch Tearnait**. In the centre of the loch is a 1,500 year-old crannog, an artificial island built for defensive purposes. This walk is detailed in the tourist board's *Great Walks* leaflet, along with the Ariundle Nature Trail, available from local tourist offices.

Ardnamurchan Peninsula → *Phone code: 01972 & 01967. Colour map 3, grid B4.*

The main places of interest in this area are to be found on the rugged Ardnamurchan peninsula, the end of which is the most westerly point on the British mainland. The winding A861 runs west from Strontian along the north shore of Loch Sunart to **Salen**, where the single-track B8007 branches west and runs all the way out to the tip of the peninsula. The A861 meanwhile turns north to Acharacle.

The first settlement you reach heading west out to Ardnamurchan Point is **Glenborrodale**. Before you reach the tiny hamlet look out on the left for the castellated late-Victorian towers of **Glenborrodale Castle**, once the property of a certain Jesse Boot, who founded a chain of chemist shops which you may have heard of. Just west of Glenborrodale is the excellent **Glenmore Natural History Centre** ⓘ *T01967-500254, Apr-Oct 1030-1730 (Sun 1200-1730), £2.50, concession £2, children £1.50*, local photographer Michael McGregor's interactive exhibition which features some of his most stunning photographs of local wildlife. The centre is designed to interact with the environment and there's live video action of the surrounding wildlife, including pine martens, birds and even fish in the nearby river. It's a great place for kids, and adults too. There's also a café serving snacks, and a bookshop. A mile to the east is the **RSPB Reserve** where you can see golden eagles, otters and seals. You can take a two-hour wildlife trip to the seal colonies – or further afield to Tobermory on Mull or Staffa and the Treshnish Islands, see Activities and tours page 381. A few miles west of the centre, the B8007 turns away from the coast. Here you'll see the beautiful bay of **Camas nan Geall**. It's worth stopping at the car park to admire the fantastic views, or take the path down to the beach. Between Glenborrodale and Kilchoan, a road runs to the north coast of the peninsula and the beautiful beaches at **Fascadale, Kilmory** and **Ockle**.

The straggling crofting village of **Kilchoan** is the main settlement on Ardnamurchan. Shortly after passing the sign for the village, you can turn left to the scenic ruin of **Mingary Castle**, built around the 13th century. There's a tourist information centre ⓘ *T01972-510222, Easter-Oct daily*, which provides information on local scenic walks and will help with accommodation. Beyond Kilchoan the road leads to the lighthouse at mainland Britain's most westerly point, with stunning views (on a clear day) across to the small isles of Rùm, Eigg, Muck and Canna, with the Cuillins of Skye rising behind Rùm. The former lighthouse was designed by Alan Stevenson, father of Robert Louis, and built in 1849. The buildings have been converted into the **Ardnamurchan Visitor Centre** ⓘ *T01972-510210, 1 Apr-31 Oct daily from 1000-1800 (1700 in Oct), £2.50, concession/children £1.50*, where you can learn about the history and workings of lighthouses. There's also self-catering accommodation, a café and gift shop.

A mile northwest of Kilchoan a road branches to the right to the beautiful long, white beach at **Sanna Bay**. It's worth making the trip here just to walk on the beach, but this is also a good place to spot whales and dolphins. On the road to Sanna Bay is the tiny settlement of **Achnaha**, which is famed for its rare 'ring-dyke' system, a huge, natural rock formation which is the crater of an extinct volcano.

North of Salen on the A861 is the scattered crofting township of **Acharacle**, at the western end of Loch Shiel surrounded by rolling hills. The village has several shops, a post office, garage and plenty of places to stay. A couple of miles to the west a road

Raising standards

It all started on 19 August 1745 at Glenfinnan, 19 miles west of Fort William at the head of Loch Shiel. Less than a month earlier, Prince Charles Edward Stuart had landed on the Scottish mainland for the first time, on the shores of Loch nan Uamh, between Lochailort and Arisaig (see below). He had come to claim the British throne for his father, James, son of the exiled King James VII of Scotland and II of England.

The clan chiefs had expected French support, but when the Prince arrived with only a handful of men they were reluctant to join the cause. Undeterred, the prince raised his standard and his faith was soon rewarded when he heard the sound of the pipes and Cameron of Lochiel, along with 800 men, came marching down the valley to join them. It must have been an incredible moment.

leads to beautiful **Kentra Bay**. Cross the wooden bridge, follow the footpath round the side of Kentra Bay and then follow the signs for Gortenfearn, where you'll find the famous 'singing sands'. Not only is the beach music to the ears as you walk its length, but the view across to Skye and the small isles is a feast for the eyes.

Three miles north of Acharacle is **Loch Moidart**. Here, perched on a rocky promontory in the middle of the loch, is the 13th-century ruin of **Castle Tioram** (pronounced 'Cheerum'), one of Scotland's truly great castles. This was the seat of the MacDonalds of Clanranald, until it was destroyed by their chief in 1715 to prevent it from falling into Hanoverian hands while he was away fighting for the Jacobites. There are plans to restore the castle, but you can visit it (free) via the sandy causeway that connects it to the mainland at low tide.

The Road to the Isles

The 46-mile stretch of the A830 from Fort William to Mallaig is known as 'The Road to the Isles'. It's a very beautiful journey, particularly by train – see page 365 – through a landscape that resonates with historical significance. This is Bonnie Prince Charlie country, where the ill-fated Jacobite Rising not only began, but also ended, with the Prince's flight to France.

Glenfinnan → *Phone code: 01397. Colour map 4, grid B5.*

There's a powerful sense of history here. You don't have to be Scottish to feel a shiver run down the spine and a tear well in the eye as you gaze across stunning Loch Shiel stretching into the distance, veiled by steep mountains. You can almost hear the wail of the bagpipes in the distance. A commemorative tower stands proudly at the head of the loch, erected in 1815 by Alexander MacDonald of Glenaladale in memory of the clansmen who fought and died for the Prince. You can climb to the top of the tower (mind your head, though) for even better views down the loch. The **Glenfinnan Games** are held here in mid-August. On the other side of the road is the **National Trust for Scotland Visitor Centre** ⓘ *T01397-722250, 1 Apr-18 May and 1 Sep-31 Oct daily 1000-1700, 19 May-31 Aug 0930-1800, £2.50, concession £1*, which has displays and an audio programme of the Prince's campaign, from Glenfinnan to its grim conclusion at Culloden. There's also a café.

A mile away, in Glenfinnan Village, is the **Station Museum** ⓘ *T01397-722295, Apr-Oct daily 0930-1630, £0.50*, which is housed in the railway station on the magnificent Fort-William to Mallaig railway line. It has displays of memorabilia from the line's 100-year history. You can also sleep and eat here (see below). The 1,000-ft span of the **Glenfinnan Viaduct**, between the visitor centre and the village, is one of the most spectacular sections of the famous West Highland Railway, see page 365.

About 10 miles west of Glenfinnan the road passes through the village of **Lochailort**, where the A861 branches south to the remote Ardnamurchan Peninsula, see above. A couple of miles further on, is **Loch nan Uamh**, where Prince Charles first landed on the Scottish mainland and from where, a year later, he fled for France following the disastrous defeat at Culloden, see page 346. A path leads down from the car park to the Prince's Cairn, which marks the beginning and the end of the Jacobite cause.

Arisaig and Morar → *Phone code: 01687. Colour map 4, grid A4.*

At the western end of the Morar Peninsula is the little village of Arisaig, scattered round a sandy bay. This was the birthplace of Long John Silver, who worked on the construction of the nearby lighthouse at **Barrahead**, which happened to be one of many such lighthouses designed by the father of Robert Louis Stevenson. Silver met Robert Louis on a few occasions, and so impressed the young writer that he immortalized him in his classic novel *Treasure Island*.

There are some nice beaches around, and the road west from the village out to the **Rhue Peninsula** is great for seal spotting. You can also take a cruise from Arisaig to the islands of Rùm, Eigg and Muck, see Transport page 381.

Between Arisaig and Morar is a string of glorious beaches of white sand backed by machair, washed by turquoise seas and enjoying the kind of views, across to Rùm and the Cuillins of Skye, that bring a smile to the face. This is one of the most stunning stretches of coastline in Britain, despite the presence of too many ugly holiday bungalows and caravan sites. Eight miles north of Arisaig is Morar, where the famous beach scenes from the movie *Local Hero* were filmed – with not a caravan in sight.

This coastline gets very busy in summer but, like so much of the Highlands, it's easy to get away from it all. A single-track road leads up behind the village of Morar to dark, mysterious **Loch Morar**, the deepest inland loch in the country and home of Morag, Scotland's other, lesser-known monster. Two locals reported seeing her in August 1969 and a scientific investigation two years later uncovered a remarkable number of eye-witness accounts. You could always try to elicit further information from the locals over a wee dram in the bar of the **Morar Hotel**. The road runs along the north shore of the loch for three miles till it reaches the pretty little hamlets of **Bracora** and **Bracorina**. Here the road stops, but a footpath continues all the way to **Tarbet** on the shores of Loch Nevis, from where it's possible to catch a boat back to Mallaig, see Transport page 381. It takes about three hours to walk to Tarbet – where there's now a bothy – and you'll need to get there by 1530 for the boat.

Mallaig → *Phone code: 01687. Colour map 4, grid A4.*

The end of the road is Mallaig, a busy fishing port huddled round its harbour and main departure point for the ferry to Skye. It's not a particularly appealing place, but it's always busy with people waiting for the ferry or the train to Fort William. The train and bus stations and CalMac ferry office are all within a few yards of each other. Also close by are banks with ATMs and the post office. The tourist information centre is by the harbour ⓘ *T01687-462170, Apr-Oct daily, Nov-Mar Mon, Tue, Fri.*

If you have some time to kill you could visit **Mallaig Marine World** ⓘ *T01687-462292, Jun-Sep Mon-Sat 0900-2100, Sun 1000-1800, Oct-May Mon-Sat 1200-1730, £2.75, children £1.35*, an aquarium with indigenous marine creatures as well as displays on the history of the local fishing industry. Beside the train station is the

Glenfinnan Viaduct featured in Harry Potter and the Chamber of Secrets, in the famous scene where he tried to board the Hogwarts Express from a flying Ford Anglia Lochailort.

Mallaig Heritage Centre ⓘ *May-Sep Mon-Sat 0930-1700, Sun 1300-1700. £1.80, children £1*, with interesting descriptions of the local Clearances, the railway line and the fishing industry.

For something a bit more energetic, there are a couple of good walks around the village. An easy one, which should take around 45 minutes, goes to the little village of **Mallaig Bheag** (Mallaigviag), further east along the coast. Just before the car park at the eastern end of the harbour you'll see a sign, on the right as you head east, which points you towards the old road to Mallaig Bheag. Follow the path up behind the houses and continue into a small glen behind the hill that overlooks the port. The path then rises gradually till you're rewarded with great views of Loch Nevis. It continues through Mallaig Bheag then joins up with the main road back to Mallaig. Follow this till the end of the row of houses on your right, turn right and then left and back down to Mallaig bay and the start of the walk.

There are great views over the Sound of Sleat from the indoor swimming pool at the top of Frank Brae.

Knoydart Peninsula

→ *Phone code: 01867. Colour map 3, grid A5.*

The Knoydart Peninsula, the most remote and unspoilt region in Britain and one of Europe's last great wildernesses, literally lies between Heaven and Hell, for it is bordered to the north by Loch Hourn (Loch of Hell) and to the south by Loch Nevis (Loch of Heaven). Knoydart is not for wimps. It can only be reached on foot or by boat and consequently attracts walkers, who can wander for days around a network of trails without seeing another soul.

A two-day hiking route starts from Kinloch Hourn, reached by bus from Invergarry, see page 354. The trail winds its way around the coast to Barrisdale and on to Inverie. Another route into Knoydart starts from the west end of Loch Arkaig, see page 356, and runs through Glen Dessarry. Both are tough hikes and only for fit, experienced and well-equipped hillwalkers. An easier way in is by boat, see Transport page 381.

The peninsula's only settlement of any size is tiny **Inverie**, with just 60 inhabitants, one of only a few villages in Scotland which can't be reached by road, but still has a post office, a shop, a few places to stay and Britain's most remote pub. Much of the peninsula is mountain, with four peaks over 3,000 ft. Its 85 square miles is a mix of private sporting estate, conservation trust and community partnership. Five years ago one chunk of the peninsula, the 17,000 acre **Knoydart Estate**, was rescued from a succession of indifferent landlords by a community buy-out, funded by public money and individual donations. The Knoydart Foundation's trustees include the conservationist, Chris Brasher and the impresario Cameron Mackintosh, and if you sit outside the Old Forge long enough, one of them might pass by, or stop for a chat. Equally possible is the sighting of otters in the Sound of Sleat or golden eagles soaring overhead.

Sleeping

Ardgour *p375*

L-A Kilcamb Lodge Hotel, Strontian, T01967-402257, www.kilcamblodge.com, open Mar-Nov. Luxurious Victorian country house standing in its own grounds on the shores of Loch Sunart with its own private beach. The perfect bolthole with only the occasional otter or eagle to disturb the peace, also serves superb food.

D-E The Inn at Ardgour, Corran, T01855-841225, www.ardgour.biz.

E Kinloch House, Strontian, T01967-402138, open Jan-Nov. A very comfortable B&B.

Morvern *p375*

L Lochaline Hotel, Lochaline, T01967-421657, which serves decent bar meals. There are a couple of B&Bs in Lochaline too.

Ardnamurchan Peninsula *p376*

B Far View Cottage, Kilchoan, T01972-510357, www.ardamurchan.com/farview. Open Mar-Nov. Superior and friendly B&B with great views and excellent food (**££**, also for non-residents, but booking is essential).

B Meall Mo Chridhe, Kilchoan, T/F01972-510328. Open Apr-Oct. A beautiful 18th-century converted manse with great sea views and fine cooking. Full board also available (**A**). Dinner available for non-residents (**£££**), but booking essential.

C Belmont House, Acharacle, T01967-431266. A good B&B.

C Feorag House, T01972-500248, F500285. A great place to stay in Glenborrodale.

C Kilchoan House Hotel, Kilchoan, T01972-510200. Another decent option in Kilchoan where both lunch (**£**) and dinner (**££**) is served.

C Loch Shiel House Hotel, Acharacle, T01967-431224. 10 rooms. Comfortable and decent bar meals (**££-£**). Contact them for details of cruises on Loch Shiel.

D Dalilea House, T01967-431253, open Apr-Oct. About 5 miles east of Acharacle, on a side road off the A861 north to Lochailort and Mallaig, is this very beautiful option.

D Sonachan Hotel, a few miles beyond Kilchoan, on the road to Ardnamurchan Point, T/F01972-510211, darie@sonachan.u-net.com.

D-E Ardshealach House, Acharacle, T01967-431301, open Apr-Sep. A good B&B.

E Salen Hotel, Salen, T01972-431661, salenhotel@aol.com, a decent hotel which serves food (**££**) and has information on local walks.

E-F Hillview, Achnaha, T01972-510322. A good-value B&B.

Camping

Resipole Farm Caravan Park, a mile or so east of Salen, Resipole, T01972-431235. You can pitch a tent here and there's also a restaurant and bar on site.

Glenfinnan *p377*

A The Prince's House, on the main road, half a mile past the monument on the right, heading west, T01397-722246, princeshouse@glenfinnan.co.uk. 9 rooms, open Mar-Nov. Comfortable old coaching inn which offers good food (**££**).

B-C Glenfinnan House Hotel, just off the main road, T/F01397-722235. 17 rooms, open Apr-Oct. Historic house with lots of charm, which is more than can be said for the staff. Overpriced. Dinner served from 1930 (**£££**). You can also walk in the vast grounds or fish on the loch.

F Glenfinnan Sleeping Car, at the train station, T01397-722400. Bunkhouse accommodation for 10 people, also mountain bike hire. You can eat here, too, in the Glenfinnan Dining Car (**££-£**).

Arisaig and Morar *p378*

Arisaig has plenty of accommodation and a decent range of services.

B Arisaig Hotel, Arisaig, T01687-450210, www.arisaighotel.co.uk. They serve meals (**££**) 1200-1400 and 1800-2100.

B The Old Library Lodge, Arisaig, T01687-450651, open Apr-Oct. Highly-acclaimed restaurant with rooms.

Mallaig *p378*

There are lots of other B&Bs to choose from.

C Marine Hotel, T01687-462217, www.marinehotel-mallaig.co.uk. Next to the train station and much nicer inside than it appears. Their restaurant also serves the best food in town (**££**).

E Glencairn, T01687-462412, open Apr-Sep. Decent B&B.

E-F Western Isles Guesthouse, T/F01687-462320, open Jan-Nov. Follow the road round the harbour to East Bay, where you'll find this excellent-value guest house which serves dinner to guests.

F Sheena's Backapackers Lodge, T01687-462764. The cheapest place to stay is this friendly, easy-going independent hostel, with dorm beds, double rooms and kitchen facilities.

Knoydart Peninsula *p379*

B Doune Stone Lodge, 3-4 miles up the peninsula's only road, standing in splendid isolation, T01687-462667, www.doune-marine.co.uk. 3 en suite rooms, all with bunk beds for 2 children. Minimum stay 3 nights. Price includes breakfast, packed lunch and dinner. The food is superb and cannot be praised highly enough. Guests are picked up by boat from Mallaig, where you can leave your car. The owners also run the nearby

Doune Bay Lodge, with shared facilities, for parties of up to 14. Can be self-catered, fully-catered, or somewhere in between. £40 per person for fully-catered.

C **Pier House**, Inverie, T01687-462347, www.thepierhouseknoydart. 4 rooms, 2 en suite, 2 with extra beds for children. Price includes dinner. Good, old-fashioned hospitality and wonderful local seafood (££).

F **Torrie Shieling**, T01687-462669. It's a bit more expensive than most other hostels, but is very comfortable, and popular with hikers. They also have their own transport for trips around the peninsula and will collect guests from Mallaig by arrangement.

F **Knoydart Hostel**, T01687-462242, near Inverie House. This is the only alternative hostel to **Torrie Shieling**. Much cheaper, but less appealing.

Eating

Ardnamurchan Peninsula *p376*

££-£ **Clanranald Hotel**, at Mingarry, T01967-431202. Food is available here.

Malliag *p378*

££-£ **Cabin Seafood Restaurant**, by the harbour, serves decent meals and a great value 'teatime special'.

£ **Cornerstone Café** for meals and snacks.

£ **Fisherman's Mission**, at the pier, cheapest of the lot is this cafetería.

Knoydart Peninsula *p379*

££ **The Old Forge**, T01687-462267, the most remote pub on mainland Britain. You can enjoy some tasty local seafood and a pint of real ale in front of an open fire. There's even the occasional impromptu ceilidh. Dress code is 'wellies, waterproofs and midge cream'.

Activities and tours

Ardnamurchan Peninsula *p376*

Outdoor activities The Achnanellan Centre, cross from Dalilea Pier, T02967-431265, is an outdoor activities centre on the south shore of Loch Shiel at the foot of Beinn Resipol (2,772 ft). They hire out mountain bikes, canoes, sail boats and camping equipment, as well as providing cheap, basic bunkhouse accommodation (F). It was from Dalilea Pier that Bonnie Prince Charlie left to sail up Loch Shiel to raise his standard at Glenfinnan, see p377.

Wildlife cruises Ardnamurchan Charters, T01972-500208, offers a 2-hr wildlife trip to the seal colonies – or further afield to Tobermory on Mull or Staffa and the Treshnish Islands.

Glenfinnan *p377*

Loch Shiel Cruises, Glenfinnan House Hotel, see Sleeping p379. You can take a cruise down Loch Shiel, from Glenfinnan to Acharacle. Sailings most days from Apr-Oct.

Arisaig to Morar *p378*

Murdo Grant, T01687-450224, see also p453, operates sailings from Arisaig to the Small Isles daily Mon-Fri, and also Sat-Sun during the summer months.

Transport

Ardgour, Ardnamurchan and Morvern *p375*

Boat For details of the ferry from Lochaline to Fishnish on Mull and from Kilchoan to Tobermory, see p323.

Bus Shiel Buses, T01967-431272, run most of the bus services. There's a bus once a day on Tue, Thu and Sat from **Fort William** to **Lochaline** (2 hrs), via the **Corran Ferry**. There's a bus once a day (Mon-Sat) from **Fort William** to **Acharacle** (1½ hrs), via Lochailort. There's also a bus (Mon-Fri) to **Acharacle** from **Mallaig** (1½ hrs). There's a bus once a day (Mon-Sat) from **Fort William** to **Kilchoan** (2 hrs 25 mins), via **Strontian** (1 hr), **Salen** and **Glenborrodale**.

Car If you're travelling by car, access is via the A861, leaving the A830 before Glenfinnan or at Lochailort. You can also make the 5-min ferry crossing to Ardgour from the Corran Ferry, about 8 miles south of Fort William on the A82, see p368.

Mallaig *p378*

Boat CalMac, T01687-462403, ferries run throughout the year to **Armadale** on Skye (see p432), to **Lochboisdale** and **Castlebay** (see p458), and to the **Small Isles** (see p451).

Bus Shiel Buses, T01967-431272, run 2 buses daily Mon-Sat from **Mallaig** to **Fort William** (1½ hrs, £4.50) from Jul-Sep, and on Mon, Thu and Fri the rest of the year.

Train The best way to arrive in **Mallaig** is by train. There are several services daily (1 on Sun) to and from **Fort William**, with connections to **Glasgow** (see p368). There's also a steam train which runs in the summer months (see p365).

Knoydart Peninsula *p379*

Boat Bruce Watt Sea Cruises, T01687-462320, have trips to the remote village of **Inverie**, on the Knoydart Peninsula, and **Tarbet** on Loch Nevis. They sail on Mon, Wed and Fri throughout the year, departing at 1015 (to Inverie only) and 1415, and returning at 1155 and 1745. They also sail on Sat during Jun-Aug to **Inverie**, departing at 1030 and returning at 1215. There's also a ferry service from **Arnisdale**, on the north shore of Loch Hourn, to **Barrisdale**. To arrange a crossing, contact Len Morrison, Croftfoot, Arnisdale, T01599-522352. It's a small open boat which takes 5 passengers, and all sailings are subject to weather.

Great Glen to Kyle of Lochalsh

The A87 is one of the main Highland tourist routes, connecting the Great Glen with the west coast and the Isle of Skye. It runs west from Invergarry between Fort Augustus and Fort William, through Glen Moriston and Glen Shiel to Shiel Bridge, at the head of Loch Duich, and on to Kyle. At Shiel Bridge a road branches off to Glenelg, from where you can sail across to Skye. It's a beautiful journey and by far the best way to reach the island. *▸▸ For Sleeping, Eating and other listings, see pages 384-386.*

Glen Shiel → *Colour map 3, grid A5. OS Landranger No33.*

The journey from Invergarry to Shiel Bridge is worth it for the views alone. Glen Shiel is a sight to make the heart soar as high as the 3,000 ft-high peaks that tower overhead on either side. This is one of the most popular hiking areas in Scotland, with the magnificent and much-photographed Five Sisters of Kintail on the north side of the glen, and the equally beautiful South Glen Shiel Ridge on the other.

There are several excellent hiking routes in Glen Shiel, but these mountains are to be treated with great respect. They require fitness, experience and proper equipment and planning. None of the routes should be attempted without a map, compass and detailed route instructions. You should be aware of the notoriously unpredictable weather conditions and also check locally about deer stalking. The season runs from August to October, but for more details contact the local stalkers, T01599-511282. A good trekking guide is the *SMC's Hill Walks in Northwest Scotland*.

The **Five Sisters Traverse** is a classic ridge route. It starts at the first fire break on the left as you head southeast down the glen from Shiel Bridge and finishes at Morvich, on the other side of the ridge. Allow a full day (eight to 10 hours). You can also hike from Morvich to **Glen Affric Youth Hostel** at Cannich. It's a strenuous 20-mile walk, but you can stop off midway at the remote **Allt Beithe Youth Hostel**. For details, see Glen Affric page 349.

The magnificent **South Glen Shiel Ridge** is one of the world's great hikes. It starts from above the **Cluanie Inn**, see Sleeping. From here, follow the old public road to Tomdoun which meets up with a good stalking path which climbs to the summit of the first Munro, Creag a' Mhaim (3,108 ft). The ridge then runs west for almost nine miles and gives you the chance to pick off no fewer than seven Munros. Allow a full day for the walk (nine to 10 hours), and you'll need to set off early.

Glenelg and around → *Phone code: 01599. Colour map 3, grid A5.*

One of the most beautiful journeys in Scotland is the road from Shiel Bridge to the picturesque little village of Glenelg on the Sound of Sleat, only a short distance opposite Kylerhea on Skye, for Transport details see page 385. The unclassified single-track road turns off the A87 and climbs steeply and dramatically through a series of sharp switchbacks to the top of the **Mam Ratagan Pass** (1,115 ft). From here the view back across Loch Duich to the Five Sisters of Kintail is simply amazing, and the all-time classic calendar shot.

The road then drops down through Glen More to Glenelg, the main settlement on the peninsula, which lies on the old drovers' route which ran from Skye to the cattle markets in the south. This little-known corner of the Western Highlands is Gavin Maxwell country and was featured in Ring of Bright Water, his novel about otters. He disguised the identity of this beautiful, unspoiled stretch of coastline, calling it Camusfearna, and today it remains a quiet backwater.

You can see the famous otters at **Sandaig**, on the road running from Glenelg, where Gavin Maxwell lived. The site of his cottage is now marked with a cairn. As well as otters, you can see numerous seabirds, seals and porpoises in the Sound of Sleat, and around the peninsula you may be lucky enough to catch a glimpse of wildcats, pine martens, golden eagles and the recently reintroduced sea eagles. The village itself consists of a row of whitewashed cottages surrounded by trees and overlooked by the ruins of the 18th-century **Bernera Barracks**. Just before the village the road forks. The right turning leads to the Glenelg-Kylerhea ferry, which makes the ten-minute crossing to Skye, see page 385.

A road runs south from Glenelg to Arnisdale. About a mile and a half along this road, a branch left leads to the **Glenelg Brochs** – Dun Telve and Dun Dun Troddan – two of the best-preserved Iron-Age buildings in the country. Dun Telve stands to a height of over 30 ft and the internal passages are almost intact. The road south from Glenelg continues past Sandaig Bay and runs along the north shore of unearthly Loch Hourn, with great views across the mountains of Knoydart. The road ends at the impossibly cute little fishing hamlet of **Arnsidale,** from where you can take a boat across the loch to Barrisdale on the Knoydart Peninsula. For details, see page 379. A bit further along the coast, the road ends at the even tinier hamlet of **Corran**.

Eilean Donan Castle → *Phone code: 01599. Colour map 3, grid A5.*

ⓘ *T01599-555202, Apr-Oct 0900-1700. £3.95, concession £3.20, group rates £2.95.* Some 10 miles west of Shiel Bridge on the A87 is the little village of Dornie, home to the one of Scotland's most photographed sights, the stunningly located Eilean Donan Castle. It stands on a tiny islet at the confluence of Loch Duich and Loch Alsh, joined to the shore by a narrow stone bridge and backed by high mountains. This great calendar favourite has also featured in several movies, including *Highlander*, which starred Sean Connery.

The original castle dates from 1230 when Alexander III had it built to protect the area from marauding Vikings. It was destroyed by King George in 1719 during its occupation by Spanish Jacobite forces sent to help the 'Old Pretender', James Stuart. It then lay in ruins, until one of the Macraes had it rebuilt between 1912 and 1932. Inside, the Banqueting Hall with its Pipers' Gallery is most impressive, and there's an exhibition of military regalia and interesting displays of the castle's history. The views from the battlements are also worthwhile.

Kyle of Lochalsh → *Phone code: 01599. Colour map 3, grid A5.*

Before the coming of the controversial Skye Bridge a mile to the north, see page 432, the little town of Kyle, as it is known, was the main ferry crossing to Skye and consequently a place which attracted a busy tourist trade. Now though, the tourist traffic bypasses Kyle, which is probably the most sensible thing to do as it's not the most attractive of places. There are a couple of banks with ATMs, two small supermarkets and a post office in the village. The tourist information centre ⓘ *T01599-534276, Apr-late Oct*, is at the main seafront car park.

Plockton → *Phone code: 01599. Colour map 3, grid A4.*

If there were a poll taken of visitors' favourite Highland villages then you can bet your bottom dollar that Plockton would come top with most folk. If you look for a definition of picturesque in your dictionary, it'll say 'see Plockton'. Maybe not – but it should.

Plockton's neat little painted cottages are ranged around the curve of a wooded bay, with flowering gardens and palm trees. Yachts bob up and down in the harbour and there are views across the island-studded waters of Loch Carron to the hills beyond. Even on the telly Plockton's charms proved irresistible, and millions of viewers tuned in each week to watch the TV series *Hamish Macbeth*, which featured Robert Carlyle as the local bobby. Plockton's a popular place with artists who are drawn by the village's setting and the wonderful light. A good place to find some of their work, as well as other souvenirs, is **The Studio Craft Shop,** on the corner of the seafront and the road leading out of town.

▲ There are lots of good walks around the village. One of the best ways to appreciate it is to head up to **Frithard Hill,** from where there are great views of the bay. Another good walk is along the beach, starting from the High School playing fields at the top of the village.

Sleeping

Glen Shiel *p382*
C Cluanie Inn, 9 miles east of Shiel Bridge, T0320-340238. This is one of the Highlands' classic hotels. It's a firm favourite with hikers and climbers and it's easy to see why. After a hard day's ridge walking, what could be better than jumping into the jacuzzi, then having a hot dinner and a good pint beside a log fire.
C Kintail Lodge Hotel, T01599-511275, www.kintaillodgehotel.co.uk. Small, cosy hotel, dinner also available. Bunkhouse attached with 12 beds (**F**). You can also camp nearby, but why deny yourself the pleasure if you can afford it?
E Fisherbeck, 3 Macinnes Place, T01599-511365. One of the several B&Bs in the village of Ratagan.
F Ratagan Youth Hostel, T01599-511243, just outside Shiel Bridge. A less salubrious option than the above but it's popular with hikers, and is open all year except Jan.

Camping
Morvich Caravan Club Site, T01599-511354, open late Mar to late Oct.
Shiel Bridge, T01599-511211.

Glenelg and around *p382*
E Glenelg Inn, T01599-522273. It's worth stopping in Glenelg, if you've got the time, to experience a night in this wonderfully cosy placer. Even if you can't spend the night, at least spend an hour or two enjoying the atmosphere, good ale and fine seafood. It's one of those places that almost makes you glad it's raining. If you're really lucky, you may even chance upon an impromptu folk jam.
E-F Mrs Nash, T01599-522336. B&B accommodation in Arnisdale where there's also a tea hut serving cakes and hot drinks.

Eilean Donan Castle *p383*
There are several places to stay in the nearby village of Dornie.
B Conchra House Hotel, cross the bridge in Dornie and turn right for Killilan, a tiny hamlet at the head of Loch Long, the hotel is about ¾ mile up this road, T01599-555233, conchra@aol.com. 6 rooms. This historic 18th-century hunting lodge is peaceful, has lovely views and boasts a reputation for good food.
D Dornie Hotel, T01599-555205, is a good option and serves very good food (**££**).
D Loch Duich Hotel, across the bridge from Dornie Hotel, T01599-555213. It offers comfortable accommodation, meals and live music in the bar on a Sun evening.
E Tigh Tasgaidh, T01599-555242, and
F Fasgadale, T01599-588238, are two of the several B&Bs in the village.
F Silver Fir Bunkhouse, Carndubh, T01599-555264. The cheapest place to stay is this 6-bed bunkhouse.
F Tigh Iseabeal, near Cochra House Hotel, at Camasluinie, T01599-588205, a 6-bed independent hostel.

Kyle of Lochalsh *p383*
It's a good idea to get the TIC to book a room for you, as there's not much choice.
B Lochalsh Hotel, T01599-534202. The most luxurious of the of couple of hotels here. Great views across to Skye and good food.
D Old Schoolhouse, Erbusaig, T01599-534 369. A very comfortable option offering dinner for guests (24 hrs notice required).
E Crowlin View, T01599-534286. A mile and a half north of Kyle.
F Cuchulainn's, T01599-534492, on Station Rd. Cheap hostel accommodation.

Camping
Reraig Caravan Site, T01599-566215, 4 miles east of Kyle, at Balmacara.

Plockton *p384*
C The Haven Hotel, Innes St, T01599-544223. 15 rooms, open Feb-Dec. The best place to stay and the food in the restaurant is quite superb (**£££**).
D Plockton Hotel, T01599-544274. There are quite a few places on Harbour St along the waterfront, including this wonderful and busy hotel. Serves good food (**££**) and has a great little beer garden at the front where you can sit and enjoy a drink on a balmy summer evening.
D Plockton Inn, T01599-544222. Near The Haven Hotel is this cosy, comfortable place.
E An Caladh, T01599-544356. This B&B is on the seafront.
E Craig Highland Farm, T01599-544205, on the road to Achmore, this farm offers B&B accommodation and self-catering cottages from £235 per week. The farm is also a conservation centre, where you can see and feed rare and ancient breeds of domestic animals.
E Shieling, T01599-544282, at the far end of the harbour. There are lots of B&Bs to choose from, this is one of the nicest.
F Plockton Station Bunkhouse, Nessun Dorma, Burnside, T01599-544235. A few miles out of Plockton. Cheapest option.

Eating

Eilean Donan Castle *p383*
Aside from the hotels listed above, there are a couple of places in Dornie serving decent food.
££ Clachan Pub where you can enjoy a good-value 3-course evening meal.
££ Jenny Js, across the bridge, T01599-555362.

Kyle of Lochalsh *p383*
£££-££ Seagreen Restaurant & Bookshop, T01599-534388. Just outside the village, on the road to Plockton is this bistro-cum-bookshop and gallery serving wholefood and local seafood throughout the day.
£££-££The Seafood Restaurant, at the railway station, T01599-534813, has a good reputation for seafood, open Easter-Oct 1000-1500 and 1830-2100.

Plockton *p384*
Apart from the hotels listed above, this option is a good place to eat in Plockton.
££ Off the Rails, at the railway station, T01599-544423. It's open from 0830 for breakfast, snacks, lunch and evening meals.

Activities and tours

Kyle of Lochalsh *p383*
Boat trips There are a couple of interesting boat trips from Kyle. One is on board the *Seaprobe Atlantis*, which is fitted with underwater windows. Check sailing times at the pier. If you prefer, you could take a seafood cruise - a 2½-hr wildlife-spotting and seafood-eating boat trip. Contact Neil MacRae, T01599-577230.

Plockton *p384*
Leisure Marine, T01599-544306, runs 1-hr seal- and otter-watching cruises in the summer. They also hire out boats.
Sea Trek Marine, T01599-544346. Similar trips are run by this outfit.

Transport

Glen Shiel *p382*
Citylink buses between **Fort William**, **Inverness** and **Skye** pass through Glen Shiel several times daily in each direction. There's a **postbus** service between **Kyle** and **Glenelg** (see below) and **Highland Country** Buses run from Ratagan Youth Hostel to **Kyle** (30 mins) and on to **Plockton** (50 mins), on schooldays only, departing at 0755 and returning at 1640.

Glenelg and around *p382*
There's a postbus service from **Kyle of Lochalsh** to **Arnisdale** and **Corran** via Glenelg at 0945 Mon-Sat. It takes 3¾ hrs. The return bus from **Corran** departs at 0725. The Glenelg-Kylerhea ferry provides the most scenic connection to Skye. 10-min crossing from Oct Mon-Sat 0900-1800 till mid-May; Mon-Sat 0900-2000, Sun 1000-1800 from mid-May to end-Aug; Mon-Sat 0900-1800, Sun 1000-1800 end-Aug to end-Oct. Per car with up to 4 passengers, £6; day return £10, T01599-511302.

Eilean Donan Castle *p383*
Citylink buses between **Fort William** and **Inverness** and **Skye** stop by the castle.

Kyle of Lochalsh *p383*
Bus Scottish Citylink buses, T0990-505050, run to Kyle from **Inverness** (3 daily, 2 hrs); **Glasgow** via **Fort William** (4 daily, 5 hrs); and **Edinburgh** via **Fort William** (1 daily, 6½ hrs). These buses continue to **Portree** (a further hour) and **Uig** (1½ hrs), for ferries to **Tarbert** on Harris and Lochmaddy on North Uist. There's also a regular shuttle service across the bridge to **Kyleakin** (every 30 mins).
Train The train journey from **Inverness** to Kyle, though not as spectacular as the West Highland line, is very scenic. It runs 3-4 times Mon-Sat (2½ hrs) and once or twice on Sun from May to Sep. There's also an observation car and dining car in the summer.

Wester Ross

From Loch Carron north to Ullapool, is the region of Wester Ross, an area of dramatic mountain massifs, fjord-like sea lochs and remote coastal villages. Here lies some of Europe's most spectacular scenery, from the isolated peninsula of Applecross to Tolkien-esque peaks of Torridon, which offer some of Scotland's best climbing and hillwalking. There are also gentler attractions such as the vast, sprawling gardens at Inverewe and the beguiling pink sands of Gruinard Bay. ▸▸ *For Sleeping, Eating and other listings, see pages 392-395.*

Loch Carron and around

Along Loch Carron

East of Plockton, just before the road meets the A890 at **Achmore** is the **West Highland Dairy,** where you can pick up some good local cheese for a picnic – weather permitting of course. The road passes the turn-off for Stromeferry and continues along the east shore of Loch Carron to **Strathcarron** at its northeastern end, on the Inverness to Kyle of Lochalsh rail line.

Lochcarron village → *Phone code: 01520. Colour map 1, grid C4. Population: 870.*

Lochcarron village consists of little more than a main street along the shore of the loch, but it has more facilities and services than most other places in these parts. Here you should take the opportunity to withdraw cash at the Bank of Scotland ATM, fill up with petrol and buy some supplies at the small self-service store. The TIC ⓘ *T01520-722357, Apr-Oct*, has details of some excellent walks in the surrounding hills.

Two miles south of the village on the road to the 15th-century ruins of **Strome Castle** is **Lochcarron Weavers,** where you can see tartan being made and also buy from a vast range of woven goods.

Loch Kishorn to Applecross → *Colour map 1, grid C4.*

There are many scenic routes in the Highlands but the road from Kishorn, west of Lochcarron to Applecross beats them all. The **Bealach na Ba** ('Pass of the Cattle') is the highest road in Scotland and is often closed during the winter snows. It climbs relentlessly and dramatically through a series of tortuous switchbacks – both spectacular and terrifying in equal measure. The high plateau, at 2,053 ft, is cold and desolate, but from here you have the most amazing views: from Ardnamurchan Peninsula to Loch Torridon, taking in Eigg, Rùm, the Cuillins of Skye, the Old Man of Storr and the Quirang.

The narrow, single-track road then begins its gradual descent to the isolated little village of **Applecross**, site of one Scotland's first Christian monasteries, founded in AD 673. The village consists of a row of whitewashed fishermen's cottages looking across to the island of Raasay and backed by wooded slopes. It's a beautifully tranquil place where you can explore beaches and rock pools or enjoy a stroll along sylvan lanes – and then of course there's the peerless **Applecross Inn**, see Sleeping page 394.

Torridon and around → *Phone code: 01445. Colour map 1, grid C4.*

Torridon is perhaps the most striking skyline in the Scottish Highlands. The multi-peaked mountains of Beinn Alligin, Liathach (pronounced 'Lee-ahakh') and Beinn Eighe ('Ben-eay') form a massive fortress of turrets, spires and pinnacles that provides an awesome backdrop to Loch Torridon, as well as the most exhilarating walking and climbing on the Scottish mainland. The straggly little village of Torridon makes the ideal base from which to tackle these mountains.

Ins and outs

Torridon offers some of the most spectacular walking on the Scottish mainland but also presents some of the most serious challenges. You need to be fit, experienced and well prepared and also be aware of the notoriously unpredictable weather, see page 56. You should have a compass and the relevant map. OS Outdoor Leisure series No 8 covers the area. For recommended mountain guides, see page 394.

Around Loch Torridon

The coast road from Applecross meets the A896 from Lochcarron at the lovely little village of **Shieldaig** on the southern shore of Loch Torridon. There's a shop, a post office, a campsite, a couple of B&Bs. Several miles east, a side road turns off the A896 by **Torridon village** and winds its way along the northern shore of the loch, then climbs through dramatic scenery before dropping to the beautiful little village of **Diabaig** (pronounced 'Jee-a-beg'), 10 miles from Torridon village. It's a worthwhile side trip, as the views across to the Applecross peninsula and Raasay are fantastic. There's also a great seven-mile coastal walk from Diabaig to Redpoint (see below).

Much of the Torridon massif is in the care of the National Trust for Scotland, and just before Torridon village is the **NTS countryside centre** ⓘ *T01445-791221*, where you can get information and advice on walks in the area, as well as books and maps. About 400 yds past the centre is the **Deer Museum**, which has a small display describing the management of red deer in the Highlands as well as some live specimens outside.

▲ Beinn Alligin

Beinn Alligin (3,232 ft) is the most westerly of the Torridon peaks and probably the least demanding. The **Allt a'Bhealaich Walk** is a steep but short walk of about two hours. It starts from the car park just beyond the stone bridge that crosses the Abhainn Coire Mhic Nobuil. Follow the path that runs beside the river gorge until you reach the first bridge, cross it and follow the east bank of the Allt a' Bhealaich burn. Higher up, cross the second bridge and continue to follow the track up to the 380-m contour line, then turn back retracing your steps. This walk doesn't include the ascent of the peak but the views are magnificent. Those who wish to climb the three **Horns of Beinn Alligin** can continue from the 380-m contour line above the second bridge. The track that follows their ridge is exposed and requires rock scrambling experience.

Liathach

Seven-peaked Liathach (3,460 ft) stretches over five miles, and the magnificent ridge walk is considered by many to be the most impressive in Britain. This walk requires a high level of stamina and will take at least seven to eight hours. It also helps if you have a car waiting at the end.

A good place to start this long and strenuous challenge is about half a mile or so east of Glen Cottage, which is just over two miles east of the Countryside Centre. A steep climb takes you to a point just west of Stuc a'Choire Dhuibh Bhig (3,000 ft). Then retrace your route to climb the twin tops of Bidein Toll a'Mhuic (3,200 ft), linked by a narrow ridge. The path from here descends to the head of a deep ravine and keeps to the crest of the ridge around the rim of Coireag Dubh Beag which plunges steeply to the north. The ridge then rises across a field of huge and unstable boulders to the highest peak – Spidean a'Choire Leith. The view from this point is stunning, with Coire na Caime before you, surrounded by 2,000 ft sheer cliffs. From here, the path follows a narrow exposed ridge for over a mile towards Mullach an Rathain (3,358 ft). Unless you are an experienced scrambler with a good head for heights, the best way from here is to take the path to the south, below the sharp pinnacles. Beyond the pinnacles the climb to Mullach an Rathain is straightforward. The track from here to Sgorr a'Chadail is a long but fairly easy walk and ends on the path in Coire Mhic Nobuil, see Beinn Alligin above.

Coire Walk

A less difficult walk, but still requiring a fair degree of fitness and taking most of the day, is the Coire Walk. It follows the River Coire Mhic Nobuil to its watershed and down again by the Allt a'Choire Dhuibh Mhoir to the main road in Glen Torridon. Again, two cars will shorten the distance considerably.

The walk starts at the same point as the Beinn Alligin walk above. It follows the path up to the first bridge then branches east and continues on the path that runs north of the river, all the way to its source in the pass between Liathach and Beinn Dearg. Here the ground is boggy between the string of pools and lochans and the path is less distinct, but it becomes clear again in the upper reaches of the Coire Dubh Mor, a huge gully that separates Liathach from Beinn Eighe. A little further on, the track joins a stalkers' path which curves round Sail Mhor to the famous Coire Mhic Fhearchair, considered to be the most spectacular corrie in Scotland (see Beinn Eighe below). The Coire path leads to a ford, which is crossed by stepping stones, then descends following the west side of the burn down to the car park on the Torridon road, from where it's about 4½ miles to Torridon village.

Diabaig to Red Point Walk → *OS Landranger No 19.*

An excellent low-level coastal walk is from Diabaig to Red Point. It is far less strenuous or daunting than the others described above and there is a clear path. It starts at the wooden gate to the right of the post office in Diabaig and ends at Red Point Farm, seven miles away.

After four miles the coastal path reaches the derelict croft houses in the Craig Valley. One of these has been converted into a **SYHA Hostel.** There are two possible routes from here. You can follow the footpath above the coastline, or leave the footpath after crossing the wooden bridge over the Craig river and climb through an area of woodland. Take a reference from your OS map and you'll reach the highest point, Meall na h-Uamha, from where there are superb views. You can then descend to rejoin the coastal path and continue till you reach the glorious golden sands of Red Point, with wonderful views across to Skye and Raasay. Keep to the path through the farm till you reach the car park. Unless you've arranged your own transport here, you'll have to walk back the way you came, or catch the schoolbus to Gairloch, see page 395.

▲ Beinn Eighe National Nature Reserve

While most of the Torridon massif is managed by the National Trust of Scotland, Beinn Eighe (which means 'File Peak' in Gaelic) is under the control of Scottish Natural Heritage. It is Britain's oldest National Nature Reserve, set up in 1951 to protect the ancient Caledonian pine forest west of Kinlochewe. It has since been designated an International Biosphere Reserve and extended to cover 30 square miles. The reserve is the home of a great variety of rare Highland wildlife, including pine martens, wildcats, buzzards, Scottish crossbills and golden eagles. There's also a wide range of flora which can best be appreciated on the excellent mountain trail described below which climbs from the ancient pine woods through alpine vegetation to the tundra-like upper slopes.

About half a mile northwest of Kinlochewe on the A832, is the Beinn Eighe Visitor Centre, which has information on the flora and fauna in the reserve and sells pamphlets on the trails described below. Note that camping is restricted to the official campsite at Taangan Farm, see Sleeping page 392.

Beinn Eighe (3,309 ft) has nine peaks and is the largest of the Torridon Mountains. To traverse its ridge is a mighty undertaking and can take two days. A much shorter and easier walk around the base of the mountain is described here. The mountain and woodland trails both start and end in the car park at the side of Loch Maree, about two miles beyond the visitor centre. The woodland trail heads west along the lochside then crosses the road and climbs for about a mile up to the Conservation cabin before descending back to the starting point. It should take about an hour and is easy to follow, though quite steep in parts, and you'll need a good pair of walking boots. The mountain trail is four miles long and rough and steep in parts. You should be well equipped with good walking boots, waterproofs, food and warm clothing. It should take around three to four hours. The route is well marked with cairns and you should not stray from the path. The trail heads south from the car park and begins a gentle ascent through woodland to a boggy area and then begins to zigzag up a very steep and rugged section, climbing to over 1,000 ft in less than half a mile. This is the steepest section of the trail, but the views back across Loch Maree to Slioch are fabulous. The summit of the mountain trail is Conservation cairn (1,800 ft) from where you can see the tops of 31 Munros on a clear day and enjoy a close-up view of the impressive Beinn Eighe ridge a few miles to the south. The trail now begins to descend as it heads northwest towards An t-Allt (1,000 ft), turns northwards down to a small enclosure, then heads east to the deep Allt na h-Airidhe gorge. From here the trail continues down to the treeline and runs through woodland to join up with the top of the Woodland Trail. Follow the path to the right and this takes you back to the car park.

Kinlochewe and Loch Maree → *Phone code: 01445. Colour map 1, grid C5.*

On the north side of the Torridon Mountains is the sprawling village of Kinlochewe, at the southeastern end of beautiful Loch Maree. The loch is dotted with islands and bordered by the mass of Slioch (3,215 ft) to the north and ancient Caledonian pine forest to the south. Running along its northern shore, from **Slioch** almost as far as **Poolewe**, is the remote **Letterewe Estate**, one of Scotland's great deer forests. The A832 skirts the south shore of the loch, running northwest from Kinlochewe, and passes the **Victoria Falls**, a mile or so beyond Talladale. The falls commemorate Queen Victoria's visit in 1877. To find them, look for the Hydro Power signs.

Gairloch and around → *Phone code: 01445. Colour map 1, grid C4.*

Gairloch consists of a string of tiny crofting townships scattered around the northeastern shore of the loch of the same name. It's a great place which attracts a large number of visitors who come for the many beautiful beaches, excellent walks, golf and fishing, and the chance of seeing seals, porpoises, dolphins and whales in the surrounding waters. » *For Sleeping, Eating and other listings, see pages 392-395.*

Ins and outs

Getting there and around There are buses to and from Inverness three times a week, also buses to Kinlochewe and a local postbus service. A passenger ferry service now operates from Gairloch to Portree on Skye. » *For further details, see Transport page 394.*
Tourist information TIC ⓘ *T01445-712130, open year round, Apr-Oct daily*, is at the car park in Auchtercairn, where the road branches off to Strath. They will book accommodation for you and sell a wide range of books and maps. There are shops and takeaways in Strath and Auchtercairn, a petrol station in Auchtercairn, and a bank with ATM near the harbour at Charleston.

Gairloch Heritage Museum

ⓘ *T01445-712287, Apr-Oct Mon-Sat 1000-1700, £2.50, concession £2, children £0.50.*
If you are interested in local history, or the weather is bad – not unknown – then this museum may entertain for a hour or so. Included are archaeological finds, a mock-up of a crofthouse room, schoolroom and shop, the interior of the local lighthouse and an archive of old photographs. It is found beside the tourist office on the A832 to Poolewe, a few yards beyond the turn-off to Strath.

Big Sand, Melvaig and Midtown

The beach by the golf course at Gairloch is nice, but the beach at Big Sand, a few miles northwest of Strath, is better, and quieter. Further north is Melvaig, from where you can walk to **Rubha Reidh Lighthouse**, see Sleeping page 392. Around the headland from the lighthouse is the beautiful, secluded beach at **Camas Mor**. This is a good place for spotting sea birds, and there's a great walk from here on a marked footpath to Midtown, four miles northwest of Poolewe. You'll have to walk or hitch from here as there's no public transport to Poolewe.

The waters around Gairloch are home to a wide variety of **marine mammals** such as seals, otters, porpoises, dolphins, minke whales and even killer whales. For details of wildlife cruises, see page 394.

Destitution Road

Many of the roads in the area were built during the Potato Famine of 1840 in order to give men work, with funds supplied by Dowager Lady Mackenzie of Gairloch. These became know as the 'Destitution Roads', and one of these is the narrow B8056 which runs west for nine miles to Red Point from the junction three miles south of Gairloch, at Kerrysdale. This is a lovely little side trip and well worth it, especially on a clear evening to enjoy the magnificent sunsets at **Red Point beach**. The beach itself is extremely seductive, backed by steep dunes and looking across to the Trotternish peninsula on Skye. So romantic is this spot that some people (naming no names) have been known to plight their troth here. Red Point is also the start or finish point for the excellent coastal walk to or from Diabaig, see page 388. On the road to Red Point is the picturesque little hamlet of **Badachro,** tucked away in a wooded, sheltered bay with fishing boats moored in its natural harbour. It's worth stopping off here on the way back from Red Point for a wee dram at the **Badachro Inn**.

There are lots of other good walks in the area, including to **Flowerdale Falls** and the **Fairy Lochs** and the **USAAF Liberator**. The TIC has a selection of walking guides and OS maps.

Poolewe → *Phone code: 01445. Colour map 1, grid B4.*

Five miles east of Gairloch on the other side of the peninsula is the neat little village of Poolewe, straddling the mouth of the River Ewe, where it cascades into sheltered Loch Ewe. There are some good walks around Poolewe, including the one around Loch Kernsary described below. There's also a nice little drive up the side road running along the west shore of Loch Ewe to Cove. You can walk from Midtown, midway along the road, to Rubha Reidh, north of Gairloch (see above).

Loch Kernsary → *OS Landranger Map No 19.*

This straightforward but rewarding walk covers six miles and should take around 2½ to three hours. The track is very boggy underfoot in places, especially after rain, so you'll need good boots.

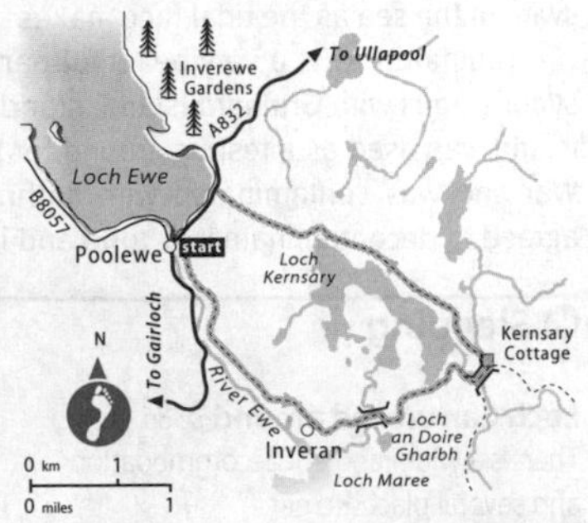

Start in Poolewe, from the car park by the school near the bridge over the Ewe. Head up the single-track road with the river on your right. Go through the gate, then the track heads away from the river and up into woodland. At the Letterewe Estate gate cross the stile and continue to the next fork. Turn left here to Kernsary Estate, with views of Loch Maree and Beinn Eighe to the south. Follow the track to the next gate, go through and cross the wooden bridge. Continue along the track and you'll see Loch Kernsary on your left. At the next fork, turn left over the bridge and pass Kernsary Cottage on the right. Beyond the cottage, go through the gate and immediately head left down towards the burn, where the ground may be boggy. There's no path here, but cross the wooden footbridge and continue straight on, past the piles of stones on your left. Cross the stile, and the path follows the length of Loch Kernsary. At the head of the loch, the path climbs to give you views down to Poolewe. Follow the path down till it eventually takes you to the main road. Turn left and follow the road back to the car park.

Inverewe Garden

ⓘ *T01445-781200, garden 15 Mar-31 Oct daily 0930-2100, 1 Nov-14 Mar daily 0930-1700 (guided garden walks 15 Apr to 15 Sep Mon-Thu at 1330); visitor centre 15 Mar to 31 Oct 0930-1730, £7, concession £5.25, family £19.*

The reason most people come this way is to visit Inverewe Garden where you'll find an astonishing collection of exotic subtropical plants growing on the same latitude as Siberia, thanks to the mild climate created by the North Atlantic Drift. This wonderful 50-acre oasis of colour is a mecca for garden lovers, but even those who flinch at the mere sight of a lawn-mower will be bowled over by the sheer scale and diversity of plants and flowers on view. The garden was created from a treeless wilderness by Osgood Mackenzie, starting in 1862. By the time of his death in 1922 he had produced an internationally renowned walled and woodland garden. His work was continued by his daughter, who then gave the garden to the National Trust for Scotland in 1952. Since then, the plant collection has diversified even more and an intricate maze of paths leads you through ever-changing displays of Himalayan rhododendrons, Tasmanian eucalyptus, many Chilean and South African species, together with a large collection of New Zealand plants.

The garden is well worth visiting in any weather and at any time of the year, but especially from the end of April through the summer when the rhododendrons are in bloom. You should allow at least a couple of hours to do it justice. The garden is about a mile north of Poolewe on the main A832. There's a visitor centre and gift shop and a good restaurant, which serves snacks and hot meals.

Gruinard Bay → *Phone code: 01445. Colour map 1, grid B5.*

North of Poolewe the A832 passes Aultbea on its way to Laide, where it then skirts the shores of Gruinard Bay, with its lovely coves of pink sand. From Laide Post Office a side road branches north to **Mellon Udrigle** and **Opinan**, both with great beaches. Between Laide and Mellon Udrigle, at **Achgarve**, a road branches left for about half a mile. From the end of this road you can walk all the way to **Slaggan**, a ruined village on the other side of the peninsula. It's a nice spot for a picnic but don't be tempted to swim in the sea as the tidal race makes it dangerous.

Gruinard Bay is a very beautiful part of the northwest coast but will always be synonymous with **Gruinard Island**, standing ominously in the middle of the bay. The island was used as a testing ground for biological warfare during the Second World War and was contaminated with anthrax spores. The Ministry of Defence finally agreed to decontaminate it in 1990 and it has now been declared 'safe'.

Sleeping

Loch Carron and around *p386*

There's a wide range of accommodation and several places to eat.

B Applecross Inn, Applecross, T01520-744262. There are, sadly, too few authentic Highland hostelries where you could quite happily while away a few hours, or even an entire afternoon, but if you have to be holed up somewhere to escape the rotten weather, then this place is as good as any and better than most. The welcome is warm, the crack is good and the seafood is so fresh you can almost see it swimming past as you order (try a half pint of prawns for a fiver or scallops for £7.50). Bar food served 1200-2100, children welcome till 2030, ceilidhs on Fri evening. The rooms upstairs have recently been refurbished to a high standard and all have sea views. If there's no room at the Inn there are a few B&Bs a mile to the south, see Torridon and around below.

C Shore House, Ardarroch, Kishorn, a few miles west of Lochcarron on the A896, T01520-733333, www.shorehouse.co.uk. 3 rooms. Comfortable with traditional Celtic character and superb food also on offer. Best of the bunch.

D Rockvilla Hotel, Lochcarron village T01520-722379, rockvilla@btinternet.com. Small, family-run hotel offering very good food (££).

E Bank House, Lochcarron village, T01520-722332, in the same building as the Bank of Scotland.

E Jam Factory, contact Cottages and Castles, T01463-226990, www.cottages-and-castles. Co.uk. An excellent self-catering option is this 18th-century building once used for jam making, 10 mins walk from Lochcarron village. It sleeps 2 and costs from £170-235 per week.

Torridon and around *p387*

L Loch Torridon Hotel, a mile south of the turn-off to Torridon village, T01445-791242, www.lochtorridonhotel.com. 22 rooms. This fairytale Gothic pile sits on the lochside surrounded by mountains and offers the ultimate in style and comfort. Rooms are sumptuous, with enormous beds and romantic bathrooms. Breakfast is positively Olympian in proportion and the restaurant is one of the finest in the area (**£££**). The views cap it all, though.

A The Old Mill Highland Lodge, on Loch Maree at Talladale, halfway between Kinlochewe and Gairloch, T01445-760271, open mid-Dec to mid-Oct. The best accommodation around here is this converted mill set in its own gardens. It's friendly and comfortable, offers great food (price includes dinner), seclusion and great views.

B Loch Maree Hotel, on Loch Maree, T01445-760288, lochmaree@easynet.co.uk. This beautifully located hotel is being returned to its former glory. Queen Victoria was here! It also offers superb cuisine (**A** including dinner).

B Tigh-an-Eilean Hotel, in Shieldaig, T01520-755251, where you can get reasonable meals.

D Cromasaig, Torridon Rd, Kinlochewe, T01445-760234, cromasaig@msn.com. A decent B&B.

E Kinlochewe Hotel, T01445-760253, offers B&B as well as cheaper bunkhouse beds and cheap bar meals. Kinlochewe is a good base for walking in and around Loch Maree. It has a post office, shop and garage.

E Upper Diabaig Farm, T01445-790227, open Apr-Sep, in Upper Diabaig. This an excellent choice.

F SYHA hostels, T01445-791284. There are two of these. One is in Torridon village, open 29 Jan-31 Oct, with an adjacent campsite. The other is much smaller and more basic, 4 miles north of Diabaig on the trail to Redpoint, at the disused crofting township of Craig (no phone; open 14 May-3 Oct).

Camping

There is a basic campsite at Taangan Farm, at the head of Loch Maree.

Gairloch and around *p390*

There are numerous B&Bs scattered throughout the area. Most of the owners will provide maps and information on local walks.

L Pool House Hotel, Poolewe, T01445-781272, poolhouse@inverewe.co.uk, open Mar-Dec. On the Cove road by the lochside is this former home of Osgood Mackenzie. It enjoys great views and serves good food (**£££**).

B-C Myrtle Bank Hotel, T01445-712004, MyrtleBank@email.msn.com. 12 rooms. Modern hotel in the centre of Gairloch overlooking the loch, very good food and service in the restaurant (**£££-££**).

C The Old Inn, by the harbour, T01445-712006, www.theoldinn.co.uk. 14 rooms. Staying here gives the advantage of not having to move far after enjoying the best pint of real ale and pub grub for miles around.

D Old Smiddy Guest House, in Laide, near Gruinard Bay, T01445-731425, www.oldsmiddy.co.uk. Open Apr-Oct. Its excellent restaurant (**£££**) is open to non-residents, but it's best to book well in advance.

E Bruach Ard, near Poolewe, T01445-781214, open Apr-Oct. At Inverasdale, a few miles up the Cove road.

E Lochside, T01445-741295. Further afield, at Badachro, south of Gairloch on the road to Red Point, is this B&B.

E Mrs A MacIver, T01445-712388, open Feb-Nov. In Charleston, B&B by the harbour.

E Mrs MacDonald, T01445-781354, open Apr-Oct. Further up this road from Bruarch Ard, near Cove. B&B.

E Mrs MacIver, T01445-781389, open Apr-Oct. Above Poolewe, reached by a path that leads from the road beside the campsite. B&B.

E-F Duisary, T01445-712252, open Apr-Oct. On the road that turns off to the right by the Millcroft Hotel, beyond the fire station.

F Auchtercairn Hostel, T01445-712131, open Mar-Nov, is at Gairloch Sands Apartments, just before the turn-off to Strath.

F Badachro Bunkhouse, T07760-344008. Also at Badachro, is this cheap bunkhouse.

F Bains House, T01445-712472. On the main street in Strath, near the shops, is this friendly and great value B&B.

F Carn Dearg Youth Hostel, T01445-712219, open 15 May-3 Oct. 3 miles beyond Gairloch, on the road to Melvaig.

F Rubha Reidh Lighthouse, T/F01445-771263, ruareidh@netcomuk.co.uk. 3 miles north of Gairloch, at the end of the road is this comfortable B&B (**D** including dinner) and hostel accommodation. It's best to book ahead in the high season. They also have a tearoom serving home baking, snacks and light lunches; open Easter-Oct Sun, Tue and Thu 1100-1700. Self-catering is also available for private rooms or the hostel. There are buses from Gairloch as far as Melvaig (see below), then it's a 3-mile hike along the road to the lighthouse.

For an explanation of sleeping and eating price codes used in this guide, see inside the front cover. Other relevant information is found in Essentials, see pages 43-51.

F Sail Mhor Croft Independent Hostel, south of Ullapool in Camusnagaul, T01854-633224, sailmhor@btinternet.com. Call before arriving.

Camping

There are a couple of campsites: **Gairloch Caravan & Camping Park**, T01445-712373, is at Strath, with full facilities and close to all amenities; **Sands Holiday Centre**, T01445-712152, open Easter-Oct, is at Big Sand, about a mile beyond Strath.
Camping and Caravan Club Site, T01445-781249, is between Poolewe village and Inverewe Garden. An excellent site.
Gruinard Bay Caravan Park, in Laide near Gruinard Bay, T01445-731225, open Apr-Oct.
Badrallach Bothy & Camp Site, T01445-633281. Near Gruinard Ba, this campsite is situated in the tiny, remote hamlet of Badrallach. A few miles east of Dundonnell, take a side road which branches left and runs for 7 miles.

Eating

Loch Carron and around *p386*

££ Carron Restaurant, T01520-722488. About 5 mins' drive from the village, across the loch on the A890, is this excellent option.

Gairloch and around *p390*

££ Scottish Seafood Restaurant, T01445-712137, next to Gairloch filling station, is good for seafood but is unlicensed.
££-£ Inverewe Garden, see Sights, daily 1000-1700. The best place to eat in Poolewe is probably the licensed restaurant here.
££-£ Myrtle Bank Hotel, see Sleeping, serves very good, expensive, meals, and good value bar lunches.
£ Bridge Cottage Café, left at the turn-off to Cove, Poolewe. If you need to grab a quick snack, or fancy a coffee, try here.
£ Gino's Italian Restaurant at the friendly Millcroft Hotel in Strath, T01445-712376.
£ Mountain Restaurant, Strath Sq, Gairloch, T01445-712316, has a terrace overlooking Gair Loch. It is run by mountaineers and offers an interesting menu, as well as accommodation in several themed rooms.
£ The Steading Restaurant, T01445-712449, next to the Heritage Museum, Gairloch, open daily 0930-2100.

Activities and tours

Climbing and hillwalking

For those who are not experienced hillwalkers, there's a Ranger Service for visitors. During Jul and Aug the ranger, **Seamus McNally**, takes guided walks up into the mountains 3 times a week. For more details call, T01445-791221. A recommended local mountain guide is **Steve Chadwick**, T01445-712455. For guided walks around Lochcarron, contact **Island Horizons**, Kirkton Rd, T01520-722238.

Fishing

For information on sea angling trips, contact the chandlery shop at the harbour, T01445-712458.

Quad biking

For those who prefer dry land, try a quad bike tour of the Flowerdale Deer Forest with **Highland Trails**. Book at The Anchorage post office/craft shop at the harbour or at Flowerdale estate office, T01445-712378.

Wildlife cruises

You can take a wildlife-spotting cruise with **Sail Gairloch**, T01445-712636. The cruise lasts 2 hrs and leaves daily from Gairloch Pier (subject to weather conditions). It can be booked at the **Gairloch Marine Life Centre** by the pier.

Transport

Loch Carron and around *p386*

There's a postbus service from **Strathcarron** to **Shieldaig** and **Torridon** twice a day Mon-Sat.

It's possible to reach **Applecross** by public transport, but only just. A postbus service leaves **Strathcarron** train station daily (except Sun) at 0955, arriving in **Shieldaig** at 1040. Another postbus then leaves **Shieldaig** at 1130 and arrives in Applecross at 1300, via the beautiful and winding coast road. No buses run over the Bealach na Ba. A postbus leaves **Applecross** at 0915 and arrives in **Shieldaig** at 1010. It continues to **Torridon** (see below) and arrives at 1030. Another postbus leaves **Shieldaig** at 1045 and arrives at **Strathcarron** train station at 1130. There are train connections from

Strathcarron to **Inverness** and **Kyle** (for times T08457-484950).

Torridon and around *p387*
The postbus from **Applecross** to **Shieldaig** continues to **Torridon village** (see above). There's a postbus from **Strathcarron** station at 0955 which arrives in **Shieldaig** at 1040. Duncan Maclennan buses, T01520-755239, have a service which leaves **Strathcarron** at 1230 and arrives in **Torridon** at 1330 (daily except Sun). There's also a daily (Mon-Sat) postbus service from **Diabaig** to **Kinlochewe** and **Achnasheen**, via **Torridon**, at 0955. There are also Duncan Maclennan buses between **Torridon** and **Shieldaig** and **Strathcarron**.

For **Loch Maree**, **Kinlochewe** is 9 miles west of **Achnasheen** rail station which is on the Inverness-Kyle line. There's a daily (except Sun) postbus service. There's also a postbus (Mon-Sat) from **Kinlochewe** to **Torridon** and **Diabaig**, and a bus to **Torridon** and **Shieldaig**, T01520-755239. Buses between **Gairloch** and **Inverness** (see below) stop in **Kinlochewe**.

Gairloch and around *p390*
There's a bus from **Inverness** to **Gairloch** 3 times a week (Mon, Wed and Sat) at 1705 with **Westerbus**, T01445-712255. The return bus is at 0805. **Westerbus** also have services to **Kinlochewe** (Mon-Sat, 0730) and to **Mellon Charles/Laide**, via **Poolewe** (Mon-Sat). There's a **Melvaig-Gairloch-Red Point** postbus service Mon-Sat which leaves Gairloch at 0820 heading north to **Melvaig** and leaves Gairloch heading south to **Red Point** at 1035. On Fri only there's a taxi service between **Gairloch** and **Melvaig** 1030-1230 (to book T01445-712559). A passenger ferry sails between **Gairloch** and **Portree** (Skye) 1½ hrs, £10 one way, operated by West Highland Seaways, T07771-667658, www.overtheseatoskye.com.

For **Gruinard Bay**, daily buses go to **Laide** from **Gairloch** with Westerbus, T01445-712255. Some continue to **Mellon Udrigle**. Buses between **Laide** and **Inverness** 3 times a week (Tue, Thu and Fri), leaving at 0805 and returning at 1705. There are also buses on other days between **Gairloch** and **Inverness** which stop at **Laide** (see above).

Ullapool and around

The attractive little fishing port of Ullapool, on the shores of Loch Broom, is the largest settlement in Wester Ross. The grid-pattern village, created in 1788 at the height of the herring boom by the British Fisheries Society, is still an important fishing centre as well as being the major tourist centre in the northwest of Scotland and one of the main ferry terminals for the Outer Hebrides. At the height of the busy summer season the town is swamped by visitors passing through on their way to or from Stornoway on Lewis, heading north into the wilds, or south to Inverness. It has excellent tourist amenities and services and relatively good transport links, making it the ideal base for those exploring the northwest coast and a good place to be if the weather is bad.

North of Ullapool you enter a different world. The landscape becomes ever more dramatic and unreal – a huge emptiness of bleak moorland punctuated by isolated peaks and shimmering lochs. A narrow and tortuously twisting road winds its way up the coast, past deserted beaches of sparkling white sand washed by turquoise sea. There's not much tourist traffic this far north and once you get off the main road and on to the backroads, you can enjoy the wonderful sensation of having all this astonishingly beautiful scenery to yourself. ▸▸ *For Sleeping, Eating and other listings, see pages 401-405.*

Ins and outs

Getting there and around Ullapool is the mainland terminal for ferries to Stornoway (Lewis). Scottish Citylink buses, T08705-505050, to and from Inverness (twice daily Monday to Saturday, just under 1½ hour; £12.10 return) connect with the ferry to and from Stornoway, see page 458. The local CalMac office on Shore Street, opposite the pier, T01854-612358, also has details. There are also buses to places further north, and south along the coast. Buses stop at the pier near the ferry dock. » *For further details, see Transport page 405.*

Tourist information The tourist information centre ⓘ *6 Argyle St, T01854-612135, Easter-Oct daily, Nov-Easter Mon-Fri 1300-1630*, is well run and provides an accommodation booking service as well as information on local walks and trips, and has a good stock of books and maps. To find out what's on locally, tune in to Loch Broom FM (102.2 and 96.8) or pick up a copy of the *Ullapool News* on Fridays.

Ullapool → *Phone code: 01854. Colour map 1, grid B5. Population: 1,800.*

Sights

Ullapool's attractions are very much of the outdoor variety and include the Falls of Measach, Achiltibuie and Stac Pollaidh. However, whist in town it's worth taking a stroll around the harbour to watch the comings and goings of the fishing fleet and you might even see the occasional seal or otter swimming close to the shore. The only real 'sight' as such is the **Ullapool Museum and Visitor Centre** ⓘ *T01854-612987, Apr-Oct Mon-Sat 0930-1730, Jul and Aug also 1930-2130, Nov-Mar 1200-1600, £3, children free*, in a converted church in West Argyle Street. It has some interesting displays on

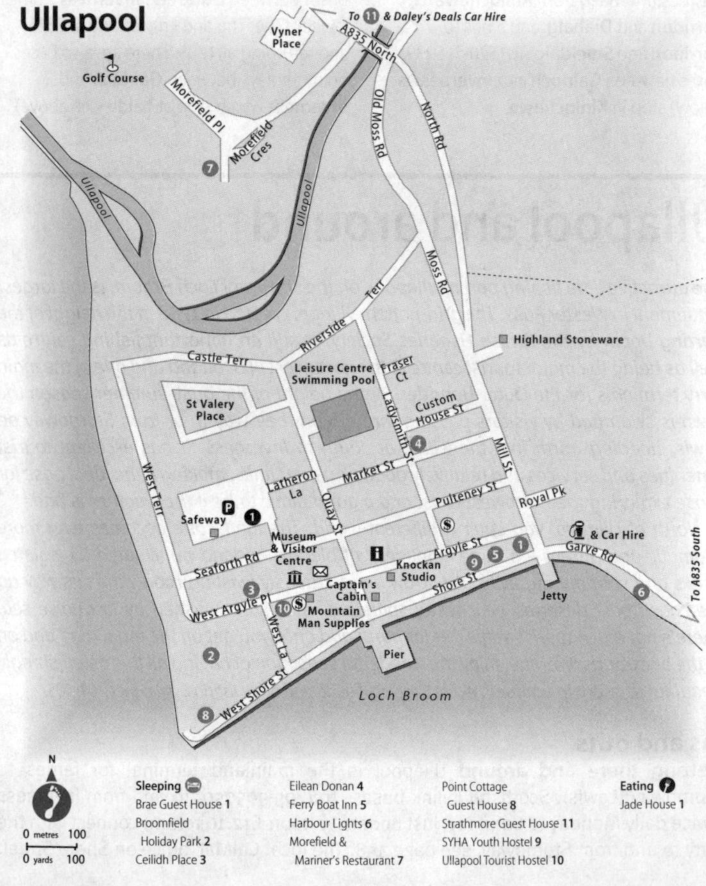

local history, including the story of those who set sail from here in 1773 on board *The Hector*, the first ship to carry emigrants from the Highlands to Nova Scotia in Canada.

Walks → *All routes are covered by OS Maps Nos 15, 19 and 20.*

There are several good walking trails which start in Ullapool. One of these is to the top of **Ullapool Hill**, or **Meall Mhor** (886 ft). Starting from the tourist office, head to the end of Argyle Street, turn left on to North Road and then cross the road at the Far Isles Restaurant. Walk down the lane between Broom Court and the Hydro sub-station and then follow the path which zigzags up the hillside. There's a good cairned path up to the top of the hill. The views from the top over Glen Achall, and on a clear day, the mountains of Sutherland, are superb. You can return by traversing the hillside to the top of the Braes, or take a track leading to Loch Achall and follow the Ullapool river through the quarry road back to the village. The return trip takes one to two hours.

A relatively easy, but much longer walk, of five to six hours, is to **Rhidorroch Estate**. Take the A835 north out of Ullapool. Opposite the petrol station and before the bridge, take the road on the right signed 'Quarry'. Go through the quarry keeping to the left, and follow the Ullapool river till you see Loch Achall. Continue along the north bank of the loch for another six miles. East Rhidorroch Lodge is on the right; cross the bridge to get there, then skirt the lodge fences and cross to the track which leads up the southwestern hill. This brings you out to Leckmelm, about four miles south of Ullapool on the A835. This last section offers wonderful views across Loch Broom to An Teallach. From Leckmelm you can also climb Beinn Eilideach (1,837 ft).

A good coastal walk is to **Rhue Lighthouse** and back. From the north end of Quay Street go down the steps to the river. Cross the bridges and head left by the football field. Follow the path to the left by the duck pond and cross in front of the bungalow. Then follow the shoreline north for about two miles, climbing up the hillside when the tide is high. Follow the path till you reach the little white lighthouse at Rhue Point. To return, take the single-track road out of Rhue back to the main road and up over the hill to Ullapool. It's about six miles in total.

There are many more strenuous hiking routes around Ullapool. The A835 south of town gives access to **Beinn Dearg** (3,556 ft) and the **Fannichs**, a range of hills on the southern side of Dirrie More. There's also **An Teallach**, a favourite with Scottish climbers, see page 397. North of Ullapool are the mountains within the Inverpolly National Nature Reserve (see below).

All routes require hillwalking experience and you should be well prepared for the unpredictable weather conditions. A good guidebook is *The Northern Highlands*, SMC District Guide, by Tom Strang. ›› *For details of a tour operator offering trips, see page 404.*

South of Ullapool → *Colour map 1, grid B5.*

On the southern shore of Little Loch Broom is the village of **Dundonnell**, from where there are spectacular views of awesome An Teallach (3,483 ft), a mountain of almost mythical status amongst Scottish climbers and spoken of in hushed, reverential tones. The path to the highest of its summits is clear and begins southeast of the **Dundonell Hotel**. It will take a full day and you'll need to be well prepared (OS map No 19) and heed the usual advice.

The A832 coastal road meets the A835 Ullapool-Inverness main road at Braemore junction, 12 miles south of Ullapool. Before heading on to Ullapool it's worth stopping at the very impressive **Falls of Measach**, just by the junction. The falls plunge 150 ft into the spectacular **Corrieshalloch Gorge** (or 'ugly/fearsome gorge' in Gaelic) and can be crossed by a distinctly wobbly suspension bridge (not for vertigo sufferers). The falls can be reached from the A835, but the most dramatic approach is from the A832 Gairloch road.

North of Ullapool → *Colour map A5, B5-6.*

The region immediately north of Ullapool is called Assynt, and is heaven for serious hillwalkers and climbers. Though most are not Munros, and not particularly difficult by Scottish standards, they can attract some of the worst weather imaginable, even in the height of summer, see page 56. Amongst the most spectacular of Assynt's distinctive 'island peaks' are Suilven (2,398 ft), Ben More Assynt (3,275 ft), Quinag (2,650 ft) and Canisp (2,775 ft). Much of this region is protected in the Inverpolly and Inchnadamph National Nature Reserves, home to an extremely rich and diverse wildlife.

Remember to check access locally during the deer-stalking season which runs from mid-August to mid-October.

Inverpolly National Nature Reserve → *Phone code: 01854. OS Landranger No 15.*

About 12 miles north of Ullapool on the main A835 is the exceptional **SNH Visitor Centre** ⓘ *T01854-666234, open all year round 24 hours a day,* at Knockan Crag. It's an interactive display of the geology, flora and fauna of the area. From the visitor centre there's a marked trail which leads up to the **Crag**, and the views from the clifftop are excellent, across to Inverpolly's 'island' peaks of Cul Mór, Cul Beag and Stac Pollaidh.

A few miles north of here is the village of **Knockan**. Nearby, at **Elphin**, is the **Highland and Rare Breeds Farm** ⓘ *mid-May to end of Sep, 1000-1700*. Beyond Elphin is **Ledmore**, where the A837 branches east towards Lairg and Bonar Bridge. There's a good craft shop at Ledmore where you can buy hand-knitted sweaters.

▲ Between Ullapool and Knockan Crag is the turn-off west (left) to the distinctive craggy peak of **Stac Pollaidh**. A new path has been recently established by the John Muir Trust, which takes you on a circular walk around the peak from the car park. Take the right-hand path and go round at the same level, or climb up the rear to the top, go around the summit and descend by the same path. You'll need a head for heights to reach the summit as much of the route is exposed, but the stunning views are worth it. Be careful not to stray from the path; it's been put there because of the damage inflicted by tens of thousands of pairs of boots each year, resulting in serious erosion on the south face. It's a fairly easy 2½-hour walk.

Achiltibuie → *Phone code: 01854.*

The unclassified single-track road winds its way west past Stac Pollaidh to the turn-off for Achiltibuie. This old crofting village, with whitewashed cottages set back from the sea views across to the beautiful Summer Isles, is home to one of the northwest's main tourist attractions, **Hydroponicum** ⓘ *T01854-622202, www.thehydroponicum, Apr-Sep daily 1000-1800, guided tours every hour on the hour, £4.75, concession £3.50, children £2.75*. This 'Garden of the Future' is a gigantic greenhouse which is pioneering the system of hydroponics to grow plants from all over the world. Hydroponics uses water instead of soil to carry nutrients to the plants and can be carried out anywhere. Here you can see an incredible variety of subtropical trees, orchids, flowers, vegetables, herbs and fruits. A guided tour takes you through the different climatic zones, and you can taste their produce, including the famous strawberries, in the **Lilypond Café**, which serves meals and snacks.

Another worthwhile attraction is the **Achiltibuie Smokehouse** ⓘ *T01854-622353, May-Sep Mon-Sat 0930-1700, free, 5 miles north*, at Altandhu. Here you can watch the salmon, herring, trout and other fish being cured before buying some afterwards.

Lochinver and around → *Phone code: 01571.*

The road from Achiltibuie north to Lochinver is known locally as the 'wee mad road', and you'd be mad to miss this thrilling route which twists and winds its way through some the northwest's most stunning scenery. The village of Lochinver is a working fishing port and the last sizeable village before Thurso. It has a good tourist office, lots of accommodation, a bank with ATM, post office and petrol station.

The best place to start is the **Assynt Visitor Centre** ⓘ *T01854-844330, Apr-Oct Mon-Fri 1000-1700 and Sun 1000-1600*, which houses the tourist information centre. It has displays on the local geology, history and wildlife and there's also a ranger service with guided walks throughout the summer. Those looking for local souvenirs should head for **Highland Stoneware**, see page 404.

▲ A few miles south of Lochinver, beyond Inverkirkaig, is the trail along the river to the **Kirkaig Falls**. The path starts near the **Achins Bookshop**, which has a good stock of Scottish titles and a café. Follow the path for about two miles till it branches right to the falls in the gorge below. Continue along the main path for about another ¾ mile till you reach Fionn Loch, with superb views of mighty Suilven. The walk up to the falls and back should take around 1½ hours. This is one of the main approaches to the foot of the mountain.

Loch Assynt and Inchnadamph → *Phone code: 01571.*

The area east of Lochinver is a remote wilderness of mountains and moorland dotted with lochs and lochans. As well as being a favourite haunt of hardy climbers and walkers, Assynt is a paradise for anglers. Most of the lochs are teeming with brown trout, and fishing permits are readily available throughout the area from the TIC in Lochinver or at local hotels, guest houses and B&Bs. There's also salmon fishing on the River Kirkaig, available through the **Inver Lodge Hotel** and on Loch Assynt through the **Inchnadamph Hotel**, see Sleeping page 401.

The A837 Lochinver-Lairg road meets the A894 to Durness 10 miles east of Lochinver at Skiag Bridge by Loch Assynt. Half a mile south of here, by the loch, are the ruins of **Ardvreck Castle**. The castle dates from 1597 and was the stronghold of the Macleods of Assynt until a siege of the castle in 1691, when it was taken by the Seaforth Mackenzies. Before that, the Marquis of Montrose had been imprisoned here following his defeat at Carbisdale in 1650. Access to the castle is free, but the ruins are in a dangerous state and should be approached with care.

To the east of the road lies the **Inchnadamph National Nature Reserve**, dominated by the massive peaks of Ben More Assynt and Conival, which should only be attempted by experienced hillwalkers. A few miles south of the village of Inchnadamph, at the fish farm, is a steep, but well-marked footpath up to the **Bone Caves**. This is one of Scotland's oldest historical sites, where the bones of humans and animals such as lynx and bear were found together with sawn-off deer antlers dating from over 8,000 years ago.

Lochinver to Kylesku → *Phone code: 01571.*

The quickest way north from Lochinver is the A837 east to the junction with the A894 which heads to Kylesku. But by far the most scenic route is the B869 coast road that passes moorland, lochs and beautiful sandy bays. It's best travelled from north to south, giving you the most fantastic views of Suilven. Untypically, most of the land in this part of Assynt is owned by local crofters who, under the aegis of the Assynt Crofters' Trust, bought 21,000 acres of the North Assynt Estate, thus setting a precedent for change in the history of land ownership in the Highlands.

The trust now owns the fishing rights to the area and sells permits through local post offices and the tourist office in Lochinver. It has also undertaken a number of conservation projects, including one at **Achmelvich**, a few miles north of Lochinver, at the end of a side road which branches off the coast road. It's worth a detour to see one of the loveliest beaches on the west coast, with sparkling white sand and clear turquoise waters straight out of a Caribbean tourist brochure.

▲ From the beach car park below the hostel a path leads northwest along the coast. Bear left off the sandy path shortly after the white cottage on the hill ahead comes into view, and follow the footpath until the road is reached at Alltan na Bradhan, where there are the remains of an old meal mill. Continue north from here along the coast for about a mile till you reach a small bay just before Clachtoll, the **Split Rock**. Close by are the remains of an Iron-Age Broch, but don't cause further damage by clambering over the ruins. Return to the beach by the same path. The walk there and back should take about 1½ hours.

A side road turns left off the B869 north of Stoer and runs out to **Stoer lighthouse**. From here you can walk across the Stoer Peninsula to the **Old Man of Stoer**, a dramatic rock pillar standing offshore, surrounded by sheer cliffs. Allow about three hours for the circular walk which starts and ends in the lighthouse car park. There is no public transport to the lighthouse, but the Lochinver-Drumbeg postbus runs to Raffin, one mile away. A clear path runs from the car park to the cliffs then follows the line of the cliffs northwards. The path heads inland for a short distance as it bypasses a deep gully then meets the clifftop again, and after a mile or so you can see the Old Man tucked away in a shallow bay, battered by huge waves. Beyond the Old Man the path continues to the headland, the **Point of Stoer**, from where it turns back on itself and climbs **Sidhean Mór** (532 ft). The views from here are fantastic, across to Harris and Lewis and south to the mountains of Assynt. From here, follow the faint path south, back towards the lighthouse, passing a small loch below Sidhean Beag on your left and an abvious cairn on your right. Then you pass a radio mast and follow the clear track back to the lighthouse car park. OS Landranger Map No 15 covers the route.

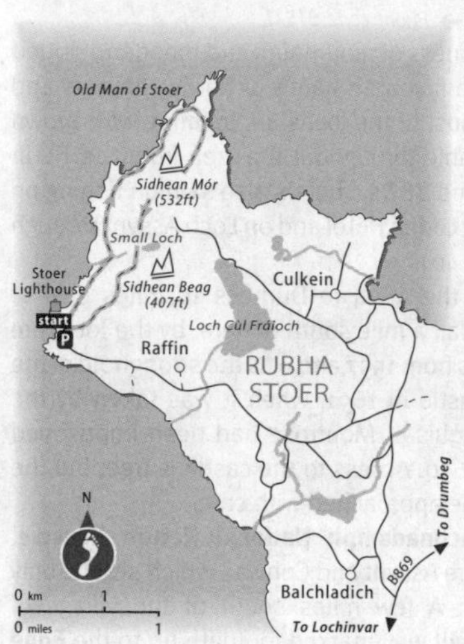

Nine miles further on, in beautiful **Eddrachillis Bay**, is **Drumbeg**, a popular place for anglers who come to fish in the many lochs of North Assynt.

Kylesku → *Phone code: 01971. Colour map 1, grid B5.*

The road runs east from Drumbeg, under the shadow of towering Quinag (2,654 ft), to meet the A894 heading north to Kylesku, site of the sweeping modern road bridge over Loch a'Cháirn Bháin. From Kylesku you can visit Britain's highest waterfall, the 650-ft high **Eas a'Chùal Aluinn**, near the head of Loch Glencoul. Cruises leave from the old ferry jetty below the **Kylesku Hotel** to the falls, see Activities and tours page 404.

There's also a trail to the top of the falls. It starts at the south end of Loch na Gainmhich, about three miles north of Skiag Bridge. Skirting the loch, follow the track in a southeasterly direction up to the head of the Bealach a Bhuirich (the Roaring Pass). Continue until you meet a stream, with several small lochans on your right. Follow this stream until it plunges over the Cliffs of Dubh (the Dark Cliffs). You can get a better view of the falls by walking to the right about 100 yds and descending a heather slope for a short distance. Allow about three to four hours for the round trip.

Scourie and Handa Island → *Phone code: 01971. Colour map 1, grid A5.*

Ten miles north of Kylesku is the little crofting community of Scourie, sitting above a sandy bay. Anyone remotely interested in wildlife is strongly advised to make a stop here to visit Handa Island, a sea bird reserve run by the Scottish Wildlife Trust, and one of the best places in the country for bird life. The island is now deserted, except for the warden, but once supported a thriving community of crofters, until the potato famine of 1846 forced them to leave, most emigrating to Canada's Cape Breton. Now it's home to huge colonies of shags, fulmars, razorbills, guillemots and puffins. The best time to visit is during the summer breeding season, from late May to August. There's a footpath right round the island, which is detailed in the free SWT leaflet available at the warden's office when you arrive. You should allow three to four hours. There's a ferry service to the island, see Transport page 405.

Another excellent wildlife boat trip leaves from Fanagmore, a mile from Tarbet on the other side of the peninsula, see Activities and tours page 404.

Kinlochbervie and around → *Phone code: 01971. Colour map 1, grid A5.*

The road north from Scourie passes Laxford Bridge, where it meets the A838 running southeast to Lairg, see page 416. The A838 also runs north to Durness, on the north coast (see below). At Rhiconich, the B801 branches northwest to Kinlochbervie, a small village with a very big fish market. This is one of the west coast's major fishing ports, and huge container lorries thunder along the narrow single-track roads carrying frozen fish and seafood to all corners of Europe. It's worth heading down to the fish market in the evenings to see the day's catch being landed and sold.

A few miles beyond Kinlochbervie is **Oldshoremore**, a tiny crofters' village scattered around a stunning white beach, and a great place to swim. The less hardy can instead explore the hidden rocky coves nearby.

At the end of the road is **Blairmore**, from where a footpath leads to **Sandwood Bay,** the most wonderful beach on the entire west coast. It's a long walk, but because of its isolation you'll probably have this glorious mile-long stretch of white sand all to yourself. The beach is flanked at one end by a spectacular rock pinnacle and is said to be haunted by the ghost of an ancient shipwrecked mariner. Allow three hours for the walk there and back, plus time at the beach. You could take a tent and watch the sunset. Sandwood Bay can also be reached from Cape Wrath, a day's hike to the north, see page 407.

Sleeping

Ullapool *p395, map p396*

There is no shortage of places to stay in Ullapool ranging from one of the very finest hotels in the UK to numerous guest houses and B&Bs, a couple of good youth hostels and a campsite. Garve Rd, heading south out of town, has several guest houses, and there are lots of B&Bs along Seaforth Rd and Pulteney St. Unfortunately the famous Altnaharrie Inn has closed though the ferry from Ullapool to the other side of Loch Broom is running; for details T01854-612656.

A Tanglewood House, T01854-612059, www.tanglewoodhouse.co.uk. 3 rooms. Chalet-style house overlooking Loch Broom. Part of the Wolsey Lodge scheme so you dine with the hostess, Anne Holloway, who offers superb cooking in a civilized atmosphere. Wonderful views across the loch.

B The Ceilidh Place, 14 West Argyle Pl, T01854-612103, www.theceilidhplace.com. 23 rooms. This former boat-shed has grown over the years to become one of the most refreshingly different hotels in the country, with comfortable bedrooms, cosy lounge, bookshop, restaurant, bar and coffee shop. They also host a varied programme of arts events such as live music, plays, poetry readings, exhibitions and ceilidhs (see below); a great place to relax and soak up some local culture. Across the road is their clubhouse, with basic but comfortable dorms (**E-F**).

C-D Harbour Lights Hotel, Garve Rd (on the left, heading into Ullapool on the A835), T01854-612222, harbour-lights.co.uk. 22 rooms, 1 Mar-31 Oct. Modern hotel offering good service and very good food available all day (**££**).

C-D Morefield Hotel, North Rd, T01854-612161. Open May-Oct. On the edge of town heading north, in the middle of a housing estate, motel-style accommodation and a superb seafood restaurant, see Eating below.

D Ferry Boat Inn, Shore St, T01854-612366, www.ferryboat-inn.com. On the lochside, decent accommodation and food and the best pub in town.

D Point Cottage Guest House, 22 West Shore St, T01854-612494, www.pointcottage.co.uk. Lovely old fishing cottage at the quieter end of the loch-front.

E Brae Guest House, Shore St, T01854-612421. 8 rooms, open May-Oct. Comfortable guest house on the loch-front.

E Eilean Donan Hotel, 14 Market St, T01854-612524. Friendly and central.

E Strathmore House, Strathmore, Morefield, 1 mile north of town, T01854-612423, murdo@strathmore.fsnet.co.uk. Open Apr-Oct. Friendly, comfortable and good value.

F SYHA youth hostel on Shore St, T01854-612254, open Mar-Dec, is very good. You can pick up some information on local walks, also bike hire, internet and laundry facilities.

F Ullapool Tourist Hostel, West House, West Argyle St, T01854-613126, open all year. This independent hostel has the full range of facilities, including free internet for guests, hires out mountain bikes and runs local bus tours.

Camping

Broomfield Holiday Park, T01854-6120020, on Shore St at the west end of the village, the only campsite, has great views across to the Summer Isles and a laundrette on site. It's open Easter-Sep.

South of Ullapool *p397*

B Dundonnell Hotel, south of Ullapool, T01854-633204, selbie@dundonnellhotel.co.uk, open Feb-Dec, good meals (**£££-££**).

E Mrs Ross, T01854-633237, south of Ullapool in Camusnagaul, a few miles back up the loch. B&B.

Achiltibuie *p398*

L Summer Isles Hotel, near the Hydroponicum, T01854-622282, www.summerislesyhotel.com. Open Easter to mid Oct. This relaxing, civilized hotel enjoys magnificent views across to the Summer Isles. Mark and Geraldine Irvine also boast a Michelin-starred restaurant serving some of the best seafood on the planet. Dinner will set you back around £40 a head but you can enjoy delicious bar lunches for a fraction of the price. Even if you're not staying or eating here, it's worth stopping to have a drink on the terrace and watch the sun set over the islands.

E Culross, T01854-622426, 2 rooms, a vegetarian B&B run by Mary King, who also runs the Picture Shack, a gallery featuring highland landscapes. The best bet for an otpion in the lower ranges.

F SYHA Youth Hostel, a few miles south at Achininver, T01854-622254, open mid-May to early Oct. Basic and very cheap.

Lochinver and around *p398*

L Inver Lodge Hotel, Iolaire Rd, T01571-844496, stay@inverlodge.com. 20 rooms, open Apr-Oct. A modern luxury hotel standing above the village with great views and excellent restaurant (**£££-££**).

L The Albannach Hotel, Baddidaroch, T01571-844407, F844285. This wonderful 18th-century house overlooking Loch Inver is one of the very best places to stay in the northwest, and the food offered in the award-winning restaurant is sublime. The price includes dinner. Non-residents are also welcome but booking is essential.

E Ardglas Guest House, T01571-844257, ardglass@btinternet.com. Comfortable.

E Polcraig, T01571-844429, cathelmac@aol.com. Clean and friendly.

E Tigh-Na-Sith, T01571-844740, Apr-Sep. A comfortable choice.

Loch Assynt and Inchnadamph *p399*

C Inchnadamph Hotel, T01571-822202, www.inchnadamphhotel. co.uk. An old-fashioned Highland hotel on the shores of Loch Assynt, catering for the hunting and fishing fraternity, see p399.

F Inchnadamph Lodge, T01571-822218, assynt@presence.co.uk, or Assynt Field Centre, offers basic hostel accommodation in bunk rooms, as well as twin, double and family rooms. Continental breakfast is included. It's open all year, but phone ahead

For an explanation of sleeping and eating price codes used in this guide, see inside the front cover. Other relevant information is found in Essentials, see pages 43-51.

Nov-Mar. It's ideally situated for climbing Ben More Assynt and guides are available.

Lochinver to Kylesku *p399*

There's not much accommodation around here other than self-catering cottages.

Camping

Shore Caravan Site, T01571-844393, open Apr-Sep.

Kylesku *p400*

B **Kylesku Hotel**, T01971-502231, kyleskuhotel@lycos.co.uk. Mar-Oct. Comfortable rooms and renowned for its delicious and great-value pub seafood. There's also a more formal and expensive restaurant next door.

D **Newton Lodge**, T/F01971-502070, newtonlge@aol.com, mid-Mar to mid-Oct. Non-smoking hotel with great views.

F **Kylesku Lodges**, T01971-502003, open Easter-Oct. A small hostel.

Scourie and Handa Island *p400*

There is lots of accommodation in and around Scourie.

C **Eddrachilles Hotel**, Badcall Bay, T01971-502080, www.eddrachilles.com. Mar-Oct. 11 rooms, this is one of the most magnificently situated hotels in the country. The 200 year-old building stands in 300 acres of grounds overlooking the bay, the food on offer is superb, though the atmosphere is a little stuffy (their Eddrachilles heel, you might say).

B **Scourie Hotel**, T01971-502396, www.scourie-hotel.co.uk, open Apr-Oct. 17th-century former coaching inn popular with anglers. Also an excellent place to eat (lunch **££**; dinner **£££**).

C **Scourie Lodge**, T01971-502248, open Mar-Oct. There are several B&Bs in the village, but none better than this welcoming lodge. Also does good evening meals.

Camping

A campsite, T01971-502060, Harbour Rd.

Kinlochbervie and around *p401*

B **The Kinlochbervie Hotel**, T01971-521275, F521438, www.kinlochberviehotel.com. In Kinlochbervie village, a decent hotel.

C **Rhiconich Hotel**, Rhiconich, T01971-521224, www.rhiconichhotel.com. 10 en suite rooms. Modern functional hotel with good facilities and surrounded by superb scenery. **B** for half board.

D **Old School Hotel**, halfway between Kinlochbervie and the A838 at Rhiconich, T/F01971-521383, www.host.co.uk. This is the best place to stay. It used to be a school, as the name implies, and this only adds to the charm. They also serve great food (**££**) daily 1200-1400 and 1800-2000.

E **Benview**, T01971-521242, open Apr-Sep. A friendly B&B.

Camping

There's a good campsite at Oldshoremore, T01971-521281.

Eating

Ullapool *p395, map p396*

££ **Mariner's Restaurant**, Morefield Hotel, see Sleeping. The setting may be a little incongruous but there's nothing wrong with the food. The seafood is sensational, which is why people travel from miles around and it's always busy. Excellent value.

££ **The Ceilidh Place**, see Bars and clubs, is one of those places that tourists seem to hang around for hours or even days. It exudes a laid-back, cultured ambience. The self- service coffee shop does cheap wholefood all day during the summer, while the restaurant serves more expensive full meals, with an emphasis on vegetarian and seafood at night. There's even outdoor seating. Open 1100-2300. Also live music and various other events, see Bars and clubs.

££ **Jade House**, beside Safeway, Latheron La, good Chinese food at reasonable prices.

£ **Ferry Boat Inn**, the **Seaforth Inn** and the **Arch Inn**, see Bars and clubs, for cheap pub food at lunchtime and early evening.

£ **Mountain Man supplies**, see Shopping, has a good coffee shop above the shop. Serves snacks and light meals.

£ **Ullapool Catering**, T01854-612969, make up great picnics from local organic produce at good value prices.

£ There's a good 'chippie' on West Shore St.

Lochinver and around *p398*

££ **Lochinver's Larder Riverside Bistro**, T01571-844356, on the way into town on the A837. Apart from the hotels listed above, the best food can be found here. You can eat in or takeaway.

£ Caberfeidh, T01571-844321. Near to the bistro, this option is the cheap and cheerful

Scourie and Handa Island *p400*

££ Seafood Restaurant, just above the jetty at Tarbet. Run by Julian Pearce, who also runs **Laxford Cruise**, see Activities and tours. If you're up this way, don't miss a visit to this restaurant which serves seafood caught by Julian during his boat trips. It's a great place and you can stay here, in the self-catering caravan next door, which sleeps up to six.

Bars and clubs

Ullapool *p395, map p396*

Arch Inn, Shore St, is good place for a drink.

The Ceilidh Place, see Sleeping, for something a wee bit more sedate and civilized than the other choices, head here where you can enjoy a quiet drink in the cosy **Parlour Bar** or take advantage of their varied programme of events. There's live music nightly (except Sun) throughout the summer and on a Mon in winter, also ceilidhs and poetry readings. The clubhouse opposite stages plays.

Ferry Boat Inn (or 'FBI' as it's known locally), on Shore St. Is Ullapool's favourite pub. It has a Thu night live music session year round and during the summer you can sit outside on the sea wall and watch the sun go down as you drain your glass

Seaforth Inn, Quay St, has live music on a Fri night, which has been described by one local as 'raucous'.

Shopping

Ullapool *p395, map p396*

The town is well supplied with shops.

The Captain's Cabin, on the corner of Quay St and Shore St, also sells books, as well as crafts and souvenirs.

The Ceilidh Place, see Bars and clubs, has the best bookshop in the northwest.

Highland Stoneware, T01854-612980, on Mill St, heading north towards Morefield. Look no further than here for pottery. You can wander round the studios before browsing in their gift shop, which is pricey but you may have luck in their bargain baskets. They also have a factory in Lochinver, T01854-844376, www.highlandtrail.co.uk/stoneware, Mon-Fri 0900-1800 (Easter-Oct also Sat 0900-1700), a local pottery factory just outside the village of Lochinver. See p399.

Knockan Studio, opposite the TIC on Argyle St, T01854-613365, open Mar-Oct, Mon-Sat 0900-1800, is an excellent jewellers.

Mountain Man Supplies, opposite the museum on West Argyle St, is a good outdoor equipment shop.

Activities and tours

Ullapool *p395, map p396*

During the summer the *MV Summer Queen* runs 4-hr cruises to the Summer Isles, with a 45-min landing on Tanera Mór. These leave Mon-Sat at 1000 from the pier and cost £14 per person. There are also 2-hr wildlife cruises around Loch Broom, Annat Bay and Isle Martin, which leave daily at 1415 and also on Sun at 1100, and cost £8 per person. Cruises can be booked at the booth by the pier or by calling, T01854-612472.

Walking tours around Ullapool and throughout the Northwest Highlands can be arranged daily with **Northwest Frontiers**, NWF@compuserve.com, ourworld.compuserve.com/homepages/NWF, T01854-612628, with the very experienced Andy Cunningham, and **Celtic Horizons**, T01854-612429.

Achiltibuie *p398*

I Macleod, Achiltibuie Post Office, T01854-622200, or at home, T018754-622315, for cruises to the Summer Isles from Achiltibuie pier on board the *Hectoria*. Cruises leave Mon-Sat at 1030 and 1415 and last 3½ hrs, with 1 hr ashore on the islands. They cost £12 per person (half price for children). There are also deep-sea angling trips (1800-2100).

Kylesku *p400*

On board the *MV Statesman*, T01571-844446, cruises go to Eas a'Chùal Aluinn waterfall leaving from the old ferry jetty below the **Kylesku Hotel**. You can also see porpoises, seals and minke whales en route. The 2-hr round trip runs Apr-Sep daily at 1100 and 1400 (Jul and Aug also at 1600), and costs £9, children £3. You may be able to get closer to the falls by getting off the boat and walking to the bottom, then getting on the next boat.

Scourie and Handa Island *p400*

Laxford Cruises, T01971-502251, sail around beautiful Loch Laxford, where you can see lots of birds from nearby Handa Island, as well as seals, porpoises and otters. Trips leave Easter till the end of Sep daily except Sun at 1000, 1200 and 1400 (also at 1600 in Jul and Aug). The trips last 1¾ hrs and cost £10 for adults, £5 for children. For bookings contact Julian Pearce, who also runs the wonderful **Seafood Restaurant**, see Eating, just above the jetty at Tarbet.

Transport

Ullapool *p395, map p396*

Scottish Citylink buses run 2-3 times daily (except Sun) between Ullapool and **Inverness**, connecting with the ferry to **Stornoway**. There are also buses daily (except Sun) to and from **Inverness** with Rapson's Coaches, T01463-710555, and **Spa** Coaches, T01997-421311. There's a service to **Lochinver** (1-2 times daily except Sun, 1 hr) with **Spa Coaches** and **Rapson's of Brora**, T01408-621245, and to **Achilitibuie** (twice daily Mon-Thu, once on Sat, 1 hr) with **Spa** Coaches. There's also a daily bus to and from **Gairloch**, which continues to **Inverness**, during the summer only.

Car hire from **Daley's Deals**, Morefield Industrial Estate, T01854-612848. Cycle hire at the hostels, (see Sleeping p401.

Achiltibuie *p398*

There are 2 buses daily (Mon-Thu) to **Ullapool** with Spa Coaches, T01997-421311, leaving Achiltibuie Post Office at 0800 and 1300. The early bus starts in Reiff (at 0740) and the other one leaves from Badenscallie. The journey takes an hour. There's also a bus on Sat, leaving at 0750.

Lochinver and around *p398*

There's a postbus service from **Lochinver** to and from **Drumbeg**, via the coast road, which continues to **Lairg**. It runs once a day, Mon-Sat. There are also buses to and from **Drumbeg** and on to **Ullapool**, once or twice daily except Sun, with **Rapsons of Brora**, T01408-621245, and **Spa Coaches**, T01997-421311.

Scourie and Handa Island *p400*

There's a postbus service to Scourie from **Durness** and **Lairg** once a day, Mon-Sat. It leaves Durness at 0820 and arrives at 0935 and continues to Lairg. It returns at 1245 and arrives at 1420. There's also a postbus service between Scourie and **Elphin**, with connections to **Lochinver**. There's a ferry service to Handa Island from **Tarbet Beach**, 3 miles northwest off the A894, about three miles north of Scourie. It sails continuously, depending on demand, Apr-Sep Mon-Sat 0930-1700. The 15-min crossing costs £7.50 return, T01971-502077.

Kinlochbervie and around *p401*

A postbus leaves Kinlochbervie harbour at 0900 and goes to **Scourie** (35 mins) and on to Lairg (1 hr 50 mins) from where there are connections to Inverness. The same postbus returns from **Lairg** at 1245, arrives in Kinlochbervie at 1448, then continues to **Durness** (35 mins).

Directory

Ullapool *p395, map p396*

Bank **Royal Bank of Scotland** on Ladysmith St, and **Bank of Scotland** with ATM, on West Argyle St.

North coast

Scotland's rugged north coast attracts few visitors, but those who do venture this far find that's there's plenty to write home about. This is some of Britain's most spectacular and undisturbed coastline from the wild and remote Cape Wrath in the far northwest to John O'Groats, that perennial favourite of sponsored walkers, in the far northeast. In between lie over 100 miles of storm-lashed cliffs, sheer rocky headlands and deserted sandy coves, all waiting to be explored. It's also a great place for birdwatching, with vast colonies of seabirds, and there's a good chance of seeing seals, porpoises and minke whales in the more sheltered estuaries. » *For Sleeping, Eating and other listings, see pages 410-412.*

Ins and outs

Getting there and around

Getting around the far north without your own transport can be a slow process. Getting to Thurso, the main town, by bus or train is easy, but beyond that things get more difficult. » *For further details, see Transport page 411.*

Tourist information

Tourist information centre in Durness ⓘ *T01971-511259, Apr-Oct Mon-Sat, daily Jul and Aug*, arranges guided walks and has a small visitor centre with displays on local history, flora and fauna and geology. tourist information centre in Thurso ⓘ *Riverside Rd, T01847-892371, Apr-Oct Mon-Sat 0900-1800, Jul and Aug also Sun 1000-1800*, has a leaflet on local surfing beaches.

Durness and around

→ *Phone code: 01971. Colour map 1, grid A5.*

Durness is not only the most northwesterly village on the British mainland, but also one of the most attractively located, surrounded by sheltered coves of sparkling white sand and machair-covered limestone cliffs. It's worth stopping here for a few days to explore the surrounding area.

Smoo Cave

A mile east of the village is the vast 200 ft-long Smoo Cave. A path from near the youth hostel leads down to the cave entrance which is hidden away at the end of a steep, narrow inlet. Plunging through the roof of the cathedral-like cavern is an 80-ft waterfall which can be seen from the entrance, but the more adventurous can take a boat trip into the floodlit interior.

A few miles east of the Smoo Cave are a couple of excellent beaches, at **Sangobeg** and **Rispond**, where the road leaves the coast and heads south along the west shore of stunning **Loch Eriboll**.

Balnakeil

About a mile northwest of Durness is the tiny hamlet of Balnakeil, overlooked by a ruined 17th-century church. In the south wall is a graveslab with carved skull-and-crossbones marking the grave of the notorious highwayman Donald MacMurchow. If you're looking for souvenirs, or an escape from the rat race, then head for the **Balnakeil Craft Village** ⓘ *Apr-Oct daily 1000-1800*, an alternative artists' community set up in the 1960s in a former RAF radar station. Here you can buy weavings, pottery, paintings, leatherwork and woodwork in the little prefab huts. There's also a café. Balnakeil has also become well-known in golfing circles. The nine-hole course, T511364, is the most northerly in mainland Britain, and its famous ninth hole involves a drive over the Atlantic Ocean. The beach here is glorious, especially in fine weather when the sea turns a brilliant shade of turquoise. Even better, walk north along the bay to **Faraid Head**, where you can see puffin colonies in

Loch Eriboll, Britain's deepest sea loch, was used by the Royal Navy during the Second World War as a base for protecting Russian convoys.

early summer. The views from here, across to Cape Wrath in the west and Loch Eriboll in the east, are stupendous.

Cape Wrath

There are several excellent trips around Durness, but the most spectacular is to Cape Wrath, Britain's most northwesterly point. It's a wild place and the name seems entirely appropriate, though it actually derives from the Norse word hwarf, meaning 'turning place'. Viking ships used it as a navigation point during their raids on the Scottish west coast. Now a lighthouse stands on the cape, above the 1,000 ft-high Clo Mor Cliffs, the highest on the mainland, and breeding ground for huge colonies of seabirds.

You can walk south from here to **Sandwood Bay**, see page 401. It's an exhilarating but long coastal walk, and will take around eight hours. It's safer doing this walk from north to south as the area around the headland is a military firing range and access may be restricted, which could leave you stranded.

Tongue to Thurso → *Phone code: 01847-01641. Colour map 2, grid A1-2.*

The road east from Durness runs around Loch Eriboll on its way to the lovely little village of **Tongue**. A causeway runs across the beautiful Kyle of Tongue, but a much more scenic route is the single-track road around its southern side, with great views of Ben Hope (3,041 ft) looming to the southwest. The village of Tongue is overlooked by the 14th-century ruins of **Varick Castle**, and there's a great beach at **Coldbackie**, two miles northeast.

The A836 runs south from Tongue through Altnaharra to Lairg, see page 416. It also continues east to the crofting community of **Bettyhill**, named after the Countess of Sutherland who ruthlessly evicted her tenants from their homes in Strathnaver to make way for more profitable sheep. The whole sorry saga is told in the interesting **Strathnaver Museum** ⓘ *T01641-521418, Apr-Oct Mon-Sat 1000-1300 and 1400-1700, £1.90, concession £1.20, children £0.50*, housed in an old church in the village. There are also Pictish stones in the churchyard behind the museum.

The museum sells a leaflet detailing the many prehistoric sites in the Strathnaver Valley which runs due south from Bettyhill. There are a couple of great beaches around Bettyhill, at **Farr Bay** and at **Torrisdale Bay**, which is the more impressive of the two and forms part of the **Invernaver Nature Reserve**. There's a small tourist information centre in Bettyhill ⓘ *T01641-521342, Easter-Sep Mon-Sat.*

East from Bettyhill the hills of Sutherland begin to give way to the fields of Caithness. The road passes the turn-off to Strathy Point before reaching **Melvich**, another wee crofting settlement overlooking a lovely sandy bay.

South from Melvich the A897 heads to Helmsdale, see page 418, through the **Flow Country**, a vast expanse of bleak bog of major ecological importance. About 15 miles south of Melvich at Forsinard is an **RSPB Visitor Centre** ⓘ *T01641-571225, Easter-Oct daily 0900-1800*, guided walks through the nature reserve leave from the visitor centre. The peatlands here are a breeding ground for black- and red-throated divers, golden plovers and merlins as well as other species. Otters and roe deer can also be spotted.

Thurso and around

Thurso is the most northerly town on the British mainland and by far the largest settlement on the north coast. In medieval times it was Scotland's chief port for trade with Scandinavia, though most of the town dates from the late 18th century when Sir John Sinclair built the 'new' extension to the old fishing port. The town increased in size to accommodate the workforce of the new nuclear power plant at nearby Dounreay, but the plant's demise has threatened the local economy. Today Thurso is a fairly nondescript place, mostly visited by people catching the ferry to Stromness in Orkney, or the occasional hardcore surfer.

Thurso → *Phone code: 01847. Colour map 2, grid A3. Population: 9,000.*

There's little of real interest in the town centre. Near the harbour are the 17th-century ruins of **Old St Peter's Church**, which stand on the site of the original 13th-century church founded by the Bishop of Caithness. In the town hall on the High Street is the **Heritage Museum** ⓘ *T01847-892459, Jun-Sep Mon-Sat 1000-1300 and 1400-1700, £0.50*, which features some Pictish carved stones. There may little in the way of activity in the town, but 10 miles west of Thurso you might say there's plenty of radioactivity at the **Dounreay Nuclear Power Station**. Though its fast breeder reactors were decommissioned in 1994, the plant is still a major local employer and now reprocesses spent nuclear fuel. There's a permanent exhibition at the visitor centre ⓘ *T01847-802572, Easter-Sep daily 1000-1700, free*, where you learn all about the 'benefits' of nuclear power.

Strathmore to Braemore → *OS sheet No 11 covers the route.*

This walk gives a flavour of the bleak but beautiful landscape of the Caithness hinterland. The 16-mile linear route starts from **Strathmore Lodge**. To get there, head south from Thurso on the B874. After a short distance turn on to the B870 and follow it for 10 miles to the little hamlet of Westerdale, which stands on the River Thurso. Turn

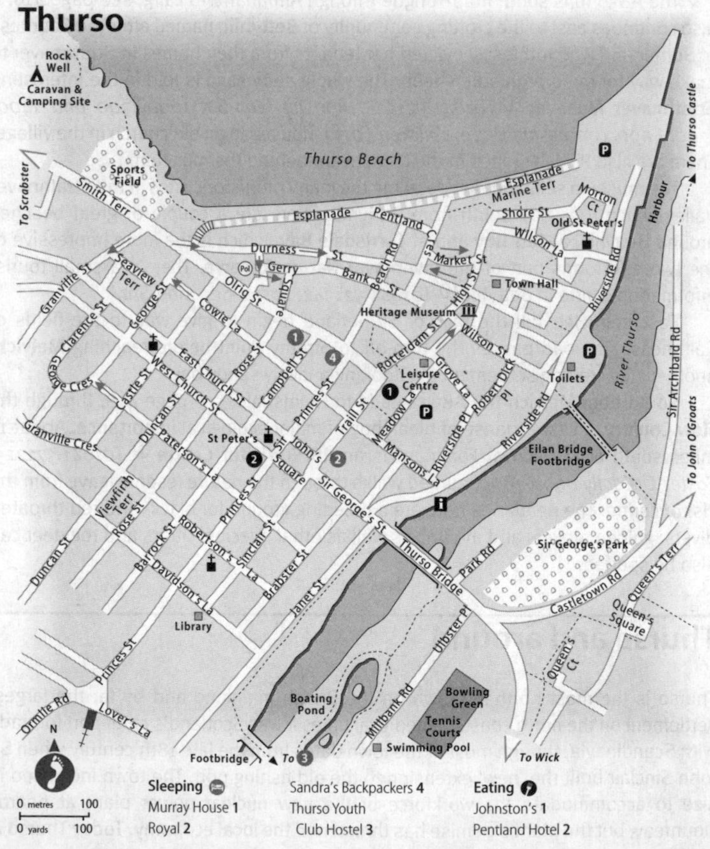

right here on to an unnumbered road and follow this road for about five miles. Just past the white **Strathmore Lodge** the road splits. Follow the right-hand track which runs through commercial forestry, before emerging on to open moor with Loch More on the left.

Where the forestry begins again on the right, the track swings left across an arm of the loch and heads southwards. At the southern end of the loch a track runs left to **Dalnaha**, but keep going straight ahead, along the valley of the River Thurso. You then reach a cluster of buildings at **Dalnawillan Lodge**. Ignore the track which heads off to the right and carry straight on, past the house at **Dalganachan**, over Rumsdale Water and on to the junction before **The Glutt**, which is a series of buildings. Turn left here and follow the track for a further four miles till you reach the junction beside Lochan nan Bò Riabach. Continue down the valley of Berriedale Water to Braemore. There is no public transport from here, so you'll have to arrange your own transport if you don't want to retrace your steps.

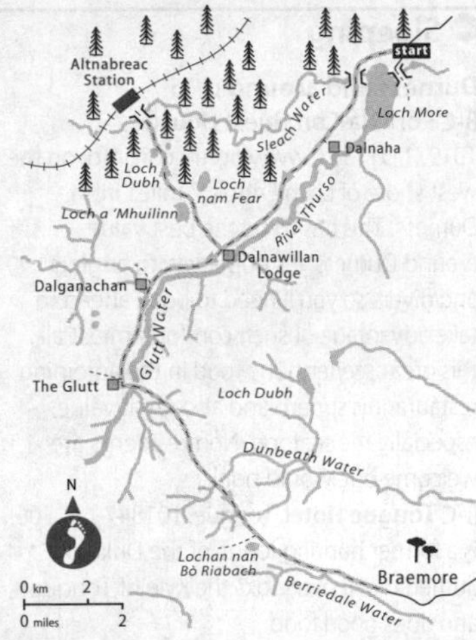

Dunnet Head → *Phone code: 01847. Colour map 2, grid A3-4.*

About 10 miles northeast of Thurso is the most northerly point on the British mainland. No, not John O'Groats, but Dunnet Head. It's reached by turning off the Thurso-John O'Groats road at Dunnett, at the east end of Dunnett Bay, a three-mile-long sandy beach that's popular with surfers who come to tackle the gigantic waves of the Pentland Firth, the wild and treacherous strait between the mainland and Orkney. Dunnet Bay has an excellent reef break and there's another good reef break, at Brims Ness to the west. Further west, at Strathy Bay you'll find rollers that can match anything in Hawaii (though the water's a lot colder). Dunnett Head is a much nicer place than John O'Groats, with marvellous views across to Orkney and along the entire north coast (on a clear day). There's a Victorian lighthouse out at the point, and the dramatic seacliffs are teeming with seabirds. There's also a great little café, see Eating page 411.

The area's newest attraction are the **Castle and Gardens of Mey** ⓘ *T01847-851473, www.castleofmey.org.uk, mid May-end Sep (closed from 29 Jul-11 Aug) Tue-Fri 1100-1630, Sun 1400-1700, £7, concessions £6, children £3, under 12 free, family £18, 15 miles east of Thurso*. This was the holiday home of the late Queen Mother and Prince Charles still holidays here each summer.

John O'Groats → *Phone code: 01955. Colour map 2, grid A4.*

If you still feel inclined to visit this dreary tourist trap, then that's your prerogative, but don't say we didn't warn you. It's boring at best and pretty miserable most of the time. It gets its name from the Dutchman Jan de Groot, who was commissioned by King James IV to run a ferry service to Orkney in 1496. Ferries still operate from here to Burwick in Orkney, see Transport page 411. There's a tourist information centre ⓘ *T01955-611373, Apr-Oct Mon-Sat*, as well as a post office, craft shops and a chippie.

Two miles east of John O'Groats is **Duncansby Head**, which is far more rewarding. South of the headland a path leads to the spectacular **Duncansby Stacks**, a series of dramatic rock formations. The 200-ft cliffs are home to countless seabirds and you can see the narrow, sheer-sided inlets known locally as geos.

Sleeping

Durness and around *p406*

B-C Port-Na-Con Guest House, T01971-511367, www.portnacon.info, on the west shore of Loch Eriboll, 7 miles from Durness. This has to be the best value around Durness. It's popular with anglers and divers so you'll need to book ahead to take advantage of such comfort amidst all this great scenery. The food in the adjoining restaurant is superb and also great value, especially the seafood. Non-residents are welcome but should book.

B-C Tongue Hotel, Tongue, T01847-611206, is a former hunting lodge of the Duke of Sutherland. It overlooks the Kyle of Tongue and does good food.

C Ben Loyal Hotel, Tongue, T01847-611216, benloyalhotel@btinternet.com, is also recommended for its food. There are cheaper options, such as the excellent-value

C Cape Wrath Hotel, just off the A838 on the road to the ferry at Keoldale, T01971-511212, jack@capewrathhotel.co.uk, overlooks the loch and is popular with fishermen and passing tourists who stop here to enjoy the great food and superb views.

D Bighouse Lodge, T01641-531207, open May-Oct. There's some excellent places to stay in Melvich including this 18th-century mansion sitting at the mouth of the Halladale river in 4 acres of its own grounds.

E Cloisters, Talmine, T01847-601286, www.cloisteral.demon.co.uk, is a lovely 19th-century converted church.

E Farr Bay Inn, Bettyhill, T01641-521230, www.bettyhill.com, decent bar food too.

E Puffin Cottage, T01971-511208, www.puffincottage.com, open Apr-Sep. There are also several B&Bs in Durness, the best of which is this one.

E Rhian Cottage, Tongue, T01847-611257, jenny.anderson@tesco.net. Excellent value.

E Shieling Guest House, Melvich, T/F01641-531256, theshieling@btinternet .com, open Apr-Oct. Recommended.

F Bruachmor, Bettyhill, T01641-521265, open Apr-Oct. A good value B&B.

F SYHA Youth Hostel, at Smoo, to the east of the village, T01971-511244; open mid-Mar to early Oct. Basic.

F SYHA Youth Hostel, Tongue, T01847-611301, open mid-Mar to late Oct, beautifully situated at the east end of the causeway.

Camping

Kincraig Camping and Caravan Site, Tongue, T01847-611218, just to the south of the village.

Salgo Sands Caravan Park, T01971-511222, caravans and camping.

Talmine, T01847-601225, 5 miles north of Tongue by the beach.

Thurso and around *p407, map p408*

Thurso has a wide variety of accommodation, most of it fairly average.

A Forss Country House Hotel, 4 miles out of Thurso at Bridge of Forss, T01847-861201, www.forsshousehotel.co.uk. The nicest place to stay by far. Price includes dinner. This small family-run hotel is set in 20 acres of lovely woodland and has an excellent restaurant, open to non-residents (**£££**).

B Royal Hotel, Traill St, Thurso, T01847-893191. 102 rooms. Central, and upgraded to include indoor pool and leisure facilities.

E Annandale, 2 Rendel Govan Rd, Thurso, T01847-893942, thomson@annandale2. freeserve.co.uk. B&B.

E Bencorragh House, Upper Gills in Canisbay, a few miles west of John O'Groats, T01955-611449, www.bencorraghhouse. com, open Mar-Oct. A very decent B&B.

E Mrs C Murray, 1 Granville Cresent, Thurso, T01847-892993. B&B.

E Murray House, 1 Campbell St, Thurso, T01847-895759, www.murrayhousebb. com. B&B.

F SYHA Youth Hostel, John O'Groats, T01955-611424, open 19 Mar-31 Oct.

F Sandra's Backpackers, 24-26 Princes St, Thurso, T01847-894575, www.sandras-back packers@ukf.net. A decent hostel.

F Thurso Youth Club Hostel, Old Mill, Millbank, Thurso, T/F01847-892964, www. tyc-hostel.com, open 1 Jul-30 Aug.

Camping

Thurso Camping Site, T01847-607771, north of town on the road to Scrabster is the nearest to Thurso. There are a couple of campsites, John O'Groats and further west by the beach at Huna. Ask at the TIC.

Eating

Durness and around *p406*
See Sleeping for options.

Thurso and around *p407, map p408*
£££ The Bower Inn, T01955-661292, between Thurso and Wick. This comes a close second to the hotel. To get there, turn off the coast road at Castletown and follow the B876 till you see the sign for Gillock.
£££ Forss Country House Hotel, see Sleeping, is the best place to eat in the area.
££ The Upper Deck, Scrabster, T01847-892814, by the harbour. A surf'n'turf menu.
£ Dunnett Head Tearoom, Dunnett Head, T01847-851774, open Apr-Oct daily 1500-2000, a few miles from the lighthouse, which serves snacks and meals.
£ Johnston's, Traill St, Thurso, a decent café.
£ Pentland Hotel, Thurso, T01847-893202. Does a decent bar meal.
£ There are also the ubiquitous Indian and Chinese restaurants and fish and chip shops in Thurso.

Entertainment

Thurso and around *p407, map p408*
Bowling **Viking Bowl**, Ormlie Rd, T01847-895050.
Cinema At Viking Bowl, see above.

Activities and tours

Thurso and around *p407, map p408*
John O'Groats Ferries, Ferry Office, John O'Groats, T01955-611353, www.jogferry.co.uk, operate **Orkney Islands Day Tours**, which leave daily 1 May-30 Sep at 0900, and return at 1945 (£35, children £17.50, under 5 free). A shorter day tour departs daily from 1 Jun-2 Sep 1030, and returns at 1800 (£32, children £16). There's also a wildlife cruise 20 Jun-31 Aug, which departs at 1430, £14, children £7.

Transport

Durness and around *p406*
A daily bus runs to and from **Thurso**, via **Tongue** and **Bettyhill** (Jun-Aug, Mon-Sat) with **Highland Country Buses**, T01847-893123, leaving Thurso at 1130 and Durness at 1500. There's also a daily bus service (May to early Oct) to and from **Inverness** via **Ullapool** and **Lochinver**, with Bluebird/ Inverness Traction, T01463-239292. There's a postbus service to **Lairg** via **Tongue** and **Altnaharra**, Mon-Sat at 1115; also via **Kinlochbervie** and **Scourie** Mon-Sat at 0820.

To get to **Cape Wrath**, first take the passenger ferry across the Kyle of Durness from Keoldale, 3 miles south of Durness, T01971-511376. It runs May-Sep hourly 0930-1630. The ferry connects with a minibus, T01971-511287, for the 11 miles to the cape (40 mins).

Thurso and around *p407, map p408*
Boat Northlink Ferries, www.northlinkferries.co.uk, to **Stromness** in **Orkney** leave from **Scrabster**, 2 miles north of Thurso. For details, see p550). John O'Groats Ferries (see above for details) sail to **Burwick** (Orkney) twice daily from Jun to Sep (45 mins, £16 one way). A connecting bus takes passengers on to **Kirkwall** (40 mins, price included in ferry ticket).
Bus Citylink buses run to and from **Inverness** (3½ hrs) 4 times daily, T0870-5505050, continuing to **Scrabster** to connect with the ferries to and from **Stromness** in **Orkney**. Citylink buses to **Inverness** connect with buses to **Edinburgh**. Highland Country Buses, T01847-893123, run local services to **Bettyhill** (3 times daily Mon-Thu, twice on Sat; 1 hr 10 mins) and to **Reay** (4 times daily Mon-Thu, 3 times on Sat). There are regular daily buses to and from **Wick** via **Halkirk** or **Castletown**. Highland Country Buses also run the service between Thurso train station and **Scrabster** ferry pier (5-10 mins). Harrold Coaches, T01955-631295, run a service to and from **John O'Groats** (4 times daily Mon-Thu, twice on Sat; 1 hr). Also from **Wick** (5 daily Mon-Fri, 4 on Sat) with **Highland Country Buses**. There's also a **postbus** service to Wick airport, leaving Riverside Rd at 0920 and arriving at 1000. Buses arrive at Sir George's St Port Office and depart from Sir George's St Church.
Car and cycle hire Car hire at William Dunnett & Co, T01847-893101. Cycle hire at The Bike & Camping Shop, the Arcade, 34 High St, T01847-896124, rents mountain bikes for £8 per day.

Train Three trains leave daily from **Inverness** (3½ hrs), 2 of them connecting with the ferries from **Scrabster** to **Stromness** in **Orkney**. Trains continue to **Wick** (30 mins) and return trains to **Inverness** leave from **Wick**. The train station is at the south end of Princes St.

East Coast

The east coast of the Highlands, from Inverness north to Wick, doesn't have the same draw as the west coast and attracts far fewer visitors, but it has its own, gentler appeal, and there are many lovely little seaside towns to explore. The sea lochs and estuaries of the inner Moray Firth are fringed with fields and woods, a fertile lowland landscape dotted with farms and crofts. Fast-flowing rivers drop from the hills through deep, wooded straths. The bulk of Ben Wyvis dominates the horizon northwest of Dingwall.

The Black Isle → *Phone code: 01381. Colour map 2, grid C2.*

Across the Kessock Bridge from Inverness is the Black Isle, which is neither an island nor black. It shares with the Moray coast long hours of sunshine and low rainfall, rolling acres of barley and stately woods of oak and beech dropping down to the shores. It also has a compelling atmosphere – a combination perhaps of its soft microclimate, lush vegetation and attractive architecture. Its main attractions are the picturesque town of Cromarty and Chanonry Point, on the southern side near Rosemarkie, which is one of the best dolphin-spotting sites in Europe. » *For Sleeping, Eating and other listings, see pages 420-422.*

North Kessock to Tore

On the north side of the Kessock Bridge, just north of the village, is the North Kessock Tourist Information Centre ⓘ *T01463-731505, daily from Easter to Oct*. Next door is the Dolphin and Seal Visitor Centre, which gives details of accredited dolphin cruises. You can see dolphins from the village of North Kessock just to the south.

One of the many sacred wells (and caves) in the area is the unmissable **Clootie Well**, on the verge of the main road between Tore and Munlochy Bay Nature Reserve. It was once blessed by St Curitan (see below under Rosemarkie) and is thought to cure sick children. Thousands of rags still flutter from the surrounding trees, though well-worshippers are in danger of being mown down by traffic. Despite the presence of traffic, it's an eerie place. Go at night – if you dare.

Fortrose and Chanonry Point

Further east on this road, beyond Munlochy and Avoch (pronounced 'Och') is the village of Fortrose, on the east shore. The magnificent cathedral at Fortrose is now largely a ruin where rainwashed carved faces of rose-coloured sandstone peer down from roof bosses, and snapped-off stumps of window tracery are redolent of Reformation vandalism. On the golf course at **Chanonry Point**, see box, overlooking the Moray Firth, a plaque marks the spot where the Brahan Seer was boiled in a barrel of tar. Chanonry Point is also a great place for seeing dolphins. They come close to shore at high tide and there's a good chance of seeing them leaping above the waves.

Rosemarkie

A few miles from Fortrose on the north side of Chanonry Point is the tiny village of Rosemarkie. Celtic saints Curitan and Boniface selected this sheltered spot on the southern shore for their Christian mission in the seventh century. St Boniface is

A seerious crime

The Brahan Seer was boiled in a barrel of tar in 1660 but not before he had foretold the building of the Caledonian Canal and Kessock Bridge, the Highland Clearances and the Second World War. He also predicted the demise of the local lairds and the Seaforths. It was Lady Seaforth who ordered his execution, after the seer had a vision of her husband in the arms of another woman. Apparently the precise spot where he met his end is now the 13th hole of the golf course at Chanonry Point, which just goes to prove that it is indeed unlucky for some.

remembered at nearby St Bennet's Well. **Groam House Museum** ⓘ *T01381-620961, Easter-Sep Mon-Sat 1000-1700, Sun 1400-1630, Oct-Apr Sat and Sun 1400-1600, free*, houses a huge collection of Pictish sculptured stones found locally, imaginatively displayed alongside contemporary artwork inspired by them. A year -round programme of events and lectures is devoted to the study of Pictish culture.

Beware of fairies, last sighted in the 1970's in Fairy Glen, now a nature reserve. A lovely marked trail leads into the glen from the top end of the High Street, through a wooded gorge where you may spot woodpeckers and treecreepers.

Cromarty → *Phone code: 01381.*

On the northeastern tip of the Black Isle Peninsula, at the mouth of the Cromarty Firth, is the gorgeous village of Cromarty, one of the east coast's major attractions. Its neat white-harled houses interspersed with gracious merchants' residences are almost unchanged since the 18th century when it was a sea port thriving on trade as far afield as Russia and the Baltic. Many emigrants bound for the New World embarked here. A prosperity based on textiles and fishing led to decline and dereliction. Although restored and much inhabited, Cromarty now has the atmosphere of a backwater, but a very attractive one at that, where you feel as if you're stepping back in time, in stark contrast to the numerous oil rigs moored on the opposite shore in Nigg Bay.

For a fascinating insight into the history of the area, visit the 18th-century **Cromarty Courthouse** ⓘ *Church St, T01381-600418, Apr-Oct daily 1000-1700, Nov, Dec and Mar daily 1200-1600, £3, concession/children £2, includes loan of headset for recorded tour of the town's other historic buildings*, which houses the town's museum. Next to the courthouse is the thatch-roofed **Hugh Miller's Cottage** ⓘ *T01381-600245, 1 May-30 Sep daily 1100-1300 and 1400-1700 (Sun afternoon only), £5, concession £2.50, family £10*, birthplace of the eminent local geologist and author. Also worth seeing is the elegant 17th-century **East Church**.

There's a good walk along a coastal path from the east end of the village through woodland to the top of the South Sutor headland, one of the two steep headlands guarding the narrow entrance to the Cromarty Firth. There are excellent views from here across the Moray Firth. Leaflets describing this and other local walks are available at the Cromarty Courthouse.

One of Cromarty's main attractions is its **dolphins**. They can be seen from the shore, or with a boat trip, see Activities and tours page 422. To the west, the mudflats of **Udale Bay** are an RSPB reserve and a haven for wading birds and wintering duck and geese, which can be viewed from a hide. In the winter other birds such as pinkfooted geese and whooper swans use the bay as a roost.

Poyntzfield Herb Garden is an organic plant nursery specializing in rare and native medicinal herbs. Worth visiting if only for a glimpse of the house, and the view from the car park over the Cromarty Firth through massive beech trees.

The Cromarty Firth → *Colour map 2, grid C1-2.*

Dingwall and around → *Phone code: 01349.*

Dingwall, at the head of the Cromarty Firth, has two major claims to fame. Not only is it believed to be the birthplace of Macbeth, it was also the home for many years of Neil Gunn (1891-1973), perhaps the Highlands' greatest literary figure, see also page 613. It's a fairly dull, though functional town, with good shops and banks lining its long main street. **Dingwall Museum** ⓘ *T01349-865366, May-Sep Mon-Sat 1000-1700, £1.50, concession £1, children £0.50*, tells the history of this Royal Burgh.

East of Dingwall, before Evanton, is **Clanland and Sealpoint** ⓘ *T01349-830033, all year daily 0930-1730*, which has history and wildlife exhibitions and offers the chance to see the local seal population. Standing on a hill above **Evanton** is the Fyrish Monument, a replica of the Gate of Negapatam in India, built by local men and funded by local military hero, Sir Hector Munro, to commemorate his capture of the Indian town, in 1781. To get there, turn off the B9176 towards Boath. It's a stiff two-hour climb up to the top.

The Cromarty Firth is a centre for repairing North Sea oil rigs, and many of the villages along its north shore have benefited from the oil industry. One of these is **Invergordon**, just west of Nigg Bay, which has suffered in recent years due to the closure of the local aluminium factory. Beyond Invergordon, a road branches south to Nigg Ferry. The ferry from Cromarty to **Nigg** was once a major thoroughfare, and now a tiny two-car ferry makes the 20-minute crossing in the summer months, see Transport page 422. From the ferry you get a good view of Nigg Bay, a vast natural harbour used in both world wars by the Royal Navy. Its entry is guarded by the dramatic headlands of the Sutors, identified in folklore as friendly giants. Also gigantic are the oil rigs ranged along the firth and the oil terminal at Nigg, a dramatic and not unpleasant contrast with Lilliputian Cromarty.

Strathpeffer and around → *Phone code: 01997.*

Just along from the Cromarty Firth is Strathpeffer, which gets busy in the summer with coach parties, but it's a pleasant place and there are some excellent walks in the surrounding hills. The little village gained recognition in 1819 when Doctor Morrison, a physician from Aberdeen, bathed in its sulphur springs and cured himself of rheumatoid arthritis. He quickly spread the word and Strathpeffer became a fashionable spa resort attracting thousands of visitors. Two world wars intervened and the town's popularity declined. Today the only reminder of its past is the **Water Sampling Pavilion** in the square where you can test the waters. There's a seasonal TIC ⓘ *main square, T01997-421415, Easter-Nov Mon-Sat 1000-1700*.

Just outside Strathpeffer on the road to Dingwall is the **Highland Museum of Childhood** ⓘ *T01997-421031, Mar-Oct Mon-Sat 1000-1700, Sun 1400-1700, Jul and Aug Mon-Thu 1000-1700 and 1900-2100, Sat 1000-1700, Sun 1400-1700, £1.50, concession £1*, which has many historical displays on childhood in the highlands, as well as collections of dolls, toys and games.

▲ A fine walk is to **Knock Farrel** and the **Touchstone Maze**, site of an Iron-Age vitrified fort which lies at the north end of a ridge known locally as the **Cat's Back**. A marked trail starts from Blackmuir Wood car park. Head up the hill from town, turn left up a road immediately before the youth hostel, and the car park is on the left. The walk is six miles in total and takes about three hours. Aside from OS Landranger sheet 26, the route is also described in a Forestry Commission leaflet Forests of Easter Ross, available from tourist offices.

Another excellent side trip is to **Rogie Falls**, near Contin, which is three miles southwest of Strathpeffer on the main A835 Inverness-Ullapool road. The short walk up to the falls starts from the car park three miles north of Contin on the A835. There

Saintly beginnings

Tain was the birthplace of the 11th-century missionary St Duthac. Pilgrims flocked here in the Middle Ages to his shrine, and a ruin near the links is thought to be the original chapel. His head and heart, encapsulated in gold and silver reliquaries, were later kept in the still extant medieval Collegiate church until their disappearance during the Reformation. The shrine was much favoured by the Stewart kings, notably James IV who on one of his frequent pilgrimages reputedly approached walking penitentially barefoot along the King's Causeway. Tain's status as a place of sanctuary probably explains why Bruce's family fled here during the Wars of Independence.

are also some pleasant woodland walks around here. Experienced hikers can tackle magnificent **Ben Wyvis** (3,432 ft). The route to the summit starts four miles north of Garve, seven miles northwest of Contin.

Tain and around → *Phone code: 01862. Colour map2, grid B2-C2.*

Squeezed between the Cromarty Firth to the south and the Dornoch Firth to the north is the Tain Peninsula, whose largest town is Tain, a place with a 1950's time-warp feel. It has an impressive historical portfolio. Its backstreets are an intriguing jigsaw of imposing merchants' houses, steep vennels, secret gardens and dormer windows. The town of Tain serves a vast hinterland. Inland the hills are little-visited backwoods and farm towns, narrow valleys lined with crofts where cattle graze in boggy haughs and, to the west, glens and moorland. Along the seaboard are the windswept fields of the Tarbat Peninsula. Good sea angling is to be had from the harbours of the otherwise dull coastal villages such as Balintore, and at Shandwick is a massive Pictish stone. It is said that unbaptized children were buried near the stone which is now in the Museum of Scotland in Edinburgh. ►► *For Sleeping, Eating and other listings, see pages 420-422.*

Tain

The **Collegiate church**, see box, is on Castle Brae, just off the High Street, and inside is a 17th-century panel painted with the badges of the trade guilds, a reminder of the town's busy international trade. Another reminder is the imposing 16th-century **Tolbooth** in the High Street. Next to the church is **Tain through Time** ⓘ *T01862-894089, Apr-Oct daily 1000-1800, Nov, Dec and Mar 1200-1600, £3.50, concession £2.50,* a museum housed in the Pilgrimage which charts the town's medieval history. One of Tain's main attractions is the very fine **Glenmorangie whisky distillery** ⓘ *T01862-892477, www.glenmorangie.com, all year Mon-Fri 0900-1700, Jun-Aug also Sat 1000-1600 and Sun 1200-1600, tours from 1030-1530, £2,* just off the A9 to the north of town, where you can see how the world-famous whisky is made and try a sample. Also out of town, just to the south off the A9, is the **Aldie Water Mill**, a restored 16th-century mill in working order, with various high-quality craft shops attached. Nearby is **The Tain Pottery** ⓘ *T01862-893786, 1000-1700,* which you can also visit.

Portnahomack

The seaside village of Portnahomack, or 'port of Colman', is named after the missionary who was keen as mustard to found a religious settlement here. Archaeological work is revealing the importance of this area in Pictish times. The **Tarbat Discovery Centre** ⓘ *T01862-871790,* in Tarbat Old Church, displays recently discovered Pictish stonecarving. From the harbour, with its 18th-century girnals (grain warehouses) and sheltered sandy beach, you can see a huge stretch of the Sutherland coast, and the great sandbanks – the 'gizzen brigs' – at the mouth of the Dornoch Firth. Boat trips are available from the harbour for sea angling. A worthwhile trip is out to Tarbat Ness lighthouse, about three miles north.

Hill of Fearn

South from Portnahomack, just west of the junction of the B9165 and the B9166, is Hill of Fearn. Fearn Abbey was moved here around 1250 from its original site near Edderton, where it was too vulnerable to sea raiders. It later became the parish church, but in 1742 lightning struck the roof which fell in, killing 38 Sunday worshippers. A tragedy was preceded by a fairy harbinger sighted at nearby Loch Eye. In Hill of Fearn is the excellent **Anta Factory Shop** ⓘ *Mon-Sat 1000-1700, Jun-Sep also Sun 1000-1600*, one of the very best places in the country for classy tartan furnishing fabrics, as well as tartan rugs and throws, and pottery.

The Dornoch Firth → *Colour map 2, grid B2.*

Fairies were said to cross the Dornoch Firth on cockle shells and were once seen building a bridge of fairy gold, perhaps a forerunner of the Dornoch Bridge which carries the A9 across the Firth just north of Tain. A more pleasant and interesting route is to follow the A836 along the south shore. From The Struie, reached by the B9176 which branches south at Easter Fearn, there's a panoramic view over the Dornoch Firth and the Sutherland hills. ⏩ *For Sleeping, Eating and other listings, see pages 420-422.*

Edderton to the Kyle of Sutherland

In the churches of Edderton and Kincardine are Pictish stones. Another stands in a field northwest of Edderton, but don't disturb the crops or livestock. A quartz boulder at **Ardgay**, the 'Clach Eiteag', commemorates the cattle tryst and fair which once took place locally.

Ten miles from Ardgay, at the end of lovely Strathcarron, is the isolated **Croick church**, one of the most poignant reminders of the infamous Clearances. Here in 1845, 90 local folk took refuge in the churchyard after they had been evicted from their homes in Glencalvie by the Duke of Sutherland to make way for flocks of sheep. A reporter from *The Times* described the 'wretched spectacle' as men, women and children were carted off, many never to return. The report is there to read. Far more evocative and harrowing, though, are the names and messages the people scratched in spidery copperplate in the window panes.

North of Ardgay is the **Kyle of Sutherland**, where several rivers converge to flood into the sea through lush water meadows. Montrose was defeated here, at Carbisdale, in 1651. Overlooking the Kyle, at Culrain, is the 19th-century **Carbisdale Castle**, once home of the exiled King of Norway, which now houses a youth hostel, see Sleeping page 420. After the Dornoch Ferry disaster of 1809, a bridge was built over the Kyle at **Bonar Bridge**, from where the A949 runs eastwards to join the main A9 just before Dornoch, while the A836 continues north to Lairg (see below). A few miles north of Invershin are the **Falls of Shin**, an excellent place to watch salmon battling upstream on their way to their spawning grounds (best seen June to September). A visitor centre and café/shop – which serves food daily till 1730 – has information about six easy walks in the immediate area; all are under an hour long.

Lairg → *Phone code: 01549.*

Eleven miles north of Bonar Bridge is the uninspiring village of Lairg, the region's main transport hub. Lairg is best known for its annual lamb sale, when young sheep

“” Fairies were said to cross the Dornoch Firth on cockle shells and were once seen building a bridge of fairy gold...

from all over the north of Scotland are bought and sold. It is said that all roads meet at Lairg, and it's certainly a hard place to avoid. From here the A839 heads east to meet the A9 between Dornoch and Golspie, and west to meet the A837 which runs out to Lochinver. The A836 heads north to Tongue, and south to Bonar Bridge. The A838 meanwhile heads northwest to Laxford Bridge and on to Durness, near Cape Wrath. There's a tourist information centre ⓘ *T01549-402160, Apr-Oct daily.*

There are several interesting walks around the village, some of which lead to prehistoric sites such as the Neolithic hut circles at nearby **Ord Hill**. These walks, and many others in the region, are described with maps in the Forestry Commission's leaflet Forests of the Far North, which is available at the Ferrycroft Countryside Centre and the TIC.

Dornoch and around → *Phone code: 01862. Colour map 2, grid B2.*

Dornoch is another architectural delight, with its deep, golden sandstone houses and leafy cathedral square. Bishop Gilbert of Moravia (Moray) built the cathedral circa 1245. His family's success in gaining a foothold in Northeast Scotland against the Norsemen was rewarded with the Earldom of Sutherland. It was trouble with the Jarls which prompted Gilbert to move his power base here from Caithness, mindful that his predecessor had been boiled in butter by the locals. The tourist information centre ⓘ *T01862-810400, Apr-Oct Mon-Sat*, is on the main square.

The 13th-century **cathedral** ⓘ *Mon-Fri 0730-2000, you can climb the cathedral tower during Jul and Aug*, was badly damaged in 1570, then subjected to an ill-conceived 'restoration' by the Countess of Sutherland in 1835. Among the few surviving features is a series of gargoyles, including a green man, and the effigy of an unknown knight. Opposite the cathedral is the 16th-century Bishop's Palace, now a hotel, see Sleeping page 420.

Nowadays Dornoch is famous for its links golf course, rated as one of the world's finests and relatively easy to get on. It overlooks miles of dunes and pristine sandy beach. A stone near the links marks the spot where the last witch in Scotland was burned in 1722. Folklore recounts a bloody battle against raiding Vikings in 1259 on the beach at Embo, just to the north, in which Sir Richard Murray was killed. The battle is commemorated at the Earl's Cross. Trout fishing is available on Dornoch Lochans; enquire locally.

Straggling crofting townships such as **Rogart** are scattered through the glens and around the coast, all occupied and worked vigorously. The coastal population was swollen in the 19th century by tenants evicted from the inland glens, resettled here and encouraged to try fishing at such villages as Embo. Others joined the eager flood of emigrants to the New World already under way. Crofting tenancies still exist, but crofters now enjoy more protection, see page 465.

North of Dornoch is **Loch Fleet**, a river estuary with a ferocious tide race at its mouth and an SNH reserve protecting rare birds and plants. The rotting skeletons of the fishing fleet abandoned in the First World War lie in the sand on the south shore west of the car park. Nearby **Skibo Castle** is where Madge and Mr Ritchie tied the knot, in relative secrecy. It is an exclusive club, but details of accommodation are available from the Dornoch tourist office. There are several walks in the forestry plantations in the area.

Far northeast coast

North of Dornoch, the A9 follows the coast of Sutherland into the neighbouring county of Caithness through a series of straggling villages, still haunted by the memories of the Duke of Sutherland, one of Scotland's most odious landowners. The chief town in these parts is Wick, once the busiest herring port in Europe. ▸▸ *For Sleeping, Eating and other listings, see pages 420-422.*

Golspie → *Phone code: 01408. Colour map 2, grid B2. Population: 1,650.*

There is little to recommend the dull little town of Golspie, though it does have a couple of banks and supermarkets. There's an 18-hole golf course, and the **Orcadian Stone Company** has a large display of fossils and geological specimens from the Highlands and beyond. The town lives in the dark shadow of the Sutherlands. On **Beinn a'Bhraggaidh** (1,293 ft), to the southwest, is a huge, 100 ft-high monument to the Duke of Sutherland. Those who make it up to the monument and who know something of the Duke's many despicable acts may find the inscription risible, as it describes him as "a judicious, kind and liberal landlord". There's no reference to the fact that he forcibly evicted 15,000 tenants from his estate. Not surprisingly, locals would like to see this eyesore removed from the landscape, broken into tiny pieces and then scattered far and wide. Unfortunately, they have thus far been unsuccessful.

The aptly named **Dunrobin Castle** ⓘ *T01408-633177, Apr-May and 1-15 Oct Mon-Sat 1030-1630, Sun 1200-1630, 1 Jun-30 Sep Mon-Sat 1030-1730, Sun 1200-1730, £6.70, 1 mile north of the village*, is the ancient seat of the Dukes of Sutherland, who once owned more land than anyone else in the British Empire. Much enlarged and aggrandized in the 19th century with fairytale turrets, the enormous 189-room castle, the largest house in the Highlands, is stuffed full of fine furniture, paintings, tapestries and objets d'art and bears witness to their obscene wealth. The castle overlooks beautiful gardens laid out with box hedges, ornamental trees and fountains. In stormy weather you should listen to the sea crashing on the beach beyond the walls. The museum is an animal-lover's nightmare and almost a caricature of the aristocracy, with a spectacular Victorian taxidermy collection. There are also local antiquities, some from ancient brochs, and Pictish stonecarvings.

Brora → *Phone code: 01408. Colour map 2, grid B2. Population: 1,860.*

Brora sits at the mouth of the River Brora which, as everywhere on this coast, is the site of a once-lucrative salmon netting industry. At the harbour, the ice house is a relic of the herring boom. Coal mines, opened in the 16th century, salt pans and a brickworks are all defunct. Still very much alive, however, is **Hunter's**, the local weavers of heavyweight traditional tweeds, and a good place to invest in some natty headwear. A mile or so north of town is the fairly ordinary **Clynelish distillery** ⓘ *T01408-623000, Easter-Sep Mon-Fri 1000-1700, Oct 1100-1600, Nov-Easter by appointment, £4*. **Castle Cole** in lovely Strath Brora, eight miles northwest, is one of several ruined brochs. Another, **Carn Liath** (signposted), is by the main road, three miles south of Brora.

Whether you're staying or just passing through don't miss Capaldi's, on the High Street, for exquisite home-made Italian ice cream.

Helmsdale → *Phone code: 01431. Colour map 2, grid B2.*

North of Brora is the former herring port of Helmsdale, which gets busy in the summer. The village is most notable for its excellent **Timespan Heritage Centre** ⓘ *T01431-821327, Easter-Oct Mon-Sat 0930-1700, Sun 1400-1700, £4, concession £2, children £1.75*, which brings the history of the Highlands to life through a series of high-tech displays, sound effects and an audiovisual programme. The TIC ⓘ *T01431-821640, Apr-Sep Mon-Sat 1000-1700*, is on the south side of the village, by the A9.

After goldrush

A short drive from Helmsdale, up the Strath of Kildonan (or Strath Ullie), is Baile an Or (Gaelic for 'goldfield'), site of the great Sutherland Gold Rush of 1869. It all started after local man Robert Gilchrist returned home from the Australian gold fields only to discover gold here, on his doorstep. His success brought others rushing to Kildonan, and soon a shanty town had sprung up to accommodate them.

Within a year the gold rush was over, but small amounts are still found today. Anyone who fancies their luck can try a bit of gold panning in the Kildonan Burn at Baile an Or, about a mile from Kildonan train station. You can rent out gold panning kits at Strath Ullie Crafts & Fishing Tackle, opposite the Timespan Heritage Centre in Helmsdale, for £2.50 per day, and licences are free.

North from Helmsdale the A9 climbs spectacularly up the **Ord of Caithness** and over the pass enters a desolate, treeless landscape; an area devastated during the Clearances. To get some idea of the hardships people had to endure, stop at the ruined crofting village of **Badbea**, just beyond Ousdale. At **Berriedale**, a farm track leads west to the Wag, from where you can climb **Morven** (2,313 ft), the highest hill in Caithness, with amazing views across the whole county.

Dunbeath → *Phone code: 01593. Colour map 2, grid B3.*

The A9 coast road then drops down into Dunbeath, a pleasant little village at the mouth of a small *strath* (or glen). This was the birthplace of one of Scotland's foremost writers, Neil Gunn (1891-1973). His finest works, such as *The Silver Darlings* and *Highland River*, reflect his experiences of growing up in the northeast and are fascinating accounts of life here during the days of the herring boom, though the sleepy harbour of today is barely recognizable as the erstwhile bustling fishing port. The villages of Dunbeath, and Latherton to the north, are included on the Neil Gunn Trail, as is the beautiful walk up the glen, described in the leaflet available at the **Dunbeath Heritage Centre** ⓘ *T01593-731233, Apr-Sep daily 1100-1700, £2, concession £1, children free*. Here, you can learn all about the life and works of the famous novelist as well as the history of Caithness. Just outside the village is the **Laidhay Croft Museum** ⓘ *T01593-731370, Apr-Oct daily 1000-1800, £1, children £0.50*, a restored traditional longhouse with stable, house and byre all under the same roof.

Wick and around → *Phone code: 01955. Colour map 2, grid A4.*

A century ago Wick was Europe's busiest herring port, its harbour jam-packed with fishing boats and larger ships exporting tons of salted fish to Russia, Scandinavia and the West Indian slave plantations. The fishing industry has long since gone, and the demise of the nearby nuclear power station at Douneray has only added to the sense of a place that's past its best. However, there are some interesting archaeological sites in Caithness, as well as the dramatic landscapes, and Wick makes a useful base for exploring the area. There is a tourist information centre ⓘ *Whitechapel Rd (just off the High St), T01955-602596, all year Mon-Fri 0900-1700, Sun 0900-1300.*

Wick is actually two towns. On one side of the river is Wick proper and on the other is Pulteneytown, the model town planned by Thomas Telford for the British Fisheries Society in 1806 to house evicted crofters who came to work here. Now it's one great living museum of fishermen's cottages and derelict sheds and stores around the near-deserted quays. It gives a good idea of the scale of the herring trade during its heyday in the mid-19th century, when over 1,000 boats set sail to catch the 'silver darlings'. Here, on Bank Row, is the superb **Wick Heritage Centre** ⓘ *T01955-605393, May-Sep Mon-Sat 1000-1700, £2, children £0.50*. The highlight of the centre is its massive photographic collection dating from the late 19th century.

Three miles north of Wick are the impressive 15th-century clifftop ruins of **Sinclair and Girnigoe Castle**. On the A99 heading north out of town is the **Caithness Glass Visitors Centre** ⓘ *T01955-602286, Mon-Thu 0900-1630*, where you can watch the famous glass being blown. There is a good walk along the rocky shore east of town to The Trinkie, and about a mile further on to the Brig o' Trams. Ask for details at the TIC. Before Wick, at Ulbster, is another archaeological site, the **Cairn o' Get**. Opposite the sign are the precipitous **Whaligoe Steps**, which lead to a tiny, picturesque harbour.

One of the most fascinating archaeological sites in the north are the well-preserved **Grey Cairns of Camster**. These chambered cairns, dating from the third and fourth millenia BC, are burial mounds of stone raised around carefully structured circular chambers with narrow entrance passages. To get there, head a mile east of Lybster on the A9, then turn left on to the minor road leading north to Watten. The cairns are five miles along this road, on the left-hand side. They comprise two enormous prehistoric burial chambers dating from 2500 BC. They are amazingly complete, with corbelled ceilings, and can be entered on hands and knees through narrow passageways.

Sleeping

Cromarty *p413*
For such an appealing place, there's precious little accommodation, so it's advisable to book ahead during the summer.
C Royal Hotel, Marine Terr, T01381-600217, www.royalcromartyhotel.co.uk. The best place to stay, with a good restaurant (**£££**), and cheaper meals are available in the bar.
E Beechfield House, 4 Urquhart Ct, T01381-600308, faericketts@btinternet.com. Out of a couple of B&Bs, this is a very good option.

Dingwall and around *p414*
B Tulloch Castle Hotel, T01349-861325, www.tullochcastle.co.uk. This 12th-century castle is the smartest place around.
F Blackrock Bunkhouse, Evanton, T01349-830917, open 1 Apr-31 Oct. Basic.

Strathpeffer and around *p414*
The best accommodation is in Contin, 3 miles southwest of Strathpeffer.
B Coull House Hotel, T01997-421487, www.milford.co.uk/go/coulhouse.html. Top of the list is this elegant 19th-century country house offering fine food. Excellent choice.
C Brunstane Lodge Hotel, Golf Course Rd, Strathpeffer, T01997-421261, www.brunstanelodge.com, open Mar-Dec, which serves decent cheap bar meals.
D Craigvar, on the Square, Strathpeffer, T01997-421622, www.craigvar.com. Elegant, good value B&B.
D-E Dunraven Lodge, Golf Course Rd, T01997-421210, sandra.iddon@ntlworld.com. Good value B&B.
E Inver Lodge, T01997-421392, open Mar-Dec. A decent B&B.
E Taigh an Eilein, T01997-421009, lorna.mac@talk21.com, open Apr-Sep. There are several B&Bs in Contin, including the very grand-looking house.

Tain *p415*
L Mansfield House Hotel, Scotsburn Rd, T01862-892052, www.mansfield-house.co.uk. 19th-century baronial splendour and superb cuisine. Restaurant also open to non-residents (**£££**).
C Morangie House Hotel, Morangie Rd, T01862-892281, www.morangiehotel.com. It's popular locally for its food (**££**) and is open for lunch and dinner. Excellent value.
E Golf View House, at 13 Knockbreck Rd, T01862-892856, www.golfview.co.uk. A modest B&B.

Lairg *p416*
D-E The Nip Inn, on the main street, T01549-402243, www.nipinn.co.uk. Also does bar meals.

F **Sleeperzzz.com**, T01408-641343, www.sleeperzzz.com. There are several B&Bs and a campsite too, but the most interesting place to stay is 9 miles east at Rogart train station, where you can get cheap hostel accommodation at the 2 old rail carriages that have been converted to sleep 16 people. There's a 10% discount for bike or train users.

Dornoch and around *p417*

There are also lots of good B&Bs and a campsite, in addition to these options.

L **The Royal Golf Hotel**, T/F01862-810283, www.morton-hotels.com, next to the first tee. Plush hotel catering to golfers. Good restaurant (**£££-££**).

B **The Two Quails**, Castle St, T01862-811811, www.2quail.com. 3 rooms. Restaurant with rooms run by Michael and Kerensa Carr. Well-equipped rooms and superb cuisine (**£££**).

B-D **Dornoch Castle Hotel**, T01862-810216, www.dornochcastle.com, open Apr-Oct. Formerly the Bishop's Palace, this 16th-century building is full of character and boasts excellent food (**£££**).

F **Carbisdale Castle Youth Hostel**, T01549-421232, open end Feb-end Oct (except the first 2 weeks in May). The largest and most sumptuous hostel in Scotland, and possibly anywhere else, is half a mile up a steep hill from the station.

Brora *p418*

D **Glenaveron**, on Golf Rd, T/F01408-621601, www.glenaveron.com. Among the many B&Bs here this is excellent.

Helmsdale *p418*

B-C **Navidale House Hotel**, T01431-821258, open Feb-Nov. A good place to eat.

D **Broomhill House**, T01431-821259. A B&B with a distinctive turret.

E **Torbuie**, T01431-821424, Navidale.

F **SYHA Youth Hostel**, T01431-821577, open mid-May to early Oct.

Wick and around *p419*

A-B **Portland Arms Hotel**, 15 miles south, in Lybster, T01593-721208, www.portlandarms.co.uk. Best around, a 19th-century coaching inn, full of character serving great food (**£££**).

C **Mackay's Hotel**, Union St, T01955-602323, www.mackayshotel.co.uk. Nothing fancy but handy for the train station.

The best of the guest houses and B&Bs are:

E **The Clachan**, on South Rd, T01955-605384; and

E **Wellington Guest House**, 41-43 High St, T01955-603287, open Mar-Oct.

Eating

Cromarty *p413*

££ **Binnie's Tearoom**, Church St, a great place for tea and scones.

££ **Cromarty Arms**, opposite the Cromarty Courthouse, for cheap bar food. Also has live music some nights.

££ **Thistle's Restaurant**, Church St, T01381-600471. Has an imaginative menu, including interesting vegetarian dishes.

Portnahomack *p415*

££ **The Oyster Catcher**, T01862-871560. A great place to eat out here is this small café-restaurant serving snacks and lunches, and dinner from 1930 (if booked). Crêpes are a speciality, but it also does pasta, seafood and fish.

Helmsdale *p418*

££ **La Mirage**, opposite the TIC. Daily 1200-2045 (Dec-Apr till 1900). Famous tearoom whose erstwhile proprietrix, the inimitable Nancy Sinclair, modelled herself, and her tearoom, on Barbara Cartland, queen of romantic novels. The whole effect is pure kitsch. Good fish and chips.

Wick and around *p419*

The best places to eat are out of town.

££ **Bower Inn**, see p411.

££ **Old Smiddy Inn**, in Thrumster, 5 miles south of Wick, T01955-651256, open daily 1200-2100.

££ **Queen's Hotel**, Francis St, T01955-602992. Probably the best place in town. It has a varied menu.

£ **Cabrelli's**, 134 High St, also in town is a great caff serving pizza and fish and chips.

Shopping

Tain *p415*

Bannerman's, a fish and seafood wholesalers, sells local mussels.

Brown's Gallery, Castle Brae. Showcases work by Highland artists.

Dornoch and around *p417*
The Dornoch Bookshop, High St, T01862-810165, is the only bookshop in the area and stocks local books.

Activities and tours

Cromarty *p413*
Dolphin-spotting boat trips leave from Cromarty, but make sure you go with an accredited operator.
Dolphin Ecosse, T01381-600323. Half- and full-day trips leave from the harbour to see porpoises, seals, dolphins, and perhaps even killer whales further out. Accredited operator.

Transport

Cromarty *p413*
Highland Bus & Coach, T01463-233371, runs a bus service from **Inverness** to **Fortrose** and **Cromarty** (4-7 times daily Mon-Sat). There is also a bus service to and from **Dingwall** on Wed and Thu.

A 2-car ferry crosses to **Nigg** every half hour from Apr to Oct, 0900-1800.

Dingwall and around *p414*
There are hourly buses between **Inverness** and **Invergordon**, via Dingwall. There are also hourly buses between **Inverness** and Dingwall via **Muir of Ord**. There are buses between Dingwall and **Rosemarkie** (twice a day Mon-Thu), and between Dingwall and **Cromarty** (Wed and Thu).

Dingwall is on the rail line between **Inverness** and **Kyle of Lochalsh** and **Thurso**. There are several trains daily in each direction (30 mins to Inverness).

Strathpeffer and around *p414*
There are regular buses between Strathpeffer and **Dingwall** (see above).

Tain *p415*
Citylink buses between **Inverness** and **Thurso** pass through Tain 4 times a day. There are also buses to **Portmahomack** (4 times daily Mon-Thu), **Balintore** (5-6 times daily Mon-Sat), **Lairg** via **Bonar Bridge** (3 times daily Mon-Sat) and **Dornoch** via **Bonar Bridge** (once a day Mon-Thu) with Inverness Traction, T01463-239292, and Rapson's of Brora, T01408-621245.

Tain is on the **Inverness-Thurso** rail line and there are 3 trains daily in each direction.

Lairg *p416*
Inverness Traction buses, T01463-239292, run from here to **Ullapool**, with connections to **Lochinver** and **Durness**, from May to early Oct (Mon-Sat). Lairg is also the central point for several **postbus** routes, T01463-256228.

Trains between **Inverness** and **Thurso** stop at Lairg and Rogart stations 3 times daily.

Dornoch and around *p417*
Buses (hourly Mon-Sat, 5 times on Sun) between **Inverness** and **Lairg** stop in **Ardgay** and **Bonar Bridge**. **Citylink** buses between Inverness and Thurso also stop in Dornoch 4 daily.

Trains between **Inverness** and **Thurso** stop at **Ardgay** and **Culrain**.

Helmsdale *p418*
Buses and trains are the same as for Wick (see below). Helmsdale is on the Inverness-Wick/Thurso rail line.

Wick and around *p419*
Air A few miles north of town, is Wick airport, T01955-602215. Daily direct flights to and from **Kirkwall** (Orkney), **Sumburgh** (Shetland), **Aberdeen** and **Edinburgh** with and British Airways Express, T08457-733377. Also direct flights to/from **Newcastle** with Eastern Airways, T01955-603914. There's a **postbus** service to Wick airport Mon-Sat at 1015.
Bus Scottish Citylink, T08705-505050, buses between **Inverness** and **Thurso** stop en route in **Wick** (3 daily). There are also regular local buses to **Thurso**, via **Halkirk** or **Castletown**, and buses to **Helmsdale** (2-6 times daily Mon-Sat, 1-4 on Sun) and **John O'Groats** (5 daily Mon-Sat, 4 on Sun). The train and bus stations are next to each other behind the hospital.
Car/bike hire **Richard's Garage**, Francis St, T01955-604123.
Train Trains leave for **Inverness** (3 daily Mon-Sat, 2 on Sun; 3¾ hrs) via **Thurso**, **Helmsdale**, **Golspie**, **Lairg** and **Dingwall**. The train station is behind the hospital.

Strathspey and the Cairngorms

One of Scotland's busiest tourist areas is Strathspey, the broad valley of the River Spey, Scotland's second longest river, which rises high in the hills above Loch Laggan and flows northeast to its mouth on the Moray Firth. The lower reaches are famous for salmon fishing and whisky and are covered in the Speyside section of this guide (see page 533), while the upper reaches attract outdoor sports enthusiasts in droves. Hemmed in between the mighty Monadhliath Mountains to the north and the magnificent Cairngorms, Britain's second highest range, to the south, this is an area which offers excellent hiking, watersports, mountain biking and above all, winter skiing. The Cairngorms were officially declared a national park in September 2003, the largest in Britain, which extends from Grantown on Spey to the heads of the Angus Glens. *▸▸ For Sleeping, Eating and other listings, see pages 425-428.*

Ins and outs

Getting there and around This part of the Highland region is easily accessible by public transport as Aviemore is one of the main hubs, with regular buses and trains to and from Inverness, Perth, Edinburgh and Glasgow. *▸▸ For further details, see page 428.*

Tourist information The TIC in Aviemore ⓘ *Grampian Rd, about 400 yds south of the train station, T01479-810363, Apr-Oct Mon-Fri 0900-1800, Sat 1000-1700, Sun 1000-1600, Nov-Mar Mon-Fri 0900-1700, Sat 1000-1700*, will book accommodation as well as provide free maps and leaflets on local attractions and change foreign currency. The train station, banks, restaurants and pretty much everything else are all found along Grampian Road. Buses stop here too.

Aviemore → *Phone code: 01479. Colour map 4, grid A3. Population: 2,500.*

The main focus of the area is the tourist resort of Aviemore, a name synonymous with winter sports. In the 1960s Aviemore was transformed from a sleepy Highland village into the jumble of concrete buildings, tacky gift shops and sprawling coach parks that it is today. The extent of the tourist tat here is so awful it makes Fort William seem charmingly understated by comparison, however it is working hard at turning itself around and was recently described as 'most improved' resort. It is certainly more pleasant than it used to be and the range of accommodation is improving.

There's nothing of real interest in Aviemore. The real enjoyment lies in the surrounding mountains and forests, though there are a few interesting places close at hand. A great place for kids is the **Cairngorm Reindeer Centre** ⓘ *Glen More Forest Park, on the road from Coylumbridge, 7 miles from Aviemore, T01479-861228£6, children £3*, where there are guided walks to see the herd and feed them leave daily at 1100 and also at 1430 during the summer.

Around Aviemore

Aviemore is surrounded by towering peaks, lochs, rivers and forests of native Caledonian pine which are home to rare wildlife such as pine martens, wildcats, red squirrels, ospreys and capercaillie, and Britain's only herd of wild reindeer. Most of upper Strathspey is privately owned by the Glen More Forest Park and Rothiemurchus Estate which has been in the possession of the Grant family since the 16th century, but both owners allow free access to their lands and provide generous outdoor facilities.

Much of this area is better known to many as Monarch of the Glen *country, where the successful BBC TV series is filmed. The fictional Glenbogle is actually Ardverikie, near Loch Laggan, but many places like Aviemore, Grantown-on-Spey, Newtonmore and Kingussie have featured in the series.*

An easy circular walk of about four hours around Loch an Eilean in Rothiemurchus Estate starts from the end of the side road which turns east off the B970 two miles south of Aviemore. From the car park at the end of the road head for the lochside. The route around the loch is clearly marked and it's difficult to lose your way as it follows the loch shore. It's a very pleasant walk through woodland with views of a 14th-century castle ruin on an island in the middle of the loch. You can extend the walk by around a mile by including the circuit around Loch Gamhna. The paths around Loch an Eilein are also connected with the massive network of trails around Rothiemurchus. OS Sheet 36 covers the route.

Lairig Ghru

The famous Lairig Ghru is an ancient route through the Cairngorms which passes between Ben Macdui and Braeriach. It is a very strenuous walk and only for fit and experienced hikers. An easier propostion is a 12-mile loop which leads to the start of the Lairig Ghru pass, starting from Loch Morlich.

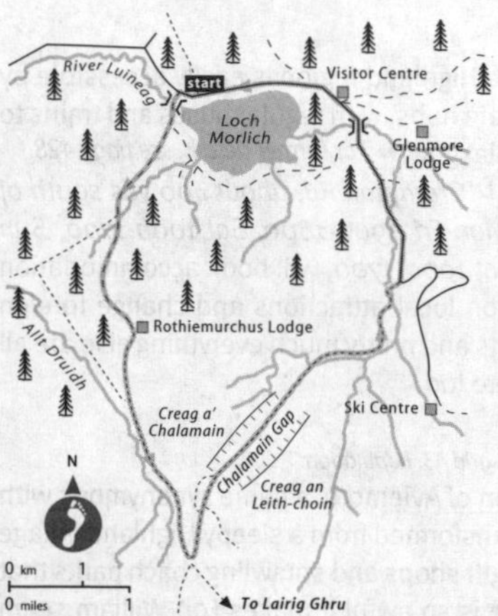

To reach Loch Morlich take the B970 east from the southern end of Aviemore, beyond Coylumbridge. The route starts at the western end of Loch Morlich where a forestry track runs south from the road. It leads to a bridge over the River Luineag. Cross the bridge and continue along the track, keeping straight on where another track heads off left. About a mile further on, another track heads off to the right, but keep to the left fork, signposted for Rothiemurchus Lodge.

The track climbs up towards the lodge. Just before it, turn right on to a clear track which leads up to a reservoir. Soon another track heads off to the right signposted for the Lairig Ghru. Follow this path through heather moorland. The path then heads left, climbing up through open moorland to the lip of the glen. The entrance to the Lairig Ghru is straight ahead.

After about a mile, as the hills begin to encroach on either side, a rough path almost doubles back to the left. Follow this path up the slope to the gap between Creag a' Chalamain and Creag an Leith- choin. The deep gully, the Chalamain Gap, is filled with huge boulders and requires great care when clambering through it. Beyond the gully a path leads through heather and pine saplings, dropping down to the side of a burn, then climbing up on the other side of the burn. Continue on this path, which then drops steeply down to the side of the burn. Cross the footbridge and climb the slope beyond to reach the main road. Turn left along the road to return to the start of the route.

Boat of Garten → *Phone code: 01479. Colour map 4, grid A3.*

Eight miles northeast of Aviemore is the tiny village of Boat of Garten which suddenly shot to fame when a pair of ospreys, which had disappeared from these shores, reappeared on nearby Loch Garten, two miles east of the village. Now these beautiful birds of prey have established themselves here and elsewhere and there are thought be well over 100 pairs throughout the Highlands. **Abernethy Forest RSPB Reserve** ⓘ *T01479-821409, daily in season 1000-1800, £2.50 for non-members, on the shore of Loch Garten*, is best visited during the nesting season, between late April and August, when the RSPB opens an observation centre. This is the only place in the world to see Scottish crossbills. You can also see ospreys at the Rothiemurchus trout loch at Inverdruie, and maybe even on Loch Morlich and Loch Insh. The reserve is also home to several other rare species such as capercaillie, whooper swans and red squirrels. 'Caperwatch' takes place from April-mid May 0530-0800.

Carrbridge → *Phone code: 01479. Colour map 4, grid A3.*

At Carrbridge, a pleasant little village seven miles north of Aviemore, is the **Landmark Forest Heritage Park** ⓘ *T01479-841613, Apr to mid-Jul daily 0930-1800, mid-Jul to Aug 0930-1900, Sep and Oct 0930-1800, Nov-Mar 1000-1700, £7.95, children £5.95*, a woodland theme park which combines entertainment, education and shopping. There's a raised Treetop Trail for viewing wildlife, a fire tower, maze and various nature trails and fun rides. It manages to avoid being tacky and is good fun for kids. In the village itself is the decidedly fragile-looking 18th-century **Bridge of Carr**, which is not for vertigo sufferers.

Kingussie → *Phone code: 01540. Colour map 4, grid A2. Population: 1,500.*

The quiet village of Kingussie (pronounced King-yoosie) lies 12 miles southwest of Aviemore and makes a pleasant alternative as a place to stay. The main attraction here is the excellent **Highland Folk Museum** ⓘ *T01540-661307, May-Aug Mon-Fri 0930-1730, Sat and Sun 1300-1700; Apr, Sep and Oct guided tours only Mon-Fri 1030-1630, £4, concession and children £2.40*, which contains a fascinating collection of traditional highland artefacts, as well as a farming museum, an old smokehouse, a water mill and traditional Hebridean 'blackhouse'. During the summer there are also demonstrations of spinning, woodcarving and peat-fire baking.

Another worthwhile attraction is **Ruthven Barracks**, standing on a hillock across the river. This former barracks was built by the English Redcoats as part of their campaign to tame the Highlands after the first Jacobite rising in 1715. It was destroyed by the Jacobites in the wake of defeat at Culloden to prevent it from falling into enemy hands, and it was from here that Bonnie Prince Charlie sent his final order which signalled the end of his doomed cause. Access is free and the ruins are particularly attractive at night when floodlit.

At nearby Kincraig village, between Kingussie and Aviemore, is the **Highland Wildlife Park** ⓘ *T01540-651270, Apr, May, Sep and Oct daily 1000-1800, Jun-Aug till 1900, Nov-Mar 1000-1600, park tours £7.50, concession £6, children £5*, which has a captive collection of rare native animals. Those who mourn the loss of the hit TV show, *One Man and His Dog*, will be excited at the prospect of visiting the **Working Sheepdogs Show** ⓘ *T01540-651310, Apr-end Oct, £4, at the nearby Leault Farm*, where you can see demonstrations of dogs rounding up a flock of sheep.

The tourist information centre ⓘ *T01540-661297*, is housed in the Folk Museum and has the same opening hours.

Grantown-on-Spey → *Phone code: 01479. Colour map 4, grid A3. Population: 3,250.*

This genteel Georgian holiday town is 15 miles northeast of Aviemore and attracts the more mature tourist by the coach-load. Everything here is geared towards fishing, and anyone wishing to get kitted out in proper style should get themselves down to either **Mortimers** or **Ritchies** on the High Street. The tourist information centre ⓘ *T01479-872773, Apr to Oct 0900-1800*, is also here.

Sleeping

Aviemore *p423*
D Vermont Guest House, T01479-810470; **D Ravenscraig Guest House**, T01479-810278, www.aviemoreonline.com, B&Bs both on Grampian Rd.

F Aviemore Independent Bunkhouse and Backpackers Hostel, T01479-811137, on Dalfaber Rd.

F SYHA hostel, T01479-810345, Grampian Rd, near the tourist office and open all year.

Around Aviemore *p423*

A **Corrour House Hotel**, Inverdruie, 2 miles southeast of Aviemore, T01479- 810220, www.corrourhouse.co.uk, open Dec-Oct. This Victorian country house oozes charm, enjoys wonderful views and offers superb cuisine. The best choice in the area.

C **Rowan Tree Restaurant & Guest House**, Loch Alvie, 1½ miles south of Aviemore on the B9152, T01479-810207, enquiries@ rowantreehotel.com, open Jan-Dec. This is one of the oldest hotels in the area and offers excellent food (lunch **£**, dinner **££**).

C **Lynwilg House**, T01479-811685, 1 mile south of Aviemore at Lynwilg, marge@lyn wilg.co.uk. Set in a beautiful house, this charming and friendly guest house also has a reputation for good food.

C **Old Minister's House**, Rothiemurchus, T01479-812181, www.theoldministers house.co.uk, set in its own grounds.

Camping

Forest Enterprise site, Glenmore, T01479-861271.

Rothiemurchus Camping & Caravan Park, Coylumbridge, T01479-812800.

Boat of Garten *p424*

B-C **Boat Hotel**, T01479-831258, www.boat hotel.co.uk, offers cheap and tasty meals.

C **Heathbank - The Victorian House**, T01479-831234, www.heathbankhotel.co.uk, is a must for art nouveau lovers. Good food.

C **Glenavon House**, T01479-831213, is a lovely guest house on Kinchurdy Rd.

C **Moorfield House**, Deshar Rd, T01479-831646, www.moorfieldhouse.com, is also a good choice.

Camping

Boat of Garten Caravan and Camping Park, T01479-831652.

Carrbridge *p425*

A-B **Dalrachney Lodge Hotel**, T01479-841252, www.dalrachney.co.uk. Top of the range is this stylish hotel. A former Victorian hunting lodge with a good restaurant.

D **Cairn Hotel**, T01479-841212, cairn.carrbrid ge@lineone.net. A comfortable option serving good-value bar meals.

F **Carrbridge Bunkhouse Hostel**, T01479-841250, Dalrachney House, half a mile north.

Kingussie *p425*

C **Arden House**, Newtonmore Rd, T01540-661369, www.arden-house.info. A good guest house.

C **The Osprey Hotel**, Ruthven Rd, T01540-661510, www.ospreyhotel.co.uk, is a comfortable little hotel with a very good restaurant (**£££**).

C **Scot House Hotel**, Newtonmore Rd, T01540-661351, www.scothouse.com, is another good choice and also offers great food (lunch **£**; dinner **££-£££**).

D **Avondale House**, Newtonmore Rd, T01540-661731, avondalehouse@talk21. com. Comfortable guest house.

D **Glengarry**, East Terrace, T01540-661386, www.scot89.freeserve.co.uk. A B&B.

D **Greystones**, on Acres Rd, T01540-661052, greystones@ lineone.net. Comfortble B&B.

D **Homewood Lodge**, Newtonmore Rd, T01540-661507, www.homewood-lodge -kingussie.co.uk. Friendly and good value.

F **Bothan Airigh Bunkhouse**, T01540-661051, is at Insh, a few miles east of Ruthven Barracks on the B970.

F **Kirkbeag Hostel**, T01540-651298, is in Kincraig, between Kingussie and Aviemore.

F **The Laird's Bothy**, T01540-661334, High St, next to **Tipsy Laird** pub. A decent hostel.

Grantown-on-Spey *p425*

As you'd expect in such a respectable place, there's a wide range of upmarket accommodation and a number of very good places to eat. The best places in town are all on Woodland Terr.

L **Culdearn House**, Woodlands Terr, T01479-872106, www.culdearn.com. Best place to stay, offering wonderful food.

A-B **Muckrach Lodge Hotel & Restaurant**, a few miles southwest of town at Dulnain Bridge, T01479-851257, www.muckrach. co.uk, is this handsome hotel, with a well-regarded restaurant.

C **Ardconnell House**, Woodlands Terr, T01479-872104, info@ardconnel.com. Another great choice offering excellent food.

C **Auchendean Lodge Hotel**, a few miles southwest of town, T01479-851347, www. auchendean.com. An elegant hotel at Dulnain Bridge with a superb restaurant.

F **Speyside Backpackers**, T01479-873514, an independent hostel, also known as The Stop-Over, at 16 The Square. Great value.

Eating

Aviemore *p423*

££ Old Bridge Inn, T01479-811137, on Dalfaber Rd. Apart from the hotels and guest houses listed in Sleeping, this is the best place to eat in Aviemore. A lovely old pub, it serves excellent-value food and hosts ceilidhs and Highland dinner dances in the summer months.

££ Cairngorm Hotel, T01479-810233, also has a good reputation for food locally.

Around Aviemore *p423*

££ Loch Insh Watersports Centre, at Kincraig, between Aviemore and Kingussie, a good lochside restaurant which doubles as a café during the day.

Kingussie *p425*

£££ The Cross, T01540-661166, on Tweed Mill Brae, a private drive leading off Ardbroilach Rd. This is an outstanding place to eat. Award-winning, it is expensive but it is worth it. They also have rooms (**A** for dinner, B&B). Open Tue-Sat, Feb just before Christmas.

££ Osprey Hotel and **££ Scot House Hotel** both have very good restaurants.

£ La Cafetière is a nice café.

£ Tipsy Laird pub serves good meals and real ales.

Activities and tours

Fishing

Fishing is a major pursuit in the area. You can fish for trout and salmon on the River Spey, and the Rothiemurchus Estate has trout fishing on its stocked loch at Inverdruie, where you can hire rods. Fishing permits cost around £10-15 per day for the stocked lochs and £20-30 per day for the River Spey. They are sold at local shops such as **Speyside Sports** in Aviemore, and at **Monster Activities** which also hires out rods and tackle. **Alvie Estate**, T01540-651255, near Kingussie also hires rods.

Horse riding

Horse riding and pony trekking are on offer at various places throughout Strathspey.

Alvie Stables, Alvie, near Kincraig, T01540-651409, T0831-495397 (mob).

Carrbridge Trekking Centre, Station Rd, Carrbridge, T01479-841602.

Strathspey Highland Pony Centre, Rowanlea, Faebuie, Grantown-on-Spey, T01479-873073.

Mountain biking

Rothiemurchus and Glen More estates are great areas for this, with lots of great trails.

Bothy Bikes, Unit 7, Grampian Rd, Aviemore, T01479-810111, daily 0900-1800. Bike hire and good advice on routes is available here.

Rothiemurchus Visitor Centre (see Walking below) at Inverdruie has route maps and you can also hire bikes.

Skiing

Cairngorm is Scotland's longest-established ski resort and, though it cannot compare to anything in the Alps or North America, it remains Scotland's largest ski area, with 28 runs and over 20 miles of pistes. When the sun shines, the snowfall is good and the crowds are thin, it can be a very satisfying experience. The season normally runs from Jan until the snow disappears, which can be as late as Apr.

Cairngorm Ski Area, 9 miles southeast of Aviemore, above Loch Morlich in Glen More Forest Park, is reached by a frequent bus service. You can rent skis etc (£13 per day, and snowboard hire is £16) and buy a lift pass (£21 per day) from the **Day Lodge**, T01479-861261, at the foot of the ski area.

Cairngorm Mountain Railway, T01479-861261, www.cairngorm mountain.com, is a funicular railway that runs to the top of Cairn Gorm from May-Oct, 1000-1630, on demand in winter, £8.00 adult, concessions available. For more information, T01479-873535, www.cairngorms.co.uk.

Loch Morlich and Rothiemurchus Estate and around provide good cross-country skiing if there's enough snow, though in recent years snowfall has been below average. For more information, see p61. TIC provides a free *Cairngorm Piste Map & Ride Guide* leaflet and a *Ski Scotland* brochure which lists ski schools and rental facilities.

Walking

The walks around Strathspey are covered by OS Landranger map No 36 (1:50,000 scale) or OS Outdoor Leisure Map No 3 (1:25,000 scale).

The Cairngorms provide some of Scotland's most challenging walking, with no fewer than 49 Munros and half of Britain's eight mountains over 4,000 ft (Ben MacDrui, Braeriach, Cairn Toul and Cairn Gorm). These mountains come into their own in winter, providing experienced climbers with a wide range of classic ice climbs. They should not be taken lightly. They require a high degree of fitness, experience and preparation (see p56 for safety precautions).

The summit of **Cairn Gorm** (4,084 ft) is readily accessible as you take the mountain railway up to the **Ptarmigan Restaurant**. However the railway cannot be used to access the high mountain plateau beyond the ski area and mountain walkers may not use the railway for their return journey.

There are 50 miles of footpaths through this area, including some lovely walks through the forests. There are also ranger-led guided walks. You can find out more at the **Rothiemurchus Estate Visitor Centre**, T01479-810858, which is a mile from Aviemore along the Ski Rd. It's open daily 0900-1700 and can provide a free *Visitor Guide and Footpath Map*.

Another good area for walking is around **Glen More Forest Park**. The visitor centre, T01479-861220, near Loch Morlich, has a Glen More Forest Guide Map which details local walks.

The best known of the long-distance trails is the **Lairig Ghru**, a 25-mile hike from Aviemore over the Lairig Ghru Pass to Braemar. The trail is well marked but can take at least 8 hrs and is very tough in parts, so you'll need to be properly equipped and prepared. See p424.

Watersports

In summer, the main activities are water-sports, and there are 2 centres which offer sailing, canoeing and windsurfing tuition and equipment hire.

Loch Morlich Watersports Centre, T01479-861221, lochmorlichw-s@sol.co.uk, open Apr-Oct, is 3 miles east of Aviemore. **Loch Insh Watersports Centre**, T01479-651272, user@lochinsh.dial.netmedia.co.uk, open Apr-Oct, offers the same facilities, plus fishing, mountain bike hire and ski instruction on a dry ski slope.

Transport

Aviemore *p423*

There are **Scottish Citylink** buses, T0990-505050, between Aviemore and **Inverness** (45 mins), **Kingussie** (20 mins), **Pitlochry** (1¼ hrs), **Perth** (2 hrs), **Glasgow** (3½ hrs) and **Edinburgh** (3½ hrs). For **Aberdeen**, change at Inverness.

Car hire from **MacDonald's Self Drive**, 13 Muirton, T01479-811444.

There are direct trains to and from **Glasgow** and **Edinburgh** (3 hrs) and **Inverness** (40 mins). Strathspey Steam Railway, T01479-810725, www.strathspeyrailway.co.uk, runs between **Aviemore**, **Boat of Garten** and **Broomhill**. The station is just to the east of the main train station.

Boat of Garten *p424*

The best way to get to Boat of Garten is on the **Strathspey Steam Railway** which runs at least 5 times daily from **Aviemore**, T01479-810725. **Loch Garten** is not easy to reach without your own transport, but check with one of the local TICs about tours.

Carrbridge *p425*

There are several buses daily (except Sun) to **Carrbridge** from **Inverness** and **Grantown-on-Spey** with Highland Country Buses, T01463-233371.

Kingussie *p425*

Kingussie is on the main **Inverness** to **Perth/Glasgow/Edinburgh** routes. All Perth-Inverness trains stop here and most Citylink buses. There's also an infrequent school bus service run by Highland Country Buses between **Kingussie**, **Aviemore**, **Newtonmore** and **Dalwhinnie**.

Grantown-on-Spey *p425*

There are several buses daily (Mon-Sat) between Grantown and **Aviemore** (35 mins), and 2 or 3 buses daily, except Sun, to and from **Inverness** (1¼ hrs).

Skye & the Small Isles

Footprint features

Introduction

The **Isle of Skye** (An t-Eilean Sgitheanach), the most scenically spectacular of all the Scottish islands, gets its name from the Norse word for cloud (skuy) and is commonly known as Eilean a Cheo (the Misty Isle), so it obviously rains a lot here. But when the rain and mist clear, the views make the heart soar. Despite the unpredictable weather, tourism is an important part of the island's economy, and has been since Victorian times when climbers returned home extolling its beauty. In the busy summer months the main roads become choked with coach tours and caravans, but the island is large enough to escape the worst of the crowds if you take the time to explore it. It offers a range of excellent walks from low-level strolls to tougher routes requiring experience and ahead for heights. In the centre of the island stand the proud, implacable **Cuillins**, the greatest concentration of peaks in Britain. They provide Scotland's best climbing and have become a mecca for all serious and experienced walkers. Equally spectacular, but easier to negotiate, are the bizarre rock formations of the **Trotternish Peninsula** in the north.

The **Small Isles** is the collective name given to the four islands of **Eigg**, **Muck**, **Rùm** and **Canna**, lying south of Skye. Seen from the mainland, they look a very tempting prospect, especially the jagged outline of Rùm and the curiously shaped Eigg. But visiting the islands is not easy, as ferry transport is purely designed for the inhabitants and not geared towards the convenience of island-hopping tourists. Furthermore, the island populations are small, and accommodation and facilities are limited. But the determined traveller with time on their hands will be well rewarded, particularly on mountainous Rùm, with its superb walking and abundant wildlife.

★ Don't miss...

1. **Loch Coruisk** Take a boat trip into the gaping mouth of this loch, page 449.
2. **Three Chimneys restaurant** Sample some of the finest food in the country, page 448.
3. **Raasay** Sail to this island, only a few miles off Skye's east coast yet well and truly off the beaten track, and climb to the top Dun Caan, page 443.
4. **Eigg** Walk across the 'Singing Sands' on this tiny island, page 451.
5. **Rùm** Brave the wilds of this island, home to the rare white-tailed sea eagle, and then explore the bizarre and extravagant interior of Kinloch Castle, page 451.

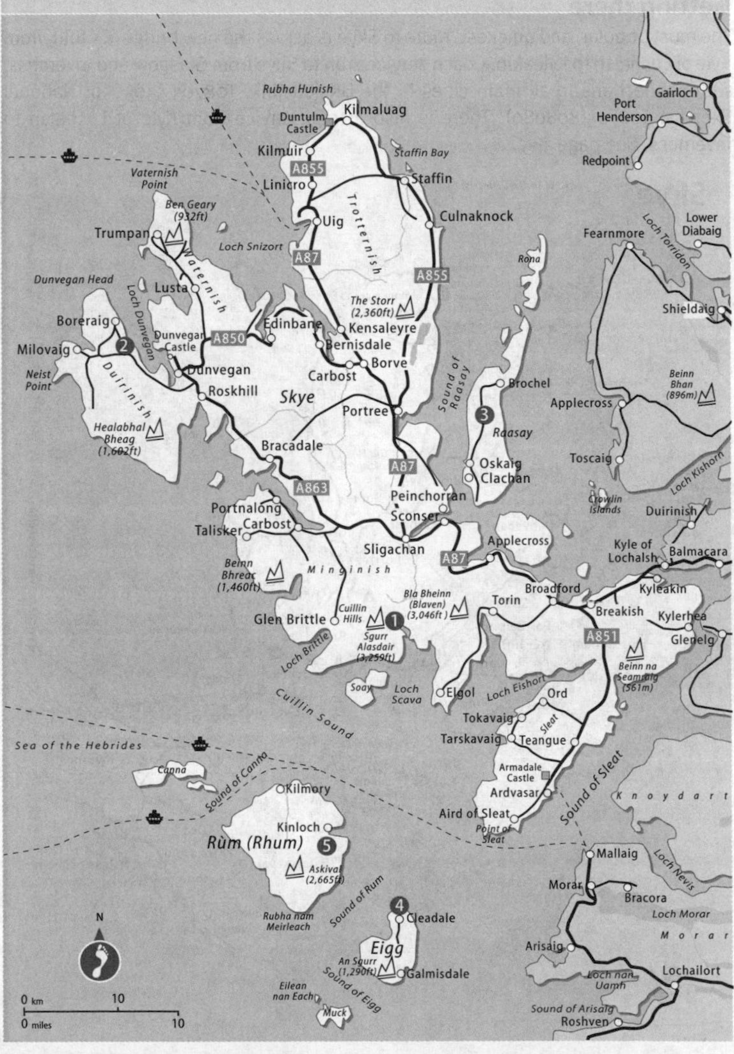

Isle of Skye

Aside from swooning at the island's natural beauty, the most popular destination is Dunvegan Castle, stronghold of the Macleod clan, while their old enemies, the MacDonalds hail from the Sleat Peninsula in the south of the island. The most famous Macdonald, Flora, who helped Bonnie Prince Charles flee to France, hailed from the northern tip of the island and is buried there. Away from all the tartan and genealogy, Skye is one of the best places in Scotland for outdoor types. » For Sleeping, Eating and other listings, see pages 445-451.

Ins and outs

Getting there

The most popular, and quickest, route to Skye is across the new bridge (£5 toll), from Kyle of Lochalsh to Kyleakin. Coach services run to Skye from Glasgow and Inverness, with connections to all main cities in the UK (Citylink, T08705-5505050; National Express, T08705-808080). There is also a train service from Kyle of Lochalsh to Inverness. See page 385.

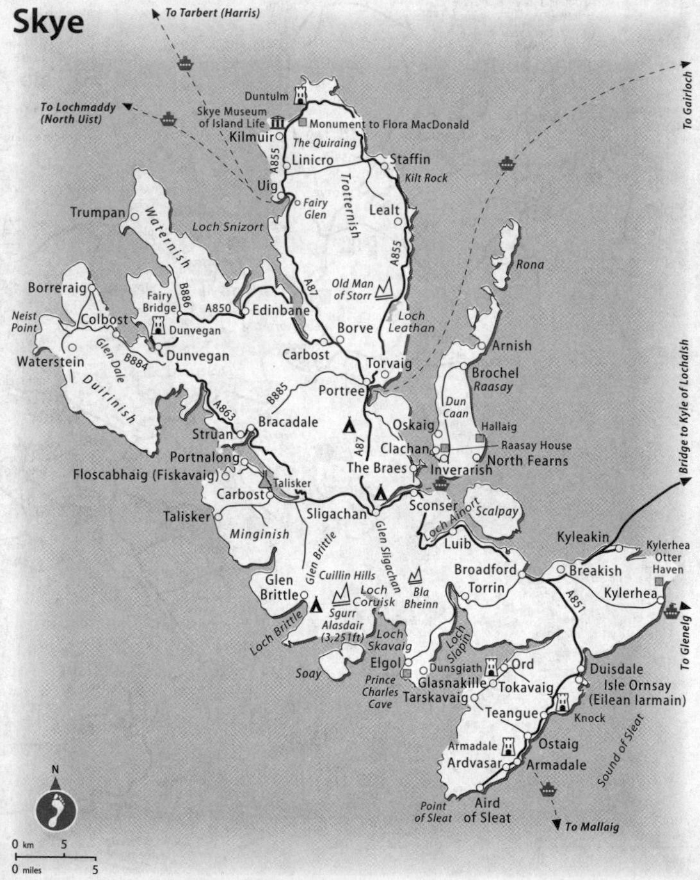

A more scenic approach is by ferry from Mallaig to Armadale, on the southern Sleat Peninsula. The car and passenger ferry makes the 20-minute crossing eight to nine times daily each way (Monday-Saturday only from mid September to mid May). Booking is recommended during the summer months, T08705-650000. The one-way trip costs £3 per passenger and £16.50 per car. Five-day saver return is £5.10 and £28.50. Trains to and from Fort William and Glasgow Queen Street connect with some of the ferries, see page 378.

The best way to Skye is from Glenelg to Kylerhea, south of Kyleakin. The tiny private car ferry makes the 10-minute crossing when required from Easter to October daily, see page 385 for details. There is also a passenger ferry from Gairloch to Portree, sailing twice daily, see page 394. For more details and ticket bookings, visit www.overtheseatoskye.com. ▸▸ *For further details, see Transport page 450.*

Getting around

Skye is the largest of the Hebridean islands, at almost 50 miles long and between seven and 25 miles wide. It is possible to run up a hefty mileage as the extensive road system penetrates to all but the most remote corners of its many peninsulas. It is possible to get around by public transport midweek, with postbuses supplementing the normal services, but, as everywhere in the Highlands and Islands, buses are few and far between at weekends, especially Sunday, and during the winter months. Buses run between Portree, Broadford, Uig (for ferries to the Western Isles), Kyleakin, Armadale (for ferries to Mallaig), Dunvegan and Carbost, and a more limited service runs from Broadford to Elgol and Portree to Glen Brittle. Getting around by public transport is virtually impossible in winter (October-March) as bus and postbus services are severely limited. ▸▸ *For further details, see Activities and tours page 449 and Transport page 450.*

Tourist information

Skye is well served by all types of accommodation: B&Bs, guest houses, hostels, bunkhouses, campsites and some very fine hotels. During the peak summer months advance bookings are recommended. These can be made directly or through the island's tourist information centres in Portree (open all year), Broadford, Uig and Dunvegan. See also www.isleofskye.com. For local tourist information centres see individual sections.

Portree → *Phone code: 01478. Colour map 1, grid C3.*

Portree is the island's capital and main settlement. It's a fairly attractive little fishing port, built around a natural harbour, with a row of brightly painted houses along the shorefront and the rest of the town rising steeply up to the central Somerled Square. ▸▸ *For Sleeping, Eating and other listings, see pages 445-451.*

Ins and outs

Getting there and around Portree is ideally placed for trips to all parts of the island. Buses leave from the bus station in Somerled Square to Dunvegan, Uig, Broadford, Kyleakin, Armadale, the Talisker Distillery and Glenbrittle. There are also services to the mainland. The CalMac ferry office is on Park Road, just off Somerled Square, T01478-612075. The town is compact enough to get around easily on foot, though there is a regular town bus service for those needing to get into the centre from the outskirts.

Tourist information The TIC ⓘ *Bridge St, T01478-612137, daily mid-May to mid-Aug, mid-Aug to mid-May Mon-Sat*, has bus timetables and a good selection of books and maps.

Aros Experience ⓘ *Viewfield Rd, T01478-613649, www.scotlandcreates.com/aros, daily 0900-2100 (off season 0900-1800), £3, concession £2, children £1, under 12 free, half a mile from the town centre on the road to Broadford*, is an exhibition and audio-visual display of the island's history and cultural heritage. The island's only theatre is housed here and features a varied programme of events, including drama, traditional music and movies, see Entertainment page 449. There's also a restaurant serving good value snacks and main meals, a gift shop and a network of forest trails to explore.

An Tuireann Arts Centre ⓘ *Struan Rd, T01478-613306, www.antuireann.org.uk, Mar-Oct Mon-Sat 1000-1700, Nov-Feb Tue-Sat 1000-1700, free*, hosts exhibitions of contemporary visual arts and crafts. It has a fine café, see Eating page 448.

▲ A nice, gentle introduction to walking in the area, and an opportunity to stretch your legs before tackling more strenuous routes such as the Old Man of Storr or the

Portree

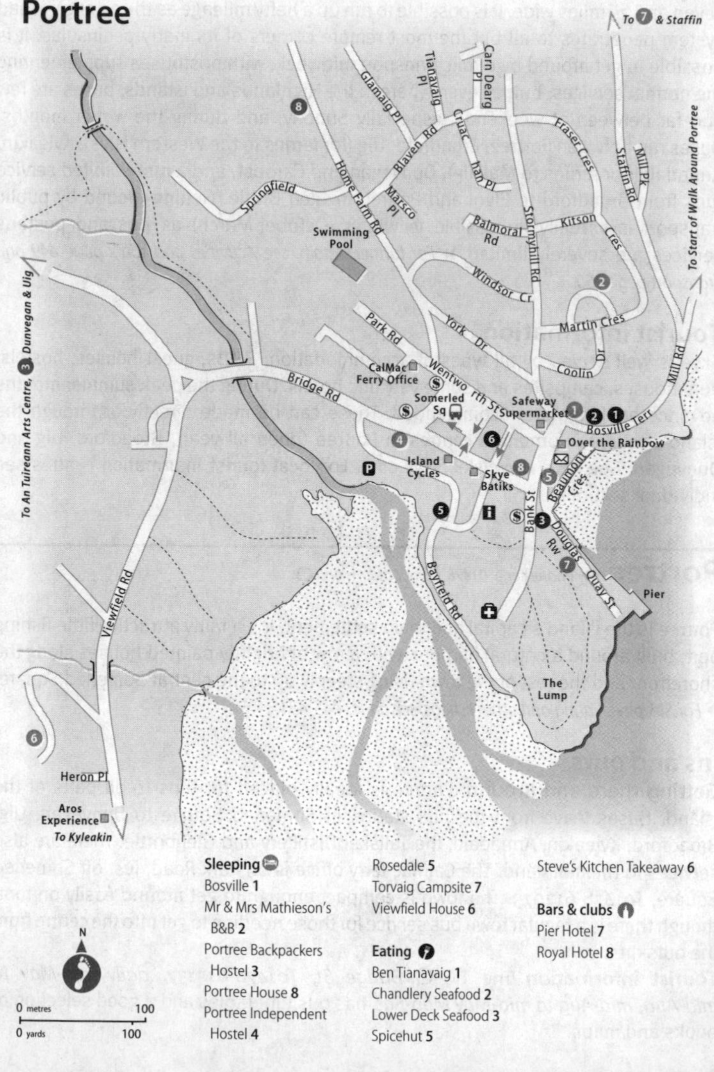

Things to do on Skye when it's raining

Just in case you didn't know, it can rain quite often on Skye and unless you're one of those hardy souls who's prepared to brave the elements, you'll need to know about the island's main indoor attractions. There are numerous opportunities to shelter from the rain, but most of them cost money, and many will leave you regretting it, so here's our list of the top ten things to do. Details of opening times and admission prices are given under each relevant destination.

Beginning in Portree, there's the **Aros Experience**, which gives a good introduction to the island's history. North of Uig, at Kilmuir on the Trotternish Peninsula, is the **Skye Museum of Island Life**, which pretty much does what it says on the sign. Northwest from Portree is **Dunvegan Castle**, home of the Clan Macleod and top of most visitors' itineraries. On the road to Dunvegan is **Edinbane Pottery**, where you can buy pots of every shape and size and watch them being made.

Travelling south from Dunvegan, you'll reach the turn-off to the **Talisker Distillery**, the island's only whisky distillery, where you can sample the distinctive peaty taste. While you're there you can visit nearby **Carbostcraft Pottery**, in the village of Carbost, and indulge in some more gift buying. If you're in need of some refreshment after all that culture and shopping, you could do a lot worse than the bar at the **Sligachan Hotel**, which boasts an impressive array of whiskies and climbers' beards. In the southern peninsula of Sleat, near the Armadale ferry terminal, is **Armadale Castle**, with a visitor centre that is actually worth visiting. Nearby is one of the branches of **Skye Batiks**, with a huge selection of these 'new age' style fabrics in a range of original Celtic designs (the other branch is in Portree). And for that final drink before boarding the ferry to Mallaig, why not pop into the cosy bar of the **Hotel Eilean Iarmain**, which also happens to serve wonderful food.

Quiraing, starts out from Bosville Terrace. Follow the street as it curves round then take the right fork at the first junction, down towards the shore. Just after the car park to the right the road splits: follow the path to the right along the northern shore of the bay. The path follows the shore and passes a viewpoint and flagpole. It then becomes rougher as it swings round the headland and reaches a gate in a dyke. Go through the gate and cross the muddy field, then follow the fence up to the left till you reach another gate. Climb over the gate and continue along the edge of the next field, then cross a stile at the top of the field. Walk up the slope to the clear track and follow this left as it heads uphill. You'll then see some houses; take the track beyond the house on the left and follow it down between two large farm buildings. The path heads down across rough moorland towards Portree. Cross the stile and continue downhill through some woods, then you'll see a hotel on your left before rejoining the original road near the car park. It's about 2½ miles and takes about an hour and a half at an easy pace. The path can get very muddy in places.

Trotternish Peninsula → *Phone code: 01470. Colour map 1, grid C3.*

North from Portree is the 30-mile long Trotternish Peninsula, sticking out like a giant thumb hitching a lift from a passing ferry. The interior of the peninsula is a basaltic

Faithful Flora

In Kilmuir graveyard is the memorial which marks the grave of Flora MacDonald, one of the most famous characters in Skye's long history. The memorial bears Dr Johnson's fitting epitaph: *A name that will be mentioned in history, and if courage and fidelity be virtues, mentioned with honour.*

It was Flora MacDonald who helped Bonnie Prince Charlie to escape capture following the Jacobite defeat at Culloden in 1746. Pursued by government troops, the prince fled from South Uist 'over the sea to Skye' aboard Flora's boat, disguised as an Irish servant girl by the name of Betty Burke. He then made his way to Portree, where he bade his farewell to the young woman who had risked her own life to protect his.

When Flora's part in the prince's escape became known, she was immediately arrested and sent to the Tower of London. She was released a year later, married a Skye man and then emigrated to North Carolina where she spent the next 12 years of her life. They returned to her husband's house in Kingsburgh in 1786. Flora died in Skye in 1790, and it is said that her funeral was the largest ever witnessed in the Highlands.

lava wilderness full of bizarre rock formations. A 20-mile long escarpment of sheer cliffs and towering pinnacles dominates the landscape. The best known of these strange formations, the **Quiraing** and **Old Man of Storr**, can be explored on foot (see below). The A855 and A87 roads follow the coast around the peninsula, and a spectacular minor road bisects the ridge from Staffin Bay to Uig. Trotternish is best explored with your own transport, but there a few daily buses covering the circular route from Portree. ▸▸ *For Sleeping, Eating and other listings, see pages 445-451.*

Uig

The A87 runs northwest from Portree to the tiny ferry port of Uig, dramatically set in a horseshoe bay and the departure point for ferries to **Tarbert** (Harris) and **Lochmaddy** (North Uist). Everything in the village revolves around the ferry timetables, and the regular bus service to and from Portree coincides with the arrival and departure of the ferries. The TIC ⓘ *T01470-542404, 1 Apr-31 Oct, Mon-Sat, also Sun Jul-Sep*, is inside the CalMac office at the ferry pier, and will book accommodation anywhere on the island.

Just outside the village is the magical **Fairy Glen**. Turn right just before the **Uig Hotel** coming down the hill from the Portree direction. About a mile up the single track road you enter an eerie, mysterious world of perfect conical hills, some up to 60-ft high. It's almost inconceivable that these are natural formations and the inevitable mist only adds to the spooky strangeness of the place.

Uig to Duntulm

At **Kilmuir**, is the **Skye Museum of Island Life** ⓘ *Easter to Oct Mon-Sat 0930-1700, £2, children £1*. The group of thatched houses give a fascinating insight into the way of life of a crofting community at the end of the last century, and is the most authentic of several such museums on Skye. Behind the museum, at the end of the road, is **Flora MacDonald's Monument**, which marks the grave of Skye's most famous daughter, with her husband buried alongside. The rather austere memorial is inscribed with Dr Johnson's poignant tribute.

At the northwest tip of the peninsula, 15 minutes' drive from Uig, is **Duntulm Castle**, a fairytale ruin dramatically perched on a steep cliff. This 15th-century

“” It’s almost inconceivable that these are natural formations and the inevitable mist only adds to the spooky strangeness of the place…

structure, built on the site of an ancient Norse stronghold, became the chief Skye residence of the powerful MacDonalds and was the most imposing castle in the Hebrides. According to local legend, the castle was abandoned around 1732 when a nursemaid accidentally let the baby heir fall from a window on to the cliffs below.

▲ The Quiraing

Beyond Duntulm the A855 heads across the tip of the peninsula to the east coast, where the famous bizarre rock scenery is found. At the north end of **Staffin Bay**, a minor road cuts across the peninsula to Uig. This road is the access point for the Quiraing, the famous jumble of strangely shaped hills and rocks that is one of the island's classic walks. This four-mile walk is quite demanding, but the dramatic scenery more than compensates. To get to the starting point, drive 19 miles north from Portree on the A855. At Brogaig, just north of Staffin, take the single-track road to Uig. Follnd, just after the road has zigzagged its way up the face of the ridge, park in the car park to the left. Cross the road and follow the well-defined path along the base of the cliffs, with a steep grassy slope down to the right. After about one mile you'll start to see some of the well-known rocky features on the far side of a rough valley. The most imposing of these is **The Prison**, a huge, tilted square block. On the left, among the towering cliffs, is **The Needle**, a shaft of rock about 120-ft high. Scramble up the narrow gully to the left of The Needle to reach **The Table**, an area of flat grassland surrounded by high cliffs (local shinty teams used to play here!). From The Table continue along the path at the foot of the cliffs, past a small lochan on the right and through a stone dyke, until you reach the lowest point of the ridge on your left. Scramble up on to the ridge and make your way back along the tops of the cliffs (take care at this point). There's a hard climb up the slopes of Meall na Suirmamach, but the views from the top are spectacular. Continue along the top of the cliffs for just over a mile and you'll see the car park.

! Even if you don't attempt the walk, the road over the back of the Trotternish ridge from Uig makes a worthwhile detour.

Kilt Rock

A few miles south of Staffin Bay is Kilt Rock, an impressive sea cliff which gets its name from the vertical columnar basalt strata overlying horizontal ones beneath. A rather tenuous comparison perhaps, but the cliffs south of Staffin are particularly spectacular, as are the **Lealt Falls**, a torrent of mountain water at the head of a gorge, a few miles south of Kilt Rock. The falls are signposted by the road, so all you have to do is park the car and peer over. Just before the turn for Kilt Rock is a wee museum sporting such finds as a dinosaur bone and bronze age artefacts (open May-October).

▲ Old Man of Storr

A few miles further south, and seven miles north of Portree, is a car park which is the starting point for another of Skye's famous walks: up to the Old Man of Storr, the distinctive pinnacle which has detached itself from the cliffs of the Storr behind. This basalt finger of rock, 165 ft high, stands beneath the steep cliffs of The Storr (2,360 ft) and is visible from the A855. The starting point for the 3½-mile walk up and back (1½ hours) is the car park on the left, just over six miles north of Portree, near the northern end of Loch Leathan, which can be reached by bus from Portree. Cross the stile over the wall by the Forestry Commission sign and follow the clear track up through the conifer plantation. The track is a gradual uphill climb until you come out into open grassland. Go through the gate in the fence and then it's a steep climb up the grassy slope with the massive pinnacle towering overhead. Once at the top you enter an area of weird and impressive rock formations. You can follow any of the dozens of paths that lead between the rocks, or just enjoy the fantastic views across to Raasay and the mainland beyond. You can follow the same path back down to the car park.

Waternish, Dunvegan and Duirinish → *Phone code: 01470.*

Colour map 1, grid C2-3.

In the northwest of Skye the peninsulas of Waternish (or Vaternish) and Duirinish point out into the Minch towards the Western Isles. The larger Duirinish Peninsula holds more interest for the visitor, featuring the beautiful green valley of **Glendale**, an area brimming with history, the dramatic walk to **Neist Point** and **Dunvegan Castle**, Skye's most famous landmark. ⏩ *For Sleeping, Eating and other listings, see pages 445-451.*

Edinbane

The turn-off to this much-visited part of the island is four miles northwest of Portree. The A850 swings west towards Dunvegan, by-passing the tiny village of Edinbane, where there's a campsite, two hotels, several B&Bs, a petrol station and the renowned **Edinbane Pottery** ⓘ *T01470-582234, Easter-Oct 0900-1800 workshop and showroom*, which is a must for souvenir hunters.

Waternish Peninsula

The A850 continues west, and those with their own transport and time on their hands might wish to make an interesting little detour at the **Fairy Bridge**, where the B886 runs north to **Trumpan**, near the tip of the Waternish Peninsula. If the weather's good (and it is, occasionally) this is the best place to watch the sun set, in a blaze of red over the Outer Hebrides. If there's no sunset, then you could always visit **Skyeskins** ⓘ *T01470-592237, www.skyeskins.co.uk, daily 1000-18000*, in Loch Bay, the country's only traditional exhibition tannery. While here, you could also pop into the island's oldest pub at **Stein**.

The ruined church at Trumpan, at the end of the road, has some grisly skeletons in its cupboard (see box). In the graveyard is the 'trial stone'. A hole in the stone was used to test whether or not an accused person was telling the truth. If they could quickly find the hole and stick their arm through it while blindfolded, they were found innocent, but if not, they were guilty. The church is also the starting point for the strenuous eight-mile walk out to **Waternish point** and back.

Dunvegan

A few miles further on from the turn-off to Waternish is the little village of Dunvegan. Just to the north of the village is proud **Dunvegan Castle** ⓘ *www.dunvegancastle.com, mid-Mar to Nov daily 1000-1730, rest of the year 1100-1600, castle £6.50, £3.50 children, gardens only £4.50*, the island's most important tourist attraction. This is the home of the chiefs of the Clan Macleod who have lived here for over seven centuries, making it the oldest inhabited castle in Britain. The present structure dates from the 15th and 16th centuries and, though the Victorian restoration has left it looking more like a baronial house, a look inside reveals its true age. Among the few genuinely interesting relics on display is Rory Mor's horn, a huge drinking vessel which the chief's heir must drain 'without setting down or falling down', when filled

Take no prisoners

Violent conflict between neighbouring clan chiefs was so commonplace on Skye and in the rest of the Western Highlands that it was almost accepted as part of the very fabric of society. One particularly gruesome example took place on Eigg in 1577. The Macleod's had taken refuge in a cave but their presence was discovered by the MacDonalds, who piled brushwood at the entrance and set fire to it, burning alive the 395 people sheltering inside, almost the entire population of the island. Revenge came the following year, at Trumpan church in Ardmore Bay. The Macleods landed under cover of the early morning fog and set light to the church, burning the congregation inside.

with claret (about 1½ bottles). There's also a lock of Bonnie Prince Charlie's hair, clipped from his head by Flora MacDonald as a keepsake, but pride of place goes to the Fairy Flag. The flag has been dated to between the fourth and seventh centuries and is made of Middle Eastern silk. It is said to have been given to the clan chief by a fairy, and has the power to ensure victory in battle for the clan on three occasions. It has been used twice so far. The lovely castle gardens lead down to the lochside jetty, from where you can take a seal-spotting cruise or a boat trip around the loch. There's also a busy restaurant and gift shop by the castle gates.

In the village of Dunvegan is **Giant Angus MacAskill Museum** ⓘ *T01470 -521296, Mar-Oct daily 0930-1830, £1*, housed in a thatched, whitewashed cottage, which relates the life story of the tallest ever Scotsman, Angus MacAskill, who grew to 7 ft and 9 ins tall. He emigrated to Novia Scotia and toured the United States with the midget General Tom Thumb, who is said to have danced on his outstretched hand. More interesting than the museum, though, are the stories of its owner, Peter MacAskill, in particular the one about the replica coffin, which is worth the admission fee alone. Peter is a descendent of Angus and also runs the museum at Colbost (see below).

Duirinish Peninsula

West of Dunvegan is the Duirinish Peninsula. The northern half is populated along the western shores of **Loch Dunvegan** and in the beautiful and green **Glendale**, an area brimming with history but with hardly an island family left. Glendale is now dubbed 'Little England', owing to the large number of incoming settlers from the south. The area is famed throughout the Highlands and Islands, for it was here in 1882 that local crofters, spurred on by the **Battle of the Braes**, see page 443, resisted the cruel and petty tyranny of their estate manager. The authorities sent a gunboat to deal with the uprising and arrested the ringleaders, some of whom were imprisoned in Edinburgh and became known as 'the Glendale Martyrs'. This episode sparked a radical movement throughout the Highlands and led to the **Crofter's Holdings Act of 1886** which gave the crofters a more secure tenure and fair rent, see page 465. The uninhabited southern half of the peninsula is dominated by the flat-topped hills, Healabhal Bheag (1,601 ft) and Healabhal Mhor (1,538 ft), known as **Macleod's Tables.**

The **Glendale Visitor Route** is signposted from just before Dunvegan village and leads westwards along the shores of the loch and across the peninsula. There are several interesting little sights along the way. Those interested in finding out more

Macleod's Tables are so named because legend has it that the clan chief held a huge open-air feast for King James V on one of the hilltops.

about the region's history, and crofting on the island, should head for the fascinating **Colbost Folk Museum** ⓘ *Easter-Oct daily 0900-1800, £1.50, children free*, housed in a restored 'black house' and with a peat fire burning and an illicit still out the back. The museum is four miles from Dunvegan on the B884 to Glendale. A little further on is **Skye Silver** ⓘ *www.skyesilver.com, daily 1000-1800*, where you can buy silver jewellery in traditional Celtic designs. Further north is the **Borreraig Park Exhibition Croft** ⓘ *daily 0900-1800, £1.50*, which features a huge display of farm equipment from days gone by.

At **Borreraig** is the **MacCrimmon Piping Heritage Centre** ⓘ *T01470-511369, daily all year 1000-1700, £1.50*, a fascinating place which is more of a shrine to the famous MacCrimmons, who were hereditary pipers to the Macleod Chiefs and the first composers, players and teachers of *piobaireachd* (pibroch), which can be heard in the museum (there's an annual recital at Dunvegan Castle in early August). Opposite are the ruins of the ancient piping college. Moving from the sublime to the ridiculous, in the village of **Glendale** is a **Toy Museum** ⓘ *T01470-511240, Mon-Sat 1000-1800, £2.50, children £1*, which should appeal to kids of all ages.

▲▲ The B884 continues west, then a road turns off left for Waterstein. At the end of this road (just over two miles) is a car park which is the starting point for the walk out to the lighthouse at **Neist Point**, the most westerly point on Skye and one of the most pleasant walks on the island. It's about 1½ miles there and back and well worth the effort. The path is easy to follow and the views of the sea cliffs are wonderful. There are lots of nesting seabirds around and you might even spot whales offshore. The **lighthouse**, built in 1909, is now unmanned, and you can stay in one of the self-catering cottages ⓘ *T/F01470-511200*.

The Cuillins and Minginish → *Colour map 3, grid A3-4. OS Landranger No 32 & OS Outdoor Leisure No 8.*

The district of Minginish is the wildest and least-populated part of the island, but for many it is the greatest attraction, for this is where the Cuillins are to be found. This hugely impressive mountain range, often shrouded in rain or cloud, is the spiritual heartland of the island, and when it's clear their heart-aching grandeur can be appreciated from every other peninsula on Skye. Though officially called the Cuillin 'Hills', these are the most untamed mountains in Britain. The magnificent scenery and vast range of walks and scrambles have attracted climbers and walkers for centuries, but have also claimed many lives. It cannot be stressed too strongly that the Cuillins are the most dangerous mountains in Britain and only for experienced climbers, see further page 56. ▸▸ *For Sleeping, Eating and other listings, see pages 445-451.*

▲▲ The Cuillins

There are three routes into the Cuillins: from the Sligachan Hotel, from Glen Brittle, and from Elgol. The eastern part of the range is known as the **Red Cuillins**. Their smoother, conical granite peaks contrast sharply with the older, darker gabbro of the jagged-edged **Black Cuillins** to the west. The latter are particularly suitable for rock climbing and best approached from Glen Brittle, while the former are accessed from the Sligachan Hotel. There are 20 'Munros' (mountains over 3,000 ft in height) in the Cuillins, with the highest being Sgurr Alasdair, at 3,251 ft. Though the sheer majesty of the mountains can only be appreciated at close quarters by the climber, there are impressive views from Elgol, from the road into Glen Brittle and, more distantly, from the west coast of Sleat. **Glen Sligachan** is one of the most popular routes into the Cuillin range and the main access point for the more forgiving Red Cuillins, the walk to **Loch Coruisk**, or the ascent of **Marsco**.

Law of the land

One of the most significant incidents in the island's history took place in April, 1882, when a group of around 100 local crofters and their families fought a pitched battle against a force of 60 police sent by the government from Glasgow. The 'Battle of the Braes', as it became known, was caused, like many other such uprisings throughout the Highlands and Islands, by threatened evictions. The local crofters were so incensed by the injustice of the eviction notices served on them that they destroyed the offending documents, leading the government to dispatch its police force. The defeat of the government forces of law and order by a bunch of men, women and children with sticks and stones is often described as the last battle fought on British soil, and led eventually to the setting up of a Royal Commission to look into the crofters' grievances.

Glen Brittle → *Phone code: 01478.*

Six miles along the A863 to Dunvegan from Sligachan is a turning left to Portnalong, Carbost and the Talisker Distillery (B8009), which soon leads to the entrance to Glen Brittle. The road down Glen Brittle affords great views of the western side of the imposing Black Cuillins, until it ends at the campsite and shore at the foot of the glen. From Glen Brittle there are numerous paths leading up to the corries of the Black Cuillins. There are many alternative options for those wishing to continue up to the upper corries or to the Main Ridge. One of the finest of the Cuillin corries is **Coire Lagan.** This walk starts from the beach at Glen Brittle village and takes you up to the lochan in the upper coire, with Sgurr Alasdair, the most difficult of the Munros, towering overhead. A fine Cuillin sampler is the short walk to the spectacular **Eas Mor** waterfall.

Talisker → *Phone code: 01478.*

A recommended trip for whisky drinkers, or if it's raining, is to the excellent **Talisker Distillery** ⓘ *T01478-614308, www.malts.com, Easter-Oct Mon-Sat 0930-1700, Nov-Easter Mon-Fri 1400-1700, tours every 15-20 mins, £4*, at **Carbost** on the shores of Loch Harport, on the B8009 (not in the village of Talisker itself, which is on the west coast). This is Skye's only whisky distillery and produces a very smoky, peaty single malt.

Near the distillery is **Carbostcraft Pottery** ⓘ *T01478-640259, Mon-Sat 0900-1700 from Feb-Dec, also Sun in summer*, which produces a wide range of traditional and original pottery, including the famous 'torn pots'. They also have a shop in Portree.

Elgol → *Phone code: 01471.*

One of the most rewarding drives on Skye is the 14-mile single-track road from Broadford to Elgol (Ealaghol), a tiny settlement near the tip of the Strathaird Peninsula, from where you can enjoy the classic view of the Cuillins from across Loch Scavaig and of the islands of Soay, Rùm and Canna. It was from here, on 4 July 1746, that the Young Pretender finally left the Hebrides. Before leaving, he was given a farewell banquet by the MacKinnons in what is now called **Prince Charlie's Cave.** There's also the added attraction of a dramatic boat trip, see page 449, to the mouth of **Loch Coruisk**, in the heart of the Black Cuillin. The glacial sea loch, romanticized by Walter Scott and painted by Turner, is over two miles long but only

Every year there's a hill race up Glamaig, near Glen Sligachan. In 1899, it was climbed in 55 minutes (up and down) by a Gurkha soldier – in bare feet!

 a few hundred yards wide, closed in by the sheer cliffs on either side and overshadowed by the towering mountains of black basalt and gabbro. The road to Elgol also gives great views of Bla Bheinn (pronounced Blaven), best seen from Torrin, at the head of Loch Slapin.

▲ Elgol to Camasunary Bay

Elgol is the starting point for the walk to Camasunary Bay. This nine-mile coastal walk is quite demanding, but on a clear day the views of the Cuillins make it well worth the effort. It starts from the car park in Elgol. From here, walk back up the road for a short distance, then turn left along a track behind some houses, signposted for 'Garsbheinn'. Beside the last of these houses is a sign for the path to Coruisk. Follow this path along a steep grassy slope. The views across Loch Scavaig to the island of Soay and the Cuillins behind are marvellous. The slope gets even steeper beneath Ben Cleat, and you'll need a good head for heights to continue, across the foot of Glen Scaladal, crossing a burn in the process (which can be tricky if it's in spate). Then it's on along the path beyond Beinn Leacach to Camasunary Bay, with its backdrop of mighty Sgurr na Stri and Bla Bheinn. The shortest way back is to retrace your steps, but as an alternative, follow the clear track from Camasunary up the right side of Abhainn nan Lean over the hills to the east until it joins the B8083 from Broadford. From here it's about 3½ miles back along the road to Elgol.

Broadford and the east coast → *Colour map 3, grid A4-5.*

Broadford (An t-Ath Leathann), Skye's second largest village, basically consists of a mile-long main street strung out along a wide bay. The village may be low on charm but it's high on tourist facilities and makes a good base for exploring the south and east of the island. The road north from Broadford to Portree passes through Sconser, departure point for the short ferry ride to the little-visited island of Raasay. » *For Sleeping, Eating and other listings, see pages 445-451.*

Broadford

Broadford has plenty of accommodation and places to eat. Next to the Esso station is a Co-op, and there's a laundrette in the petrol station shop (open 24 hours), and bank with ATM. There is no tourist office as such, just an information point housed in the **Otter Shop** in the main car park (with erratic opening hours). It is also home to one of the most incongruous attractions on the island, or elsewhere in the Highlands, the **Skye Serpentarium** ⓘ *T01471-822209, www.skyeserpentarium.org.uk, Apr-Oct Mon-Sat 1000-1700 (also Sun in Jul/Aug), £2.50, children £1.50*, where you can see, and touch, all kinds of snakes, lizards and other reptiles. A welcome retreat if it's raining. When the weather's clear you can take a trip on a glass-bottomed boat from the pier, see Activities and tours page 449.

Kyleakin

The opening of the Skye Bridge, linking the island with the Kyle of Lochalsh, see page 383, has turned the former ferry terminal of Kyleakin (Caol Acain) into something of a backwater, as well as infuriating the locals with its £6 per car toll. The absence of road traffic, though, makes it a quiet place to stay, and it's now a favourite with backpackers, judging by the number of hostels. The bridge is supported in the middle on the small islet of **Eilean Ban**, erstwhile home of author and naturalist, Gavin Maxwell, and now home to an otter sanctuary. It can be visited as part of tour from the **Bright Water Visitor Centre** ⓘ *T01599-530040, Apr-Oct Mon-Fri 1000-1700, free (tour costs £8)*, in Kyleakin. The centre is worth a visit, especially if you have kids. There's precious little else to do here, other than look at the small ruin of **Castle Moil**.

Gaelic, Gaelic, Gaelic

Outside the Outer Hebrides, Skye is the most important centre of Gaelic culture, with a large proportion of the island's population speaking the Gaelic language in everyday life. This in itself is remarkable given the significant drop in population during the Clearances and the continued undermining of the Gaelic culture ever since, especially through the State education system.

Today, as in other parts of the Hebrides, the native culture is again under threat, this time from the huge influx of 'white settlers' from the south, but there is also a new-found pride and interest in the Gaelic language. This has been helped by the existence of the Gaelic college on Sleat, through Gaelic writers such as the late Sorley Maclean, a radical local newspaper (*The West Highland Free Press*), economic support from Highlands and Islands Enterprise, and spiritual underpinning from the Sabbatarian Free Church. Gaelic is being taught again in schools and can be heard on television. The ancient heritage of the Highlands and Islands is fighting back and reasserting itself as a major European culture.

Kylerhea

About four miles out of Kyleakin a road turns left off the A87 and heads southeast to Kylerhea (pronounced Kile-ray). The bridge may be the most convenient route to Skye, but the best way to cross is on the small car and passenger ferry that makes the 10-minute crossing to Kylerhea from Glenelg, see page 382. For full details of times and prices, see page 432. Near Kylerhea is the Forestry Commission **Otter Haven** ⓘ *T01320-366322, daily 0900 till 1 hr before dusk, free*. An hour-long nature trail takes you to an observation hide where you can look out for these elusive creatures.

Broadford to Portree

The road north to Portree runs between the fringes of the Red Cuillins and the coast, giving good views across to the **Isle of Scalpay**. The road then turns west along the shores of Loch Ainort to the turn-off for the **Luib Folk Museum** ⓘ *0900-1800, £1*, another of Peter MacAskill's island museums. The restored croft house has a smoky atmosphere and has old newspaper cuttings telling of the 'Battle of the Braes' and the 'Glendale Martyrs'.

The road runs north to **Sconser**, departure point for the ferry to Raasay (see below), then runs around Loch Sligachan and heads north to Portree. On the opposite side of the loch from Sconser are the crofting communities known as **The Braes**, who successfully opposed their landlords' eviction notices and brought the crofters' cause to the public's attention.

Isle of Raasay → *OS Landranger No 24.*

The lush and beautiful island of Raasay lies only a few miles off the east coast of Skye yet remains well and truly off the tourist trail. The island is a nature conservancy, and you may see seals, eagles and otters. Its hilly terrain and superb cliff scenery also offer numerous walking opportunities and the views from the highest point, **Dun Caan** (1,456 ft), with the Cuillins on one side and Torridon on the other, are, quite simply, beyond compare.

▲ The walk to the distinctive flat-topped summit of the extinct volcano, Dun Caan, via an old iron mine, is relatively straightforward and one of the most rewarding anywhere in the islands. So much so, in fact, that Boswell was inspired to dance a Highland jig on reaching the top, in 1773, during his grand tour with Dr Johnson.

Another excellent walk starts from North Fearns, at the end of a road running east from **Inverarish**, to the deserted township of **Hallaig**, down the side of Beinn na Leac and back to North Fearns. The circular route is five miles long.

Raasay was for much of its history the property of the Macleods of Lewis, whose chief residence was the ruined **Brochel Castle**, before moving to **Clachan**, where **Raasay House** is now located (see below). The original Raasay House was torched by government troops after Culloden, along with all the island's houses and its boats, as punishment for the Macleods giving refuge to Bonnie Prince Charlie. After the Macleods sold the island in 1843, the Clearances began in earnest and Raasay suffered a long period of emigration, depopulation and poverty. It is not surprising, then, that the island's most famous son, the great poet **Sorley Maclean**, writes so passionately about this lost society. Born in Oskaig in 1911, he writes in his native Gaelic as well as in English, and is highly regarded internationally. Raasay's population now numbers around 150 and the island is a bastion of the Free Church, whose strict Sabbatarian beliefs should be respected by visitors.

Those who make it to the north of the island may wish to note that the two miles of road linking **Brochel** to **Arnish** were the work of one man, Calum Macleod. He decided to build the road himself after the council turned down his requests for proper access to his home. He spent between 10 and 15 years building it with the aid of a pick, a shovel, a wheelbarrow and a road-making manual which cost him three shillings. He died in 1988, soon after its completion, and it coninues to be known as 'Calum's Road'.

Sleat Peninsula → *Phone code: 01471. Colour map 3, grid A4.*

East of Broadford is the turn-off to the peninsula of Sleat (pronouned 'slate'), a part of the island so uncharacteristically green and fertile that it's known as 'The Garden of Skye'. Sleat is another entry point to the island. Ferries cross from Mallaig on the mainland to Armadale on the southeastern shore of the peninsula. While the rest of the island is the preserve of the Macleods, Sleat is MacDonald country. The MacDonalds of Sleat are one of the major surviving branches of Clan Donald, and have the right to use the title Lord MacDonald (but not Lord of the Isles, which is now used by the heir to the throne). » *For Sleeping, Eating and other listings, see pages 445-451.*

Isle Ornsay

South of Duisdale is the signed turning for Isle Ornsay, or Eilean Iarmain (pronounced eelan yarman) in Gaelic, a very beautiful place in a small rocky bay overlooking the tidal Isle of Ornsay with the mountains of Knoydart in the background. This was once Skye's main fishing port, and the neat whitewashed cottages and tiny harbour are still there. It is also largely Gaelic-speaking, thanks mainly to the efforts of its landlord, Sir Iain Noble, who owns the hotel and his own local Gaelic whisky company as well as the northern half of the peninsula, which is known as Fearan Eilean Iarmain.

A few miles further on is a turn-off to the left to the villages of **Ord**, **Tokavaig** and **Tarskavaig**, on the west coast of the peninsula, from where, on a clear day, there are views across to the Cuillins. Near Tokavaig is the ruin of **Dunsgaith Castle**, home of the MacDonalds of Sleat until the 17th century. Tarskavaig is a typical crofting township. In the early 19th century the MacDonalds wanted the more fertile glens inland for their sheep farms and so evicted the people to coastal townships like Tarskavaig. Just beyond the turn-off to Ord are the remains of **Knock Castle**, yet another MacDonald stronghold.

Ostaig

At Ostaig is the Gaelic College, **Sabhal Mor Ostaig** ① *T01471-844373*, where all subjects are taught in Gaelic, including full-time courses in business studies and media, as well as short courses in Gaelic music and culture during the summer months. The bookshop has a good selection of books and tapes for those wishing to learn the language. The college was founded by Sir Iain Noble (see above). Ostaig is also the beginning or end (depending on which direction you're heading) of the detour to Tarskavaig, Tokavaig and Ord.

Armadale to the Point of Sleat

Just before the ferry pier at Armadale is **Armadale Castle** ⓘ *T01471-844305, www.highlandconnection.org/clandonaldcentre.htm, Apr-Oct daily 0930-1730, £4.50*, which was built in 1815 as the main residence of the MacDonalds of Sleat. Most of the castle is now a roofless ruin but the servants' quarters contain an excellent exhibition and accompanying video explaining the history of the Lordship of the Isles. The Clan Donald Lords of the Isles took over from their Norse predecessors in ruling the Hebrides until their power was broken in 1493. The former stables at the entrance comprise offices, a restaurant and bookshop, while the estate manager's house has been converted to accommodate an extensive library and archives. The castle is surrounded by 40 acres of handsome gardens and woodland, and there are ranger-led walks along nature trails with fine views across to the mainland.

Just beyond Armadale Castle is the tiny village of **Armadale** which is strung out along the wooded shoreline and merges into the neighbouring village of **Ardvasar** (pronounced Ard-vaa-sar), which has a post office, general store. Armadale's raison d'être is the ferry pier and there's not a huge amount to keep you occupied, but there are a couple of good handicraft shops. At the turn-off to the pier is **Skye Batiks** ⓘ *T01471-844396*, which also has a shop in Portree, see page 449. Here you'll find the colourful cotton garments which make a unique souvenir of the island. They also now have B&B accommodation. On the ferry pier is **Ragamuffin** ⓘ *T01471-844217, daily 0900-1800*, which sells a wide range of knitwear. About four or five miles past the ferry port, at the end of the road, is **Aird of Sleat**, a crofting township, from where you walk out to the lighthouse at the **Point of Sleat**. It's a five-mile walk on a clear path across moorland with fine coastal scenery.

Sleeping

Portree *p433, map p434*
There are numerous hotels, guest houses and B&Bs in Portree, but accommodation can be hard to find in the busy summer season. There are several guest houses on Bosville Terr and many B&Bs on Stormyhill Rd and the streets running off it.

For a small fee the tourist office will book accommodation for you. Prices tend to be slightly higher in Portree than the rest of the island, though B&Bs on the outskirts of town are usually cheaper.

B Rosedale Hotel, Beaumont Cres, T01478-613131. 23 rooms. Open May-Sep. Cosy little hotel by the harbour, converted from fishermen's houses.

C Bosville Hotel, Bosville Terr, T01478-612846, www.macleodhotels.co.uk/bosville 18 rooms. Comfortable and stylish accommodation with friendly service. Boasts 2 award-winning restaurants (see Eating).

C Viewfield House Hotel, on the road into Portree from the south, T01478-612217, www.skye.co.uk/viewfield. 9 rooms. Open mid-Apr to mid-Oct. Grand old country house full of antiques, set in 20 acres of woodland garden. Log fire adds to the welcoming atmosphere; great value.

E Mr & Mrs Mathieson, 'Grenitote', 9 Martin Cres, T01478-612808, on Viewfield Rd heading south out of town. Good value.

E Portree House, Home Farm Rd, T01478-613713, nigel@potreehouse.demon.co.uk. 5 rooms. B&B with reduction on meals in the restaurant.

F Portree Backpackers Hostel, 6 Woodpark, Dunvegan Rd, T01478-613641, F613643. 26 beds.

F Portree Independent Hostel, Old Post Office, The Green, T01478-613737. 60 beds. Right in the centre of town, with laundrette (£3 per wash) and email facilities (£3 per hr).

Camping

There's a campsite at Torvaig, just outside the town, T01478-612209, open Apr-Oct.

Trotternish Peninsula *p435*

A **Flodigarry Country House Hotel**, a few miles north of Staffin and 20 miles north of Portree, T01470-552203, F552301. Beautifully located at the foot of the mighty Quiraing and with stunning views across Staffin Bay, this is one of the great country house hotels, with a relaxing old-world atmosphere and excellent restaurant. Flora MacDonald's actual cottage is in the grounds and has been tastefully refurbished, giving the chance to stay in a place steeped in the island's history. The lively bar is a good place to enjoy a laugh and a jig.

B **Uig Hotel**, on the right of the road into the village from Portree, beside a white church and opposite Frazer's Folly, Uig, T01470-542205, F542308. 17 rooms, open year round. Classy accommodation with great views across the bay, good food and a friendly island welcome. Offers clay pigeon shooting and fly fishing.

C **Duntulm Castle Hotel**, near Duntulm Castle, T01470-552213, www.duntulmcastle.co.uk. Open Mar-Nov. Friendly and homely with great views across the Minch to the Outer Hebrides. Idyllic and good value. Restaurant is open to non-residents.

D **The Ferry Inn**, Uig, T01470-542242, joycemary@supanet.com. Close to the ferry pier and serves bar meals.

D **Glenview Inn and Restaurant**, at Culnacnoc, just north of the Lealt Falls, T01470-562248. 5 rooms. Cosy and relaxed accommodation with a very fine restaurant.

E **Idrigill House**, Uig, T01470-542398, s.watkins@lineone.net. Good value B&B.

F **Dun Flodigarry Backpackers Hostel**, T/F01470-552212. 66 beds. Open Mar-Oct. Only 100 yds from the bar of the **Flodigarry Country House Hotel**. Those who can't afford the luxury of the **Flodigarry House Hotel** can always opt for this more modest alternative. Laundry facilities, breakfast.

F **SYHA Youth Hostel**, Uig, T01470-542211, is high above the port on the south side of the village and is open mid-Mar to Oct.

Camping

There's a campsite south of Staffin Bay, T01470-562213, open mid Apr-end Sep.

Waternish, Dunvegan and Duirinish *p438*

There are numerous places to stay in and around Dunvegan, and the tourist information centre in the village will arrange accommodation for you, T01470-521581

A **The House Over-By**, a few yds away from the very wonderful **Three Chimneys**, see Eating, on Duirnish Peninsula, and run by the same folk. 6 sumptuous rooms, all with sea views.

B **Atholl House Hotel**, Dunvegan, T01470-521219, www.athollhotel.co.uk. Very comfortable accommodation.

B **Harlosh House Hotel**, just beyond Roskhill is a turning south off the A863 to T/F01470-521367, harlosh.house@virgin.net. 6 rooms. Open Easter to mid-Oct. Cosy, comfortable, great views and a reputation for superb food (evenings only).

D **Roskhill House**, 3 miles south of Dunvegan Castle on the A863, T01470-521317, stay@roskhill.demon.co.uk. 5 cosy rooms, peaceful setting, great food. Recommended.

The Cuillins and Minginish *p440*

C **Sligachan Hotel**, 7 miles south of Portree, where the A87 Kyleakin-Portree road meets the A863 to Dunvegan, T01471-8650204, F650207. The legendary rallying point for climbers who come to Skye for the Cuillins. The hotel's **Seamus** bar stocks an impressive selection of malts and also serves the island's real ales as well as meals.

C **Talisker House**, in the village of Talisker, T01471-640245, jon_and_ros.wathen@virgin.net. 4 rooms. This excellent guest house makes an ideal retreat from the summer hordes, and serves fine food.

D **Coruisk House**, on the righthand side just after the Elgol village sign on the road from Broadford, T01471-866330, www.seafood-skye.co.uk. Restaurant with rooms. No smoking, all rooms en suite. Worth coming here for the freshest of seafood (lunch **££**, dinner **£££**). Also have a

For an explanation of sleeping and eating price codes used in this guide, see inside the front cover. Other relevant information is found in Essentials, see pages 43-51.

self-catering cottage and traditional crofthouse for rent.

D **Rowan Cottage**, a mile east at Glasnakille, T01471-866287, www.rowancottage-skye.co.uk. Open mid-Mar to end Nov. Attractive B&B offering the best of home cooking (lunch **££**, dinner **£££**, restaurant closed Tue).

F **Croft Bunkhouse & Bothies**, north of Carbost, near Portnalong, T/F01471-640254, pete@skyehostel.free-online.co.uk. Sleeps 26. Also room for camping, transport from Sligachan or Portree, rents mountain bikes, pub and shop nearby.

F **Skyewalker Independent Hostel**, T640250, skyewalker@easynet.co.uk. In a converted school beyond Portnalong on the road to Fiscavaig. 32 beds.

F **SYHA Hostel**, Glen Brittle, T01471-640278, in the village. It's open mid-Mar to end of Oct and has 39 beds.

Camping

The campsite opposite **Sligachan Hotel** is the most popular place to stay in the area. A campsite by the shore in Glen Brittle, T01471-640404.

Broadford and the east coast *p442*

D **Lime Stone Cottage**, 4 Lime Park (behind the Serpentarium), Broadford, T01471-822142, kathielimepark@btinternet.com. One of the best places to stay around here, full of rustic charm.

D **Ptarmigan**, Broadford, T01471-822744, www.ptarmigan-cottage.com. Modern and comfortable B&B overlooking the bay.

E **Churchton House**, Isle of Raasay, T01478-660260, open all year.

E **Isle of Raasay Hotel**, on the Isle of Raasay nearby to the Outdoor Centre, T/F01478-660222. Open all year.

E **Mrs Mackay**, at Oskaig on the Isle of Raasay, T01478-660207. A good B&B including dinner.

E **Raasay Outdoor Centre**, T01478-660266, the main settlement on the island is Inverarish, a 15-min walk from the ferry dock. Half a mile further is this centre housed in the huge Georgian mansion that was Raasay House, which runs many and various adventure courses, from climbing to windsurfing, as well as offering basic accommodation from Mar to mid-Oct, and a campsite.

F **Dun Caan Hostel**, near the old ferry quay, Kyleakin, T01599-534087, www.skyerover.co.uk. Open all year and also hires bikes.

F **Fossil Bothy**, a mile or so south of Broadford, at Lower Breakish off the A87 to Kyleakin, T01471-822297. Has 8 beds and is open Easter-Oct, book in advance.

F **SYHA Hostel**, Broadford, is by the new pier, T01471-822422. Open all year.

F **SYHA Hostel**, Kyleakin, T01599-534585. Large, modern building a few hundred yards from the pier. Open all year.

F **Skye Backpackers Hostel**, Kyleakin, T/F01599-534510, skye@scotlands-top-hostels.co.uk. More relaxed option. Open all year, breakfast £1.50.

F **SYHA Hostel**, T01478-660240, open mid-Mar to end-Oct. Reached via a rough track leading up a steep hill from tiny Oskaig.

Sleat Peninsula *p444*

L **Hotel Eilean Iarmain**, at Isle Ornsay, T01471-833332, www.eileanarmain.co.uk. 12 rooms. Award-winning Victorian hotel full of charm and old-world character, with wonderful views. It is utterly lovely and romantic and an absolute must if you're in the area and can afford it. Award-winning restaurant features local shellfish landed only yards away (open to non-residents). A cheaper option is to eat in the cosy bar next door, which serves pub grub of an impossibly high standard in a more informal atmosphere. The hotel also offers winter shooting on the local estate, and you can enjoy a tasting of the local whisky.

L **Kinloch Lodge**, at the head of Loch na Dal, T01471-833214, www.kinloch lodge.com. Lord and Lady MacDonald's family home is also an award-winning restaurant, offering the rare chance to enjoy superb food in the grandest of settings. The track that leads to the 19th-century Sporting Lodge turns off the A851 about 8 miles south of Broadford. Lady Claire MacDonald is one of the best known cooks in Scotland and author of several cookbooks, and if you do decide to treat yourself make sure you leave enough room for their exquisite puddings. The 5-course fixed menu is in our expensive range, but well worth it. Accommodation is in 10 en suite rooms. Open Mar-Nov.

B **Duisdale Hotel**, Duisdale, T01471-833202, www.duisdale.com. 19 rooms (2 with

4-poster beds). Country house hotel set in lovely grounds with great views across the Sound of Sleat. The restaurant serves good traditional Scottish cooking, and a 5-course meal is in the expensive range.

C **Ardvasar Hotel**, in Ardvasar, near the ferry terminal, T01471-844223, www.ardvasar.com. Traditional whitewashed coaching inn with 9 rooms, an excellent restaurant and the liveliest pub in the vicinity.

F **Flora MacDonald Hostel**, at Kilmore, between the turning for Isle Ornsay and Armadale, T01471-844440, www.isle-of-skye-tour-guide.co.uk. Newly refurbished with all facilities, 32 beds, open all year, and free transport to and from Armadale Pier.

F **SYHA Hostel**, just before the turn-off to the ferry pier, T01471-844260. 42 beds. Open mid-Mar to end Oct, rents bikes.

Eating

With the notable exception of the magnificent **Three Chimneys** restaurant the best food on Skye is normally served in hotel dining rooms, so also check the Sleeping section for places to eat. Many B&Bs also provide evening meals on request.

Portree *p433, map p434*

£££ **Chandlery Seafood Restaurant**, next door to the **Bosville Hotel**, see Sleeping. Superb French/Scottish cuisine using local produce.

£££ **Lower Deck Seafood Restaurant**, on the harbour front at the foot of Quay Brae, T01478-613611. Freshest of seafood and a contender with the **Chandlery** for the best food in town. Open Apr-Oct daily 1100-2200. For a budget treat try the excellent fish and chips from their takeaway next door.

£££ **Skeabost House Hotel**, 4 miles north of Portree on the Dunvegan Rd, T01470-532202, skeabost@sol.co.uk. This peaceful country house in lovely grounds on the shores of Loch Snizort has a reputation for fine food using the best local produce.

££ **Ben Tianavaig**, 5 Bosville Terr, T01478-612152. Excellent vegetarian bistro. Seating is limited so you'll need to book. Open lunchtimes at weekends, and Tue-Sun 1800-2130.

££ **Bosville Restaurant**, in the **Bosville Hotel**, see Sleeping. Also recommended. They offer a lunchtime special (soup, sandwich and coffee for £5) which is great value.

£ **Portree House**, Home Farm Rd, see Sleeping, serves good value food, daily 1200-1545, 1730-2000.

£ **Spicehut**, Bayfield Rd, T01478-612681. Indian restaurant and takeaway. Open daily 1200-1430 and 1700-2400.

£ **Steve's Kitchen Takeaway**, on Bayfield Rd, opposite the library. For cheap Chinese takeaway food.

£ **Tuireann Café**, part of the arts centre, see Sights p433. Natural whole-foods and organic produce, home-made bread, cakes and pastries. Excellent quality and value. Open Mar-Oct Mon-Sat 1000-1800, Nov-Feb Tue-Sat 1000-1630.

Trotternish Peninsula *p435*

££ **Oystercatcher Restaurant**, in the village of Staffin, T01470-562384, closed Sun. A good place for food.

£ **Pub on the Pier**, Uig, serves cheap bar meals, and the famous Cuillin ales are brewed at the nearby Skye Brewery. You can also change foreign currency here. Open till 2300.

Waternish, Dunvegan and Duirinish *p438*

£££ **The Three Chimneys**, Duirnish Peninsula, T01470-511258, www.threechimneys.co.uk. Considered by many to be the best restaurant in the north of Scotland and, judging by the numerous awards they've won, that judgement can't be far wrong. Local seafood, meat, veg and dairy produce and a great wine list. Open daily 1230-1400 (except Sun) and 1830-2130.

££ **Lochbay Seafood**, Waternish Peninsula, T01470-592235. You should finish off the day with a meal at the this wonderful restaurant where you can almost see your dinner being landed. Open Apr-Oct for lunch and till 2030 (closed Sat).

Broadford and the east coast *p442*

£££ **Rendezvous**, at Breakish, south of Broadford on the main road to Kyleakin, T01471-822001. Expensive place to eat but excellent food.

££-£ **Claymore Bar-Restaurant**, at the south end of the village, T01471-822333. Decent bar meals.

££ The Crofter's Kitchen, outside the village of Kyleakin on the road to Broadford, T01599-534134. Good food, from snacks to 3-course meals. Open Mon-Sat 1000-2100, Sun 1230-2100.

Bars and clubs

Portree *p433, map p434*
The town's nightlife is mainly confined to eating and drinking.
Pier Hotel, Quay St, T01478-612094, by the harbour. The bar in this hotel is a real fishermen's drinking den.
Royal Hotel, Bank St, T01478-612525. Also popular is the bar here.

Entertainment

Portree *p433, map p434*
Portree Community Centre, Camanahd Sq, Park Rd, T01478-613736. This is the place to come if you fancy a wild Fri night ceilidh.
Aros Experience, see Sights p433, has a theatre which shows drama, movies and live music. Call the box office for details of their monthly programme, T01478-613750.

Festivals and events

Portree *p433, map p434*
Early Aug: **Highland Games** are a 1-day event held in Portree.

Shopping

Portree *p433, map p434*
Carbostcraft Pottery, Bayfield Rd, which sells pottery with a huge variety of designs (they also have a shop near the Talisker Distillery, see p441).
Jackson's Wholefoods, at Park Pl, opposite the council offices, a wholefood store.
Outdoor Sports, Bridge Rd, next to Skye Batiks, Portree. Good for mountain gear.
Over the Rainbow, at the top of Quay Brae, T01478-612555. Open 0900-2200 in the high season. A good place to buy woollens.
Safeway supermarket, diagonally opposite the Bosville Hotel.
Skye Batiks, The Green, near the TIC, T01478-613331. Sells handmade 'batiks' (colourful cotton fabrics), which are pricey but unique souvenirs of Skye, see also p445.
Skye Woollen Mill, Dunvegan Rd, T01478-612889. Knitwear and tartan souvenirs can be found here.

The Cuillins and Minginish *p440*
Cioch Direct, 4 Ullinish, Struan, T01470-572307. For mountain gear.

Activities and tours

Portree *p433, map p434*
If the weather's good, Portree offers many opportunities for a wide variety of outdoor activities.
Boat trips, T01478-613718, or ask for Peter Urquhart at the pier, can be made to the island of Rona, north of Raasay, with the *MV Brigadoon*. Trips leave from the pier (Apr-Sep) and cost from £10 per person. Full-day charters are also available for £75-150 (12 passengers).
Island Cycles, on The Green, Mon-Sat 1000-1700, T01478-613121. Mountain bikes for hire here.
Portree Riding and Trekking Stables, T01478-582419, are a couple of miles from the town centre. Follow the Struan Rd (B885) for 2 miles, then bear right at the fork towards Peiness. Offer horse riding.
Skye Riding Centre, T01470-532439, 2 miles north of Portree, at Borve on the road to Uig. Offer horse riding.
Swimming pool, Camanahd Sq, T01478-612655.

Trotternish Peninsula *p435*
Whitewave Activities, a few miles north of Uig, on the A855 at Linicrowhere, T01471-542414, info@white-wave.co.uk. Here you can try windsurfing and sea kayaking. There's also a café specializing in vegetarian, seafood and celtic music, and a B&B.

The Cuillins and Minginish *p440*
The Bella Jane, T0800-7313089 (freephone 0730-2200), www.bellajane.co.uk, makes the spectacular trip from Elgol into the gaping maw of Loch Coruisk, one of the highlights of any trip to Skye. It lasts 3 hrs, including about 1½ hrs ashore, and cost £15, £7.50 children. You should be able to see seals and porpoises en route. There's also a one-way trip for experienced walkers/climbers who wish to make the return journey on foot or to

explore the Cuillins. There are also trips on the **Aquaxpolre** to Rùm or Canna.

For **climbing** the following guides have all been recommended:

Colin Threlfall, Outdoor Sports (see below).

Cuillin Guides, Gerry Achroyd, Stac Lee, Glen Brittle, T01478-640289.

Hugh Evans, 4d Wentworth St, Portree, T01478-612682.

Richard MacGuire, 4 Matheson Place, Portree, T01478-613180.

Skye Highs, Mike Lates, 3 Luib, Broadford, T01471-822116.

Broadford and the east coast *p442*

Wildlife cruises, T0800-7832175, www.glassbottomboat.co.uk, run from Broadford pier. You can choose the glass-bottomed *Family's Pride II*, or the much faster *SkyeJet*, a Rigid Inflatable Boat (RIB) which has the advantage of taking you farther afield.

Kyleakin Private Hire, T01599-534452, run a taxi service and guided tours of the island.

Transport

Portree *p433, map p434*

There are 4 buses daily (Mar-Oct) Mon-Fri (2 on Sat) around the Trotternish Peninsula, in each direction, via **Uig**. There are daily buses (4 Mon-Sat, 3 on Sun) to **Kyleakin**, and 3 buses daily Mon-Sat to **Armadale** via **Broadford**. There are 2 daily buses to **Carbost** (for the Talisker Distillery) and Mon-Fri (1 on Sat), and 2 daily buses to **Glenbrittle** (in the summer only). There are 3 buses daily Mon-Fri to **Glendale** via **Dunvegan** (1 on Sat), and 3 buses to **Waternish** via **Dunvegan** (Mon-Sat). For taxis call **Ace Taxis**, T01478-613600 or **A2B Taxis**, T01478-613456.

There's a **Scottish Citylink** service from **Inverness** (3 Mon-Sat, 2 on Sun, 3 hrs) and also from **Glasgow** via **Fort William** to **Kyleakin**, **Portree** and **Uig** 3-4 times daily (3 hrs from Fort William to Portree). Winter services are severely limited with only a few buses in each direction each day.

Trotternish Peninsula *p435*

Scottish **Citylink** runs a service to/from **Inverness**, **Fort William** and **Glasgow**.

Ferries leave from **Uig** to **Lochmaddy** on **North Uist** (1¾ hrs) and to **Tarbert** on **Harris** (1¾ hrs). For details see p432, or contact Uig, T01470-542219.

Waternish, Dunvegan and Duirinish *p438*

There are 3 buses daily (Mar-Oct, Mon-Fri) from **Glendale** to and from **Portree** via **Dunvegan**. The bus leaves Portree at 1000, arrives at the castle at 1048 and returns at 1252 (Mar-Oct only). There is 1 bus on Sat and a daily bus from Dunvegan to Glendale (not Sun).

The Cuillins and Minginish *p440*

There are 2 daily buses from **Portree** to **Glen Brittle** Mon-Sat during the summer only. Otherwise, take the **Portree-Carbost-Fiscavaig** bus, which leaves twice Mon-Fri and once on Sat, and get off at the turn-off, then walk the remaining 7 miles, or hitch, though it can be slow. The only public transport to **Elgol** is the **postbus** from **Broadford**, which runs twice Mon-Sat and once on Sun, and takes 2 hrs. There's a regular bus service (weekdays only) from **Portree** and **Sligachan** to **Portnalong**, T01470-532240.

Broadford and the east coast *p442*

Daily **Citylink** buses run from **Broadford** to and from **Portree**, **Inverness** and **Fort William**. Waterloo buses run daily to and from **Kyleakin**, **Portree** (£6 return) and **Armadale/Ardvasar**. There are buses from **Kyleakin** to **Portree** via **Broadford** (4 daily), to **Armadale** and **Ardvasar** via Broadford (3 daily Mon-Sat) and half hourly to **Kyle of Lochalsh**, see p383, via the Skye Bridge.

CalMac car and passenger ferry runs from **Sconser** daily Mon-Sat every hour. It takes 15 mins and costs £4.40 per person return, plus £17.65 per car and £1 per bicycle.

Car hire at **Sutherlands** at the Esso Garage, Broadford, T01471-822225. From £30 per day. Bikes can be hired from **Fairwinds Bicycle Hire**, just past the Broadford Hotel, T01471-822270. Mar-Oct

Sleat Peninsula *p444*

For full details of ferry crossings to Mallaig, see p432. There are 3 buses daily, except Sun, from **Armadale Pier** to **Portree** (1 hr 20 mins) and **Kyleakin** (1 hr) via **Broadford** (40 mins). The first bus leaves at 0935.

Directory

Portree *p433, map p434*
Banks **Bank of Scotland** and **Clydesdale Bank**, both on Somerled Sq. **Royal Bank of Scotland** is on Bank St. All have ATMs.
Internet **Portree Independent Hostel**, see Sleeping p445, at the post office and at Portree Backpacker's Hostel, Dunvegan Rd.
Laundry At the **Portree Independent Hostel**.
Post At the top of Quay Brae.

Broadford and the east coast *p442*
Banks **Bank of Scotland** with ATM by the shops opposite the road to the new pier in Broadford.

The Small Isles

These four tenacious little siblings are a world away from the Scottish mainland and not for the faint or fickle traveller. It takes longer to reach them from London than it does to fly to Australia, so you have to be pretty determined. Those who do make it are rewarded with perfect peace and an almost primeval silence and solitude. This is nature in its purest form, free from the fripperies of the 21st century. ▸▸ *For Sleeping, Eating and other listings, see pages 453-454.*

Ins and outs

A CalMac passenger-only ferry sails from Mallaig to all four islands once daily Monday to Thursday and twice on Friday and Saturday, returning on the same days. There aren't any transport connections with Skye. ▸▸ *For further details, see Transport page 453.*

Eigg → *Phone code: 01687. Colour map 3, grid A3-B3.*

Little Eigg (pronounced 'egg'), only five miles long by three miles wide, has had something of a chequered past. In 1577 it was the scene of one of the bloodiest episodes in the history of Clan warfare, when 395 MacDonalds, almost the entire population, were trapped in a cave and suffocated by a raiding party of Macleods from Skye, who lit a fire at the entrance. More recently it has been at the heart of a bitter land ownership debate. Having endured a succession of absentee landlords, ranging from the merely eccentric to the criminally negligent, the 70 remaining islanders seized the moment in 1997 and bought the island themselves, in conjunction with the Scottish Wildlife Trust. Now everyone can enjoy the island's wildlife, which includes otters, seals, eagles and many other birds, such as the Manx shearwater, guillemots and black-throated divers. It's worth tagging along on one of the regular walks organized by the Scottish Wildlife Trust warden, John Chester.

The island is dominated by **An Sgurr**, a distinctive 1,289 ft flat-topped basalt peak with three vertical sides. It can be climbed fairly easily by its western ridge, though the last few hundred feet is precipitous, and there are superb views of the Inner Hebrides and mountains of Knoydart from the summit. Sitting in the shadow of the Sgurr, at the southeastern corner, is the main settlement, **Galmisdale**. This is where the ferries drop anchor (passengers are transferred to a smaller boat), and there's a post office, shop and tearoom, all by the pier. At the northern end is the small township of **Cleadale**, on the Bay of Laig. Just to the north are the **'Singing Sands'**, a beach that makes a strange sound as you walk across it. At the end of the island's only road you'll find its most famous property, **Howlin' House**, which apparently once belonged to JRR Tolkein. More details on the island are available at www.isleofeigg.org.

Muck → *Phone code: 01687. Colour map 3, grid B3.*

Tiny Muck, just two miles long by one mile wide, is the smallest of the four islands and is flat and fertile, with a beautiful shell beach. It has been owned by the MacEwan family since 1879. The island gets its unfortunate name (*muc* is Gaelic for pig) from the porpoises, or 'sea pigs', that swim round its shores. The ferry drops anchor near **Port Mór**, where there's accommodation. The tearoom here does snacks and sells fresh bread. Visit the island's website, www.islemuck.com.

Rùm → *Phone code: 01687. Colour map 3, grid A3.*

Rùm is the largest of the islands and the most wild, beautiful and mountainous. The island is owned and run by Scottish Natural Heritage as an enormous outdoor laboratory and research station, and most of the 30 or so inhabitants are employed by them. Studies of the red deer population are among the most important areas of their work, and access to parts of the island is restricted. This is not prohibitive, though, and there are many marked nature trails, walks and birdwatching spots. The island is a haven for wildlife, and perhaps its most notable resident is the magnificent white-tailed sea eagle, successfully re-introduced on to Rùm in the 1980s and now spreading beyond the island. Rùm is also home to golden eagles, Manx shearwaters and, less appealingly, millions of midges. The island is the wettest of the Small Isles and a haven for the little pests.

Rùm's other great attraction is its mountain range, which rivals that of the Cuillins of Skye. The highest point is **Askival** (2,664 ft), which can be reached by the main ridge from **Hallival**, though the route involves some rock scrambling and is only advised for fit and experienced walkers. Before setting out, ask permission from the manager of the reserve office at the White House ⓘ *T01687-462026, Mon-Fri 0900-1230*.

Though it looks like a wilderness, Rùm once supported a population of 300. Most of them were shipped off to Canada in the mid-19th century, leaving behind an uninhabited deer forest for sporting millionaires. One of these, John Bullough, a cotton millionaire from Accrington, bought it in 1888 and passed it on to his son, Sir George Bullough, who built the extravagant and extraordinary **Kinloch Castle** ⓘ *guided tours of the castle are run most days at 1400, £4*, in 1900 and then promptly deserted it in the mid 1920s. No expense was spared on this massive late-Victorian mansion, constructed of red sandstone from Arran in a bizarre combination of styles; to describe it as over-the-top would be a gross understatement. It was a finalist in the BBC's recent *Restoration* series and is currently undergoing a major refurbishment. Visitors take their shoes off as they are escorted round the lavish rooms, which echo to the ghostly sound of a mechanical organ tucked away under the stairs. The castle stands at the head of narrow Loch Scresort by the little hamlet of **Kinloch**, where you'll find a well-stocked shop, a post office and a coffee shop in the community hall. Ferries are anchored in the loch and passengers are transferred to a smaller craft and dropped a few minutes' walk along the shore from Kinloch.

The Bullough family mausoleum, built in the style of a Greek Doric temple, stands incongruously on the west coast at **Harris Bay**. It's an interesting 7½-mile walk across to the mausoleum from Kinloch.

Canna → *Colour map 3, grid A3.*

Canna is the most westerly of the Small Isles and is owned by the National Trust for Scotland. It's a small island, five miles long by one mile wide, bounded by cliffs and with a rugged interior, fringed by fertile patches. It's attached to its smaller neighbour, **Sanday**, by a narrow isthmus which is covered, except at low tide. The main attraction for visitors is some fine walking. It's about a mile from the ferry jetty up to the top of **Compass Hill** (458 ft), so called because its high metallic content distorts compasses. The highest point on the island is **Carn a' Ghaill** (690 ft). During the summer, a day trip from Mallaig allows you over nine hours in which to explore Canna and enjoy the fantastic views across to Rùm and Skye.

The population of 20 mostly work on the island's farm. Canna was gifted to the National Trust by its benevolent owner, Dr John Lorne, a notable Gaelic scholar who still lives there. The island continues to be run as a single working farm and, since it was sold in 1938, has been an unofficial bird sanctuary with 157 recorded bird species, including Manx shearwater and puffins.

Sleeping

Eigg *p451*
D **Kildonan House**, T01687-482446. The island's only guest house, price includes dinner and the food is superb.
F **The Glebe Barn**, T01687-482417, Apr-Oct.
F **Hostel**, independent with 24 beds
Self-catering cottages, for details www.isleofeigg.org, are alsoavailable.

Muck *p452*
D **Port Mór House**, T01678-462365. The price includes dinner which is also available to non-residents. Alternatively, you can ask permission to camp at the tearoom.

Rùm *p452*
E **Bay View**, T01687-462023. The only B&B. Book well in advance.
E-F **Kinloch Castle**, for bookings and more information, T01687-462037, castleman ager@rumcastle.free_/online.co.uk. They no longer have rooms but there is cheap hostel accommodation in the old servants' quarters, including double rooms, open Mar-Oct.

Camping
F **Bothies**, and camping is allowed at Kinloch. Contact the reserve manager at the White House, T01687-462026.

Canna *p452*
Those wishing to stay can **camp rough**, with permission from the **National Trust for Scotland**, or rent out their self-catering cottage, T0131-226 5922, www.nts.org.uk.

Eating

There is a tearoom and shop on each island with the exception of Canna, where there are no shops so you'll need to bring your own supplies. Most of the B&Bs and guest houses serve food. The well-stocked shop on Eigg is at the jetty, T01687-482432, open Mon-Sat.

Transport

CalMac operates the passenger-only ferry from **Mallaig** to all 4 islands once daily Mon-Thu and twice on Fri and Sat, returning on the same days. There's also a **non-landing cruise** around all the islands which costs £13 but you can sail to all 4 islands if you catch the 0620 ferry on Sat. A second ferry leaves on Sat, making it possible to spend time on one of the islands. Bicycles cost £2 for any trip.

To **Eigg** 1 hr 10 mins direct, £5.05 one way) on Mon, Tue (via **Muck**), Thu, Fri and Sat. To **Muck** (1 ½ hrs direct, £7.65 one way) on Tue, Thu (via Eigg), Fri and Sat (via Eigg). To **Rùm** (1 hr 10 mins direct, £7.50 one way) on Mon (via Eigg), Wed, Fri and Sat. To **Canna** (2 hrs direct, £8.55 one way) on Mon (via **Eigg** and **Rùm**), Wed (via **Rùm**), Fri (via Rùm) and Sat.

At Muck and Rùm passengers are transferred to small boats as there are no suitable piers. For more details contact the **CalMac** office in Mallaig, T01687-462403.

From May-Sep the **CalMac** ferries from Mallaig are supplemented by cruises from Arisaig with **Arisaig Marine**, T01687-450224, www.airsaig.co.uk, run by Murdo Grant. See p381. For a bus/taxi service on Eigg, call **Davie Robertson**, T01687-482494, and bike hire from **Eigg Bikes**, call Stuart Thomson, T01687-482469.

Outer Hebrides

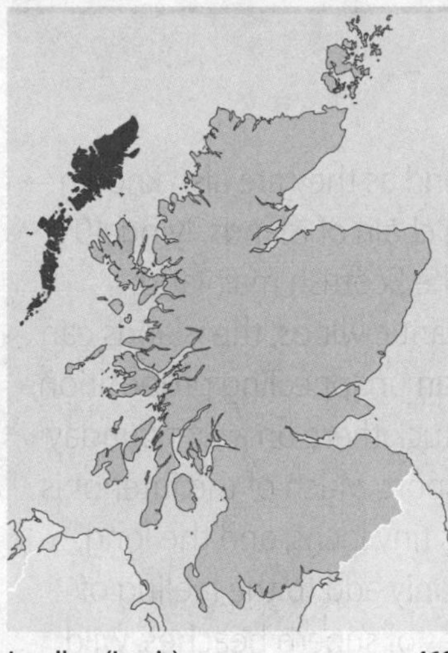

Footprint features

Introduction

The Outer Hebrides – or Long Island as they are also known – consist of a narrow 130-mile long chain of islands, lying 40 miles off the northwest coast of the Scottish mainland. Relentlessly battered by fierce Atlantic winds, the islands can seem a hostile environment and an unappealing proposition, particularly if you happen to be stuck there on a wet Sunday without your own means of transport. Much of the interior is bleak peat bog, rocks and endless tiny lochs, and the long, straggling crofting communities only add to the feeling of desolation. But there are also miles of superb beaches, wild mountain scenery, numerous archaeological treasures and long hours of summer daylight in which to appreciate it all.

Despite the frequency of transport connections with the mainland, the Outer Hebrides remain remote in every sense. Unlike Skye and the Inner Hebrides, tourism is of far less importance to the local economy. In many ways, the islands are the last bastion of the old Highland life. Though newer industries such as fish farming have been introduced, the traditional occupations of crofting, fishing and weaving still dominate, and outside Stornoway on Lewis (the only decent-sized town in the islands) life is very much a traditional one, revolving around the seasons and the tides. Almost every islander has more than one occupation, so don't be surprised if the landlady of your guest house also weaves Harris Tweed, or if her husband drives the postbus as well as doing a bit of fishing on the side. This creates a network of relationships where everyone knows everyone else.

★ Don't miss...

1. **Calanais** Visit the standing stones here, preferably at night when there's a spooky atmosphere, page 466.
2. **Uig sands** Take a stroll along these wonderful sands, the loveliest beach on Lewis page 467.
3. **Bays** Hire a car and drive through the weird lunar landscape at Bays, on the east coast of Harris, page 475.
4. **Barra** Fly to this island, where the planes land on the beach, page 478.
5. **St Kilda** Take a trip here, home to some of the largest seabird colonies in Europe, page 488.

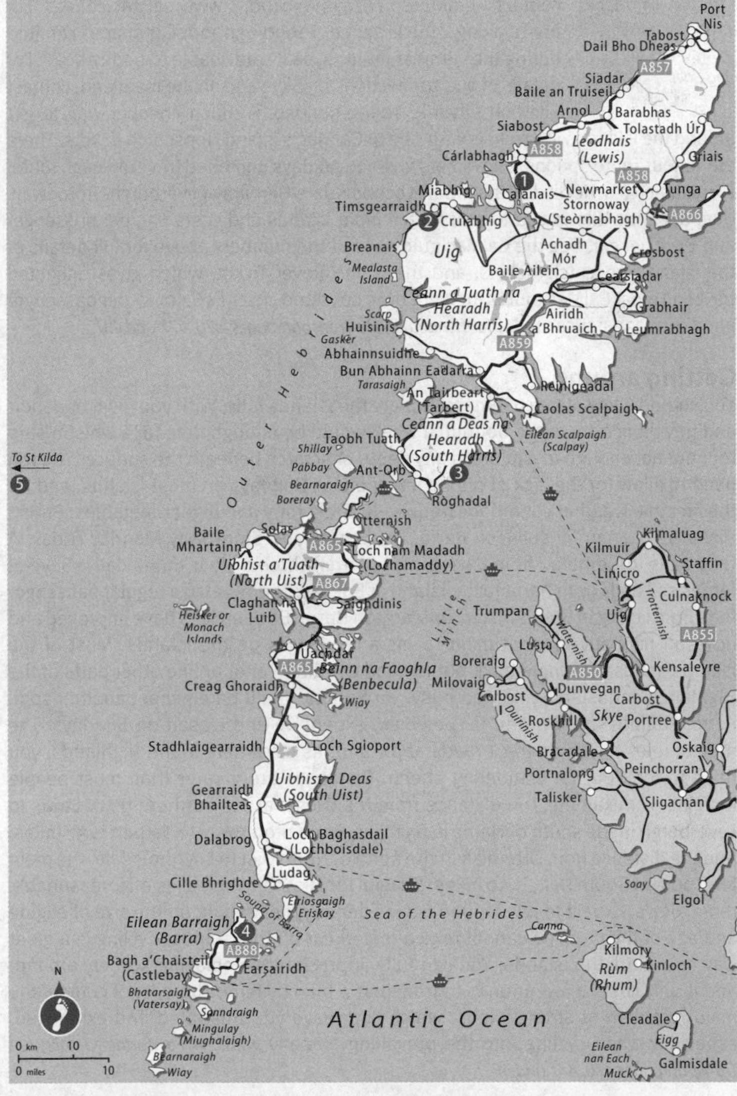

Ins and outs

Getting there

British Airways/Loganair flies from Glasgow to Stornoway on Lewis, Barra and Benbecula on North Uist. There are also flights from Edinburgh to Stornoway, Inverness to Stornoway, and from Benbecula to Barra and Stornoway. CalMac car and passenger ferries sail to and from Stornoway (Lewis), Tarbert (Harris), Lochmaddy (North Uist), Lochboisdale (South Uist) and Castlebay (Barra). Ferry times change according to the day of the week and time of the year, so they aren't listed in full below. For full details of ferry timetables contact CalMac, T01475-650100, www.calmac.co.uk. For pre-booking vehicle space, T0990-650000. Car space is limited during the summer months, so it's advisable to book ahead. For details of bus connections on Skye and on the mainland, contact Scottish Citylink, T0990-505050. A much cheaper way to get around the islands with a car is with one of CalMac's Island Hopscotch tickets. There are various route options, and tickets give you 30 days unlimited travel on each route. For example, a ticket for the Oban-Lochboisdale-Bernaray-Leverburgh-Stornoway-Ullapool route allows you to visit all the main islands and costs £35 per passenger and £147 per car. See the CalMac guide or call the numbers above for full details of the Island Hopscotch Tickets, and the Island Rover Ticket, which gives unlimited travel on most CalMac routes for eight or 15 days and costs £46.50/67 per passenger and £222/332 per car. ▸▸ *For further details, see Transport pages 470, 477 and 487.*

> *Weather conditions are so changeable that flights are prone to delay and can be very bumpy. Flights to Barra have an added complication. They land on the beach, meaning that the runway disappears twice a day under the incoming tide.*

Getting around

You should allow plenty of time to explore the islands fully. With your own transport and travelling from top to bottom, a week would be enough time for a whistle-stop tour but not enough to explore in any depth or scratch beneath the surface. You will need to allow for the lack of public transport on Sundays on most islands, and for the fact that weather conditions frequently affect ferry and flight timetables. British Airways/Loganair fly between Barra, Benbecula and Stornoway Monday-Friday. A ferry sails to Berneray from Leverburgh (Harris) three or four times daily. Several ferries sail daily from Barra to the island of Eriskay. There's also a regular passenger ferry from Ludag in South Uist to Eoligarry on Barra. Bus services have improved and now run regularly to most main towns and villages on the islands. Most of the islands' roads are single track but in good condition and, unlike other parts of the Highlands and Islands, not too busy. On Sunday you'll barely meet another soul. Petrol stations are few and far between, expensive and closed on Sundays. The normal rules for single track roads apply and, as elsewhere in the Highlands, you need to look out for wandering sheep. Distances are greater than most people imagine. For example, the distance from Nis (Ness) at the northern tip of Lewis to Leverburgh in the south of Harris is 85 miles. From Stornoway to Tarbert is 37 miles. And the distance from Otternish in the north of North Uist to Lochboisdale, the main ferry port on South Uist, is 50 miles. Several local car hire agencies offer reasonable rental deals. Expect to pay around £15-25 per day, depending on the size of engine and age of the car. You cannot take a rented car off the islands. Cycling is a great way to explore the islands. You can fully appreciate the amazing scenery around, and it only costs a few pounds to transport a bike by ferry. There is, of course, the major problem of strong winds, which can leave you frustrated and exhausted, especially when cycling into the prevailing easterly wind. ▸▸ *For further details, see Transport pages 470, 477 and 487.*

Never on a Sunday

The islands are the 'Gaidhealtachd', the land of the Gael. Gaelic culture has remained more prominent here than in any other part of Scotland, and the way of life and philosophy of the islanders will seem totally alien and fascinating to many visitors. Gaelic is the first language for the majority of the islanders – and the only one for the older generation – but the all-pervading influence of the English media has taken its toll and the language is under threat. Though Gaelic is still taught in schools, the younger generation tends to speak to each other in English. Visitors will not have any language problems, as the Gaelic-speaking inhabitants are so polite they will always change to English when visitors are present, though place names and signposts are in Gaelic.

The church is also an important factor in preserving the language, and services are usually held in Gaelic. In fact, religion is one of the most pervasive influences of Hebridean life, and the islanders' faith is as strong as the winds that pound their shores. The islands are split between the Presbyterian Lewis, Harris and North Uist, and the predominantly Roman Catholic South Uist and Barra. Benbecula, meanwhile, has a foot in either camp. On Lewis and Harris the Free Church is immensely powerful and the Sabbath is strictly observed. Don't expect to travel anywhere by public transport, shops and petrol stations will be closed and you'll be hard pressed to find a place to eat. Even the swings in the playgrounds are padlocked! Things are changing, however, and October 2002 saw the revolutionary move to allow Loganair to fly to Stornoway on a Sunday. Despite protests of tsunami-like proportions from the church, who described the idea as "a breach of God's moral law", Loganair's tourisy-friendly flights went ahead.

Tourist information

The Outer Hebrides is made up of more than 200 islands, only 10 of which are populated: Lewis and Harris; Scalpay; Berneray; North Uist; Benbecula; South Uist; Eriskay; Barra; and Vatersay; giving a total population of just under 30,000. The main population centre is Stornoway on Lewis, the only major town in the islands. The rest of the population is scattered throughout the islands in much smaller villages, mostly strung out along the coast. There are tourist information centres in Stornoway and Tarbert which are open all year round, and also in Lochmaddy, Lochboisdale and Castlebay which are open early April to mid October. Full details are given under each destination. The Western Isles Tourist Board produces an accommodation brochure as well as the essential *Western Isles Official Tourist Map* (Estate Publications; £3.95), which gives place names in English and Gaelic. They also have their own website, www.witb.co.uk, which provides lots of information on the islands, including up and coming events. Information about the islands can also be obtained at the excellent www.visit.hebrides.com. You should also invest in a copy of the *Highlands & Islands Travel Guide* which is available from the local tourist information centres. Accommodation on the islands is generally not difficult to find, except perhaps at the height of the summer when you should book in advance, either directly or through the local tourist office. It's also a good idea to book ahead if you're staying on a Sunday, and if you're staying in the countryside, you should check if there's a convenient pub or hotel to eat in, and if not, make arrangements to eat at your B&B. ➤➤ *For further accommodation information, see page 467.*

Leodhas (Lewis)

➔ *Phone code: 01851. Colour map 1.*

Lewis constitutes the northern two thirds of the most northerly island in the Outer Hebrides. It is by far the most populous of the Outer Hebridean islands and, with over 20,000 inhabitants, makes up two thirds of the total population. Just over 8,000 people live in Stornoway, the largest town in the Hebrides and the administrative capital of the Western Isles. The majority of the rest of the population live in the long line of crofting townships strung out along the west coast between Port Nis (Ness) and Càrlabhagh (Carloway). The west coast is also where you'll find the island's most interesting sites, the prehistoric remains of Dùn Chàrlabhaigh (Carloway) Broch and the impressive Calanais (Callanish) Standing Stones, the restored blackhouse village

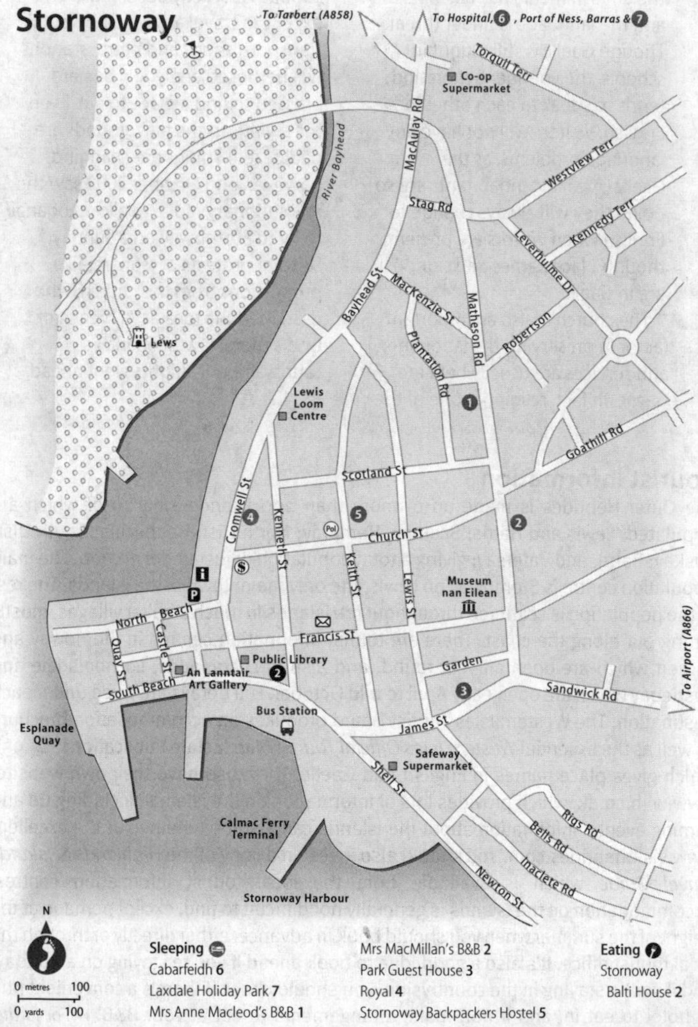

of Garenin and the Arnol Blackhouse. These can all be visited as a day trip from Stornoway, either as an organized tour or on the 'West Side Circular' bus service. The interior of the northern half is flat peat bog, hence the island's name which means 'marshy' in Gaelic. Further south, where Lewis becomes Harris, the scenery is more dramatic as the relentlessly flat landscape gives way to rocky hills, providing the backdrop to the sea-lochs that cut deep into the coast and the beautiful beaches around Uig. ▸▸ *For Sleeping, Eating and other listings, see pages 467-470.*

History

Lewis was dominated by the Vikings, and the Norse influence can be seen in many of the place names, such as Uig (which is Norse for 'a bay'). After the end of Norwegian sovereignty in 1266, the island was ruled by the Macleods, said to be descendants of early settlers from Iceland. Control of the island was wrested from them by the Mackenzies, who then proceeded to sell it, in 1844, to Sir James Matheson. The new owner built Lews Castle in Stornoway and began to develop the infrastructure of the island as well as investing in new industries. Though many crofts were cleared and families sent to Canada, the people of Lewis fared well and certainly much better than their counterparts in the Southern Isles.

The next proprietor was Lord Leverhulme, founder of Lever Brothers, who bought the island (along with Harris) in 1918. He planned to turn Lewis into a major fishing centre and ploughed money into developing the infrastructure. He was forced to abandon his plans, however, partly because of the decline of the fishing industry, and partly owing to the growing conflict between him and the islanders returning from the war who wanted land of their own to farm. As a final benevolent gesture, Lord Leverhulme offered Lewis to the islanders, but only Stornoway Council accepted. The island was then divided into estates and sold, and hundreds emigrated.

Today the economy of Lewis is still based on the traditional industries of crofting, fishing and weaving, though there are other economic activities such as fish farming, which is now a major employer, service industries, tourism, construction and the onshore oil yard at Stornoway.

Steòrnabhagh (Stornoway) → *Colour map 1, grid B3. Population: 8,132.*

The fishing port of Stornoway, the only town in the Outer Hebrides, is the islands' commercial capital and as such boasts more services and facilities than you might expect in any town of comparable size. It's not a pretty place, dominated as it is by the oil industry, but has the full range of banks, shops, hotels, guest houses, pubs and restaurants, garages, car hire firms, sports facilities, an airport and ferry terminal, and for the visiting tourist it presents a rare opportunity to stock up on supplies.

Stornoway is also the administrative capital and home to the Comhairle nan Eilean (Western Isles Council), which has done much to broaden the local economy and to promote and protect Gaelic language and culture, but is probably best known for its disastrous financial dealings with the Bank of Credit and Commerce International (BCCI), which collapsed in 1991, losing the islands a cool £23 million. ▸▸ *For Sleeping, Eating and other listings, see pages 467-470.*

Ins and outs

Getting there and around Stornoway is the island's transport hub. The airport is 4 miles east of the town centre, a £5 taxi ride away. The CalMac ferry terminal is just beyond the bus station, which is on South Beach, a short walk from the town centre. Buses leave from Stornoway to all parts of the island and also to Tarbert and Leverburgh on Harris. Bus timetables are available from the tourist office. The town is compact and most of what you need is within easy walking distance of the tourist office. Some of the B&Bs in the residential areas are quite a distance from the centre, but there's an hourly town bus service, or hire a taxi. » *For further details, see Transport page 470.*

Tourist information The TIC ⓘ *26 Cromwell St, T01856-703088, Apr-May and Sep-Oct Mon-Fri 0900-1800, Sat 0900-1700, Jun-Aug Mon-Fri 0900-2000, Oct-Mar Mon-Fri 0900-1700*, stocks maps, bus timetables and various books and brochures, and sell tickets for minibus tours to Calanais and for wildlife trips around Lewis and Harris.

Sights

Stornoway is short on conventional tourist sights and once you've been to the tourist office and bought the necessities from the local supermarkets, there's not much else to do. The focal point of the town has always been its sheltered deep-water **harbour** and, though the fishing industry has declined since its peak at the end of the last century, there's still a fair amount of activity, especially at the fish market on North Beach on Tuesday and Thursday evenings. The harbour is usually full of seals, giving the town its nickname of Portrona (port of seals). There's a good view across the harbour to **Lews Castle**, a 19th-century edifice built by Sir James Matheson with money earned from opium and tea. The castle now houses a college and its real attraction is the wooded grounds, the only place you'll see trees on the islands.

Museum nan Eilean ⓘ *Francis St, T01851-703773, Apr to Sep Mon-Sat 1000-1730, Oct-Mar Tue 1000-1700 and Sat 1000-1300, free*, features a range of temporary exhibitions on island life and history. Anyone remotely interested in Harris Tweed should visit the **Lewis Loom Centre** ⓘ *T01851-703117, Mon-Sat 1000-1700, £2*, housed in the Old Grainstore at the northern end of Cromwell Street, just off Bayhead. The 40-minute guided tour includes demonstrations of traditional methods of warping, dyeing and spinning, and a detailed lecture on the history of Harris Tweed. There's also a craft shop.

The impressive baronial Town Hall on South Beach currently houses the **An Lanntair Art Gallery** ⓘ *T01851-703307, www.lanntair.co.uk, Mon-Sat 1000-1730, free*, though plans are afoot to move the gallery into a new arts centre. The gallery features the work of local, national and international artists and also stages various musical events. The coffee shop serves home baking and tasty snacks.

North to Nis (Ness) → *Colour map 1, grid A3.*

The A857 leaves Stornoway and runs northwest through barren, treeless and relentlessly bleak moorland to **Barabhas (Barvas).** The landscape is scarred by deep gashes caused by peat digging, and the unfamiliar smell you detect in your nostrils is peat burning – a strange mixture of burning grass, whisky and coffee. Peat is the main source of domestic fuel used on the islands, and outside most houses you'll see large stacks of peat, or *cruachs*.

The road from Barabhas northeast to Nis runs through a series of forlorn-looking, scrawny settlements that all look identical and merge into one. They consist of modern, characterless grey pebble-dash cottages with the ubiquitous piles of peat in the gardens, and the abandoned cars and vans scattered around everywhere only adds to the ugly and depressing scene.

Just beyond Barabhas a sign points left to the **Morvern Art Gallery,** which has a café, making it a welcome refuge in bad weather. A few miles further on is a turning right to **Baile an Trùiseil (Ballantrushel),** site of the huge **Clach an Trùiseil**, a 20-ft monolith (the largest in Europe), which was the scene of the last major battle on the island, fought between the Morrisons of Nis and the MacAuleys of Uig. This is the first

Gatliff Trust

The Gatliff Hebridean Hostels Trust (GHHT) is a non-profit making charitable organization run entirely by volunteers, working with the island community to establish, maintain and develop a chain of 'value-for-money' hostels offering clean, cheap, simple, safe, welcoming and traditional croft-style accommodation in dramatic and beautiful locations for visitors to the Outer Hebrides.

The GHHT is independent of the SYHA but has adopted status. Visitors do not have to be members of either organization to use and stay in the hostels. First established as the Gatliff Trust in 1961 by Herbert Gatliff, the Trust was originally intended to provide young persons of limited means with the opportunity to meet local people and enjoy the unique natural environment and cultural heritage of the islands. However, in recent years visitors of all incomes, ages, nationalities and interests have been encouraged to use the facilities.

The Trust is currently involved in the operation of four hostels situated at Garenin (Isle of Lewis), Rhenigidale (Isle of Harris), Berneray (Isle of North Uist) and Howmore (South Uist). Further hostels may be opened on other islands in the future.

The hostels are open all year and looked after by non-resident wardens who live and practise crofting nearby. No advance bookings are accepted but it is very unlikely that visitors will find themselves turned away and without a bed for the night. There is also limited space for camping at the hostels. Hostels provide bunk/camp beds, cooking facilities and cutlery, piped water, toilets and coal/wood fires, but visitors should bring their own food and a sleeping bag is recommended.

Charges for 2004 are: £8 per night, under 18 £5.50, camping £4.50, day visitors £1. Annual membership £10, under 18 £7.50. Further information, including membership and contact details, hostel locations and photographs, a reading list and places of interest to visit in the surrounding area can be found at the GHHT website: www.gatliff.ic24.net.

of a number of prehistoric sights between here and **Siadar (Shader)** which may be of interest to the keen archaeologist, but otherwise there's little of note on the road north to Nis as it passes through the typical crofting townships of **Coig Peighinnean Buirgh (Five Penny Borve), Gàbhsann bho Dheas (South Galson), Dail (Dell), Suainebost (Swainbost), Tàbost (Habost)** and **Lìonal (Lionel)**. In saying that, those interested in buying souvenirs should look in at the **Borgh Pottery** ⓘ *T01856-850345, Mon-Sat 0930-1800*, by the bridge at Coig Peighinnean. Here you'll find a wide range of beautiful and original domestic and decorative ware.

The road continues north, passing through a number of straggling villages that collectively make up **Nis (Ness)**, until it ends at the fishing village of **Port Nis (Port of Ness)**. It's a lovely spot, with a picturesque little harbour and golden sweep of beach enclosed by steep cliffs. Each September the locals head out to the island of **Sula Sgeir**, 30 miles to the north, for the annual cull of young gannets (or *gugas*), which are considered something of a delicacy by the people of Lewis. A few minutes to the northwest, the Butt of Lewis lighthouse forms the most northerly tip of the Outer Hebrides.

▲ Just before Port Nis, is Lìonal, where the B8015 turns off right and leads to the start of the 10-mile coastal trail that works it way round to **Tòlstadh (Tolsta North)** and the beautiful beaches of Traigh Mhor and Garry. Numerous shielings pepper the landscape from an earlier era when local crofters drove their cattle to the summer pastures in the island's interior. The beaches can be reached much more easily by road north from Stornoway. For details of the coastal walk, see the tourist information centre in Stornoway.

Another minor road heads northwest to the tiny hamlet of **Eòropaidh (Eoropie)** (pronounced 'Yor-erpee'). By the road junction that leads to Rubha Robhanais is the ancient **Teampull Mholuaidh (St Moluag's Church)**, thought to date from the 12th century and restored to its present state in 1912. It is now used on certain Sundays by Stornoway's Episcopal Church. From Eòropaidh a narrow road runs to the lighthouse at **Rubha Robhanais (Butt of Lewis)**, which marks the nothernmost tip of the Outer Hebrides. It's a great place for spotting seabirds or whales and dolphins, but also very wild and windy. Just don't tell any visiting Americans where you've been. Half a mile back down the road a path leads down to the tiny beach of **Port Sto**, which is more sheltered.

The West Coast → *Phone code: 01851. Colour map 1, grid A2-3 & B2.*

Arnol

At the end of the village of Arnol is the **Blackhouse Museum** ⓘ *T01851-710395, Apr-Sep Mon-Sat 0930-1830 Oct-Mar Mon-Sat 0930-1630, Sun 1400-1630, £3, concession £2.30, children £1*, one of the best surviving examples of an original blackhouse in Scotland and well worth visiting. These traditional thatched houses were once common throughout the Highlands and Islands, and inhabited until the 1960s. They were built in the tradition of 'longhouses' which can be traced back 1,000 years to the time of the Viking invaders. The name 'blackhouses' dates back to the 1850s when modern buildings were introduced. These were known as 'white houses' and the older style houses were called 'blackhouses'. The blackhouses were well adapted to the harsh local climate. They had no windows or chimney and were built with local materials – stone, turf and thatch of oat, barley or marram grass, and with a peat fire burning continually in the central hearth – and attached to the living quarters was the cattle byre. This particular blackhouse was built in 1885 and lived in until 1964. **Hebridean Replicas** ⓘ*T01851-710562, in the village, offers quality handmade Lewis chess sets from local stone, and provides a welcome alternative to much of the tacky tourist paraphernalia to be found in Stornnoway.*

The west coast of Lewis contains most of what you'll want to see and can be covered in a day trip from Stornoway, either with your own transport, by public bus or as part of a minibus tour.

Siabost and around

Two miles south of the Arnol turn-off, at **Bragar**, look out for an archway, formed from the jawbone of a blue whale which was washed up on the coast nearby in 1920. A few miles further on is the township of Siabost (Shawbost), where the charmingly ramshackle **folk museum** ⓘ *Mon-Sat 0900-1800, free*, which was started originally as a project by local schoolchildren, now contains an interesting collection of Hebridean artefacts.

Just south of Siabost, beside a small loch, is the sign for the recently restored **Norse Mill and Kiln**, which are a half-mile walk over the hill from the car park. There's not much to see as yet, but it's worth getting out of the car if you want to stretch your legs. A little further on is the turning for **Dail Beag (Dalbeg)**, a lovely secluded beach.

Gearrannan (Garenin)

The landscape gradually becomes more undulating and scenically interesting as the road then passes through the village of **Càrlabhagh (Carloway)**, Lord Leverhume's proposed fishing port. Here, a branch road leads to the ruined and deserted

Croft conversion

The word 'croft' is derived from the Gaelic croit, meaning a small area of land, and crofting has been the traditional way of life in the Scottish Highlands for many centuries. Its emotive hold on the psyche of the Highlander comes from the long, hard struggle for security of tenure, see page 602.

A croft is aptly described as a parcel of land entirely surrounded by regulations. Most crofts consist of a few acres of arable land with a proportion of grazing land shared with other crofts. Each crofter is, in effect, a kind of small tenant-farmer, the distinction being that he has almost absolute security of tenure and has the right to assign the croft to a member of his family whether the landlord agrees or not. In fact, over the years the crofter has managed to acquire most of the rights of ownership with few of the disadvantages.

The croft is the area of land involved and not the house which is called the 'croft house'. Crofts can vary in size, from a quarter of an acre upwards. Those on Lewis are small and relatively unproductive, with an average size of only about five acres, while on the Uists, where the land is more fertile, crofts are up to 50 acres or more.

As well as having the sole tenancy of the croft, the crofter usually also has a share in a huge area of 'common grazing' along with the other members of the crofting community – commonly called a township. They also work together in such activities as fencing, sheep dipping or cutting peat.

In reality, crofting does not provide a viable means of living. Very few crofters rely solely on their smallholding for an income and most need to have several occupations (including running a B&B) to make ends meet. But without the family croft whole communities would just pack up and leave, so crofting functions as a means of preventing the depopulation of remote rural areas.

The crofter's lot may change for the better, however, thanks to the Scottish Parliament's new Land Reform Bill which includes a special right to buy for crofting communities.

'blackhouse' village of Gearrannan (Garenin). The old village has been undergoing extensive renovation in recent years with the aid of EU funding, and several derelict crofts have now been painstakingly restored to their original style of stone walls and thatched roofs. An old cart track leads down to the bay and wonderful sunsets out at sea. The village now boasts a Gatliff Trust hostel, heritage centre, café and holiday dwellings. Above the village a footpath can be followed through the lazybeds and above the sea cliffs to reveal a stunning view of beautiful **Dal More Bay**. The Atlantic waves seem to break relentlessly on golden sands and the beach is, not surprisingly, a favourite haunt of surfers from Stornoway and farther afield. Swimmers and bathers should be careful, however, because as with many of the west coast beaches there can be a fierce rip-current carrying the unwary into deeper water out at sea.

Dùn Chàrlabhaigh (Doune Carloway) Broch

A little further on, standing a few hundred yards from the main road, is the Dùn Chàrlabhaigh Broch, the best-preserved building of its type in the Outer Hebrides. The impressive 2,000 year-old drystone habitation is beautifully situated on a rocky outcrop, commanding great views across Loch Carloway to the sea beyond. The remaining outer wall is 30-ft high and slopes inwards, with an inner wall which rises vertically, leaving chambers between the walls. Parts of the inner wall have collapsed, revealing the interior stairs and galleries. There's also the **Doune Broch Visitor Centre** ⓘ *T01851-643338, Apr-Oct Mon-Sat 1000-1800, free*, which tastefully complements the architectural style of the site, and which gives a good audio-visual description of how life must have been in one of these structures around 50 BC.

Calanais (Callanish)

ⓘ *T01851-621422, site Apr-Sep 1000-1900, Oct-Mar 1000-1600, free; visitor centre closed Sun, £1.75, concession £1.25, children £0.75.*

Five miles south of Dun Chàrlabhaigh is the jewel in the islands' prehistoric crown, the Calanais **Standing Stones**, which are unique in Scotland and the equal of Stonehenge in historical value. The stones are in a beautiful setting overlooking Loch Roag and are very atmospheric, especially at sunset or at night, when no one's around. They are in the form of a Celtic cross, and in the centre is a circle of 13 stones with a central monolith over 12-ft tall, and a chambered burial cairn. The oldest part of this great ceremonial site – probably the stone circle – dates from around 3,000 BC (older than Stonehenge) and continued in use until about 800 BC. The full significance of the site is not yet known, though it is probably connected to the seasonal cycle, as many of the stones are aligned with the rising and setting moon. There are also a number of smaller and more isolated stone circles a few miles south of Calanais on the road to Gearraidh na h-Aibhne (Garynahine).

Next to the stones is the Calanais Visitor Centre, which features 'The Story of the Stones' exhibition, a restaurant and gift shop. On the other side of the stones is the Blackhouse tearoom and craft shop, run by the MacBears and better value if you fancy a bite.

The Uig Peninsula

→ *Colour map 1, grid B2.*

From Gearraidh na h-Aibhne the main A858 runs back to Stornoway, while the B8011 forks west to the remote Uig Peninsula in the southwest of the island. » *For Sleeping, Eating and other listings, see pages 467-470.*

Bearnaraigh (Great Bernera) to Cnip

Four miles down this road is a turning to the right onto the B8059, which leads to the island of Bearnaraigh, now connected to the mainland of Lewis by a single-track road bridge. The main settlement on the island is **Breacleit (Breaclete)**, where you can find out about the island's history in the **Bernera Museum** ⓘ *Jun-Sep Mon-Sat 1100-1800, £1.50*. The rest of the island is fairly interesting with tiny fishing villages, and one or two brochs and some standing stones. The nicest part, though, is on the north coast, near the tiny hamlet of **Bostadh (Bosta)**, where a lovely little sandy bay looks out to the nearby island of **Bearnaraigh Beag (Little Bernera)**.

The B8011 continues across bleak moorland, then cuts north to **West Loch Roag**, which is fringed by some fine sandy beaches and backed by a much hillier landscape. Just beyond **Miabhag (Miavaig)** is the turn-off right to **Cliobh (Cliff)**, with its picturesque beach which is unsafe for swimming. A mile further on is the little village of **Cnip (Kneep)**, to the east of which is the beautiful **Traigh na Berie**, a long sandy beach backed by flat machair which is ideal for camping.

Gallan Head

Beyond Miabhag, the eerie peninsula of Gallan Head provides a setting befitting of a science fiction drama or Cold War Orwellian novel, with empty, decaying Ministry of Defence buildings battered by the Atlantic storms. Wandering around the abandoned site it is easy to form ideas of bizarre, top-secret government experiments and

Room at the inn?

There are plenty of B&Bs and guest houses scattered throughout the islands, many of which offer better value than the hotels. Most don't have private bathrooms, but they're comfortable, very welcoming and will offer evening meals. There are numerous self-catering style cottages across the islands, many of which are advertised in the Western Isles brochure published annually by the Western Isles Tourist Board. Also check out the websites listed on page xxx. There are several official youth hostels in converted crofts scattered around the islands in isolated locations. Some are difficult to get to without your own transport, but you can always hitchhike. They are run by the SYHA or the Gatliff Hebridean Hostels Trust, see page 463.

early-warning missile tracking in this seemingly edge-of-the-world place far removed from the unwanted prying eyes of everyday society.

Mangersta and the Flannan Islands

Beyond Ardroil the road continues to Mangersta where at Aird Fenish is some of the most spectacular and photogenic coastal scenery in the Outer Hebrides. The cliffs plunge dramatically beyond the road to the inaccessible beach below with a series of crumbling sea stacks battered by the fearsome waves and seabirds riding the updraughts adding to the sense of natural beauty, energy and power. Further south at **Brenish**, about a 10-minute walk from the road, is a menacing blowhole connected to the sea by an underground passage.

Far out into the Atlantic are the haunting Flannan Islands, scene of an unsolved mystery in 1900 following the disappearance of three lighthouse keepers. Various explanations have been put forward over the years, ranging from a freak-wave in stormy weather to a monster sea serpent or even a dispute and fight between the men, but whatever the real reason the legend continues. See page 469 for boat trips.

Timsgearraidh (Timsgarry)

At Timsgearraidh (Timsgarry) are the **Traigh Chapadail (Uig sands)** at the village of **Eadar Dha Fhadhail (Adroil)**. This is the loveliest of all the beaches on Lewis, with miles of sand dunes and machair, but it is famous for an entirely different reason. It was here in 1831 that a crofter dug up the 'Lewis Chessmen', 78 pieces carved from walrus ivory and belonging to at least eight incomplete chess sets from 12th-century Scandinavia. Some are now in the Museum of Scotland in Edinburgh, but most can be found in the British Museum in London.

Sleeping

Stornoway *p461, map p460*
As the largest settlement on the islands, Stornoway has a good selection of accommodation from which to choose, though you should book in advance in the peak summer season. The TIC will do this for you, for a small fee.
B Cabarfeidh Hotel, Perceval Rd South, T01851-702604, F705572. 46 rooms. On the outskirts of town and not as convenient as the Royal but with the full range of facilities and a decent restaurant.
B Park Guest House, 30 James St, T01851-702485, F703482. 10 rooms. This Victorian townhouse is comfortable, only 500 yds from the ferry terminal, and the best of the guest houses. It also has an excellent restaurant, recommended even if you're not staying.
B Royal Hotel, Cromwell St, T01851-702109, www.calahotels.com. 24 rooms. Best of

several centrally located hotels. Good value, and good food in its restaurant and bistro (see Eating below).

There are many B&Bs in and around the town centre, most of which offer a 'room only' rate for those requiring an early start to catch the first ferry. There are several along Matheson Rd, which is close to the town centre and the ferry terminal, including:

E Mrs Anne Maclead, at No 12, T01851-702673; and

E Mrs M MacMillan, 'Fernlea' No 9, T01851-702125. **F** room only.

F Fairhaven, 17 Keith St, T01851-705862, which can also do meals.

F Laxdale Holiday Park, Laxdale La, about a mile out of town on the road to Barabhas, T01851-703234. This bunkhouse has 16 beds, basic facilities and is open all year.

F Stornoway Backpackers Hostel, 47 Keith St, T01851-703628. Includes breakfast, open all year. Basic.

North to Nis *p462*

D Galson Farm Guest House, Gàbhsann bho Deas (South Galson), halfway between Barabhas and Port Nis, T01851-850492, www.galsonfarm.freeserve.com. Friendly and beautifully restored 18th-century house.

F Galson Farm Bunkhouse, is cheaper, more basic accommodation run by the same owners.

D Ms Catriona Macleod, at Coig Peighinnean Buirgh (Five Penny Borve), T01851-810240.

The West Coast *p464*

If you want to stay near the stones and visit them after dark, there are several inexpensive B&Bs in the village of Calanais.

E-F Mrs Morrison, 27 Callanish (200 yds from the site), T01851-621392 (open Mar-Sep). Friendly.

E Aros, T01851-621266, kateblue@yahoo.com. Again convenient for the stones, owned by Kate Kirby.

E Debbie Nash, a few miles north at 19 Tolsta Chaolais, T01851-621321. Recommended vegetarian B&B .

Uig Peninsula *p466*

C Baile Na Cille Guest House, Timsgarry, T01851-672242, F672241. Apr-Sep. Best of the places to stay around Uig bay, this restored 18th-century manse is beautifully located overlooking a 2-mile stretch of sand. Superb home cooking and one of the warmest welcomes in the islands.

There are a couple of good B&Bs on the island of Great Bernera which both offer evening meals:

E Mrs Macauley, in Circebost (Kirkibost), on the east coast, T01851-612341.

E Mrs MacDonald, in Tobson, on the west coast, T01851-612347.

Eating

Stornoway *p461, map p460*

The pubs and hotels serve the usual range of bar meals. Note that pubs are closed on Sun and hotels cater only for residents. There are plenty of takeaways offering the standard fare of pizza, kebabs, fish and chips etc.

£££ The Boatshed, in the **Royal Hotel**, see Sleeping above. Also recommended, specializes in seafood. Less upmarket and cheaper is their Barnacle Bistro.

£££-££ Park Guest House, see Sleeping above. Probably the best restaurant in town. Top-class modern Scottish cooking using local fish, lamb and venison. It also caters for vegetarians. Open Tue-Sat.

£ Ann Lanntair Gallery, see Sights p461. Good, cheap snacks and light lunches.

£ Co-op supermarket. If you are on a budget the all-day breakfast served here is one of the cheapest dishes on the island.

£ Deep Sea Fishermen's Mission, North Beach. A cheap cafeteria.

£ Stornoway Balti House, near the bus station on South Beach. For a touch of non-Scottish fare.

North to Nis *p462*

£ Harbour View Gallery & Café, Port Nis, T01851-810735. Also offers B&B.

The West Coast *p464*

££ Copper Kettle, overlooking a small lochan beside the car park at Dalbeg, T01851-710592. An unassuming little house which is actually a superb restaurant. Meals must be booked at least 24 hrs in advance (last booking 2000). Open 1030 till 1730 for tea, coffee, snacks and home baking (all year Mon-Sat). Next door is a self-catering bungalow for rent (same phone number).

Music to your ears

As the heartland of Gaelic culture, the Outer Hebrides are host to many music events throughout the year ranging from a spontaneous ceilidh to one of the three local mods. Mods usually consist of three days of competition in piping, singing, instrumental music, drama and poetry, and are an opportunity to see the best of the local talent. More information can be obtained from An Comunn Gaidhealach, T01851-703487.

Also listed below are the various Highland Games and agricultural shows, where you can also see piping competitions and Highland dancing.

Late March Feis nan Coisir, Stornoway, Lewis.
First Friday in April Donald Macleod Memorial Piping Competition, Stornoway, Lewis.
May-June Highland Festival, held in various locations.
Early June Harris Mod, Tarbert, Harris.
Second week in June Lewis Mod, Stornoway, Lewis.
Mid June Uist Mod, Iochdar, South Uist.
May-June Lochmaddy Boat Festival, Lochmaddy, North Uist.
Mid July Berneray Week, Bearnaraigh (Berneray), North Uist.
July Ceolas Music School, South Uist.
Early July Barra Festival lasting for 2 weeks.
Early/mid July Feis Tir an Eorna, Paibeil, North Uist; Barra Highland Games, Borgh (Borve), Barra, lasting for a week.
11-14 July Hebridean Celtic Music Festival, Stornoway, Lewis.
Mid July North Uist Highland Games, Hosta, North Uist.
Mid/late July Harris Gala; South Uist Highland Games, Aisgeirnis (Askernish), South Uist; Lewis Highland Games, Tong, Lewis.
Mid July Barra Highland Games.
Third week of July Harris Festival
Late July Barra Live, Barra; West Side Agricultural Show, Barabhas (Barvas), Lewis; South Uist Agricultural Show, Iochdar, South Uist; South Harris Agricultural Show, Leverburgh, Harris.
July Feis Eilean an Fhraoich, Stornoway, Lewis.
Late July/early August North Uist Agricultural Show, Hosta, North Uist.
Early August Carloway Agricultural Show, Càrlabhagh (Carloway), Lewis; Fies Tir a Mhurain, Lionacleit, Benbecula; Lewis Carnival, Stornoway; Fish Festival, Stornoway; Twin Peaks Hill Race, North Uist.
Second week August Harris Arts Festival, Tarbert.

££ **Tigh Mealros**, a few miles south of the stones, Gearraidh na h-Aibhne, T01851-621333. They serve good local grub in a cosy, relaxed atmosphere, with scallops a speciality (closes at 2100).
£ **Calanais Visitor Centre** and **Blackhouse tearoom**, are places to eat near the stones.

The Uig Peninsula *p466*
££ **Bonaventure**, north of Timsgarry, at Aird Uig, T01851-672474. Restaurant and B&B serving lunches and dinners of a French/Scottish style.

Shopping

Stornoway *p461, map p460*
Safeway is beside the ferry terminal and the **Co-op** is by the first roundabout on the road out to Barabhas. There's also a smaller supermarket opposite the TIC.

Activities and tours

Elena C, 5a Knock, Point, T01851-870537, F706384. Wildlife trips from Stornoway harbour.

Galson Motors, T01851-840269, leaving from Stornoway bus station they run day trips to Calanais.
Hebridean Exploration, 19 Westview Tce, T01851-705655, T0374-292746 (mob). Sea kayak tours.
Island Cruising, Uig, T01851-672381. For boat trips to the Flannan Islands.
MacDonald's Coaches, at the Ferry Terminal, T01851-706267. Coach tours.
W. MacDonald, T01851-706267, day trips to Calanais leaving from the pier.

Transport

Lewis *p460*
Local Buses leave from Stornoway to all parts of the island. Note that buses do not run on Sun. To **Port Niss (Ness)** via **Barabhas (Barvas)** 4-6 times per day; to **Arnol**, **Siabost (Shawbost)**, **Càrlabhagh (Carloway)**, **Calanais (Callanish)**, and back to Stornoway ('West Side Circular') 4-6 times per day; to **Bearnaraigh (Great Bernera)** via **Gearraidh na h-Aibhne (Garynahine)** 4 per day; to **Uig District** 3-4 per day; to **Ranais (Ranish)** 6-8 times per day. Contact the tourist office in Stornoway, or the bus station, T01851- 704327, for further details. There are also buses from Stornoway to **Tarbert** and on to **Leverburgh** (for the ferry to North Uist) 4-5 times per day, T01859-502441.

Car and bike rental is available at good rates from **Lewis Car Rentals**, 52 Bayhead St, T01851-703760, F705860. Also **Arnol Motors**, in Arnol (see p464), T01851-710548, T0831-823318 (mob). You can rent bikes at **Alex Dan's Cycle Centre**, 67 Kenneth St, T01851-704025, F701712.

Taxis from **Central Cabs**, T01851-706900.

Long distance British Airways/Loganair, T08708-509850, www.ba.com, flies from **Glasgow** to Stornoway (Mon-Sat 2 daily, 1 hr). There are also flights from **Edinburgh** to Stornoway (Mon-Sun 1 daily, 1 hr), **Inverness** to Stornoway (Mon-Sat 4 daily, 40 mins).

CalMac ferry runs a service from **Ullapool** to Stornoway (2 hrs 40 minutes) 2-3 times daily Mon-Sat in the summer (Jun-Sep) and twice daily Mon-Sat in the winter. One-way ticket costs £13.70 per passenger and £67 per car. A 5-day saver return costs £23.50 per passenger and £114 per car. Contact CalMac offices Ullapool, T01854-612358, and Stornoway, T01851-702361, for further details.

Directory

Stornoway *p461, map p460*
Banks **Bank of Scotland** is directly opposite the tourist office and has an ATM. The other major banks are also in the centre of town and also have ATMs.
Internet **Captions**, 27 Church St, T01851-702238, www.captions.co.uk. Open Mon- Sat till late in the summer months. Internet facilities also available at the public library on Cromwell St.
Post On Francis St.

Na Hearadh (Harris)

→ *Phone code: 01859. Colour map 1.*

Harris is not an island, but together with Lewis forms the largest of the Outer Hebrides, with Harris taking up the southern third. The two parts are divided by the long sea lochs of Loch Seaforth in the east and Loch Resort in the west, though this division is rarely shown on maps. Though joined, the two are very different in terms of geography. Harris is largely mountain and rock whereas Lewis is flat moorland.

The largest town and site of the ferry terminal is An Tairbeart (Tarbert). To the north are the highest peaks in the Outer Hebrides, surrounded by some of the finest unspoilt wilderness in the whole country, while to the south are miles of wonderful sandy beaches and, on the east coast, a preternaturally strange lunar landscape straight out of a science fiction film. With your own transport you could 'do' Harris in a day quite comfortably, but if the weather's good enough you'll want to spend more time and appreciate its precious natural beauty. ▸▸ *For Sleeping, Eating and other listings, see pages 476-477.*

Wee free

The Forest of Harris is a vast tract of mountain wilderness extending north from West Loch Tarbert to Loch Resort that forms the de facto boundary with Lewis. It is one of the most isolated and unspoilt upland landscapes in Scotland and, because of its remoteness, receives very few visitors. For experienced hillwalkers, however, it is a paradise offering rugged mountains, dramatic escarpments, airy ridges and desolate glens. There are endless walking possibilities including a horseshoe walk around Clisham and a long walk through Glen Ulladale to Kinlochresort, a former crofting community now abandoned, but once described as the remotest habitation in Britain. Known as the North Harris Estate, this 22,000 acre tract of land was owned and managed by the family of the Bulmer cider empire – until 2003. In a move that had Scottish lairds incandescent with rage, the 800 residents of the estate were granted the right to take over the land on which they live, for more than £2 million, and finally throw off the shackles of feudal rule. Now that they have become masters of their own destiny, the community can relish the thought of a prosperous future, with energy development plans, sporting rights and tourism top of the agenda.

Background

The separation of Harris and Lewis dates back to Norse times, when the island was divided between the two sons of Leod, progenitor of the Macleods. Harris remained in Macleod hands until 1834. The recent history of Harris is closely bound up with that of Lewis. Both were bought by the soap magnate, Lord Leverhulme, see page 461, whose grandiose schemes for Lewis came to nothing. Leverhulme then turned his attentions to Harris, where the peaceful little village of An t-Ob (Obbe) was renamed Leverburgh and transformed into a bustling port with all manner of public works programmes under development. His death in 1925 brought an end to all his plans for Harris, and instead of becoming a town with a projected population of 10,000, Leverburgh reverted to being a sleepy village, with only the harbour, the roads and the change of name to show for it all.

Since the Leverhulme era there has been no main source of employment for the population of 2,400 on Harris, though a successful fishing industry continues on Scalpaigh (Scalpay). There is still some crofting supplemented by the Harris Tweed industry, though most production is now in Lewis, and whatever employment can be found: road-works, crafts and tourism. The most recent project proposed for Harris, to create one of Europe's largest superquarries, is highly controversial and would involve destroying an area of outstanding natural beauty for the sake of perhaps only a few dozen jobs, see page 475, with potentially disastrous consequences for the island's fragile tourist economy.

Ceann a Tuath na Hearadh (North Harris)

→ *Phone code: 01859. Colour map 1, grid B2.*

North Harris is the most mountainous part of the Outer Hebrides and its wild, rugged peaks are ideal for hillwalking. The A859 south from Lewis gets progressively more scenic as it skirts **Loch Siophort (Seaforth)** and the mountains rise before you like a giant barrier. The road then climbs past **Bogha Glas (Bowglass)** and **Aird a Mhulaidh (Ardvourlie)** with **Clisham** (2,619 ft), the highest peak in the Outer Hebrides, and **Sgaoth Aird** (1,829 ft) towering overhead on either side.

Just off the A859 near Ardvourlie is **Ardvourlie Castle Guest House**, see Sleeping page 476. If you can't afford such luxury but still crave the isolation, then carry on south until you reach the turn-off to **Reinigeadal (Rhenigidale)**, which was the most remote community on Harris and accessible only by sea or by a rough hill track until the access road was built. Here you'll find a **Gatliff Trust youth hostel**, see Sleeping page 476. From Reinigeadal an ascent of shapely **Toddun** (528 m) provides exhilarating exercise rewarded with fine views east across the Minch to the mainland and in the other direction to the mountain wilderness of North Harris.

The A859 continues west across the crest of the craggy hills then drops down to the turn-off for the single-track B887 which winds its way all the way out to Huisinis (Hushinish) between the impressive mountains of the Forest of Harris on one side and the northern shore of West Loch Tarbert on the other, with views across to the Sound of Taransay and the beaches of South Harris. Immediately beyond the turn-off you pass through **Bun Abhainn Eadarra (Bunavoneadar)**, which was a thriving whaling station until 1930 and one of Lord Leverhulme's many schemes for the island. The old whaling station is worth a visit even though the site has not been developed as a tourist attraction.

▲ Just before the village of **Miabhag (Meavaig)**, a defined footpath heads north into the hills up Glen Meavaig to Loch Voshimid. Further on, though, is a better opportunity for walking. Just before the gates of **Amhuinnsuidhe Castle** (pronounced 'Avan-soo-ee') is a signpost for Chliostair Power Station. From here you can walk two miles up to the dam, then follow the right-hand track round the reservoir and the left-hand track round the upper loch, before you arrive in a wild and remote glen. Just beyond the castle gates you'll see a beautiful waterfall spilling straight into the sea. The road then runs right past the front door of the castle, built in 1868 by the Earl of Dunmore, and still a private residence, before passing through an archway and continuing to the tiny crofting township of **Huisinis (Hushinish)**, beautifully situated in a sandy bay. This is where the road ends; next stop the USA. Follow the track to the right across the machair where a footpath above the jetty and rocky beach can be followed to the old fishing lodge at **Cravadale** and Loch Cravadale beyond. Make a detour to the golden sands and turquoise waters of **Traigh Mheilein** overlooking Scarp. From the coast strong walkers can follow Glen Cravadale inland eventually rejoining the main road near Amhuinnsuidhe Castle.

The rocky island of **Scarp** supported a population of more than 100 as late as the 1940s but was abandoned in 1971, and now the crofters' cottages are used as holiday homes. The island was the scene of a bizarre experiment in 1934, when a German rocket scientist, Gerhard Zucher, tried to prove that rockets could be used to transport mail and medical supplies to remote communities. His theory went up in smoke, however, when the rocket exploded before it even got off the ground, with 30,000 letters on board.

An Tairbeart (Tarbert) and around

→ *Phone code: 01859. Colour map 1, grid B2. Population: 500.*

Tarbert, the largest settlement on Harris, lies in a sheltered bay on the narrow isthmus that joins North and South Harris. It's a tiny place and there's not much to do, but as it's the main ferry port for Harris it has more facilities than anywhere else, with shops, a bank and post office. Tarbert's relatively wide range of accommodation and location makes it the ideal base from which to explore. The TIC ⓘ *T01859-502011, Apr-Oct Mon-Sat 0900-1700, also in winter (check times)*, is close to the ferry terminal.

Material girl

Few visitors to Harris will not have heard of its most famous export, Harris Tweed. But how did it emerge from its humble origins to become a product synonymous with high-quality craftsmanship and a de rigeur item of clothing for any self-respecting aristocrat?

Traditionally the tweed was made by fishermen's wives to clothe their own families using wool from their own sheep. They carried out the whole process themselves by hand. First the wool was washed, then dyed using native plants and bushes, tree bark and lichen, then carded, spun, warped, woven and finally waulked, or made soft, by beating it on a table. Many women could produce more than they needed and the surplus was available for sale or barter. The cloth was made throughout the Outer Hebrides and originally was not known as Harris Tweed, but simply as *clo mòr* (or big cloth).

All that changed in 1842 when the Countess of Dunmore, who owned a large part of Harris, took great interest and introduced many of her aristocratic friends to Harris Tweed. Very soon, much of the surplus tweed was being sold and becoming quite a fashion statement in high places. By the beginning of the 20th century demand was exceeding supply, stimulated by Royal patronage, and faster and more efficient ways of carrying out the ancillary processes were being developed by some of the larger producers. This led, in 1909, to the setting up of the Harris Tweed Association Ltd, to ensure quality control and to protect the interests of the independent crofter/ weavers. So Harris Tweed came officially into being, with its famous Orb trademark, originating from the Coat of Arms of the Countess of Dunmore.

To earn this official stamp of authenticity Harris Tweed must be made from pure Scottish wool, dyed, spun and finished in the Outer Hebrides, and hand woven by the islanders in their own homes. There are now about 750 independent weavers and about 400 millworkers employed in the islands, and each weaver can produce three webs of tweed a week (a web measures 80-90 yds in length). In total the industry produces around 5,000,000 yds of tweed annually, depending on demand. The main production centre is now Lewis, but all over the island you can see the woven tweed lying at the gates of crofts waiting to be collected and sent all over the world.

An interesting little excursion from Tarbert is the 10-mile return route that runs east through the tiny villages of **Urgha** and **Caolas Scalpaigh** to **Carnach** at the end of the road. Just beyond Urgha, on the north side of the road, is a path which leads across the hills to the **Reinigeadal**. It was originally used by the community in Reinigeadal, and the children would make the daily journey across the hills to Tarbert before the village was connected to the A859 by the new road. The wonderfully engineered zigzag path passes through enchanting scenery above **Loch Trollamarig** in a setting more reminiscent of Scandinavia's Fjordland. A visit can easily be made to the deserted village of **Molinginish** nestled snugly in a small valley above the loch.

The island of **Scalpaigh (Scalpay)**, now connected to Harris by a road bridge opened by Prime Minister Tony Blair in 1998, is a thriving fishing community with a population of over 400. It's a pleasant three-mile walk across the island to Eilean Glas Lighthouse, built by the Stevensons and the first ever on the Outer Hebrides. There are diving trips here, see page 477.

Ceann a Deas na Hearadh (South Harris)

An absolute must while you're in the Outer Hebrides is the 45-mile circular route around South Harris. If you only do one thing while you're here, then make sure this is it, for the change in scenery from the west coast to the east is utterly astounding. One thing you're sure to puzzle over as you travel round is the fact that most people live on the harsh and inhospitable east coast, known as Na Baigh (Bays), while the beautiful west coast with its miles of glorious golden sands is scarcely populated. This is not through choice. The fertile west coast housed most of the population until the end of the 18th century when they were cleared to make way for sheep farms. Some emigrated to Cape Breton, while others chose instead to stay in Harris and moved to the east side.

The West Coast

The main road from Tarbert runs south, skirting East Loch Tarbert, then cuts inland and heads west through a dramatic lunar landscape of rocks dotted with tiny lochans. It then begins to descend towards the sea and you can see the vast expanse of **Losgaintir (Luskentyre)** beach directly ahead. A single-track road turns off to the right and runs out to the tiny settlement of Losgaintir. The road cuts through the rich machair as it follows the magnificent stretch of bleached white sand that fills the entire bay, washed by turquoise sea and backed by steep dunes. All this set against the backdrop of the mountains to the north. Paradise!

A short distance offshore is the island of **Tarasaigh (Taransay)**, which was well populated at the beginning of the 1900s but was recently abandoned. The island gained national prominence a few years ago as the setting for the popular BBC television series *Castaway* where an assortment of supposedly normal people from a variety of backgrounds were challenged to pit their wits against the elements and themselves for a period of a full year in 2000.

The road follows the coast, passing through the tiny settlements of **Seilebost**, **Horgabost** and **Burgh (Borve)**. There's B&B accommodation at Seilebost and Horgabost, but a few miles further on is another beautiful stretch of white sands at **Sgarasta Bheag (Scaristabeg).**

Beyond Sgarasta Bheag, the village of **Taobh Tuath (Northton)** provides access to the scenic promontory of **Toe Head**, almost cut off from the rest of Harris by the huge expanse of the golden sands of Sgarasta. At the **MacGillivary Machair Centre** you can learn about the ecology of the local machair which forms such a distinctive and attractive element of the landscape of the west coast of the Hebrides. A ruined chapel of 16th-century origin is situated on the machair below **Chaipaval** (365 m), whose heathery slopes can be climbed for one of the best views out to sea towards St Kilda some 40 miles distant.

Ant-Ob (Leverburgh)

The road then runs along the south shore till it reaches An t-Ob (Leverburgh), site of Lord Leverhulme's ambitious plan to turn a sleepy crofting township into a major fishing port, see page 471. The present village consists of little more than a row of incongruous Scandinavian-style wooden houses. A few of the original buildings can be seen near the pier, which is the departure point for CalMac's car ferry to Berneray.
▸▸ *For further details, see Transport page 477.*

Rumour has it that during the Castaway *television series, the bar in the Harris Hotel in Tarbert had never seen such good business suggesting that some participants were more committed than others.*

Rock 'n' roll suicide

Like Newbury Bypass in England, the proposed Lingarabay superquarry represents a cause célèbre in the classic debate between the clashing interests of environment and development. Redland Aggregates originally proposed to develop the east face of Roineabhal (460 m) as a huge quarry providing a vast source of aggregate material for the construction industry in an economically impoverished part of Scotland perceived to be far removed from the mass tourism market. However, the proposal provoked a local, national and international outcry as environmental groups objected to the likely visual, landscape and ecological impacts in a unique and essentially unspoilt mountain environment designated a National Scenic Area and representative of some of the oldest rock in the world. A Public Enquiry followed in 1994-95 at which Redland presented the case for long-term local employment and the preference of one large quarry in a remote area rather than many smaller projects on the highly populated mainland. Objectors set out the concerns for the damage to a resource of national importance and the precedent it would set for environmental protection both within and outwith the industry in the future if planning legislation were to be overcome. Following a lengthy follow up the Secretary of State rejected the proposal in 2000. Redland Aggregates who have now been taken over by French company, Lafarge, are now appealing against the decision. In the latest twist in the saga Scottish Natural Heritage and other action groups are now believed to be lobbying the UK government and European Parliament to reinforce the environmental value of the site by designation as a Special Area for Conservation under the EC Habitats Directive, thereby making it illegal to develop the site for industrial purposes. In a case where each side attempts to out-manoeuvre the other the outcome is still far from clear and the saga continues.

Ròghadal (Rodel)

Three miles east of Leverburgh, at the southeastern tip of Harris, is Ròghadal (Rodel), dominated by the beautiful 12th-century **St Clement's Church**, something of an unusual sight in such a remote spot and one of the most impressive religious building in the Hebrides (only the Benedictine abbey on Iona is larger). The church stands on a site which goes back 1,500 years and was built by Alastair Crotach (Hunchback) Macleod of Harris in the 1520s. Though impressive from the outside, particularly the huge tower, the real interest lies inside, with a collection of remarkable carved wall tombs. There are three tombs, the most notable of which is that of the founder, Alastair Crotach. The one in the south wall of the choir is also worth a close look.

Na Baigh (Bays)

Running north from Ròghadal up the east coast of South Harris is the **Golden Road**, so named by the locals because the of the huge expense of building it. This twisting, tortuous single-track road runs through a bizarre and striking moonscape, and driving through it is a unique experience (but keep your eyes on the road or you'll end up in one of the many narrow sea lochs). It seems inconceivable that anyone could survive in such an environment, but the road passes through a string of townships created in the 19th century by the people evicted from the west coast, see page 474. People here have spent years eking a meagre living from the thin soil by building 'lazy beds' (thin strips of piled-up earth between the rocks) for planting potatoes. Weaving and fishing also provide much-needed income.

At **Lingreabhagh (Lingarabay)** the road skirts the foot of **Roinebhal**, the proposed site of one of the largest superquarries in Europe, which would demolish virtually the entire mountain over many decades. Local people and environmentalists are up in arms at the prospect of losing precious fishing grounds, not to mention a precious natural asset. The road passes through a succession of tiny settlements before joining the A859 just south of Tarbert.

Sleeping

North Harris *p471*

B **Ardvourlie Castle Guest House**, just off the A859 near Ardvourlie, T01859-502307, F502348. 4 rooms. Open Apr-Oct. This lovingly restored Victorian hunting lodge on the shores of Loch Seaforth just oozes charm and elegance and can't be recommended highly enough. As if that weren't enough, they also happen to serve excellent food. There can be no better end to a day spent walking in the surrounding mountains.

F **Gatliff Trust youth hostel**, Reinigeadal (Rhenigidale). Here you'll find a converted croft house (no phone) which sleeps 11 and is open all year (for details on how to get there on foot, see Sights p471).

Tarbert and around *p472*

C **Harris Hotel**, on the main road from Stornoway on the left before the turning for the ferry, Tarbert, T01859-502154, F502281. An old established favourite, but more importantly the only place serving food on a Sun, see Eating. The bar next door also serves meals and is the social hub of the village.

C **Leachin House**, 1 mile out of Tarbert on the Stornoway road, T/F01859-502157. Luxurious Victorian home with great views and superb home cooking (for residents only). **B** including dinner. Only 2 rooms so book ahead.

D **Allan Cottage Guest House**, on the left after the turning into Tarbert, T01859-502146. Open Apr-Sep. Close to the ferry, very comfortable rooms and exceptional food. **B** including dinner. Book ahead.

E **Hirta House**, Scalpay, T01859-540394.

E **Macleod Motel**, right beside the ferry pier, T01859-502364. Very handy for the early-morning ferry, also has room-only rate.

There are also several B&Bs within 5 mins' walk of the ferry pier, including the very friendly and welcoming

E **Mrs Mackinnon**, Tarbert, T01859-502095. Another good B&B.

E **Mrs Morrison**, Tarbert, T01859-502334. B&B also near the pier. Comfortable.

E **Mrs Miller**, Tarbert, T01859-502140. A friendly and clean B&B.

E-F **Mrs Flora Morrison**, Tigh na Mara, Tarbert, T01859-502270. A B&B within 5 mins' walk of the ferry pier, very friendly and welcoming.

F **New Haven**, Scalpay, T01859-540325.

F **Rockview Bunkhouse**, on the main street, Tarbert, T/F01859-5022211. Open all year.

F **Seafield**, Scalpay, T01859-540250.

South Harris *p474*

There is a wide range of accommodation in Leverburgh but on the east coast it is limited.

B **Scarista House**, Scaristabeg, T01859-550238, www.scaristahouse.com. Five rooms, open May-Sep. Overlooking the beach in a wonderful setting, To add to the peace and quiet, there's no TV, only an extensive library and drawing room with open fires. The food on offer is amongst the best on the islands, particularly the seafood. Even if you're not staying, you should treat yourself to dinner here. Breakfast is a majesterial feast of kippers, kedgeree, Stornoway black pudding and Ayrshire bacon. Expensive but well worth it. There are also self-catering cottages in the grounds. The golf course over the road is so scenic the views may put you off your swing.

E **Mrs Paula Williams**, Leverburgh, T01859-520319, F520146. Caters for vegetarians.

For an explanation of sleeping and eating price codes used in this guide, see inside the front cover. Other relevant information is found in Essentials, see pages 43-51.

Out to lunch

Travelling in the Outer Hebrides can be a very different experience from visiting other parts of Scotland. The pace of life is very different here and the needs of tourists have to come second to the ways of local people. Take the example of a passenger flight from Glasgow to Benbecula, which was delayed for 30 minutes when the plane had to circle because the air traffic controller was out to lunch!

E Mrs Catherine Mackenzie, Leverburgh, T01859-520246, situated on Ferry Rd, a few mins from the ferry terminal.
E Shieldaig House, Leverburgh, T01859-520378, kwhettall@aol.com. More secluded and with free cycle hire.
E-F Caberfeidh House, Leverburgh, T01859-520276. Close to the ferry and also offers room only (**F**). One of the best B&Bs.
E-F Hillhead, T01859-511226, at Scadabhagh (Scadabay), Bays, between Stocinis and Drinisiadar. There's also the independent
E-F Moravia, Luskentyre, T01859-550262, open Mar-Oct. B&B.
E-F Seaview, Luskentyre, T01859-550263, open Apr-Oct.
F Am Bothan Bunkhouse, Leverburgh, T01859-520251, close to the ferry, has full facilities, space for tents and is open all year.
F Drinishader Bunkhouse, at Drinisiader (Drinishader), 3 miles south of Tarbert, Bays, T01859-511255, open all year.

Camping

In Luskentyre, you can camp on the machair, but ask for permission at the first house.

Eating

Options on places to eat are limited. Most guest houses and B&Bs provide dinner on request, check if they do so on a Sun.

Tarbert and around *p472*

££ Firstfruits Tearoom, Tarbert, T01859-502349. Aside from the guest houses, this is probably the best food here, a cosy joint by the ferry pier. Open Apr, May and Sep Mon-Sat 1030-1630 and till 1830 Jun, Jul and Aug.
££ Harris Hotel, see Sleeping, serves food every day till around 2030. They do a 3-course fixed menu or basic and cheap bar meals, as does the bar next door Mon-Sat.
£ The only other option is the **chippy** next door to the **Rockview Bunkhouse**, Tarbert, open for lunch and in the evening.

South Harris *p474*

£ An Clachan, Leverburgh, T01859-520370, café/restaurant and shop, not far from the bunkhouse.

Activities and tours

Tarbert and around *p472*

Scalpay Diving Services, T01859-540328, for diving.

Transport

Harris *p470*

Local There's a regular bus service between **Tarbert** and **Stornoway** (1¼ hrs, which continues to **Leverburgh** (for the ferry to North Uist) via the west coast of South Harris. There's a also bus service 3-4 times per day from **Tarbert** to **Leverburgh** via the east coast (45 mins), along the so-called 'Golden Road'. There are also services to **Huisinis** (2-4 per day on school days, 45 mins), to **Reinigeadal** (2 per day on school days) and to **Scalpaigh** (2-5 per day, 10 mins).
Long distance Bus timetables are available at the TIC. Ferries sails from **Uig** (Skye) to **Tarbert** (1 hr 35 mins) 1-2 times daily Mon-Sat. One-way ticket £8.95 per passenger, £43 per car (£15.25 and £73 for 5-day saver return). Contact Uig, T01470-542219, or Tarbert, T01859-502444. A ferry sails from **Leverburgh** to **Berneray** 3 or 4 times daily. The trip takes 1 hr 10 mins and a one-way ticket costs £5 per passenger, £23.05 per car (£8.60 and £39.50 for 5-day saver return). See above for details of services to Leverburgh.

The Uists, Benbecula and Barra

South from Harris lies the southern 'half' of the Outer Herbides. The Uists, north and south, and Benbecula, are all connected by a series of causeways and you can drive their length, past a never-ending series of fish-filled lochs and windswept beaches, tiny, straggling crofting communities and the bizarre giant 'golf balls' of Space City, on South Uist. The road ends at the southerly tip of South Uist, where you'll have to board a ferry to cross to the more relaxed island of Barra, or, better still, fly there from Glasgow, landing on the famous cockle strand – at low tide, of course! » *For Sleeping, Eating and other listings, see pages 485-488.*

Uibhist a Tuath (North Uist) → *Phone code: 01876. Colour map 1, grid C1. Population: 1,815.*

North Uist is the largest of the southern chain of the Outer Hebrides, about 13 miles from north to south and 18 miles east to west at its widest point. At first sight it comes as something of a disappointment after the dramatic landscapes of Harris. In fact, it's barely a landscape at all, as over a third of the island's surface is covered by water. The east coast around Lochmaddy, the main settlement, is so peppered with lochs it resembles a giant sieve. But heading west from Lochmaddy the island's attractions become apparent, particularly the magnificent beaches on the north and west coast. Also on the west coast, the Balranald Nature Reserve is the ideal place for bird watching. You're also likely to see otters. There are numerous prehistoric sites scattered across the island, and with all that water around there's obviously plenty of good fishing to be had. » *For Sleeping, Eating and other listings, see pages 485-488.*

Ins and outs

Getting there There are three car ferry services to North Uist. One is to Otternish from Leverburgh on South Harris, the others are to Lochmaddy from Uig on Skye, and from Tarbert on Harris. North Uist is joined to the islands of Benbecula and South Uist to the south by causeway and bridge. There are several buses daily (Monday-Saturday) from Otternish to Lochmaddy and on to Lochboisdale on South Uist. » *For further details, see Transport pages 458 and 487.*

Getting around There are four to six buses per day (except Sunday) from Otternish to Lochmaddy. These buses continue to Baile a Mhanaich (Balivanich) on Benbecula, where there is an airport, see page 480, and Lochboisdale and Ludag on South Uist, see page 481. There are four to seven buses per day from Lochmaddy to Otternish. These continue via the new causeway to the island of Bearnaraigh (Berneray) just off the north coast in the sound of Harris. There are three buses per day from Lochmaddy to Clachan na Luib (Clachan-a-Luib) which run in an anti-clockwise direction around the north and west coasts. Two buses per day connect Clachan-a-Luib with Baile Sear (Baleshare) and also with Saighdinis (Sidinish). There are also postbuses linking the main settlements. Bus timetables are available at the tourist office in Lochmaddy.

Loch nam Madadh (Lochmaddy)

Lochmaddy, the island's main village and ferry port, is a tiny place, so small you're almost through it before you realize. Though it's on the east coast and not close to the beaches, it is the best base for exploring the island as it boasts most facilities. It has a bank (next to the tourist office), a hotel and pub, a tourist office, a few shops, post office, hospital and petrol station.

If you have time the **Taigh Chearsabhagh Museum and Arts Centre** ⓘ *T/01876-500293, www.taigh-chearsabhagh.com*, is worth visiting and has a café. The tourist information centre ⓘ *near the ferry pier, T01876-500321, Mid-Apr to mid-Oct Mon-Sat 0900-1700, and for the arrival of the evening ferry*, will provide transport timetables.

Around the island

There are a number of interesting archaeological sites of different periods dotted around the island. The most notable is **Barpa Langass**, seven miles southwest of Lochmaddy on the slope of Ben Langass, just off the A867 which cuts across the bleak peaty hinterland of North Uist. This is a huge chambered burial cairn dating from around 3,000 BC. Unfortunately, it is now too dangerous to enter. About a mile away, on the southern side of Ben Langass, is the small stone circle known as **Pobull Fhinn**, standing on the edge of Loch Langass. Three miles northwest of Lochmaddy on the A865 are three Bronze Age standing stones called **Na Fir Bhreige** (The False Men), said to be the graves of three spies who were buried alive.

The real charms of North Uist, though, are its fabulous beaches on the north and west coasts. Heading anti-clockwise from Lochmaddy, the A865 runs northwest, passing the turning for Otternish and Bearnaraigh (see below), which is now connected to North Uist by a causeway. It continues west through the township of **Sollas (Solas)**, where there are a couple of B&Bs, and then past the beautiful sands of **Bhalaigh (Vallay) Strand**. Near the northwestern tip of the island is **Scolpaig Tower**, standing on an islet in Loch Scolpaig, a 'folly' built for famine relief in the 19th century.

▲ Three miles south of here is the turning to Balranald RSPB Reserve, an area of rocky coast, sandy beaches and dunes, machair and lochs. The reserve is ideal for bird watching, especially waders. A two-hour guided walk along the headland allows you to see Manx shearwaters, gannets, skuas and storm petrels, and during the summer you can listen out for the distinctive rasping call of the corncrake, one of the rarest birds in Britain. There's a basic visitor centre ⓘ *Apr-Sep*.

In Ceann a Bhaigh is the **Uist Animal Visitors Centre** ⓘ *Mon-Sat 1000-2200, £2*, where you can see Highland cattle and other rare native breeds, as well as more exotic species such as llamas. The road continues south to **Clachan na Luib**, at the crossroads of the A865 and A867 which heads east back to Lochmaddy. Offshore is the tidal island of **Baile Sear (Baleshare)**, now connected by a causeway to North Uist, with its three-mile long beach on the west coast. A further five miles west are the **Monach Isles** (also known by their old Norse name of Heisker), which were once connected to North Uist at low tide, until the 16th century when a huge tidal wave swept away the sand bridge, thus isolating them. Even so, the islands were still populated until as recently as the 1930s. Now they are populated by the largest breeding colony of grey seals in Europe.

South of Clachan, the road runs past **Cairinis (Carinish)** over a series of causeways to the little-visited lobster-fishing island of **Griomasaigh (Grimsay)**, before heading across another causeway to Benbecula. Near Cairinis is **Feith na Fala** (Field of Blood), site of the last battle fought in Scotland solely with swords and bows and arrows, in 1601, between the MacDonalds of Sleat and Macleods of Harris. The bloodshed was provoked by one of the MacDonalds divorcing his Macleod wife. When 60 Skye Macleods set off to North Uist to wreak revenge, they were met by 16 MacDonalds who literally chopped them to pieces, proving that divorce was a messy affair even then.

Bearnaraigh (Berneray) → *Phone code: 01876. Colour map 1, grid C1.*

Ferries from Leverburgh on Harris arrive at the low-lying island of Bearnaraigh, now connected by a causeway to North Uist. The island is famous as the place where

A fishy tale

In the 1820s a dead body was washed up in Culla Bay, near Griminish on Benbecula. It was said to have had the upper body of a well-developed four-year-old child, with long, dark glossy hair, and the lower half was like a salmon, but without scales. Many people came from all around to look at the bizarre creature, before the landlord of the estate ordered a coffin and shroud and it was given a decent burial on the shore of Culla Bay. What exactly this creature was has remained a mystery to this day.

Prince Charles spent a holiday helping out on a croft. It's also the birthplace of the giant Angus MacAskill, see page 439. Its real attraction, though, apart from the splendid isolation, is the three-mile-long sandy beach along its north and west coast.

A *Western Isles Walks* booklet for Bearnaraigh, available from Lochmaddy TIC, describes an enjoyable eight-mile walk around the island visiting all the main places of interest including the 16th-century gunnery at **Baile**, the beaches and machair of the north and west coast, and archaeological sites dating from the Viking period near **Borgh**.

Beinn na Faoghla (Benbecula)

→ *Phone code: 01870. Colour map 1, grid C1. Population: 1,803.*

Tiny Benbecula may be suffering from delusions of stature. Its Gaelic name means 'mountain of the fords', but the highest point is a mere 407 ft, with the rest of the island as flat as a pancake. It lies between Protestant North Uist and Catholic South Uist, and most visitors use it solely as a means of getting from one to the other via the A865 which cuts straight through the middle.

Ins and outs

Benbecula's airport is at Balivanich and there are direct flights to Glasgow, Barra and Stornoway, see page 487. The island is connected by causeways to both North and South Uist, and buses travelling to and from Lochmaddy and Lochboisdale pass through the villages of Balivanich, Lionacleit (Liniclate) and Creag Ghoraidh (Creagorry). There are also regular island buses which run between these settlements.

Sights

Like North Uist, the east of the island is so pitted with lochs that most people live on the west coast. A large percentage of the population are Royal Artillery personnel and their families stationed at **Baile a Mhanaich (Balivanich)**, a sprawling army base of utilitarian buildings in the northwest of the island. The influx of so many English-speakers has had a less than positive impact on Gaelic culture, and the military facilities have blighted much of the island's natural beauty, but Benbecula has benefited economically from the army's presence. Not only is there an airport here, but also a relatively large number of shops and amenities, including the only NAAFI supermarket in the UK that's open to the public, a Bank of Scotland (with ATM) and post office. There are worries, however, that the base may be scaled or closed, which would have a devastating effect on the local economy.

South of Balivanich the B892 runs around the west coast before joining the main A865 at the southern end of the island. It runs past **Culla Bay**, overlooked by **Baille**

nan Cailleach (Nunton). It was from here in 1746 that Bonnie Prince Charlie set off with Flora MacDonald over the sea to Skye, disguised as her maid, see page 436. To the south is **Poll-na-Crann**, better known as 'stinky bay' because of the piles of seaweed deposited there by fierce Atlantic storms. From the mid-18th century this kelp was used extensively in making glass, and provided a source of income for many communities. By 1820 the so-called kelp boom was over, though it is still gathered today and used for fertilizer.

The B892 ends at **Lionacleit (Liniclate)**, where the new community school serves the Uists and Benbecula. It has extensive facilities, including internet, a swimming pool, library, theatre and even a small local history **museum** ⓘ *Mon, Tue and Thu 0900-1600, Wed 0900-1230 and 1330-1600, Fri 0900-2000, Sat 1100-1300 and 1400-1600, free.*

Uibhist a Deas (South Uist) → *Phone code: 01870. Colour map 3, grid A1.*

Population: 2,285.

South Uist is the largest of the southern chain of Outer Hebridean islands and the most scenically attractive. Like its southern neighbour, Barra, South Uist is Roman Catholic and generally more relaxed about Sunday openings. Its 20 miles of west coast is one long sandy beach, backed by dunes with a mile or two of beautiful, flowering machair behind. To the east of the main A865 that runs the length of the island rises a central mountainous spine of rock and peat dotted with numerous lochs. Its two highest peaks, **Beinn Mhor** (2,034 ft) and **Hecla** (1,988 ft), tower over the rocky cliffs of an inaccessible eastern coastline indented by sea lochs. » *For Sleeping, Eating and other listings, see pages 485-488.*

Ins and outs

Getting there The island's main ferry port is Lochboisdale, which is reached from Oban (via Castlebay on Barra), arriving late at night. A private passenger-only ferry sails from Barra to Ludag, at the southern tip of South Uist . There are passenger ferry sailings on Sunday to and from Barra and a car ferry to Castlebay and Oban, but no ferry arrival from Oban or Castlebay and no bus services. » *For further details, see Transport pages 458 and 487.*

Getting around A causeway connects South Uist to Benbecula by road and regular buses (four to six per day daily except Sunday) run between Lochboisdale and Lochmaddy on North Uist, stopping en route at Dalabrog (Daliburgh), Tobha Mòr (Howmore) and Lionacleit and Balinavich on Benbecula. There is also a regular bus service between Lochboisdale and Ludag (for ferries to Barra). A new causeway, completed in August 2001, now links Eriskay to South Uist. There are ferries to Eriskay from Barra, see page 487.

History

The dominant family in South Uist was Clanranald, who also owned Benbecula. They were descendants of the first Lord of the Isles, who was a MacDonald. The island's connections with Clanranald came to a sorry end, however, in 1837 when it was sold, along with Benbecula, to pay off bad debts, and became the property of the infamous Lieutenant-Colonel John Gordon Cluny. Though all the southern isles suffered during the brutal clearances of the 19th century, the experiences of people on South Uist were particularly cruel and inhumane. Between 1849 and 1851 over 2,000 were forcibly shipped to Quebec in Canada. Those who refused to board the transport ships were hunted down by dogs and bound, before being thrown on board and shipped to Canada, where they were left to starve.

Tight little island

Between Eriskay and South Uist is the wreck of the famous *SS Politician*, the island's other claim to fame. In 1941 the 12,000 ton ship went aground just off the island of Calvey and sank with its cargo, which included 20,000 cases of whisky. This not only provided many islanders with a supply of whisky for many years, but also provided the plot for Compton Mackenzie's book *Whisky Galore!*, which was later made into the famous Ealing comedy of the same name (it was called Tight Little Island in the US) and filmed on Barra. Part of the wreck can be seen at low tide, and there's more information on the famous incident on display in the appropriately named Am Politician pub (open 1230-1430), in the main settlement of Baile (Balla).

Loch Baghasdail (Lochboisdale) → *Phone code: 01878. Colour map 3, grid A1. Population: 300.*

South Uists's largest settlement is set on a rocky promontory in a beautiful island-dotted sea loch. The imposing entrance is guarded by Calvay Island with its 13th-century castle ruin. Lochboisdale is a tiny place, with little in the way of tourist sights, though it does have a hotel, bank, post office and tourist information centre ⓘ *Pier Rd, T01878-700286, early Apr to mid-Oct.*

About 10 miles south of Lochboisdale, on the southern coast of the island, is **Ludag jetty**, the departure point for the small private passenger ferry to **Eòlaigearraidh (Eoligarry)** on Barra. At **Cille Bhrìghde (West Kilbride)** nearby is **Hebridean Croft Originals**, which has a wide range of local crafts on show, as well as a photographic display of local history. It's open daily and has a tearoom.

Around the island

At the north of the island a causeway leads across **Loch Bi** (pronounced 'Bee') to the distinctive modern statue of **Our Lady of the Isles**, standing by the main road on the lower slopes of **Rueval Hill**. Further up the hill is the Royal Artillery control centre, known by the locals as 'Space City', due to its forest of aerials and 'golf balls', which tracks the missiles fired from a range on the northwestern corner of the island out into the Atlantic.

Just to the south of here is **Loch Druidibeag Nature Reserve**, on the site of the large freshwater loch, one of the largest breeding grounds in the British Isles for greylag geese and also a favourite haunt for mute swans (there's a warden nearby at Groigearraidh Lodge). From here the main road runs down the spine of the island, and all along the way little tracks branch off to the west, leading down to lovely beaches.

Not far south of Loch Druidibeag is the turning to the tiny village of **Tobha Mòr (Howmore)**, where you can see a collection of old traditional thatched 'blackhouses' beside the seemingly endless stretch of golden sand. One of the houses has been converted into a **Gatliff Trust Youth Hostel**, see Sleeping page 485. From the hostel it's a five-minute walk across the machair to the sandy beach which stretches almost the entire length of South Uist.

From Tobha Mòr, there are superb walks through the lonely hills of **Beinn Mhor** (620 m), **Beinn Corodale** (527 m) and **Hecla** (606 m) to the picturesque and dramatic valleys of Glen Hellisdale, Glen Corodale and Glen Usinish on the east coast. In 1746 that ubiquitous troglodyte, Bonnie Prince Charlie is reputed to have taken refuge in a cave above **Corodale Bay** for three weeks following his defeat and escape from Culloden.

Near **Bornais (Bornish)** another minor road can be followed east of the A865 to **Loch Eynort** that penetrates far inland from the Minch. An old stalkers path can be followed along the north shore of the loch towards the sea, with views of numerous seals and the occasional otter and the steep upper slopes of Beinn Mhor towering above to the north.

A few miles south, at **Gearraidh Bhailteas (Milton)**, a cairn marks the birthplace of that famous Heridean lass, Flora MacDonald, see page 436. Nearby is the **Kildonan Museum**, which has a tearoom. The A865 continues south for a few miles to the village of Dalabrog (Daliburgh), then heads east to the island's main ferry port, **Lochboisdale**.

Eirisgeidh (Eriskay) → *Phone code: 01878. Colour map 3, grid A1.*

The tiny island of Eriskay, with a population of less than 200, gives its name to the native breed of pony, said to have been ridden by King Robert the Bruce at the Battle of Bannockburn in 1314. In the late 1970s it nearly became extinct, but one surviving stallion saved the breed and numbers are growing. A series of paths take you around the island in about three hours. For more details, see the Cuairt Eirisgeidh leaflet published by the Western Isles Tourist Board and available at the Lochboisdale Tourist Information Centre.

Most people come to Eriskay to pay a visit to **Coilleag a' Phrionnsa (Prince's beach)**, the sandy beach on the west coast. This is where Bonnie Prince Charlie first stepped on to Scottish soil on 23 July 1745, at the start of the ill-fated Jacobite Rebellion. The rare pink convolvulus which grows there today is said to have been planted by the Prince himself from seeds brought from France. A small memorial cairn situated in the dunes behind the beach was erected by the local school to commemorate the occasion.

As well as the wreck of the *SS Politician*, see box page 482, another sight worth seeing is **St Michael's**, the Roman Catholic church built in 1903 and funded by the local fishing fleet.

Bharraigh (Barra) → *Phone code: 01871. Colour map 3, grid A1. Population: 1,316.*

It may be tempting to overlook the little island of Barra, only about eight miles long by five miles wide, but this would be a great mistake, as it's one of the most beautiful of all the islands in the Outer Hebrides. Here you'll find the best of the islands in miniature – beaches, machair, peat-covered hills, tiny crofting communities and Neolithic remains – and a couple of days spent on Barra gives a real taster of Hebridean life. Gaelic culture is also strong here but, with its Catholic tradition, Barra is a bit more laid-back than many of the other islands in the Outer Hebrides and doesn't follow the others' strict Sabbatarianism. ▸▸ *For Sleeping, Eating and other listings, see pages 485-488.*

Ins and outs

Getting there The best way to arrive is by air at Tràigh Mhòr ('Cockle Strand'), the famous airstrip on the beach at the north end of the island. This is the only airport in the UK where flight schedules are shown as 'subject to tides'. Barra is reached by car ferry from Oban on the mainland, by car ferry from Lochboisdale on South Uist, and from Tiree. A private passenger-only ferry sails from Ludag on South Uist. ▸▸ *For further details, see Transport pages 458 and 487.*

Getting around There is a regular bus/postbus service (five to eight times per day Monday-Saturday) that runs from Castlebay to the ferry port of Eòlaigearraidh, via the airport. There are also buses (three to four per day Monday-Saturday) from Castlebay

Sand lends a hand

Machair is the name given to the strips of land that lie behind the many wonderful beaches of northwest Scotland and the islands. Machair is notable for its fertility, in sharp contrast to the poor, acid peat of the interior. In summer these strips are transformed into a blaze of colour when a multitude of wild flowers bloom – primroses, buttercups, orchids, gentian and wild iris – and this provides good grazing for sheep. The fertility of the machair comes from the calcium-rich shell sand which is blown inshore from the beaches and neutralizes the acidity of the peaty soil.

to Bhatarsaigh (Vatersay). You can also hire a car or a bicycle to tour the island at your leisure. » *For further details, see Transport pages 458 and 487.*

Bàgh a' Chaisteil (Castlebay)

The main settlement is Castlebay, on the southern side of the island, situated in a wide sheltered bay and overlooked by **Sheabhal** (383 m), on top of which is a marble statue of the Blessed Virgin and Child. It's a short but steep walk up to the top from the town, and the views are well worth it. The once-thriving herring port is also overlooked by the large Roman Catholic church, Our Lady, Star of the Sea.

As the main ferry port, Castlebay provides the full range of services: hotels, B&Bs, shops, a bank (with ATM) and post office. The tourist information centre ⓘ *T01871-810223, Apr to mid-Oct Mon-Sat 0900-1700, also open for the arrival of the evening ferry*, is on the main street near the ferry terminal. It has information on local walks and will book accommodation.

Castlebay's most notable feature is the impressive 15th-century **Kisimul Castle** ⓘ *T01871-810313, Apr-Sep daily 0930-1830, Oct Mon-Wed 0930-1630, Thu 0930-1230, Sat 0930-1630, Sun 1400-1630, £3.30, concession £2.50, children £1*, reached by boat from Castlebay pier (five minutes), weather permitting, built on an island in the middle of the harbour. This was the ancient home of the Chief of the MacNeils, one of the oldest Scottish clans, who owned the island from 1427 till 1838. It was then sold to the notorious Colonel Gordon of Cluny, along with neighbouring South Uist and Benbecula, see page 481, and the poor people of Barra suffered the same cruel fate, 600 of them being shipped to Canada to starve. One hundred years later the castle and much of the island was bought back for the MacNeils by an American architect, Robert Lister MacNeil, who became the 45th Clan Chief and restored the castle to its present state before his death in 1970. His son, the new Clan Chief, uses it as his residence when visiting, though it is now in the care of Historic Scotland.

If you're interested in finding out about the island's history, you should visit the Barra Heritage Centre, known as **Dualchas** ⓘ *T01871-810403, Apr-Sep Mon-Fri 1100-1700, £1.*

Around the island

The A888 follows a circular route of 14 miles around the island, making an ideal day's bike tour from Castlebay. Heading west, it passes the turning for the causeway to **Vatersay** (see below), then runs northwest between two hills (Sheabhal to the east and Beinn Tangabhal to the west) to the west coast, where you'll find the nicest beaches. One of these is at **Halaman Bay**, near the village of **Tangasdal (Tangasdale)**, overlooked by the **Isle of Barra Hotel**, see Sleeping page 485. At the turning for **Borgh (Borve)** there are standing stones. Next is the turning for the small settlement of **Baile Na Creige**

(Craigston), where you'll find the **Thatched Cottage Museum** ⓘ *Easter-Oct Mon-Fri 1100-1700, £1*, an original 'blackhouse' and the chambered burial cairn of **Dun Bharpa.** From Dun Bharpa there are pleasant walks into the surrounding hills, with the summit of **Sheabhal** offering tremendous views from the highest point on the island.

North of the turning, near **Allathsdal (Allasdale)**, is another lovely beach, and just beyond are the remains of **Dun Cuier**, an Iron-Age fort. Make a short detour at Greian, and follow the headland to the rugged cliffs at **Greian Head**.

The A888 then heads east to **Bagh a Tuath (Northbay)**, where a branch left leads to the village of **Eòlaigearraidh (Eoligarry)**, near the northern tip, surrounded by sandy bays washed by Atlantic rollers. A private passenger ferry leaves from here to Ludag on South Uist.

The road to Eoligarry passes the island's airport at **Tràigh Mhòr**, the 'cockle strand', which once provided 100 to 200 cartloads of delicious cockles each day. Now the cockleshells are gathered and used for harling, the roughcast wall covering used on many Scottish houses. By the beach is the house that was once the home of Compton MacKenzie, author of *Whisky Galore!*, see page 483. He lies buried at **Cille Bhara**, to the west of the village of Eòlaigearraidh, along with members of the MacNeil clan. This was one of the most important religious complexes in the Outer Hebrides, built in the 12th century, and consists of a church and two chapels. One of these, St Mary's, has been re-roofed and houses several carved medieval tombstones and a copy of a runic stone. The original is in the **Museum of Scotland** in Edinburgh.

Bhatarsaigh (Vatersay) and Mingulay

A worthwhile trip from Castlebay is to the island of Vatersay, now linked to Barra by a causeway built in an effort to stabilize the island community (the present population is around 70). The island boasts two lovely shell-sand beaches backed by beautiful machair, only a few hundred yards apart on either side of the narrow isthmus that leads to the main settlement of Vatersay. On the west beach, Bagh Siar, is the **Annie Jane Monument**, which commemorates the terrible tragedy in 1853, when the emigrant ship Annie Jane was wrecked off the coast of Vatersay, with the loss of 333 lives, many of them islanders.

On a clear day from Vatersay you can enjoy the view of the smaller islands to the south – Sandray, Pabbay and Mingulay. The latter was inhabited until 1912, and can still be visited from Barra. It has recently been acquired by the National Trust for Scotland. ▸▸ *For details of tours, see Activities and tours page 487.*

Sleeping

North Uist *p478*

B Langass Lodge, near Pobhull Fhinn (see above), T01876-580285, langars@btinternet.com. Their restaurant specializes in local seafood and game.

C Lochmaddy Hotel, Lochmaddy, T01876-500332, F500210. Right by the ferry terminal. Open all year. Their restaurant serves great seafood, and the lively bar serves snacks. This is also the place to ask about fishing, as they rent out boats and sells permits for trout and salmon fishing.

C Temple View Hotel, at Grimsay, T01876-580676.

D-E The Old Courthouse, Lochmaddy, T01876-500358. One of a couple of good B&Bs.

D-E The Stag Lodge, Lochmaddy, T01876-500364, F500417, is a restaurant which also does B&B.

E Mrs Kathy Simpson, near Balranald, in Hogha Gearraidh (Houghgarry), overlooking the beautiful beach, T01876-510312.

E The Old Bank House, Lochmaddy, T01876-500275. Another good choice and also open all year.

E-F Mrs Morag Nicholson, in Ceann a Bhaigh (Bayhead), T01876-510395.

F Lochmaddy Uist Outdoor Centre, half a mile from the ferry pier, Lochmaddy, T01876-500480. Independent hostel, open all year, offers a wide range of outdoor activities including kayaking, windsurfing and rock climbing.

F Taigh Mo Sheannair, a few miles south of Clachan, at Cladach a Bhaile Shear (Claddach-baleshare), T01876-580246. Renovated crofthouse on a working farm which offers good hostel accommodation all year round, rents out bicycles and has space for camping.

Berneray *p479*

There are a couple of options for those wishing to stay.

E Burnside Croft, T01876-540235, splashmackilloop@burnsidecroft.fsnet.co.uk. Here you can share the prince's crofting experience with Donald (Splash) MacKillop. It also offers cycle hire and stories round the fire for evening entertainment.

F Gatliff Trust Hostel, in 2 restored blackhouses overlooking a lovely sandy beach and old Viking pier about a mile up the east coast from the old ferry pier. 12 beds, no phone, open all year.

Benbecula *p480*

A Dark Island Hotel, Lionacleit, T01870-603030, F602347. Functional hotel but a lot nicer inside than its name may suggest, has a good restaurant.

D Inchyra Guest House, Lionacleit, T01870-602176. Reliable and much cheaper alternative to the hotel.

F Tigh-na-Cille Bunkhouse, Balivanich, T01870-602522, open all year and sleeps 10 in 2 dorms and 2 twin rooms.

Camping

Shellbay Caravan and Camping Park, Lionacleit, T01870-602447, open Apr-Oct.

South Uist *p481*

You should book accommodation in advance, as the ferry arrives in Lochboisdale late in the evening.

C Lochboisdale Hotel, Lochboisdale, T01870-700332, F700367. This fishing hotel is right by the ferry terminal, and the best place to stay and the only place to have a drink or a meal.

C Polachar Inn, a few miles to the west of Ludag, at Pol a' Charra (Pollachar), T01870-700215, F700768. Charming place with great views across the Sound of Barra and its own beach close by.

D Brae Lea Guest House, about a mile from the terminal, Lochboisdale, T/F01870-700497. Will collect you from the ferry.

D Orosay Inn, T01870- 610298, www.orosayinn.com. Small, modern hotel at Loch a' Chairnain (Lochcarnan). Open all year and offers fine Scottish cooking (££).

E Bayview, Lochboisdale, T01870-700329. B&B accommodation at the ferry terminal.

E-F Lochside Cottage, Lochboisdale, T01870-700472. B&B accommodation at the ferry terminal.

F Gatliff Trust Youth Hostel, at Tobha Mòr (Howmore), converted blackhouse which overlooks the ruins of an ancient church and graveyard, beside the seemingly endless stretch of golden sand, 13 beds, open all year, no phone. The warden lives at Ben More House, at the junction with the main road.

Barra *p483*

It's a good idea to book in advance if arriving on the evening ferry from Oban.

B-C Isle of Barra Hotel a few miles west of Castlebay, T01871-810383, www.barrahotel.com. 30 rooms, open Apr-Oct. Modern, purpose-built hotel overlooking a lovely beach with fantastic sea views.

D Castlebay Hotel, by the ferry terminal in Castlebay, T01871-810223. 14 rooms. The best place to stay on the island. Friendly, good food, good value and a great bar.

D Craigard Hotel, in Castlebay, T01871-810200, is a family-run hotel with hearty home cooking.

There are also several guest houses and B&Bs in and around Castlebay, including:

E Ceol Mara, T01871-810294;

E Grianamul, T01871-810416, ronnie.macneil@virgin.net; and

E Terra Nova, T01871-810458, which is situated a 10-min walk from the ferry in Nask.

At the moment there are no independent hostels or a Gatliff Trust Hostel on Barra.

Camping

Although there are also no official campsites on Barra, there are endless opportunities for wild camping across the island, with the most popular spots to be found on the machair at Traigh Mhor (north Barra), Borve Point (west Barra) and Ledaig (Castlebay). Generally no permission is required from the landowner, but ensure all waste and litter is removed when you leave the site. For campers, there are 2 or 3 well-stocked mini-supermarkets in Castlebay.

Eriskay *p483*
There is a **B&B**, T01870-720232, and a **self-catering flat**, T01870-720274, or you can wild camp – though there are few amenities, other than a shop, pub and post office.

Eating

See Sleeping for further options.

Benbecula *p480*
£££-££ Stepping Stone Restaurant, Balivanich, T01870-603377. By far the best place to eat on the island. Good wholesome Scottish food every day from 1000 till 2100. Snacks, sandwiches, takeaways and home baking are all available, as well as 3- or 5-course meals.

Barra *p483*
££ Castelbay Hotel and **Isle of Barra Hotel**, both offer excellent local fish and seafood.
£ Kismul Galley, on the main street in Castlebay, T01871-810645, offers all-day breakfasts, snacks and home baking, and is open Mon-Sat 0900-2100 and Sun 1000-1800.
£ There's also a tearoom at the airport.

Activities and tours

Barra *p483*
Mr John Allan MacNeil in Castlebay, T01871-810449 (approximately £15 per person), can arrange boat trips to Mingulay. He sails to the island in settled weather when sufficient people can be found to fill the boat. It is one of the most rewarding excursions in the Outer Hebrides, particularly during the puffin season from Jun to early Aug. The trip normally includes a 2-hr sail from Barra past the neighbouring islands of Sandray and Pabbay, a circumnavigation of Mingulay to view the spectacularly high western sea cliffs, and a landing on the east coast for a 3-hr exploration of the beautiful beach of Mingulay Bay, the deserted village and surrounding hills and coast. There are also fine views to the lighthouse on Barra Head, the most southerly outpost of the Outer Hebrides island chain.
Mr George McLeod, at the Castlebay Hotel, T01871-810223, can arrange a similar tour to that outlined above, or ask at the tourist office in Castlebay.
Hatcher's Taxis, T01871-810486; and **Nellie's Taxi**, T01871-810302, conduct island tours.

Transport

Air
British Airways/Loganair, T08708-509850, www.ba.com, flies from **Glasgow** to **Barra** (Mon-Sat 1 daily, 1 hr 5 mins) and **Benbecula** on North Uist (Mon-Sat 1 daily, 1 hr). There are also flights from **Benbecula** to **Barra** (Mon-Fri 1 daily, 20 mins). To North Uist from **Uig** to **Lochmaddy** (1 hr 40 mins) 1-2 times daily. One-way ticket £8.95 per passenger, £43 per car. Contact Lochmaddy, T01876-5000337. To **Barra** and **South Uist**, from **Oban** to **Castlebay** (5 hrs) and on to **Lochboisdale** (a further 1 hr 40 mins) once daily except Wed, plus an extra sailing on Thu to **Castlebay** only, via **Tiree**. **Oban** to **Castlebay** or **Lochboisdale**, one-way ticket £19.70 per passenger, £72 per car, 5-day saver return £9.50 and £55. **Castlebay** to **Lochboisdale**, £5.60 one way per passenger, £32.50 per car. **Tiree** to **Castlebay**, £9.25 per passenger, £41 per car.

Boat
There's also a regular passenger ferry from **Ludag** in **South Uist** to **Eoligarry** on **Barra**, T01878-720238. Ferries sail from **Barra** to **Eriskay** 5 times daily (4 on Sun). A one-way ticket costs £5.35 per passenger and £15.80 per car. 5-day return is £9.10 and £27. Bicycles £1.

For an explanation of sleeping and eating price codes used in this guide, see inside the front cover. Other relevant information is found in Essentials, see pages 43-51.

Car and bike hire
Car hire at **Maclennan Self Drive**, Balivanich on Beinn na Faoghla, T01870-602191, F603191. Also at **Ask Car Hire**, Lionacleit, Beinn na Faoghla, T01870-602818, F602933. Car hire on South Uist is possible from **Laing Motors**, Lochboisdale, T01870-700267, and cycle hire from **Rothan Cycles**, Lochboisdale, T01870-620283.

St Kilda

Over 40 miles west of the Outer Hebrides lie the spectacular and isolated islands of St Kilda, Scotland's first UNESCO World Heritage Site. St Kilda consists of several islands and manages to capture the imagination of most visitors to the Outer Hebrides, whether they actually get there or just dream about romantic voyages to mysterious lands across perilous seas. Now owned by the National trust for Scotland, St Kilda is a National Nature reserve. Each year, during the brief summer months, when travel to the islands is possible, teams of volunteers work on Hirta, maintaining what remains of the abandoned houses, studying the wildlife and glorying in the peace and isolation of the place.

Ins and outs

The biggest problem apart from accessibility is cost, although it is definitely possible if you're prepared to break the bank. Island Cruising in Uig, on Lewis, T01851-672381, F672212, arranges boat trips to St Kilda from April to October starting from about £300 (four-day all-inclusive). The tour comprises the journey to and from St Kilda and a landing on Hirta with a visit to the museum, the old village and a wider exploration of the island including a climb up to the highest sea cliffs in the British Isles at Conachair (430 m). A 70-ft converted lifeboat also makes the trip, operated by Northern Light in Oban, T01680-814260. A seven-day expedition costs £650 per person. For more details of tours, ask at one of the main tourist information centres in the Outer Hebrides.

National Trust for Scotland also organizes two-week long voluntary Work Parties throughout the summer every year to undertake restoration, maintenance and archaeology projects around the old village on Hirta. The groups are very popular, and each volunteer must complete an application form, so apply early. The fortnight costs between £450 and £500 and this covers transport from Oban to St Kilda and all food and lodging costs while on the island. For details contact National Trust for Scotland in Oban, T01631-570000, stkilda@nts.org.uk. For more information, contact Scottish Natural Heritage ⓘ *135 Stilligarry, South Uist, HS8 5RS, T01870-620238.*

Sights

In 1957 the islands become the property of the National Trust for Scotland, who in turn leased them to the Nature Conservancy (the forerunner of Scottish Natural Heritage) as a National Nature Reserve. St Kilda is the most important seabird breeding station in northwest Europe. The islands are home to the largest colony of gannets in the world, the largest colony of fulmars in Britain, and one the largest colonies of puffins in Scotland. These huge numbers of seabirds were vital to the islanders' survival. Their eggs provided food in the summer, and gannets and fulmers were caught each season to be plucked, dried and stored for the winter. Their feathers and oil were kept for export to generate income, whilst their bones were shaped into useful tools and their skins into shoes.

The largest of the islands, **Hirta**, was the remotest community in Britain, if not Europe, until 1930, when the remaining 36 Gaelic-speaking inhabitants were

How St Kilda was killed off

Friday 29 August 1930 was the end of the life of St Kilda as it had been for centuries. For a least 1,000 years the inhabitants of this remote group of islands had been tenants of the Macleods of Dunvegan on Skye. In earlier days the trip from Skye, undertaken in longboats, would require 16 hours of rigorous rowing and sailing. Even now, the trip to St Kilda is no easy matter.

Until 1930 the islanders had been supported by the mainland by the provision of a nurse and a post office. But the Scottish Office decided that their subsidy of the islands was no longer economic. This meant that life for the residents without those facilities would be untenable.

But in 1930, to the younger of the 36 residents, including a man with nine children, evacuation was an attractive prospect. There would be better schooling for the children, and better health care. Although many had never seen a tree, a new life in forestry appealed. The more elderly residents, most of whom had never left the island and who could not speak English, must have viewed the drastic change with alarm. But the younger majority view prevailed and evacuation was planned.

There were 500 Soay sheep to be moved first. Their coats of fine wool were not sheared but plucked by the inhabitants using only a penknife. The resultant locally woven tweed, either shipped ashore or sold to rare visitors, had provided the inhabitants' only contact with actual money. No taxes on income or on anything else were paid. Their internal economy took the form of barter. The plentiful supply of gannets, when dried, provided winter food. No inhabitant had ever fought in any war. Their distance and isolation earned them no consideration by the rest of Scotland.

Despite protestations by The Canine Defence League, all dogs were destroyed. Just two were put down by injections of hydrocyanic acid. The rest, at the islanders' insistence, had stones tied around their necks and were hurled from the jetty. Small boats, holding only a dozen or so sheep, were used to ferry them out to the *SS Dunara Castle*. Ten cows with four calves were also evacuated. Then *HMS Harebell*, of the Fishery Protection Service, came on the final day to take the islanders to the mainland. The Under Secretary of State for Scotland imposed a ban on photography, thus ensuring the people of St Kilda privacy during the evacuation. It was not possible to house all of the inhabitants in Argyll, as had been hoped, so the community was split, their communal lives coming to an end.

The history of the island has been documented in a number of scholarly works, including *The Life and Death of St Kilda* by Tom Steel, and *Island on the Edge of the World* by Charles Maclean.

evacuated at their own request, in one of the most poignant episodes of Scottish history.Today Hirta is partly occupied by the army as a radar-tracking station for the rocket range on South Uist and managed by Scottish Natural Heritage. Across a narrow channel lies **Dun**. Nearby **Boreray** is home to the world's largest colony of gannets, and **Soay** virtually completes the group. There are several dramatic 'stacs' rising sheer from the Atlantic Ocean. At 430 m, the sea cliffs at Conachair are the highest in the British Isles.

Northeast Scotland

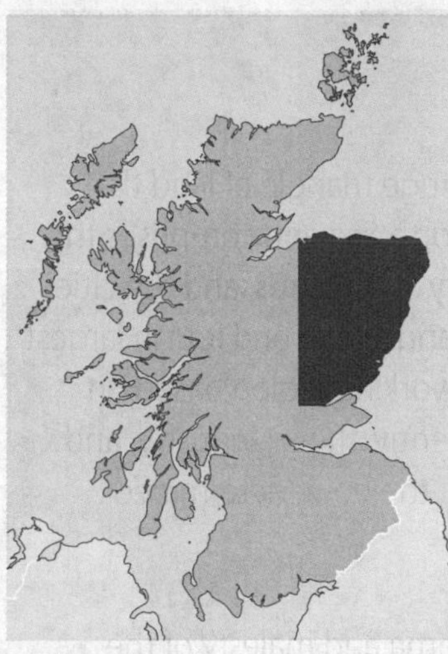

Footprint features

Introduction

The northeast of Scotland is the huge triangle of land that thrusts defiantly into the harsh North Sea and comprises the regions of **Aberdeenshire**, **Moray** and **Angus**, and the cities of **Aberdeen** and **Dundee**, Scotland's third and fourth largest cities respectively. This is a hard-working region based on agriculture, fishing and, more recently, the oil industry, and its people typify the stereotype of the dour, determined and thrifty Scot.

The region may lack the sheer drama and majesty of the northwest, but countryside between the Firth of Tay and the Moray Firth has its own, more subtle charms – and better weather. The **Moray Firth**, from the hardy fishing port of **Fraserburgh** west to the **Findhorn community**, has some of the country's most dramatic coastal scenery, lined with little fishing villages clinging, limpet-like to storm-battered cliffs. There are also long stretches of apricot-coloured beaches, long hours of sunshine, and even dolphins frolicking in the waters offshore. Flowing into the Moray Firth is the **River Spey**, whose gentle, wooded valley is a major centre of Scotland's malt whisky industry.

Another of the region's assets is its rich history. This is castle country and there are over 70 in Aberdeenshire and Moray alone. One of the most famous is **Balmoral Castle**, forever linked to the royal family since Queen Victoria came, saw and purchased in 1852. So strong is the connection that this area is better known as 'Royal Deeside' and visitors can indulge in a bit of royal spotting at the annual **Braemar Gathering**, the local Highland Games.

★ Don't miss...

❶ **Auchmithie** Head down to this attractive little fishing village and enjoy some superb seafood at the But'n'Ben restaurant, page 503.

❷ **Dufftown** Visit the self-proclaimed 'Malt Whisky Capital of the World' and begin the tour of the region's many distilleries, page 533.

❸ **Crathes** If you're not all castled-out, then crack on down to this perfect fairytale castle, which, unbelievably, is almost overshadowed by its gorgeous gardens, page 525.

❹ **Lonach Highland Gathering** If all that royal-spotting leaves you cold, then head here, held in August and frequented by the likes of Billy Connolly and Judi Dench, page 532.

Ins and outs

Dundee and Aberdeen are connected by the fast A90 which runs inland through Angus before linking up with the coastal A92 near Stonehaven. Regular buses run between the two cities, and there's a good rail link, connecting Aberdeen and Dundee to Edinburgh. Trains also run northwest from Aberdeen to Inverness, passing through Elgin and other inland towns. There's a fairly good bus service throughout the northeast, as well as a limited network of postbuses (www.royalmail.com/postbus) serving the Angus glens. Only the most remote and mountainous parts of the region cannot be reached by public transport. ▸▸ *For further details, see the respective transport sections.*

Dundee

→ *Phone code: 01382. Colour map 4, grid B4. Population: 14,300.*

Scotland's fourth largest city sits on two prominent hills, Balgay and the Law, overlooking the River Tay. Few cities in Britain can match Dundee's impressive setting, seen at its breathtaking best from across the Tay, in Fife. But, despite the common consensus that the views of the city are indeed spectacular, certain guidebooks have suggested that visitors keep their distance. This just goes to show how out of touch they are, for Dundee has transformed itself into a vibrant, thriving city and an increasingly popular destination for tourists.

One of Dundee's big attractions is Captain Scott's ship, the Discovery, *and such is the civic pride engendered by its return home that Dundee has become widely known through its slogan – City of Discovery. There are other, less publicized, attractions, such as the Law Hill, which commands fantastic views over the city and the Tay estuary, and the attractive seaside suburb of Broughty Ferry. Dundee also has a thriving arts scene and plenty of good shops, bars and restaurants. But the city's best kept secret is its people. The accent may at first be somewhat impenetrable, but Dundonians have an endearing earthy humour and are the friendliest bunch of people you'll find anywhere on the east coast of Scotland.* ▸▸ *For Sleeping, Eating and other listings, see pages 498-501.*

Ins and outs

Getting there

Dundee's airport, T01382-643242, is on Riverside Drive, about a five-minute drive west of the city centre. Scot Airways run daily services to and from London City airport T0870-6060707. There are no buses to the centre. A taxi will cost around £4. The bus station, T01382-228345, is on Seagate, a few hundred yards east of the City Square. All regional and national buses arrive here. Trains into Dundee arrive at Taybridge Station, a few hundred yards south of the High Street, across the dual carriageway at the foot of Union Street. By car the best approach is from the south, across the Tay Road Bridge (£0.80 toll; payable heading south only), which gives a spectacular introduction to the city. Alternatively, the city is reached via the A90, from Aberdeen to the north or Perth to the west. Coming from Perth, turn on to Riverside Drive at the Invergowrie roundabout for the city centre. ▸▸ *For further details, see page 501.*

Getting around

Dundee city centre is fairly compact and most of the sights are within walking distance of each other. For outlying sights, the city is served by an efficient bus service. Buses heading west along the Perth Road pass along the High Street, stopping at the city square. Heading northwards, buses leave from Albert Square, behind the McManus Galleries, and buses heading east towards Broughty Ferry leave from outside Littlewoods on the High Street.

Tourist information

The very helpful tourist information centre ⓘ *21 Castle St, T01382-527527, www.angusanddundee.co.uk, Jun-Sep Mon-Sat 0900-1800, Sun 1200-1600, Oct-May Mon-Sat 0900-1700*, is a short walk from the train station. It provides extensive details and free leaflets for all Dundee's attractions. They also book accommodation and have a good souvenir shop. You can pick up a free copy of the monthly *What's On* listings magazine here. The two local newspapers, the *Courier* and the *Evening Telegraph*, are good sources of information.

History

Dundee has been settled since prehistoric times, and Pictish earthworks and chambers can still be seen at Tealing, Ardestie and Carlungie, just beyond the city's boundaries. The city was an important trading port as long ago as the 12th century, and it was here that Robert the Bruce was proclaimed King of Scots in 1309. Its importance, however, made it a prime target for a succession of English invaders. It was captured by Edward I, besieged by Henry VIII, destroyed by Royalists and Cromwell's army during the Civil War, and then again by Viscount Dundee prior to the Battle of Killiecrankie. The young William Wallace, the fiery Scottish patriot, was educated in Dundee, and during its occupation by Edward's forces Wallace stabbed the son of an English overlord for daring to insult him, and had to flee south. A plaque on the High Street marks the spot where the incident took place.

Dundee is famous within Scotland as the city of the three J's: Jute, Jam and Journalism. These three industries were part of the city's commercial success, and the jute mills in particular, from the early 19th century, were the foundation of the city's wealth. Along with Edinburgh, Dundee became a centre for investment trusts which sunk cash into ventures all over the world, particularly the USA. In 1873 Dundee jute man Robert Fleming set up the Scottish Investment Trust to channel money into US cattle ranches, mining companies and railways. The biggest cattle ranch in the USA was run from Dundee until 1951 and the Texas oil industry was largely financed by Dundee jute wealth. The jam-making came about almost by accident, when a ship carrying a cargo of oranges was forced to put into Dundee harbour during a storm. A local grocer bought the oranges, which his wife then made into marmalade, and an industry was born. Journalism is the only 'J' still in operation in the city. DC Thomson is now the city's largest employers outside the health and leisure industries, and continues to produce many newspapers and magazines. Perhaps their most famous creations are the children's comics *The Dandy* and *The Beano*, begun in 1937 and 1938 respectively and still going strong. Generations of British children have been brought up on the antics of Dennis the Menace, Desperate Dan, The Bash Street Kids et al, and the popularity of these cartoon characters is reflected in the choice of the comic-inspired lettering for Dundee's promotional logo.

While the three 'J's' were undoubtedly important to Dundee, other industries also played a substantial role in the city's history. Dundee was a major centre for shipbuilding and ships were built for both the whaling industry and for the import and export of jute and other cargoes. Dundee has a proud maritime heritage and for many years was the capital of the British whaling industry. In these more enlightened times

The name Dundee is derived from the Gaelic words 'dun' meaning hill or fort and 'daig', who was thought to be an early local chieftain.

 we may shudder at the decimation of the whale stocks that led to the demise of the industry, but whale oil was a very valuable commodity, and the men who sailed the freezing Arctic seas to catch whales suffered terrible privations and hardships. On one famous occasion the whalers did not have to travel very far in search of their quarry. In December 1883 a humpback whale swam into the Tay estuary and foundered on the sandbanks. Large crowds gathered to watch the doomed animal's attempts to return to the sea, and it was harpooned on 7 December before finally being landed, completely exhausted, on 8 January the following year. It was put on public display before being sold, and the skeleton of the 'Tay whale' now resides in the city's McManus Galleries (see below).

Sights

Discovery Point

ⓘ *T01382-201245, www.rsdiscovery.com, Apr-Oct 1000-1800 (Sun 1100-1800), Nov-Mar till 1700, £6.25, £3.85 child, £4.45 concession, £10.95/£8.15 for joint ticket with Verdant Works.*

The obvious place to begin your tour of the city is Discovery Point, the impressive riverside location of Dundee's main attraction, the Royal Research Ship *Discovery*. This excellent facility, which attracts tens of thousands of visitors each year, is across the road from the train station, next to the Leisure Centre and Hilton Hotel. When Dundee was an important shipbuilding centre its speciality was wooden ships, and it was the Royal Geographical Society who commissioned the *Discovery*, which was launched on the Tay on 21 March 1901. She was the first specially designed scientific

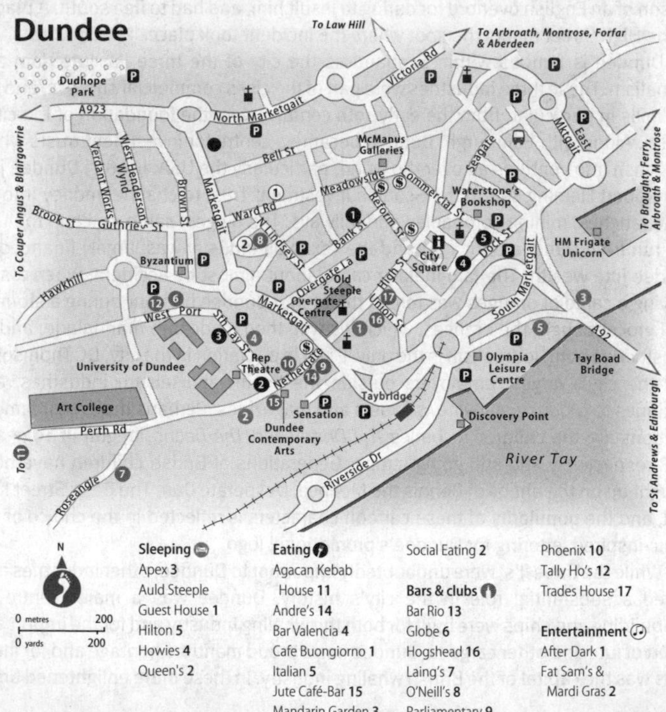

research ship and spent two winters in the Antarctic, where her wooden hull was able to withstand the enormous pressures of the pack ice. Famous as Captain Scott's ship, the *Discovery* and Scott parted company after his expedition in 1904. Another Dundee-built vessel, the *Terra Nova*, carried Scott to the South Pole in 1911 – the fateful expedition from which he never returned. After being purchased by the Maritime Trust, the *Discovery* was returned to Dundee in 1986 and moored at its present specially built quay with an excellent visitor centre at her side. The state-of-the-art centre presents an entertaining introduction, with audio-visual displays and an exhibition. On board the vessel you can see the cabins used by Scott and his crew, and hear some interesting anecdotes from the enthusiastic guides.

A short distance west of the *Discovery*, in Victoria Dock on the other side of the road bridge, is Dundee's other major floating attraction, the HM Frigate *Unicorn* ⓘ *T01382-200900, Mar-Oct daily 1000-1700, Nov-Feb Wed-Fri 1200-1600 1000-1600, £3.50, £2.50 child/concession*, built in 1824, this is the oldest British warship still afloat, probably because it never fired a shot in anger. It was used variously as a gunpowder store and a training vessel, until it was rescued from the scrapyard in 1968 by a preservation society. A tour of the ship gives some idea of the cramped conditions in which the 300 men had to live and work, and the unused cannons are still on display.

Around the centre

The focal point of the city centre is City Square, which is surrounded by shops and cafés, the imposing **Caird Hall**, the city's main concert hall, and the City Chambers, scene of much shady dealing in the 1960s and 1970s, which led to the demolition of the city's medieval core. The resulting shopping mall, the infamous Overgate, has itself been replaced by a brand new **Overgate retail complex**. In front is the **Old Steeple** ⓘ *not open to the public*, the highest surviving medieval tower in the country.

The pedestrianized Reform Street leads north from City Square to Albert Square, site of the **McManus Galleries** ⓘ *T01382-432350, Mon-Sat 1030-1700 (1900 on Thu) and 1230-1600 Sun, free*, housed in Gilbert Scott's impressive Victorian Gothic edifice. Inside are some very fine exhibits detailing the city's history from the Iron Age to the Tay Bridge Disaster. The latter event was chronicled by the inimitable William McGonagall, the 'World's Worst Poet', and here you can read his excruciatingly awful verse, along with an equally painful account of the famous 'Tay Whale', the skeleton of which is also on display. Upstairs is the superb Albert Hall, which contains various antique collections, and the Victoria Gallery, whose 19th- and 20th-century collections include some notable Scottish painters such as McTaggart. Also in Albert Square are the huge red sandstone offices of local publishing giant, **DC Thomson**, who have entertained generations of British kids with their *Beano* and *Dandy* comics.

A five-minute walk west, along Meadowside and Ward Road, across the dual carriageway and up Guthrie Street, is the excellent **Verdant Works** ⓘ *West Henderson's Wynd, T01382-225282, www.verdantworks.com, Apr-Oct Mon-Sat 1000-1800, Sun 1100-1800; Nov-Mar Wed-Sat 1030-1630, Sun 1100-1630, £5.95, £3.95 child/concessions)*. This former jute mill gives a rare insight into what life was like for mill workers, and details the history of the jute industry.

Behind the **Dundee Contemporary Arts** (see page 500) is **Sensation Dundee** ⓘ *Greenmarket, T01382-228800, 1000- 1800 summer, shuts earlier in winter, £6.50, £4.50 child*, one of those hands-on, interactive kind of places, so loved by kids.

Law Hill and Balgay Hill

The most prominent feature of the city is the Law Hill, a 571-ft high ancient volcanic plug. The views from the summit, over the entire city and south to Fife across the River Tay and its two bridges, are fantastic. It's a steep climb to the foot of the Law from the city centre, up the Hilltown, so it's best to take a bus (Nos 3 or 4) from Albert Square.

 The 1½-mile-long Tay Road Bridge was opened in 1966, while the **Tay Rail Bridge** is over two miles long and the longest railway bridge in Europe. It was built in 1878 but the following year the final section collapsed during a terrible storm. No one could alert the driver of the approaching train and it plunged into the cold, dark waters of the Tay, killing the crew and 75 passengers. A replacement section was built in 1887 and still stands today.

About a mile west of the Law, is Balgay Hill, site of the **Mills Observatory** ⓘ *T01382-435967, Apr-Sep Tue-Fri 1100-1700, Sat, Sun 1230-1600, Oct-Mar Mon-Fri 1600-2200, Sat, Sun 1230-1600, free, take bus Nos 2, 36 or 37 to Balgay Rd*, at the entrance to Balgay Park, a free public facility which houses a planetarium as well as displays on astronomy and space exploration.

West of Balgay Hill is the huge **Ninewells Hospital**, site of Maggie's Centre, one of a series of cancer-support centres established around the country. This one is notable as the very first building in the UK to be designed by US architect, Frank Gehry, who is best known as the inspiration behind Bilbao's Guggenheim Museum. Buses 9 and 22 go to the hospital from the city centre.

Broughty Ferry

Four miles east of Dundee, is the attractive seaside resort of Broughty Ferry. 'The Ferry' was once a separate settlement, with fishermen's cottages lining the shore and the large villas of wealthy jute barons climbing the hills behind, but it has since been swallowed up by the city's eastern suburbs. There's a long sandy beach, which is now much cleaner than it used to be, and several good pubs and places to eat, as well as some good individual shops. The 15th-century **Broughty Castle** ⓘ *T01382-436916, Apr-Sep Mon-Sat 1000-1600, Sun 1230-1600, Oct-Mar closed Mon, free*, stands on the seafront, guarding the mouth of the Tay, and now houses an interesting museum of local history which includes a detailed description of the whaling industry. There are frequent buses to Broughty Ferry leaving from outside Littlewoods on the High Street.

Sleeping

Dundee *p494, map p496*
The range of upmarket accommodation in Dundee has improved recently, although many of the best hotels are still outside the city. There are plenty of good-value guest houses, particularly in the West End, on and around the Perth Rd, in the eastern suburb of Broughty Ferry and along Arbroath Rd which heads east towards Broughty Ferry from the centre.

B **Hilton Hotel**, Earl Grey Place, T01382-229271, www.hilton.com.uk. 54 double and 74 twin rooms. Reliable 4-star chain with car parking, a leisure club with a pool and a restaurant.

C **Apex City Quay Hotel**, West Victoria Dock Rd, T01382-202404, www.apexhotels.co.uk. 153 rooms. Contemporary style comes to Dundee. This multi storey hotel has 4-star rooms with CD/DVD players, modem points as well as a restaurant and a brasserie. Yu Spa includes Japanese hot tubs, a pool and sauna.

C **Howies**, 25 South Tay St, T01382-200399, www.howies.uk.com. Small but cool restaurant with 4 stylish and comfortable rooms on the top floor.

C **Queen's Hotel**, 160 Nethergate, T01382-322515, www.queenshotel-dundee.com. 47 rooms. Perennial old favourite, conveniently located for all the main sights and with car parking. Also handy for West End pubs and restaurants, the Rep Theatre and its almost next door to the DCA.

C **Swallow Hotel**, Kingsway West, T01382-631200, F631201. 107 rooms. Conveniently situated by the large roundabout where Riverside Dr meets the city ringroad (Kingsway) and A90 to Perth, tastefully refurbished and extended Victorian mansion with full leisure facilities and extensive grounds.

C **Woodlands Hotel**, 13 Panmure Terr, Brought Ferry, T01382-480033, www.redwoodleisure.co.uk. 38 rooms. Set in extensive grounds and with pool and gym.

D Auld Steeple Guest House, 94 Nethergate, T/F01382-200302. 11 rooms. Nothing fancy but clean and tidy. Smack in the centre, only a few mins' walk from the train station.
D Bracklinn, 5 Fort St (off Richmond Terr), T/F01382-566563. Good West End choice.
D Cullaig Guest House, Rosemount Terr, Upper Constitution St, T01382-322154. A short walk north of the city centre. Victorian building with 1 en suite and 2 rooms with shared facilities.
D Invermark House, 23 Monifieth Rd, T01382-739430, www.invermarkhouse.com. A Victorian house with a private car park and comfortable, en suite rooms.
D Nelson Guest House, 8 Nelson Terr (off Victoria Rd), T01382-225354. A 10-min walk from the bus station.
D Redwood Guest House, 89 Monifieth Rd, T01382-736550. En suite rooms, quiet garden.
D Shaftesbury Hotel, 1 Hyndford St, T01382-669216, F641598. 12 rooms. In a converted jute baron's mansion just off the Perth Rd about a mile from the city centre. Comfy, relaxed, with a decent restaurant.
E University of Dundee, West Park, 319 Perth Rd, T01382-647181, g.anderson@dundee.ac.uk. Offers B&B accommodation (shared bathrooms) from Jun-Sep in its halls of residence. It also has self-catering flats for weekly rental, T01382-344039.

Camping

Woodlands Caravan Park, T01241-854430, open Apr-Oct. A campsite at Carnoustie, 10 miles east of Dundee city centre.

Eating

Dundee *p494, map p496*

There's no shortage of places to eat from the ubiquitous burger bars, pizza parlours, fish and chip shops to upmarket continental cuisine. Many of the city's pubs provide excellent value meals. Most of the better restaurants, bars and pubs are to be found in the West End, around the University and Perth Rd, and there's also a wide selection of places to eat in Broughty Ferry.
££ Agacan Kebab House, 113 Perth Rd, T01382-644227. Closed Mon. Brightly decorated and cosy Turkish restaurant, nice ambience and tasty grills.
££ Andre's, 134A Nethergate, T01382-224455. Tue-Sun 1200-1500 and from 1700. Classic French dishes like coq au vin and good value prix fixe menu for £7.95 for 3 courses at lunch.
££ Byzantium, 13 Hawkhill, T01382-228866. Tue-Sun 1730-2400. Popular Mediterranean eaterie with lots of seafood dishes.
££ Café Buongiorno, 11 Bank St, T01382-221179. Small, intimate Italian, popular as a café by day and restaurant by night.
££ Howies, 25 South Tay St, T01382-200339. 1200-1430, 1730-2200. Classy contemporary restaurant with dark wood and bright, white tablecloths. The set lunches for £12.50 for 3 courses are good value. Mains feature dishes like thyme baked pheasant or steak, and there's always a veggie choice. Cheaper meals in the basement bar.
££ The Italian, 38 Commercial St, T01382-205444. Not surprisingly serves Italian food in sleek surroundings.
££ Jute Café-bar, 152 Nethergate, in DCA. Daily 1030-2400 (Sun till 2300). So stylish you could be in Glasgow, and a great vibe. Small but interesting menu.
££ Mandarin Garden, 40-44 South Tay St, T01382-227733. Daily except Sun for lunch and 1700-2300. Excellent Chinese cuisine, served by friendly, efficient staff. Try the house banquet.
££ Nawab, 43a Gray St, Broughty Ferry, T01382-731800. An excellent Indian Balti house that's a cut above the rest.
££ Social Eating, 10 South Tay St, T01382-202070. 1200-1500, 1700-2230. Café-bar/restaurant with a cool, laid-back atmosphere and Asian influenced mains.
£ Visocchi's, 40 Gray St, Broughty Ferry, T01382-779297. A genuine Italian café serving the best cappuccino in town and the best ice cream for miles.

Bars and clubs

Dundee *p494, map p496*

Dundee's nightlife is concentrated in a relatively small area of the city centre, based around the West Port and Nethergate.

For an explanation of sleeping and eating price codes used in this guide, see inside the front cover. Other relevant information is found in Essentials, see pages 43-51.

Bars

For something lively, try any of the busy bars along the Nethergate. At the top of South Tay St is the West Port, where you'll find a clutch of student bars. Broughty Ferry is a good place for a drink on a summer's evening.

Bar Rio, the Nethergate, is a contemporary bar which also serves food.

Bar Valencia, Dock St, Shore Terrace, a tapas bar with some outside seating.

Fisherman's Tavern, 12 Fort St, Broughty Ferry, popular with nautical types and rightly famed for its superb real ales and good pub food. Now has comfy rooms upstairs (www.fishermans-tavern-hotel.co.uk).

Hogshead, Union St, serves several ales and decent bar grub.

Jute Café-bar, Nethergate, see Eating, a civilized places to chill.

Laing's, Roseangle, is hugely popular with the 20-30s and boasts a beer garden with views across the Tay. It also serves pretty decent grub.

O'Neill's Irish Bar, 80 North Lindsay St, a cheap and cheerful pub with a wide range of good-value pub food and live folk music.

Phoenix and **Parliamentary Bar**, on opposite sides of the Nethergate by the junction with West Marketgait, are both lively.

Ship Inn, Broughty Ferry, is a cosy old pub right on the seafront with a reputation for fine food.

Social Eating, South Tay St, see Eating.

Tally Ho's and **The Globe**, South Tay St, two studenty bars on this studenty street.

Trades House, at the top of Union St, a sumptuous option in a converted bank which has received some favourable accounts.

Clubs

There's no shortage of post-pub venues, though the best places are to be found around the West Port area.

After Dark, Ward Rd, Dundee's newest and biggest club.

Fat Sam's, 31 South Ward Rd, attracts a slightly older crowd (ie out of short trousers), and has a large chill-out area.

Mardi Gras, South Ward Rd, a vast club open every night except Tue. It's popular with teenagers.

Entertainment

Dundee *p494, map p496*

Cinema **UGC** multiplex, Kingsway West near the entrance to Camperdown Park, T0870-9020407, shows mainstream movies. **The Odeon**, Douglasfield, T0870-5050007. Also see DCA, below.

Theatre **Dundee Contemporary Arts**, 152 Nethergate, T01382-909900, www.dca.org.uk, is Dundee's cultural hub, housed in a superb modern building, with 2 cinema screens showing current arthouse releases, also exhibition spaces, print studio, visual research centre and the **Jute Café-bar**.

Rep Theatre, Tay Sq, off South Tay St, T01382-223530. Dundee's excellent theatre stages locally produced contemporary productions and hosts various national touring companies. It is also a jazz venue and has a good café-restaurant in the foyer.

Shopping

Dundee *p494, map p496*

The new **Overgate Centre** is on Nethergate and has all the usual High Street shops, including Debenhams, Mango, Morgan, Gap, Warehouse, Oasis and H&M.

The main bookshops are **Ottakars**, 7 High St, and **Waterstone's**, 34 Commercial St.

Westport Gallery, on West Port is good for crafts and gifts, while **The Appletree** on Nethergate has lovely accessories and jewellery. For outdoor gear try **Blacks** on the corner of Seagate or **Tiso** on Whitehall St.

Activities and sport

Dundee *p494, map p496*

Football Dundee has two Premier League football clubs, the cash-strapped **Dundee FC**, who strut their stuff at Dens Park, T01382-826104, and their bitter rivals **Dundee United** (aka the 'Arabs'), who reside at Tannadice, T01382-833166, which is just across the street.

Golf There are two public courses. Dundee is also within 30 mins' drive of **Carnoustie** and **St Andrews**, both of which have famous championship courses.

Caird Park, Mains Loan, T01382-438871. Public course.

Camperdown, Camperdown Park, T01382-432688. Public course.

Downfield Golf Club, Turnberry Av, T01382-825595, a fine private course which allows visitors.

Leisure centres **Dundee Ice Arena**, Camperdown Leisure Centre, T01382-608060, www.dundeeice arena.co.uk, offers skating and curling. **Olympia Leisure Centre**, Earl Grey Place (next to the *Discovery*), T01382-434888. Pool with water slides and wave machines, also gym, sauna and climbing wall. Mon-Fri 0900-2100, Sat-Sun 0900-1700. **Stack Leisure Park**, Harefield Rd. 10-pin bowling.

Transport

Dundee *p494, map p496*

Air There are direct flights to Dundee from London City Airport, 4 times daily, with Scot Airways, T0870-6060707.

Bus For information on city buses, phone Dundee District Council Transport Division, T01382-433125. Local services are run by Travel Dundee, T01382-201121, and Strathtay Scottish, T01382-228054. Day passes (£2.20) can be bought on board buses or at the Travel Dundee shop at the top of Commercial St.

For long-distance services National Express, runs 4 services daily to and from **London** (10 hrs direct). Scottish Citylink, operates an hourly service to and from **Edinburgh** (2 hrs) and **Glasgow** (2¼ hrs). Most Edinburgh and Glasgow buses stop en route in **Perth** (35 mins). There are also hourly buses to **Aberdeen** (2 hrs). Some Aberdeen buses go via **Forfar** (25 mins) and others go via **Arbroath** (30 mins). Strathtay Scottish, T01382-228054, runs buses at least every 30 mins to **Blairgowrie** (1 hr), **Forfar** (30 mins), **Brechin** (via **Forfar**, 1¼ hrs) and **Arbroath** (1 hr); and hourly to **Perth** (1 hr), **Kirriemuir** (1 hr 10 mins) and **Montrose** (1¼ hrs). Their Rover ticket (£5.50) gives unlimited travel for 1 day.

Car hire Enterprise, T01382-666400, Arnold Clark, 14-22 Trades Lane, T01382-225382. Hertz, 18 Marketgait, T01382-223711.

Cycle hire Just Bikes, 57 Gray St, T01382-732100. Nicholson's, 2-4 Forfar Rd, T01382-461212.

Taxi There are taxi ranks on Nethergate and High Street, or call **City Cabs**, T01382-566666, or **Tele Taxis**, T01382-889333.

Train There are trains at least every hour, Mon-Sat, to and from **Glasgow** (1½ hrs) and **Edinburgh** (1½ hrs). Trains run less frequently on Sun. Trains run every 30 mins to and from **Aberdeen** (1¼ hrs), via **Arbroath**, **Montrose** and **Stonehaven**.

Directory

Dundee *p494, map p496*

Banks **Bank of Scotland**, 2 West Marketgait, T01382-317500. **Lloyds TSB**, 96 Albert St, T01382-453535. **Royal Bank of Scotland**, 133 Albert St, T01382-462256. Currency exchange at **Thomas Cook**, City Sq, T01382-200204. Mon-Fri 0900-1730, Sat 0900-1700. Also at the TIC.

Hospital Ninewells Hospital T01382-660111, 24-hr accident and emergency.

Internet **Megabyte Internet Bistro**, 31 Hilltown (behind Wellgate Centre), T01382-200134; **Mailboxes etc**, 17 Union St, T01382-228999, and the **Inter Café** in Debenhams. The library at the Wellgate Centre has free access.

Pharmacy **Boots**, High St. Mon-Wed, Fri-Sat 0830-1745, Thu till 1900. Sun opening on rota basis; check local press.

Post Post office at 4 Meadowside, T01382-203532. Mon-Fri 0900-1730, Sat 0900-1900.

Useful addresses Police Tayside Police HQ, Bell St, T01382-223200.

Angus

→ *Colour map 4, grid B4-5.*

The fishing and farming county of Angus was formerly part of the giant Tayside region but is now a separate authority with its own distinct identity. Angus isn't a name that rolls off many tourists' tongues, but it has much to recommend it to those who prefer to escape the summer hordes. The east coast, from Arbroath north to Montrose, is particularly attractive with its sheer red cliffs punctuated by sweeping bays of golden

 sand. In the north are the Angus Glens, stretching deep into the heart of the Grampian peaks and offering excellent walking opportunities. The heart of the county is the wide valley of Strathmore, with its string of neat market towns. This was part of the ancient Pictish Kingdom and there are still many interesting carved stones scattered around the area. ▸▸ *For Sleeping, Eating and other listings, see pages 508-510.*

Ins and outs

Getting there and around

The towns along the main Dundee-Aberdeen routes are easy to get to by bus or train, but public transport to the more remote parts is limited. For more information pick up a copy of Angus Council's *Public Transport Map & Guide*, available from tourist offices, or call the Transport Team, T01307-461775, or Strathtay Scottish, T01382-228054. ▸▸ *For further details, see Transport page 510.*

Tourist information

Angus is covered by the Angus & Dundee Tourist Board, which has offices in Arbroath, Brechin, Carnoustie, Forfar, Kirriemuir and Montrose. They have a website: www.angusanddundee.co.uk.

Arbroath and around → *Colour map 4, grid B5. Population: 23,500.*

Arbroath, 17 miles northeast of Dundee, is the home of that great Scottish delicacy, the Arbroath smokie – haddock smoked over oak chips – which you can buy in the tiny smokehouses around the harbour. But though Arbroath was once a thriving fishing and trading port, today it has the look of a place that's down on its luck, with high unemployment and a town centre blighted by insensitive planning. On the way, the A92 coast road bypasses the little coastal town of Carnoustie, whose championship golf course is revered worldwide. ▸▸ *For Sleeping, Eating and other listings, see pages 508-510.*

Sights

The chief attraction is undoubtedly **Arbroath Abbey** ⓘ *Abbey St, T01241-878756, Apr-Sep 0930-1830, Oct-Mar Mon-Wed and Sat till 1630, Thu till 1230, Sun 1400-1630, £3, £2.30 concession, £1 child.* Founded by William the Lion in 1178 (who's buried here), it went on to become one of the wealthiest monasteries in the country. It is also one of the most important sites in Scottish history. It was here, on 6 April 1320, that the Declaration of Arbroath was issued, asking Rome to reverse its excommunication of Robert the Bruce and recognize him as King, thus asserting Scotland's independence from England. Pope John XXII finally agreed to the claim four years later. You can buy copies of the declaration (the original is in Edinburgh) which contains the stirring words: "For so long as a hundred of us remain alive, we will yield in no least way to English dominion. For we fight, not for glory, not for riches, nor honour, but only for freedom, which no good man surrenders but with his life". After the Reformation the abbey suffered badly and, like so many other important ecclesiastical buildings in Scotland, was used as a quarry for the building of the town. However, enough of the abbey survives to give you a good idea of just how magnificent it must have been; in particular the massive west front and the south transept (containing a circular window which was once lit up as a beacon to guide ships). In 1951 the Stone of Destiny found a temporary home here following its theft from Westminster Abbey by Scottish Nationalists. It was duly returned, where it stayed until its recent move to Edinburgh Castle, see page 79.

Beside the harbour is the **Arbroath Museum** ⓘ *T01241-875598, Mon-Sat 1000-1700, also Sun 1400-1700 in Jul-Aug, free*, housed in the elegant Signal Tower, the Regency building that was once the shore base and family living quarters for the keepers of the Bell Rock Lighthouse, 12 miles offshore. The museum has some interesting local history displays, including re-creations of a fisherman's cottage and a schoolroom. The TIC ⓘ *Market Place, T01241-872609, seasonal hours, Apr-Oct.*

Around Arbroath

A mile northwest of the town centre is **St Vigeans**, where the red sandstone church is perched right on top of a hill in the centre of the village. Beside the hill is tiny **St Vigeans Museum** ⓘ *Apr-Sep Mon-Sat 0930-1830 (collect the key from No 7)*, which contains an excellent collection of Pictish and medieval carved stones.

Five miles north of Arbroath by road is the attractive little fishing village of **Auchmithie**, perched precariously on the cliff-top with a steep descent to the harbour and quay. Auchmithie is the true home of the smokie and, though Arbroath later took the credit, the village can at least lay claim to the region's best seafood restaurant, the **But'n'Ben**, see page 509. You can walk to the foot of Auchmithie along a marvellous cliff path which starts at the far end of Victoria Park. There are numerous caves to explore and lots of seabirds to see along the three-mile route. You should pick up a free copy of *The Arbroath Cliffs Nature Trail Guide* from the tourist office.

Montrose and around → *Colour map 4, grid B5.*

Fourteen miles north of Arbroath is the elegant town of Montrose, the most pleasant and interesting of the Angus towns, rich in history and with great beaches to the north and south, especially Lunan Bay. It stands at the mouth of a vast tidal basin, covering 2,000 acres and bordered by 17 miles of roads. The basin is home to a multitude of wild birds such as ducks, geese, swans and waders who come here to search for food on the wide expanse of mud flats. ▸▸ *For Sleeping, Eating and other listings, see pages 508-510.*

Sights

Montrose was once a thriving port, trading with various European countries, and the wealthy 18th- and 19th-century merchants built their houses gable-end to the street, in imitation of the Continental style. This earned the townsfolk the nickname of 'gable-endies', which has stuck to this day. The sole remaining gable-ended houses can be seen on the High Street, which is the widest in Scotland. The south end of the High Street is overlooked by a statue of Sir Robert Peel, a local man who was British Prime Minister and founder of the present-day Police Force. From his name came the old slang term for police, 'The Peelers'.

A few blocks from the High Street, on Panmure Place, is **Montrose Museum and Art Gallery** ⓘ *T01674-673232, Mon-Sat 1000-1700, free*, housed in a fine neoclassical Victorian building and one of the first purpose-built museums in Scotland. Among the displays are Bronze-Age axe-heads, Montrose pottery and silver (the town had its own assay mark, a rose, and pieces are much sought after). The Maritime Gallery has a fleet of model ships, relics of the once-thriving whaling industry, and Napoleonic items, including a cast of his death mask. Outside the museum is a lifesize bronze sculpture of a boy by local sculptor, William Lamb (1893-1951). More of his work can be seen at the **William Lamb Sculpture Studio** ⓘ *Market St, Jul-Sep Tue-Sun 1400-1700, free*, where his famous subjects include the Queen, Queen Mother and the great Scots poet Hugh McDiarmid. The studio was left by the artist as his memorial gift to the town. Near the museum, on the same side of the street, up an alley (or *close*), are **Taylor's Auction Rooms** ⓘ *T01674-672775*. Every second Saturday, people come from far and wide to bid for paintings, jewellery, furniture and many other items. It's well worth a visit, and you might even come away with a piece of locally hall-marked silver. The tiny tourist information centre ⓘ *T01674-672000, Apr-Sep*, next to the library.

Around Montrose

On the A92 heading north out of town is the **Montrose Air Station Museum** ⓘ *T01674-674210, Sun 1200-1700, or at other times by appointment.* Montrose was Scotland's first airport, used in both world wars for the training of pilots. The museum documents the lives of many of the men who lost their lives, including the chilling tale of Lieutenant Desmond Arthur whose ghost is said to haunt the former air base. There are also assorted aircraft on display outside.

Traill Drive leads to the town's impressive **beach**, which stretches all the way north to St Cyrus, see page 520. About four miles south of Montrose, reached by turning off the A92, is the great sweep of **Lunan Bay**, a stunningly beautiful, and usually deserted, sandy beach, once popular with smugglers. Like many beaches on the northeast coast, there are strong currents, so do not swim beyond your capabilities. There's a variety of wildlife around, including nesting puffins on the red sandstone cliffs. Overlooking the beach is the 12th-century ruin of Red Castle, which was originally a royal hunting lodge.

Montrose Basin Wildlife Centre ⓘ *T01674-676336, Apr-Oct 1030-1730, Nov-Mar 1030-1600, £2.50*, is at Rossie Braes, a mile out of town on the A92. They have superb viewing facilities, with binoculars and high-powered telescopes as well as remote-control video cameras. There are also guided walks around the reserve.

Three miles west of Montrose on the A935 is the **House of Dun** ⓘ *T01674-810264, Apr-30 Jun, Sep Fri-Tue 1200-1700, 1 Jul-31 Aug daily 1200-1700, garden and grounds all year daily 0930 to sunset, £7, concession £5.25, garden and grounds only £1*, built in 1730 for David Erskine, Lord Dun. It is a very attractive Georgian building in the Palladian style, designed by William Adam, who was at the forefront of Scottish architecture between the Jacobite risings of 1715 and 1745, but otherwise somewhat eclipsed by his sons Robert and James. Lady Augusta Kennedy-Erskine, daughter of William IV and the actress Mrs Jordan, also lived there, and the house contains many royal mementos. Alas, the huge sword which was driven into a tree in the grounds by one of the Erskines was removed by the present owners, the National Trust, for safety reasons. The courtyard has recently been restored, and Angus Handloom Weavers, Scotland's last handloom linen weavers, are based there. Fine linen is for sale by the yard, as well as linen goods. There's an attractive café and shop. Strathtay bus No 30 to Brechin passes the entrance.

Brechin and Edzell → *Colour map 4, grid B5. Population: 7,500.*

Nine miles west of Montrose is Brechin, a quiet little town on the banks of the River South Esk, whose main attraction is its 14th-century cathedral, in Bishop's Close off the High Street. There's been a church here since the ninth century though most of what you see dates from the beginning of the 20th century when major restoration work was carried out. The adjacent 106-ft high round tower dates from the 11th century and is one of only two such structures in the country. Five miles north of Brechin on the B966 is Edzell, an impossibly neat and picturesque planned village lying at the foot of Glen Esk. ▸▸ *For Sleeping, Eating and other listings, see pages 508-510.*

Sights

The small **Brechin Museum** ⓘ *Mon, Tue, Thu-Fri 0930-1800, Wed 0930-1900, Sat 0930-1700, free*, is housed in The Townhouse, High Street and is the usual collection of local curiosities and memorabilia. Also on St Ninian's Square is the terminus of the

Caledonian Railway ⓘ *T01356-810318, trains run 6 times daily on Sun only, from Jun to early Sep, £5 return, child/concession £3*, which runs steam trains on a four-mile section of line between Brechin station and Bridge of Dun, a mile from the House of Dun (see under Montrose above).

Just off the A90, is the **Brechin Castle Centre**, which is a country park with garden centre, pets corner, miniature railway ⓘ *Apr-Sep*, picnic areas and waterside walks. There's also a coffee shop. Part of the centre is **Pictavia** ⓘ *T01307-473750, www.pictavia.org.uk, daily in summer 0900-1730, £3.25, child/ concession £2.25*, which gives a fascinating glimpse into Scotland's Celtic past. You'll help to solve the riddles of the stones, see the mysterious Pictish standing stones and hear the sounds of battle in the Tower of Sound.

At the entrance to the village of Edzell is the impressive **Dalhousie Arch** which leads on to the wide main street, lined with quaint little tea rooms and shops selling Victoriana. A mile west of the village is the red sandstone ruin of **Edzell Castle** ⓘ *T01356-648631, Apr-Sep 0930-1830, Oct-Mar Mon-Wed and Sat 0930-1630, Thu 0930-1200, Fri and Sun 1400-1630, £3, concession £2.30, child £1*, a 16th-century tower house which, over the course of its life, has been visited by Mary, Queen of Scots, James VI and, less happily, Cromwell's troops. But it is the magnificent garden, or 'Pleasance', which is the real attraction. Created by Sir David Lindsay in 1604, the superb heraldic and symbolic sculpted wall panels are rare examples of European Renaissance Art in Scotland.

Three miles southwest of Edzell, on either side of the road, are the **Brown Caterthun and White Caterthun**, two remarkable Iron-Age forts, defended by ditches and ramparts over 900-ft high. These were occupied by the Picts around the first few centuries AD and the views from the top are amazing. To get there, follow the road west of the castle and turn left at Bridgend, then take the left fork. Or take the road southwest from Edzell and take the first right after Dunlappie. There's no public transport. It's an easy walk from the road to either fort.

The tourist information centre ⓘ *Brechin Castle Centre, Haughmuir, Brechin, T01356-623050, Apr-Sep Mon-Sat*, have information on hiking in Glen Esk.

Forfar and Glamis → *Colour map 4, grid B4. Population: 12,650.*

Fourteen miles north of Dundee, just off the main A90, is Forfar, the county capital of Angus. Forfar was the ancient capital of the Picts and, though it wouldn't be picked as a top tourist destination today, it is only a few miles from the county's star attraction, Glamis Castle. The town is best known for its contribution to Scottish cuisine, the famous Forfar Bridie, a gigantic shortcrust pastie filled with mince and onions. ▸▸ *For Sleeping, Eating and other listings, see pages 508-510.*

There are several places to stay in Forfar, but Kirriemuir is nicer and equally convenient for Glamis Castle.

Sights

Meffan Gallery and Museum ⓘ *20 West High St, T01307-464123, Mon-Sat 1000-1700, free*, illustrates the colourful history of town and county, and includes Pictish remains and a grisly account of the witch-hunts of the 17th century. Two miles east of town, off the B9113, are the ruins of **Restenneth Priory** ⓘ *open at all times, free*, the 12th-century Augustinian priory was chosen by King Robert the Bruce as the last resting place of his son, Prince John. About four miles southeast, on the road to Letham, is **Dunnichen Hill**, once known as Nechtansmere, scene of a Pictish victory in AD 685 over Ecgfrith, King of the Angles, thus assuring Scotland's independence.

Five miles northeast of Forfar, along the B9134, is the tiny village of **Aberlemno**, home to some of the country's best Pictish stones ⓘ *open access except Nov-Mar, free*. The best example can be found in the churchyard, just off the main road, an eighth-century cross-slab with a Celtic cross, entwined beasts on one side and an elaborate depiction of the Battle of Nechtansmere on the other. There are three other stones with Pictish and early-Christian symbols by the roadside.

In the village of Glamis, just off the square, is the **Angus Folk Museum** ⓘ *T01307-840233, Easter and 1 May-Sep daily 1100-1700, weekends only in Oct 1100-1700, £2.40, £1.60 child/concession*. It's housed in a picturesque row of 18th-century cottages which are divided into domestic and agricultural sections. The changes in living and farming in Angus over the last 200 years are vividly illustrated with the help of a vast collection of local artefacts.

Information for Forfar and around can be found at the tourist information centre in Forfar ⓘ *45 East High St, T01307-467876, Apr-Sep Mon-Sat.*

Glamis Castle

ⓘ *T01307-840393, late Mar to end Oct daily 1030-1730 (Jul-Aug from 1000), last admission 1645. Guided tours last 1 hr and leave every 15 mins. £6.70, £5 concession, £3.50 child.*

Five miles southwest of Forfar is the county's star attraction, Glamis Castle (pronounced Glamz), the fabulous family home of the Earls of Strathmore and Kinghorne. Glamis is every inch the archetypal Scottish castle, and one of the most famous. This was the setting for Shakespeare's *Macbeth*, but its royal connection doesn't end there. It was the childhood home of the late Queen Elizabeth, the Queen Mother, and the birthplace of the late Princess Margaret. The setting matches the impeccable pedigree. As you approach down the long, tree-lined drive, the castle suddenly appears in all its glory, the jumble of turrets, towers and conical roofs rising up against the backdrop of the Grampian Mountains like one of Walt Disney's fairytale fantasies. Most of the building you see dates from the 15th century, though the glamorous touches were added in the 17th century.

The five-storey, L-shaped castle grew from its humble beginnings as a mere hunting lodge, used by the Kings of Scotland in the 11th century. In 1372 King Robert II gave it to his son-in-law, Sir John Lyon, whose descendants, the Earls of Strathmore and Kinghorne, have lived here ever since. The 14th Earl was the Queen Mother's father.

Highlights of the tour include the 17th-century drawing room, with its impressive plasterwork ceilings, and the ghostly crypt, haunted by Lord Glamis and Crawford who was entombed within its walls as punishment for playing a few hands of gin rummy with the Devil on the Sabbath. The 17th-century chapel, with its biblical frescoes, is also haunted, this time by the 'grey lady', the ghost of the sixth Lady Glamis, who was burnt as a witch by James V. Duncan's Hall is reputedly where King Duncan was murdered by Macbeth, though, like much else in the play, this is very doubtful. You can also see the Royal Apartments, including the Queen Mother's bedroom, and the extensive grounds are also well worth exploring. There's a restaurant on site.

Kirriemuir

→ *Colour map 4, grid B4. Population: 5,300.*

Kirriemuir, or Kirrie as it's known locally, is the ideal spot for those wishing to explore the beautiful Angus Glens, or visit Glamis Castle, only five miles south, or simply for those who wish to get off the tartan trail and stay in a lovely, unspoiled wee town.

▸▸ *For Sleeping, Eating and other listings, see pages 508-510.*

Sights

Kirrie's claim to fame is as the birthplace of JM Barrie (1860-1937), creator of Peter Pan, the little boy who never grew up. Barrie was the son of a hand-loom weaver and ninth of 10 children. His classic tale of *Peter Pan and the Lost Boys*, written in 1904, is said to have been inspired by the memory of his older brother, who died while still young. Kirrie is the fictional Thrums of Barrie's autobiographical novel, *A Window in Thrums*. **Barrie's birthplace** ⓘ *T01575-572646, 1 Apr-30 Jun, Sep Fri-Tue 1200-1700, Jul, Aug daily 1200-1700, £5, concession £3.75, child £1*, can be visited at 9 Brechin Road. The humble little weaver's cottage is now managed by the NTS, and the upper floor is furnished as it would have been when he lived there. The adjacent house features an exhibition of his literary and theatrical works. The outside wash-house is said to have been his first theatre and the model for the house built for Wendy by the Lost Boys in Never-Never Land. Barrie is also buried in Kirrie, at the nearby St Mary's Episcopal Church.

At the top of Kirriemuir Hill is a camera obscura, which offers a panorama of the surrounding Strathmore countryside and the glens to the north. At the southern end of town, at Bellies Brae, is the **Aviation Museum** ⓘ *Apr-Sep Mon-Sat 1000-1700, Sun 1100-1700, other times by arrangement, free (donations welcome)*, which houses a large, eclectic collection of Second World War memorabilia. Birdwatchers should head a few miles west of town, just off the B951, to the **Loch of Kinnordy** and **RSPB Reserve**, where there are two hides overlooking the loch and wetlands.

The TIC ⓘ *Cumberland Close, T01575-574097, Apr-Sep Mon-Sat.*

The Angus Glens → *Colour map 4, grid B4.*

East of Perthshire, south of the Grampians and north of Dundee are the Angus Glens, a series of five glens running parallel to each other and all of them beautiful, peaceful and offering plenty of relatively painless hillwalking opportunities.

Glen Isla

Running parallel to Glenshee, see page 245, lovely Glen Isla is the furthest west of the Angus Glens and can also be reached from the little town of **Alyth**, east of Blairgowrie. At the southern end of the glen, five miles north of Alyth by Bridge of Glenisla, is **Reekie Linn**, a series of waterfalls that plunge through a deep, wooded gorge. A path leads for 200 yds from the car park and picnic site on the road between Bridge of Glenisla and Bridge of Lintrathen. Nearby is the excellent **Lochside Lodge** restaurant and **Peel Farm Coffee and Craft Shop**.

Six miles north, at Kirkton of Glenisla, on the B951, is the **Glenisla Hotel**, see Sleeping page 509. Further north a side road turns off the B951 and runs to **Auchavan**, at the head of the glen. There are paths from here into the wild and mountainous **Caenlochan Forest**. A postbus runs once daily except Sunday from Blairgowrie to Auchavan. At the mouth of the glen is the tiny village of **Meigle**, home to Scotland's most important collection of early-Christian and Pictish carved stones. They are housed in the superb **Meigle Museum** ⓘ *Apr-Sep daily 0930-1830, £1.80*.

Glen Prosen

Five miles north of Kirriemuir is the tiny village of Dykehead, at the foot of Glen Clova, where a side road branches northwest and runs into Glen Prosen. Both glens penetrate deep into the Grampian Mountains and are blessed with a rugged beauty, but Glen Prosen carries little of the cachet of its neighbour and is consequently a much more peaceful option for hillwalkers. The little road runs deep into the glen but it's best explored on foot.

A good walk is the relatively straightforward four-mile **Minister's Path**, which connects the two glens. It starts from behind the kirk in Glenprosen village and heads over the hilly moorland and down to the B955 just before Clova village. You can catch the postbus back to Kirriemuir from the **Clova Hotel**, see Sleeping page 509. The Kirriemuir to Glen Prosen postbus runs once daily except Sunday.

Glen Clova and Glen Doll → *OS Landranger Nos 43 & 44.*

Glen Clova is only 30 miles north of Dundee yet you could be in the heart of the Highlands, with craggy mountains towering overhead and heather-clad slopes populated by deer and grouse. Glen Clova leads north into Glen Doll, from where you can follow the old drove roads which lead to Ballater and Braemar in Deeside. These ancient routes were used by whisky smugglers, government troops and rebels, as well as cattle drovers, and though they may look straightforward on the map, they can be as treacherous as any of the Scottish mountains. Only fit and experienced walkers should attempt these walks.

One excellent walk is the **Loops of Brandy**, which starts from behind the **Clova Hotel** and climbs up into the mountains, around Loch Brandy and back again. It's a four-hour walk there and back.

Drivers should note that the B955 from Dykehead divides just before the bridge of the River South Esk. The west branch is traditionally used by vehicles heading up the glen, while the east branch should be for traffic returning down the glen. The two roads meet up again six miles further on, at the tiny hamlet of **Clova**, which consists of little more than the **Clova Hotel**, see Sleeping page 509. There's a postbus service to Glen Clova from Kirriemuir twice a day Monday to Friday and once on Saturday. The 0830 departure runs as far as the hostel and the 1500 departure (Monday to Friday only) stops at the **Clova Hotel**. The afternoon service leaves from the hotel at 1555.

Glen Esk → *OS Landranger No 44.*

North from Edzell, the road runs 13 miles to the head of beautiful Glen Esk, the most easterly of the Angus Glens and, like the others, quiet and empty. Nine miles north of Edzell along the Glen road is the **Glenesk Folk Museum** ⓘ *T01356-670254, Easter-May Sat-Mon 1200-1800, Jun to mid-Oct 1200-1800, £2*, housed in an old shooting lodge known as 'The Retreat'. The museum's extensive local folk history collection gives a fascinating insight into the lives of the Glen's inhabitants. It also has a good tea room (try their rhubarb jam and home baking).

Four miles further on, beyond Tarfside village, the public road ends at **Invermark Castle**. This is the start of one of the Mounth Roads, ancient rights of way leading from the Angus Glens across the mountains to Deeside. This route leads eventually to Ballater or Glen Tanar, near Aboyne. For a description of the latter route in reverse, see Deeside page 528. You can also hike from here to the summit of **Mount Keen** (3,081 ft), Scotland's most easterly Munro, but – like the Mounth Road – this is a tough walk and you'll need full hill-walking equipment and a map. An easier walk is to the **Queen's Well**, three miles from the car park across the river from Invermark Castle. It's about three hours there and back. Alternatively, you can head west from the castle, past the lovely old church and along the north shore of Loch Lee.

Sleeping

Arbroath and around *p502*

D-E Five Gables, a mile south of town on the A92 to Dundee, T01241-871632. A former clubhouse overlooking golf course.

E Harbour Nights Guesthouse, 4 The Shore, by the harbour, T01241-434343, www.harbournightsguesthouse.com. One of several guest houses around the centre. Modern, clean and comfortable.

Montrose and around *p503*

B Woodston, on the coast road north to St Cyrus, T01674-850226, info@woodstonfishingstation.co.uk, is a B&B in the old fishing station at Woodston. An evening meal is available and there is great bird watching down on the sands.

C The Links Hotel, Mid Links, T01674-671000, www.linkshotel.com. A short walk from

For an explanation of sleeping and eating price codes used in this guide, see inside the front cover. Other relevant information is found in Essentials, see pages 43-51.

the beach, comfortable town house hotel offering good Scottish/French cooking (**££**).

E Limes Guesthouse, 15 King St, T01674-677236, www.thelimesmontrose.co.ukco.uk. Good B&B choice.

E Lunan Lodge, T01241-830679, www.cix.co.uk/~jules/lunanlodge. An 18th-century country house in the village of Lunan overlooking Lunan Bay. Can cater for a variety of food intolerances.

Brechin and Edzell *p504*

C Glenesk Hotel, Edzell, T01356-648319, pleasant place to spend the night and does bar and restaurant meals.

E-F Inchcape, High St, Edzell, T01356-647266. B&B, late Victorian house with 3 en suite rooms.

E-F Mrs Mackintosh, Ramsey St, Edzell, T01356-648051. Good B&B.

Kirriemuir *p506*

There's not a huge choice of accommodation in Kirrie.

D Airlie Arms Hotel, St Malcom's Wynd, T01575-572847. The best option is this converted medieval monastery, now a small, comfortable hotel. It offers cheap bar meals and decent, moderately priced evening meals.

E Crepto, 1 Kinnordy Pl, T01575-572746. A B&B, good value, modern house 10 mins walk from centre, with off-street parking.

E Woodlands, at Lisden Gdns, T01575-572582. A B&B in a modern bungalow with good views. Evening meal on request.

Those wishing to stay longer can rent a self-catering cottage next door to Barrie's birthplace, for £250-320 per week for up to 4 people. Contact the National Trust for Scotland head office, see p36.

The Angus Glens *p507*

C Glenisla Hotel, Kirkton of Glenisla, on the B951, Glen Isla, T01575-582223, glenislahotel @sol.co.uk. An impossibly cosy 17th-century inn with log fires, real ales, good grub and plenty of local characters. It's worth the trip just to spend a night here.

C Clova Hotel, Glen Clova, T01575-550222. Very friendly and popular climbers' retreat. As well as bar meals, the hotel lays on regular barbecues, ceilidhs and a multitude of various activities. There's also an 8-bed bunkhouse outside (**F**) which is open all year. It has a kitchen, but no shower.

Eating

Arbroath and around *p502*

££ But'n'Ben, T01241-877223, by the harbour in Auchmithie (see p503). The best place to eat is this cosy option. Their seafood is superb and great value. Daily except Tue 1200-1500 for lunch, 1600-1730 for high tea and 1900-2200 for dinner.

££ Gordon's Restaurant with Rooms, Main St, Inverkeilor, T01241-830364, www.gordonsrestaurant.co.uk, is worth trying. It has 2 AA rosettes and en suite rooms.

£ Peppo's, 51 Ladybridge St, by the harbour (closed Sat).It will come as no surprise that Arbroath has this excellent fish and chip shop.

Montrose and around *p503*

Apart from the hotels, eating options are limited.

££ Murray Lodge Hotel at the end of Murray St, does a tasty lunch.

££ Roos Leap 2 Traill Dr, T01674-672157. Aussie eaterie on Montrose Golf Course. Mon-Sat 1130-1430, 1700-2200 and Sun 1130-2100.

Forfar and Glamis *p505*

££ Baxters Bistro, 41-43 West High St, T01307-464350. Bar-bistro offering great food with an inventive twist and real ales. Food served Mon-Sat lunch and evening.

££ Chapelbank House Hotel, 69 East High St, T01307-463151. They serve a good, cheap lunch daily except Mon, and mid-range dinner daily except Sun and Mon.

£ Several bakeries in town sell bridies, but the locals will tell you that the best place to sample this delight is **McLaren's**, next to the Queen's Hotel, West High St.

Kirriemuir *p506*

£££ Lochside Lodge, by the Loch of Lintrathen, 6 miles along the B951, then take the turning left for Bridge of Lintrathen, T01575-560340. This converted farmstead is the best restaurant in the area, serving modern Scottish cooking and also rents rooms (**C**).

££ Airlie Arms Hotel, see Sleeping.
££ Thrums Hotel, Bank St, T01575-572758, decent food.
££ Visocchi's, on the main street, is a great café which has been serving delicious ice cream since 1953.

Festivals and events

Kirriemuir *p506*
Kirriemuir is well known for its **Folk Festival**, held on the first weekend in Sep. The best venues for live music are the **Airlie Arms**, the **Roods Bar** nearby, and **Three Bellies Brae**, which may be an unusual name for a pub, but is a very welcoming watering hole.

Transport

Arbroath and around *p502*
The bus station is nearby, on Catherine St, T01241-870646. There are **Scottish Citylink** buses every 2 hrs to **Aberdeen** (1½ hrs) via **Montrose** and **Stonehaven**, and to **Dundee** (25 mins). **Strathtay Scottish**, T01382-228054, runs regular buses to **Brechin** via **Montrose**, and less frequently to **Auchmithie**.

The train station is on Keptie St, 5 mins' walk from the TIC. Arbroath is on the Dundee-Aberdeen rail line, there are trains every 30 mins to and from **Dundee** (20 mins).

Montrose and around *p503*
Buses stop in the High St. There are frequent buses to and from **Aberdeen** (1¾ hrs), though you have to change at **Stonehaven**. **Strathtay Scottish**, T01382-228054, runs regular buses to and from **Brechin** and **Forfar**. The train station is on Western Rd, 1 block from the High St. There are trains every 30 mins to Aberdeen and Dundee.

Brechin and Edzell *p504*
Scottish Citylink buses run every 2 hrs to **Aberdeen** (1 hr), **Dundee** (50 mins) and **Forfar** (20 mins). Buses leave from Panmure St. **Strathtay Scottish**, T01382-228054, has services to **Edzell** several times daily (20 mins) and daily every hr to **Montrose** (20 mins), from South Esk St.

Forfar and Glamis *p505*
Scottish Citylink buses run to and from **Dundee** every 2 hrs (25 minutes) and **Aberdeen** (1 hr 20 mins), via **Brechin** (20 mins). Buses stop opposite the church in East High St. **Strathtay Scottish**, T01382-228054, runs buses every hr to Kirriemuir (25 mins) and to Brechin via **Aberlemno**. There's a limited bus service from Dundee, Forfar and Kirriemuir to **Glamis**.

Kirriemuir *p506*
Strathtay Scottish, T01382-228054, runs hourly buses (Mon-Sat, less frequently on Sun) to and from **Dundee** (1 hr 10 mins). There are also buses every hr to **Forfar** (25 mins) and twice a day (except Sun) to Glamis. There's a postbus service, T01463-256200, from **Kirriemuir** to **Glen Prosen** (once daily except Sun) and **Glen Clova** (twice on weekdays, once on Sat).

The Angus Glens *p507*
Kirriemuir is the gateway to glens Isla, Prosen and Clova, while the other two, Glens Lethnot and Esk, are reached via Brechin. There are regular buses to Brechin and Kirriemuir from Dundee, but getting around the glens is not easy without your own transport as there is only a limited postbus service.

Aberdeen

→ *Colour map 4, grid A6. Population: 217,260.*

Scotland's third largest city is a tough place. Tough because of the grey granite of its buildings, and tough because of the nature of its people, who are industrious, thrifty, proud and uncompromising. First impressions are often determined by the weather: when it rains it's about as appealing as cold porridge, when the sky's blue and clear it has a salty grandeur and when the sun shines down, the tiny mica chips – which form a natural part of granite – sparkle and glisten like a display in a jewellers' window. Whatever the impression, it is a place that elicits a strong response. Lewis Grassic Gibbon, the northeast's most famous writer, wrote: "One detests Aberdeen with the detestation of a thwarted lover. It is the one haunting and exasperatingly lovable city in Scotland." ⏩ *For Sleeping, Eating and other listings, see pages 516-520.*

Ins and outs

Getting there

Aberdeen airport is seven miles northwest of the city centre, at Dyce, off the A96 to Inverness. There are regular domestic flights to Scottish and UK destinations, including Orkney and Shetland, as well as international flights to several European destinations. For airport information, T01224-722331. There's car hire and currency exchange at the airport. Buses 27 run at peak times to and from the city centre (35 minutes, £1.35 single). For more information, T01224-650065. Alternatively, take a train to Dyce station and a bus or taxi from there. A taxi from the airport to Dyce railway station costs around £5, and £14 to the city centre.

Aberdeen is linked to Lerwick in Shetland and Kirkwall in Orkney by Northlink ferries, T0845-6000449, www.northlinkferries.co.uk. There are regular sailings from the passenger terminal in the harbour, a short walk east of the train and bus stations.

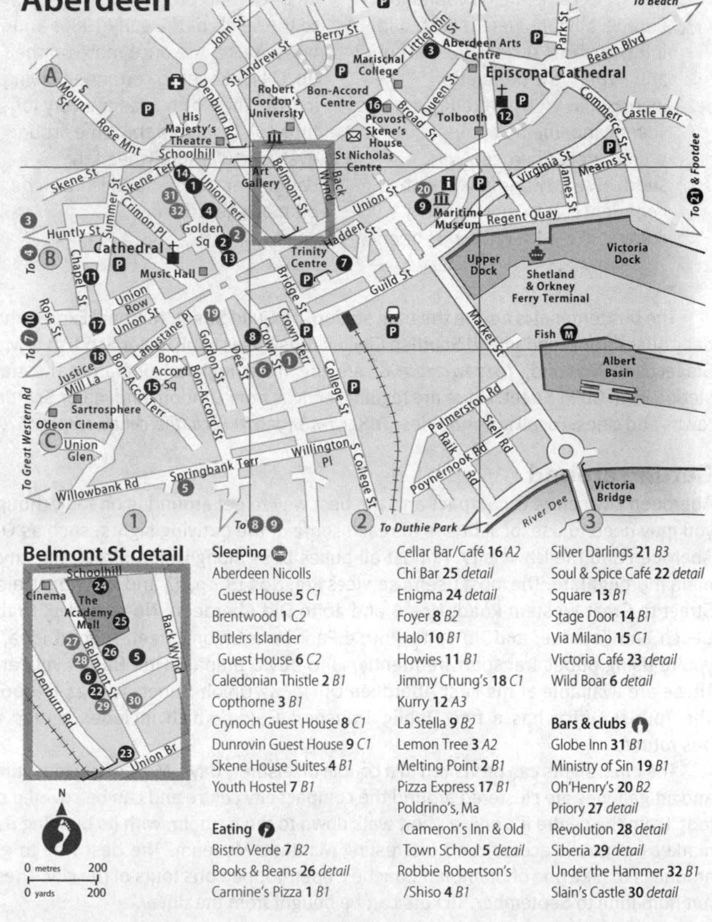

City slickers

When oil was discovered in the North Sea in 1970, it was assumed that 'black gold' would bring nationwide prosperity. But while many in the country would argue that the huge oil revenues flowed south with little benefit accruing to the Scottish people, the people of Aberdeen have a different tale to tell.

Oil transformed Aberdeen from a relatively impoverished northern backwater to a flourishing and prosperous city, where every oil company, exploration firm, tool manufacturer and diving supplier now base themselves. Aberdeen quickly became the oil capital of Europe. Millions were invested in infrastructure, such as the harbour and airport, the population increased rapidly, average earnings soared and unemployment plummeted. Aberdeen was suddenly a city brimming with confidence. New, upmarket restaurants, bars and shops opened to cater for a population with money to burn. Ironic really, in a city whose people have a reputation for being less than extravagant with their cash.

But it couldn't last. In the mid-1980s the price of oil slumped from US$80 a barrel to US$10 and recession struck the northeast. Jobs vanished, house prices dropped and Aberdonians woke up to the realization that they were completely dependent on oil for their economic well-being. But predictions of the city's demise were greatly exaggerated. In recent years oil prices and production have risen to the levels of the early 1980s and house prices are once more on the up. Oil looks set to continue flowing in from the North Sea for a very long time to come. And this time around everyone will surely heed the dangers of the past and learn to be a bit more Aberdonian.

The bus terminal is next to the train station, on Guild Street. National Express has daily buses from London and Scottish Citylink runs buses to all major Scottish towns. Stagecoach Bluebird, T01224-212266, are the main regional operator. The train station is on Guild Street. There are regular services from London, and major Scottish towns and cities. For all rail enquiries, T08457-484950. ▸▸ *For further details, see page 520.*

Getting around

Aberdeen city centre is compact and the best way to get around is on foot, though you may need to use local buses to reach some of the outlying sights, such as Old Aberdeen and the University. Almost all buses pass along Union Street, the city's main thoroughfare. The most useful services are: Nos 18, 19, 24 and 24A from Union Street to Great Western Road; Nos 6 and 20 to Old Aberdeen; No 14 and 15 to the Beach and Footdee; and No 17 to Duthie Park from Union Street. A good idea, if you're using public transport frequently, is to buy a prepaid First Bus travel card. These are available at the First Aberdeen Office, 47 Union Street, T01224-650065. The Tourist Office has a free Public Transport Guide which includes a map of bus routes.

The main sights can be visited in a couple of leisurely days. Most of the museums and art galleries are clustered around the compact city centre and can be covered on foot. From the centre it's only a short walk down to the harbour, with its bustling fish market (no public access) and interesting Maritime Museum. The best way to get around is to take one of Grampian Coaches' open-topped bus tours of the city. These run from June to September. Tickets can be bought from the driver.

Tourist information

The very helpful tourist information centre ⓘ *23 Union St, T01224-288828, www.aberdeen-grampian.com, Mon-Sat 0930-1730 (1900 mid Jun-mid Sep), Sun 1000-1600*, has, as well as the usual accommodation booking service, a wide selection of leaflets on walks in Aberdeen, and run bus tours. Another good source of information on current events are the local newspapers, the *Press and Journal* and *Evening Express*.

Background

Aberdeen lies between two rivers, the Don to the north and the Dee to the south, backed by a fertile hinterland and facing the wild North Sea, which has brought the city great wealth since the discovery of oil in the early 1970s. Its maritime history, however, dates back to its foundation as a Royal Burgh in 1124. In the past Aberdeen had strong trading links with Scandinavia and the Low Countries. Fast clipper ships, built in the city, brought tea from India and other goods from all over the world. Until some years after the Second World War, Aberdeen's lifeblood was fishing and shipping. It was the biggest fish market in the country and still lands considerable catches. Then came the discovery of North Sea oil and gas and Aberdeen became Boom City, flaunting its new-found wealth with an almost unseemly fervour. The glory years of the early 1980s may have gone, but Aberdeen still exudes an air of self-confidence and prosperity rare in other regional UK cities.

Aberdonians also have an inordinate amount of civic pride, which can verge on the overweening. This may have been enhanced in recent years by its new-found status and wealth, but has its roots in the 14th century, when the townsfolk offered protection to Robert the Bruce during the Wars of Independence. In return, Bruce rewarded the town with 'Freedom Lands' for which he had previously received rent. The money saved was diverted into a Common Good Fund, to be spent on amenities. Today this money is still used to pay for the upkeep of its many fine parks and to keep the city looking its best. This sense of pride in its parks and public buildings makes Aberdeen an extremely pleasant place to visit. It's also a very lively place, and its many bars, restaurants, nightclubs, theatres and shops are as vibrant and thriving as you'd expect in any city with money in its pockets.

Sights

City centre

Aberdeen's main artery is **Union Street**, one mile long and built on pillars (an amazing and expensive engineering feat). The street is a fascinating mix of Victorian Gothic and modern glass and concrete and is perpetually packed with buses, cars and pedestrians. The oldest part of the city is the 13th-century **Castlegate**, at the eastern end of Union Street, now dominated by the 17th-century **Mercat Cross**, which was the focus of Aberdeen's long history as a major market town and trading centre. Opposite, at the corner of Union Street and King Street, in the Town House, is the **Tolbooth** ⓘ *open by appointment, T01224-622906*, which dates from the 14th century. Not only did it serve as a collection point for tolls and taxes but it was also used as the Wardhouse, housing prisoners held on remand. Northeast of the Mercat Cross, towards the beach, is **Satrosphere** ⓘ *179 Constitution St, T01224-640340, Mon-Sat 1000-1700, Sun 1130-1700, £5, £3 child/concession*, a hands-on science and technology discovery centre that's great for kids.

A little further west down Union Street is Broad Street off which, at 45 Guestrow, is Aberdeen's oldest surviving private house, the 16th-century **Provost Skene's House**

A rose by any other name

Aberdeen is known as the 'Granite City', and Rubislaw Quarry still bears testament to the vast quantities of granite hewn there and used to build its striking Victorian Gothic buildings. But it has a softer side, and is also known as the 'City of Roses'. There is a profusion of blooming flowers that fill the parks, gardens, traffic islands and roadways, creating a stark contrast to the grey streets and buildings. In fact, flower power is so prevalent here that Aberdeen has been debarred from entering the 'Britain in Bloom' competition, in order to give other places a chance!

ⓘ *T01224-641086, Mon-Sat 1000-1700, Sun 1300-1600, free.* Its distinctive style, with boldly pointed stone and little turrets, stands out from the adjacent modern buildings. It was only the intervention of the late Queen Mother which saved this little historical gem from the same fate as its neighbours. The interior features a series of ornate tempera-painted ceilings dating from 1622, which somehow survived the orgy of vandalism in the wake of the Reformation. There are also furnished period rooms and an interesting display of memorabilia, including mementos of John Brown, ghillie and companion of Queen Victoria. There is a pocket watch given to him by the widowed queen, also a silver pipe and case from the same donor. Down in the cellar is a good little café.

Also off Broad Street is the imposing **Marischal College** (pronounced 'Marshall'), the second largest granite building in the world, after the Escorial in Madrid. This massive neo-Gothic sculpture is loved and loathed in equal measure, but cannot be ignored. Aberdeen was the seat of two universities, the Catholic King's College (see 'Old Aberdeen' below) and the Protestant Marischal College, founded in 1593 by the 5th Earl of Marischal. The two colleges combined in 1860 to form Aberdeen University. The **museum** ⓘ *T01224-274301, Mon-Fri 1000-1700, Sun 1400-1700, free*, entered through the main quadrangle and up the stairs, is open to visitors and worth visiting. It is divided into two exhibitions, the 'Encylopaedia of the Northeast', which depicts the region's distinctive culture, and 'Collecting the World', which features many wonderfully diverse items collected from around the globe.

From Marischal College, head down Upperkirkgate, past the Bon Accord and St Nicholas Shopping Centres, and up Schoolhill to the city's magnificent **Art Gallery**, ⓘ *T01224-523700, Mon-Sat 1000-1700, Sun 1400-1700, free*, a most elegant building of marble steps with a pillared gallery overlooking a central well. At the top of the stairs stands a showcase of lovely Meissen china. There are changing displays of costumes and applied arts. All the big names are here; there's a Degas bronze, and paintings by Dante Gabriel Rossetti, Monet, Pissarro, Millais, Legros, Sargent, Sisley, Russell Flint, Holman Hunt, Landseer, Augustus John, Raeburn, McTaggart and Sir George Reid, amongst many others. William Roelofs' large oil of Waterlilies is a fitting rival to Monet. There are also several works by Joan Eardley, who lived near Stonehaven. A large number of the paintings were bequeathed by local granite merchant, Alex MacDonald, in 1900. Downstairs is a white-walled circular room which commemorates the 167 people who lost their lives in the Piper Alpha oil rig disaster in 1988. There's also a well-stocked shop, café and craft gallery.

West of the Art Gallery are the sunken **Union Terrace Gardens**, which make a pleasant escape from the traffic on Union Street. Here, at the end of Union Terrace,

Legend has it that Machar, a follower of Columba, was sent to establish a church at a place near the sea where the river was shaped like the crook on a Bishop's crozier, hence the site of the cathedral in Old Aberdeen.

stand three buildings at right angles: the **Central Library, His Majesty's Theatre** and **St Mark's Church**, always known locally as 'Education, Damnation and Salvation'. They are obligingly pointed out by a huge statue of William Wallace, brandishing his sword. Anyone interested in military history should not miss the **Gordon Highlanders Museum** ⓘ *T01224-311200, Apr-Oct Tue-Sat 1030-1630, Sun 1330-1630, for the rest of the year by appointment, £2.50, £1.50 concession, £1 child, at St Luke's in Viewfield Rd, which is off Queen's Rd (buses 14 or 15 from Union St).*

The harbour

From the Castlegate, Shiprow, a steep cobbled street, leads down to the harbour and the gleaming glass and steel of the excellent new **Maritime Museum** ⓘ *T01224-337700, Mon-Sat 1000-1700, Sun 1200-1500, free*, which traces Aberdeen's long seafaring history from earliest times up to the present day. In the entrance is a list, updated daily, of ships in harbour. The Lloyd's register is there if you ask. As you go up the stairs (there's a lift, if needed), the first things that you will see are the lenses from Rattray Head lighthouse. The sounds are authentic: the cry of seagulls and the crash of the sea on shale. A huge board lists all the ships built in Aberdeen from 1811 until 1991, including the famous fast clippers. Most dramatically, down the stairwell hangs a model of an oil rig. The methods in use in oil and gas exploration and production are explained. The auditorium (which has an induction loop system) features good explanatory videos. There is a hands-on children's area and a layout of bunks. The museum spills over into the adjoining Provost Ross' House dating from 1593, the oldest building in the city. There's also a shop and a good licensed café.

At the foot of Shiprow is **Market Street**, which runs the length of the harbour. It's still a busy place and on any one day you'll see a huge variety of vessels from all over the world. Follow your nose and the screech of seagulls down to the fish market, where fish has been landed and traded since the 13th century (no public access). The best time to see it is early in the morning, before 0800. At the northeast corner of the harbour is the old fishing village of **Footdee** (pronounced 'Fittie'), which is interesting to explore and an easy walk from Market Street, via Regent and Waterloo Quays and York Street, or south from the Beach Esplanade. Ask at the tourist office about guided walks, or pick up one of their leaflets.

At the southern end of Market Street, North Esplanade leads to **Duthie Park**, a 10-minute bus ride from town, on the banks of the Dee. The park features a beautiful rose garden, known as 'Rose Mountain', which is best seen in summer. Also in the park are the Winter Gardens, a gigantic hothouse full of tropical plants and birds. It covers an amazing two acres and is the second largest of its kind in Europe.

Old Aberdeen

A 20-minute bus ride northwest of the city centre, on the banks of the Don, is the beautifully preserved suburb of Old Aberdeen, with its cobbled streets and peaceful atmosphere. An independent burgh until 1891, Old Aberdeen is clustered around **St Machar's Cathedral** ⓘ *T01224-485988, 0900-1700, free, services on Sun at 1100 and 1800*, with its soaring twin spires. The cathedral was founded in the sixth century and is one of the oldest granite buildings in the city, dating from the 15th century. It is also one of the few examples in the country of a fortified cathedral. Inside, the heraldic ceiling is particularly impressive.

Next to the cathedral is the **Cruickshank Botanic Garden** ⓘ *Mon-Fri 0900-1700, free*, with beautiful floral displays. A short walk south of St Machar's is **King's College**, founded in 1495 by Bishop Elphinstone. The most notable of the college buildings is the 16th-century **King's College Chapel** ⓘ *T01224-272137, Mon-Fri 0900-1700, free*, with its distinctive crowned spire. The interior is remarkably well preserved and features some rare and beautiful medieval woodcarving in the ceiling and choir stalls. The King's College Visitor Centre ⓘ *T01224-273702, Mon-Fri 0930-1700, Sat 1100-*

 1600, free, houses a multimedia display on the university's often turbulent history. There are guided walks around the cathedral and University from June to August, leaving from King's College on Wednesday at 1900 and Sunday at 1430. The guides are extremely helpful and well informed.

Just to the north of St Machar's Cathedral, on the banks of the Don, is **Seaton Park**, another of the city's fine open spaces. North of the park, the Don is spanned by the **Brig o' Balgownie**, completed in the 14th century with money from the Common Good Fund. It is the oldest Gothic bridge in Scotland, and over the years has charmed the likes of Byron. On the north bank of the Don is **Bridge of Don**, home to the city's two finest golf courses, the Royal Aberdeen and Murcar.

The beach

Between the mouths of the rivers Don and Dee, and less than a mile east of Union Street, is Aberdeen's beach, a two-mile stretch of glorious golden sand. But though the northeast gets a large share of Scotland's sunshine, don't expect to sunbathe comfortably as the beach is exposed to the bitter North Sea winds. And as you watch parents coaxing their reluctant children into the water, note that a few miles offshore, oil rig workers are being warned of the dangers of perishing in these freezing seas. At the southern end of the esplanade is **Aberdeen Fun Beach**, a huge leisure complex with multi sports facilities, swimming pool, bar and cafés, ice arena, multiplex cinema and Scotland's largest permanent fun fair. Nearby is **Pittodrie Stadium**, home of Aberdeen FC. The northern end of the long, long beach is backed by a succession of golf links.

Sleeping

Aberdeen *p510, map p511*
Aberdeen has plenty of accommodation but its hotels are relatively expensive. Having said that, full of transient oil workers and business people during the week, many do offer discounts at the weekend, when prices can fall by up to 50 per cent. Single rooms are at premium and very poor value. The best value are the B&Bs and guest houses, many of which can be found on Bon Accord St, Springbank Terrace and Crown St, both running south off Union St, and along Great Western Rd. Serviced apartments also offer very good value. The cheapest options are the youth hostel and university residences left vacant during summer vacation. There's also a campsite in the suburbs. The tourist office has a free guide and will book accommodation.

L-A The Marcliffe at Pitfodels, North Deeside Rd, T01224-861000, www.marcliffe.com. 40 rooms. This outstanding, luxurious country house hotel on the outskirts of town offers an unbeatable mix of baronial elegance and modern comforts, as well as exceptional hospitality and service, and superb cuisine.

A Caledonian Thistle Hotel, Union Terrace, T01224-640233, F641627. 76 rooms. Superior city-centre hotel in a grand old Victorian building. Full facilities, friendly service and good restaurants.

A-B Simpson's Hotel Bar/Brasserie, 59 Queen's Rd, T01224-327777, reservations@simpsonshotel.com. 50 rooms. Very stylish, modern hotel with a Mediterranean look and feel. The attached restaurant has won many plaudits for its excellent Scottish/international cuisine, see Eating.

A-B Copthorne Hotel, 122 Huntly St, T01224-630404, www.millenniumhotels.com. 89 rooms. Reliable chain in the city centre. Special breaks available reducing the price considerably at weekends.

B Atholl Hotel, 54 King's Gate, T01224-323505, info@atholl-aberdeen.com. 35 rooms. One of many elegant granite mansions in the West End, this one has an excellent reputation for its reliability, service and good food.

For an explanation of sleeping and eating price codes used in this guide, see inside the front cover. Other relevant information is found in Essentials, see pages 43-51.

B-C Brentwood Hotel, 101 Crown St, T01224-595440, www.brentwood-hotel.co.uk. 65 rooms. Good-value business hotel and therefore often full on weekdays. Better than most and close to the action on Union St, its cellar bar does very good bar meals.
C Craiglynn Hotel, 36 Fonthill Rd, T01224-584050, www.craiglynn.co.uk. 8 rooms. Intimate and comfortable Victorian house close to the town centre, also has a good reputation for its food.
C Mannofield Hotel, 447 Great Western Rd, T01224-315888, www.hotels-rus.co.uk. 9 rooms. Small, friendly and elegant hotel about a mile west of Union St.
C Speedbird Inns, Argyll Rd, Dyce, T01224-772884, www.speedbirdinns.co.uk. 159 rooms. Large, purpose-built hotel chain at the airport, good value.
There are many guest houses including:
C Dunrovin Guest House, 168 Bon Accord St, T01224-586081, www.dunrovin.freeservers.com;
C Crynoch Guesthouse, 164 Bon Accord St, T01224-582743;
C The Jays Guesthouse, 422 King St, T01224-638295, www.jaysguesthouse.co.uk, which is very highly rated.
D Aberdeen Nicoll's Guest House, 63 Springbank Terr, T01224-572867, wwwaberdeennicollsguest house.com;
D Butler's Islander Guest House, 122 Crown St, T01224-212411, www.butlersguesthouse.com, clean, comfortable accommodation, also offers free internet access; and
D Campbell's Guesthouse, 444 King St, T01224-625444, info@campbellsguesthouse.com.
There are also numerous small, family-run guest houses along Great Western Rd:
D Aberdeen Springdale Guesthouse, No 404, T01224-316561;
D Kildonan Guesthouse, No 410, T01224-316115; and
D The Noble Guesthouse, No 376, T01224-313678.
C-D Skene House Suites, www.skene-house.co.uk, are an outfit providing high quality serviced apartments. They offer good value with 1, 2 or 3 bedrooms, bathrooms, kitchen, lounge and reception, maid and breakfast facilities and are clean and bright. The cheapest are at the Rosemount site (T01224-645971), more luxurious are the Whitehall (T01224- 646600) and Holburn (T01224-580000) sites.
E-D Kings Hall (open all year); and
E-D Crombie Johnston Hall (Mar-Apr and Jun-Sep), contact Conference Office, Regent Walk, Old Aberdeen, T01224-272664, j.m.pirie@admin.abdn.ac.uk, are university campuses both well situated in Old Aberdeen.
F Aberdeen Youth Hostel, 8 Queen's Rd, T01224-646988, a mile west of the bus and train stations (take buses 14 or 15 from the bus station). It's open all year till 0200 and has 116 beds.
Robert Gordon's University, T01224-262134, www.scotland2000.com/rgu, also has self-catering flats throughout the city. For more details check with the TIC.

Camping

Lower Deeside Holiday Park, Maryculter, T01224-733860, is the nearest site.

Eating

Aberdeen *p510, map p511*
There's no shortage of good places to eat in Aberdeen, though prices tend to be higher than elsewhere in the region. Many of the city's pubs and bars serve good-value meals, though many don't serve food in the evening. Golden Square area is home to some of the city's slickest restaurants, while many of the buzzy bars on Belmont St also serve food.
£££ Courtyard on the Lane, Alford La, T01224-213795, just off the west end of Union St. Highly rated bistro serving imaginative Scottish/European menu, with a more formal restaurant upstairs. Tue-Sat.
£££ Melting Point, 3 Golden Sq, T01224-639944, is a fondue restaurant with meat, fish and vegetarian fondues to choose from. Mon-Sat 1200-1500, 1800-late.
£££ Robbie Robertson's, 8 Golden Sq, T01224-624324, is the city's newest restaurant and already highly acclaimed. With only 7 tables (it's upstairs above **Shiso**) there's an intimate, stylish atmosphere while food is modern Mediterranean with an Asian twist. Open every evening from 1900.
£££ Silver Darlings Restaurant, Pocra Quay, North Pier, Footdee, at the southern end of the Beach Esplanade, T01224-576229. Highly

recommended as serving the best seafood in town (try the oysters or turbot), and perhaps the best seaside location in the country, in a conservatory on the roof of an old granite house overlooking the harbour entrance. Best to book in advance. Mon-Fri 1200-1400, Mon-Sat 1900-2130.

£££ Simpson's, 59 Queen's Rd, T01224-327777, see also Sleeping. Designer brasserie serving superb Scottish cuisine with an international flavour. Open daily.

££ Bistro Verde, The Green, T01224-586180 serves lots of fish and French style dishes. Tue-Sat 1200-1400, 1800-2200.

££ Foyer, 82A Crown St, T01224-582277. Contemporary restaurant/gallery in a former church that helps to fund Foyer, a young person's charity. It offers some imaginative veggie choices as well as meaty dishes. Tue-Sat 1100-2400 (food until 2200).

££ Halo, 470 Union St, T01224-622107. New kid on the Aberdeen block - one of those cool, contemporary places with lots of blonde wood and blonde waitresses, serving modern Mediterranean dishes.

££ Howies, 50 Chapel St, T01224-639500. Yellow walls and a cosy, contemporary exterior and offers modern Scottish/French food. Set 3 course dinners for £17.95. Daily 1200-1430, 1800-2230.

££ Kurry, 22/24 King St, T01224-645015. Contemporary styled Indian eaterie (not a speck of flock wallpaper to be seen) serving old favourites as well as speciality dishes. Sun-Thu 1700-2300, Fri, Sat 1700-2330, Sun brunch 1600-1900.

££ La Stella, 28 Adelphi, T01224-211414. Mediterranean restaurant/café tucked away down a side street off Union St.

££ Little Italy, 79 Holborn St, T01224-515227, near the west end of Union St. Usual pasta and pizza fare. Open late (till 2400 Mon-Wed and till 0200 Thu-Sat).

££ Poldino's, 7 Little Belmont St, T01224-647777. One of the city's most established Italian restaurants, so it's always busy. Mon-Sat 1200-1430, 1800-2245.

££ Shiso, 8 Golden Sq, T01224-624324. Chic brasserie offering mains like fillet of monkfish or pumpkin risotto. Daily 1100-0100.

££ The Royal Thai, Crown Terr (off Crown St), T01224-212922. Long-established Thai restaurant with wide-ranging menu. Open daily for lunch and 1900-2300.

££ The Square, 1 Golden Sq, T01224-646362. Restaurant/bar offering good value lunches as well as evening meals. Mon-Thu 1130-2330, Fri 1130-2400, Sat 1100-2400.

££ The Wild Boar, 19 Belmont St, T01224-625357. Popular bar-bistro serving good-value food, plenty of vegetarian choices, and just look at those cakes! Mon-Thu 1200-2400, Fri, Sat 1200-0100, Sun 1230-2400, food until 2000, 1800 on Sun.

££ Via Milano, The Galleria, Bon Accord St, T01224-593222. Popular Italian restaurant offering pizza, pasta and other Italian dishes. Mon-Sat 1200-2200, Sun 1700-2200.

£ Ashvale, 46 Great Western Rd, T01224-596981.The northeast's most famous, and best, fish and chips, quite simply unmissable. This is the original branch and it's huge, with seating for 300; also takeaway. Open daily till late.

£ Books and Beans, 22 Belmont St, T01224-646438, offers sandwiches, paninis, drinks – and secondhand books upstairs. Mon-Sat 0800-1800, Sun 1100-1700.

£ Café 52, The Green, T01224-590094, is a dark bar/café offering light dishes like goat's cheese fritters and moussaka, as well as tapas between 1600-1900. Tue-Thu 1200-2400, Fri, Sat 1200-0100, Sun 1200-1800.

£ Carmine's Pizza, 32 Union Terr, T01224-624145. Best pizza in town and excellent-value 3-course lunches. Mon-Sat 1200-1730.

£ Jimmy Chung's Bar and Chinese Buffet, almost opposite Carmine's, T01224-593838, has all you can eat Chinese food buffets. Open daily.

£ Soul and Spice, 15/17 Belmont St, T01224-645200. Relaxed African/Caribbean restaurant. Tue-Fri 1800-late, Sat 1200-late.

£ The Cellar Café Bar, Provost Skene's House, Guestrow, T01224-522743, has a low stone ceiling, a glass floor revealing the old cellar steps and a good range of paninis, baguettes, soup and cakes. Mon-Sat 1000-1630.

£ The Dolphin, Chapel St. Another superb chippie, some say better than the Ashvale. Mostly takeaway and open till 0100 (0300 at weekends).

£ The Lemon Tree, 5 West North St, T01224-642230, see also Entertainment.

Café inside the excellent arts centre. Relaxed and laid-back place for a light vegetarian lunch, or coffee and cakes. Wed-Sun 1200-1500.

£ Victoria Restaurant, Union St, upstairs in a jewellery shop. Great scones, teas and light lunches – very popular with Aberdeen's lady shoppers. Mon-Sat 0900-1700 (1830 on Thu). For picnic food **Terroir** is a good deli and **La Gourmandise** is a French patisserie, both on Thistle St.

Bars and clubs

Aberdeen *p510, map p511*

Like most busy ports, Aberdeen has a large transient population with lots of cash to spend. Consequently, its numerous loud, flashy bars and traditional pubs are usually packed with people out for a good time. Aberdeen also has numerous nightclubs to choose from, most of which close at 0200.

Bars

There are lots of trendy bars in Belmont St, off Union St, the most happening area in the city.

Bar Shiso, 8 Golden Sq, is a new basement bar that serves food.

Beluga Bar, Union St, has art deco lights, terracotta walls and serves food like nachos and wraps.

Enigma, in The Academy shopping centre on Belmont St, offers a wide range of food as well as drinks

Chi Bar, Belmont St, as well as drinks this place offers Thai and Chinese dishes.

The Globe, 13 North Silver St. Down-to-earth café-bar which serves decent food at lunchtime.

The Globe Inn, North Silver St, a basement wine bar which attracts a more mature crowd. Open evenings only.

Ma Cameron's Inn, Little Belmont St. The city's oldest pub, though the old bit now constitutes only a small section, serves food at lunch and early evening.

The Old Town School, Little Belmont St, which is more of a modern theme bar but has a good selection of ales and does food.

O'Neill's, 9 Back Wynd. An Irish theme pub which serves decent grub, a good selection of Irish beers, stout and whiskeys, and has live folk music at weekends.

The Prince of Wales, 7 St Nicholas La, just off Union St, T01224-640597. The best pub in the city, with a great selection of real ales and a real flagstone floor. Also does very cheap bar food and gets very crowded. Traditional fiddle music on Sun evenings.

Siberia, Belmont St, is a vodka bar that serves food.

Under the Hammer, North Silver St, is noted for its good beers.

Clubs

Frankenstein's, Union St, is a themed gothic club.

Jumpin' Jaks, at the western end of Union St, caters for a 30 something crowd.

Ministry, 16 Dee St, T01224-211661, off Union St. Pick of the bunch. The faithful congregate in this converted church for a heavenly mix of cool sounds and atmosphere. Popular with students and oldies. Often has big-name guest DJs and open 7 days.

Oh'Henry's, 20 Adelphi Close, just off Union St. Very studenty and therefore very retro (1970s and 1980s).

The Priory, Belmont St, also in a converted church which has the original stained-glass windows.

Revolution, Belmont St.

Slain's Castle, Belmont St, a popular club in a former church.

Entertainment

Aberdeen *p510, map p511*

Tickets for most plays and concerts can be booked at the box office, next to the Music Hall on Union St, T01224-641122. Mon-Sat 1000-1800, www.abdnboxoffice.com.

Cinema Belmont Cinema, Belmont St, is a small cinema showing mainly general release.

Lighthouse, Shiprow, is another muliplex.

UGC, T0870 1550502. Among the city's mainstream cinemas is this huge 9-screen complex on Beach Esplanade.

Theatre Aberdeen Arts Centre, 33 King St, T01224-635208. Stages a variety of theatrical productions and exhibitions, and also shows art house movies.

Aberdeen Exhibition and Conference Centre, outside the city centre hosts big name pop /rock acts.

His Majesty's, Rosemount Viaduct, T01224-637788. Aberdeen's main theatre, featuring opera, ballet, musicals and panto (closed for renovations opening again Spring 2005).
The Lemon Tree, 5 West North St, T01224-642230. The hub of the city's arts scene, with a wide and varied programme of events, including live jazz and folk, comedy and contemporary drama. Also has a good café/bar-restaurant, see Eating.
Music Hall, Union St, T01224-632508. The main venue for classical music concerts, as well as big-name comedy acts.

Transport

Aberdeen *p510, map p511*
Air There are domestic flights to and from London and several provincial airports, and to a few European destinations.
Boat Northlinkferries, T0845-6000449, have daily evening departures (Mon-Fri) to Lerwick on Shetland. They also sail to Kirkwall on Orkney. See also under Orkney and Shetland, see p550.
Bus Scottish Citylink runs direct buses to **Dundee** (2 hrs), **Perth** (2½ hrs), **Edinburgh** (4 hrs), **Stirling** (3½ hrs) and **Glasgow** (4½ hrs). Stagecoach Bluebird Buses, T01224-212266, is the major local bus operator. Service No 10 goes every hour to **Inverness** via **Huntly** and **Elgin**. Service No 201 goes every 30 mins (hourly on Sun) to **Banchory**, every hour (Mon-Sat; less frequently on Sun) to **Ballatar** and several times daily to **Braemar**. There are also buses to **Stonehaven** (Service No 107), **Alford** (Service No 220), **Peterhead** (No 263), **Fraserburgh** (Nos 267/268) and **Ellon** (Nos 290/291). For more details pick up a free copy of the *Aberdeenshire & Moray Public Transport Guide* at the bus station or tourist office, or call the Public Transport Unit, T01224-664581.
Car hire **Arnold Clark**, Girdleness Rd, T01224-249159, **Lang Stracht**, T01224-663723, and **Thrifty**, 76 Huntly St, T01224-621033.
Cycle hire **Aberdeen Cycle Centre**, 188 King St, T01224-644542. **Alpine Bikes**, 64 Holburn St, T01224-211455. From £12 per day. Open daily.
Taxi Call **Comcabs**, T01224-353535.
Train There are services to **Edinburgh** (2½ hrs), **Glasgow** (2¾ hrs), **Dundee** (1¼ hrs), **Perth** (1¾ hrs), **Stirling** (2¼ hrs) and **Inverness** (2¼ hrs).

Directory

Aberdeen *p510, map p511*
Banks All the major banks have branches with ATMs on and around Union St. Currency exchange at **Thomas Cook**, 335-337 Union St, T01224-212271. Mon-Sat 0930-1730, and there is an **American Express** office at **Lunn Poly**, 3-5 St Nicholas St, T01224-633119. Mon-Fri 0900-1730, Sat 0900-1700.
Internet Internet facilities at the **Central Library**, also at the TIC, Union St and **Costa Coffee**, near John Lewis on George St.
Medical services **Aberdeen Royal Infirmary**, T01224-681818, is on Foresthill, northeast of the town centre. 24-hr A&E.
Pharmacy **Boots**, 161 Union St, T01224-211592. Mon-Sat 0800-1800.
Post The main post office is in the St Nicholas Centre, T01224-633065.
Tour operators **Grampian Coaches**, T01358-789513, run various day tours around the region, leaving from Shiprow. **STA Travel**, 30 Kirkgate, T01224-658222.
Useful addresses **Left luggage** at Aberdeen Bus Station 0830-1630. 24-hr lockers at the train station. **Police** at Queen St, T01224-639111.

South Aberdeenshire

The main A90 runs north from Dundee to Aberdeen and passes through the Howe of the Mearns, an agricultural district so evocatively described by local author, Lewis Grassic Gibbon, in his brilliant trilogy A Scots Quair. *His home can be visited at Arbuthnott. The coastal route (A92) from Dundee runs north from Montrose and meets the A90 by the little fishing port of Stonehaven, which is close to the dramatic ruins of*

Dunnotar Castle, one of the area's main attractions. Other places of interest include Fasque House, family home of Victorian prime minister Gladstone. ▸▸ *For Sleeping, Eating and other listings, see pages 523-524.*

St Cyrus ➔ *Colour map 4, grid B5.*

North of Montrose on the A92, is the little coastal village of St Cyrus, whose church steeple is seen to great effect for miles around. Thanks to a bequest in the will of one John Orr in 1844, four local brides benefit each year in the most unusual way. The eldest, the youngest, the tallest and the shortest (all of them carefully measured by the local minister) receive a dowry from the interest on the money which he left for that purpose. Thus they are known as **The Dowry Brides**. The annual interest is in fact divided in five. The final fifth is used to buy comforts for the poor. The town is also known for its strict enforcement of the 30 mph speed limit (this applies to Kincardine O'Neil on Deeside too). There's a wonderful sandy **beach** here, and the **National Nature Reserve** ⓘ *T01674-830736, May-Sep*, complete with marine-life tank and visitor centre, is interesting.

Johnshaven ➔ *Phone code: 01561. Colour map 4, grid B5.*

A few miles further on is the old fishing village of Johnshaven, a thriving fishing port until quite recently, and in the early 18th century probably the largest in Scotland. The village is unusual because of the great number of people who are called **McBay**. They are all mostly descended from two cousins, Long Ned and Little Ned, one of whom had seven sons, and the other 10. Johnshaven is a good spot for buying lobster and crab, and its annual **Fish Festival** is getting more and more popular. It takes place on either the first or second Saturday in August. The date depends upon the tides, which have to be suitable for visiting craft.

▲ The three-mile walk north along the shore to **Gourdon**, is one of the most pleasant and one of the easiest in the area. Very often, cormorants bask in the sun out on the rocks, spreading their wings to dry. Rather less often dolphins tumble past. In Gourdon you can buy fish from several fish houses on the harbour.

Inverbervie ➔ *Colour map 4, grid B6.*

A few miles further on from Johnshaven lies Inverbervie, birthplace of **Hercules Linton**, designer of the *Cutty Sark*. The village is probably better known for the **Bervie Chipper**, see Eating page 524. By decree of King David, son of Robert the Bruce, Inverbervie is a Royal Burgh and residents enjoy several privileges, such as free fishing in the local river. Many anglers know this, but the fish seem to know as well as they are not very plentiful. For full-blooded fishing make for either the North Esk River at Edzell, see page 504, or somewhere along its length before it flows out to the sea by the two bridges just north of Montrose. The old bridge in **Inverbervie**, built in 1799, is the oldest single span bridge in the British Isles. To see it, turn left to the north of the village, just before the memorial to Linton. In the village square is **Mingei**, which has a good selection of Japanese and European antiques.

Just to the south of the village, on the left heading north, is the **Mill of Benholm** (pronounced 'Ben-um'). This is a water mill powered by the water from the miller's dam. There's also a little tea room and an easy signed walk nearby.

Arbuthnott ➔ *Colour map 4, grid B6.*

Five miles inland from Inverbervie, between the A92 and A90, is Arbuthnott, birthplace of the amazingly prolific author Lewis Grassic Gibbon (1901-1935), and where he spent his formative years. From 1928 till his untimely death at the age of 34, he wrote an astonishing 17 books. *Sunset Song*, the first part of the Scots Quair trilogy, is his best-known work. It remains one of the true classics of Scottish literature and is an absolute must for anyone exploring this area. **Grassic Gibbon Centre**

 ⓘ *T01561-361668, Mar-Oct daily 1000-1630, £2.50, £1.75 child/concession*, at the east end of the village, traces his life and points out the places he wrote about. There is also a café and bookshop. Grassic Gibbon is also buried here, under his real name of James Leslie Mitchell, in a corner of the churchyard, about half a mile away at the other end of the village. The parish church itself is one of the few intact pre-Reformation churches in Scotland and is notable for its 13th-century chancel. Near the centre of the village is **Arbuthnott House** ⓘ *www.arbuthnott.co.uk, gardens are open all year daily 0900-1700,£2, the house on certain days in the summer, £4*, a fortified manorhouse dating from the 15th century.

Kinneff → *Colour map 4, grid B6.*

A few miles north of Inverbervie, on the road to Stonehaven, you'll see a sign on the right to the Old Church, Kinneff, where the Scottish Crown Jewels – the Royal Regalia – were hidden in 1651 to protect them from Cromwell's greedy paws. Here they lay buried under the church floor for nearly 10 years. It's a mile and a half down to the church, where there's a memorial to the Reverend James Grainger, who hid the treasures and thus saved the 'Honours of Scotland': the crown, sceptre and sword. There are various stories of how they were smuggled out of nearby Dunnottar Castle (see below). In *Tales of a Grandfather*, Sir Walter Scott relates how Christian Grainger, the minister's wife, accompanied by her serving maid, carried them out of Dunnottar in collaboration with the Governor and his wife. Another version tells how they were lowered on ropes down the castle wall. There, on the beach, a fishwife gathering seaweed hid the sword in a bundle of flax and the crown in her creel (used for catching lobsters). Thus were the 'Honours' saved and are now displayed in Edinburgh castle.

Just to the north of Kinneff, at **Crawton**, is the **Fowlsheugh RSPB Reserve**. The spectacular 250-ft high cliffs are home to tens of thousands of seabirds, including shags, guillemots, kittiwakes, fulmars, razorbills and puffins. They're best seen in early summer (May-July). You can see them from the top of the cliffs, but take great care. Better still, take a boat trip from Stonehaven (May-July).

Stonehaven → *Phone code: 01569. Colour map 4, grid B6. Population: 9,000.*

The solid and tidy old fishing port of Stonehaven lies 15 miles south of Aberdeen, where the coastal A92 joins the main A90 from Dundee. Nowadays Stonehaven is better known as a seaside resort, attracting a fair few visitors in the summer months. Not least of the town's attractions is its wonderful art deco outdoor, heated salt-water **swimming pool** ⓘ *first Sat in Jun till end Aug, 1100-1930 (there's also a midnight swim; ask for details at the TIC), day ticket £3.20*, one of only two in Scotland (the other is at Gourock). It is kept at a constant 82°F. By the harbour is the **Tolbooth** ⓘ *May-Oct Wed-Mon 1330-1630, free, built around 1600*, and the town's oldest building. It now houses a seafood restaurant (see below) and local history museum. Away from the harbour and old town is the market square, where you'll find banks with ATMs and most of the shops. Stonehaven Tourist Information Centre ⓘ *66 Allardice St, the main street past the square, T01569-762806, Apr-Oct Mon-Sat, Jul-Aug daily.*

Dunnottar Castle

ⓘ *T01569-762173, Easter-Oct Mon-Sat 0900-1800, Sun 1400-1700, Nov-Mar Fri-Mon 0930-sunset, £3.50, £1 child, 2 miles south of town just off the A92, the castle can also be reached by a footpath from Stonehaven, contact the TIC for the leaflet.*

The main reason for coming to Stonehaven is to visit the impressive and impregnable Dunnottar Castle. Dating from the 12th century, this ancient ruin was a stronghold for the Earls Marischal of Scotland. Standing 160 ft high, with the sea on three sides and a huge drop and 'curtain wall' on the fourth, it is not far short of an island. It is worth devoting considerable time to exploring one of the country's most outstanding castles, which is approached by a steep 400-yd walk from the car park. So dramatic is its setting, that it was used as the backdrop for Zeffirelli's film version of *Hamlet*, starring Mel Gibson. But the fortress has a dramatic and bloody history all of its own. In 1297 William Wallace (another of Mel Gibson's characters, strangely enough) burnt alive an entire English garrison here; later, in 1685, a large group of Covenanters was imprisoned, tortured and then left to rot in the castle dungeons. The castle was reduced to its present state in 1716, during reprisals for the Earl Marischal's Jacobite activities.

Howe of the Mearns to Deeside → *Colour map 4, grid B5.*

Fourteen miles south of Stonehaven, just off the main A90 is **Laurencekirk**. A few miles east, off the tiny B9120, is the **Hill of Garvock** (908 ft), which gives great views over the Howe of the Mearns. It is topped by the **Tower of Johnston** (which lies up a footpath), built to commemorate Britain's victory over Napoleon in the Peninsula Wars. On the other side of the hill is a depression called the **Sheriff's Kettle**. Here, at Baileys Farm in 1420, disgruntled local lairds boiled the Sheriff and 'supped the brew'.

Four miles west of Laurencekirk on the B9120 is the village of **Fettercairn**, famous for its handsome arch, built in 1861 following a visit from Queen Victoria. A mile west of the village is the distillery ⓘ *T01561-340205, May-Sep Mon-Sat 1000-1430, free*, one of the oldest in Scotland, with an excellent video presentation on the whole process and the obligatory dram at the end. The village holds its annual **Highland Games** on the first Saturday in July. They're authentic and the setting is lovely.

A few miles north on the B974 is the 18th-century **Fasque House** ⓘ *T01561-340569, May-Sep daily 1100-1730, £4, £3 concession*, erstwhile home of four-times British prime minister, William Gladstone. The family still lives in the west wing. Closed at the outbreak of the Second World War and only reopened in the 1970s, the faded grandeur of the place is wonderfully tangible. Though the house is interesting because of its historic connections with the former prime minister, it is also an excellent example of an 'Upstairs-Downstairs' country house and gives a fascinating insight into the lifestyle of a wealthy Victorian landowner. The estate also includes extensive grounds filled with deer.

Beyond Fasque the B974 wends its way through rich farming country, with its distinctive red soil, up to the **Cairn O' Mount** (1,492 ft) and on to Banchory. Before you start the actual steep ascent, the road to the right, over a water splash, leads to the **Glen of Drumtochty**. This is a delightful detour, ending up in the little town of **Auchinblae**. If you decide not to divert and feel like some refreshment, park on the left and climb the steps to the **Clatterin' Brig restaurant**, T01561-340297. Opened originally by a Bowes-Lyon, kinswoman of Queen Elizabeth the Queen Mother, it is open all year round. When you eventually reach the summit of the Cairn O' Mount, stop for a moment to admire the view. The cairn dates from 2000 BC.

> *Take your mountain bike in May and enter the Great Drumtochty Challenge, www.drumtochty challenge.co.uk.*

Sleeping

St Cyrus *p521*

D Woodston Fishing Station, T01674-850226, www.woodstonfishingstation.co.uk. 7 en suite rooms. Former Victorian icehouse, spectacularly sited on the clifftops with great sea views. Something a bit different.

East Bowstrips Caravan Park, T01674-850328, a campsite with decent facilities. At Lauriston, turn right at the Bush Hotel for Milton Haven.

Stonehaven *p522*

C Heugh Hotel, Westfield Rd, T01569-762379, wwwheughhotel.com. A granite baronial mansion with its own private grounds, giving a real sense of luxury.

C-D **Arduthie House**, Ann St, T01569-762381, www.arduthieguesthouse.com. A well-equipped, recommended guest house.

Howe of Mearns to Deeside *p523*
Drumtochty Castle Stables, near the village of Auchinblae, T01561-320082. Sleeps up to four, from £250/350 per week.

Eating

Inverbervie *p521*
£ **Bervie Chipper**, the region's best fish and chip shop. Eat in or takeaway; just don't leave town without finding out what all the fuss is about.

Stonehaven *p522*
£££ **Tolbooth Restaurant**, upstairs from the museum on the harbour, T01569-762287. The best place to eat in town. Expensive but worth it for the excellent seafood. Tue-Sat 1830-2130 (1730-2200 Sat).
££ **Lairhillock Inn & Restaurant**, 6 miles north of town at Netherley, on the B979, T01569-730001. A charming old coaching inn which offers excellent local produce in beautifully rustic surroundings. Friendly and welcoming. Also has rooms.
£ **Carron Tearooms**, in town, serves traditional high tea Wed-Mon 1330-1600 and boasts a wonderful art deco interior.

Dunnotar Castle *p522*
££ **Creel**, a few miles south of the castle, at Catterline, T01569-750254. Wonderfully cosy and renowned for its seafood.

Festivals and events

Stonehaven *p522*
Stonehaven is famous for its strange fireball-swinging festival on **Old Year's Night**, an ancient pagan ritual. Another attraction is the town's highly respected folk festival, held over 3 days in **mid-Jul**.

Transport

South Aberdeenshire *p520*
Stonehaven is served by buses 101, 107 and 707 from **Aberdeen**. Bluebird Buses, service No 101 between **Stonehaven** and **Montrose**, pass through **St Cyrus**, **Johnshaven**, **Inverbervie** and **Kinneff** hourly Mon-Fri (less frequently Sat-Sun).

Stonehaven is on the **Aberdeen-Dundee** rail line and there are regular trains in either direction. The train station is a 15-min walk from the square.

It's possible to head straight from Stonehaven to **Deeside** by taking the A957 (known as 'The Slug') to Crathes, see p525.

Deeside

→ *Colour map 4, grid A4-6.*

The River Dee rises in the Cairngorms and flows down through the surrounding hills, eastwards to the sea at Aberdeen. The valley of the Dee is known as Deeside, or rather Royal Deeside, for its connections with the royal family, who have holidayed here, at Balmoral, since Queen Victoria first arrived in 1848. Originally, Queen Victoria and Prince Albert were looking for an estate further west, but were advised that the Deeside climate would be better for Albert's delicate constitution. The queen fell in love with this area and its people, and following Albert's death she sought out the company of straight-talking northerners, preferring their down-to-earth honesty to the two-faced toadies she endured at court.

Today, Deeside's royal associations have made it the tourist honeypot of the northeast, but the royal presence has also saved it from mass development. There's an air of understated affluence and refinement in the villages strung out along the A93 that runs along the north bank of the Dee and, as well as the obvious attraction of Balmoral, there are many other fine examples of baronial castles. Deeside is also a great area for various outdoor activities, such as hiking in the surrounding mountains, mountain biking, canoeing and skiing. ▸▸ *For Sleeping, Eating and other listings, see pages 528-530.*

Ins and outs

For details of the Castle Trail, Victorian Heritage Trail and Deeside Tourist Route, contact the TIC in Aberdeen, or in any of the towns along the way. Banchory TIC is in the local museum ⓘ *Bridge St, behind the High St, Apr-late Oct*, can provide information on walking and fishing in the area. Ballater TIC ⓘ *T01339-755306, ballater@agtb.org, daily Jan-end May 1000-1700, end May-end Sep 0900-1800, end Sep-end Dec 1000-1700*, is housed in the Old Royal Station. Braemar TIC ⓘ *Balmoral Mews, on Mar Rd, T01339-741600, braemar@agtb.org, daily all year, 1000-1800 end May-end Sep, closes earlier and for lunch rest of year, Sun afternoons only end Sep-end May.* » *For transport details, see page 530.*

Sights in Deeside

Aberdeen to Banchory → *Colour map 4, grid A5-6.*

The first sight of interest heading west from Aberdeen is **Drum Castle** ⓘ *T01330-811204, www.drum-castle.org.uk, Apr-31 May and 1-30 Sep daily 1230-1730, 1 Jun-31 Aug daily 1000-1730, gardens same dates daily 1000-1800, grounds all year daily 0930 till dusk, castle, gardens and grounds £7, £5.25 concession, car park £2, garden and grounds only £2.50, £1.90 concession, three miles west of Peterculter (pronounced 'Petercooter')*. It's a combination of a 13th-century square tower, Jacobean mansion house and later Victorian additions. It was given to one William de Irvine by Robert the Bruce for service rendered at Bannockburn and was in the family's hands for over 650 years, until it was taken over by the National Trust for Scotland in 1976. There's a beautiful walled garden and a trail through the 100-acre ancient Wood of Drum which forms part of the castle grounds.

A few miles southeast of Peterculter is its sister village, Maryculter (pronounced 'Marycooter'), where you'll find **Storybook Glen** ⓘ *T01224-732491, www.storybookglen.aberdeen.co.uk, Mar-Oct 1000-1800, Nov-Feb 1000-1600, £3.95, children £2.95*, the northeast's answer to Disneyland. This very attractive and tasteful 'theme park' is a great place to take the kids and features giant tableaux and lifesize characters from many childhood fairy tales and nursery rhymes.

Fifteen miles west of Aberdeen, where the A93 meets the A957 from Stonehaven, is **Crathes Castle** ⓘ *T01330-844525, castle 1 Apr-30 Sep 1030-1730, 1-31 Oct 1030-1630 (last admission to castle 45 mins before closing); licensed restaurant 1 Apr-31 Oct 1030-1730, less often rest of year; grounds and garden open all year daily 0900-dusk; gardens only £4.50, concession £3; castle and grounds combined £7, concession £5*, a perfect 'fairytale' castle built over 40 years in the mid-16th century. The turreted tower house is still furnished with many period pieces and wall hangings, and is notable for its superb painted ceilings. There are narrow spiral staircases leading to tiny rooms, one of which is said to be inhabited by the obligatory ghost. The castle is well worth exploring but is almost overshadowed by the exceptional gardens, which shouldn't be missed. There are no fewer than eight of them, so take your time. There's also a visitor centre, restaurant and shop.

Banchory to Alford → *Phone code: 01330. Colour map 4, grid A5.*

Banchory makes a very pleasant base for exploring the area, with the River Dee burbling through, but there's not a great deal to do here, apart from salmon fishing, which is popular in these parts. You can watch salmon leaping spectacularly at the Bridge of Feugh, to the south of town. There is a sad tale, though, of a lady-in-waiting who was staying at Balmoral when the royal family were in residence some years ago. She was standing fishing in the river, in quite deep water, and wearing chest-height waders, when the sovereign rode by. Seeing the king, she curtsied, whereupon the water flowed quickly into her waders and she sank beneath the water and drowned.

From Banchory you can head northwest on the A980 to Alford, in the Don Valley, see page 530. Roughly halfway is the village of **Lumphanan**, which was thought to be the burial place of Macbeth, the Scottish king so misrepresented by Shakespeare (he is actually buried on Iona). Macbeth's Cairn is instead a prehistoric cairn. Just to the south of the village is the **Peel Ring**, a 12th-century Motte, or castle mound, and one of Scotland's earliest medieval sites.

West of Banchory → *Colour map 4, grid A5.*

The attractive little village of Aboyne is 30 miles west of Banchory on the A93. A few miles further on is Dinnet. In the Muir of Dinnet National Nature Reserve you can explore the Burn o' Vat, a sheltered valley which attracts many butterflies and dragonflies. During the walk, you'll come to a huge circular stone chamber and, in nearby Loch Kinord, there are crannogs, which are ancient man-made islands.

Ballater and Balmoral → *Colour map 4, grid A4.*

The neat little town of Ballater is proud of its royal connections. You can buy meat from the butcher with his 'By Royal Appointment' sign, or clothes from royal outfitters. This is where Lizzie and Phil pop down to the shops for a pint of milk or perhaps to choose a DVD for a quiet night in. Ever since Queen Victoria first arrived by train from Aberdeen in 1848, the royal family have been spending their holidays here in their summer residence, Balmoral. She was not amused at the prospect of having an unsightly rail station on her doorstep, so the line ended eight miles east, at Ballater. The line has been closed for some time, but you can still visit the old train station, which now houses an elegant tea room.

The royals are not the only famous summer visitors. The poet **Byron** (who attended Aberdeen Grammar School) spent many childhood summer holidays at **Ballaterach**, a few miles east of Ballater. He had a narrow escape when he slipped and nearly fell into the fast flowing stream at the Linn of Dee, beyond Braemar. He was rescued just in time and went on to wax poetic about the beautiful hills which are Ballater's other great attraction. The town makes the ideal base for **hiking** (see below) as well as a number of other outdoor activities. Many of the walks set off from **Loch Muick** (pronounced 'Mick'), nine miles southwest of Ballater, at the head of Glen Muick. There's a visitor centre and car park at Spittal of Glenmuick. From here a track leads along the west shore of the loch to the lodge where Queen Victoria met John Brown. For guides and equipment for canoeing, climbing, mountain biking and skiing, contact **Adventure Scotland** in Banchory, see page 530.

Balmoral Castle → *Colour map 4, grid A4.*

ⓘ *T01339-742334, Apr to end Jul, 1000-1700, last admission 1600, £5, concession £4, children £1.*

Eight miles west of Ballater is the area's main attraction, Balmoral Castle. The 16th-century tower house, formerly owned by the local Gordon family, was bought for Queen Victoria by Prince Albert in 1852 and converted into today's baronial mansion. It has been the royal family's summer retreat ever since. Only the ballroom and the grounds are open to the likes of you and me, and only for three months of the year. Pony trekking and pony cart rides are available around the estate grounds and are favourite ways of enjoying the wonderful scenery. Opposite the castle gates is **Crathie Church**, which is used by the family when they're in residence. There's a small souvenir shop next to the main gates and a visitor centre which gives a lot of information on the castle and its owners.

Braemar → *Colour map 4, grid A3.*

Nine miles west of Balmoral, is Braemar, the final town on Deeside, lying at the foot of the awesome, brooding **Cairngorm massif,** which dominates the Eastern Highlands.

Good old-fashioned fun

There has been a gathering (or games) of some sort at Braemar for 900 years, ever since Malcolm Canmore set contests for the local clans so that he could pick the strongest and bravest of men for his army. These events take place up and down the country throughout the summer, but none is as famous, or well attended, as Braemar's. Queen Victoria attended in 1848 and the Gathering is still patronized by the royal family. Crowds come from all over the world to proclaim the monarch as Chieftain of the Braemar Gathering.

At the gathering the visitor will see contests in traditional Scottish events, such as tossing the caber, Highland dancing and bagpipe competitions and displays. There is an inter-services tug o' war championship, a medley relay race and a hill race up Morrone. The sounds of the massed pipes echoing around the encircling heather-clad hills and a plethora of tartan also help to make this a real tourist highlight. The royal connection (and the crowds) apart, many other local communities hold similar games.

Even at the height of summer you can see a dab of snow still lying in a hollow in the surrounding mountains, and Braemar is an excellent base for hiking, see below, and winter skiing at Glenshee, see page 245. It's an attractive little place, much loved by Queen Victoria and much visited during its annual **Braemar Gathering** (or games), which attracts tens of thousands of visitors each year, amongst them members of the royal family. **Braemar Highland Heritage Centre** ⓘ *Balmoral Mews by the tourist office, T01339-741944, Apr-Sep 0900-1800 (Jul-Aug till 2000), Oct-Mar 1000-1700, free,* includes informative talks (in several languages) on the area, an exhibition and shops.

Just north of the village, and well signposted, is **Braemar Castle** ⓘ *T01339- 741219, Mid-Apr to end Oct Sat-Thu 1000-1800, £3.50, concession £3, children £1,* dating from 1628. This impressive fortress was used by Hanoverian troops after the Jacobite Rising of 1745. It is L-shaped, with a star-shaped defensive wall and a central round tower with a spiral stair. There are barrel-vaulted ceilings and an underground prison. The world's largest cairngorm – a semi-precious stone, a variety of quartz, which is yellow, grey or brown in colour – weighing 52 lbs is on display in the morning room. There's also a piece of tartan worn by Prince Charles Edward, Bonnie Prince Charlie.

A very scenic side trip from Braemar is to the **Linn of Dee**, six miles west of the village, at the end of the road. Here, the river thunders through a narrow gorge to spectacular effect. There are numerous walks from here along the river, or for the more adventurous, the famous **Lairig Ghru**, which runs through the Cairngroms to Aviemore, see page 423. Between the Linn of Dee and the tiny settlement of **Inverey**, a mile to the east, there's a very basic youth hostel (open mid-May to early October), which has no phone, so book through **Braemar youth hostel**, see page 528. A postbus runs in the afternoon (Monday to Saturday) from Braemar to the Linn of Dee, via the hostel.

Walks in Deeside

Ballater and Braemar are ideal bases for walking in the surrounding Grampian Mountains, and if you feel like 'bagging a Munro' (ie climbing a mountain over 3,000 ft), there are some close at hand. All of this area is included in the new Cairngorms National Park, which opened in 2003. This is the largest national park in Britain, covering a vast 4,500 sq km, from Aboyne in the east to Dalwhinnie in the west, and from Blair Atholl north to Grantown-on-Spey.

Lochnagar → *OS Landranger No 44.*

The best walk in the area is to the summit of Lochnagar (3,786 ft), made famous by Prince Charles in the book he wrote for his brothers when young, *The Old Man of Lochnagar*. The noble and mysterious mountain dominates the Royal Forest of Balmoral and takes its name from a small loch at its foot (it's also known as the White Mounth). This fine granite mass is approached from the car park by the Rangers' Visitor Centre at Spittal of Glen Muick. The path to the top is well trodden and well marked, though steep as you near the summit. It's 10 miles there and back, so allow a full day for the climb. You'll need to be properly equipped and take a map.

Cambus o' May and Morrone → *OS Landranger No 43.*

An easier walk is to Cambus o' May, on the river, about four miles east of Ballater. It's a great spot for a picnic, or to swim in the river, or to enjoy a stroll along the riverbank. A good walk from Braemar is to the summit of Morrone (2,818 ft), the mountain to the southwest. The walk takes about four hours in total.

Glen Tanar to Glen Esk → *OS Landranger No 44.*

Another good climb is the route up **Mount Keen** (3,077 ft), the most easterly Munro, which lies between Deeside and Glen Esk, the loveliest of the Angus glens, see page 508. Again, you should allow a whole day for this expedition. It can be approached from the visitor centre in Glen Tanar, at the end of the little road that runs southwest off the B976, across the river from Aboyne. You can climb to the summit and return by the same route but, if your party has two cars, it is well worth walking over to Glen Esk, 14 miles away. Drive around to the Invermark car park at the head of Glen Esk and park one car there. From Glen Tanar follow the old drove road which at times runs with the Mounth road. Skirting the **Home Farm** with its Arboretum and its dammed lake, the fairly flat track winds along Glen Tanar through the forest for about four miles. Then comes the Halfway Hut, used for rest and repast by former shooting parties. You will pass shooting butts en route. The next stretch is through open country with the **Clachan Yell** (626 ft) on the left.

The walk proper then begins to take shape. Cross the stone bridge of **Etnach**, and then the path begins to lead up to the **Shiel of Glentanar**. The second bridge forks left and the track heads for the summit. The rough path continues along a ridge, the shoulder of Mount Keen. From the summit with its stone marker, **Dinnet**, see page 526, and its two lakes is visible to the north, and the River Esk glints its way down the valley to the south. Watch out for adders around here. On the descent, you'll pass the **Queen's Well**, used by Queen Victoria when she and her party went down to Fettercairn posing as a wedding party. The well is decorated with a graceful granite crown which was erected in 1861. The royal party covered much of the climb on hill ponies. The stone arch at Fettercairn commemorates this visit.

Sleeping

Banchory *p525*
There are some very fine places to stay in and around Banchory.
B Banchory Lodge Hotel, T01330-822625. An excellent choice is this sporting lodge-type hotel superbly situated on the banks of the river near the town centre. It's also a great place to stop and have a bite to eat for lunch. The river runs past the lawn and you can watch the salmon leap as you perhaps enjoy the fruits of their labour.
B Raemoir House Hotel, T01330-824884, www.raemoir.com. Three miles north of town on the A980 is this wonderful country mansion set in 3,500 acres of woods and parkland with 20 rooms.

B Tor-na-Coille Hotel, T01330-822242, www.tornacoille.com, outside town on the Inchmarlo Rd. This tastefully furnished Victorian country house hotel is set in lovely grounds and boasts a considerable reputation for its modern Scottish cooking (**£££-££**).

There are also plenty of good guest houses and B&Bs, including:

E Towerbank House, at 93 High St, T01330-824798, diane@dawps.fsnet.co.uk; and

E June Little, 73 High St, T01330-824666, and excellent choice.

Camping

Silver Ladies Caravan Park, T01330-822800, at Strachan, just outside Banchory.

Ballater and Balmoral *p526*

There's plenty of accommodation in Ballater, from expensive hotels to reasonably priced B&Bs.

A Balgonie Country House Hotel, T/F01339-755482, on the western outskirts of town, off the A93. 9 rooms, open Feb-Dec. Friendly and comfortable country house hotel, excellent food (**£££**).

A-B Hilton Craigendarroch, Braemar Rd, T01339-755858, www.hilton.com. 45 rooms. Victorian country house converted into a modern resort hotel with full leisure and sports facilities, 2 good restaurants.

B Darroch Learg Hotel, T01339-755443, darroch.learg@exoams.wk.com, half a mile from town, off the A93 heading west to Braemar. 18 rooms, open Feb-Dec. Pick of the bunch. Friendly country house hotel with fine views and a reputation for superb food (**£££**), good value.

C Deeside Hotel, set back from the A93 heading out of town towards Braemar, T01339-755420, www.deesidehotel.co.uk. Friendly, good value and good food (**££**).

C Glen Lui Hotel, Invercauld Rd, T01339-755402, www.glen-lui-hotel.co.uk. 19 rooms. Another comfortable hotel offering fine food (**££-£**).

C Inverdeen House, 11 Bridge Sq, T01339-755759, www.inverdeen.com. Amoung the many B&Bs, this one is recommended. French, German and Polish spoken, great breakfasts, no smoking.

D Moorside House, T/F01339-755492, on the Braemar Rd. This B&B is also good.

Camping

Anderson Road Caravan Park, T01339-755727, open Apr-Oct.

Braemar *p526*

Accommodation is hard to find before and during the Braemar Gathering, but at other times of the year there's plenty to choose from including many B&Bs and guest houses.

A-C Braemar Lodge Hotel, T01339-741627, www.braemarlodge.co.uk, on the outskirts of the village on the road south to Glenshee and Blairgowrie. This is the best choice in the area.

C Callater Lodge Hotel, Glenshee Rd, T01339-741275, www.hotel-braemar.co.uk. Small and comfortable.

C Invercauld Arms Hotel, T01339-741605. 68 rooms. Large Victorian landmark on the edge of the village.

D Clunie Lodge, T01339-741330, on Cluniebank Rd. 5 rooms, 3 en suite. Good value guesthouse with good views.

D Schiehallion House, T01339-741679, open Jan-Oct on Glenshee Rd. 6 rooms, 5 en suite. Traditional Highland welcome in this friendly house.

F Rucksacks, 15 Mar Rd, T01339-741517, a cheap and friendly bunkhouse that's popular with hikers and rents out mountain bikes.

F SYHA Youth Hostel, T01339-741659, open all year, at Corrie Feragie on Glenshee Rd.

Camping

Invercauld Caravan Site, T01339-741373, open Dec-Oct, on Glenshee Rd.

Eating

Banchory *p525*

££ Burnett Arms Hotel, High St, T01330-824944. Aside from the hotels listed above, this is the best place to eat.

££ Le Bistroquet, has a varied menu.

££ The Milton Restaurant, opposite the gates of Drum Castle, T01330-844566, serves excellent food daily till 2100 (lunch only on Sun and Mon).

£ The Shieling, a good café and gift shop.

Ballatar and Balmoral *p526*

See also Sleeping.

£££ The Green Inn, on the green in the town centre, T/F01339-755701. It boasts a well-deserved reputation as one of the very best restaurants in the region, classic Scottish cooking with an imaginative and health-conscious twist; also has 3 rooms upstairs (**C** full board).

££ La Mangiatoia, on Bridge Sq, T/F01339-755999. Serves tasty fare in its family-friendly restaurant.

££ Inver, Crathie, T01339-742345, an 18th-century inn which serves good, honest food (best to book).

Braemar *p526*

The only decent places to eat are the bars of the larger hotels, which are a bit on the expensive side.

££ Braemar Lodge serves meals 1200-1400 and 1800-2100.

Activities and sport

Adventure Scotland, T01330-850332, dlatham@netcomuk.co.uk, is a Banchory-based company offering a wide range of adventure activities, including white-water rafting, mountain biking, skiing and hiking. For rental of ski equipment, try the The Braemar Ski School Hire, in Victoria Hall on Glenshee Rd.

Glen Tanar Equestrian Centre, south of Aboyne, in Glen Tanar (see Walks in Deeside), T01339-886448, offers riding in the forests and hills.

Festivals and events

Braemar games are held on the first Sat in Sep. Booking is essential and tickets can be bought in advance from the Booking Secretary, BRHS, Coilacreich, Ballater, AB35 5UH, T01339-755377, info@braemargathering.org.

Transport

Deeside *p530*

All the main tourist attractions on Deeside can be reached by bus from Aberdeen. To reach **Balmoral** by bus from Aberdeen catch the one destined for **Braemar**. Contact Bluebird Northern, T01224-212266, or Traveline, T0870-6082608, for information.

If you wish to explore Deeside along a less popular route (though even in the summer, crowds are never great) take the B976 along the south bank of the River Dee.

The Don Valley

→ *Colour map 4, grid A4-5.*

North of Royal Deeside is the lesser-known valley of the Don, Aberdeen's second river. This relatively little-visited corner of the northeast is an historian's and archaeologist's dream, as it's littered with medieval castles, Pictish stone circles and Iron-Age hillforts. A quarter of all Britain's stone circles can be found here (if you look hard enough). Local tourist offices have free leaflets on the region's archaeological sites, with background information and details of how to find them. The main sites are included in the tourist board's 'Stone Circle Trail'. There's also a well-signposted 'Castle Trail', which includes the area's main castles. One of these castles, Corgarff, stands at the southern end of the notorious Lecht Road, which runs from Cock Bridge to Tomintoul. This area, known as The Lecht, is one of Scotland's main ski centres.

▸▸ *For Sleeping, Eating and other listings, see pages 532-533.*

Inverurie and around → *Colour map 4, grid A5.*

The solid farming town of Inverurie is 17 miles northwest of Aberdeen on the A96 to Inverness. It makes a useful base for visiting the numerous castles and ancient relics dotted around the area. The **Thainstone Mart**, south of town just off the A96, is one of the largest livestock markets in the country, and interesting if you like that sort of thing. It's held Monday, Wednesday and Friday around 1000. There's a tourist information centre ⓘ *18 High St, T01467-625800, inverurie@agtb.org, Apr-Sep.*

About six miles southwest of Inverurie, off the B993 (turn first left after the village of Kemnay), is the magnificent **Castle Fraser** ⓘ *T01330-833463, castle Apr-end June* *and 1-30 Sep Fri-Tue 1200-1730, 1 Jul-31 Aug daily 1100-1730; garden and grounds all year daily 0800 till dusk, castle, garden and grounds £7 concession £5.25*, built in 1575 by the 6th Earl of Mar and similar in style to Crathes and Craigievar. The interior was remodelled in 1838 and many of the furnishings date from that period. There's a walled garden, tea room and trails through the estate.

▲ Close by, and signed off the B993, is the 4,000 year-old **Easter Aquhorthies Stone Circle**. This archaeological site is overshadowed by Bennachie (1,732 ft), by far the best hill in the area and thought to be the site of Mons Graupius, in 83 AD, when the Romans defeated the Picts. It's a straightforward two-hour walk to the summit and the views from the top are great. There are various trails, though the most commonly used route starts from the **Bennachie Centre** ⓘ *a mile beyond Chapel of Garioch, signposted off the A96 at Pitcaple, 5 miles northwest of Inverurie, T01467-681470, Apr-Oct Tue-Sun 1000-1700, Nov-Mar Wed-Sun 1000-1700*. Near here is the **Maiden Stone**, a 10-ft high Pictish gravestone with relief carvings showing what looks like an elephant, along with other creatures not normally found around these parts.

A few miles west of the turn-off to Chapel of Garioch, the B9002 heads west off the A96 to the village of Oyne, site of the **Archaeolink Prehistory Park** ⓘ *T01464-851500, www.archaeolink.co.uk, Apr-Oct daily 1000-1700, £4.25, children £3*. This state-of-the-art interpretative centre takes you on a journey back in time. It's a great introduction to the numerous ancient sites in the area and explains why the stone circles were built and what the various carved symbols mean. The 40-acre park includes various interesting features such as a reconstructed Iron Age farm, Stone-Age settlement and Roman camp, as well as a hilltop Iron-Age fort. The Archeodrome features audio-visual presentations which bring to life the ancient history of the area.

Near the village of Daviot, north of the A96 off the B9001 from Inverurie, or reached via the A920 west of Oldmeldrum, is the **Loanhead of Daviot Stone Circle**. This impressive 6,000 year-old site is 500 yds from the village and consists of two stone circles, the smaller of which encloses a cremation cemetery dating from 1500 BC. Thirteen miles north of Inverurie is **Fyvie Castle**, off the A947 between Oldmeldrum and Turriff, see page 538.

Alford → *Colour map 4, grid A5.*

The main tourist centre on Donside is the little country town of Alford (pronounced 'Ah-ford'), 25 miles west of Aberdeen. The principal point of interest in town is the **Grampian Transport Museum** ⓘ *T01975-562292, end Mar to end Oct daily, 1000-1700, £4, £3.10 concession, £1.60 child*, which features a comprehensive and fascinating display of transport history, with collections of cars, buses, trams, steam engines and some more unusual exhibits. Almost next door is the terminus for the **Alford Valley Railway** ⓘ *T01975-562811, steam engine runs 1st Sun of month, diesel engine runs Apr-May and Sep Sat-Sun 1300-1700, Jun-Aug daily 1300-1700, £2, £1 child*, a narrow-gauge passenger steam railway that runs for about a mile to Murray Park and back again (total journey time one hour). The railway station is also where you'll find the tourist information centre ⓘ *T01975-562052, daily Apr-Sep*. Also in town is the **Alford Heritage Centre** ⓘ *Mart Rd, T01975-562906, Apr-Oct Mon-Sat 1000-1700, Sun 1300-1700, £3, concession £0.50*, which has a large display of agricultural and domestic items. Alford is close to Lecht ski centre, see page 536, but you can ski here year round on the local dry ski slope, **Alford Ski Centre** ⓘ *Greystone Rd, T01975-563024*. There's also snowboarding, instruction and equipment hire.

Craigievar Castle

ⓘ *T01339-883280, castle open mid-Apr-30 Sep Fri-Tue 1200-1730 (last admission 1645); grounds open all year daily 0930-dusk, £9, £5.25 concession.*

Six miles south of Alford is one of the northeast's most gorgeous castles, the classic tower house of Craigievar, with its impressive turrets, balustrades and cupolas. The castle remains much as it was when it was built in 1626 by wealthy local merchant, William Forbes. Unfortunately, though, its popularity led to its deterioration and the NTS now restricts entry to only a small number of visitors at a time to prevent further damage. The castle stands in well-tended grounds.

Kildrummy Castle → *Phone code: 01975.*

ⓘ *T01975-571331. Apr-Sep daily 0930-1830. £2.20, £1.60 concession, £0.75 child.* Six miles west of Alford, the A944 meets the A97 which heads north towards the town of Huntly on Speyside, see page 535. A few miles south of the junction stand the extensive and impressive ruins of Kildrummy Castle, Scotland's most complete 13th-century castle. Amongst the most infamous events in the castle's long and bloody history was the treacherous betrayal of Robert the Bruce's family to the English during the Wars of Independence. It was the seat of the Earls of Mar and used as an HQ for the Jacobite rebellion of 1715, after which the 6th Earl of Mar ('Bobbing John') fled to exile in France and the castle fell into ruin.

Strathdon and Corgarff Castle

The tiny village of Strathdon, 10 miles southwest of Kidrummy, is famous for the **Lonach Highland Gathering**. Held on the third Saturday in August, it has a healthy blast of authenticity in comparison to the more glitsy affair in Braemar on Deeside.

Five miles west of Strathdon the A944 meets the A939 Ballater-Tomintoul road. A few miles beyond the junction is the austere Corgarff Castle, a 16th-century tower house, later turned into a garrison post, with an eventful and gruesome history. Here Margaret Forbes and her family were burned alive by the Gordons in 1571 during the bitter feud between the two families. In the wake of the ill-fated 1745 rebellion the government remodelled the castle, building a star-shaped defensive wall, and garrisoned 60 men to maintain order and communications in this part of the Highlands. Corgarff continued in use into the 19th century when English Redcoats were stationed here in order to prevent whisky smuggling.

Tomintoul → *Colour map 4, grid A4. Altitude: 1,600 ft.*

Beside Corgarff is the hamlet of **Cock Bridge**, standing at the end of one the most beautiful and notorious stretches of road in the country. In winter, the Tomintoul to Cock Bridge road is almost always the first road in Scotland to be blocked by snow (you have been warned!). From Cock Bridge the A939 rises steeply to the Lecht Pass (2,089 ft) before dropping dramatically to Tomintoul, the highest village in the Highlands. Tomintoul is well-placed for both the Whisky and Castle Trails. It is also the nearest settlement of any size to The Lecht, one of Scotland's top five ski resorts (see below), and it marks the end of the long-distance Speyside Way (see page 540), so is popular with walkers and skiers. TheTIC ⓘ *T01807-580285, tomintoul@agtb.org, Apr-end Oct,* is on the village square, as is the Museum and Visitor Centre ⓘ *T01807-673701, Jun-Sep Mon-Sat 1000-1600, Oct-May Mon-Fri 1000-1600, free*, which has a display of local history, wildlife, landscape and outdoor activities. Ten miles north of Tomintoul on the B9008 is the **Glenlivet Crown Estate** ⓘ *T01807-580283, www.crownestate.co.uk/glenlivet,* with an extensive network of hiking paths and cycle trails, as well as lots of wildlife, including reindeer, see also page 534.

Sleeping

Inverurie and around *p530*

A-B Pittodrie House Hotel, near Chapel of Garioch, T01467-681444, www.macdonald.hotels.co.uk. 27 rooms. This is best place to stay around Inverurie. A magnificent baronial mansion, it originally belonged to the Earls of Mar. The 2,000-acre estate was granted to them by Robert the Bruce for their loyalty at the Battle of Bannockburn. The opulent surroundings are matched by superb cuisine.

B Thainstone House Hotel, to the south of Inverurie off the A96, T01467-621643, is a luxurious country mansion offering excellent cuisine and leisure facilities.
D Breaslann Guest House, Old Chapel Rd, T01467-621608. One of a decent selection.

Alford *p531*
B-C Frog Marsh, Mossat, Alford, T01975-571355, www.frogmarshcafe.com. Good.
D Bydand, 18 Balfour Rd, T01975-563613. One of a selection of good B&Bs.
D Forbes Arms Hotel, a mile west, Bridge of Alford, T01975-562108, decent bar fod (**££-£**).

Kildrummy Castle *p532*
L Kildrummy Castle Hotel, T01975-571288, www.kildrummycastelhotel.co.uk. A baronial country mansion spectacularly sited set in beautiful grounds across the river from the castle ruins. One of the very best hotels in the northeast. It also has an excellent restaurant.

Corgarff Castle *p532*
F Jenny's Bothy, T01975-651449, open all year. Just before the castle an old military road leads for about a mile to this basic but wonderfully remote bunkhouse.

Tomintoul *p532*
C Glenavon Hotel, T01807-580218. There are a few hotels around the main square, the nicest of which is this option. It is also the best place for a drink, and popular with après-skiers, tired walkers and locals.
D Livet House, Main St, T01807-580205. A pleasant B&B.
F SYHA Youth Hostel, on Main St, T0870-0041152.

Transport

The Don Valley *p530*
Travelling around the Don Valley without your own transport is not easy. There are regular trains and buses to **Inverurie** from **Aberdeen** and **Inverness**. Bluebird Northern, T01224-212266, No 220 runs regularly every day from **Aberdeen** to **Alford** (1¼ hrs). Bus No 219 runs from **Alford** to **Strathdon** (Mon-Sat), but services beyond Strathdon are virtually non-existent. There are buses to **Tomintoul** from **Keith** via **Dufftown** (Tue and Sat only), from **Elgin** (Thu only) and from **Aberlour** (on schooldays, with connection to Elgin). For details call Roberts of Rothiemay, T01466-711213.

Speyside

→ *Colour map 2, grid C3-4.*

The River Spey is Scotland's second longest river, rising in the hills above Loch Laggan and making its way northeast to where it debouches at Spey Bay, on the Moray Coast. Speyside is one of Scotland's loveliest valleys and is synonymous with two of Scotland's greatest products, salmon and whisky. The upper part, Strathspey, is equally famous for its hiking, skiing and watersports. It is covered in the Highlands chapter (see page 423). This section covers the lower part of the valley and comprises the famous Malt Whisky Trail. There are more malt whisky distilleries in this small area than in any other part of the country, including some famous brands such as Glenlivet and Glenfiddich. However, it's not all whisky in these parts: there's also some fine walking along the Speyside Way which runs from Spey Bay south to Tomintoul. ▸▸ *For Sleeping, Eating and other listings, see pages 536-537.*

Dufftown and around

→ *Colour map 2, grid C4.*

A good place to start your whisky tour is Dufftown, founded in 1817 by James Duff, the fourth Earl of Fife, and the self-proclaimed 'Malt Whisky Capital of the World'. There's more than a grain of truth in that assertion, for there are no fewer than seven working distilleries here. This is indeed the town that was built on seven stills.

Just outside of town, on the A941 to Craigellachie, is the **Glenfiddich Distillery**, the town's most famous distillery and one of the best known of all malt whiskies, see

Whisky-a-go-go

Speyside is Scotland's most prolific whisky-producing region and the Malt Whisky Trail is a well-signposted 70-mile tour around seven of the most famous distilleries, plus the Speyside Cooperage. Most of the distilleries offer guided tours, and most (with the exception of Glenfiddich) charge an entry fee, which can then be discounted, in full or in part, from the cost of a bottle of whisky in the distillery shop. Tours also include a free dram. Those listed below are the most interesting. For more information, visit www.maltwhiskytrail.com.

Strathisla, *Keith, T01542-783044. Open Apr to Nov Mon-Sat 0930-1600, Sun 1230-1600. £4 (includes £2 discount voucher)*, is the oldest working distillery in the Highlands (1786) and perhaps the most atmospheric, in a beautiful setting on the River Isla. This is a relatively rare malt, which is also used in the better-known Chivas Regal blend.

Speyside Cooperage, *T01340-871108, all year Mon-Fri 0900-1600, £3.10, concessions £2.50, children £1.80*, is near Craigellachie, four miles north of Dufftown. Here you can watch the oak casks for whisky being made.

Cardhu, *T01340-872555, Jan-Mar Mon-Fri 1100-1500, Apr-Jun 1000-1700, Jul-Sep Mon-Sat 1000-1700, Sun 1200-1600, Oct Mon-Fri 1100-1600, Nov/Dec Mon-Fri 1100-1500, tours every 30 mins, £4*, is seven miles west of Craigellachie, at Knockando on the B9102. This lovely little distillery is now owned by United Distillers, and their fine malt is one of many used in the famous Johnny Walker blend.

Glen Grant, *T01542-783318, Apr-Oct Mon-Sat 1000-1600, Sun 1230-1600, free*, is in Rothes, on the A941 to Elgin. This distillery tour has the added attraction of a Victorian garden and orchard, woodland walks by the burn and the rebuilt 'Dram Pavilion'.

Glenfiddich, *T01340-820373, www.glenfiddich.com, Apr to mid-Oct Mon-Sat 0930-1630 and Sun 1200-1630, mid-Oct to Mar Mon- Fri only, free*, is just north of Dufftown, on the A941. Probably the best known of all the malts and the most professionally run operation. It's the only distillery where you can see the whisky being bottled on the premises, and the only major distillery that's free (including the obligatory dram).

Glenlivet, *T01542-783220, www.theglenlivet.com, Apr-Oct, free*, is 10 miles north of Tomintoul on the B9008. This was an illicit whisky until it was licensed in 1824. The distillery was later founded in 1858 and this malt has gone on to become one of the world's favourites. It was then taken over in 1978 by Seagram's.

box. Behind the distillery are the 13th-century ruins of **Balvenie Castle** ⓘ *T01340-820121, Apr-Sep daily 0930-1830, £1.80, £1.30 concession, £0.50 child*, built by Alexander 'Black' Comyn, then added to in the 15th and 16th centuries, and visited by Mary, Queen of Scots in 1562. Four miles north of Dufftown, at the junction of the A941 and A95, is the little village of Craigellachie, site of the Speyside Cooperage, see box, and where you can see Thomas Telford's beautiful bridge over the River Spey.

At nearby village of **Aberlour** is the home of **Walkers Shortbread** ⓘ *T01340-871555*. Also here is the expensive but superb **Aberlour Distillery** ⓘ *T01340-881249, www.aberlour.com, tours at 1030 and 1400 Apr-Nov Mon-Sat, and 1130 and 1500 on Sun, £7.50*. Close by is the exclusive **Macallan Distillery** ⓘ *T01340-872280, www.themacallan.com, tours every hour Mar-Oct Mon-Sat 0900-1530, Nov-Easter Mon-Fri, booking essential, free (incredibly)*.

About eight miles southwest of Craigellachie, on the A95 to Grantown-on- Spey, is beautiful **Ballindalloch Castle** ⓘ *T01807-500206, Easter-Sep Sun-Fri 1030-1700. £5 entry, £4.00 concessions, child £2.00*, a mile west of the village of **Marypark**. The castle is one of the loveliest in the northeast and has been lived in continuously by its original family, the Macpherson-Grants, since 1546. It houses a fine collection of Spanish paintings and the extensive grounds are home to the famous Aberdeen-Angus herd of cattle, which have been bred here since 1860. Also in Ballindalloch is the **Glenfarclas Distillery** ⓘ *T01807-500257, www.glenfarclas.co.uk, tours Apr-Sep Mon-Fri 1000-1700, Jun-Sep also Sat 1000-1700, Oct-Mar Mon-Fri 1000-1600, £3.50, children free*, which despite the relatively high entrance fee is a worthwhile experience.

Dufftown's Tourist Information Centre ⓘ *clock tower, centre of the main square, T01340-820501, Apr-Oct*, has maps and information on the whisky trail.

Huntly and around

→ *Colour map 2, grid C5.*

Ten miles east of Dufftown is the pleasant and prosperous-looking little town of Huntly. Close to the Whisky Trail and on the main Aberdeen to Inverness train route, it makes a convenient base from which to explore this area. The town also boasts a lovely little castle all of its own. The 16th-century **Huntly Castle** ⓘ *T01466-793191, Apr-Sep daily 0930-1830, Oct-Mar Mon-Wed and Sat 0930-1630, Thu 0930-1200, Fri and Sun 1400-1630, £3, £2.30 concession, children £1*, stands in a beautiful setting on the banks of the River Deveron, on the northern edge of town. It was built by the powerful Gordon family and is notable for its fine heraldic sculpture and inscribed stone friezes, particularly over the main door. Near the castle is the **Nordic Ski Centre** ⓘ *T01466-794428*, the only year-round cross-country ski centre in the UK. The centre also hires out ski equipment and mountain bikes. Huntly Tourist Information Centre ⓘ *T01466-792255, huntly@agtb.org, Apr-Oct.*

Seven miles south of town, near the village of Kennethmont, is **Leith Hall** ⓘ *T01464-831216, Easter 1200-1700, and 1 May-30 Sep Fri-Tue 1200-1700, garden and grounds open all year daily 0930-dusk, £7, £5.25 concession, £1.90 child*, an unprepossessing mid-17th-century mansion house. The house contains the personal possessions of successive Leith lairds, most of whom saw military service overseas, but more interesting are the extensive grounds which include a six-acre garden, 18th-century stables and ice house, two ponds, a bird observation hide and countryside walks.

▲ The Tap o' Noth walk

→ *Colour map 4, grid A5. OS Landranger No 37.*

Eight miles south of Huntly on the A97 is the village of Rhynie, where you turn off for one of the best walks in the northeast. The Tap o' Noth (1,851 ft) dominates this part of rural Aberdeenshire and the panoramic views from the top make it a worthwhile climb. It's also a fairly easy walk to the conical summit, where there's a vitrified fort. The total distance is of this walk is three miles. Allow at least two hours there and back.

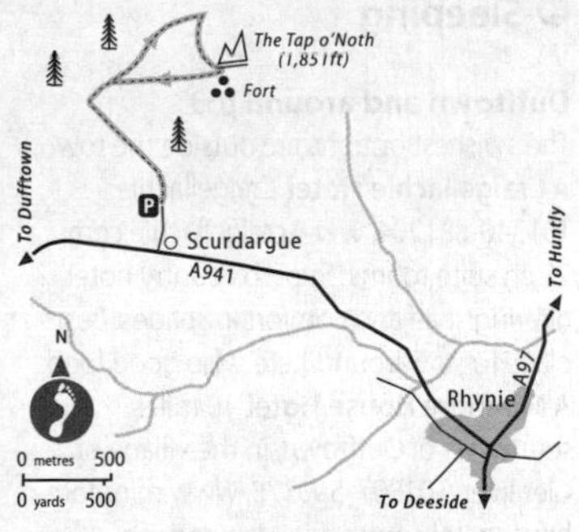

It's believed that the name, Tap o' Noth, derives from the Gaelic taip a'nochd, which translates as look-out top. But there's also a local legend that the hill's giant, Jack o'Noth, stole the sweetheart of his neighbour, Jack o'Bennachie. In retaliation, the cuckolded neighbour hurled a huge boulder and flattened Jack on his own hilltop.

Start the walk from the car park at Scurdargue, a few miles west of Rhynie, off the A941. Leave the car park and head straight up the track to a gate. Go through the gate and cross some rough pasture into woodland. At the northwest corner of the wood, go through another gate and turn left onto a track. Follow this grassy track uphill beside a fence until you see another area of forestry ahead, with rough pastureland on the right. Follow the faint track across the pasture to the broad track which then climbs up the Tap's western slopes. Follow this all the way to the top, up the tight zigzag on the southern flank and through the eastern entry to the hillfort, into a large enclosure. On the way back down look out for a subsidiary path under the fort's western ramparts. This path descends steeply to the left, south of the main track. It then joins the main track and you can retrace your steps back to the car park.

▲ The Speyside Way

The Speyside Way follows the River Spey from its mouth at Spey Bay inland as far as Ballindalloch, then crosses high moorland to Tomintoul. The 45-mile route takes three to five days to complete. Much of it is on an old railway line and passes close to several small villages, meaning that it can easily be broken down into shorter walks. It also passes several distilleries along the way. There are plans to extend the route in the next few years, from Buckie, on the Moray coast, to Aviemore.

There is no guidebook to the Speyside Way, but OS Landranger maps Nos 28 & 36 cover the entire route. Further information and route leaflets are available from the Moray Council Ranger Service ⓘ *Boat of Fiddich, Craigellachie, T01340-881266, www.moray.org/area.speyway/webpages/swhome.htm, open Easter-Oct 0900-1700.*

The Lecht → *Colour map 4, grid A5.*

ⓘ *Day ticket £15 adults, £8 for children; half-day ticket £12. There's a ski school and equipment hire at the base station, T01975-651440, thelecht@sol.co.uk. For latest snow and weather conditions call the base station, or the Ski Hotline, T09001-654657.*
The Lecht is a ski resort for all seasons. It offers dry-slope skiing throughout the year and its snowmaking facilities mean that the winter season can be extended beyond January and February. The Lecht's gentler slopes make it ideal for beginners and intermediates and the emphasis is on family skiing. There's a snowboard fun park with half pipe, log slide, gap jump and table top. However, there are also more difficult runs for the more experienced skier, and extensive off piste skiing. There's also a summer acitvity area with quad bikes, a tubing slope and funkarts.

Sleeping

Dufftown and around *p533*
The swishest options are outside the town.

A Craigellachie Hotel, Craigellachie, T01340-881204, www.craigellachie.com. 25 en suite rooms. Superb country hotel offering style and comfort in spades. Best place to stay around here. Also good food.

A Minmore House Hotel, 10 miles southwest of Dufftown, in the village of Glenlivet, T01807-590378, www.minmorehousehotel.com, open May-end Jan. Right beside the distillery and is the former home of the owner. Recommended.

C Highlander Inn, on Victoria St, Craigellachie, T/F01340-881446. Popular and serves decent bar meals.

D Gowanbrae Guest House, Dufftown, T01340-820461, www.gowanbrae-dufftown.co.uk. A good B&B.

D Tannoch Brae, Dufftown, T01340-820541, www.tannochbrae.co.uk. 6 en suite rooms. Very comfortable guest house with a reputation for fine food (**££**).

Huntly and around *p535*
There's a decent selection of places to stay in and around Huntly.

C The Castle Hotel, T01466-792696, castlehot@enterprise.net. The most impressive place to stay is this former home of the Duke of Gordon, approached through the castle entrance and then over the river.

D Greenmount Guesthouse, 43 Gordon St, T01340-792482; **D New Marnoch**, 48 King St, T01340-792018; and **D Strathlene**, on MacDonald St, T01340-792664, decent B&Bs.

Eating

Dufftown and around *p533*
££ A Taste of Speyside, Balvenie St, T01340-820860, is good choice.
££ La Faisandarie, T01340-821273, has a good reputation, book first.
£ The Fife Arms Hotel, on the square, bar fod.

Huntly and around *p535*
Auld Pit is a good pub.
Borve Brew House, Ruthven, a few miles off the A96 to Keith, good food and fine real ale.

Entertainment

Dufftown and around *p533*
Commercial Hotel, T01340-820313, Church St, has ceilidhs second Thu during summer.

Festivals and events

Speyside *p533*
Spirit of Speyside Whisky Festival, held in **May**, is a celebration of 'the water of life' with various whisky-related events taking place throughout the region. For details visit www.spiritofspeyside.com.

Transport

Speyside *p533*
A restored old train powered by a diesel engine runs from Dufftown to Drummuir (5 miles) and on to Keith (10 miles) on Sat and Sun, at 1330 and 1500, £6, T01340-821181.

Bluebird Buses, T01224-212266, run a daily service from **Elgin** (No 336). There's also a service (Nos 360 & 361) which connects **Dufftown** with **Keith** and **Aberlour** (Mon-Fri). For details call WW Smith, T01542-882113.

The Northeast Coast

→ *Colour map 2, grid C3-6.*

The northeast coast holds some of Scotland's best coastal scenery, particularly the Moray Coast from Spey Bay to Fraserburgh. Here you'll find some picturesque little villages clinging to the cliffs like limpets, and miles of windswept, deserted sandy beaches. Portsoy, Pennan, Gardenstown and Crovie are all well worth visiting, and there are great beaches at Cullen, Lossiemouth, Rosehearty and Sunnyside. Other highlights in the region include the beautiful Duff House, the working abbey at Pluscarden, and Findhorn, famous worldwide for its alternative, spiritual community.

▸▸ *For Sleeping, Eating and other listings, see pages 544-546.*

Ins and outs

The two largest towns are the hard-working, no-nonsense fishing ports of Peterhead and Fraserburgh, both linked by a regular bus service from Aberdeen. Fochabers, Elgin and Forres are all on the main Aberdeen-Inverness bus route and served regularly, and trains between Aberdeen and Inverness stop at Elgin and Forres. Otherwise, public transport is somewhat limited and it can be difficult getting to the more out-of-the-way places without your own transport. ▸▸ *For further details, see page 545.*

Pitmedden

The A90 runs north to Peterhead. Fifteen miles north of Aberdeen is the turn-off to Ellon, and five miles west of Ellon, on the A920 to Oldmeldrum, are **Pitmedden Gardens** ① *T01651-842352, 1 May-30 Sep daily 1000-1730. £5, £4 concession, £1 child*. The centrepiece of the property, the Great Garden, was originally laid out in 1675 by Sir Alexander Seton, and the elaborate, orderly floral patterns have been lovingly recreated. Also on the 100-acre site is the Museum of Farming Life, where you can see how the estate workers lived. There's a visitor centre, tea room and a woodland walk.

A mile north of Pitmedden, a side road turns left off the B999 to **Tolquhon Castle Roman** ⓘ *T01651-851286, Apr-Sep daily 0930-1830, Oct-Mar weekends only, Sat 0930-1630, Sun 1400-1630, £2.20, £1.60 concession*, (pronounced 'tee-hon'). This early 15th-century tower was built for the Forbes family and later extended with a large mansion around a courtyard. The most impressive feature is the ornamental gatehouse, but there are also other interesting original features to discover.

Haddo House

ⓘ *T01651-851440 (NTS), House Jun, Fri-Mon 1100-1630, Jul-end Aug daily 1100-1630; garden and country park open all year 0930-dusk, £7, £5.25 concession/child.*
Four miles north of Pitmedden, reached via the B9005 from Ellon, is the elegant Palladian mansion of Haddo House, one of the most impressive of Scotland's country houses. Designed by William Adam for the 2nd Earl of Aberdeen in 1732, and later refurbished in the 1880s, the house beautifully marries graceful Georgian architecture with sumptuous late-Victorian interiors. Home of the Gordon family for over 400 years, Haddo is a wonderfully tasteful legacy of how the other half lived. The house sits in 177 acres of country park, where you can stroll around the woodland and lakes, home to abundant wildlife such as deer, red squirrels and pheasants. Haddo also hosts a varied programme of music, drama and arts events. For details of forthcoming productions, contact the Haddo Arts Trust ⓘ *T01651-851770*, or the National Trust.

Fyvie Castle

ⓘ *T01651-891266 (NTS), Apr-30 Jun and Sep Fri-Tue 1200-1700, Jul-Aug daily 1100-1730, grounds open all year daily 0930-dusk, £7, £5.25 concession/child.*
Seven miles west of Haddo House is Fyvie Castle, off the A947 between Oldmeldrum and Turriff. This grandest of Scottish baronial piles is a major feature on the 'Castle Trail' and shouldn't be missed if you're in the vicinity. The castle's five towers are each named after one of the five families who have had the pleasure of living here over the centuries. The last lot only moved out in 1980 so it has a rare lived-in feel to it. The oldest part of the castle dates from the 13th century and, apart from the great wheel-stair and the 17th-century morning room, the extravagantly opulent interior largely dates from the Edwardian era. There's a superb collection of portraits including works by the likes of Raeburn, Batoni, Gainsborough and Hoppner, as well as 17th-century tapestries and collections of arms and armour. The landscaped grounds and Fyvie Loch are also worth exploring and even the tea room is great.

Newburgh to Cruden Bay

Eleven miles north of Aberdeen, the A975 turns off the A90 and makes an interesting little detour along the coast before rejoining the A90 a few miles south of Peterhead. The road crosses the mouth of the River Ythan at Newburgh and passes the dramatic Sands of Forvie, which are now part of the **Forvie National Nature Reserve**, one of Britain's largest dune systems and home to a vast array of birdlife.

Eight miles north is the little town of Cruden Bay, at the northern end of a wide sweep of sandy beach. Close by, perched on the clifftop, are the gaunt, storm-lashed ruins of **Slains Castle**, built in 1597 by the Earls of Errol. So eerily evocative is the ruin that it fired the imagination of Bram Stoker and inspired him to write *Dracula* during one of his holiday visits. The castle ruin is a 15-minute walk from Cruden Bay. From the car park at the end of the main street, head along the cliffs.

Three miles north of Slains Castle is the **Bullers of Buchan**, an amazing 245-ft deep circular basin of rocky cliff where the sea boils in through an eroded archway. In spring and summer the cliffs are home to countless thousands of seabirds. You can also reach this point from the A975, via the footpath from the car park. Take great care near the edge of the chasm and watch out for kamikaze seabirds. Cruden Bay also has a terrific **golf course** ⓘ *T01779-812285*, rated as one of the best links courses in the UK.

Peterhead and around → *Colour map 2, grid C6. Population: 18,500.*

Thirty miles north of Aberdeen is the harsh, uncompromising town of Peterhead, Europe's busiest white-fish port. Fish is Peterhead's raison d'être and everything revolves around its huge harbour. Local fishermen have not been having it so good in recent years, however, as North Sea fish stocks have become dangerously depleted and EU quotas have threatened livelihoods. The town's alternative sources of income are the power station and the high-security prison.

Peterhead may not be the most appealing prospect, but the town is rightly proud of its seafaring heritage. **Peterhead Maritime Heritage Museum** ⓘ *T01779-473000, Apr-Oct Mon-Sat 1000-1700, Sun 1200-1700, Nov-Mar Sat 1000-1600, Sun 1200-1600, £2.50, £1.50 child*, is housed in an attractive new building on South Road. It tells the story of the whaling and fishing industries and depicts the life and times of the townsfolk through a series of interactive displays and a video presentation. At the north end of town on Golf Road, at the mouth of the River Ugie, is the **Ugie Fish House** ⓘ *T01779-476209, all year Mon-Fri 0900-1700, Sat 0900-1200, free*, Scotland's oldest working fish house. Salmon and trout have been smoked here since 1585 and you can still see traditional methods being employed, and then purchase the finished product.

Nine miles west of town at **Mintlaw**, is the **Aden Country Park** (pronounced 'Ah-den'). It's a great place for kids, with numerous walks around the estate, various organized activities and events, and the **Aberdeenshire Farming Museum** ⓘ *T01771-622906, May-Sep daily 1100-1700, Apr and Oct weekends only 1200-1630, free, bus No 286 daily to and from Peterhead*, which features a semi-circular farmstead built in the early 19th century and a working farm dating from the 1950s.

Fraserburgh → *Colour map 4, grid C6. Population: 13,000.*

Eighteen miles north of Peterhead, at the very northeastern tip of the northeast coast, is the hardy, windswept fishing town of Fraserburgh. At the northern tip of the town is Kinnaird Head Castle and Lighthouse, which now houses **Scotland's Lighthouse Museum** ⓘ *T01346-511022, Apr-Oct Mon-Sat 1000-1700, Sun 1200-1700 – 1800 in summer, Nov-Mar till 1600*. This bizarre structure started out as a 16th-century castle which was then converted by the Northern Lighthouse Company in 1787 into one of mainland Scotland's first lighthouses. The museum offers a truly fascinating illumination of the engineering skill and innovation involved in the design and workings of the lighthouse, with displays of the huge lenses and prisms, as well as a history of the Stevenson family (Robert Louis' father and grandfather) who designed many of Scotland's lighthouses. The highlight is the guided tour to the top of Kinnaird Head Lighthouse itself. There's a tourist information centre ⓘ *3 Saltoun Sq, T01346-518315, fraserburgh@agtb.org, Apr-Oct Mon-Sat 1000-1300 and 1400-1700*.

Pennan, Crovie and Gardenstown → *Colour map 2, grid C5-6.*

Between Fraserburgh and Macduff/Banff lies a trio of interesting little coastal villages, clinging hungrily to the sea cliffs like babies to their mothers' breasts. The most easterly is Pennan, which shot to fame in 1982 when the hit British movie Local Hero was filmed here. The tiny hamlet lies just off the road, at the foot of a very steep hill, and consists of little more than a row of neat, whitewashed cottages, bravely challenging the North Sea. A few miles west, on the other side of Troup Head, is the equally lovely little fishing village of Gardenstown (or Gamrie, pronounced 'Game-ree'), whose streets are so precipitous you almost need to be roped up to get around on foot, never mind trying to drive a car. A stone's throw away is the even tinier village of Crovie (pronounced 'Crivvie'), which is so narrow its residents have to walk sideways.

Banff and Macduff → *Colour map 2, grid C5.*

The road west from Pennan leads on to the busy fishing port of Macduff, separated only by a bridge from neighbouring Banff, whose town centre still retains its faded

 Georgian elegance. The great attraction in the area is **Duff House** ⓘ *T01261-818181, Apr-Oct daily 1100-1700, Nov-Mar Thu-Sun 1100-1600, £4, £3 child/concession*, on the Banff side of the River Deveron, a short walk upstream from the bridge. This magnificent Georgian mansion was designed by William Adam in 1735 for local entrepreneur William Duff, who later became Earl of Fife. The house was supposed to act as the capital of Duff's huge estate, but the whole project collapsed after a major disagreement between architect and patron and ended with a lawsuit in 1747. The wings were never built but Duff House remains one of the finest Georgian baroque houses in Britain. After a variety of uses and a period of dereliction, the house has been meticulously restored and reopened as an important outpost of the National Gallery of Scotland. The extensive collection on display includes works by Scottish artists Ramsay and Raeburn, as well as an El Greco.

The house is surrounded by extensive grounds with some lovely walks through sylvan settings. The best, though, is along the banks of the River Deveron to the beautiful **Bridge of Alvah**, spanning the river across a deep gorge. It's about four miles there and back from Duff House. Leaflets showing the route are available free from Banff Tourist Information Centre ⓘ *Collie Lodge, opposite the gates of Duff House, T01261-812419, banff@agtb.org, Apr-Oct daily 1000-1300 and 1400-1700*. They offer a free hour-long walkman tour (£1 deposit) which takes you around the elegant Georgian upper town.

A mile southwest from Banff, on the A97 to Huntly, is the **Colleonard Sculpture Garden** ⓘ *daily 0930-1700, free*, a peaceful space populated by wooden sculptures carved out of tree trunks, the work of Frank Bruce, who lives in the house and can often be seen around the site.

In Macduff is the **Macduff Marine Aquarium** ⓘ *11 High Shore, T01261-833369, daily 1000-1700, £2.75, £1.50 child*. Various weird and wonderful specimens from the Moray Firth are displayed in Britain's deepest aquarium tank.

Portsoy and Cullen → *Colour map 2, grid C4-5.*

West of Banff are two of the most attractive towns on the Moray coast, Portsoy and Cullen. Portsoy is particularly lovely, with its 17th-century harbour, restored merchants' houses and narrow streets. The famous Portsoy marble, used in the building of Versailles, was quarried nearby. Six miles west is the town of Cullen, dramatically sited beneath a series of striking 19th-century railway viaducts and fronting an impressive sweep of sand. Walk east from Cullen harbour along the coast for a few miles to the lovely, deserted beach at **Sunnyside**, overlooked by the lemming-like ruin of **Findlater Castle**. There's another great beach at **Sandend**, between Portsoy and Cullen.

Fochabers and around → *Phone code: 01343. Colour map 2, grid C4.*

The A98 runs inland, bypassing the coastal town of Buckie, to reach the pleasant little town of Fochabers, 12 miles west of Cullen. The town is best known as the home of the famous Baxter family, whose name has become synonymous with food, especially soup. The Baxters factory now stands west of the bridge over the Spey by the A98, and the Baxter's Visitor Centre ⓘ *T01343-820666, www.baxters.com, factory tours Mon-Fri 1000-1130 and 1230-1600, free*, tells the story of the famous food-producing family from 1868, when George and Margaret Baxter opened their grocery shop in Spey Street. There are also factory tours on weekdays, and cooking demonstrations. **Baxter's Spey Restaurant** serves good cheap meals and snacks.

Five miles north of Fochabers, at the mouth of the River Spey, is **Spey Bay**, site of the **Tugnet Ice House** ⓘ *T01309-673701, May-Sep daily 1100-1600, free*, which was built in 1830 to store ice for packing salmon, and now houses an exhibition on the salmon industry and the wildlife of the Spey Estuary. Next door is the **Moray Firth Wildlife Centre** ⓘ *T01343-820339, www.mfwc.co.uk, Mar-Dec daily 1100-1630,*

Jul-Aug 1030-1900, £1.50, £0.75 concession, which has an exhibition on the Moray Firth dolphins, as well as other local wildlife, including grey and common seals, otters and ospreys. The centre organize wildlife cruises. The centre also houses a research unit studying the resident bottlenose dolphins. For more on the dolphins, see page 343.

Fochabers to Spey Bay

There's an excellent walk from Fochabers to Spey Bay, along the first section of the Speyside Way. Start by the old Spey Bridge and follow the B9104 for about 800 yds until you reach the 'Speyside Way' sign which takes you away from the road on to the riverside footpath. Follow this path for two miles, then, as the river swings left, look for the sign on the right showing where you leave the riverside track. Continue along this path for 500 yds, then turn left on to a minor track and, after a further 400 yds, you join a wider track and follow this all the way to Spey Bay.

You can take an alternative route back to Fochabers by turning right at the old railway track (Scottish Wildlife Trust sign) on to a track leading down to the river and then up on to the old railway viaduct and across the river. At the road bridge, take the steps on the left and go up to the road, then turn left and follow this minor road all the way back to the A98, about half a mile west of Baxters.

Instead of turning left at the end of the viaduct, you can make a short diversion into the little village of Garmouth. Here, a plaque marks the spot where King Charles II signed the Solemn League and Covenant in June 1650, thus accepting the proposed Reformation of the Church.The total distance covered is nine miles, and you should allow between four and five hours. There's no public transport to Spey Bay.

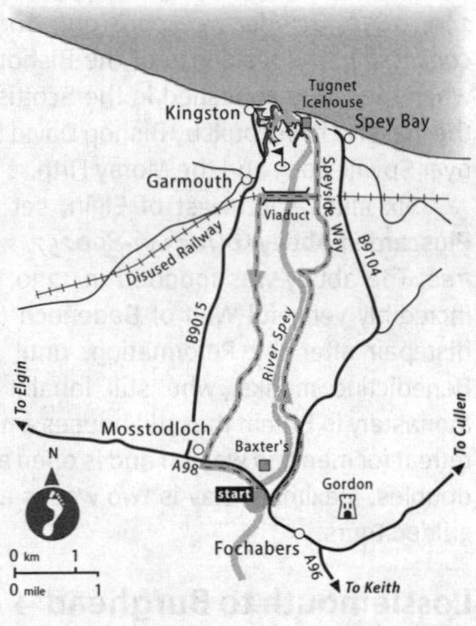

Elgin and around → *Colour map 2, grid C3. Population: 20,000.*

Nine miles west of Fochabers and 38 miles east of Inverness, is the busy market town of Elgin, which dates back to the 13th century. Elgin has retained much of its medieval streetplan, making it one of the loveliest towns in the country. There's also a good range of shops, and banks with ATMs, in the town centre.

The main tourist attraction is **Elgin Cathedral** ⓘ *North College St, T01343-547171, Apr-Sep daily 0930-1830, Oct-Mar Mon-Wed and Sat 0930-1630, Thu 0930-1200, Sun 1400-1630, £3, concession £2.30*. Though partially ruined, the scattered remains still bear testament to what was once a majestic and beautiful cathedral. Founded in 1224, the cathedral was considered the finest in Scotland until 1390 when it was burned to the ground by the big, bad 'Wolf of Badenoch', the name given to Alexander Stewart, the illegitimate son of Robert II, following his excommunication by the bishop. And if that weren't bad enough, it was rebuilt, only to suffer further damage during the orgy of vandalism that followed the Reformation. There are still some 13th-century features remaining amongst the ruins, particularly the Pictish cross-slab and the octagonal chapterhouse.

Also in town is the **Elgin Museum** ⓘ *1 High St, T01343-543675, Apr-Oct Mon-Fri 1000-1700, Sat 1100-1600, Sun 1400-1700, £2, £1 concession*. It has excellent displays of fossils and Pictish relics, as well as some interesting anthropological collections. A new distillery not yet on the Malt Whisky Trail is the friendly and highly

The light fantastic

A feature of visiting the far north of Scotland in winter is the chance of seeing the *Aurora Borealis*, or Northern Lights, which decorate the night skies like a gigantic laser show. The best time to see them is between October and March – especially during December and January. Try to get as far north as you can, though there are no guarantees of a sighting as cloud cover can obscure visibility. Any of the north-facing coastal villages are a good bet.

recommended **Glen Moray Distillery** ⓘ *Bruceland Rd, western outskirts of town, T01343-542577, www.glenmoray.com, tours all year hourly 0930-1130, 1330-1530 Mon-Fri (Sat Jun-Sep), £2*. Elgin TIC ⓘ *17 High St, T01343-542666, Apr-Oct.*

Two miles north of Elgin is **Spynie Palace** ⓘ *Apr-Sep Mon-Sat 0930-1830, Sun 1400-1830, Oct-Mar weekends only Sat 0930- 1630, Sun 1400-1630, £2.20, £1.60 concession*, the residence of the Bishops of Moray from the 14th century till 1686, when they were abolished in the Scottish Church. The palace is now a ruin, though the massive tower built by Bishop David Stewart remains, affording spectacular views over Spynie Loch and the Moray Firth.

Six miles southwest of Elgin, set in a sheltered valley, is the giant hulk of **Pluscarden Abbey** ⓘ *T01343-890257, www.pluscardenabbey.org, daily 0445-2045, free*. The abbey was founded in 1230, but in 1390 became another victim of the incredibly vengeful Wolf of Badenoch (see above). It recovered, but then fell into disrepair after the Reformation, until 1948 when it was rebuilt by an order of Benedictine monks, who still inhabit the abbey, making it the only medieval monastery in Britain that still houses a monastic community. Today it is a residential retreat for men and women and is open all year round. It has 26 single rooms and two doubles. Maximum stay is two weeks and charges are by donation. There are also guided tours.

Lossiemouth to Burghead → *Colour map 2, grid C4.*

Six miles north of Elgin is **Lossiemouth**, funnily enough at the mouth of the River Lossie. The old fishing port is blessed with two fine beaches, to the east and west of town, and an excellent golf course, making it a popular seaside resort in summer. The town's real claim to fame, though, is as the birthplace of James Ramsay MacDonald (1866-1937), Britain's first Labour prime minister.

Between 'Lossie' and Burghead, south of the coast road, is the scattered village of **Duffus**. The old part is home to a ruined 14th-century motte and bailey castle and an interesting 13th-century church, while the newer part is better known for its close neighbour, Gordonstoun School, the public school favoured (but not necessarily loved) by the royal family.

Six miles west of Lossie is the fishing village of **Burghead**, ancient Pictish capital of Moray and site of an important Iron-Age fort. The only real surviving feature is the well in King Street (you have to get the the key from No 69 King Street). The village gave its name to the **Burghead Bulls**, a series of remarkable Pictish stone carvings, some of which can be seen in the Elgin Museum (the others are in the Royal Museum in Edinburgh and the British Museum in London). The old Pictish New Year is still celebrated in the village on 11 January, when a burning tar barrel – the Clavie – is carried around. To the west of the village a wide sweep of sandy beach stretches all the way west to Findhorn, see box. There's a good chance of seeing the Moray Firth's resident population of bottlenose dolphins from here.

Garden of Findhorn

A combination of hard work and serendipity led three hard-pressed caravan dwellers in the early sixties – Peter and Eileen Caddy and Dorothy Maclean – to establish a garden in the Kinloss dunes which quickly became renowned far and wide for its miraculous abundance, owing, they claim, not only to organic methods but directions from the kingdom of nature spirits. Attracting the like-minded and curious, it grew into a pioneering community where, with an emphasis on the spiritual, the philosophy of the ecological movement was put into practice, following angelic guidance regularly channelled by two of the founding fathers.

Caravans are slowly being replaced by energy efficient houses using environmentally safe building materials, including upturned whisky barrels salvaged from a nearby distillery, with reed bed sewage systems and turf roofs. A strong educational bias brings 4,000 people annually from all over the world to participate in residential courses in personal development, community living and ecological building, or to complete a year-long 'foundation course'. In a vibrant, hot-house atmosphere overshadowed by pine trees in a warren of densely packed houses, is a community centre and a stone and timber arts centre/café architecturally inspired by the tenets of Rudolph Steiner, all giving shelter against the sea winds in order to promote plant life and greenery.

Extending worldwide by reputation, the influence of the Findhorn Foundation has also spread locally, attracting kindred spirits to settle in the area and establish initiatives such as native reforestation of the Highlands, a Steiner School and complementary health practices.

All but the most world-weary of cynics will find the Foundation a fascinating, and possibly enlightening, experience. There are guided tours around the site daily at 1400 throughout the summer.

Forres and around → *Colour map 2, grid C3.*

Twelve miles west of Elgin is the solid little town of Forres. On Invererne Road is **Benromach Distillery** ⓘ *T01309-675968, www.benromach.com, Oct-Mar Mon-Fri 1000-1600, Apr-Sep Mon-Sat 0930-1700, also Sun Jun-Aug 1200-1600, £3.* On the eastern edge of town is the 20-ft high **Sueno's Stone**, one of the most remarkable and important Pictish carved stones in Scotland. There's a tourist information centre ⓘ *116 High St, T01309-672938, Easter-Oct.*

About six miles south of Forres is one of the northeast's best-kept secrets, the very beautiful **Randolph's Leap**, a spectacular gorge on the River Findhorn which is the perfect place for a picnic, or a swim in the river. To get there, head south on the A940 and just beyond Logie Steading take the right fork (the B9007) for a half a mile. It's on the right side of the road as you head south. It's also worth stopping at **Logie Steading** ⓘ *May-Oct daily 1100-1700, weekends from 1200,* where you can buy good-value arts and crafts. A few miles west of Forres is Brodie Castle, see page 348.

Findhorn → *Colour map 2, grid C3.*

A few miles northeast of Forres is **Kinloss**, site of a major RAF base. The B9011 heads north from Kinloss and past the RAF base; on the right is a sign to the Findhorn Bay Caravan Park. In the shadow of the RAF base in a landscape of gorse and pine-clad dunes, the caravan park is the original site and nucleus of the Findhorn Foundation, a world-renowned spiritual community.

A mile north of the caravan park is the traditional fishing village of Findhorn, sparkling white under a huge sky, on the eastern shore of Findhorn Bay. The bay provides sheltered waters for boating and watersports, which can all be arranged from the village. On the other side of the bay you can walk on the dunes of **Culbin Sands**, explore the forest and look for dolphins in the Moray Firth. You may even see osprey fishing for trout or salmon. In the village itself is the **Findhorn Heritage Centre** ⓘ *Easter, Jun, Jul-Aug daily (except Tue) 1400-1700, May and Sep also weekends 1400-1700.*

Sleeping

Peterhead and around *p539*
A Waterside Inn, T01779-471121, on the road heading out of town to Fraserburgh, by the River Ugie. The best place to stay is this modern option.
E Carrick Guesthouse, 16 Merchant St, T01779-470610. Cheaper and pleasant.

Fraserburgh *p539*
Accommodation is fairly thin on the ground.
E-F Clifton House, 131 Charlotte St, T01346-518365. A comfortable B&B.

Camping
There's a campsite 5 miles west of town at Rosehearty, which has a good beach.

Pennan, Crovie and Gardenstown *p539*
E Pennan Inn, Pennan, T01466-561201. Pennan Inn is the only place to eat in the village. Good for local fish.
E Bankhead Croft, Gardenstown, T01261-851584, can provide dinner.
E The Palace Farm, Gardenstown, T01261-851261, open March-Nov. Dinner can also be provided.
Self-catering cottages in Pennan can be booked through Mrs Anne Anderson, T01466-792260, puffinspennant@btinternet.co.uk, from £150-350 per week.

Banff and Macduff *p539*
B Banff Springs Hotel, Banff, T01261-812881, is on the western outskirts of town on the A98 to Elgin. It's a friendly, modern hotel with a good restaurant (**££**).
There are several very good guest houses and B&Bs, including:
D Bryvard Guesthouse, Seafield St, Banff, T01261-818090, www.byvardguesthouse.co.uk; **D Durno House**, Netherwood, Banff, T01261-821203, www.durnohouse-scotland.co.uk; **D The Highland Haven**, Shore St, Macduff, T01261-832408; **D The Orchard**, Duff House, Banff, T01261- 812146, www.orchardbanff.co.uk; and **D-E Knowes Hotel**, Market St, Macduff, T01261-832229.

Camping
There's a campsite at **Banff Links Caravan Park**, on Boyndie Bay, T01261-812228, open Mar-Oct.

Portsoy and Cullen *p540*
The best places to stay in Cullen are:
B-C The Seafield Arms Hotel, T01542-840791, www.theseafieldarms.co.uk; **D The Bayview Hotel**, T01542-841031, both on Seafield St. There are also several B&Bs.

Elgin and around *p541*
There's a wide range of accommodation in Elgin including many fine guest houses and B&Bs.
A Mansion House Hotel, The Haugh, north of the High St, overlooking the river, T01343-548811. 23 rooms. Full leisure facilities and a good restaurant in an elegant and comfortable town house. Best of the hotels.
A-B Mansfield House Hotel, Mayne Rd (1 block south of the High St), T01343- 540883. 35 rooms. Centrally located, elegant town house. Its restaurant is very popular with locals and reputed to be the best in town (expensive). Recommended.
C The Lodge, 20 Duff Av, T01343-549981. A good guest house.
C-D Carrick House, 13 South Guildry St, T01343-569321.
C-D The Croft, 10 Institution Rd, T01343-546004. A decent guest house.
C-D The Old Church of Urquhart, T01343-843063, www.oldkirk.co.uk. For something a bit different stay at this converted church in the tiny village of Urquhart, 5 miles east of Elgin, off the A96 to Aberdeen.

C-D The Pines Guesthouse, East Rd, a short walk from the town centre T01343-552495, www.thepinesguest house.com. A highly rated guest house.

Lossiemouth to Burghead *p542*
There are a few campsites between Lossiemouth and Burghead.
Hopeman Sands Caravan Park, T01343-830880, open Apr-Nov, a couple of miles east of Burghead.
Silver Sands Leisure Park, T01343-813262, open Apr-Oct. Overlooking the beach to the west of Lossiemouth.

Forres and around *p543*
There's a surprisingly wide range of accommodation in Forres.
A Knockomie Hotel, overlooking the town on the A940 south to Grantown, T01309-673146. An excellent hotel, the best in town with a highly acclaimed restaurant.
B Ramnee Hotel, Victoria Rd, T01309-672410. Also with a highly reputed restaurant. Among the many fine guest houses and B&Bs: **D-E Sherston House**, Hillhead, T01309-671087; **D-E Springfield**, Croft Rd, T01309-676965, hbain@globalnet.co.uk.

Findhorn *p543*
You can join the community as a short-term guest, eating and working on-site and staying at local recommended B&Bs. There's a full programme of courses and residential workshops on spiritual growth and healing etc. For more information, T01309-690311.

Camping
The caravan park is open to the public and you can camp beside the Foundation, T01309-690203, caravan@findhorn.org.

Eating

Fraserburgh *p539*
££ Findlays, Smiddyhill Rd and Boothby Rd, this is the best place to eat, especially good for fish and Aberdeen Angus steaks.

Banff and Macduff *p539*
££ Fagin's, a few miles west of Banff in the little village of Whitehills, T01261-861321. Highly-rated. Fri-Sun for lunch and Wed-Sat 1900-2200.

Portsoy and Cullen *p540*
The local delicacy (and delicious it is, too) is Cullen Skink, a soup made with smoked haddock and cream. For food try the hotels listed in Sleeping.
££-£ Royal Oak and **Cullen Bay**, both on the A98 east towards Banff, are two good pubs for food.

Elgin and around *p541*
£££ Mansfield House Hotel, Elgin, see Sleeping. The best place to eat in town.
££ Littlejohn's, 193 High St, a Tex-Mex/Cajun restaurant chain that's child-friendly.
£ Ca'Dora, 181 High St, Elgin, a good fish and chip shop.
£ Gordon and McPhail, 50-60 South St, is an excellent deli, with a lip-smacking variety of fine foods and a huge range of malt whiskies.
£ Thunderton House, Thunderton Pl, off the High St. A good pub is this 17th-century option.

Findhorn *p543*
££ Crown & Anchor, off the A96, a very child-friendly pub offering good value food.
££ Kimberley Inn, T01309-690492. A good place to eat in the village is this pub which serves seafood and real ales in a colourful atmosphere.
£ Findhorn Foundation, by the car park, is the excellent on-site shop/deli at the sells a huge variety of organic food. Open Mon-Fri till 1800; weekends till 1700. There's also a very good vegetarian café. The shop also sells books and new-age paraphernalia.

Festivals and events

Portsoy and Cullen *p540*
The best time to visit Portsoy is in late **Jun**, when you can enjoy the town's excellent **Scottish Traditional Boat Festival** which features local food, street theatre and music.

Transport

Peterhead and around *p539*
Bluebird Buses, T01224-212266, run every 30 mins (Mon-Sat; every hour on Sun) from **Aberdeen**, via **Ellon** (No 260) and **Cruden Bay** (No 263).

Fraserburgh *p539*
Bluebird Buses, T01224-212266, runs regular buses to and from **Aberdeen**, via **Mintlaw**, and **Peterhead**. Buses to **Banff** via **Pennan** and **Gardenstown** (No 273; Mon-Sat).

Banff and Macduff *p539*
Bluebird Buses, T01224-212266, run services from **Banff** to **Fraserburgh** (Mon-Sat) via **Gardenstown** and **Pennan**, and from **Macduff** to **Huntly/Keith** (Mon-Sat). Bus No 305 leaves hourly (Mon-Sat; less frequent on Sun) to **Aberdeen**, and to **Elgin** via **Portsoy**, **Cullen** and **Buckie**.

Fochabers and around *p540*
Fochabers is on the main A96 Aberdeen-Inverness route and there are regular buses to and from various towns en route, such as **Elgin**, **Forres** and **Nairn**. There are also Bluebird Buses, T01224-212266, to **Banff**, via **Cullen** and **Portsoy**.

Elgin and around *p541*
The bus station is central, on Alexandra Rd, 1 block north of the High St. The train station is about 750 yds south of town, on Station Rd, off Moss St, which runs south from the High St. Elgin is well-served by public transport.

Bluebird Buses, T01224-212266, run hourly to **Aberdeen** (3 hrs) and **Inverness** (1¼ hrs) via **Nairn** (40 mins) and **Forres** (25 mins). There are buses every 30 mins to **Lossiemouth** (20 mins) and hourly to **Burghead** (Mon-Sat, 30 mins). There are buses along the coast to **Banff** and **Macduff**, hourly to **Dufftown** (1 hr) and to **Findhorn** (Mon-Sat, 20 mins). There's also a bus once a day (schooldays only) to **Pluscarden**, T01542-882482.

Trains run hourly every day to **Aberdeen** and **Inverness**, stopping at **Forres** and **Nairn**.

Forres and around *p543*
Forres is on the main Aberdeen to Inverness bus route and rail line, and there are regular buses and trains in either direction.

Bluebird Buses Nos 310 and 311 run from **Elgin** to Forres, via **Kinloss** and **Findhorn** several times daily (Mon-Sat).

Orkney & Shetland

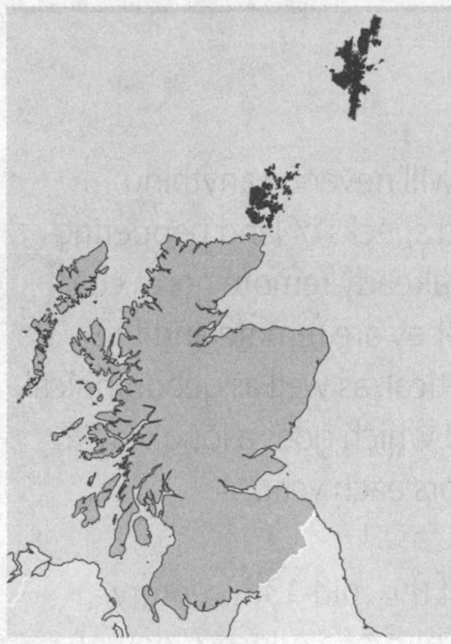

Footprint features

Introduction

To some these two archipelagos will never be anything more than distant and overlooked specks of land peppering the wild north Atlantic, above an already remote north coast of mainland Scotland. It is true – they are remote and they have maintained a social and political, as well as geographical, distance from the rest of Scotland which goes a long way to explaining the relatively few visitors each year.

Orkney was under Norse rule until the mid-13th century, and Shetland was only 'given' (as part of a princess' dowry) to Scotland in 1469. Somehow, seeing them as a part of Scotland can be very misleading and each must be seen within the context of its own unique cultural background and unusual geography.

It is these two qualities that make the islands worth visiting and the ones that the tourist boards are keen to plug. Both Orkney and Shetland are littered with outstanding archaeological evidence, not just of Norse occupation, such as at **Jarlshof** at the very southern tip of Shetland, but also of life back in 3000 BC at **Skara Brae** and the **Knap of Howar** in the Orkneys. They are also the best places in Britain to see **wildlife** as yet untamed by the 21st century. Here you can sail alongside porpoises and seals, and watch a million migratory seabirds nest and bring up their young during the summer months. And, thanks to fast and frequent transport links, it doesn't take an Arctic expedition to get here.

★ Don't miss...

❶ **Stromness** Explore the winding streets of one of the most fascinating fishing villages in Scotland, page 555.

❷ **Maes Howe and Skara Brae** Visit these amazing archaeological wonders, page 557 and 558.

❸ **Island of Lamb Holm** Visit the incredible little Italian Chapel, page 560.

❹ **Old Man of Hoy** Take the spectacular clifftop walk to meet the Old Man of Hoy, page 563.

❺ **Westray to Papa Westray** Fly to one island from the other, it takes all of two minutes, page 566.

❻ **Mousa** Visit the best-preserved broch in Scotland, page 581.

❼ **Fair Isle** Brave the white-knuckle boat trip to one of the best places on earth for birdwatching, page 583.

❽ **Hermaness National Nature Reserve** Explore the dramatic coastal scenery of this nature reserve, page 586.

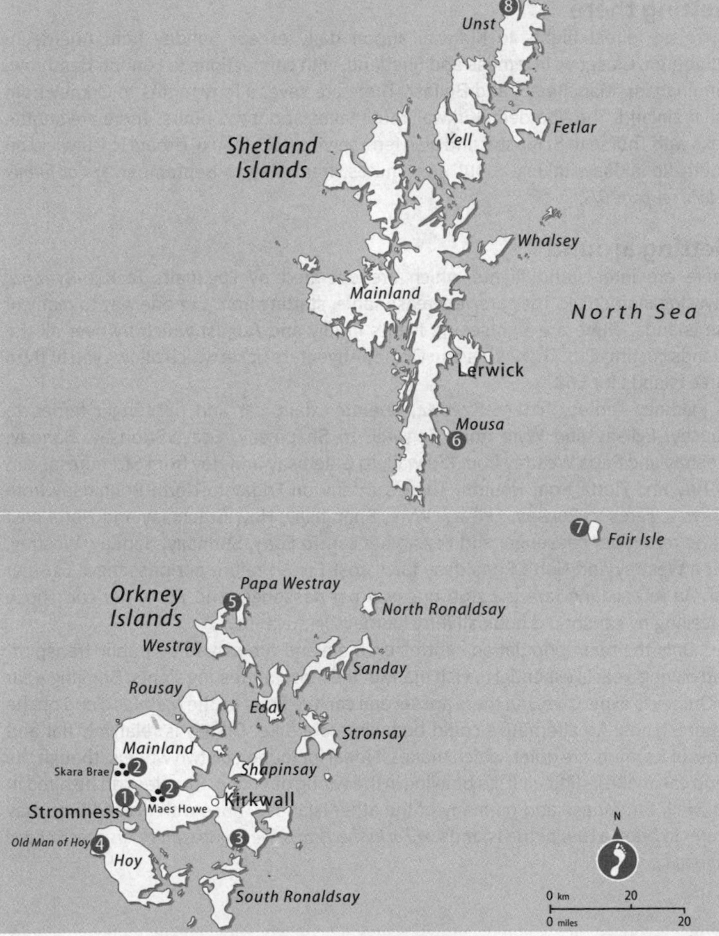

Orkney

Orkney may only be a short step away from John O' Groats, but to the fiercely independent Orcadians, 'Mainland' means the largest of the Orkney islands and not the Scottish mainland. Mainland is also the site of the two main towns and ferry terminals: the capital Kirkwall and the beautiful old fishing port of Stromness. Here, you'll also find many of Orkney's most precious archaeological treasures: the Stones of Stenness, Maes Howe, the Broch of Gurness and the remarkable Neolithic village of Skara Brae. Aside from Mainland, there are a dozen smaller islands to explore, including Hoy, with its wild, spectacular coastal scenery. The even more remote northerly islands offer miles of deserted beaches, and nothing but the calls of myriad birds to shatter the all-pervading peace and quiet. ▸▸ *For Sleeping, Eating and other listings, see pages 568-574.*

Ins and outs

Getting there

There are direct flights to Kirkwall airport daily except Sunday from Aberdeen, Edinburgh, Glasgow, Inverness and Shetland, with connections to London Heathrow, Birmingham, Manchester and Belfast. There are several ferry routes to Orkney from the mainland. The Aberdeen-Kirkwall route takes about 7½ hours. There are shuttle links with Thurso to Scrabster and also ferry service from John o' Groats to Burwick, on South Ronaldsay, taking about 40 minutes, from May to September. ▸▸ *For further details, see page 572.*

Getting around

There are inter-island flights which are operated by Loganair, T01856-872494, www.loganair.co.uk. They are very reasonable, starting from £12 one way to many of the islands. There are sightseeing flights in July and August which fly over all the islands costing £30. There's also an Orkney Adventure ticket which allows you to fly to three islands for £68.

Orkney Ferries, T01856-872044, operates daily car and passenger ferries to Rousay, Egilsay and Wyre from Tingwall; to Shapinsay, Eday, Stronsay, Sanday, Westray and Papa Westray from Kirkwall; to Graemsay and Hoy from Stromness; and to Hoy and Flotta from Houton. There's a ferry on Friday to North Ronaldsay from Kirkwall. Fares to Rousay, Egilsay, Wyre, Shapinsay, Hoy, Graemsay and Flotta cost £5.80 return per passenger and £17.50 per car. To Eday, Stronsay, Sanday, Westray, Papa Westray and North Ronaldsay fares cost £11.60 return per passenger £26 per car. An inter-island fare is £2.90 one-way per passenger and £6.55 per car. Those travelling by car should book all ferry journeys in advance.

Only the main population centres on Mainland are served by public transport, and having a car is essential to visit many of the most interesting sights. Bringing a car to Orkney is expensive, but there are several car hire firms on the Mainland and on the other islands. An alternative could be taking to a bike. Orkney is relatively flat and most of its roads are quiet, which makes it ideal for touring on two wheels, though the wind can make it difficult if it's blowing in the wrong direction. Bicycles can be hired in Kirkwall, Stromness and on many of the other islands. Those with limited time may prefer to book a tour of the islands. ▸▸ *For further details, see Activities and tours page 571 and Transport page 572.*

Learning the lingo

Despite the disappearance of the Norse language, many of the Viking place names have survived. Here are some of the most common Old Norse elements which will help explain the meaning of many place names:

A(y)	island	holm	small island
a, o	stream	houb	lagoon
aith	isthmus	howe	mound
ayre	beach	kirk	church
bard	headland	lax	salmon
bister	farm	ler	mud, clay
brae, brei	broad	lyng	heather
fell, field	hill	minn	mouth
fors	waterfall	mool, noup	headland
garth	farm	setter	farm
geo	creek	ting	parliament
grind	gate	toft	house site
ham(n)	anchorage	voe	sea inlet

Tourist information

Orkney Tourist Board, www.visitorkney.com, has tourist offices in Kirkwall and Stromness. They will book accommodation for you, or provide a list of what's available, though many B&Bs are not included in the tourist board scheme. They can also provide information on various sights, walks and the islands' wildlife. Those wishing to leave Mainland and visit the smaller islands should pick up a free copy of the tourist board's excellent information and travel guide, *The Islands of Orkney*.

Many of Orkney's monuments are managed by Historic Scotland. They include the Bishop and Earl's Palaces, Broch of Gurness, Maes Howe, Skara Brae and Skaill House, Brough of Birsay and Hackness Martello Tower. If you plan to visit all or most of these sights, it may be cheaper to buy a three, seven or 10-day Historic Scotland Explorer Ticket, which costs £16, £22 and £25 respectively.

Kirkwall → *Phone code: 01856. Population: 7,000.*

Orkney's capital is built around a wide sheltered bay and is the main departure point for ferries to the northern islands. First impressions are a little misleading, as the harbour area has been blighted by modern development. More appealing, however, are the narrow winding streets and lanes of the old town, which has not changed much over the centuries. There are many houses dating from the 16th, 17th and 18th centuries, as well as Kirkwall's greatest attraction, its magnificent cathedral, the finest medieval building in northern Scotland. ▸▸ *For Sleeping, Eating and other listings, see pages 568-574.*

Ins and outs

Getting there and around The airport, T01856-872421, is three miles southeast of Kirkwall on the A960. There are no buses to and from town. A taxi will cost around £6. The bus station is five minutes' walk west of the town centre. The town is compact and it's easy to get around on foot. The main street changes its name from Bridge Street to Albert Street, to Broad Street and Victoria Street as it twists its way south from the

Orkney

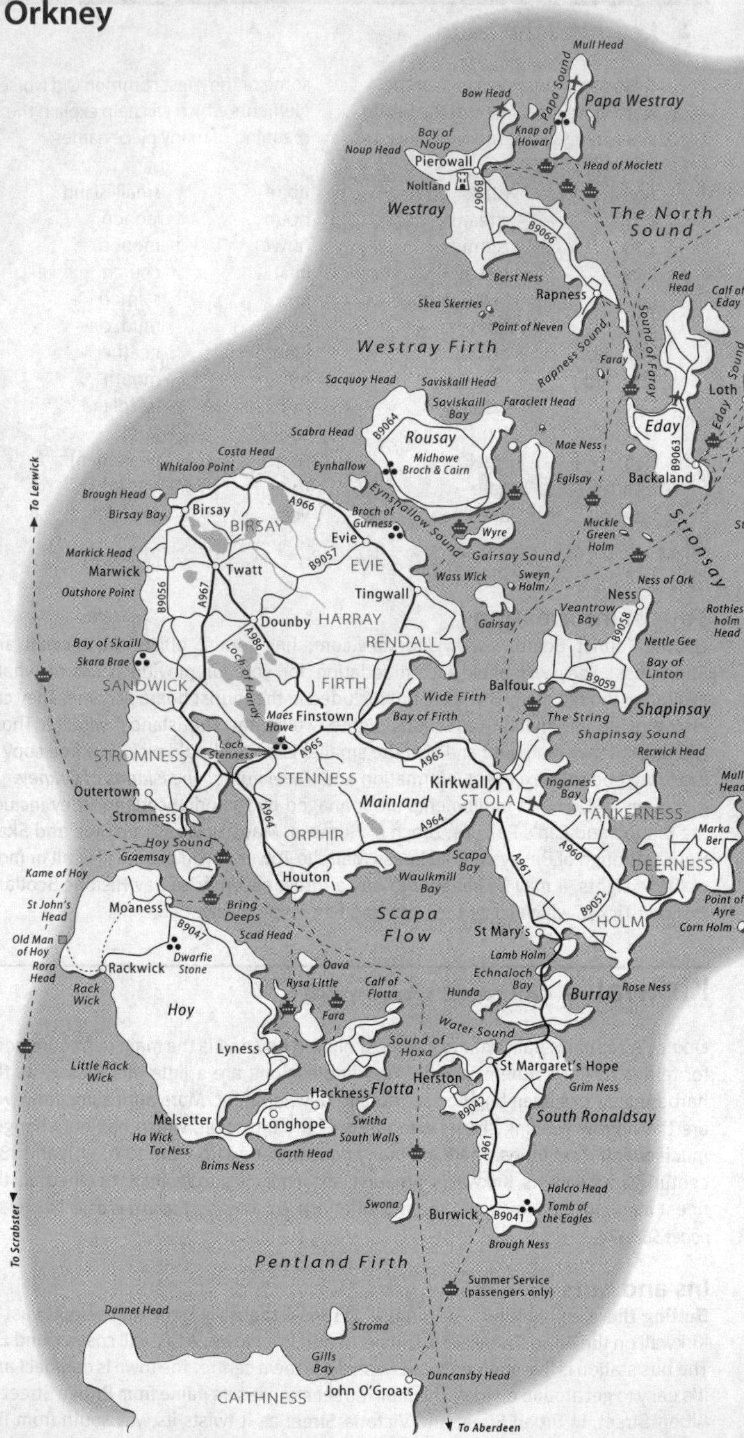

Orkney & Shetland Kirkwall

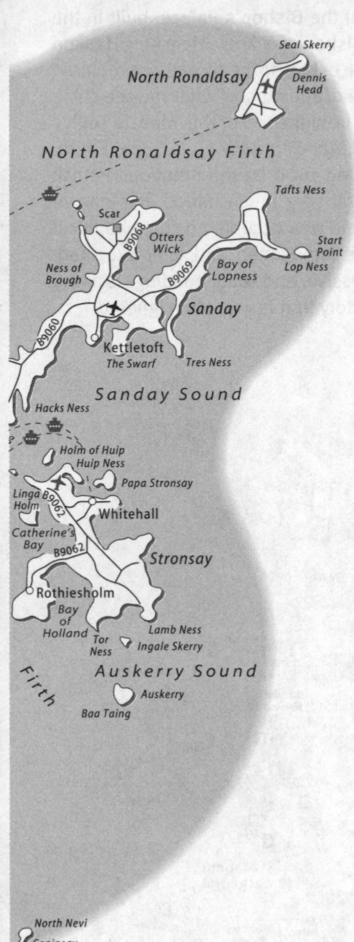

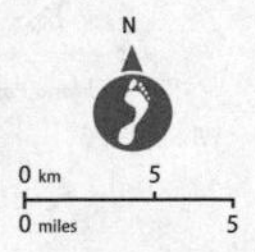

busy harbour. The cathedral is on Broad Street, and most of the shops and banks are on Broad Street and Albert Street.

▸▸ *For further details, see Transport page 572.*

Tourist information On Broad Street, near the cathedral, is the very helpful TIC ⓘ *T01856-872856, info@otb.ossian.net, Apr-Sep 0830-2000, Oct-Mar Mon-Sat 0930-1700*. Service they provide include booking accommodation and changing money, and they also has various useful free leaflets including *The Islands of Orkney and the Kirkwall Heritage Guide*. They also stock a wide range of guidebooks and maps, and have details of forthcoming events. Another good source is the weekly newspaper *The Orcadian*.

Sights

The town's outstanding sight is the huge and impressive red sandstone **St Magnus Cathedral** ⓘ *Apr-Sep Mon-Sat 0900-1800, Sun 1400-1800, Oct-Mar Mon-Sat 0900-1300 and 1400-1700, Sun service at 1115*, built by masons who had worked on Durham Cathedral in the north of England. It was founded in 1137 by Rognvald Kolson, Earl of Orkney, in memory of his uncle, Magnus Erlendson, who was slain by his cousin, Haakon Paulson, on Egilsay in 1115. Magnus was buried at Birsay and it is said that heavenly light was seen over his grave. It soon became a shrine, attracting pilgrims from as far afield as Norway. Magnus was canonized in 1133, and four years later his nephew commissioned construction of the cathedral. The building wasn't completed until the 14th century, and major additions were made during the intervening centuries. The most recent addition was a new west window for the nave, to celebrate the cathedral's 850th anniversary in 1987. The bones of St Magnus now lie in the north choir pillar, while those of St Rognvald lie in the south one. There's also a memorial to John Rae, the 19th-century Arctic explorer who is buried in the graveyard, as well as a monument to the 833 men of the *HMS Royal Oak* who died when it was torpedoed in Scapa Flow in 1939.

Looming impressively nearby are the ruins of the **Bishop's Palace**, built in the 12th century as the first Kirkwall residence of the Bishop of Orkney. Here King Haakon of Norway died in 1263 after his defeat at the Battle of Largs. The palace was repaired and extended in the mid-16th century by Bishop Reid, and most of what you see dates from that period. There's a good view of the town from the top of the 'Moosie Too'r'.

The adjacent **Earl's Palace** ⓘ *T01856-871918, Apr-Sep daily 0930-1830, £2.20, concession £1.60, children £0.75*, was built around 1600 by the notorious Patrick Stewart, Earl of Orkney, using forced labour. Still very much intact, it is one of Scotland's most elegant Renaissance buildings and was occupied by the tyrannical Stewart only for a very short time, until he was imprisoned and later executed. Wandering around both these spectacularly impressive, and solid, buildings is a very good way to get a feel for a period of Orkney's history that is very often ignored.

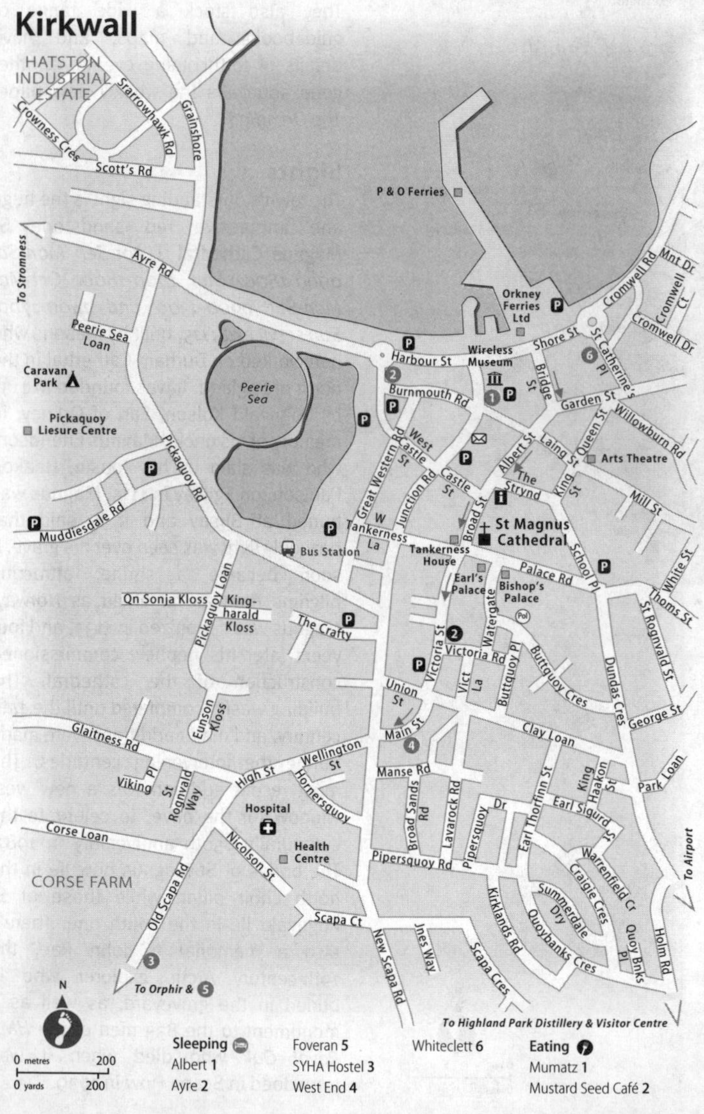

Opposite St Magnus Cathedral is **Tankerness House and Gardens**, a 16th-century former manse which has been restored and now houses the **Orkney Museum** ⓘ *T01856-873191, Oct-Mar Mon-Sat 1030-1230, 1330-1700, Apr-Sep 1030-1700, May-Sep also Sun 1400-1700, free*, which features various archaeological artefacts from Neolithic times to the Vikings. If you are spending any time in Kirkwall at the beginning of your stay, then this is an exceedingly worthwhile exhibition. It is a great way to whet your appetite for the archaeological gems that are lying in wait for you all over the islands, and it also puts them into a useful chronological context.

Old radio buffs should not miss the **Orkney Wireless Museum** ⓘ *Apr-Sep Mon-Sat 1000-1630, Sun 1400-1630, £2, children £1*, at Kiln Corner, at the harbour end of Junction Road, which houses a jumble of domestic and wartime communications equipment from the 1930s onwards.

A mile south of the town centre on the road to South Ronaldsay is the 200-year-old **Highland Park Distillery** ⓘ *T01856-874619, www.highlandpark.co.uk, tours every half hour Apr, Sep and Oct Mon-Fri 1000-1700, May-Aug Mon-Sat 1000-1700, Sun 1200-1700, Nov-Mar Mon-Fri at 1400 only, £4*, the most northerly of Scotland's whisky distilleries and one of the very best. It's one of the few that still has its own floor maltings – as well as it's own mouser cat – and there's a dram of this particularly fine single malt at the end.

Stromness and West Mainland → *Phone code: 01856.*

Ferries from Scrabster arrive in Stromness, and the newcomer is greeted by rows of stone-built houses hugging the shore, each with their own jetty. Stromness is a much more attractive town than Kirkwall, and its narrow, winding main street, its *wynds* and *closes*, its fascinating shops, and its unique atmosphere make it the ideal base for exploring the West Mainland, the name given to everything west of Kirkwall. It's an area of rich farmland, rolling hills and moorland, fringed by spectacular cliffs along the Atlantic coastline and with the greatest concentration of prehistoric monuments in Britain. Here you'll find, amongst many others, the well-preserved Neolithic village of **Skara Brae**, silent monuments to human endeavour in the form of the standing **Stones of Stenness** and the **Ring of Brodgar**, and the chambered tomb of **Maes Howe**, with its many still unresolved mysteries. ›› *For Sleeping, Eating and other listings, see pages 568-574.*

Ins and outs

Stromness Tourist Information Centre ⓘ *T01856-850716, Apr-Oct Mon-Sat 0800-1800, Sun 0900-1600, Nov-Mar Mon-Fri 0900-1700*, is at the new ferry terminal. Its exhibition, This Place Called Orkney, is a useful introduction to the islands, and its free *Stromness Heritage Guide* takes you round all the buildings of interest in the town. ›› *For details of Transport, see pages 550 and 562.*

Stromness

Stromness is one of the classic Scottish fishing villages and a perfect introduction to Orkney. Though referred to in the Viking Saga as Hamnavoe, the town in fact dates from the 17th century. Its importance as a trading port grew in the 18th century when wars and privateers made the English Channel too dangerous and ships used the northern route across the Atlantic, calling in at Stromness to take on food and water and to hire local men as crew. Until the late 19th century, ships of the Hudson Bay Company made Stromness their main base for supplies, and used **Login's Well** as a source of fresh water. Whaling ships bound for Greenland also hired local labour. By the late 19th century the herring boom had reached Stromness and there were 400 boats using its harbour, but within two decades the boom was over due to

Scandanavian settlements

The history of Orkney and Shetland is bound up with the history of the Vikings, who first came to the islands in the latter half of the ninth century and stayed for about 650 years. This was part of a great Viking expansion westwards, and in less than a century emigrants from Norway and Denmark settled in Orkney, Shetland, Iceland, Greenland, Caithness, the Western Isles, Isle of Man and parts of Ireland and the northern half of England.

In 872 the King of Norway set up a Norse earldom in Orkney, from which the Vikings ruled Orkney, Shetland and the Western Isles and took part in raids around Britain and Europe, creating the popular image of Vikings as aggressive, bloodthirsty invaders. At home, however, they lived a peaceful life, adhering to the laws of their parliament, the ting, and many converted to Christianity.

In the late 14th century Norway, Denmark and Sweden were united under a Danish king. In 1469 the Royal estates and prerogatives in Orkney and Shetland were pledged to Scotland as part of the marriage dowry of Margaret, daughter of the King of Denmark, on her marriage to Prince James of Scotland, later to become King James III. Orkney and Shetland were to revert to rule by the kings of Norway when the debt was paid, but the pledge was never redeemed and the islands remained under Scottish control.

Soon after assuming control, the Scots began to change the old Norse laws which they had agreed to maintain, and Scottish influence grew. In 1564 Mary, Queen of Scots granted the control and revenues from Orkney and Shetland to her half-brother, Robert Stewart. His prime motivation, however, was to extract as much money as possible through taxes. He was succeeded by his son, the infamous Patrick Stewart, who demanded even more rents, dues and fines. Earl Patrick eventually got his come-uppance when he was executed in Edinburgh for treason, but the changes he had made continued and Scots and English gradually began to usurp Old Norse as the native language of the islands.

over-fishing. Today Stromness remains a fishing port, as well as Orkney's main ferry terminal and the headquarters of the Northern Lighthouse Board.

Stromness consists largely of one narrow, winding main street, paved with flagstones, which hugs the shoreline. Running off the street are numerous little lanes and alleyways, many with fascinating names such as **Khyber Pass**, and full of interesting buildings which reflect the town's proud maritime heritage. The houses on the seaward side of the street are gable end to the waterfront and each has its own jetty. The town is not designed for the car, so you'll have to park by the harbour and explore its delights on foot. The main street changes its name from Victoria Street to Graham Place, Dundas Street, Alfred Street and South End as it runs south from the harbour.

Stromness Museum ⓘ *52 Albert St, T01856-850025, May-Sep daily 1000-1700, Oct-Apr Mon-Sat 1030-1230 and 1330-1700, £2.50, children £0.50*, has exhibitions on natural and maritime history, and contains artefacts from Scapa Flow and the days of the Hudson Bay company. Opposite the museum is the house where **George Mackay Brown** (1921-1996), Orkney's most famous poet and story-writer, spent the last two decades of his life, see also page 613. On a jetty to the south of the new harbour is the excellent **Pier Arts Centre** ⓘ *Tue-Sat 1030-1230 and 1330-1700, Jul and*

Aug also Sun 1400-1700, free, housing a permanent collection of works of the St Ives school, including Barbara Hepworth, Ben Nicholson and Patrick Heron, amongst others, in a lovely gallery.

Skara Brae and Skaill House

ⓘ *T01956-841815, Apr-Sep daily 0930-1830. £5, concession £3.75, children £1.30. Oct-Mar (Skara Brae only) Mon-Sat 0930-1630 and Sun 1400-1630. £4, concessions £3, children £1.20.*

Eight miles north of Stromness, in the magnificent setting of the dazzling white sands of the Bay of Skaill, is Skara Brae, the best-preserved Stone-Age village in northern Europe. First revealed in 1850 after a violent storm blew away the dunes, the site dates from around 5,000 years ago and was occupied for about 600 years.

The houses contain stone furniture, fireplaces, drains, beds, dressers and even have damp-proof coursing in the foundations. The whole complex presents a unique picture of the lifestyle of its inhabitants, and there's also a replica 'house' that you can enter, and wander around in through the gloom, empathizing with that 3000 BC lifestyle.

The swish, modern visitor centre has a useful introductory video and exhibition which is definitely worth seeing before you look round the site (and it's also worth buying their guidebook). After leaving the visitor centre, you walk down a 'path of time', which takes you back through landmark achievements of the last seven millennia, gradually building up the suspense and putting the achievements of Skara Brae in perspective – they may only be rudimentary buildings that once had turf for their rooves, but they were built 2,000 years before the pyramids of Egypt, and in one of the world's most northerly outposts.

During the summer a ticket to Skara Brae includes admission to nearby **Skaill House**, an early 17th-century mansion which contains a few old artefacts, including Captain Cook's dinner service from the Resolution, but is a bit of a let-down after what you will have just witnessed, not 300 yds away at Skara Brae.

Sandwick and Yesnaby

A short distance inland from here, at Sandwick, is Orkney's only brewery, housed in the old Quoyloo School. It brews the island's Raven Ale and various bottled beers, including Skull-splitter, named after the Viking Earl, Thorfinn Skull-splitter.

South of the Bay of Skaill is Yesnaby, one of the most spectacular places on the islands, where the cliffs have been eroded into a series of stacks and geos by the fierce Atlantic seas. An exhilarating, and precarious, half-mile walk south from the car park and old Second World War lookout post brings you to **Yesnaby Castle**, a huge sea stack similar to the Old Man of Hoy. It's a dramatic sight, especially in a full force gale.

Standing Stones of Stenness and Ring of Brodgar

Northeast of Stromness on the road to Kirkwall is the tiny village of **Stenness**, near some of Orkney's most interesting prehistoric sites. The Standing Stones of Stenness comprise the four remaining stones from an original circle of 12 stones, dating from 3000 BC. The largest of the stones stands over 15 ft high. A path leads from the stones to the nearby **Barnhouse Settlement**, a recently excavated Neolithic village.

About a mile northwest of Stenness is another stone circle, the **Ring of Brodgar**. This is a particularly impressive henge monument. It is over 100 yds in diameter and 27 of the original 60 stones are still standing, some of them up to 15 ft high. Given the importance of these sites, it is particularly refreshing to realize when you get there that you can walk about amongst the stones in the still calm of a summer evening, with only a few oyster catchers for company, but both do get busy with coach parties during the day.

Maes Howe

ⓘ *T01856-761606, Apr-Sep daily 0930-1830, Oct-Mar Mon-Sat 0930-1630 and Sun 1400-1630. £3, concession £2.30, children £1, tickets bought from Tormiston Mill, on the other side of the road, where there's an exhibition, introductory video and café.*

Less than a mile northeast of the Stones of Stenness is Maes Howe, the finest Neolithic burial chamber in Europe. It was built around 2750 BC, making it contemporary with the Standing Stones and Skara Brae, and is amazingly well preserved. A huge mound covers a stone-built entrance passage which leads into a central chamber – over 12 ft square and the same in height – with three smaller cells built into the walls of the tomb.

When it was opened in 1861, no human remains or artefacts were found, giving no clues as to its usage. However, in the 12th century Vikings returning from the Crusades broke into the tomb searching for treasure. They found nothing but left behind one of the largest collections of runic graffiti anywhere in the world, as well as carvings of a dragon, serpent and walrus. Many of the inscriptions are pretty basic, along the lines of 'Thorfinn wrote these runes', but some are more intriguing, such as 'Many a woman has come stooping in here no matter how pompous a person she was'.

A guide gives you an excellent overview of the chamber's mysterious architectural attributes, but the fact remains that the history of this extraordinary place is still largely unsolved – something that obviously adds to the site's attraction. Unfortunately, you do not get the chance to spend very much time in the chamber, so you are unlikely to uncover any great secrets.

Orphir

On the southern shores of West Mainland, overlooking Scapa Flow, is the scattered community of Orphir, which has a few sights worth visiting, especially if you're heading across to Hoy from the ferry terminal at **Houton**, a little further west. The main point of interest in Orphir is the **Orkneyinga Saga Centre** ⓘ *all year daily 0900-1700, free*, where a small exhibition and video introduces the saga, written circa 1200, possibly by an Icelander, which tells the history of the Viking Earls of Orkney from around AD 900 to AD 1200, when the islands became a part of Scotland rather than Norway. As you would expect, there's plenty of gore and Machiavellian goings-on, including an assassination attempt that went disastrously wrong, when a poisoned shirt meant for Earl Harold was unwittingly and fatally worn by his brother Paul instead.

For details of ferries to Hoy and Flotta, see page 562. For details of buses to Houton, see page 572.

Behind the centre is **The Earl's Bu**, looking out across Orphir Bay south to Cava Island. These are the 12th-century foundations of the home of the Norse Earls of Orkney written about in the saga. Inside the cemetery gates is a section of the circular church built by Haakon and modelled on the rotunda of the Church of the Holy Sepulchre in Jerusalem.

Markwick Head

At the southern end of Birsay Bay are the wild and spectacular 300 ft-high cliffs of Marwick Head, topped by the distinctive **Kitchener Memorial**, erected after the First World War to commemorate Lord Kitchener and the crew of the *HMS Hampshire*, which was sunk by a German mine off the coast in 1916 with the loss of all but 12 of her crew. Marwick Head is also an **RSPB Reserve**, and during the nesting season in early summer is home to many thousands of guillemots, razorbills, kittiwakes and fulmars, as well as a few puffins.

A fascinating feature of Maes Howe is that the winter solstice sun sets directly over the Barnhouse Stone, half a mile away, and shines down the entrance passage of Maes Howe and on to the back wall of one of the cells.

A mile inland, by the Loch of Isibister, is another RSPB reserve, **The Loons**, an area of marshland where you can see breeding and migrating wildfowl and waders. Further east, between Boarhouse Loch and Hundland Loch, is the **Kirbuster Farm Museum** ⓘ Mar-Oct Mon-Sat 1030-1300 and 1400-1700, Sun 1400-1900, free, the last surviving Orkney 'black house' which was inhabited till the 1960s and gives an insight into 19th-century rural life on the islands.

Birsay

At the far northwestern corner of the Mainland is the parish of Birsay, which was a favourite residence of the Earls of Orkney in Viking times as well as the first seat of the Bishop, before the building of St Magnus Cathedral in Kirkwall. Earl Thorfinn the Mighty lived here (1014-1064) and built Orkney's first cathedral, **Christchurch**, for the new Bishop.

In the centre of the village are the ruins of the **Earl's Palace** ⓘ *T01856-721205, open at all times, free*, built by the infamous Earl Robert Stewart in the late 16th century, and once described as "a sumptuous and stately dwelling". Not much remains today, but enough to give some idea of the sheer scale of the place. Close by is **St Magnus church**, built in 1760 on the site of an earlier church, which in turn was built on the foundations of what is believed to be the original Christchurch. Also in Birsay, just south of the A966 and A967 junction, is **Barony Mills** ⓘ *Apr-Sep daily 1000-1300 and 1400-1700, £1.50*, the last working water-powered mill in Orkney.

Lying half a mile off the coast near the village is the **Brough of Birsay** ⓘ *open (when tides permit) 11 Jun-30 Sep daily 0930-1830, £1.80, concession £1.30, children £0.50, phone the Earl's Palace (see above)*. The tidal island, now managed by Historic Scotland, jutts out into the north Atlantic and is visible from several other points all the way down the west cost of the mainland. It is only accessible for a couple of hours at low tide (times available from Kirkwall and Stromness tourist offices) but, if possible, it is best seen at the end of the day, as the sun sets – and you'll probably have the whole island to yourself. Pick your way over the shell- and bladderack-strewn causeway and wander at your leisure (but don't forget the tide!) amongst the remnants of a Pictish, and then Viking, community. The island was an important Pictish settlement from around the sixth century, and many artefacts have been found here. Some of these can be seen at the small ticket office at the entrance to the island. The Brough was also the site of an important Viking settlement, and there are extensive remains, including the 12th-century **St Peter's church** where St Magnus was buried after his murder on Egilsay. You can also walk out to the island's lighthouse along the top of the cliffs and see puffins – amongst other migrating seabirds – and possibly Minke whales, Pilot whales and Killer whales.

Evie and the Broch of Gurness

Nine miles northwest of Kirkwall is the tiny village of Evie. A track leads from the village towards the coast, past a sandy beach, to the **Broch of Gurness** ⓘ *T01856-751414, Apr-Sep daily 0930-1830, £3, concession £2.30, children £1*. Standing on a lonely, exposed headland on the north coast, with warm, gentle views across towards the island of Rousay, this is the best-preserved broch on Orkney, thought to date from around 100 BC. It is surrounded by an Iron-Age village whose houses are also remarkably well-preserved, with the original hearths, beds, cupboards and even a toilet still in evidence. The broch and village were occupied by the Picts right up till Viking times, around AD 900. Many Pictish artefacts have been found on the site, and the grave of a ninth-century Norse woman was also discovered.

To the southwest of Evie is the **Birsay Moors RSPB Reserve**, and at **Lowrie's Water** on Burgar Hill there's a bird-hide from where you can watch breeding red-throated divers. Also on Burgar Hill you'll see several huge aerogenerators built to take advantage of Orkney's fierce winds.

East Mainland and South Ronaldsay → *Phone code: 01856.*

The East Mainland is mainly agricultural land and though it contains little of the amazing archaeological wealth of its western counterpart, there are some attractive fishing villages, fine coastal walks and many poignant reminders of Orkney's important wartime role. Linked to East Mainland by a series of causeways, South Ronaldsay is the southernmost of the Orkney islands, only six miles from the Scottish mainland across the stormy Pentland Firth, the most dangerous stretch of water in the British Isles. A small passenger ferry crosses to Burwick on the southern tip of the island from John O' Groats. » *For Sleeping, Eating and other listings, see pages 568-574.*

Deerness

There is not much to see inland on the road running southeast from Kirkwall past the airport, but head on towards the Deerness Peninsula and you will be richly rewarded by a truly serene, gentle beauty. There are sandy bays, which make for very pleasant short walks and picnics (if you can find a sheltered spot), jutting cliffs and a great variety of birdlife. The peninsula makes the West Mainland seem positively crowded by comparison, and is one of the best places on the Mainland to 'get away from it all'.

▲ When the weather's good, the view southwest from Sandside Bay to the Isle of **Copinsay** (an RSPB reserve) is glorious, and, as it emerges slowly and gracefully from the wild North Sea, is a perfect example of the whale-like properties that have been attributed to the Orkneys by the islands' most famous poet George Mackay Brown. There is a footpath following the coast from Sandside Bay to Mull Head (a Nature Reserve) and round the tip of the peninsula to the Covenanters Memorial (1679), a five-mile circular walk.

▲ If you continue along the B9050, the road ends at The Gloup car park at Skaill Bay, from where it's a 200-yd walk to **The Gloup**, a dramatic collapsed sea cave, separated from the sea by a land bridge about 80 yds wide. The word comes from the Old Norse 'gluppa', meaning chasm, the local name for a blow-hole. A network of signposted footpaths covers the northeastern part of the peninsula and there are circular walks of between two and five miles which start from The Gloup car park. At the northeastern tip is **Mull Head**, a clifftop nature reserve which is home to guillemots, shags, fulmars, razorbills, terns and skuas.

On the south coast of East Mainland, near the northern end of the Churchill Barriers, is the old fishing village of **St Mary's**, once a busy little place but largely forgotten since the building of the causeways. To the east of the village is the **Norwood Museum** ⓘ *T01856-781217, May-Sep Tue-Thu and Sun 1400-1700 and 1800-2000, £3, children £1,* which features the large and eclectic antique collection of local stonemason Norris Wood.

The Churchill Barriers

East Mainland is linked to a string of islands to the south by four causeways, known as the Churchill Barriers, built on the orders of Prime Minister Winston Churchill during the Second World War as anti-submarine barriers to protect the British Navy which was based in Scapa Flow at the time. His decision was prompted by the sinking of the battleship *HMS Royal Oak* in October 1939 by a German U-boat which had slipped between the old blockships, deliberately sunk during the First World War to protect Scapa Flow, and the shore. After the war, a road was built on top of the causeways, linking the islands of Lamb Holm, Glimps Holm, Burray and South Ronaldsay to Mainland.

On the island of **Lamb Holm** camps were built to accommodate the men working on the construction of the barriers, many of whom were Italian Prisoners of War. The camps have long since gone, but the Italians left behind the remarkable **Italian**

Chapel ⓘ *open all year during daylight hours, free*, fittingly known as 'The Miracle of Camp 60'. It is difficult to believe that such a beautiful building could have been made using two Nissen huts, concrete and bits of scrap metal, and the chapel's enduring popularity with visitors is a tribute to the considerable artistic skill of the men involved. One of them, Domenico Chiochetti, returned in 1960 to restore the interior paintwork.

Burray

On the island of Burray the road passes the **Orkney Fossil and Vintage Centre** ⓘ *Apr-Sep daily 1000-1800, Oct Wed-Sun 1030-1800, £2*, which houses a bizarre collection of old furniture, various relics and 350 million-year-old fish fossils found locally. There's also an archive room where you can browse through old books and photographs, and a coffee shop. Not really something to go out of your way for, but worth a look if it's raining.

South Ronaldsay

The main settlement is the picturesque little village of **St Margaret's Hope** on the north coast. It is said to be named after Margaret, Maid of Norway, who died near here in 1290 at the age of seven while on her way to marry Prince Edward, later Edward II of England. She had already been proclaimed Queen of Scotland, and her premature death was a major factor in the long Wars of Independence with England. The word 'hope' comes from the Old Norse word 'hjop' meaning bay.

The village smithy has been turned into the **Smiddy Museum** ⓘ *May and Sep daily 1400-1600, Jun-Aug 1200-1600, Oct Sun 1400-1600, free*, with lots of old blacksmith's tools to try out. The museum also features a small exhibition on the annual **Boys' Ploughing Match**, a hugely popular event first held circa 1860. Each year in August, boys from the village (and now girls as well) dress up as horses and parade in the village square (prizes are given for the best costume). Afterwards the boys and their fathers, or grandfathers, head for the **Sand of Wright**, a few miles west, and have a ploughing match with miniature ploughs, which are usually family heirlooms. The categories are: best ploughed ring, best feering or guiding furrow, neatest ends and best kept plough. This sheltered beach is well worth a visit anyway, ploughing or no ploughing. The views stretch in a spectacular 180 degree panorama, south across the Pentland Firth to Caithness on mainland Scotland, west to South Walls and Cantick Head on Hoy, and northwest to Flotta and the west Mainland. It is also yet another good place to spot snipe, lapwing, curlew and redshank. Arctic terns also nest nearby and you can spot them diving dramatically as they fish in the bay.

To the north of the beach is the **Howe of Hoxa**, a ruined broch where Earl Thorfinn Skull-Splitter was buried in AD 963, according to the Orkneyinga saga. South Ronaldsay is a good place to buy local arts and crafts, and there are several workshops dotted around the island. One of these is the **Hoxa Tapestry Gallery** ⓘ *T/F01856-831395, Apr-Sep Mon-Fri 1000-1730, Sat and Sun 1400-1800, £2, concession £1.50, children under 12 free*, three miles west of the village on the way to Hoxa Head. Local artist Leila Thompson's huge tapestries are well worth a visit; you may not like the style, but you cannot help but marvel at the extraordinary amount of work and dedication involved in their creation; many of them take years to finish.

At the southeastern corner of South Ronaldsay is the recently excavated **Tomb of the Eagles** ⓘ *Apr-Oct daily 1000-2000, Nov-Mar 1000-1200, £3.50*, one of the most interesting archaeological sights on Orkney. The 5,000-year-old chambered cairn was discovered by local farmer and amateur archaeologist, Ronald Simison, whose family now runs the privately owned site and museum. The interior contents of the tomb were practically intact and there were up to 340 people buried here, along with carcasses and talons of sea eagles, hence the name. Various objects were also found outside the tomb, including stone tools and polished stone axes.

The graveyard of Scapa Flow

The huge natural harbour of Scapa Flow has been used since Viking times, and in the years leading up to the First World War the Royal Navy held exercises there, sometimes involving up to 100 ships. But Scapa was vulnerable to attack, and over the course of the war defences were improved with 21 blockships sunk at the eastern approaches. Scapa Flow continued to be used as the main naval base in the Second World War, but the blockships were not enough to prevent a German U-boat from torpedoing *HMS Royal Oak*, and the huge task of building the Churchill Barriers began, see page 560.

Scapa Flow's most famous incident happened at the end of the First World War, when, under the terms of the Armistice, Germany agreed to surrender most of her navy. Seventy-four German ships were interred in Scapa Flow, awaiting the final decision, but as the deadline approached the German commander, Admiral Von Reuter, gave the order for all the ships to be scuttled, and every ship was beached or sank.

The scuttled German fleet, however, proved a hazard for fishing and a massive salvage operation began. Today seven German ships remain at the bottom of Scapa Flow – three battleships and four light cruisers – along with four destroyers and a U-boat and the Royal Navy battleships *HMS Royal Oak* and *HMS Vanguard*, which blew up in 1917.

Before visiting the tomb you can handle the skulls and various other artefacts at the small 'museum' in the family home, which actually means their front porch! Then you walk for about five to 10 minutes through a field to visit a **burnt mound**, a kind of Bronze-Age kitchen, where Ronald Simison will regail you with all manner of fascinating insider information about the excavation process, before walking out along the cliff edge to the spectacularly sited tomb which you must enter by lying on a trolley and pulling yourself in using an overhead rope. It is particularly eerie being here because there is generally no-one else around, and as you haul yourself into the tomb, with the sound of the North Sea crashing into the cliffs nearby, you wonder to yourself how those buried here met their fate. There is also a lovely, but generally wild and windy, walk back along the cliffs, via a different route, to the car park.

Hoy → *Phone code: 01856.*

To the southwest of the Mainland is Hoy, the second largest of the Orkney islands. The name is derived from the Norse Ha-ey, meaning High Island, which is appropriate as much of the island is more reminiscent of the Scottish Highlands than Orkney, with only the southern end being typically low and fertile. » *For Sleeping, Eating and other listings, see pages 568-574.*

Ins and outs

There are two ferry services to Hoy, both run by Orkney Ferries, T01856-850624. Transport on Hoy is limited to a minibus between Moaness Pier and Rackwick. » *For further details, see Transport page 572.*

Sights

Orkney's highest point, **Ward Hill** (1,571 ft) is in the north of the island, and the north and west coasts are bounded by spectacular cliffs. At **St John's Head**, the sheer cliffs rise out of the sea to a height of 1,150 ft, the highest vertical cliffs in Britain. The island is most famous for its **Old Man of Hoy**, a great rock stack rising to 450 ft. This northern part of Hoy forms the **North Hoy RSPB Reserve** which has a variety of habitats ranging from woodland to tundra-like hill-tops and sea cliffs. The reserve is home to a huge variety of birds including great skuas and Arctic skuas, Manx shearwaters and puffins. On the hills there are red grouse, curlews, golden plovers and dunlins, peregrine falcons, merlins, kestrels and even golden eagles. Mountain hares are quite common and, if you are lucky, you can also see otters along the Scapa Flow coastline.

On the southeast coast of the island is **Lyness**, site of a large naval base during both world wars when the British fleet was based in Scapa Flow. Many of the old dilapidated buildings have gone, but the harbour area is still scarred with the scattered remains of concrete structures, and there's also the unattractive sight of the huge oil terminal on **Flotta**. Lyness has a large **Naval Cemetery**, last resting place of those who died at Jutland, of Germans killed during the scuttle and of the crew of *HMS Royal Oak*. The old pump house opposite the new ferry terminal is now the **Scapa Flow Visitor Centre** ⓘ *T01856-791300, Mon-Fri 0900-1630, Sat and Sun 0930-1630, free*, a fascinating naval museum with old photographs, various wartime artefacts, a section devoted to the scuttling of the German Fleet, and an audio-visual feature on the history of Scapa Flow. Well worth a visit. At South Walls, overlooking Longhope Bay, is **Hackness Martello Tower and Battery** ⓘ *T01856-811397, Apr-Sep daily 0930-1830, £3, concessions £2.50, children £1*, which, along with another tower on the north side at Crockness, was built in 1815 to protect British ships in Longhope Bay against attack by American and French privateers while they waited for a Royal Navy escort on their journey to Baltic ports.

▲ Hoy's great attraction is its many excellent walking opportunities. A minibus runs between **Moaness Pier**, where the ferry from Stromness docks (see Transport page 572), and **Rackwick**, on the opposite side of the island, but it's a lovely two-hour walk by road through beautiful **Rackwick Glen**, once populated by crofters and fishermen, but now quiet and isolated. On the way you'll pass the **Dwarfie Stone**, a huge, lonely block of sandstone which is the only rock-cut tomb in Britain, dating from around 3000 BC. Be careful, though, because according to Sir Walter Scott this is the residence of the Trolld, a dwarf from Norse legend. On your return you can take a different route through a narrow valley between the **Cuilags** (1,421 ft) and **Ward Hill** and **Berriedale Wood**, the most northerly woodland in Britain. The most popular walk on Hoy is the spectacular three-hour hike from Rackwick to the cliffs facing the **Old Man of Hoy**. The path climbs steeply westwards from the old crofting township, then turns northwards before gradually descending to the cliff edge.

Rousay, Egilsay and Wyre

These three islands lie a short distance off the northeast coast of Mainland and, together with Shapinsay to the southeast, are the closest of Orkney's North Isles to Kirkwall. ▸▸ *For Sleeping, Eating and other listings, see pages 568-574.*

Rousay

Rousay is a hilly island about five miles in diameter and known as the 'Egypt of the North' due to the large number of archaeological sites. It also has the important **Trumland RSPB Reserve**, home to merlins, hen harriers, peregrine falcons, short-eared owls and red-throated divers, and its three lochs offer good trout fishing.

A road runs right around the island, and makes a pleasant 13-mile bike run, but most of the sights are within walking distance of the ferry pier on the southeast side of the island, where most of the 200 inhabitants live. A short distance west of the pier by the road is **Tavershoe Tuick**, an unusual two-storey burial cairn, which was discovered in the late 19th century by Mrs Burroughs, wife of General Traill Burroughs who lived at nearby Trumland House. A mile further west, to the north of the road, is **Blackhammer**, a stalled Neolithic burial cairn. Further west, and a steep climb up from the road, is **Knowe of Yarso**, another stalled cairn, which contained the remains of at least 21 people. The tomb dates from around 2900 BC.

Most of the island's archaeological sights are to be found along the **Westness Walk**, a mile-long walk which starts from Westness Farm, about four miles west of the ferry pier, and ends at the remarkable Midhowe Cairn. The walk is described in detail in a leaflet available from the tourist offices on Mainland. **Midhowe Cairn** is the largest and longest thus far excavated on Orkney – over 100 ft long and 40 ft wide – and, like the others, dates from around 3000 BC. Housed in a large building to protect it, the 'Great Ship of Death', as it is known, contained the remains of 25 people in crouched position on or under the eastern shelves of the chamber, which is divided into 12 sections. Standing nearby, with fine views across to Eynehallow island, is **Midhowe Broch**, one of the best-preserved brochs on Orkney, occupied from around 200 BC to AD 200. The outer walls are about 60 ft in diameter and up to 14 ft high in places.

Another fine walk on the island is around the **RSPB Reserve**. A footpath leads from beside Trumland House and heads up towards the island's highest point, **Blotchnie Fiold** (821 ft). A leaflet describing the walk is available from the tourist offices on Mainland or the **Trumland Orientation Centre** by the pier.

Egilsay and Wyre

These two small islands lie to the east of Rousay and have a couple of interesting sights of their own. Egilsay's claim to fame is the murder here of St Magnus in 1115, and a **cenotaph** marks the spot where he was slain. The island is dominated by the 12th-century **St Magnus church**, built on the site of an earlier church, possibly as a shrine to St Magnus. It is the only surviving example on Orkney of a round-towered Viking church. Much of Egilsay has been bought by the RSPB as a reserve to preserve the habitat of the very rare **corncrake**, whose distinctive rasping call may be heard.

Tiny Wyre features strongly in the Viking saga as the domain of Kolbein Hruga, and the remains of his 12th-century stronghold, **Cubbie Roo's Castle**, and nearby **St Mary's chapel** can be still be seen. Kolbein's home, or Bu, was on the site of the nearby Bu Farm, where the poet Edwin Muir (1887-1959) spent part of his childhood. The far westerly point of the island, known as **the Taing**, is a favourite haunt of seals, and a great place to enjoy a summer sunset.

Shapinsay → *Phone code: 01856.*

Less than 30 minutes by ferry from Kirkwall is the fertile, low-lying island of Shapinsay. The main attraction is **Balfour Castle** ⓘ *guided tour only which leaves from Kirkwall on Wed and Sun, May-Sep, 1415 ferry, arrange in advance at the tourist office in Kirkwall, cost £15 per person including ferry ticket, guided tour of the castle and gardens (at 1500) and complimentary tea and cakes in the servants' quarters*, an imposing baronial pile which is in fact a Victorian extension to a much older house called 'Cliffdale'. The house, and the rest of the island, was bought by successive generations of the Balfour family who had made their fortune in India. Today the castle is the home of the Zawadski family and can only be visited as part of an inclusive half-day tour. You can take an earlier ferry if you wish to explore the island.

In the village, built by the Balfours to house their estate workers, is the **Shapinsay Heritage Centre** ⓘ *T01856-711258, Mon, Tue and Thu-Sat 1200-1630, Wed and Sun till 1730, free*, in the old Smithy. It has displays on the island's history and a tearoom upstairs. There's a **pub** in the village, in the old gatehouse. Also a couple of shops and a post office.

A mile north of the village is the **Mill Dam RSPB Reserve**, where there's a hide overlooking a loch from which you can see many species of wildfowl and waders. Four miles from the pier, at the far northeast corner of the island, is the well-preserved **Burroughston Broch**, with good views of seals sunning themselves on the nearby rocks. West of here, at **Quholme**, is the original birthplace of the father of Washington Irving, author of *Rip Van Winkle*.

Eday → *Phone code: 01857.*

The long, thin and sparsely populated island of Eday lies at the centre of the North Isles group. It is less fertile than the other islands, but its heather-covered hills in the centre have provided peat for the other peatless Orkney islands. Eday's sandstone has also been quarried, and was used in the building of St Magnus Cathedral in Kirkwall. » *For Sleeping, Eating and other listings, see pages 568-574.*

Ins and outs

There are flights from Kirkwall to Eday airport, called London Airport. There are also ferries from Kirkwall. The ferry pier is at Backaland, on the southeast of the island, a long way from the main sights. Orkney Ferries, T01856-872044, also run the Eday Heritage Tour. » *For further details, see Transport page 572.*

Sights

The island has numerous chambered cairns and these, along with the other attractions, are concentrated in the northern part. They are all covered in the signposted five-mile **Eday Heritage Walk**, which starts from the Community Enterprises Shop and leads up to the Cliffs of Red Head at the northern tip. The walk takes about three hours to complete, and it's worth picking up the *Eday Heritage Walk* leaflet.

The walk starts at Mill Bay and heads past **Mill Loch**, where an RSPB hide allows you to watch rare red-throated divers breeding in spring and summer. Further north is the huge, 15-ft tall **Stone of Setter**, the largest standing stone in Orkney and visible from most of the chambered cairns. Close by are the **Fold of Setter**, a circular enclosure dating back to 2000 BC, and the **Braeside** and **Huntersquoy** chambered cairns. Further north along the path is **Vinquoy Chambered Cairn**, one of the finest in Orkney and similar to the better-known tomb at Maes Howe, dating from around the same time. An acrylic dome provides light to the main chamber, which can be entered by a narrow underground passage.

The path continues to the summit of **Vinquoy Hill**, which commands excellent views of the surrounding islands of Westray and Sanday. From here you can continue north to the spectacular red sandstone cliffs at **Red Head**, home to nesting guillemots, razorbills and puffins in summer, or head southeast along the coast to **Carrick House** ⓘ *T01856-622260, Mid-Jun to mid-Sep guided tour at 1400, £2*. Built for Lord Kinclaven, Earl of Carrick, in 1633, the house is best known for its associations with the pirate, John Gow, whose ship ran aground during a failed attack on the house. He was captured and taken to London for trial and hanged. Sir Walter Scott's novel, *The Pirate*, is based on this story.

Sanday → *Phone code: 01857.*

Sanday is the largest of the North Isles, 12 miles long and flat as a pancake except for the cliffs at Spurness. It is well-named, as its most notable feature is its sweeping bays of sparkling white sand backed by machair, and turquoise seas.

There are numerous burial mounds all over the island, the most impressive being **Quoyness Chambered Cairn**, a 5,000 year-old tomb similar to Maes Howe. The 13 ft-high structure contains a large main chamber with six smaller cells opening through low entrances. Most of the burial tombs remain unexcavated, such as those at **Tofts Ness** at the far northeastern tip, where there are over 500 cairns, making it potentially one of the most important prehistoric sites in Britain. At **Scar**, in Burness, a spectacular Viking find was made recently, and at **Pool** a major excavation has uncovered the remains of at least 14 Stone-Age houses.

Sanday is known for its **knitwear**, though the factory unfortunately closed down recently. You can still visit the **Orkney Angora craft shop**, in Upper Breckan, near the northern tip of the island.

Stronsay → *Phone code: 01857.*

The peaceful, low-lying island of Stronsay has some fine sandy beaches and cliffs which attract large colonies of grey seals and nesting seabirds. There are few real sights on this largely agricultural island, but the coastline has some pleasant walks. One of the best is to the **Vat of Kirbister** in the southeast, a spectacular 'gloup' or blow-hole spanned by the finest natural arch in Orkney. To the south of here, at **Burgh Head**, you'll find nesting puffins and the remains of a ruined broch, and at the southeastern tip, at **Lamb Head**, is a large colony of grey seals, lots of seabirds and several archaeological sites.

The main settlement is the quiet village of **Whitehall**, on the northeast coast where the ferry arrives. It's hard to believe it now, but this was one of the largest herring ports in Europe. During the boom years of the early 20th century 300 steam drifters were working out of Whitehall and nearly 4,000 fishing crew and shore workers were employed. In the peak year of 1924 over 12,000 tons of herring were landed here, to be cured (salted) and exported to Russia and Eastern Europe. Whitehall developed considerably and the Stronsay Hotel was said to have the longest bar in Scotland. On Sundays during July and August there were so many boats tied up that it was possible to walk across them to the little island of Papa Stronsay. By the 1930s, however, herring stocks were severely depleted and the industry was in decline. The old Fish Mart by the pier houses a **heritage centre** ⓘ *T01856-616360, May-Sep 1100-1700, free*, with photos and artefacts from the herring boom days. It also has a café and hostel. » *For Sleeping, Eating and other listings, see pages 568-574.*

Westray → *Phone code: 01857.*

Westray is the second largest of the North Isles, with a varied landscape of farmland, hilly moorland, sandy beaches and dramatic cliffs. It is also the most prosperous of the North Isles, producing beef, fish and seafood, and supports a population of 700.

The main settlement is **Pierowall**, in the north of the island, but, though it has one of the best harbours in Orkney, the main ferry terminal is at Rapness, on the south coast. Pierowall is a relatively large village for the North Isles and there are several shops, a post office, a hotel and the **Westray Heritage Centre** ⓘ *early May to late Sep Tue-Sat 0930-1230 and 1400-1700, £2*, with displays on local and natural history, and a tearoom. Also in the village is the ruined 17th-century **St Mary's church**. About a mile west of the village is Westray's most notable ruin, the impressive **Notland Castle**,

Prior to the herring boom, Stronsay's economic mainstay was the kelp industry. By the end of the 18th century 3,000 people were employed in the collection of seaweed and production of kelp for export, to be used in making iodine, soap and glass.

a fine example of a 16th-century fortified Z-plan tower-house. To explore the interior, pick up the key from the back door of the nearby farm.

There are some great coastal **walks** on the island, particularly to the spectacular sea cliffs at **Noup Head**, at the far northwestern tip, which are an **RSPB Reserve** and second only to St Kilda in terms of breeding seabirds, with huge colonies of guillemots, razorbills, kittiwakes and fulmars, as well as puffins. The cliffs on the west coast of Westray are five miles long and there's an excellent walk down the coast from Noup Head, past **Gentleman's Cave**, used as a hiding place by four Jacobite lairds in 1746. Near the southern end of the walk is **Fitty Hill** (554 ft), the highest point on the island, which you can climb for great views, and the walk ends at **Inga Ness**, where you can also see puffins. The best place to see puffins is at **Castle o' Burrian**, a sea stack on **Stanger Head**, on the southeastern coast near the Rapness ferry terminal. » *For Sleeping, Eating and other listings, see pages 568-574.*

There are guided minibus tours of Westray which connect with the ferry at Rapness. *See page 571.*

Papa Westray → *Phone code: 01857.*

Tiny Papa Westray, known locally as 'Papay', can be reached on the world's shortest scheduled flight – all of two minutes – from Westray, but there are other reasons to visit this little island, one of the most remote of the Orkney group.

Papay is home to Europe's oldest house, the **Knap of Howar** ⓘ *open at all times, free*, which was built around 5,500 years ago and is still standing (they knew how to build 'em in those days). It's on the west coast, just south of the airport. Half a mile north is **St Boniface Kirk**, one of the oldest Christian sites in the north of Scotland, founded in the eighth century, though most of the recently restored building dates from the 12th century. Inland from the Knap of Howar is **Holland Farm**, former home of the lairds of the island, where you can rummage around the farm buildings and the small museum.

Papay is famous for its birds, and **North Hill**, on the north of the island, is an important RSPB Reserve. The cliffs are home to many thousands of breeding seabirds, and at **Fowl Craig** on the east coast you can see nesting puffins. The interior is home to the largest arctic tern colony in Europe, as well as many arctic skuas. If you wish to explore you have to contact the warden at **Rose Cottage** ⓘ *T01857-644240*, who runs regular guided walks.

It's worth taking a boat trip to the even tinier, deserted **Holm of Papay**, off the east coast. This is the site of several Neolithic burial cairns, including one of the largest **chambered cairns** on Orkney. You enter the tomb down a ladder into the main chamber which is nearly 70 ft long, with a dozen side-cells. Contact Jim Davidson, T01856-644259, for boat trips between May and September. » *For Sleeping, Eating and other listings, see pages 568-574.*

North Ronaldsay

Remote and storm-battered, North Ronaldsay is the most northerly of the Orkney islands and a place where old Orcadian traditions remain. It seems remarkable that anyone should live here at all in these extreme conditions, but 'North Ron' – as it is known locally – has been inhabited for many centuries and continues to be heavily farmed. The island's sheep are a hardy lot and live exclusively off the seaweed on a narrow strip of beach, outside a 13-mile stone dyke which surrounds the island. This gives their meat a unique, 'gamey' flavour.

This small, flat island, only three miles long, has few real attractions, except to keen ornithologists who flock here to catch a glimpse of its rare migrants. From late

March to early June and mid-August to early November there are huge numbers of migratory birds. The **Bird Observatory**, in the southwest corner of the island by the ferry pier, gives information on which species have been sighted, as well as providing accommodation. There are also colonies of grey seals and cormorants at **Seal Skerry**, on the northeast tip of the island. » *For Sleeping, Eating and other listings, see pages 568-574.*

Sleeping

Kirkwall *p551, map p553*
There are plenty of cheap B&Bs, though most rooms are small without en suite.
B-C Ayre Hotel, on the harbour front, T01856-873001, www.ayrehotel.co.uk. The best hotel in Kirkwall, very comfortable.
B-D Albert Hotel, Mounthoolie La, T01856-876000, enquiries@alberthotel.co.uk. Another good option, in the centre of town with a restaurant and a couple of lively bars.
D Foveran Hotel, 2 miles from town on the A964 Orphir road at St Ola, T01856-872389, www.foveranhotel.com. Overlooking Scapa Flow. It is friendly and comfortable, and also offers very good food, including vegetarian.
D West End Hotel, Main St, T01856-872368, www.orkneyisles.co.uk/westendhotel. Central and serves good bar meals.
E Whiteclett, St Catherine's Pl, T01856-874193. This B&B is a 200-year-old listed house near the harbour.
E-F Arundel, Inganess Rd, T01856-873148. A modern bungalow offering B&B on a quiet road about a mile from the town centre.
F SYHA Youth Hostel, Old Scapa Rd, T01856-872243, open Apr-Sep. This large, well-equipped youth hostel about 15 mins' walk from the town centre.

Camping
Pickaquoy Caravan & Camping Site, on the western outskirts of Kirkwall, off the A965, T01856-873535. Open May-Sep.

Stromness and West Mainland *p555*
B Merkister Hotel, on the shores of Loch Harray, Stenness, T01856-771366, merkisterhotel@ecos.co. A favourite with anglers. It has a very good restaurant and a popular bar.
C-D Standing Stones Hotel, on the shores of Loch Stenness, Stenness, T01856-850449, standingstones@sol.co.uk.
C-D Stromness Hotel, Stromness, T01856-850298, www.stromnesshotel.com. The best hotel in town is this imposing old building overlooking the harbour. Recently refurbished and offering good-value meals.
D-E Barony Hotel, on the north shore of Boardhouse Loch, Marwick Head, T01856-721327, baronyhotel@btinternet.com. Open May-Sep. It specializes in fishing holidays and is about the only place offering food in these parts.
D-E Mill of Eyreland, Stenness, T01856-850136, ww.orknet.co.uk/mill. Lovely a converted mill 3 miles from Stromness.
D-E Stenigar, T01856-850438. Open Apr-Oct. Converted boatyard on Ness Rd, just before the campsite, with views of Hoy.
E Ferry Inn, near the ferry terminal, John St, T01856-850280, www.ferryinn.com. Serves food and has a lively bar.
E Kierfiold House, near Loch Harray, T/F01856-841583. There are a few B&Bs close to Skara Brae, including this one.
E Orca Hotel, on Victoria St near the harbour, T01856-850447, www.theoakleigh.com. Also has a cellar bistro, **Bistro 76**, serving good food.
E Thira, a few miles behind Stromness, at Innertown, T01856-851181. Comfortable, friendly and non-smoking modern bungalow with spectacular views of Hoy. Also serves an excellent cooked breakfast, and will provide a fantastic dinner made from the finest local ingredients on request.
E-F Netherstove, T/F01856-841625, ann.poke@virgin.net. A B&B near Skara Brae, overlooking the Bay of Skaill.
E-F Primrose Cottage, Marwick Head, T/F01856-721384, i.clouston@talk21.com. A comfortable B&B overlooking Marwick Bay.
F Brown's Hostel, 45 Victoria St, T01856-850661. This popular independent hostel has no curfew and is open all year round.

For an explanation of sleeping and eating price codes used in this guide, see inside the front cover. Other relevant information is found in Essentials, see pages 43-51.

F SYHA Hostel, on Hellihole Rd, a 10-min walk south from the ferry terminal, T01856-850589. Open Mar-Oct.

Camping

F Eviedale Centre, beside the junction of the road to Dounby, T01856-751270, Apr-Oct, has a small bothy and campsite. There's a campsite, T01856-873535, open May to mid-Sep, at Ness Point, a mile south of the ferry terminal. It's well equipped and has incomparable views, but is very exposed.

East Mainland and South Ronaldsay *p560*

There's a good selection of accommodation in St Margaret's Hope.

D Creel Restaurant & Rooms, Front Rd, St Margaret's Hope, T01856-831311, www.thecreel.co.uk. Best of the lot. Offers comfortable rooms and superb, though expensive, food using deliciously fresh, locally grown ingredients. Dinner only.

E Bellevue Guest House, St Margaret's Hope, T01856-831294. Good B&B choice.

E Commodore Motel, Deerness, T01856-781319. Only place to stay or eat in Deerness.

E The Fisher's Gill, St Margaret's Hope, T01856-831711. Another good B&B and also offers seafood dishes.

E Murray Arms Hotel, Back Rd, St Margaret's Hope, T01856-831205. Good value bar meals.

E Vestlaybanks, Burray village, on the south coast, T01856-731305, vestlaybanks@btinternet.com. B&B also providing evening meals.

F Wheems Bothy, at Wheems, Eastside, a few miles southeast of St Margaret's Hope, T01856-831537, open Apr-Oct. Organic farm offering cheap and basic hostel accommodation.

Hoy *p562*

There's not much accommodation in the north of the island, except for the 2 SYHA hostels. There are a few very good B&Bs in the south of the island.

E The Hoy Hotel, near the ferry terminal in Lyness, T01856-791377. Open Apr-Oct. Also serves meals.

E Stoneyquoy, south of Lyness, T/F01856-791234, www.visithoy.com. The owner, Louise Budge, also runs guided tours of the island for £40 for up to 4 people with lunch.

E-F Burnhouse, on the other side of the bay in Longhope, T01856-701263.

E-F Old Custom House, also in Longhope, T01856-701358.

F Hoy Youth Hostel, is the larger of the two, about a mile from Moaness Pier. It's open from May-Sep.

F Rackwick Youth Hostel in Rackwick Glen (open mid-Mar to mid-Sep). To book ahead for both hostels, contact Orkney Council, T01856-873535, ext 2404.

Rousay, Egilsay and Wyre *p563*

Accommodation is very limited on Rousay, and non-existent on Egilsay and Wyre.

D-E Taversoe Hotel, near Knowe of Yarso, about 2 miles west of the pier, T01857-821325. Offers excellent-value meals. The seafood is particularly recommended (closed Mon to non-residents).

F Rousay Hostel, Trumland Organic Farm, T01857-821252, open all year and half a mile from the ferry. It has laundry facilities and you can also camp.

Shapinsay *p564*

C Balfour Castle, T01857-711282, www.balfourcastle.co.uk. Stay here and enjoy all that Victorian splendour. The price includes dinner. The castle has a private chapel and a boat is available for bird watching and fishing trips for residents.

E Girnigoe, T01857-711256, near the northern end of Veantro Bay. This B&B is a little humbler but comfortable. Also offers evening meals.

Eday *p565*

E Mrs Poppelwell's, T01857-622248, Blett, Carrick Bay, opposite the Calf of Eday. Very friendly. Evening meal and packed lunch provided if you wish. Mrs Poppelwell also has a self-catering cottage for up to 3 nearby.

D Mrs Cockram, T01857-622271. Open Jun-Mar, at Skaill Farm, just south of the airport. Price includes dinner.

F Youth Hostel, T01857-622206, open Apr-Sep, run by Eday Community Enterprises, just north of the airport. Basic lodging.

Sanday *p565*

E Belsair Hotel, Kettletoft, where the ferry used to dock, T01857-600206, joy:@sanday.quista.net. Serves meals.

E **Kettletoft Hotel**, Kettletoft, T/F01857-600217. Serves meals and has a lively bar.
E-F **Quivals**, T01857-600467. One of a handful of B&Bs, this one is run by Tina and Bernie Flett. In addition to the B&B between them they operate a ferry service, run a car and bike hire service (T01857-600418), and Bernie also takes out tours, see Activities and tours p571.

Stronsay *p566*
F **Stronsay Fish Mart Hostel**, T01857-616360. Open all year, is well-equipped and comfortable, see p566. Their café does cheap meals.
E **Stronsay Hotel**, T01857-616213, www.stronsayhotel.com, has been refurbished and offers cheap bar food.
F **Stronsay Bird Reserve**, Mill Bay, south of Whitehall, T01857-616363. B&B or you can camp overlooking the wide sandy bay.
F **Torness Camping Barn**, at the southern end of the island, on the shore of Holland Bay near Lea-shun Loch, T01857-616314. Very basic and very cheap. They also organize nature walks to the nearby seal-hide. Phone for pick-up from the ferry.

Westray *p566*
C-D **Cleaton House Hotel**, about 2 miles southeast of Pierowall, T01857-677508, www.orknet.co.uk/cleaton. This converted Victorian manse is the best place to stay. It serves excellent meals in the restaurant (1900-2100) and in the bar (1200-1400, 1800-2100).
E **Pierowall Hotel**, in the village, T01857-677208, www.orknet.co.uk/pierwall. Less stylish, but comfortable and friendly. It also serves good-value bar meals.
E-F **Sand o' Gill**, T01857-677374. One of several B&Bs. You can also camp or hire their self-catering caravan.

Papa Westray *p567*
D-E **Beltane House Guest House**, T01857-644267. A row of converted farm workers' cottages to the east of Holland House. It offers dinner (**££**). Run by the island community co-operative.
F **Papa Westray Hostel**, T01857-644267. Open all year, housed in the same complex at Beltane. A 16-bed hostel run by the island community co-operative which also runs a shop and restaurant serving lunch and evening meals. They have a minibus which takes ferry passengers from the pier to anywhere on the island.

North Ronaldsay *p567*
E **North Ronaldsay Bird Observatory**, T01857-633200, alison@nrbo.prestel.co.uk. Offers wind-and solar-powered full-board accommodation in private rooms or dorms.
D-E **Garso House**, T01857-633244, christine.muir@virgin.net, about 3 miles from the ferry pier. Full-board. They also have a self-catering cottage (up to 5 people) and can arrange car hire, taxis or minibus tours.

Camping
Contact, T01857-633222, for informtion.

Eating

Eating options are very limited on the islands but most B&Bs and guest houses will provide evening meals. Even in Kirkwall you'll be hard-pushed to find a decent meal.

Kirkwall *p551, map p553*
Kirkwall is no gastronome's paradise and you'll be hard-pushed to find somewhere decent to eat in town.
£££-££ **Foveran Hotel**, see Sleeping, is perhaps the best place to eat.
££-£ **Albert Hotel**, see Sleeping, serves bar meals made with home-grown produce.
££ **Mumtaz**, on Bridge St. The islands' only Indian restaurant.
£ **The Mustard Seed Café**, 65 Victoria St. The best place for a snack is this cafeteria-style café, serving substantial soups and main courses in a bustling and very friendly atmosphere.

Stromness and West Mainland *p555*
££ **Coffee Shop**, near the ferry terminal, on John St, Stromness. Popular place for good, cheap grub. Open Mon-Sat 0900-1830, Sun 0900-1700 (Mon-Sat till 1700 in winter).
££ **Hamnavoe Restaurant**, 35 Graham Pl, Stromness, T01856-850606. The best place to eat in town. It specializes in local seafood but also offers good vegetarian dishes. Open Mar-Oct Tue-Sun from 1900.
££-£ **Stromness Hotel**, see Sleeping, Stromness, good bar meals.

£ Ferry Inn, see Sleeping, Stromness, also serves decent bar food.

Hoy *p562*
££-£ Hoy Inn, near the pier and post office, T01856-791313, a bar and restaurant which serves good seafood (closed Mon). There's also an RSPB information centre here.
£ Anchor Bar, T01856-791356, in Lyness serves lunches. There are shops/petrol stations in Lyness and Longhope.

Rousay, Egilsay and Wyre *p563*
££-£ Pier Restaurant, beside the pier, serves food at lunchtime.

North Ronaldsay *p567*
Burrian Inn and Restaurant is the island's pub, and also serves food.

Bars and clubs

Kirkwall *p551, map p553*
Nightlife in Kirkwall revolves around its lively pubs. Check in *The Orcadian* for folk nights etc.
Ayre Hotel stages folk music nights.
Bothy Bar, Albert Hotel, is a good place for a drink, and sometimes has live folk music.
Matchmakers Bar, also at the Albert Hotel, has a disco at weekends.

Stromness and West Mainland *p555*
Stromness Hotel, the **Ferry Inn** and the bar of the **Royal Hotel** are the best places for a drink are in Stromness.
The Mistra, Evie, is the local village shop, post office and pub.

Entertainment

For details of what's going on, buy *The Orcadian*, which comes out on Thu, or pick up a free copy of the Tourist Board's guide.

Kirkwall *p551, map p553*
The town's **New Phoenix cinema** is housed in the **Pickaquoy Leisure Centre**, Pickaquoy Rd, T01856-879900. It also has sports and fitness facilities, and a café and bar.

Festivals and events

There are numerous events which take place throughout the year.

The Ba' (ball): Christmas Day and New Year's Day in Kirkwall Amongst the best-known annual events it is a bit like rugby, basketball and a full-scale riot all rolled into one, and is contested between two sides – the Uppies and the Doonies – representing different districts of the town. As many as 200 'players' may be involved, and a game can last up to 7 hrs as both sides attempt to jostle the ball along the streets until one reaches their 'goal' to win the prized ba'.
Orkney Folk Festival: 3 days at the end of May This excellent event takes place at various locations throughout the islands. It is one of the most entertaining events of all.
St Magnus Festival: Jun This acclaimed festival is the most prestigious and popular. Held in Kirkwall, it consists of 6 days of music, drama, literature and the visual arts, and features many internationally renowned performers.
Regattas: Jul During this month there are several regattas held on most of the islands.
Festival of the Horse and Boys' Ploughing Match on South Ronaldsay: Aug There are numerous agricultural shows in Aug which culminate in this festival, see p561.
Orkney Science Festival: first week in Sep, T01856-876214.

Activities and tours

Both general sightseeing tours and special interest tours are available.
Go-Orkney, South Cannigall, St Ola, T01856-871871, www.orknet.co.uk/orkney-tours, runs a series of tours of Mainland, and also to Hoy and Rousay.
Wildabout Orkney, 5 Clouston Corner, Stenness, T01856- 851011, www.wildabout.orknet.co.uk, offers highly rated wildlife, historical, folklore and environmental tours of Mainland for around £16 per person for a full day.
Discover Orkney Tours, T/F01856-872865, offers tours of Mainland as well as trips to Westray and Papa Westray.

Stromness and West Mainland *p555*
For a full list, check out www.subaqua.co.uk.
The Diving Cellar, 4 Victoria St, Stromness, T01856-850055, divescapaflow.co.uk, and

To dive for

Orkney offers some of the best scuba diving in the world, thanks to the part played by Scapa Flow in both world wars, see page 317. The wreckage on the sea bed, combined with the wildlife that teems around it – sea anemones, seals, whales and porpoises – make for great diving. Visibility is sharp and the water is not as cold as you expect, thanks to the Gulf Stream. Several companies offer diving courses for beginners and wreck diving for more experienced divers. This can be as a dive package, including accommodation, meals and boat charter, or simply as a boat charter. Most companies are based in Stromness. See page 571.

Scapa Flow Diving Holidays, Stromness, T01856-851110, offer liveaboard packages or day trips on the *MV Invincible*, complete with its own bar.

East Mainland and South Ronaldsay *p560*
Orkney Divers, based at the Crowsnest bunkhouse, St Margaret's Hope, South Ronaldsay, T01856-831205, www.orkneydivers.com. Scuba diving.

Rousay, Egilsay and Wyre *p563*
Rousay Traveller, T01856-821234, run very informative minibus tours from Jun-early Sep Tue-Fri, meeting the 1040 ferry from Tingwall, they last 6 hrs and cost £15, children £6.

Eday *p565*
Orkney Ferries, T01856-872044, also run the Eday Heritage Tour every Sun from mid-Jun to mid-Sep. It leaves Kirkwall at 0920 and return at 1955 and costs around £30 per person, which includes ferries, guided walks or minibus tour, entry to Carrick House and lunch. Book with **Orkney Ferries** or at the tourist office in Kirkwall.

Sanday *p565*
Quivals, see also Sleeping, T01856-600467. A B&B, the owners also run full-day tours of the island, on Wed and Fri, from mid-May to early Sep, departing from Kirkwall pier at 1010 and returning at 1940 (around £30 per person, minimum of 4 people).

Westray *p566*
Discover Orkney, T/F01856-872865, run day tours on a Sun to Westray from Kirkwall, leaving at 0940 and returning at 2015, and costing around £30 per person including ferry. They also run a day tour on a Mon to Papa Westray.
Island Explorer, T01856-677355. There are guided minibus tours of Westray with Alex Costie. They connect with the ferry at Rapness and cost £20 for a full day.
J & M Marcus, Pierowall, also runs bus tours and offers car hire.
Tom Rendall, T01856-677216, for boat trips to Papa Westray.

Transport

Kirkwall *p551, map p553*
Local Eight-seater aircraft fly from Kirkwall daily except Sun to **Stronsay**, **Sanday**, **North Ronaldsay**, **Westray** and **Papa Westray**, and on Wed to **Eday**. To Papa Westray and North Ronaldsay costs only £15 one way (£12 with a one-night stay), and to the other islands listed costs £31 one way.

There's a limited bus service around the Mainland. Peace Coaches, T01856-872866, runs regular buses Mon-Sat from Kirkwall bus station to **Stromness**, 30 mins. They also run 3-5 buses a day, Mon-Sat, to **Houton**, 30 mins, which connect with ferries to **Hoy**; and a daily bus, Mon-Sat, to **East Holm**, 25 mins, and **Stromness** via **Dounby**, 55 mins. Causeway Coaches, T01856-831444, runs 2-4 buses a day, Mon-Sat, to **St Margaret's Hope**, 30 mins. Rosie Coaches, T01856-751227, runs buses to **Tingwall** and **Evie**. The bus service between Kirkwall and **Burwick** is run by Shalders Coaches, T01856-850809. Note that there is no Sun bus service on Orkney.

Car hire from **Scarth Car Hire**, Great Western Rd, T01856-872125; **WR Tullock**, Castle St, T01856-876262, and Kirkwall airport, T01856-875500. Cycle hire from **Bobby's Cycle Centre**, Tankerness La, T/F01856-875777. Mountain bikes from £8 per day.

Long distance Daily flights from **Scotland** and **England** are operated by **Loganair/ British Regional Airlines** and can be booked through **British Airways**, T08708-509850 or **Loganair**, T01856-872494.

Northlink Ferries, T01856-885500, www.northlinkferries.co.uk, sail from **Aberdeen** to **Kirkwall** (7½ hrs) on Tue, Thu, Sat and Sun at 1700, returning to Aberdeen on Mon, Wed and Fri at 2330. A return passenger fare costs from £32 up to £48 (peak season, Jul-Aug). A car and driver costs from £142 up to £200, plus £25-40 per additional passenger.

Northlink Ferries sail from **Lerwick** (Shetland) to **Kirkwall** (7 hrs) on Mon, Wed and Fri at 1800, returning on Tue, Thu, Sat and Sun at 2345. A passenger fare costs £26-39 return. A car with driver costs £112-178, plus £22-20 per additional passenger. Single fares are 50 per cent of return fares and children under 16 travel for 50% discount. Cars should be booked in advance and all passengers must check in at least 30 mins before departure. 2- and 4-berth cabins are available on all journeys, from £42 up to £78 per journey.

John o'Groats Ferries, T01955-611353, www.jogferry.co.uk, operate a passenger-only (and bicycles) ferry service from **John o' Groats** to **Burwick** (twice a day, 4 times Jul-Aug, 40 mins) on South Ronaldsay, from May to Sep. There are bus connections between **Burwick** and **Kirkwall** (45 mins) for all ferry sailings. Return fare including bus is £24 (bicycles an extra £3). No bookings required. A free bus meets the afternoon train from Thurso at 1445 and connects with the 1600 or 1800 ferry to Orkney. They also operate the **Orkney Bus**, a daily direct bus/ferry/bus service between **Inverness** and **Kirkwall**, via **John o' Groats**. It leaves Inverness at 0730 and 1420 from Jun-Sep (at 1420 only in May). It costs £40 return. Journey time 5 hrs. Advance booking is essential.

Stromness and West Mainland *p555*

Local There are several buses daily (Mon-Sat) between **Stromness** and **Kirkwall**, 30 mins. On Mon there's a bus between Kirkwall and Birsay with **Shalder Coaches**, T01856- 850809. To get to Skara Brae you'll need your own transport, or you can visit as part of a guided tour (see the TIC), or walk north along the coast from Stromness, via Yesnaby.

Car hire from **Brass's Car Hire**, Blue Star Garage, North End Rd, Stromness, T01856-850850. Cycle hire from **Orkney Cycle Hire**, 54 Dundas St, Stromness, T01856-850255.

Long distance **Northlink Ferries** sail from **Scrabster** to **Stromness** (1½ hrs) 3 times a day Mon-Fri and twice a day on Sat and Sun. Passenger fare is £27-33 return and a car costs £98-112 with a driver plus £20-22 per addi- tional passenger.

A shuttle bus links Scrabster with the nearby town of Thurso, on the north coast. There are regular bus and train services to Thurso from Inverness, see p411.

East Mainland and South Ronaldsay *p560*

See Kirkwall Transport section for details of the ferry service from **John o' Groats** to **Burwick**.

Hoy *p562*

Local Transport on Hoy is very limited. **North Hoy Transport**, T01856-791315, runs a minibus service between **Moaness Pier** and **Rackwick**, which meets the 1000 ferry from Stromness. Call the same number for a taxi around the island.

Car and bike hire is available from **Halyel Car Hire**, Lyness, T01856-791240.

Long distance A passenger ferry sails between **Stromness** and **Moaness Pier** in the north (30 mins) 3 times a day Mon-Fri and twice on Fri evenings, twice daily Sat and Sun. There's a reduced winter service (mid-Sep to mid-May). There's also a car and passenger service between **Houton** and **Lyness** and **Longhope** (45 mins) up to 6 times daily (Mon-Sat). There's a limited Sun service from mid-May to mid-Sep.

Rousay, Egilsay and Wyre *p563*
A small car ferry sails from **Tingwall** (20 mins) to **Rousay** 6 times a day (Mon-Sat; 5 times on Sun). Most of the ferries call in at **Egilsay** and **Wyre**, but some are on demand only and should be booked in advance, T01856-751360. A bus connects **Tingwall** and **Kirkwall** (see p572).

Cycle hire is available from **Arts, Crafts & Bike Hire**, at the pier, T01856-821398.

Shapinsay *p564*
The small car ferry makes 6 sailings daily (including Sun in summer) from Kirkwall (25 mins).

Eday *p565*
You can hire a taxi from **Mr A Stewart** by the pier, T01857-622206, or hire bikes from **Mr Burkett** at Hamarr, near the post office south of Mill Loch.

There are flights from **Kirkwall** to Eday with **Loganair**, T01856-872494, on Wed only. There are ferries from **Kirkwall** (1¼ hr to 2 hrs) twice daily via **Sanday** or **Stronsay**.

Sanday *p565*
There are **Loganair** flights to Sanday from **Kirkwall** twice daily Mon-Fri and once on Sat. There's a ferry service twice daily from **Kirkwall** (1½ hrs). The ferry arrives at Loth, at the southern tip of the island, and is met by a minibus which will take you to most places.

Stronsay *p566*
Taxis and island minibus tours are available from **M Williamson**, T01857-616255. Car hire and taxis are available from **DS Peace**, T01857-616335.

There are **Loganair** flights to Stronsay from **Kirkwall**, twice daily Mon-Fri. A ferry service runs from **Kirkwall** (1½ hr) twice daily Mon-Sat (once on Sun), and once daily Mon-Sat from Eday (35 mins).

Westray *p566*
For cycle hire contact **Mrs Groat** at **Sand o' Gill** (see above); or **Mrs Bain** at **Twiness**, T01856-677319. Flights to Westray with **Loganair** depart Kirkwall twice daily Mon-Fri and once on Sat. There's a car ferry service from **Kirkwall** to **Rapness**, on the south coast of the island (1½ hrs). It sails twice daily in summer (mid-May to mid-Sep) and once daily in winter. There's also a passenger ferry from **Pierowall** to **Papa Westray** (see below).

Papa Westray *p567*
The famous 2-min flight from Westray leaves twice daily Mon-Sat (£14 one-way). There is also a direct flight to Papay from **Kirkwall** daily Mon-Sat, except Fri (£15 one-way). There's a passenger ferry from **Pierowall** on Westray 3-6 times daily (25 mins). The car ferry from **Kirkwall** to Westray continues to Papa Westray on Tue and Fri (2¼ hrs).

North Ronaldsay *p567*
There are **Loganair** flights from **Kirkwall** twice daily Mon-Sat, T01856-872494. There's a car and passenger ferry which sails from **Kirkwall** (2 hrs 40 mins) once a week (usually Fri) and also on some Sun between May and Sep. Contact **Orkney Ferries** for details, T01856-872044.

Directory

Kirkwall *p551, map p553*
Banks Branches of the 3 main Scottish banks with cash machines are on Broad St and Albert St. Exchange also at the tourist office.
Hospitals **Balfour Hospital**, Health Centre and Dental Clinic, New Scapa Rd, T01856-885400.
Laundry **The Launderama**, Albert St, T01856-872982. Open Mon-Fri 0830-1730, Sat 0900-1700.
Post Junction Rd. Open Mon-Fri 0900-1700, Sat 0930-1230.

Stromness and West Mainland *p555*
Banks There are branches of **Bank of Scotland** and **Royal Bank of Scotland**, both with ATMs, on Victoria St, Stromness.
Laundry Next to the **Coffee Shop**, Stromness, T01856-850904. Self-service or service washes.

Shetland

Shetland is so far removed from the rest of Scotland it can only be shown as an inset on maps. In fact, it is easier and quicker to get there from Norway than it is from London. This seems entirely appropriate, for Shetland is historically and culturally closer to Scandinavia than Britain. Many of its place-names are of Norse origin, and people here still celebrate ancient Viking festivals, such as Up Helly-Aa. Modern-day visitors tend to come by plane rather than longboat, and usually bring binoculars, for Shetland is a birdwatchers' paradise. It is home to countless species, many of them seeking refuge from the madding crowds. And, let's face it, there's no better place than here to get away from it all. ▸▸ *For Sleeping, Eating and other listings, see pages 586-592.*

Ins and outs

Getting there

Shetland has good air connections with the rest of the UK. There are regular flights to and from several mainland airports which are operated by British Airways' franchise partners Loganair and British Regional Airlines. There are daily car ferry sailings from Aberdeen to Lerwick taking 12 hours and as well as ferries arriving from Kirkwall (Orkney). ▸▸ *For further details, see Transport page 590.*

Getting around

There is a regular scheduled inter-island service from Tingwall Airport near Lerwick with Loganair to Foula, Fair Isle, Papa Stour and Out Skerries. There are also frequent ferry service links many of the islands with the Shetland Mainland. Booking is essential for all journeys. Shetland has around 500 miles of good roads, and an extensive public bus service links Lerwick with all towns, villages and tourist sights. There are several bus operators. A Shetland Transport Timetable, published by Shetland Islands Council, contains details of all air, sea and bus services throughout the islands. It is available from the tourist office in Lerwick. The best way to explore the islands is with your own private car. It is cheaper to hire a car in Lerwick rather than at the airport. Hitching is a feasible way to get around and is relatively safe. Cycling is a good way to experience the islands, though most places are very exposed and the winds can be strong. ▸▸ *For further details, see Transport page 590.*

Lerwick and around → *Phone code: 01595. Population: 7,600.*

Lerwick is the capital and administrative centre of Shetland and the only sizeable town. Though the islands have been inhabited for many centuries, Lerwick only dates from the 17th century, when it began to grow as a trading port for Dutch herring fishermen, thanks to its superb natural sheltered harbour, the Bressay Sound. The town spread along the waterfront, where merchants built their lodberries, which were houses and warehouses with their own piers so that they could trade directly with visiting ships. By the late 19th century Lerwick had become the main herring port in northern Europe. Lerwick has continued to grow and is now home to a third of Shetland's population. The discovery of oil in the North Sea in the early 1970s led to the building of the Sullom Voe Oil Terminal, and the effect on Lerwick has been dramatic. It is now the main transit point to the North Sea oil rigs and there have been major extensions to the harbour area, bringing increased shipping and prosperity to the town. ▸▸ *For Sleeping, Eating and other listings, see pages 586-592.*

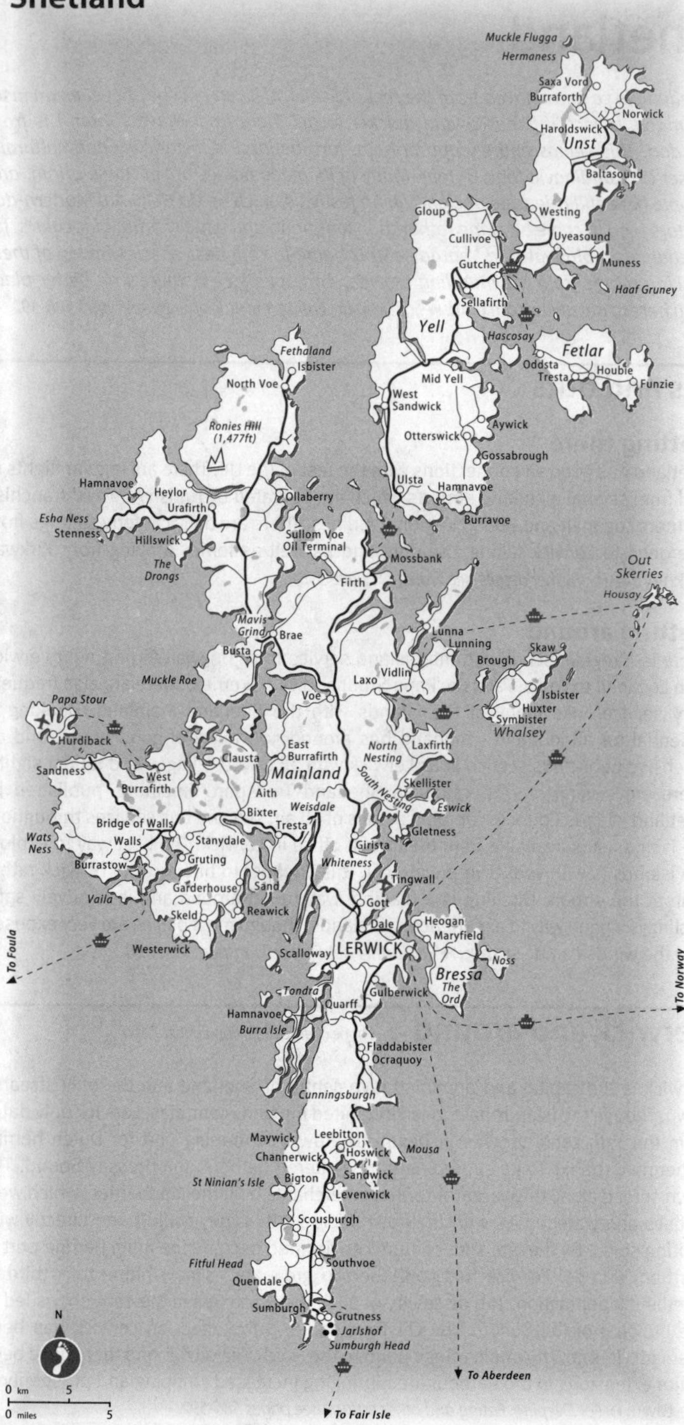
Muckle Flugga
Hermaness
Saxa Vord
Burrafirth
Norwick
Haroldswick
Unst
Baltasound
Westing
Uyeasound
Muness
Haaf Gruney
Gloup
Cullivoe
Gutcher
Sellafirth
Yell
Hascosay
Fetlar
Oddsta
Tresta
Houbie
Funzie
Mid Yell
West Sandwick
Aywick
Otterswick
Gossabrough
Ulsta
Hamnavoe
Burravoe
Fethaland
Isbister
North Voe
Ronies Hill (1,477ft)
Hamnavoe
Heylor
Urafirth
Ollaberry
Esha Ness
Stenness
Hillswick
The Drongs
Sullom Voe Oil Terminal
Mossbank
Firth
Out Skerries
Housay
Lunna
Lunning
Mavis Grind
Brae
Busta
Skaw
Brough
Isbister
Huxter
Symbister
Whalsey
Muckle Roe
Laxo
Vidlin
Voe
Papa Stour
Hurdiback
East Burrafirth
Clausta
North Nesting
Laxfirth
Sandness
West Burrafirth
Mainland
Aith
South Nesting
Skellister
Eswick
Bridge of Walls
Bixter
Weisdale
Tresta
Gletness
Wats Ness
Walls
Stanydale
Girlsta
Burrastow
Gruting
Whiteness
Tingwall
Garderhouse
Sand
Vaila
Skeld
Reawick
Gott
Dale
Heogan
Maryfield
Westerwick
LERWICK
Scalloway
Noss
Bressa
To Foula
The Ord
Gulberwick
To Norway
Tondra
Hamnavoe
Quarff
Burra Isle
Fladdabister
Ocraquoy
Cunningsburgh
Maywick
Leebitton
Mousa
Channerwick
Hoswick
Sandwick
St Ninian's Isle
Bigton
Levenwick
Scousburgh
Fitful Head
Southvoe
Quendale
Sumburgh
Grutness
Jarlshof
Sumburgh Head
N
To Aberdeen
0 km 5
0 miles 5
To Fair Isle

Ins and outs

Getting there and around Ferries from Aberdeen arrive at the main Holmsgarth terminal, which is about a mile north of the old harbour. There's a regular bus service between Lerwick and Sumburgh airport (50 minutes) run by John Leask & Son, T01595-693162. Taxis (around £25) and car hire are also available. All island bus services start and end at the Viking bus station, which is on Commercial Road, a short distance north of the town centre. The town is small and everything is within easy walking distance.

Tourist information The main TIC ⓘ *Market Cross, Commercial St, T01595-693434, www.shetland-tourism.co.uk, May-Sep Mon-Fri 0800-1800, Sat 0800-1600, Sun 1000-1300, Oct-Apr Mon-Fri 0900-1700*, are an excellent source of information, books, maps and leaflets. They will also change foreign currency and book accommodation.

Lerwick

The town's heart is the attractive **Commercial Street**, which runs parallel to the Esplanade. At the southern end are many old houses and lodberries, and you can continue south along the cliffs to the **Knab** or to lovely **Bain's beach**. *Lerwick Walks* is a leaflet detailing many interesting walks in and around town.

Overlooking the north end of Commercial Street is **Fort Charlotte** ⓘ *Jun-Sep daily 0900-2200, Oct-May 0900-1600, free*, built in 1665 and later rebuilt in 1780 and named after Queen Charlotte, George III's consort. It has since been used as a prison and Royal Naval Reserve base and, though there's little to see in the fort, there are fine views of the harbour from the battlements. One of Lerwick's most impressive buildings is the Victorian **town hall** ⓘ *Mon-Fri 1000-1200 and 1400-1530, free*, on Hillhead. The stained-glass windows of the main hall depict episodes from Shetland's history. Opposite the town hall, above the library, is

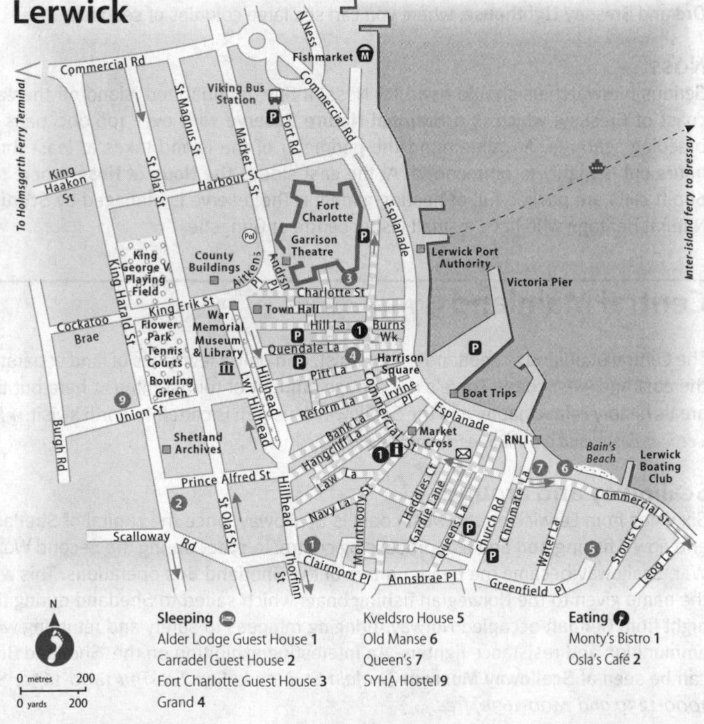

the **Shetland Museum** ⓘ *T01595-695057, Mon, Wed and Fri 1000-1900, Tue, Thu and Sat till 1700, free*, which gives a useful introduction to the islands' history. Amongst the artefacts on display is a replica of the St Ninian's Isle treasure.

Also in town is the **Up Helly-Aa Exhibition** ⓘ *mid-May to mid-Sep Tue 1400-1600 and 1700-1900, Fri 1700-1900, Sat 1400-1600, £3, concession £1.50*, in the Galley Shed off St Sunniva Street. This gives a taste of the famous Viking fire festival held annually in Lerwick on the last Tuesday in January, when a torch-lit procession through the town by hundreds of people dressed in Viking costumes (guizers) is followed by a replica Viking longship built especially for the event. At the end of the procession the ship is set ablaze when the guizers throw their flaming torches on to it.

A mile west of town are the substantial remains of **Clickimin Broch**, a fortified site occupied from 700 BC to around the fifth or sixth century AD. A path leads to the site from opposite the Safeway supermarket on the A970. About a mile north of the ferry terminal is the **Böd of Gremista** ⓘ *Jun to mid-Sep Wed and Sun 1000-1300 and 1400-1700*, free, a restored 18th-century fishing böd (booth) which was the birthplace of Arthur Anderson (1791-1868), co-founder of the Peninsular and Oriental Steam Navigation Company, now P&O. One of the rooms features an exhibition on Anderson's life and involvement with P&O.

Bressay

Lying to the east of Lerwick across the Bressay Sound is the island of Bressay (pronounced 'bressah'), which creates a sheltered harbour for the capital and led to its establishment as a major trading port. Seven miles long by three miles wide, it makes an ideal day trip for cyclists. Another good way to get around is on foot, and there's a fine walk to the top of **Ward Hill** (742 ft), the highest point, from where you get great views of the island and as far afield as Foula and Out Skerries. There are also good coastal walks, particularly along the cliffs from Noss Sound south to **Bard Head, The Ord** and **Bressay Lighthouse,** where you can see large colonies of seabirds.

Noss

Serious birdwatchers should head for Noss, a tiny, uninhabited island off the east coast of Bressay, which is a **National Nature Reserve** with over 100,000 pairs of breeding seabirds. A walk around the perimeter of the island takes at least three hours but is highly recommended. At the east side is the **Noup of Noss,** where the 600-ft cliffs are packed full of nesting gannets. The reserve is managed by Scottish Natural Heritage who have a small visitor centre at Gungstie.

Central Mainland → *Phone code: 01595.*

The Central Mainland is Shetland's slim waist, and only a few miles of land separates the east and west coast. There's not a huge amount of tourist interest here but the area's history is fascinating and the Scalloway Museum is certainly worth a visit. ▸▸ *For Sleeping, Eating and other listings, see pages 586-592.*

Scalloway and around

Six miles from Lerwick on the west coast is Scalloway, once the capital of Shetland and now a fishing port and fish-processing centre. In 1942, during the Second World War, Scalloway became the headquarters of the **Shetland Bus** operations. This was the name given to the Norwegian fishing boats which sailed to Shetland during the night from German-occupied Norway, bringing refugees to safety and returning with ammunition and resistance fighters. An interesting exhibition on the 'Shetland Bus' can be seen at **Scalloway Museum** ⓘ *Main St, May to Sep Tue-Thu 1400-1630, Sat 1000-1230 and 1400-1630, free.*

The harbour is dominated by the ruins of **Scalloway Castle**, built in 1600 by the notorious Earl Patrick Stewart using local slave labour, see page 556. After his execution the castle fell into disrepair, though the four-storey main block and one wing remain. Inside, an interpretative display explains its history.

South of Scalloway lie the islands of **Trondra** and **Burra**, now connected to the Mainland by bridges. At Burland on Trondra is the **Spirit of Shetland**, where you can buy Shetland knitwear, while on West Burra is the attractive little fishing village of **Hamnavoe**.

Tingwall

North of Scalloway, the B9074 runs through the fertile Tingwall Valley, past a nine-hole **golf course** at Asta, and the **Loch of Tingwall**, which is good for brown trout fishing and also home to swans and otters. At the northern end of the loch is a promontory called **Law Ting Holm**, which was the site of the Althing, or parliament, during the period of Norse rule. Overlooking the loch is **Tingwall Kirk**, built in the late 18th century on the site of the earlier church of St Magnus which dated back to the early period of Norse Christianity. In the graveyard is the old burial vault with several interesting old grave slabs. Nearby is **Tingwall Agricultural Museum** ⓘ *Jun-Aug Mon-Sat 1000-1300 and 1400-1700, £1.50*, which houses a collection of old crofting implements.

Weisdale

The A971 continues northwest towards Weisdale, a district with some worthwhile attractions. At the head of **Weisdale Voe** the B9075 branches north to **Weisdale Mill** ⓘ *T01595-830400, Wed-Sat 1030-1630, Sun 1200-1630, free*, which now houses the **Bonhoga Gallery**, a purpose-built art gallery featuring varied exhibitions of local, national and international works. There's also a nice café serving snacks. Weisdale Mill was part of the Kergord Estate, known until 1945 as Flemington, and was built from the stones of evacuated crofthouses. Over 300 crofters were forcibly evicted in the mid-19th century during the 'Clearances', when lairds expanded their more profitable sheep-farming activities. In 1940 the mill was requisitioned as the intelligence and administrative HQ for the 'Shetland Bus' operations (see Scalloway above). The Kergord estate today is the largest area of woodland in Shetland, and attracts a variety of migratory birds.

On the west shore of Weisdale Voe, south of the mill, are the ruins of the house where **John Clunies Ross** (1786-1854) was born. He settled in the Cocos Islands in the Indian Ocean in 1827 and the islands were owned by the Estate of the Clunies Ross family until purchased by the Australian government in 1978. In 1984 the islanders voted to become part of Australia.

The Westside

→ *Phone code: 01595. OS Landranger Nos 3 & 4.*

The western Mainland of Shetland, stretching west from Weisdale to Sandness, is known as The Westside. This part of Shetland is notable for its varied landscape of spectacular sea cliffs, rolling green hills, bleak moorland, peaty freshwater lochs and numerous long sea lochs, or voes. This is excellent **walking** country, with many fine coastal routes, especially around **Culswick** and **Dale of Walls**. It is also great for birdwatching and trout fishing, and there are many opportunities for spotting whales, dolphins and otters. » *For Sleeping, Eating and other listings, see pages 586-592.*

Stanydale, Walls and Sandness

There are a few interesting archaeological sites here, too. At Stanydale, signposted from the road between the villages of **Bixter** and **Walls**, is the site of a Neolothic settlement with the remains of houses, field boundaries and clearance cairns. Near

Battling Betty

Betty Mouat was quite a woman. In 1886, at the age of 60, she was on a boat heading for Lerwick when the captain was swept overboard and the two crewmen went to rescue him, leaving Betty alone. They were unable to get back to the boat which drifted for nine days before ending up in Norway. Betty survived the ordeal.

the **Brig o' Waas**, just north of Walls, is the **Scord of Brouster**, a prehistoric farm site which has been excavated.

The pretty little village of **Walls** (pronounced 'waas') is set around a sheltered natural harbour and is a popular spot with visiting yachts. It also attracts many visitors during its **Agricultural Show** in August, the biggest such event on Shetland. Walls is the departure point for ferries to the remote island of Foula, below.

Northwest of Walls, the A971 crosses bleak moorland before descending to the crofting township of **Sandness** (pronounced 'saa-ness'), surrounded by fertile land and facing little Papa Stour, about a mile offshore. There's a good beach here and also a **woollen spinning mill** ⓘ *Mon-Fri 0800-1700, free*, where you can watch how they spin the famously fine wool into yarn.

Foula

Lying 15 miles west of the Shetland Mainland, tiny Foula – whose name derives from the Norse fugl ey, meaning 'bird island' – is the second most remote inhabited island after Fair Isle. It supports a population of around 40 people, who are greatly out-numbered by the many thousands of seabirds, including a small colony of gannets and the rare Leach's petrel. There are also about 2,500 pairs of great skuas, the largest colony in the UK. The island is dominated by its sheer cliffs, which reach their most awe-inspiring peak at **The Kame** (1,220 ft), the second highest sea cliffs in Britain after St Kilda.

An interesting feature of the island's people is that they still observe the old **Julian calendar**, replaced in 1752 in Britain by the present Gregorian system which deleted 11 days from the year. Remote areas of the country kept to the old calendar, adding an extra day in 1800, which was a leap year, and some parts of Shetland continued to observe festivals 12 days after the dates in the new calendar. The most remote areas kept to the old calendar longest, and the people of Foula still celebrate Christmas on 6 January and New Year's Day on 13 January.

Papa Stour

A ferry sails from West Burrafirth on the Westside, near Sandness, to the little island of Papa Stour, only a mile offshore. The island, which has a population of around 30, is mostly made up of volcanic rock which has been eroded to form an amazing coastline of stacks, arches and caves, most spectacular of which is **Kirstan's Hole**. The island is home to large colonies of auks, terns and skuas, and also has a fascinating history of its own. Pick up the island trails leaflet from the tourist office in Lerwick.

South Mainland → *Phone code: 01950.*

From Lerwick a long, narrow finger of land points south. The main road runs down the east coast for 25 miles till it ends at Sumburgh Head, near Shetland's main airport. This southern part of the Shetland Mainland holds the islands' two most important archaeological sights and main tourist attractions. ▸▸ *For Sleeping, Eating and other listings, see pages 586-592.*

Isle of Mousa

ⓘ *T01950-431367, www.mousaboattrips.co.uk, entry to the broch is free, a ferry sails to the island from Leebitton harbour in Sandwick twice daily from mid-Apr to mid-Sep, weather permitting, allowing visitors 2½ hours to see the island, the trip takes 15 mins and costs £8 per adult.*

Fifteen miles south of Lerwick, the scattered crofting communities of Sandwick look across to the Isle of Mousa, site of the best-preserved broch in Scotland. This fortified tower was built around 2,000 years ago and still stands close to its original height of 45 ft. It's a very impressive structure when you see it from the inside and has chambers, galleries, an internal staircase and a parapet. The broch features in a Viking saga of the 12th century when the mother of Harald, Earl of Orkney, took refuge there with her lover. The Earl, who did not approve of the liaison, laid siege to the broch, but it proved impregnable and he gave up.

Mousa island is also home to many seabirds and waders, most notably the Storm Petrel, which is best seen at dusk as they return to their nests amongst the beach rocks. You can also see seals on the white-sand beach at West Voe. If you have time, it's a good idea to walk right around the coast, starting from the landing stage at West Ham and first heading south to the broch. Watch out for dive-bombing terns.

South of Sandwick

At Hoswick, between Sandwick and Levenwick, is **Da Warp and Weft Visitor Centre** ⓘ *May-Sep Mon-Sat 1000-1700, Sun 1200-1700, free*, which houses an exhibition on weaving, crofting, fishing and island life. Next door is the **Shetland Woollen Company**, where you can buy knitwear. Further south on the east coast, at Boddam, is the **Shetland Crofthouse Museum** ⓘ *May-Sep daily 1000-1300 and 1400-1700, £2*, a restored thatched crofthouse with 19th-century furniture and utensils.

St Ninian's Isle to Quendale

On the west coast, near Bigton village, a signposted track leads to the spectacular sandy causeway (known as a tombolo) which leads to St Ninian's Isle. The tombolo is the best example of its kind in Britain, and you can walk across to the island which is best known for the hoard of Pictish treasure which was discovered in 1958 in the ruins of the 12th-century church. The 28 silver objects included bowls, a spoon and brooches, probably dating from around AD 800, and are now on display in the Royal Scottish Museum in Edinburgh, though you can see replicas in the Shetland Museum in Lerwick.

The west coast south of Bigton is beautiful with long, sandy beaches interspersed with dramatic cliff scenery. On the other side of the road from the long, sheltered beach at **Scousburgh Sands** is the **Loch of Spiggie RSPB Reserve**. The loch is an important winter wildfowl refuge, particularly for Whooper Swans, and during the summer you can see various ducks, waders, gulls, terns and skuas. There's a hide on the northern shore with an information board. Nearby is the **Spiggie Hotel** which offers bar meals, afternoon tea or dinner.

A few miles south of the loch is the village of **Quendale**, overlooking a wide, sandy bay. Here you'll find the beautifully restored and fully working 19th-century **Quendale Mill** ⓘ *May-Sep daily 1000-1700, £2*, the last of Shetland's watermills. Not far from here, between Garth's Ness and Fitful Head, lies the wreck of the Braer oil

Catpund Quarries, 10 miles south of Lerwick, to the south of Cunningsburgh, is where soft soapstone was quarried from Neolithic to medieval times, making a variety of stone implements and utensils for these times.

Close encounters of the bird kind

Shetland is famous for its birds. As well its huge seabird colonies, the islands attract Arctic species and are an important crossroads for migrating birds. Over 340 species have been recorded on Fair Isle, including rare and exotic birds from Asia and America. Twenty-one out of the 24 seabirds common to Britain breed in Shetland. These can be found around the coastline, but the largest colonies are at the Hermaness and Noss reserves.

Amongst the many species which can be seen are the puffin. About one fifth of Scotland's puffins breed in Shetland. Its cousins in the auk family, guillemots, and razorbills, are also here in abundance during the summer months, along with kittiwakes, shags and that most common of seabirds, the fulmar. Britain's largest seabird, the gannet, can be seen diving spectacularly for fish at Hermaness, Noss, Fair Isle and Foula, while its smallest seabird, the storm petrel, is best seen around dusk on the tiny island of Mousa.

Summer heralds the return of the Arctic tern which breeds along low coastlines, as do the eider, oystercatcher, ringed plover and black guillemot, or tystie, which stays here all year round. The best place to see waders and shelduck are the nutrient-rich tidal mudflats at the Pool of Virkie in the South Mainland.

Many birds breed on agricultural land, and these include the lapwing, skylark, meadow pipit and wheater. The hills and moorland provide breeding grounds for many summer visitors such as that pirate of the skies, the great skua, or bonxie, and the Arctic skua. Another Arctic species, the whimbrel, also nests here, mainly in Unst, Yell and Fetlar. Moorland habitats are also favoured by the curlew, golden plover and merlin, Shetland's only bird of prey, while the lochs are home to large numbers of red-throated divers. Fetlar is home to 90 per cent of the population of one of Britain's rarest birds, the red-necked phalarope.

Many of Shetland's bird habitats are protected as RSPB Reserves and National Nature Reserves, and it is an offence to disturb the birds and their young at or near their nests. You also risk being dive-bombed by some of the more aggressively protective species. For a full list of all species recorded on the islands and more practical birdwatching information, be sure to get a copy of the *Shetland Bird Chart* by Joyce Gammack, available from the tourist office in Lerwick.

tanker which ran on to the rocks in 1993. A disaster of epic proportions was averted by the hurricane-force gales which dispersed the huge oil spillage.

Sumburgh and Jarlshof

At the southern tip of Mainland is the village of Sumburgh, site of Shetland's main airport for external passenger flights and for helicopters and planes servicing the North Sea oil industry. South of the airport is Shetland's prime archaeological site, **Jarlshof** ⓘ *T01950-460112, Apr-Sep daily 0930-1830, £3.30, concession £2.50, children £1*, a hugely impressive place which spans 4,000 years of occupation from Neolithic times through Norse settlement to the 16th century. The original Stone-Age dwellings are topped by a medieval broch, Pictish wheelhouses, Viking longhouses and, towering over the whole complex, the ruins of a 16th-century mansion. This remarkable site was only discovered at the end of the 19th century when a violent storm ripped off the top layer of turf. Jarlshof is, in fact, not a genuine name, but the exotic invention of Sir Walter Scott in his novel *The Pirate*. A helpful guidebook available from the visitor centre helps to bring the place to life.

South of Jarlshof the Mainland ends abruptly at **Sumburgh Head**, an RSPB Reserve. The **lighthouse** on top of the cliff was built by Robert Stevenson in 1821, and the keepers' cottages are now rented out as self-catering accommodation. The lighthouse isn't open to the public, but from its grounds you can see many nesting seabirds such as puffins, kittiwakes, fulmars, guillemots and razorbills. Just to the east of the airport is **Pool of Virkie**, another good birdwatching area.

Fair Isle → *Phone code: 01595.*

Fair Isle, 24 miles southwest of Sumburgh and 27 miles northeast of North Ronaldsay in Orkney, is the most isolated of Britain's inhabited islands. Only three miles long by 1½ miles wide, the island has a population of around 70 and is best known for its intricately patterned knitwear, which is still produced by a co-operative, **Fair Isle Crafts**. Co-operative could be said to sum up the friendly islanders, whose lifestyle is based on mutual help and community effort. ▸▸ *For Sleeping, Eating and other listings, see pages 586-592.*

Ins and outs

Getting to Fair Isle requires patience, persistence and a strong stomach to survive the white-knuckle 4 ½-hour ferry sailing. There are also flights from Tingwall Airport. For more information visit on Fair Isle visit www.fairisle.org.uk, or call the National Trust for Scotland, T0141-616 2266, www.thenationaltrustforscotland.org.uk. ▸▸ *For further details, see Transport page 590.*

Sights

Fair Isle is a paradise for birdwatchers, and keen ornithologists form the majority of the island's visitors. Celebrity birdwatcher and former Goodie, Bill Oddie, has dubbed it the "the Hilton of the bird world". It stands in the flight path of many thousands of migrating birds, and over 340 species have been recorded here at the **Fair Isle Bird Observatory**, which also offers accommodation and where visitors are welcome to take part. As well as the almost obscenely rich birdlife there are around 240 species of flowering plants, making the island an especially beautiful haven for naturalists. Fair Isle's coastline, especially in the north and west, also boasts some outstanding cliff scenery.

The bird observatory was the brainchild of George Waterston, an ornithologist who first visited in 1935 and then bought the island in 1948 to begin his task of building the observatory. The island was given to the National Trust for Scotland in 1954 and declared a National Scenic Area. It was recently designated a place of outstanding natural beauty and cultural heritage by the Council of Europe. The **George Waterston Memorial Centre** ⓘ *May to mid-Sep Mon and Fri 1400-1600, Wed 1030-1200, donations welcome*, has exhibits and photographs detailing the island's natural history, as well as the history of crofting, fishing, archaeology and knitwear.

North Mainland → *Phone code: 01806.*

The main road north from Lerwick branches at **Voe**, a peaceful and colourful little village nestling in a bay at the head of the Olna Firth. One branch leads to the Yell car and passenger ferry terminal at **Toft**, past the turn-off to the massive **Sullom Voe Oil Terminal**, the largest oil and liquefied gas terminal in Europe. The other road heads northwest to Brae (see below). ▸▸ *For Sleeping, Eating and other listings, see pages 586-592.*

Brae

Brae is not a very pretty place and was built to accommodate workers at the nearby Sullom Voe oil terminal. It does boast a good selection of accommodation and decent facilities, though, and makes a good base from which to explore the wild and wonderful coastal scenery around the Northmavine peninsula to the north. There's also good walking and spectacularly good westerly views around the island of **Muckle Roe** to the southwest, and up the island's small hill, **South Ward** (554 ft). But be careful of the overly protective bonxies, or great skuas, which will attack if you get too close. The island is attached to the mainland by a bridge.

Northmavine

Mavis Grind, the narrow isthmus where it's claimed you can throw a stone from the Atlantic to the North Sea, leads into Northmavine, the northwest peninsula of North Mainland. It is one of Shetland's most dramatic and beautiful areas, with rugged scenery, spectacular coastline and wide empty spaces. This is wonderful walking country, and it's a good idea to abandon the car and explore it on foot. **Hillswick Ness**, to the south of **Hillswick** village, is a nice walk, but further west, around the coastline of **Eshaness**, is the most spectacular cliff scenery and amazing natural features, all with unusual and evocative names.

North of the lighthouse are the **Holes of Scraada**, **Grind o' da Navir** and the **Villians of Hamnavoe**, which are not the local gangs but eroded lava cliffs with blowholes, arches and caves. East of Eshaness are the **Heads of Grocken** and **The Drongs**, a series of exposed sea stacks, which offer superb diving. Further north, overlooking the deep sea inlet of **Ronies Voe**, is the dramatic red granite bulk of **Ronies Hill** (1,477 ft), with a well-preserved burial cairn at the summit. The coastal scenery to the north and west of here is even more breathtaking, but very remote and exposed. You should be well equipped before setting out.

Between Eshaness and Hillswick, a side road leads south to the **Tangwick Haa Museum** ⓘ *May-Sep Mon-Fri 1300-1700, Sat and Sun 1100-1900, free*, which features displays and photographs on the history of fishing and whaling and the hardships of life in these parts.

Whalsay and Out Skerries → *Phone code: 01806.*

South of Voe, the B9071 branches east to Laxo, the ferry terminal for the island of **Whalsay**, one of Shetland's most prosperous small islands owing to its thriving fishing industry, which helps support a population of around 1,000. The fleet is based at **Symbister**, the island's main settlement. Beside the harbour at Symbister is the **Pier House** ⓘ *Mon-Sat 0900-1300 and 1400-1700, Sun 1400-1700, free*, a restored böd which was used by the Hanseatic League, a commercial association of German merchants who traded in Shetland from the Middle Ages to the early 18th century. Inside is an exhibition explaining the history of the Hanseatic trade, and general information on the island. One of Scotland's great poets, **Hugh McDiarmid** (Christopher Grieve), spent most of the 1930s in Whalsay, where he wrote much of his finest poetry, until he was called for war work in 1942, never to return. His former home, at Sodom near Symbister, is now a camping böd, see Sleeping page 587.

The Out Skerries is a small group of rocky islands about five miles from Whalsay and 10 miles east of Shetland Mainland. It's made up of three main islands: the larger islands of **Housay** and **Bruray**, which are connected by a road bridge; and the

In the seas around Whalsay you can see porpoises, dolphins, minke whales and orcas, hence its Viking name which means 'island of whales'.

uninhabited island of **Grunay**. The Skerries boast some spectacular and rugged sea cliffs which are home to many rare migrant seabirds in spring and autumn. » *For Sleeping, Eating and other listings, see pages 586-592.*

Yell, Fetlar and Unst → *Phone code: 01957.*

Yell

Yell, the second largest of the Shetland islands, was described rather damningly by Shetland-born writer Eric Linklater as 'dull and dark'. And it's true that the interior is consistently desolate peat moorland. But the coastline is greener and more pleasant and provides an ideal habitat for the island's large **otter** population. Yell is also home to a rich variety of birds, and offers some good coastal and hill walks, especially around the rugged coastline of **The Herra**, a peninsula about half way up the west coast.

At **Burravoe**, about five miles east of the ferry terminal at **Ulsta**, is the **Old Haa Museum** ⓘ *T01957-722339, late Apr-Sep Tue-Thu and Sat 1000-1600, Sun 1400-1700, free*, housed in Yell's oldest building which dates from 1672. It contains an interesting display on local flora and fauna and history.

The island's largest village, **Mid Yell**, has a couple of shops, a pub and a leisure centre with a good swimming pool. About a mile northwest, on the hillside above the main road, are the reputedly haunted ruins of **Windhouse**, dating from 1707. To the north is the **RSPB Lumbister Reserve**, where red-throated divers, merlins, great and Arctic skuas and many other bird species come to breed. The reserve is also home to a large number of otters. A pleasant walk leads along the nearby steep and narrow gorge, known as the **Daal of Lumbister**, filled with many colourful flowers. The area to the north of the reserve provides good walking over remote moorland and coastline.

The road continues north past the reserve and around **Basta Voe,** where you can see otters. North of **Gutcher**, the ferry port for Unst, is the village of **Cullivoe**, with some good walks along the attractive coastline.

Fetlar

Fetlar is the smallest of the North Isles but the most fertile, and known as 'the garden of Shetland'. Indeed, the name derives from Norse meaning 'fat land', as there is good grazing and croftland and a rich variety of plant and bird life. The whole island is good for birdwatching, but the prime place is the 1,700 acres of **North Fetlar RSPB Reserve** around Vord Hill (522 ft) in the north of the island. This area has restricted access during the summer months, and visitors should contact the warden at Bealance, T01957-733246. The warden will also let you know if and when you can see the one or two female Snowy Owls which sometime visit.

The north cliffs of the reserve are home to large colonies of breeding seabirds, including auks, gulls and shags, and you can also see common and grey seals on the beaches in late autumn. Fetlar is home to one of Britain's rarest birds, the **red-necked phalarope**, which breeds in the loch near **Funzie** (pronounced 'finnie') in the east of the island. You can watch them from the RSPB hide in the nearby marshes. Red-throated divers and whimbrel also breed here. The island is also good for walking, and a leaflet describing some of the walks is available from the tourist office in Lerwick.

The main settlement on the island is **Houbie**; on the south coast. Here you'll see a house called Leagarth, which was built by the island's most famous son, Sir William Watson Cheyne, who with Lord Lister pioneered antiseptic surgery. Nearby is the excellent **Fetlar Interpretive Centre** ⓘ *May-Sep Tue-Sun 1200-1700, free*, which presents the island's history and gives information on its bounteous birdlife.

With nothing between you and the North Pole but water, this is the place to sit and contemplate what it feels like to be at the end of the world...

Unst

Unst is the most northerly inhabited island in Britain, but there is more to the island than its many 'most northerly' credentials. It is scenically one of the most varied of the Shetland islands, with spectacular cliffs, sea stacks, sheltered inlets, sandy beaches, heather-clad hills, fertile farmland, freshwater lochs and even a sub-arctic desert. Such a variety of habitats supports over 400 plant species and a rich variety of wildlife. Unst is a major breeding site for gannets, puffins, guillemots, razorbills, kittiwakes, shags, Arctic and great skuas and whimbrels, amongst others, and in the surrounding waters you can see seals, porpoises, otters and even killer whales.

In the east of the island, north of **Baltasound**, is the **Keen of Hamar National Nature Reserve**, 74 acres of serpentine rock which breaks into tiny fragments known as 'debris', giving the landscape a strange, lunar-like appearance. This bleak 'desert' is actually home to some of the rarest plants in Britain. Baltasound is the island's main settlement, with an airport, hotel, pub, post office, leisure centre with pool and Britain's most northerly brewery, the **Valhalla Brewery** which can be visited by appointment, T01975-711348.

To the north of here is the village of **Haroldswick**, home of Britain's most northerly post office, where your postcards are sent with a special stamp to inform everyone of this fact. Here also is **Unst Boat Haven** ⓘ *May-Sep daily 1400-1700, free*, where you can see a beautifully presented collection of traditional boats and fishing artefacts. A little way further north is the **Unst Heritage Centre** ⓘ *same opening hours as Boat Haven and also free*, which has a museum of local history and island life. Nearby is an RAF radar-tracking station at Saxa Vord. The road ends at Skaw, where there's a lovely beach and Britain's most northerly house. The road northwest from Haroldswick leads to the head of **Burra Firth**, a sea inlet flanked by high cliffs, and site of Britain's most northerly golf course.

To the west of Burra Firth is the remote **Hermaness National Nature Reserve**, 2,422 acres of dramatic coastal scenery and wild moorland which is home to over 100,000 nesting seabirds including gannets, and the largest number of puffins and great skuas (or 'bonxies') in Shetland. There's an excellent **visitor centre** ⓘ *T01975-711278, daily late Apr to mid-Sep 0830-1800*, in the former lighthouse keeper's shore station, where you can pick up a leaflet which shows the marked route into the reserve, and see the artistic efforts of many of Unst's children. Whilst in the reserve, make sure you keep to the marked paths to avoid being attacked by bonxies; they are highly protective and rest assured that they will attack if they think that their territory is being threatened.

The views from Hermaness are wonderful, out to the offshore stacks and skerries including **Muckle Flugga**, and then to the wide open north Atlantic Ocean. Muckle Flugga is the site of the most northerly lighthouse in Britain, built in 1857-1858 by Thomas Stevenson, father of Robert Louis Stevenson. The writer visited the island in 1869, and the illustrated map in his novel *Treasure Island* bears a striking similarity to the outline of Unst. Beyond the lighthouse is **Out Stack**, which marks the most northerly point on the British Isles. With nothing between you and the North Pole but water, this is the place to sit and contemplate what it feels like to be at the end of the world.

A böd for the night

There is only one youth hostel in Shetland, but budget travellers shouldn't panic. Shetland Camping Böd project has developed a network of camping böds (pronounced 'burd') which provide basic and cheap digs throughout the islands.

A böd was a building used to house fishermen and their gear during the fishing season and the name has been used to describe these types of accommodation which are similar to English 'camping barns'. They are all located in scenically attractive places and each has its own fascinating history. They are very basic and the more remote ones have no electricity or lighting. You'll need to bring a stove, cooking and eating utensils, sleeping bag and torch (flashlight). All böds must be booked in advance through the tourist office in Lerwick. They cost £5 per person per night, though they can also be booked for exclusive use by large groups. They are open from the beginning of April till the end of September. There are at present six camping böds on Shetland and these are listed in the relevant places.

Sleeping

Lerwick and around *p575, map p577*
Shetland's best accommodation is outside Lerwick, whose hotels are mostly geared towards the oil industry. During the peak months of Jul and Aug and the Folk Festival in Apr, it's a good idea to book in advance.

B Grand Hotel, Commercial St, T01595-692826. Features Shetland's only nightclub.

B Kveldsro House Hotel, Greenfield Pl, T01595-692195, www.kghotels.co.uk. The most luxurious hotel in town. Pronounced 'kel-ro', it overlooks the harbour and has an upmarket (and **£££**) restaurant as well as cheaper bar food.

B Lerwick Hotel, 15 South Rd, T01595-692166, rcception@lerwickhotel.co.uk. 10 mins from the centre, has a reputation for fine cuisine.

B Shetland Hotel, directly opposite the ferry terminal, T01595-695515. Modern and functional.

B-C Queen's Hotel, Commercial St, T01595-692826. By the harbour. Rather faded.

There are several pleasant guest houses and B&Bs, including:

D Alder Lodge Guest House, 6 Clairmont Pl, T01595-695705;

D-E Fort Charlotte Guest House, 1 Charlotte St, T01595-695956;

D The Old Manse, 9 Commercial St, T01595-696301;

D-E Carradel Guest House, 36 King Harald St, T01595-692251;

D-E Maryfield House Hotel, on the little island of Bressay, T01595-820207, near the ferry terminal.

D-E Solheim Guest House, next door to Maryfield House Hotel, T01595-695275.

F SYHA hostel, Islesburgh House, King Harald St, T01595-692114, open Apr-Sep. Clean and well-run.

Camping

Clickimin Caravan & Camp Site, T01595-741000, near Clickimin Leisure Centre and loch on the western edge of town.

Central Mainland *p578*

E Hildasay Guest House, Scalloway, in the upper part of the village, T01595-880822. Has disabled facilities and arranges fishing trips.

C Herrislea House Hotel, Tingwall, near the airport, by the crossroads, T01595-840208, www.herrislea-house.shetland.co.uk. Offers good home cooking daily till 2100, and live music in its Starboard Tack bar.

For an explanation of sleeping and eating price codes used in this guide, see inside the front cover. Other relevant information is found in Essentials, see pages 43-51.

C-D **Westings Hotel**, in Wormadale, near Tingwall, T01595-840242, www.westings.shetland.co.uk. Modern hotel which is a good place to stop for lunch.

The Westside *p579*

The best accommodation on the Westside is in Walls.

B **Burrastow House**, 2 miles southwest of Walls, T01595-809307, burr.hs.hotel@zetnet.co.uk. A restored 18th-century house overlooking Vaila Sound, it's full of character and has a reputation for serving superb cuisine (some say the best on the islands, so you'll need to book ahead).

D **North House**, Papa Stour, T01595-873238, which offers full board. There's no shop on the island.

E **Leraback**, Foula, T01595-753226, which includes dinner in the price. There is also self-catering accommodation available on the island, £90-150 per week for a cottage sleeping 4-6 people. Contact Mr R Holbourn, T01595-753232.

E **Skeoverick**, a mile or so north of Walls, T01595-803349. Friendly B&B.

E-F **Pomona**, Gruting, east of Brig o' Waas, T01595-810438.

Camping

Voe House, Walls, is a camping **böd** – a restored 18th-century house overlooking the village. Open Apr-Sep. Book through Lerwick tourist office.

South Mainland *p580*

There's accommodation in Sandwick, around Sumburgh however it is limited.

C **Sumburgh Hotel**, T01950-460201, next to Jarlshof, in a converted laird's house, has a bar and restaurant.

E **Barclay Arms Hotel**, Sandwick, T01950-431226, offers evening meals.

E-F **Solbrekke**, Sandwick, T01950-431410.

Camping

Betty Mouat's Cottage, next to a excavated site at Scatness, next to the airport, is this camping böd. It sleeps up to 8 and is open Apr-Sep. Book through Lerwick tourist office.

Fair Isle *p583*

There are a few places to stay on the island, but accommodation must be booked in advance and includes meals. There are no hotels, pubs or restaurants.

C **Fair Isle Lodge and Bird Observatory**, T01595-760258, www.fairislebirdobs.co.uk, offers full-board accommodation in private rooms or in a dormitory (**E**).

D **Schoolton**, T01595-760250. Full board.

D **Upper Leogh**, T01595-760248, kathleen.coull@lineone.net. Full board.

Self-catering cottage, T01595-760248, for 4 from £210 weekly.

North Mainland *p583*

B **Busta House Hotel**, Brae, T01806-522506, www.mes.co.uk/busta. The best place to stay around Brae, or anywhere else on Shetland, is this luxurious and wonderfully atmospheric 16th-century country house overlooking Busta Voe about 1½ miles from Brae village. The superb restaurant (**£££**) is the finest on Shetland, with a selection of malts to match, and there are also meals in the bar.

D **Valleyfield Guest House**, Brae, T01806-522563. B&B with the option of dinner.

E **Almara**, T01806-503261, Upper Urafirth. Comfortable B&B.

E **Drumquin Guest House**, Brae, T01806-522621, dinner available.

E **Westayre**, T01806-522368. On Muckle Roe, a working croft.

Camping

Sail Loft, in Voe by the pier, is this former fishing store and now Shetland's largest camping böd. Open Apr-Sep.

Johnny Notion's Camping Böd, in Hamnavoe, Northmavine, is reached by a side road which branches north from the road between Hillswick and Eshaness. This is birthplace of John Williamson, known as 'Johnny Notion', an 18th-century craftsman who developed an effective innoculation against smallpox. It's open Apr-Sep and has no electricity. Book through Lerwick TIC.

Whalsay and Out Skerries *p584*

Hugh Mc Diarmid's Camping Böd, near Symbister, open Apr-Sep, with no electricity. The former home of this great poet, see p584.

Yell, Fetlar and Unst *p585*

There's a decent selection of accommodation on Unst.

D Buness House, T01975-711315,Unst, buness@zetnet.co.uk. Top choice has to be this lovely old 17th-century Haa in Baltasound. Staying here is a bizarre and rather surreal experience, given that you are on the most northerly island in Britain. The house is crammed full of Indian Raj relics, and the stuffed eagle, tiger and leopard skins hanging in the hallway are a wildlife close-up almost as impressive, though considerably more unsettling and un-'PC', as the Hermaness Nature Reserve in the north of the island that the family own. The food is excellent and taccommodation comfortable.
E Cligera Guest House, Baltasound, Unst, T01975-711579. Friendly.
E Gerratoun, Haroldswick, Unst, T01975-711323. B&B.
E The Glebe, Fetlar, T01975-733242, a lovely old house overlooking Papil Water.
E The Gord, in Houbie, Fetlar, T01975-733227.
E Hillhead, in Burravoe, Yell, T01975-722274.
E Pinewood Guest House, in South Aywick, between Burravoe and Mid Yell,Yell, T01975-702427.
E Prestegaard, Unst, T01975-755234. Another good place is this Victorian house at Uyeasound on the south coast near the ferry.
E-F Post Office, in Gutcher, Yell, T01975-744201. Friendly and welcoming.
F Gardiesfauld Hostel, Baltasound, Unst, T01975-755259; open Apr-Sep. An independent hostel which also hires bikes.

Camping
Windhouse Lodge, Yell, a camping böd below the ruins of haunted Windhouse. It's well-equipped and open Apr-Sep.
Gerth's Campsite, Fetlar, T01975-733227, overlooks the beach at Tresta and has good facilities.

Eating

Lerwick and around *p575, map p577*
Despite a ready supply of fresh local produce, Shetland is a gastronomic desert.
££ Kveldsro Hotel and **Lerwick Hotel** (see Sleeping) are the next best choices after Monty's for dinner or bar lunch.
££ Monty's Bistro & Deli, 5 Mounthooly St, T01595-696655. The best place to eat in Lerwick. It offers good modern Scottish cooking in a cosy, informal setting. Closed Sun.
£ Osla's Café, 88 Commercial St, T01595-696005. Cosy café serving a wide range of coffees, pancakes and other snacks and boasting the islands' only beer garden. Open Mon-Sat till at least 1900, Sun 1200-1600.

Central Mainland *p578*
£ Da Haaf Restaurant, T01595-880328, is a canteen-style restaurant in the North Atlantic Fisheries college and specializes in (yes, you guessed it) seafood. Does a good fish supper, as well as having a more up-market menu for the evenings. Open Mon-Fri 0900-2000.
£ Scalloway Hotel and **Kiln Bar**, both offer bar meals.

North Mainland *p583*
££ Busta House, Brae, see Sleeping, serves fine good.
££-£ Mid Brae Inn, Brae, is a good place to eat serving great food daily till 2100.
££-£ Pierhead Restaurant and Bar, Voe, T01806-588332, serves meals.
££ The Booth, Hillswick, is Shetland's oldest pub serving food daily in summer.

Yell, Fetlar and Unst *p585*
Eating options on very limited, though most B&Bs will serve evening meals on request.
Baltasound Hotel, Unst, T01975-711334, serves meals and drinks to non-residents.
Hilltop Restaurant and Bar, Mid Yell, Yell.
Old Haa Museum, Yell, has a café.
Seaview Café, Gutcher, Yell.

Bars and clubs

Lerwick and around *p575, map p577*
Lounge, Mounthooly St near the tourist office. The upstairs bar here is best place for a drink. Local musicians usually play on Sat lunchtimes and some evenings.
Posers, at the Grand Hotel, is the town's only nightclub.

Festivals and events

Lerwick and around *p575, map p577*
For details of both events, contact the Folk Festival office, 5 Burns La, Lerwick, T01595-694757. The *Shetland Times* (Fri), www. Shetland-times.co.uk, also details what is

going on. Also check the tourist board's Events phoneline, T01595-694200.

Folk music has a strong following in Shetland and the islands play host to 2 of Scotland's top folk events.

Shetland Folk Festival: mid-Apr The islands are alive with the sound of music as musicians from around the globe come to play at this event.

Shetland Accordion and Fiddle Festival: mid-Oct.

Shopping

Central Mainland *p578*

Shetland Woollen Company, next to Scalloway Castle, T01595-880243, where you can buy the famous Shetland wool and Fair Isle sweaters.

Activities and tours

Lerwick and around *p575, map p577*

Shetland Wildlife Tours,T01950-422483, www.shetland-wildlife-tours.zetnet.co.uk. Offer a number of guided tours to see the islands' outstandingly rich selection of wildlife; ranging from the excellent-value £20 trip around Noss and Bressay, where, if you go at the right time of year, you are almost guaranteed to see seals, porpoises and the astounding gannetry on the spectacular cliffs of Noss' east coast, to the more upmarket week-long 'Ultimate Shetland' tour, at around £700.

Noss & Bressay Wildlife Cruises, with Bressaboats, T01595-693434, and **Shetland Sea Charters** (same phone number), also offer cruises which cost around £20. **Bressaboats** and **Shetland Wildlife Tours** both run a full-day Hermaness and Muckle Flugga Cruise which costs around £70 per person.

John Leask & Son, The Esplanade, Lerwick, T01595-693162, offers a variety of bus tours costing from around £10 up to £20 depending on the destination.

Transport

Lerwick and around *p575, map p577*

Local For detailed information on all bus services, call T01595-694100 (Mon-Sat 0900-1715). There are regular daily buses (Nos 3 and 4) to and from **Sumburgh airport** which connect with flights. These buses also stop at several main sights, including **Jarlshof**, **Sandwick** (for Mousa Broch) and **St Ninian's Isle**. Bus No 2 runs to **Scalloway** (Mon-Sat). There are also buses (daily except Sun) to **Walls**, **Sandness**, **Aith**, **Skeld**, **North Roe**, **Hillswick**, **Vidlin**, **Toft** and **Mossbank**. Buses depart from the Viking bus station.

There is car hire at Bolts Car Hire, Toll Clock Shopping Centre, 26 North Rd, T01595-693636; John Leask & Son, Esplanade, T01595-693162; and Star Rent-a-Car, 22 Commercial Rd, T01595-692075. They have offices at Sumburgh Airport too. Cycle hire from Grantfield Garage, North Rd, T692709, Mon-Sat 0800-1300 and 1400-1700.

There are several taxi companies in Lerwick: **6050 Cabs**, T01595-696050; Sheilds Taxis, T01595-695276; and Abbys Taxis, T01595-696666.

Long distance Loganair, T01595-840246, operates a regular service from Lerwick to the islands of **Foula** (£43.60 return), **Fair Isle** (£76 return), **Papa Stour** (£33 return) and **Out Skerries** (£37 return). Also from Out Skerries to **Whalsay** (£21 return) and Sumburgh to **Fair Isle** (£76).

Getting to Shetland by air is expensive. From Aberdeen fares range from around £150 one way, depending on the day and time of year. A return flight from Orkney is around £186. For details of the excellent value Highland Rover Pass, see p39. Flights from several mainland airports in Scotland and England can be booked through British Airways, T08708-509850, or by calling Loganair in Lerwick, T01595-840246. Shetland's main airport is at Sumburgh, 25 miles south of Lerwick, T01950-460654. Bus services operate linking Sumburgh with Lerwick. There are direct daily flights from **Aberdeen** (4 Mon-Fri; 2 on Sat and Sun), which has frequent services to all other major British airports. There are also direct flights from **Glasgow** (daily), **Edinburgh** (daily except Sun), **London Heathrow** (daily), **Inverness** (Mon-Fri), **Orkney** (daily except Sun), **Wick** (Mon-Sat) and **Belfast** (daily except Sat). There are also international flights to and from **Bergen** and **Oslo** (Norway) on Thu and Sun.

There are regular daily car ferries between **Lerwick** and **Bressay** (5 mins), **East Mainland** and **Whalsay** (30 mins), **North Mainland** and **Yell** (20 mins), **Yell** and **Unst** (10 mins), and **Yell** and **Fetlar** (25 mins). **Noss** can only be visited from late May to late Aug daily, except Mon and Thu, from 1000-1700. From the 'Wait here' sign overlooking Noss sound on the east side of Bressay an inflatable dinghy shuttles back and forth to Noss during the island's opening hours. The trip costs £3 return. In bad weather, call the tourist office, T01595-693434, to check if it's sailing. A postcar service runs once a day (except Sun) from Maryfield ferry terminal to Noss Sound, T01595-820200. There's a less frequent car ferry service between **East Mainland** and **Skerries** (Mon, Fri, Sat and Sun; 1½ hrs), and **Lerwick** and **Skerries** (Tue and Thu; 2½ hrs). There's also a passenger/cargo ferry service between **West Mainland** and **Papa Stour** (Mon, Wed, Fri, Sat and Sun; 40 mins), **West Mainland** and **Foula** (Tue, Sat and alternate Thu; 2 hrs), **Scalloway** and **Foula** (alternate Thu; 3 hrs), **South Mainland** and **Fair Isle** (Tue, Sat and alternate Thu; 2½ hrs), and **Lerwick** and **Fair Isle** (alternate Thu; 4 ½ hrs). These services are operated by **Shetland Council**, T01595- 744866, www.shetland.gov.uk. Fares vary according the route. Bookings are also essential. Times and fares are also available from the TIC in Lerwick (see below).

Ferry links with the UK are provided mostly by **Northlink Ferries**, T0845-6000449, www.northlinkferries.co.uk. They operate car ferries to **Lerwick** from **Aberdeen** (and to Kirkwall, Orkney). There are sailings from Aberdeen once a day Mon-Sun at 1900, the journey takes 12 hrs. Passenger fares for a seat with no accommodation cost from £43-63 return, depending on the times of year. A car and driver costs from £190-263 return. A 2-berth cabin costs £50-78 per journey. Children aged 4-16 travel for half price and under 4s go free. There are also ferries from **Norway**, **Iceland** and the **Faroe Isles**, see p35.

Central Mainland *p578*

Tingwall Airport, T01595-840246, has flights to most of the smaller islands, see the Lerwick transport. Getting to and from the airport is straightforward, as regular buses between Lerwick and Westside (see below) stop in Tingwall. There are several daily buses (except Sun) between **Lerwick** and **Scalloway**, operated by Shalder Coaches, T01595-880217.

The Westside *p579*

There are daily buses to **Walls** from Lerwick, Mon-Sat, with Shalder Coaches, T01595-880217. A minibus runs to **Sandness** from **Walls** once a day (except Sun). Contact Mr P Isbister, T01595-809268. Ferries should be booked with W Clark, T01595-810460. See Lerwick transport section for details of flights and ferries to the area.

South Mainland *p580*

There are several daily buses (Mon-Sat; 2-3 on Sun) between **Lerwick**, **Sandwick** and **Sumburgh Airport**. Two buses daily (Mon-Sat) run to **Quendale** from **Lerwick**, with a change at **Channerwick junction**. There are regular daily buses from **Lerwick**, which stop at the Sumburgh Hotel, **Scatness** and **Grutness Pier** (for Fair Isle) en route to the airport. See the Lerwick transport section for details of flights and ferries to the area.

Fair Isle *p583*

For details of ferries and flights, see the Lerwick transport section. A day-return flight allows about 6 hrs on the island. You can also fly from **Kirkwall** on Orkney, which allows 2½ hrs on the island, T01856-872420. Ferries should be booked with J W Stout, T01595-760222.

North Mainland *p583*

Regular buses from **Lerwick** to **Brae** and **Hillswick** to the northwest, and **Toft** and **Mossbank** to the north, pass through **Voe** daily except Sun. Buses from **Lerwick** to **Hillswick** (see below) and to Toft/ Mossbank (see under Yell below) stop in **Brae**. There is a daily bus service from **Lerwick** to **Hillswick** (Mon-Sat), departing at 1710 and arriving at 1825. From there, a feeder service continues to **Eshaness** (20 mins). Contact Whites Coaches, T01806-809443.

Whalsay and Out Skerries *p584*

There are regular daily car and passenger ferries between **Laxo** and **Symbister**. To book, call T01806-566259. There are daily buses to **Laxo** and and **Vidlin** (see below) from Lerwick, run by Whites Coaches, T01595-809443.

There are ferries to the Skerries from Lerwick and also from Vidlin, about 3 miles northeast of Laxo. For bookings, call G W Henderson, T01806-515226. There are also flights from Tingwall Airport. See the Lerwick transport section for further details.

Yell, Fetlar and Unst *p585*

There are frequent car and passenger ferries from **Toft** on North Mainland to **Ulsta** on the south coast of **Yell**. It's not essential, but a good idea to book in advance, T01975-722259. Three buses daily (Mon-Fri; 2 on Sat, 1 on Sun) run between Lerwick and Toft (1 hr). There's a bus service on Yell which runs between Ulsta and Cullivoe and stops at villages in between, T01975-744214.

There are regular car and passenger ferries between **Oddsta** in the northwest of **Fetlar** and Gutcher on Yell and Belmont on Unst. There's a post car service which runs around the Fetlar from the ferry once a day on Mon, Wed and Fri, T01975-733227.

There are regular car and passenger ferries to **Belmont** on **Unst** from Gutcher on Yell. Booking is advised, T01975-722259. Also on Unst, there's an island bus service which runs a few times daily (except Sun) between **Baltasound**, **Belmont** and **Haroldswick**, T01975-711666.

For further details of ferries and flights see the Lerwick transport section above.

Directory

Lerwick and around *p575, map p577*

Banks **Bank of Scotland**, **Clydesdale** and **Royal** are on Commercial St. **Lloyds TSB** is on the Esplanade.

Embassies and consulates **Denmark**, **Iceland**, **Netherlands** and **Sweden** at Hay & Company, 66 Commercial Rd, T01595-692533; **Finland**, **France**, **Germany** and **Norway** at Shearer Shipping Services, Garthspool, T01595-692556.

Hospitals **Gilbert Bain Hospital**, Scalloway Rd, T01595-743000. Opposite is the **Lerwick Health Centre**, T01595-693201.

Laundry **Lerwick Laundry**, 36 Market St, T01595-693043, closed Sun. Service washes only.

Post Commercial St (Mon-Fri 0900-1700, Sat 0900-1200), also in Toll Clock Shopping Centre, 26 North Rd.

Travel agents **John Leask & Son**, Esplanade, T01595-693162.

Background

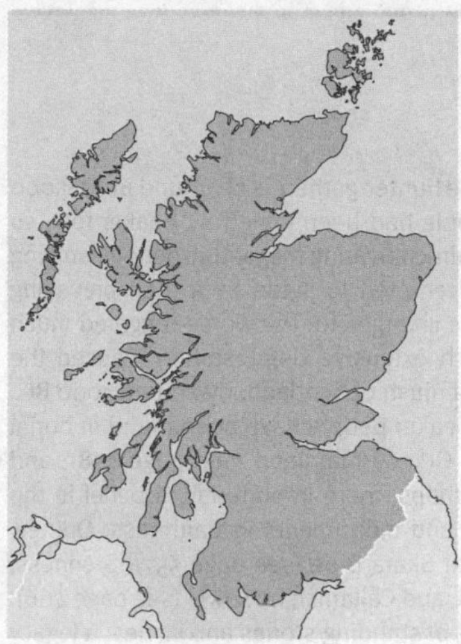

Footprint features

History

Prehistoric times

Scotland's earliest known inhabitants are the hunter-gatherers of around 6000-5000 BC. By 2000-1500 BC these Mesolithic people had been joined by Beaker folk, so named from their distinctive pottery, and grain-cultivating Megalithic people, arriving by sea via Spain and Portugal, who were tempted to settle by a then prevailing near-Mediterranean climate. Several climate changes for the worse triggered much population movement and also, along with extensive deforestation, caused the formation of peaty soil, now characteristic of much of Scotland, by around 1000 BC.

The pottery and other artefacts of the Beaker people have been found in burial mounds or cairns, such as Maeshowe on Orkney Mainland (see page 558), and suggest a complex social structure and perhaps, more importantly, a belief in the afterlife, as do the prehistoric settlements and monuments in Caithness, Orkney, Shetland and the Outer Hebrides, notably at Skara Brae (see page 557), Stenness, and the Ring of Brodgar on Orkney Mainland, and Callanish on Lewis (see page 466). But throughout Scotland there are hundreds of standing stones and circles, a legacy of the megalithic peoples. In Aberdeenshire surveys reveal precise orientations indicating their use as observatories charting lunar cycles and eclipses. The layout of Clava Cairns, near Inverness (see page 347), bears similarities to the great temple at Newgrange in Ireland. And at Kilmartin in Argyll (see page 347), cup and ring marks, stone alignments and burial cairns, formed in a complete 'landscape temple', suggest a geomantic sophistication that has now been forgotten.

At the beginning of the first millennium BC, Bronze-Age traders from far afield were busy around the coasts. Celts arrived from Germany, bringing with them new agricultural technology and weaponry such as swords and shields, which in turn necessitated impressive earthwork defences in the form of hillforts and crannogs (see page 606) as competition for land increased. In about 200-100 BC more Celts arrived with superior iron-working skills, and consequently, more fortifications were also built. The brochs, or towers, the remains of many of which can still be seen dotted along the west coast and in the islands, date from this time (see also page 606).

The Picts and the Romans

Indigenous Iron-Age tribes inhabited most of the country and were identified by the Romans as 'Picts' – possibly meaning 'painted, or tattooed, people'. They thwarted Roman imperial ambition in Alba, the land north of the Forth and Clyde, in around AD 80, and a string of Roman military outposts along the Highland line remain from this abandoned campaign. At Fortingall near Aberfeldy, the ancient yew tree is said to mark the birthplace of Pontius Pilate, possibly the son of a Roman soldier who later found preferment in Rome. To add credence to this theory, a gravestone marked 'PP' was found.

Defensive walls built by Emperors Hadrian (circa AD 123 from the Solway Firth to the Tyne) and Antoninus (from the Clyde to the Forth circa AD 143) against the Picts inadvertently set a precedent for the eventual polarization of Scotland and England, beginning around the ninth century, out of the mass of tribal kingdoms. An endlessly disputed border led to centuries of retaliatory raids and devastation on either side.

Picts south of the Antonine wall became semi-Romanized and were known as Britons, kin to the Welsh. Their kingdom of Strathclyde, with a stronghold on Dumbarton Rock near Glasgow, once extended into Lancashire and retained a separate identity into the 11th century. The Lothians, territory of the British Gododdin, was overrun by Anglians from Northumbria. In the seventh century the Anglians challenged the Picts in Alba and were finally defeated at Dunnichen.

Meanwhile an Irish tribe, the Scots, who claimed descent from an Egyptian Pharaoh's daughter, had been settling in Pictish territory in Argyll from around the fourth century. Once in Argyll, the sons of the Scots' leader, Erc, established a kingdom called Dalriada, sharing it between themselves under a high king at Dunadd (see page 298). When their fellow countryman, Columba, arrived in the sixth century on Iona, they were aided in their cause by his diplomatic skills at the hostile Pictish court of King Brude, in Inverness. In the ninth century the Scots under Kenneth MacAlpin took over the Picts. Although their written records were destroyed, or falsified by the conquering Scots, they left a rich legacy of unique sculptured stones denoting a civilized and artistic culture. When Kenneth set up at Scone, and Alba became Scotland, the seven kingdoms of Pictland in the north and east survived as great earldoms.

The early Church

Some claim Joseph of Arimathea brought Christianity to Whithorn in Galloway, which had been a religious centre since the first century. Around AD 397 Ninian founded a Christian Mission in Whithorn, along eastern Mediterranean monastic lines vastly different from the Roman model. From here he and countless missionaries such as Kentigern, Moluag and Comgan went north to convert the Picts, as far as St Ninian's Isle in Shetland. Their communities, oak churches and cells are remembered in innumerable place names, wells and simple cross-marked stones, often established on pre-Christian sacred sites.

In AD 563 Columba arrived on Iona (see page 318), where he went on to found the Celtic Church, or the Church of the Culdees, with centres throughout Scotland, which differed in many ways from the Church of Rome. Iona became known as the 'Cradle of Christianity in Scotland', but the arrival of the Vikings inhibited sea travel and the monks were driven from Iona. About this time, the Scots took over the Pictish nation and the Columban church moved to Dunkeld, with Columba's relics transported in the breacbannoch, or Monymusk reliquary. This was carried at Bannockburn and is now in the Museum of Scotland in Edinburgh.

St Andrews later became the principal seat of the church, although Iona retained special status. Communities of Culdees (one of which was at St Andrews) survived into the 13th century, outwith the Columban and later Roman church. These were thought to be adherents of Ninian's church, preserving elements of pre-Christian druid religion.

A common origin for the cross symbol found on both the Pictish cross slabs and the free standing crosses of Iona and Islay is the chi-ro, or wheeled cross, as found at Whithorn. However, the enigmatic symbols, vivid hunting scenes and mythical beasts of the Pictish stones found throughout Pictland are unique, and their function remains a mystery. Another mystery is the brief flourishing in the early 13th century of an accomplished school of sculptors around Loch Awe, in Argyll. In ancient burial grounds throughout Knapdale are found grave slabs depicting swords, warriors, and foreign ships, thought to mark the graves of the Knights Templar who fled here from France.

The Vikings

Pagan Norsemen in dragonships are first heard of in Argyll in AD 795, the first of many such coastal raids of unimaginable savagery, which included ritual killings. Colonies of monks were not spared; 68 suffered the 'red martyrdom' on Iona in 807, and its library, 'a shop window crammed with the loot of centuries' was a magnet for raiders. By the late ninth century Norsemen had colonized Orkney (see page 556), and from Birsay Palace Earl Sigurd wielded power as far south as Moray. Arenegade bunch of mixed Norse and Gaelic ancestry, the Gall-Gaels, appeared in the Hebrides and Galloway. Some of these, like chieftain Ketil Flatnose's family, became early settlers of Iceland.

Once surrounded by aggressive Norse colonies, now also in Dublin and York, the newly formed 'Scotland' survived through a combination of fighting spirit and a network of shifting alliances with the various Norse powers. Some of these alliances were enduring. In the ninth century 'Torf' Einar, credited with introducing peat cutting, founded a dynasty from which sprang the Earls of Angus.

After the Dublin colony collapsed in 1014, a Viking kingdom of 'Man and the Sudreys' (Hebrides) filled the vacuum, and the isles continued to be ravaged by warring Norsemen. By around 1100 Norwegian king Magnus Barelegs' empire included the entire northern and western seaboard. Against this backdrop, pursuing his own interests, appears Somerled, Hebridean hero of Norse-Gaelic blood, progenitor of Clan Donald and the powerful Lordship of the Isles. In 1153 he supported a rebellion against the Scottish crown. Later, in the early 13th century, he built a series of castles around the coast, such as Sween, Tioram, Mingary and Dunstaffnage, which foiled the intermittent attempts made by the Scottish crown to assert control.

The last of the great Norse kings, Hakon, was defeated by the Scots in 1263 at Largs, with the aid of bad winter weather. Orkney and Shetland were only returned to Scotland in the 15th century. A Norse dialect was spoken there into the 18th century, and vestiges of Norwegian law still survive, as does the Viking St Magnus Cathedral in Kirkwall.

Macbeth and the battle for kingship

Macbeth, the earl-king of the vast land of Moray, rose to high kingship with popular support, reigning for a relatively long (1040-1057) and peaceful time with his queen Gruoch, grand-daughter of Kenneth III of Scots. The popular image of Macbeth as portrayed by Shakespeare is, in fact, a false one. The great bard vilified Macbeth in order to please his James VI, who claimed descent from Duncan, Macbeth's rival. But it was Duncan who was the nasty piece of work, and he was slain not at Glamis, as in the famous play, but on the battlefield, while invading Macbeth's territory. Indeed Duncan is remembered in the Orkneyinga saga, the 'bible' of Viking history, as Karl Hundason, 'low-born son of the hound'.

Competition for the throne was a part of Pictish custom. A suitable 'tanist' or candidate was elected from anyone whose great-grandfather had been king, and the candidates would then fight it out: in practice survival of the fittest. This competition for the right to be king was complicated by the ancient dynastic rivalry among the Dalriadic Scots and perpetuated when they merged with the Picts under Kenneth MacAlpin. This later precipitated the Wars of Independence.

One part of Shakespeare's Macbeth which is historical fact is the Birnam Wood incident, when Malcolm, Duncan's son, and his Northumbrian allies used tree branches as camouflage to advance on Macbeth in his Dunsinnan stronghold near Perth. He was later hunted down and slain at Lumphanan by Malcolm's ally, MacDuff, Earl of Fife, and is buried on Iona.

Macbeth, the last truly Celtic king, was also one of the most able early kings. He was the first to establish and implement a fair legal system and, a firm supporter of the Celtic church, he went on pilgrimage to Rome where an Irish monk observed him liberally scattering money to the poor. Further evidence of the great disservice done to his memory by Shakespeare.

The Canmores and the Norman conquest

Macbeth's usurper, the uncouth Malcolm III, Canmore (meaning 'big head'), was an illegitimate son of Duncan and a miller's daughter. In 1067 Malcolm married Margaret, a Saxon princess born in Hungary and sister of Edgar Atheling, the English heir to the throne, who had fled north with his family to escape William the Conqueror and the Norman conquest. Margaret was a devout Catholic and was largely responsible for introducing the religious ideas of the Roman Catholic Church into Scotland, for which she was canonized in 1251. In 1072 she founded Dunfermline

Abbey and introduced southern manners to the Scottish court. Her private chapel survives in Edinburgh Castle, and is one of the oldest surviving buildings in Scotland.

Malcolm's belligerent instincts were not curbed by the influence of the saintly Margaret, however, and one of his many raids into Northumberland provoked a visit from William the Conqueror. The result was that Malcolm was forced to swear allegiance to William, an oath he didn't take too seriously, as he continued to raid England at whim, but one which would lead to a greater degree of southern interference in Scottish constitutional matters.

The Normans began to exert their influence over Scotland in many other ways. They were granted land as far as the Highland fringes, establishing a feudal system based on loyalty to the crown. The traditional patriarchal tribal culture was eroded, causing constant rebellions in the North and Galloway. The Norman successor to the Scottish throne, David I, like many of his Norman friends, had English estates, acquired through his wife. This wealth built the great Border abbeys and established the Roman church more fully. New parishes and dioceses revolutionized administration, and burghs were founded to develop international trade, attracting Flemish settlers. Society in medieval Scotland became more typically European than England or even France.

One of the depressingly familiar themes running through Scottish history has been the unwillingness of the Scots nobility to resist English ambitions towards Scotland. This has always been their Achilles heel and, in 1290, it provoked a crisis of succession, when the new child queen, Margaret, Maid of Norway, died en route from Norway. Margaret had been recognized as heiress of Scotland, the Hebrides and the Isle of Man, and the planned child marriage to the prince who would become Edward II, son of Edward I, was not to be. Following her death, no fewer than 13 rival contestants materialized. Two main factions emerged: the Balliols and Comyns against the Bruces. But instead of reverting to the traditional method of tanistry, or 'natural selection', the pusillanimous Scots nobles appealed to Edward I of England to adjudicate.

Wallace and Bruce: the Wars of Succession

Edward eventually chose John Balliol, and he was crowned king at Scone in June 1292. Balliol was anxious to prove to his fellow Scots that he was not as weak as they claimed him to be. He negotiated a defensive agreement with the French, the beginning of the Auld Alliance. He then invaded Cumberland in 1296, but in retaliation Edward attacked Berwick and slaughtered its inhabitants. The Scottish army was then defeated at Dunbar, and thereafter the castles of Edinburgh, Roxburgh, Perth and Stirling were captured.

In the same year, Balliol abdicated at Stracathro and went into exile. Edward then destroyed the great Seal of Scotland and, worse still, moved the Stone of Destiny, the traditional crowning throne for all Scottish kings, to Westminster Abbey, where it lay under the Coronation Chair for 700 years. Scotland, as a result, was left in disarray.

However, resistance found a leader in William Wallace, son of a Renfrew laird. He began a revolt against the English in 1297 and built up a substantial army. By September of that year he he had secured a small but strategic victory against English forces at Stirling Bridge. This galvanized support, and he was quickly declared 'Guardian of the Realm'. Following his defeat at Falkirk he was betrayed to Edward by one of the Scots noblemen, captured and taken south to be executed (disembowelled, then hung, drawn and quartered) in Smithfield, London, in 1305.

This stirred Robert the Bruce to take up the cause of independence. Encountering his treacherous rival, 'Red' Comyn, in a Dumfries church, he seized the initiative, stabbing him at the altar. With Comyn dead, and the support of patriotic church leaders, as well as Sir James, 'The Black Douglas', Bruce was able to consolidate his gains, and he was crowned king with full ceremony at Scone before the inevitable blow of Papal excommunication fell. But it was not only that Rome refused to recognize Bruce as king. Edward I, the self-proclaimed 'Hammer of the Scots', was not best pleased, and for the next seven years Bruce was a virtual outlaw fighting a guerrilla campaign against Edward from hiding in the west.

During this time the indomitable Edward died, and Bruce felt bold and confident enough to raid the northern counties of England as far south as Appleby and Richmond. Of his castles captured by the English, only Stirling remained to be wrested from Edward's successor, Edward II. So the scene was set for the most significant battle in Scottish history, at Bannockburn, near Stirling, in 1314, where Bruce confronted Edward II's vastly superior army. His incredible victory, aided by Angus Og of the Isles, and a number of Knights Templar recently arrived seeking sanctuary from persecution in France, has ensured him a place in the heart of every patriotic Scot.

Bannockburn brought the Scots a rare victory over their southern enemy, and led to the signing of the Declaration of Arbroath, manifesto of Scotland's independence, in 1320. There followed a temporary peace with England, and Bruce was finally recognized as king by the Pope, before he died in 1329. His friend Douglas, as requested, took Bruce's heart on pilgrimage to the Holy Land, but when Douglas died en route it was returned to Melrose Abbey.

The Stewart Dynasty

From Robert the Bruce's title of 'High Steward' sprang the dynasty of Stewart kings. The early Jameses (of whom there were seven in all) all followed a tragic pattern: succeeding as infant kings, imprisoned throughout childhood, and suffering untimely deaths. James I and III were both murdered, and James II blew himself up accidentally with a cannon. Unscrupulous regents frequently took charge, and hugely powerful nobles like the house of Douglas competed both amongst themselves and against the king. James II hot-bloodedly murdered the Earl of Douglas over dinner at Stirling Castle by throwing him out of the window. The Lords of the Isles were put down by the Earl of Mar and his followers in one of the bloodiest battles of all, 'Red Harlaw' near Inverurie. Like the Douglases, they too were finally forfeited, in 1543.

However, the early Stewarts made progress towards rescuing the country from anarchy by laying the foundations for a modern state through a series of constitutional reforms. They embodied the democratic 'Kings of Scots', answerable first to the common people. Mostly cultured and progressive, they found time to write poetry (James I wrote the King's Quair), to build Renaissance palaces, and to father sufficient illegitimate 'James Stewarts' to fill numerous ecclesiastical sinecures (James IV and V). James IV was a true Renaissance prince with a glittering court, but a self-destructive streak led to his early death – along with most of the nobility – at Flodden, in 1513, sacrificed for the long-standing 'Auld Alliance' with France.

Mary, Queen of Scots

There is no more tragic and romantic figure in Scottish history than Mary, Queen of Scots. Raised in France for safekeeping as a Catholic, her brief reign was dogged by bad luck, bad judgement and bad timing. She arrived back in Scotland in 1561, a young widow, at the height of Reformation turmoil in which both France and Catholicism were inimical. Something of a loose cannon, she was embroiled in a power struggle not helped by her disastrous choice of husbands. Implicated in the celebrated murder of the first one, her cousin, Henry Lord Darnley, she then swiftly married one of the chief suspects, the Earl of Bothwell, incurring the fury of everyone else. Imprisoned after the Battle of Carberry on the island fortress of Loch Leven, she escaped only to throw herself on the mercy of her cousin Queen Elizabeth I, who, mindful that in Catholic eyes Mary had the better claim to the English throne, locked her up at Fotheringhay for 19 years before deciding to do away with her altogether.

Reformation and the roots of Scottish education

The Reformation, converting the Catholic church to Protestant, came relatively late to Scotland and the motives were as much political as religious, though, of course, in 16th-century terms the two were inextricably linked. A pro-English Protestant faction had grown over decades, opposing the French Catholic Regent, Mary of Guise, and in 1560 a rebel parliament banned Catholic Mass, thus shattering for good the Auld Alliance with France, first formalized in 1295.

The casualties of the Reformation were countless, and included religious buildings, works of art and even whole libraries. It amounted to a complete obliteration of the past over which even today amnesia prevails, though, unlike in England, there were very few martyrs. So began 100 years of bitter struggle to establish the reformed church. Cue the Protestant exile, John Knox, a Calvinist rabble-rouser of dubious character and little diplomacy who was prone to blasting his trumpet off against the 'monstrous regiment of women,' namely Mary, Queen of Scots. Knox's skills as a colourful orator, and his self-appointed role as official historian of the Reformation, have allowed him to eclipse the real hero, Andrew Melville, who sacrificed his career of reforming university education to devote himself to the nuts and bolts of church reform.

Schooling for all as a passport to intellectual freedom and moral probity was a dream of the reformers. While grammar and song schools already existed, by the end of the 17th century most parishes had schools using the bible as textbook. The 'Dominie' (schoolmaster) was, until recently, a hugely influential community figure. Prior to the Reformation the Universities of St Andrews (1412), Glasgow (1451) and Aberdeen (1495) had been established, and Edinburgh University was added to the list in the 1580's.

James VI and the Union of Crowns

After Elizabeth's death, Mary's son became James VI of Scotland. Jacobean Scotland was vibrant and vigorously European. Religious extremists were checked by James VI, the 'Wisest fool in Christendom,' and unprecedented peace allowed Renaissance culture to blossom. But trouble was brewing. In 1603 James VI ascended to the English throne as James I, with the Union of Crowns. At this time the Scottish Parliament had so little power that James VI/I was able to write from his palace in London: "Here I sit and govern Scotland with my pen. I write and it is done." In contrast, the English parliament had begun to assume some genuine power.

Charles I and the Covenanters

James believed in the Divine Right of Kings – the God-given right of monarchs to rule their subjects. It was a belief that he passed on to his son Charles I, who succeeded in 1625 and quickly proved that he had little desire to consult parliament in either Scotland or England. Although he was born in Dunfermline, he showed little interest in Scotland and was essentially an absentee monarch. He did not even bother to come to Scotland to be crowned until 1633, calling a parliament at the same time – and then overseeing proceedings, making sure that the voting went his way.

Charles also showed little tact and diplomacy in matters ecclesiastical, and by reasserting the powers of the bishops he rode roughshod over the authority of the General Assembly of the Church of Scotland. Not surprisingly, the rumblings of revolution could soon be heard.

The struggle of the kirk (church) against the king erupted into full scale civil war, with hostility towards bishops the recurrent theme. A riot in St Giles in Edinburgh expressed public feeling and resulted in The National Covenant, signed in Edinburgh in 1638, pledging faith to 'the true religion' and affirming the authority of the powerful General Assembly of the Church of Scotland in all matters spiritual. Covenanters and king came to blows, followed by an extremist group of Presbyterians allying with the

 English parliament against the king, in the Solemn League and Covenant. Battle-hardened Scots flooded back from European campaigns to take up arms.

A supporter of the original Covenant, Montrose, led a spirited but doomed campaign for the king against the extremists. At Ardvreck in Assynt he was betrayed to his arch-enemy 'King Campbell', Duke of Argyll, who gave him a traitor's death in Edinburgh. After the Restoration Argyll found himself on the wrong side and met the same end on the same spot.

Civil War

Throughout the 17th century the dark side of religious idealism – fanaticism and paranoia – were epitomized by the 'kirk sessions': courts in which the church conducted an orgy of scapegoating and witch-hunts. Fundamental differences of ideology, constitution and culture between two countries only recently 'twinned', opened cracks in the alliance with the Parliamentarians. The following year Civil War broke out in England, with parliamentarians led by Oliver Cromwell fighting to wrest power from the king. In 1649 Charles was executed and England became a republic. The Scots, however, wanted to keep the monarchy and proclaimed his son, Charles II as their king, despite falling under Cromwell's military 'Protectorate'. Cromwell acted swiftly to bring the country under his control. In 1651 he forbade the Scots from holding their own parliament – forcing them to send representatives to Westminster instead.

Charles II and Restoration

The Commonwealth under Cromwell lasted until 1660, when Charles II was restored to the English throne. The Scottish Parliament was revived and met again in 1661. This time the Presbyterian Covenanters, who had gained such control of Parliament prior to the Commonwealth, were tamed. The Scottish Parliament was again largely run by nobles loyal to the king.

Although Charles II's was greeted with wild rejoicing, the reinstatement of the bishops once again proved problematic. Some unconsenting ministers of the church were outlawed and, finding a loyal following, especially in the southwest, they held illegal services, 'Conventicles', in the open air. Crippling fines and brutal persecution from officers of the crown, including Graham of Claverhouse, merely increased their resistance, and many died in the 'Killing Times' as martyrs to high principle.

Religion and the Monarchy

Scotland and England continued to disagree, both about the succession and about religion. Charles II's brother and successor, James VII/II, was a Roman Catholic, and in 1687 he tried to introduce more tolerant policies towards Catholics. His actions were seen as a threat to the privileged position held by the Church of England, which since the time of Henry VIII had been the official church in England, and also displeased Presbyterians in Scotland. At first the feeling was that this state of affairs wouldn't last: James was ageing, and as both his daughters were Protestants, the Protestant succession seemed safe. However, when his heir James Francis Edward was born and brought up as a Catholic, a crisis was precipitated, James was ousted from the throne, and fled ignominiously in 1689. His Protestant daughter, Mary, and her husband William of Orange, were invited to take the throne of England, and were later reluctantly accepted by the Scots under the terms of the Revolution Settlement.

The Darién Scheme

Although both countries shared a monarch, England was growing significantly wealthier than Scotland. Like other European countries, it was thriving economically through trade generated by its colonies. Scotland, however, had no colonies of its own. To remedy this, a monopoly company was founded with the approval of the King, modelled on the English East India Company. Wealthy Scots helped to fund it, but much of the capital was raised in England. However, the English East India Company exercised its considerable power to protect its monopoly. Strings were pulled and the House of Commons soon threatened to prosecute the Scottish company's English directors. The King, who had agreed to its establishment, now came under pressure to oppose it. Not surprisingly, most of the English backers withdrew and Scotland saw it as a matter of national pride to raise the starting capital itself – a sum of £400,000, roughly half the nation's capital.

The intention of the scheme was to establish a permanent colony at Darién, on the Panama Isthmus in Central America. Darién was a strategically important site, and the plan was that goods sent to and from Europe would sail to Panama, be carried overland across the isthmus, then reshipped – the new Scottish company carrying out this lucrative work.

However, the project had not been thoroughly researched. For one thing, the land was owned by Spain, a major world power who King William could not afford to offend. Consequently, he ordered English colonists in the area not to help the Scottish settlers defend their new home against the Spanish. In addition the terrain was hostile (which was why the Spanish had not set up a similar scheme already), and diseases like malaria and yellow fever were rife. Within months large numbers of colonists had died. Another attempt was made and was also unsuccessful, and by 1700 the colony had been abandoned.

The consequences were far reaching. Scotland lost a vast proportion of her wealth; national pride and confidence were dented; and the country lost faith in the dual monarchy. The King had sided with his wealthiest subjects – and Scotland felt betrayed.

Union of Parliaments

While Darién produced much anti-English feeling, a number of Scots began to feel that greater co-operation with England could be economically advantageous. At around the same time a further constitutional crisis was brewing. William of Orange had no children and was to be succeeded by James VII/II's daughter, Anne, who was Protestant. However, Anne had no surviving children and English politicians began to search for an heir – who had to be both Protestant and have Stuart blood. They decided on the Hanoverians, who were descended from the daughter of James VI/I. In 1701 the English parliament passed the Act of Settlement, ruling that on Anne's death the throne should pass to the House of Hanover. In 1702 William died and the throne passed to Anne.

The assumption was that the Scots would follow England's lead and accept the Hanoverian succession. But the nation was still smarting over Darién and, as Anne turned out to have little interest in Scotland, relations were strained. The difficulties over having two separate governments under one monarch would not go away. In 1703 the Scottish parliament passed the Act of Security which declared that on Anne's death Scotland would take a different successor to England, unless some settlement could be agreed upon that restored 'the honour and sovereignty of this Crown and Kingdom'. They wanted to guarantee the power of the Scottish parliament; the freedom of Scottish religion; and freedom of trade. In addition Parliament ordered people to arm themselves and prepare to fight. It was sabre rattling that the English could hardly ignore.

Although Anne signed the Act of Security, Scotland's triumph was shortlived. England passed the Alien Act, which declared that all Scots except those resident in England should be treated as aliens, and Scottish trade with England was to be blocked. The Act was to remain in force until Scotland agreed to make moves towards parliamentary union, or accepted Hanoverian succession.

 There were obvious economic advantages to closer ties with England, and Scotland was in a vulnerable position. Not only had the Darién venture weakened the economy, the country was also suffering from several years of harvest failure which had led to famine. Although public opinion was against union with England, it counted for little. It certainly appealed to many in parliament. Financial inducements were offered – and accepted, causing Robert Burns to comment later that Scotland had been "bought and sold for English gold". The Church of Scotland, initially suspicious of Union, withdrew its objections when it was assured that Presbyterianism would be safeguarded. A propaganda campaign was carried out on both sides of the border, many of the pamphlets being written by the author Daniel Defoe. The English were assured that union would end the threat of invasion from Scotland; the Scots assured of great economic benefits.

The people were not swayed. There were violent demonstrations in the streets, and riots in Glasgow, Dumfries and Edinburgh. Opponents even went as far as claiming that union would be sinful. The riots in Edinburgh were particularly violent, causing Defoe, who was acting as a spy for the English government, to say: "A Scots rabble is the worst of its kind. 'The Scots', he said, 'were a hardened and terrible people'. Pro union MPs were attacked, and plans were made in Lanarkshire to raise an army to march on Edinburgh. But public opinion was not of consequence. The Duke of Argyll, for instance, made paper kites out of anti-union petitions and flew them around Parliament. Although some members, notably Andrew Fletcher of Saltoun, were opposed to union, the treaty was comfortably passed by the Scottish Parliament on 16 January 1707. It had to be signed in secret in Edinburgh to protect politicians from the mob.

In April the act was passed in the English Parliament, and on 1 May 1707 the Union came into effect. The Kingdoms of Scotland and England were united into Great Britain, though Scotland preserved its separate legal system, educational system and church. Despite the vigorous opposition, threats and bribery assured that a bankrupt and exhausted Scotland was, in popular mythology, sold to England for £398,085 – part compensation for Darién, part wages for the Commissioners who closed the deal.

Jacobite rebellion and the Clearances

Rebellion against the imposition of William of Orange began in 1689, when William's government redcoats clashed with supporters of James II (the Jacobites) at Killiecrankie (see page 242). They were led by Graham of Claverhouse, 'Bonnie Dundee', who was killed in the battle. In 1692 an expedition to weed out the Jacobites in the Highlands resulted in the Glencoe massacre, which provoked unprecedented public outcry (see page 372).

The Act of Settlement was not forgotten, and dwindling trade and increased taxation fuelled dissatisfaction with the Union. A lively underground resistance, aided by long-standing French connections, revolved around the Jacobite court in exile at St Germain. Sympathy also came from English quarters.

Four attempts ensued to reinstate a Stewart monarchy, supported erratically by France, and culminating at Culloden in 1746 (see page 346). Much support came from north of the Tay, which was Catholic and Episcopalian country. The term 'Jacobite' popularly denoted anti-establishment and Episcopalian. Also, pejoratively, Highlander, and was evocative of a linguistic, social and cultural divide between Lowlander and Highlander which had grown since the 15th century.

Highland culture and independence was not diminished after the demise of the Lords of the Isles, hence the rise of the Campbells to enormous power as government agents, dealing for instance with the troublesome MacGregors. Claiming descent from Kenneth MacAlpin, the MacGregors were almost annihilated in 1603, and outlawed until 1774. They played a significant part in the Jacobite rebellions (see also page 261).

Clans and tartans

Before Culloden and the Clearances, Highland tradition decreed that a person's loyalty lay first and foremost with their own particular clan, or family group. There were two classes of clan: clansmen of the clan who were related by blood and shared the same family name, and individuals and groups who sought and obtained the protection of the clan. This resulted in a clan having septs, or sub-groups, of different surnames. Most Scottish surnames can be traced to a clan name, each with their own particular tartan.

Clan tartans are patterns for general use by clanspeople, but there are also variations of clan tartans which are used for specific purposes. Dress tartans were originally worn by the women of the clan who preferred light-coloured patterns, and were woven on a white background. Hunting tartans are worn for sport and outdoor activities, with brown or some other dark hue as the predominant colour, in order to give some form of camouflage. Rather confusingly, ancient clan tartan does not signify an older pattern, but is merely a term used to describe a tartan woven in lighter-coloured shades.

Those wishing to trace their Scottish ancestry should start at the Scots Ancestry Research Society, 20 York Place, Edinburgh.

Although traditionally indifferent to the monarchy, many clans came out in support of Prince Charles (of 'Bonnie Prince Charlie' fame) in 1745. After defeat at Culloden, savage reprisals were led by the 'Butcher' Cumberland. Rebels were beheaded or hanged, estates confiscated, and the pipes and Highland dress proscribed until 1782. Clansmen were enlisted into Highland regiments and 1,150 were exiled, swelling the ranks of emigrants to the colonies. Gaelic culture was effectively expunged and Scotland as a whole suffered disgrace.

Rise and fall of Bonnie Prince Charlie

Charles Edward Stuart, the 'Young Pretender', grandson of James II, was born in Italy. First setting foot on Scottish soil aged 23 with seven companions (the Seven Men of Moidart), his forceful personality persuaded reluctant clan chiefs to join him in raising the Standard for his father at Glenfinnan in 1745. Inadequately prepared government troops under 'Johnny Cope' (of ballad fame) enabled his swift progress to Edinburgh, where he held court at Holyrood, dazzling the populace with a grand ball. Edinburgh was charmed but embarrassed.

With sights set on the English throne, he reached Derby. Encouraging reports about panic in London were offset by news of advancing government troops which prompted retreat. The pursuing redcoats were outwitted as far as Inverness, and the ensuing bloodbath at Culloden, though Charles' only defeat, was decisive. Fleeing to the Hebrides, he was given shelter by Flora MacDonald (see page 436) and then spent a summer as a lone fugitive. Despite a £30,000 reward for his capture, he managed to escape on a French frigate in 1746. Too late by just a fortnight, 40,000 louis d'ors then arrived from France, enough to have revived the whole campaign.

This failure has been ascribed to a fatal weakness of character and a collapse of resolve at Derby. He ended his days a degenerate and broken man, ensuring the complete collapse of the Jacobite cause. But Bonnie Prince Charlie is remembered in numerous nostalgic songs, a toast to 'the King over the Water', and a host of memorabilia.

“” Sir Walter Scott's best-selling historical novels worked miracles for Scotland's public image. It was he who stage-managed the visit of George IV, who sportingly donned a kilt and, for modesty's sake, pink tights for the occasion...

The Enlightenment

Intellectual life flourished in late 18th-century Scotland. Embracing all the arts, its roots lay in the philosophical nature, shaped by European thought, underlying Scots law, education and the church. The sceptic David Hume (1711-1776) was the foremost of a school of philosophers, best known for his *Treatise on Human Nature and Essays, Moral and Political*. Kirkcaldy-born Adam Smith pioneered political economy in his *Wealth of Nations* (1776), a powerful impetus to later political reform.

An emphasis on research and practicality in the sciences fostered inventiveness in applied science, contributing much to industry and agriculture. James Watt (1736-1819) developed the steam engine which powered the machinery of the Industrial Revolution, medicine flourished at Edinburgh University, and further generations spawned engineers and inventors like Alexander Graham Bell and John Logie Baird, inventors of the telephone and television respectively.

Classicism was espoused in architecture and by painters like Allan Ramsay, Raeburn and Naysmth, and gave way in literature to the Romanticism of Robert Burns whose work profoundly influenced popular culture and notions of democracy.

Sir Walter Scott's best selling historical novels worked miracles for Scotland's public image. It was he who stage-managed the visit of George IV, who sportingly donned a kilt and, for modesty's sake, pink tights for the occasion. Later on, Queen Victoria was inspired to adopt a Highland home and, with the craze for 'Balmorality', the Highlands assumed a romantic glamour, becoming a fashionable resort for southern sportsmen.

Industrial revolution

Until around 1750 a large percentage of Scotland's population lived north of the Clyde and Tay. Emigration to the Lowlands or North America was already a problem, as a money economy threatened traditional ways of life. The decision of landlords to resettle their tenants on the coasts, replacing black cattle with sheep, was a disastrous economic and social experiment, with brutal evictions in some areas – although popular myth forgets that famine, disease and overpopulation were rife and many went willingly. Eventually, in 1886, crofters' rights were to some extent recognized (see also page 465).

The gap between Highland and Lowland life continued to widen as overgrazing, deforestation for industry, and deer 'forests', led to desolation in the Highlands, while improvements and drainage transformed Lowland agriculture.

At the same time industrialization was soon to bring a massive population shift. Wool, cloth and linen, long established as cottage industries, were undergoing mechanization. By 1820 mills were established in the coalfields of Lanark, Renfrew and Ayr. Linen declined in favour of cotton, spun and woven in Paisley and New Lanark, while tweed was first woven in Galashiels in 1830. Dundee substituted jute for linen and Kirkcaldy developed linoleum. Thriving on trade with America,

Glasgow's population mushroomed, absorbing many from the Highlands, as well as thousands of Irish refugees from the potato famine of the 1840's. Poor housing, overcrowding and disease became chronic.

20th-century Scotland

By 1900 iron and later steel, mainly in the west, had become manufacturing mainstays, serviced by new canals, railways and roads. As well as emigrants, Scotland supplied goods to North America: locomotives, girders, bridges, textile machinery and tools. Shipyards flourished on the Clyde. The first iron steam ships were launched around 1800, although fast wooden clippers like the *Cutty Sark* were still competitive in the mid-19th century, when major shipping companies such as Cunard came to the fore. From 1880 skilled labour built steel ships for world markets as well as for the Royal Navy. Business boomed during the First World War, when political activity among skilled workers inspired by the Bolshevik revolution, led by Marxist and Scottish Nationalist John Maclean, gave rise to the myth of 'Red Clydeside'.

Post-war slump hit all industries in the 1920s, from which they never really recovered. A dangerous dependency on mining, metalworking and heavy engineering was a crucial factor in industrial decline, and the innovative spirit of the 19th century is only now re-emerging among pioneering computer software development companies in the central belt.

In a long Liberal tradition dedicated to political reform, the issue of Home Rule reared its head repeatedly after the 1880s. The first stirrings of nationalism were heard after the First World War and voiced by writers in the 1920's, such as Lewis Spence, Hugh MacDiarmid, Grassic Gibbon and Neil Gunn. These sentiments took political shape as the Scottish National Party (SNP) in 1934. Support grew through the 1950s and 1960s, and in 1967 the SNP was revealed as a potent political force when Winifred Ewing won the Hamilton by-election.

Nationalist fervour reached its height in the 1970s, roused by expectations that revenue from the oil and gas recently discovered in the North Sea would reverse economic decline. These hopes were dashed by oil revenues disappearing into the British Treasury at Westminster. In 1974, 11 SNP MPs were elected to Westminster – and, although many felt that this was a protest vote, Labour felt concerned. In 1979 it held a referendum on the establishment of a Scottish Assembly. Turnout was low and support was lukewarm, so no assembly was established.

Labour were soon ousted from office and the Thatcher government swept to power in 1979, bringing with them a disdain for Scotland that was to have far reaching consequences. The new Conservative government also introduced policies that did not sit easily with most Scots. When the unpopular Poll Tax, which notoriously taxed 'dukes the same as dustmen', was introduced in Scotland a year earlier than in the rest of Britain, the country felt that it was increasingly being governed by politicians who cared little for its people. Years of Tory rule served only to widen the gap between Scotland and Westminster, and it was almost inevitable that some form of devolution would follow.

The new parliament

Twenty years on, the Scots voted emphatically in favour of devolution, and the Scottish Parliament reconvened after 292 years on 12 May, 1999. The new Parliament has 129 MSPs (Members of the Scottish Parliament) who were elected by proportional representation. It has the power to pass legislation and to alter the rate of taxation. However, defence and foreign affairs are still handled by Westminster. The early years of the Parliament have not been without controversy, and its relationship with Westminster has at times proved frosty. The most pressing issue is the so-called 'West Lothian Question', the anomaly that allows Scottish MPs at

 Westminster to vote on issues solely affecting England, while English MPs cannot vote on solely Scottish issues. MSPs, for example, recently voted to fund all care for all elderly people in Scotland. Yet this went against the policy of the Labour government, leading to the possible scenario of Scottish Labour MPs at Westminster voting against such funding for the elderly in England. As one commentator said: "The English have been the silent and uninvited guests at the devolutionary feast". In addition, Scotland still benefits from higher spending per head than any other part of Britain – a situation which is almost certain to change.

The new parliamentary building has attracted controversy as its estimated £50 mn construction costs have spiralled to over £400 mn, and, although it was due to be completed in summer 2001, it still remains unfinished at the time of going to press (May 2004) and is not due to be officially opened until October 2004. Further controversy followed the tragic and sudden death of Donald Dewar, the first First Minister, when his successor Henry McLeish resigned in the face of allegations of financial shenanigans. His own successor, Jack McConnel, immediately had to contend with the tidal wave of tabloid sex scandal. Despite these teething troubles, Scotland's Parliament is finding its feet. Whether devolution is a step on the road to full independence remains to be seen but at least the Scots now have their own set of politicians to moan about.

Culture

Architecture

Early structures: from brochs to towers

A thousand years before Stonehenge, a Neolithic architect was supervising the construction of Maes Howe (see page 558) in Orkney. Dramatically accompanied by two stone circles, its massive precision-cut stonework houses a tomb. Religious architecture evolved into the Bronze Age, and over 22 centuries of chambered tombs survive, notably at Camster and Kilmartin. Henges and stone circles, as at Cairnpapple, also abound. At Skara Brae (see page 557) is a 5,000 year-old village, a Neolithic Pompeii where stone furniture and utensils survive in rooms straight out of the 'Flintstones'.

Brochs, fortresses not dissimilar to diminutive industrial cooling towers such as at Mousa on Shetland (see page 582), appeared around 75 BC. A staircase ascended within double walls and a well often provided water for the besieged within. On duns and hilltops, timber laced forts, built from 700 BC into the Middle Ages, are sometimes found to have been fired to such an extent that stonework fused solid or vitrified. Whether this was intentional, or the result of attack, remains a mystery.

Ninth-century wheelhouses, with stone piers radiating from a central hearth, are visible at Jarlshof on Shetland, and appeared later in the Hebrides. Timber began to be used for Pictish hall houses, crannogs – lake dwellings on wooden rafts – and early churches (such as at Whithorn).

In the 11th century round towers, such as those at Brechin and Abernethy, were used for defence and as belfries by Culdee communities. Around this time the first cathedrals were built. The one at Birsay on Orkney, founded in 1050 by Earl Thorfinn, was soon replaced by another in Kirkwall commemorating the Norse St Magnus (see page 553). This was built by masons from Durham Cathedral after working at Dunfermline Abbey, also Romanesque, built for St Margaret. She also commissioned St Rule's in St Andrews, whose tall square tower suggests Northumbrian influence, echoed in those at Muthill, Dunning (in Strathearn) and Dunblane.

Great Scots

For such a small country, Scotland has produced a remarkable number of intellectual geniuses who have been peculiarly influential. Many of them were great scientists, like James Clerk Maxwell, described by Einstein as the most important physicist after Newton, and who paved the way for Einstein's theory of relativity. There was also John Napier, the inventor of logarithms, Lord Kelvin, who devised the second law of thermodynamics, and James Hutton, Roderick Murchison and Charles Lyell, who together created modern geology.

In medicine, Scotland led the world. Robert Liston and James Young Simpson discovered the benefits of chloroform, and Alexander Fleming discovered penicillin, the most effective antibiotic ever devised. The number of technologists is incredible, and includes James Watt, who developed the steam engine, R W Thomson, who invented the fountain pen and pneumatic tyre, John Macadam, who gave the world the metalled road, Charles Mackintosh, who invented waterproof fabric, Alexander Graham Bell, who invented the telephone, and not forgetting John Logie Baird, the father of television.

Scotland has also given the world the Bank of England, the decimal point, colour photographs, the fax machine, the photocopier, the bicycle, the bus, the thermos flask, the thermometer, the gas mask, the gravitating compass, the fridge, the grand piano, fingerprinting, Bovril, interferon, insulin, the gel-filled bra and Dolly, the cloned sheep.

Abbeys and cathedrals

David I (1124-1153) granted land to Roman monastic orders and two centuries of abbey and cathedral building ensued, though mostly in the Lowlands. Years of neglect and depredations by English troops and iconoclastic reformers leave many as picturesque ruins, stripped of magnificent wood and stone carving, stained glass and wallpainting. The wallpaintings at Fowlis Easter, 15th-century collegiate churches, are a rare survivor. The ruins of Oronsay Priory and the Valerian clad cloisters of Iona's nunnery (see page 320) are the legacy of the Augustinians.

Medieval castles

Symbols of feudalism built by Norman settlers appear in the form of timber motte and bailey fortresses – timber towers with defensive earthworks – though they are found mostly south of the Forth and Clyde.

Square or oblong tower houses, with a defensive entry at first floor level, barrel vaulting and great hall, were to be an enduring form of dwelling, evolving from the 14th century into the 17th. More elaborate are L-plan and Z-plan versions, with one or two towers added at the corners to defend the entry.

Renaissance palaces

While ordinary folk lived in thatched turf and stone hovels (some into the 20th century), the cosmopolitan and cultured Stewart kings set about building new palaces and improving existing residences. The old castle at Linlithgow had emerged by 1540, a wholly residential Renaissance palace ranged around a quadrangle, which even impressed the French Mary of Guise. While the Great Hall at Stirling is a triumph of late Gothic, the later Palace block (1540-1542) reveals many Renaissance features, such as the recessed bays along the exterior with sculpted figures, and the famous carved wooden ceiling medallions, the 'Stirling Heads'.

The Tower house

A minor building boom in the late 16th century was a result of church land being transferred over a long period into private hands. The old tower house formula found favour, preferred over earlier royal examples of Renaissance innovation. Everyone from nobility to minor gentry was afforded both defence against troublesome neighbours as well as gracious living. Claypotts in Dundee is a good example of 'the castle with a country house built on top', while at Craigievar (see page 531), finished as late as 1626, idiosyncratic inventiveness reaches its apogée where the roofline explodes in a flurry of fairytale turrets. Families of masons developed individual styles detectable in Aberdeenshire where many tower houses, great and small, are still inhabited or have been recently revived. Defensive features like gun loops (apertures for guns) survived less out of necessity than as status symbols, and interiors, especially timber ceilings, were vividly painted, with exuberant imagery, as at Crathes (see page 525).

16- to 18th-century townhouses

'New towns' to promote trade were established by David I and settled with English and Flemish merchants, with a strict hierarchy of trading rights and privileges. Stone houses first replaced wood in the east coast burghs in the 16th century, setting a precedent for future urban design. Every burgh had its symbols of commerce and government at its centre: the Mercat (market) cross and the Tolbooth (town hall).

Two centuries later, the spirit of vernacular architecture had not changed dramatically. Nor had urban layout, many houses still being built gable end on to the street. The multi-storey tenement became a distinctive feature of urban living, pioneered in Edinburgh's Canongate, where buildings such as Gladstone's Land are still intact. Culross Palace and Argyll's Ludgings in Stirling are outstanding examples of grand town houses.

William Bruce and the 17th-century mansion

The country mansion was a concept pioneered by Alexander Seton, paragon of a new kind of architectural patron, at Pinkie House in Musselburgh, a daring essay in elegance and erudition. Post Restoration, William Bruce exemplifies a new concept: the architect. Introducing classical symmetry to existing buildings such as Holyrood and Thirlestane, he also designed Hopetoun in 1699-1703. The innovative oblong shape and hipped roof of Kinross are characteristic of his many other country house designs with their Anglo-Dutch interiors and plasterwork. He also revolutionized garden and landscape design. Bruce's protégé, James Smith, was a pioneer of British Palladianism. Rising from master mason to King's Master of Works and private architect, his own house, Newhailes (circa 1690), was the inspiration for countless lairds' houses, both grand and humble, built throughout Scotland in the 18th century.

Victorian Baronial

Not content with Classicism, architects raided the Gothic, Tudor, Jacobean and Scottish past, even Asia and Europe, for ideas. Late 18th-century country houses by Gillespie Graham were asymmetrical and castellated. Inspired by the picturesque movement, they are the harbingers of the High Victorian revival of Scottish baronial which reached its peak in the 1860s. New and unprecedented wealth found industrial tycoons and landowners beating a path to the doors of fashionable architects like Burn and Bryce, to build colossal and fantastic country seats with room for entertaining on a huge scale, and the latest in comforts – like plumbing. Some followed Queen Victoria's example at Balmoral, building extravagant Highland shooting lodges. Most eclectic of all is Mount Stuart on Bute (1870s) a neo-Gothic/Renaissance palace whose sumptuous interior even includes details from Charlemagne's tomb (see page 304).

Flamboyant design extended to monumental industrial buildings like textile mills and foundries, also railway stations, viaducts and bridges.

Glasgow's heyday: Thomson and Mackintosh

Glasgow grew phenomenally through the 19th century to become the 'Second City of the Empire'. While acres of tenements housed artisans and middle-class families, earlier Georgian suburbs were abandoned for commodious villas for the prosperous, designed by leading architects in areas like Kelvingrove. Many, especially on the south side, were designed by Alexander 'Greek' Thomson using Classical Greece and Egypt as inspiration. The best known of his public works is the Greek Revival church in St Vincent St (1858). The originality of his work is itself currently enjoying a long-overdue revival.

While Glasgow University (1870) by Gilbert Scott was inspired by medieval Flemish cloth halls, banks were modelled on Renaissance palazzos. Thomson designed Egyptian-style warehouses, and Burnet in the 1890s returned from New York to design tall, narrow-fronted buildings with steel frames. By 1896 and Charles Rennie Mackintosh's debut, Glasgow had the most exciting architecture in Europe.

20th century: Traditionalism and modernism

The forward-looking Beaux-Arts rationalism of Burnet and company was challenged by Traditionalists reacting against aggressive modernity and advocating traditional building materials and craftsmanship, and referring back to 16th- and 17th-century vernacular architecture. Rennie Mackintosh was a leading, if independent exponent, as exemplified at Hill House in Helensburgh (see page 303), while a more mainstream Arts and Crafts aesthetic was adopted by Robert Lorimer who 'restored' many early houses, as well as designing anew.

In contrast, art deco was favoured by architects such as Glasgow's Jack Coia and, by the mid-century, Basil Spence was a champion of modernism. Traditionalism versus modernism was to become an enduring theme.

Economic depression and dramatic social change brought an urgent need for solutions to both rural depopulation, and urban overpopulation and decay. Already by the 1930s two contrasting visions of social progress were being proposed: restoration of organic unity versus modernist utopia.

Post-war to present day

A desperate need for housing resulted in massive building projects into the 1970's transforming cities. Many historic buildings were demolished and city centres gutted in an effort to remedy post-war dereliction. Edinburgh had the worst slums in Europe, where overpopulated tenements were literally collapsing. The first residential towerblocks, the epitome of the Modern Functionalist brave new world, appeared, most notoriously in Glasgow's Gorbals. Urban over-spill was re-housed in New Towns such as Cumbernauld which, although internationally acclaimed in the 1960s, was unpopular with its inhabitants.

Traditionalists meanwhile continued to advocate experiments in vernacular style, and a move was made to protect historic buildings. Most prominent of recent public buildings is the new wing of the Museum of Scotland in Edinburgh. Completed at a time of renewed national confidence and cultural awareness, historical references are foremost. The sandstone-clad exterior is reminiscent of a medieval fortress, and from within the view over the adjacent Greyfriar's church, scene of the signing of the National Covenant in 1638, has been emphasized.

With the building of the Scottish Parliament at Holyrood by Eric Miralles still under way, it is not inappropriate that its temporary home is in the Assembly Rooms of the Church of Scotland, that most democratic of institutions. The Parliament building, due to be opened by HM The Queen on 9 October 2004, is the most

Some recommended Scottish poetry

Norman McCaig, *Selected Poems.* Challenging poet whose work is deeply rooted in the landscapes of the Highlands.
Hugh McDiarmid, *Selected poems.* A huge figure on the Scottish literary landscape. His nationalist views and use of Scots have been as influential as they have been provocative.
Ian Crichton-Smith *Collected poems.* Bi-lingual (English and Gaelic) poet writing passionately about life in the Outer Hebrides.
Edwin Muir, *Collected Poems.* Recognized as one of the most distinguished poets of the last century, received an MBE in 1953 for his significant contribution to Scottish poetry.
Edwin Morgan, *New Selected Poems.* Scotland's new poet laureate is one of the country's foremost living writers and both entertaining and experimental.
Don Paterson, *Landing Light.* This is the latest work of a genuinely innovative new voice in Scottish poetry.
For an excellent overview, see *The New Penguin Book of Scottish Verse*, editied by Robert Crawford and Mick Imlah (2000).

important architectural structure in over 300 years in Scotland and will surely silence the critics when it opens (though a public inquiry into the spiralling cost and delay is being held). It is a project that has a reach far beyond this country. Like the Museum building, it reflects many aspects of Scottish history, but also, stunningly, was designed to appear to be growing organically from the surrounding landscape. It is a tragedy that its architect died, aged just 45, only a month after construction, and will never see the realisation of his ambition of creating a functioning work of art. The most extraordinary thing about the project is not the cost, nor the delay, but the fact that the Parliament looks set to prove just how much Miralles, and the team led by Benedetta Tagliabue and RMJM, the Edinburgh practice that took on the building after his death, have succeeded in achieving that ambition.

Literature

Any overview, no matter how brief, of Scotland's literary tradition must begin with a poet who has become inextricably linked with the image of Scotland and all things Scottish across the globe. **Robert Burns** was born on 25 January 1759 in Alloway, Ayrshire, in very humble surroundings, later referring to himself as 'a very poor man's son'. Burns wrote in the dialect of plain country people and about the lives they led, but the emotions he described were so genuine that they appealed to all classes.

His poetry mainly concerned itself with life as he was living it. He was also keen to point out what he saw as a kinship between all living things, such as in his famous *To A Mouse*. The most frequently quoted lines of this poem; 'The best laid schemes o' mice an' men – Gang aft a-gley,' has entered the language, as have many sayings originated by Burns, and is a perfect summing up of his point of view. His most celebrated work, *Auld Lang Syne* expresses the joys of human companionship and is practically an anthem when friends gather to celebrate New Year around the world. His love of the companionship of friends is also a focus of *Tam O'Shanter*, which also serves as a cautionary warning against overindulgence and is a ghost story in the tradition of the mythic, while his irritation against the assumed superiority of some was put into words in *A Man's A Man For A' That*, which also returns to his theme of kinship.

The 'heav'n-taught' Ayrshire ploughman died on 21 July 1796, and was buried in St Michael's Churchyard, Dumfries. Such is his standing that his memory is celebrated every year on 25 January, his date of birth, now referred to as Burns Night.

Another writer forever associated with the Borders is **Sir Walter Scott**, who not only ruled the roost of his native Scotland but the world of literature in general. Born in 1771, the son of a wealthy Edinburgh lawyer, Scott spent much of his childhood in the Borders during which time he immersed himself in tales and ballads of Jacobites and Border heroes, giving him a passion for history which would infuse his later work.

It was this material which would eventually become poems in his three volumes of *Minstrelsy Of The Scottish Border* which established his name as a literary figure. Other romantic poetic works followed, such as *The Lady Of The Lake*, as with Burns, employing the Scottish dialect.

In 1811 Scott purchased Abbotsford, a farmhouse near Melrose (see page 191), and during the following years developed the style which would remain his best-remembered contribution to literature, the historical novel. Collectively known as the Waverley novels, these included *Old Mortality*, *Rob Roy* and *The Heart Of Midlothian*. The original Waverley was a romantic tale of the Jacobite Rebellion of 1745 and the Highland society of the time. By 1819 Scott had moved beyond purely Scottish history and wrote Ivanhoe, set in 12th-century England. It remains his most enduring work, and he followed it with Kenilworth, Redgauntlet and The Talisman.

Scott died in ill health on 21 September 1832. His huge popularity was believed to have kept the spirit of Scotland alive and he is commemorated by the Scott Monument in Princes Street, Edinburgh.

A contemporary of Scott's, though far less well known, was **James Hogg**, the Ettrick Shepherd, born at Ettrickhall Farm in Selkirkshire in 1770. Like Burns before him, Hogg was of humble origins and did not receive a proper education he but inherited a vast store of balladry from his mother, Margaret, some of which Scott published in his *Minstrelsy Of The Scottish Border*. Like Burns, Hogg was lionised by the Edinburgh elite as another heaven-taught rustic with a flair for poetry, but that is to severely undermine his importance to the world of philosophy and psychology as well as literature. His writings dealt with the notion of a divided nature within a single individual, reflecting Hogg's own double life as rough Border shepherd and sophisticated urban intellectual. Hogg's thinking and writing reached their apotheosis is his extraordinary *The Private Memoirs and Confessions of a Justified Sinner*, published in 1824 and one of the true masterpieces of Scottish literature. There is nothing else like it and, prior to the Freudian era, nothing to match its insight into fractures of human nature.

This exploration of the dual nature of man received its quintessential expression in **Robert Louis Stevenson's** *The Strange Case of Doctor Jekyll and Mister Hyde*, published some 50 years after Hogg's death and one of the classics of horror literature. The tale was inspired by Edinburgh's notorious Deacon Brodie, a seemingly respectable pillar of the community by day and a criminal, gambler and womaniser by night.

Stevenson's fondness of the macabre is also stories like *The Bottle Imp* and *The Bodysnatcher*, but it is for his romantic historical adventures that he is best known. Born at 8 Howard Place, Edinburgh, on 13 November 1850, Stevenson was fond of travel which led to his employment as a writer of travel articles and essays. While staying in Braemar in 1881, Stevenson drew pirate maps of an island, and these became the basis of his tale, *Treasure Island*, published two years later. For Stevenson it was just the first of the many adventure tales, including *Kidnapped*, its sequel, *Catriona* and *The Master of Ballantrae*, he wrote before his death in Samoa on 3 December 1894. The tradition of the adventure story has continued throughout the 20th century in the works of Perth-born **John Buchan**, author of *The Thirty-Nine Steps*.

One of Stevenson's contemporaries at Edinburgh University was **Sir Arthur Conan Doyle**. Born at Picardy Place, Edinburgh, on 22 May 1859, Conan Doyle was

Essential selection: contemporary Scottish fiction

1 Ian Banks, *The Crow Road*
2 James Kelman, *The Busconductor Hines*
3 Alan Warner, *Morvern Callar*
4 Louise Welsh, *The Cutting Room*
5 Irvine Welsh, *Trainspotting*

schooled in Lancashire before returning to study medicine at Edinburgh University in 1876. It was while serving as an out-patient clerk at Edinburgh Royal Infirmary that Doyle met Doctor Joseph Bell, the man who was to influence most the creation of his famous character. "His strong point", Doyle later noted, "was diagnosis, not only of disease, but of occupation and character".

Doyle was living in London and had published several short stories and essays when memories of his former mentor, combined with a love of the detective fiction of Edgar Allan Poe, inspired him to write *A Study In Scarlet*, which first appeared in the 1887 edition of *Beeton's Christmas Annual*. Doctor Watson recounted Sherlock Holmes' unique detective skills in this, followed by a further three novels and 56 short stories, with all but *The Sign Of Four* making their initial appearance in *The Strand Magazine*.

Holmes became a phenomenon that not even Doyle could control. In fact, by 1893 he was so annoyed that his more serious literary endeavours were being neglected that he achieved what many criminals had failed to do. He killed Holmes. Following publication of *The Final Problem*, in which Holmes and his mortal foe, Professor Moriarty plunged over the Reichenbach Falls, there were public displays of grief and mourning. It was clear that the public were not going to let Holmes rest in peace, and eventually Doyle was forced to find an ingenious way of reviving the character. He penned his last Holmes story in 1927, a mere three years before his own death. Doyle's other famous character was Professor Challenger, who famously discovered the Lost World, which later inspired Steven Spielberg's *Jurassic Park*.

Another classic of literature was written by Doyle's 'older literary friend', **JM Barrie.** Born in Kirriemuir in 1860, James Matthew Barrie was the son of a weaver. Educated at Glasgow Academy and Edinburgh University, Barrie spent some years in Nottingham as a journalist before returning to Kirriemuir to write. He moved to London in 1885, and it was there that he wrote his first novel, *Better Dead*. More novels and plays followed, best known of which is *Peter Pan* and *The Lost Boys*. First published in 1904, it was written for the children of a friend, Llewelyn Davis. Barrie returned to Kirriemuir. Before his death in 1937, he bequeathed the copyright for Peter Pan to Great Ormond Street Hospital in London.

20th century

A common criticism of 19th and early 20th-century Scottish literature was the relative absence of novels dealing with the whole issue of industrialization, growing social division and immigration. Rather than explore the vexed issues of poverty, class division and the growing Celtic influence, most writers belonged to the 'Kailyard School', which presented a romantic, sentimental and completely unrealistic image of Scotland, perhaps reflecting the overwhelmingly middle-class background of novelists at that time.

The Kailyard came to be detested by a growing band of writers in the 20th century, and a new phase of realistic literature began in the 1920s, inspired by one of the greatest novels to emerge from Scotland, **George Douglas Brown**'s ground-breaking *House of the Green Shutters*. Published in 1901, the novel brings

Greek tragedy to 19th-century rural Ayrshire and, more than any other, destroyed the bucolic escapism of the Kailyard School.

In the same year **James Leslie Mitchell** was born in rural Aberdeenshire. Better known by his pseudonym **Lewis Grassic Gibbon**, his novel, *Sunset song*, published in 1932 (only three years before his untimely death), has become one of the mainstays of modern Scottish literature, and taught as part of the national curriculum. It was written as the first book in the trilogy, *A Scots Quair*, which charts the life of Chris Guthrie, from late 19th century through to the 1920s. Written from the girl's perspective, it is remarkable not only for its strong evocation of this part of Scotland, but also for its uncanny emotional resonance.

Another renowned northeast writer is **Neil Gunn**, born in Dunbeath, Caithness, in 1891. His writings, which deal with the disintegration of the old Highland way of life in the wake of the Clearances and the struggle to adapt to new conditions, also convey a strong sense of place and are as important to Scottish literature and identity as Faulkner and Dostoevsky are to the USA and Russia. Amongst his best-known works is *Silver Darlings* (1939), the title of which refers to the booming herring industry. Gunn died in 1973.

For its size, Orkney has produced a disproportionate number of well-loved and much-read authors. The poet, novelist and playwright, **George Mackay Brown**, gained even more popularity after the posthumous publication of his autobiography, following his death in 1996. Like Gunn and Grassic Gibbon before him, Brown is inextricably linked to his homeland and evokes the spirit and landscapes of his beloved Orkney with a deft sensitivity, bringing a strong poetic impulse to bear on the social realism of his novels. Amongst his best is *Greenvoe*, published in 1972. **Eric Linklater** (1899-1974) is another Orcadian whose copious output of books and poems gained him international recognition. *The Dark of Summer* best represents his compelling style.

One of the most important 20th-century Scottish novelists is **Robin Jenkins**, referred to as "the Scottish Thomas Hardy". It was Jenkins who put his native city of Glasgow firmly on the literary map. His most Glaswegian of novels, *A Very Scotch Affair* (Gollancz, 1968), is still regarded as a highpoint in pre-1970s Glasgow fiction. Jenkins is also recognized as the founder of new Scottish fiction and a precursor to Kelman and Welsh as portraying an unsentimental view of Scottish life. Among his other novels are *The Cone Gatherers* (MacDonald 1955), *Fergus Lamont* (Edinburgh Canongate 1979) and *Childish Things* (Canongate 2001).

Another Glasgow literary talent of this time is **William McIlvanney**. Though he had already published two Glasgow novels in the 1960s, it was the following decade which saw him emerge as one the city's greats. In *Laidlaw* (Hodder and Stoughton, 1977), McIlvanney explored Glasgow's seedy, criminal underbelly through the eyes of the eponymous police Detective-Inspector, who became as much a part of the city as Ian Rankin's Rebus has become a part of Edinburgh. Two subsequent crime thrillers featuring Laidlaw, *The Papers of Tony Veitch* (Hodder and Stoughton, 1983) and *Strange Loyalties* (Hodder and Stoughton, 1991) helped McIlvanney transcend the crime novel genre, in the same way that Ian Rankin has done today.

Writers, of course, are interested in people and as Ian Rankin says: "Edinburgh's dualism makes it perfect for tales of people who are not what they seem. It's a very secretive place, its residents reticent.". It was this characteristic that **Muriel Spark** captured in her classic novel *The Prime of Miss Jean Brodie* (1965). Spark was born and educated in Edinburgh, attending James Gillespie's School for Girls. The eponymous Jean Brodie teaches at a girls' school in the city in the 1930s and is the very model of respectability. She loves art and culture, and instils in her pupils the need to cultivate an air of 'composure'. She could be the stereotyped lady from the still genteel suburb of Morningside. A place where, as one writer recently said: "The nearest thing you'd find to a drugs war is two old ladies fighting over a bottle of

 Sanatogen in a chemist's shop." Yet Brodie also relishes the power she has over her pupils and has an alarming regard for the fascist teachings of Hitler and Mussolini.

If the 1970s were good for the image of Glasgow literature, then the 1980s were nothing short of earth-shattering. In 1981 **Alasdair Gray**'s totally original debut novel, *Lanark: A Life in Four Books* (Canongate, 1981), changed everything. It single- handedly raised the profile of Scottish fiction. Suddenly, the outside world stood up and took notice. Since then, Scottish writers have gone from strength to strength, most notably with **James Kelman**, a giant on the literary scene, whose brilliant fourth novel, *How Late It Was, How Late* (Secker and Warburg, 1994), won the Booker Prize. A one-time bus conductor, Kelman is a committed and uncompromising writer whose use of dialect has attracted as much criticism from the literary establishment as it has praise from fellow writers at home. When some reviewers accused him of insulting literature, he retorted that "a fine line can exist between elitism and racism. On matters concerning language and culture the distinction can sometimes cease altogether."

Kelman has revolutionized Scottish fiction by writing not just dialogue but his entire novels in his own accent, and the debt owed to him by young contemporaries is immense. Writers such as **Duncan Mclean**, **Alan Warner** and **Irvine Welsh** all cite Kelman as a major influence on their writing. Cairns Craig, who has written widely on the modern Scottish novel, states that Kelman's real importance lies in his original use of the English language. "He can be seen as a post-colonial writer who has displaced and reformed English in a regional mode". Among Kelman's finest is his first novel, *The Busconductor Hines* (Polygon Books, 1984) and *A Disaffection* (Secker and Warburg, 1989). Kelman's most recent work, *Translated Accounts* (Secker and Warburg, 2001) is his most 'difficult' to date. One literary critic claimed that, while it took Kelman three years to write, it might take the reader three years to understand it.

There are many other notable Glasgow novelists who began to make their name from the 1980s onwards. **Jeff Torrington**, the Linwood car-plant shop steward who was discovered by Kelman, won the Whitbread Prize for his debut novel *Swing Hammer Swing* (Secker and Warburg, 1992), which is set in the Gorbals of the late 1960s. **Janice Galloway** received much praise for her first novel, *The Trick is to Keep Breathing* (Vintage, 1990), which was on the short-list for Whitbread First Novel, and followed it up with an excellent collection of short stories, *Blood* (Secker and Warburg, 1991). Another brilliant collection of mostly Glasgow short stories is **AL Kennedy**'s *Night Geometry and the Garscadden Trains* (Edinburgh: Polygon, 1991), while *So I am Glad* (Jonathan Cape, 1995) is a Glaswegian take on Magic Realism.

The same year that Kelman's debut was published saw the death of one of Glasgow's forgotten literary sons, **Alexander Trocchi**. Born in 1925 to Italian immigrant parents, Trocchi moved to Paris where he rubbed shoulders with the likes of Samuel Beckett, William Burroughs and Alan Ginsberg and published his brilliant and influential debut novel, *Young Adam* (1954), which soon became a beat cult classic and which was recently made into a film starring Ewan MacGregor, Tilda Swinton and Peter Mullan. Trocchi's initial literary talents were soon diluted by his prodigious drug consumption and he became better known as a counter-culture icon than a literary figure. Nonetheless, he was an inspiration to a new generation of Scottish writers led by Irvine Welsh, who began publishing in magazines such as *Rebel Inc* in the early 1990s.

Scottish literature has long been known for its dark hue. Crime, poverty and social dysfunction have provided rich copy for writers in a world where detectives are never less than hardened and profanity is as prevalent as punctuation. **Irvine Welsh** whose 1994 cult novel, *Trainspotting* shone a spotlight on the city's drug-ridden underbelly and spawned an entire generation of gritty, realist writing. After a succession of hit and miss follow ups, Welsh is back to rude health with his latest, *Porno* (2002), a sequel to *Trainspotting*, which sees the return of Renton, Sick Boy, Spud and Begbie.

From the same stable is **Alan Warner**, whose bleakly humorous *Morvern Callar* not only put Oban on the literary map but also signalled the arrival of a major and serious new talent, and **Laura Hird**, whose debut novel, *Born Free* (Rebel Inc 1999), tells the tale of a dysfunctional family trying to cope with life in one of West Edinburgh's most notorious housing schemes.

One of the most successful and best-known Scottish authors is **Iain Banks**, whose shocking debut, *The Wasp Factory* (1984), heralded a new Scottish writer of considerable imagination and wit. Banks has gone on to become one of the most prolific writers around, penning his best-seller, *The Crow Road*, and many others, as well as science fiction novels written under the name **Iain M Banks**.

Perhaps the most successful current Scottish writer is Fife-born **Ian Rankin**, currently the finest exponent of so-called 'Tartan Noir'. Rankin's Inspector Rebus novels give a striking depiction of contemporary Edinburgh. Rankin lives in Edinburgh and walks around the city a lot while researching new titles. He uses real locations and gruesome historical events in his books. Rebus drinks in a real city pub, the Oxford Bar, and in one book *Set in Darkness*, Rankin uses the story of an act of cannibalism which took place in the 18th century Scottish Parliament. Like the rest of Rankin's Inspector Rebus novels, this paints a stark, honest picture of contemporary Edinburgh through the eyes of a cynical detective straight out of the Philip Marlowe school of hard cops. His other Rebus novels include *The Falls* (2001), *Black and Blue* (1998) and *A Question of Blood* (2003), his most recent. Rumour has it that, like Conan Doyle with Sherlock Holmes, Rankin is planning to get rid of Rebus.

Another fine exponent of the so-called 'tartan noir' genre is **Christopher Brookmyre**, hailed as the Scottish Carl Hiaasen and a satirist of considerable standing. His first novel, *Quite Ugly One Morning* (Little, Brown, 1996) received brickbats and blandishments in equal measure. His latest, *Be my Enemy* (Little, Brown, 2004), features the usual violence and scatological humour.

A recent addition to the Tartan Noir fold is **Louise Walsh**, whose much acclaimed debut novel, *The Cutting Room* (Canongate, 2002) explores the dark recesses of Glasgow through the eyes of a gay, middle-aged auctioneer.

Music

It could easily be argued that, in its music, Scotland produces the finest and clearest expression of its culture. All tastes are currently catered for within its music scene, reflecting the cosmopolitan nature of a country standing at the threshold of a new era with its own parliament and a deep sense of love of its history and traditions, while keeping a weather eye on the future. Although the words 'Scottish music' often conjure up images of a tartan-clad piper on a mist-covered moor, that same piper is just as likely to be found supplying stirring melodies to the decidedly nineties edge of 'drums and bass' styles heard in clubs around the country. And that's not all – the sheer number of options available to those seeking any style of music, ranging from folk to funk, from 'Tattoo' to 'T In The Park', is truly remarkable.

Yet, despite the fact a new millennium has come and gone, bringing with it so many changes in music and technology, Scotland as a nation still responds, virtually as one, to the skirl of a full set of **Highland bagpipes**. Little wonder the pipes have been a dominant instrument for centuries – in celebration, in battle, in mourning – and are never far from the traveller's notion of all things Scottish. The pipes' unique sound is enjoyed the world over, not just in Scotland – witness the large numbers of pipe bands in the USA, Canada, across Europe, Australia and New Zealand. However, perhaps the best way to enjoy the pipes is to visit the country in summer when, accompanied by a full complement of drummers, many pipe bands can be seen taking part in competitions or playing at Highland Games in the open air. It would also

Essential selection: Scottish pop and rock

1 Aztec Camera, *High Land, Hard Rain* (1982)
2 Blue Nile, *A Walk Across The Rooftops* (1984)
3 The Jesus and Mary Chain, *Pyschocandy* (1984)
4 Teenage Fanclub, *Banwagonesque* (1991)
5 Franz Ferdinand, *Franz Ferdinand* (2004)

be totally remiss not to mention the **Edinburgh Military Tattoo**, which takes place annually during August at the world-renowned Edinburgh Festival on the esplanade of Edinburgh Castle (see page 79).

Traditional Scottish music can be passionate or jocular, mournful or joyous. In the hands of a good player, few instruments compare to the violin, or **'fiddle'**. For confirmation, simply seek out the work of Ally Bain. With The Boys Of The Lough, Phil Cunningham or solo, his handling of all traditional Scottish styles is superb. Delving a little deeper into Scotland's music, one may come across Strathspey and Reel societies. These are groups of fiddlers, large or small, which are well attended across the length and breadth of Scotland. Most welcome visitors to their meetings to enjoy the music and, as most of these take place in pubs and hotels, to enjoy the local brew. On a more informal level, there are also ceilidhs which often employ the help of a 'caller' to call out the moves, and Scottish Country Dances which usually feature a more traditional dance band and require at least a basic understanding of the steps.

There are also numerous Scottish music festivals, which range from the massive **Celtic Connections** (see page 53) and the well-respected **Shetland Folk Festival**, to smaller events which feature ceilidhs and more informal jam sessions.

Folk fusion

Scottish folk music struggled hard to shake off its couthy image, no doubt fuelled by too many dreadful hogmanay TV shows and shameless shysters in kilts. Things then took a turn for the better in the 1970s with the emergence of bands such as North Uist's **Runrig**, who married Gaelic lyrics to rock stylings and even reached the UK Top 10, and **Capercaillie**, whose reworkings of traditional West Highland songs with Karen Mattheson's haunting vocals have brought them significant commercial success. These two in particular have managed to promote Gaelic language and culture as well as promoting the image of traditional music as an exciting, innovative and relevant medium.

Others have followed in their footsteps, including **Silly Wizard** (featuring Phil Cunnigham), **Salsa Celtica, The Easy Club, Mouth Music, Deaf Shepherd** and, most controversially, **Shooglenifty**, whose radical mixing of folk music with trance – 'acid croft' as they call it – has made a huge impact internationally. One of the most successful marriages of traditional and contemporary Scottish music has been **Eddi Reader**, former lead singer with Fairground Attraction, singing the songs of Robert Burns.

Scottish rock, pop and dance

The Scots may be stereotyped as a bunch of kilt-wearing, haggis-munching bagpipe players, but there's so much more to the country's musical heritage. This is the country that gave the world **Lonnie Donegan, Lulu, Donovan** and **The Incredible String Band**. Ex-Faces lead singer and sun-tanned bad-hair boy, **Rod Stewart**, though born in England, still remembers his roots and wraps himself in tartan every time Scotland (used to) qualify for a World Cup. And speaking of tartan, there's the **Bay City Rollers**, who blazed a trail in the 1970s as the forefathers of the teeny-bop market. The 1970s were also notable for the peerless white funk of **Average White**

Band, whose singles *Pick up the Pieces* and *Let's Go round Again*, dented the charts. Glasgow-born **Sheena Easton** made it big stateside in the 1980s, while that decade was dominated by the **Eurythmics**, led by Aberdeen-born singer, **Annie Lennox** and **Dave Stewart**. Also big in the 1980s were **Simple Minds**, whose early post-punk sound and look gave no hint of their later stadium rock credentials.

One of the most influential bands of the 1980s were the **Jesus and Mary Chain**, whose distinctive feedback-drenched sound and notoriously shambolic live gigs brought them a huge cult following. Their drummer, **Bobby Gillespie** went on to form the equally influential **Primal Scream**, whose prodigious alcohol and drug consumption was only matched by the size of their egos.

The 1980s also saw the emergence of the innovative Postcard label, which launched the careers of **Orange Juice**, whose frontman **Edwyn Collins** went on to huge international solo success with A Girl Like You, Josef K, the Bluebells (featuring Lonnie Donegan's son) and the 16-year old **Roddy Frame** and his band, **Aztec Camera**. Also big in the 80s was the Celtic-influenced guitar sound of **Big Country**, fronted by former Skids man, **Stuart Adamson, Wet Wet Wet,** who still hold the record for the number of weeks at number one (15) with 'Love is all around', and who could forget **The Proclaimers** who released the unashamedly sentimental 'Letter from America'. Other notable Scots names from that decade include **The Cocteau Twins, Love & Money, Altered Images, Texas, Del Amitri, Blue Nile, Billy Mackenzie** and **The Associates, Waterboys, Danny Wilson, Goodbye Mr Mackenzie** (who featured Shirley Manson on vocals, later of Garbage). As dance began to take hold in the latter half of the decade, another Scottish band provided one of the key albums of the period, namely **Primal Scream**'s epic Screamadelica.

The 1990s were no less productive with **Bronski Beat, The Shamen, Soup Dragons,** the hugely important **Teenage Fanclub**, and the bizarre and enigmatic **KLF**, who produced one of the soundtracks of the time with their 1990 ambient classic, 'Chill Out'. The 90s also saw the arrival of **Travis**, whose 1999, 'The Man Who', brought them massive commercial success.

Behind the scenes, too, Scots have been influential, and none more so than **Alan McGee**, whose Creation label signed up the cream of talent north of the border in The Jesus and Mary Chain, Primal Scream and Teenage Fanclub (as well as a bunch of Mancunian upstarts by the name of Oasis). And Glasgow's fecund indie scene continues to produce a stream of contenders. There are established favourites like **Belle and Sebastian, Idlewild, Mogwai, Arab Strap, Idlewild, The Delgados, Bis, The Cosmic Roughrider** and **Uresei Yatsura**, and now the fabulous avant garde funk of **Franz Ferdinand,** who appear to be on the verge of world domination.

Language

Though the vast majority of Scots speak English, one ancient Scottish language which survives is Scottish Gaelic (Gaidhlig, pronounced 'Gallic'). Preceded by the speech of the Celts, it is now Scotland's oldest surviving language. Often referred to as the national language, it has been spoken the longest. Introduced to the country by Irish immigrants in the third and fourth centuries, its use soon spread and became well established. The language is spoken by about 85,000 people in Scotland (about two per cent of the population). This is in the Gaidhealtachd, the Gaelic-speaking areas of the Outer Hebrides, parts of Skye and a few of the smaller Hebridean islands. Gaelic is one of the Celtic languages, which has included Irish Gaelic, Manx, Welsh, Cornish and Breton. Today only Scottish and Irish Gaelic, Welsh and Breton survive.

Argyll takes its name from the Irish, Dal Rioda, and was the prime Gaelic-speaking area from the time Columba landed there in 563. Scottish Gaelic expanded

Some useful Gaelic

abhainn	river	eilean	island
aonach	ridge	fin or fionn	white
aros	dwelling	gare or gear	short
ault or allt	stream	garv or garbh	rough
Bagh	bay	geodha	cove
bal or baile	town or village	glen or glean	valley
ban or beinn	mountain	inch or innis	meadow or island
bealach	mountain pass	inver or inbhir	river mouth
beg or beag	small	kyle or caolas	narrow strait
cairn	heap of stones marking particular spot	liath	grey
		loch	lake
		more or mór	great, large
camas	bay or harbour	rannoch	bracken
cnoc or knock	hill	ross or rubha	promontory
coll or coille	wood or forest	sgeir	sea rock
corran	point jutting into the sea	sgurr	sharp point
		strath	wide valley
corrie or coire	hollow in mountainside or whirlpool	tarbet/tairbeart	isthmus
		tigh	house
		tir or tyre	land
craig, from creag	rock, crag	torr	hill, castle
drum	ridge	tràigh	shore
dubh	black	uig	shelter
dun	fort	uige	water
eas	waterfall		

greatly from the fifth century to around the 12th century and became the national language, spoken throughout most of the country with the exception of the Norse-speaking Orkney and Shetland isles. Galloway had a Gaelic community which was separated from the Highlands, but the language died out there about the 17th century.

From that point, Gaelic began a steady decline over the following centuries and, even before Union with England, was being usurped by English as more and more wealth and power passed into non-Gaelic hands. This transfer of power was given a major boost by the Reformation in the mid-16th century, as strong anti-Gaelic feeling was to the fore in the Church of Scotland.

Gaelic culture still flourished in the Highlands, but the failure of two successive Jacobite rebellions in the 18th century helped to seal its fate. In the wake of Culloden, all features of traditional Gaelic culture were proscribed and the clean sweep by government and landlords culminated in the Highland Clearances of the 19th century. The final nail in the coffin came in 1872, with the Education Act that gave no official recognition to Gaelic.

After two centuries of decline, Gaelic is now staging a comeback, thanks to financial help from government agencies and the EU which has enabled the introduction of bilingual primary and nursery schools and a massive increase in broadcasting time given to Gaelic language programmes. This renaissance can also be seen, and heard, in the fields of music and literature, and the recent return of the Scottish Parliament can surely only help to strengthen the position of Gaelic in Scottish society.

Land and environment

Geographically, Scotland can be divided into three areas: Southern Uplands, Central Lowlands and Highlands. The Southern Uplands is the area south from Edinburgh and Glasgow to the English border, and consists of a series of hill ranges sandwiched between fertile coastal plains. The Central Lowlands, the triangle formed by Edinburgh, Glasgow and Dundee to the north, contains most of the population, and is the country's industrial heartland. The Highland Boundary Fault is the geographical division running northeast from Helensburgh (west of Glasgow) to Stonehaven (south of Aberdeen). To the north of this line lie the Highlands and Islands, which comprise roughly two-thirds of the country. This is an area of high mountain ranges punctuated by steep-sided valleys, or glens, and deep lochs. The northwest coastline is indented by numerous steep, fjord-like sea lochs, and offshore are some 790 islands, 130 of which are inhabited. These are grouped into the Outer Hebrides, or Western Isles, the Inner Hebrides, and, to the north, the Orkney and Shetland Islands.

Much of Scotland was long ago covered by the Caledonian forest, which consisted mainly of the Scots pine, along with oak, birch and other hardwoods. Over the centuries, the trees were felled for timber and to accommodate livestock, and now only around one per cent of this ancient forest still remains. Small pockets of native Scots pine can be found scattered around the Highlands, at Rothiemurchus, near Aviemore, at Glen Tanar, near Ballater in Deeside, around Braemar, at Strathytre near Callander and Achray Forest near Aberfoyle, at Rowardennan on Loch Lomond, in Glen Affric and on the shores of Loch Maree.

Several decades ago the Forestry Commission, a government body, set about fencing off large areas of moorland for reforestation. Now much of the landscape is dominated by regimented rows of fast-growing sitka spruce, which are not particularly attractive. There are also serious concerns over the damage coniferization causes to the unique habitats in many areas, in particular to large areas of bogland in the 'Flow Country' of Caithness and Sutherland, a unique natural environment as precious as any tropical rainforest. This and other endangered habitats are registered as an SSSI – a Site of Special Scientific Interest – but this has proved less than adequate. The only real guarantee of protection is for such areas to be owned or managed by environmental organizations such as Scottish Natural Heritage, the Scottish Wildlife Trust, the Royal Society for the Protection of Birds, the Woodland Trust and John Muir Trust (see page 63).

In recognition of this, the new Scottish Parliament produced a draft bill to establish a series of national parks, based on advice from Scottish National Heritage. This is aimed to reduce the conflict between social and economic development and long-term protection of the natural and cultural environment. The first new park to open, in April 2002, was Loch Lomond and Trossachs National Park, and the other was Cairngorms National Park, which opened in early 2003.

Wildlife

The Scottish countryside plays host to some of Europe's rarest and most celebrated wildlife, though much of it has disappeared over the centuries. The ancient Caledonian forests were once home to wildlife that we now identify with other far-flung countries: the brown bear, lynx, wolf, reindeer and beaver to name but a few. Small numbers of beaver and reindeer have been reintroduced in recent years and there is the ongoing controversial debate regarding the reintroduction of the wolf.

Coastal wildlife

Scotland boasts over 13,000 km of the British coastline. As a result seabirds and some sea mammals abound and both the resident and visitor list is impressive. Some of the more notable avian 'stars' include the eider duck, most famous for its feather 'down' which the birds use to keep their eggs warm and we use in quilts to keep us cosy. Both sexes are about the size of a small goose yet are quite different in appearance. The male, for courting purposes, looks very regal, being predominantly black and white with lime green cheeks and a pastel pink breast, while the female, for the purposes of camouflage, is a dull brown colour. During the breeding season on the coast fringes and off-shore islands it is not unusual to encounter the females at very close quarters while she is on the nest. They are very confident about their camouflage and will stay perfectly still even when you are within a few feet.

During the winter the firths (large coastal inlets) and estuaries play host to large numbers of predominantly arctic seaduck including the beautiful jet black common and velvet scoter, the scaup (very similar to the common tufted duck) and the spectacular and rare king eider. Waders too are present in large numbers around the coast and again, especially in winter. Knot, dunlin and turnstones are also common along the beaches and mudflats. During the summer perhaps the most commonly seen coastal wader is the oystercatcher which is black and white with a conspicuous orange beak. While around estuaries keep your ears open for the high pitched call of the curlew. The Firths of Forth, Tay, Moray and Dornoch on Scotland's east coast are prime wader and sea-duck watching areas along with excellent lesser known venues like St Andrews Bay and the Eden Estuary in Fife.

These firths and estuaries, along with many of the offshore islands also play host to Scotland's two resident seal species, the common seal and the grey seal. Although the two are at long range quite hard to distinguish, the common is generally lighter in colour and smaller with more delicate dog-like facial features. The common seal breeds in summer and generally independent of one another, while the grey breeds in mid-winter in rookeries predominantly on offshore islands. Both species can be seen throughout the year with the common most common on the west coast and the grey on the east. The Isle of May in the Firth of Forth is a well known breeding location for greys and an excellent place to see them in the wild.

Dolphins, porpoises, basking sharks and some species of whale can also been seen regularly around the Scottish coastline. The resident pod of bottlenose dolphins in the Moray Firth is best viewed between May and September, while minke whales, basking sharks and even orca (killer whales) are not entirely unusual off the west coast and Western Isles.

Island wildlife

The many offshore islands scattered around the Scottish coast provide sanctuary to a wide variety of seabirds, often in huge numbers. These islands are important both nationally and internationally for many breeding species and as such are designated National Nature Reserves (NNRs) and Sites of Special Scientific Interest (SSSIs). On the east coast the most noted are the Bass Rock and The Isle of May in the Firth of Forth, while to the north are the islands around Orkney and Shetland and on the west coast Handa Island near Cape Wrath

To visit these islands and the massive seabird colonies that inhabit their towering cliffs in the breeding season (April to September) is an unforgettable experience. Classic residents include members of the auk family, including the guillemot, razorbill and the puffin, without doubt the most colourful and charming seabird in Britain. Unlike the hardy guillemots and razorbills that nest precariously on the cliff ledges, the puffin nests in burrows, which they excavate with razor-sharp claws. After the eggs are incubated and the eggs hatch the chicks are raised in the burrow and this is the best time to view the birds.

The best places to see puffin and the seabird colonies are on a day trip to the Isle of May in the Firth of Forth, in Orkney and Shetland, or Handa Island in the far north west of the country, near Cape Wrath. Several other species inhabit other neighbourhoods within these seabird cities including the Manx shearwater and fulmar, which are both specialist pelagic petrels. The fulmar is worth special mention because it has the admirable habit of vomiting all over you should you stray too close. One of the most famous seabirds around Scotland is the large and very stern looking gannet which is black and white in colour with a 2 m wing span and an ochre coloured head. Its most famous international breeding site is the Bass Rock in the Firth of Forth where over 50,000 pairs breed annually. So famous is the Bass that it lends its name to the Northern or Atlantic gannet's official scientific name, Morus bassanus.

Other more unusual rare and resident species you might be very lucky to see on the coast is the white-tailed sea eagle around the Western Isles or the beautiful snowy owl on Fetlar in Shetland. The sea eagle used to be fairly common but was wiped out in Scotland by early last century. Now, after a successful reintroduction on the Isle of Rùm on the west coast, several pairs breed. The specific nesting locations are understandably keep secret but you may still see one on a fishing foray over its huge territorial range. Like the golden eagle its sheer size is an instant give away while the tail of course distinguishes it from its more common relative. The snowy owl is rarely seen outside Shetland and of course is instantly recognizable.

Some islands around the coast of Scotland are also well known internationally as migratory stopovers for vagrant species. The Isle of May in the Firth of Forth and Fair Isle between Shetland and Orkney are particularly important and well known often providing life saving shelter in spring and autumn storms for such exotically named species as the jack snipe or black redstart.

Rivers, lochs and wetlands

Otters are more commonly found along riverbanks in Europe but in Scotland are best observed on the tidal fringes searching for seafood. The Isle of Skye and Shetland are the best venues. The otter was for decades almost hunted to extinction in Britain but is now fully protected. It is often confused with the feral mink or ferret, which is far more commonly seen in the countryside throughout Britain.

Loch Garten in Speyside near Aviemore is the home to the Osprey and the venue of one of Scotland's most successful avian conservation stories. After being absent for many years the Loch Garten breeding site became a catalyst for what is now the successful national comeback of the species. You can view the birds nesting in summer at Loch Garten but if you are really lucky you will see one catching fish in a spectacular display of aerial acrobatics on the lochs and rivers of the region. The rivers Tay and Spey are world famous for their salmon. Some of the hydroelectric dams in Scotland have fish ladders where you can observe this archetype of inherent motivation as the fish struggle relentlessly upstream to breed. Pitlochry is one such venue.

Although not endemic to Scotland one of the most beautiful bird species you may encounter on the more remote lochs are divers (or loons as they are called in North America) – most commonly the red throated diver, the rarer black throated diver and occasionally the largest, the great northern diver. All three can be seen on the coast in winter. The best time to see these birds is in their superb summer breeding attire but it is perhaps their call that is most memorable. The haunting cry of the great northern or black throat that carries for miles across the moors and wide-open spaces is quite simply unforgettable. Red throated divers breed on lochs throughout the highlands while black throated divers can be found in the far north, especially round Lochinver and in Caithness. Also both rare and beautiful is the delicate black neck grebe which supports a headpiece in the breeding season to beat any human fashion label at the annual Royal Ascot horse races. Loch Ruthven near Inverness is an excellent place to observe this particular avian fashion parade.

For any Scot who is in tune with the countryside the first calls of greylag and pink footed geese are a sure sign that summer has ended. Huge numbers winter in Scotland especially in the central lowlands and parts of the west coast. Similarly, barnacle geese invade the Solway Firth in the south in their thousands. The V-shaped flying formations and constant honking of course make the type of bird if not the actual species instantly identifiable. Of course no mention of Scotland's waterways and wildlife would be complete without mention of Scotland's most famous aquatic creature – the Loch Ness Monster. Nessie does of course exist but like the wild haggis is very very shy and elusive.

Forests and lowlands

As opposed to its introduced North American cousin the native red squirrel is a delicate and shy creature. Their beautiful rustic colours can often herald their occasional public appearance in the forests of the Central Highlands, especially Speyside. If it were not for the grey squirrel pushing them out of former habitats and man destroying the habitat itself they could once again be classed as common. Even rarer is the elusive and rarely seen wildcat and pine marten. The wildcat is larger than the domestic 'moggy' and has a much courser, thicker fur coat, piercing, wild eyes and untamed attitude. Over the years the feral cat and wild variety have interbred and now it is very unusual to see the species in its rawest form. The pine marten is about the size of a mink and is occasionally seen in forested areas of more remote and unpopulated areas of the country.

The forests and lowlands are also home to some familiar bird species. The quite bizarre and wonderfully named capercaille (pronounced 'capper-kay-lee') is a member of the grouse family and the largest of the three species found in Scotland. It is the handsome black male that is most often seen deep in the forests, most commonly crossing forest paths and fire breaks while guarding his extensive territory. This is necessary not so much as protection from predators, but invasion by other highly sexed males intent on one thing and one thing only. An encounter and subsequent dispute results in audible threats and much puffing up of the plumage. Even more spectacular are the fights between the capercaillie's smaller relative the black grouse. Their version of a 'boxing ring' is called a 'lek' and can be the sight of spectacular displays of male hormonal overload.

Other unusual birds of the forest includes the crossbill, which is about the size of a overweight canary and has a beak that intersects, which it uses to expertly extract pine seeds from the cone. Crossbills can regularly be seen in the central highlands with National Nature Reserves like Loch Garten being a good bet. While in the Loch Garten area you may also see the delicate little crested tit, which although not endemic, only breeds in this part of Scotland. In much of western Scotland the hooded crow, or 'hoodie' replaces the common crow found throughout Britain. The hooded crow can be distinguished by the diagnostic grey patches on its plumage.

Britain's only venomous snake the adder is relatively common throughout Scotland and is mainly found on open ground covered in bracken or heather. They are rarely seen and generally keep well out of your way, though you may be lucky enough to encounter one sunning itself on rocks early in the day.

Highlands

The red deer are as much an environmental problem as a feature of the Scottish landscape. They now number over 300,000 and in the absence of natural predators are essentially out of control in the central highlands. Extensive management through hunting and culling has so far failed to keep numbers in check. In summer they remain in herds on high ground and, despite their size, they are actually very hard to spot. In winter however you can often see them in large numbers on lower ground in the glens and beside the main roads. During the 'rut' in autumn the males (stags) become highly aggressive and use their impressive antlers in fierce combat to win the females (hinds). This fighting is often accompanied by a loud roar that carries for miles. Other deer species seen commonly in Scotland in the Highlands, Central Lowlands and Borders are the roe, sitka and fallow deer.

Another famous Highlands inhabitant is the golden eagle. After periods of decline they are now present in relatively healthy numbers especially in the central and western highlands but are not exactly widespread or commonly seen. To the uninitiated the eagle is very often confused with the common buzzard, though the latter is actually much smaller. The golden eagle also dwarfs the large and menacing raven that is also a regular sight in central and western Scotland-usually accompanied by a raucous, 'throaty' call. Another regal and masterful lord of the highland skies is the peregrine falcon. In both flight and appearance they are the epitome of power. To watch a peregrine hunting other birds in flight is to witness one of the most spectacular acts in nature.

Two quite common masters of camouflage on the mountain slopes are the mountain hare and the ptarmigan, a bird similar in size and appearance to a red grouse. Both go through an incredible phase of moult from dark browns in summer to pure white in winter. They do this of course in order to blend in with their surroundings and avoid predators like the peregrine. Any time spent around the ski-fields in summer or winter should reveal one or both species.

Other rarer birds found breeding on the inhospitable high tops, especially in the Cairngorms, are the dotterel, a small attractive wading bird and the sparrow sized snow bunting‹$]1C Text Bold›. The snow bunting, like the mountain hare and ptarmigan, assumes a predominantly white plumage in summer. Few breed in Scotland as it is predominantly a winter visitor to the coast. On the lower slopes the red grouse is a common sight. Vast tracks of land are maintained to provide the ideal breeding habitat for this 'game bird' which are then hunted for sport.

Books

→ *See also page 610.*

History, politics and culture

The best general overview of Scottish social history is given by **Professor Chris Smout** in his excellent *A History of the Scottish People* (1560-1830) and *A Century of the Scottish People* (1830-1950). A worthy new contender is *Scotland A New History*, by **Michael Lynch** (Pimlico, 1999). Also *Scotland the Story of a Nation*, by **Magnus Manusson** (Harper Collins, 2000) is a mighty tome, and after reading it you're unlikely to pass on any questions on Scottish history. For a more emotive and subjective view of highland history, read any of **John Prebble**'s books, including *1,000 years of Scotland's History*, *The Lion in the North*, *Glen Coe*, *Culloden* and *The Highland Clearances* (Penguin), or **Nigel Tranter**'s *The Story of Scotland*. An entertaining account of Scotland's often turbulent relationship with England is given by **Sir Ludovic Kennedy**'s *In Bed with an Elephant*. **Tom Nairn**'s *The Break-up of Britain* gives a radical perspective of Scottish independence and *Scotland's Story* (Fontana) is also insightful. A comprehensive guide to Scottish culture is **David Daiches**' *The New Companion to Scottish Culture* (Arnold). For an overview, *Scottish Art* by **Murdo Macdonald** (Thames & Hudson, 2000). **James Buchan**'s *Capital of the Mind: How Edinburgh Changed the World* (John Murray, 2003) is a captivating study of enlightenment Edinburgh.

Biographies, travelogues & memoirs

Two excellent biographies of the most romantic figures in Scottish history are **Antonia Fraser**'s *Mary, Queen of Scots* (UK

Mandarin) and **Fitzroy Maclean**'s *Bonnie Prince Charlie* (Canongate). For a fascinating study of the life and works of one of Scotland's most enigmatic literary figures look no further than **Karl Miller**'s *Electric Shepherd: A Likeness of James Hogg* (Faber & Faber, 2003).

If you only read one travelogue, then make it **James Boswell and Samuel Johnson**'s *A Journey to the Western Islands of Scotland* (UK Penguin). Other notables include *In Search of Scotland* by **HV Morton** (Methuen), *A High and Lonely Place and Gulfs of Blue Air – A Highland Journey* (Mainstream) by **Jim Crumley and Elizabeth Grant of Rothiemurchus**, *Memoirs of a Highland Lady* (Canongate). One of the best known Highland memoirs is *A Ring of Bright Water* by **Gavin Maxwell**; a tale of otters and other wildlife set in Glenelg. *A Last Wild Place* by naturalist **Mike Tomkies** is a fascinating account of life in a remote West Highland croft. Another interesting read is *Queen Victoria's Highland Journal*, edited by **David Duff** (UK Hamlyn). Also worth mentioning is **Bella Bathurst**'s *The Lighthouse Stevensons* (HarperCollins, 1999), a well-documented account of the fascinating story of Robert Louis Stevenson's family, who built many of the lighthouses around Scotland's coast.For a selection of the best, including **Daniel Defoe**, **Edwin Muir** and **Jan Morris**, there's *The Road North - 300 years of Classic Scottish Travel Writing*, edited by **June Skinner Sawyers** (The Inn Pinn, 2000).

Outdoor activities

There are numerous walking guides available and this is only the briefest of selections. Two of the best are *Great Walks Scotland* by **Hamish Brown** and *100 Best Routes on Scottish Mountains* by **Ralph Storer**. Two helpful hillwalking guides published by the **Scottish Mountaineering Trust** are *The Munros* by **Donald Bennett** and *The Corbetts* by **Scott Johnstone et al**. The SMT also publishes a range of district guides listing mainly high level walks. Also useful are *The Munro Almanac* and *The Corbett Almanac* by **Cameron McNeish**. A healthy antidote to all those climbing anoraks is **Muriel Gray**'s entertaining and clean-shaven *The First Fifty: Munro Bagging without a Beard* (UK Corgi).

Those wishing to attempt one of the long-distance walks should read *The West Highland Way* or *The Southern Upland Way*, both highly informative guides by **Roger Smith** (HM Stationery Office). An excellent guide for both walkers and mountain bikers is **Ralph Storer**'s *Exploring Scottish Hill Tracks*. Other recommended cycling guides include: *The Scottish Cycling Guide* by **Brendan Walsh**; *101 Bike Routes in Scotland* by **Henry Henniker** (Mainstream); *Cycling in Scotland* by **John Hancox** (Collins Pocket Reference, Harper Collins); and *Cycling in Great Britain: Bicycle Touring Adventures in England, Scotland and Wales* by **Tim Hughes & Jo Cleary** (Bicycle Books, US). For a comprehensive guide to Scotland's golf courses try *Scotland – Home of Golf*, a Pastime publication produced by the **Scottish Tourist Board** and *The Scottish Golf Guide* by **David Hamilton** (Canongate Press). An outsider's view of golf in Scotland can be found in American **Michael Bamberger**'s highly entertaining book *To the Linksland* (Mainstream Publishing), ideal if the Scottish weather keeps you from playing! A good birdwatching guide is *Where to Watch Birds in Scotland* by **Michael Madders and Julia Welstead** (UK Christopher Helm).

Miscellaneous

For a comprehensive history of Scottish clans and families, see *Scottish Family History*, by **Margaret Stuart and James Balfour Paul** (Edinburgh, 1930), or *The Surnames of Scotland: their origin, meaning and history* by **George Black** (New York, 1940). These books are available in most public libraries. For more detailed genealogical study, look at *Tracing your Ancestors* by **Cecil Sinclair** (HM Stationery Office). *Exploring Scotland's Heritage* is a beautifully-illustrated series of books on historic buildings and archaeological sites in different regions of Scotland (HM Stationery Office). Those wishing to bone up on their malt whiskies should refer to the *Malt Whisky Companion* by **Michael Jackson** (UK Dorling Kindersley). An excellent Scottish recipe book is the *Claire MacDonald Cookbook* by **Lady Claire MacDonald** (UK Bantam) who runs a hotel on Skye.

Footnotes

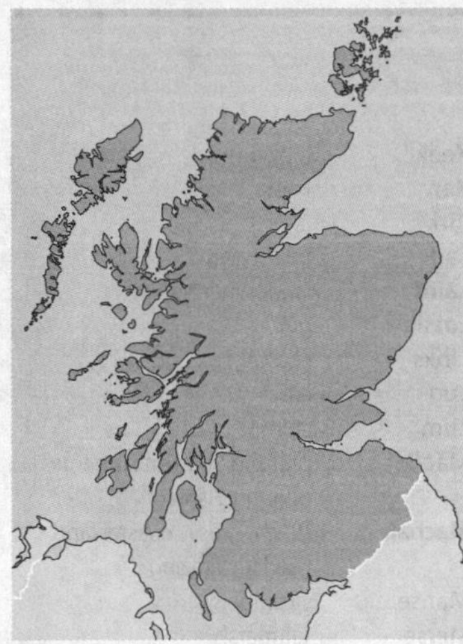

Glossary

Auld	old
Aye	yes
Bairn	child
Ben	hill or mountain
Besom	cheeky/rascal
Blether	to talk nonsense
Bonny	pretty
Bothy	farm cottage/mountain hut
Brae	hill or slope
Braw	beautiful
Breeks	trousers
Brig	bridge
Burn	brook
Canny	careful
Ceilidh	social gathering involving singing, dancing and drinking
Clan	tribe bearing same surname
Clearances	evictions of tenant crofters by landowners in the Highlands in late 18th and early 19th centuries in order to create space for more profitable sheep
Close	narrow passage between buildings
Clype	tell-tale
Couthy	cosy
Crannog	Celtic lake or bog dwelling
Croft	small plot of farmland and house
Cuddie	horse
Doo	dove
Dour	hard/stubborn
Dram	small measure of whisky
Drouthy	thirsty
Dunt	bump
Elder	office bearer in Presbyterian church
Factor	manager of estate/landlord
Firth	estuary
Fash	trouble/bother
Gallus	cheeky/forward
Ghillie	personal hunting or fishing guide
Glaikit	gormless
Girn	moan/whinge
Greet	cry
Haar	sea mist
Hen	dear (female person)
Howff	traditional pub/haunt
Keek	look furtively
Ken	know
Kirk	church
Lade	mill stream
Laird	landowner/squire
Lassie	girl
Links	coastal golf course
Lug	ear
Lum	chimney
Mac/Mc	prefix in Scottish surnames denoting 'son of'
Machair	sandy, grassy coastal land used for grazing
Manse	vicarage
Merse	saltmarsh
Mind	remember
Muckle	big
Munro	mountain over 3,000 ft
Neep	turnip
Nicht	night
Nippit	tight fitting
Oxter	armpit
Partan	large crab
Peely wally	pale/wan
Pend	alleyway
Pinkie	little finger
Poke	paper bag
Provost	mayor
Puddock	frog
Reek	smoke
Sair	sore
Sassenach	literally 'southerner' though commonly used to describe English
Scunner	nuisance/disgust
Sept	branch of clan
Shoogle	shake
Sleekit	sly/cunning
Smirr	fine rain
Sort	fix/mend
Tattie bogle	scarecrow
Thole	endure
Trauchled	tired and bothered
Wabbit	exhausted
Wean	child
Wee	small
Wee Frees	Followers of the Free Church of Scotland
Wynd	lane
Yett	gate or door

Index

C

D

E

Footnotes Index

Map index

Map symbols

Administration

- Capital city
- Other city/town
- International border
- Regional border
- Disputed border

Roads and travel

- National highway, motorway
- Main road
- Minor road
- Track
- Footpath
- Railway with station
- Airport
- Bus station
- Metro station
- Cable car
- Funicular
- Ferry
- Pedestrianized street
- Tunnel
- One way street
- Steps
- Bridge
- Fortified wall
- Park, garden, stadium
- Sleeping
- Eating
- Bars & clubs
- Entertainment
- Building
- Sight
- Cathedral, church
- Chinese temple
- Hindu temple
- Meru
- Mosque
- Stupa
- Synagogue
- Tourist office
- Museum
- Post office
- Police
- Bank
- Internet
- Telephone
- Market
- Hospital
- Parking
- Petrol
- Golf
- Detail map
- Related map

Water features

- River, canal
- Lake, ocean
- Seasonal marshland
- Beach, sand bank
- Waterfall

Topographical features

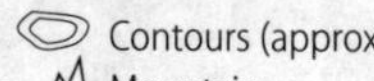

- Contours (approx)
- Mountain
- Volcano
- Mountain pass
- Escarpment
- Gorge
- Glacier
- Salt flat
- Rocks

Cities and towns

- Main through route
- Main street
- Minor street

Other symbols

- Archaeological site
- National park, wildlife reserve
- Viewing point
- Campsite
- Refuge, lodge
- Castle
- Diving
- Deciduous/coniferous/palm trees
- Hide
- Vineyard
- Distillery
- Shipwreck
- Historic battlefield

Acknowledgements

I would like to thank those who contributed to this book. Rebecca Ford is a full-time travel writer, who specializes in Britain and Italy. Her work has appeared in publications such as the *Daily Telegraph*, the *Evening Standard* and *Scotland on Sunday*. Rebecca researched and updated the Glasgow, Northeast and Central Scotland chapters, as well as contributing to the Edinburgh chapter and History section. John Murphy updated the pubs and clubs of Edinburgh, while Jane Hamilton and John Binney updated the Glasgow pubs and clubs and gay listings. Suzy Kennard wrote the History and Architecture sections, Duncan Lindsay wrote Music, Frank Nicholas wrote Literature and Darroch Donald wrote Wildlife.

Thanks go to the staff of the many local and regional tourist offices for their invaluable advice and assistance, to Francoise Van Buuren at the National Trust for Scotland, Deborah Brown at Caledonian McBrayne, and the staff at Historic Scotland. Thanks also to the many travellers, and Scottish residents, who wrote in with their helpful comments, tips and suggestions. It's nice to be appreciated.

A special thank you to everyone at Footprint, especially Stephanie Lambe for all her hard work, patience and good ideas.

As always , this book is dedicated to Philippa, for her unfailing love and support, and to Rosa and Ruben for providing (not always welcome) diversions and helping me to keep things in perspective.

Credits

Footprint credits
Editor: Stephanie Lambe
Map editor: Sarah Sorensen
Publisher: Patrick Dawson
Editorial: Sophie Blacksell, Sarah Thorowgood, Claire Boobbyer, Felicity Laughton, Davina Rungasamy, Laura Dixon
Cartography: Robert Lunn, Claire Benison, Kevin Feeney
Series development Rachel Fielding
Design: Mytton Williams and Rosemary Dawson (brand)
Advertising: Debbie Wylde
Finance and administration: Sharon Hughes, Elizabeth Taylor

Photography credits
Front and back cover: Alamy
Inside colour section: POWERSTOCK

Print
Manufactured in Italy by LegoPrint
Pulp from sustainable forests

Footprint feedback
We try as hard as we can to make each Footprint guide as up to date as possible but, of course, things always change. If you want to let us know about your experiences – good, bad or ugly – then don't delay, go to **www.footprintbooks.com** and send in your comments.

Ordnance Survey® This product includes mapping data licensed from Ordnance Survey® with the permission of the Controller of Her Majesty's Stationery Office. © Crown Copyright. All rights reserved. Licence No. 100027877.

Publishing information
Footprint Scotland
3rd edition

June 2004

ISBN 1 903471 94 X
CIP DATA: A catalogue record for this book is available from the British Library

® Footprint Handbooks and the Footprint mark are a registered trademark of Footprint Handbooks Ltd

Published by Footprint
6 Riverside Court
Lower Bristol Road
Bath BA2 3DZ, UK
T +44 (0)1225 469141
F +44 (0)1225 469461
discover@footprintbooks.com
www.footprintbooks.com

Distributed in the USA by
Publishers Group West

Neither the black and white nor coloured maps are intended to have any political significance.

Every effort has been made to ensure that the facts in this guidebook are accurate. However, travellers should still obtain advice from consulates, airlines etc about travel and visa requirements before travelling. The authors and publishers cannot accept responsibility for any loss, injury or inconvenience however caused.

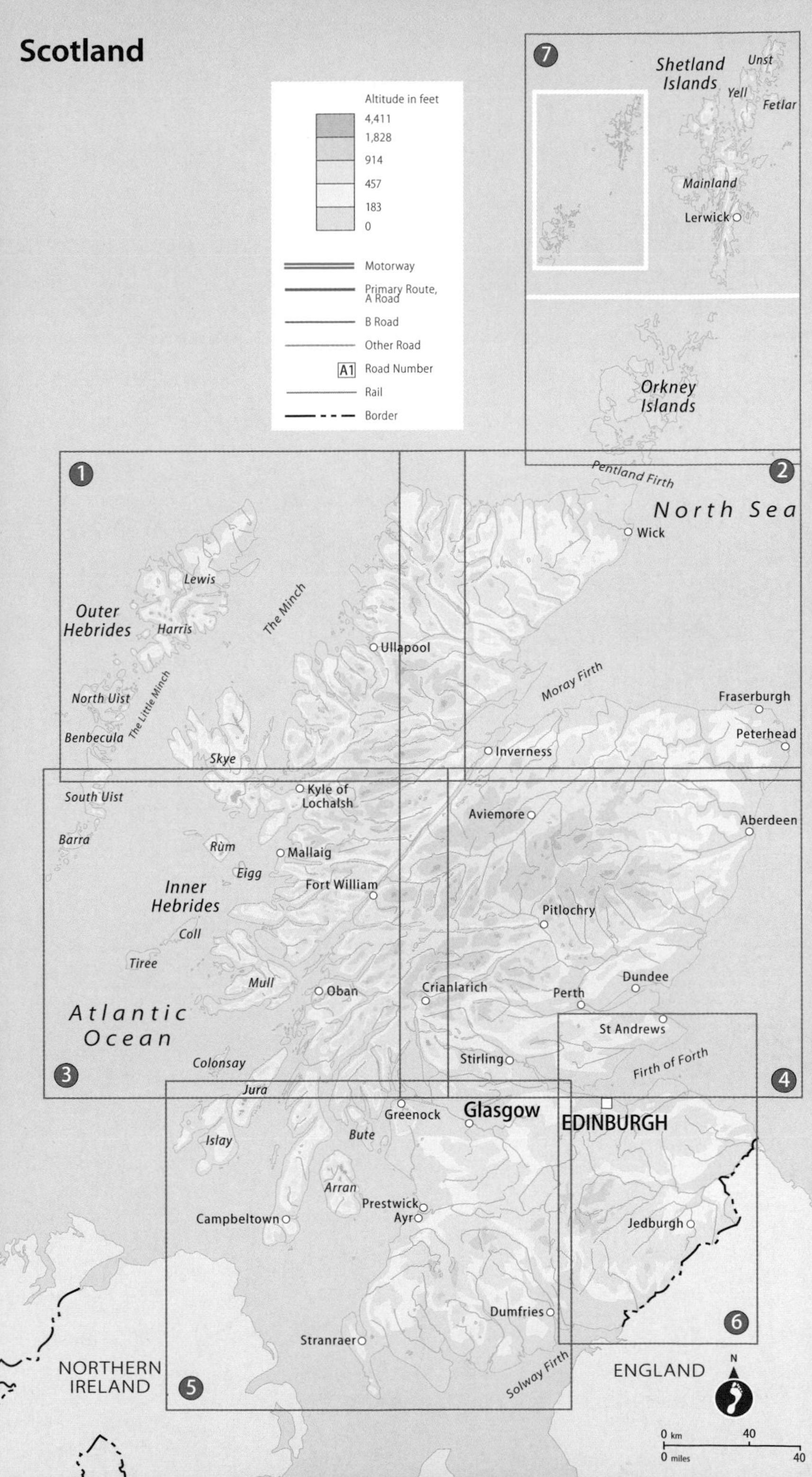
Scotland
Altitude in feet
4,411
1,828
914
457
183
0
Motorway
Primary Route, A Road
B Road
Other Road
A1
Road Number
Rail
Border
7
Shetland Islands
Unst
Yell
Fetlar
Mainland
Lerwick
Orkney Islands
1
2
Pentland Firth
North Sea
Wick
Lewis
Outer Hebrides
Harris
The Minch
Ullapool
North Uist
The Little Minch
Benbecula
Moray Firth
Fraserburgh
Peterhead
Inverness
Skye
South Uist
Kyle of Lochalsh
Aviemore
Aberdeen
Barra
Rùm
Mallaig
Eigg
Inner Hebrides
Fort William
Pitlochry
Coll
Tiree
Mull
Oban
Crianlarich
Perth
Dundee
St Andrews
Atlantic Ocean
Colonsay
Stirling
Firth of Forth
3
4
Jura
Greenock
Glasgow
EDINBURGH
Islay
Bute
Arran
Prestwick
Ayr
Campbeltown
Jedburgh
Dumfries
Stranraer
6
NORTHERN IRELAND
5
Solway Firth
ENGLAND
N
0 km
40
0 miles
40

Map 1

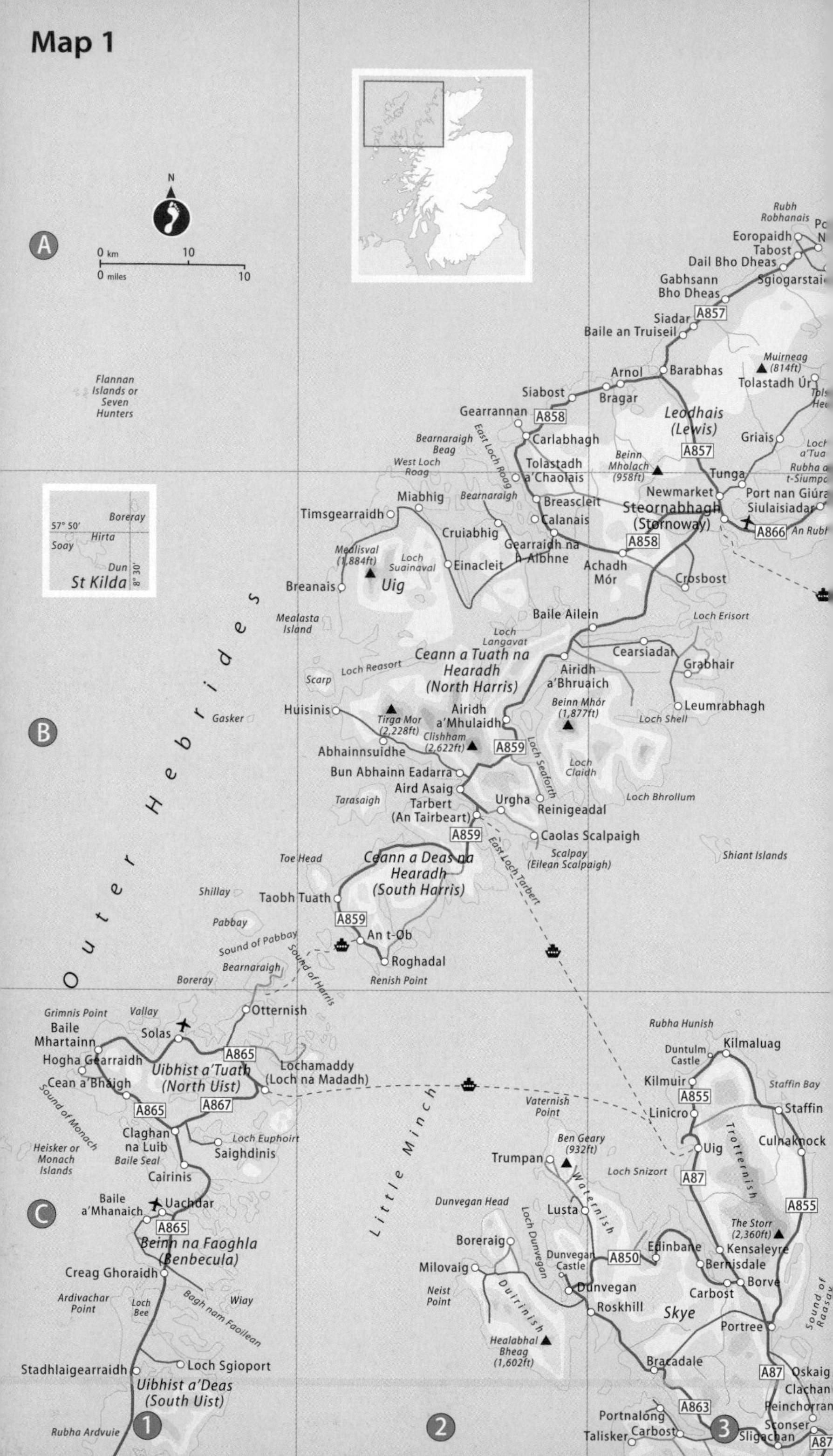

A
B
C
1
2
3
0 km 10
0 miles 10
N
Flannan Islands or Seven Hunters
St Kilda
Boreray
Hirta
Soay
Dun
57° 50'
8° 30'
Outer Hebrides
Little Minch
Rubh Robhanais
Eoropaidh
Tabost
Dail Bho Dheas
Sgiogarstai
Gabhsann Bho Dheas
Siadar
A857
Baile an Truiseil
Muirneag (814ft)
Arnol
Barabhas
Tolastadh Úr
Siabost
Bragar
Gearrannan
A858
Leodhais (Lewis)
Carlabhagh
Bearnaraigh Beag
East Loch Roag
West Loch Roag
Griais
Beinn Mholach (958ft)
Tolastadh a'Chaolais
Tunga
Newmarket
Port nan Giúra
Siulaisiadar
Miabhig
Bearnaraigh
Breascleit
Steornabhagh (Stornoway)
Timsgearraidh
Calanais
A866
Cruiabhig
Gearraidh na h-Aibhne
Mealisval (1,884ft)
Loch Suainaval
Einacleit
Achadh Mór
Crosbost
Breanais
Uig
Baile Ailein
Loch Erisort
Mealasta Island
Loch Langavat
Cearsiadar
Ceann a Tuath na Hearadh (North Harris)
Loch Reasort
Airidh a'Bhruaich
Grabhair
Scarp
Beinn Mhór (1,877ft)
Leumrabhagh
Huisinis
Airidh a'Mhulaidh
Loch Shell
Gasker
Tirga Mor (2,228ft)
Clishham (2,622ft)
A859
Abhainnsuidhe
Loch Seaforth
Loch Claidh
Bun Abhainn Eadarra
Aird Asaig
Tarasaigh
Tarbert (An Tairbeart)
Urgha
Reinigeadal
Loch Bhrollum
Caolas Scalpaigh
East Loch Tarbert
Toe Head
Ceann a Deas na Hearadh (South Harris)
Scalpay (Eilean Scalpaigh)
Shiant Islands
Shillay
Taobh Tuath
Pabbay
An t-Ob
Sound of Pabbay
Sound of Harris
Roghadal
Bearnaraigh
Boreray
Renish Point
Grimnis Point
Vallay
Otternish
Baile Mhartainn
Solas
A865
Hogha Gearraidh
Uibhist a'Tuath (North Uist)
Lochamaddy (Loch na Madadh)
Cean a'Bhàigh
A867
Sound of Monach
Claghan na Luib
Loch Euphoirt
Saighdinis
Heisker or Monach Islands
Baile Seal
Cairinis
Baile a'Mhanaich
Uachdar
Beinn na Faoghla (Benbecula)
Creag Ghoraidh
Bagh nam Faoilean
Wiay
Ardivachar Point
Loch Bee
Loch Sgioport
Stadhlaigearraidh
Uibhist a'Deas (South Uist)
Rubha Ardvuie
Rubha Hunish
Duntulm Castle
Kilmaluag
Kilmuir
Staffin Bay
A855
Vaternish Point
Linicro
Staffin
Trotternish
Culnaknock
Ben Geary (932ft)
Uig
Trumpan
Waternish
Loch Snizort
A87
Dunvegan Head
Lusta
The Storr (2,360ft)
Loch Dunvegan
Boreraig
Edinbane
Kensaleyre
Dunvegan Castle
A850
Bernisdale
Milovaig
Duirinish
Dunvegan
Borve
Neist Point
Carbost
Roskhill
Skye
Portree
Sound of Raasay
Healabhal Bheag (1,602ft)
Bracadale
Oskaig
Clachan
A863
Peinchorran
Portnalong
Sconser
Talisker
Carbost
Sligachan

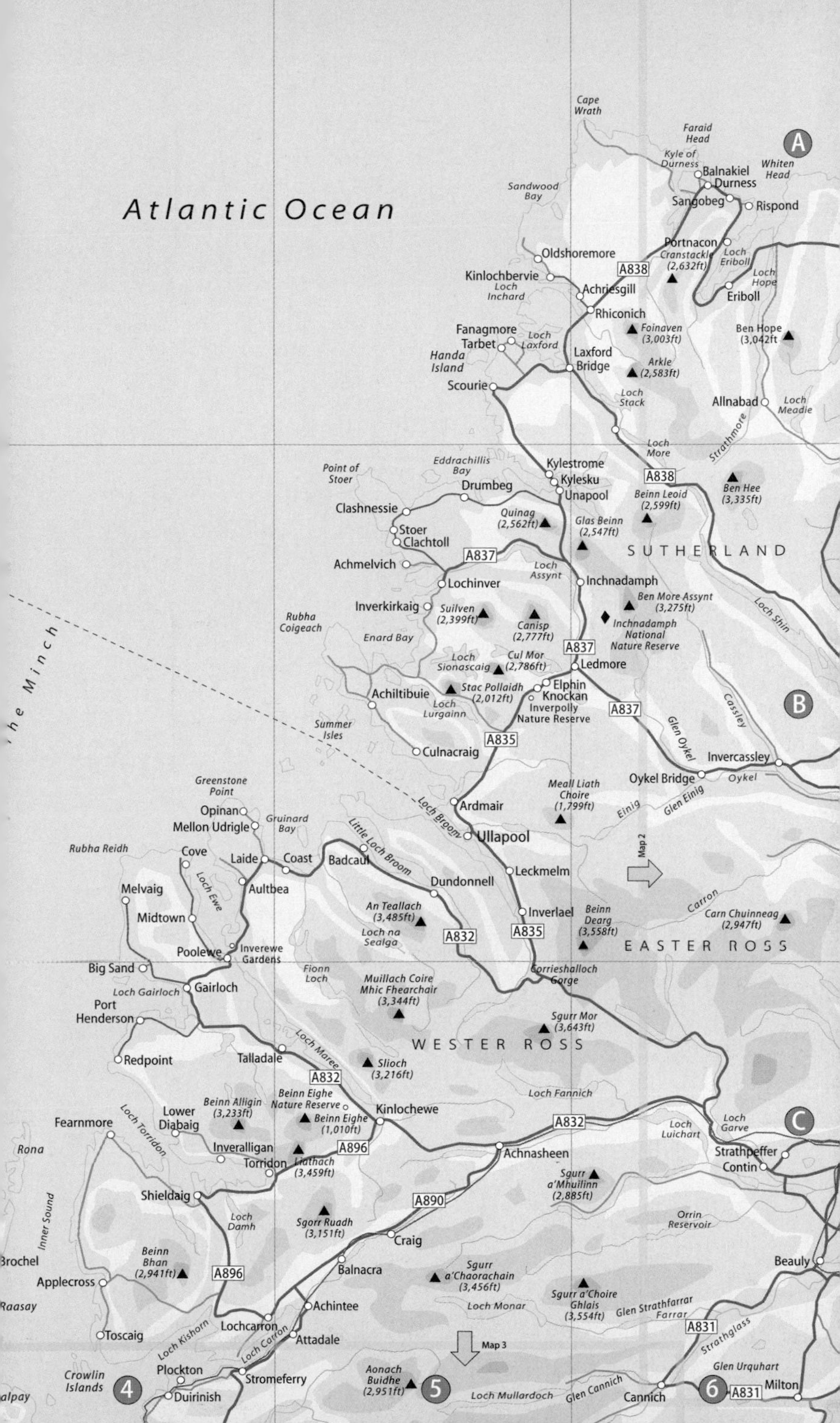

Atlantic Ocean
Cape Wrath
Faraid Head
Kyle of Durness
Balnakiel
Durness
Whiten Head
Sandwood Bay
Sangobeg
Rispond
Portnacon
Cranstackle (2,632ft)
Loch Eriboll
Loch Hope
Eriboll
Oldshoremore
A838
Kinlochbervie
Loch Inchard
Achriesgill
Rhiconich
Foinaven (3,003ft)
Ben Hope (3,042ft)
Fanagmore
Tarbet
Loch Laxford
Handa Island
Laxford Bridge
Arkle (2,583ft)
Scourie
Loch Stack
Allnabad
Loch Meadie
Strathmore
Loch More
Point of Stoer
Eddrachillis Bay
Kylestrome
Kylesku
Unapool
A838
Ben Hee (3,335ft)
Drumbeg
Beinn Leoid (2,599ft)
Clashnessie
Quinag (2,562ft)
Glas Beinn (2,547ft)
Stoer
Clachtoll
SUTHERLAND
A837
Achmelvich
Loch Assynt
Inchnadamph
Lochinver
Ben More Assynt (3,275ft)
Inverkirkaig
Suilven (2,399ft)
Canisp (2,777ft)
Inchnadamph National Nature Reserve
Loch Shin
Rubha Coigeach
Enard Bay
the Minch
A837
Loch Sionascaig
Cul Mor (2,786ft)
Ledmore
Stac Pollaidh (2,012ft)
Elphin
Knockan
Achiltibuie
Loch Lurgainn
Inverpolly Nature Reserve
A837
Cassley
Glen Oykel
Summer Isles
A835
Culnacraig
Invercassley
Oykel Bridge
Oykel
Greenstone Point
Meall Liath Choire (1,799ft)
Einig
Glen Einig
Opinan
Mellon Udrigle
Gruinard Bay
Ardmair
Loch Broom
Little Loch Broom
Ullapool
Rubha Reidh
Cove
Laide
Coast
Badcaul
Map 2
Leckmelm
Loch Ewe
Aultbea
Dundonnell
Melvaig
An Teallach (3,485ft)
Inverlael
Beinn Dearg (3,558ft)
Carron
Carn Chuinneag (2,947ft)
Midtown
Loch na Sealga
A832
A835
EASTER ROSS
Poolewe
Inverewe Gardens
Big Sand
Fionn Loch
Corrieshalloch Gorge
Gairloch
Loch Gairloch
Muillach Coire Mhic Fhearchair (3,344ft)
Port Henderson
Sgurr Mor (3,643ft)
Loch Maree
WESTER ROSS
Talladale
Redpoint
Slioch (3,216ft)
A832
Loch Fannich
Beinn Eighe Nature Reserve
Beinn Alligin (3,233ft)
Lower Diabaig
Kinlochewe
Beinn Eighe (1,010ft)
A832
Loch Luichart
Loch Garve
Fearnmore
Loch Torridon
Rona
Inveralligan
A896
Achnasheen
Strathpeffer
Torridon
Liathach (3,459ft)
Contin
Sgurr a'Mhuilinn (2,885ft)
Shieldaig
A890
Inner Sound
Loch Damh
Sgorr Ruadh (3,151ft)
Orrin Reservoir
Craig
Brochel
Beinn Bhan (2,941ft)
Beauly
Balnacra
Sgurr a'Chaorachain (3,456ft)
A896
Applecross
Sgurr a'Choire Ghlais (3,554ft)
Achintee
Loch Monar
Glen Strathfarrar
Farrar
Raasay
Lochcarron
A831
Strathglass
Toscaig
Loch Kishorn
Loch Carron
Attadale
Map 3
Glen Urquhart
Crowlin Islands
Plockton
Aonach Buidhe (2,951ft)
Stromeferry
Loch Mullardoch
Glen Cannich
Milton
A831
Cannich
Duirinish
A
B
C
4
5
6

Map 2

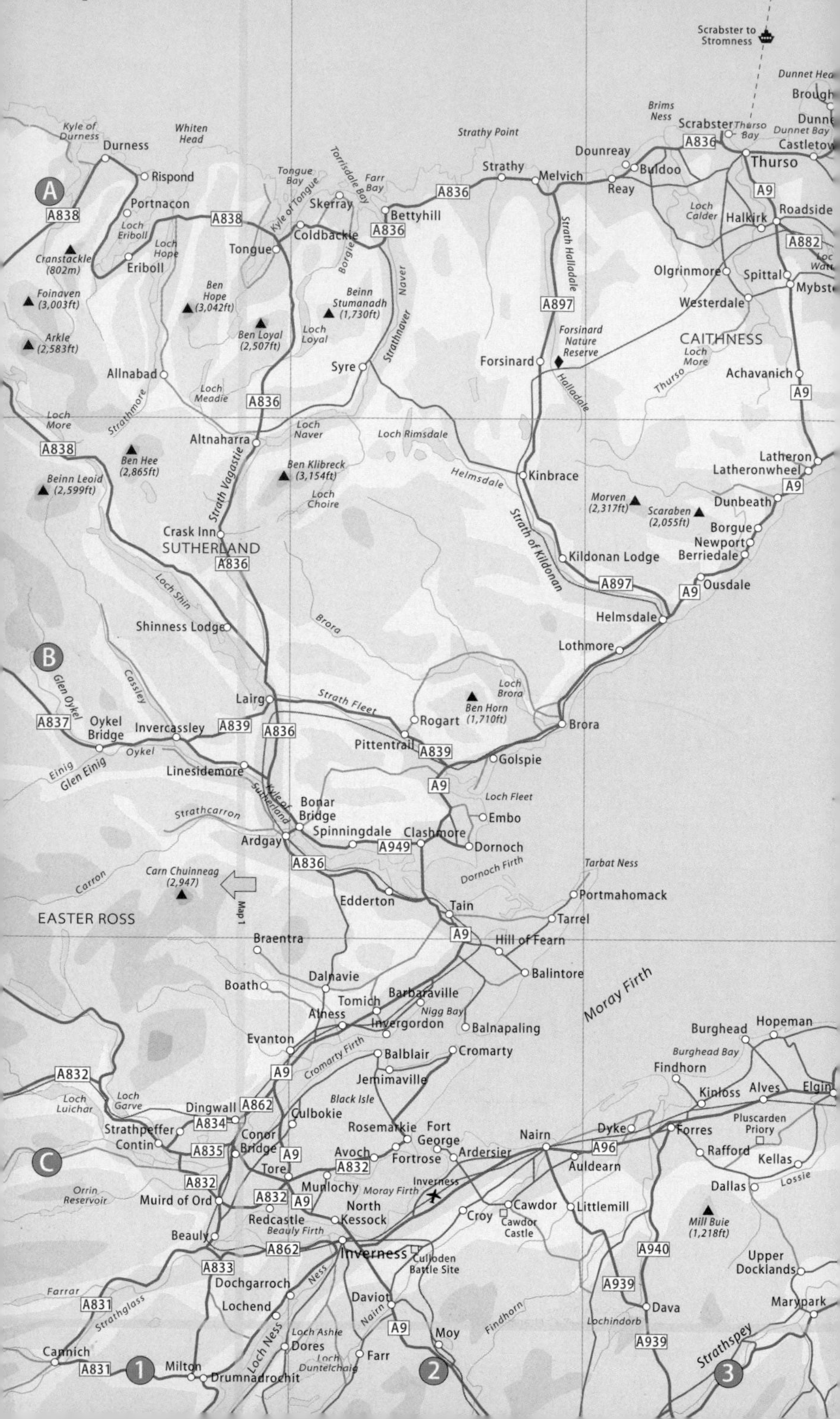

Scrabster to Stromness
Dunnet Head
Brough
Dunnet
Dunnet Bay
Castletown
Brims Ness
Scrabster
Thurso Bay
A836
Thurso
Kyle of Durness
Whiten Head
Strathy Point
Dounreay
Buldoo
Reay
Durness
Rispond
Strathy
Melvich
A
A838
Portnacon
Tongue Bay
Torrisdale Bay
Farr Bay
A836
A9
Roadside
Kyle of Tongue
Skerray
Bettyhill
Loch Calder
Halkirk
Loch Eriboll
A838
Coldbackie
A836
Strath Halladale
A882
Loch Hope
Tongue
Loch Watten
Cranstackle (802m)
Eriboll
Borgie
Olgrinmore
Spittal
Naver
Mybster
Foinaven (3,003ft)
Ben Hope (3,042ft)
Beinn Stumanadh (1,730ft)
A897
Westerdale
Ben Loyal (2,507ft)
Loch Loyal
Forsinard Nature Reserve
CAITHNESS
Arkle (2,583ft)
Strathnaver
Loch More
Syre
Forsinard
Achavanich
Allnabad
Thurso
Halladale
A9
Loch Meadie
A836
Loch More
Strathmore
Loch Naver
Loch Rimsdale
Altnaharra
A838
Ben Hee (2,865ft)
Latheron
Latheronwheel
Helmsdale
Kinbrace
Beinn Leoid (2,599ft)
Ben Klibreck (3,154ft)
Strath Vagastie
A9
Loch Choire
Morven (2,317ft)
Dunbeath
Scaraben (2,055ft)
Borgue
Crask Inn
Strath of Kildonan
Newport
SUTHERLAND
Kildonan Lodge
Berriedale
A836
A897
Ousdale
Loch Shin
A9
Helmsdale
Shinness Lodge
Brora
Lothmore
B
Glen Oykel
Cassley
Loch Brora
Lairg
Strath Fleet
Ben Horn (1,710ft)
A837
Oykel Bridge
Invercassley
A839
A836
Rogart
Brora
Pittentrail
A839
Oykel
Golspie
Einig
Glen Einig
Linesidemore
Kyle of Sutherland
A9
Loch Fleet
Bonar Bridge
Embo
Strathcarron
Spinningdale
Clashmore
Ardgay
A949
Dornoch
A836
Tarbat Ness
Dornoch Firth
Carron
Carn Chuinneag (2,947)
Map 1
Portmahomack
Edderton
Tain
Tarrel
EASTER ROSS
A9
Hill of Fearn
Braentra
Balintore
Dalnavie
Boath
Barbaraville
Moray Firth
Tomich
Nigg Bay
Alness
Invergordon
Balnapaling
Burghead
Hopeman
Evanton
Burghead Bay
Balblair
Cromarty
Cromarty Firth
A9
Findhorn
A832
Jemimaville
Kinloss
Alves
Elgin
Black Isle
Loch Luichar
Loch Garve
Dingwall
A862
Culbokie
Pluscarden Priory
A834
Rosemarkie
Fort George
Nairn
Dyke
Forres
Strathpeffer
Contin
Conon Bridge
A835
A9
Avoch
Ardersier
A96
Rafford
C
Tore
A832
Fortrose
Auldearn
Kellas
A832
Inverness
Lossie
Orrin Reservoir
Munlochy
Moray Firth
Dallas
Muird of Ord
A832
A9
North Kessock
Cawdor
Croy
Littlemill
Mill Buie (1,218ft)
Redcastle
Cawdor Castle
Beauly Firth
Beauly
A862
Inverness
A940
Culloden Battle Site
Upper Docklands
A833
Dochgarroch
Ness
A939
Farrar
Daviot
Marypark
A831
Lochend
Nairn
Findhorn
Dava
Strathglass
A9
Loch Ness
Loch Ashie
Moy
Lochindorb
Dores
A939
Strathspey
Cannich
Farr
Loch Duntelchaig
A831
1
Milton
Drumnadrochit
2
3

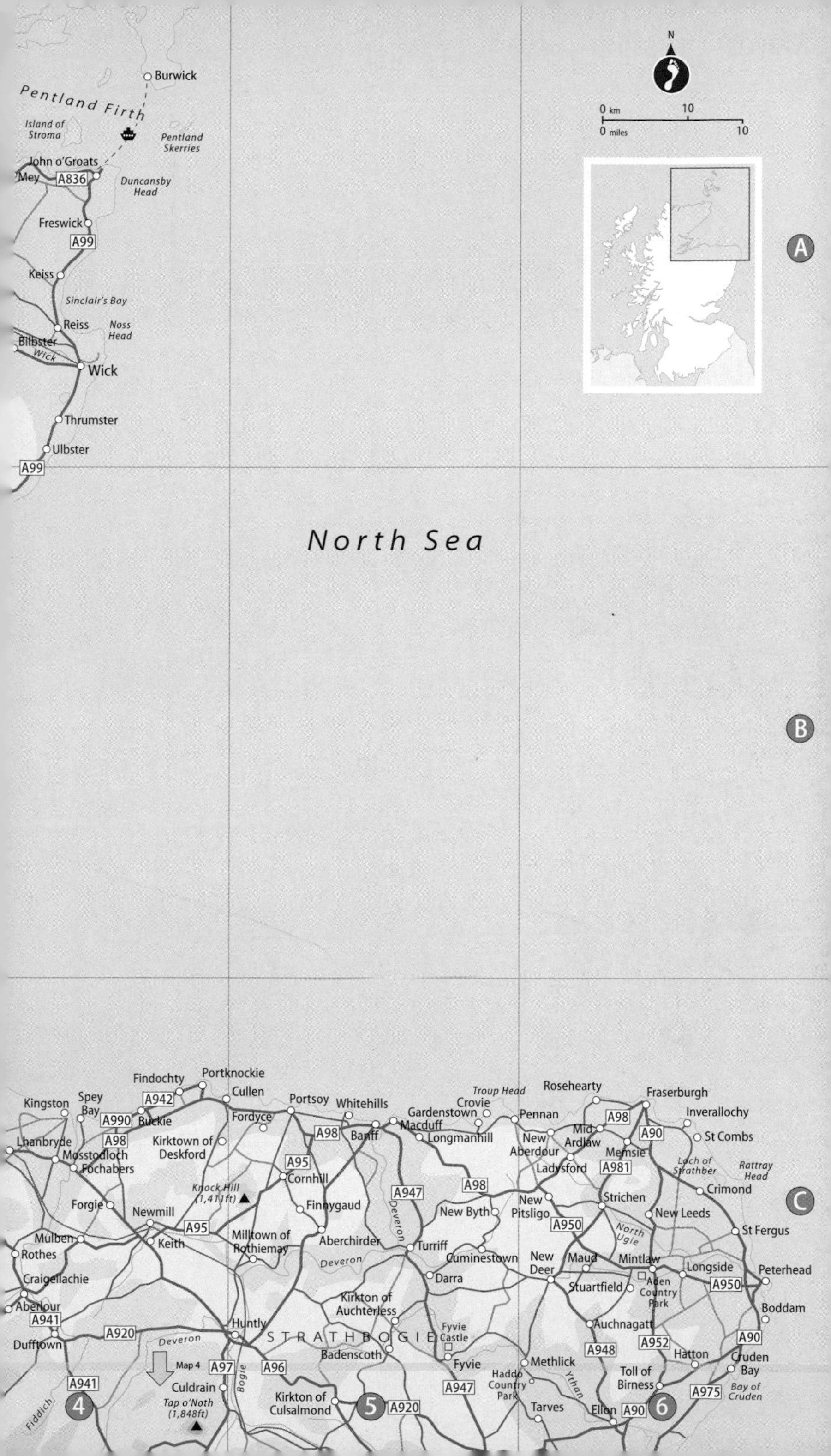

N
0 km
10
0 miles
10
A
B
C
Burwick
Pentland Firth
Island of Stroma
Pentland Skerries
John o'Groats
Mey
A836
Duncansby Head
Freswick
A99
Keiss
Sinclair's Bay
Reiss
Noss Head
Bilbster
Wick
Wick
Thrumster
Ulbster
A99
North Sea
Findochty
Portknockie
Cullen
Portsoy
Whitehills
Troup Head
Crovie
Gardenstown
Rosehearty
Fraserburgh
Inverallochy
St Combs
Kingston
Spey Bay
A942
A990
Buckie
A98
Fordyce
A98
Banff
Macduff
Longmanhill
Pennan
New Aberdour
Mid Ardlaw
A98
A90
Memsie
A981
Ladysford
Loch of Strathbeg
Rattray Head
Crimond
Lhanbryde
Mosstodloch
Fochabers
Kirktown of Deskford
A95
Cornhill
Knock Hill (1,411ft)
A947
A98
Strichen
New Leeds
Forgie
Newmill
Finnygaud
Deveron
New Byth
New Pitsligo
A950
North Ugie
St Fergus
Mulben
Keith
A95
Milltown of Rothiemay
Aberchirder
Turriff
Cuminestown
New Deer
Maud
Mintlaw
Longside
Peterhead
Rothes
Deveron
Darra
Aden Country Park
A950
Craigellachie
Stuartfield
Aberlour
Kirkton of Auchterless
Boddam
A941
Huntly
STRATHBOGIE
Fyvie Castle
Auchnagatt
A920
Deveron
A90
Dufftown
Badenscoth
A948
A952
Hatton
Map 4
A97
A96
Fyvie
Methlick
Cruden Bay
A941
Culdrain
Bogie
Haddo Country Park
Ythan
Toll of Birness
4
Tap o'Noth (1,848ft)
Kirkton of Culsalmond
5
A920
A947
Tarves
Ellon
A90
6
A975
Bay of Cruden
Fiddich

Map 3

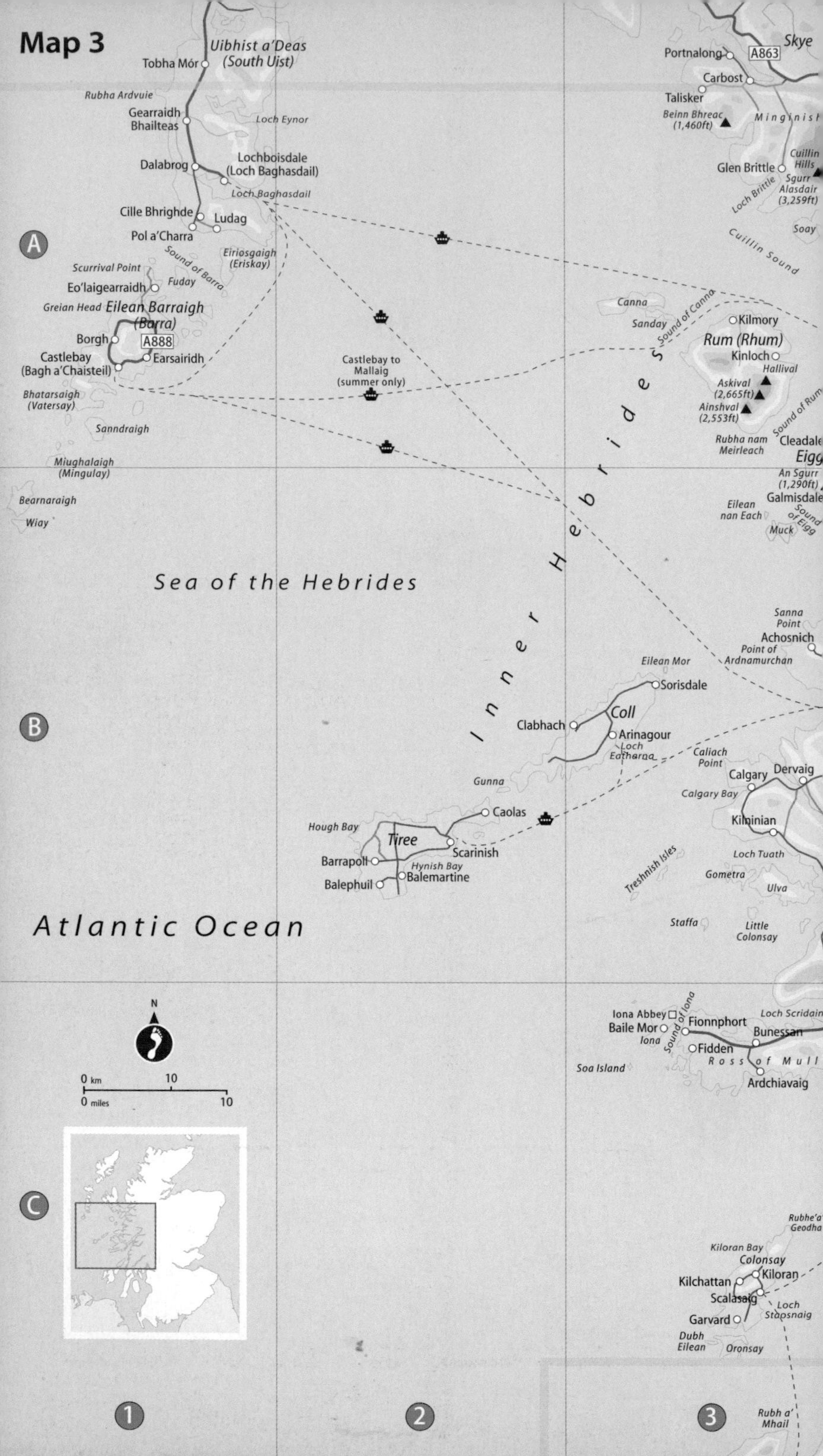

Uibhist a'Deas
(South Uist)
Tobha Mór
Rubha Ardvuie
Gearraidh
Bhailteas
Loch Eynor
Dalabrog
Lochboisdale
(Loch Baghasdail)
Loch Baghasdail
Cille Bhrighde
Ludag
Pol a'Charra
Sound of Barra
Eiriosgaigh
(Eriskay)
Scurrival Point
Fuday
Eo'laigearraidh
Greian Head
Eilean Barraigh
(Barra)
Borgh
A888
Earsairidh
Castlebay
(Bagh a'Chaisteil)
Bhatarsaigh
(Vatersay)
Sanndraigh
Miughalaigh
(Mingulay)
Bearnaraigh
Wiay
Castlebay to
Mallaig
(summer only)
Sea of the Hebrides
Inner Hebrides
Skye
Portnalong
A863
Carbost
Talisker
Beinn Bhreac
(1,460ft)
Minginish
Cuillin
Hills
Glen Brittle
Sgurr
Alasdair
(3,259ft)
Loch Brittle
Soay
Cuillin Sound
Canna
Sanday
Sound of Canna
Kilmory
Rum (Rhum)
Kinloch
Hallival
Askival
(2,665ft)
Ainshval
(2,553ft)
Sound of Rum
Rubha nam
Meirleach
Cleadale
Eigg
An Sgurr
(1,290ft)
Galmisdale
Eilean
nan Each
Sound
of Eigg
Muck
Sanna
Point
Achosnich
Point of
Ardnamurchan
Eilean Mor
Sorisdale
Coll
Clabhach
Arinagour
Loch
Eatharna
Caliach
Point
Gunna
Calgary
Dervaig
Calgary Bay
Caolas
Hough Bay
Tiree
Kilninian
Scarinish
Barrapoll
Hynish Bay
Balemartine
Balephuil
Loch Tuath
Treshnish Isles
Gometra
Ulva
Atlantic Ocean
Staffa
Little
Colonsay
N
Iona Abbey
Baile Mor
Iona
Sound of Iona
Fionnphort
Loch Scridain
Bunessan
Fidden
Ross of Mull
Soa Island
Ardchiavaig
0 km
10
0 miles
10
Rubha'a'
Geodha
Kiloran Bay
Colonsay
Kiloran
Kilchattan
Scalasaig
Loch
Staosnaig
Garvard
Dubh
Eilean
Oronsay
Rubh a'
Mhail
A
B
C
1
2
3

Clachan
Raasay
Peinchorran
Sconser
Scalpay
Sligachan
A87
Applecross
Bla Bheinn (Blaven) (3,046ft)
Broadford
Torrin
Crowlin Islands
Loch Kishorn
Plockton
Duirinish
Loch Carron
Stromeferry
Kyle of Lochalsh
Kyleakin
Balmacara
Loch Alsh
A87
Dornie
Eilean Donan Castle
Map 1
Aonach Buidhe (2,951ft)
Loch Mullardoch
Glen Cannich
A831
Cannich
Carn Eighe (3,883ft)
Glen Affric
Loch Affric
Breakish
A851
Kylerhea
Beinn na Seamraig (1,841ft)
Glenelg
Kintail
Loch Duich
Shiel Bridge
Five Sisters
Invermoriston
Loch Scavaig
Elgol
Loch Eishort
Ord
Duisdale
Loch na Dal
Beinn Sgritheall (3,220ft)
Glen Shiel
A87
A'Chralaig (3,676m)
Dundreggan
Glen Moriston
A887
Fort Augustus
Tokavaig
Tarskavaig
Sleat
Teangue
Arnisdale
Loch Hourn
Corran
Kinloch Hourn
Loch Cluanie
Armadale Castle
Ardvasar
Sound of Sleat
Ladhar Bheinn (3,348ft)
Knoydart
Loch Loyne
A87
Aird of Sleat
Inverie
Loch Quoich
Tomdoun
Loch Garry
Invergarry
Loch Oich
Glen More
Point of Sleat
Mallaig
Meall Buidhe (3,105ft)
Sgurr na Ciche (3,413ft)
Glen Garry
Kingie
Laggan
Carn Dearg (2,678ft)
Loch Nevis
Morar
Bracora
Loch Morar
Loch Arkaig
Loch Lochy
Roy
Clunes
Achnacarry
Morar
Sgurr Thuilm (3,164ft)
Arisaig
Loch Beoraid
A82
Gairlochy
Spean Bridge
Roybridge
A86
Tulloch
Glen Spean
Loch nan Uamh
Loch Ailort
Glenfinnan
Kinlocheil
A830
Sound of Arisaig
Roshven
Loch Eil
Corpach
A861
Blaich
Fort William
Aonach Mor (4,007ft)
Stob Choire Claurigh (3,863ft)
Moidart
Eilean Shona
Loch Sheil
Glen Nevis
Ben Nevis (4,411ft)
Fascadale
Ockle
Ardtoe
Ardgour
Kentra Bay
Acharacle
Kilmory
Polloch
Sgurr Dhomhnuill (2,914ft)
A82
Ardnamurchan
Binnein Mor (3,702ft)
Map 4
Kilchoan
Salen
A861
Beinn Resipol (2,773ft)
Corran
North Ballachulish
Ben Hiant (1,732ft)
Glenbeg
Loch Sunart
Strontian
Oinch
Kinlochleven
Glenborrodale
Kentallen
Blackwater Reservoir
Glencoe
Aonach Eagach
Fuar Bheinn (2,514ft)
Kilmalieu
Ballachulish
Altnafeadh
Tobermory
Drimnin
A828
Glen Coe
Morvern
A884
Loch Linnhe
Bidean Nam Bian (3,768ft)
Glencoe Ski Centre
Loch Laidon
Loch Arienas
Camasnacroise
Rannoch Moor
Killundine
Claggan
Meall a'Bhuiridh (3,636ft)
Loch Frisa
Fiunary
Loch Teàrnait
Portnacroish
Glen Etive
Stob Ghabhar (3,568ft)
Water of Tulla
A82
Salen
Lochaline
A849
Fishnish
Lismore
Port Appin
Sea Life Centre
Loch Na Keal
Knock
Achnacroish
A828
Loch Etive
Loch Ba
Dun da Ghaoithe (2,514ft)
Ledaig
Craignure
Mull
Bonawe Quarries
A82
Lochdon
Ben Cruachan (3,696ft)
Ben More (3,170ft)
A849
A85
Connel
Bonawe
Glen Lochy
Oban
Taynuilt
A85
Lochawe
A85
Tyndrum
A82
Ben Buie (2,353ft)
Loch Spelve
Kerrera
A816
Dalmally
Pennyghael
Firth of Lorn
Loch Nant
A819
Crianlarich
Carsaig
Loch Buie
Kilninver
Beinn Chapuli (1,690ft)
Kilchrenan
Cladich
A82
Malcolm's Point
Inverinan
Inverarnan
Seil
Easdale
Balvicar
A816
Loch Awe
Beinn Bhreac (1,726ft)
Ardlui
Sound of Luing
Cullipool
Kilmelford
Loch Avich
Luing
Loch Melfort
Inveraray Castle
A83
Cairndow
Garvellachs
Arduaine
Inveraray
Toberonochy
Oban to Colonsay
Cruach Scarba (1,474ft)
A815
Scarba
Ardfern
Arrochar
Ben Lomond (3,197ft)
Tarbet
A816
Ford
Auchindrain
Strachur
Lochgoilhead
Kirkton
Loch Long
Loch Lomond
Kilmartin
Argyll Forest Park
Furnace
Craignish Point
Kilmartin House
A886
Newton
Invernoaden
Minard
Loch Gail
A814
Loch Lomond Regional Park
Crinan
Bridgend
Beinn Bhreac (1,533ft)
Loch Eck
Garelochead
Luss
Cairnbaan
Glendaruel
Cowal Peninsula
A815
A82
Balmaha
Jura
Ardlussa
Lochgilphead
A83
Glendaruel
Coulport
A817
Shian Bay
Loch Righ Mor
Tayvallich
Map 5
Ardentinny
Rhu
Arden
A846
Ardrishaig
Clachan of Glendaruel
Cove
Balloch
Rubh' an t-Sailein
Tarbert
Loch Sween
Loch Fyne
Otter Ferry
Craigandaive
A880
Helensburgh
Loch Tarbert
Keillmore
A8003
Auchenbreck
Strone
Kilcreggan
A83
Kilfinan
A886
Hunter's Quay
Craigendoran
A
B
C
4
5
6

Map 4
A833
Loch Ashie
Dores
Nairn
A9
Moy
Lochindorb
A939
A831
Milton
Drumnadrochit
Urqhart Castle
Loch Duntelchaig
Farr
Findhorn
Map 2
Tormatin
Strathspey
Granton-on-Spey
Dulnain Bridge
Glen Affric
Meal Fuarmhonaidh (2,284ft)
Loch Ness
Inverfarigaig
Errogie
Strath Dearn
Carrbridge
Lynemore
Foyers
Loch Mhor
A9
Nethy Bridge
A939
Invermoriston
Carn Odhar (2,632ft)
Boat of Garten
Dundreggan
Stratherrick
A887
Glen Morriston
Monadhliath Mountains
Glenmore Forest Park
A
Fort Augustus
Cnoc Fraing (2,445ft)
Aviemore
Loch
Alvie
Inverdruie
Glen More
A87
Carn a'Chuilinn (2,678ft)
Feshiebridge
Cairn Gorm (4,086ft)
Loch Garry
Invergarry
Loch Oich
Carn Dearg (3,101ft)
Kingussie
Lairig Ghru
Cairgorm Mountains
Braeriach (4,250ft)
Ben Macdui (4,296ft)
Ben Avon (3,843ft)
A82
Laggan
Carn Dearg (2,678ft)
Cairn Toul (4,001ft)
Loch Lochy
Spey
Garvamore
Laggan
A86
Roy
Etteridge
Beinn Bhrotain (3,797ft)
Braemar
Glen Roy
A86
A889
Linn of Dee
Inverey
Auchallater
Map 3
Loch Laggan
Roy Bridge
Dhalwhinnie
Mountains
An Sgarsoch (3,479ft)
A86
Tulloch
Geal Charn (3,443ft)
Carn na Caim (3,008ft)
Glen Spean
Beinn a'Chlachair (3,571ft)
Grampian
A'Bhuidheanach Bheag (3,072ft)
Beinn Dearg (3,308ft)
Glenshee Ski Centre
Tilt
Stob Choire Claurigh (3,863ft)
Aonach Beag (3,650ft)
Loch Eric
Pass of Drumochter
A9
Glas Tulaichean (3,449ft)
Ben Alder (3,768ft)
Beinn Udlamain (3,069ft)
Carn nan Gabhar (3,679ft)
Loch Garry
Spittal of Glenshee
Glen Gary
A93
Glen Shee
Loch Errochty
Calvine
Pitagowan
Blair Atholl
Straloch
Tay Forest Park
Kinloch Rannoch
Tummel Bridge
Killiecrankie
Pass of Killiecrankie
Blacklunans
Blackwater Reservoir
Rannoch
Killichonan
Tressait
Loch Tummel
Kirkmichael
B
Loch Rannoch
Pitlochry
A924
Loch Laidon
Tay Forest Park
Schiehallion (3,547ft)
Ballintuim
Glencoe Ski Centre
Rannoch Moor
Grandtully
Coshieville
Weem
Ballinluig
Water of Tulla
Glen Lyon
Fortingall
Bridge of Cally
Strath Tay
Dowally
A82
Aberfeldy
Bridge of Balgie
Kenmore
Dunkeld
A923
Blairgowrie
Loch of the Lawes
Loch Lyon
Ben Lawers (3,984ft)
Meikleour
Loch Tay
Trochry
Milton
Beinn Heasgarnich (3,531ft)
Braan
Amulree
Lochay
Morenish
Bankfoot
A82
A93
Stanley
Glen Lochy
Killin
Almond
Guildtown
A85
Tyndrum
Harrietfield
Balbeggie
Ben Chonzie (3,056ft)
Luncarty
Scone Palace
Glen Lednock
A82
Dochart
A85
A85
A822
Methven
Crianlarich
St Fillans
Gilmerton
A85
New Scone
Ben More (3,853ft)
Lochearnhead
Loch Earn
A85
Comrie
Tibbermore
Perth
A82
Earn
Crieff
A9
Glencarse
Strathearn
Kingshouse
Loch Voil
Inverarnan
Strathyre
Ben Vorlich (3,233ft)
Glen Artney
Earn
Forgandenny
Muthill
Bridge of Earn
A84
Aberuthven
Dunning
Ardlui
Path of Condie
Ben Ledi (2,882ft)
A822
A823
Ben A'an (1,851ft)
Loch Lubnaig
Auchterarder
Blackford
Loch Katrine
Braco
Glenfarg
C
Inversnaid
Brig o'Turk
Callander
Gleneagles
Ben Venue (2,386ft)
Greenloaning
A9
A823
Hills
Milnathort
A821
Ochi
Tarbet
Carnbo
A91
A911
Loch Long
Arrochar
Ben Lomond (3,197ft)
Aberfoyle
A81
A84
Doune
Dunblane
Kinross
Queen Elizabeth Forest Park
A873
Yetts o'Muckhart
A977
A814
Port of Menteith
Thornhill
Bridge of Allan
Loch Leven
Loch Lomond Regional Park
Rowardennan Forest
Teith
Dollar
M90
M9
Alva
Powmill
Lochore Meadows Country Park
Menstrie
Tillicoultry
Amprior
Kippen
Luss
A811
Alloa
A823
Balmaha
Stirling
Fallin
Clackmannan
A82
Loch Lomond
Drymen
A875
Gargunnock Hills
Bannockburn
Cowdenbeath
A817
Map 5
Airth
A977
A907
Dunfermline
M9
Arden
A811
Killearn
Carron Valley Reservoir
Plean
Kincardine
A985
Cairneyhill
Rhu
Craighat
Fintry
M80
Stenhousemuir
Culross
Aberdour
Helensburgh
Campsie Fells
M876
Grangemouth
Limekilns
Dalgety Bay
Balloch
Kilpatrick Hills
A81
Kilsyth Hills
Denny
Inverkeithing
Bonnybridge
Bo'ness
Craigendoran
1
Strathblane
Milltown of Campsie
Kilsyth
2
3
N Queensferry
Alexandria
A809
A891
A80
Falkirk
Polmont
S Queensferry

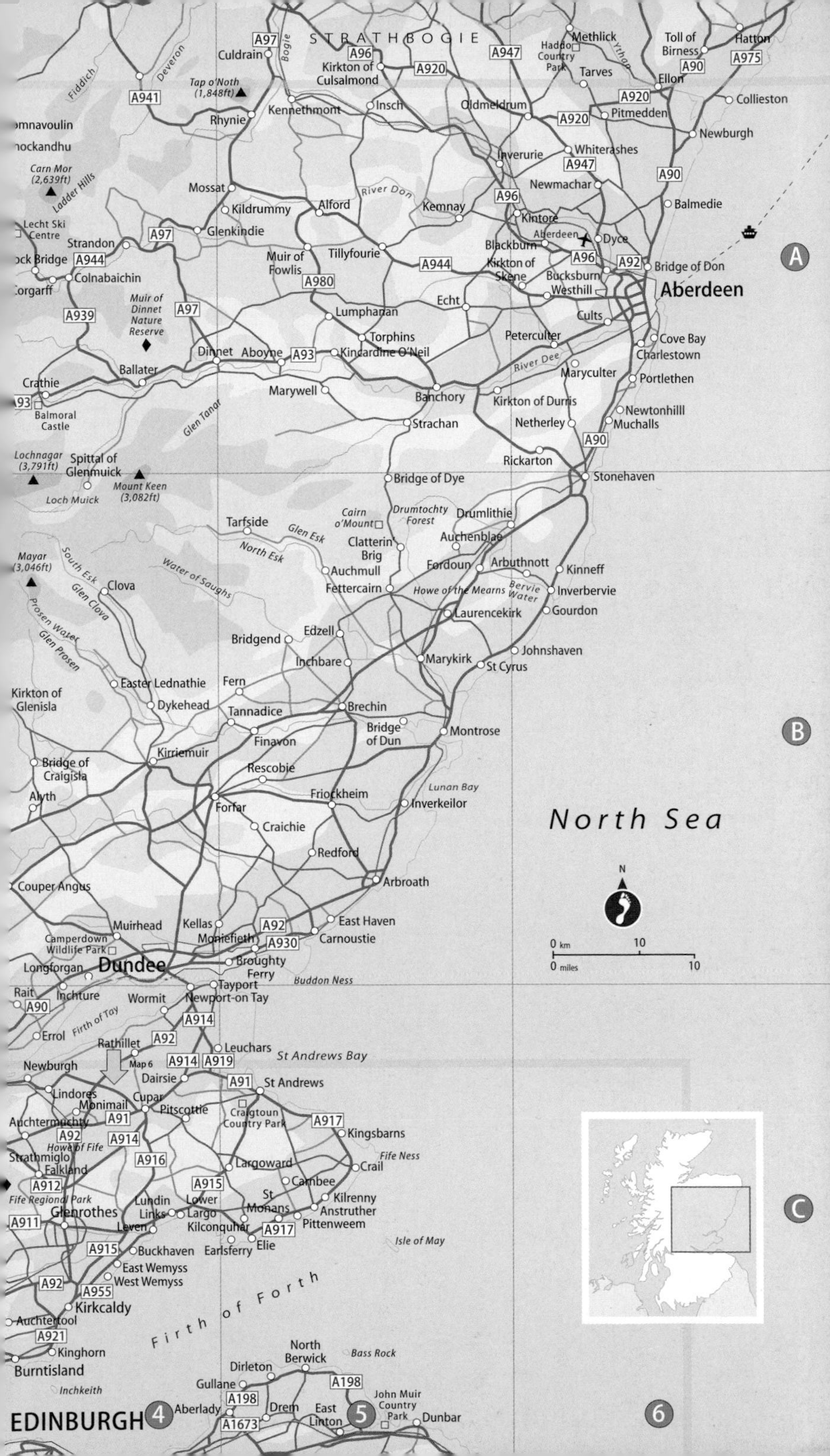
STRATHBOGIE
A97
Culdrain
Bogie
Deveron
Fiddich
Tap o'Noth (1,848ft)
A941
A96
Kirkton of Culsalmond
A920
A947
Haddo Country Park
Methlick
Ythan
Toll of Birness
Hatton
A975
A90
Tarves
Ellon
Rhynie
Kennethmont
Insch
Oldmeldrum
A920
Pitmedden
Collieston
Newburgh
Carn Mor (2,639ft)
Ladder Hills
Inverurie
Whiterashes
A947
A90
Newmachar
Mossat
Kildrummy
River Don
Alford
Kemnay
A96
Balmedie
Lecht Ski Centre
A97
Glenkindie
Kintore
Aberdeen
Dyce
Strandon
Tillyfourie
Blackburn
A96
A92
Bridge of Don
A944
Muir of Fowlis
A944
Kirkton of Skene
Bucksburn
Colnabaichin
A980
Westhill
Aberdeen
Muir of Dinnet Nature Reserve
A97
Echt
A939
Lumphanan
Cults
Torphins
Peterculter
Cove Bay
Dinnet
Aboyne
A93
Kincardine O'Neil
Charlestown
Ballater
River Dee
Maryculter
Portlethen
Crathie
Marywell
Banchory
Kirkton of Durris
Balmoral Castle
Glen Tanar
Strachan
Newtonhill
Netherley
Muchalls
A90
Lochnagar (3,791ft)
Spittal of Glenmuick
Rickarton
Stonehaven
Mount Keen (3,082ft)
Bridge of Dye
Loch Muick
Cairn o'Mount
Drumtochty Forest
Drumlithie
Tarfside
Glen Esk
Clatterin' Brig
Auchenblae
North Esk
Mayar (3,046ft)
South Esk
Water of Saughs
Auchmull
Fordoun
Arbuthnott
Kinneff
Clova
Glen Clova
Fettercairn
Howe of the Mearns
Bervie Water
Inverbervie
Prosen Water
Gourdon
Laurencekirk
Glen Prosen
Bridgend
Edzell
Inchbare
Marykirk
Johnshaven
St Cyrus
Kirkton of Glenisla
Easter Lednathie
Fern
Dykehead
Tannadice
Brechin
Bridge of Dun
Montrose
Finavon
Kirriemuir
Bridge of Craigisla
Rescobie
Alyth
Forfar
Friockheim
Lunan Bay
Inverkeilor
North Sea
Craichie
Redford
Arbroath
N
Couper Angus
Muirhead
Kellas
A92
East Haven
Camperdown Wildlife Park
Monifieth
A930
Carnoustie
0 km 10
0 miles 10
Dundee
Broughty Ferry
Longforgan
Buddon Ness
Tayport
Rait
Inchture
Wormit
Newport-on Tay
A90
Firth of Tay
A914
Errol
Rathillet
A92
Leuchars
Map 6
A914
A919
St Andrews Bay
Newburgh
Dairsie
A91
St Andrews
Lindores
Monimail
Cupar
Pitscottie
Craigtoun Country Park
A91
A917
Auchtermuchty
Kingsbarns
A92
A914
Howe of Fife
Fife Ness
Strathmiglo
A916
Falkland
Largoward
Crail
A912
A915
Cambee
Fife Regional Park
Lundin Links
Lower Largo
St Monans
Kilrenny
Anstruther
Glenrothes
A911
Leven
Kilconquhar
A917
Pittenweem
A915
Buckhaven
Earlsferry
Elie
Isle of May
East Wemyss
West Wemyss
A92
A955
Kirkcaldy
Firth of Forth
Auchtertool
A921
Kinghorn
North Berwick
Bass Rock
Burntisland
Dirleton
Gullane
A198
A198
Inchkeith
John Muir Country Park
EDINBURGH
Aberlady
Drem
East Linton
Dunbar
A1673
A
B
C
4
5
6

Map 5

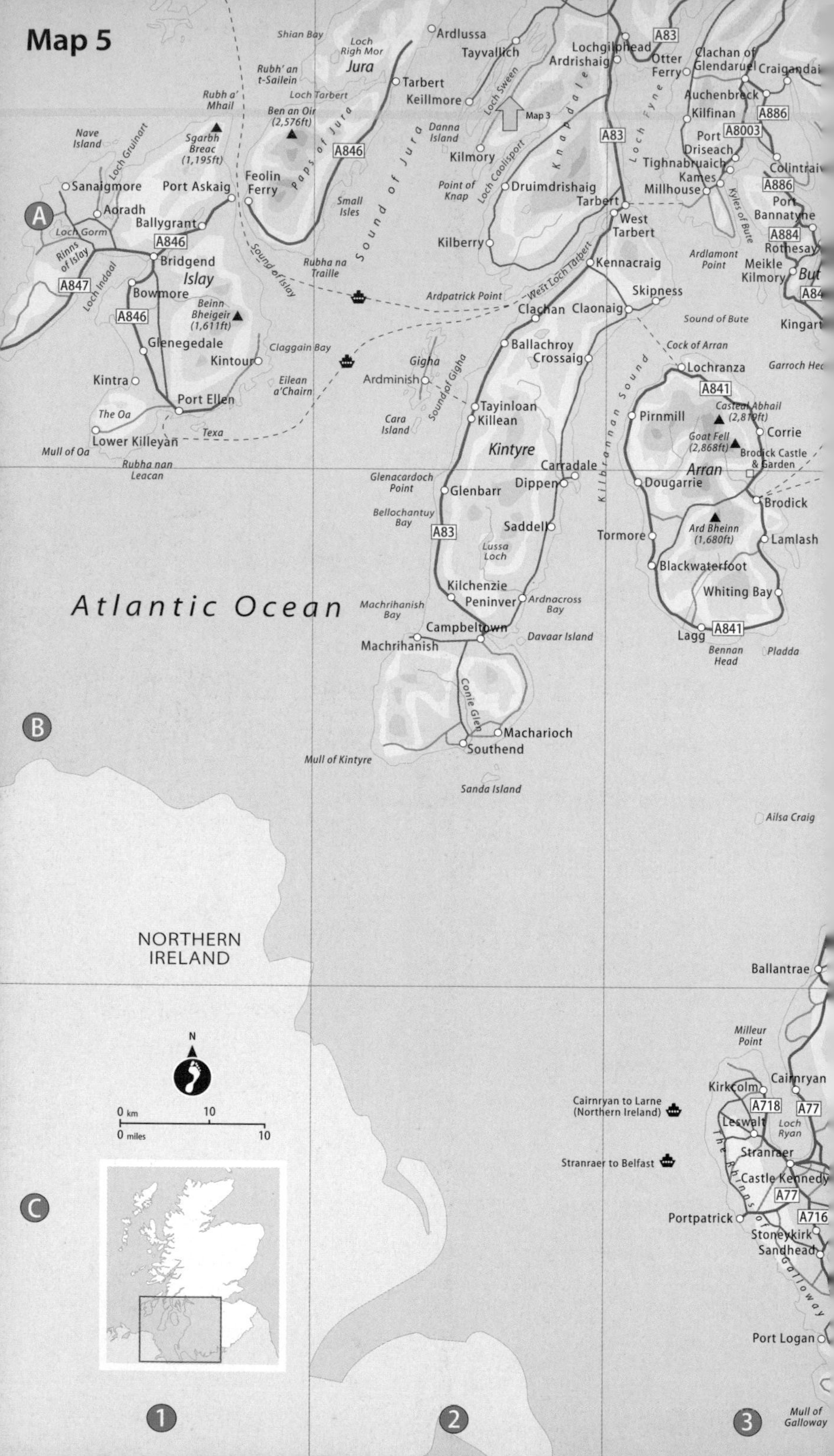
Map 5
Atlantic Ocean
NORTHERN IRELAND
Islay
Jura
Kintyre
Arran
Gigha
Sound of Jura
Sound of Islay
Sound of Gigha
Kilbrannan Sound
Sound of Bute
Paps of Jura
Knapdale
Loch Fyne
Kyles of Bute
The Rhinns of Galloway
Shian Bay
Loch Righ Mor
Ardlussa
Tayvallich
Lochgilphead
Ardrishaig
Otter Ferry
Clachan of Glendaruel
Craigandai
Rubh' an t-Sailein
Tarbert
Keillmore
Loch Tarbert
Loch Sween
Map 3
Rubh a' Mhail
Ben an Oir (2,576ft)
Danna Island
Auchenbreck
Kilfinan
Nave Island
Sgarbh Breac (1,195ft)
Loch Gruinart
Kilmory
Loch Caolisport
Port Driseach
Tighnabruaich
Colintraiv
Kames
Millhouse
Sanaigmore
Port Askaig
Feolin Ferry
Small Isles
Point of Knap
Druimdrishaig
Aoradh
Ballygrant
West Tarbert
Port Bannatyne
Loch Gorm
Rinns of Islay
Bridgend
Kilberry
Rothesay
Meikle Kilmory
Loch Indaal
Rubha na Traille
Ardlamont Point
Kennacraig
West Loch Tarbert
Bowmore
Beinn Bheigeir (1,611ft)
Ardpatrick Point
Skipness
Clachan
Claonaig
Kingart
Glenegedale
Kintour
Claggain Bay
Ballachroy
Crossaig
Cock of Arran
Garroch Head
Kintra
Eilean a'Chairn
Ardminish
Lochranza
The Oa
Port Ellen
Tayinloan
Killean
Pirnmill
Casteal Abhail (2,819ft)
Corrie
Lower Killeyan
Texa
Cara Island
Goat Fell (2,868ft)
Brodick Castle & Garden
Mull of Oa
Rubha nan Leacan
Carradale
Dippen
Dougarrie
Glenacardoch Point
Glenbarr
Brodick
Bellochantuy Bay
Saddell
Ard Bheinn (1,680ft)
Tormore
Lamlash
Lussa Loch
Blackwaterfoot
Kilchenzie
Peninver
Ardnacross Bay
Whiting Bay
Machrihanish Bay
Campbeltown
Davaar Island
Machrihanish
Lagg
Bennan Head
Pladda
Conie Glen
Macharioch
Southend
Mull of Kintyre
Sanda Island
Ailsa Craig
Ballantrae
Milleur Point
Cairnryan
Kirkcolm
Cairnryan to Larne (Northern Ireland)
Leswalt
Loch Ryan
Stranraer
Stranraer to Belfast
Castle Kennedy
Portpatrick
Stoneykirk
Sandhead
Port Logan
Mull of Galloway
A83
A886
A8003
A884
A846
A847
A841
A718
A77
A716
N
0 km
10
0 miles
10
A
B
C
1
2
3

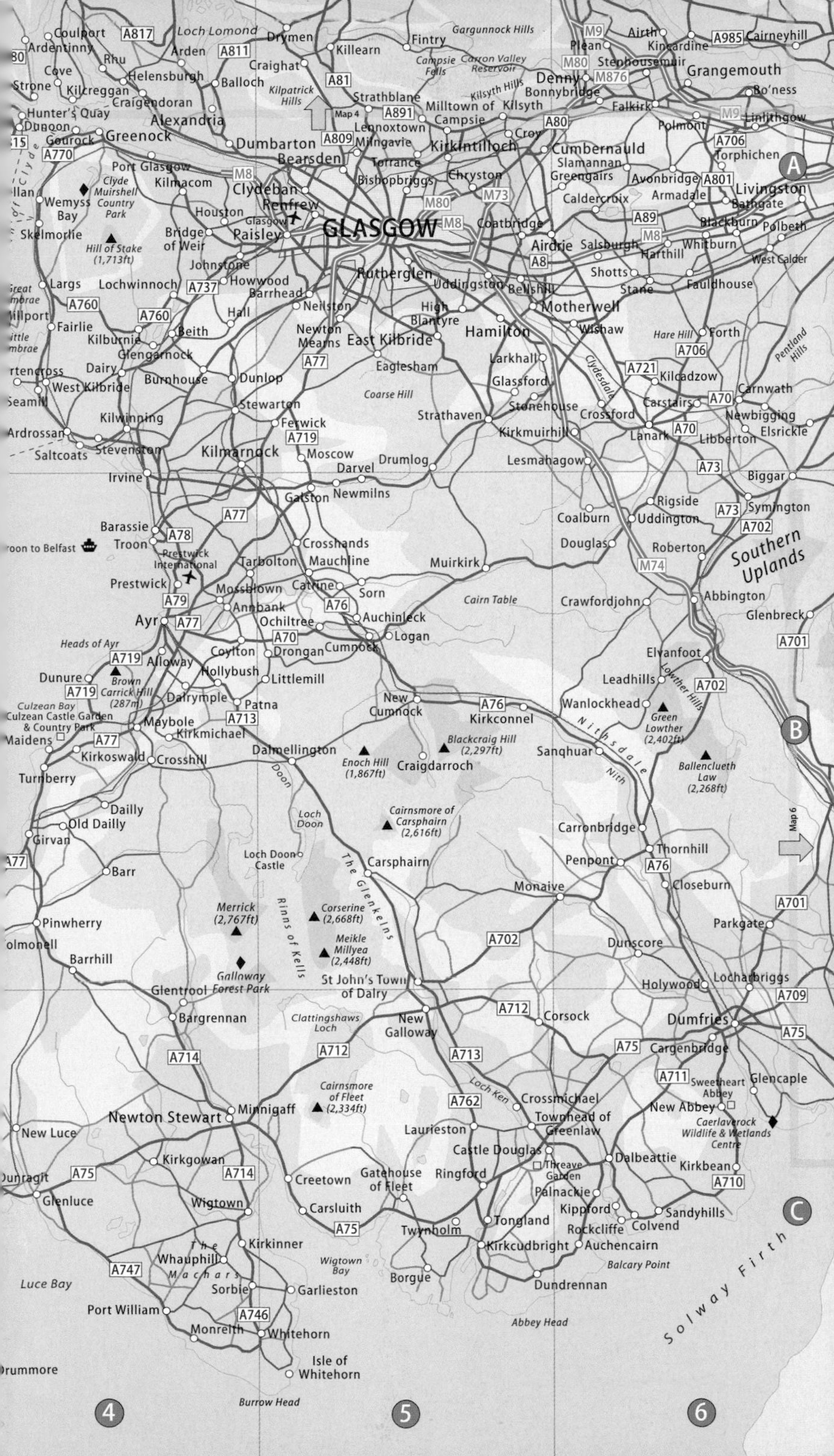
Coulport
Ardentinny
Cove
Strone
Kilcreggan
Rhu
Helensburgh
Hunter's Quay
Dunoon
Gourock
Greenock
Craigendoran
Alexandria
Balloch
Arden
Loch Lomond
Drymen
Killearn
Fintry
Craighat
Kilpatrick Hills
Strathblane
Campsie Fells
Carron Valley Reservoir
Gargunnock Hills
Kilsyth Hills
Milltown of Campsie
Kilsyth
Lennoxtown
Milngavie
Map 4
Dumbarton
Bearsden
Kirkintilloch
Croy
Cumbernauld
Denny
Bonnybridge
Falkirk
Plean
Airth
Kincardine
Stenhousemuir
Grangemouth
Cairneyhill
Bo'ness
Linlithgow
Polmont
Torphichen
Slamannan
Greengairs
Avonbridge
Armadale
Livingston
Bathgate
Caldercruix
Blackburn
Polbeth
Whitburn
West Calder
Harthill
Salsburgh
Airdrie
Coatbridge
Chryston
Bishopbriggs
Torrance
Port Glasgow
Clyde Muirshell Country Park
Kilmacom
Clydebank
Renfrew
Glasgow
GLASGOW
Wemyss Bay
Skelmorlie
Houston
Bridge of Weir
Paisley
Hill of Stake (1,713ft)
Johnstone
Howwood
Barrhead
Neilston
Rutherglen
Uddingston
Bellshill
Motherwell
Shotts
Stane
Fauldhouse
Largs
Lochwinnoch
Great Cumbrae
Millport
Little Cumbrae
Fairlie
Kilburnie
Hall
Beith
Glengarnock
High Blantyre
Hamilton
Wishaw
Newton Mearns
East Kilbride
Hare Hill
Forth
Pentland Hills
Eaglesham
Larkhall
Kilcadzow
Glassford
Carnwath
Dairy
Burnhouse
Dunlop
West Kilbride
Seamill
Ardrossan
Saltcoats
Stevenston
Kilwinning
Stewarton
Fenwick
Coarse Hill
Strathaven
Stonehouse
Crossford
Carstairs
Newbigging
Clydesdale
Lanark
Elsrickle
Libberton
Kirkmuirhill
Kilmarnock
Moscow
Drumlog
Darvel
Newmilns
Galston
Lesmahagow
Biggar
Irvine
Rigside
Symington
Coalburn
Uddingston
Barassie
Troon
Troon to Belfast
Crosshands
Douglas
Roberton
Southern Uplands
Prestwick International
Tarbolton
Mauchline
Muirkirk
Prestwick
Mossblown
Catrine
Sorn
Cairn Table
Crawfordjohn
Abbington
Annbank
Auchinleck
Glenbreck
Ayr
Ochiltree
Logan
Cumnock
Heads of Ayr
Coylton
Drongan
Alloway
Elvanfoot
Dunure
Brown Carrick Hill (287m)
Hollybush
Littlemill
Leadhills
Lowther Hills
Culzean Bay
Culzean Castle Garden & Country Park
Dalrymple
Patna
New Cumnock
Kirkconnel
Wanlockhead
Green Lowther (2,402ft)
Maidens
Maybole
Kirkmichael
Blackcraig Hill (2,297ft)
Nithsdale
Kirkoswald
Crosshill
Dalmellington
Enoch Hill (1,867ft)
Craigdarroch
Sanqhuar
Ballencleuth Law (2,268ft)
Turnberry
Doon
Nith
Dailly
Old Dailly
Girvan
Loch Doon
Cairnsmore of Carsphairn (2,616ft)
Carronbridge
Map 6
Loch Doon Castle
Carsphairn
Thornhill
Penpont
Barr
The Glenkens
Closeburn
Monaive
Merrick (2,767ft)
Corserine (2,668ft)
Pinwherry
Parkgate
Colmonell
Meikle Millyea (2,448ft)
Rinns of Kells
Dunscore
Barrhill
Galloway Forest Park
St John's Town of Dalry
Holywood
Locharbriggs
Glentrool
Bargrennan
Clattingshaws Loch
New Galloway
Corsock
Dumfries
Cargenbridge
Cairnsmore of Fleet (2,334ft)
Loch Ken
Crossmichael
Glencaple
Sweetheart Abbey
New Abbey
Minnigaff
Newton Stewart
Laurieston
Townhead of Greenlaw
Caerlaverock Wildlife & Wetlands Centre
New Luce
Castle Douglas
Threave Garden
Dalbeattie
Kirkbean
Kirkgowan
Creetown
Gatehouse of Fleet
Ringford
Palnackie
Dunragit
Glenluce
Wigtown
Carsluith
Tongland
Kippford
Sandyhills
Colvend
Rockcliffe
Auchencairn
Twynholm
Kirkcudbright
Kirkinner
The Machars
Whauphill
Wigtown Bay
Borgue
Balcary Point
Solway Firth
Luce Bay
Sorbie
Garlieston
Dundrennan
Port William
Monreith
Whitehorn
Abbey Head
Isle of Whitehorn
Drummore
Burrow Head
A817
A811
A81
A891
A809
A80
M9
M80
M876
A985
A706
A801
M8
M80
M73
A89
A8
A770
A737
A760
A77
A721
A706
A70
A719
A73
A702
A78
M74
A79
A76
A701
A713
A702
A712
A709
A75
A714
A762
A711
A710
A747
A746
A
B
C
4
5
6

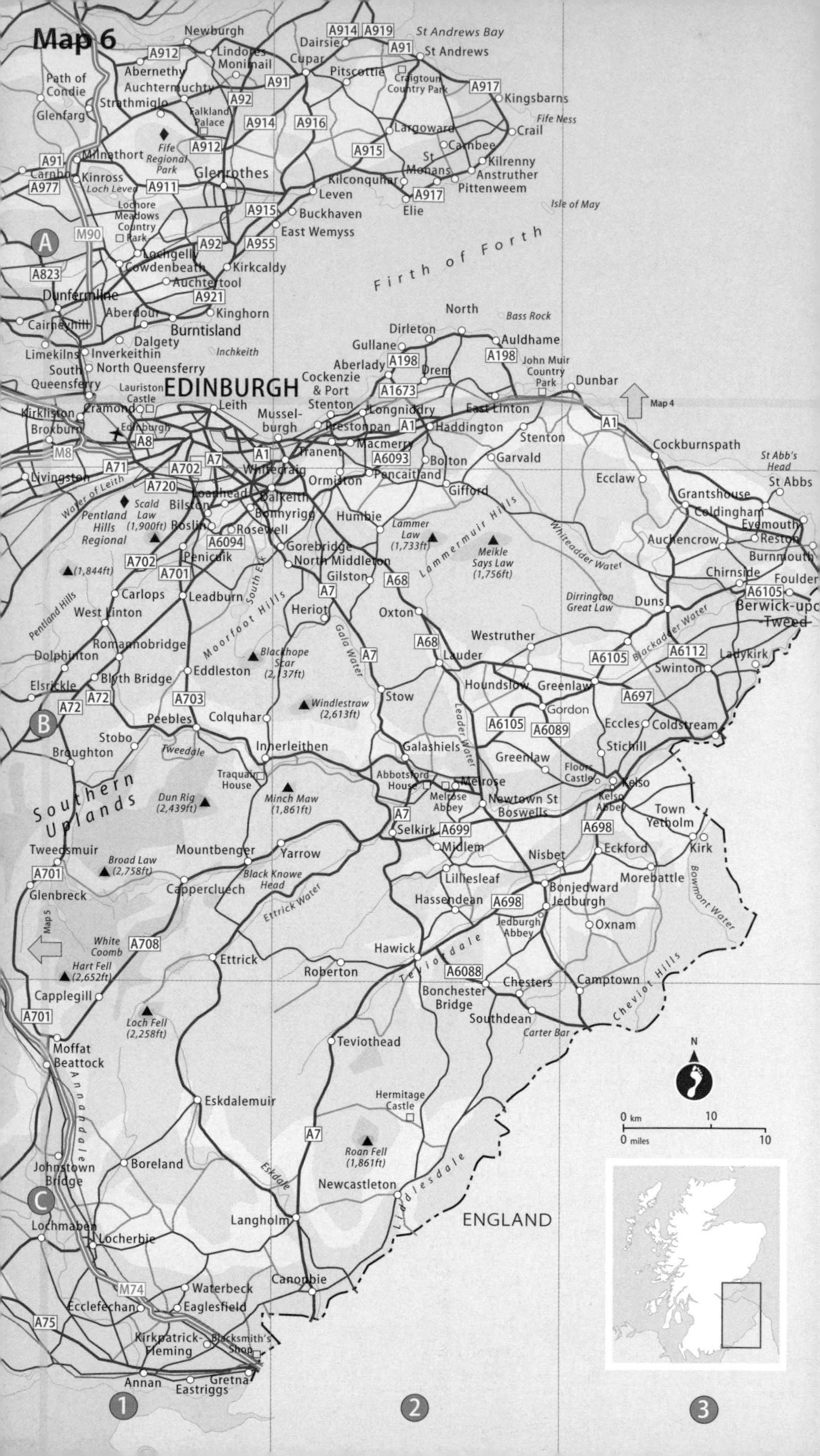
Map 6
Newburgh
A914
A919
St Andrews Bay
Dairsie
A912
Lindores
Cupar
A91
St Andrews
Path of Condie
Abernethy
Monimail
Pitscottie
Craigtoun Country Park
Auchtermuchty
A91
A917
Strathmiglo
A92
Kingsbarns
Glenfarg
Falkland Palace
A914
A916
Fife Ness
Largoward
Crail
Fife Regional Park
A912
A915
Carnbee
A91
Milnathort
St Monans
Kilrenny
Carnbo
Kinross
Glenrothes
Anstruther
A977
Loch Leven
A911
Kilconquhar
Pittenweem
Leven
A917
Lochore Meadows Country Park
A915
Buckhaven
Elie
Isle of May
M90
East Wemyss
A
Lochgelly
A92
A955
Firth of Forth
Cowdenbeath
Kirkcaldy
A823
Auchtertool
Dunfermline
A921
Aberdour
Kinghorn
North
Cairneyhill
Burntisland
Bass Rock
Dirleton
Dalgety
Auldhame
Limekilns
Inverkeithin
Inchkeith
Gullane
A198
A198
John Muir Country Park
South Queensferry
North Queensferry
Aberlady
Drem
Cockenzie & Port
A1673
Dunbar
Lauriston Castle
EDINBURGH
Stenton
Map 4
Kirkliston
Cramond
Leith
Longniddry
East Linton
Musselburgh
Prestonpan
A1
Haddington
A1
Broxburn
Edinburgh
Stenton
A8
Macmerry
M8
Tranent
A6093
Bolton
Garvald
Cockburnspath
A1
A7
Whitecraig
St Abb's Head
Livingston
A71
A702
Ormiston
Pencaitland
Ecclaw
St Abbs
Water of Leith
A720
Loanhead
Dalkeith
Gifford
Grantshouse
Bilston
Coldingham
Scald Law (1,900ft)
Bonnyrigg
Humbie
Eyemouth
Pentland Hills Regional
Roslin
Rosewell
Lammer Law (1,733ft)
Lammermuir Hills
Whiteadder Water
Auchencrow
Reston
A6094
Meikle Says Law (1,756ft)
Penicuik
Gorebridge
Burnmouth
A702
North Middleton
(1,844ft)
A701
Gilston
A68
Chirnside
Foulder
South Esk
A7
A6105
Carlops
Leadburn
Dirrington Great Law
Duns
Berwick-upon-Tweed
Pentland Hills
Heriot
Oxton
West Linton
Moorfoot Hills
Gala Water
Blackadder Water
Westruther
Romannobridge
A68
A6112
Blackhope Scar (2,137ft)
Lauder
A6105
Ladykirk
Dolphinton
A7
Swinton
Eddleston
Blyth Bridge
Houndslow
Greenlaw
Elsrickle
A703
Windlestraw (2,613ft)
Stow
A697
A72
A72
Gordon
Leader Water
A6105
A6089
B
Peebles
Colquhar
Eccles
Coldstream
Stobo
Innerleithen
Broughton
Tweedale
Galashiels
Stichill
Greenlaw
Traquair House
Floors Castle
Southern Uplands
Abbotsford House
Melrose
Kelso
Minch Maw (1,861ft)
Melrose Abbey
Newtown St Boswells
Kelso Abbey
Town Yetholm
Dun Rig (2,439ft)
A7
Selkirk
A699
A698
Kirk
Tweedsmuir
Mountbenger
Yarrow
Midlem
Eckford
Broad Law (2,758ft)
Nisbet
A701
Black Knowe Head
Lilliesleaf
Morebattle
Glenbreck
Cappercluech
Bonjedward
Bowmont Water
Ettrick Water
Hassendean
A698
Jedburgh
Map 5
Jedburgh Abbey
Oxnam
White Coomb
A708
Hawick
Teviotdale
Ettrick
Hart Fell (2,652ft)
Roberton
A6088
Chesters
Camptown
Cheviot Hills
Capplegill
Bonchester Bridge
A701
Loch Fell (2,258ft)
Southdean
Carter Bar
Moffat
Teviothead
N
Beattock
Annandale
Hermitage Castle
Eskdalemuir
0 km
10
A7
0 miles
10
Roan Fell (1,861ft)
Boreland
Johnstown Bridge
Eskdale
Newcastleton
Liddlesdale
C
ENGLAND
Langholm
Lochmaben
Locherbie
M74
Canonbie
Waterbeck
Ecclefechan
Eaglesfield
A75
Kirkpatrick-Fleming
Blacksmith's Shop
Annan
Gretna
Eastriggs
1
2
3

Map 7

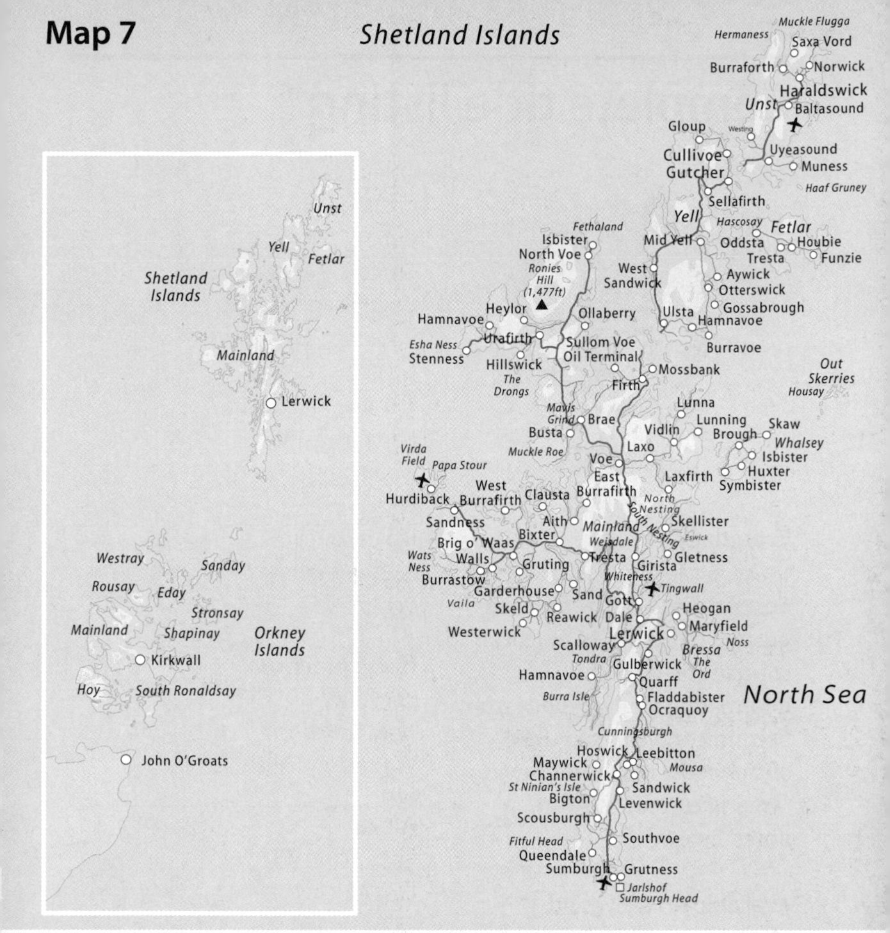

Shetland Islands
Muckle Flugga
Hermaness
Saxa Vord
Burraforth
Norwick
Haraldswick
Unst
Baltasound
Gloup
Westing
Cullivoe
Gutcher
Uyeasound
Muness
Haaf Gruney
Sellafirth
Yell
Hascosay
Fetlar
Fethaland
Isbister
Mid Yell
Oddsta
Houbie
North Voe
Tresta
Funzie
Ronies Hill (1,477ft)
West Sandwick
Aywick
Otterswick
Heylor
Ollaberry
Ulsta
Gossabrough
Hamnavoe
Hamnavoe
Urafirth
Sullom Voe Oil Terminal
Burravoe
Esha Ness
Stenness
Hillswick
The Drongs
Mossbank
Firth
Out Skerries
Housay
Lunna
Mavis Grind
Brae
Lunning
Skaw
Busta
Vidlin
Brough
Whalsey
Virda Field
Muckle Roe
Laxo
Isbister
Papa Stour
Voe
Huxter
East Burrafirth
Laxfirth
Symbister
West Burrafirth
Hurdiback
Clausta
North Nesting
South Nesting
Sandness
Aith
Skellister
Mainland
Eswick
Brig o' Waas
Bixter
Weisdale
Gletness
Wats Ness
Walls
Gruting
Tresta
Girista
Burrastow
Whiteness
Tingwall
Garderhouse
Sand
Gott
Vaila
Skeld
Reawick
Dale
Heogan
Westerwick
Lerwick
Maryfield
Scalloway
Noss
Bressa
Tondra
Gulberwick
The Ord
Hamnavoe
Quarff
Burra Isle
Fladdabister
Ocraquoy
North Sea
Cunningsburgh
Hoswick
Leebitton
Maywick
Mousa
Channerwick
St Ninian's Isle
Sandwick
Bigton
Levenwick
Scousburgh
Southvoe
Fitful Head
Queendale
Grutness
Sumburgh
Jarlshof
Sumburgh Head
Unst
Yell
Fetlar
Shetland Islands
Mainland
Lerwick
Westray
Sanday
Rousay
Eday
Stronsay
Mainland
Shapinay
Orkney Islands
Kirkwall
Hoy
South Ronaldsay
John O'Groats

Orkney Islands
Mull Head
Noup Head
Papa Westray
North Ronaldsay Firth
North Ronaldsay
The North Sound
Westray
Sanday
Westray Firth
Sanday Sound
Eday
Rousay
Egilsay
Birsay
Brough Head
Wyre
Stronsay Firth
Twatt
Tingwall
Stronsay
Gairsay
Skaill House
Dounby
Skara Brae
Wide Firth
Shapinsay
Loch of Harray
Bimbister
Auskerry
Loch of Stenness
Finstown
Kirkwall
Stromness
Mainland
Skaill
Clestrain
Greamsay
Greenigo
Gritley
Houton
St Mary's
Old Man of Hoy
Scapa Flow
Copinsay
Hoy
Burray
Flotta
St Margaret's Hope
Longhope
South Ronaldsay
South Walls
Swona
Burwick
Pentland Firth
Brough Ness
N
0 km 10
0 miles 10

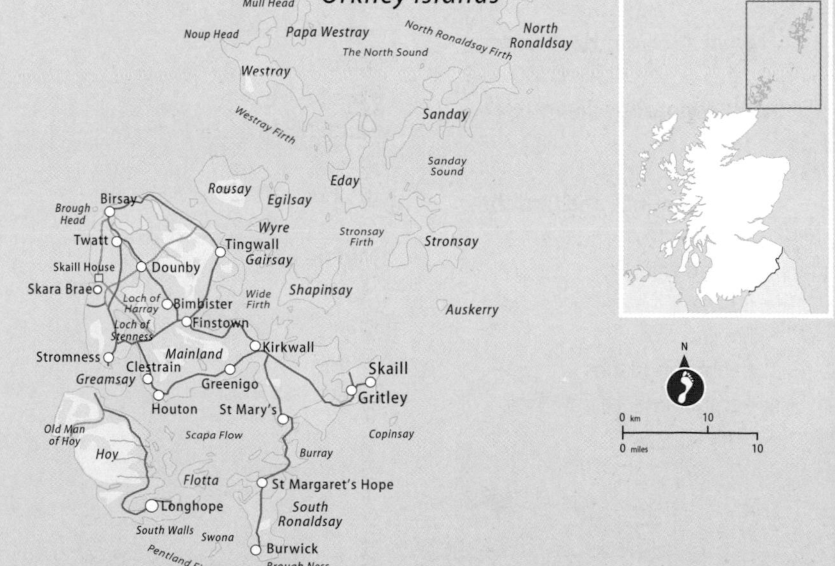

Complete title listing

Footprint publishes travel guides to over 150 destinations worldwide. Each guide is packed with practical, concise and colourful information for everybody from first-time travellers to travel aficionados. The list is growing fast and current titles are noted below.

Available from all good bookshops and online

www.footprintbooks.com

(P) denotes pocket guide

Latin America and Caribbean
Argentina
Barbados (P)
Bolivia
Brazil
Caribbean Islands
Central America & Mexico
Chile
Colombia
Costa Rica
Cuba
Cusco & the Inca Trail
Dominican Republic
Ecuador & Galápagos
Guatemala
Havana (P)
Mexico
Nicaragua
Peru
Rio de Janeiro
South American Handbook
Venezuela

North America
Vancouver (P)
New York (P)
Western Canada

Africa
Cape Town (P)
East Africa
Libya
Marrakech & the High Atlas
Marrakech (P)
Morocco
Namibia
South Africa
Tunisia
Uganda

Middle East
Egypt
Israel
Jordan
Syria & Lebanon

Australasia

Australia
East Coast Australia
New Zealand
Sydney (P)
West Coast Australia

Asia

Bali
Bangkok & the Beaches
Cambodia
Goa
Hong Kong (P)
India
Indian Himalaya
Indonesia
Laos
Malaysia
Nepal
Pakistan
Rajasthan & Gujarat
Singapore
South India
Sri Lanka
Sumatra
Thailand
Tibet
Vietnam

Europe

Andalucía
Barcelona
Barcelona (P)
Berlin (P)
Bilbao (P)
Bologna (P)
Britain
Cardiff (P)
Copenhagen (P)
Croatia
Dublin
Dublin (P)
Edinburgh
Edinburgh (P)
England
Glasgow
Glasgow (P)
Ireland
Lisbon (P)
London
London (P)
Madrid (P)
Naples (P)
Northern Spain
Paris (P)
Reykjavík (P)
Scotland
Scotland Highlands & Islands
Seville (P)
Spain
Tallinn (P)
Turin (P)
Turkey
Valencia (P)
Verona (P)

Also available
Traveller's Handbook (WEXAS)
Traveller's Healthbook (WEXAS)
Traveller's Internet Guide (WEXAS)